Lectur

T0140062

Founding

Gerhard Go
Karlsruh

Juris Hartm
Cornell U

Editorial I

Elisa Ber n
Purdue

Wen Gao
Peking U

Bernhard S
TU Dort

Moti Yung
Columbi

More information about this series at https://link.springer.com/bookseries/558

Shai Avidan · Gabriel Brostow ·
Moustapha Cissé · Giovanni Maria Farinella ·
Tal Hassner (Eds.)

Computer Vision – ECCV 2022

17th European Conference
Tel Aviv, Israel, October 23–27, 2022
Proceedings, Part IX

 Springer

Editors
Shai Avidan
Tel Aviv University
Tel Aviv, Israel

Gabriel Brostow ⓘ
University College London
London, UK

Moustapha Cissé
Google AI
Accra, Ghana

Giovanni Maria Farinella ⓘ
University of Catania
Catania, Italy

Tal Hassner ⓘ
Facebook (United States)
Menlo Park, CA, USA

ISSN 0302-9743   ISSN 1611-3349 (electronic)
Lecture Notes in Computer Science
ISBN 978-3-031-20076-2   ISBN 978-3-031-20077-9 (eBook)
https://doi.org/10.1007/978-3-031-20077-9

This Springer imprint is published by the registered company Springer Nature Switzerland AG
The registered company address is: Gewerbestrasse 11, 6330 Cham, Switzerland

Foreword

Organizing the European Conference on Computer Vision (ECCV 2022) in Tel-Aviv during a global pandemic was no easy feat. The uncertainty level was extremely high, and decisions had to be postponed to the last minute. Still, we managed to plan things just in time for ECCV 2022 to be held in person. Participation in physical events is crucial to stimulating collaborations and nurturing the culture of the Computer Vision community.

There were many people who worked hard to ensure attendees enjoyed the best science at the 16th edition of ECCV. We are grateful to the Program Chairs Gabriel Brostow and Tal Hassner, who went above and beyond to ensure the ECCV reviewing process ran smoothly. The scientific program includes dozens of workshops and tutorials in addition to the main conference and we would like to thank Leonid Karlinsky and Tomer Michaeli for their hard work. Finally, special thanks to the web chairs Lorenzo Baraldi and Kosta Derpanis, who put in extra hours to transfer information fast and efficiently to the ECCV community.

We would like to express gratitude to our generous sponsors and the Industry Chairs, Dimosthenis Karatzas and Chen Sagiv, who oversaw industry relations and proposed new ways for academia-industry collaboration and technology transfer. It's great to see so much industrial interest in what we're doing!

Authors' draft versions of the papers appeared online with open access on both the Computer Vision Foundation (CVF) and the European Computer Vision Association (ECVA) websites as with previous ECCVs. Springer, the publisher of the proceedings, has arranged for archival publication. The final version of the papers is hosted by SpringerLink, with active references and supplementary materials. It benefits all potential readers that we offer both a free and citeable version for all researchers, as well as an authoritative, citeable version for SpringerLink readers. Our thanks go to Ronan Nugent from Springer, who helped us negotiate this agreement. Last but not least, we wish to thank Eric Mortensen, our publication chair, whose expertise made the process smooth.

October 2022

Rita Cucchiara
Jiří Matas
Amnon Shashua
Lihi Zelnik-Manor

Preface

Welcome to the proceedings of the European Conference on Computer Vision (ECCV 2022). This was a hybrid edition of ECCV as we made our way out of the COVID-19 pandemic. The conference received 5804 valid paper submissions, compared to 5150 submissions to ECCV 2020 (a 12.7% increase) and 2439 in ECCV 2018. 1645 submissions were accepted for publication (28%) and, of those, 157 (2.7% overall) as orals.

846 of the submissions were desk-rejected for various reasons. Many of them because they revealed author identity, thus violating the double-blind policy. This violation came in many forms: some had author names with the title, others added acknowledgments to specific grants, yet others had links to their github account where their name was visible. Tampering with the LaTeX template was another reason for automatic desk rejection.

ECCV 2022 used the traditional CMT system to manage the entire double-blind reviewing process. Authors did not know the names of the reviewers and vice versa. Each paper received at least 3 reviews (except 6 papers that received only 2 reviews), totalling more than 15,000 reviews.

Handling the review process at this scale was a significant challenge. To ensure that each submission received as fair and high-quality reviews as possible, we recruited more than 4719 reviewers (in the end, 4719 reviewers did at least one review). Similarly we recruited more than 276 area chairs (eventually, only 276 area chairs handled a batch of papers). The area chairs were selected based on their technical expertise and reputation, largely among people who served as area chairs in previous top computer vision and machine learning conferences (ECCV, ICCV, CVPR, NeurIPS, etc.).

Reviewers were similarly invited from previous conferences, and also from the pool of authors. We also encouraged experienced area chairs to suggest additional chairs and reviewers in the initial phase of recruiting. The median reviewer load was five papers per reviewer, while the average load was about four papers, because of the emergency reviewers. The area chair load was 35 papers, on average.

Conflicts of interest between authors, area chairs, and reviewers were handled largely automatically by the CMT platform, with some manual help from the Program Chairs. Reviewers were allowed to describe themselves as senior reviewer (load of 8 papers to review) or junior reviewers (load of 4 papers). Papers were matched to area chairs based on a subject-area affinity score computed in CMT and an affinity score computed by the Toronto Paper Matching System (TPMS). TPMS is based on the paper's full text. An area chair handling each submission would bid for preferred expert reviewers, and we balanced load and prevented conflicts.

The assignment of submissions to area chairs was relatively smooth, as was the assignment of submissions to reviewers. A small percentage of reviewers were not happy with their assignments in terms of subjects and self-reported expertise. This is an area for improvement, although it's interesting that many of these cases were reviewers hand-picked by AC's. We made a later round of reviewer recruiting, targeted at the list of authors of papers submitted to the conference, and had an excellent response which helped provide enough emergency reviewers. In the end, all but six papers received at least 3 reviews.

The challenges of the reviewing process are in line with past experiences at ECCV 2020. As the community grows, and the number of submissions increases, it becomes ever more challenging to recruit enough reviewers and ensure a high enough quality of reviews. Enlisting authors by default as reviewers might be one step to address this challenge.

Authors were given a week to rebut the initial reviews, and address reviewers' concerns. Each rebuttal was limited to a single pdf page with a fixed template.

The Area Chairs then led discussions with the reviewers on the merits of each submission. The goal was to reach consensus, but, ultimately, it was up to the Area Chair to make a decision. The decision was then discussed with a buddy Area Chair to make sure decisions were fair and informative. The entire process was conducted virtually with no in-person meetings taking place.

The Program Chairs were informed in cases where the Area Chairs overturned a decisive consensus reached by the reviewers, and pushed for the meta-reviews to contain details that explained the reasoning for such decisions. Obviously these were the most contentious cases, where reviewer inexperience was the most common reported factor.

Once the list of accepted papers was finalized and released, we went through the laborious process of plagiarism (including self-plagiarism) detection. A total of 4 accepted papers were rejected because of that.

Finally, we would like to thank our Technical Program Chair, Pavel Lifshits, who did tremendous work behind the scenes, and we thank the tireless CMT team.

October 2022

Gabriel Brostow
Giovanni Maria Farinella
Moustapha Cissé
Shai Avidan
Tal Hassner

Organization

General Chairs

Rita Cucchiara	University of Modena and Reggio Emilia, Italy
Jiří Matas	Czech Technical University in Prague, Czech Republic
Amnon Shashua	Hebrew University of Jerusalem, Israel
Lihi Zelnik-Manor	Technion – Israel Institute of Technology, Israel

Program Chairs

Shai Avidan	Tel-Aviv University, Israel
Gabriel Brostow	University College London, UK
Moustapha Cissé	Google AI, Ghana
Giovanni Maria Farinella	University of Catania, Italy
Tal Hassner	Facebook AI, USA

Program Technical Chair

Pavel Lifshits	Technion – Israel Institute of Technology, Israel

Workshops Chairs

Leonid Karlinsky	IBM Research, Israel
Tomer Michaeli	Technion – Israel Institute of Technology, Israel
Ko Nishino	Kyoto University, Japan

Tutorial Chairs

Thomas Pock	Graz University of Technology, Austria
Natalia Neverova	Facebook AI Research, UK

Demo Chair

Bohyung Han	Seoul National University, Korea

Social and Student Activities Chairs

Tatiana Tommasi   Italian Institute of Technology, Italy
Sagie Benaim   University of Copenhagen, Denmark

Diversity and Inclusion Chairs

Xi Yin   Facebook AI Research, USA
Bryan Russell   Adobe, USA

Communications Chairs

Lorenzo Baraldi   University of Modena and Reggio Emilia, Italy
Kosta Derpanis   York University & Samsung AI Centre Toronto,
                           Canada

Industrial Liaison Chairs

Dimosthenis Karatzas   Universitat Autònoma de Barcelona, Spain
Chen Sagiv   SagivTech, Israel

Finance Chair

Gerard Medioni   University of Southern California & Amazon,
                           USA

Publication Chair

Eric Mortensen   MiCROTEC, USA

Area Chairs

Lourdes Agapito   University College London, UK
Zeynep Akata   University of Tübingen, Germany
Naveed Akhtar   University of Western Australia, Australia
Karteek Alahari   Inria Grenoble Rhône-Alpes, France
Alexandre Alahi   École polytechnique fédérale de Lausanne,
                           Switzerland
Pablo Arbelaez   Universidad de Los Andes, Columbia
Antonis A. Argyros   University of Crete & Foundation for Research
                           and Technology-Hellas, Crete
Yuki M. Asano   University of Amsterdam, The Netherlands
Kalle Åström   Lund University, Sweden
Hadar Averbuch-Elor   Cornell University, USA

Matthijs Douze	Facebook AI Research, USA
Mohamed Elhoseiny	King Abdullah University of Science and Technology, Saudi Arabia
Sergio Escalera	University of Barcelona, Spain
Yi Fang	New York University, USA
Ryan Farrell	Brigham Young University, USA
Alireza Fathi	Google, USA
Christoph Feichtenhofer	Facebook AI Research, USA
Basura Fernando	Agency for Science, Technology and Research (A*STAR), Singapore
Vittorio Ferrari	Google Research, Switzerland
Andrew W. Fitzgibbon	Graphcore, UK
David J. Fleet	University of Toronto, Canada
David Forsyth	University of Illinois at Urbana-Champaign, USA
David Fouhey	University of Michigan, USA
Katerina Fragkiadaki	Carnegie Mellon University, USA
Friedrich Fraundorfer	Graz University of Technology, Austria
Oren Freifeld	Ben-Gurion University, Israel
Thomas Funkhouser	Google Research & Princeton University, USA
Yasutaka Furukawa	Simon Fraser University, Canada
Fabio Galasso	Sapienza University of Rome, Italy
Jürgen Gall	University of Bonn, Germany
Chuang Gan	Massachusetts Institute of Technology, USA
Zhe Gan	Microsoft, USA
Animesh Garg	University of Toronto, Vector Institute, Nvidia, Canada
Efstratios Gavves	University of Amsterdam, The Netherlands
Peter Gehler	Amazon, Germany
Theo Gevers	University of Amsterdam, The Netherlands
Bernard Ghanem	King Abdullah University of Science and Technology, Saudi Arabia
Ross B. Girshick	Facebook AI Research, USA
Georgia Gkioxari	Facebook AI Research, USA
Albert Gordo	Facebook, USA
Stephen Gould	Australian National University, Australia
Venu Madhav Govindu	Indian Institute of Science, India
Kristen Grauman	Facebook AI Research & UT Austin, USA
Abhinav Gupta	Carnegie Mellon University & Facebook AI Research, USA
Mohit Gupta	University of Wisconsin-Madison, USA
Hu Han	Institute of Computing Technology, Chinese Academy of Sciences, China

Bohyung Han	Seoul National University, Korea
Tian Han	Stevens Institute of Technology, USA
Emily Hand	University of Nevada, Reno, USA
Bharath Hariharan	Cornell University, USA
Ran He	Institute of Automation, Chinese Academy of Sciences, China
Otmar Hilliges	ETH Zurich, Switzerland
Adrian Hilton	University of Surrey, UK
Minh Hoai	Stony Brook University, USA
Yedid Hoshen	Hebrew University of Jerusalem, Israel
Timothy Hospedales	University of Edinburgh, UK
Gang Hua	Wormpex AI Research, USA
Di Huang	Beihang University, China
Jing Huang	Facebook, USA
Jia-Bin Huang	Facebook, USA
Nathan Jacobs	Washington University in St. Louis, USA
C. V. Jawahar	International Institute of Information Technology, Hyderabad, India
Herve Jegou	Facebook AI Research, France
Neel Joshi	Microsoft Research, USA
Armand Joulin	Facebook AI Research, France
Frederic Jurie	University of Caen Normandie, France
Fredrik Kahl	Chalmers University of Technology, Sweden
Yannis Kalantidis	NAVER LABS Europe, France
Evangelos Kalogerakis	University of Massachusetts, Amherst, USA
Sing Bing Kang	Zillow Group, USA
Yosi Keller	Bar Ilan University, Israel
Margret Keuper	University of Mannheim, Germany
Tae-Kyun Kim	Imperial College London, UK
Benjamin Kimia	Brown University, USA
Alexander Kirillov	Facebook AI Research, USA
Kris Kitani	Carnegie Mellon University, USA
Iasonas Kokkinos	Snap Inc. & University College London, UK
Vladlen Koltun	Apple, USA
Nikos Komodakis	University of Crete, Crete
Piotr Koniusz	Australian National University, Australia
Philipp Kraehenbuehl	University of Texas at Austin, USA
Dilip Krishnan	Google, USA
Ajay Kumar	Hong Kong Polytechnic University, Hong Kong, China
Junseok Kwon	Chung-Ang University, Korea
Jean-Francois Lalonde	Université Laval, Canada

Ivan Laptev   Inria Paris, France
Laura Leal-Taixé   Technical University of Munich, Germany
Erik Learned-Miller   University of Massachusetts, Amherst, USA
Gim Hee Lee   National University of Singapore, Singapore
Seungyong Lee   Pohang University of Science and Technology,
                                  Korea
Zhen Lei   Institute of Automation, Chinese Academy of
                                  Sciences, China
Bastian Leibe   RWTH Aachen University, Germany
Hongdong Li   Australian National University, Australia
Fuxin Li   Oregon State University, USA
Bo Li   University of Illinois at Urbana-Champaign, USA
Yin Li   University of Wisconsin-Madison, USA
Ser-Nam Lim   Meta AI Research, USA
Joseph Lim   University of Southern California, USA
Stephen Lin   Microsoft Research Asia, China
Dahua Lin   The Chinese University of Hong Kong,
                                  Hong Kong, China
Si Liu   Beihang University, China
Xiaoming Liu   Michigan State University, USA
Ce Liu   Microsoft, USA
Zicheng Liu   Microsoft, USA
Yanxi Liu   Pennsylvania State University, USA
Feng Liu   Portland State University, USA
Yebin Liu   Tsinghua University, China
Chen Change Loy   Nanyang Technological University, Singapore
Huchuan Lu   Dalian University of Technology, China
Cewu Lu   Shanghai Jiao Tong University, China
Oisin Mac Aodha   University of Edinburgh, UK
Dhruv Mahajan   Facebook, USA
Subhransu Maji   University of Massachusetts, Amherst, USA
Atsuto Maki   KTH Royal Institute of Technology, Sweden
Arun Mallya   NVIDIA, USA
R. Manmatha   Amazon, USA
Iacopo Masi   Sapienza University of Rome, Italy
Dimitris N. Metaxas   Rutgers University, USA
Ajmal Mian   University of Western Australia, Australia
Christian Micheloni   University of Udine, Italy
Krystian Mikolajczyk   Imperial College London, UK
Anurag Mittal   Indian Institute of Technology, Madras, India
Philippos Mordohai   Stevens Institute of Technology, USA
Greg Mori   Simon Fraser University & Borealis AI, Canada

Vittorio Murino	Istituto Italiano di Tecnologia, Italy
P. J. Narayanan	International Institute of Information Technology, Hyderabad, India
Ram Nevatia	University of Southern California, USA
Natalia Neverova	Facebook AI Research, UK
Richard Newcombe	Facebook, USA
Cuong V. Nguyen	Florida International University, USA
Bingbing Ni	Shanghai Jiao Tong University, China
Juan Carlos Niebles	Salesforce & Stanford University, USA
Ko Nishino	Kyoto University, Japan
Jean-Marc Odobez	Idiap Research Institute, École polytechnique fédérale de Lausanne, Switzerland
Francesca Odone	University of Genova, Italy
Takayuki Okatani	Tohoku University & RIKEN Center for Advanced Intelligence Project, Japan
Manohar Paluri	Facebook, USA
Guan Pang	Facebook, USA
Maja Pantic	Imperial College London, UK
Sylvain Paris	Adobe Research, USA
Jaesik Park	Pohang University of Science and Technology, Korea
Hyun Soo Park	The University of Minnesota, USA
Omkar M. Parkhi	Facebook, USA
Deepak Pathak	Carnegie Mellon University, USA
Georgios Pavlakos	University of California, Berkeley, USA
Marcello Pelillo	University of Venice, Italy
Marc Pollefeys	ETH Zurich & Microsoft, Switzerland
Jean Ponce	Inria, France
Gerard Pons-Moll	University of Tübingen, Germany
Fatih Porikli	Qualcomm, USA
Victor Adrian Prisacariu	University of Oxford, UK
Petia Radeva	University of Barcelona, Spain
Ravi Ramamoorthi	University of California, San Diego, USA
Deva Ramanan	Carnegie Mellon University, USA
Vignesh Ramanathan	Facebook, USA
Nalini Ratha	State University of New York at Buffalo, USA
Tammy Riklin Raviv	Ben-Gurion University, Israel
Tobias Ritschel	University College London, UK
Emanuele Rodola	Sapienza University of Rome, Italy
Amit K. Roy-Chowdhury	University of California, Riverside, USA
Michael Rubinstein	Google, USA
Olga Russakovsky	Princeton University, USA

Mathieu Salzmann	École polytechnique fédérale de Lausanne, Switzerland
Dimitris Samaras	Stony Brook University, USA
Aswin Sankaranarayanan	Carnegie Mellon University, USA
Imari Sato	National Institute of Informatics, Japan
Yoichi Sato	University of Tokyo, Japan
Shin'ichi Satoh	National Institute of Informatics, Japan
Walter Scheirer	University of Notre Dame, USA
Bernt Schiele	Max Planck Institute for Informatics, Germany
Konrad Schindler	ETH Zurich, Switzerland
Cordelia Schmid	Inria & Google, France
Alexander Schwing	University of Illinois at Urbana-Champaign, USA
Nicu Sebe	University of Trento, Italy
Greg Shakhnarovich	Toyota Technological Institute at Chicago, USA
Eli Shechtman	Adobe Research, USA
Humphrey Shi	University of Oregon & University of Illinois at Urbana-Champaign & Picsart AI Research, USA
Jianbo Shi	University of Pennsylvania, USA
Roy Shilkrot	Massachusetts Institute of Technology, USA
Mike Zheng Shou	National University of Singapore, Singapore
Kaleem Siddiqi	McGill University, Canada
Richa Singh	Indian Institute of Technology Jodhpur, India
Greg Slabaugh	Queen Mary University of London, UK
Cees Snoek	University of Amsterdam, The Netherlands
Yale Song	Facebook AI Research, USA
Yi-Zhe Song	University of Surrey, UK
Bjorn Stenger	Rakuten Institute of Technology
Abby Stylianou	Saint Louis University, USA
Akihiro Sugimoto	National Institute of Informatics, Japan
Chen Sun	Brown University, USA
Deqing Sun	Google, USA
Kalyan Sunkavalli	Adobe Research, USA
Ying Tai	Tencent YouTu Lab, China
Ayellet Tal	Technion – Israel Institute of Technology, Israel
Ping Tan	Simon Fraser University, Canada
Siyu Tang	ETH Zurich, Switzerland
Chi-Keung Tang	Hong Kong University of Science and Technology, Hong Kong, China
Radu Timofte	University of Würzburg, Germany & ETH Zurich, Switzerland
Federico Tombari	Google, Switzerland & Technical University of Munich, Germany

James Tompkin	Brown University, USA
Lorenzo Torresani	Dartmouth College, USA
Alexander Toshev	Apple, USA
Du Tran	Facebook AI Research, USA
Anh T. Tran	VinAI, Vietnam
Zhuowen Tu	University of California, San Diego, USA
Georgios Tzimiropoulos	Queen Mary University of London, UK
Jasper Uijlings	Google Research, Switzerland
Jan C. van Gemert	Delft University of Technology, The Netherlands
Gul Varol	Ecole des Ponts ParisTech, France
Nuno Vasconcelos	University of California, San Diego, USA
Mayank Vatsa	Indian Institute of Technology Jodhpur, India
Ashok Veeraraghavan	Rice University, USA
Jakob Verbeek	Facebook AI Research, France
Carl Vondrick	Columbia University, USA
Ruiping Wang	Institute of Computing Technology, Chinese Academy of Sciences, China
Xinchao Wang	National University of Singapore, Singapore
Liwei Wang	The Chinese University of Hong Kong, Hong Kong, China
Chaohui Wang	Université Paris-Est, France
Xiaolong Wang	University of California, San Diego, USA
Christian Wolf	NAVER LABS Europe, France
Tao Xiang	University of Surrey, UK
Saining Xie	Facebook AI Research, USA
Cihang Xie	University of California, Santa Cruz, USA
Zeki Yalniz	Facebook, USA
Ming-Hsuan Yang	University of California, Merced, USA
Angela Yao	National University of Singapore, Singapore
Shaodi You	University of Amsterdam, The Netherlands
Stella X. Yu	University of California, Berkeley, USA
Junsong Yuan	State University of New York at Buffalo, USA
Stefanos Zafeiriou	Imperial College London, UK
Amir Zamir	École polytechnique fédérale de Lausanne, Switzerland
Lei Zhang	Alibaba & Hong Kong Polytechnic University, Hong Kong, China
Lei Zhang	International Digital Economy Academy (IDEA), China
Pengchuan Zhang	Meta AI, USA
Bolei Zhou	University of California, Los Angeles, USA
Yuke Zhu	University of Texas at Austin, USA

Todd Zickler   Harvard University, USA
Wangmeng Zuo   Harbin Institute of Technology, China

Technical Program Committee

Davide Abati
Soroush Abbasi
  Koohpayegani
Amos L. Abbott
Rameen Abdal
Rabab Abdelfattah
Sahar Abdelnabi
Hassan Abu Alhaija
Abulikemu Abuduweili
Ron Abutbul
Hanno Ackermann
Aikaterini Adam
Kamil Adamczewski
Ehsan Adeli
Vida Adeli
Donald Adjeroh
Arman Afrasiyabi
Akshay Agarwal
Sameer Agarwal
Abhinav Agarwalla
Vaibhav Aggarwal
Sara Aghajanzadeh
Susmit Agrawal
Antonio Agudo
Touqeer Ahmad
Sk Miraj Ahmed
Chaitanya Ahuja
Nilesh A. Ahuja
Abhishek Aich
Shubhra Aich
Noam Aigerman
Arash Akbarinia
Peri Akiva
Derya Akkaynak
Emre Aksan
Arjun R. Akula
Yuval Alaluf
Stephan Alaniz
Paul Albert
Cenek Albl

Filippo Aleotti
Konstantinos P.
  Alexandridis
Motasem Alfarra
Mohsen Ali
Thiemo Alldieck
Hadi Alzayer
Liang An
Shan An
Yi An
Zhulin An
Dongsheng An
Jie An
Xiang An
Saket Anand
Cosmin Ancuti
Juan Andrade-Cetto
Alexander Andreopoulos
Bjoern Andres
Jerone T. A. Andrews
Shivangi Aneja
Anelia Angelova
Dragomir Anguelov
Rushil Anirudh
Oron Anschel
Rao Muhammad Anwer
Djamila Aouada
Evlampios Apostolidis
Srikar Appalaraju
Nikita Araslanov
Andre Araujo
Eric Arazo
Dawit Mureja Argaw
Anurag Arnab
Aditya Arora
Chetan Arora
Sunpreet S. Arora
Alexey Artemov
Muhammad Asad
Kumar Ashutosh

Sinem Aslan
Vishal Asnani
Mahmoud Assran
Amir Atapour-Abarghouei
Nikos Athanasiou
Ali Athar
ShahRukh Athar
Sara Atito
Souhaib Attaiki
Matan Atzmon
Mathieu Aubry
Nicolas Audebert
Tristan T.
  Aumentado-Armstrong
Melinos Averkiou
Yannis Avrithis
Stephane Ayache
Mehmet Aygün
Seyed Mehdi
  Ayyoubzadeh
Hossein Azizpour
George Azzopardi
Mallikarjun B. R.
Yunhao Ba
Abhishek Badki
Seung-Hwan Bae
Seung-Hwan Baek
Seungryul Baek
Piyush Nitin Bagad
Shai Bagon
Gaetan Bahl
Shikhar Bahl
Sherwin Bahmani
Haoran Bai
Lei Bai
Jiawang Bai
Haoyue Bai
Jinbin Bai
Xiang Bai
Xuyang Bai

Yang Bai
Yuanchao Bai
Ziqian Bai
Sungyong Baik
Kevin Bailly
Max Bain
Federico Baldassarre
Wele Gedara Chaminda
  Bandara
Biplab Banerjee
Pratyay Banerjee
Sandipan Banerjee
Jihwan Bang
Antyanta Bangunharcana
Aayush Bansal
Ankan Bansal
Siddhant Bansal
Wentao Bao
Zhipeng Bao
Amir Bar
Manel Baradad Jurjo
Lorenzo Baraldi
Danny Barash
Daniel Barath
Connelly Barnes
Ioan Andrei Bârsan
Steven Basart
Dina Bashkirova
Chaim Baskin
Peyman Bateni
Anil Batra
Sebastiano Battiato
Ardhendu Behera
Harkirat Behl
Jens Behley
Vasileios Belagiannis
Boulbaba Ben Amor
Emanuel Ben Baruch
Abdessamad Ben Hamza
Gil Ben-Artzi
Assia Benbihi
Fabian Benitez-Quiroz
Guy Ben-Yosef
Philipp Benz
Alexander W. Bergman

Urs Bergmann
Jesus Bermudez-Cameo
Stefano Berretti
Gedas Bertasius
Zachary Bessinger
Petra Bevandić
Matthew Beveridge
Lucas Beyer
Yash Bhalgat
Suvaansh Bhambri
Samarth Bharadwaj
Gaurav Bharaj
Aparna Bharati
Bharat Lal Bhatnagar
Uttaran Bhattacharya
Apratim Bhattacharyya
Brojeshwar Bhowmick
Ankan Kumar Bhunia
Ayan Kumar Bhunia
Qi Bi
Sai Bi
Michael Bi Mi
Gui-Bin Bian
Jia-Wang Bian
Shaojun Bian
Pia Bideau
Mario Bijelic
Hakan Bilen
Guillaume-Alexandre
  Bilodeau
Alexander Binder
Tolga Birdal
Vighnesh N. Birodkar
Sandika Biswas
Andreas Blattmann
Janusz Bobulski
Giuseppe Boccignone
Vishnu Boddeti
Navaneeth Bodla
Moritz Böhle
Aleksei Bokhovkin
Sam Bond-Taylor
Vivek Boominathan
Shubhankar Borse
Mark Boss

Andrea Bottino
Adnane Boukhayma
Fadi Boutros
Nicolas C. Boutry
Richard S. Bowen
Ivaylo Boyadzhiev
Aidan Boyd
Yuri Boykov
Aljaz Bozic
Behzad Bozorgtabar
Eric Brachmann
Samarth Brahmbhatt
Gustav Bredell
Francois Bremond
Joel Brogan
Andrew Brown
Thomas Brox
Marcus A. Brubaker
Robert-Jan Bruintjes
Yuqi Bu
Anders G. Buch
Himanshu Buckchash
Mateusz Buda
Ignas Budvytis
José M. Buenaposada
Marcel C. Bühler
Tu Bui
Adrian Bulat
Hannah Bull
Evgeny Burnaev
Andrei Bursuc
Benjamin Busam
Sergey N. Buzykanov
Wonmin Byeon
Fabian Caba
Martin Cadik
Guanyu Cai
Minjie Cai
Qing Cai
Zhongang Cai
Qi Cai
Yancheng Cai
Shen Cai
Han Cai
Jiarui Cai

Bowen Cai
Mu Cai
Qin Cai
Ruojin Cai
Weidong Cai
Weiwei Cai
Yi Cai
Yujun Cai
Zhiping Cai
Akin Caliskan
Lilian Calvet
Baris Can Cam
Necati Cihan Camgoz
Tommaso Campari
Dylan Campbell
Ziang Cao
Ang Cao
Xu Cao
Zhiwen Cao
Shengcao Cao
Song Cao
Weipeng Cao
Xiangyong Cao
Xiaochun Cao
Yue Cao
Yunhao Cao
Zhangjie Cao
Jiale Cao
Yang Cao
Jiajiong Cao
Jie Cao
Jinkun Cao
Lele Cao
Yulong Cao
Zhiguo Cao
Chen Cao
Razvan Caramalau
Marlène Careil
Gustavo Carneiro
Joao Carreira
Dan Casas
Paola Cascante-Bonilla
Angela Castillo
Francisco M. Castro
Pedro Castro

Luca Cavalli
George J. Cazenavette
Oya Celiktutan
Hakan Cevikalp
Sri Harsha C. H.
Sungmin Cha
Geonho Cha
Menglei Chai
Lucy Chai
Yuning Chai
Zenghao Chai
Anirban Chakraborty
Deep Chakraborty
Rudrasis Chakraborty
Souradeep Chakraborty
Kelvin C. K. Chan
Chee Seng Chan
Paramanand Chandramouli
Arjun Chandrasekaran
Kenneth Chaney
Dongliang Chang
Huiwen Chang
Peng Chang
Xiaojun Chang
Jia-Ren Chang
Hyung Jin Chang
Hyun Sung Chang
Ju Yong Chang
Li-Jen Chang
Qi Chang
Wei-Yi Chang
Yi Chang
Nadine Chang
Hanqing Chao
Pradyumna Chari
Dibyadip Chatterjee
Chiranjoy Chattopadhyay
Siddhartha Chaudhuri
Zhengping Che
Gal Chechik
Lianggangxu Chen
Qi Alfred Chen
Brian Chen
Bor-Chun Chen
Bo-Hao Chen

Bohong Chen
Bin Chen
Ziliang Chen
Cheng Chen
Chen Chen
Chaofeng Chen
Xi Chen
Haoyu Chen
Xuanhong Chen
Wei Chen
Qiang Chen
Shi Chen
Xianyu Chen
Chang Chen
Changhuai Chen
Hao Chen
Jie Chen
Jianbo Chen
Jingjing Chen
Jun Chen
Kejiang Chen
Mingcai Chen
Nenglun Chen
Qifeng Chen
Ruoyu Chen
Shu-Yu Chen
Weidong Chen
Weijie Chen
Weikai Chen
Xiang Chen
Xiuyi Chen
Xingyu Chen
Yaofo Chen
Yueting Chen
Yu Chen
Yunjin Chen
Yuntao Chen
Yun Chen
Zhenfang Chen
Zhuangzhuang Chen
Chu-Song Chen
Xiangyu Chen
Zhuo Chen
Chaoqi Chen
Shizhe Chen

Xiaotong Chen
Xiaozhi Chen
Dian Chen
Defang Chen
Dingfan Chen
Ding-Jie Chen
Ee Heng Chen
Tao Chen
Yixin Chen
Wei-Ting Chen
Lin Chen
Guang Chen
Guangyi Chen
Guanying Chen
Guangyao Chen
Hwann-Tzong Chen
Junwen Chen
Jiacheng Chen
Jianxu Chen
Hui Chen
Kai Chen
Kan Chen
Kevin Chen
Kuan-Wen Chen
Weihua Chen
Zhang Chen
Liang-Chieh Chen
Lele Chen
Liang Chen
Fanglin Chen
Zehui Chen
Minghui Chen
Minghao Chen
Xiaokang Chen
Qian Chen
Jun-Cheng Chen
Qi Chen
Qingcai Chen
Richard J. Chen
Runnan Chen
Rui Chen
Shuo Chen
Sentao Chen
Shaoyu Chen
Shixing Chen

Shuai Chen
Shuya Chen
Sizhe Chen
Simin Chen
Shaoxiang Chen
Zitian Chen
Tianlong Chen
Tianshui Chen
Min-Hung Chen
Xiangning Chen
Xin Chen
Xinghao Chen
Xuejin Chen
Xu Chen
Xuxi Chen
Yunlu Chen
Yanbei Chen
Yuxiao Chen
Yun-Chun Chen
Yi-Ting Chen
Yi-Wen Chen
Yinbo Chen
Yiran Chen
Yuanhong Chen
Yubei Chen
Yuefeng Chen
Yuhua Chen
Yukang Chen
Zerui Chen
Zhaoyu Chen
Zhen Chen
Zhenyu Chen
Zhi Chen
Zhiwei Chen
Zhixiang Chen
Long Chen
Bowen Cheng
Jun Cheng
Yi Cheng
Jingchun Cheng
Lechao Cheng
Xi Cheng
Yuan Cheng
Ho Kei Cheng
Kevin Ho Man Cheng

Jiacheng Cheng
Kelvin B. Cheng
Li Cheng
Mengjun Cheng
Zhen Cheng
Qingrong Cheng
Tianheng Cheng
Harry Cheng
Yihua Cheng
Yu Cheng
Ziheng Cheng
Soon Yau Cheong
Anoop Cherian
Manuela Chessa
Zhixiang Chi
Naoki Chiba
Julian Chibane
Kashyap Chitta
Tai-Yin Chiu
Hsu-kuang Chiu
Wei-Chen Chiu
Sungmin Cho
Donghyeon Cho
Hyeon Cho
Yooshin Cho
Gyusang Cho
Jang Hyun Cho
Seungju Cho
Nam Ik Cho
Sunghyun Cho
Hanbyel Cho
Jaesung Choe
Jooyoung Choi
Chiho Choi
Changwoon Choi
Jongwon Choi
Myungsub Choi
Dooseop Choi
Jonghyun Choi
Jinwoo Choi
Jun Won Choi
Min-Kook Choi
Hongsuk Choi
Janghoon Choi
Yoon-Ho Choi

Yukyung Choi
Jaegul Choo
Ayush Chopra
Siddharth Choudhary
Subhabrata Choudhury
Vasileios Choutas
Ka-Ho Chow
Pinaki Nath Chowdhury
Sammy Christen
Anders Christensen
Grigorios Chrysos
Hang Chu
Wen-Hsuan Chu
Peng Chu
Qi Chu
Ruihang Chu
Wei-Ta Chu
Yung-Yu Chuang
Sanghyuk Chun
Se Young Chun
Antonio Cinà
Ramazan Gokberk Cinbis
Javier Civera
Albert Clapés
Ronald Clark
Brian S. Clipp
Felipe Codevilla
Daniel Coelho de Castro
Niv Cohen
Forrester Cole
Maxwell D. Collins
Robert T. Collins
Marc Comino Trinidad
Runmin Cong
Wenyan Cong
Maxime Cordy
Marcella Cornia
Enric Corona
Huseyin Coskun
Luca Cosmo
Dragos Costea
Davide Cozzolino
Arun C. S. Kumar
Aiyu Cui
Qiongjie Cui

Quan Cui
Shuhao Cui
Yiming Cui
Ying Cui
Zijun Cui
Jiali Cui
Jiequan Cui
Yawen Cui
Zhen Cui
Zhaopeng Cui
Jack Culpepper
Xiaodong Cun
Ross Cutler
Adam Czajka
Ali Dabouei
Konstantinos M. Dafnis
Manuel Dahnert
Tao Dai
Yuchao Dai
Bo Dai
Mengyu Dai
Hang Dai
Haixing Dai
Peng Dai
Pingyang Dai
Qi Dai
Qiyu Dai
Yutong Dai
Naser Damer
Zhiyuan Dang
Mohamed Daoudi
Ayan Das
Abir Das
Debasmit Das
Deepayan Das
Partha Das
Sagnik Das
Soumi Das
Srijan Das
Swagatam Das
Avijit Dasgupta
Jim Davis
Adrian K. Davison
Homa Davoudi
Laura Daza

Matthias De Lange
Shalini De Mello
Marco De Nadai
Christophe De
    Vleeschouwer
Alp Dener
Boyang Deng
Congyue Deng
Bailin Deng
Yong Deng
Ye Deng
Zhuo Deng
Zhijie Deng
Xiaoming Deng
Jiankang Deng
Jinhong Deng
Jingjing Deng
Liang-Jian Deng
Siqi Deng
Xiang Deng
Xueqing Deng
Zhongying Deng
Karan Desai
Jean-Emmanuel Deschaud
Aniket Anand Deshmukh
Neel Dey
Helisa Dhamo
Prithviraj Dhar
Amaya Dharmasiri
Yan Di
Xing Di
Ousmane A. Dia
Haiwen Diao
Xiaolei Diao
Gonçalo José Dias Pais
Abdallah Dib
Anastasios Dimou
Changxing Ding
Henghui Ding
Guodong Ding
Yaqing Ding
Shuangrui Ding
Yuhang Ding
Yikang Ding
Shouhong Ding

Haisong Ding
Hui Ding
Jiahao Ding
Jian Ding
Jian-Jiun Ding
Shuxiao Ding
Tianyu Ding
Wenhao Ding
Yuqi Ding
Yi Ding
Yuzhen Ding
Zhengming Ding
Tan Minh Dinh
Vu Dinh
Christos Diou
Mandar Dixit
Bao Gia Doan
Khoa D. Doan
Dzung Anh Doan
Debi Prosad Dogra
Nehal Doiphode
Chengdong Dong
Bowen Dong
Zhenxing Dong
Hang Dong
Xiaoyi Dong
Haoye Dong
Jiangxin Dong
Shichao Dong
Xuan Dong
Zhen Dong
Shuting Dong
Jing Dong
Li Dong
Ming Dong
Nanqing Dong
Qiulei Dong
Runpei Dong
Siyan Dong
Tian Dong
Wei Dong
Xiaomeng Dong
Xin Dong
Xingbo Dong
Yuan Dong

Samuel Dooley
Gianfranco Doretto
Michael Dorkenwald
Keval Doshi
Zhaopeng Dou
Xiaotian Dou
Hazel Doughty
Ahmad Droby
Iddo Drori
Jie Du
Yong Du
Dawei Du
Dong Du
Ruoyi Du
Yuntao Du
Xuefeng Du
Yilun Du
Yuming Du
Radhika Dua
Haodong Duan
Jiafei Duan
Kaiwen Duan
Peiqi Duan
Ye Duan
Haoran Duan
Jiali Duan
Amanda Duarte
Abhimanyu Dubey
Shiv Ram Dubey
Florian Dubost
Lukasz Dudziak
Shivam Duggal
Justin M. Dulay
Matteo Dunnhofer
Chi Nhan Duong
Thibaut Durand
Mihai Dusmanu
Ujjal Kr Dutta
Debidatta Dwibedi
Isht Dwivedi
Sai Kumar Dwivedi
Takeharu Eda
Mark Edmonds
Alexei A. Efros
Thibaud Ehret

Max Ehrlich
Mahsa Ehsanpour
Iván Eichhardt
Farshad Einabadi
Marvin Eisenberger
Hazim Kemal Ekenel
Mohamed El Banani
Ismail Elezi
Moshe Eliasof
Alaa El-Nouby
Ian Endres
Francis Engelmann
Deniz Engin
Chanho Eom
Dave Epstein
Maria C. Escobar
Victor A. Escorcia
Carlos Esteves
Sungmin Eum
Bernard J. E. Evans
Ivan Evtimov
Fevziye Irem Eyiokur
  Yaman
Matteo Fabbri
Sébastien Fabbro
Gabriele Facciolo
Masud Fahim
Bin Fan
Hehe Fan
Deng-Ping Fan
Aoxiang Fan
Chen-Chen Fan
Qi Fan
Zhaoxin Fan
Haoqi Fan
Heng Fan
Hongyi Fan
Linxi Fan
Baojie Fan
Jiayuan Fan
Lei Fan
Quanfu Fan
Yonghui Fan
Yingruo Fan
Zhiwen Fan

Zicong Fan
Sean Fanello
Jiansheng Fang
Chaowei Fang
Yuming Fang
Jianwu Fang
Jin Fang
Qi Fang
Shancheng Fang
Tian Fang
Xianyong Fang
Gongfan Fang
Zhen Fang
Hui Fang
Jiemin Fang
Le Fang
Pengfei Fang
Xiaolin Fang
Yuxin Fang
Zhaoyuan Fang
Ammarah Farooq
Azade Farshad
Zhengcong Fei
Michael Felsberg
Wei Feng
Chen Feng
Fan Feng
Andrew Feng
Xin Feng
Zheyun Feng
Ruicheng Feng
Mingtao Feng
Qianyu Feng
Shangbin Feng
Chun-Mei Feng
Zunlei Feng
Zhiyong Feng
Martin Fergie
Mustansar Fiaz
Marco Fiorucci
Michael Firman
Hamed Firooz
Volker Fischer
Corneliu O. Florea
Georgios Floros

Wolfgang Foerstner
Gianni Franchi
Jean-Sebastien Franco
Simone Frintrop
Anna Fruehstueck
Changhong Fu
Chaoyou Fu
Cheng-Yang Fu
Chi-Wing Fu
Deqing Fu
Huan Fu
Jun Fu
Kexue Fu
Ying Fu
Jianlong Fu
Jingjing Fu
Qichen Fu
Tsu-Jui Fu
Xueyang Fu
Yang Fu
Yanwei Fu
Yonggan Fu
Wolfgang Fuhl
Yasuhisa Fujii
Kent Fujiwara
Marco Fumero
Takuya Funatomi
Isabel Funke
Dario Fuoli
Antonino Furnari
Matheus A. Gadelha
Akshay Gadi Patil
Adrian Galdran
Guillermo Gallego
Silvano Galliani
Orazio Gallo
Leonardo Galteri
Matteo Gamba
Yiming Gan
Sujoy Ganguly
Harald Ganster
Boyan Gao
Changxin Gao
Daiheng Gao
Difei Gao

Chen Gao
Fei Gao
Lin Gao
Wei Gao
Yiming Gao
Junyu Gao
Guangyu Ryan Gao
Haichang Gao
Hongchang Gao
Jialin Gao
Jin Gao
Jun Gao
Katelyn Gao
Mingchen Gao
Mingfei Gao
Pan Gao
Shangqian Gao
Shanghua Gao
Xitong Gao
Yunhe Gao
Zhanning Gao
Elena Garces
Nuno Cruz Garcia
Noa Garcia
Guillermo
    Garcia-Hernando
Isha Garg
Rahul Garg
Sourav Garg
Quentin Garrido
Stefano Gasperini
Kent Gauen
Chandan Gautam
Shivam Gautam
Paul Gay
Chunjiang Ge
Shiming Ge
Wenhang Ge
Yanhao Ge
Zheng Ge
Songwei Ge
Weifeng Ge
Yixiao Ge
Yuying Ge
Shijie Geng

Zhengyang Geng
Kyle A. Genova
Georgios Georgakis
Markos Georgopoulos
Marcel Geppert
Shabnam Ghadar
Mina Ghadimi Atigh
Deepti Ghadiyaram
Maani Ghaffari Jadidi
Sedigh Ghamari
Zahra Gharaee
Michaël Gharbi
Golnaz Ghiasi
Reza Ghoddoosian
Soumya Suvra Ghosal
Adhiraj Ghosh
Arthita Ghosh
Pallabi Ghosh
Soumyadeep Ghosh
Andrew Gilbert
Igor Gilitschenski
Jhony H. Giraldo
Andreu Girbau Xalabarder
Rohit Girdhar
Sharath Girish
Xavier Giro-i-Nieto
Raja Giryes
Thomas Gittings
Nikolaos Gkanatsios
Ioannis Gkioulekas
Abhiram
    Gnanasambandam
Aurele T. Gnanha
Clement L. J. C. Godard
Arushi Goel
Vidit Goel
Shubham Goel
Zan Gojcic
Aaron K. Gokaslan
Tejas Gokhale
S. Alireza Golestaneh
Thiago L. Gomes
Nuno Goncalves
Boqing Gong
Chen Gong

Yuanhao Gong
Guoqiang Gong
Jingyu Gong
Rui Gong
Yu Gong
Mingming Gong
Neil Zhenqiang Gong
Xun Gong
Yunye Gong
Yihong Gong
Cristina I. González
Nithin Gopalakrishnan
    Nair
Gaurav Goswami
Jianping Gou
Shreyank N. Gowda
Ankit Goyal
Helmut Grabner
Patrick L. Grady
Ben Graham
Eric Granger
Douglas R. Gray
Matej Grcić
David Griffiths
Jinjin Gu
Yun Gu
Shuyang Gu
Jianyang Gu
Fuqiang Gu
Jiatao Gu
Jindong Gu
Jiaqi Gu
Jinwei Gu
Jiaxin Gu
Geonmo Gu
Xiao Gu
Xinqian Gu
Xiuye Gu
Yuming Gu
Zhangxuan Gu
Dayan Guan
Junfeng Guan
Qingji Guan
Tianrui Guan
Shanyan Guan

Denis A. Gudovskiy
Ricardo Guerrero
Pierre-Louis Guhur
Jie Gui
Liangyan Gui
Liangke Gui
Benoit Guillard
Erhan Gundogdu
Manuel Günther
Jingcai Guo
Yuanfang Guo
Junfeng Guo
Chenqi Guo
Dan Guo
Hongji Guo
Jia Guo
Jie Guo
Minghao Guo
Shi Guo
Yanhui Guo
Yangyang Guo
Yuan-Chen Guo
Yilu Guo
Yiluan Guo
Yong Guo
Guangyu Guo
Haiyun Guo
Jinyang Guo
Jianyuan Guo
Pengsheng Guo
Pengfei Guo
Shuxuan Guo
Song Guo
Tianyu Guo
Qing Guo
Qiushan Guo
Wen Guo
Xiefan Guo
Xiaohu Guo
Xiaoqing Guo
Yufei Guo
Yuhui Guo
Yuliang Guo
Yunhui Guo
Yanwen Guo

Akshita Gupta
Ankush Gupta
Kamal Gupta
Kartik Gupta
Ritwik Gupta
Rohit Gupta
Siddharth Gururani
Fredrik K. Gustafsson
Abner Guzman Rivera
Vladimir Guzov
Matthew A. Gwilliam
Jung-Woo Ha
Marc Habermann
Isma Hadji
Christian Haene
Martin Hahner
Levente Hajder
Alexandros Haliassos
Emanuela Haller
Bumsub Ham
Abdullah J. Hamdi
Shreyas Hampali
Dongyoon Han
Chunrui Han
Dong-Jun Han
Dong-Sig Han
Guangxing Han
Zhizhong Han
Ruize Han
Jiaming Han
Jin Han
Ligong Han
Xian-Hua Han
Xiaoguang Han
Yizeng Han
Zhi Han
Zhenjun Han
Zhongyi Han
Jungong Han
Junlin Han
Kai Han
Kun Han
Sungwon Han
Songfang Han
Wei Han

Xiao Han
Xintong Han
Xinzhe Han
Yahong Han
Yan Han
Zongbo Han
Nicolai Hani
Rana Hanocka
Niklas Hanselmann
Nicklas A. Hansen
Hong Hanyu
Fusheng Hao
Yanbin Hao
Shijie Hao
Udith Haputhanthri
Mehrtash Harandi
Josh Harguess
Adam Harley
David M. Hart
Atsushi Hashimoto
Ali Hassani
Mohammed Hassanin
Yana Hasson
Joakim Bruslund Haurum
Bo He
Kun He
Chen He
Xin He
Fazhi He
Gaoqi He
Hao He
Haoyu He
Jiangpeng He
Hongliang He
Qian He
Xiangteng He
Xuming He
Yannan He
Yuhang He
Yang He
Xiangyu He
Nanjun He
Pan He
Sen He
Shengfeng He

Songtao He
Tao He
Tong He
Wei He
Xuehai He
Xiaoxiao He
Ying He
Yisheng He
Ziwen He
Peter Hedman
Felix Heide
Yacov Hel-Or
Paul Henderson
Philipp Henzler
Byeongho Heo
Jae-Pil Heo
Miran Heo
Sachini A. Herath
Stephane Herbin
Pedro Hermosilla Casajus
Monica Hernandez
Charles Herrmann
Roei Herzig
Mauricio Hess-Flores
Carlos Hinojosa
Tobias Hinz
Tsubasa Hirakawa
Chih-Hui Ho
Lam Si Tung Ho
Jennifer Hobbs
Derek Hoiem
Yannick Hold-Geoffroy
Aleksander Holynski
Cheeun Hong
Fa-Ting Hong
Hanbin Hong
Guan Zhe Hong
Danfeng Hong
Lanqing Hong
Xiaopeng Hong
Xin Hong
Jie Hong
Seungbum Hong
Cheng-Yao Hong
Seunghoon Hong

Yi Hong
Yuan Hong
Yuchen Hong
Anthony Hoogs
Maxwell C. Horton
Kazuhiro Hotta
Qibin Hou
Tingbo Hou
Junhui Hou
Ji Hou
Qiqi Hou
Rui Hou
Ruibing Hou
Zhi Hou
Henry Howard-Jenkins
Lukas Hoyer
Wei-Lin Hsiao
Chiou-Ting Hsu
Anthony Hu
Brian Hu
Yusong Hu
Hexiang Hu
Haoji Hu
Di Hu
Hengtong Hu
Haigen Hu
Lianyu Hu
Hanzhe Hu
Jie Hu
Junlin Hu
Shizhe Hu
Jian Hu
Zhiming Hu
Juhua Hu
Peng Hu
Ping Hu
Ronghang Hu
MengShun Hu
Tao Hu
Vincent Tao Hu
Xiaoling Hu
Xinting Hu
Xiaolin Hu
Xuefeng Hu
Xiaowei Hu

Yang Hu
Yueyu Hu
Zeyu Hu
Zhongyun Hu
Binh-Son Hua
Guoliang Hua
Yi Hua
Linzhi Huang
Qiusheng Huang
Bo Huang
Chen Huang
Hsin-Ping Huang
Ye Huang
Shuangping Huang
Zeng Huang
Buzhen Huang
Cong Huang
Heng Huang
Hao Huang
Qidong Huang
Huaibo Huang
Chaoqin Huang
Feihu Huang
Jiahui Huang
Jingjia Huang
Kun Huang
Lei Huang
Sheng Huang
Shuaiyi Huang
Siyu Huang
Xiaoshui Huang
Xiaoyang Huang
Yan Huang
Yihao Huang
Ying Huang
Ziling Huang
Xiaoke Huang
Yifei Huang
Haiyang Huang
Zhewei Huang
Jin Huang
Haibin Huang
Jiaxing Huang
Junjie Huang
Keli Huang

Lang Huang
Lin Huang
Luojie Huang
Mingzhen Huang
Shijia Huang
Shengyu Huang
Siyuan Huang
He Huang
Xiuyu Huang
Lianghua Huang
Yue Huang
Yaping Huang
Yuge Huang
Zehao Huang
Zeyi Huang
Zhiqi Huang
Zhongzhan Huang
Zilong Huang
Ziyuan Huang
Tianrui Hui
Zhuo Hui
Le Hui
Jing Huo
Junhwa Hur
Shehzeen S. Hussain
Chuong Minh Huynh
Seunghyun Hwang
Jaehui Hwang
Jyh-Jing Hwang
Sukjun Hwang
Soonmin Hwang
Wonjun Hwang
Rakib Hyder
Sangeek Hyun
Sarah Ibrahimi
Tomoki Ichikawa
Yerlan Idelbayev
A. S. M. Iftekhar
Masaaki Iiyama
Satoshi Ikehata
Sunghoon Im
Atul N. Ingle
Eldar Insafutdinov
Yani A. Ioannou
Radu Tudor Ionescu

Umar Iqbal
Go Irie
Muhammad Zubair Irshad
Ahmet Iscen
Berivan Isik
Ashraful Islam
Md Amirul Islam
Syed Islam
Mariko Isogawa
Vamsi Krishna K. Ithapu
Boris Ivanovic
Darshan Iyer
Sarah Jabbour
Ayush Jain
Nishant Jain
Samyak Jain
Vidit Jain
Vineet Jain
Priyank Jaini
Tomas Jakab
Mohammad A. A. K.
   Jalwana
Muhammad Abdullah
   Jamal
Hadi Jamali-Rad
Stuart James
Varun Jampani
Young Kyun Jang
YeongJun Jang
Yunseok Jang
Ronnachai Jaroensri
Bhavan Jasani
Krishna Murthy
   Jatavallabhula
Mojan Javaheripi
Syed A. Javed
Guillaume Jeanneret
Pranav Jeevan
Herve Jegou
Rohit Jena
Tomas Jenicek
Porter Jenkins
Simon Jenni
Hae-Gon Jeon
Sangryul Jeon

Boseung Jeong
Yoonwoo Jeong
Seong-Gyun Jeong
Jisoo Jeong
Allan D. Jepson
Ankit Jha
Sumit K. Jha
I-Hong Jhuo
Ge-Peng Ji
Chaonan Ji
Deyi Ji
Jingwei Ji
Wei Ji
Zhong Ji
Jiayi Ji
Pengliang Ji
Hui Ji
Mingi Ji
Xiaopeng Ji
Yuzhu Ji
Baoxiong Jia
Songhao Jia
Dan Jia
Shan Jia
Xiaojun Jia
Xiuyi Jia
Xu Jia
Menglin Jia
Wenqi Jia
Boyuan Jiang
Wenhao Jiang
Huaizu Jiang
Hanwen Jiang
Haiyong Jiang
Hao Jiang
Huajie Jiang
Huiqin Jiang
Haojun Jiang
Haobo Jiang
Junjun Jiang
Xingyu Jiang
Yangbangyan Jiang
Yu Jiang
Jianmin Jiang
Jiaxi Jiang

Jing Jiang
Kui Jiang
Li Jiang
Liming Jiang
Chiyu Jiang
Meirui Jiang
Chen Jiang
Peng Jiang
Tai-Xiang Jiang
Wen Jiang
Xinyang Jiang
Yifan Jiang
Yuming Jiang
Yingying Jiang
Zeren Jiang
ZhengKai Jiang
Zhenyu Jiang
Shuming Jiao
Jianbo Jiao
Licheng Jiao
Dongkwon Jin
Yeying Jin
Cheng Jin
Linyi Jin
Qing Jin
Taisong Jin
Xiao Jin
Xin Jin
Sheng Jin
Kyong Hwan Jin
Ruibing Jin
SouYoung Jin
Yueming Jin
Chenchen Jing
Longlong Jing
Taotao Jing
Yongcheng Jing
Younghyun Jo
Joakim Johnander
Jeff Johnson
Michael J. Jones
R. Kenny Jones
Rico Jonschkowski
Ameya Joshi
Sunghun Joung

Felix Juefei-Xu
Claudio R. Jung
Steffen Jung
Hari Chandana K.
Rahul Vigneswaran K.
Prajwal K. R.
Abhishek Kadian
Jhony Kaesemodel Pontes
Kumara Kahatapitiya
Anmol Kalia
Sinan Kalkan
Tarun Kalluri
Jaewon Kam
Sandesh Kamath
Meina Kan
Menelaos Kanakis
Takuhiro Kaneko
Di Kang
Guoliang Kang
Hao Kang
Jaeyeon Kang
Kyoungkook Kang
Li-Wei Kang
MinGuk Kang
Suk-Ju Kang
Zhao Kang
Yash Mukund Kant
Yueying Kao
Aupendu Kar
Konstantinos Karantzalos
Sezer Karaoglu
Navid Kardan
Sanjay Kariyappa
Leonid Karlinsky
Animesh Karnewar
Shyamgopal Karthik
Hirak J. Kashyap
Marc A. Kastner
Hirokatsu Kataoka
Angelos Katharopoulos
Hiroharu Kato
Kai Katsumata
Manuel Kaufmann
Chaitanya Kaul
Prakhar Kaushik

Yuki Kawana
Lei Ke
Lipeng Ke
Tsung-Wei Ke
Wei Ke
Petr Kellnhofer
Aniruddha Kembhavi
John Kender
Corentin Kervadec
Leonid Keselman
Daniel Keysers
Nima Khademi Kalantari
Taras Khakhulin
Samir Khaki
Muhammad Haris Khan
Qadeer Khan
Salman Khan
Subash Khanal
Vaishnavi M. Khindkar
Rawal Khirodkar
Saeed Khorram
Pirazh Khorramshahi
Kourosh Khoshelham
Ansh Khurana
Benjamin Kiefer
Jae Myung Kim
Junho Kim
Boah Kim
Hyeonseong Kim
Dong-Jin Kim
Dongwan Kim
Donghyun Kim
Doyeon Kim
Yonghyun Kim
Hyung-Il Kim
Hyunwoo Kim
Hyeongwoo Kim
Hyo Jin Kim
Hyunwoo J. Kim
Taehoon Kim
Jaeha Kim
Jiwon Kim
Jung Uk Kim
Kangyeol Kim
Eunji Kim

Daeha Kim
Dongwon Kim
Kunhee Kim
Kyungmin Kim
Junsik Kim
Min H. Kim
Namil Kim
Kookhoi Kim
Sanghyun Kim
Seongyeop Kim
Seungryong Kim
Saehoon Kim
Euyoung Kim
Guisik Kim
Sungyeon Kim
Sunnie S. Y. Kim
Taehun Kim
Tae Oh Kim
Won Hwa Kim
Seungwook Kim
YoungBin Kim
Youngeun Kim
Akisato Kimura
Furkan Osman Kınlı
Zsolt Kira
Hedvig Kjellström
Florian Kleber
Jan P. Klopp
Florian Kluger
Laurent Kneip
Byungsoo Ko
Muhammed Kocabas
A. Sophia Koepke
Kevin Koeser
Nick Kolkin
Nikos Kolotouros
Wai-Kin Adams Kong
Deying Kong
Caihua Kong
Youyong Kong
Shuyu Kong
Shu Kong
Tao Kong
Yajing Kong
Yu Kong

Zishang Kong
Theodora Kontogianni
Anton S. Konushin
Julian F. P. Kooij
Bruno Korbar
Giorgos Kordopatis-Zilos
Jari Korhonen
Adam Kortylewski
Denis Korzhenkov
Divya Kothandaraman
Suraj Kothawade
Iuliia Kotseruba
Satwik Kottur
Shashank Kotyan
Alexandros Kouris
Petros Koutras
Anna Kreshuk
Ranjay Krishna
Dilip Krishnan
Andrey Kuehlkamp
Hilde Kuehne
Jason Kuen
David Kügler
Arjan Kuijper
Anna Kukleva
Sumith Kulal
Viveka Kulharia
Akshay R. Kulkarni
Nilesh Kulkarni
Dominik Kulon
Abhinav Kumar
Akash Kumar
Suryansh Kumar
B. V. K. Vijaya Kumar
Pulkit Kumar
Ratnesh Kumar
Sateesh Kumar
Satish Kumar
Vijay Kumar B. G.
Nupur Kumari
Sudhakar Kumawat
Jogendra Nath Kundu
Hsien-Kai Kuo
Meng-Yu Jennifer Kuo
Vinod Kumar Kurmi

Yusuke Kurose
Keerthy Kusumam
Alina Kuznetsova
Henry Kvinge
Ho Man Kwan
Hyeokjun Kweon
Heeseung Kwon
Gihyun Kwon
Myung-Joon Kwon
Taesung Kwon
YoungJoong Kwon
Christos Kyrkou
Jorma Laaksonen
Yann Labbe
Zorah Laehner
Florent Lafarge
Hamid Laga
Manuel Lagunas
Shenqi Lai
Jian-Huang Lai
Zihang Lai
Mohamed I. Lakhal
Mohit Lamba
Meng Lan
Loic Landrieu
Zhiqiang Lang
Natalie Lang
Dong Lao
Yizhen Lao
Yingjie Lao
Issam Hadj Laradji
Gustav Larsson
Viktor Larsson
Zakaria Laskar
Stéphane Lathuilière
Chun Pong Lau
Rynson W. H. Lau
Hei Law
Justin Lazarow
Verica Lazova
Eric-Tuan Le
Hieu Le
Trung-Nghia Le
Mathias Lechner
Byeong-Uk Lee

Chen-Yu Lee
Che-Rung Lee
Chul Lee
Hong Joo Lee
Dongsoo Lee
Jiyoung Lee
Eugene Eu Tzuan Lee
Daeun Lee
Saehyung Lee
Jewook Lee
Hyungtae Lee
Hyunmin Lee
Jungbeom Lee
Joon-Young Lee
Jong-Seok Lee
Joonseok Lee
Junha Lee
Kibok Lee
Byung-Kwan Lee
Jangwon Lee
Jinho Lee
Jongmin Lee
Seunghyun Lee
Sohyun Lee
Minsik Lee
Dogyoon Lee
Seungmin Lee
Min Jun Lee
Sangho Lee
Sangmin Lee
Seungeun Lee
Seon-Ho Lee
Sungmin Lee
Sungho Lee
Sangyoun Lee
Vincent C. S. S. Lee
Jaeseong Lee
Yong Jae Lee
Chenyang Lei
Chenyi Lei
Jiahui Lei
Xinyu Lei
Yinjie Lei
Jiaxu Leng
Luziwei Leng

Jan E. Lenssen
Vincent Lepetit
Thomas Leung
María Leyva-Vallina
Xin Li
Yikang Li
Baoxin Li
Bin Li
Bing Li
Bowen Li
Changlin Li
Chao Li
Chongyi Li
Guanyue Li
Shuai Li
Jin Li
Dingquan Li
Dongxu Li
Yiting Li
Gang Li
Dian Li
Guohao Li
Haoang Li
Haoliang Li
Haoran Li
Hengduo Li
Huafeng Li
Xiaoming Li
Hanao Li
Hongwei Li
Ziqiang Li
Jisheng Li
Jiacheng Li
Jia Li
Jiachen Li
Jiahao Li
Jianwei Li
Jiazhi Li
Jie Li
Jing Li
Jingjing Li
Jingtao Li
Jun Li
Junxuan Li
Kai Li

Kailin Li
Kenneth Li
Kun Li
Kunpeng Li
Aoxue Li
Chenglong Li
Chenglin Li
Changsheng Li
Zhichao Li
Qiang Li
Yanyu Li
Zuoyue Li
Xiang Li
Xuelong Li
Fangda Li
Ailin Li
Liang Li
Chun-Guang Li
Daiqing Li
Dong Li
Guanbin Li
Guorong Li
Haifeng Li
Jianan Li
Jianing Li
Jiaxin Li
Ke Li
Lei Li
Lincheng Li
Liulei Li
Lujun Li
Linjie Li
Lin Li
Pengyu Li
Ping Li
Qiufu Li
Qingyong Li
Rui Li
Siyuan Li
Wei Li
Wenbin Li
Xiangyang Li
Xinyu Li
Xiujun Li
Xiu Li

Xu Li
Ya-Li Li
Yao Li
Yongjie Li
Yijun Li
Yiming Li
Yuezun Li
Yu Li
Yunheng Li
Yuqi Li
Zhe Li
Zeming Li
Zhen Li
Zhengqin Li
Zhimin Li
Jiefeng Li
Jinpeng Li
Chengze Li
Jianwu Li
Lerenhan Li
Shan Li
Suichan Li
Xiangtai Li
Yanjie Li
Yandong Li
Zhuoling Li
Zhenqiang Li
Manyi Li
Maosen Li
Ji Li
Minjun Li
Mingrui Li
Mengtian Li
Junyi Li
Nianyi Li
Bo Li
Xiao Li
Peihua Li
Peike Li
Peizhao Li
Peiliang Li
Qi Li
Ren Li
Runze Li
Shile Li

Sheng Li
Shigang Li
Shiyu Li
Shuang Li
Shasha Li
Shichao Li
Tianye Li
Yuexiang Li
Wei-Hong Li
Wanhua Li
Weihao Li
Weiming Li
Weixin Li
Wenbo Li
Wenshuo Li
Weijian Li
Yunan Li
Xirong Li
Xianhang Li
Xiaoyu Li
Xueqian Li
Xuanlin Li
Xianzhi Li
Yunqiang Li
Yanjing Li
Yansheng Li
Yawei Li
Yi Li
Yong Li
Yong-Lu Li
Yuhang Li
Yu-Jhe Li
Yuxi Li
Yunsheng Li
Yanwei Li
Zechao Li
Zejian Li
Zeju Li
Zekun Li
Zhaowen Li
Zheng Li
Zhenyu Li
Zhiheng Li
Zhi Li
Zhong Li

Zhuowei Li
Zhuowan Li
Zhuohang Li
Zizhang Li
Chen Li
Yuan-Fang Li
Dongze Lian
Xiaochen Lian
Zhouhui Lian
Long Lian
Qing Lian
Jin Lianbao
Jinxiu S. Liang
Dingkang Liang
Jiahao Liang
Jianming Liang
Jingyun Liang
Kevin J. Liang
Kaizhao Liang
Chen Liang
Jie Liang
Senwei Liang
Ding Liang
Jiajun Liang
Jian Liang
Kongming Liang
Siyuan Liang
Yuanzhi Liang
Zhengfa Liang
Mingfu Liang
Xiaodan Liang
Xuefeng Liang
Yuxuan Liang
Kang Liao
Liang Liao
Hong-Yuan Mark Liao
Wentong Liao
Haofu Liao
Yue Liao
Minghui Liao
Shengcai Liao
Ting-Hsuan Liao
Xin Liao
Yinghong Liao
Teck Yian Lim

Che-Tsung Lin
Chung-Ching Lin
Chen-Hsuan Lin
Cheng Lin
Chuming Lin
Chunyu Lin
Dahua Lin
Wei Lin
Zheng Lin
Huaijia Lin
Jason Lin
Jierui Lin
Jiaying Lin
Jie Lin
Kai-En Lin
Kevin Lin
Guangfeng Lin
Jiehong Lin
Feng Lin
Hang Lin
Kwan-Yee Lin
Ke Lin
Luojun Lin
Qinghong Lin
Xiangbo Lin
Yi Lin
Zudi Lin
Shijie Lin
Yiqun Lin
Tzu-Heng Lin
Ming Lin
Shaohui Lin
SongNan Lin
Ji Lin
Tsung-Yu Lin
Xudong Lin
Yancong Lin
Yen-Chen Lin
Yiming Lin
Yuewei Lin
Zhiqiu Lin
Zinan Lin
Zhe Lin
David B. Lindell
Zhixin Ling

Zhan Ling
Alexander Liniger
Venice Erin B. Liong
Joey Litalien
Or Litany
Roee Litman
Ron Litman
Jim Little
Dor Litvak
Shaoteng Liu
Shuaicheng Liu
Andrew Liu
Xian Liu
Shaohui Liu
Bei Liu
Bo Liu
Yong Liu
Ming Liu
Yanbin Liu
Chenxi Liu
Daqi Liu
Di Liu
Difan Liu
Dong Liu
Dongfang Liu
Daizong Liu
Xiao Liu
Fangyi Liu
Fengbei Liu
Fenglin Liu
Bin Liu
Yuang Liu
Ao Liu
Hong Liu
Hongfu Liu
Huidong Liu
Ziyi Liu
Feng Liu
Hao Liu
Jie Liu
Jialun Liu
Jiang Liu
Jing Liu
Jingya Liu
Jiaming Liu

Jun Liu
Juncheng Liu
Jiawei Liu
Hongyu Liu
Chuanbin Liu
Haotian Liu
Lingqiao Liu
Chang Liu
Han Liu
Liu Liu
Min Liu
Yingqi Liu
Aishan Liu
Bingyu Liu
Benlin Liu
Boxiao Liu
Chenchen Liu
Chuanjian Liu
Daqing Liu
Huan Liu
Haozhe Liu
Jiaheng Liu
Wei Liu
Jingzhou Liu
Jiyuan Liu
Lingbo Liu
Nian Liu
Peiye Liu
Qiankun Liu
Shenglan Liu
Shilong Liu
Wen Liu
Wenyu Liu
Weifeng Liu
Wu Liu
Xiaolong Liu
Yang Liu
Yanwei Liu
Yingcheng Liu
Yongfei Liu
Yihao Liu
Yu Liu
Yunze Liu
Ze Liu
Zhenhua Liu

Zhenguang Liu
Lin Liu
Lihao Liu
Pengju Liu
Xinhai Liu
Yunfei Liu
Meng Liu
Minghua Liu
Mingyuan Liu
Miao Liu
Peirong Liu
Ping Liu
Qingjie Liu
Ruoshi Liu
Risheng Liu
Songtao Liu
Xing Liu
Shikun Liu
Shuming Liu
Sheng Liu
Songhua Liu
Tongliang Liu
Weibo Liu
Weide Liu
Weizhe Liu
Wenxi Liu
Weiyang Liu
Xin Liu
Xiaobin Liu
Xudong Liu
Xiaoyi Liu
Xihui Liu
Xinchen Liu
Xingtong Liu
Xinpeng Liu
Xinyu Liu
Xianpeng Liu
Xu Liu
Xingyu Liu
Yongtuo Liu
Yahui Liu
Yangxin Liu
Yaoyao Liu
Yaojie Liu
Yuliang Liu

Yongcheng Liu
Yuan Liu
Yufan Liu
Yu-Lun Liu
Yun Liu
Yunfan Liu
Yuanzhong Liu
Zhuoran Liu
Zhen Liu
Zheng Liu
Zhijian Liu
Zhisong Liu
Ziquan Liu
Ziyu Liu
Zhihua Liu
Zechun Liu
Zhaoyang Liu
Zhengzhe Liu
Stephan Liwicki
Shao-Yuan Lo
Sylvain Lobry
Suhas Lohit
Vishnu Suresh Lokhande
Vincenzo Lomonaco
Chengjiang Long
Guodong Long
Fuchen Long
Shangbang Long
Yang Long
Zijun Long
Vasco Lopes
Antonio M. Lopez
Roberto Javier
    Lopez-Sastre
Tobias Lorenz
Javier Lorenzo-Navarro
Yujing Lou
Qian Lou
Xiankai Lu
Changsheng Lu
Huimin Lu
Yongxi Lu
Hao Lu
Hong Lu
Jiasen Lu

Juwei Lu
Fan Lu
Guangming Lu
Jiwen Lu
Shun Lu
Tao Lu
Xiaonan Lu
Yang Lu
Yao Lu
Yongchun Lu
Zhiwu Lu
Cheng Lu
Liying Lu
Guo Lu
Xuequan Lu
Yanye Lu
Yantao Lu
Yuhang Lu
Fujun Luan
Jonathon Luiten
Jovita Lukasik
Alan Lukezic
Jonathan Samuel Lumentut
Mayank Lunayach
Ao Luo
Canjie Luo
Chong Luo
Xu Luo
Grace Luo
Jun Luo
Katie Z. Luo
Tao Luo
Cheng Luo
Fangzhou Luo
Gen Luo
Lei Luo
Sihui Luo
Weixin Luo
Yan Luo
Xiaoyan Luo
Yong Luo
Yadan Luo
Hao Luo
Ruotian Luo
Mi Luo

Tiange Luo
Wenjie Luo
Wenhan Luo
Xiao Luo
Zhiming Luo
Zhipeng Luo
Zhengyi Luo
Diogo C. Luvizon
Zhaoyang Lv
Gengyu Lyu
Lingjuan Lyu
Jun Lyu
Yuanyuan Lyu
Youwei Lyu
Yueming Lyu
Bingpeng Ma
Chao Ma
Chongyang Ma
Congbo Ma
Chih-Yao Ma
Fan Ma
Lin Ma
Haoyu Ma
Hengbo Ma
Jianqi Ma
Jiawei Ma
Jiayi Ma
Kede Ma
Kai Ma
Lingni Ma
Lei Ma
Xu Ma
Ning Ma
Benteng Ma
Cheng Ma
Andy J. Ma
Long Ma
Zhanyu Ma
Zhiheng Ma
Qianli Ma
Shiqiang Ma
Sizhuo Ma
Shiqing Ma
Xiaolong Ma
Xinzhu Ma

Gautam B. Machiraju
Spandan Madan
Mathew Magimai-Doss
Luca Magri
Behrooz Mahasseni
Upal Mahbub
Siddharth Mahendran
Paridhi Maheshwari
Rishabh Maheshwary
Mohammed Mahmoud
Shishira R. R. Maiya
Sylwia Majchrowska
Arjun Majumdar
Puspita Majumdar
Orchid Majumder
Sagnik Majumder
Ilya Makarov
Farkhod F.
   Makhmudkhujaev
Yasushi Makihara
Ankur Mali
Mateusz Malinowski
Utkarsh Mall
Srikanth Malla
Clement Mallet
Dimitrios Mallis
Yunze Man
Dipu Manandhar
Massimiliano Mancini
Murari Mandal
Raunak Manekar
Karttikeya Mangalam
Puneet Mangla
Fabian Manhardt
Sivabalan Manivasagam
Fahim Mannan
Chengzhi Mao
Hanzi Mao
Jiayuan Mao
Junhua Mao
Zhiyuan Mao
Jiageng Mao
Yunyao Mao
Zhendong Mao
Alberto Marchisio

Diego Marcos
Riccardo Marin
Aram Markosyan
Renaud Marlet
Ricardo Marques
Miquel Martí i Rabadán
Diego Martin Arroyo
Niki Martinel
Brais Martinez
Julieta Martinez
Marc Masana
Tomohiro Mashita
Timothée Masquelier
Minesh Mathew
Tetsu Matsukawa
Marwan Mattar
Bruce A. Maxwell
Christoph Mayer
Mantas Mazeika
Pratik Mazumder
Scott McCloskey
Steven McDonagh
Ishit Mehta
Jie Mei
Kangfu Mei
Jieru Mei
Xiaoguang Mei
Givi Meishvili
Luke Melas-Kyriazi
Iaroslav Melekhov
Andres Mendez-Vazquez
Heydi Mendez-Vazquez
Matias Mendieta
Ricardo A. Mendoza-León
Chenlin Meng
Depu Meng
Rang Meng
Zibo Meng
Qingjie Meng
Qier Meng
Yanda Meng
Zihang Meng
Thomas Mensink
Fabian Mentzer
Christopher Metzler

Gregory P. Meyer
Vasileios Mezaris
Liang Mi
Lu Mi
Bo Miao
Changtao Miao
Zichen Miao
Qiguang Miao
Xin Miao
Zhongqi Miao
Frank Michel
Simone Milani
Ben Mildenhall
Roy V. Miles
Juhong Min
Kyle Min
Hyun-Seok Min
Weiqing Min
Yuecong Min
Zhixiang Min
Qi Ming
David Minnen
Aymen Mir
Deepak Mishra
Anand Mishra
Shlok K. Mishra
Niluthpol Mithun
Gaurav Mittal
Trisha Mittal
Daisuke Miyazaki
Kaichun Mo
Hong Mo
Zhipeng Mo
Davide Modolo
Abduallah A. Mohamed
Mohamed Afham
Mohamed Aflal
Ron Mokady
Pavlo Molchanov
Davide Moltisanti
Liliane Momeni
Gianluca Monaci
Pascal Monasse
Ajoy Mondal
Tom Monnier

Aron Monszpart
Gyeongsik Moon
Suhong Moon
Taesup Moon
Sean Moran
Daniel Moreira
Pietro Morerio
Alexandre Morgand
Lia Morra
Ali Mosleh
Inbar Mosseri
Sayed Mohammad
    Mostafavi Isfahani
Saman Motamed
Ramy A. Mounir
Fangzhou Mu
Jiteng Mu
Norman Mu
Yasuhiro Mukaigawa
Ryan Mukherjee
Tanmoy Mukherjee
Yusuke Mukuta
Ravi Teja Mullapudi
Lea Müller
Matthias Müller
Martin Mundt
Nils Murrugarra-Llerena
Damien Muselet
Armin Mustafa
Muhammad Ferjad Naeem
Sauradip Nag
Hajime Nagahara
Pravin Nagar
Rajendra Nagar
Naveen Shankar Nagaraja
Varun Nagaraja
Tushar Nagarajan
Seungjun Nah
Gaku Nakano
Yuta Nakashima
Giljoo Nam
Seonghyeon Nam
Liangliang Nan
Yuesong Nan
Yeshwanth Napolean

Dinesh Reddy
    Narapureddy
Medhini Narasimhan
Supreeth
    Narasimhaswamy
Sriram Narayanan
Erickson R. Nascimento
Varun Nasery
K. L. Navaneet
Pablo Navarrete Michelini
Shant Navasardyan
Shah Nawaz
Nihal Nayak
Farhood Negin
Lukáš Neumann
Alejandro Newell
Evonne Ng
Kam Woh Ng
Tony Ng
Anh Nguyen
Tuan Anh Nguyen
Cuong Cao Nguyen
Ngoc Cuong Nguyen
Thanh Nguyen
Khoi Nguyen
Phi Le Nguyen
Phong Ha Nguyen
Tam Nguyen
Truong Nguyen
Anh Tuan Nguyen
Rang Nguyen
Thao Thi Phuong Nguyen
Van Nguyen Nguyen
Zhen-Liang Ni
Yao Ni
Shijie Nie
Xuecheng Nie
Yongwei Nie
Weizhi Nie
Ying Nie
Yinyu Nie
Kshitij N. Nikhal
Simon Niklaus
Xuefei Ning
Jifeng Ning

Yotam Nitzan
Di Niu
Shuaicheng Niu
Li Niu
Wei Niu
Yulei Niu
Zhenxing Niu
Albert No
Shohei Nobuhara
Nicoletta Noceti
Junhyug Noh
Sotiris Nousias
Slawomir Nowaczyk
Ewa M. Nowara
Valsamis Ntouskos
Gilberto Ochoa-Ruiz
Ferda Ofli
Jihyong Oh
Sangyun Oh
Youngtaek Oh
Hiroki Ohashi
Takahiro Okabe
Kemal Oksuz
Fumio Okura
Daniel Olmeda Reino
Matthew Olson
Carl Olsson
Roy Or-El
Alessandro Ortis
Guillermo Ortiz-Jimenez
Magnus Oskarsson
Ahmed A. A. Osman
Martin R. Oswald
Mayu Otani
Naima Otberdout
Cheng Ouyang
Jiahong Ouyang
Wanli Ouyang
Andrew Owens
Poojan B. Oza
Mete Ozay
A. Cengiz Oztireli
Gautam Pai
Tomas Pajdla
Umapada Pal

Simone Palazzo
Luca Palmieri
Bowen Pan
Hao Pan
Lili Pan
Tai-Yu Pan
Liang Pan
Chengwei Pan
Yingwei Pan
Xuran Pan
Jinshan Pan
Xinyu Pan
Liyuan Pan
Xingang Pan
Xingjia Pan
Zhihong Pan
Zizheng Pan
Priyadarshini Panda
Rameswar Panda
Rohit Pandey
Kaiyue Pang
Bo Pang
Guansong Pang
Jiangmiao Pang
Meng Pang
Tianyu Pang
Ziqi Pang
Omiros Pantazis
Andreas Panteli
Maja Pantic
Marina Paolanti
Joao P. Papa
Samuele Papa
Mike Papadakis
Dim P. Papadopoulos
George Papandreou
Constantin Pape
Toufiq Parag
Chethan Parameshwara
Shaifali Parashar
Alejandro Pardo
Rishubh Parihar
Sarah Parisot
JaeYoo Park
Gyeong-Moon Park

Hyojin Park
Hyoungseob Park
Jongchan Park
Jae Sung Park
Kiru Park
Chunghyun Park
Kwanyong Park
Sunghyun Park
Sungrae Park
Seongsik Park
Sanghyun Park
Sungjune Park
Taesung Park
Gaurav Parmar
Paritosh Parmar
Alvaro Parra
Despoina Paschalidou
Or Patashnik
Shivansh Patel
Pushpak Pati
Prashant W. Patil
Vaishakh Patil
Suvam Patra
Jay Patravali
Badri Narayana Patro
Angshuman Paul
Sudipta Paul
Rémi Pautrat
Nick E. Pears
Adithya Pediredla
Wenjie Pei
Shmuel Peleg
Latha Pemula
Bo Peng
Houwen Peng
Yue Peng
Liangzu Peng
Baoyun Peng
Jun Peng
Pai Peng
Sida Peng
Xi Peng
Yuxin Peng
Songyou Peng
Wei Peng

Weiqi Peng
Wen-Hsiao Peng
Pramuditha Perera
Juan C. Perez
Eduardo Pérez Pellitero
Juan-Manuel Perez-Rua
Federico Pernici
Marco Pesavento
Stavros Petridis
Ilya A. Petrov
Vladan Petrovic
Mathis Petrovich
Suzanne Petryk
Hieu Pham
Quang Pham
Khoi Pham
Tung Pham
Huy Phan
Stephen Phillips
Cheng Perng Phoo
David Picard
Marco Piccirilli
Georg Pichler
A. J. Piergiovanni
Vipin Pillai
Silvia L. Pintea
Giovanni Pintore
Robinson Piramuthu
Fiora Pirri
Theodoros Pissas
Fabio Pizzati
Benjamin Planche
Bryan Plummer
Matteo Poggi
Ashwini Pokle
Georgy E. Ponimatkin
Adrian Popescu
Stefan Popov
Nikola Popović
Ronald Poppe
Angelo Porrello
Michael Potter
Charalambos Poullis
Hadi Pouransari
Omid Poursaeed

Shraman Pramanick
Mantini Pranav
Dilip K. Prasad
Meghshyam Prasad
B. H. Pawan Prasad
Shitala Prasad
Prateek Prasanna
Ekta Prashnani
Derek S. Prijatelj
Luke Y. Prince
Véronique Prinet
Victor Adrian Prisacariu
James Pritts
Thomas Probst
Sergey Prokudin
Rita Pucci
Chi-Man Pun
Matthew Purri
Haozhi Qi
Lu Qi
Lei Qi
Xianbiao Qi
Yonggang Qi
Yuankai Qi
Siyuan Qi
Guocheng Qian
Hangwei Qian
Qi Qian
Deheng Qian
Shengsheng Qian
Wen Qian
Rui Qian
Yiming Qian
Shengju Qian
Shengyi Qian
Xuelin Qian
Zhenxing Qian
Nan Qiao
Xiaotian Qiao
Jing Qin
Can Qin
Siyang Qin
Hongwei Qin
Jie Qin
Minghai Qin

Yipeng Qin
Yongqiang Qin
Wenda Qin
Xuebin Qin
Yuzhe Qin
Yao Qin
Zhenyue Qin
Zhiwu Qing
Heqian Qiu
Jiayan Qiu
Jielin Qiu
Yue Qiu
Jiaxiong Qiu
Zhongxi Qiu
Shi Qiu
Zhaofan Qiu
Zhongnan Qu
Yanyun Qu
Kha Gia Quach
Yuhui Quan
Ruijie Quan
Mike Rabbat
Rahul Shekhar Rade
Filip Radenovic
Gorjan Radevski
Bogdan Raducanu
Francesco Ragusa
Shafin Rahman
Md Mahfuzur Rahman
  Siddiquee
Hossein Rahmani
Kiran Raja
Sivaramakrishnan
  Rajaraman
Jathushan Rajasegaran
Adnan Siraj Rakin
Michaël Ramamonjisoa
Chirag A. Raman
Shanmuganathan Raman
Vignesh Ramanathan
Vasili Ramanishka
Vikram V. Ramaswamy
Merey Ramazanova
Jason Rambach
Sai Saketh Rambhatla

Clément Rambour
Ashwin Ramesh Babu
Adín Ramírez Rivera
Arianna Rampini
Haoxi Ran
Aakanksha Rana
Aayush Jung Bahadur
  Rana
Kanchana N. Ranasinghe
Aneesh Rangnekar
Samrudhdhi B. Rangrej
Harsh Rangwani
Viresh Ranjan
Anyi Rao
Yongming Rao
Carolina Raposo
Michalis Raptis
Amir Rasouli
Vivek Rathod
Adepu Ravi Sankar
Avinash Ravichandran
Bharadwaj Ravichandran
Dripta S. Raychaudhuri
Adria Recasens
Simon Reiß
Davis Rempe
Daxuan Ren
Jiawei Ren
Jimmy Ren
Sucheng Ren
Dayong Ren
Zhile Ren
Dongwei Ren
Qibing Ren
Pengfei Ren
Zhenwen Ren
Xuqian Ren
Yixuan Ren
Zhongzheng Ren
Ambareesh Revanur
Hamed Rezazadegan
  Tavakoli
Rafael S. Rezende
Wonjong Rhee
Alexander Richard

Christian Richardt
Stephan R. Richter
Benjamin Riggan
Dominik Rivoir
Mamshad Nayeem Rizve
Joshua D. Robinson
Joseph Robinson
Chris Rockwell
Ranga Rodrigo
Andres C. Rodriguez
Carlos Rodriguez-Pardo
Marcus Rohrbach
Gemma Roig
Yu Rong
David A. Ross
Mohammad Rostami
Edward Rosten
Karsten Roth
Anirban Roy
Debaditya Roy
Shuvendu Roy
Ahana Roy Choudhury
Aruni Roy Chowdhury
Denys Rozumnyi
Shulan Ruan
Wenjie Ruan
Patrick Ruhkamp
Danila Rukhovich
Anian Ruoss
Chris Russell
Dan Ruta
Dawid Damian Rymarczyk
DongHun Ryu
Hyeonggon Ryu
Kwonyoung Ryu
Balasubramanian S.
Alexandre Sablayrolles
Mohammad Sabokrou
Arka Sadhu
Aniruddha Saha
Oindrila Saha
Pritish Sahu
Aneeshan Sain
Nirat Saini
Saurabh Saini

Takeshi Saitoh
Christos Sakaridis
Fumihiko Sakaue
Dimitrios Sakkos
Ken Sakurada
Parikshit V. Sakurikar
Rohit Saluja
Nermin Samet
Leo Sampaio Ferraz
    Ribeiro
Jorge Sanchez
Enrique Sanchez
Shengtian Sang
Anush Sankaran
Soubhik Sanyal
Nikolaos Sarafianos
Vishwanath Saragadam
István Sárándi
Saquib Sarfraz
Mert Bulent Sariyildiz
Anindya Sarkar
Pritam Sarkar
Paul-Edouard Sarlin
Hiroshi Sasaki
Takami Sato
Torsten Sattler
Ravi Kumar Satzoda
Axel Sauer
Stefano Savian
Artem Savkin
Manolis Savva
Gerald Schaefer
Simone Schaub-Meyer
Yoni Schirris
Samuel Schulter
Katja Schwarz
Jesse Scott
Sinisa Segvic
Constantin Marc Seibold
Lorenzo Seidenari
Matan Sela
Fadime Sener
Paul Hongsuck Seo
Kwanggyoon Seo
Hongje Seong

Dario Serez
Francesco Setti
Bryan Seybold
Mohamad Shahbazi
Shima Shahfar
Xinxin Shan
Caifeng Shan
Dandan Shan
Shawn Shan
Wei Shang
Jinghuan Shang
Jiaxiang Shang
Lei Shang
Sukrit Shankar
Ken Shao
Rui Shao
Jie Shao
Mingwen Shao
Aashish Sharma
Gaurav Sharma
Vivek Sharma
Abhishek Sharma
Yoli Shavit
Shashank Shekhar
Sumit Shekhar
Zhijie Shen
Fengyi Shen
Furao Shen
Jialie Shen
Jingjing Shen
Ziyi Shen
Linlin Shen
Guangyu Shen
Biluo Shen
Falong Shen
Jiajun Shen
Qiu Shen
Qiuhong Shen
Shuai Shen
Wang Shen
Yiqing Shen
Yunhang Shen
Siqi Shen
Bin Shen
Tianwei Shen

Xi Shen
Yilin Shen
Yuming Shen
Yucong Shen
Zhiqiang Shen
Lu Sheng
Yichen Sheng
Shivanand Venkanna
   Sheshappanavar
Shelly Sheynin
Baifeng Shi
Ruoxi Shi
Botian Shi
Hailin Shi
Jia Shi
Jing Shi
Shaoshuai Shi
Baoguang Shi
Boxin Shi
Hengcan Shi
Tianyang Shi
Xiaodan Shi
Yongjie Shi
Zhensheng Shi
Yinghuan Shi
Weiqi Shi
Wu Shi
Xuepeng Shi
Xiaoshuang Shi
Yujiao Shi
Zenglin Shi
Zhenmei Shi
Takashi Shibata
Meng-Li Shih
Yichang Shih
Hyunjung Shim
Dongseok Shim
Soshi Shimada
Inkyu Shin
Jinwoo Shin
Seungjoo Shin
Seungjae Shin
Koichi Shinoda
Suprosanna Shit

Palaiahnakote
   Shivakumara
Eli Shlizerman
Gaurav Shrivastava
Xiao Shu
Xiangbo Shu
Xiujun Shu
Yang Shu
Tianmin Shu
Jun Shu
Zhixin Shu
Bing Shuai
Maria Shugrina
Ivan Shugurov
Satya Narayan Shukla
Pranjay Shyam
Jianlou Si
Yawar Siddiqui
Alberto Signoroni
Pedro Silva
Jae-Young Sim
Oriane Siméoni
Martin Simon
Andrea Simonelli
Abhishek Singh
Ashish Singh
Dinesh Singh
Gurkirt Singh
Krishna Kumar Singh
Mannat Singh
Pravendra Singh
Rajat Vikram Singh
Utkarsh Singhal
Dipika Singhania
Vasu Singla
Harsh Sinha
Sudipta Sinha
Josef Sivic
Elena Sizikova
Geri Skenderi
Ivan Skorokhodov
Dmitriy Smirnov
Cameron Y. Smith
James S. Smith
Patrick Snape

Mattia Soldan
Hyeongseok Son
Sanghyun Son
Chuanbiao Song
Chen Song
Chunfeng Song
Dan Song
Dongjin Song
Hwanjun Song
Guoxian Song
Jiaming Song
Jie Song
Liangchen Song
Ran Song
Luchuan Song
Xibin Song
Li Song
Fenglong Song
Guoli Song
Guanglu Song
Zhenbo Song
Lin Song
Xinhang Song
Yang Song
Yibing Song
Rajiv Soundararajan
Hossein Souri
Cristovao Sousa
Riccardo Spezialetti
Leonidas Spinoulas
Michael W. Spratling
Deepak Sridhar
Srinath Sridhar
Gaurang Sriramanan
Vinkle Kumar Srivastav
Themos Stafylakis
Serban Stan
Anastasis Stathopoulos
Markus Steinberger
Jan Steinbrener
Sinisa Stekovic
Alexandros Stergiou
Gleb Sterkin
Rainer Stiefelhagen
Pierre Stock

Ombretta Strafforello
Julian Straub
Yannick Strümpler
Joerg Stueckler
Hang Su
Weijie Su
Jong-Chyi Su
Bing Su
Haisheng Su
Jinming Su
Yiyang Su
Yukun Su
Yuxin Su
Zhuo Su
Zhaoqi Su
Xiu Su
Yu-Chuan Su
Zhixun Su
Arulkumar Subramaniam
Akshayvarun Subramanya
A. Subramanyam
Swathikiran Sudhakaran
Yusuke Sugano
Masanori Suganuma
Yumin Suh
Yang Sui
Baochen Sun
Cheng Sun
Long Sun
Guolei Sun
Haoliang Sun
Haomiao Sun
He Sun
Hanqing Sun
Hao Sun
Lichao Sun
Jiachen Sun
Jiaming Sun
Jian Sun
Jin Sun
Jennifer J. Sun
Tiancheng Sun
Libo Sun
Peize Sun
Qianru Sun

Shanlin Sun
Yu Sun
Zhun Sun
Che Sun
Lin Sun
Tao Sun
Yiyou Sun
Chunyi Sun
Chong Sun
Weiwei Sun
Weixuan Sun
Xiuyu Sun
Yanan Sun
Zeren Sun
Zhaodong Sun
Zhiqing Sun
Minhyuk Sung
Jinli Suo
Simon Suo
Abhijit Suprem
Anshuman Suri
Saksham Suri
Joshua M. Susskind
Roman Suvorov
Gurumurthy Swaminathan
Robin Swanson
Paul Swoboda
Tabish A. Syed
Richard Szeliski
Fariborz Taherkhani
Yu-Wing Tai
Keita Takahashi
Walter Talbott
Gary Tam
Masato Tamura
Feitong Tan
Fuwen Tan
Shuhan Tan
Andong Tan
Bin Tan
Cheng Tan
Jianchao Tan
Lei Tan
Mingxing Tan
Xin Tan

Zichang Tan
Zhentao Tan
Kenichiro Tanaka
Masayuki Tanaka
Yushun Tang
Hao Tang
Jingqun Tang
Jinhui Tang
Kaihua Tang
Luming Tang
Lv Tang
Sheyang Tang
Shitao Tang
Siliang Tang
Shixiang Tang
Yansong Tang
Keke Tang
Chang Tang
Chenwei Tang
Jie Tang
Junshu Tang
Ming Tang
Peng Tang
Xu Tang
Yao Tang
Chen Tang
Fan Tang
Haoran Tang
Shengeng Tang
Yehui Tang
Zhipeng Tang
Ugo Tanielian
Chaofan Tao
Jiale Tao
Junli Tao
Renshuai Tao
An Tao
Guanhong Tao
Zhiqiang Tao
Makarand Tapaswi
Jean-Philippe G. Tarel
Juan J. Tarrio
Enzo Tartaglione
Keisuke Tateno
Zachary Teed

Ajinkya B. Tejankar
Bugra Tekin
Purva Tendulkar
Damien Teney
Minggui Teng
Chris Tensmeyer
Andrew Beng Jin Teoh
Philipp Terhörst
Kartik Thakral
Nupur Thakur
Kevin Thandiackal
Spyridon Thermos
Diego Thomas
William Thong
Yuesong Tian
Guanzhong Tian
Lin Tian
Shiqi Tian
Kai Tian
Meng Tian
Tai-Peng Tian
Zhuotao Tian
Shangxuan Tian
Tian Tian
Yapeng Tian
Yu Tian
Yuxin Tian
Leslie Ching Ow Tiong
Praveen Tirupattur
Garvita Tiwari
George Toderici
Antoine Toisoul
Aysim Toker
Tatiana Tommasi
Zhan Tong
Alessio Tonioni
Alessandro Torcinovich
Fabio Tosi
Matteo Toso
Hugo Touvron
Quan Hung Tran
Son Tran
Hung Tran
Ngoc-Trung Tran
Vinh Tran

Phong Tran
Giovanni Trappolini
Edith Tretschk
Subarna Tripathi
Shubhendu Trivedi
Eduard Trulls
Prune Truong
Thanh-Dat Truong
Tomasz Trzcinski
Sam Tsai
Yi-Hsuan Tsai
Ethan Tseng
Yu-Chee Tseng
Shahar Tsiper
Stavros Tsogkas
Shikui Tu
Zhigang Tu
Zhengzhong Tu
Richard Tucker
Sergey Tulyakov
Cigdem Turan
Daniyar Turmukhambetov
Victor G. Turrisi da Costa
Bartlomiej Twardowski
Christopher D. Twigg
Radim Tylecek
Mostofa Rafid Uddin
Md. Zasim Uddin
Kohei Uehara
Nicolas Ugrinovic
Youngjung Uh
Norimichi Ukita
Anwaar Ulhaq
Devesh Upadhyay
Paul Upchurch
Yoshitaka Ushiku
Yuzuko Utsumi
Mikaela Angelina Uy
Mohit Vaishnav
Pratik Vaishnavi
Jeya Maria Jose Valanarasu
Matias A. Valdenegro Toro
Diego Valsesia
Wouter Van Gansbeke
Nanne van Noord

Simon Vandenhende
Farshid Varno
Cristina Vasconcelos
Francisco Vasconcelos
Alex Vasilescu
Subeesh Vasu
Arun Balajee Vasudevan
Kanav Vats
Vaibhav S. Vavilala
Sagar Vaze
Javier Vazquez-Corral
Andrea Vedaldi
Olga Veksler
Andreas Velten
Sai H. Vemprala
Raviteja Vemulapalli
Shashanka
    Venkataramanan
Dor Verbin
Luisa Verdoliva
Manisha Verma
Yashaswi Verma
Constantin Vertan
Eli Verwimp
Deepak Vijaykeerthy
Pablo Villanueva
Ruben Villegas
Markus Vincze
Vibhav Vineet
Minh P. Vo
Huy V. Vo
Duc Minh Vo
Tomas Vojir
Igor Vozniak
Nicholas Vretos
Vibashan VS
Tuan-Anh Vu
Thang Vu
Mårten Wadenbäck
Neal Wadhwa
Aaron T. Walsman
Steven Walton
Jin Wan
Alvin Wan
Jia Wan

Jun Wan
Xiaoyue Wan
Fang Wan
Guowei Wan
Renjie Wan
Zhiqiang Wan
Ziyu Wan
Bastian Wandt
Dongdong Wang
Limin Wang
Haiyang Wang
Xiaobing Wang
Angtian Wang
Angelina Wang
Bing Wang
Bo Wang
Boyu Wang
Binghui Wang
Chen Wang
Chien-Yi Wang
Congli Wang
Qi Wang
Chengrui Wang
Rui Wang
Yiqun Wang
Cong Wang
Wenjing Wang
Dongkai Wang
Di Wang
Xiaogang Wang
Kai Wang
Zhizhong Wang
Fangjinhua Wang
Feng Wang
Hang Wang
Gaoang Wang
Guoqing Wang
Guangcong Wang
Guangzhi Wang
Hanqing Wang
Hao Wang
Haohan Wang
Haoran Wang
Hong Wang
Haotao Wang

Hu Wang
Huan Wang
Hua Wang
Hui-Po Wang
Hengli Wang
Hanyu Wang
Hongxing Wang
Jingwen Wang
Jialiang Wang
Jian Wang
Jianyi Wang
Jiashun Wang
Jiahao Wang
Tsun-Hsuan Wang
Xiaoqian Wang
Jinqiao Wang
Jun Wang
Jianzong Wang
Kaihong Wang
Ke Wang
Lei Wang
Lingjing Wang
Linnan Wang
Lin Wang
Liansheng Wang
Mengjiao Wang
Manning Wang
Nannan Wang
Peihao Wang
Jiayun Wang
Pu Wang
Qiang Wang
Qiufeng Wang
Qilong Wang
Qiangchang Wang
Qin Wang
Qing Wang
Ruocheng Wang
Ruibin Wang
Ruisheng Wang
Ruizhe Wang
Runqi Wang
Runzhong Wang
Wenxuan Wang
Sen Wang

Shangfei Wang
Shaofei Wang
Shijie Wang
Shiqi Wang
Zhibo Wang
Song Wang
Xinjiang Wang
Tai Wang
Tao Wang
Teng Wang
Xiang Wang
Tianren Wang
Tiantian Wang
Tianyi Wang
Fengjiao Wang
Wei Wang
Miaohui Wang
Suchen Wang
Siyue Wang
Yaoming Wang
Xiao Wang
Ze Wang
Biao Wang
Chaofei Wang
Dong Wang
Gu Wang
Guangrun Wang
Guangming Wang
Guo-Hua Wang
Haoqing Wang
Hesheng Wang
Huafeng Wang
Jinghua Wang
Jingdong Wang
Jingjing Wang
Jingya Wang
Jingkang Wang
Jiakai Wang
Junke Wang
Kuo Wang
Lichen Wang
Lizhi Wang
Longguang Wang
Mang Wang
Mei Wang

Min Wang
Peng-Shuai Wang
Run Wang
Shaoru Wang
Shuhui Wang
Tan Wang
Tiancai Wang
Tianqi Wang
Wenhai Wang
Wenzhe Wang
Xiaobo Wang
Xiudong Wang
Xu Wang
Yajie Wang
Yan Wang
Yuan-Gen Wang
Yingqian Wang
Yizhi Wang
Yulin Wang
Yu Wang
Yujie Wang
Yunhe Wang
Yuxi Wang
Yaowei Wang
Yiwei Wang
Zezheng Wang
Hongzhi Wang
Zhiqiang Wang
Ziteng Wang
Ziwei Wang
Zheng Wang
Zhenyu Wang
Binglu Wang
Zhongdao Wang
Ce Wang
Weining Wang
Weiyao Wang
Wenbin Wang
Wenguan Wang
Guangting Wang
Haolin Wang
Haiyan Wang
Huiyu Wang
Naiyan Wang
Jingbo Wang

Jinpeng Wang
Jiaqi Wang
Liyuan Wang
Lizhen Wang
Ning Wang
Wenqian Wang
Sheng-Yu Wang
Weimin Wang
Xiaohan Wang
Yifan Wang
Yi Wang
Yongtao Wang
Yizhou Wang
Zhuo Wang
Zhe Wang
Xudong Wang
Xiaofang Wang
Xinggang Wang
Xiaosen Wang
Xiaosong Wang
Xiaoyang Wang
Lijun Wang
Xinlong Wang
Xuan Wang
Xue Wang
Yangang Wang
Yaohui Wang
Yu-Chiang Frank Wang
Yida Wang
Yilin Wang
Yi Ru Wang
Yali Wang
Yinglong Wang
Yufu Wang
Yujiang Wang
Yuwang Wang
Yuting Wang
Yang Wang
Yu-Xiong Wang
Yixu Wang
Ziqi Wang
Zhicheng Wang
Zeyu Wang
Zhaowen Wang
Zhenyi Wang

Zhenzhi Wang
Zhijie Wang
Zhiyong Wang
Zhongling Wang
Zhuowei Wang
Zian Wang
Zifu Wang
Zihao Wang
Zirui Wang
Ziyan Wang
Wenxiao Wang
Zhen Wang
Zhepeng Wang
Zi Wang
Zihao W. Wang
Steven L. Waslander
Olivia Watkins
Daniel Watson
Silvan Weder
Dongyoon Wee
Dongming Wei
Tianyi Wei
Jia Wei
Dong Wei
Fangyun Wei
Longhui Wei
Mingqiang Wei
Xinyue Wei
Chen Wei
Donglai Wei
Pengxu Wei
Xing Wei
Xiu-Shen Wei
Wenqi Wei
Guoqiang Wei
Wei Wei
XingKui Wei
Xian Wei
Xingxing Wei
Yake Wei
Yuxiang Wei
Yi Wei
Luca Weihs
Michael Weinmann
Martin Weinmann

Congcong Wen
Chuan Wen
Jie Wen
Sijia Wen
Song Wen
Chao Wen
Xiang Wen
Zeyi Wen
Xin Wen
Yilin Wen
Yijia Weng
Shuchen Weng
Junwu Weng
Wenming Weng
Renliang Weng
Zhenyu Weng
Xinshuo Weng
Nicholas J. Westlake
Gordon Wetzstein
Lena M. Widin Klasén
Rick Wildes
Bryan M. Williams
Williem Williem
Ole Winther
Scott Wisdom
Alex Wong
Chau-Wai Wong
Kwan-Yee K. Wong
Yongkang Wong
Scott Workman
Marcel Worring
Michael Wray
Safwan Wshah
Xiang Wu
Aming Wu
Chongruo Wu
Cho-Ying Wu
Chunpeng Wu
Chenyan Wu
Ziyi Wu
Fuxiang Wu
Gang Wu
Haiping Wu
Huisi Wu
Jane Wu

Jialian Wu
Jing Wu
Jinjian Wu
Jianlong Wu
Xian Wu
Lifang Wu
Lifan Wu
Minye Wu
Qianyi Wu
Rongliang Wu
Rui Wu
Shiqian Wu
Shuzhe Wu
Shangzhe Wu
Tsung-Han Wu
Tz-Ying Wu
Ting-Wei Wu
Jiannan Wu
Zhiliang Wu
Yu Wu
Chenyun Wu
Dayan Wu
Dongxian Wu
Fei Wu
Hefeng Wu
Jianxin Wu
Weibin Wu
Wenxuan Wu
Wenhao Wu
Xiao Wu
Yicheng Wu
Yuanwei Wu
Yu-Huan Wu
Zhenxin Wu
Zhenyu Wu
Wei Wu
Peng Wu
Xiaohe Wu
Xindi Wu
Xinxing Wu
Xinyi Wu
Xingjiao Wu
Xiongwei Wu
Yangzheng Wu
Yanzhao Wu

Yawen Wu
Yong Wu
Yi Wu
Ying Nian Wu
Zhenyao Wu
Zhonghua Wu
Zongze Wu
Zuxuan Wu
Stefanie Wuhrer
Teng Xi
Jianing Xi
Fei Xia
Haifeng Xia
Menghan Xia
Yuanqing Xia
Zhihua Xia
Xiaobo Xia
Weihao Xia
Shihong Xia
Yan Xia
Yong Xia
Zhaoyang Xia
Zhihao Xia
Chuhua Xian
Yongqin Xian
Wangmeng Xiang
Fanbo Xiang
Tiange Xiang
Tao Xiang
Liuyu Xiang
Xiaoyu Xiang
Zhiyu Xiang
Aoran Xiao
Chunxia Xiao
Fanyi Xiao
Jimin Xiao
Jun Xiao
Taihong Xiao
Anqi Xiao
Junfei Xiao
Jing Xiao
Liang Xiao
Yang Xiao
Yuting Xiao
Yijun Xiao

Yao Xiao
Zeyu Xiao
Zhisheng Xiao
Zihao Xiao
Binhui Xie
Christopher Xie
Haozhe Xie
Jin Xie
Guo-Sen Xie
Hongtao Xie
Ming-Kun Xie
Tingting Xie
Chaohao Xie
Weicheng Xie
Xudong Xie
Jiyang Xie
Xiaohua Xie
Yuan Xie
Zhenyu Xie
Ning Xie
Xianghui Xie
Xiufeng Xie
You Xie
Yutong Xie
Fuyong Xing
Yifan Xing
Zhen Xing
Yuanjun Xiong
Jinhui Xiong
Weihua Xiong
Hongkai Xiong
Zhitong Xiong
Yuanhao Xiong
Yunyang Xiong
Yuwen Xiong
Zhiwei Xiong
Yuliang Xiu
An Xu
Chang Xu
Chenliang Xu
Chengming Xu
Chenshu Xu
Xiang Xu
Huijuan Xu
Zhe Xu

Jie Xu
Jingyi Xu
Jiarui Xu
Yinghao Xu
Kele Xu
Ke Xu
Li Xu
Linchuan Xu
Linning Xu
Mengde Xu
Mengmeng Frost Xu
Min Xu
Mingye Xu
Jun Xu
Ning Xu
Peng Xu
Runsheng Xu
Sheng Xu
Wenqiang Xu
Xiaogang Xu
Renzhe Xu
Kaidi Xu
Yi Xu
Chi Xu
Qiuling Xu
Baobei Xu
Feng Xu
Haohang Xu
Haofei Xu
Lan Xu
Mingze Xu
Songcen Xu
Weipeng Xu
Wenjia Xu
Wenju Xu
Xiangyu Xu
Xin Xu
Yinshuang Xu
Yixing Xu
Yuting Xu
Yanyu Xu
Zhenbo Xu
Zhiliang Xu
Zhiyuan Xu
Xiaohao Xu

Yanwu Xu
Yan Xu
Yiran Xu
Yifan Xu
Yufei Xu
Yong Xu
Zichuan Xu
Zenglin Xu
Zexiang Xu
Zhan Xu
Zheng Xu
Zhiwei Xu
Ziyue Xu
Shiyu Xuan
Hanyu Xuan
Fei Xue
Jianru Xue
Mingfu Xue
Qinghan Xue
Tianfan Xue
Chao Xue
Chuhui Xue
Nan Xue
Zhou Xue
Xiangyang Xue
Yuan Xue
Abhay Yadav
Ravindra Yadav
Kota Yamaguchi
Toshihiko Yamasaki
Kohei Yamashita
Chaochao Yan
Feng Yan
Kun Yan
Qingsen Yan
Qixin Yan
Rui Yan
Siming Yan
Xinchen Yan
Yaping Yan
Bin Yan
Qingan Yan
Shen Yan
Shipeng Yan
Xu Yan

Yan Yan
Yichao Yan
Zhaoyi Yan
Zike Yan
Zhiqiang Yan
Hongliang Yan
Zizheng Yan
Jiewen Yang
Anqi Joyce Yang
Shan Yang
Anqi Yang
Antoine Yang
Bo Yang
Baoyao Yang
Chenhongyi Yang
Dingkang Yang
De-Nian Yang
Dong Yang
David Yang
Fan Yang
Fengyu Yang
Fengting Yang
Fei Yang
Gengshan Yang
Heng Yang
Han Yang
Huan Yang
Yibo Yang
Jiancheng Yang
Jihan Yang
Jiawei Yang
Jiayu Yang
Jie Yang
Jinfa Yang
Jingkang Yang
Jinyu Yang
Cheng-Fu Yang
Ji Yang
Jianyu Yang
Kailun Yang
Tian Yang
Luyu Yang
Liang Yang
Li Yang
Michael Ying Yang

Yang Yang
Muli Yang
Le Yang
Qiushi Yang
Ren Yang
Ruihan Yang
Shuang Yang
Siyuan Yang
Su Yang
Shiqi Yang
Taojiannan Yang
Tianyu Yang
Lei Yang
Wanzhao Yang
Shuai Yang
William Yang
Wei Yang
Xiaofeng Yang
Xiaoshan Yang
Xin Yang
Xuan Yang
Xu Yang
Xingyi Yang
Xitong Yang
Jing Yang
Yanchao Yang
Wenming Yang
Yujiu Yang
Herb Yang
Jianfei Yang
Jinhui Yang
Chuanguang Yang
Guanglei Yang
Haitao Yang
Kewei Yang
Linlin Yang
Lijin Yang
Longrong Yang
Meng Yang
MingKun Yang
Sibei Yang
Shicai Yang
Tong Yang
Wen Yang
Xi Yang

Xiaolong Yang
Xue Yang
Yubin Yang
Ze Yang
Ziyi Yang
Yi Yang
Linjie Yang
Yuzhe Yang
Yiding Yang
Zhenpei Yang
Zhaohui Yang
Zhengyuan Yang
Zhibo Yang
Zongxin Yang
Hantao Yao
Mingde Yao
Rui Yao
Taiping Yao
Ting Yao
Cong Yao
Qingsong Yao
Quanming Yao
Xu Yao
Yuan Yao
Yao Yao
Yazhou Yao
Jiawen Yao
Shunyu Yao
Pew-Thian Yap
Sudhir Yarram
Rajeev Yasarla
Peng Ye
Botao Ye
Mao Ye
Fei Ye
Hanrong Ye
Jingwen Ye
Jinwei Ye
Jiarong Ye
Mang Ye
Meng Ye
Qi Ye
Qian Ye
Qixiang Ye
Junjie Ye

Sheng Ye
Nanyang Ye
Yufei Ye
Xiaoqing Ye
Ruolin Ye
Yousef Yeganeh
Chun-Hsiao Yeh
Raymond A. Yeh
Yu-Ying Yeh
Kai Yi
Chang Yi
Renjiao Yi
Xinping Yi
Peng Yi
Alper Yilmaz
Junho Yim
Hui Yin
Bangjie Yin
Jia-Li Yin
Miao Yin
Wenzhe Yin
Xuwang Yin
Ming Yin
Yu Yin
Aoxiong Yin
Kangxue Yin
Tianwei Yin
Wei Yin
Xianghua Ying
Rio Yokota
Tatsuya Yokota
Naoto Yokoya
Ryo Yonetani
Ki Yoon Yoo
Jinsu Yoo
Sunjae Yoon
Jae Shin Yoon
Jihun Yoon
Sung-Hoon Yoon
Ryota Yoshihashi
Yusuke Yoshiyasu
Chenyu You
Haoran You
Haoxuan You
Yang You

Quanzeng You
Tackgeun You
Kaichao You
Shan You
Xinge You
Yurong You
Baosheng Yu
Bei Yu
Haichao Yu
Hao Yu
Chaohui Yu
Fisher Yu
Jin-Gang Yu
Jiyang Yu
Jason J. Yu
Jiashuo Yu
Hong-Xing Yu
Lei Yu
Mulin Yu
Ning Yu
Peilin Yu
Qi Yu
Qian Yu
Rui Yu
Shuzhi Yu
Gang Yu
Tan Yu
Weijiang Yu
Xin Yu
Bingyao Yu
Ye Yu
Hanchao Yu
Yingchen Yu
Tao Yu
Xiaotian Yu
Qing Yu
Houjian Yu
Changqian Yu
Jing Yu
Jun Yu
Shujian Yu
Xiang Yu
Zhaofei Yu
Zhenbo Yu
Yinfeng Yu

Zhuoran Yu
Zitong Yu
Bo Yuan
Jiangbo Yuan
Liangzhe Yuan
Weihao Yuan
Jianbo Yuan
Xiaoyun Yuan
Ye Yuan
Li Yuan
Geng Yuan
Jialin Yuan
Maoxun Yuan
Peng Yuan
Xin Yuan
Yuan Yuan
Yuhui Yuan
Yixuan Yuan
Zheng Yuan
Mehmet Kerim Yücel
Kaiyu Yue
Haixiao Yue
Heeseung Yun
Sangdoo Yun
Tian Yun
Mahmut Yurt
Ekim Yurtsever
Ahmet Yüzügüler
Edouard Yvinec
Eloi Zablocki
Christopher Zach
Muhammad Zaigham
    Zaheer
Pierluigi Zama Ramirez
Yuhang Zang
Pietro Zanuttigh
Alexey Zaytsev
Bernhard Zeisl
Haitian Zeng
Pengpeng Zeng
Jiabei Zeng
Runhao Zeng
Wei Zeng
Yawen Zeng
Yi Zeng

Yiming Zeng
Tieyong Zeng
Huanqiang Zeng
Dan Zeng
Yu Zeng
Wei Zhai
Yuanhao Zhai
Fangneng Zhan
Kun Zhan
Xiong Zhang
Jingdong Zhang
Jiangning Zhang
Zhilu Zhang
Gengwei Zhang
Dongsu Zhang
Hui Zhang
Binjie Zhang
Bo Zhang
Tianhao Zhang
Cecilia Zhang
Jing Zhang
Chaoning Zhang
Chenxu Zhang
Chi Zhang
Chris Zhang
Yabin Zhang
Zhao Zhang
Rufeng Zhang
Chaoyi Zhang
Zheng Zhang
Da Zhang
Yi Zhang
Edward Zhang
Xin Zhang
Feifei Zhang
Feilong Zhang
Yuqi Zhang
GuiXuan Zhang
Hanlin Zhang
Hanwang Zhang
Hanzhen Zhang
Haotian Zhang
He Zhang
Haokui Zhang
Hongyuan Zhang

Hengrui Zhang
Hongming Zhang
Mingfang Zhang
Jianpeng Zhang
Jiaming Zhang
Jichao Zhang
Jie Zhang
Jingfeng Zhang
Jingyi Zhang
Jinnian Zhang
David Junhao Zhang
Junjie Zhang
Junzhe Zhang
Jiawan Zhang
Jingyang Zhang
Kai Zhang
Lei Zhang
Lihua Zhang
Lu Zhang
Miao Zhang
Minjia Zhang
Mingjin Zhang
Qi Zhang
Qian Zhang
Qilong Zhang
Qiming Zhang
Qiang Zhang
Richard Zhang
Ruimao Zhang
Ruisi Zhang
Ruixin Zhang
Runze Zhang
Qilin Zhang
Shan Zhang
Shanshan Zhang
Xi Sheryl Zhang
Song-Hai Zhang
Chongyang Zhang
Kaihao Zhang
Songyang Zhang
Shu Zhang
Siwei Zhang
Shujian Zhang
Tianyun Zhang
Tong Zhang

Tao Zhang
Wenwei Zhang
Wenqiang Zhang
Wen Zhang
Xiaolin Zhang
Xingchen Zhang
Xingxuan Zhang
Xiuming Zhang
Xiaoshuai Zhang
Xuanmeng Zhang
Xuanyang Zhang
Xucong Zhang
Xingxing Zhang
Xikun Zhang
Xiaohan Zhang
Yahui Zhang
Yunhua Zhang
Yan Zhang
Yanghao Zhang
Yifei Zhang
Yifan Zhang
Yi-Fan Zhang
Yihao Zhang
Yingliang Zhang
Youshan Zhang
Yulun Zhang
Yushu Zhang
Yixiao Zhang
Yide Zhang
Zhongwen Zhang
Bowen Zhang
Chen-Lin Zhang
Zehua Zhang
Zekun Zhang
Zeyu Zhang
Xiaowei Zhang
Yifeng Zhang
Cheng Zhang
Hongguang Zhang
Yuexi Zhang
Fa Zhang
Guofeng Zhang
Hao Zhang
Haofeng Zhang
Hongwen Zhang

Hua Zhang
Jiaxin Zhang
Zhenyu Zhang
Jian Zhang
Jianfeng Zhang
Jiao Zhang
Jiakai Zhang
Lefei Zhang
Le Zhang
Mi Zhang
Min Zhang
Ning Zhang
Pan Zhang
Pu Zhang
Qing Zhang
Renrui Zhang
Shifeng Zhang
Shuo Zhang
Shaoxiong Zhang
Weizhong Zhang
Xi Zhang
Xiaomei Zhang
Xinyu Zhang
Yin Zhang
Zicheng Zhang
Zihao Zhang
Ziqi Zhang
Zhaoxiang Zhang
Zhen Zhang
Zhipeng Zhang
Zhixing Zhang
Zhizheng Zhang
Jiawei Zhang
Zhong Zhang
Pingping Zhang
Yixin Zhang
Kui Zhang
Lingzhi Zhang
Huaiwen Zhang
Quanshi Zhang
Zhoutong Zhang
Yuhang Zhang
Yuting Zhang
Zhang Zhang
Ziming Zhang

Zhizhong Zhang
Qilong Zhangli
Bingyin Zhao
Bin Zhao
Chenglong Zhao
Lei Zhao
Feng Zhao
Gangming Zhao
Haiyan Zhao
Hao Zhao
Handong Zhao
Hengshuang Zhao
Yinan Zhao
Jiaojiao Zhao
Jiaqi Zhao
Jing Zhao
Kaili Zhao
Haojie Zhao
Yucheng Zhao
Longjiao Zhao
Long Zhao
Qingsong Zhao
Qingyu Zhao
Rui Zhao
Rui-Wei Zhao
Sicheng Zhao
Shuang Zhao
Siyan Zhao
Zelin Zhao
Shiyu Zhao
Wang Zhao
Tiesong Zhao
Qian Zhao
Wangbo Zhao
Xi-Le Zhao
Xu Zhao
Yajie Zhao
Yang Zhao
Ying Zhao
Yin Zhao
Yizhou Zhao
Yunhan Zhao
Yuyang Zhao
Yue Zhao
Yuzhi Zhao

Bowen Zhao
Pu Zhao
Bingchen Zhao
Borui Zhao
Fuqiang Zhao
Hanbin Zhao
Jian Zhao
Mingyang Zhao
Na Zhao
Rongchang Zhao
Ruiqi Zhao
Shuai Zhao
Wenda Zhao
Wenliang Zhao
Xiangyun Zhao
Yifan Zhao
Yaping Zhao
Zhou Zhao
He Zhao
Jie Zhao
Xibin Zhao
Xiaoqi Zhao
Zhengyu Zhao
Jin Zhe
Chuanxia Zheng
Huan Zheng
Hao Zheng
Jia Zheng
Jian-Qing Zheng
Shuai Zheng
Meng Zheng
Mingkai Zheng
Qian Zheng
Qi Zheng
Wu Zheng
Yinqiang Zheng
Yufeng Zheng
Yutong Zheng
Yalin Zheng
Yu Zheng
Feng Zheng
Zhaoheng Zheng
Haitian Zheng
Kang Zheng
Bolun Zheng

Haiyong Zheng
Mingwu Zheng
Sipeng Zheng
Tu Zheng
Wenzhao Zheng
Xiawu Zheng
Yinglin Zheng
Zhuo Zheng
Zilong Zheng
Kecheng Zheng
Zerong Zheng
Shuaifeng Zhi
Tiancheng Zhi
Jia-Xing Zhong
Yiwu Zhong
Fangwei Zhong
Zhihang Zhong
Yaoyao Zhong
Yiran Zhong
Zhun Zhong
Zichun Zhong
Bo Zhou
Boyao Zhou
Brady Zhou
Mo Zhou
Chunluan Zhou
Dingfu Zhou
Fan Zhou
Jingkai Zhou
Honglu Zhou
Jiaming Zhou
Jiahuan Zhou
Jun Zhou
Kaiyang Zhou
Keyang Zhou
Kuangqi Zhou
Lei Zhou
Lihua Zhou
Man Zhou
Mingyi Zhou
Mingyuan Zhou
Ning Zhou
Peng Zhou
Penghao Zhou
Qianyi Zhou

Shuigeng Zhou
Shangchen Zhou
Huayi Zhou
Zhize Zhou
Sanping Zhou
Qin Zhou
Tao Zhou
Wenbo Zhou
Xiangdong Zhou
Xiao-Yun Zhou
Xiao Zhou
Yang Zhou
Yipin Zhou
Zhenyu Zhou
Hao Zhou
Chu Zhou
Daquan Zhou
Da-Wei Zhou
Hang Zhou
Kang Zhou
Qianyu Zhou
Sheng Zhou
Wenhui Zhou
Xingyi Zhou
Yan-Jie Zhou
Yiyi Zhou
Yu Zhou
Yuan Zhou
Yuqian Zhou
Yuxuan Zhou
Zixiang Zhou
Wengang Zhou
Shuchang Zhou
Tianfei Zhou
Yichao Zhou
Alex Zhu
Chenchen Zhu
Deyao Zhu
Xiatian Zhu
Guibo Zhu
Haidong Zhu
Hao Zhu
Hongzi Zhu
Rui Zhu
Jing Zhu

Jianke Zhu
Junchen Zhu
Lei Zhu
Lingyu Zhu
Luyang Zhu
Menglong Zhu
Peihao Zhu
Hui Zhu
Xiaofeng Zhu
Tyler (Lixuan) Zhu
Wentao Zhu
Xiangyu Zhu
Xinqi Zhu
Xinxin Zhu
Xinliang Zhu
Yangguang Zhu
Yichen Zhu
Yixin Zhu
Yanjun Zhu
Yousong Zhu
Yuhao Zhu
Ye Zhu
Feng Zhu
Zhen Zhu
Fangrui Zhu
Jinjing Zhu
Linchao Zhu
Pengfei Zhu
Sijie Zhu
Xiaobin Zhu
Xiaoguang Zhu
Zezhou Zhu
Zhenyao Zhu
Kai Zhu
Pengkai Zhu
Bingbing Zhuang
Chengyuan Zhuang
Liansheng Zhuang
Peiye Zhuang
Yixin Zhuang
Yihong Zhuang
Junbao Zhuo
Andrea Ziani
Bartosz Zieliński
Primo Zingaretti

Nikolaos Zioulis
Andrew Zisserman
Yael Ziv
Liu Ziyin
Xingxing Zou
Danping Zou
Qi Zou

Shihao Zou
Xueyan Zou
Yang Zou
Yuliang Zou
Zihang Zou
Chuhang Zou
Dongqing Zou

Xu Zou
Zhiming Zou
Maria A. Zuluaga
Xinxin Zuo
Zhiwen Zuo
Reyer Zwiggelaar

Contents – Part IX

BEVFormer: Learning Bird's-Eye-View Representation
from Multi-camera Images via Spatiotemporal Transformers 1
    Zhiqi Li, Wenhai Wang, Hongyang Li, Enze Xie, Chonghao Sima,
    Tong Lu, Yu Qiao, and Jifeng Dai

Category-Level 6D Object Pose and Size Estimation Using Self-supervised
Deep Prior Deformation Networks 19
    Jiehong Lin, Zewei Wei, Changxing Ding, and Kui Jia

Dense Teacher: Dense Pseudo-Labels for Semi-supervised Object
Detection 35
    Hongyu Zhou, Zheng Ge, Songtao Liu, Weixin Mao, Zeming Li,
    Haiyan Yu, and Jian Sun

Point-to-Box Network for Accurate Object Detection via Single Point
Supervision 51
    Pengfei Chen, Xuehui Yu, Xumeng Han, Najmul Hassan, Kai Wang,
    Jiachen Li, Jian Zhao, Humphrey Shi, Zhenjun Han, and Qixiang Ye

Domain Adaptive Hand Keypoint and Pixel Localization in the Wild 68
    Takehiko Ohkawa, Yu-Jhe Li, Qichen Fu, Ryosuke Furuta,
    Kris M. Kitani, and Yoichi Sato

Towards Data-Efficient Detection Transformers 88
    Wen Wang, Jing Zhang, Yang Cao, Yongliang Shen, and Dacheng Tao

Open-Vocabulary DETR with Conditional Matching 106
    Yuhang Zang, Wei Li, Kaiyang Zhou, Chen Huang, and Chen Change Loy

Prediction-Guided Distillation for Dense Object Detection 123
    Chenhongyi Yang, Mateusz Ochal, Amos Storkey, and Elliot J. Crowley

Multimodal Object Detection via Probabilistic Ensembling 139
    Yi-Ting Chen, Jinghao Shi, Zelin Ye, Christoph Mertz, Deva Ramanan,
    and Shu Kong

Exploiting Unlabeled Data with Vision and Language Models for Object
Detection 159
    Shiyu Zhao, Zhixing Zhang, Samuel Schulter, Long Zhao,
    B.G Vijay Kumar, Anastasis Stathopoulos, Manmohan Chandraker,
    and Dimitris N. Metaxas

CPO: Change Robust Panorama to Point Cloud Localization 176
  Junho Kim, Hojun Jang, Changwoon Choi, and Young Min Kim

INT: Towards Infinite-Frames 3D Detection with an Efficient Framework 193
  Jianyun Xu, Zhenwei Miao, Da Zhang, Hongyu Pan, Kaixuan Liu,
  Peihan Hao, Jun Zhu, Zhengyang Sun, Hongmin Li, and Xin Zhan

End-to-End Weakly Supervised Object Detection with Sparse Proposal
Evolution 210
  Mingxiang Liao, Fang Wan, Yuan Yao, Zhenjun Han, Jialing Zou,
  Yuze Wang, Bailan Feng, Peng Yuan, and Qixiang Ye

Calibration-Free Multi-view Crowd Counting 227
  Qi Zhang and Antoni B. Chan

Unsupervised Domain Adaptation for Monocular 3D Object Detection
via Self-training 245
  Zhenyu Li, Zehui Chen, Ang Li, Liangji Fang, Qinhong Jiang,
  Xianming Liu, and Junjun Jiang

SuperLine3D: Self-supervised Line Segmentation and Description
for LiDAR Point Cloud 263
  Xiangrui Zhao, Sheng Yang, Tianxin Huang, Jun Chen, Teng Ma,
  Mingyang Li, and Yong Liu

Exploring Plain Vision Transformer Backbones for Object Detection 280
  Yanghao Li, Hanzi Mao, Ross Girshick, and Kaiming He

Adversarially-Aware Robust Object Detector 297
  Ziyi Dong, Pengxu Wei, and Liang Lin

HEAD: HEtero-Assists Distillation for Heterogeneous Object Detectors 314
  Luting Wang, Xiaojie Li, Yue Liao, Zeren Jiang, Jianlong Wu, Fei Wang,
  Chen Qian, and Si Liu

You Should Look at All Objects 332
  Zhenchao Jin, Dongdong Yu, Luchuan Song, Zehuan Yuan, and Lequan Yu

Detecting Twenty-Thousand Classes Using Image-Level Supervision 350
  Xingyi Zhou, Rohit Girdhar, Armand Joulin, Philipp Krähenbühl,
  and Ishan Misra

DCL-Net: Deep Correspondence Learning Network for 6D Pose Estimation ... 369
  Hongyang Li, Jiehong Lin, and Kui Jia

Monocular 3D Object Detection with Depth from Motion 386
   Tai Wang, Jiangmiao Pang, and Dahua Lin

DISP6D: Disentangled Implicit Shape and Pose Learning for Scalable 6D
Pose Estimation 404
   *Yilin Wen, Xiangyu Li, Hao Pan, Lei Yang, Zheng Wang, Taku Komura,
   and Wenping Wang*

Distilling Object Detectors with Global Knowledge 422
   *Sanli Tang, Zhongyu Zhang, Zhanzhan Cheng, Jing Lu, Yunlu Xu,
   Yi Niu, and Fan He*

Unifying Visual Perception by Dispersible Points Learning 439
   Jianming Liang, Guanglu Song, Biao Leng, and Yu Liu

PseCo: Pseudo Labeling and Consistency Training for Semi-Supervised
Object Detection 457
   *Gang Li, Xiang Li, Yujie Wang, Yichao Wu, Ding Liang,
   and Shanshan Zhang*

Exploring Resolution and Degradation Clues as Self-supervised Signal
for Low Quality Object Detection 473
   *Ziteng Cui, Yingying Zhu, Lin Gu, Guo-Jun Qi, Xiaoxiao Li,
   Renrui Zhang, Zenghui Zhang, and Tatsuya Harada*

Robust Category-Level 6D Pose Estimation with Coarse-to-Fine
Rendering of Neural Features 492
   Wufei Ma, Angtian Wang, Alan Yuille, and Adam Kortylewski

Translation, Scale and Rotation: Cross-Modal Alignment Meets
RGB-Infrared Vehicle Detection 509
   Maoxun Yuan, Yinyan Wang, and Xingxing Wei

RFLA: Gaussian Receptive Field Based Label Assignment for Tiny Object
Detection 526
   Chang Xu, Jinwang Wang, Wen Yang, Huai Yu, Lei Yu, and Gui-Song Xia

Rethinking IoU-based Optimization for Single-stage 3D Object Detection 544
   *Hualian Sheng, Sijia Cai, Na Zhao, Bing Deng, Jianqiang Huang,
   Xian-Sheng Hua, Min-Jian Zhao, and Gim Hee Lee*

TD-Road: Top-Down Road Network Extraction with Holistic Graph
Construction 562
   Yang He, Ravi Garg, and Amber Roy Chowdhury

Multi-faceted Distillation of Base-Novel Commonality for Few-Shot
Object Detection   578
   Shuang Wu, Wenjie Pei, Dianwen Mei, Fanglin Chen, Jiandong Tian,
   and Guangming Lu

PointCLM: A Contrastive Learning-based Framework for Multi-instance
Point Cloud Registration   595
   Mingzhi Yuan, Zhihao Li, Qiuye Jin, Xinrong Chen, and Manning Wang

Weakly Supervised Object Localization via Transformer with Implicit
Spatial Calibration   612
   Haotian Bai, Ruimao Zhang, Jiong Wang, and Xiang Wan

MTTrans: Cross-domain Object Detection with Mean Teacher Transformer   629
   Jinze Yu, Jiaming Liu, Xiaobao Wei, Haoyi Zhou, Yohei Nakata,
   Denis Gudovskiy, Tomoyuki Okuno, Jianxin Li, Kurt Keutzer,
   and Shanghang Zhang

Multi-domain Multi-definition Landmark Localization for Small Datasets   646
   David Ferman and Gaurav Bharaj

DEVIANT: Depth EquiVarIAnt NeTwork for Monocular 3D Object
Detection   664
   Abhinav Kumar, Garrick Brazil, Enrique Corona, Armin Parchami,
   and Xiaoming Liu

Label-Guided Auxiliary Training Improves 3D Object Detector   684
   Yaomin Huang, Xinmei Liu, Yichen Zhu, Zhiyuan Xu, Chaomin Shen,
   Zhengping Che, Guixu Zhang, Yaxin Peng, Feifei Feng, and Jian Tang

PromptDet: Towards Open-Vocabulary Detection Using Uncurated Images   701
   Chengjian Feng, Yujie Zhong, Zequn Jie, Xiangxiang Chu, Haibing Ren,
   Xiaolin Wei, Weidi Xie, and Lin Ma

Densely Constrained Depth Estimator for Monocular 3D Object Detection   718
   Yingyan Li, Yuntao Chen, Jiawei He, and Zhaoxiang Zhang

Polarimetric Pose Prediction   735
   Daoyi Gao, Yitong Li, Patrick Ruhkamp, Iuliia Skobleva,
   Magdalena Wysocki, HyunJun Jung, Pengyuan Wang, Arturo Guridi,
   and Benjamin Busam

Author Index   753

BEVFormer: Learning Bird's-Eye-View Representation from Multi-camera Images via Spatiotemporal Transformers

Zhiqi Li[1,2], Wenhai Wang[2], Hongyang Li[2], Enze Xie[3], Chonghao Sima[2], Tong Lu[1], Yu Qiao[2], and Jifeng Dai[2(✉)]

[1] Nanjing University, Nanjing, China
[2] Shanghai AI Laboratory, Shanghai, China
daijifeng@sensetime.com
[3] The University of Hong Kong, Pokfulam, Hong Kong

Abstract. 3D visual perception tasks, including 3D detection and map segmentation based on multi-camera images, are essential for autonomous driving systems. In this work, we present a new framework termed BEVFormer, which learns unified BEV representations with spatiotemporal transformers to support multiple autonomous driving perception tasks. In a nutshell, BEVFormer exploits both spatial and temporal information by interacting with spatial and temporal space through predefined grid-shaped BEV queries. To aggregate spatial information, we design spatial cross-attention that each BEV query extracts the spatial features from the regions of interest across camera views. For temporal information, we propose temporal self-attention to recurrently fuse the history BEV information. Our approach achieves the new state-of-the-art 56.9% in terms of NDS metric on the nuScenes test set, which is 9.0 points higher than previous best arts and on par with the performance of LiDAR-based baselines. The code is available at https://github.com/zhiql-li/BEVFormer.

Keywords: Autonomous driving · Bird's-Eye-View · 3D object detection · Map segmentation · Transformer

1 Introduction

Perception in 3D space is critical for various applications such as autonomous driving, robotics, *etc.* Despite the remarkable progress of LiDAR-based methods [8,20,41,48,52], camera-based approaches [28,30,43,45] have attracted extensive attention in recent years. Apart from the low cost for deployment, cameras

---

Z. Li, W. Wang and H. Li—Equal contribution.

Supplementary Information The online version contains supplementary material available at https://doi.org/10.1007/978-3-031-20077-9_1.

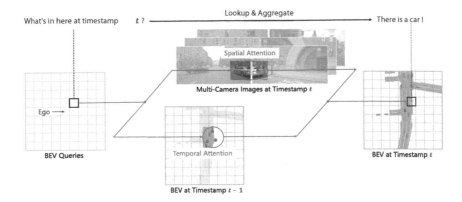

Fig. 1. BEVFormer leverages queries to lookup spatial/temporal space and aggregate spatiotemporal information correspondingly, hence benefiting stronger representations for perception tasks.

own the desirable advantages to detect long-range distance objects and identify vision-based road elements (*e.g.*, traffic lights, stoplines), compared to LiDAR-based counterparts.

Visual perception of the surrounding scene in autonomous driving is expected to predict the 3D bounding boxes or the semantic maps from 2D cues given by multiple cameras. The most straightforward solution is based on the monocular frameworks [3,29,33,42,43] and cross-camera post-processing. The downside of this framework is that it processes different views separately and cannot capture information across cameras, leading to low performance and efficiency [30,45].

As an alternative to the monocular frameworks, a more unified framework is extracting holistic representations from multi-camera images. The bird's-eye-view (BEV) is a commonly used representation of the surrounding scene since it clearly presents the location and scale of objects and is suitable for various autonomous driving tasks, such as perception and planning [27]. Although previous map segmentation methods demonstrate BEV's effectiveness [18,27,30], BEV-based approaches have not shown significant advantages over other paradigm in 3D object detections [29,32,45]. The underlying reason is that the 3D object detection task requires strong BEV features to support accurate 3D bounding box prediction, but generating BEV from the 2D planes is ill-posed. A popular BEV framework that generates BEV features is based on depth information [30,32,44], but this paradigm is sensitive to the accuracy of depth values or the depth distributions. The detection performance of BEV-based methods is thus subject to compounding errors [45], and inaccurate BEV features can seriously hurt the final performance. Therefore, *we are motivated to design a BEV generating method that does not rely on depth information and can learn BEV features adaptively rather than strictly rely on 3D prior.* Transformer, which uses an attention mechanism to aggregate valuable features dynamically, meets our demands conceptually.

Another motivation for using BEV features to perform perception tasks is that BEV is a desirable bridge to connect temporal and spatial space. For the human visual perception system, temporal information plays a crucial role in inferring the motion state of objects and identifying occluded objects, and many works in vision fields have demonstrated the effectiveness of using video data [2,19,24,25,31]. However, the existing state-of-the-art multi-camera 3D detection methods rarely exploit temporal information. The significant challenges are that autonomous driving is time-critical and objects in the scene change rapidly, and thus simply stacking BEV features of cross timestamps brings extra computational cost and interference information, which might not be ideal. Inspired by recurrent neural networks (RNNs) [10,17], *we utilize the BEV features to deliver temporal information from past to present recurrently, which has the same spirit as the hidden states of RNN models.*

To this end, we present a transformer-based bird's-eye-view (BEV) encoder, termed **BEVFormer**, which can effectively aggregate spatiotemporal features from multi-view cameras and history BEV features. The BEV features generated from the BEVFormer can simultaneously support multiple 3D perception tasks such as 3D object detection and map segmentation, which is valuable for the autonomous driving system. As shown in Fig. 1, our BEVFormer contains three key designs, which are (1) grid-shaped BEV queries to fuse spatial and temporal features via attention mechanisms flexibly, (2) spatial cross-attention module to aggregate the spatial features from multi-camera images, and (3) temporal self-attention module to extract temporal information from history BEV features, which benefits the velocity estimation of moving objects and the detection of heavily occluded objects, while bringing negligible computational overhead. With the unified features generated by BEVFormer, the model can collaborate with different task-specific heads such as Deformable DETR [54] and mask decoder [22], for end-to-end 3D object detection and map segmentation.

Our main contributions are as follows:

- We propose BEVFormer, a spatiotemporal transformer encoder that projects multi-camera/timestamp input to BEV representations. With the unified BEV features, our model can simultaneously support multiple autonomous driving perception tasks, including 3D detection and map segmentation.
- We designed learnable BEV queries along with a spatial cross-attention layer and a temporal self-attention layer to lookup spatial features from cross cameras and temporal features from history BEV, respectively, and then aggregate them into unified BEV features.
- We evaluate the proposed BEVFormer on multiple challenging benchmarks, including nuScenes [4] and Waymo [38]. Our BEVFormer consistently achieves improved performance compared to the prior arts. For example, under a comparable parameters and computation overhead, BEVFormer achieves 56.9% NDS on nuScenes `test` set, outperforming previous best detection method DETR3D [45] by 9.0 points (56.9% *vs.* 47.9%). For the map segmentation

task, we also achieve the state-of-the-art performance, more than 5.0 points higher than Lift-Splat [30] on the most challenging lane segmentation. We hope this straightforward and strong framework can serve as a new baseline for following 3D perception tasks.

2   Related Work

Transformer-Based 2D Perception. Recently, a new trend is to use transformer to reformulate detection and segmentation tasks [7,22,54]. DETR [7] uses a set of object queries to generate detection results by the cross-attention decoder directly. However, the main drawback of DETR is the long training time. Deformable DETR [54] solves this problem by proposing deformable attention. Different from vanilla global attention in DETR, the deformable attention interacts with local regions of interest, which only samples K points near each reference point and calculates attention results, resulting in high efficiency and significantly shortening the training time. The deformable attention mechanism is calculated by:

$$\text{DeformAttn}(q, p, x) = \sum_{i=1}^{N_{\text{head}}} \mathcal{W}_i \sum_{j=1}^{N_{\text{key}}} \mathcal{A}_{ij} \cdot \mathcal{W}_i' x(p + \Delta p_{ij}), \tag{1}$$

where q, p, x represent the query, reference point and input features, respectively. i indexes the attention head, and N_{head} denotes the total number of attention heads. j indexes the sampled keys, and N_{key} is the total sampled key number for each head. $W_i \in \mathbb{R}^{C \times (C/H_{\text{head}})}$ and $W_i' \in \mathbb{R}^{(C/H_{\text{head}}) \times C}$ are the learnable weights, where C is the feature dimension. $A_{ij} \in [0, 1]$ is the predicted attention weight, and is normalized by $\sum_{j=1}^{N_{\text{key}}} A_{ij} = 1$. $\Delta p_{ij} \in \mathbb{R}^2$ are the predicted offsets to the reference point p. $x(p + \Delta p_{ij})$ represents the feature at location $p + \Delta p_{ij}$, which is extracted by bilinear interpolation as in Dai *et al.* [12]. In this work, we extend the deformable attention to 3D perception tasks, to efficiently aggregate both spatial and temporal information.

Camera-Based 3D Perception. Previous 3D perception methods typically perform 3D object detection or map segmentation tasks independently. For the 3D object detection task, early methods are similar to 2D detection methods [1,26,37,47,51], which usually predict the 3D bounding boxes based on 2D bounding boxes. Wang *et al.* [43] follows an advanced 2D detector FCOS [39] and directly predicts 3D bounding boxes for each object. DETR3D [45] projects learnable 3D queries in 2D images, and then samples the corresponding features for end-to-end 3D bounding box prediction without NMS post-processing. Another solution is to transform image features into BEV features and predict 3D bounding boxes from the top-down view. Methods transform image features into BEV features with the depth information from depth estimation [44] or categorical depth distribution [32]. OFT [34] and ImVoxelNet [35] project the predefined voxels onto image features to generate the voxel representation of the

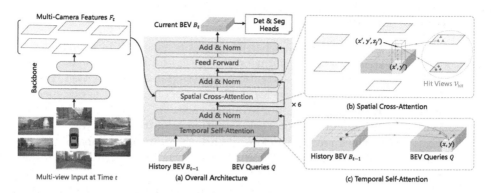

Fig. 2. Overall architecture of BEVFormer. (a) The encoder layer of BEVFormer contains grid-shaped BEV queries, temporal self-attention, and spatial cross-attention. (b) In spatial cross-attention, each BEV query only interacts with image features in the regions of interest. (c) In temporal self-attention, each BEV query interacts with two features: the BEV queries at the current timestamp and the BEV features at the previous timestamp.

scene. Recently, M^2BEV [46] futher explored the feasibility of simultaneously performing multiple perception tasks based on BEV features.

Actually, generating BEV features from multi-camera features is more extensively studied in map segmentation tasks [28,30]. A straightforward method is converting perspective view into the BEV through Inverse Perspective Mapping (IPM) [5,33]. In addition, Lift-Splat [30] generates the BEV features based on the depth distribution. Methods [9,16,28] utilize multilayer perceptron to learn the translation from perspective view to the BEV. PYVA [49] proposes a cross-view transformer that converts the front-view monocular image into the BEV, but this paradigm is not suitable for fusing multi-camera features due to the computational cost of global attention mechinism [40]. In addition to the spatial information, previous works [6,18,36] also consider the temporal information by stacking BEV features from several timestamps. Stacking BEV features constraints the available temporal information within fixed time duration and brings extra computational cost. In this work, the proposed spatiotemporal transformer generates BEV features of the current time by considering both spatial and temporal clues, and the temporal information is obtained from the previous BEV features by the RNN manner, which only brings little computational cost.

3 BEVFormer

Converting multi-camera image features to bird's-eye-view (BEV) features can provide a unified surrounding environment representation for various autonomous driving perception tasks. In this work, we present a new transformer-based framework for BEV generation, which can effectively aggregate spatiotemporal features from multi-view cameras and history BEV features via attention mechanisms.

3.1 Overall Architecture

As illustrated in Fig. 2, BEVFormer has 6 encoder layers, each of which follows the conventional structure of transformers [40], except for three tailored designs, namely BEV queries, spatial cross-attention, and temporal self-attention. Specifically, BEV queries are grid-shaped learnable parameters, which is designed to query features in BEV space from multi-camera views via attention mechanisms. Spatial cross-attention and temporal self-attention are attention layers working with BEV queries, which are used to lookup and aggregate spatial features from multi-camera images as well as temporal features from history BEV, according to the BEV query.

During inference, at timestamp t, we feed multi-camera images to the backbone network (*e.g.*, ResNet-101 [15]), and obtain the features $F_t = \{F_t^i\}_{i=1}^{N_{\text{view}}}$ of different camera views, where F_t^i is the feature of the i-th view, N_{view} is the total number of camera views. At the same time, we preserved the BEV features B_{t-1} at the prior timestamp $t-1$. In each encoder layer, we first use BEV queries Q to query the temporal information from the prior BEV features B_{t-1} via the temporal self-attention. We then employ BEV queries Q to inquire about the spatial information from the multi-camera features F_t via the spatial cross-attention. After the feed-forward network [40], the encoder layer output the refined BEV features, which is the input of the next encoder layer. After 6 stacking encoder layers, unified BEV features B_t at current timestamp t are generated. Taking the BEV features B_t as input, the 3D detection head and map segmentation head predict the perception results such as 3D bounding boxes and semantic map.

3.2 BEV Queries

We predefine a group of grid-shaped learnable parameters $Q \in \mathbb{R}^{H \times W \times C}$ as the queries of BEVFormer, where H, W are the spatial shape of the BEV plane. To be specific, the query $Q_p \in \mathbb{R}^{1 \times C}$ located at $p = (x, y)$ of Q is responsible for the corresponding grid cell region in the BEV plane. Each grid cell in the BEV plane corresponds to a real-world size of s meters. The center of BEV features corresponds to the position of the ego car by default. Following common practices [14], we add learnable positional embedding to BEV queries Q before inputting them to BEVFormer.

3.3 Spatial Cross-attention

Due to the large input scale of multi-camera 3D perception (containing N_{view} camera views), the computational cost of vanilla multi-head attention [40] is extremely high. Therefore, we develop the spatial cross-attention based on deformable attention [54], which is a resource-efficient attention layer where each BEV query Q_p only interacts with its regions of interest across camera views. However, deformable attention is originally designed for 2D perception, so some adjustments are required for 3D scenes.

As shown in Fig. 2(b), we first lift each query on the BEV plane to a pillar-like query [20], sample N_{ref} 3D reference points from the pillar, and then project these points to 2D views. For one BEV query, the projected 2D points can only fall on some views, and other views are not hit. Here, we term the hit views as $\mathcal{V}_{\text{hit}}$. After that, we regard these 2D points as the reference points of the query Q_p and sample the features from the hit views $\mathcal{V}_{\text{hit}}$ around these reference points. Finally, we perform a weighted sum of the sampled features as the output of spatial cross-attention. The process of spatial cross-attention (SCA) can be formulated as:

$$\text{SCA}(Q_p, F_t) = \frac{1}{|\mathcal{V}_{\text{hit}}|} \sum_{i \in \mathcal{V}_{\text{hit}}} \sum_{j=1}^{N_{\text{ref}}} \text{DeformAttn}(Q_p, \mathcal{P}(p, i, j), F_t^i), \qquad (2)$$

where i indexes the camera view, j indexes the reference points, and N_{ref} is the total reference points for each BEV query. F_t^i is the features of the i-th camera view. For each BEV query Q_p, we use a project function $\mathcal{P}(p, i, j)$ to get the j-th reference point on the i-th view image.

Next, we introduce how to obtain the reference points on the view image from the projection function $\mathcal{P}$. We first calculate the real world location (x', y') corresponding to the query Q_p located at $p = (x, y)$ of Q as Eq. 3.

$$x' = (x - \frac{W}{2}) \times s; \quad y' = (y - \frac{H}{2}) \times s, \qquad (3)$$

where H, W are the spatial shape of BEV queries, s is the size of resolution of BEV's grids, and (x', y') are the coordinates where the position of ego car is the origin. In 3D space, the objects located at (x', y') will appear at the height of z' on the z-axis. So we predefine a set of anchor heights $\{z_j'\}_{j=1}^{N_{\text{ref}}}$ to make sure we can capture clues that appeared at different heights. In this way, for each query Q_p, we obtain a pillar of 3D reference points $(x', y', z_j')_{j=1}^{N_{\text{ref}}}$. Finally, we project the 3D reference points to different image views through the projection matrix of cameras, which can be written as:

$$\mathcal{P}(p, i, j) = (x_{ij}, y_{ij})$$
$$\text{where } z_{ij} \cdot \begin{bmatrix} x_{ij} & y_{ij} & 1 \end{bmatrix}^T = T_i \cdot \begin{bmatrix} x' & y' & z_j' & 1 \end{bmatrix}^T. \qquad (4)$$

Here, $\mathcal{P}(p, i, j)$ is the 2D point on i-th view projected from j-th 3D point (x', y', z_j'), $T_i \in \mathbb{R}^{3 \times 4}$ is the known projection matrix of the i-th camera.

3.4   Temporal Self-attention

In addition to spatial information, temporal information is also crucial for the visual system to understand the surrounding environment [25]. For example, it is challenging to infer the velocity of moving objects or detect highly occluded objects from static images without temporal clues. To address this problem, we design temporal self-attention, which can represent the current environment by incorporating history BEV features.

Given the BEV queries Q at current timestamp t and history BEV features B_{t-1} preserved at timestamp $t-1$, we first align B_{t-1} to Q according to ego-motion to make the features at the same grid correspond to the same real-world location. Here, we denote the aligned history BEV features B_{t-1} as B'_{t-1}. However, from times $t-1$ to t, movable objects travel in the real world with various offsets. It is challenging to construct the precise association of the same objects between the BEV features of different times. Therefore, we model this temporal connection between features through the temporal self-attention (TSA) layer, which can be written as follows:

$$\text{TSA}(Q_p, \{Q, B'_{t-1}\}) = \sum_{V \in \{Q, B'_{t-1}\}} \text{DeformAttn}(Q_p, p, V), \tag{5}$$

where Q_p denotes the BEV query located at $p = (x, y)$. In addition, different from the vanilla deformable attention, the offsets Δp in temporal self-attention are predicted by the concatenation of Q and B'_{t-1}. Specially, for the first sample of each sequence, the temporal self-attention will degenerate into a self-attention without temporal information, where we replace the BEV features $\{Q, B'_{t-1}\}$ with duplicate BEV queries $\{Q, Q\}$.

Compared to simply stacking BEV in [6,18,36], our temporal self-attention can more effectively model long temporal dependency. BEVFormer extracts temporal information from the previous BEV features rather than multiple stacking BEV features, thus requiring less computational cost and suffering less disturbing information.

3.5   Applications of BEV Features

Since the BEV features $B_t \in \mathbb{R}^{H \times W \times C}$ is a versatile 2D feature map that can be used for various autonomous driving perception tasks, the 3D object detection and map segmentation task heads can be developed based on 2D perception methods [22,54] with minor modifications.

For 3D object detection, we design an end-to-end 3D detection head based on the 2D detector Deformable DETR [54]. The modifications include using single-scale BEV features B_t as the input of the decoder, predicting 3D bounding boxes and velocity rather than 2D bounding boxes, and only using L_1 loss to supervise 3D bounding box regression. With the detection head, our model can end-to-end predict 3D bounding boxes and velocity without the NMS post-processing.

For map segmentation, we design a map segmentation head based on a 2D segmentation method Panoptic SegFormer [22]. Since the map segmentation based on the BEV is basically the same as the common semantic segmentation, we utilize the mask decoder of [22] and class-fixed queries to target each semantic category, including the car, vehicles, road (drivable area), and lane.

3.6   Implementation Details

Training Phase. For each sample at timestamp t, we randomly sample another 3 samples from the consecutive sequence of the past 2 s, and this random sampling strategy can augment the diversity of ego-motion [55]. We denote the timestamps of these four samples as $t-3$, $t-2$, $t-1$ and t. For the samples of the first three timestamps, they are responsible for recurrently generating the BEV features $\{B_{t-3}, B_{t-2}, B_{t-1}\}$ and this phase requires no gradients. For the first sample at timestamp $t-3$, there is no previous BEV features, and temporal self-attention degenerate into self-attention. At the time t, the model generates the BEV features B_t based on both multi-camera inputs and the prior BEV features B_{t-1}, so that B_t contains the temporal and spatial clues crossing the four samples. Finally, we feed the BEV features B_t into the detection and segmentation heads and compute the corresponding loss functions.

Inference Phase. During the inference phase, we evaluate each frame of the video sequence in chronological order. The BEV features of the previous timestamp are saved and used for the next, and this online inference strategy is time-efficient and consistent with practical applications. Although we utilize temporal information, our inference speed is still comparable with other methods [43,45].

4   Experiments

4.1   Datasets

We conduct experiments on two challenging public autonomous driving datasets, namely nuScenes dataset [4] and Waymo open dataset(WOD) [38] and experiments on WOD were introduced in the supplementary.

The nuScenes dataset [4] contains 1000 scenes of roughly 20 s duration each, and the key samples are annotated 2 Hz. Each sample consists of RGB images from 6 cameras and has 360° horizontal FOV. For the detection task, there are 1.4M annotated 3D bounding boxes from 10 categories. We follow the settings in [30] to perform BEV segmentation task. This dataset also provides the official evaluation metrics for the detection task. The mean average precision (mAP) of nuScenes is computed using the center distance on the ground plane rather than the 3D Intersection over Union (IoU) to match the predicted results and ground truth. The nuScenes metrics also contain 5 types of true positive metrics (TP metrics), including ATE, ASE, AOE, AVE, and AAE for measuring translation, scale, orientation, velocity, and attribute errors, respectively. The nuScenes also defines a nuScenes detection score (NDS) as $\text{NDS} = \frac{1}{10}[5\text{mAP} + \sum_{\text{mTP} \in \text{TP}}(1 - \min(1, \text{mTP}))]$ to capture all aspects of the nuScenes detection tasks.

4.2   Experimental Settings

Following previous methods [29,43,45], we adopt two types of backbone: ResNet101-DCN [12,15] that initialized from FCOS3D [43] checkpoint, and VoVnet-99 [21] that initialized from DD3D [29] checkpoint. By default, we utilize the output multi-scale features from FPN [23] with sizes of $\frac{1}{16}$, $\frac{1}{32}$, $\frac{1}{64}$ and the dimension of $C = 256$. For experiments on nuScenes, the default size of

Table 1. 3D detection results on nuScenes test set. ∗ notes that VoVNet-99 (V2-99) [21] was pre-trained on the depth estimation task with extra data [29]. "BEVFormer-S" does not leverage temporal information in the BEV encoder. "L" and "C" indicate LiDAR and Camera, respectively.

Method	Modality	Backbone	NDS↑	mAP↑	mATE↓	mASE↓	mAOE↓	mAVE↓	mAAE↓
SSN [53]	L	–	0.569	0.463	–	–	–	–	–
CenterPoint-Voxel [50]	L	–	0.655	0.580	–	–	–	–	–
PointPainting [41]	L&C	–	0.581	0.464	0.388	0.271	0.496	0.247	0.111
FCOS3D [43]	C	R101	0.428	0.358	0.690	0.249	0.452	1.434	**0.124**
PGD [42]	C	R101	0.448	0.386	**0.626**	**0.245**	0.451	1.509	0.127
BEVFormer-S	C	R101	0.462	0.409	0.650	0.261	0.439	0.925	0.147
BEVFormer	C	R101	**0.535**	**0.445**	0.631	0.257	**0.405**	**0.435**	0.143
DD3D [29]	C	V2-99∗	0.477	0.418	**0.572**	**0.249**	0.368	1.014	**0.124**
DETR3D [45]	C	V2-99∗	0.479	0.412	0.641	0.255	0.394	0.845	0.133
BEVFormer-S	C	V2-99∗	0.495	0.435	0.589	0.254	0.402	0.842	0.131
BEVFormer	C	V2-99∗	**0.569**	**0.481**	0.582	0.256	0.375	**0.378**	0.126

Table 2. 3D detection results on nuScenes val set. "C" indicates Camera.

Method	Modality	Backbone	NDS↑	mAP↑	mATE↓	mASE↓	mAOE↓	mAVE↓	mAAE↓
FCOS3D [43]	C	R101	0.415	0.343	0.725	0.263	0.422	1.292	**0.153**
PGD [42]	C	R101	0.428	0.369	0.683	**0.260**	0.439	1.268	0.185
DETR3D [45]	C	R101	0.425	0.346	0.773	0.268	0.383	0.842	0.216
BEVFormer-S	C	R101	0.448	0.375	0.725	0.272	0.391	0.802	0.200
BEVFormer	C	R101	**0.517**	**0.416**	**0.673**	0.274	**0.372**	**0.394**	0.198

BEV queries is 200×200, the perception ranges are $[-51.2\,\text{m}, 51.2\,\text{m}]$ for the X and Y axis and the size of resolution s of BEV's grid is $0.512\,\text{m}$. We adopt learnable positional embedding for BEV queries. The BEV encoder contains 6 encoder layers and constantly refines the BEV queries in each layer. The input BEV features B_{t-1} for each encoder layer are the same and require no gradients. For each local query, during the spatial cross-attention module implemented by deformable attention mechanism, it corresponds to $N_{\text{ref}} = 4$ target points with different heights in 3D space, and the predefined height anchors are sampled uniformly from -5 m to 3 m. For each reference point on 2D view features, we use four sampling points around this reference point for each head. By default, we train our models with 24 epochs, a learning rate of 2×10^{-4}.

Baselines. To eliminate the effect of task heads and compare other BEV generating methods fairly, we use VPN [28] and Lift-Splat [30] to replace our BEV-Former and keep task heads and other settings the same. We also adapt BEV-Former into a static model called **BEVFormer-S** via adjusting the temporal self-attention into a vanilla self-attention without using history BEV features.

4.3   3D Object Detection Results

We train our model on the detection task with the detection head only for fairly comparing with previous state-of-the-art 3D object detection methods. In Table 1 and Table 2, we report our main results on nuScenes `test` and `val` splits. Our method outperforms previous best method DETR3D [45] over 9.2 points on `val` set (51.7% NDS *vs.* 42.5% NDS), under fair training strategy and comparable model scales. On the `test` set, our model achieves 56.9% NDS without bells and whistles, 9.0 points higher than DETR3D (47.9% NDS). Our method can even achieve comparable performance to some LiDAR-based baselines such as SSN (56.9% NDS) [53] and PointPainting (58.1% NDS) [41].

Previous camera-based methods [29,43,45] were almost unable to estimate the velocity, and our method demonstrates that temporal information plays a crucial role in velocity estimation for multi-camera detection. The mean Average Velocity Error (mAVE) of BEVFormer is 0.378 m/s on the `test` set, outperforming other camera-based methods by a vast margin and approaching the performance of LiDAR-based methods [41].

Table 3. 3D detection and map segmentation results on nuScenes `val` set. Comparison of training segmentation and detection tasks jointly or not. *: We use VPN [28] and Lift-Splat [30] to replace our BEV encoder for comparison, and the task heads are the same. †: Results from their paper.

Method	Task Head		3D Detection		BEV Segmentation (IoU)			
	Det	Seg	NDS↑	mAP↑	Car	Vehicles	Road	Lane
Lift-Splat† [30]	✗	✓	–	–	32.1	32.1	72.9	20.0
FIERY† [18]	✗	✓	–	–	–	38.2	–	–
VPN* [28]	✓	✗	0.333	0.253	–	–	–	–
VPN*	✗	✓	–	–	31.0	31.8	76.9	19.4
VPN*	✓	✓	0.334	0.257	36.6	37.3	76.0	18.0
Lift-Splat*	✓	✗	0.397	0.348	–	–	–	–
Lift-Splat*	✗	✓	–	–	42.1	41.7	77.7	20.0
Lift-Splat*	✓	✓	0.410	0.344	43.0	42.8	73.9	18.3
BEVFormer-S	✓	✗	0.448	0.375	–	–	–	–
BEVFormer-S	✗	✓	–	–	43.1	43.2	**80.7**	21.3
BEVFormer-S	✓	✓	0.453	0.380	44.3	44.4	77.6	19.8
BEVFormer	✓	✗	0.517	**0.416**	–	–	–	–
BEVFormer	✗	✓	–	–	44.8	44.8	80.1	**25.7**
BEVFormer	✓	✓	**0.520**	0.412	**46.8**	**46.7**	77.5	23.9

4.4   Multi-tasks Perception Results

We train our model with both detection and segmentation heads to verify the learning ability of our model for multiple tasks, and the results are shown in Table 3. While comparing different BEV encoders under same settings, BEV-Former achieves higher performances of all tasks except for road segmentation results is comparable with BEVFormer-S. For example, with joint training, BEV-Former outperforms Lift-Splat* [30] by 11.0 points on detation task (52.0% NDS *v.s.* 41.0% NDS) and IoU of 5.6 points on lane segmentation (23.9% *v.s.* 18.3%). Compared with training tasks individually, multi-task learning saves computational cost and reduces the inference time by sharing more modules, including the backbone and the BEV encoder. In this paper, we show that the BEV features generated by our BEV encoder can be well adapted to different tasks, and the model training with multi-task heads performs even better on detection tasks and vehicles segmentation. However, the jointly trained model does not perform as well as individually trained models for road and lane segmentation, which is a common phenomenon called *negative transfer* [11,13] in multi-task learning

4.5   Ablation Study

To delve into the effect of different modules, we conduct ablation experiments on nuScenes `val` set with detection head. More ablation studies are in Appendix.

Effectiveness of Spatial Cross-attention. To verify the effect of spatial cross-attention, we use BEVFormer-S to perform ablation experiments to exclude the interference of temporal information, and the results are shown in Table 4. The default spatial cross-attention is based on deformable attention. For comparison, we also construct two other baselines with different attention mechanisms: (1) Using the global attention to replace deformable attention; (2) Making each query only interact with its reference points rather than the surrounding local regions, and it is similar to previous methods [34,35]. For a broader comparison, we also replace the BEVFormer with the BEV generation methods proposed by VPN [28] and Lift-Spalt [30]. We can observe that deformable attention significantly outperforms other attention mechanisms under a comparable model scale. Global attention consumes too much GPU memory, and point interaction has a limited receptive field. Sparse attention achieves better performance because it interacts with a priori determined regions of interest, balancing receptive field and GPU consumption.

Effectiveness of Temporal Self-attention. From Table 1 and Table 3, we can observe that BEVFormer outperforms BEVFormer-S with remarkable improvements under the same setting, especially on challenging detection tasks. The effect of temporal information is mainly in the following aspects: (1) The introduction of temporal information greatly benefits the accuracy of the velocity estimation; (2) The predicted locations and orientations of the objects are more accurate with temporal information; (3) We obtain higher recall on heavily occluded objects since the temporal information contains past objects clues,

Table 4. The detection results of different methods with various BEV encoders on nuScenes val set. "Memory" is the consumed GPU memory during training. *: We use VPN [28] and Lift-Splat [30] to replace BEV encoder of our model for comparison. †: We train BEVFormer-S using global attention in spatial cross-attention, and the model is trained with fp16 weights. In addition, we only adopt single-scale features from the backbone and set the spatial shape of BEV queries to be 100 × 100 to save memory. ‡: We degrade the interaction targets of deformable attention from the local region to the reference points only by removing the predicted offsets and weights.

Method	Attention	NDS↑	mAP↑	mATE↓	mAOE↓	#Param.	FLOPs	Memory
VPN* [28]	-	0.334	0.252	0.926	0.598	111.2M	924.5G	∼20G
List-Splat* [30]	-	0.397	0.348	0.784	0.537	74.0M	1087.7G	∼20G
BEVFormer-S†	Global	0.404	0.325	0.837	0.442	62.1M	1245.1G	∼36G
BEVFormer-S‡	Points	0.423	0.351	0.753	0.442	68.1M	1264.3G	∼20G
BEVFormer-S	Local	**0.448**	**0.375**	**0.725**	**0.391**	68.7M	1303.5G	∼20G

as showed in Fig. 3. To evaluate the performance of BEVFormer on objects with different occlusion levels, we divide the validation set of nuScenes into four subsets according to the official visibility label provided by nuScenes. In each subset, we also compute the average recall of all categories with a center distance threshold of 2 m during matching. The maximum number of predicted boxes is 300 for all methods to compare recall fairly. On the subset that only 0–40% of objects can be visible, the average recall of BEVFormer outperforms BEVFormer-S and DETR3D with a margin of more than 6.0%.

Model Scale and Latency. We compare the performance and latency of different configurations in Table 5. We ablate the scales of BEVFormer in three aspects, including whether to use multi-scale view features, the shape of BEV queries, and the number of layers, to verify the trade-off between performance and inference latency. We can observe that configuration C using one encoder layer in BEVFormer achieves 50.1% NDS and reduces the latency of BEVFormer from the original 130 ms to 25 ms. Configuration D, with single-scale view features, smaller BEV size, and only 1 encoder layer, consumes only 7 ms during inference, although it loses 3.9 points compared to the default configuration. However, due to the multi-view image inputs, the bottleneck that limits the efficiency lies in the backbone, and efficient backbones for autonomous driving deserve in-depth study. Overall, our architecture can adapt to various model scales and be flexible to trade off performance and efficiency.

4.6   Visualization Results

We show the detection results of a complex scene in Fig. 4. BEVFormer produces impressive results except for a few mistakes in small and remote objects. More qualitative results are provided in Appendix.

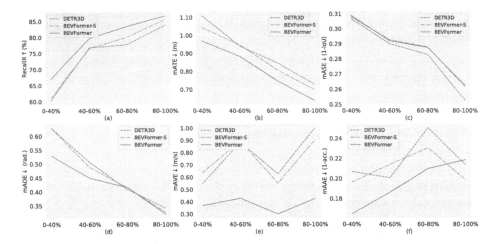

Fig. 3. The detection results of subsets with different visibilities. We divide the nuScenes `val` set into four subsets based on the visibility that {0–40%, 40–60%, 60–80%, 80–100%} of objects can be visible. (a): Enhanced by the temporal information, BEVFormer has a higher recall on all subsets, especially on the subset with the lowest visibility (0–40%). (b), (d) and (e): Temporal information benefits translation, orientation, and velocity accuracy. (c) and (f): The scale and attribute error gaps among different methods are minimal. Temporal information does not work to benefit an object's scale prediction.

5   Discussion and Conclusion

In this work, we have proposed BEVFormer to generate the bird's-eye-view features from multi-camera inputs. BEVFormer can efficiently aggregate spatial and temporal information and generate powerful BEV features that simultaneously support 3D detection and map segmentation tasks.

Table 5. Latency and performance of different model configurations on nuScenes `val` set. The latency is measured on a V100 GPU, and the backbone is R101-DCN. The input image shape is 900×1600. "MS" notes multi-scale view features.

| Method | Scale of BEVFormer | | | Latency (ms) | | | FPS | NDS↑ | mAP↑ |
	MS	BEV	#Layer	Backbone	BEVFormer	Head			
BEVFormer	✓	200×200	6	391	130	19	1.7	**0.517**	**0.416**
A	✗	200×200	6	387	87	19	1.9	0.511	0.406
B	✓	100×100	6	391	53	18	2.0	0.504	0.402
C	✓	200×200	1	391	25	19	2.1	0.501	0.396
D	✗	100×100	1	387	**7**	18	**2.3**	0.478	0.374

Fig. 4. Visualization results of BEVFormer on nuScenes val set. We show the 3D bboxes predictions in multi-camera images and the bird's-eye-view.

Limitations. At present, the camera-based methods still have a particular gap with the LiDAR-based methods in effect and efficiency. Accurate inference of 3D location from 2D information remains a long-stand challenge for camera-based methods.

Broader Impacts. BEVFormer demonstrates that using spatiotemporal information from the multi-camera input can significantly improve the performance of visual perception models. The advantages demonstrated by BEVFormer, such as more accurate velocity estimation and higher recall on low-visible objects, are essential for constructing a better and safer autonomous driving system and beyond. We believe BEVFormer is just a baseline of the following more powerful visual perception methods, and vision-based perception systems still have tremendous potential to be explored.

Acknowledgement. This work is supported by the Natural Science Foundation of China under Grant 61672273 and Grant 61832008, the Shanghai Committee of Science and Technology (Grant No. 21DZ1100100) and Shanghai AI Laboratory. This work is done when Zhiqi Li is an intern at Shanghai AI Lab.

References

1. Brazil, G., Liu, X.: M3D-RPN: monocular 3D region proposal network for object detection. In: Proceedings of the IEEE/CVF International Conference on Computer Vision, pp. 9287–9296 (2019)
2. Brazil, G., Pons-Moll, G., Liu, X., Schiele, B.: Kinematic 3D object detection in monocular video. In: Vedaldi, A., Bischof, H., Brox, T., Frahm, J.-M. (eds.) ECCV 2020. LNCS, vol. 12368, pp. 135–152. Springer, Cham (2020). https://doi.org/10.1007/978-3-030-58592-1_9
3. Bruls, T., Porav, H., Kunze, L., Newman, P.: The right (angled) perspective: improving the understanding of road scenes using boosted inverse perspective mapping. In: 2019 IEEE Intelligent Vehicles Symposium (IV), pp. 302–309. IEEE (2019)
4. Caesar, H., et al.: nuScenes: a multimodal dataset for autonomous driving. In: Proceedings of the IEEE/CVF Conference on Computer Vision and Pattern Recognition, pp. 11621–11631 (2020)

5. Can, Y.B., Liniger, A., Paudel, D.P., Van Gool, L.: Structured bird's-eye-view traffic scene understanding from onboard images. In: Proceedings of the IEEE/CVF International Conference on Computer Vision, pp. 15661–15670 (2021)
6. Can, Y.B., Liniger, A., Unal, O., Paudel, D., Van Gool, L.: Understanding bird's-eye view semantic HD-maps using an onboard monocular camera. arXiv preprint arXiv:2012.03040 (2020)
7. Carion, N., Massa, F., Synnaeve, G., Usunier, N., Kirillov, A., Zagoruyko, S.: End-to-end object detection with transformers. In: Vedaldi, A., Bischof, H., Brox, T., Frahm, J.-M. (eds.) ECCV 2020. LNCS, vol. 12346, pp. 213–229. Springer, Cham (2020). https://doi.org/10.1007/978-3-030-58452-8_13
8. Chen, X., Ma, H., Wan, J., Li, B., Xia, T.: Multi-view 3D object detection network for autonomous driving. In: Proceedings of the IEEE Conference on Computer Vision and Pattern Recognition, pp. 1907–1915 (2017)
9. Chitta, K., Prakash, A., Geiger, A.: Neat: neural attention fields for end-to-end autonomous driving. In: Proceedings of the IEEE/CVF International Conference on Computer Vision, pp. 15793–15803 (2021)
10. Cho, K., Van Merriënboer, B., Bahdanau, D., Bengio, Y.: On the properties of neural machine translation: encoder-decoder approaches. arXiv preprint arXiv:1409.1259 (2014)
11. Crawshaw, M.: Multi-task learning with deep neural networks: a survey. arXiv preprint arXiv:2009.09796 (2020)
12. Dai, J., et al.: Deformable convolutional networks. In: Proceedings of the IEEE International Conference on Computer Vision, pp. 764–773 (2017)
13. Fifty, C., Amid, E., Zhao, Z., Yu, T., Anil, R., Finn, C.: Efficiently identifying task groupings for multi-task learning. In: Advances in Neural Information Processing Systems, vol. 34 (2021)
14. Gehring, J., Auli, M., Grangier, D., Yarats, D., Dauphin, Y.N.: Convolutional sequence to sequence learning. In: International Conference on Machine Learning, pp. 1243–1252. PMLR (2017)
15. He, K., Zhang, X., Ren, S., Sun, J.: Deep residual learning for image recognition. In: Proceedings of the IEEE Conference on Computer Vision and Pattern Recognition, pp. 770–778 (2016)
16. Hendy, N., et al.: Fishing net: future inference of semantic heatmaps in grids. arXiv preprint arXiv:2006.09917 (2020)
17. Hochreiter, S., Schmidhuber, J.: Long short-term memory. Neural Comput. 9(8), 1735–1780 (1997)
18. Hu, A., et al.: Fiery: future instance prediction in bird's-eye view from surround monocular cameras. In: Proceedings of the IEEE/CVF International Conference on Computer Vision, pp. 15273–15282 (2021)
19. Kang, K., Ouyang, W., Li, H., Wang, X.: Object detection from video tubelets with convolutional neural networks. In: Proceedings of the IEEE Conference on Computer Vision and Pattern Recognition, pp. 817–825 (2016)
20. Lang, A.H., Vora, S., Caesar, H., Zhou, L., Yang, J., Beijbom, O.: Pointpillars: fast encoders for object detection from point clouds. In: Proceedings of the IEEE/CVF Conference on Computer Vision and Pattern Recognition, pp. 12697–12705 (2019)
21. Lee, Y., Hwang, J.W., Lee, S., Bae, Y., Park, J.: An energy and GPU-computation efficient backbone network for real-time object detection. In: Proceedings of the IEEE/CVF Conference on Computer Vision and Pattern Recognition Workshops (2019)
22. Li, Z., et al.: Panoptic segformer: delving deeper into panoptic segmentation with transformers. arXiv preprint arXiv:2109.03814 (2021)

23. Lin, T.Y., Dollár, P., Girshick, R.B., He, K., Hariharan, B., Belongie, S.J.: Feature pyramid networks for object detection. In: 2017 IEEE Conference on Computer Vision and Pattern Recognition (CVPR), pp. 936–944 (2017)
24. Luo, W., Yang, B., Urtasun, R.: Fast and furious: real time end-to-end 3D detection, tracking and motion forecasting with a single convolutional net. In: Proceedings of the IEEE Conference on Computer Vision and Pattern Recognition, pp. 3569–3577 (2018)
25. Ma, X., Ouyang, W., Simonelli, A., Ricci, E.: 3D object detection from images for autonomous driving: a survey. arXiv preprint arXiv:2202.02980 (2022)
26. Mousavian, A., Anguelov, D., Flynn, J., Kosecka, J.: 3D bounding box estimation using deep learning and geometry. In: Proceedings of the IEEE Conference on Computer Vision and Pattern Recognition, pp. 7074–7082 (2017)
27. Ng, M.H., Radia, K., Chen, J., Wang, D., Gog, I., Gonzalez, J.E.: BEV-seg: bird's eye view semantic segmentation using geometry and semantic point cloud. arXiv preprint arXiv:2006.11436 (2020)
28. Pan, B., Sun, J., Leung, H.Y.T., Andonian, A., Zhou, B.: Cross-view semantic segmentation for sensing surroundings. IEEE Robot. Autom. Lett. **5**(3), 4867–4873 (2020)
29. Park, D., Ambrus, R., Guizilini, V., Li, J., Gaidon, A.: Is pseudo-lidar needed for monocular 3D object detection? In: Proceedings of the IEEE/CVF International Conference on Computer Vision, pp. 3142–3152 (2021)
30. Philion, J., Fidler, S.: Lift, splat, shoot: encoding images from arbitrary camera rigs by implicitly unprojecting to 3D. In: Vedaldi, A., Bischof, H., Brox, T., Frahm, J.-M. (eds.) ECCV 2020. LNCS, vol. 12359, pp. 194–210. Springer, Cham (2020). https://doi.org/10.1007/978-3-030-58568-6_12
31. Qi, C.R., et al.: Offboard 3D object detection from point cloud sequences. In: Proceedings of the IEEE/CVF Conference on Computer Vision and Pattern Recognition, pp. 6134–6144 (2021)
32. Reading, C., Harakeh, A., Chae, J., Waslander, S.L.: Categorical depth distribution network for monocular 3D object detection. In: Proceedings of the IEEE/CVF Conference on Computer Vision and Pattern Recognition, pp. 8555–8564 (2021)
33. Reiher, L., Lampe, B., Eckstein, L.: A Sim2Real deep learning approach for the transformation of images from multiple vehicle-mounted cameras to a semantically segmented image in bird's eye view. In: 2020 IEEE 23rd International Conference on Intelligent Transportation Systems (ITSC), pp. 1–7. IEEE (2020)
34. Roddick, T., Kendall, A., Cipolla, R.: Orthographic feature transform for monocular 3D object detection. In: BMVC (2019)
35. Rukhovich, D., Vorontsova, A., Konushin, A.: Imvoxelnet: image to voxels projection for monocular and multi-view general-purpose 3D object detection. In: Proceedings of the IEEE/CVF Winter Conference on Applications of Computer Vision, pp. 2397–2406 (2022)
36. Saha, A., Maldonado, O.M., Russell, C., Bowden, R.: Translating images into maps. arXiv preprint arXiv:2110.00966 (2021)
37. Simonelli, A., Bulo, S.R., Porzi, L., Lopez-Antequera, M., Kontschieder, P.: Disentangling monocular 3D object detection. In: Proceedings of the IEEE/CVF International Conference on Computer Vision (ICCV), October 2019
38. Sun, P., et al.: Scalability in perception for autonomous driving: waymo open dataset. In: Proceedings of the IEEE/CVF Conference on Computer Vision and Pattern Recognition, pp. 2446–2454 (2020)

39. Tian, Z., Shen, C., Chen, H., He, T.: FCOS: fully convolutional one-stage object detection. In: Proceedings of the IEEE/CVF International Conference on Computer Vision, pp. 9627–9636 (2019)
40. Vaswani, A., et al.: Attention is all you need. In: Advances in Neural Information Processing Systems, vol. 30 (2017)
41. Vora, S., Lang, A.H., Helou, B., Beijbom, O.: Pointpainting: sequential fusion for 3D object detection. In: Proceedings of the IEEE/CVF Conference on Computer Vision and Pattern Recognition, pp. 4604–4612 (2020)
42. Wang, T., Xinge, Z., Pang, J., Lin, D.: Probabilistic and geometric depth: detecting objects in perspective. In: Conference on Robot Learning, pp. 1475–1485. PMLR (2022)
43. Wang, T., Zhu, X., Pang, J., Lin, D.: FCOS3D: fully convolutional one-stage monocular 3D object detection. In: Proceedings of the IEEE/CVF International Conference on Computer Vision, pp. 913–922 (2021)
44. Wang, Y., Chao, W.L., Garg, D., Hariharan, B., Campbell, M., Weinberger, K.Q.: Pseudo-lidar from visual depth estimation: bridging the gap in 3D object detection for autonomous driving. In: Proceedings of the IEEE/CVF Conference on Computer Vision and Pattern Recognition, pp. 8445–8453 (2019)
45. Wang, Y., Guizilini, V.C., Zhang, T., Wang, Y., Zhao, H., Solomon, J.: DETR3D: 3D object detection from multi-view images via 3D-to-2D queries. In: Conference on Robot Learning, pp. 180–191. PMLR (2022)
46. Xie, E., et al.: M2BEV: multi-camera joint 3D detection and segmentation with unified birds-eye view representation. arXiv preprint arXiv:2204.05088 (2022)
47. Xu, B., Chen, Z.: Multi-level fusion based 3D object detection from monocular images. In: Proceedings of the IEEE Conference on Computer Vision and Pattern Recognition, pp. 2345–2353 (2018)
48. Yan, Y., Mao, Y., Li, B.: Second: sparsely embedded convolutional detection. Sensors **18**(10), 3337 (2018)
49. Yang, W., et al.: Projecting your view attentively: monocular road scene layout estimation via cross-view transformation. In: Proceedings of the IEEE/CVF Conference on Computer Vision and Pattern Recognition, pp. 15536–15545 (2021)
50. Yin, T., Zhou, X., Krahenbuhl, P.: Center-based 3D object detection and tracking. In: Proceedings of the IEEE/CVF Conference on Computer Vision and Pattern Recognition, pp. 11784–11793 (2021)
51. Zhou, X., Wang, D., Krähenbühl, P.: Objects as points. arXiv preprint arXiv:1904.07850 (2019)
52. Zhou, Y., Tuzel, O.: Voxelnet: end-to-end learning for point cloud based 3D object detection. In: Proceedings of the IEEE Conference on Computer Vision and Pattern Recognition, pp. 4490–4499 (2018)
53. Zhu, X., Ma, Y., Wang, T., Xu, Y., Shi, J., Lin, D.: SSN: shape signature networks for multi-class object detection from point clouds. In: Vedaldi, A., Bischof, H., Brox, T., Frahm, J.-M. (eds.) ECCV 2020. LNCS, vol. 12370, pp. 581–597. Springer, Cham (2020). https://doi.org/10.1007/978-3-030-58595-2_35
54. Zhu, X., Su, W., Lu, L., Li, B., Wang, X., Dai, J.: Deformable detr: deformable transformers for end-to-end object detection. In: International Conference on Learning Representations (2020)
55. Zhu, X., Xiong, Y., Dai, J., Yuan, L., Wei, Y.: Deep feature flow for video recognition. In: Proceedings of the IEEE Conference on Computer Vision and Pattern Recognition, pp. 2349–2358 (2017)

Category-Level 6D Object Pose and Size Estimation Using Self-supervised Deep Prior Deformation Networks

Jiehong Lin[1,2] , Zewei Wei[1] , Changxing Ding[1] , and Kui Jia[1,3(✉)]

[1] South China University of Technology, Guangzhou, China
{lin.jiehong,eeweizewei}@mail.scut.edu.cn, {chxding,kuijia}@scut.edu.cn
[2] DexForce Co. Ltd., Shenzhen, China
[3] Peng Cheng Laboratory, Shenzhen, China

Abstract. It is difficult to precisely annotate object instances and their semantics in 3D space, and as such, synthetic data are extensively used for these tasks, e.g., category-level 6D object pose and size estimation. However, the easy annotations in synthetic domains bring the downside effect of synthetic-to-real (Sim2Real) domain gap. In this work, we aim to address this issue in the task setting of Sim2Real, unsupervised domain adaptation for category-level 6D object pose and size estimation. We propose a method that is built upon a novel *Deep Prior Deformation Network*, shortened as DPDN. DPDN learns to deform features of categorical shape priors to match those of object observations, and is thus able to establish deep correspondence in the feature space for direct regression of object poses and sizes. To reduce the Sim2Real domain gap, we formulate a novel self-supervised objective upon DPDN via consistency learning; more specifically, we apply two rigid transformations to each object observation in parallel, and feed them into DPDN respectively to yield dual sets of predictions; on top of the parallel learning, an inter-consistency term is employed to keep cross consistency between dual predictions for improving the sensitivity of DPDN to pose changes, while individual intra-consistency ones are used to enforce self-adaptation within each learning itself. We train DPDN on both training sets of the synthetic CAMERA25 and real-world REAL275 datasets; our results outperform the existing methods on REAL275 test set under both the unsupervised and supervised settings. Ablation studies also verify the efficacy of our designs. Our code is released publicly at https://github.com/JiehongLin/Self-DPDN.

Keywords: 6D pose estimation · Self-supervised learning

1 Introduction

The task of category-level 6D object pose and size estimation, formally introduced in [24], is to estimate the rotations, translations, and sizes of unseen object instances of certain categories in cluttered RGB-D scenes. It plays a crucial role

© The Author(s), under exclusive license to Springer Nature Switzerland AG 2022
S. Avidan et al. (Eds.): ECCV 2022, LNCS 13669, pp. 19–34, 2022.
https://doi.org/10.1007/978-3-031-20077-9_2

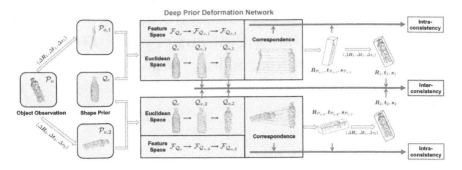

Fig. 1. An illustration of our proposed self-supervised Deep Prior Deformation Network (DPDN). DPDN deforms categorical shape priors in the feature space to pair with object observations, and establishes deep correspondence for direct estimates of object poses and sizes; upon DPDN, a novel self-supervised objective is designed to reduce synthetic-to-real domain gap via consistency learning. Specifically, we apply two rigid transformations to the point set $\mathcal{P}_o$ of an object observation, and feed them into DPDN in parallel to make dual sets of predictions; on top of the parallel learning, an inter-consistency term between dual predictions is then combined with individual intra-consistency ones within each learning to form the self-supervision. For simplicity, we omit the image input of object observation. Notations are explained in Sect. 3.

in many real-world applications, such as robotic grasping [17,27], augmented reality [2], and autonomous driving [5,6,12,26].

For this task, existing methods can be roughly categorized into two groups, i.e., those based on direct regression and those based on dense correspondence learning. Methods of the former group [4,14,15] are conceptually simple, but struggle in learning pose-sensitive features such that direct predictions can be made in the full $SE(3)$ space; dense correspondence learning [3,11,20,24,25] makes the task easier by first regressing point-wise coordinates in the canonical space to align with points of observations, and then obtaining object poses and sizes via solving of Umeyama algorithm [21]. Recent works [3,11,20,25] of the second group exploit strong categorical priors (*e.g.*, mean shapes of object categories) for improving the qualities of canonical point sets, and constantly achieve impressive results; however, their surrogate objectives for the learning of canonical coordinates are one step away from the true ones for estimating object poses and sizes, making their learning suboptimal to the end task.

The considered learning task is further challenged by the lack of real-world RGB-D data with careful object pose and size annotations in 3D space. As such, synthetic data are usually simulated and rendered whose annotations can be freely obtained on the fly [7,24]. However, the easy annotations in synthetic domains bring a downside effect of synthetic-to-real (Sim2Real) domain gap; learning with synthetic data with no consideration of Sim2Real domain adaptation would inevitably result in poor generalization in the real-world domain. This naturally falls in the realm of Sim2Real, unsupervised domain adaptation (UDA) [1,11,16,19,23,28–30].

In this work, we consider the task setting of Sim2Real UDA for category-level 6D object pose and size estimation. We propose a new method of *self-supervised Deep Prior Deformation Network*; Fig. 1 gives an illustration. Following dense correspondence learning, we first present a novel *Deep Prior Deformation Network*, shortened as **DPDN**, which implements a deep version of shape prior deformation in the feature space, and is thus able to establish deep correspondence for direct regression of poses and sizes with high precision. For a cluttered RGB-D scene, we employ a 2D instance segmentation network (*e.g.*, Mask RCNN [8]) to segment the objects of interest out, and feed them into our proposed DPDN for pose and size estimation. As shown in Fig. 2, the architecture of DPDN consists of three main modules, including a Triplet Feature Extractor, a Deep Prior Deformer, and a Pose and Size Estimator. For an object observation, the Triplet Feature Extractor learns point-wise features from its image crop, point set, and categorical shape prior, respectively; then Deep Prior Deformer deforms the prior in feature space by learning a feature deformation field and a correspondence matrix, and thus builds deep correspondence from the observation to its canonical version; finally, Pose and Size Estimator is used to make reliable predictions directly from those built deep correspondence.

On top of DPDN, we formulate a self-supervised objective that combines an inter-consistency term with two intra-consistency ones for UDA. More specifically, as shown in Fig. 1, we apply two rigid transformations to an input point set of object observation, and feed them into our DPDN in parallel for making dual sets of predictions. Upon the above parallel learning, the inter-consistency term enforces cross consistency between dual predictions w.r.t. two transformations for improving the sensitivity of DPDN to pose changes, and within each learning, the individual intra-consistency term is employed to enforce self-adaptation between the correspondence and the predictions. We train DPDN on both training sets of the synthetic CAMERA25 and real-world REAL275 datasets [24]; our results outperform the existing methods on REAL275 test set under both unsupervised and supervised settings. We also conduct ablation studies that confirm the advantages of our designs. Our contributions can be summarized as follows:

– We propose a *Deep Prior Deformation Network*, termed as DPDN, for the task of category-level 6D object pose and size estimation. DPDN deforms categorical shape priors to pair with object observations in the feature space, and is thus able to establish deep correspondence for direct regression of object poses and sizes.

– Given that the considered task largely uses synthetic training data, we formulate a novel self-supervised objective upon DPDN to reduce the synthetic-to-real domain gap. The objective is built upon enforcing consistencies between parallel learning w.r.t. two rigid transformations, and has the effects of both improving the sensitivity of DPDN to pose changes, and making predictions more reliable.

– We conduct thorough ablation studies to confirm the efficacy of our designs. Notably, our method outperforms existing ones on the benchmark dataset of real-world REAL275 under both the unsupervised and supervised settings.

2 Related Work

Fully-Supervised Methods. Methods of fully-supervised category-level 6D pose and size estimation could be roughly divided into two groups, *i.e.*, those based on direct regression [4,14,15] and those based on dense correspondence learning [3,20,24,25].

Direct estimates of object poses and sizes from object observations suffer from the difficulties in the learning of the full $SE(3)$ space, and thus make demands on extraction of pose-sensitive features. FS-Net [4] builds an orientation-aware backbone with 3D graph convolutions to encode object shapes, and makes predictions with a decoupled rotation mechanism. DualPoseNet [15] encodes pose-sensitive features from object observations based on rotation-equivariant spherical convolutions, while two parallel pose decoders with different working mechanisms are stacked to impose complementary supervision. A recent work of SS-ConvNet [14] designs Sparse Steerable Convolutions (SS-Conv) to further explore SE(3)-equivariant feature learning, and presents a two-stage pose estimation pipeline upon SS-Convs for iterative pose refinement.

Another group of works first learn coordinates of object observations in the canonical space to establish dense correspondence, and then obtain object poses and sizes by solving Umeyama algorithm from the correspondence in 3D space. NOCS [24], the first work for our focused task, is realized in this way by directly regressing canonical coordinates from RGB images. SPD [20] then makes the learning of canonical points easier by deforming categorical shape priors, rather than directly regressing from object observations. The follow-up works also confirm the advantages of shape priors, and make efforts on the prior deformation to further improve the qualities of canonical points, *e.g.*, via recurrent reconstruction for iterative refinement [25], or structure-guided adaptation based on transformer [3].

Unsupervised Methods. Due to the time-consuming and labor-intensive annotating of real-world data in 3D space, UDA-COPE [11] presents a new setting of unsupervised domain adaptation for the focused task, and adapts a teacher-student scheme with bidirectional point filtering to this setting, which, however, heavily relies on the qualities of pseudo labels. In this paper, we exploit inter-/intra-consistency in the self-supervised objective to explore the data characteristics of real-world data and fit the data for the reduction of domain gap.

3 Self-supervised Deep Prior Deformation Network

Given a cluttered RGB-D scene, the goal of *Category-Level 6D Object Pose and Size Estimation* is to detect object instances of interest with compact 3D bounding boxes, each of which is represented by rotation $\boldsymbol{R} \in SO(3)$, translation $\boldsymbol{t} \in \mathbb{R}^3$, and size $\boldsymbol{s} \in \mathbb{R}^3$ *w.r.t.* categorical canonical space.

A common practice to deal with this complicated task is decoupling it into two steps, including 1) object detection/instance segmentation, and 2) object pose and size estimation. For the first step, there exist quite mature techniques to accomplish it effectively, *e.g.*, employing an off-the-shelf MaskRCNN [8] to segment object instances of interest out; for the second step, however, it is still challenging to directly regress poses of unknown objects, especially for the learning in $SO(3)$ space. To settle this problem, we propose in this paper a novel *Deep Prior Deformation Network* Φ, shortened as **DPDN**, which deforms categorical shape priors to match object observations in the feature space, and estimates object poses and sizes from the built deep correspondence directly; Fig. 2 gives an illustration. We will detail the architecture of Φ in Sect. 3.1.

Another challenge of this task is the difficulty in precisely annotating real-world data in 3D space. Although synthetic data at scale are available for the learning of deep models, their results are often less precise than those trained with annotated real-world data, due to downside effect of large domain gap. To this end, we take a mixture of labeled synthetic data and unlabeled real-world one for training, and design a novel self-supervised objective for synthetic-to-real (Sim2Real), unsupervised domain adaptation. Specifically, given a mini batch of B training instances $\{\mathcal{V}_i\}_{i=1}^B$, we solve the following optimization problem on top of Φ:

$$\min_{\Phi} \sum_{i=1}^B \frac{1}{B_1} \alpha_i \mathcal{L}_{supervised}^{\mathcal{V}_i} + \frac{1}{B_2}(1-\alpha_i)\mathcal{L}_{self-supervised}^{\mathcal{V}_i}, \tag{1}$$

with $B_1 = \sum_{i=1}^B \alpha_i$ and $B_2 = \sum_{i=1}^B 1 - \alpha_i$. $\{\alpha_i\}_{i=1}^B$ is a binary mask; $\alpha_i = 1$ if the observation of $\mathcal{V}_i$ is fully annotated and $\alpha_i = 0$ otherwise. In Sect. 3.2, we will give a detailed illustration on the self-supervised objective $\mathcal{L}_{self-supervised}$, which learns inter-consistency and intra-consistency upon DPDN, while the illustration on the supervised objective $\mathcal{L}_{supervised}$ is included in Sect. 3.3.

3.1   Deep Prior Deformation Network

For an object instance $\mathcal{V}$ belonging to a category c of interest, we represent its RGB-D observation in the scene as $(\mathcal{I}_o, \mathcal{P}_o)$, where $\mathcal{I}_o \in \mathbb{R}^{H \times W \times 3}$ denotes the RGB segment compactly containing the instance with a spatial size of $H \times W$, and $\mathcal{P}_o \in \mathbb{R}^{N \times 3}$ denotes the masked point set with N object surface points. Direct regression of object pose and size from $(\mathcal{I}_o, \mathcal{P}_o)$ struggles in the learning of SO(3) space without object CAD model [4,14,15].

Alternatively, a recent group of works [3,11,20,25] achieve impressive results by taking advantages of strong categorical priors to establish dense point-wise correspondence, from which object pose and size could be obtained by solving of Umeyama algorithm [21]. Specifically, assuming $\mathcal{Q}_c \in \mathbb{R}^{M \times 3}$ is a sampled point set from the shape prior of c with M points, a point-wise deformation field $\boldsymbol{D} \in \mathbb{R}^{M \times 3}$ and a correspondence matrix $\boldsymbol{A} \in \mathbb{R}^{N \times M}$ are learned from a triplet of $(\mathcal{I}_o, \mathcal{P}_o, \mathcal{Q}_c)$. $\boldsymbol{D}$ contains point-wise deviations with respect to $\mathcal{Q}_c$, deforming $\mathcal{Q}_c$ to $\mathcal{Q}_v \in \mathbb{R}^{M \times 3}$, which represents a complete shape of $\mathcal{V}$ in the canonical space. $\boldsymbol{A}$ models relationships between points in $\mathcal{Q}_v$ and $\mathcal{P}_o$, serving

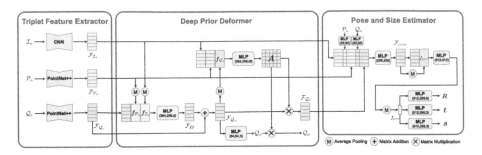

Fig. 2. An illustration of our Deep Prior Deformation Network (DPDN). For an object observation $\mathcal{V}$, we take its image crop $\mathcal{I}_o$, point set $\mathcal{P}_o$, and shape prior $\mathcal{Q}_c$ of the same category as inputs of a **Triplet Feature Extractor**, for the learning of their point-wise features $\mathcal{F}_{\mathcal{I}_o}$, $\mathcal{F}_{\mathcal{P}_o}$, and $\mathcal{F}_{\mathcal{Q}_c}$, respectively; then a **Deep Prior Deformer** is employed to learn a feature deformation field $\mathcal{F}_D$ and a correspondence matrix $\boldsymbol{A}$ to deform $\mathcal{F}_{\mathcal{Q}_c}$, yielding a feature map $\mathcal{F}_{\mathcal{Q}_o}$ in the canonical space to pair with $\mathcal{F}_{\mathcal{P}_o}$; a **Pose and Size Estimator** makes final predictions $(\boldsymbol{R}, \boldsymbol{t}, \boldsymbol{s})$ directly from the built deep correspondence between $\mathcal{F}_{\mathcal{P}_o}$ and $\mathcal{F}_{\mathcal{Q}_o}$.

as a sampler from $\mathcal{Q}_v$ to generate a partial point set $\mathcal{Q}_o \in \mathbb{R}^{N \times 3}$, paired with $\mathcal{P}_o$, as follows:

$$\mathcal{Q}_o = \boldsymbol{A} \times \mathcal{Q}_v = \boldsymbol{A} \times (\mathcal{Q}_c + \boldsymbol{D}). \tag{2}$$

Finally, solving of Umeyama algorithm to align $\mathcal{Q}_o$ with $\mathcal{P}_o$ gives out the target pose and size.

However, surrogate objectives for the learning of $\boldsymbol{A}$ and $\boldsymbol{D}$ are a step away from the true ones for estimates of pose and size; for example, small deviations of $\boldsymbol{A}$ or $\boldsymbol{D}$ may lead to large changes in the pose space. Thereby, we present a Deep Prior Deformation Network (DPDN), which implements a deep version of (2) as follows:

$$\mathcal{F}_{\mathcal{Q}_o} = \boldsymbol{A} \times \mathcal{F}_{\mathcal{Q}_v} = \boldsymbol{A} \times (\mathcal{F}_{\mathcal{Q}_c} + \mathcal{F}_D), \tag{3}$$

where $\mathcal{F}_{\mathcal{Q}_c}$, $\mathcal{F}_{\mathcal{Q}_v}$, and $\mathcal{F}_{\mathcal{Q}_o}$ denote point-wise features of $\mathcal{Q}_c$, $\mathcal{Q}_v$, and $\mathcal{Q}_o$, respectively, and $\mathcal{F}_D$ is a feature deformation field $w.r.t.$ $\mathcal{F}_{\mathcal{Q}_c}$. The deep version (3) deforms $\mathcal{Q}_c$ in the feature space, such that features of $\mathcal{Q}_o$ and $\mathcal{P}_o$ are paired to establish deep correspondence, from which object pose and size $(\boldsymbol{R}, \boldsymbol{t}, \boldsymbol{s})$ could be predicted via a subsequent network. Direct regression from deep correspondence thus alleviates the difficulties encountered by that from object observation. We note that upon the correspondence and the predictions, a self-supervised signal of intra-consistency could also be built for unlabeled data (see Sect. 3.2).

As depicted in Fig. 2, the architecture of DPDN consists of three main modules, including **Triplet Feature Extractor**, **Deep Prior Deformer**, and **Pose and Size Estimator**. We will give detailed illustrations shortly.

Triplet Feature Extractor. Given the inputs of object observation $(\mathcal{I}_o, \mathcal{P}_o)$ and categorical shape prior $\mathcal{Q}_c$, we firstly extract their point-wise features

$(\mathcal{F}_{\mathcal{I}_o}, \mathcal{F}_{\mathcal{P}_o}) \in (\mathbb{R}^{N \times d}, \mathbb{R}^{N \times d})$ and $\mathcal{F}_{\mathcal{Q}_c} \in \mathbb{R}^{M \times d}$, where d denotes the number of feature channels. Following [22], we firstly employ a PSP network [31] with ResNet-18 [9] to learn pixel-wise appearance features of $\mathcal{I}_o$, and then select those corresponding to $\mathcal{P}_o$ out to form $\mathcal{F}_{\mathcal{I}_o}$. For both $\mathcal{P}_o$ and $\mathcal{Q}_c$, two networks of PointNet++ [18] decorated with 4 set abstract levels are individually applied to extract their point-wise geometric features $\mathcal{F}_{\mathcal{P}_o}$ and $\mathcal{F}_{\mathcal{Q}_c}$.

Deep Prior Deformer. After obtaining $\mathcal{F}_{\mathcal{I}_o}$, $\mathcal{F}_{\mathcal{P}_o}$ and $\mathcal{F}_{\mathcal{Q}_c}$, the goal of Deep Prior Deformer is to learn the feature deformation field $\mathcal{F}_D \in \mathbb{R}^{M \times d}$ and the correspondence matrix $\boldsymbol{A} \in \mathbb{R}^{N \times M}$ in (3), and then implement (3) in the feature space to establish deep correspondence.

Specifically, as shown in Fig. 2, we obtain global feature vectors $\boldsymbol{f}_{\mathcal{I}_o} \in \mathbb{R}^d$ and $\boldsymbol{f}_{\mathcal{P}_o} \in \mathbb{R}^d$ of $\mathcal{I}_o$ and $\mathcal{P}_o$, respectively, by averaging their point-wise features $\mathcal{F}_{\mathcal{I}_o}$ and $\mathcal{F}_{\mathcal{P}_o}$; then each point feature of $\mathcal{F}_{\mathcal{Q}_c}$ is fused with $\boldsymbol{f}_{\mathcal{I}_o}$ and $\boldsymbol{f}_{\mathcal{P}_o}$, and fed into a subnetwork of Multi-Layer Perceptron (MLP) to learn its deformation. Collectively, the whole feature deformation field $\mathcal{F}_D$ could be learned as follows:

$$\mathcal{F}_D = \mathrm{MLP}([\mathcal{F}_{\mathcal{Q}_c}, \mathrm{Tile}^M(\boldsymbol{f}_{\mathcal{I}_o}), \mathrm{Tile}^M(\boldsymbol{f}_{\mathcal{P}_o})]),$$
$$s.t. \quad \boldsymbol{f}_{\mathcal{I}_o} = \mathrm{AvgPool}(\mathcal{F}_{\mathcal{I}_o}), \quad \boldsymbol{f}_{\mathcal{P}_o} = \mathrm{AvgPool}(\mathcal{F}_{\mathcal{P}_o}), \qquad (4)$$

where $[\cdot, \cdot]$ denotes concatenation along feature dimension, $\mathrm{MLP}(\cdot)$ denotes a trainable subnetwork of MLP, $\mathrm{AvgPool}(\cdot)$ denotes an average-pooling operation over surface points, and $\mathrm{Tile}^M(\cdot)$ denotes M copies of the feature vector.

$\mathcal{F}_D$ is used to deform the deep prior $\mathcal{F}_{\mathcal{Q}_c}$ to match $\mathcal{V}$ in the feature space. Thereby, according to (3), we have $\mathcal{F}_{\mathcal{Q}_v} = \mathcal{F}_{\mathcal{Q}_c} + \mathcal{F}_D$, with a global feature $\boldsymbol{f}_{\mathcal{Q}_v}$ generated by averaging $\mathcal{F}_{\mathcal{Q}_v}$ over M points. Then $\boldsymbol{A}$ could be learned from the fusion of $\mathcal{F}_{\mathcal{I}_o}$, $\mathcal{F}_{\mathcal{P}_o}$, and N copies of $\boldsymbol{f}_{\mathcal{Q}_v}$, via another MLP as follows:

$$\boldsymbol{A} = \mathrm{MLP}([\mathcal{F}_{\mathcal{I}_o}, \mathcal{F}_{\mathcal{P}_o}, \mathrm{Tile}^N(\boldsymbol{f}_{\mathcal{Q}_v})]),$$
$$s.t. \quad \boldsymbol{f}_{\mathcal{Q}_v} = \mathrm{AvgPool}(\mathcal{F}_{\mathcal{Q}_v}) = \mathrm{AvgPool}(\mathcal{F}_{\mathcal{Q}_c} + \mathcal{F}_D). \qquad (5)$$

Compared to the common practice in [3,20,25] to learn $\boldsymbol{A}$ by fusing $\mathcal{F}_{\mathcal{I}_o}$ and $\mathcal{F}_{\mathcal{P}_o}$ with N copies of $\boldsymbol{f}_{\mathcal{Q}_c} = \mathrm{AvgPool}(\mathcal{F}_{\mathcal{Q}_c})$, our deformed version of the deep prior $\boldsymbol{F}_{\mathcal{Q}_c}$ via adding $\mathcal{F}_D$ could effectively improve the quality of $\boldsymbol{A}$.

We also learn $\mathcal{Q}_v$ in (2) from $\mathcal{F}_{\mathcal{Q}_v}$ as follows:

$$\mathcal{Q}_v = \mathrm{MLP}(\mathcal{F}_{\mathcal{Q}_v}) = \mathrm{MLP}(\mathcal{F}_{\mathcal{Q}_c} + \mathcal{F}_D), \qquad (6)$$

such that according to (2) and (3), we have $\mathcal{Q}_o = \boldsymbol{A} \times \mathcal{Q}_v$ and $\mathcal{F}_{\mathcal{Q}_o} = \boldsymbol{A} \times \mathcal{F}_{\mathcal{Q}_v}$, respectively. Supervisions on $\mathcal{Q}_v$ and $\mathcal{Q}_o$ could guide the learning of $\mathcal{F}_D$ and $\boldsymbol{A}$.

Pose and Size Estimator. Through the module of Deep Prior Deformer, we establish point-to-point correspondence for the observed $\mathcal{P}_o$ with $\mathcal{F}_{\mathcal{P}_o}$ by learning $\mathcal{Q}_o$ in the canonical space with $\mathcal{F}_{\mathcal{Q}_o}$. As shown in Fig. 2, for estimating object pose and size, we firstly pair the correspondence via feature concatenation and apply an MLP to lift the features as follows:

$$\mathcal{F}_{corr} = \mathrm{MLP}([\mathcal{F}_{\mathcal{I}_o}, \mathrm{MLP}(\mathcal{P}_o), \mathcal{F}_{\mathcal{P}_o}, \mathrm{MLP}(\mathcal{Q}_o), \mathcal{F}_{\mathcal{Q}_o}]). \qquad (7)$$

We then inject global information into the point-wise correspondence in $\mathcal{F}_{corr}$ by concatenating its averaged feature $\boldsymbol{f}_{corr}$, followed by an MLP to strengthen the correspondence; a pose-sensitive feature vector $\boldsymbol{f}_{pose}$ is learned from all the correspondence information via an average-pooling operation:

$$\boldsymbol{f}_{pose} = \texttt{AvgPool}(\texttt{MLP}([\mathcal{F}_{corr}, \texttt{Tile}^N(\boldsymbol{f}_{corr})])),$$
$$s.t. \quad \boldsymbol{f}_{corr} = \texttt{AvgPool}(\mathcal{F}_{corr}). \tag{8}$$

Finally, we apply three parallel MLPs to regress $\boldsymbol{R}$, $\boldsymbol{t}$, and $\boldsymbol{s}$, respectively:

$$\boldsymbol{R}, \boldsymbol{t}, \boldsymbol{s} = \rho(\texttt{MLP}(\boldsymbol{f}_{pose})), \texttt{MLP}(\boldsymbol{f}_{pose}), \texttt{MLP}(\boldsymbol{f}_{pose}), \tag{9}$$

where we choose a 6D representation of rotation [32] as the regression target of the first MLP, for its continuous learning space in $SO(3)$, and $\rho(\cdot)$ represents transformation from the 6D representation to the 3×3 rotation matrix $\boldsymbol{R}$.

For the whole DPDN, we could summarize it as follows:

$$\boldsymbol{R}, \boldsymbol{t}, \boldsymbol{s}, \mathcal{Q}_v, \mathcal{Q}_o = \Phi(\mathcal{I}_o, \mathcal{P}_o, \mathcal{Q}_c). \tag{10}$$

3.2 Self-supervised Training Objective $\mathcal{L}_{self-supervised}$

For an observed point set $\mathcal{P}_o = \{\boldsymbol{p}_o^{(j)}\}_{j=1}^N$, if we transform it with $(\Delta\boldsymbol{R}_1, \Delta\boldsymbol{t}_1, \Delta s_1)$ and $(\Delta\boldsymbol{R}_2, \Delta\boldsymbol{t}_2, \Delta s_2)$, we can obtain $\mathcal{P}_{o,1} = \{\boldsymbol{p}_{o,1}^{(j)}\}_{j=1}^N = \{\frac{1}{\Delta s_1}\Delta\boldsymbol{R}_1^T(\boldsymbol{p}_o^{(j)} - \Delta\boldsymbol{t}_1)\}_{j=1}^N$ and $\mathcal{P}_{o,2} = \{\boldsymbol{p}_{o,2}^{(j)}\}_{j=1}^N = \{\frac{1}{\Delta s_2}\Delta\boldsymbol{R}_2^T(\boldsymbol{p}_o^{(j)} - \Delta\boldsymbol{t}_2)\}_{j=1}^N$, respectively. When inputting them into DPDN in parallel, we have

$$\boldsymbol{R}_{\mathcal{P}_{o,1}}, \boldsymbol{t}_{\mathcal{P}_{o,1}}, s_{\mathcal{P}_{o,1}}, \mathcal{Q}_{v,1}, \mathcal{Q}_{o,1} = \Phi(\mathcal{I}_o, \mathcal{P}_{o,1}, \mathcal{Q}_c), \tag{11}$$
$$\text{and} \quad \boldsymbol{R}_{\mathcal{P}_{o,2}}, \boldsymbol{t}_{\mathcal{P}_{o,2}}, s_{\mathcal{P}_{o,2}}, \mathcal{Q}_{v,2}, \mathcal{Q}_{o,2} = \Phi(\mathcal{I}_o, \mathcal{P}_{o,2}, \mathcal{Q}_c), \tag{12}$$

with $\mathcal{Q}_{v,1} = \{\boldsymbol{q}_{v,1}^{(j)}\}_{j=1}^M$, $\mathcal{Q}_{o,1} = \{\boldsymbol{q}_{o,1}^{(j)}\}_{j=1}^N$, $\mathcal{Q}_{v,2} = \{\boldsymbol{q}_{v,2}^{(j)}\}_{j=1}^M$, and $\mathcal{Q}_{o,2} = \{\boldsymbol{q}_{o,2}^{(j)}\}_{j=1}^N$.

There exist two solutions to $(\boldsymbol{R}, \boldsymbol{t}, \boldsymbol{s})$ of $\mathcal{P}_o$ from (11) and (12), respectively; for clarity, we use subscripts '1' and '2' for $(\boldsymbol{R}, \boldsymbol{t}, \boldsymbol{s})$ to distinguish them:

1) $\boldsymbol{R}_1, \boldsymbol{t}_1, \boldsymbol{s}_1 = \Delta\boldsymbol{R}_1\boldsymbol{R}_{\mathcal{P}_{o,1}}, \Delta\boldsymbol{t}_1 + \Delta s_1\Delta\boldsymbol{R}_1\boldsymbol{t}_{\mathcal{P}_{o,1}}, \Delta s_1 s_{\mathcal{P}_{o,1}}$;
2) $\boldsymbol{R}_2, \boldsymbol{t}_2, \boldsymbol{s}_2 = \Delta\boldsymbol{R}_2\boldsymbol{R}_{\mathcal{P}_{o,2}}, \Delta\boldsymbol{t}_2 + \Delta s_2\Delta\boldsymbol{R}_2\boldsymbol{t}_{\mathcal{P}_{o,2}}, \Delta s_2 s_{\mathcal{P}_{o,2}}$.

Upon the above parallel learning of (11) and (12), we design a novel self-supervised objective for the unlabeled real-world data to reduce the Sim2Real domain gap. Specifically, it combines an inter-consistency term $\mathcal{L}_{inter}$ with two intra-consistency ones $(\mathcal{L}_{intra,1}, \mathcal{L}_{intra,2})$ as follows:

$$\mathcal{L}_{self-supervised} = \lambda_1\mathcal{L}_{inter} + \lambda_2(\mathcal{L}_{intra,1} + \mathcal{L}_{intra,2}), \tag{13}$$

where λ_1 and λ_2 are superparameters to balance the loss terms. $\mathcal{L}_{inter}$ enforces consistency across the parallel learning from $\mathcal{P}_o$ with different transformations, making the learning aware of pose changes to improve the precision of predictions, while $\mathcal{L}_{intra,1}$ and $\mathcal{L}_{intra,2}$ enforce self-adaptation between correspondence and predictions within each learning, respectively, in order to realize more reliable predictions inferred from the correspondence.

Inter-consistency Term. We construct the inter-consistency loss based on the following two facts: 1) two solutions to the pose and size of $\mathcal{P}_o$ from those of $\mathcal{P}_{o,1}$ and $\mathcal{P}_{o,2}$ are required to be consistent; 2) as representations of a same object $\mathcal{V}$ in the canonical space, $\mathcal{Q}_{v,1}$ and $\mathcal{Q}_{v,2}$ should be invariant to any pose transformations, and thus keep consistent to each other, as well as $\mathcal{Q}_{o,1}$ and $\mathcal{Q}_{o,2}$. Therefore, with two input transformations, the inter-consistency loss $\mathcal{L}_{inter}$ could be formulated as follows:

$$\mathcal{L}_{inter} = \mathcal{D}_{pose}(\boldsymbol{R}_1, \boldsymbol{t}_1, \boldsymbol{s}_1, \boldsymbol{R}_2, \boldsymbol{t}_2, \boldsymbol{s}_2) + \beta_1 \mathcal{D}_{cham}(\mathcal{Q}_{v,1}, \mathcal{Q}_{v,2}) + \beta_2 \mathcal{D}_{L2}(\mathcal{Q}_{o,1}, \mathcal{Q}_{o,2}),$$
(14)

where λ_1 and λ_2 are balanced parameters, and

$$\mathcal{D}_{pose}(\boldsymbol{R}_1, \boldsymbol{t}_1, \boldsymbol{s}_1, \boldsymbol{R}_2, \boldsymbol{t}_2, \boldsymbol{s}_2) = ||\boldsymbol{R}_1 - \boldsymbol{R}_2||_2 + ||\boldsymbol{t}_1 - \boldsymbol{t}_2||_2 + ||\boldsymbol{s}_1 - \boldsymbol{s}_2||_2,$$

$$\mathcal{D}_{cham}(\mathcal{Q}_{v,1}, \mathcal{Q}_{v,2}) = \frac{1}{2M}\left(\sum_{j=1}^{M} \min_{\boldsymbol{q}_{v,2}} ||\boldsymbol{q}_{v,1}^{(j)} - \boldsymbol{q}_{v,2}||_2 + \sum_{j=1}^{M} \min_{\boldsymbol{q}_{v,1}} ||\boldsymbol{q}_{v,1} - \boldsymbol{q}_{v,2}^{(j)}||_2\right),$$

$$\mathcal{D}_{L2}(\mathcal{Q}_{o,1}, \mathcal{Q}_{o,2}) = \frac{1}{N}\sum_{j=1}^{N} ||\boldsymbol{q}_{o,1}^{(j)} - \boldsymbol{q}_{o,2}^{(j)}||_2.$$

Chamfer distance $\mathcal{D}_{cham}$ is used to restrain the distance of two complete point sets $\mathcal{Q}_{v,1}$ and $\mathcal{Q}_{v,2}$, while for the partial $\mathcal{Q}_{o,1}$ and $\mathcal{Q}_{o,2}$, we use a more strict metric of L2 distance $\mathcal{D}_{L2}$ for point-to-point constraints, since their points should be ordered to correspond with those of $\mathcal{P}_o$.

Intra-consistency Terms. For an observation $(\mathcal{I}_o, \mathcal{P}_o)$, DPDN learns deep correspondence between $\mathcal{P}_o = \{\boldsymbol{p}_o^{(j)}\}_{j=1}^{N}$ and $\mathcal{Q}_o = \{\boldsymbol{q}_o^{(j)}\}_{j=1}^{N}$ to predict their relative pose and size $(\boldsymbol{R}, \boldsymbol{t}, \boldsymbol{s})$; ideally, for $\forall j = 1, \cdots, N$, $\boldsymbol{q}_o^{(j)} = \frac{1}{||\boldsymbol{s}||_2} \boldsymbol{R}^T(\boldsymbol{p}_o^{(j)} - \boldsymbol{t})$. Accordingly, the predictions $\mathcal{Q}_{o,1}$ and $\mathcal{Q}_{o,2}$ in (11) and (12) should be restrained to be consistent with $\mathcal{Q}_{o,1}' = \{\frac{1}{||\boldsymbol{s}_1||_2} \boldsymbol{R}_1^T(\boldsymbol{p}_o^{(j)} - \boldsymbol{t}_1)\}_{j=1}^{N}$ and $\mathcal{Q}_{o,2}' = \{\frac{1}{||\boldsymbol{s}_2||_2} \boldsymbol{R}_2^T(\boldsymbol{p}_o^{(j)} - \boldsymbol{t}_2)\}_{j=1}^{N}$, respectively, which gives the formulations of two intra-consistency terms based on Smooth-L1 distance as follows:

$$\mathcal{L}_{intra,1} = \mathcal{D}_{SL1}(\mathcal{Q}_{o,1}, \mathcal{Q}_{o,1}'), \quad \mathcal{L}_{intra,2} = \mathcal{D}_{SL1}(\mathcal{Q}_{o,2}, \mathcal{Q}_{o,2}'),$$
(15)

where

$$\mathcal{D}_{SL1}(\mathcal{Q}_1, \mathcal{Q}_2) = \frac{1}{N}\sum_{j=1}^{N}\sum_{k=1}^{3} \begin{cases} 5(q_1^{(jk)} - q_2^{(jk)})^2, & \text{if} |q_1^{(jk)} - q_2^{(jk)}| \leq 0.1 \\ |q_1^{(jk)} - q_2^{(jk)}| - 0.05, & \text{otherwise} \end{cases},$$

with $\mathcal{Q}_1 = \{(q_1^{(j1)}, q_1^{(j2)}, q_1^{(j3)})\}_{j=1}^{N}$ and $\mathcal{Q}_2 = \{(q_2^{(j1)}, q_2^{(j2)}, q_2^{(j3)})\}_{j=1}^{N}$.

3.3 Supervised Training Objective $\mathcal{L}_{supervised}$

Given a triplet of inputs $(\mathcal{I}_o, \mathcal{P}_o, \mathcal{Q}_c)$ along with the annotated ground truths $(\hat{\boldsymbol{R}}, \hat{\boldsymbol{t}}, \hat{\boldsymbol{s}}, \hat{\mathcal{Q}}_v, \hat{\mathcal{Q}}_o)$, we generate dual input triplets by applying two rigid transformations to $\mathcal{P}_o$, as done in Sect. 3.2, and use the following supervised objective on top of the parallel learning of (11) and (12):

$$\mathcal{L}_{supervised} = \mathcal{D}_{pose}(\boldsymbol{R}_1, \boldsymbol{t}_1, \boldsymbol{s}_1, \hat{\boldsymbol{R}}, \hat{\boldsymbol{t}}, \hat{\boldsymbol{s}}) + \mathcal{D}_{pose}(\boldsymbol{R}_2, \boldsymbol{t}_2, \boldsymbol{s}_2, \hat{\boldsymbol{R}}, \hat{\boldsymbol{t}}, \hat{\boldsymbol{s}})$$
$$+ \gamma_1(\mathcal{D}_{cham}(\mathcal{Q}_{v,1}, \hat{\mathcal{Q}}_v) + \mathcal{D}_{cham}(\mathcal{Q}_{v,2}, \hat{\mathcal{Q}}_v))$$
$$+ \gamma_2(\mathcal{D}_{SL1}(\mathcal{Q}_{o,1}, \hat{\mathcal{Q}}_o) + \mathcal{D}_{SL1}(\mathcal{Q}_{o,2}, \hat{\mathcal{Q}}_o)). \quad (16)$$

We note that this supervision also implies inter-consistency between the parallel learning defined in (14), making DPDN more sensitive to pose changes.

4 Experiments

Datasets. We train DPDN on both training sets of synthetic CAMERA25 and real-world REAL275 datasets [24], and conduct evaluation on REAL275 test set. CAMERA25 is created by a context-aware mixed reality approach, which renders 1,085 synthetic object CAD models of 6 categories to real-world backgrounds, yielding a total of 300,000 RGB-D images, with 25,000 ones of 184 objects set aside for validation. REAL275 is a more challenging real-world dataset, which includes 4,300 training images of 7 scenes and 2,754 testing ones of 6 scenes. Both datasets share the same categories, yet impose large domain gap.

Implementation Details. To obtain instance masks for both training and test sets of REAL275, we train a MaskRCNN [8] with a backbone of ResNet101 [9] on CAMERA25; for settings of available training mask labels, we use the same segmentation results as [14,15,20] to make fair comparisons. We employ the shape priors released by [20].

For DPDN, we resize the image crops of object observations as 192×192, and set the point numbers of shape priors and observed point sets as $M = N = 1,024$, respectively. In Triplet Feature Extractor, a PSP Network [31] based on ResNet-18 [9] and two networks of PointNet++ [18] are employed, sharing the same architectures as those in [3,10]. To aggregate multi-scale features, each PointNet++ is built by stacking 4 set abstract levels with multi-scale grouping. The output channels of point-wise features ($\mathcal{F}_{\mathcal{I}_o}, \mathcal{F}_{\mathcal{P}_o}, \mathcal{F}_{\mathcal{Q}_c}$) are all set as $d = 128$; other network specifics are also given in Fig. 2. We use ADAM to train DPDN with a total of 120,000 iterations; the data size of a mini training batch is $B = 24$ with $B_1 : B_2 = 3 : 1$. The superparameters of $\lambda_1, \lambda_2, \beta_1, \beta_2, \gamma_1$ and γ_2 are set as 0.2, 0.02, 5.0, 1.0, 5.0 and 1.0, respectively. For each pose transformation, $\Delta\boldsymbol{R}$ is sampled from the whole SO(3) space by randomly generating three euler angles, while $\Delta\boldsymbol{t} \in \mathbb{R}^3$ with each element $\Delta t \sim U(-0.02, 0.02)$, and $\Delta s \sim U(0.8, 1.2)$.

Evaluation Metrics. Following [24], we report mean Average Precision (mAP) of Intersection over Union (IoU) for object detection, and mAP of $n°m$ cm for 6D pose estimation. IoU_x denotes precision of predictions with IoU over a threshold of $x\%$, and $n°m$ cm denotes precision of those with rotation error less than $n°$ and transformation error less than m cm.

Table 1. Quantitative comparisons of different methods for category-level 6D pose and size estimation on REAL275 [24]. 'Syn' and 'Real' denote the uses of training data of synthetic CAMERA25 and real-world REAL275 datasets, respectively. '$*$' denotes training with mask labels

Method	Syn	Real w/o label	Real with label	mAP					
				IoU$_{50}$	IoU$_{75}$	5°	5°	10°	10°
Unsupervised									
NOCS [24]	✓			36.7	3.4	-	3.4	-	20.4
SPD [24]	✓			71.0	43.1	11.4	12.0	33.5	37.8
DualPoseNet [15]	✓			68.4	49.5	15.9	27.1	33.1	56.8
DPDN (Ours)	✓			71.7	60.8	29.7	37.3	53.7	67.0
Self-DPDN (Ours)	✓	✓		**72.6**	**63.8**	**37.8**	**45.5**	**59.8**	**71.3**
UDA-COPE [11]	✓	✓*		82.6	62.5	30.4	34.8	56.9	66.0
Self-DPDN (Ours)	✓	✓*		**83.0**	**70.3**	**39.4**	**45.0**	**63.2**	**72.1**
Supervised									
NOCS [24]	✓		✓	78.0	30.1	7.2	10.0	13.8	25.2
SPD [20]	✓		✓	77.3	53.2	19.3	21.4	43.2	54.1
CR-Net [25]	✓		✓	79.3	55.9	27.8	34.3	47.2	60.8
DualPoseNet [15]	✓		✓	79.8	62.2	29.3	35.9	50.0	66.8
SAR-Net [13]	✓		✓	79.3	62.4	31.6	42.3	50.3	68.3
SS-ConvNet [14]	✓		✓	79.8	65.6	36.6	43.4	52.6	63.5
SGPA [3]	✓		✓	80.1	61.9	35.9	39.6	61.3	70.7
DPDN (Ours)	✓		✓	**83.4**	**76.0**	**46.0**	**50.7**	**70.4**	**78.4**

4.1 Comparisons with Existing Methods

We compare our method with the existing ones for category-level 6D object pose and size estimation under both unsupervised and supervised settings. Quantitative results are given in Table 1, where results under supervised setting significantly benefit from the annotations of real-world data, compared to those under unsupervised one; for example, on the metric of 5°2 cm, SPD [20] improves the results from 11.4% to 19.3%, while DualPoseNet [15] improves from 15.9% to 29.3%. Therefore, the exploration of UDA for the target task in this paper is of great practical significance, due to the difficulties in precisely annotating real-world object instances in 3D space.

Unsupervised Setting. Firstly, a basic version of DPDN is trained on the synthetic data and transferred to real-world domain for evaluation; under this setting, our basic DPDN outperforms the existing methods on all the evaluation metrics, as shown in Table 1. To reduce the Sim2Real domain gap, we further include the unlabeled Real275 training set via our self-supervised DPDN for UDA; results in Table 1 verify the effectiveness of our self-supervised DPDN (dubbed **Self-DPDN** in the table), which significantly improves the precision

Table 2. Ablation studies on the variants of our proposed DPDN under supervised setting. Experiments are evaluated on REAL275 test set [24].

Input		Deep prior deformer	Pose & size estimator	mAP					
$\mathcal{P}_{o,1}$	$\mathcal{P}_{o,2}$			IoU$_{50}$	IoU$_{75}$	5° 2 cm	5° 5 cm	10° 2 cm	10° 5 cm
✓	✗	✗	✓	79.9	65.4	26.7	35.6	47.2	63.9
✓	✓	✗	✓	83.3	72.9	35.2	43.9	57.3	70.8
✓	✗	✓	✓	**83.4**	**76.2**	39.6	46.1	65.5	76.7
✓	✓	✓	✓	**83.4**	76.0	**46.0**	**50.7**	**70.4**	**78.4**
✓	✓	✓	✗	59.6	45.6	27.9	33.0	50.2	63.9

of the basic version, *e.g.*, a performance gain of 8.1% on 5°2 cm from 29.7% to 37.8%.

UDA-COPE [11] is the first work to introduce the unsupervised setting, which trains deep model with a teacher-student scheme to yield pseudo labels for real-world data; in the process of training, pose annotations of real-world data are not employed, yet mask labels are used for learning instance segmentation. To fairly compare with UDA-COPE, we evaluate DPDN under the same setting; results in Table 1 also show the superiority of our self-supervised DPDN over UDA-COPE, especially for the metrics of high precisions, *e.g.*, an improvement of 10.2% on 5°5 cm. The reason for the great improvement is that UDA-COPE heavily relies on the qualities of pseudo labels, while our self-supervised objective could guide the optimization moving for the direction meeting inter-/intra- consistency, to make the learning fit the characteristics of REAL275 and decrease the downside effect of the synthetic domain.

Supervised Setting. We also compare our DPDN with the existing methods, including those of direct regression [14,15], and those based on dense correspondence learning [3,13,20,24,25], under supervised setting. As shown in Table 1, DPDN outperforms the existing methods on all the evaluation metrics, *e.g.*, reaching the precisions of 76.0% on IoU$_{75}$ and 78.4% on 10°5 cm. Compared with the representative SS-ConvNet [14], which directly regresses object poses and sizes from observations, our DPDN takes the advantages of categorical shape priors, and achieves more precise results by regressing from deep correspondence; compared with SGPA [3], the recent state-of-the-art method based on correspondence learning (*c.f.* Eq. (2)), our DPDN shares the same feature extractor, yet benefits from the direct objectives for pose and size estimation, rather than the surrogate ones, *e.g.*, for regression of D and A in Eq. (2); DPDN thus achieves more reliable predictions.

4.2 Ablation Studies and Analyses

In this section, we conduct experiments to evaluate the efficacy of both the designs in our DPDN and the self-supervision upon DPDN.

Table 3. Ablation studies of our proposed self-supervised objective upon DPDN under unsupervised setting. Experiments are evaluated on REAL275 test set [24].

$\mathcal{L}_{inter}$	$\mathcal{L}_{intra,1}$ $\mathcal{L}_{intra,2}$	mAP					
		IoU_{50}	IoU_{75}	$5°\ 2\,cm$	$5°\ 5\,cm$	$10°\ 2\,cm$	$10°\ 5\,cm$
✗	✗	71.7	60.8	29.7	37.3	53.7	67.0
✓	✗	**72.6**	63.2	36.9	43.7	58.7	68.7
✗	✓	70.9	58.6	35.8	43.6	56.6	69.3
✓	✓	**72.6**	**63.8**	**37.8**	**45.5**	**59.8**	**71.3**

Effects of the Designs in DPDN. We verify the efficacy of the designs in DPDN under supervised setting, with the results of different variants of our DPDN shown in Table 2. Firstly, we confirm the effectiveness of our Deep Prior Deformer with categorical shape priors; by removing Deep Prior Deformer, the precision of DPDN with parallel learning on $5°2$ cm drops from 46.0% to 35.2%, indicating that learning from deep correspondence by deforming priors in feature space indeed makes the task easier than that directly from object observations.

Secondly, we show the advantages of using true objectives for direct estimates of object poses and sizes, over the surrogate ones for the learning of the canonical point set $\mathcal{Q}_o$ to pair with the observed $\mathcal{P}_o$. Specifically, we remove our Pose and Size Estimator, and make predictions by solving Umeyama algorithm to align $\mathcal{P}_o$ and $\mathcal{Q}_o$; precisions shown in the table decline sharply on all the evaluation metrics, especially on IoU_x. We found that the results on IoU_x are also much lower than those methods based on dense correspondence learning [3,20,25], while results on $n°m$ are comparable; the reason is that we regress the absolute coordinates of $\mathcal{Q}_c$, rather than the deviations D in Eq. (2), which may introduce more outliers to affect the object size estimation.

Thirdly, we confirm the effectiveness of the parallel supervisions in (16), *e.g.*, inputting $\mathcal{P}_{o,1}$ and $\mathcal{P}_{o,2}$ of the same instance with different poses. As shown in Table 2, results of DPDN with parallel learning are improved (with or without Deep Prior Deformer), since the inter-consistency between dual predictions is implied in the parallel supervisions, making the learning aware of pose changes.

Effects of the Self-supervision upon DPDN. We have shown the superiority of our novel self-supervised DPDN under the unsupervised setting in Sect. 4.1; here we include the evaluation on the effectiveness of each consistency term in the self-supervised objective, which is confirmed by the results shown in Table 3. Taking results on $5°, 2$ cm as examples, DPDN with inter-consistency term $\mathcal{L}_{inter}$ improves the results of the baseline from 29.7% to 36.9%, and DPDN with the intra-consistency ones $\mathcal{L}_{intra,1}$ and $\mathcal{L}_{intra,2}$ improves to 35.8%, while their combinations further refresh the results, revealing their strengths on reduction of domain gap. We also show the influence of data size of unlabeled real-world images on the precision of predictions in Fig. 3, where precisions improve along with the increasing ratios of training data.

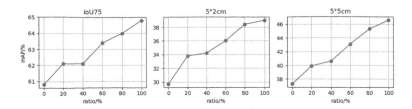

Fig. 3. Plottings of mAP versus the ratio of unlabeled REAL275 training data under unsupervised setting. Experiments are evaluated on REAL275 test set [24]

Fig. 4. Qualitative results of DPDN on REAL275 test set [24]. 'Syn' and 'Real' denote the uses of synthetic CAMERA25 and real-world REAL275 training sets, respectively.

4.3   Visualization

We visualize in Fig. 4 the qualitative results of our proposed DPDN under different settings on REAL275 test set [24]. As shown in the figure, our self-supervised DPDN without annotations of real-world data, in general, achieves comparable results with the fully-supervised version, although there still exist some difficult examples, *e.g.*, cameras in Fig. 4(a) and (b), due to the inaccurate masks from MaskRCNN trained on synthetic data. Under the unsupervised setting, our self-supervised DPDN also outperforms the basic version trained with only CAMERA25, by including unlabeled real-world data with self-supervision; for example, more precise poses of laptops are obtained in Fig. 4(c) and (d).

Acknowledgements. This work is supported in part by Guangdong R&D key project of China (No.: 2019B010155001), and the Program for Guangdong Introducing Innovative and Enterpreneurial Teams (No.: 2017ZT07X183).

References

1. Ajakan, H., Germain, P., Larochelle, H., Laviolette, F., Marchand, M.: Domain-adversarial neural networks. arXiv preprint arXiv:1412.4446 (2014)
2. Azuma, R.T.: A survey of augmented reality. Presence Teleoperators Virtual Environ. **6**(4), 355–385 (1997)
3. Chen, K., Dou, Q.: SGPA: structure-guided prior adaptation for category-level 6D object pose estimation. In: Proceedings of the IEEE/CVF International Conference on Computer Vision, pp. 2773–2782 (2021)
4. Chen, W., Jia, X., Chang, H.J., Duan, J., Shen, L., Leonardis, A.: FS-Net: fast shape-based network for category-level 6D object pose estimation with decoupled rotation mechanism. In: Proceedings of the IEEE/CVF Conference on Computer Vision and Pattern Recognition, pp. 1581–1590 (2021)
5. Chen, X., Ma, H., Wan, J., Li, B., Xia, T.: Multi-view 3D object detection network for autonomous driving. In: Proceedings of the IEEE Conference on Computer Vision and Pattern Recognition, pp. 1907–1915 (2017)
6. Deng, S., Liang, Z., Sun, L., Jia, K.: Vista: boosting 3D object detection via dual cross-view spatial attention. In: Proceedings of the IEEE/CVF Conference on Computer Vision and Pattern Recognition, pp. 8448–8457 (2022)
7. Denninger, M., et al.: Blenderproc: reducing the reality gap with photorealistic rendering. In: International Conference on Robotics: Science and Systems, RSS 2020 (2020)
8. He, K., Gkioxari, G., Dollár, P., Girshick, R.: Mask R-CNN. In: Proceedings of the IEEE International Conference on Computer Vision, pp. 2961–2969 (2017)
9. He, K., Zhang, X., Ren, S., Sun, J.: Deep residual learning for image recognition. In: Proceedings of the IEEE Conference on Computer Vision and Pattern Recognition, pp. 770–778 (2016)
10. He, Y., Sun, W., Huang, H., Liu, J., Fan, H., Sun, J.: PVN3D: a deep point-wise 3D keypoints voting network for 6DoF pose estimation. In: Proceedings of the IEEE/CVF Conference on Computer Vision and Pattern Recognition, pp. 11632–11641 (2020)
11. Lee, T., et al.: UDA-COPE: unsupervised domain adaptation for category-level object pose estimation. In: Proceedings of the IEEE/CVF Conference on Computer Vision and Pattern Recognition, pp. 14891–14900 (2022)
12. Levinson, J., et al.: Towards fully autonomous driving: systems and algorithms. In: 2011 IEEE Intelligent Vehicles Symposium (IV), pp. 163–168. IEEE (2011)
13. Lin, H., Liu, Z., Cheang, C., Fu, Y., Guo, G., Xue, X.: SAR-Net: shape alignment and recovery network for category-level 6D object pose and size estimation. In: Proceedings of the IEEE/CVF Conference on Computer Vision and Pattern Recognition, pp. 6707–6717 (2022)
14. Lin, J., Li, H., Chen, K., Lu, J., Jia, K.: Sparse steerable convolutions: an efficient learning of se (3)-equivariant features for estimation and tracking of object poses in 3D space. In: Advances in Neural Information Processing Systems, vol. 34 (2021)
15. Lin, J., Wei, Z., Li, Z., Xu, S., Jia, K., Li, Y.: Dualposenet: category-level 6D object pose and size estimation using dual pose network with refined learning of pose consistency. In: Proceedings of the IEEE/CVF International Conference on Computer Vision, pp. 3560–3569 (2021)
16. Long, M., Cao, Y., Wang, J., Jordan, M.: Learning transferable features with deep adaptation networks. In: International Conference on Machine Learning, pp. 97–105. PMLR (2015)

17. Mousavian, A., Eppner, C., Fox, D.: 6-DOF GraspNet: variational grasp generation for object manipulation. In: Proceedings of the IEEE/CVF International Conference on Computer Vision, pp. 2901–2910 (2019)
18. Qi, C.R., Yi, L., Su, H., Guibas, L.J.: Pointnet++: deep hierarchical feature learning on point sets in a metric space. In: Advances in Neural Information Processing Systems, vol. 30 (2017)
19. Qin, C., You, H., Wang, L., Kuo, C.C.J., Fu, Y.: Pointdan: a multi-scale 3D domain adaption network for point cloud representation. In: Advances in Neural Information Processing Systems, vol. 32 (2019)
20. Tian, M., Ang, M.H., Lee, G.H.: Shape prior deformation for categorical 6D object pose and size estimation. In: Vedaldi, A., Bischof, H., Brox, T., Frahm, J.-M. (eds.) ECCV 2020. LNCS, vol. 12366, pp. 530–546. Springer, Cham (2020). https://doi.org/10.1007/978-3-030-58589-1_32
21. Umeyama, S.: Least-squares estimation of transformation parameters between two point patterns. IEEE Trans. Pattern Anal. Mach. Intell. **13**(04), 376–380 (1991)
22. Wang, C., et al.: Densefusion: 6D object pose estimation by iterative dense fusion. In: Proceedings of the IEEE/CVF Conference on Computer Vision and Pattern Recognition, pp. 3343–3352 (2019)
23. Wang, G., Manhardt, F., Shao, J., Ji, X., Navab, N., Tombari, F.: Self6D: self-supervised monocular 6D object pose estimation. In: Vedaldi, A., Bischof, H., Brox, T., Frahm, J.-M. (eds.) ECCV 2020. LNCS, vol. 12346, pp. 108–125. Springer, Cham (2020). https://doi.org/10.1007/978-3-030-58452-8_7
24. Wang, H., Sridhar, S., Huang, J., Valentin, J., Song, S., Guibas, L.J.: Normalized object coordinate space for category-level 6D object pose and size estimation. In: Proceedings of the IEEE/CVF Conference on Computer Vision and Pattern Recognition, pp. 2642–2651 (2019)
25. Wang, J., Chen, K., Dou, Q.: Category-level 6d object pose estimation via cascaded relation and recurrent reconstruction networks. In: 2021 IEEE/RSJ International Conference on Intelligent Robots and Systems (IROS), pp. 4807–4814. IEEE (2021)
26. Wang, Z., Jia, K.: Frustum convnet: sliding frustums to aggregate local pointwise features for amodal 3D object detection. In: 2019 IEEE/RSJ International Conference on Intelligent Robots and Systems (IROS), pp. 1742–1749. IEEE (2019)
27. Wu, C., et al.: Grasp proposal networks: an end-to-end solution for visual learning of robotic grasps. Adv. Neural. Inf. Process. Syst. **33**, 13174–13184 (2020)
28. Zhang, Y., Deng, B., Jia, K., Zhang, L.: Label propagation with augmented anchors: a simple semi-supervised learning baseline for unsupervised domain adaptation. In: Vedaldi, A., Bischof, H., Brox, T., Frahm, J.-M. (eds.) ECCV 2020. LNCS, vol. 12349, pp. 781–797. Springer, Cham (2020). https://doi.org/10.1007/978-3-030-58548-8_45
29. Zhang, Y., Deng, B., Tang, H., Zhang, L., Jia, K.: Unsupervised multi-class domain adaptation: theory, algorithms, and practice. IEEE Trans. Pattern Anal. Mach. Intell. (2020)
30. Zhang, Y., Tang, H., Jia, K., Tan, M.: Domain-symmetric networks for adversarial domain adaptation. In: Proceedings of the IEEE/CVF Conference on Computer Vision and Pattern Recognition, pp. 5031–5040 (2019)
31. Zhao, H., Shi, J., Qi, X., Wang, X., Jia, J.: Pyramid scene parsing network. In: Proceedings of the IEEE Conference on Computer Vision and Pattern Recognition, pp. 2881–2890 (2017)
32. Zhou, Y., Barnes, C., Lu, J., Yang, J., Li, H.: On the continuity of rotation representations in neural networks. In: Proceedings of the IEEE/CVF Conference on Computer Vision and Pattern Recognition, pp. 5745–5753 (2019)

Dense Teacher: Dense Pseudo-Labels for Semi-supervised Object Detection

Hongyu Zhou[1,3], Zheng Ge[1], Songtao Liu[1], Weixin Mao[1,2], Zeming Li[1],
Haiyan Yu[3(✉)], and Jian Sun[1]

[1] MEGVII Technology, Beijing, China
[2] Waseda University, Tokyo, Japan
[3] Harbin Institute of Technology, Harbin, China
haiyanyu@hit.edu.cn

Abstract. To date, the most powerful semi-supervised object detectors (SS-OD) are based on pseudo-boxes, which need a sequence of post-processing with fine-tuned hyper-parameters. In this work, we propose replacing the sparse pseudo-boxes with the dense prediction as a united and straightforward form of pseudo-label. Compared to the pseudo-boxes, our Dense Pseudo-Label (DPL) does not involve any post-processing method, thus retaining richer information. We also introduce a region selection technique to highlight the key information while suppressing the noise carried by dense labels. We name our proposed SS-OD algorithm that leverages the DPL as Dense Teacher. On COCO and VOC, Dense Teacher shows superior performance under various settings compared with the pseudo-box-based methods. Code is available at https://github.com/Megvii-BaseDetection/DenseTeacher.

Keywords: Semi-supervised object detection · Dense pseudo-label

1 Introduction

Current high-performance object detection neural networks rely on a large amount of labeled data to ensure their generalization capability. However, labeling samples takes a high cost of human effort. Thus the industry and academia pay extensive attention to the use of relatively easy-to-obtain unlabeled data. An effective way to use these data is Semi-Supervised Learning (SSL), where at the training time, only part of the data is labeled while the rest are unlabeled. On image classification tasks, the dominated method of mining information from unlabeled data is "Consistency-based Pseudo-Labeling" [3–5,23]. Pseudo-Labeling [12] is a technique that utilizes trained models to generate labels for unlabeled data. Meanwhile, the Consistency-based regularization [1], from another perspective, forces a model to have similar output when giving a normal and a perturbed input with different data augmentations and perturbations like Dropout [25].

H. Zhou and Z. Ge—Authors contributed equally to this work.

© The Author(s), under exclusive license to Springer Nature Switzerland AG 2022
S. Avidan et al. (Eds.): ECCV 2022, LNCS 13669, pp. 35–50, 2022.
https://doi.org/10.1007/978-3-031-20077-9_3

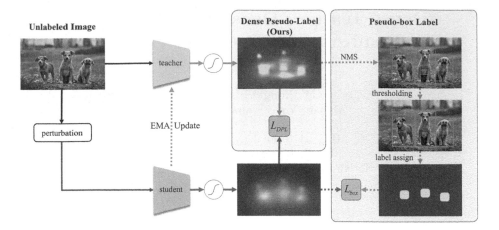

Fig. 1. The overview of our purposed pipeline for unlabeled data compared with traditional pseudo-box based pipeline. For each iteration, Dense Pseudo-Label (DPL) are generated by the teacher model on unlabeled images. The student model then calculates unsupervised loss on perturbed images and corresponding DPLs. By removing post-processing steps, DPL contains rich information from the teacher model. Note that the vanilla learning approach uses only labeled data (not plotted in the figure) and the total loss is the sum of both supervised and unsupervised loss.

This pipeline has been successfully transferred to Semi-Supervised Object Detection (SS-OD) [18,24,30]. Specifically, the predicted boxes from a pre-trained "teacher" detector are used as the annotations of unlabeled images to train the "student" detector, where the same images are applied with different augmentations for the teacher and student model. This instinctive method has proven to be effective in SS-OD and has achieved state-of-the-art scores on benchmarks such as COCO [17] and Pascal VOC [6]. However, it is not reasonable to replicate all the empirics directly from the classification task. While the generated pseudo-label is a single and united class label for an image in classification, the object detectors predict a set of pseudo-boxes as the annotation of an image. As shown in Fig. 1, making direct supervision on the unlabeled image with these pseudo-boxes requires several additional steps, including Non-Maximum-Suppression (NMS), Thresholding, and Label Assignment. Such a lengthy label-generating procedure introduces many hyper-parameters, such as NMS threshold σ_{nms} and score threshold σ_t, substantially affecting the SS-OD performance.[1] This motivates us to explore a more simple and effective form of pseudo-labels for SS-OD.

In this work, we propose a new SS-OD pipeline named Dense Teacher with a *united* form of pseudo-label—Dense Pseudo-Label (DPL), which enables more efficient knowledge transfer between the teacher and student models. DPL is an integral label. Different from the existing box-like labels in a human-readable form, it is the original output from the network without ordinary post-processing. Our Dense Teacher, following existing Pseudo-Labeling paradigms, works in the

---

[1] See also in Sect. 3.2 for a related discussion.

following way: For each iteration, labeled and unlabeled images are randomly sampled to form a data batch. The "teacher" model, which is an Exponential Moving Average of the "student" model, generates DPL for unlabeled data. And the student model is trained on both ground truth on labeled images and DPL on unlabeled images. Since the DPL does not require any post-processing, the pipeline of Dense Teacher is extremely simple. The overall pipeline of Dense Teacher can be seen in Fig. 1.

Although DPL provides more information than pseudo-box labels, it contains high-level noise (*e.g.*, low-scoring predictions) as well. We show in Sect. 4.2 that learning to make those low-scoring predictions can distract the student model, resulting in poor detection performance. Therefore, we propose a region division method to suppress noise and highlight key regions where the student model should concentrate on. According to our experiments, the region division strategy can effectively utilize the rich information contained in hard negative regions to enhance training. As a result, our proposed Dense Teacher, together with the region division strategy, shows state-of-the-art performance on MS-COCO and Pascal VOC.

Our main contributions in this paper are:

– We conduct a thorough analysis on the drawbacks of pseudo-boxes in the SS-OD task.
– We propose a united form of pseudo-label named DPL to better fit the semi-supervised setting and the Dense Teacher framework to apply the DPL on one-stage detector.
– The proposed Dense Teacher achieves state-of-the-art performance on MS-COCO and Pascal VOC benchmarks under various settings. Gain analysis and ablation study are provided to verify the effectiveness of each part in Dense Teacher.

2   Related Works

2.1   Semi-supervised Learning

sSemi-Supervised Learning (SSL) means that a portion of the data is labeled at training time while the other is not. Currently, there are two main approaches to achieve this goal: pseudo-labeling and consistency regularization. Pseudo-label-based methods [12] first train a network on labeled data, then use the trained network as a teacher to make inferences on unlabeled data. This prediction result is then assigned to a specific class according to a threshold based on the predicted confidence and used as labeled data to train another student network. In [27], the teacher model is replaced by the Exponential Moving Average (EMA) of the student to conduct online pseudo-labeling. Consistency regularization based methods [1] construct a regularization loss to force predictions under a set of perturbations $\{T_i\}$ to be same. Perturbations can be implemented using augmentation [5,21,29], dropout [11]), or adversarial training [19]. This approach does not require annotation and can be used in combination with other methods; therefore, it is widely adopted in many SSL frameworks [2,4,23].

2.2 Object Detection

Object detectors can be divided into Anchor-based and Anchor-free paradigms. Anchor-based detectors predict the offsets and scales of target boxes from pre-defined anchor boxes. Although this approach has succeeded on many tasks, one needs to redefine new anchor boxes when applying such models to new data. In contrast to anchor-based detectors, predefined anchor boxes are not required for anchor-free detectors. These detectors directly predict the box size and location on the feature map. Take FCOS model as an example; this detector predicts the classification score, distances to four boundaries, and a quality score on each pixel of Feature Pyramid Network (FPN) [15]. A variety of subsequent improvements, such as the adaptive label assigning while training [33], boundary distribution modeling [14] were proposed to improve its performance. Considering the wide application, streamlined architecture, and excellent performance of FCOS, we will conduct our experiments under this framework.

2.3 Semi-supervised Object Detection

The label type is the main difference between Semi-Supervised Object Detection (SS-OD) and SSL. Previous studies have transferred a great deal of experience from SSL works to the SS-OD domain. CSD [10] use a flipped image I' to introduce a consistency loss between $F(I)$ and $F(I')$, this regularization can be applied to unlabeled image. STAC [24] train a teacher detector on labeled images and generate pseudo-labels on unlabeled data using this static teacher. These pseudo-labels will then be selected and used for training like labeled data. Unbiased Teacher [18] use thresholding to filter pseudo-labels, Focal Loss [16] is also applied to address the pseudo-labeling bias issue. Adaptive Class-Rebalancing [32] artificially adds foreground targets to images to achieve inter-class balance. *Li, et al.* [13] propose dynamic thresholding and loss re-weighting for each category. Soft Teacher [30] proposed a score-weighted classification loss and box jittering approach to select and utilize regression loss of pseudo-boxes. While these methods successfully transferred paradigms from SSL to SS-OD, they ignored the unique characteristics of SS-OD. These pseudo-box-based strategies treat pseudo-boxes, or selected pseudo-boxes, as ordinary target boxes, and thus they invariably follow the detector's label assign strategy.

3 Dense Teacher

In Sect. 3.1, we first introduce the existing Pseudo-Labeling SS-OD framework. Then we analyze the disadvantages of utilizing pseudo-boxes in Sect. 3.2. In the remaining part, we propose Dense Pseudo-Label to overcome the issues mentioned above and introduce our overall pipeline in detail, including the label generation, loss function, and the learning region selection strategy. Since our primary motivation is to show the superiority of dense pseudo-labels compared to pseudo-box labels, we naturally choose to verify our idea on dense detectors (*i.e.*, one-stage detectors).

3.1   Pseudo-Labeling Framework

Our Dense Teacher follows the existing pseudo-labeling framework [18,30] as shown in Fig. 1. Within each iteration:

1. Labeled and unlabeled images are randomly sampled to form a data batch.
2. The teacher model, an exponential moving average (EMA) of the student, takes the augmented unlabeled images to generate pseudo-labels.
3. The student model then takes the labeled data for vanilla training and calculates supervised loss $\mathcal{L}_s$, while the unlabeled data together with pseudo-labels are used to produce unsupervised loss $\mathcal{L}_u$.
4. Two losses are weighted and learned to update parameters of the student model. The student model updates the teacher model in an EMA manner.

Finally, the overall loss function is defined as:

$$\mathcal{L} = \mathcal{L}_s + w_u\mathcal{L}_u, \tag{1}$$

where w_u is the unsupervised loss weight. Traditionally, the unsupervised loss $\mathcal{L}_u$ is calculated with pseudo-boxes. However, in the following section, we point out that using processed boxes as pseudo-labels can be inefficient and sub-optimal.

3.2   Disadvantages of Pseudo-Box Labels

In this part, we study the behavior of pseudo-box-based SS-OD algorithms on COCO [17], as well as CrowdHuman[2] [22] since the impact of the NMS threshold can be more clearly demonstrated in the crowd situation. We adopt Unbiased Teacher [18] as a representative algorithm to FCOS for these experiments.

Dilemma in Thresholding. In SS-OD algorithms [18,30], the output of the teacher model is expected to play the role of ground-truth labels for unsupervised images. To this end, Thresholding is a key operation to screen out low-scoring boxes so that the quality of pseudo-box labels can be improved. However, our preliminary experiments show that the threshold σ_t introduced by this operation may substantially affect the entire training process. In Fig. 2(a), we present the training results of Unbiased Teacher under different σ_t. It shows that the detection performance fluctuates significantly on both datasets as the σ_t varies. Moreover, when σ_t is set to a high value (e.g., 0.7 and 0.9), the training process even fails to converge. Such a phenomenon is possibly caused by a large number of false negatives in the teacher's prediction, as shown in Fig. 2(c) and (d). When this is the case, Thresholding will eliminate many high-quality predictions and mislead the learning process of the student model. Conversely, when set σ_t to a low value such as 0.3, the performance shows apparent degradation due to the increasing number of false positives (see in Fig. 2(c) and (d) as well). As a result, one can not find a perfect threshold to ensure the quality of generated pseudo-boxes.

---

[2] CrowdHuman is a benchmark for detecting humans in a crowded situation, performance is measured by Log-average Miss Rate (mMR). The lower the better.

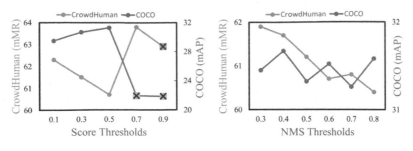

(a) Detection Performance v.s. σ_t (b) Detection Performance v.s. σ_{nms}

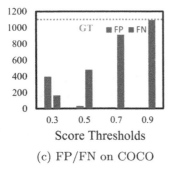
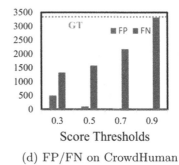

(c) FP/FN on COCO   (d) FP/FN on CrowdHuman

Fig. 2. Analysis of Pseudo-box based approaches. (a) and (b): Performances under different σ_t and σ_{NMS}. Note that the gray $\boxtimes$ represents the training fails to converge. (c) and (d): False Positive and False Negative boxes on 128 images under different threshold on COCO and CrowdHuman, the green line denotes the ground truth box number

Dilemma in Non-Maximum Suppression (NMS). NMS is adopted on the detector's original outputs for most object detection algorithms to remove redundant predictions. It is also indispensable to the teacher model in existing SS-OD frameworks, without which the resulting pseudo-labels will be a mess. NMS introduces a threshold σ_{nms} to control the degree of suppression. According to our experiments, we find that σ_{nms} also has a non-negligible effect on the SS-OD algorithms. Figure 2(b) shows the relationship between σ_{nms} and performance of Unbiased Teacher. From this figure, we can tell that 1). different σ_{nms} may lead to fluctuations in the detection performance (especially on CrowdHuman). 2). the optimal σ_{nms} values for different datasets are different (*i.e.*, 0.7 on COCO and 0.8 on CrowdHuman), which will bring in extra workload for developers to tune the optimal σ_{nms} on their custom datasets. Moreover, previous works [7,8] show that in a crowd scene like in the CrowdHuman dataset, there does not exist a perfect σ_{nms} that can keep all true positive predictions while suppressing all false positives. As a result, with NMS adopted, the unreliability of pseudo-box labels is further exacerbated.

(a) Raw Image   (b) Ground Truth Positives   (c) Pseudo-Box Positives

● True   ⦂ Miss   ● False

Fig. 3. Comparisons between (b) foreground pixels assigned by ground truth boxes and (c) foreground pixels assigned by pseudo-boxes

Inconsistent Label Assignment. As shown in Fig. 1, existing pseudo-label-based algorithms convert the sparse pseudo-boxes into a dense form by label assignment to form the final supervision. An anchor box (or point) will be assigned as either positive or negative during label assignment based on a particular pre-defined rule. Although this process is natural in the standard object detection task, we believe it is harmful to SS-OD tasks. The reason is quite simple: the pseudo-boxes may suffer from the inaccurate localization problem, making the label assigning results inconsistent with the potential ground-truth labels. In Fig. 3, we can find that although the predicted box matches the actual box under IoU threshold 0.5, a severe inconsistent assigning result appears due to the inaccurate pseudo-box. This inconsistency with the ground truth is likely to degrade the performance.

Due to the above three issues, we challenge the convention of using pseudo-box as the middle-ware of unsupervised learning and propose a new form of pseudo-label that is dense and free of post-processing.

3.3   Dense Pseudo-Label

To address the problems mentioned above, we propose Dense Pseudo-Label (DPL) that encompasses richer and undistorted supervising signals. Specifically, we adopt the post-sigmoid logits predicted by the trained model as our desired dense pseudo-label, as shown in the green box in Fig. 1. After bypassing those lengthy post-processing methods, one can naturally discover that our proposed DPL reserves more detailed information from the teacher than its pseudo-box counterpart.

Since DPL represents information in continuous values (value between 0 and 1) and the standard Focal Loss [16] can only deal with discrete binary values (0 or 1), we adopt Quality Focal Loss [14] to conduct learning between dense pseudo-labels and the student's predicting results. Let us denote $\vec{y_i} \triangleq \vec{p_i^t}$ as DPL (*i.e.*, teacher's prediction) and denote $\vec{p_i^s}$ as student's prediction for i-th anchor[3], we hope the prediction and the target to be similar for the same anchor. Therefore, we can write the classification loss on the i-th anchor for an unlabeled image as:

$$\mathcal{L}_i^{cls} = -|\vec{y_i} - \vec{p_i^s}|^\gamma * \left[\vec{y_i}log(\vec{p_i^s}) + (1 - \vec{y_i})log(1 - \vec{p_i^s})\right] \tag{2}$$

where γ is the suppression factor.

While DPL contains rich information, it also keeps many low-scoring predictions due to the absence of the thresholding operation. Since those low-scoring predictions usually involve the background regions, intuitively, the knowledge encompassed in them shall be less informative. In Sect. 4.4, we experimentally prove that learning to mimic the teacher's response in those regions will hurt the SS-OD algorithm's performance. Therefore, we propose to divide the whole input image into a learning region and a suppressing region (e.t., negative region in positive-negative division) based on the teacher's Feature Richness Score (FRS [34]). With the help of this richness score, we select the pixels with top $k\%$ scores as the learning region and the other regions will be suppressed to 0. As result, our DPL is extended to:

$$S_i = \max_{c \in [1,C]} (p_{i,c}^t) \tag{3}$$

$$\vec{y_i} = \begin{cases} \vec{p_i^t}, & \text{if } S_i \text{ in top } k\%, \\ \vec{0}, & \text{otherwise.} \end{cases} \tag{4}$$

where $p_{i,c}^t$ denotes the score prediction of c-th class for i-th sample from the teacher, C denotes the total number of classes.

Besides, this design has other advantages:

1. By modifying the learning region, we can easily achieve Hard Negative Mining by selecting extra samples (see Fig. 4). In Sect. 4.4 we will analyze the gain from this part in detail.
2. Since the learning region is selected, unsupervised learning for regression branch can be easily achieved. We apply IoU Loss on this branch and analyze its gain in Sect. 4.2.

---

[3] "Anchor" stands for "anchor point" in anchor-free detectors and "anchor box" in anchor-based detectors.

4   Experiments

4.1   Datasets and Experiment Settings

Datasets. We present our experimental results on MS-COCO [17] and Pascal VOC [6] benchmarks. For MS-COCO, both labeled and unlabeled training datasets will be used. The `train2017` set contains 118k images with target bounding boxes and the `unlabeled2017` contains 123k unlabeled images. Validation is performed on the subset `val2017`. For Pascal VOC, training set uses `VOC07 train` and `VOC12 train` and validation set uses `VOC07 test`. The following three experimental settings are mainly studied:

- **COCO-Standard:** 1%, 2%, 5% and 10% of the `train2017` set are sampled as labeled data, respectively. The rest of images are viewed as unlabeled data while training. For fairness of comparison, we follow the same dataset division as in [18] which contains 5 different data folds. Mean score of all 5 folds are taken as the final performance.
- **COCO-Full:** `train2017` is used as labeled data while `unlabeled2017` is used as unlabeled data.
- **VOC Mixture:** `VOC07 train` is used as labeled data, while `VOC12 train` and `COCO20cls`[4] are taken as unlabeled data.

Implementation Details. Without loss of generality, we take FCOS [28] as the representative anchor-free detector for experiments. ResNet-50 [9] pre-trained on ImageNet [20] is used as the backbone. We use batch-size 16 for both labeled and unlabeled images. The base learning rate and γ in QFL are set to 0.01 and 2 in all of our experiments. Loss weight w_u on unlabeled data is set to 4 on COCO-Standard and 2 on the other settings. Following previous works [18,24], we adopt "burnin" strategy to initialize the teacher model, same data augmentations as in [18] are applied.

4.2   Main Results

In this section, we progressively improve the Dense Teacher and analyze the performance gain from each part in detail. We adopt Unbiased Teacher as our baseline. Results on the COCO-Standard 10% setting are shown in Table 1. We first replace Unbiased Teacher's pseudo-boxes with our proposed Dense Pseudo-Labels without the region division strategy. It shows that this improves the mAP from 31.52% to 32.0%. Then, we apply our region division strategy on DPL and the mAP is further improved by 1.34%. Finally, we extend the unsupervised learning scheme to the regression branch as done by [30], and our final mAP comes to 35.11%. To the best of our knowledge, this is the new state-of-the-art under the COCO-Standard 10% setting. According to these results, we can attribute the advantages of Dense Teacher over existing methods to two major improvements:

---

[4] `COCO20cls` is the sampled COCO `train2017` set, only 20 classes same as in VOC are included.

Table 1. Performance under different model configurations on COCO-Standard 10%.
* denotes our re-implemented result on FCOS. "Our Division" means the learning/suppression region division based on FRS score

Method	Learning region	Cls	Reg	AP	AP50	AP75
Supervised	-	-	-	26.44	42.69	28.11
Unbiased Teacher* [18]	Predicted Positive	✓	×	31.52	48.80	33.57
Dense Teacher	All	✓	×	32.00	50.29	34.17
Dense Teacher	Our Division	✓	×	**33.34**	52.14	35.53
Unbiased Teacher* [18]	Predicted Positive	✓	✓	33.13	49.96	35.36
Dense Teacher	Our Division	✓	✓	**35.11**	53.35	37.79

(a) Ground Truth   (b) Pseudo-Box Label   (c) Dense Pseudo-Label

Fig. 4. Illustration of (c) our Dense Pseudo-Label compared with (b) pseudo-box label and its assigning result. Blue areas denote the assigned negative samples. In Dense Pseudo-Label, red means high quality scores, which denotes positive samples in pseudo-box label. It can be seen that Dense Pseudo-Label is able to leverage more hard negative regions compared to the Pseudo-Box based method (Color figure online)

1) The new form of pseudo-label resolves the deterioration problem of the pseudo-box label as mentioned in Sect. 3.2. It is worth mentioning that by getting rid of the lengthy post-processing procedure, our Dense Teacher forms a much simpler SS-OD pipeline but still with better performance. However, the resulting improvement (from 31.52% to 32.00%) remains marginal without the advanced learning region division strategy.

2) Our region division strategy can efficiently utilize hard negative regions to enhance training. Specifically, we conduct label assignment on FCOS using ground truth annotation of COCO, finding that there are only about 0.4% of positive samples in the COCO train2017 set. By specifying $k = 1$, we take a fair amount of hard negative samples for unsupervised training. In Fig. 4, we can see that hard negatives samples distribute on meaningful background objects (chair cushion, cabinet, and other parts of the dog) in the image. These responses from the teacher are valuable in improving the student's performance.

4.3   Comparison with State-of-the-Arts

Table 2. Experimental results on COCO-Standard. * means our re-implemented results on FCOS, ⊚ means large scale jittering is adopted when training

| | COCO-Standard | | | |
	1%	2%	5%	10%
Supervised	11.24 ± 0.18	15.04 ± 0.31	20.82 ± 0.13	26.44 ± 0.11
CSD [10]	10.51 ± 0.06	13.93 ± 0.12	18.63 ± 0.07	22.46 ± 0.08
STAC [24]	13.97 ± 0.35	18.25 ± 0.25	24.38 ± 0.12	28.64 ± 0.21
Instant teaching [35]	18.05 ± 0.15	22.45 ± 0.30	26.75 ± 0.05	30.40 ± 0.05
ISMT [31]	18.88 ± 0.74	22.43 ± 0.56	26.37 ± 0.24	30.52 ± 0.52
Unbiased teacher [18]	$\mathbf{20.75 \pm 0.12}$	24.30 ± 0.07	28.27 ± 0.11	31.50 ± 0.10
Humble teacher [26]	16.96 ± 0.38	21.72 ± 0.24	27.70 ± 0.15	31.61 ± 0.28
Li, et al. [13]	19.02 ± 0.25	23.34 ± 0.18	28.40 ± 0.15	32.23 ± 0.14
Unbiased teacher* [18]	18.31 ± 0.44	22.39 ± 0.26	27.73 ± 0.13	31.52 ± 0.15
Ours	19.64 ± 0.34	$\mathbf{25.39 \pm 0.13}$	$\mathbf{30.83 \pm 0.21}$	$\mathbf{35.11 \pm 0.12}$
Soft teacher⊚ [30]	20.46 ± 0.39	–	30.74 ± 0.08	34.04 ± 0.14
Ours⊚	$\mathbf{22.38 \pm 0.31}$	$\mathbf{27.20 \pm 0.20}$	$\mathbf{33.01 \pm 0.14}$	$\mathbf{37.13 \pm 0.12}$

COCO-Standard. We compare Dense Teacher with several existing methods under the COCO-Standard setting in Table 2. When the labeled data varies from 2% to 10% our model consistently shows superior results. Whereas Under the 1% labeled setting, the performance of Dense Teacher is lower than Faster R-CNN based Unbiased Teacher. However, a more direct comparison between our method and Unbiased Teacher under the 1% setting on FCOS shows that Dense Teacher still leads by 1.2% mAP. Moreover, when applying large-scale jittering for augmentation following the implementation of Soft Teacher, our method obtains more significant improvements and becomes new the state-of-the-art.

VOC & COCO-Full. Results in Table 3 and Table 4 show that Dense Teacher lead the performance in both settings. On VOC dataset, Dense Teacher improves its supervised baseline by 8.2% and 10.0% on AP50 and mAP (*i.e.*, from AP50 to AP95). Under the COCO-Full setting, since the baseline reported in other works are not the same, we list the performance of each method in the form of "baseline→result". Our approach obtains a boost of 3.1% from the 2017unlabeled set, which is much higher than CSD, STAC, and Unbiased Teacher. We finally apply the large-scale jittering trick and a longer training scheduler for a fair comparison with Soft Teacher, where Dense Teacher boosts mAP by 4.9%, reaching 46.12% mAP.

Table 3. Comparison with existing methods on Pascal VOC. Evaluations are performed on **VOC07 test**

Method	Labeled	Unlabeled	AP_{50}	$AP_{50:95}$
Supervised(Ours)	VOC07	None	71.69	45.87
CSD [10]	VOC07	VOC12	74.7	-
STAC [24]			77.45	44.64
ISMT [31]			77.23	46.23
Unbiased teacher [18]			77.37	48.69
Li, et al. [13]			79.00	54.60
Instant teaching [35]			79.20	50.00
Ours			**79.89**	**55.87**
CSD [10]	VOC07	VOC12 + COCO20cls	75.1	-
STAC [24]			79.08	46.01
ISMT [31]			77.75	49.59
Unbiased teacher [18]			78.82	50.34
Li, et al. [13]			79.60	56.10
Instant teaching [35]			79.90	55.70
Ours			**81.23**	**57.52**

4.4   Ablation and Key Parameters

Effect of Hard Negative Samples. In Dense Teacher, hard negative samples/anchors can be better utilized. We explore three different strategies to study the impact of these hard negative regions[5], including "suppressing", "ignoring" and "selecting". Results are shown in Table 5. We first suppress these samples to 0 and find a significant performance drop on both classification and regression branches compared to the original setting. Then, we ignore these samples when calculating loss. It turns out that this setting performs better than the "suppress" setting but still falls short when they are selected for training, indicating that learning to predict those hard negative samples can positively affect the model performance.

Regression Branch. We have shown that unsupervised learning on the regression branch effectively improves model performance. However, since the output of deltas in the background region is not meaningful in FCOS, the quality of pseudo-labels in this branch is highly dependent on the design of the learning region. As can be seen in Table 1, in our region division and pseudo-box based method, the model can obtain gains of 1.8% mAP and 1.6% mAP. When using ground truth positives as learning region (see Table 5 "suppress" and "ignore"), the model gains about 2% mAP. Therefore, our region division strategy can produce sufficiently reliable regions for this task.

---

[5] Since the "unlabeled images" under the COCO-Standard setting actually come with annotations, we can perform label assignments on images using these annotations.

Table 4. Experimental results on COCO-Full. Evaluations are done on COCO val2017. Note that 1x represents 90K training iterations, Nx represents Nx90K iterations. ⊙ means training with large scale jittering

Method	mAP
CSD [10] (3x)	$40.20 \xrightarrow{-1.38} 38.82$
STAC [24] (6x)	$39.48 \xrightarrow{-0.27} 39.21$
ISMT [31]	$37.81 \xrightarrow{+1.83} 39.64$
Instant-teaching [35]	$37.63 \xrightarrow{+2.57} 40.20$
Unbiased teacher [18] (3x)	$40.20 \xrightarrow{+1.10} 41.30$
Humble teacher [26] (3x)	$37.63 \xrightarrow{+4.74} 42.37$
Li, et al. [13] (3x)	$40.20 \xrightarrow{+3.10} 43.30$
Ours(3x)	$41.22 \xrightarrow{+2.66} 43.90$
Ours(6x)	$41.22 \xrightarrow{+3.70} \mathbf{44.94}$
Soft teacher⊙ [30] (8x)	$40.90 \xrightarrow{+3.70} 44.60$
Ours(8x)⊙	$41.24 \xrightarrow{+4.88} \mathbf{46.12}$

Effectiveness on Other Detectors and Datasets. Apart from comparison with state-of-the-arts, we also validate the effectiveness of our method on anchor-based detector and on CrowedHuman [22] dataset. For anchor-based detector, we take RetinaNet as representation. When comparing with pseudo-box based Unbiased Teacher, our method stay ahead of the curve as show in Table 6, Dense Teacher achieved a 2.2% mAP improvement over Unbiased Teacher. On the CrowedHuman dataset with FCOS detector, our method obtains a 2.1% mMR improvement as well.

Size of Learning Region. We compare Dense Teacher's performance under different selecting ratio k in Table 7(a). As shown in the table, we obtain the best

Table 5. Impact of strategies dealing with hard negatives

HN samples	Cls	Reg	AP
Suppress	✓	✗	31.56
Ignore	✓	✗	32.64
Select	✓	✗	**33.34**
Suppress	✓	✓	33.47
Ignore	✓	✓	34.72
Select	✓	✓	**35.11**

Table 6. Extensive comparison on different detectors and datasets

Method	Anchor	Dataset	AP/MR
UT [18]	✓	COCO	28.9
Ours	✓	COCO	**31.1**
UT [18]	✗	CH [22]	62.8
Ours	✗	CH [22]	**60.7**

The difference between our division ($k = 1$) and the assigned foreground is defined as hard negatives.

Table 7. Ablation study on hyper-parameters introduced by our method. COCO 10% stands for COCO-Standard 10%

Setting	$k(\%)$	AP	AP50	AP75	Setting	w_u	AP	AP50	AP75
COCO 10%	0.1	25.76	41.79	27.34	COCO 10%	2	34.86	53.22	37.34
	0.5	34.11	51.94	36.80		4	**35.11**	53.35	37.79
	1	**35.11**	53.35	37.79		8	33.81	51.97	36.34
	3	34.47	53.13	36.87	COCO- Full	2	**44.92**	63.71	48.79
	5	33.85	53.00	36.03		4	43.04	61.60	46.87

performance when selecting 1% of the samples (5 layers of FPN) for unsupervised learning. According to statistics, there are about 0.4% of positive samples in COCO under the label assigning rule of FCOS. Therefore, the optimal learning region not only contains ground truth positives, but also encompasses hard negatives that are valuable. This also suggests that although the model performance is affected by this hyperparameter, the statistical characteristics of the data set can help us determine the optimal value of this hyperparameter, mitigate model migration and deployment challenges.

Unsupervised Loss Weight. The weight of unsupervised data also has an important impact on the training results. The experimental results in Table 7(b) turn out that: for a limited amount of supervised data like in the COCO-Standard 10% setting, a relatively large weight of 4 is favorable. Meanwhile, for the COCO-Full setting where much more labeled data are available, weight of 2 is enough. We attribute this phenomenon to the different degrees of overfitting. When only a small amount of annotations are available, a relatively large weight of unsupervised parts could introduce stronger supervision. In contrast, when given a large amount of labeled data, a small unsupervised weight could address and better utilize supervision.

5   Conclusion

In this paper, we revisit the form of pseudo-labels in existing semi-supervised learning. By analyzing various flaws caused by the lengthy pseudo-box generation pipeline, we point out that pseudo-box is a sub-optimal choice for unlabeled data. To address this issue, we propose the Dense Teacher, a SS-OD framework which adopts dense predictions from the teacher model as pseudo-labels for unlabeled data. Our approach is simpler but stronger. We demonstrate its efficacy by comparing Dense Teacher with other pseudo-box based SS-OD algorithms on MS-COCO and Pascal VOC benchmarks. Results on both benchmarks show that our Dense Teacher achieves state-of-the-art performance.

References

1. Bachman, P., Alsharif, O., Precup, D.: Learning with pseudo-ensembles. In: Advances in Neural Information Processing Systems, vol. 27 (2014)

2. Bachman, P., Alsharif, O., Precup, D.: Learning with pseudo-ensembles. In: Advances in Neural Information Processing Systems, vol. 27 (2014)

3. Berthelot, D., et al.: Remixmatch: semi-supervised learning with distribution alignment and augmentation anchoring. arXiv preprint arXiv:1911.09785 (2019)

4. Berthelot, D., Carlini, N., Goodfellow, I., Papernot, N., Oliver, A., Raffel, C.A.: Mixmatch: a holistic approach to semi-supervised learning. In: Advances in Neural Information Processing Systems, vol. 32 (2019)

5. Chen, T., Kornblith, S., Norouzi, M., Hinton, G.: A simple framework for contrastive learning of visual representations. In: International Conference on Machine Learning, pp. 1597–1607. PMLR (2020)

6. Everingham, M., Van Gool, L., Williams, C.K.I., Winn, J., Zisserman, A.: The PASCAL Visual Object Classes Challenge 2012 (VOC 2012) Results. www.pascal-network.org/challenges/VOC/voc2012/workshop/index.html

7. Ge, Z., Hu, C., Huang, X., Qiu, B., Yoshie, O.: Dualbox: generating bbox pair with strong correspondence via occlusion pattern clustering and proposal refinement. In: 2020 25th International Conference on Pattern Recognition (ICPR), pp. 2097–2102. IEEE (2021)

8. Ge, Z., Jie, Z., Huang, X., Xu, R., Yoshie, O.: PS-RCNN: detecting secondary human instances in a crowd via primary object suppression. In: 2020 IEEE International Conference on Multimedia and Expo (ICME), pp. 1–6. IEEE (2020)

9. He, K., Zhang, X., Ren, S., Sun, J.: Deep residual learning for image recognition. In: Proceedings of the IEEE Conference on Computer Vision and Pattern Recognition, pp. 770–778 (2016)

10. Jeong, J., Lee, S., Kim, J., Kwak, N.: Consistency-based semi-supervised learning for object detection. In: Advances in Neural Information Processing Systems, vol. 32 (2019)

11. Laine, S., Aila, T.: Temporal ensembling for semi-supervised learning. arXiv preprint arXiv:1610.02242 (2016)

12. Lee, D.H., et al.: Pseudo-label: the simple and efficient semi-supervised learning method for deep neural networks (2013)

13. Li, H., Wu, Z., Shrivastava, A., Davis, L.S.: Rethinking pseudo labels for semi-supervised object detection. arXiv preprint arXiv:2106.00168 (2021)

14. Li, X., et al.: Generalized focal loss: learning qualified and distributed bounding boxes for dense object detection. Adv. Neural. Inf. Process. Syst. **33**, 21002–21012 (2020)

15. Lin, T.Y., Dollár, P., Girshick, R., He, K., Hariharan, B., Belongie, S.: Feature pyramid networks for object detection. In: Proceedings of the IEEE Conference on Computer Vision and Pattern Recognition, pp. 2117–2125 (2017)

16. Lin, T.Y., Goyal, P., Girshick, R., He, K., Dollár, P.: Focal loss for dense object detection. In: Proceedings of the IEEE International Conference on Computer Vision, pp. 2980–2988 (2017)

17. Lin, T.-Y., et al.: Microsoft COCO: common objects in context. In: Fleet, D., Pajdla, T., Schiele, B., Tuytelaars, T. (eds.) ECCV 2014. LNCS, vol. 8693, pp. 740–755. Springer, Cham (2014). https://doi.org/10.1007/978-3-319-10602-1_48

18. Liu, Y.C., et al.: Unbiased teacher for semi-supervised object detection. arXiv preprint arXiv:2102.09480 (2021)

19. Miyato, T., Maeda, S.I., Koyama, M., Ishii, S.: Virtual adversarial training: a regularization method for supervised and semi-supervised learning. IEEE Trans. Pattern Anal. Mach. Intell. **41**(8), 1979–1993 (2018)

20. Russakovsky, O., et al.: ImageNet large scale visual recognition challenge. Int. J. Comput. Vision **115**(3), 211–252 (2015). https://doi.org/10.1007/s11263-015-0816-y
21. Sajjadi, M., Javanmardi, M., Tasdizen, T.: Regularization with stochastic transformations and perturbations for deep semi-supervised learning. In: Advances in Neural Information Processing Systems, vol. 29 (2016)
22. Shao, S., et al.: Crowdhuman: a benchmark for detecting human in a crowd. arXiv preprint arXiv:1805.00123 (2018)
23. Sohn, K., et al.: Fixmatch: simplifying semi-supervised learning with consistency and confidence. Adv. Neural. Inf. Process. Syst. **33**, 596–608 (2020)
24. Sohn, K., Zhang, Z., Li, C.L., Zhang, H., Lee, C.Y., Pfister, T.: A simple semi-supervised learning framework for object detection. arXiv preprint arXiv:2005.04757 (2020)
25. Srivastava, N., Hinton, G., Krizhevsky, A., Sutskever, I., Salakhutdinov, R.: Dropout: a simple way to prevent neural networks from overfitting. J. Mach. Learn. Res. **15**(1), 1929–1958 (2014)
26. Tang, Y., Chen, W., Luo, Y., Zhang, Y.: Humble teachers teach better students for semi-supervised object detection. In: Proceedings of the IEEE/CVF Conference on Computer Vision and Pattern Recognition, pp. 3132–3141 (2021)
27. Tarvainen, A., Valpola, H.: Mean teachers are better role models: weight-averaged consistency targets improve semi-supervised deep learning results. In: Advances in Neural Information Processing Systems, vol. 30 (2017)
28. Tian, Z., Shen, C., Chen, H., He, T.: FCOS: fully convolutional one-stage object detection. In: Proceedings of the IEEE/CVF International Conference on Computer Vision, pp. 9627–9636 (2019)
29. Xie, Q., Luong, M.T., Hovy, E., Le, Q.V.: Self-training with noisy student improves imagenet classification. In: Proceedings of the IEEE/CVF Conference on Computer Vision and Pattern Recognition, pp. 10687–10698 (2020)
30. Xu, M., et al.: End-to-end semi-supervised object detection with soft teacher. In: Proceedings of the IEEE/CVF International Conference on Computer Vision, pp. 3060–3069 (2021)
31. Yang, Q., Wei, X., Wang, B., Hua, X.S., Zhang, L.: Interactive self-training with mean teachers for semi-supervised object detection. In: Proceedings of the IEEE/CVF Conference on Computer Vision and Pattern Recognition, pp. 5941–5950 (2021)
32. Zhang, F., Pan, T., Wang, B.: Semi-supervised object detection with adaptive class-rebalancing self-training. arXiv preprint arXiv:2107.05031 (2021)
33. Zhang, S., Chi, C., Yao, Y., Lei, Z., Li, S.Z.: Bridging the gap between anchor-based and anchor-free detection via adaptive training sample selection. In: Proceedings of the IEEE/CVF Conference on Computer Vision and Pattern Recognition, pp. 9759–9768 (2020)
34. Zhixing, D., Zhang, R., Chang, M., Liu, S., Chen, T., Chen, Y., et al.: Distilling object detectors with feature richness. In: Advances in Neural Information Processing Systems, vol. 34 (2021)
35. Zhou, Q., Yu, C., Wang, Z., Qian, Q., Li, H.: Instant-teaching: an end-to-end semi-supervised object detection framework. In: Proceedings of the IEEE/CVF Conference on Computer Vision and Pattern Recognition, pp. 4081–4090 (2021)

Point-to-Box Network for Accurate Object Detection via Single Point Supervision

Pengfei Chen[1], Xuehui Yu[1], Xumeng Han[1], Najmul Hassan[2], Kai Wang[2], Jiachen Li[3], Jian Zhao[4], Humphrey Shi[2,3,5], Zhenjun Han[1(✉)], and Qixiang Ye[1]

[1] University of Chinese Academy of Sciences, Beijing, China
{chenpengfei20,yuxuehui17,hanxumeng19}@mails.ucas.ac.cn,
{hanzhj,qxye}@ucas.ac.cn
[2] SHI Lab, University of Oregon, Eugene, USA
[3] UIUC, Champaign, USA
[4] Institute of North Electronic Equipment, Beijing, China
zhaojian90@u.nus.edu
[5] Picsart AI Research (PAIR), Princeton, USA

Abstract. Object detection using single point supervision has received increasing attention over the years. However, the performance gap between point supervised object detection (PSOD) and bounding box supervised detection remains large. In this paper, we attribute such a large performance gap to the failure of generating high-quality proposal bags which are crucial for multiple instance learning (MIL). To address this problem, we introduce a lightweight alternative to the off-the-shelf proposal (OTSP) method and thereby create the Point-to-Box Network (P2BNet), which can construct an inter-objects balanced proposal bag by generating proposals in an anchor-like way. By fully investigating the accurate position information, P2BNet further constructs an instance-level bag, avoiding the mixture of multiple objects. Finally, a coarse-to-fine policy in a cascade fashion is utilized to improve the IoU between proposals and ground-truth (GT). Benefiting from these strategies, P2BNet is able to produce high-quality instance-level bags for object detection. P2BNet improves the mean average precision (AP) by more than 50% relative to the previous best PSOD method on the MS COCO dataset. It also demonstrates the great potential to bridge the performance gap between point supervised and bounding-box supervised detectors. The code will be released at www.github.com/ucas-vg/P2BNet.

Keywords: Object detection · Single point annotation · Point supervised object detection

1 Introduction

Object detectors [4, 13, 23, 25, 29, 30, 38, 46] trained with accurate bounding box annotations have been well received in academia and industry. However,

---

Supplementary Information The online version contains supplementary material available at https://doi.org/10.1007/978-3-031-20077-9_4.

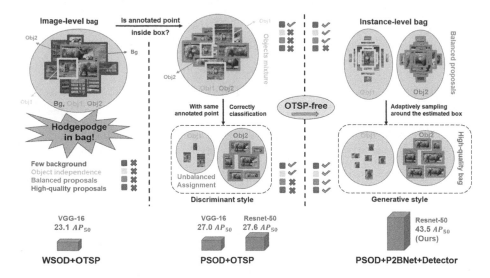

Fig. 1. Based on OTSP methods, the image-level bag in WSOD shows many problems: Too much background, mixture of different objects, unbalanced and low-quality proposals. With point annotation, the previous work UFO² filters most background in first stage and splits bags for different objects in refinement. Our P2BNet produces balanced instance-level bags in coarse stage and improves bag quality improves by adaptively sampling proposal boxes around the estimated box of the former stage for better optimization. The performance is the performance in COCO-14. The 27.6 AP_{50} is conducted on UFO² with ResNet-50 and our point annotation for a fair comparison.

collecting quality bounding box annotations requires extensive human efforts. To solve this problem, weakly supervised object detection [2,6,8,39–41,49,51] (WSOD) replace bounding box annotations using low-cost image-level annotations. However, lacking crucial location information and experiencing the difficulty of distinguishing dense objects, WSOD methods perform poorly in complex scenarios. Point supervised object detection (PSOD), on the other hand, can provide distinctive location information about the object and is much cheaper compared with that via bounding box supervision.

Recently, point-based annotations are widely used in many tasks including object detection [28,32] and localization [33,37,45], instance segmentation [7], and action localization [21]. However, the performance gap between point supervised detection methods [28,32] and bounding box supervised detectors remain large. Although it is understandable that location information provided by bounding boxes is richer than the points, we argue that this is not the only reason. We believe most PSOD methods do not utilize the full potential of point-based annotations. Previous works use off-the-shelf proposal (OTSP) methods (*e.g.*, Selective Search [34], MCG [1], and EdgeBox [53]) to obtain proposals for constructing bags. Despite the wide adaptation of these OTSP-based methods in weakly supervised detectors, they suffer from the following problems in Fig. 1: 1) There are too many background proposals in the bags. OTSP methods generate

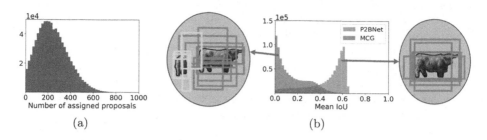

Fig. 2. (a) The number of assigned proposal boxes per object produced by MCG (OTSP -based) is unbalanced, which is unfair for training. (b) Histogram of mIoU_{prop} for different proposal generation methods. mIoU_{prop} denotes the mean IoU between proposal boxes and ground-truth for an object. Small mIoU_{prop} in MCG brings semantic confusion. Whereas for our P2BNet with refinement, large mIoU_{prop} is beneficial for optimization. Statistics are on COCO-17 training set, and both figures have 50 bins.

too many proposal boxes that do not have any intersection with any of the foreground objects; 2) Positive proposals per object are unbalanced. The positive proposals per object produced by MCG on the COCO-17 training set are shown in Fig. 2(a), which is clearly off-balance; 3) Majority of the proposals in bags have very low IoU indicating low-quality proposals (Fig. 2(b)). Also, as the previous PSOD methods only construct image-level bags, they can not utilize the point annotations during MIL training leading to a mixture of different objects in the same bag. All these problems limit the overall quality of the constructed bags, which contributes to the poor performance of the model.

In this paper, we propose P2BNet as an alternative to the OTSP methods for generating high-quality object proposals. The number of proposals generated by P2BNet is balanced for each object, and they cover varied scales and aspect ratios. Additionally, the proposal bags are instance-level instead of image-level. This preserves the exclusivity of objects for a given proposal bag which is very helpful during MIL training. To further improve the quality of the bag, a coarse-to-fine procedure is designed in a cascade fashion in P2BNet. The refinement stage consists of two parts, the coarse pseudo-box prediction (CBP) and the precise pseudo-box refinement (PBR). The CBP stage predicts the coarse scale (width and height) of objects, whereas the PBR stage iteratively finetunes the scale and position. Our P2BNet generates high-quality, balanced proposal bags and ensures the contribution of point annotations in all stages (before, during, and after MIL training). The detailed experiments on COCO suggest the effectiveness and robustness of our model outperforming the previous point-based detectors by a large margin. Our main contributions are as follows:

– P2BNet, a generative and OTSP-free network, is designed for predicting pseudo boxes. It generates inter-objects balanced instance-level bags and is beneficial for better optimization of MIL training. In addition, P2BNet is much more time-efficient than the OTSP-base methods.

- A coarse-to-fine fashion in P2BNet with CBP and PBR stage is proposed for higher-quality proposal bags and better prediction.
- The detection performance of our proposed P2BNet-FR framework with P2BNet under single quasi-center point supervision improves the mean average precision (AP) of the previous best PSOD method by more than 50% (relative) on COCO and bridges the gap between bounding box supervised detectors achieving comparable performance on AP_{50}.

2   Related Work

In this section, we briefly discuss the research status of box-supervised, image-level and point-level supervised object detection.

2.1   Box-Supervised Object Detection

Box-supervised object detection [4,13,23,25,29,30,38,46] is a traditional object detection paradigm that gives the network a specific category and box information. One-stage detectors based on sliding-window, like YOLO [29], SSD [25], and RetinaNet [23], predict classification and bounding-box regression through setting anchors. Two-stage detectors predict proposal boxes through OTSP methods (like selective search [34] in Fast R-CNN [13]) or deep networks (like RPN in Faster R-CNN [30]) and conduct classification and bounding-box regression with filtered proposal boxes sparsely. Transformer-based detectors (DETR [4], Deformable-DETR [52], and Swin-Transformer [26]) come, utilizing global information for better representation. Sparse R-CNN [38] combines the advantages of transformer and CNN to a sparse detector. [9,14,43] study on oriented object detection in aerial scenario. However, box-level annotation requires high costs.

2.2   Image-Supervised Object Detection

Image-supervised object detection [2,6,8,27,35,39–41,48,49,51] is the traditional field in WSOD. The traditional image-supervised WSOD methods can be divided into two styles: MIL-based [2,6,39–41], and CAM-based [8,49,51].

In MIL-based methods, a bag is positively labelled if it contains at least one positive instance; otherwise, it is negative. The objective of MIL is to select positive instances from a positive bag. WSDDN [2] introduced MIL into WSOD with a representative two-stream weakly supervised deep detection network that can classify positive proposals. OICR [39] introduces iterative fashion into WSOD and attempts to find the whole part instead of a discriminative part. PCL [40] develops the proposal cluster learning and uses the proposal clusters as supervision to indicate the rough locations where objects most likely appear. Subsequently, SLV [6] brings in spatial likelihood voting to replace the max score proposal, further looking for the whole context of objects. Our paper produces the anchor-like [30,35] proposals around the point annotation as a bag and uses instance-level MIL to train the classifier. It moves the fixed pre-generated proposals (e.g. OICR, PCL and UWSOD [35]) to achieve the coarse to fine purpose.

In CAM-based methods, the main idea is to produce the class activation maps (CAM) [51], use threshold to choose a high score region, and find the smallest circumscribed rectangle of the largest general domain. WCCN [8] uses a three-stage cascade structure. The first stage produces the class activation maps and obtains the initial proposals, the second stage is a segmentation network for refining object localization, and the last stage is a MIL stage outputting the results. Acol [49] introduces two parallel-classifiers for object localization using adversarial complementary learning to alleviate the discriminative region.

2.3   Point-Supervised Object Detection

Point-level annotation is a fairly recent innovation. The average time for annotating a single point is about $1.87\,s$ per image, close to image-level annotation ($1.5\,s$/image) and much lower than that for bounding box ($34.5\,s$/image). The statistics [11,28] are performed on VOC [10], which can be analogized to COCO [24].

[28] introduces center-click annotation to replace box supervision and estimates scale with the error between two times of center-click. [32] designs a network compatible with various supervision forms like tags, points, scribbles, and boxes annotation. However, these frameworks are based on OTSP methods and are not specially designed for point annotation. Therefore, the performance is limited and performs poorly in complex scenarios like the COCO [24] dataset. We introduce a new framework with P2BNet which is free of OTSP methods.

3   Point-to-Box Network

The P2BNet-FR framework consists of Point-to-Box Network (P2BNet) and Faster R-CNN (FR). P2BNet predicts pseudo boxes with point annotations to train the detector. We use standard settings for Faster R-CNN without any bells and whistles. Hence, we go over the proposed P2BNet in detail in this section.

The architecture of P2BNet is shown in Fig. 3, which includes the coarse pseudo box prediction (CBP) stage and the pseudo box refinement (PBR) stage. The CBP stage predicts the coarse scale (width and height) of objects, whereas the PBR stage iteratively finetunes the scale and position. The overall loss function of P2BNet is the summation of the losses of these two stages, *i.e.*,

$$\mathcal{L}_{p2b} = \mathcal{L}_{cbp} + \sum_{t=1}^{T} \mathcal{L}_{pbr}^{(t)}, \tag{1}$$

where PBR includes T iterations, and $\mathcal{L}_{pbr}^{(t)}$ is the loss of t-th iteration.

3.1   Coarse Pseudo Box Prediction

In the CBP stage, firstly, proposal boxes of different widths and heights are generated in an anchor-style for each object, taking the annotated point as the

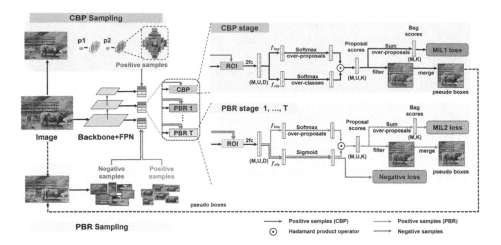

Fig. 3. The architecture of P2BNet. Firstly, to predict coarse pseudo boxes in CBP stage, proposal bags are fixedly sampled around point annotations for classifier training. Then, to predict refined pseudo boxes in PBR stage, high-quality proposal bags and negative proposals are sampled with coarse pseudo boxes for training. Finally, the pseudo boxes generated by the trained P2BNet serve as supervision for the training the classic detector. (Best viewed in color.) (Color figure online)

box center. Secondly, features of the sampled proposals are extracted to train a MIL classifier for selecting the best fitted proposal of objects. Finally, the top-k merging policy are utilized to estimate coarse pseudo boxes.

CBP Sampling: fixed sampling around the annotated point. With the point annotation $p = (p_x, p_y)$ as the center, s as the size, and v to adjust the aspect ratio, the proposal box $b = (b_x, b_y, b_w, b_h)$ is generated, *i.e.* $b = (p_x, p_y, v \cdot s, \frac{1}{v} \cdot s)$. The schematic diagram of proposal box sampling is shown in Fig. 4 (Left). By adjusting s and v, each point annotation p_j generates a bag of proposal boxes with different scales and aspect ratios, denoted by $\mathcal{B}_j$ ($j \in \{1, 2, \ldots, M\}$, where M is the amount of objects). The details of the settings of s and v are given in supplemental. All proposal bags are utilized for training the MIL classifier in the CBP module with the category labels of points as supervision.

There is a minor issue that oversized s may lead most of b outside the image and introduce too many meaningless padding values. In this case, we clip b to guarantee that it is inside the image (see Fig. 4 (Left)), *i.e.*,

$$b = \left(p_x, p_y, min(v \cdot s, 2(p_x - 0), 2(W - p_x)), min(\frac{1}{v} \cdot s, 2(p_y - 0), 2(H - p_y)) \right), \quad (2)$$

where W and H denote the image size. $(p_x - 0)$ and $(W - p_x)$ are the distances from the center to the left and right edges of the image, respectively.

CBP Module. For a proposal bag $\mathcal{B}_j$, features $\mathbf{F}_j \in \mathbb{R}^{U \times D}$ are extracted through 7×7 RoIAlign [15] and two fully connected (fc) layers, where U is the number of proposals in $\mathcal{B}_j$, and D is the feature dimension. We refer to

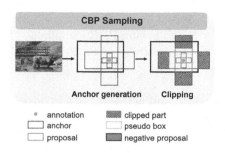

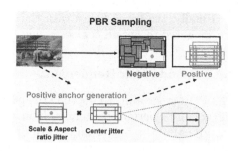

Fig. 4. Details of sampling strategies in the CBP stage and the PBR stage. The arrows in PBR sampling mean the offset of center jitter. Samples are obtained through center jitter following scale and aspect ratio jatter in PBR sampling

WSDDN [2] and design a two-stream structure as a MIL classifier to find the best bounding box region to represent the object. Specifically, applying the classification branch f_{cls} to $\mathbf{F}_j$ yields $\mathbf{O}_j^{cls} \in \mathbb{R}^{U \times K}$, which is then passed through the activation function to obtain the classification score $\mathbf{S}_j^{cls} \in \mathbb{R}^{U \times K}$, where K represents the number of instance categories. Likewise, instance score $\mathbf{S}_j^{ins} \in \mathbb{R}^{U \times K}$ is obtained through instance selection branch f_{ins} and activation function, *i.e.*,

$$\mathbf{O}_j^{cls} = f_{cls}(\mathbf{F}_j), \quad [\mathbf{S}_j^{cls}]_{uk} = e^{[\mathbf{O}_j^{cls}]_{uk}} / \sum_{i=1}^{K} e^{[\mathbf{O}_j^{cls}]_{ui}}; \tag{3}$$

$$\mathbf{O}_j^{ins} = f_{ins}(\mathbf{F}_j), \quad [\mathbf{S}_j^{ins}]_{uk} = e^{[\mathbf{O}_j^{ins}]_{uk}} / \sum_{i=1}^{U} e^{[\mathbf{O}_j^{ins}]_{ik}}, \tag{4}$$

where $[\cdot]_{uk}$ denotes the value at row u and column k in the matrix. The proposal score $\mathbf{S}_j$ is obtained by computing the Hadamard product of the classification score and the instance score, and the bag score $\widehat{\mathbf{S}}_j$ is obtained by the summation of the proposal scores of U proposal boxes, *i.e.*,

$$\mathbf{S}_j = \mathbf{S}_j^{cls} \odot \mathbf{S}_j^{ins} \in \mathbb{R}^{U \times K}, \quad \widehat{\mathbf{S}}_j = \sum_{u=1}^{U} [\mathbf{S}_j]_u \in \mathbb{R}^{K}. \tag{5}$$

$\widehat{\mathbf{S}}_j$ can be seen as the weighted summation of the classification score $[\mathbf{S}_j^{cls}]_u$ by the corresponding selection score $[\mathbf{S}_j^{ins}]_u$.

CBP Loss. The MIL loss in the CBP module (termed $\mathcal{L}_{mil1}$ to distinguish it from the MIL loss in PBR) uses the form of cross-entropy loss, defined as:

$$\mathcal{L}_{cbp} = \alpha_{mil1}\mathcal{L}_{mil1} = -\frac{\alpha_{mil1}}{M} \sum_{j=1}^{M} \sum_{k=1}^{K} [\mathbf{c}_j]_k \log([\widehat{\mathbf{S}}_j]_k) + (1 - [\mathbf{c}_j]_k) \log(1 - [\widehat{\mathbf{S}}_j]_k),$$
$$\tag{6}$$

where $\mathbf{c}_j \in \{0,1\}^K$ is the one-hot category label, α_{mil1} is 0.25. The CBP loss is to make each proposal correctly predict the category and instance it belongs to.

Finally, the top-k boxes with the highest proposal scores $\mathbf{S}_j$ of each object are weighted to obtain coarse pseudo boxes for the following PBR sampling.

3.2 Pseudo Box Refinement

The PBR stage aims to finetune the position, width and height of pseudo boxes, and it can be performed iteratively in a cascaded fashion for better performance. By adjusting the height and width of the pseudo box obtained in the previous stage (or iteration) in a small span while jittering its center position, finer proposal boxes are generated as positive examples for module training. Further, because the positive proposal bags are generated in the local region, negative samples can be sampled far from the proposal bags to suppress the background. The PBR module also weights the top-k proposals with the highest predicted scores to obtain the refined pseudo boxes, which are the final output of P2BNet.

PBR Sampling. Adaptive sampling around estimated boxes. As shown in Fig. 4 (Right), for each coarse pseudo box $b^* = (b_x^*, b_y^*, b_w^*, b_h^*)$ obtained in the previous stage (or iteration), we adjust its scale and aspect ratio with s and v, and jitter its position with o_x, o_y to obtain the finer proposal $b = (b_x, b_y, b_w, b_h)$:

$$b_w = v \cdot s \cdot b_w^*, \quad b_h = \frac{1}{v} \cdot s \cdot b_h^*, \tag{7}$$

$$b_x = b_x^* + b_w \cdot o_x, \quad b_y = b_y^* + b_h \cdot o_y. \tag{8}$$

These finer proposals are used as positive proposal bag $\mathcal{B}_j$ to train PBR module.

Furthermore, to better suppress the background, negative samples are introduced in the PBR sampling. We randomly sample many proposal boxes, which have small IoU (by default set as smaller than 0.3) with all positive proposals in all bags, to compose the negative sample set $\mathcal{N}$ for the PBR module. Through sampling proposal boxes by pseudo box distribution, high-quality proposal boxes are obtained for better optimization (shown in Fig. 5).

PBR Module. The PBR module has a similar structure to the CBP module. It shares the backbone network and two fully connected layers with CBP, and also has a classification branch f_{cls} and an instance selection branch f_{ins}. Note that f_{cls} and f_{ins} do not share parameters between different stages and iterations. For instance selection branch, we adopt the same structure as the CBP module, and utilize Eq. 4 to predict the instance score $\mathbf{S}_j^{ins}$ for the proposal bag $\mathcal{B}_j$. Differently, the classification branch uses the *sigmoid* activation function $\sigma(x)$ to predict the classification score $\mathbf{S}_j^{cls}$, i.e.,

$$\sigma(x) = 1/(1 + e^{-x}), \quad \mathbf{S}_j^{cls} = \sigma(f_{cls}(\mathbf{F}_j)) \in \mathbb{R}^{U \times K}. \tag{9}$$

This form makes it possible to perform multi-label classification, which can distinguish overlapping proposal boxes from different objects. According to the form of Eq. 5, bag score $\widehat{\mathbf{S}}_j^*$ is calculated using $\mathbf{S}_j^{cls}$ and $\mathbf{S}_j^{ins}$ of the current stage.

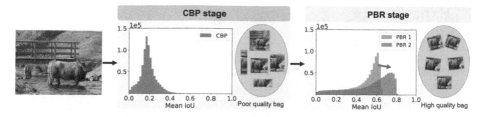

Fig. 5. The progression of the mIoU$_{prop}$ during refinement. By statistics, the mIoU$_{pred}$ is gradually increasing in the PBR stage, indicating that the quality of the proposal bag improves in iterative refinement

For the negative sample set $\mathcal{N}$, we calculate its classification score as:

$$\mathbf{S}_{neg}^{cls} = \sigma(f_{cls}(\mathbf{F}_{neg})) \in \mathbb{R}^{|\mathcal{N}| \times K}. \tag{10}$$

PBR Loss. The PBR loss consists of MIL loss $\mathcal{L}_{mil2}$ for positive bags and negative loss $\mathcal{L}_{neg}$ for negative samples, *i.e.*,

$$\mathcal{L}_{pbr} = \alpha_{mil2}\mathcal{L}_{mil2} + \alpha_{neg}\mathcal{L}_{neg}, \tag{11}$$

where $\alpha_{mil2} = 0.25$ and $\alpha_{neg} = 0.75$ are the settings in this paper.

1) **MIL Loss.** The MIL loss $\mathcal{L}_{mil2}$ in the PBR stage is defined as:

$$\text{FL}(\zeta, \tau) = -\sum_{k=1}^{K} [\tau]_k (1 - [\zeta]_k)^{\gamma} \log([\zeta]_k) + (1 - [\tau]_k)([\zeta]_k)^{\gamma} \log(1 - [\zeta]_k),$$
$$\tag{12}$$

$$\mathcal{L}_{mil2} = \frac{1}{M} \sum_{j=1}^{M} \langle \mathbf{c}_j^{\mathrm{T}}, \widehat{\mathbf{S}}_j^* \rangle \cdot \text{FL}(\widehat{\mathbf{S}}_j, \mathbf{c}_j), \tag{13}$$

where $\text{FL}(\zeta, \tau)$ is the focal loss [23], and γ is set as 2 following [23]. $\widehat{\mathbf{S}}_j^*$ represents the bag score of the last PBR iteration (for the first iteration of PBR, using the bag score in CBP). $\langle \mathbf{c}_j^{\mathrm{T}}, \widehat{\mathbf{S}}_j^* \rangle$ represents the inner product of the two vectors, which means the predicted bag score of the previous stage or iteration on ground-truth category. Score is used to weight the FL of each object for stable training.

2) **Negative Loss.** Conventional MIL treats proposal boxes belonging to other categories as negative samples. In order to further suppress the backgrounds, we sample more negative samples in the PBR stage and introduce the negative loss (γ is also set to 2 following FL), *i.e.*,

$$\beta = \frac{1}{M} \sum_{j=1}^{M} \langle \mathbf{c}_j^{\mathrm{T}}, \widehat{\mathbf{S}}_j^* \rangle, \quad \mathcal{L}_{neg} = -\frac{1}{|\mathcal{N}|} \sum_{\mathcal{N}} \sum_{k=1}^{K} \beta \cdot ([\mathbf{S}_{neg}^{cls}]_k)^{\gamma} \log(1 - [\mathbf{S}_{neg}^{cls}]_k).$$
$$\tag{14}$$

4   Experiments

4.1   Experiment Settings

Datasets and Evaluate Metrics. For experiments, we use the public available MS COCO [24] dataset. COCO has 80 different categories and two versions. COCO-14 has 80K training and 40K validation images whereas COCO-17 has 118K training and 5K validation images. Since the ground truth on the test set is not released, we train our model on the training set and evaluate it on the validation set reporting AP_{50} and AP (averaged over IoU thresholds in [0.5 : 0.05 : 0.95]) on COCO. The $mIoU_{pred}$ is calculated by the mean IoU between predicted pseudo boxes and their corresponding ground-truth bounding-boxes of all objects in the training set. It can directly evaluate the ability of P2BNet to transform annotated points into accurate pseudo boxes.

Implementation Details. Our codes of P2BNet-FR are based on MMDetection [5]. The stochastic gradient descent (SGD [3]) algorithm is used to optimize in 1× training schedule. The learning rate is set to 0.02 and decays by 0.1 at the 8-th and 11-th epochs, respectively. In P2BNet, we use multi-scale (480, 576, 688, 864, 1000, 1200) as the short side to resize the image during training and single-scale (1200) during inference. We choose the classic Faster R-CNN FPN [22,30] (backbone is ResNet-50 [16]) as the detector with the default setting, and single-scale (800) images are used during training and inference. More details are included in the supplementary section.

Quasi-Center Point Annotation. We propose a quasi-center (QC) point annotation that is friendly for object detection tasks with a low cost. In practical scenarios, we ask annotators to annotate the object in the non-high limit center region with a loose rule. Since datasets in the experiment are already annotated with bounding boxes or masks, it is reasonable that the manually annotated points follow Gaussian distribution in the central region. We utilize Rectified Gaussian Distribution (RG) defined in [45] with central ellipse constraints. For a bounding box of $b = (b_x, b_y, b_w, b_h)$, its central ellipse can be defined as $Ellipse(\kappa)$, using (b_x, b_y) as the ellipse center and $(\kappa \cdot b_w, \kappa \cdot b_h)$ as the two axes of the ellipse. In addition, in view of the fact that the absolute position offset for a large object is too large under the above rule, we limit the two axes to no longer than 96 pixels. If the object's mask $Mask$ overlaps with the central ellipse $Ellipse(\kappa)$, V is used to denote the intersection. If there is no intersecting area, V represents the entire $Mask$. When generated from bounding box annotations, the boxes are treated as masks. Then RG is defined as,

$$RG(p; \mu, \sigma, \kappa) = \begin{cases} \frac{Gauss(p;\mu,\sigma)}{\int_V Gauss(p;\mu,\sigma)dp}, & p \in V \\ 0, & p \notin V \end{cases} \tag{15}$$

where μ and σ are mean and standard deviation of RG. κ decides the $Ellipse(\kappa)$. In this paper, $RG(p; 0, \frac{1}{4}, \frac{1}{4})$ is chosen to generate the QC point annotations.

Table 1. The performance comparison of box-supervised, image-supervised, and point-supervised detectors on COCO dataset. * means UFO^2 with image-level annotation. † means the performance we reproduce with the original setting. ‡ means we re-implement UFO^2 with our QC point annotation. The performance of P2BNet-FR, UFO^2, and the box-supervised detector is tested on a single scale dataset. Our P2BNet-FR is based on P2BNet with top-4 merging and one PBR stage. SS is selective search [34], PP means proposal box defined in [38], and Free represents OTSP-free based method.

Method	Backbone	Proposal	COCO-14		COCO-17	
			AP	AP$_{50}$	AP	AP$_{50}$
Box-supervised detectors						
Fast R-CNN [13]	VGG-16	SS	18.9	38.6	19.3	39.3
Faster R-CNN [30]	VGG-16	RPN	21.2	41.5	21.5	42.1
FPN [5]	R-50	RPN	**35.5**	**56.7**	37.4	**58.1**
RetinaNet [5,23]	R-50	-	34.3	53.3	36.5	55.4
Reppoint [5,44]	R-50	-	-	-	37.0	56.7
Sparse R-CNN [5,38]	R-50	PP	-	-	**37.9**	56.0
Image-supervised detectors						
OICR+Fast [13,39]	VGG-16	SS	7.7	17.4	-	-
PCL [40]	VGG-16	SS	8.5	19.4	-	-
PCL+Fast [13,40]	VGG-16	SS	9.2	19.6	-	-
MEFF+Fast [12,13]	VGG-16	SS	8.9	19.3	-	-
C-MIDN [42]	VGG-16	SS	9.6	21.4	-	-
WSOD2 [47]	VGG-16	SS	10.8	22.7	-	-
UFO^2* [32]	VGG-16	MCG	10.8	23.1	-	-
GradingNet-C-MIL [18]	VGG-16	SS	11.6	25.0	-	-
ICMWSD [31]	VGG-16	MCG	11.4	24.3	-	-
ICMWSD [31]	R-50	MCG	12.6	26.1	-	-
ICMWSD [31]	R-101	MCG	13.0	26.3	-	-
CASD [17]	VGG-16	SS	12.8	26.4	-	-
CASD [17]	R-50	SS	**13.9**	**27.8**	-	-
Point-supervised detectors						
Click [28]	AlexNet	SS	-	18.4	-	-
UFO^2 [32]	VGG-16	MCG	12.4	27.0	-	-
UFO^{2†} [32]	VGG-16	MCG	12.8	26.6	13.2	27.2
UFO^{2‡} [32]	VGG-16	MCG	12.7	26.5	13.5	27.9
UFO^{2‡} [32]	R-50	MCG	12.6	27.6	13.2	28.9
P2BNet-FR (Ours)	R-50	Free	**19.4**	**43.5**	**22.1**	**47.3**

4.2 Performance Comparisons

Unless otherwise specified, the default components of our P2BNet-FR framework are P2BNet and Faster R-CNN. We compare the P2BNet-FR with the existing PSOD methods while choosing the state-of-the-art UFO^2 [32] framework as the baseline for comprehensive comparisons. In addition, to demonstrate the perfor-

Table 2. Ablation study (Part I)

CBP stage		PBR stage			Performance		
$\mathcal{L}_{pos}$	$\mathcal{L}_{mil1}$	$\mathcal{L}_{mil2}$	$\mathcal{L}_{neg}$	$\mathcal{L}_{pesudo}$	mIoU$_{pred}$	AP	AP$_{50}$
✓					25.0	2.9	10.3
	✓				50.2	13.7	37.8
	✓	✓			52.0	12.7	35.4
	✓	✓	✓		**57.4**	**21.7**	**46.1**
	✓	✓	✓	✓	56.7	18.5	44.1

(a) The effectiveness of training loss in P2BNet: $\mathcal{L}_{mil1}$ in CBP stage, $\mathcal{L}_{mil2}$ and $\mathcal{L}_{neg}$ in PBR stage. $\mathcal{L}_{pos}$ and $\mathcal{L}_{pesudo}$ is for comparison.

top-k	mIoU$_{pred}$	AP	AP$_{50}$
1	49.2	12.2	35.9
3	54.7	21.3	46.6
4	**57.5**	**22.1**	**47.3**
7	57.4	21.7	46.1
10	57.1	21.5	46.0

(b) The top-k policy for box merging. k is set the same for all stages.

T	mIoU$_{pred}$	AP	AP$_{50}$
0	50.2	13.7	37.8
1	**57.4**	21.7	**46.1**
2	57.0	**21.9**	**46.1**
3	56.2	21.3	45.6

(c) The number of iterations T in the PBR stage. $T = 0$ means only the CBP stage is conducted.

mance advantages of the PSOD methods, we compare them with the state-of-the-art WSOD methods. At the same time, we compare the performance of the box-supervised object detectors to reflect their performance upper bound.

Comparison with PSOD Methods. We compare the existing PSOD methods Click [28] and UFO^2 [32] on COCO, as shown in Table 1. Both Click and UFO^2 utilize OTSP-based methods (SS [34] or MCG [1]) to generate proposal boxes. Since the point annotation used by UFO^2 is different from the QC point proposed in this paper, for a fair comparison, we re-train UFO^2 on the public code with our QC point annotation. In addition, the previous methods are mainly based on VGG-16 [36] or AlexNet [20]. For consistency, we extend the UFO^2 to the ResNet-50 FPN backbone and compare it with our framework. In comparison with Click and UFO^2, our P2BNet-FR framework outperforms them by a large margin. On COCO-14, P2BNet-FR improves AP and AP$_{50}$ by 6.8 and 15.9, respectively. Also, our framework significantly outperforms state-of-the-art performance by 8.9 AP and 18.4 AP$_{50}$ on COCO-17. In Fig. 6, the visualization shows our P2BNet-FR makes full use of the precise location information of point annotation and can distinguish dense objects in complex scenes.

Comparison with WSOD Methods. We compare the proposed framework to the state-of-the-art WSOD methods on the COCO-14 in Table 1. The performance of P2BNet-FR proves that compared with WSOD, PSOD significantly improves the detection performance with little increase in the annotation cost, showing that the PSOD task has great prospects for development.

Comparison with Box-Supervised Methods. In order to verify the feasibility of P2BNet-FR in practical applications and show the upper bound under this supervised manner, we compare the box-supervised detector [30] in Table 1. Under AP$_{50}$, P2BNet-FR-R50 (47.3 AP$_{50}$) is much closer to box-supervised

Table 3. Ablation study (Part II)

Methods	AR$_1$	AR$_{10}$	AR$_{100}$
UFO^2	14.7	22.6	23.3
P2BNet-FR	**21.3**	**32.8**	**34.2**

(a) Comparisons of average recall for UFO^2 and P2BNet-FR.

Detectors	GT box		Pseudo box	
	AP	AP$_{50}$	AP	AP$_{50}$
RetinaNet [23]	36.5	55.4	21.0	44.9
Reppoint [44]	37.0	56.7	20.8	45.1
Sparse R-CNN [38]	**37.9**	56.0	21.1	43.3
FR-FPN [22,30]	37.4	**58.1**	**22.1**	**47.3**

(d) Performance of different detectors on ground-truth box annotations and pseudo boxes generated by P2BNet. We use the top-4 for box merging.

Balance	AP	AP$_{50}$
✓	**21.7**	**46.1**
-	12.9	36.0

(b) Unbalance issue.

Jitter	AP	AP$_{50}$
✓	**21.7**	**46.1**
-	14.2	38.2

(c) Jitter strategy.

detector FPN-R50 (58.1 AP$_{50}$) than previous WSOD and PSOD method. It shows that PSOD can be applied in industries that are less demanding on box quality and more inclined to find objects [19,50], with greatly reduced annotation cost.

4.3 Ablation Study

In this section, all the ablation studies are conducted on t he COCO-17 dataset. The top-k setting is $k = 7$ except for the box merging policy part in Table 2(b) and different detectors part ($k = 4$) in Table 3(d).

Training Loss in P2BNet. The ablation study of the training loss in P2BNet is shown in Table 2(a). **1) CBP loss.** Only with $\mathcal{L}_{mil1}$ in the CBP stage, we can obtain 13.7 AP and 37.8 AP$_{50}$. For comparison, we conduct $\mathcal{L}_{pos}$, which views all the proposal boxes in the bag as positive samples. We find it hard to optimize, and the performance is bad, demonstrating the effectiveness of our proposed $\mathcal{L}_{mil1}$ for pseudo box prediction. Coarse proposal bags can cover most objects in high IoU, resulting in a low missing rate. However, the performance still has the potential to be refined because the scale and aspect ratio are coarse, and the center position needs adjustment. **2) PBR loss.** With a refined sampling of proposal bag (shown in Fig. 5), corresponding PBR loss is introduced. Only with $\mathcal{L}_{mil2}$, the performance is just 12.7 AP. The main reasons of performance degradation are error accumulation in a cascade fashion and lacking negative samples for focal loss. There are no explicit negative samples to suppress background for *Sigmoid* activation function, negative sampling and negative loss $\mathcal{L}_{neg}$ is introduced. Performance increases by 9.0 AP and 10.7 AP$_{50}$, indicating that it is essential and effectively improves the optimization. We also evaluate the mIoU$_{pred}$ to discuss the predicted pseudo box's quality. In the PBR stage with $\mathcal{L}_{mil2}$ and $\mathcal{L}_{neg}$, the mIoU increases from 50.2 to 57.4, suggesting better quality of the pseudo box. Motivated by [45], we conduct $\mathcal{L}_{pesudo}$, viewing pseudo boxes from the CBP stage as positive samples. However, the $\mathcal{L}_{pesudo}$ limits the refinement and the performance decreases. In Table 3(c), if we remove the jitter strategy of proposal boxes in PBR stage, the performance drops to 14.2 AP.

Fig. 6. Visualization of detection results of P2BNet-FR and UFO^2. Our P2BNet-FR can distinguish dense objects and perform well in complex scene. (Best viewed in color.) (Color figure online)

Number of Refinements in PBR. Refining pseudo boxes is a vital part of P2BNet, and the cascade structure is used for iterative refinement to improve performance. Table 2(c) shows the effect of the refining number in the PBR stage. One refinement brings a performance gain of 8.0 AP, up to a competitive 21.7 AP. The highest 21.9 AP is obtained with two refinements, and the performance is saturated. We choose one refinement as the default configuration.

Box Merging Policy. We use the top-k score average weight as our merging policy. We find that the hyper-parameter k is slightly sensitive and can be easily generalized to other datasets, as presented in Table 2(b), and only the top-1 or top-few proposal box plays a leading role in box merging. The best performance is 22.1 AP and 47.3 AP$_{50}$ when $k = 4$. The mIoU$_{pred}$ between the pseudo box and ground-truth box is 57.5. In inference, if bag score $\mathbf{S}$ is replaced by classification score $\mathbf{S}^{cls}$ for merging, the performance drops to 17.4 AP (vs 21.7 AP).

Average Recall. In Table 3(a), the AR in UFO^2 is 23.3, indicating a higher missing rate. Whereas the P2BNet-FR obtains 34.2 AR, far beyond that of the UFO^2. It shows our OTSP-free method is better at finding objects.

Unbalance Sampling Analysis. To demonstrate the effect of unbalance sampling, we sample different numbers of proposal boxes for each object and keep them constant in every epoch during the training period. The performance drops in Table 3(b) suggests the negative impact of unbalanced sampling.

Different Detectors. We train different detectors [22,23,30,38,44] for the integrity experiments, all of which are conducted on R-50, as shown in Table 3(d). Our framework exhibits competitive performance on other detectors. Box supervised performances are listed to demonstrate the upper bound of our framework.

5 Conclusion

In this paper, we give an in-depth analysis of shortcomings in OTSP-based PSOD frameworks, and further propose a novel OTSP-free network termed P2BNet to obtain inter-objects balanced and high-quality proposal bags. The coarse-to-fine strategy divides the prediction of pseudo boxes into CBP and PBR stages. In the CBP stage, fixed sampling is performed around the annotated points, and coarse pseudo boxes are predicted through instance-level MIL. The PBR stage performs adaptive sampling around the estimated boxes to finetune the predicted boxes in a cascaded fashion. As mentioned above, P2BNet takes full advantage of point information to generate high-quality proposal bags, which is more conducive to optimizing the detector (FR). Remarkably, the conceptually simple P2BNet-FR framework yields state-of-the-art performance with single point annotation.

Acknowledgements. This work was supported in part by the Youth Innovation Promotion Association CAS, the National Natural Science Foundation of China (NSFC) under Grant No. 61836012, 61771447 and 62006244, the Strategic Priority Research Program of the Chinese Academy of Sciences under Grant No.XDA27000000, and Young Elite Scientist Sponsorship Program of China Association for Science and Technology YESS20200140.

References

1. Arbeláez, P.A., Pont-Tuset, J., et al.: Multiscale combinatorial grouping. In: CVPR (2014)
2. Bilen, H., Vedaldi, A.: Weakly supervised deep detection networks. In: CVPR (2016)
3. Bottou, L.: Stochastic gradient descent tricks. In: Montavon, G., Orr, G.B., Müller, K.-R. (eds.) Neural Networks: Tricks of the Trade. LNCS, vol. 7700, pp. 421–436. Springer, Heidelberg (2012). https://doi.org/10.1007/978-3-642-35289-8_25
4. Carion, N., Massa, F., Synnaeve, G., Usunier, N., Kirillov, A., Zagoruyko, S.: End-to-end object detection with transformers. In: Vedaldi, A., Bischof, H., Brox, T., Frahm, J.-M. (eds.) ECCV 2020. LNCS, vol. 12346, pp. 213–229. Springer, Cham (2020). https://doi.org/10.1007/978-3-030-58452-8_13
5. Chen, K., Wang, J., Pang, J.E.: MMDetection: open MMLab detection toolbox and benchmark. arXiv preprint arXiv:1906.07155 (2019)
6. Chen, Z., Fu, Z., et al.: SLV: spatial likelihood voting for weakly supervised object detection. In: CVPR (2020)
7. Cheng, B., Parkhi, O., Kirillov, A.: Pointly-supervised instance segmentation. CoRR (2021)
8. Diba, A., Sharma, V., et al.: Weakly supervised cascaded convolutional networks. In: CVPR (2017)
9. Ding, J., Xue, N., Long, Y., Xia, G., Lu, Q.: Learning RoI transformer for oriented object detection in aerial images. In: CVPR (2019)
10. Everingham, M., Gool, L.V., et al.: The pascal visual object classes (VOC) challenge. In: IJCV (2010)
11. Gao, M., Li, A., et al.: C-WSL: count-guided weakly supervised localization. In: ECCV (2018)

12. Ge, W., Yang, S., Yu, Y.: Multi-evidence filtering and fusion for multi-label classification, object detection and semantic segmentation based on weakly supervised learning. In: CVPR (2018)
13. Girshick, R.B.: Fast R-CNN. In: ICCV (2015)
14. Guo, Z., Liu, C., Zhang, X., Jiao, J., Ji, X., Ye, Q.: Beyond bounding-box: convex-hull feature adaptation for oriented and densely packed object detection. In: CVPR (2021)
15. He, K., Gkioxari, G., et al.: Mask R-CNN. In: ICCV (2017)
16. He, K., Zhang, X., et al.: Deep residual learning for image recognition. In: CVPR (2016)
17. Huang, Z., Zou, Y., et al.: Comprehensive attention self-distillation for weakly-supervised object detection. In: NeurIPS (2020)
18. Jia, Q., Wei, S., et al.: Gradingnet: towards providing reliable supervisions for weakly supervised object detection by grading the box candidates. In: AAAI (2021)
19. Jiang, N., et al.: Anti-UAV: a large multi-modal benchmark for UAV tracking. IEEE TMM (2021)
20. Krizhevsky, A., Sutskever, I., Hinton, G.E.: Imagenet classification with deep convolutional neural networks. In: NIPS (2012)
21. Lee, P., Byun, H.: Learning action completeness from points for weakly-supervised temporal action localization. In: ICCV (2021)
22. Lin, T., Dollár, P., et al.: Feature pyramid networks for object detection. In: CVPR (2017)
23. Lin, T., Goyal, P., et al.: Focal loss for dense object detection. In: ICCV (2017)
24. Lin, T.-Y., et al.: Microsoft COCO: common objects in context. In: Fleet, D., Pajdla, T., Schiele, B., Tuytelaars, T. (eds.) ECCV 2014. LNCS, vol. 8693, pp. 740–755. Springer, Cham (2014). https://doi.org/10.1007/978-3-319-10602-1_48
25. Liu, W., et al.: SSD: single shot MultiBox detector. In: Leibe, B., Matas, J., Sebe, N., Welling, M. (eds.) ECCV 2016. LNCS, vol. 9905, pp. 21–37. Springer, Cham (2016). https://doi.org/10.1007/978-3-319-46448-0_2
26. Liu, Z., Lin, Y., et al.: Swin transformer: hierarchical vision transformer using shifted windows. In: ICCV (2021)
27. Meng, M., Zhang, T., Yang, W., Zhao, J., Zhang, Y., Wu, F.: Diverse complementary part mining for weakly supervised object localization. IEEE TIP **31**, 1774–1788 (2022)
28. Papadopoulos, D.P., Uijlings, J.R.R., et al.: Training object class detectors with click supervision. In: CVPR (2017)
29. Redmon, J., Divvala, S.K., et al.: You only look once: unified, real-time object detection. In: CVPR (2016)
30. Ren, S., He, K., et al.: Faster R-CNN: towards real-time object detection with region proposal networks. IEEE TPAMI **39**(6), 1137–1149 (2017)
31. Ren, Z., Yu, Z., et al.: Instance-aware, context-focused, and memory-efficient weakly supervised object detection. In: CVPR (2020)
32. Ren, Z., Yu, Z., Yang, X., Liu, M.-Y., Schwing, A.G., Kautz, J.: UFO^2: a unified framework towards omni-supervised object detection. In: Vedaldi, A., Bischof, H., Brox, T., Frahm, J.-M. (eds.) ECCV 2020. LNCS, vol. 12364, pp. 288–313. Springer, Cham (2020). https://doi.org/10.1007/978-3-030-58529-7_18
33. Ribera, J., Guera, D., Chen, Y., Delp, E.J.: Locating objects without bounding boxes. In: CVPR (2019)
34. van de Sande, K.E.A., Uijlings, J.R.R., et al.: Segmentation as selective search for object recognition. In: ICCV (2011)

35. Shen, Y., Ji, R., Chen, Z., Wu, Y., Huang, F.: UWSOD: toward fully-supervised-level capacity weakly supervised object detection. In: NeurIPS (2020)
36. Simonyan, K., Zisserman, A.: Very deep convolutional networks for large-scale image recognition. In: ICLR (2015)
37. Song, Q., et al.: Rethinking counting and localization in crowds: a purely point-based framework. In: ICCV (2021)
38. Sun, P., Zhang, R., et al.: Sparse R-CNN: end-to-end object detection with learnable proposals. In: CVPR (2021)
39. Tang, P., et al.: Multiple instance detection network with online instance classifier refinement. In: CVPR (2017)
40. Tang, P., Wang, X., et al.: PCL: proposal cluster learning for weakly supervised object detection. IEEE TPAMI **42**(1), 176–191 (2020)
41. Wan, F., Wei, P., et al.: Min-entropy latent model for weakly supervised object detection. IEEE TPAMI **41**(10), 2395–2409 (2019)
42. Yan, G., Liu, B., et al.: C-MIDN: coupled multiple instance detection network with segmentation guidance for weakly supervised object detection. In: ICCV (2019)
43. Yang, X., Yan, J., Feng, Z., He, T.: R3Det: refined single-stage detector with feature refinement for rotating object. In: AAAI (2021)
44. Yang, Z., Liu, S., et al.: Reppoints: point set representation for object detection. In: ICCV (2019)
45. Yu, X., Chen, P., et al.: Object localization under single coarse point supervision. In: CVPR (2022)
46. Yu, X., Gong, Y., et al.: Scale match for tiny person detection. In: IEEE WACV (2020)
47. Zeng, Z., Liu, B., et al.: WSOD2: learning bottom-up and top-down objectness distillation for weakly-supervised object detection. In: ICCV (2019)
48. Zhang, D., Han, J., Cheng, G., Yang, M.: Weakly supervised object localization and detection: a survey. IEEE TPAMI **44**(9), 5866–5885 (2021)
49. Zhang, X., Wei, Y., et al.: Adversarial complementary learning for weakly supervised object localization. In: CVPR (2018)
50. Zhao, J., et al.: The 2nd anti-UAV workshop & challenge: methods and results. In: ICCVW 2021 (2021)
51. Zhou, B., Khosla, A., et al.: Learning deep features for discriminative localization. In: CVPR (2016)
52. Zhu, X., Su, W., et al.: Deformable DETR: deformable transformers for end-to-end object detection. In: ICLR (2021)
53. Zitnick, C.L., Dollár, P.: Edge boxes: locating object proposals from edges. In: Fleet, D., Pajdla, T., Schiele, B., Tuytelaars, T. (eds.) ECCV 2014. LNCS, vol. 8693, pp. 391–405. Springer, Cham (2014). https://doi.org/10.1007/978-3-319-10602-1_26

Domain Adaptive Hand Keypoint and Pixel Localization in the Wild

Takehiko Ohkawa[1,2]($\boxtimes$), Yu-Jhe Li[2], Qichen Fu[2], Ryosuke Furuta[1],
Kris M. Kitani[2], and Yoichi Sato[1]

[1] The University of Tokyo, Tokyo, Japan
{ohkawa-t,furuta,ysato}@iis.u-tokyo.ac.jp
[2] Carnegie Mellon University, Pittsburgh, PA, USA
{yujheli,qichenf,kkitani}@cs.cmu.edu
https://tkhkaeio.github.io/projects/22-hand-ps-da/

Abstract. We aim to improve the performance of regressing hand keypoints and segmenting pixel-level hand masks under new imaging conditions (*e.g.*, outdoors) when we only have labeled images taken under very different conditions (*e.g.*, indoors). In the real world, it is important that the model trained for both tasks works under various imaging conditions. However, their variation covered by existing labeled hand datasets is limited. Thus, it is necessary to adapt the model trained on the labeled images (source) to unlabeled images (target) with unseen imaging conditions. While self-training domain adaptation methods (*i.e.*, learning from the unlabeled target images in a self-supervised manner) have been developed for both tasks, their training may degrade performance when the predictions on the target images are noisy. To avoid this, it is crucial to assign a low importance (confidence) weight to the noisy predictions during self-training. In this paper, we propose to utilize the divergence of two predictions to estimate the confidence of the target image for both tasks. These predictions are given from two separate networks, and their divergence helps identify the noisy predictions. To integrate our proposed confidence estimation into self-training, we propose a teacher-student framework where the two networks (teachers) provide supervision to a network (student) for self-training, and the teachers are learned from the student by knowledge distillation. Our experiments show its superiority over state-of-the-art methods in adaptation settings with different lighting, grasping objects, backgrounds, and camera viewpoints. Our method improves by 4% the multi-task score on HO3D compared to the latest adversarial adaptation method. We also validate our method on Ego4D, egocentric videos with rapid changes in imaging conditions outdoors.

1 Introduction

In the real world, hand keypoint regression and hand segmentation are considered important to work under broad imaging conditions for various computer

Supplementary Information The online version contains supplementary material available at https://doi.org/10.1007/978-3-031-20077-9_5.

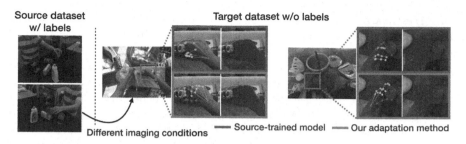

Fig. 1. We aim to adapt the model of localizing hand keypoints and pixel-level hand masks to new imaging conditions without annotation.

vision applications, such as egocentric video understanding [17, 28], hand-object interaction analysis [12, 21], AR/VR [39, 70], and assistive technology [37, 40]. For building models for both tasks, several labeled hand datasets have been proposed in laboratory settings, such as multi-camera studios [13, 34, 46, 80] and attaching sensors to hands [24, 26, 75]. However, their imaging conditions do not adequately cover real-world imaging conditions [51], consisting of various lighting, hand-held objects, backgrounds, and camera viewpoints. In addition, the annotation of keypoints and pixel-level masks are not always available in real-world environments because they are labor-intensive to acquire. As shown in Fig. 1, when localizing hand keypoints and pixels in real-world egocentric videos [28] (*e.g.*, outdoors), we may only have access to a hand dataset [13] taken under completely different imaging conditions (*e.g.*, indoors). Given these limitations, we need methods that can robustly adapt the models trained on the available labeled images (source) to unlabeled images (target) with new imaging conditions.

To enable such adaptation, the approach of self-training domain adaptation has been developed for both tasks. This approach aims to learn unlabeled target images by optimizing a self-supervised task, which exhibits effectiveness in various domain adaptation tasks [7, 15, 18, 67, 77]. For keypoint estimation, consistency training, a method that regularizes keypoint predictions to be consistent under geometric transformations, has been proposed [66, 73, 77]. As for hand segmentation, prior studies use pseudo-labeling [7, 53], which produces hard labels by thresholding a predicted class probability for updating a network. However, these self-training methods for both tasks perform well only when the predictions are reasonably correct. When the predictions become noisy due to the gap in imaging conditions, the trained network will cause over-fitting to the noisy predictions, resulting in poor performance in the target domain.

To avoid this, it is crucial to assign a low importance (confidence) weight to the loss of self-training with noisy predictions. This confidence weighting can mitigate the distractions from the noisy predictions. To this end, we propose self-training domain adaptation with confidence estimation for hand keypoint regression and hand segmentation. Our proposed method consists of (i) confidence estimation based on the divergence of two networks' predictions and (ii) an update rule that integrates a training network for self-training and the two networks for confidence estimation.

To (i) estimate confidence, we utilize the predictions of two different networks. While class probability can be used as the confidence in classification tasks, it is not trivial to obtain such a measure in keypoint regression. Thus, we newly focus on the divergence of the two networks' predictions for each target image. We design their networks to have an identical architecture but have different learning parameters. We observe that when the divergence measure is high, the predictions of both networks are noisy and should be avoided in self-training.

To (ii) integrate the estimated confidence into self-training, inspired by the single-teacher-single-student update [54,64], we develop mutual training with self-training based on consistency training for a training network (student) and distillation-based update for the two networks (teachers). For training the student network, we build a unified self-training framework that can work favorably for the two tasks. Motivated by supervised or weakly-supervised learning for jointly estimating both tasks [16,27,49,68,76], we expect that jointly adapting both tasks will allow one task to provide useful cues to the other task even in the unlabeled target domain. Specifically, we enforce the student network to generate consistent predictions for both tasks under geometric augmentation. We weight the loss of the consistency training using the confidence estimated from the divergence of the teachers' predictions. This can reduce the weight of the noisy predictions during the consistency training. To learn the two teacher networks differently, we train the teachers independently from different mini-batches by knowledge distillation, which matches the teacher-student predictions in the output level. This framework enables the teachers to update more carefully than the student and prevent over-fitting to the noisy predictions. Such stable teachers provide reliable confidence estimation for the student's training.

In our experiments, we validate our proposed method in adaptation settings where lighting, grasping objects, backgrounds, camera viewpoints, etc., vary between labeled source images and unlabeled target images. We use a large-scale hand dataset captured in a multi-camera system [13] as the source dataset (see Fig. 1). For the target dataset, we use HO3D [29] with different environments, HanCo [78] with multiple viewpoints and diverse backgrounds, and FPHA [24] with a novel first-person camera viewpoint. We also apply our method to in-the-wild egocentric video Ego4D [28] (see Fig. 1), including diverse indoor and outdoor activities worldwide. Our method improves the average score of the two tasks by 14.4%, 14.9%, and 18.0% on HO3D, HanCo, and FPHA, respectively, compared to a unadapted baseline. Our method further exhibits distinct improvements compared to the latest adversarial adaption method [33] and consistency training baselines with uncertainty estimation [7], confident instance selection [53], and the teacher-student scheme [64]. We finally confirm that our method also performs qualitatively well on the Ego4D videos.

Our contributions are summarized as follows:

– We propose a novel confidence estimation method based on the divergence of the predictions from two teacher networks for self-training domain adaptation of hand keypoint regression and hand segmentation.

- To integrate our proposed confidence estimation into self-training, we propose mutual training using knowledge distillation with a student network for self-training and two teacher networks for confidence estimation.
- Our proposed framework outperforms state-of-the-art methods under three adaptation settings across different imaging conditions. It also shows improved qualitative performance on in-the-wild egocentric videos.

2 Related Work

Hand keypoint regression is the task of regressing the positions of hand joint keypoints from a cropped hand image. 2D hand keypoint regression is trained by optimizing keypoint heatmaps [50,69,79] or directly predicting keypoint coordinates [60]. The 2D keypoints are informative for estimating 3D hand poses [5,47,61,74]. To build an accurate keypoint regressor, collecting massive hand keypoint annotations is required but laborious. While early works annotate the keypoints manually from a single view [48,56,62], recent studies have collected the annotation more densely and efficiently using synthetic hand models [30,47,48,79], hand sensors [24,26,63,75], or multi-camera setups [6,13,29,34,43,46,80]. However, these methods suffer the gap in imaging conditions with real-world images in deployment [51]. For instance, the synthetic hand models and hand sensors induce different lighting conditions from actual human hands. The multi-camera setup lacks a variety of lighting, grasping objects, and backgrounds. To tackle these problems, domain adaptation is a promising solution that can transfer the knowledge of the network trained on source data to unlabeled target data. Jiang *et al.*proposed an adversarial domain adaptation for human and hand keypoint regression, optimizing the discrepancy between regressors [33]. Additionally, self-training adaptation methods have been studied in the keypoint regression of animals [11], humans [66], and objects [77]. Unlike these prior works, we incorporate confidence estimation into a self-training method based on consistency training for keypoint regression.

Hand segmentation is the task of segmenting pixel-level hand masks in a given image. CNN-based segmentation networks [3,35,65] are popularly used. The task can be jointly trained with hand keypoint regression because detecting hand regions guides to improve keypoint localization [16,27,49,68,76]. Since hand mask annotation is laborious as hand keypoint regression, a few domain adaptation methods with pseudo-labeling have been explored [7,53]. To reduce the effect of highly noisy pseudo-labels in the target domain, Cai *et al.*incorporate the uncertainty of pseudo-labels in model adaptation [7], and Ohkawa *et al.*select confident pseudo-labels by the overlap of two predicted hand masks [53]. Unlike [7], we estimate the target confidence using two networks. Instead of using the estimated confidence for instance selection [53], we assign the confidence to weight the loss of consistency training.

Domain adaptation via self-training aims to learn unlabeled target data in a self-supervised learning manner. This approach can be divided into three categories. (i) Pseudo-labeling [7,15,53,59,81] learns unlabeled data with hard labels assigned by confidence thresholding from the output of a network. (ii) Entropy minimization [42,55,67] regularizes the conditional entropy of unlabeled data and increases the confidence of class probability. (iii) Consistency regularization [14,20,71] enforces regularization so that the prediction on unlabeled data is invariant under data perturbation. We choose to leverage this consistency-based method for our task because it works for various tasks [41,45,52] and the first two approaches cannot be directly applied. Similar to our work, Yang et al.[73] enforce the consistency for two different views and modalities in hand keypoint regression. Mean teacher [64] provides teacher-student training with consistency regularization, which regularizes a teacher network by a student's weights and avoids over-fitting to incorrect predictions. Unlike [73], we propose to integrate confidence estimation into the consistency training and adopt the teacher-student scheme with two networks. To encourage the two networks to have different representations, we propose a distillation-based update rule instead of updating the teacher with the exponential moving average [64].

3   Proposed Method

In this section, we present our proposed self-training domain adaptation with confidence estimation for adapting hand keypoint regression and hand segmentation. We first present our problem formulation and network initialization with supervised learning from source data. We then introduce our proposed modules: (1) geometric augmentation consistency, (2) confidence weighting by using two networks, and (3) teacher-student update via knowledge distillation. As shown in Fig. 2, our adaptation is done with two different networks (teachers) for confidence estimation and another network (student) for self-training of both tasks.

Problem Formulation. Given labeled images from one source domain and unlabeled images from another target domain, we aim to jointly estimate hand keypoint coordinates and pixel-level hand masks on the target domain. We have a source image x_s drawn from a set $X_s \subset \mathbb{R}^{H \times W \times 3}$, its corresponding labels (y_s^p, y_s^m), and a target image x_t drawn from a set $X_t \subset \mathbb{R}^{H \times W \times 3}$. The pose label y_s^p consists of the 2D keypoint coordinates of 21 hand joints obtained from a set $Y_s^p \subset \mathbb{R}^{21 \times 2}$, while the mask label y_s^m denotes a binary mask obtained from $Y_s^m \subset (0,1)^{H \times W}$. A network parameterized by θ learns the mappings $f^k(x; \theta) : X \to Y^k$ where $k \in \{p, m\}$ represents the indicator for both tasks.

Initialization with Supervised Learning. To initialize networks used in our adaptation, we train the network f on the labeled source data following multi-task learning. Given the labeled dataset (X_s, Y_s) and the network θ, a supervised loss function is defined as

$$\mathcal{L}_{\text{task}}(\theta, X_s, Y_s) = \sum_k \lambda^k \mathbb{E}_{(x_s, y_s^k) \sim (X_s, Y_s^k)} \left[\mathcal{L}^k(p_s^k, y_s^k) \right], \tag{1}$$

where $Y_s = \{Y_s^p, Y_s^m\}$ and $p_s^k = f^k(x_s; \theta)$. $\mathcal{L}^k(\cdot, \cdot) : Y^k \times Y^k \to \mathbb{R}^+$ is a loss function in each task and λ^k is a hyperparameter to balance the two tasks. We use a smooth L1 loss [32,58] as $\mathcal{L}^p$ and a binary cross-entropy loss as $\mathcal{L}^m$.

3.1 Geometric Augmentation Consistency

Inspired by semi-supervised learning using hand keypoint consistency [73], we advance a unified training with consistency for both hand keypoint regression and hand segmentation. We expect that joint adaption of both tasks will allow one task to provide useful cues to the other task in consistency training, as studied in supervised or weakly-supervised learning setups [16,27,49,68,76]. We design consistency training by predicting the location of hand keypoints and hand pixels in a given geometrically transformed image, including rotation and transition. This consistency under geometric augmentation encourages the network to learn against positional bias in the target domain, which helps capture the hand structure related to poses and regions. Specifically, given a paired augmentation function $(T_\mathrm{x}, T_\mathrm{y}^k) \sim \mathcal{T}$ for an image and an label, we generate the prediction on the target images $\boldsymbol{p}_\mathrm{t}^k = f^k (\boldsymbol{x}_\mathrm{t}; \boldsymbol{\theta})$ and the augmented target images $\boldsymbol{p}_{\mathrm{t,aug}}^k = f^k (T_\mathrm{x}(\boldsymbol{x}_\mathrm{t}); \boldsymbol{\theta})$. We define the loss function of geometric augmentation consistency (GAC) $\mathcal{L}_\mathrm{gac}$ between $\boldsymbol{p}_{\mathrm{t,aug}}^k$ and $T_\mathrm{y}^k(\boldsymbol{p}_\mathrm{t})$ as

$$\mathcal{L}_\mathrm{gac} (\boldsymbol{\theta}, X_\mathrm{t}, \mathcal{T}) = \mathbb{E}_{\boldsymbol{x}_\mathrm{t}, (T_\mathrm{x}, T_\mathrm{y}^\mathrm{p}, T_\mathrm{y}^\mathrm{m})} \left[\sum_{k \in \{\mathrm{p,m}\}} \tilde{\lambda}^k \tilde{\mathcal{L}}^k \left(\boldsymbol{p}_{\mathrm{t,aug}}^k, T_\mathrm{y}^k(\boldsymbol{p}_\mathrm{t}^k) \right) \right]. \qquad (2)$$

To correct the augmented prediction $\boldsymbol{p}_{\mathrm{t,aug}}^k$ by $T_\mathrm{y}^k(\boldsymbol{p}_\mathrm{t})$, we stop the gradient update for $\boldsymbol{p}_\mathrm{t}^k$, which can be viewed as the supervision to $\boldsymbol{p}_{\mathrm{t,aug}}^k$. We use the smooth L1 loss (see Eq. 1) as $\tilde{\mathcal{L}}^\mathrm{p}$ and a mean squared error as $\tilde{\mathcal{L}}^\mathrm{m}$. We introduce $\tilde{\lambda}^k$ as a hyperparameter to control the balance of the two tasks. The augmentation set $\mathcal{T}$ contains the geometric augmentation and photometric augmentation, such as color jitter and blurring. We set $T_\mathrm{y}(\cdot)$ to align geometric information to the augmented input $T_\mathrm{x}(\boldsymbol{x}_\mathrm{t})$. For example, we apply rotation $T_\mathrm{y}(\cdot)$ to the outputs $\boldsymbol{p}_\mathrm{t}^k$ with the same degree of rotation $T_\mathrm{x}(\cdot)$ to the input $\boldsymbol{x}_\mathrm{t}$.

3.2 Confidence Estimation by Two Separate Networks

Since the target predictions are not always reliable, we aim to incorporate the estimated confidence weight for each target instance into the consistency training. In Eq. 2, the generated outputs $\boldsymbol{p}_\mathrm{t}^k$ that is the supervision to $\boldsymbol{p}_{\mathrm{t,aug}}^k$ may be unstable and noisy due to the domain gap between source and target domains. Due to that, the network trained with the consistency readily overfits to the incorrect supervision $\boldsymbol{p}_\mathrm{t}^k$, which is known as confirmation bias [2,64]. To reduce the bias, it is crucial to assign a low importance (confidence) weight to the consistency training with the incorrect supervision. This enables the network to learn primarily from reliable supervision while avoiding being biased to such erroneous predictions. In classification tasks, predicted class probability can serve as the confidence, while these measures are not trivially defined and available in regression tasks. To estimate the confidence of keypoint predictions, Yang et al. [73] measure the confidence of 3D hand keypoints by the distance to the fitted 3D hand template, but the hand template fitting is an ill-posed problem

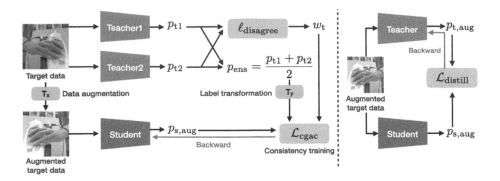

Fig. 2. Method overview. Left: Student training with confidence-aware geometric augmentation consistency. The student learns from the consistency between its prediction and the two teachers' predictions. The training is weighted by the target confidence computed by the divergence of both teachers. **Right**: Teacher training with knowledge distillation. Each teacher independently learns to match the student's predictions. The task index k is omitted for simplicity.

for 2D hands and is not applicable to hand segmentation. Dropout [7,8,22] is a generic way of estimating uncertainty (confidence), calculated by the variance of multiple stochastic forwards. However, the estimated confidence is biased to the current state of the training network because the training and confidence estimation are done by a single network. When the training network works poorly, the confidence estimation becomes readily unreliable.

To perform reliable confidence estimation for both tasks, we propose a confidence measure by computing the divergence of two predictions. Specifically, we introduce two networks (*a.k.a.*, teachers) for the confidence estimation and the estimated confidence is used to train another network (*a.k.a.*, student) for the consistency training. The architecture of the teachers is identical, yet they have different learning parameters. We observe that when the divergence of the two predictions from the teachers for a target instance is high, the predictions of both networks become unstable. In contrast, a lower divergence indicates that the two teacher networks predict stably and agree on their predictions. Thus, we use the divergence for representing the target confidence. Given the teachers $\boldsymbol{\theta}^{\mathrm{tch1}}, \boldsymbol{\theta}^{\mathrm{tch2}}$, we define a disagreement measure ℓ_{disagree} to compute the divergence as

$$\ell_{\mathrm{disagree}}\left(\boldsymbol{\theta}^{\mathrm{tch1}}, \boldsymbol{\theta}^{\mathrm{tch2}}, \boldsymbol{x}_{\mathrm{t}}\right) = \sum_{k \in \{\mathrm{p,m}\}} \tilde{\lambda}^k \tilde{\mathcal{L}}^k(\boldsymbol{p}_{\mathrm{t1}}^k, \boldsymbol{p}_{\mathrm{t2}}^k), \qquad (3)$$

where $\boldsymbol{p}_{\mathrm{t1}}^k = f^k(\boldsymbol{x}_{\mathrm{t}}; \boldsymbol{\theta}^{\mathrm{tch1}})$ and $\boldsymbol{p}_{\mathrm{t2}}^k = f^k(\boldsymbol{x}_{\mathrm{t}}; \boldsymbol{\theta}^{\mathrm{tch2}})$.

As a proof of concept, we visualize the correlation between the disagreement measure and a validation score averaged over evaluation metrics of the two tasks (PCK and IoU) in Fig. 3. We compute the score between the ensemble of the teachers' predictions $\boldsymbol{p}_{\mathrm{ens}}^k = \left(\boldsymbol{p}_{\mathrm{t1}}^k + \boldsymbol{p}_{\mathrm{t2}}^k\right)/2$ and its ground truth in the validation set on HO3D [29]. The instances with a small disagreement measure tend to

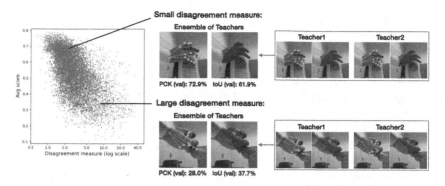

Fig. 3. The correlation between a disagreement measure and task scores. Target instances with smaller disagreement values between the two teacher networks tend to have higher task scores. (Color figure online)

have high validation scores. In contrast, the instances with a high disagreement measure entail false predictions, *e.g.*, detecting the hand-held object as a hand joint and hand class. When the disagreement measure was high at the bottom of Fig. 3, we found that both predictions were particularly unstable on the keypoints of the ring finger (yellow). This study shows that the disagreement measure can represent the correctness of the target predictions.

With the disagreement measure ℓ_{disagree}, we define a confidence weight $w_{\mathrm{t}} \in [0,1]$ for assigning importance to the consistency training. We compute the weight w_{t} as $w_{\mathrm{t}} = 2\left(1 - \mathrm{sigm}\left(\lambda_{\mathrm{d}}\ell_{\mathrm{disagree}}\left(\boldsymbol{\theta}^{\mathrm{tch1}}, \boldsymbol{\theta}^{\mathrm{tch2}}, \boldsymbol{x}_{\mathrm{t}}\right)\right)\right)$ where w_{t} is a normalized disagreement measure with sign inversion, $\mathrm{sigm}(\cdot)$ denotes a sigmoid function, and λ_{d} controls the scale of the measure. With the confidence weight w_{t}, we enforce the consistency training between the student's prediction on the augmented target images $\boldsymbol{p}^k_{\mathrm{s,aug}}$ and the ensemble of the two teachers' predictions $\boldsymbol{p}^k_{\mathrm{ens}}$. Our proposed loss function of confidence-aware geometric augmentation consistency (C-GAC) $\mathcal{L}_{\mathrm{cgac}}$ for the student $\boldsymbol{\theta}^{\mathrm{stu}}$ is formulated as

$$\mathcal{L}_{\mathrm{cgac}}\left(\boldsymbol{\theta}^{\mathrm{stu}}, \boldsymbol{\theta}^{\mathrm{tch1}}, \boldsymbol{\theta}^{\mathrm{tch2}}, X_{\mathrm{t}}, \mathcal{T}\right) = \mathbb{E}_{\boldsymbol{x}_{\mathrm{t}},(T_{\mathrm{x}},T_{\mathrm{y}}^{\mathrm{p}},T_{\mathrm{y}}^{\mathrm{m}})}\left[w_{\mathrm{t}}\sum_{k\in\{\mathrm{p,m}\}}\tilde{\lambda}^k\tilde{\mathcal{L}}^k\left(\boldsymbol{p}^k_{\mathrm{s,aug}}, T_{\mathrm{y}}^k(\boldsymbol{p}^k_{\mathrm{ens}})\right)\right],$$

$$(4)$$

where $\boldsymbol{p}^k_{\mathrm{s,aug}} = f^k\left(T_{\mathrm{x}}(\boldsymbol{x}_{\mathrm{t}}); \boldsymbol{\theta}^{\mathrm{stu}}\right)$. Following [54,64], we design the student prediction $\boldsymbol{p}^k_{\mathrm{s,aug}}$ to be supervised by the teachers. We generate the teachers' prediction by doing ensemble $\boldsymbol{p}^k_{\mathrm{ens}}$, which is better than the prediction of either teacher.

3.3 Teacher-Student Update by Knowledge Distillation

In addition to the student's training, we formulate an update rule for the two teacher networks by using knowledge distillation. Since ℓ_{disagree} would not work

if the two teachers had the same output values, we aim to learn two teachers
that have different representations yet keep high task performance as co-training
works [4,15,57,59]. In a prior teacher-student update, Tarvainen *et al.* [64] found
that the teacher's update by an exponential moving average (EMA), which averages the student's weights iteratively, makes the teacher's learning more slowly
and mitigates the confirmation bias as discussed in Sect. 3.2. While this EMA-
based teacher-student framework is widely used in various domain adaptation
tasks [9,19,25,38,72], naively applying the EMA rule to the two teachers would
produce exactly the same weights for both networks.

To prevent this, we propose independent knowledge distillation for building
two different teachers. The distillation matches the teacher-student predictions
in the output level. To let both networks have different parameters, we train the
teachers from different mini-batches and using stochastic augmentation as

$$\mathcal{L}_{\text{distill}}\left(\boldsymbol{\theta}, \boldsymbol{\theta}^{\text{stu}}, X_{\text{t}}, \mathcal{T}\right) = \mathbb{E}_{\boldsymbol{x}_{\text{t}}, T_{\text{x}}}\left[\sum_{k\in\{\text{p,m}\}} \tilde{\lambda}^k \tilde{\mathcal{L}}^k(\boldsymbol{p}_{\text{t,aug}}^k, \boldsymbol{p}_{\text{s,aug}}^k)\right], \qquad (5)$$

where $\boldsymbol{\theta} \in \{\boldsymbol{\theta}^{\text{tch1}}, \boldsymbol{\theta}^{\text{tch2}}\}$, $\boldsymbol{p}_{\text{t,aug}}^k = f^k\left(T_{\text{x}}(\boldsymbol{x}_{\text{t}}); \boldsymbol{\theta}\right)$, and $\boldsymbol{p}_{\text{s,aug}}^k = f^k(T_{\text{x}}\left(\boldsymbol{x}_{\text{t}}\right); \boldsymbol{\theta}^{\text{stu}})$.
The distillation loss $\mathcal{L}_{\text{distill}}$ is used for updating the teacher networks only. This
helps the teachers to adapt to the target domain more carefully than the student
and avoid falling into exactly the same predictions on a target instance.

3.4   Overall Objectives

Overall, the objective of the student's training consists of the supervised loss
(Eq. 1) from the source domain and the self-training with confidence-aware geometric augmentation consistency (Eq. 4) in the target domain as

$$\min_{\boldsymbol{\theta}^{\text{stu}}} \mathcal{L}_{\text{task}}\left(\boldsymbol{\theta}^{\text{stu}}, X_{\text{s}}, Y_{\text{s}}\right) + \mathcal{L}_{\text{cgac}}\left(\boldsymbol{\theta}^{\text{stu}}, \boldsymbol{\theta}^{\text{tch1}}, \boldsymbol{\theta}^{\text{tch2}}, X_{\text{t}}, \mathcal{T}\right). \qquad (6)$$

The two teachers are asynchronously trained with the distillation loss (Eq. 5) in
the target domain, which is formulated as

$$\min_{\boldsymbol{\theta}} \mathcal{L}_{\text{distill}}\left(\boldsymbol{\theta}, \boldsymbol{\theta}^{\text{stu}}, X_{\text{t}}, \mathcal{T}\right), \qquad (7)$$

where $\boldsymbol{\theta} \in \{\boldsymbol{\theta}^{\text{tch1}}, \boldsymbol{\theta}^{\text{tch2}}\}$. Since the teachers are updated carefully and can perform better than the student, we use the ensemble of the two teachers' predictions
for a final output in inference.

4   Experiments

In this section, we first present our experimental datasets and implementation
details and then provide quantitative and qualitative results along with the ablation studies. We analyze our proposed method by comparing it with several
existing methods in three different domain adaptation settings. We also show
qualitative results by applying our method to in-the-wild egocentric videos.

4.1 Experiment Setup

Datasets. We experimented with several hand datasets including a variety of hand-object interactions, the annotation of 2D hand keypoints, and hand masks as follows. We adopted **DexYCB** [13] dataset as our source dataset since it contains a large amount of training images, their corresponding labels, and natural hand-object interactions. We chose to use the following datasets as our target datasets: **HO3D** [29] captured in different environments with the same YCB objects [10] as the source dataset, **HanCo** [78] captured in a multi-camera studio and generated with synthesized backgrounds, and **FPHA** [24] captured by a first-person view. We also used **Ego4D** [28] to verify the effectiveness of our method in real-world scenarios. During training, we used cropped images of the hand regions from the original images as input.

Implementation Details. Our teacher-student networks share an identical network architecture, which consists of a unified feature extractor and task-specific branches for hand keypoint regression and hand segmentation. For training our student network, we used the Adam optimizer [36] with a learning rate of 10^{-5}, while the learning rate of the teacher networks was set to 5×10^{-6}. We set the hyperparameters ($\lambda^p (= \tilde{\lambda}^p)$, λ^m, $\tilde{\lambda}^m$, λ_d) to ($10^7, 10^2, 5, 0.5$). Since both task-specific branches have different training speeds, we began our adaptation with the backbone and keypoint regression branch. We then trained all sub-networks, including the hand segmentation branch. We report the percentage of correct keypoints (PCK) and the mean joint position error (MPE) for hand keypoint regression, and the intersection over union (IoU) for hand segmentation.

Baseline Methods. We compared quantitative performance with the following methods. **Source only** denotes the network trained on the source dataset without any adaptation. To compare with another adaptation approach with adversarial training, we trained **DANN** [23] that aligns marginal feature distributions between domains, and **RegDA** [33] with an adversarial regressor that optimizes domain disparity. In addition, we implemented several self-training adaptation methods by replacing pseudo-labeling with the consistency training. **GAC** is a simple baseline with the consistency training updated by Eq. 2. **GAC + UMA** [7] is a GAC method with confidence estimation by Dropout [22]. **GAC + CPL** [53] is a GAC method with confident instance selection using the agreement with another network. **GAC + MT** [64] is a GAC method with the single-teacher-single-student architecture using EMA for the teacher update. **Target only** indicates the network trained on the target dataset with labels, which shows an empirical performance upper bound.

Our Method. We denote our full method as **C-GAC** introduced in Sect. 3.4. As an ablation study, we present a variant of the proposed method as **GAC-Distill** with a teacher-student pair, which is updated by the consistency training (Eq. 2) and the distillation loss (Eq. 5). **GAC-Distill** is different from **GAC + MT** only in the way of the teacher update.

Table 1. DexYCB [13] → **HO3D** [29]. We report PCK (%) and MPE (px) for hand keypoint regression and IoU (%) for hand segmentation. Each score format of *val / test* indicates the validation and test scores. Red and blue letters indicate the best and second best values

Method	2D Pose		Seg	2D Pose + Seg
	PCK ↑ (%)	MPE ↓ (px)	IoU ↑ (%)	Avg. ↑ (%)
Source only	42.8/33.5	15.39/19.32	57.9/49.1	50.3/41.3
DANN [23]	49.0/46.8	12.39/13.39	52.8/54.7	50.9/50.8
RegDA [33]	48.8/48.2	12.50/12.64	55.7/55.3	52.2/51.7
GAC	47.6/47.4	12.47/12.54	58.0/56.9	52.8/52.2
GAC + UMA [7]	47.1/45.3	12.97/13.51	58.0/55.0	52.5/50.2
GAC + CPL [53]	48.1/48.1	12.74/12.61	57.2/55.6	52.7/51.8
GAC + MT [64]	45.5/44.4	13.65/14.05	54.8/52.3	50.2/48.3
GAC-Distill (Ours)	49.9/50.4	11.98/11.51	60.7/60.6	55.3/55.5
C-GAC (Ours-Full)	50.3/51.1	11.89/11.22	60.9/60.3	55.6/55.7
Target only	55.1/58.6	11.00/9.29	68.2/66.1	61.7/62.4

4.2   Quantitative Results

We show the results of three adaptation settings: DexYCB → {HO3D, HanCo, FPHA} in Tables 1 and 2. We then provide detailed comparisons of our method.

DexYCB → HO3D. Table 1 shows the results of the adaptation from DexYCB to HO3D where the grasping objects are overlapped. The baseline of the consistency training (**GAC**) was effective in learning target images in both tasks. Our proposed method (**C-GAC**) improved by 5.3/14.4 in the average task score from the source-only performance. The method also outperformed all comparison methods and achieved close performance to the upper bound.

DexYCB → HanCo. Table 2 shows the results of the adaptation from DexYCB to HanCo across laboratory setups. The source-only network less generalized to the target domain because the HanCo has diverse backgrounds, while **GAC** succeeded in adapting up to 47.4/47.9 in the average score. Our method **C-GAC** showed further improved results in hand keypoint regression.

DexYCB → FPHA. Table 2 also shows the results of the adaptation from DexYCB to FPHA, which captures egocentric users' activities. Since hand markers and in-the-wild target environments cause large appearance gaps, the source-only performance performed the most poorly among the three adaption settings. In this challenging setting, **RegDA** and **GAC + UMA** performed well for hand segmentation, while their performance on hand keypoint regression was inferior to the **GAC** baseline. Our method **C-GAC** further improved than the **GAC** method in the MPE and IoU metrics and exhibited stability in adaptation training among the comparison methods.

Table 2. DexYCB [13] → {**HanCo** [78], **FPHA** [24]}. We report PCK (%) and MPE (px) for hand keypoint regression and IoU (%) for hand segmentation. We show the validation and test results on HanCo and the validation results on FPHA. Red and blue letters indicate the best and second best values

Method	DexYCB → HanCo				DexYCB → FPHA			
	2D Pose		Seg		2D Pose		Seg	
	PCK ↑ (%)	MPE ↓ (px)	IoU ↑ (%)	Avg. ↑ (%)	PCK	MPE	IoU	Avg.
Source only	26.0/27.3	21.82/21.48	41.8/41.4	33.9/34.3	14.0	31.32	24.8	19.4
DANN [23]	32.3/33.0	19.99/19.82	56.3/56.9	44.3/45.0	24.4	25.79	28.4	26.4
RegDA [33]	33.0/33.6	19.51/19.44	57.8/58.4	45.4/46.0	23.7	24.27	41.7	32.7
GAC	36.6/37.1	16.63/16.59	58.1/58.8	47.4/47.9	37.2	17.02	33.3	35.3
GAC + UMA [7]	35.1/35.6	17.51/17.48	57.1/57.7	46.1/46.6	36.8	17.29	39.2	38.0
GAC + CPL [53]	32.7/33.5	19.85/19.62	55.8/56.4	44.2/45.0	25.7	24.99	32.7	29.2
GAC + MT [64]	33.2/33.8	18.93/18.83	54.3/55.1	43.8/44.4	31.3	20.81	38.4	34.9
GAC-Distill (Ours)	38.8/39.5	16.06/15.97	57.5/57.7	48.1/48.6	36.8	15.99	35.5	36.1
C-GAC (Ours-Full)	39.2/39.9	15.83/15.74	58.2/58.6	48.7/49.2	37.2	15.36	37.7	37.4
Target only	76.8/77.3	4.91/4.80	75.9/76.1	76.3/76.7	63.3	8.11	-	-

Comparison to Different Confidence Estimation Methods. We compare the results with existing confidence estimation methods. **GAC + UMA** and **GAC + CPL** estimate the confidence of target predictions by computing the variance of multiple stochastic forwards and the task scores between a training network and an auxiliary network, respectively. **GAC + UMA** performed effectively on DexYCB → FPHA, whereas the performance gain was thin in the other settings compared to **GAC**. **GAC + CPL** worked well for keypoint regression on DexYCB → HO3D, but it cannot address the other settings with a large domain gap well since the prediction of the auxiliary network became unstable. Although these prior methods had different disadvantages depending on the settings, our method **C-GAC** using the divergence of the two teachers for confidence estimation performed stably in the three settings.

Comparison to Standard Teacher-Student Update. We compare our teacher update with the update with an exponential moving average (EMA) [64]. The EMA-based update (**GAC-MT**) degraded the performance from the source only in hand segmentation in Table 1. This suggests that the EMA update can be sensitive to the task. In contrast, our method **GAC-Distill** matching the teacher-student predictions in the output level did not produce such performance degeneration and worked more stably.

Comparison to Adversarial Adaptation Methods. We compared our method with another major adaptation approach with adversarial training. In Tables 1 and 2, the performance of **DANN** and **RegDA** was mostly worse than the consistency-based baseline **GAC**. We found that instead of matching features between both domains [23,33], directly learning target images by the consistency training was critical in the adaptation of our tasks.

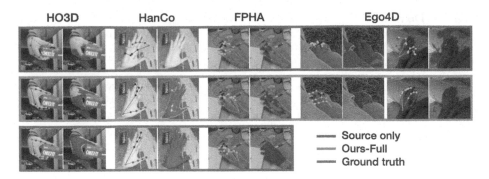

Fig. 4. Qualitative results. We show qualitative examples of the source-only network (top), the Ours-Full method (middle), and ground truth (bottom) on HO3D [29], HanCo [78], FPHA [24], and Ego4D [28] without ground truth.

Comparison to an Off-the-Shelf Hand Pose Estimator. We tested the generalization ability of an open-source library for pose estimation: **OpenPose** [31]. It resulted in 15.75/12.72, 18.31/18.42, and 29.02 in the MPE on HO3D, HanCo, and FPHA, respectively. Since it is built on multiple source datasets [1,34,44], the baseline showed higher generalization than the source-only network. However, the performance did not exceed our proposed method in the MPE. This shows that generalizing hand keypoint regression to other datasets is still challenging, and our adaptation framework supports improving target performance.

4.3   Qualitative Results

We show the qualitative results of hand keypoint regression and hand segmentation in Fig. 4. When hands are occluded in HO3D and FPHA or the backgrounds are diverse in HanCo, the keypoint prediction of the source only (top) represented infeasible hand poses and hand segmentation was too noisy or missing. However, our method **C-GAC** (middle) corrected the hand keypoint errors and improved to localize hand regions. Hand segmentation in FPHA was still noisy because visible white markers obstructed hand appearance. We can also see distinct improvements in the Ego4D dataset. We provide additional qualitative analysis in adaptation to the Ego4D beyond countries, cultures, ages, indoors/outdoors, and performing tasks with hands in our supplementary material.

4.4   Ablation Studies

Effect of Confidence Estimation. To confirm the effect of our proposed confidence estimation, we compare our full method **C-GAC** and our ablation model **GAC-Distill** without the confidence weighting. In Tables 1 and 2, while **GAC-Distill** mostly surpassed the comparison methods in most cases, **C-GAC** showed further performance gain in all three adaptation settings.

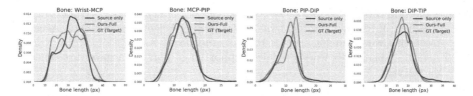

Fig. 5. Visualization of bone length distributions. We show the distributions of the bone length between hand joints, namely, Wrist, metacarpophalangeal (MCP), proximal interphalangeal (PIP), distal interphalangeal (DIP), and fingertip (TIP). Using kernel density estimation, we plotted the density of the bone length for the predictions of the source only, the Ours-Full method, and ground truth on test data of HO3D [29]. (Color figure online)

Multi-task *vs*. Single-Task Adaptation. We studied the effect of our multi-task adaptation compared with single-task adaptation on DexYCB → HO3D. The single-task adaptation results are 50.1/51.0 in the PCK and 58.2/57.7 in the IoU. Compared to Table 1, our method in the multi-task setting improved by 2.7/2.6 over the single-task adaption in hand segmentation while it provided marginal gain in hand keypoint regression. This shows that the adaptation of hand keypoint regression helps to localize hand regions in the target domain.

Bone Length Distributions. To study our adaptation results in each hand joint, we show the distributions of bone length between hand joints in Fig. 5. In Wrist-MCP, PIP-DIP, and DIP-TIP, the distribution of the source-only prediction on target images (blue) was far from that of the target ground truth (green), whereas our method (orange) improved to approximate the target distribution (green). In MCP-PIP, we could not observe such clear differences because the source-only model already represented the target distribution well. This indicates that our method improved to learn hand structure near the palm and fingertips.

5 Conclusion

In this work, we tackled the problem of joint domain adaptation of hand keypoint regression and hand segmentation. Our proposed method consists of the self-training with geometric augmentation consistency, confidence weighting by the two teacher networks, and the teacher-student update by knowledge distillation. The consistency training under geometric augmentation served to learn the unlabeled target images for both tasks. The divergence of the predictions from two teacher networks could represent the confidence of each target instance, which enables the student network to learn from reliable target predictions. The distillation-based teacher-student update guided the teachers to learn from the student carefully and mitigated over-fitting to the noisy predictions. Our method delivered state-of-the-art performance on the three adaptation setups. It also showed improved qualitative results in the real-world egocentric videos.

Acknowledgments. This work was supported by JST ACT-X Grant Number JPMJAX2007, JSPS Research Fellowships for Young Scientists, JST AIP Acceleration Research Grant Number JPMJCR20U1, and JSPS KAKENHI Grant Number JP20H04205, Japan. This work was also supported in part by a hardware donation from Yu Darvish.

References

1. Andriluka, M., Pishchulin, L., Gehler, P.V., Schiele, B.: 2D human pose estimation: new benchmark and state of the art analysis. In: Proceedings of the IEEE Conference on Computer Vision and Pattern Recognition (CVPR), pp. 3686–3693 (2014)
2. Arazo, E., Ortego, D., Albert, P., O'Connor, N.E., McGuinness, K.: Pseudo-labeling and confirmation bias in deep semi-supervised learning. In: IEEE International Joint Conference on Neural Networks (IJCNN), pp. 1–8 (2020)
3. Benitez-Garcia, G., et al.: Improving real-time hand gesture recognition with semantic segmentation. Sensors **21**(2), 356 (2021)
4. Blum, A., Mitchell, T.M.: Combining labeled and unlabeled data with co-training. In: Proceedings of the ACM Annual Conference on Computational Learning Theory (COLT), pp. 92–100 (1998)
5. Boukhayma, A., Bem, R.D., Torr, P.H.S.: 3D hand shape and pose from images in the wild. In: Proceedings of the IEEE Conference on Computer Vision and Pattern Recognition (CVPR), pp. 10843–10852 (2019)
6. Brahmbhatt, S., Tang, C., Twigg, C.D., Kemp, C.C., Hays, J.: ContactPose: a dataset of grasps with object contact and hand pose. In: Vedaldi, A., Bischof, H., Brox, T., Frahm, J.-M. (eds.) ECCV 2020. LNCS, vol. 12358, pp. 361–378. Springer, Cham (2020). https://doi.org/10.1007/978-3-030-58601-0_22
7. Cai, M., Lu, F., Sato, Y.: Generalizing hand segmentation in egocentric videos with uncertainty-guided model adaptation. In: Proceedings of the IEEE Conference on Computer Vision and Pattern Recognition (CVPR), pp. 14380–14389 (2020)
8. Cai, M., Luo, M., Zhong, X., Chen, H.: Uncertainty-aware model adaptation for unsupervised cross-domain object detection. CoRR, abs/2108.12612 (2021)
9. Cai, Q., Pan, Y., Ngo, C.-W., Tian, X., Duan, L., Yao, T.: Exploring object relation in mean teacher for cross-domain detection. In: Proceedings of the IEEE Conference on Computer Vision and Pattern Recognition (CVPR), pp. 11457–11466 (2019)
10. Çalli, B., Walsman, A., Singh, A., Srinivasa, S.S., Abbeel, P., Dollar, A.M.: Benchmarking in manipulation research: using the Yale-CMU-Berkeley object and model set. IEEE Robot. Autom. Mag. **22**(3), 36–52 (2015)
11. Cao, J., Tang, H., Fang, H., Shen, X., Tai, Y.-W., Lu, C.: Cross-domain adaptation for animal pose estimation. In: Proceedings of the IEEE International Conference on Computer Vision (ICCV), pp. 9497–9506 (2019)
12. Cao, Z., Radosavovic, I., Kanazawa, A., Malik, J.: Reconstructing hand-object interactions in the wild. In: Proceedings of the IEEE International Conference on Computer Vision (ICCV), pp. 12417–12426 (2021)
13. Chao, Y.-W., et al.: DexYCB: a benchmark for capturing hand grasping of objects. In: Proceedings of the IEEE Conference on Computer Vision and Pattern Recognition (CVPR), pp. 9044–9053 (2021)

14. Chen, C.-H., et al.: Unsupervised 3D pose estimation with geometric self-supervision. In: Proceedings of the IEEE Conference on Computer Vision and Pattern Recognition (CVPR), pp. 5714–5724 (2019)

15. Chen, M., Weinberger, K.Q., Blitzer, J.: Co-training for domain adaptation. In: Proceedings of the Advances in Neural Information Processing Systems (NeurIPS), pp. 2456–2464 (2011)

16. Chen, X., Wang, G., Zhang, C., Kim, T.-K., Ji, X.: SHPR-Net: deep semantic hand pose regression from point clouds. IEEE Access 6, 43425–43439 (2018)

17. Damen, D., et al.: Rescaling egocentric vision. Int. J. Comput. Vision (IJCV) (2021)

18. Deng, J., Li, W., Chen, Y., Duan, L.: Unbiased mean teacher for cross-domain object detection. In: Proceedings of the IEEE Conference on Computer Vision and Pattern Recognition (CVPR), pp. 4091–4101 (2021)

19. French, G., Mackiewicz, M., Fisher, M.H.: Self-ensembling for visual domain adaptation. In: Proceedings of the International Conference on Learning Representations (ICLR) (2018)

20. Fu, H., Gong, M., Wang, C., Batmanghelich, K., Zhang, K., Tao, D.: Geometry-consistent generative adversarial networks for one-sided unsupervised domain mapping. In: Proceedings of the IEEE Conference on Computer Vision and Pattern Recognition (CVPR), pp. 2427–2436 (2019)

21. Fu, Q., Liu, X., Kitani, K.M.: Sequential decision-making for active object detection from hand. CoRR, abs/2110.11524 (2021)

22. Gal, Y., Ghahramani, Z.: Dropout as a Bayesian approximation: representing model uncertainty in deep learning. In Proceedings of the International Conference on Machine Learning (ICML), pp. 1050–1059 (2016)

23. Ganin, Y., Lempitsky, V.: Unsupervised domain adaptation by backpropagation. In Proceedings of the International Conference on Machine Learning (ICML), pp. 1180–1189 (2015)

24. Garcia-Hernando, G., Yuan, S., Baek, S., Kim, T.-K.: First-person hand action benchmark with RGB-D videos and 3D hand pose annotations. In Proceedings of the IEEE Conference on Computer Vision and Pattern Recognition (CVPR), pp. 409–419 (2018)

25. Ge, Y., Chen, D., Li, H.: Mutual mean-teaching: pseudo label refinery for unsupervised domain adaptation on person re-identification. In Proceedings of the International Conference on Learning Representations (ICLR) (2020)

26. Glauser, O., Wu, S., Panozzo, D., Hilliges, O., Sorkine-Hornung, O.: Interactive hand pose estimation using a stretch-sensing soft glove. ACM Trans. Graph. 38(4), 41:1-41:15 (2019)

27. Goudie, D., Galata, A.: 3D hand-object pose estimation from depth with convolutional neural networks. In: Proceedings of the IEEE International Conference on Automatic Face & Gesture Recognition (FG), pp. 406–413 (2017)

28. Grauman, K., et al.: Ego4D: around the world in 3,000 hours of egocentric video. In: Proceedings of the IEEE Conference on Computer Vision and Pattern Recognition (CVPR), pp. 18995–19012 (2022)

29. Hampali, S., Rad, M., Oberweger, M., Lepetit, V.: Honnotate: a method for 3D annotation of hand and object poses. In: Proceedings of the IEEE Conference on Computer Vision and Pattern Recognition (CVPR), pp. 3196–3206 (2020)

30. Hasson, Y., et al.: Learning joint reconstruction of hands and manipulated objects. In: Proceedings of the IEEE Conference on Computer Vision and Pattern Recognition (CVPR), pp. 11807–11816 (2019)

31. Hidalgo, G., et al.: OpenPose. https://github.com/CMU-Perceptual-Computing-Lab/openpose
32. Huang, W., Ren, P., Wang, J., Qi, Q., Sun, H.: AWR: adaptive weighting regression for 3D hand pose estimation. In: Proceedings of the AAAI Conference on Artificial Intelligence (AAAI), pp. 11061–11068 (2020)
33. Jiang, J., Ji, Y., Wang, X., Liu, Y., Wang, J., Long, M.: Regressive domain adaptation for unsupervised keypoint detection. In: Proceedings of the IEEE Conference on Computer Vision and Pattern Recognition (CVPR), pp. 6780–6789 (2021)
34. Joo, H., et al.: Panoptic studio: a massively multiview system for social motion capture. In: Proceedings of the IEEE Conference on Computer Vision and Pattern Recognition (CVPR), pp. 3334–3342 (2015)
35. Kim, S., Chi, H.-G., Hu, X., Vegesana, A., Ramani, K.: First-person view hand segmentation of multi-modal hand activity video dataset. In: Proceedings of the British Machine Vision Conference (BMVC) (2020)
36. Kingma, D.P., Ba, J.: Adam: a method for stochastic optimization. In: Proceedings of the International Conference on Learning Representations (ICLR) (2014)
37. Lee, K., Shrivastava, A., Kacorri, H.: Hand-priming in object localization for assistive egocentric vision. In: IEEE Winter Conference on Applications of Computer Vision (WACV), pp. 3422–3432 (2020)
38. Li, Y.-J., et al.: Cross-domain object detection via adaptive self-training. CoRR, abs/2111.13216 (2021)
39. Liang, H., Yuan, J., Thalmann, D., Magnenat-Thalmann, N.: AR in hand: egocentric palm pose tracking and gesture recognition for augmented reality applications. In: Proceedings of the ACM International Conference on Multimedia (MM), pp. 743–744 (2015)
40. Likitlersuang, J., Sumitro, E.R., Cao, T., Visée, R.J., Kalsi-Ryan, S., Zariffa, J.: Egocentric video: a new tool for capturing hand use of individuals with spinal cord injury at home. J. Neuroeng. Rehabil. (JNER) **16**(1), 83 (2019)
41. Liu, Y.-C., et al.: Unbiased teacher for semi-supervised object detection. In: Proceedings of the International Conference on Learning Representations (ICLR) (2021)
42. Long, M., Zhu, H., Wang, J., Jordan, M.I.: Unsupervised domain adaptation with residual transfer networks. In: Proceedings of the Advances in Neural Information Processing Systems (NeurIPS), pp. 136–144 (2016)
43. Lu, Y., Mayol-Cuevas, W.W.: Understanding egocentric hand-object interactions from hand pose estimation. CoRR, abs/2109.14657 (2021)
44. McKee, R., McKee, D., Alexander, D., Paillat, E.: NZ sign language exercises. Deaf Studies Department of Victoria University of Wellington. http://www.victoria.ac.nz/llc/llc_resources/nzsl
45. Melas-Kyriazi, L., Manrai, A.K.: Pixmatch: unsupervised domain adaptation via pixelwise consistency training. In: Proceedings of the IEEE Conference on Computer Vision and Pattern Recognition (CVPR), pp. 12435–12445 (2021)
46. Moon, G., Yu, S.-I., Wen, H., Shiratori, T., Lee, K.M.: InterHand2.6M: a dataset and baseline for 3D interacting hand pose estimation from a single RGB image. In: Vedaldi, A., Bischof, H., Brox, T., Frahm, J.-M. (eds.) ECCV 2020. LNCS, vol. 12365, pp. 548–564. Springer, Cham (2020). https://doi.org/10.1007/978-3-030-58565-5_33
47. Mueller, F., et al.: GANerated hands for real-time 3D hand tracking from monocular RGB. In: Proceedings of the IEEE Conference on Computer Vision and Pattern Recognition (CVPR), pp. 49–59 (2018)

48. Mueller, F., Mehta, D., Sotnychenko, O., Sridhar, S., Casas, D., Theobalt, C.: Real-time hand tracking under occlusion from an egocentric RGB-D sensor. In: Proceedings of the IEEE International Conference on Computer Vision (ICCV), pp. 1163–1172 (2017)
49. Neverova, N., Wolf, C., Nebout, F., Taylor, G.W.: Hand pose estimation through semi-supervised and weakly-supervised learning. Comput. Vis. Image Underst. **164**, 56–67 (2017)
50. Newell, A., Yang, K., Deng, J.: Stacked hourglass networks for human pose estimation. In: Leibe, B., Matas, J., Sebe, N., Welling, M. (eds.) ECCV 2016. LNCS, vol. 9912, pp. 483–499. Springer, Cham (2016). https://doi.org/10.1007/978-3-319-46484-8_29
51. Ohkawa, T., Furuta, R., Sato, Y.: Efficient annotation and learning for 3D hand pose estimation: a survey. CoRR, abs/2206.02257 (2022)
52. Ohkawa, T., Inoue, N., Kataoka, H., Inoue, N.: Augmented cyclic consistency regularization for unpaired image-to-image translation. In: Proceedings of the International Conference on Pattern Recognition (ICPR), pp. 362–369 (2020)
53. Ohkawa, T., Yagi, T., Hashimoto, A., Ushiku, Y., Sato, Y.: Foreground-aware stylization and consensus pseudo-labeling for domain adaptation of first-person hand segmentation. IEEE Access **9**, 94644–94655 (2021)
54. Pham, H., Dai, Z., Xie, Q., Le, Q.V.: Meta pseudo labels. In: Proceedings of the IEEE Conference on Computer Vision and Pattern Recognition (CVPR), pp. 11557–11568 (2021)
55. Prabhu, V., Khare, S., Kartik, D., Hoffman, J.: SENTRY: selective entropy optimization via committee consistency for unsupervised domain adaptation. In: Proceedings of the IEEE International Conference on Computer Vision (ICCV), pp. 8558–8567 (2021)
56. Qian, C., Sun, X., Wei, Y., Tang, X., Sun, J.: Realtime and robust hand tracking from depth. In: Proceedings of the IEEE Conference on Computer Vision and Pattern Recognition (CVPR), pp. 1106–1113 (2014)
57. Qiao, S., Shen, W., Zhang, Z., Wang, B., Yuille, A.: Deep co-training for semi-supervised image recognition. In: Ferrari, V., Hebert, M., Sminchisescu, C., Weiss, Y. (eds.) ECCV 2018. LNCS, vol. 11219, pp. 142–159. Springer, Cham (2018). https://doi.org/10.1007/978-3-030-01267-0_9
58. Ren, P., Sun, H., Qi, Q., Wang, J., Huang, W.: SRN: stacked regression network for real-time 3D hand pose estimation. In: Proceedings of the British Machine Vision Conference (BMVC) (2019)
59. Saito, K., Ushiku, Y., Harada, T.: Asymmetric tri-training for unsupervised domain adaptation. In: Proceedings of the International Conference on Machine Learning (ICML), pp. 2988–2997 (2017)
60. Santavas, N., Kansizoglou, I., Bampis, L., Karakasis, E., Gasteratos, A.: Attention! A lightweight 2D hand pose estimation approach. CoRR, abs/2001.08047 (2020)
61. Simon, T., Joo, H., Matthews, I., Sheikh, Y.: Hand keypoint detection in single images using multiview bootstrapping. In Proceedings of the IEEE Conference on Computer Vision and Pattern Recognition (CVPR), pp. 4645–4653 (2017)
62. Sridhar, S., Mueller, F., Zollhoefer, M., Casas, D., Oulasvirta, A., Theobalt, C.: Real-time joint tracking of a hand manipulating an object from RGB-D input. In Proceedings of the European Conference on Computer Vision (ECCV), pp. 294–310 (2016)

63. Taheri, O., Ghorbani, N., Black, M.J., Tzionas, D.: GRAB: a dataset of whole-body human grasping of objects. In: Vedaldi, A., Bischof, H., Brox, T., Frahm, J.-M. (eds.) ECCV 2020. LNCS, vol. 12349, pp. 581–600. Springer, Cham (2020). https://doi.org/10.1007/978-3-030-58548-8_34

64. Tarvainen, A., Valpola, H.: Mean teachers are better role models: weight-averaged consistency targets improve semi-supervised deep learning results. In: Proceedings of the International Conference on Learning Representations (ICLR) (2017)

65. Urooj, A., Borji, A.: Analysis of hand segmentation in the wild. In: Proceedings of the IEEE Conference on Computer Vision and Pattern Recognition (CVPR), pp. 4710–4719 (2018)

66. Vasconcelos, L.O., Mancini, M., Boscaini, D., Bulò, S.R., Caputo, B., Ricci, E.: Shape consistent 2D keypoint estimation under domain shift. In: Proceedings of the International Conference on Pattern Recognition (ICPR), pp. 8037–8044 (2020)

67. Vu, T.H., Jain, H., Bucher, M., Cord, M., Perez, P.: Advent: adversarial entropy minimization for domain adaptation in semantic segmentation. In: Proceedings of the IEEE Conference on Computer Vision and Pattern Recognition (CVPR), pp. 2512–2521 (2019)

68. Wang, Y., Peng, C., Liu, Y.: Mask-pose cascaded CNN for 2D hand pose estimation from single color image. IEEE Trans. Circuits Syst. Video Technol. (TCSVT) **29**(11), 3258–3268 (2019)

69. Wei, S.-E., Ramakrishna, V., Kanade, T., Sheikh, Y.: Convolutional pose machines. In: Proceedings of the IEEE Conference on Computer Vision and Pattern Recognition (CVPR), pp. 4724–4732 (2016)

70. Wu, M.-Y., Ting, P.-W., Tang, Y.-H., Chou, E.T., Fu, L.-C.: Hand pose estimation in object-interaction based on deep learning for virtual reality applications. J. Vis. Commun. Image Represent. **70**, 102802 (2020)

71. Xie, Q., Dai, Z., Hovy, E., Luong, T., Le, Q.: Unsupervised data augmentation for consistency training. In: Proceedings of the Advances in Neural Information Processing Systems (NeurIPS) (2020)

72. Yan, L., Fan, B., Xiang, S., Pan, C.: CMT: cross mean teacher unsupervised domain adaptation for VHR image semantic segmentation. IEEE Geosci. Remote Sens. Lett. **19**, 1–5 (2022)

73. Yang, L., Chen, S., Yao, A.: Semihand: semi-supervised hand pose estimation with consistency. In: Proceedings of the IEEE International Conference on Computer Vision (ICCV), pp. 11364–11373 (2021)

74. Yang, L., Li, J., Xu, W., Diao, Y., Lu, C.: Bihand: recovering hand mesh with multi-stage bisected hourglass networks. In: Proceedings of the British Machine Vision Conference (BMVC) (2020)

75. Yuan, S., Ye, Q., Stenger, B., Jain, S., Kim, T.K.: BigHand2.2M benchmark: hand pose dataset and state of the art analysis. In: Proceedings of the IEEE Conference on Computer Vision and Pattern Recognition (CVPR), pp. 2605–2613 (2017)

76. Zhang, C., Wang, G., Chen, X., Xie, P., Yamasaki, T.: Weakly supervised segmentation guided hand pose estimation during interaction with unknown objects. In: Proceedings of the IEEE International Conference on Acoustics, Speech and Signal Processing, (ICASSP), pp. 2673–2677 (2020)

77. Zhou, X., Karpur, A., Gan, C., Luo, L., Huang, Q.: Unsupervised domain adaptation for 3D keypoint estimation via view consistency. In: Ferrari, V., Hebert, M., Sminchisescu, C., Weiss, Y. (eds.) ECCV 2018. LNCS, vol. 11216, pp. 141–157. Springer, Cham (2018). https://doi.org/10.1007/978-3-030-01258-8_9

78. Zimmermann, C., Argus, M., Brox, T.: Contrastive representation learning for hand shape estimation. CoRR, abs/2106.04324 (2021)

79. Zimmermann, C., Brox, T.: Learning to estimate 3D hand pose from single RGB images. In: Proceedings of the IEEE International Conference on Computer Vision (ICCV), pp. 4913–4921 (2017)
80. Zimmermann, C., Ceylan, D., Yang, J., Russell, B., Argus, M., Brox, T.: Frei-HAND: a dataset for markerless capture of hand pose and shape from single RGB images. In: Proceedings of the IEEE International Conference on Computer Vision (ICCV), pp. 813–822 (2019)
81. Zou, Y., Yu, Z., Kumar, B.V., Wang, J.: Unsupervised domain adaptation for semantic segmentation via class-balanced self-training. In: Proceedings of the European Conference on Computer Vision (ECCV), pp. 289–305 (2018)

Towards Data-Efficient Detection Transformers

Wen Wang[1], Jing Zhang[2], Yang Cao[1,3(✉)], Yongliang Shen[4],
and Dacheng Tao[2,5]

[1] University of Science and Technology of China, Hefei, China
`wangen@mail.ustc.edu.cn`, `forrest@ustc.edu.cn`
[2] The University of Sydney, Camperdown, Australia
`jing.zhang1@sydney.edu.au`
[3] Institute of Artificial Intelligence, Hefei Comprehensive National Science Center,
Hefei, China
[4] Zhejiang University, Hangzhou, China
`syl@zju.edu.cn`
[5] JD Explore Academy, Beijing, China

Abstract. Detection transformers have achieved competitive performance on the sample-rich COCO dataset. However, we show most of them suffer from significant performance drops on small-size datasets, like Cityscapes. In other words, the detection transformers are generally data-hungry. To tackle this problem, we empirically analyze the factors that affect data efficiency, through a step-by-step transition from a data-efficient RCNN variant to the representative DETR. The empirical results suggest that sparse feature sampling from local image areas holds the key. Based on this observation, we alleviate the data-hungry issue of existing detection transformers by simply alternating how key and value sequences are constructed in the cross-attention layer, with minimum modifications to the original models. Besides, we introduce a simple yet effective label augmentation method to provide richer supervision and improve data efficiency. Experiments show that our method can be readily applied to different detection transformers and improve their performance on both small-size and sample-rich datasets. Code will be made publicly available at https://github.com/encounter1997/DE-DETRs.

Keywords: Data efficiency · Detection transformer · Sparse feature · Rich supervision · Label augmentation

W. Wang—This work was done during Wen Wang's internship at JD Explore Academy.
J. Zhang—Co-first author.

Supplementary Information The online version contains supplementary material available at https://doi.org/10.1007/978-3-031-20077-9_6.

1   Introduction

Object detection is a long-standing topic in computer vision. Recently, a new family of object detectors, named detection transformers, has drawn increasing attention due to their simplicity and promising performance. The pioneer work of this class of methods is DETR [3], which views object detection as a direct set prediction problem and applies a transformer to translate the object queries to the target objects. It achieves better performance than the seminal Faster RCNN [31] on the commonly used COCO dataset [24], but its convergence is significantly slower than that of CNN-based detectors. For this reason, most of the subsequent works have been devoted to improving the convergence of DETR, through efficient attention mechanism [50], conditional spatial query [29], regression-aware co-attention [14], *etc.*These methods are able to achieve better performance than Faster RCNN with comparable training costs on the COCO dataset, demonstrating the superiority of detection transformers.

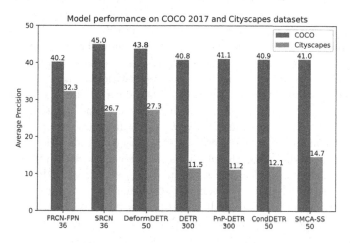

Fig. 1. Performance of different object detectors on COCO 2017 with 118K training data and Cityscapes with 3K training data. The respective training epochs are shown below the name of each method. While the RCNN family show consistently high average precision, the detection transformer family degrades significantly on the small-size dataset. FRCN-FPN, SRCN, and SMCA-SS represent Faster-RCNN-FPN, Sparse RCNN, and single-scale SMCA, respectively.

Current works seem to suggest that detection transformers are superior to the CNN-based object detector, like Faster RCNN, in both simplicity and model performance. However, we find that detection transformers show superior performance only on datasets with rich training data like COCO 2017 (118K training images), while the performance of most detection transformers drops significantly when the amount of training data is small. For example, on the commonly used autonomous driving dataset Cityscapes [7] (3K training images), the average precisions (AP) of most of the detection transformers are less than half of

Faster RCNN AP performance, as shown in Fig. 1. Moreover, although the performance gaps between different detection transformers on the COCO dataset are less than 3 AP, a significant difference of more than 15 AP exists on the small-size Cityscapes dataset.

These findings suggest that detection transformers are generally more data-hungry than CNN-based object detectors. However, the acquisition of labeled data is time-consuming and labor-intensive, especially for the object detection task, which requires both categorization and localization of multiple objects in a single image. What's more, the large amount of training data means more training iterations to traverse the dataset, and thus more computational resources are consumed to train the detection transformers, increasing the carbon footprint. In a word, it takes a lot of human labor and computational resources to meet the training requirements of existing detection transformers.

To address these issues, we first empirically analyze the key factors affecting the data efficiency of detection transformers through a step-by-step transformation from the data-efficient Sparse RCNN to the representative DETR. Our investigation and analysis show that sparse feature sampling from local area holds the key: on the one hand, it alleviates the difficulty of learning to focus on specific objects, and on the other hand, it avoids the quadratic complexity of modeling image features and makes it possible to utilize multi-scale features, which has been proved critical for the object detection task.

Based on these observations, we improve the data efficiency of existing detection transformers by simply alternating how the key and value are constructed in the transformer decoder. Specifically, we perform sparse sampling features on key and value features sent to the cross-attention layer under the guidance of the bounding boxes predicted by the previous decoder layer, with minimum modifications to the original model, and without any specialized module. In addition, we mitigate the data-hungry problem by providing richer supervisory signals to detection transformers. To this end, we propose a label augmentation method to repeat the labels of foreground objects during label assignment, which is both effective and easy to implement. Our method can be applied to different detection transformers to improve their data efficiency. Interestingly, it also brings performance gain on the COCO dataset with a sufficient amount of data.

To summarize, our contributions are listed as follows.

- We identify the data-efficiency problem of detection transformers. Though they achieve excellent performance on the COCO dataset, they generally suffer from significant performance degradation on small-size datasets.
- We empirically analyze the key factor that affects detection transformers' data efficiency through a step-by-step model transformation from Sparse RCNN to DETR, and find that sparse feature sampling from local areas holds the key to data efficiency.
- With minimum modifications, we significantly improve the data efficiency of existing detection transformers by simply alternating how key and value sequences are constructed in the cross-attention layer.

– We propose a simple yet effective label augmentation strategy to provide richer supervision and improve the data efficiency. It can be combined with different methods to achieve performance gains on different datasets.

2   Related Work

2.1   Object Detection

Object detection [13,16,23,26,30,31,35] is essential to many real-world applications, like autonomous driving, defect detection, and remote sensing. Representative deep-learning-based object detection methods can be roughly categorized into two-stage detectors like Faster RCNN [31] and one-stage object detectors like YOLO [30] and RetinaNet [23]. While effective, these methods generally rely on many heuristics like anchor generation and rule-based label assignments.

Recently, DETR [3] provides a simple and clean pipeline for object detection. It formulates object detection as a set prediction task, and applies a transformer [37] to translate sparse object candidates [33] to the target objects. The success of DETR has sparked the recent surge of detection transformers [4,8,12,14,25,29,39,40,44,50] and most of the following-up works focus on alleviating the slow convergence problem of DETR. For example, DeformDETR [50] propose the deformable attention mechanism for learnable sparse feature sampling and aggregates multi-scale features to accelerate model convergence and improve model performance. CondDETR [29] proposes to learn a conditional spatial query from the decoder embedding, which helps the model quickly learn to localize the four extremities for detection.

These works achieve better performance than Faster RCNN on the COCO dataset [24] with comparable training costs. It seems that detection transformers have surpassed the seminal Faster RCNN in both simplicity and superior performance. But we show that detection transformers are generally more data-hungry and perform much worse than Faster RCNN on small-size datasets.

2.2   Label Assignment

Label assignment [15,32,38,43,48,49] is a crucial component in object detection. It matches the ground truth of an object with a specific prediction from the model, and thereby provides the supervision signal for training. Prior to DETR, most object detectors [23,30,31] adopt the one-to-many matching strategy, which assigns each ground truth to multiple predictions based on local spatial relationships. By contrast, DETR makes one-to-one matching between ground truths and predictions by minimizing a global matching loss. This label assignment approach has been followed by various subsequent variants of the detection transformer [8,12,29,40,50]. Despite the merits of avoiding the duplicates removal process, only a small number of object candidates are supervised by the object labels in each iteration. As a result, the model has to obtain enough supervised signals from a larger amount of data or more training epochs.

2.3   Data-Efficiency of Vision Transformers

Vision Transformers [6,10,11,17,28,41,42,45,46] (ViTs) are emerging as an alternative to CNN for feature extractors and visual recognition. Despite the superior performance, they are generally more data-hungry than their CNN counterparts. To tackle this problem, DeiT [36] improves its data efficiency by knowledge distillation from pre-trained CNNs, coupled with a better training recipe. Liu et al. propose a dense relative localization loss to improve ViTs' data efficiency [27]. Unlike the prior works [2,27,36] that focus on the data efficiency issue of transformer backbones on image classification tasks, we tackle the data efficiency issue of detection transformers on the object detection task.

Table 1. Model transformation from Sparse RCNN (SRCN for short) to DETR, experimented on Ciytscapes [7]. "50E AP" and "300E AP" indicate average precision after training for 50 and 300 epochs respectively. The change in AP is shown in the brackets, where red indicates drops and blue indicates gains on AP.

Model	Added	Removed	50E AP	300E AP	Params	FLOPs
SRCN	–		29.4	35.9	106M	631G
Net1	DETR Recipe	SRCN Recipe	30.6 (+1.2)	34.4 (-1.5)	106M	294G
Net2	–	FPN	23.3 (-7.3)	26.6 (-7.8)	103M	244G
Net3	transformer encoder	–	21.0 (-2.3)	27.5 (+0.9)	111M	253G
Net4	cross-attn in decoder	dynamic conv	18.1 (-2.9)	25.4 (-2.1)	42M	86G
Net5	dropout in decoder	–	16.7 (-1.4)	26.1 (+0.7)	42M	86G
Net6	–	bbox refinement	15.0 (-1.7)	22.7 (-3.4)	41M	86G
Net7	–	RoIAlign	6.6 (-8.4)	17.7 (-5.0)	41M	86G
DETR	–	initial proposals	1.6 (-5.0)	11.5 (-6.2)	41M	86G

3   Difference Analysis of RCNNs and DETRs

As can be seen in Fig. 1, detection transformers are generally more data-hungry than RCNNs. To find out the key factors to data efficiency, we transform a data-efficient RCNN step-by-step into a data-hungry detection transformer to ablate the effects of different designs. Similar research approach has also been adopted by ATSS [47] and Visformer [5], but for different research purposes.

3.1   Detector Selection

To obtain insightful results from the model transformation, we need to choose the appropriate detectors to conduct the experiments. To this end, we choose Sparse RCNN and DETR for the following reasons. Firstly, they are representative detectors from the RCNN and detection transformer families, respectively. The observations and conclusions drawn from the transformation between them shall also be helpful to other detectors. Secondly, there is large difference between the two detectors in data efficiency, as shown in Fig. 1. Thirdly, they share many similarities in label assignment, loss design, and optimization, which helps us eliminate the less significant factors while focus more on the core differences.

3.2 Transformation from Sparse RCNN to DETR

During the model transformation, we consider two training schedules that are frequently used in detection transformers. The first is training for 50 epochs and learning rate decays after 40 epochs, denoted as 50E. And the second is training for 300 epochs and learning rate decays after 200 epochs. The transformation process is summarized in Table 1.

Alternating Training Recipe. Though Sparse RCNN and DETR share many similarities, there are still slight differences in their training Recipes, including the classification loss, the number of object queries, learning rate, and gradient clip. We first eliminate these differences by replacing the Sparse RCNN training recipe with the DETR training recipe. Eliminating the differences in training recipes helps us focus more on the key factors that affect the data-efficiency.

Removing FPN. Multi-scale feature fusion has been proved effective for object detection [22]. The attention mechanism has a quadratic complexity with respect to the image scale, making the modeling of multi-scale features in DETR non-trivial. Thus DETR only takes 32× down-sampled single-scale feature for prediction. In this stage, we remove the FPN neck and send only the 32× down-sampled feature to the detection head, which is consistent with DETR. As expected, without multi-scale modeling, the model performance degrades significantly by 7.3 AP under the 50E schedule, as shown in Table 1.

Introducing Transformer Encoder. In DETR, the transformer encoder can be regarded as the neck in the detector, which is used to enhance the features extracted by the backbone. After removing the FPN neck, we add the transformer encoder neck to the model. It can be seen that the AP result decreases at 50E schedule while improves at 300E schedule. We conjecture that similar to ViT [10], the attention mechanism in the encoder requires longer training epochs to converge and manifest its advantages, due to the lack of inductive biases.

Replacing Dynamic Convolutions with Coss-attention. A very interesting design in Sparse RCNN is the dynamic convolution [20,34] in the decoder, which acts very similar to the role of cross-attention in DETR. Specifically, they both adaptively aggregate the context from the image features to the object candidates based on their similarity. In this step, we replace the dynamic convolution with the cross-attention layer with learnable query positional embedding, and the corresponding results are shown in Table 1. Counter-intuitively, a larger number of learnable parameters does not necessarily make the model more data-hungry. In fact, the dynamic convolutions with about 70M parameters can exhibit better data efficiency than the parameter-efficient cross-attention layer.

Aligning Dropout Settings in the Decoder. A slight difference between Sparse RCNN and DETR is the use of dropout layers in self-attention and FFN layers in the decoder. In this stage, we eliminate the interference of these factors.

Removing Cascaded Bounding Box Refinement. Sparse RCNN follows the cascaded bounding box regression in Cascade RCNN [1], where each decoder layer iteratively refines the bounding box predictions made by the previous layer. We remove it in this stage and as expected, the model performance degrades to some extent.

Removing RoIAlign. Sparse RCNN, like other detectors in the RCNNs family, samples features from local regions of interest, and then makes predictions based on the sampled sparse features [33]. By contrast, each content query in DETR aggregates object-specific information directly from the global features map. In this step, we remove the RoIAlign [18] operation in Sparse RCNN, with the box target transformation [16]. It can be seen that significant degradation of the model performance occurs, especially under the 50E schedule, the model performance decreases by 8.4 AP. We conjecture that learning to focus on local object regions from the entire feature map is non-trivial. The model requires more data and training epochs to capture the locality properties.

Removing Initial Proposals. Finally, DETR directly predicts the target bounding boxes, while RCNNs make predictions relative to some initial guesses. In this step, we eliminate this difference by removing the initial proposal. Unexpectedly, this results in a significant decrease in model performance. We suspect that the initial proposal works as a spatial prior that helps the model to focus on object regions, thus reducing the need to learn locality from large training data.

3.3   Summary

By far, we have completed the model transformation from Sparse RCNN to DETR. From Table 1 and our analysis in Sect. 3.2, it can be seen that three factors result in more than 5 AP performance changes, and are key to data-efficient: (a) sparse feature sampling from local regions, *e.g.*, using RoIAlign; (b) multi-scale features which depend on sparse feature sampling to be computationally feasible; (c) prediction relative to initial spatial priors. Among them, (a) and (c) help the model to focus on local object regions and alleviate the requirement of learning locality from a large amount of data, while (b) facilitates a more comprehensive utilization and enhancement of the image features, though it also relies on sparse features.

It is worth mentioning that DeformDETR [50] is a special case in the detection transformer family, which shows comparable data efficiency to Sparse RCNN. Our conclusions drawn from the Sparse RCNN to DETR model transformation can also explain DeformDETR's data efficiency. Specifically, multi-scale deformable attention samples sparse features from local regions of the image and utilizes multi-scale features. The prediction of the model is relative to the initial reference points. Thus, all three key factors are satisfied in DeformDETR, though it was not intended to be data-efficient on small-size datasets.

4   Method

In this section, we aim to improve the data efficiency of existing detection transformers, while making minimum modifications to their original designs. Firstly, we provide a brief revisiting of existing detection transformers. Subsequently, based on experiments and analysis in the previous section, we make minor modifications to the existing data-hungry detection transformer models, like DETR [3] and CondDETR [29], to significantly improve their data efficiency. Finally, we propose a simple yet effective label augmentation method to provide richer supervised signals to detection transformers to further improve their data efficiency.

4.1   A Revisit of Detection Transformers

Model Structure. Detection transformers generally consist of a backbone, a transformer encoder, a transformer decoder, and the prediction heads. The backbone first extracts multi-scale features from the input image, denoted as $\{f^l\}_{l=1}^{L}$, where $f^l \in \mathbb{R}^{H^l \times W^l \times C^l}$. Subsequently, the last feature level with the lowest resolution is flattened and embedded to obtain $z^L \in \mathbb{R}^{S^L \times D}$ where $S^L = H^L \times W^L$ is sequence length and D is the feature dimension. Correspondingly, the positional embedding is denoted as $p^L \in \mathbb{R}^{S^L \times D}$. Afterward, The single-scale sequence feature is encoded by the transformer encoder to obtain $z_e^L \in \mathbb{R}^{S^L \times D}$.

The decoder consists of a stack of L_d decoder layers, and the query content embedding is initialized as $\mathbf{q}_0 \in \mathbb{R}^{N \times D}$, where N is the number of queries. Each decoder layer DecoderLayer$_\ell$ takes the previous decoder layer's output $\mathbf{q}_{\ell-1}$, the query positional embedding p_q, the image sequence feature $\mathbf{z}_\ell$ and its position embedding p_ℓ as inputs, and outputs the decoded sequence features.

$$\mathbf{q}_\ell = \text{DecoderLayer}_\ell\left(\mathbf{q}_{\ell-1}, p_q, \mathbf{z}_\ell, p_\ell\right), \quad \ell = 1 \ldots L_\text{d}. \tag{1}$$

In most detection transformers, like DETR and CondDETR, single-scale image feature is utilized for decoder, and thus $\mathbf{z}_\ell = z_e^L$ and $p_\ell = p^L$, where $\ell = 1 \ldots L_\text{d}$.

Label Assignment. Detection transformers view the object detection task as a set prediction problem and perform deep supervision [21] on predictions made by each decoder layer. Specifically, the labels set can be denoted as $y = \{y_1, \ldots, y_M, \varnothing, \ldots, \varnothing\}$, where M denotes the number of foreground objects in the image and the $\varnothing$ (no object) pads the label set to a length of N. Correspondingly, the output of each decoder layer can be written as $\hat{y} = \{\hat{y}_i\}_{i=1}^{N}$. During label assignment, detection transformers search for a permutation $\tau \in T_N$ with the minimum matching cost:

$$\hat{\tau} = \arg\min_{\tau \in T_N} \sum_i^N \mathcal{L}_\text{match}\left(y_i, \hat{y}_{\tau(i)}\right), \tag{2}$$

where $\mathcal{L}_\text{match}\left(y_i, \hat{y}_{\tau(i)}\right)$ is the pair-wise loss between ground truth and the prediction with index $\tau(i)$.

4.2   Model Improvement

In this section, we make slight adjustments to data-hungry detection transformers such as DETR and CondDETR, to largely boost their data efficiency.

Sparse Feature Sampling. From the analysis in Sect. 3, we can see that local feature sampling is critical to data efficiency. Fortunately, in detection transformers, the object locations are predicted after each decoder layer. Therefore, we can sample local features under the guidance of the bounding box prediction made by the previous decoder layer without introducing new parameters, as shown in Fig. 2. Although more sophisticated local feature sampling methods can be used, we simply adopt the commonly used RoIAlign [18]. Formally, the sampling operation can be written as:

$$\mathbf{z}_\ell^L = \text{RoIAlign}\left(z_e^L, \mathbf{b}_{\ell-1}\right), \quad \ell = 2 \dots L_{\mathrm{d}} \tag{3}$$

where $\mathbf{b}_{\ell-1}$ is the bounding boxes predicted by the previous layer, $\mathbf{z}_\ell^L \in \mathbb{R}^{N \times K^2 \times D}$ is the sampled feature, K is the feature resolution in RoIAlign sampling. Note the reshape and flatten operations are omitted in Eq. 3. Similarly, the corresponding positional embedding p_ℓ^L can be obtained.

The cascaded structure in the detection transformer makes it natural to use layer-wise bounding box refinement [1,50] to improve detection performance. Our experiments in Sect. 3 also validate the effectiveness of the iterative refinement and making predictions with respect to initial spatial references. For this reason, we also introduce bounding box refinement and initial reference points during our implementation, as did in CondDETR [29].

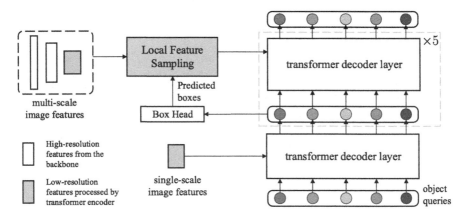

Fig. 2. The proposed data-efficient detection transformer structure. With minimum modifications, we perform sparse sampling feature on key and value feature sent to the cross-attention layers in the decoder, under the guidance of bounding boxes predicted by the previous layer. Note the box head is part of the original detection transformers, which utilize deep supervision on the predictions made by each decoder layer. The backbone, the transformer encoder, and the first decoder layer are kept unchanged.

Incorporating Multi-scale Feature. Our sparse feature sampling makes it possible to use multi-scale features in detection transformers with little computation cost. To this end, we also flatten and embed the high-resolution features extracted by the backbone to obtain $\{z^l\}_{l=1}^{L-1} \in \mathbb{R}^{S^l \times D}$ for local feature sampling. However, these features are not processed by the transformer encoder. Although more sophisticated techniques can be used, these single-scale features sampled by RoIAlign are simply concatenated to form our multi-scale feature. These features are naturally fused by the cross-attention in the decoder.

$$\mathbf{z}_\ell^{\mathrm{ms}} = \left[\mathbf{z}_\ell^1, \mathbf{z}_\ell^2, \dots, \mathbf{z}_\ell^L\right], \ell = 2 \dots L_{\mathrm{d}}, \tag{4}$$

where $\mathbf{z}_\ell^{\mathrm{ms}} \in \mathbb{R}^{N \times LK^2 \times D}$ is the multi-scale feature, and $\mathbf{z}_\ell^l = $ RoIAlign $\left(z^l, \mathbf{b}_{\ell-1}\right), l = 1 \dots L - 1$. The corresponding positional embedding $\mathbf{p}_\ell^{\mathrm{ms}}$ is obtained in a similar way. The decoding process is the same as original detection transformers, as shown in Eq. 1, where we have $\mathbf{z}_\ell = \mathbf{z}_\ell^{\mathrm{ms}}$ and $p_\ell = p_\ell^{\mathrm{ms}}$. Please refer to the Appendix for details in implementation.

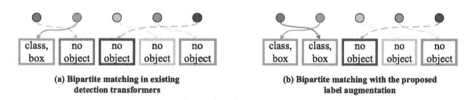

(a) Bipartite matching in existing detection transformers

(b) Bipartite matching with the proposed label augmentation

Fig. 3. Illustration of the proposed label augmentation method. The predictions and the ground truths are represented by circles and rectangles, respectively. The matching between foreground instances is represented by solid lines, while the matching between background instances is represented by dotted lines. The prediction in blue that was originally matched to a background instance in (a) is now matched to a foreground instance in our method (b), thus obtaining more abundant supervision.

4.3 Label Augmentation for Richer Supervision

Detection transformers perform one-to-one matching for label assignment, which means only a small number of detection candidates are provided with a positive supervision signal in each iteration. As a result, the model has to obtain enough supervision from a larger amount of data or more training epochs.

To alleviate this problem, we propose a label augmentation strategy to provide a richer supervised signal to the detection transformers, by simply repeating positive labels during bipartite matching. As shown in Fig. 3, we repeat the labels of each foreground sample y_i for R_i times, while keeping the total length of the label set N unchanged.

$$y = \left\{y_1^1, y_1^2, \dots, y_1^{R_1}, \dots, y_M^1, y_M^2, \dots, y_M^{R_M}, \dots, \varnothing, \dots, \varnothing\right\}. \tag{5}$$

Subsequently, the label assignment is achieved according to the operation in Eq. 2.

Two label repeat strategies are considered during our implementation as follows. (a) Fixed repeat times, where all positive labels are repeated for the same number of times, *i.e.*, $R_i = R, i = 1 \ldots M$. (b) Fixed positive sample ratio, where the positive labels are sampled repeatedly to ensure a proportion of r positive samples in the label set. Specifically, $F = N \times r$ is the expected number of positive samples after repeating labels. We first repeat each positive label for $F//M$ times, and subsequently, randomly sample $F\%M$ positive labels without repetition. By default, we use the fixed repeat times strategy, because it is easier to implement and the resultant label set is deterministic.

5   Experiments

Datasets. To explore detection transformers' data efficiency, most of our experiments are conducted on small-size datasets including Cityscapes [7] and sub-sampled COCO 2017 [24]. Cityscapes contains 2,975 images for training and 500 images for evaluation. For the sub-sampled COCO 2017 dataset, the training images are randomly sub-sampled by 0.1, 0.05, 0.02, and 0.01, while the evaluation set is kept unchanged. Besides, we also validate the effectiveness of our method on the full-size COCO 2017 dataset with 118K training images.

Implementation Details. By default, our feature sampling is implemented as RoIAlign with a feature resolution of 4. Three different feature levels are included for multi-scale feature fusion. A fixed repeat time of 2 is adopted for our label augmentation and non-maximum suppression (NMS) with a threshold of 0.7 is used for duplicate removal. All models are trained for 50 epochs and the learning rate decays after 40 epochs, unless specified. ResNet-50 [19] pre-trained on ImageNet-1K [9] is used as backbone. To guarantee enough number of training iterations, all experiments on Cityscapes and sub-sampled COCO 2017 datasets are trained with a batch size of 8. And the results are averaged over five repeated runs with different random seeds. Our data-efficient detection transformers only make slight modifications to existing methods. Unless specified, we follow the original implementation details of corresponding baseline methods [3,29]. Run time is evaluated on NVIDIA A100 GPU.

5.1   Main Results

Results on Cityscapes. In this section, we compare our method with existing detection transformers. As shown in Table 2, most of them suffer from the data-efficiency issue. Nevertheless, with minor changes to the CondDETR model, our DE-CondDETR is able to achieve comparable data efficiency to DeformDETR. Further, with the richer supervision provided by label augmentation, our DELA-CondDETR surpasses DeformDETR by 2.2 AP. Besides, our method can be combined with other detection transformers to significantly improve their data efficiency, for example, our DE-DETR and DELA-DETR trained for 50 epochs perform significantly better than DETR trained for 500 epochs.

Table 2. Comparison of detection transformers on Cityscapes. DE denotes data-efficient and LA denotes label augmentation. † indicates the query number is increased from 100 to 300.

Method	Epochs	AP	AP_{50}	AP_{75}	AP_S	AP_M	AP_L	Params	FLOPs	FPS
DETR [3]	300	11.5	26.7	8.6	2.5	9.5	25.1	41M	86G	44
UP-DETR [8]	300	23.8	45.7	20.8	4.0	20.3	46.6	41M	86G	44
PnP-DETR-α=0.33 [39]	300	11.2	11.5	8.7	2.3	21.2	25.6	41M	79G	43
PnP-DETR-α=0.80 [39]	300	11.4	26.6	8.1	2.5	9.3	24.7	41M	83G	43
CondDETR [29]	50	12.1	28.0	9.1	2.2	9.8	27.0	43M	90G	39
SMCA (single scale) [14]	50	14.7	32.9	11.6	2.9	12.9	30.9	42M	86G	39
DeformDETR [50]	50	27.3	49.2	26.3	8.7	28.2	45.7	40M	174G	28
DE-DETR	50	21.7	41.7	19.2	4.9	20.0	39.9	42M	88G	34
DELA-DETR†	50	24.5	46.2	22.5	6.1	23.3	43.9	42M	91G	29
DE-CondDETR	50	26.8	47.8	25.4	6.8	25.6	46.6	44M	107G	29
DELA-CondDETR	50	29.5	52.8	27.6	7.5	28.2	50.1	44M	107G	29

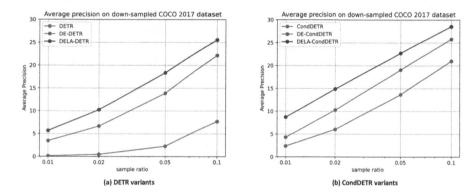

Fig. 4. Performance comparison of different methods on sub-sampled COCO 2017 dataset. Note the sample ratio is shown on a logarithmic scale. As can be seen, both local feature sampling and label augmentation consistently improve the model performance under varying data sampling ratios.

Results on Sub-sampled COCO 2017. Sub-sampled COCO 2017 datasets contain 11,828 (10%), 5,914 (5%), 2,365 (2%), and 1,182 (1%) training images, respectively. As shown in Fig. 4, our method consistently outperforms the baseline methods by a large margin. In particular, DELA-DETR trained with only ∼1K images significantly outperforms the DETR baseline with five times the training data. Similarly, DELA-CondDETR consistently outperforms the Cond-DETR baseline trained with twice the data volume.

5.2 Ablations

In this section, we perform ablated experiments to better understand each component of our method. All the ablation studies are implemented on the DELA-

CondDETR and the Cityscapes dataset, while more ablation studies based on
DELA-DETR can be found in our Appendix.

Table 3. Ablations on each component in DELA-CondDETR. "SF", "MS", and "LA"
represent sparse feature sampling, multi-scale feature fusion, and label augmentation.

Method	SF	MS	LA	AP	AP$_{50}$	AP$_{75}$	AP$_S$	AP$_M$	AP$_L$	Params	FLOPs	FPS
CondDETR [29]				12.1	28.0	9.1	2.2	9.8	27.0	43M	90G	39
			✓	14.7	31.6	12.1	2.9	12.5	32.1	43M	90G	38
	✓			20.4	40.7	17.7	2.9	16.9	42.0	44M	95G	32
DE-CondDETR	✓	✓		26.8	47.8	25.4	6.8	25.6	46.6	44M	107G	29
DELA-CondDETR	✓	✓	✓	29.5	52.8	27.6	7.5	28.2	50.1	44M	107G	29

Effectiveness of Each Module. We first ablate the role of each module in
our method, as shown in Table 3. The use of local feature sampling and multi-
scale feature fusion significantly improves the performance of the model by 8.3
and 6.4 AP, respectively. In addition, label augmentation further improves the
performance by 2.7 AP. Besides, using it alone also brings a gain of 2.6 AP.

Table 4. Ablations on multi-scale feature levels and feature resolutions for RoIAlign.
Note label augmentation is not utilized for clarity.

MS Lvls	RoI Res.	AP	AP$_{50}$	AP$_{75}$	AP$_S$	AP$_M$	AP$_L$	Params	FLOPs	FPS
1	1	14.8	35.1	11.0	2.4	11.7	31.1	44M	90G	32
1	4	20.4	40.7	17.7	2.9	16.9	42.0	44M	95G	32
1	7	20.7	40.9	18.5	2.9	16.8	42.7	44M	104G	31
3	4	26.8	47.8	25.4	6.8	25.6	46.6	44M	107G	29
4	4	26.3	47.1	25.1	6.5	24.8	46.5	49M	112G	28

Feature Resolution for RoIAlign. In general, a larger sample resolution in
RoIAlign provides richer information and thus improves detection performance.
However, sampling larger feature resolution is also more time-consuming and
increases the computational cost of the decoding process. As shown in Table 4,
the model performance is significantly improved by 5.6 AP when the resolution
is increased from 1 to 4. However, when the resolution is further increased to 7,
the improvement is minor and the FLOPs and latency are increased. For this
reason, we set the feature resolution for RoIAlign as 4 by default.

Number of Multi-scale Features. To incorporate multi-scale features, we
also sample the 8× and 16× down-sampled features from the backbone to construct multi-scale features of 3 different levels. As can be seen from Table 4, it

significantly improves the model performance by 6.4 AP. However, when we further add the 64× down-sampled features for multi-scale fusion, the performance drops by 0.5 AP. By default, we use 3 feature levels for multi-scale feature fusion.

Table 5. Ablations on label augmentation using fixed repeat time. Params, FLOPs, and FPS are omitted since they are consistent for all settings.

Time	AP	AP_{50}	AP_{75}	AP_S	AP_M	AP_L
–	26.8	47.8	25.4	6.8	25.6	46.6
2	29.5	52.8	27.6	7.5	28.2	50.1
3	29.4	52.6	28.0	7.6	28.1	50.3
4	29.0	52.0	27.7	7.8	27.9	49.5
5	28.7	51.3	27.4	7.8	27.7	49.3

Table 6. Ablations on label augmentation using fixed positive sample ratio.

Ratio	AP	AP_{50}	AP_{75}	AP_S	AP_M	AP_L
–	26.8	47.8	25.4	6.8	25.6	46.6
0.1	27.7	49.7	26.1	7.4	26.5	47.2
0.2	28.2	50.2	26.9	7.4	26.8	48.5
0.25	28.3	50.5	27.2	7.5	27.1	48.3
0.3	27.9	50.3	26.5	7.3	27.1	47.4
0.4	27.6	49.7	26.0	7.0	27.0	46.8

Strategies for Label Augmentation. In this section, we ablate the proposed two label augmentation strategies, namely fixed repeat time and fixed positive sample ratio. As shown in Table 5, using different fixed repeated times consistently improves the performance of DE-DETR baseline, but the performance gain tends to decrease as the number of repetitions increases. Moreover, as shown in Table 6, although using different ratios can bring improvement on AP, the best performance is achieved when the positive to negative samples ratio is 1:3, which, interestingly, is also the most commonly used positive to negative sampling ratio in the RCNN series detectors, e.g.Faster RCNN.

Table 7. Performance of our data-efficient detection transformers on COCO 2017. All models are trained for 50 epochs.

Method	Epochs	AP	AP_{50}	AP_{75}	AP_S	AP_M	AP_L	Params	FLOPs	FPS
DETR [3]	50	33.6	54.6	34.2	13.2	35.7	53.5	41M	86G	43
DE-DETR	50	40.2	60.4	43.2	23.3	42.1	56.4	43M	88G	33
DELA-DETR[†]	50	41.9	62.6	44.8	24.9	44.9	56.8	43M	91G	29
CondDETR [29]	50	40.2	61.1	42.6	19.9	43.6	58.7	43M	90G	39
DE-CondDETR	50	41.7	62.4	44.9	24.4	44.5	56.3	44M	107G	28
DELA-CondDETR	50	43.0	64.0	46.4	26.0	45.5	57.7	44M	107G	28

5.3   Generalization to Sample-Rich Dataset

Although the above experiments show that our method can improve model performance when only limited training data is available, there is no guarantee that our method remains effective when the training data is sufficient. To this end, we evaluate our method on COCO 2017 with a sufficient amount of data. As can be seen from Table 7, our method does not degrade the model performance on COCO 2017. Conversely, it delivers a promising improvement. Specifically, DELA-DETR and DELA-CondDETR improve their corresponding baseline by 8.3 and 2.8 AP, respectively.

6   Conclusion

In this paper, we identify the data-efficiency issue of detection transformers. Through step-by-step model transformation from Sparse RCNN to DETR, we find that sparse feature sampling from local areas holds the key to data efficiency. Based on these, we improve existing detection transformers by simply sampling multi-scale features under the guidance of predicted bounding boxes, with minimum modifications to the original models. In addition, we propose a simple yet effective label augmentation strategy to provide richer supervision and thus further alleviate the data-efficiency issue. Extensive experiments validate the effectiveness of our method. As transformers become increasingly popular for visual tasks, we hope our work will inspire the community to explore the data efficiency of transformers for different tasks.

Acknowledgement. This work is supported by National Key R&D Program of China under Grant 2020AAA0105701, National Natural Science Foundation of China (NSFC) under Grants 61872327, Major Special Science and Technology Project of Anhui (No. 012223665049), and the ARC project FL-170100117.

References

1. Cai, Z., Vasconcelos, N.: Cascade r-cnn: Delving into high quality object detection. In: Proceedings of the IEEE Conference on Computer Vision and Pattern Recognition, pp. 6154–6162 (2018)
2. Cao, Y.H., Yu, H., Wu, J.: Training vision transformers with only 2040 images. arXiv preprint arXiv:2201.10728 (2022)
3. Carion, N., Massa, F., Synnaeve, G., Usunier, N., Kirillov, A., Zagoruyko, S.: End-to-end object detection with transformers. In: Vedaldi, A., Bischof, H., Brox, T., Frahm, J.-M. (eds.) ECCV 2020. LNCS, vol. 12346, pp. 213–229. Springer, Cham (2020). https://doi.org/10.1007/978-3-030-58452-8_13
4. Chen, Z., Zhang, J., Tao, D.: Recurrent glimpse-based decoder for detection with transformer. In: Proceedings of the IEEE/CVF Conference on Computer Vision and Pattern Recognition, pp. 5260–5269 (2022)
5. Chen, Z., Xie, L., Niu, J., Liu, X., Wei, L., Tian, Q.: Visformer: the vision-friendly transformer. In: Proceedings of the IEEE/CVF International Conference on Computer Vision, pp. 589–598 (2021)
6. Chu, X., Tian, Z., Wang, Y., Zhang, B., Ren, H., Wei, X., Xia, H., Shen, C.: Twins: Revisiting the design of spatial attention in vision transformers. In: 34th Proceedings of the International Conference on Advances in Neural Information Processing Systems (2021)
7. Cordts, M., et al.: The cityscapes dataset for semantic urban scene understanding. In: Proceedings of the IEEE Conference on Computer Vision and Pattern Recognition, pp. 3213–3223 (2016)

8. Dai, Z., Cai, B., Lin, Y., Chen, J.: UP-DETR: unsupervised pre-training for object detection with transformers. In: Proceedings of the IEEE Conference on Computer Vision and Pattern Recognition (2020)

9. Deng, J., Dong, W., Socher, R., Li, L.J., Li, K., Fei-Fei, L.: ImageNet: A large-scale hierarchical image database.ac In: 2009 IEEE Conference on Computer Vision and Pattern Recognition, pp. 248–255. IEEE (2009)

10. Dosovitskiy, A., et al.: An image is worth 16x16 words: transformers for image recognition at scale. arXiv preprint arXiv:2010.11929 (2020)

11. Fang, J., Xie, L., Wang, X., Zhang, X., Liu, W., Tian, Q.: Msg-transformer: exchanging local spatial information by manipulating messenger tokens. arXiv preprint arXiv:2105.15168 (2021)

12. Fang, Y., et al.: You only look at one sequence: rethinking transformer in vision through object detection. arXiv preprint arXiv:2106.00666 (2021)

13. Felzenszwalb, P.F., Girshick, R.B., McAllester, D., Ramanan, D.: Object detection with discriminatively trained part-based models. IEEE Trans. Pattern Anal. Mach. Intell. **32**(9), 1627–1645 (2009)

14. Gao, P., Zheng, M., Wang, X., Dai, J., Li, H.: Fast convergence of DETR with spatially modulated co-attention. In: Proceedings of the IEEE International Conference on Computer Vision (2021)

15. Ge, Z., Liu, S., Li, Z., Yoshie, O., Sun, J.: OTA: optimal transport assignment for object detection. In: Proceedings of the IEEE/CVF Conference on Computer Vision and Pattern Recognition, pp. 303–312 (2021)

16. Girshick, R., Donahue, J., Darrell, T., Malik, J.: Rich feature hierarchies for accurate object detection and semaantic segmentation. In: Proceedings of the IEEE conference on Computer Vision and Pattern Recognition, pp. 580–587 (2014)

17. Han, K., Xiao, A., Wu, E., Guo, J., Xu, C., Wang, Y.: Transformer in transformer. In: 34th Proceedings of the Conference on Advances in Neural Information Processing Systems (2021)

18. He, K., Gkioxari, G., Dollár, P., Girshick, R.: Mask R-CNN. In: Proceedings of the IEEE International Conference on Computer Vision, pp. 2961–2969 (2017)

19. He, K., Zhang, X., Ren, S., Sun, J.: Deep residual learning for image recognition. In: Proceedings of the IEEE Conference on Computer Vision and Pattern Recognition, pp. 770–778 (2016)

20. Jia, X., De Brabandere, B., Tuytelaars, T., Gool, L.V.: Dynamic filter networks. In: 29th Proceedings of the Conference on Advances in Neural Information Processing Systems (2016)

21. Lee, C.Y., Xie, S., Gallagher, P., Zhang, Z., Tu, Z.: Deeply-supervised nets. In: Artificial Intelligence and Statistics, pp. 562–570. PMLR (2015)

22. Lin, T.Y., Dollár, P., Girshick, R., He, K., Hariharan, B., Belongie, S.: Feature pyramid networks for object detection. In: Proceedings of the IEEE Conference on Computer Vision and Pattern Recognition, pp. 2117–2125 (2017)

23. Lin, T.Y., Goyal, P., Girshick, R., He, K., Dollár, P.: Focal loss for dense object detection. In: Proceedings of the IEEE International Conference on Computer Vision, pp. 2980–2988 (2017)

24. Lin, T., et al.: Microsoft COCO: common objects in context. In: Fleet, D., Pajdla, T., Schiele, B., Tuytelaars, T. (eds.) ECCV 2014. LNCS, vol. 8693, pp. 740–755. Springer, Cham (2014). https://doi.org/10.1007/978-3-319-10602-1_48

25. Liu, F., Wei, H., Zhao, W., Li, G., Peng, J., Li, Z.: WB-DETR: transformer-based detector without backbone. In: Proceedings of the IEEE/CVF International Conference on Computer Vision, pp. 2979–2987 (2021)

26. Liu, W., et al.: SSD: single shot multibox detector. In: Leibe, B., Matas, J., Sebe, N., Welling, M. (eds.) ECCV 2016. LNCS, vol. 9905, pp. 21–37. Springer, Cham (2016). https://doi.org/10.1007/978-3-319-46448-0_2

27. Liu, Y., Sangineto, E., Bi, W., Sebe, N., Lepri, B., Nadai, M.: Efficient training of visual transformers with small datasets. In: 34th Proceedings of the Conference on Advances in Neural Information Processing Systems (2021)

28. Liu, Z., et al.: Swin transformer: hierarchical vision transformer using shifted windows. arXiv preprint arXiv:2103.14030 (2021)

29. Meng, D., et al.: Conditional DETR for fast training convergence. In: Proceedings of the IEEE International Conference on Computer Vision (2021)

30. Redmon, J., Divvala, S., Girshick, R., Farhadi, A.: You only look once: Unified, real-time object detection. In: Proceedings of the IEEE Conference on Computer Vision and Pattern Recognition, pp. 779–788 (2016)

31. Ren, S., He, K., Girshick, R., Sun, J.: Faster R-CNN: towards real-time object detection with region proposal networks. IEEE Trans. Pattern Anal. Mach. Intell. **39**(6), 1137–1149 (2016)

32. Shen, Y., et al.: Parallel instance query network for named entity recognition. In: Proceedings of the 60th Annual Meeting of the Association for Computational Linguistics. Association for Computational Linguistics (2022). arxiv.org/abs/2203.10545

33. Sun, P., et al.: Sparse r-CNN: end-to-end object detection with learnable proposals. In: Proceedings of the IEEE/CVF Conference on Computer Vision and Pattern Recognition, pp. 14454–14463 (2021)

34. Tian, Z., Shen, C., Chen, H.: Conditional convolutions for instance segmentation. In: Vedaldi, A., Bischof, H., Brox, T., Frahm, J.-M. (eds.) ECCV 2020. LNCS, vol. 12346, pp. 282–298. Springer, Cham (2020). https://doi.org/10.1007/978-3-030-58452-8_17

35. Tian, Z., Shen, C., Chen, H., He, T.: FCOS: fully convolutional one-stage object detection. In: Proceedings of the IEEE/CVF International Conference on Computer Vision, pp. 9627–9636 (2019)

36. Touvron, H., Cord, M., Douze, M., Massa, F., Sablayrolles, A., Jégou, H.: Training data-efficient image transformers & distillation through attention. In: International Conference on Machine Learning, pp. 10347–10357. PMLR (2021)

37. Vaswani, A., et al.: Attention is all you need. In: Conference on Neural Information Processing Systems (2017)

38. Wang, J., Chen, K., Yang, S., Loy, C.C., Lin, D.: Region proposal by guided anchoring. In: Proceedings of the IEEE/CVF Conference on Computer Vision and Pattern Recognition, pp. 2965–2974 (2019)

39. Wang, T., Yuan, L., Chen, Y., Feng, J., Yan, S.: PNP-DETR: towards efficient visual analysis with transformers. In: Proceedings of the IEEE/CVF International Conference on Computer Vision (2021)

40. Wang, W., Cao, Y., Zhang, J., Tao, D.: FP-DETR: detection transformer advanced by fully pre-training. In: International Conference on Learning Representations (2022). 'openreview.net/forum?id=yjMQuLLcGWK

41. Wang, W., et al.: Pyramid vision transformer: a versatile backbone for dense prediction without convolutions. In: Proceedings of the IEEE/CVF International Conference on Computer Vision, pp. 568–578 (2021)

42. Xu, Y., Zhang, Q., Zhang, J., Tao, D.: Vitae: vision transformer advanced by exploring intrinsic inductive bias. In: 34th Proceedings of the Conference on Advances in Neural Information Processing Systems (2021)

43. Yang, T., Zhang, X., Li, Z., Zhang, W., Sun, J.: Metaanchor: learning to detect objects with customized anchaors. In: 31st Proceedings of the Conference on Advances in Neural Information Processing Systems (2018)
44. Yuan, H., et al.: Polyphonicformer: unified query learning for depth-aware video panoptic segmentation. In: European Conference on Computer Vision (2022)
45. Yuan, L., et al.: Tokens-to-token VIT: training vision transformers from scratch on ImageNet. In: Proceedings of the IEEE/CVF International Conference on Computer Vision, pp. 558–567 (2021)
46. Zhang, Q., Xu, Y., Zhang, J., Tao, D.: Vitaev2: vision transformer advanced by exploring inductive bias for image recognition and beyond. arXiv preprint aarXiv:2202.10108 (2022)
47. Zhang, S., Chi, C., Yao, Y., Lei, Z., Li, S.Z.: Bridging the gap between anchor-based and anchor-free detection via adaptive training sample selection. In: Proceedings of the IEEE/CVF Conference ON Computer Vision and Pattern Recognition, pp. 9759–9768 (2020)
48. Zhang, X., Wan, F., Liu, C., Ji, R., Ye, Q.: Freeanchor: Learning to match anchors for visual object detection. In: 32nd Proceedings of the Conference on Advances in Neural Information Processing Systems (2019)
49. Zhu, B., et al.: Autoassign: differentiable label assignment for dense object detection. arXiv preprint arXiv:2007.03496 (2020)
50. Zhu, X., Su, W., Lu, L., Li, B., Wang, X., Dai, J.: Deformable DETR: deformable transformers for end-to-end object detection. In: International Conference on Learning and Representations (2020)

Open-Vocabulary DETR
with Conditional Matching

Yuhang Zang[1], Wei Li[1], Kaiyang Zhou[1], Chen Huang[2],
and Chen Change Loy[1(✉)]

[1] S-Lab, Nanyang Technological University, Singapore, Singapore
{zang0012,wei.l,kaiyang.zhou,ccloy}@ntu.edu.sg
[2] Carnegie Mellon University, Pittsburgh, USA
chen-huang@apple.com

Abstract. Open-vocabulary object detection, which is concerned with the problem of detecting novel objects guided by natural language, has gained increasing attention from the community. Ideally, we would like to extend an open-vocabulary detector such that it can produce bounding box predictions based on user inputs in form of either natural language or exemplar image. This offers great flexibility and user experience for human-computer interaction. To this end, we propose a novel open-vocabulary detector based on DETR—hence the name OV-DETR—which, once trained, *can detect any object given its class name or an exemplar image*. The biggest challenge of turning DETR into an open-vocabulary detector is that it is impossible to calculate the classification cost matrix of novel classes without access to their labeled images. To overcome this challenge, we formulate the learning objective as a binary matching one between input queries (class name or exemplar image) and the corresponding objects, which learns useful correspondence to generalize to unseen queries during testing. For training, we choose to condition the Transformer decoder on the input embeddings obtained from a pre-trained vision-language model like CLIP, in order to enable matching for both text and image queries. With extensive experiments on LVIS and COCO datasets, we demonstrate that our OV-DETR—*the first end-to-end Transformer-based open-vocabulary detector*—achieves non-trivial improvements over current state of the arts. Code is available at https://github.com/yuhangzang/OV-DETR.

1 Introduction

Object detection, a fundamental computer vision task aiming to localize objects with tight bounding boxes in images, has been significantly advanced in the last decade thanks to the emergence of deep learning [9,15,25,29,32]. However, most object detection algorithms are unscalable in terms of the vocabulary size, *i.e.*, they are limited to a fixed set of object categories defined in detection

Supplementary Information The online version contains supplementary material available at https://doi.org/10.1007/978-3-031-20077-9_7.

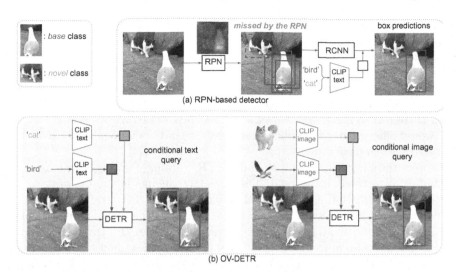

Fig. 1. Comparison between a RPN-based detector and our Open-Vocabulary Transformer-based detector (OV-DETR) using conditional queries. The RPN trained on closed-set object classes is easy to ignore novel classes (*e.g.*, the "cat" region receives little response). Hence the cats in this example are largely missed with few to no proposals. By contrast, our OV-DETR is trained to perform matching between a conditional query and its corresponding box, which helps to learn correspondence that can generalize to queries from unseen classes. Note we can take input queries in the form of either text (class name) or exemplar images, which offers greater flexibility for open-vocabulary object detection.

datasets [8,22]. For example, an object detector trained on COCO [22] can only detect 80 classes and is unable to handle new classes beyond the training ones.

A straightforward approach to detecting novel classes is to collect and add their training images to the original dataset, and then re-train or fine-tune the detection model. This is, however, both impractical and inefficient due to the large cost of data collection and model training. In the detection literature, generalization from base to novel classes has been studied as a zero-shot detection problem [1] where zero-shot learning techniques like word embedding projection [10] are widely used.

Recently, open-vocabulary detection, a new formulation that leverages large pre-trained language models, has gained increasing attention from the community [13,36]. The central idea in existing works is to align detector's features with embedding provided by models pre-trained on large scale image-text pairs like CLIP [27] (see Fig. 1(a)). This way, we can use an aligned classifier to recognize novel classes only from their descriptive texts.

A major problem with existing open-vocabulary detectors [13,36] is that they rely on region proposals that are often not reliable to cover all novel classes in an image due to the lack of training data, see Fig. 1(a). This problem has also been identified by a recent study [17], which suggests the binary nature of the region proposal network (RPN) could easily lead to overfitting to seen classes (thus fail to generalize to novel classes).

In this paper, we propose to train end-to-end an open-vocabulary detector under the Transformer framework, aiming to enhance its novel class generalization without using an intermediate RPN. To this end, we propose a novel open-vocabulary detector based on DETR [2]—hence the name OV-DETR— which is trained to *detect any object given its class name or an exemplar image*. This would offer greater flexibility than conventional open-vocabulary detection from natural language only.

Despite the simplicity of end-to-end DETR training, turning it into an open-vocabulary detector is non-trivial. The biggest challenge is the inability to calculate the classification cost for novel classes without their training labels. To overcome the challenge, we re-formulate the learning objective as binary matching between input queries (class name or exemplar image) and the corresponding objects. Such a matching loss over diverse training pairs allows to learn useful correspondence that can generalize to unseen queries during testing. For training, we extend the Transformer decoder of DETR to take conditional input queries. Specifically, we condition the Transformer decoder on the query embeddings obtained from a pre-trained vision-language model CLIP [27], in order to perform conditional matching for either text or image queries. Figure 1 shows this high-level idea, which proves better at detecting novel classes than RPN-based closed-set detectors.

We conduct comprehensive experiments on two challenging open-vocabulary object detection datasets, and show consistent improvements in performance. Concretely, our OV-DETR method achieves 17.4 mask mAP of novel classes on the open-vocabulary LVIS dataset [13] and 29.4 box mAP of novel classes on open-vocabulary COCO dataset [36], surpassing SOTA methods by 1.3 and 1.8 mAP, respectively.

2   Related Work

Open-Vocabulary Object Detection leverages the recent advances in large pre-trained language models [13,36] to incorporate the open-vocabulary information into object detectors. OVR-CNN [36] first uses BERT [6] to pre-train the Faster R-CNN detector [29] on image-caption pairs and then fine-tunes the model on downstream detection datasets. ViLD [13] adopts a distillation-based approach that aligns the image feature extractor of Mask R-CNN [15] with the image and text encoder of CLIP [27] so the CLIP can be used to synthesize the classification weights for any novel class. The prompt tuning techniques [37–39] for the pre-trained vision-language model have also been applied for open-vocabulary detectors, like DetPro [7]. Our approach differs from these works in that we train a Transformer-based detector end-to-end, with a novel framework of conditional matching.

Zero-Shot Object Detection is also concerned with the problem of detecting novel classes [1,20,28,31,40]. However, this setting is less practical due to the harsh constraint of limiting access to resources relevant to unseen classes [36].

A common approach to zero-shot detection is to employ word embeddings like GloVe [26] as the classifier weights [1]. Other works have found that using external resources like textual descriptions can help improve the generalization of classifier embeddings [20,28]. Alternatively, Zhao et al.. [31] used Generative Adversarial Network (GAN) [12] to generate feature representations of novel classes. While Zhu et al.. [40] synthesized unseen classes using a data augmentation strategy.

Visual Grounding is another relevant research area where the problem is to ground a target object in one image using natural language input [3,5]. Different from open-vocabulary detection that aims to identify all target objects in an image, the visual grounding methods typically involve a particular single object, hence cannot be directly applied to generic object detection. There is a relevant visual grounding method though, which is called MDETR [16]. This method similarly trains DETR along with a given language model so as to link the output tokens of DETR with specific words. MDETR also adopts a conditional framework, where the visual and textual features are combined to be fed to the Transformer encoder and decoder. However, the MDETR method is not applicable to open-vocabulary detection because it is unable to calculate the cost matrix for novel classes under the classification framework. Our OV-DETR bypasses this challenge by using a conditional matching framework instead.

Object Detection with Transformers. The pioneer DETR approach [2] greatly simplifies the detection pipeline by casting detection as a set-to-set matching problem. Several follow-up methods have been developed to improve performance and training efficiency. Deformable DETR [41] features a deformable attention module, which samples sparse pixel locations for computing attention, and further mitigates the slow convergence issue with a multi-scale scheme. SMCA [11] accelerates training convergence with a location-aware co-attention mechanism. Conditional DETR [24] also addresses the slow convergence issue, but with conditional spatial queries learned from reference points and the decoder embeddings. Our work *for the first time* extends DETR to the open-vocabulary domain by casting open-vocabulary detection as a conditional matching problem, and achieves non-trivial improvements over current SOTA.

3   Open-Vocabulary DETR

Our goal is to design a simple yet effective open-vocabulary object detector that can detect objects described by arbitrary text inputs or exemplar images. We build on the success of DETR [2] that casts object detection as an end-to-end set matching problem (among closed classes), thus eliminating the need of hand-crafted components like anchor generation and non-maximum suppression. This pipeline makes it appealing to act as a suitable framework to build our end-to-end open-vocabulary object detector.

However, it is non-trivial to retrofit a standard DETR with closed-set matching to an open-vocabulary detector that requires matching against unseen classes. One intuitive approach for such open-set matching is to learn a class-agnostic module (*e.g.*, ViLD [13]) to handle all classes. This is, however, still

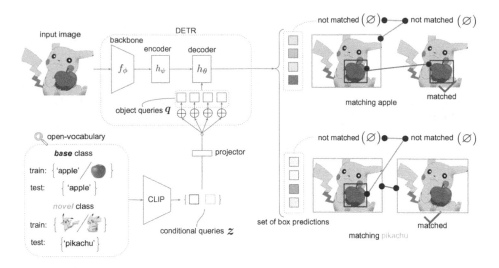

Fig. 2. Overview of OV-DETR. Unlike the standard DETR, our method does not separate 'objects' from 'non-objects' for a closed set of classes. Instead, OV-DETR performs open-vocabulary detection by measuring the matchability ('matched' vs. 'not matched') between some conditional inputs (text or exemplar image embeddings from CLIP) and detection results. We show such pipeline is flexible to detect open-vocabulary classes with arbitrary text or image inputs.

unable to match for those open-vocabulary classes that come with no labeled images. Here we provide a new perspective on the matching task in DETR, which leads us to reformulate the fixed set-matching objective into a conditional binary matching one between conditional inputs (text or image queries) and detection outputs.

An overview of our Open-Vocabulary DETR is shown in Fig. 2. At high level, DETR first takes query embeddings (text or image) as conditional inputs obtained from a pre-trained CLIP [27] model, and then a binary matching loss is imposed against the detection result to measure their matchability. In the following, we will revisit the closed-set matching process in standard DETR in Sect. 3.1. We then describe how to perform conditional binary matching in our OV-DETR in Sect. 3.2.

3.1   Revisiting Closed-Set Matching in DETR

For input image x, a standard DETR infers N object predictions $\hat{y}$ where N is determined by the fixed size of object queries q that serve as learnable positional encodings. One single pass of the DETR pipeline consists of two main steps: (i) set prediction, and (ii) optimal bipartite matching.

Set Prediction. Given an input image x, the global context representations c is first extracted by a CNN backbone f_ϕ and then a Transformer encoder h_ψ:

$$c = h_\psi(f_\phi(x)), \tag{1}$$

where the output c denotes a sequence of feature embeddings of q. Taking the context feature c and object queries q as inputs, the Transformer decoder h_θ (with prediction heads) then produce the set prediction $\hat{y} = \{\hat{y}_i\}_{i=1}^N$:

$$\hat{y} = h_\theta(c, q), \tag{2}$$

where $\hat{y}$ contains both bounding box predictions $\hat{b}$ and class predictions $\hat{p}$ for a closed-set of training classes.

Optimal Bipartite Matching is to find the best match between the set of N predictions $\hat{y}$ and the set of ground truth objects $y = \{y_i\}_{i=1}^M$ (including no object $\varnothing$). Specifically, one needs to search a permutation of N elements $\sigma \in \mathfrak{S}_N$ that has the lowest matching cost:

$$\hat{\sigma} = \arg\min_{\sigma \in \mathfrak{S}_N} \sum_i^N \mathcal{L}_{cost}(y_i, \hat{y}_{\sigma(i)}), \tag{3}$$

where $\mathcal{L}_{cost}(y_i, \hat{y}_{\sigma(i)})$ is a pair-wise *matching cost* between ground truth y_i and the prediction $\hat{y}_{\sigma(i)}$ with index $\sigma(i)$. Note $\mathcal{L}_{cost}$ is comprised of the losses for both class prediction $\mathcal{L}_{cls}(\hat{p}, p)$ and bounding box localization $\mathcal{L}_{box}(\hat{b}, b)$. The whole bipartite matching process produces *one-to-one* label assignments, where each prediction $\hat{y}_i$ is assigned to a ground-truth annotation y_j or $\varnothing$ (no object). The optimal assignment can be efficiently found by the Hungarian algorithm [18].

Challenge. As mentioned above, the bipartite matching method cannot be directly applied to an open-vocabulary setting that contains both *base* and *novel* classes. The reason is that computing the matching cost in Eq. (3) requires access of the label information, which is unavailable for *novel* classes. We can follow previous works [7,13,35] to generate class-agnostic object proposals that may cover the *novel* classes, but we do not know the ground-truth classification labels of these proposals. As a result, the predictions for the N object queries cannot generalize to novel classes due to the lack of training labels for them. As shown in Fig. 3(a), bipartite matching can only be performed for base classes with available training labels.

3.2 Conditional Matching for Open-Vocabulary Detection

To enable DETR to go beyond closed-set classification and perform open-vocabulary detection, we equip the Transformer decoder with conditional inputs and reformulate the learning objective as binary matching problem.

Conditional Inputs. Given an object detection dataset with standard annotations for all the training (*base*) classes, we need to convert those annotations to conditional inputs to facilitate our new training paradigm. Specifically, for each ground-truth annotation with bounding box b_i and class label name y_i^{class}, we use the CLIP model [27] to generate their corresponding image embedding z_i^{image} and text embedding z_i^{text}:

$$\begin{aligned} z_i^{image} &= \mathrm{CLIP}_{image}(x, b_i), \\ z_i^{text} &= \mathrm{CLIP}_{text}(y_i^{class}). \end{aligned} \tag{4}$$

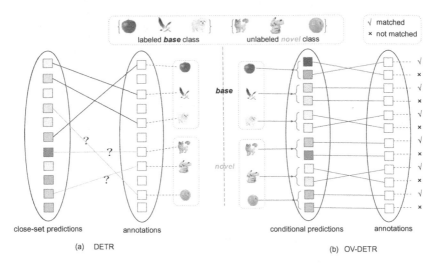

Fig. 3. Comparing the label assignment mechanisms of DETR and our OV-DETR. **(a)** In the original DETR, the set-to-set prediction is conducted via bipartite matching between predictions and closed-set annotations, in which a cost matrix in respect of the queries and categories. Due to the absence of class label annotations for *novel* classes, computing such a class-specific cost matrix is impossible. **(b)** On the contrary, our OV-DETR casts the open-vocabulary detection as a conditional matching process and formulate a binary matching problem that computes a class-agnostic matching cost matrix for conditional inputs.

Such image and text embeddings are already well-aligned by the CLIP model. Therefore, we can choose either of them as input queries to condition the DETR's decoder and train to match the corresponding objects. Once training is done, we can then take arbitrary input queries during testing to perform open-vocabulary detection. To ensure equal training conditioned on image and text queries, we randomly select z_i^{text} or z_i^{image} with probability $\xi = 0.5$ as conditional inputs. Moreover, we follow previous works [7,13,35] to generate additional object proposals for *novel* classes to enrich our training data. We only extract image embeddings z_i^{image} for such novel-class proposals as conditional inputs, since their class names are unavailable to extract text embeddings. Please refer to supplementary materials for more details.

Conditional Matching. Our core training objective is to measure the matchability between the conditional input embeddings and detection results. In order to perform such conditional matching, we start with a fully-connected layer $\mathbb{F}_{\text{proj}}$ to project the conditional input embeddings (z_i^{text} or z_i^{image}) to have the same dimension as q. Then the input to the DETR decoder q' is given by:

$$q' = q \oplus \mathbb{F}_{\text{proj}}(z_i^{\text{mod}}), \ \ \text{mod} \in \{\text{text}, \text{image}\}, \tag{5}$$

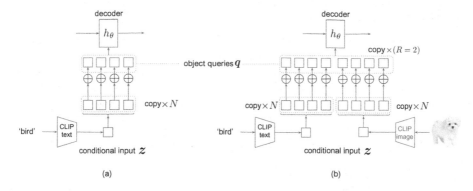

Fig. 4. DETR decoder with **(a)** single conditional input or **(b)** multiple conditional inputs in parallel.

where we use a simple addition operation $\oplus$ to convert the *class-agnostic* object queries $\boldsymbol{q}$ into *class-specific* $\boldsymbol{q}'$ informed by $\mathbb{F}_{\text{proj}}(\boldsymbol{z}_i^{\text{mod}})$.

In practice, adding the conditional input embeddings $\boldsymbol{z}$ to only one object query will lead to a very limited coverage of the target objects that may appear many times in the image. Indeed, in existing object detection datasets, there are typically multiple object instances in each image from the same or different classes. To enrich the training signal for our conditional matching, we copy the object queries $\boldsymbol{q}$ for R times, and the conditional inputs ($\boldsymbol{z}_i^{\text{text}}$ or $\boldsymbol{z}_i^{\text{image}}$) for N times before performing the conditioning in Eq. (5). As a result, we obtain a total of $N \times R$ queries for matching during each forward pass, as shown in Fig. 4(b). Experiments in the supplementary material will validate the importance of such "feature cloning" and also show how we determine N and R based on the performance-memory trade-off. Note for the final conditioning process, we further add an attention mask to ensure the independence between different query copies, as is similarly done in [4].

Given the conditioned query features $\boldsymbol{q}'$, our binary matching loss for label assignment is given as:

$$\mathcal{L}_{\text{cost}}(\boldsymbol{y}, \hat{\boldsymbol{y}}_\sigma) = \mathcal{L}_{\text{match}}(\boldsymbol{p}, \hat{\boldsymbol{p}}_\sigma) + \mathcal{L}_{\text{box}}\left(\boldsymbol{b}, \hat{\boldsymbol{b}}_\sigma\right), \tag{6}$$

where $\mathcal{L}_{\text{match}}(\boldsymbol{p}, \hat{\boldsymbol{p}}_\sigma)$ denotes a new matching loss that replaces the classification loss $\mathcal{L}_{\text{cls}}(\boldsymbol{p}, \hat{\boldsymbol{p}}_\sigma)$ in Eq. (3). Here in our case, $\boldsymbol{p}$ is a 1-dimensional sigmoid probability vector that characterizes the matchability ('matched' vs. 'not matched'), and $\mathcal{L}_{\text{match}}$ is simply implemented by a Focal loss [21] $\mathcal{L}_{\text{Focal}}$ between predicted $\hat{\boldsymbol{p}}_\sigma$ and groud-truth $\boldsymbol{p}$. For instance, with the 'bird' query as input, our matching loss should allow us to match all the bird instances in one image, while tagging instances from other classes as 'not matched'.

3.3 Optimization

After optimizing Eq. (6), we obtain the optimized label assignments σ for different object queries. This process produces a set of detected objects with assigned box coordinates $\hat{b}$ and 2-dim matching probability $\hat{p}$ that we will use to compute our final loss function for modeling training. We further attach an embedding reconstruction head to the model, which learns to predict embedding e to be able to reconstruct each conditional input embedding z^{text} or z^{image}:

$$\mathcal{L}_{\text{embed}}(e, z) = \left\| e - z^{\text{mod}} \right\|_1, \quad \text{mod} \in \{\text{text}, \text{image}\}. \tag{7}$$

2 Supplementary materials validate the effectiveness of $\mathcal{L}_{\text{embed}}$.

Our final loss for model training combines $\mathcal{L}_{\text{embed}}$ with bounding box losses $\mathcal{L}_{\text{match}}(p, \hat{p})$ and $\mathcal{L}_{\text{box}}(b, \hat{b})$ again:

$$\begin{aligned}
\mathcal{L}_{\text{loss}}(y, \hat{y}) &= \mathcal{L}_{\text{match}}(p, \hat{p}) + \mathcal{L}_{\text{box}}(b, \hat{b}) + \mathcal{L}_{\text{embed}}(e, z) \\
&= \lambda_{L_{\text{Focal}}} \mathcal{L}_{\text{Focal}} + \lambda_{L_{L1}} \mathcal{L}_{\text{L1}} + \lambda_{L_{\text{GIoU}}} \mathcal{L}_{\text{GIoU}} + \lambda_{L_{\text{embed}}} \mathcal{L}_{\text{embed}},
\end{aligned} \tag{8}$$

where $\mathcal{L}_{\text{box}}$ consists of the L1 loss and the generalized IoU (GIoU) [30] loss for boxes, while $\lambda_{L_{\text{Focal}}}$, $\lambda_{L_{L1}}$, $\lambda_{L_{\text{Giou}}}$ and $\lambda_{L_{\text{embed}}}$ are the weighting parameters.

3.4 Inference

During testing, for each image, we send the text embedding z^{text} of all the *base+novel* classes to the model and merge the results by selecting the top k predictions with highest prediction scores. We follow the prior work [13] to use $k = 100$ for COCO dataset and $k = 300$ for LVIS dataset. To obtain the context representation c in Eq. (1), we forward the input image through the CNN backbone f_ϕ and Transformer encoder h_ψ. Note c is computed only once and shared for all conditional inputs for efficiency. Then the conditioned object queries from different classes are sent to the Transformer decoder in parallel. In practice, we copy the object queries for R times as shown in Fig. 4(b).

4 Experiments

Datasets. We evaluate our approach on two standard open-vocabulary detection benchmarks modified from LVIS [14] and COCO [22] respectively. LVIS [14] contains 100K images with 1,203 classes. The classes are divided into three groups, namely frequent, common and rare, based on the number of training images. Following ViLD [13], we treat 337 rare classes as *novel* classes and use only the frequent and common classes for training. The COCO [22] dataset is a widely-used benchmark for object detection, which consists of 80 classes. Following OVR-CNN [36], we divide the classes in COCO into 48 *base* categories and 17 *novel* categories, while removing 15 categories without a synset in the WordNet hierarchy. The training set is the same as the full COCO but only images containing at least one *base* class are used. We refer to these two benchmarks as OV-LVIS and OV-COCO hereafter.

Table 1. Mask R-CNN and Def DETR on OV-LVIS, both trained on base classes. †: copied from ViLD [13].

#	Method	AP^m	AP^m_{novel}	AP^m_c	AP^m_f
1	Mask R-CNN†	22.5	0.0	22.6	32.4
2	Def DETR	22.4	0.0	22.4	32.0

Table 2. Ablation study on using object proposals (P) and our conditional binary matching mechanism (M).

#	P	M	AP^m	AP^m_{novel}	AP^m_c	AP^m_f
1			24.2	9.5	23.2	31.7
2	✓		19.9	6.3	17.4	28.6
3	✓	✓	**26.6**	**17.4**	**25.0**	**32.5**

Evaluation Metrics. For OV-LVIS, we report the mask mAP for rare, common and frequent classes, denoted by AP^m_r, AP^m_c and AP^m_f. The rare classes are treated as *novel* classes (AP^m_{novel}). The symbol AP^m denotes to the mAP of all the classes. For OV-COCO, we follow previous work that only reports the $AP50^b$ metric, which means the box mAP at IoU threshold 0.5.

Extension for Instance Segmentation. For OV-LVIS, instance segmentation results are needed for the evaluation process. Although DETR [2] and its follow-ups [24,41] are developed for the object detection task, they can also be extended to the instance segmentation task. We follow DETR [2] to add an external class-agnostic segmentation head to solve the instance segmentation task. The segmentation head employs the fully convolutional network (FCN [23]) structure, which takes features extracted from the Transformer decoder as input and produces segmentation masks.

Implementation Details. Our model is based on Deformable DETR [41]. Following ViLD [13], we also use the open-source CLIP model [27] based on ViT-B/32 for extracting text and image embeddings. Please refer to our supplementary material for more training details.

4.1 Ablation Studies

We conduct ablation study on OV-LVIS to evaluate the main components in our approach.

The Architecture Difference. Previous works such as ViLD [13] are based on the RPN-based Mask R-CNN [15], while our work is based on the Transformer-based detector Deformable DETR [41]. We first study the difference of these two detectors on the open-vocabulary setting trained with *base* classes only. As shown in Table 1 row(1-2), we observe that Mask R-CNN performs a slightly better than Deformable DETR [41]. This gap is small, indicating that we have a fair starting point compared to ViLD [13].

Object Proposals. We then replace Deformable DETR's classifier layer as text embedding provided by CLIP and trained with *base* classes only. This step is similar to the previous ViLD-text [13] method. Results is presented in Table 2 row 1. We observe that the AP^m_{novel} metric improved from 0.0 to 9.5. To further improve the AP^m_{novel} metric, we add the object proposals that may contain the region of *novel* classes into the training stage. Because we do not know the category id of these object proposals, we observe that the label assignment of these object proposals is inaccurate and will decrease the AP^m_{novel} performance from 9.5 to 6.3.

Table 3. Main results on OV-LVIS and OV-COCO. For OV-LVIS (w/ 886 base classes and 317 novel classes), we report mask mAP and a breakdown on novel (rare), common, and frequent classes. For OV-COCO (w/ 48 base classes and 17 novel classes), we report bounding box mAP at IoU threshold 0.5. †: zero-shot methods that do not use captions or image-text pairs. ‡: ensemble model.

#	Method	OV-LVIS				OV-COCO		
		AP^m	AP^m_{novel}	AP^m_c	AP^m_f	$AP50^b$	$AP50^b_{novel}$	$AP50^b_{base}$
1	SB [1]†	-	-	-	-	24.9	0.3	29.2
2	DELO [40]†	-	-	-	-	13.0	3.1	13.8
3	PL [28]†	-	-	-	-	27.9	4.1	35.9
4	OVR-CNN [36]	-	-	-	-	46.0	22.8	39.9
5	ViLD-text [13]	24.9	10.1	23.9	**32.5**	49.3	5.9	**61.8**
6	ViLD [13]	22.5	16.1	20.0	28.3	51.3	27.6	59.5
7	ViLD-ens. [13]‡	25.5	16.6	24.6	30.3	-	-	-
8	OV-DETR	**26.6**	**17.4**	**25.0**	**32.5**	**52.7**	**29.4**	61.0
	(ours vs. #6)	(+4.1)	(+1.3)	(+5.0)	(+4.2)	(+1.4)	(+1.8)	(+1.5)

Conditional Binary Matching. Now we replace DETR's default close-set labeling assignment as our proposed conditional binary matching. The comparison results between Table 2 row 2-3 shows that our binary matching strategy can better leverage the knowledge from object proposals and improve the AP^m_{novel} from 9.5 to 17.4. Such a large improvement shows that the proposed conditional matching is essential when applying the DETR-series detector for the open-vocabulary setting.

4.2 Results on Open-Vocabulary Benchmarks

Table 3 summarizes our results. We compare our method with SOTA open-vocabulary detection methods including: (1) OVR-CNN [36] (see Table 3 row

4). It pre-trains the detector's projecting layer on image-caption pairs using contrastive loss and then fine-tunes on the object detection task; (2) Variants of ViLD [13] such as ViLD-text and ViLD-ensemble (see Table 3 rows 5-7). ViLD is the first study that uses CLIP embeddings [27] for open-vocabulary detection. Compared with ViLD-text, ViLD uses knowledge distillation from the CLIP visual backbone, improves AP_{novel} at the cost of hurting AP_{base}. ViLD-ens. combines the two models and shows improvements for both metrics. Such an ensemble-based method also brings extra time and memory cost.

For completeness, we also list the results of some previous zero-shot methods such as SB [1], DELO [40] and PL [28] in Table 3 rows 1-3. On *OV-LVIS* benchmark, OV-DETR improves the previous SOTA ViLD by 4.1 on AP^m and 1.3 on AP^m_{novel}. Compared with ViLD, our method will not affect the performance of *base* classes when improve the *novel* classes. Even compared with the ensemble result of ViLD-ensemble, OV-DETR still boosts the performance by 1.5, 0.8, 1.0 and 2.2, respectively (%). Noted that OV-DETR only uses a single model and does not leverage any ensemble-based technique. On *OV-COCO* benchmark, OV-DETR improves the baseline and outperforms OVR-CNN [36] by a large margin, notably, the 6.6 mAP improvements on *novel* classes. Compared with ViLD [13], OV-DETR still achieves 1.4 mAP gains on all the classs and 1.8 mAP gains on *novel* classes. In summary, it is observed that OV-DETR achieves superior performance across different datasets compared with different methods.

Table 4. Generalization to Other Datasets. We evaluate OV-DETR trained on LVIS when transferred to other datasets such as PASCAL VOC 2007 test set and COCO validation set by simply replacing the text embeddings. The experimental setting is the same as that of ViLD [13]. We observe that OV-DETR achieves better generalization performance than ViLD [13].

#	Method	Pascal VOC		COCO		
		AP^b_{50}	AP^b_{75}	AP^b	AP^b_{50}	AP^b_{75}
1	ViLD-text [13]	40.5	31.6	28.8	43.4	31.4
2	ViLD [13]	72.2	56.7	36.6	55.6	39.8
3	OV-DETR	**76.1**	**59.3**	**38.1**	**58.4**	**41.1**
	(ours vs #2)	(+3.9)	(+2.6)	(+1.5)	(+2.8)	(+1.3)

4.3   Generalization Ability of OV-DETR

We follow ViLD [13] to test the generalization ability of OV-DETR by training the model on LVIS [14] dataset and evaluated on PASCAL VOC [8] and COCO [22]. We keep the same implementation details with ViLD [13]. We switch the text embeddings of the category names from the source dataset to new datasets. The text embeddings of new classes are used as conditional inputs during the inference phase. As shown in Table 4, we observe that OV-DETR achieves better transfer performance than ViLD. The experimental results show that the model trained by our conditional-based mechanism has transferability to other domains.

4.4 Qualitative Results

We visualize OV-DETR's detection and segmentation results in Fig. 5. The results based on conditional text queries, conditional image queries, and a mixture of conditional text and image queries are shown in the top, middle and bottom row, respectively. Overall, our OV-DETR can accurately localize and precisely segment out the target objects from novel classes despite no annotations of these classes during training. It is worth noting that the conditional image queries, such as "crape" in (d) and "fork" in (h), appear drastically different from those in the target images but OV-DETR can still robustly detect them.

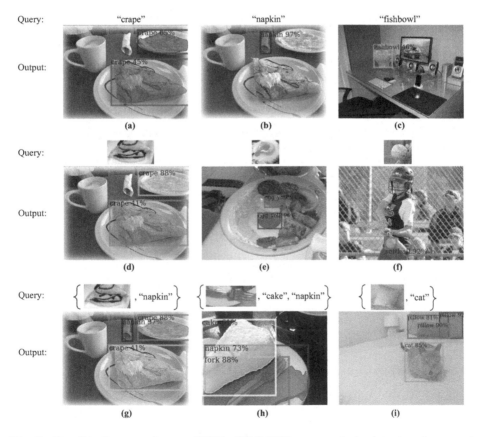

Fig. 5. Qualitative results on LVIS. OV-DETR can precisely detect and segment novel objects (*e.g.*, 'crape', 'fishbowl', 'softball') given the conditional text query (top) or conditional image query (middle) or a mixture of them (bottom).

4.5   Inference Time Analysis

OV-DETR exhibits great potential in open-vocabulary detection but is by no means a perfect detector. The biggest limitation of OV-DETR is that the inference speed is slow when the number of classes to detect is huge like 1,203 on LVIS [13]. This problem is caused by the conditional design that requires multiple forward passes in the Transformer decoder (depending on the number of classes).

We show a detailed comparison on the inference time between Deformable DETR and OV-DETR in Table 5. Without using any tricks, the vanilla OV-DETR (#2), i.e., using a single forward pass for each class, is about 2× slower than Deformable DETR (#1) on COCO (w/ 80 classes) while 16× slower on LVIS (w/ 1,203 classes). As discussed in Sect. 3.2 and shown in Fig. 4(b), we optimize the speed by forwarding multiple conditional queries to the Transformer decoder in parallel, which reduces the inference time by 12.5% on COCO and nearly 60% on LVIS (see #3 in Table 5). Still, there is much room for improvement.

Table 5. Comparison of the inference time (second per iteration) between Deformable DETR [41] and our OV-DETR before/after optimization on LVIS and COCO.

#	Method	COCO	LVIS
1	Def DETR	0.31	1.49
2	Ours	0.72	23.84
3	Ours (optimized)	0.63	9.57
	(vs #2)	(+↓ 12.5%)	(+↓ 59.9%)

It is worth noting that such a slow inference problem is not unique to our approach—most instance-conditional models would have the same issue [19], which is the common price to pay in exchange for better performance. The computation bottleneck of our method lies in the computation of the Transformer decoder in Eq. (2). A potential solution is to design more efficient attention modules [33,34], which we leave as future work. In human-computer interaction where users already have target object(s) in mind, e.g., a missing luggage or a specific type of logo, the conditional input is fixed and low in number, thus the inference time is negligible.

5   Conclusion

Open-vocabulary detection is known to be a challenging problem due to the lack of training data for unseen classes. Recent advances in large language models have offered a new perspective for designing open-vocabulary detectors. In this work, we show how an end-to-end Transformer-based detector can be turned into an open-vocabulary detector based on conditional matching and with the help of pre-trained vision-language models. The results show that, despite having a simplified training pipeline, our open-vocabulary detector based on Transformer significantly outperforms current state of the arts that are all based on two-stage detectors. We hope our approach and the findings presented in the paper can inspire more future work on the design of efficient open-vocabulary detectors.

Acknowledgments. This study is supported under the RIE2020 Industry Alignment Fund Industry Collaboration Projects (IAF-ICP) Funding Initiative, as well as cash and in-kind contribution from the industry partner(s). It is also partly supported by the NTU NAP grant and Singapore MOE AcRF Tier 2 (MOE-T2EP20120-0001). This work was supported by SenseTime SenseCore AI Infrastructure-AIDC.

References

1. Bansal, A., Sikka, K., Sharma, G., Chellappa, R., Divakaran, A.: Zero-shot object detection. In: Ferrari, V., Hebert, M., Sminchisescu, C., Weiss, Y. (eds.) ECCV 2018. LNCS, vol. 11205, pp. 397–414. Springer, Cham (2018). https://doi.org/10.1007/978-3-030-01246-5_24
2. Carion, N., Massa, F., Synnaeve, G., Usunier, N., Kirillov, A., Zagoruyko, S.: End-to-end object detection with transformers. In: Vedaldi, A., Bischof, H., Brox, T., Frahm, J.-M. (eds.) ECCV 2020. LNCS, vol. 12346, pp. 213–229. Springer, Cham (2020). https://doi.org/10.1007/978-3-030-58452-8_13
3. Chen, K., Kovvuri, R., Nevatia, R.: Query-guided regression network with context policy for phrase grounding. In: ICCV, pp. 824–832 (2017)
4. Dai, Z., Cai, B., Lin, Y., Chen, J.: UP-DETR: unsupervised pre-training for object detection with transformers. In: CVPR, pp. 1601–1610 (2021)
5. Deng, C., Wu, Q., Wu, Q., Hu, F., Lyu, F., Tan, M.: Visual grounding via accumulated attention. In: CVPR, pp. 7746–7755 (2018)
6. Devlin, J., Chang, M.W., Lee, K., Toutanova, K.: Bert: Pre-training of deep bidirectional transformers for language understanding. arXiv preprint arXiv:1810.04805 (2018)
7. Du, Y., Wei, F., Zhang, Z., Shi, M., Gao, Y., Li, G.: Learning to prompt for open-vocabulary object detection with vision-language model. In: CVPR, pp. 14084–14093 (2022)
8. Everingham, M., Van Gool, L., Williams, C.K., Winn, J., Zisserman, A.: The pascal visual object classes (VOC) challenge. IJCV 88(2), 303–338 (2010)
9. Felzenszwalb, P., McAllester, D., Ramanan, D.: A discriminatively trained, multi-scale, deformable part model. In: CVPR, pp. 1–8. Ieee (2008)
10. Frome, A., et al.: Devise: A deep visual-semantic embedding model. In: NeurIPS (2013)
11. Gao, P., Zheng, M., Wang, X., Dai, J., Li, H.: Fast convergence of DETR with spatially modulated co-attention. In: ICCV, pp. 3621–3630 (2021)
12. Goodfellow, I., et al.: Generative adversarial nets. In: NeurIPS, vol. 27 (2014)
13. Gu, X., Lin, T.Y., Kuo, W., Cui, Y.: Open-vocabulary object detection via vision and language knowledge distillation. In: ICLR (2022)
14. Gupta, A., Dollar, P., Girshick, R.: LVIS: a dataset for large vocabulary instance segmentation. In: CVPR, pp. 5356–5364 (2019)

15. He, K., Gkioxari, G., Dollár, P., Girshick, R.: Mask r-cnn. In: ICCV. pp. 2961–2969 (2017)
16. Kamath, A., Singh, M., LeCun, Y., Synnaeve, G., Misra, I., Carion, N.: Mdetr-modulated detection for end-to-end multi-modal understanding. In: ICCV. pp. 1780–1790 (2021)
17. Kim, D., Lin, T.Y., Angelova, A., Kweon, I.S., Kuo, W.: Learning open-world object proposals without learning to classify. Rob. Autom. Lett. **7**(2), :1-1 (2022)
18. Kuhn, H.W.: The Hungarian method for the assignment problem. Naval Res. Logist Q. **2**(1–2), 83–97 (1955)
19. Li, S., Xiao, T., Li, H., Zhou, B., Yue, D., Wang, X.: Person search with natural language description. In: CVPR, pp. 1970–1979 (2017)
20. Li, Z., Yao, L., Zhang, X., Wang, X., Kanhere, S., Zhang, H.: Zero-shot object detection with textual descriptions. In: AAAI, pp. 8690–8697 (2019)
21. Lin, T.Y., Goyal, P., Girshick, R.B., He, K., Dollár, P.: Focal loss for dense object detection. In: ICCV, pp. 2999–3007 (2017)
22. Liu, T.Y., et al.: Microsoft COCO: common objects in context. In: Fleet, D., Pajdla, T., Schiele, B., Tuytelaars, T. (eds.) ECCV 2014. LNCS, vol. 8693, pp. 740–755. Springer, Cham (2014). https://doi.org/10.1007/978-3-319-10602-1_48
23. Lin, T., et al.: Microsoft COCO: common objects in context. In: Fleet, D., Pajdla, T., Schiele, B., Tuytelaars, T. (eds.) ECCV 2014. LNCS, vol. 8693, pp. 740–755. Springer, Cham (2014). https://doi.org/10.1007/978-3-319-10602-1_48
24. Meng, D., et al.: Conditional DETR for fast training convergence. In: ICCV, pp. 3651–3660 (2021)
25. Papageorgiou, C., Poggio, T.: A trainable system for object detection. Int. J. Comput. Vis. **38**(1), 15–33 (2000)
26. Pennington, J., Socher, R., Manning, C.D.: Glove: Global vectors for word representation. In: EMNLP, pp. 1532–1543 (2014)
27. Radford, A., et al.: Learning transferable visual models from natural language supervision. arXiv preprint arXiv:2103.00020 (2021)
28. Rahman, T., Chou, S.H., Sigal, L., Carenini, G.: An improved attention for visual question answering. In: CVPR, pp. 1653–1662 (2021)
29. Ren, S., He, K., Girshick, R., Sun, J.: Faster r-CNN: towards real-time object detection with region proposal networks. In: NeurIPS, vol. 28, 91–99 (2015)
30. Rezatofighi, H., Tsoi, N., Gwak, J., Sadeghian, A., Reid, I., Savarese, S.: Generalized intersection over union: a metric and a loss for bounding box regression. In: CVPR, pp. 658–666 (2019)
31. Shizhen, Z., et al.: GtNet: generative transfer network for zero-shot object detection. In: AAAI (2020)
32. Szegedy, C., Toshev, A., Erhan, D.: Deep neural networks for object detection. In: NeurIPS, vol. 26 (2013)
33. Tay, Y., Bahri, D., Yang, L., Metzler, D., Juan, D.C.: Sparse sinkhorn attention. In: ICML, pp. 9438–9447. PMLR (2020)
34. Wang, S., Li, B.Z., Khabsa, M., Fang, H., Ma, H.: Linformer: self-attention with linear complexity. arXiv preprint arXiv:2006.04768 (2020)
35. Xie, J., Zheng, S.: ZSD-yolo: zero-shot yolo detection using vision-language knowledgedistillationa. arXiv preprint arXiv:2109.12066 (2021)
36. Zareian, A., Rosa, K.D., Hu, D.H., Chang, S.F.: Open-vocabulary object detection using captions. In: CVPR, pp. 14393–14402 (2021)
37. Zhang, Y., Zhou, K., Liu, Z.: Neural prompt search. arXiv (2022)
38. Zhou, K., Yang, J., Loy, C.C., Liu, Z.: Conditional prompt learning for vision-language models. In: CVPR (2022)

39. Zhou, K., Yang, J., Loy, C.C., Liu, Z.: Learning to prompt for vision-language models. In: IJCV (2022)
40. Zhu, P., Wang, H., Saligrama, V.: Don't even look once: Synthesizing features for zero-shot detection. In: CVPR, pp. 11693–11702 (2020)
41. Zhu, X., Su, W., Lu, L., Li, B., Wang, X., Dai, J.: Deformable DETR: deformable transformers for end-to-end object detection. In: ICLR (2020)

Prediction-Guided Distillation for Dense Object Detection

Chenhongyi Yang[1]([✉]), Mateusz Ochal[2,3], Amos Storkey[2],
and Elliot J. Crowley[1]

[1] School of Engineering, University of Edinburgh, Edinburgh, UK
chenhongyi.yang@ed.ac.uk
[2] School of Informatics, University of Edinburgh, Edinburgh, UK
[3] School of Engineering and Physical Sciences, Heriot-Watt University,
Edinburgh, UK

Abstract. Real-world object detection models should be cheap and accurate. Knowledge distillation (KD) can boost the accuracy of a small, cheap detection model by leveraging useful information from a larger teacher model. However, a key challenge is identifying the most informative features produced by the teacher for distillation. In this work, we show that only a very small fraction of features within a ground-truth bounding box are responsible for a teacher's high detection performance. Based on this, we propose Prediction-Guided Distillation (PGD), which focuses distillation on these *key predictive regions* of the teacher and yields considerable gains in performance over many existing KD baselines. In addition, we propose an adaptive weighting scheme over the key regions to smooth out their influence and achieve even better performance. Our proposed approach outperforms current state-of-the-art KD baselines on a variety of advanced one-stage detection architectures. Specifically, on the COCO dataset, our method achieves between +3.1% and +4.6% AP improvement using ResNet-101 and ResNet-50 as the teacher and student backbones, respectively. On the CrowdHuman dataset, we achieve +3.2% and +2.0% improvements in MR and AP, also using these backbones. Our code is available at https://github.com/ChenhongyiYang/PGD.

Keywords: Dense object detection · Knowledge distillation

1 Introduction

Advances in deep learning have led to considerable performance gains on object detection tasks [2,6,11,15,18,25–27,31]. However, detectors can be computationally expensive, making it challenging to deploy them on devices with limited resources. Knowledge distillation (KD) [1,13] has emerged as a promising approach for compressing models. It allows for the direct training of a smaller student

Supplementary Information The online version contains supplementary material available at https://doi.org/10.1007/978-3-031-20077-9_8.

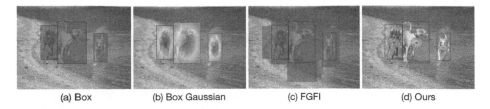

(a) Box   (b) Box Gaussian   (c) FGFI   (d) Ours

Fig. 1. A comparison between different foreground distillation regions. The ground-truth bounding box is marked in blue. The colour heatmaps indicate the distillation weight for different areas. In contrast to other methods (a)–(c) [9,30,34], Our approach (d) focuses on a few key predictive regions of the teacher.

model [17,24,28,33] using information from a larger, more powerful teacher model; this helps the student to generalise better than if trained alone.

KD was first popularised for image classification [13] where a student model is trained to mimic the *soft labels* generated by a teacher model. However, this approach does not work well for object detection [34] which consists of jointly classifying and localising objects. While soft label-based KD can be directly applied for classification, finding an equivalent for localisation remains a challenge. Recent work [8,9,30,34,35,37,41] alleviates this problem by forcing the student model to generate feature maps similar to the teacher counterpart; a process known as *feature imitation.*

However, which features should the student imitate? This question is of the utmost importance for dense object detectors [6,15,18,31,38,42] because, unlike two-stage detectors [2,11,27], they do not use the RoIAlign [11] operation to explicitly pool and align object features; instead they output predictions at every location of the feature map [16]. Recent work [30,35] has shown that distilling the whole feature map with equal weighting is sub-optimal because not all features carry equally meaningful information. Therefore, a weighting mechanism that assigns appropriate importance to different regions, particularly to *foreground* regions near the objects, is highly desirable for dense object detectors, and has featured in recent work. For example, in DeFeat [9], foreground features that lie within ground truth (GT) boxes (Fig. 1a) are distilled with equal weighting. In [30] the authors postulate that useful features are located at the centre of GT boxes and weigh the foreground features using a Gaussian (Fig. 1b). In Fine-grained Feature Imitation (FGFI) [34], the authors distil features covered by anchor boxes whose Intersection over Union (IoU) with the GTs are above a certain threshold (Fig. 1c).

In this paper, we treat feature imitation for foreground regions differently. Instead of assigning distillation weights using hand-design policies, we argue that feature imitation should be conducted on a few *key predictive regions*: the locations where the teacher model generates the most accurate predictions. Our intuition is that these regions should be distilled because they hold the information that leads to the best predictions; other areas will be less informative and can contaminate the distillation process by distracting from more essential features. To achieve our goal, we adapt the *quality* measure from [6] to score teacher predictions. Then, we conduct an experiment to visualise how these scores are distributed and verify that high-scoring *key predictive regions* contribute the most to teacher performance. Those findings drive us to propose a *Prediction-Guided Weighting* (PGW) module to weight the foreground distillation loss: inspired by recent progress in label assignment [6,20,32,38,42] for dense detectors, we sample the top-K positions with the highest quality score from the teacher model and use an adaptive Gaussian distribution to fit the *key predictive regions* for smoothly weighting the distillation loss. Figure 1d shows a visual representation of the regions selected for distillation. We call our method Prediction-Guided Distillation (PGD). Our contributions are as follows:

1. We conduct experiments to study how the *quality* scores of teacher predictions are distributed in the image plane and observe that the locations that make up the top-1% of scores are responsible for most of the teacher's performance in modern state-of-the-art dense detectors.
2. Based on our observations, we propose using the *key predictive regions* of the teacher as foreground features. We show that focusing distillation mainly on these few areas yields significant performance gains for the student model.
3. We introduce a parameterless weighting scheme for foreground distillation pixels and show that when applied to our *key predictive regions*, we achieve even stronger distillation performance.
4. We benchmark our approach on the COCO and CrowdHuman datasets and show its superiority over the state-of-the-art across multiple detectors.

2   Related Work

Dense Object Detection. In the last few years, object detection has seen considerable gains in performance [2,3,6,11,15,18,25–27,31]. The demand for simple, fast models has brought one-stage detectors into the spotlight [6,31]. In contrast to two-stage detectors, one-stage detectors directly regress and classify candidate bounding boxes from a pre-defined set of anchor boxes (or anchor points), alleviating the need for a separate region proposal mechanism. Anchor-based detectors [6,18] achieve good performance by regressing from anchor boxes with pre-defined sizes and ratios. In contrast, anchor-free methods [15,31,42] regress directly from anchor points (or locations), eliminating the need for the additional hyper-parameters used in anchor-based models. A vital challenge for detectors is determining which bounding box predictions to label as positive and negative – a problem frequently referred to as *label assignment* [42]. Anchors are commonly labelled as positives when their IoU with the GT is over a certain threshold (e.g. IoU $\geq$ 0.5) [18,31], however, more elaborate mechanisms for label assignment have been proposed [6,31,38,42]. For example, FCOS [31] applies a weighting scheme to suppress low-quality positive predictions using a "centerness" score. Other works dynamically adjust the number of positive instances according to statistical characteristics [38] or by using a differentiable confidence module [42]. In DDOD [6], the authors separate label assignment for the classification and regression branches and balance the influence of positive samples between different scales of the feature pyramid network (FPN).

Knowledge Distillation for Object Detection. Early KD approaches for classification focus on transferring knowledge to student models by forcing their predictions to match those of the teacher [13]. More recent work [34, 35, 41] claims that feature imitation, i.e. forcing the intermediate feature maps of student models to match their teacher counterpart, is more effective for detection. A vital challenge when performing feature imitation for dense object detectors is determining which feature regions to distil from the teacher model. Naively distilling all feature maps equally results in poor performance [9, 30, 35]. To solve this problem, FGFI [34] distils features that are covered by anchor boxes which have a high IoU with the GT. However, distilling in this manner is still suboptimal [8, 30, 35, 40, 41]. TADF [30] suppresses foreground pixels according to a static 2D Gaussian fitted over the GT. LD [40] gives higher priority to central locations of the GT using DIoU [39]. GID [8] propose to use the top-scoring predictions using L1 distance between the classifications scores of the teacher and the student, but do not account for location quality. In LAD [21], the authors use *label assignment* distillation where the detector's encoded labels are used to train a student. Others weight foreground pixels according to intricate adaptive weighting or attention mechanisms [8, 14, 35, 36, 41]. However, these weighting schemes still heavily rely on the GT dimensions, and they are agnostic to the capabilities of the teacher. In contrast, we focus distillation on only a few *key predictive regions* using a combination of classification and regression scores as a measure of quality. We then smoothly aggregate and weigh the selected locations using an estimated 2D Gaussian, which further focuses distillation and improves performance. This allows us to dynamically adjusts to different sizes and orientations of objects independently of the GT dimensions while accounting for the teacher's predictive abilities.

3   Method

We begin by describing how to measure the predictive quality of a bounding box prediction and find the *key predictive regions* of a teacher network (Sect. 3.1). Then, we introduce our *Prediction-Guided Weighting* (PGW) module that returns a foreground distillation mask based on these regions (Sect. 3.2). Finally, we describe our full Prediction-Guided Distillation pipeline (Sect. 3.3).

3.1   Key Predictive Regions

Our goal is to amplify the distillation signal for the most meaningful features produced by a teacher network. For this purpose, we look at the *quality* of a teacher's bounding box predictions taking both classification and localisation into consideration, as defined in [6]. Formally, the quality score of a box $\hat{b}_{(i,j)}$ predicted from a position $X_i = (x_i, y_i)$ w.r.t. a ground truth b is:

$$q(\hat{b}_{(i,j)}, b) = \underbrace{\mathbb{1}\left[X_i \in b\right]}_{\text{indicator}} \cdot \underbrace{\left(\hat{p}_{(i,j)}(b)\right)^{1-\xi}}_{\text{classification}} \cdot \underbrace{\left(\text{IoU}\left(b, \hat{b}_{(i,j)}\right)\right)^{\xi}}_{\text{localisation}} \tag{1}$$

(a) ATSS   (b) FCOS   (c) AutoAssign   (d) GFL   (e) DDOD

Fig. 2. A visualisation of quality scores for various dense object detectors with $\xi = 0.8$ following [6]. We acquire the quality heatmap by taking the maximum value at each position across FPN layers.

where $\mathbb{1}\,[X_i \in \Omega_b]$ is an indicator function that is 1 if X_i lies inside box b and 0 otherwise; $\hat{p}_{(i,j)}(b)$ is the classification probability w.r.t. the GT box's category; $\text{IoU}\big(b, \hat{b}_{(i,j)}\big)$ is the IoU between the predicted and ground-truth box; ξ is a hyper-parameter that balances classification and localisation. We calculate the quality score of location X_i as the maximum value of all prediction scores for that particular location, i.e. $\hat{q}_i = max_{j \in J_i}\, q(\hat{b}_{(i,j)}, b)$, where J_i is the set of predictions at location X_i. While this quality score has been applied for standard object detection [6], we are the first to use it to identify useful regions for distillation.

In Fig. 2 we visualise the heatmaps of prediction quality scores for five state-of-the-art detectors, including anchor-based (ATSS [38] and DDOD [6]) and anchor-free (FCOS [31], GFL [15] and AutoAssign [42]) detectors. Across all detectors, we observe some common characteristics: (1) For the vast majority of objects, high scores are concentrated around a **single region**; (2) The size of this region doesn't necessarily correlate strongly with the size of the actual GT box; (3) Whether or not the centring prior [31,42] is applied for label assignment during training, this region tends to be close to the centre of the GT box. These observations drive us to develop a *Prediction-Guided Weighting* (PGW) module to focus the distillation on these important regions.

3.2 Prediction-Guided Weighting Module

The purpose of KD is to allow a student to mimic a teacher's strong generalisation ability. To better achieve this goal, we propose to focus foreground distillation on locations where a teacher model can yield predictions with the highest quality scores because those locations contain the most valuable information for detection and are critical to a teacher's high performance. In Fig. 3 we present the results of a pilot experiment to identify how vital these high-scoring locations are for a detector. Specifically, we measure the performance of different pre-trained detectors after masking out their top-$X\%$ predictions before non-maximum suppression (NMS) during inference. We observe that in all cases the mean Averaged Precision (mAP) drops dramatically as the mask-out ratio increases. Masking out the top-1% of predictions incurs around a 50% drop in

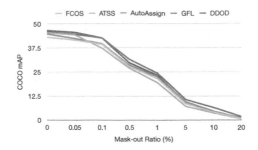

Fig. 3. COCO mAP performance of pre-trained detectors after ignoring predictions in the top-X% of quality scores during inference. We observe that the top-1% predictions within the GT box region are responsible for most performance gains.

AP. This suggests that the *key predictive regions* (responsible for the majority of a dense detector's performance) lie within the top-1% of all anchor positions bounded by the GT box.

Given their significance, how do we incorporate these regions into distillation? We could simply use all feature locations weighted by their quality score, however, as we show in Sect. 4.3 this does not yield the best performance. Inspired by recent advances in label assignment for dense object detectors [6,32], we instead propose to focus foreground distillation on the top-K positions (feature pixels) with the highest quality scores across all FPN levels. We then smooth the influence of each position according to a 2D Gaussian distribution fitted by Maximum-Likelihood Estimation (MLE) for each GT box. Finally, foreground distillation is conducted only on those K positions with their weights assigned by the Gaussian.

Formally, for an object o with GT box b, we first compute the quality score for each feature pixel inside b, then we select the K pixels with the highest quality score $T^o = \{(X_k^o, l_k^o) | k = 1, ..., K\}$ across all FPN levels, in which X_k^o and l_k^o are the absolute coordinate and the FPN level of the k-th pixel. Based on our observation in Sect. 3.1, we assume the selected pixels T_k^o are drawn as $T_k^o \sim \mathcal{N}(\mu, \Sigma | o)$ defined on the image plane and use MLE to estimate μ and Σ:

$$\hat{\mu} = \frac{1}{K} \sum_{k=1}^{K} X_k^o, \quad \hat{\Sigma} = \frac{1}{K} \sum_{k=1}^{K} (X_k^o - \hat{\mu})(X_k^o - \hat{\mu})^T \qquad (2)$$

Then, for every feature pixel $P_{(i,j),l}$ on FPN layer l with absolute coordinate $X_{i,j}$, we compute its distillation importance w.r.t. object o by:

$$I_{(i,j),l}^o = \begin{cases} 0 & P_{(i,j),l} \notin T^o \\ \exp\left(-\frac{1}{2}(X_{i,j} - \hat{\mu})\hat{\Sigma}^{-1}(X_{i,j} - \hat{\mu})^T\right) & P_{(i,j),l} \in T^o \end{cases} \qquad (3)$$

If a feature pixel has non-zero importance for multiple objects, we use its maximum: $I_{(i,j),l} = \max_o \{I_{(i,j),l}^o\}$. Finally, for each FPN level l with size $H_l \times W_l$, we assign the distillation weight $M_{(i,j),l}$ by normalising the distillation importance by the number of non-zero importance pixels at that level:

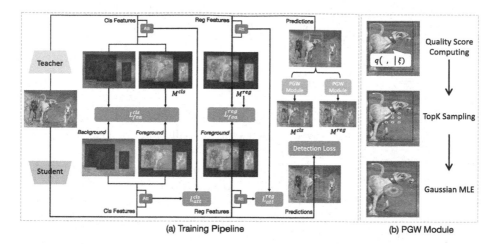

(a) Training Pipeline   (b) PGW Module

Fig. 4. Our Prediction-Guided Distillation (PGD) pipeline. The *Prediction-Guided Weighting* (PGW) modules find the teacher's *key predictive regions* and generates a foreground distillation weighting mask by fitting a Gaussian over these regions. Our pipeline also adopts the attention masks from FGD [35] and distils them together with the features. We distil the classification and regression heads separately to accommodate for these two distinct tasks [6].

$$\mathbf{M}_{(\mathbf{i,j}),\mathbf{l}} = \frac{I_{(i,j),l}}{\sum_{i=1}^{H_l} \sum_{j=1}^{W_l} \mathbb{1}_{(i,j),l}} \tag{4}$$

where $\mathbb{1}_{(i,j),l}$ is an indicator function that outputs 1 if $I_{(i,j),l}$ is not zero. The process above constitutes our *Prediction-Guided Weighting* (PGW) module whose output is a foreground distillation weight $\mathbf{M}$ across all feature levels and pixels.

3.3   Prediction-Guided Distillation

In this section, we introduce our KD pipeline, which is applicable to any dense object detector. We build our work on top of the state-of-the-art Focal and Global Distillation (FGD) [35] and incorporate their spatial and channel-wise attention mechanisms. In contrast to other distillation methods, we use the output mask from our PGW module to focus the distillation loss on the most important foreground regions. Moreover, we decouple the distillation for the classification and regression heads to better suit the two different tasks [6,22]. An illustration of the pipeline is shown in Fig. 4.

Distillation of Features. We perform feature imitation at each FPN level, encouraging feature imitation on the first feature maps of the regression and classifications heads. Taking inspiration from [6], we separate the distillation process for the classification and regression heads – distilling features of each head independently. Formally, at each feature level of the FPN, we generate two foreground distillation masks $\mathbf{M^{cls}}, \mathbf{M^{reg}} \in \mathbb{R}^{H \times W}$ with different ξ^{cls} and ξ^{reg} using PGW. Then, student features $F^{S,cls}, F^{S,reg} \in \mathbb{R}^{C \times H \times W}$ are encouraged to mimic teacher features $F^{T,cls}, F^{T,reg} \in \mathbb{R}^{C \times H \times W}$ as follows:

$$L_{fea}^{cls} = \sum_{k=1}^{C}\sum_{i=1}^{H}\sum_{j=1}^{W}(\alpha \mathbf{M}_{i,j}^{cls} + \beta N_{i,j}^{cls})P_{i,j}^{T,cls}A_{k,i,j}^{T,cls}(F_{k,i,j}^{T,cls} - F_{k,i,j}^{S,cls})^2 \qquad (5)$$

$$L_{fea}^{reg} = \sum_{k=1}^{C}\sum_{i=1}^{H}\sum_{j=1}^{W}\gamma \mathbf{M}_{i,j}^{reg}A_{k}^{T,reg}(F_{k,i,j}^{T,reg} - F_{k,i,j}^{S,reg})^2 \qquad (6)$$

where α, β, γ are hyperparameters to balance between loss weights; N^{cls} is the normalised mask over background distillation regions: $N_{i,j}^{cls} = \mathbb{1}_{i,j}^{-}/\sum_{h=1,w=1}^{H,W}\mathbb{1}_{w,h}^{-}$ where $\mathbb{1}_{a,b}^{-}$ is the background indicator that becomes 1 if pixel (a,b) does not lie within any GT box. P and A are spatial and channel attention maps from [35] as defined below. Note, we do not use the Global Distillation Module in FGD and the adaptation layer that is commonly used in many KD methods [4,9,34,35,37,41] as we find them have negligible impact to the overall performance.

Distillation of Attention. We build on the work in FGD [35] and additionally encourage the student to imitate the attention maps of the teacher. We use spatial attention as defined in [35], but we modify their channel attention by computing it independently for each feature location instead of all spatial locations. Specifically, we define spatial attention $\mathbf{P} \in \mathbb{R}^{1 \times H \times W}$ and channel attention $\mathbf{A} \in \mathbb{R}^{C \times H \times W}$ over a single feature map $F \in \mathbb{R}^{C \times H \times W}$ as follows:

$$P_{i,j} = \frac{HW \cdot \exp\left(\sum_{k=1}^{C}|F_{k,i,j}|/\tau\right)}{\sum_{i=1}^{H}\sum_{j=1}^{W}\exp\left(\sum_{k=1}^{C}|F_{k,i,j}|/\tau\right)}, \quad A_{k,i,j} = \frac{C \cdot \exp\left(|F_{k,i,j}|/\tau\right)}{\sum_{k=1}^{C}\exp\left(|F_{k,i,j}|/\tau\right)} \qquad (7)$$

Similar to feature distillation, we decouple the attention masks for classification and regression for the teacher and student: $A^{T,cls}$, $A^{T,reg}$, $P^{S,cls}$. The two attention losses are defined as follows:

$$L_{att}^{cls} = \frac{\delta}{HW}\sum_{i=1}^{H}\sum_{j=1}^{W}|P_{i,j}^{T,cls} - P_{i,j}^{S,cls}| + \frac{\delta}{CHW}\sum_{k=1}^{C}\sum_{i=1}^{H}\sum_{j=1}^{W}|A_{k,i,j}^{T,cls} - A_{k,i,j}^{S,cls}| \qquad (8)$$

$$L_{att}^{reg} = \frac{\delta}{C\sum_{i=1}^{H}\sum_{j=1}^{W}\mathbb{1}_{i,j}}\sum_{i=1}^{H}\sum_{j=1}^{W}\sum_{k=1}^{C}\mathbb{1}_{i,j}|A_{k,i,j}^{T,reg} - A_{k,i,j}^{S,reg}| \qquad (9)$$

where δ is balancing loss weight hyperparameter; and $\mathbb{1}_{i,j}$ is an indicator that becomes 1 when $\mathbf{M}_{i,j}^{reg} \neq 0$.

Full Distillation. The full distillation loss is

$$L_{distill} = L_{fea}^{cls} + L_{fea}^{reg} + L_{att}^{cls} + L_{att}^{reg} \qquad (10)$$

4   Experiments

4.1   Setup and Implementation Details

We evaluate PGD on two benchmarks: COCO [19] for general object detection and CrowdHuman [29] for crowd scene detection; this contains a large number of

Table 1. A comparison between our PGD with other state-of-the-art distillation methods on COCO *mini-val* set. All models are trained locally. We set hyper-parameters for competing methods following their paper or open-sourced code bases.

Detector	Setting	AP	AP$_{50}$	AP$_{75}$	AP$_S$	AP$_M$	AP$_L$
FCOS [31]	Teacher	43.1	62.4	46.6	25.5	47.1	54.7
	Student	38.2	57.9	40.5	23.1	41.3	49.4
	DeFeat [9]	40.7(+2.5)	60.5(+2.6)	43.5(+3.0)	24.7(+1.6)	44.4(+3.1)	52.4(+3.0)
	FRS [41]	40.9(+2.7)	60.6(+2.7)	44.0(+3.5)	25.0(+1.9)	44.4(+3.1)	52.6(+3.2)
	FKD [37]	41.3(+3.1)	60.9(+3.0)	44.1(+3.6)	23.9(+0.8)	44.9(+3.6)	53.8(+4.4)
	FGD [35]	41.4(+3.2)	61.1(+3.2)	44.2(+3.7)	25.3(+**2.2**)	45.1(+3.8)	53.8(+4.4)
	Ours	42.5(+**4.3**)	62.0(+**4.1**)	45.4(+**4.9**)	24.8(+1.7)	46.1(+**5.8**)	55.5(+**6.1**)
Auto-Assign [42]	Teacher	44.8	64.1	48.9	27.3	48.8	57.5
	Student	40.6	60.1	43.8	23.6	44.3	52.4
	DeFeat [9]	42.3(+1.7)	61.6(+1.5)	46.1(+2.3)	24.1(+0.5)	46.0(+1.7)	54.4(+2.0)
	FRS [41]	42.4(+1.8)	61.9(+1.8)	46.0(+2.2)	24.9(+1.3)	46.0(+1.7)	54.8(+2.4)
	FKD [37]	42.8(+2.2)	62.1(+2.0)	46.5(+2.7)	25.7(+2.1)	46.4(+2.1)	55.5(+3.1)
	FGD [35]	43.2(+2.6)	62.5(+2.4)	46.9(+3.1)	25.2(+1.6)	46.7(+2.4)	56.2(+3.8)
	Ours	43.8(+**3.1**)	62.9(+**2.8**)	47.4(+**3.6**)	25.8(+**2.2**)	47.3(+**3.0**)	57.5(+**5.1**)
ATSS [38]	Teacher	45.5	63.9	49.7	28.7	50.1	57.8
	Student	39.6	57.6	43.2	23.0	42.9	51.2
	DeFeat [9]	41.8(+2.2)	60.3(+2.7)	45.3(+2.1)	24.8(+1.8)	45.6(+2.7)	53.5(+2.3)
	FRS [41]	41.6(+2.0)	60.1(+2.5)	44.8(+1.6)	24.9(+1.9)	45.2(+2.3)	53.2(+2.0)
	FGFI [34]	41.8(+2.2)	60.3(+2.7)	45.3(+2.1)	24.8(+1.8)	45.6(+2.7)	53.5(+2.3)
	FKD [37]	42.3(+2.7)	60.7(+3.1)	46.2(+3.0)	26.3(+3.3)	46.0(+3.1)	54.6(+3.4)
	FGD [35]	42.6(+3.0)	60.9(+3.3)	46.2(+3.0)	25.7(+2.7)	46.7(+3.8)	54.5(+3.3)
	Ours	44.2(+**4.6**)	62.3(+**4.7**)	48.3(+**5.1**)	26.5(+**3.5**)	48.6(+**5.7**)	57.1(+**5.9**)
GFL [15]	Teacher	45.8	64.2	49.8	28.3	50.3	58.6
	Student	40.2	58.4	43.3	22.7	43.6	52.0
	DeFeat [9]	42.1(+1.9)	60.5(+2.1)	45.2(+1.9)	24.4(+1.7)	46.1(+2.5)	54.5(+2.5)
	FRS [41]	42.2(+2.0)	60.6(+2.2)	45.6(+2.3)	24.7(+2.0)	46.0(+2.4)	55.5(+3.5)
	FKD [37]	43.1(+2.9)	61.6(+3.2)	46.6(+3.3)	25.1(+2.4)	47.2(+3.6)	56.5(+4.5)
	FGD [35]	43.2(+3.0)	61.8(+3.4)	46.9(+3.6)	25.2(+2.5)	47.5(+3.9)	56.2(+4.2)
	LD [40]	43.5(+3.3)	61.8(+3.4)	47.4(+**4.1**)	24.7(+2.0)	47.5(+3.9)	57.3(+5.3)
	Ours	43.8(+**3.6**)	62.0(+**3.6**)	47.4(+**4.1**)	25.4(+**2.7**)	47.8(+**4.2**)	57.6(+**5.6**)
DDOD [6]	Teacher	46.6	65.0	50.7	29.0	50.5	60.1
	Student	42.0	60.2	45.5	25.7	45.6	54.9
	DeFeat [9]	43.2(+1.2)	61.6(+1.4)	46.7(+1.2)	25.7(+0.0)	46.5(+0.9)	57.3(+2.4)
	FRS [41]	43.7(+1.7)	62.2(+2.0)	47.6(+2.1)	25.7(+0.0)	46.8(+1.2)	58.1(+3.2)
	FGFI [34]	44.1(+2.1)	62.6(+2.4)	47.9(+2.4)	26.3(+0.6)	47.3(+1.7)	58.5(+3.6)
	FKD [37]	43.6(+1.6)	62.0(+1.8)	47.1(+1.6)	25.9(+0.2)	47.0(+1.4)	58.1(+3.2)
	FGD [35]	44.1(+2.1)	62.4(+2.2)	47.9(+2.4)	26.8(+1.1)	47.2(+1.6)	58.5(+3.6)
	Ours	45.4(+**3.4**)	63.9(+**3.7**)	49.0(+**3.5**)	26.9(+1.2)	49.2(+**3.6**)	59.7(+**4.8**)

heavily occluded objects. Our codebase is built on PyTorch [23] and the MMDetection [5] toolkit and is available at https://github.com/ChenhongyiYang/PGD. All models are trained on 8 Nvidia 2080Ti GPUs. For both COCO and CrowdHuman, all models are trained using batch sizes of 32 and with an initial learning rate of 0.02, we adopt ImageNet pre-trained backbones and freeze all

Batch Normalisation layers during training. Unless otherwise specified, on both dataset we train teacher models for 3× schedule (36 epochs) [10] with multi-scale inputs using ResNet-101 [12] as backbone, and train student models for 1× schedule (12 epochs) with single-scale inputs using ResNet-50 as backbone. The COCO models are trained using the *train2017* set and evaluated on *mini-val* set following the official evaluation protocol [19]. The CrowdHuman models are trained using the CrowdHuman *training* set, which are then evaluated on the CrowdHuman *validation* set following [7]. We set K in the top-K operation to 30 for all detectors and set α to 0.8 and 0.4 for anchor-based and anchor-free detectors respectively. Following [35], we set $\sigma = 0.0008$, $\tau = 0.8$ and $\beta = 0.5\alpha$; we set $\xi^{cls} = 0.8$ and $\xi^{reg} = 0.6$ following [6]. We empirically set $\gamma = 1.6\alpha$ with minimal tuning.

Table 2. Distillation results on COCO *mini-val* using MobileNetV2 as the student backbone.

Detector	Setting	AP	AP$_{50}$	AP$_{75}$	AP$_S$	AP$_M$	AP$_L$
FCOS	Teacher	43.1	62.4	46.6	25.5	47.1	54.7
	Student	32.8	51.3	34.5	18.4	35.4	42.6
	FGD	34.7(+1.9)	53.0(+1.7)	36.8(+2.3)	19.8(+1.4)	36.8(+1.4)	44.9(+2.3)
	Ours	37.3(+4.5)	55.6(+4.3)	39.8(+5.3)	20.5(+2.1)	40.3(+4.9)	49.9(+7.3)
ATSS	Teacher	45.5	63.9	49.7	28.7	50.1	57.8
	Student	33.5	50.1	36.0	18.7	36.2	43.6
	FGD	35.8(+2.3)	52.6(+2.5)	38.8(+2.8)	20.6(+1.9)	38.4(+2.2)	46.2(+2.6)
	Ours	38.3(+4.8)	55.1(+5.0)	41.7(+5.7)	21.3(+2.6)	41.6(+5.4)	51.6(+8.0)

4.2   Main Results

Comparison with State-of-the-Art. We compare our PGD and other recent state-of-the-art object detection KD approaches for five high-performance dense detectors on COCO; these are a mixture of anchor-based (ATSS and DDOD) and anchor-free (FCOS, GFL and AutoAssign) detectors for COCO. The results are presented in Table 1. We use the same teacher and student models and the same training settings in each case, and all training is conducted locally. For competing distillation methods, we follow the hyper-parameter settings in their corresponding papers or open-sourced code repositories. We observe that our methods surpass other KD methods with a large margin for all five detectors, which validates the effectiveness of our approach. Our approach significantly improvement over the baseline approach FGD [35] and even outperforms LD [40] when applied to GFL [15], which was specifically designed for this detector. We observe PGD is particularly good at improving the AP$_{75}$ of student models, suggesting that the student model's localisation abilities have been largely improved.

Distilling to a Lightweight Backbone. Knowledge Distillation is usually used to transfer useful information from a large model to a lightweight model suitable for deployment on the edge. With this in mind, we apply PGD using

Table 3. A comparison between our PGD with other state-of-the-art distillation methods on CrowdHuman *validation* set using DDOD as object detector.

Setting	MR ↓	AP ↑	JI ↑
Teacher	41.4	90.2	81.4
Student	46.0	88.0	79.0
FKD []	44.3(−1.7)	89.1(+1.1)	80.0(+1.0)
DeFeat [9]	44.2(−1.8)	89.1(+1.1)	79.9(+0.9)
FRS [41]	44.1(−1.9)	89.2(+1.2)	80.3(+1.3)
FGFI [34]	43.8(−2.2)	89.2(+1.2)	80.3(+1.3)
FGD [35]	43.1(−2.9)	89.3(+1.3)	80.4(+1.4)
Ours	42.8(−**3.2**)	90.0(+**2.0**)	80.7(+**1.7**)

a ResNet-101 as the teacher backbone and a MobileNet V2 [28] as the student backbone on anchor-based (ATSS) and anchor-free (FCOS) detectors. The results are provided in Table 2. Our method surpasses the baseline by a significant margin, pointing to its potential for resource-limited applications.

Distillation for Crowd Detection. We compare our approach to other KD methods on the challenging CrowdHuman dataset that features heavily crowded scenes. We use the DDOD object detector for this experiment as it achieves the strongest performance. In addition to detection AP, we report the log miss rate (MR) [7] designed for evaluation in crowded scenes as well as the Jaccard Index (JI) that evaluates a detector's counting ability. The results are available in Table 3. Our approach performs better than all competing methods. While FGD achieves comparable MR and JI scores to our method, the AP for our methods is significantly greater. We believe this is because PGD strongly favours highly accurate predictions during distillation, which directly impacts the AP metric.

Table 4. Self-distillation performance on COCO *mini-val*. ResNet-50 is adopted as teacher and student backbone, which are both trained for 1× schedule.

Detector	Setting	AP	AP_{50}	AP_{75}	AP_S	AP_M	AP_L
FCOS	S & T	38.2	57.9	40.5	23.1	41.3	49.4
	FGD	39.0(+0.8)	58.6(+0.7)	41.4(+0.9)	23.7(+0.6)	42.1(+0.8)	50.6(+1.2)
	Ours	39.5(+1.3)	59.2(+1.3)	41.9(+1.4)	24.4(+1.3)	42.8(+1.5)	50.6(+1.2)
ATSS	S & T	39.6	57.6	43.2	23.0	42.9	51.2
	FGD	40.2(+0.6)	58.6(+1.0)	43.6(+1.4)	23.3(+0.3)	43.7(+0.8)	52.3(+1.1)
	Ours	40.7(+1.1)	58.9(+1.3)	44.2(+2.0)	24.0(+0.9)	44.2(+1.3)	52.9(+1.7)

Self-distillation. Self-distillation is a special case of knowledge distillation where the teacher and student models are exactly same. It is useful as it can boost a model's performance while avoiding introducing extra parameters. We compare the our method's self-distillation performance with the baseline FGD and present results for both anchor-free FCOS and anchor-based ATSS in Table 4. The teachers and students use ResNet-50 as backbone and are trained with 1× schedule using single-scale inputs. We can see that our approach achieves a better performance than the baseline, indicating its effectiveness in self-distillation.

Table 5. Ablation study on different foreground distillation strategies on COCO *mini-val* seet using ATSS as object detector.

Setting	AP	AP_{50}	AP_{75}	AP_S	AP_M	AP_L
Teacher	45.5	63.9	49.7	28.7	50.1	57.8
Student	39.6	57.6	43.2	23.0	42.9	51.2
Box	43.3 (+3.7)	61.4(+3.8)	47.2(+4.0)	25.9(+2.9)	47.6(+4.7)	56.4(+5.2)
BoxGauss	43.7(+4.1)	61.9(+4.3)	47.6(+4.4)	26.7(+3.7)	47.8(+4.9)	56.6(+5.4)
Centre	43.1(+3.5)	61.0(+3.4)	46.9(+3.7)	25.9(+2.9)	47.3(+4.4)	56.1(+4.9)
Quality	43.8(+4.2)	61.8(+4.2)	47.8(+4.6)	25.7(+2.7)	48.2(+5.3)	56.8(+5.6)
TopkEq	43.9(+4.3)	62.0(+4.4)	47.7(+4.5)	27.1(**+4.1**)	48.0(+5.1)	56.8(+5.6)
KDE	44.0(+4.4)	62.1(+4.5)	47.8(+4.6)	26.3(+3.3)	48.5(+5.6)	56.8(+5.6)
Ours	44.2(+**4.6**)	62.3(+**4.7**)	48.3(+**5.1**)	26.5(+3.5)	48.6(+**5.7**)	57.1(+**5.9**)

Table 6. Hyper-parameter ablation studies on COCO *mini-val*.

K	1	5	9	15	30	45	60
AP	43.2	43.5	43.6	43.9	**44.2**	44.0	43.9

Ablation study on different K in the top-K operation using ATSS as detector.

α	0.005	0.01	0.03	0.05	0.07	0.1	0.2
FCOS	41.7	42.0	**42.5**	**42.5**	42.4	42.2	41.8
ATSS	42.9	43.2	43.7	43.9	**44.2**	44.1	43.2

Ablation study on distillation loss magnitude α using FCOS and ATSS.

4.3   Ablation Study

Comparing Foreground Distillation Strategies. We compare alternative strategies for distilling foreground regions to investigate how important is distilling different foreground regions. We use ATSS as our object detector and present results in Table 5. Note here we only modify the foreground distillation strategy while keeping everything else the same. We first evaluate the strategy used in FGD [35] and DeFeat [9], where regions in the GT box are distilled equally. We dub this the *Box* strategy (Fig. 1a). Compared to our method, *Box* achieves 0.9 AP worse performance. A possible reason for this is that it can include sub-optimal prediction locations that distract from more meaningful features.

Note that the *Box* strategy still outperforms the baseline FGD, we attribute this improvement to the decoupling of distillation for classification and regression branches. Several works [30, 40] postulate that most meaningful regions lie near the centre of the GT box. We evaluate the *BoxGauss* strategy that was proposed in TADF [30] (Fig. 4b). Specifically, a Gaussian distribution is used to weight the distillation loss, where its mean is the centre of the GT box, and the standard deviation is calculated from the box dimensions. This strategy yields +0.4 AP improvement over vanilla *Box* strategy, suggesting the importance of focusing on the centre area; however, it is still surpassed by our approach. We consider a *Centre* strategy, which distils a $0.2H \times 0.2W$ area at the middle of the GT box. Somewhat surprisingly, this achieves an even worse AP than the vanilla *Box* strategy in almost all instances, with comparable performance on small objects. A possible explanation is that a fixed ratio region fails to cover the full span of useful regions for different-sized objects and limits the amount of distilled information. Then we compare to an adaptive loss weighting mechanism where we directly use the quality score in Eq. 1 to weight features for the distillation loss. The strategy—which we refer to as *Quality*—improves slightly on *BoxGauss*, especially for medium and high scoring boxes. However, it significantly under-performs on small objects. In contrast, the *TopkEq* strategy, where we limit distillation to only the top-K pixels according to the quality score (we set $K = 30$ to match our method), provides a significant improvement to the detection of small objects. A possible explanation for this is that distilling on positions with lower scores still introduces considerable noise, whereas limiting distillation to only the highest-scoring pixels focuses the student towards only the most essential features of the teacher. Finally, we compare our method to one that replaces the Gaussian MLE with kernel density estimation, the *KDE* strategy. It achieves similar performance to our Gaussian MLE approach, but is more complicated.

Hyper-Parameter Settings. Here, we examine the effect of changing two important hyper-parameters used in our approach, as presented in Table 6. The first is K, which is the number of high-scoring pixels used for distillation. The best performance is obtained for $K = 30$. Small K can cause distillation to neglect important regions, whereas large K can introduce noise that distracts the distillation process from the most essential features. The second hyper-parameter we vary is α which controls the magnitude of the distillation loss. We can see how this affects performance for anchor-based ATSS and anchor-free FCOS. We find that the ATSS's performance is quite robust when α is between 0.05–0.1, and FCOS can achieve good performance when α is between 0.03–0.1. For both types of detectors, a small α will minimise the effect of distillation, and a large α can make training unstable.

Decoupled Distillation. In our pipeline, we decouple the KD loss to distil the classification and regression heads separately (see Sect. 3.3). This practice differs from previous feature imitation-based approaches where the FPN neck features are distilled. Here we conduct experiments to test this design and present the result in Table 7. Firstly, we remove the regression KD loss and only apply the classification KD loss using FPN features. The model achieves 43.6 mAP on COCO. Then we test only applying the classification KD loss using the classification feature map; the performance improves very slightly (by 0.2). Next, we only test the regression KD loss using the regression features, resulting in 41.7 COCO mAP. The performance is significantly harmed because the regression KD loss only considers foreground regions while ignoring background areas. Finally, we come to our design by combining both classification and regression KD losses, which achieves the best performance, at 44.2 COCO mAP.

(a)   (b)   (c)   (d)   (e)

Fig. 5. Visualisation of the detection results on COCO *mini-val* set using ATSS as detector and PGD for distillation. GTs are shown in blue; plain student detections are shown in red; distilled student predictions are shown in orange. (Color figure online)

Table 7. Comparison between different distillation branches.

neck	cls	reg	AP	AP_{50}	AP_{75}	AP_S	AP_M	AP_L
-	-	-	39.6	57.6	43.2	23.0	42.9	51.2
✓			43.6(+4.0)	61.8(+4.2)	47.5(+4.3)	26.1(**+3.1**)	47.8(+4.9)	56.8(+5.6)
	✓		43.8(+4.2)	62.1(+4.5)	47.5(+4.3)	26.5(3.5)	48.0(+5.1)	56.8(+5.6)
		✓	41.7(+2.1)	60.2(+2.6)	45.2(+2.0)	25.3(+2.3)	45.4(+2.5)	53.9(+2.7)
	✓	✓	44.2(**+4.6**)	62.3(**+4.7**)	48.3(**+5.1**)	26.5(+3.5)	48.6(**+5.7**)	57.1(**+5.9**)

Qualitative Studies. We visualise box predictions using ATSS as our object detector in Fig. 5, in which we show GT boxes alongside student predictions with and without distillation using PGD. While the high-performance ATSS is able to accurately detect objects in most cases, we observe some clear advantages of using our distillation approach: it outputs fewer false positives (Fig. 5b,c), improves detection recall (Fig. 5a,d), and localises objects better (Fig. 5b,d,e).

5 Conclusion

In this work, we highlight the need to focus distillation on features of the teacher that are responsible for high-scoring predictions. We find that these *key predictive regions* constitute only a small fraction of all features within the boundaries of the ground-truth bounding box. We use this observation to design a novel distillation technique—PGD—that amplifies the distillation signal from these features. We use an adaptive Gaussian distribution to smoothly aggregate those top locations to further enhance performance. Our approach can significantly improve state-of-the-art detectors on COCO and CrowdHuman, outperforming many existing KD methods. In future, we could investigate the applicability of high-quality regions to two-stage and transformer models for detection.

Acknowledgement. The authors would like to thank Joe Mellor, Kaihong Wang, and Zehui Chen for their useful comments and suggestions. This work was supported by a PhD studentship provided by the School of Engineering, University of Edinburgh as well as the EPSRC Centre for Doctoral Training in Robotics and Autonomous Systems (Grant No. EP/S515061/1) and SeeByte Ltd., Edinburgh, UK.

References

1. Ba, L.J., Caruana, R.: Do deep nets really need to be deep? In: NeurIPS (2014)
2. Cai, Z., Vasconcelos, N.: Cascade R-CNN: delving into high quality object detection. In: CVPR (2018)
3. Carion, N., Massa, F., Synnaeve, G., Usunier, N., Kirillov, A., Zagoruyko, S.: End-to-end object detection with transformers. In: Vedaldi, A., Bischof, H., Brox, T., Frahm, J.-M. (eds.) ECCV 2020. LNCS, vol. 12346, pp. 213–229. Springer, Cham (2020). https://doi.org/10.1007/978-3-030-58452-8_13
4. Chen, G., Choi, W., Yu, X., Han, T., Chandraker, M.: Learning efficient object detection models with knowledge distillation. In: NeurIPS (2017)
5. Chen, K., et al.: MMDetection: open MMLab detection toolbox and benchmark. In: arXiv preprint arXiv:1906.07155 (2019)
6. Chen, Z., Yang, C., Li, Q., Zhao, F., Zha, Z.J., Wu, F.: Disentangle your dense object detector. In: ACM MM (2021)
7. Chu, X., Zheng, A., Zhang, X., Sun, J.: Detection in crowded scenes: one proposal. In: CVPR, Multiple Predictions (2020)
8. Dai, X., et al.: General instance distillation for object detection. In: CVPR (2021)
9. Guo, J., et al.:: Distilling object detectors via decoupled features. In: CVPR (2021)
10. He, K., Girshick, R., Dollár, P.: Rethinking ImageNet pre-training. In: CVPR (2019)
11. He, K., Gkioxari, G., Dollár, P., Girshick, R.: Mask R-CNN. In: ICCV (2017)
12. He, K., Zhang, X., Ren, S., Sun, J.: Deep residual learning for image recognition. In: CVPR (2016)
13. Hinton, G., et al.: Distilling the knowledge in a neural network. In: NeurIPS 2014 Deep Learning Workshop (2014)
14. Kang, Z., Zhang, P., Zhang, X., Sun, J., Zheng, N.: Instance-conditional knowledge distillation for object detection. In: NeurIPS (2021)
15. c Kang, Z., Zhang, P., Zhang, X., Sun, J., Zheng, N.: Instance-conditional knowledge distillation for object detection. In: NeurIPS (2021)
16. Li, Y., Chen, Y., Wang, N., Zhang, Z.: Scale-aware trident networks for object detection. In: ICCV (2019)
17. Li, Z., Peng, C., Yu, G., Zhang, X., Deng, Y., Sun, J.: Light-head r-CNN: in defense of two-stage object detector. In: arXiv preprint arXiv:1711.07264 (2017)
18. Lin, T.Y., Goyal, P., Girshick, R., He, K., Dollár, P.: Focal loss for dense object detection. In: ICCV (2017)
19. Lin, T.Y., et al.: Microsoft COCO: common objects in context. In: Fleet, D., Pajdla, T., Schiele, B., Tuytelaars, T. (eds.) ECCV 2014. LNCS, vol. 8693, pp. 740–755. Springer, Cham (2014). https://doi.org/10.1007/978-3-319-10602-1_48

20. Ma, Y., Liu, S., Li, Z., Sun, J.: IQDet: instance-wise quality distribution sampling for object detection. In: CVPR (2021)
21. Nguyen, C.H., Nguyen, T.C., Tang, T.N., Phan, N.L.: Improving object detection by label assignment distillation. In: WACV (2022)
22. Oksuz, K., Cam, B.C., Akbas, E., Kalkan, S.: A ranking-based, balanced loss function unifying classification and localisation in object detection. Adv. Neural. Inf. Process. Syst. **33**, 15534–15545 (2020)
23. Paszke, A., et al.: Pytorch: an imperative style, high-performance deep learning library. In: NeurIPS (2019)
24. Qin, Z., Li, Z., Zhang, Z., Bao, Y., Yu, G., Peng, Y., Sun, J.: ThunderNet: towards real-time generic object detection on mobile devices. In: ICCV (2019)
25. Redmon, J., Divvala, S., Girshick, R., Farhadi, A.: You only look once: unified, real-time object detection. In: CVPR (2016)
26. Redmon, J., Farhadi, A.: YOLO9000: better, faster, stronger. In: CVPR (2017)
27. Ren, S., He, K., Girshick, R., Sun, J.: Faster R-CNN: towards real-time object detection with region proposal networks. In: NeurIPS (2015)
28. Sandler, M., Howard, A., Zhu, M., Zhmoginov, A., Chen, L.C.: Mobilenetv 2: Inverted residuals and linear bottlenecks. In: CVPR (2018)
29. Shao, S., et al.: CrowdHuman: a benchmark for detecting human in a crowd. In: arXiv preprint arXiv:1805.00123 (2018)
30. Sun, R., Tang, F., Zhang, X., Xiong, H., Tian, Q.: Distilling object detectors with task adaptive regularization. In: arXiv preprint arXiv:2006.13108 (2020)
31. Tian, Z., Shen, C., Chen, H., He, T.: FCOS: fully convolutional one-stage object detection. In: ICCV (2019)
32. Wang, J., Song, L., Li, Z., Sun, H., Sun, J., Zheng, N.: End-to-end object detection with fully convolutional network. In: CVPR (2021)
33. Wang, R.J., Li, X., Ling, C.X.: Pelee: a real-time object detection system on mobile devices. In: NeurIPS (2018)
34. Wang, T., Yuan, L., Zhang, X., Feng, J.: Distilling object detectors with fine-grained feature imitation. In: CVPR (2019)
35. Yang, Z., et al.: Focal and global knowledge distillation for detectors. In: arXiv preprint arXiv:2111.11837 (2021)
36. Yao, L., Pi, R., Xu, H., Zhang, W., Li, Z., Zhang, T.: G-DetKD: towards general distillation framework for object detectors via contrastive and semantic-guided feature imitation. In: ICCV (2021)
37. Zhang, L., Ma, K.: Improve object detection with feature-based knowledge distillation: towards accurate and efficient detectors. In: ICLR (2021)
38. Zhang, S., Chi, C., Yao, Y., Lei, Z., Li, S.Z.: Bridging the gap between anchor-based and anchor-free detection via adaptive training sample selection. In: CVPR (2020)
39. Zheng, Z., Wang, P., Liu, W., Li, J., Ye, R., Ren, D.: Distance-IOU loss: faster and better learning for bounding box regression. In: AAAI (2020)
40. Zheng, Z., Ye, R., Wang, P., Wang, J., Ren, D., Zuo, W.: Localization distillation for object detection. In: arXiv preprint arXiv:2102.12252 (2021)
41. Zhixing, D., , et al.: Distilling object detectors with feature richness. In: NeurIPS (2021)
42. Zhu, B., et al.: Autoassign: Differentiable label assignment for dense object detection. In: arXiv preprint arXiv:2007.03496 (2020)

Multimodal Object Detection via Probabilistic Ensembling

Yi-Ting Chen[1], Jinghao Shi[2], Zelin Ye[2], Christoph Mertz[2], Deva Ramanan[2,3],
and Shu Kong[2,4(✉)]

[1] University of Maryland, College Park, USA
ytchen@umd.edu
[2] Carnegie Mellon University, Pittsburgh, USA
{jinghaos,zeliny,cmertz}@andrew.cmu.edu, deva@cs.cmu.edu
[3] Argo AI, Pittsburgh, USA
[4] Texas A&M University, College Station, USA
shu@tamu.edu

Abstract. Object detection with multimodal inputs can improve many safety-critical systems such as autonomous vehicles (AVs). Motivated by AVs that operate in both day and night, we study multimodal object detection with RGB and thermal cameras, since the latter provides much stronger object signatures under poor illumination. We explore strategies for fusing information from different modalities. Our key contribution is a probabilistic ensembling technique, **ProbEn**, a simple non-learned method that fuses together detections from multi-modalities. We derive ProbEn from Bayes' rule and first principles that assume conditional independence across modalities. Through probabilistic marginalization, ProbEn elegantly handles missing modalities when detectors do not fire on the same object. Importantly, ProbEn also notably improves multimodal detection even when the conditional independence assumption does not hold, e.g., fusing outputs from other fusion methods (both off-the-shelf and trained in-house). We validate ProbEn on two benchmarks containing both aligned (KAIST) and unaligned (FLIR) multimodal images, showing that ProbEn outperforms prior work by more than **13%** in relative performance!

Keywords: Object detection · Multimodal detection · Infrared · Thermal · Probabilistic model · Ensembling · Multimodal fusion · Uncertainty

---

Y.-T. Chen, J. Shi and Z. Ye—Equal contribution. The work was mostly done when authors were with CMU.
D. Ramanan and S. Kong—Equal supervision.
open-source code in Github.

Supplementary Information The online version contains supplementary material available at https://doi.org/10.1007/978-3-031-20077-9_9.

1   Introduction

Object detection is a canonical computer vision problem that has been greatly advanced by the end-to-end training of deep neural detectors [23,45]. Such detectors are widely adopted in various safety-critical systems such as autonomous vehicles (AVs) [7,19]. Motivated by AVs that operate in both day and night, we study multimodal object detection with RGB and thermal cameras, since the latter can provide much stronger object signatures under poor illumination [4,12,26,32,51,57].

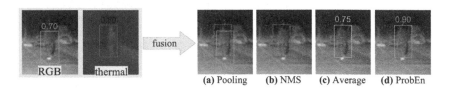

(a) Pooling   (b) NMS   (c) Average   (d) ProbEn

Fig. 1. Multimodal detection via ensembling single-modal detectors. (a) A naive approach is to pool detections from each modality, but this will result in multiple detections that overlap the same object. (b) To remedy this, one can apply non-maximal suppression (NMS) to suppress overlapping detections from different modalities, which always returns the higher (maximal) scoring detection. Though quite simple, NMS is an effective fusion strategy that has *not* been previously proposed as such. However, NMS fails to incorporate cues from the lower-scoring modality. (c) A natural strategy for doing so might average scores of overlapping detections (instead of suppressing the weaker ones) [33,36]. However, this must decrease the reported score compared to NMS. Intuitively, if two modalities agree on a candidate detection, one should *boost* its score. (d) To do so, we derive a simple probabilistic ensembling approach, **ProbEn**, to score fusion that increases the score for detections that have strong evidence from multiple modalities. We further extend ProbEn to box fusion in Sect. 3. Our *non-learned* ProbEn significantly outperforms prior work (Tables 2 and 4).

Multimodal Data. There exists several challenges in multimodal detection. One is the lack of data. While there exists large repositories of annotated single-modal datasets (RGB) and pre-trained models, there exists much less annotated data of other modalities (thermal), and even less annotations of them paired together. One often-ignored aspect is the alignment of the modalities: aligning RGB and thermal images requires special purpose hardware, e.g., a beam-splitter [26] or a specialized rack [48] for spatial alignment, and a GPS clock synchronizer for temporal alignment [42]. Fusion on *un*aligned RGB-thermal inputs (cf. Fig. 4) remains relatively unexplored. For example, even annotating bounding boxes is cumbersome because separate annotations are required for each modality, increasing overall cost. As a result, many unaligned datasets annotate only one modality (e.g., FLIR [17]), further complicating multimodal learning.

Multimodal Fusion. The central question in multimodal detection is *how* to fuse information from different modalities. Previous work has explored strategies

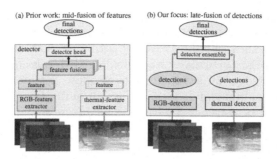

Fig. 2. High-level comparisons between mid- and late-fusion. **(a)** Past work primarily focuses on mid-fusion, e.g., concatenating features computed by single-modal feature extractors. **(b)** We focus on late-fusion via *detector ensemble* that fuses detections from independent detectors, e.g., two single-modal detectors trained with RGB and thermal images respectively.

for fusion at various stages [4,9,32,51,56,57], which are often categorized into early-, mid- and late-fusion. Early-fusion constructs a four-channel RGB-thermal input [49], which is then processed by a (typical) deep network. In contrast, mid-fusion keeps RGB and thermal inputs in different streams and then merges their features downstream within the network (Fig. 2a) [30,36,49]. The vast majority of past work focuses on architectural design of where and how to merge. Our key contribution is the exploration of an extreme variant of *very*-late fusion of detectors trained on separate modalities (Fig. 2b) through *detector ensembling*. Though conceptually simple, ensembling can be effective because one can learn from single-modal datasets that often dwarf the size of multimodal datasets. However, ensembling can be practically challenging because different detectors might not fire on the same object. For example, RGB-based detectors often fail to fire in nighttime conditions, implying one needs to deal with "missing" detections during fusion.

Probabilistic Ensembling (ProbEn). We derive our very-late fusion approach, ProbEn, from first principles: simply put, if single-modal signals are conditionally independent of each other given the true label, the optimal fusion strategy is given by Bayes rule [41]. ProbEn requires no learning, and so does not require any multimodal data for training. Importantly, ProbEn elegantly handles "missing" modalities via probabilistic marginalization. While ProbEn is derived assuming conditional independence, we empirically find that it can be used to fuse outputs that are not strictly independent, by fusing outputs from *other* fusion methods (both off-the-shelf and trained in-house). In this sense, ProbEn is a general technique for ensembling detectors. We achieve significant improvements over prior art, both on aligned and unaligned multimodal benchmarks.

Why Ensemble? One may ask why detector ensembling should be regarded as an interesting contribution, given that ensembling is a well-studied approach [3,13,18,29] that is often viewed as an "engineering detail" for improving leaderboard performance [22,25,31]. Firstly, we show that the precise ensembling technique matters, and prior approaches proposed in the (single-modal) detection literature such as score-averaging [14,31] or max-voting [52], are not as effective as ProbEn, particularly when dealing with missing modalities. Secondly, to our knowledge, we are the first to propose detector ensembling as a fusion method for multimodal detection. Though quite simple, it is remarkably effective and should be considered a baseline for future research.

2   Related Work

Object Detection and Detector Ensembling. State-of-the-art detectors train deep neural networks on large-scale datasets such as COCO [34] and often focus on architectural design [37,43–45]. Crucially, most architectures generate overlapping detections which need to be post-processed with non-maximal suppression (NMS) [5,10,47]. Overlapping detections could also be generated by detectors tuned for different image crops and scales, which typically make use of ensembling techniques for post-processing their output [1,22,25]. Somewhat surprisingly, although detector ensembling and NMS are widely studied in single-modal RGB detection, to the best of our knowledge, they have *not* been used to (very) late-fuse multimodal detections; we find them remarkably effective.

Multimodal Detection, particularly with RGB-thermal images, has attracted increasing attention. The KAIST pedestrian detection dataset [26] is one of the first benchmarks for RGB-thermal detection, fostering growth of research in this area. Inspired by the successful RGB-based detectors [37,43,45], current multimodal detectors train deep models with various methods for fusing multimodal signals [4,9,28,32,51,56,57,57,58]. Most of these multimodal detection methods work on aligned RGB-thermal images, but it is unclear how they perform on heavily unaligned modalities such as images in Fig. 4 taken from FLIR dataset [17]. We study multimodal detection under both aligned and unaligned RGB-thermal scenarios. **Multimodal fusion** is the central question in multimodal detection. Compared to early-fusion that simply concatenates RGB and thermal inputs, mid-fusion of single-modal features performs better [49]. Therefore, most multimodal methods study how to fuse features and focus on designing new network architectures [30,36,49]. Because RGB-thermal pairs might not be aligned, some methods train an RGB-thermal translation network to synthesize aligned pairs, but this requires annotations in each modality [12,27,38]. Interestingly, few works explore learning from unaligned data that are annotated only in single modality; we show that mid-fusion architectures can still learn in this setting by acting as an implicit alignment network. Finally, few fusion architectures explore (very) late fusion of single-modal detections via detector ensembling. Most that do simply take heuristic (weighted) averages of confidence scores [20,32,57]. In contrast, we introduce probabilistic ensembling (ProbEn) for late-fusion, which significantly outperforms prior methods on both aligned and unaligned RGB-thermal data.

3   Fusion Strategies for Multimodal Detection

We now present multimodal fusion strategies for detection. We first point out that **single-modal** detectors are viable methods for processing multimodal signals, and so include them as a baseline. We also include fusion baselines for **early-fusion**, which concatenates RGB and thermal as a four-channel input, and **mid-fusion**, which concatenates single-modal features inside a network (Fig. 2). As a preview of results, we find that mid-fusion is generally the most effective baseline (Table 1). Surprisingly, this holds even for unaligned data that is annotated with a single modality (Fig. 4), indicating that mid-fusion can perform some implicit alignment (Table 3).

We describe strategies for late-fusing detectors from different modalities, or detector ensembling. We begin with a naive approach (Fig. 1). Late-fusion needs to fuse scores and boxes; we discuss the latter at the end of this section.

Naive Pooling. The possibly simplest strategy is to naively pool detections from multiple modalities together. This will probably result in multiple detections overlapping the same ground-truth object (Fig. 1a).

Non-Maximum Supression (NMS). The natural solution for dealing with overlapping detections is NMS, a crucial component in contemporary RGB detectors [14,24,60]. NMS finds bounding box predictions with high spatial overlap and remove the lower-scoring bounding boxes. This can be implemented in a sequential fashion via sorting of predictions by confidence, as depicted by Algorithm 1, or in a parallel fashion amenable to GPU computation [6]. While NMS has been used to ensemble single-modal detectors [47], it has (surprisingly) *not* been advocated for fusion of *multi*-modal detectors. We find it be shockingly effective, outperforming the majority of past work on established benchmarks (Fig. 2). Specifically, when two detections from two different modalities overlap (e.g., IoU>0.5), NMS simply keeps the higher-score detection and suppresses the other (Fig. 1b). This allows each modality to "shine" where effective – thermal detections tend to score high (and so will be selected) when RGB detections perform poorly due to poor illumination conditions. That said, rather than selecting one modality at the global image level (e.g., day-time vs. night time), NMS selects one modality at the local bounding box level. However, in some sense, NMS fails to "fuse" information from multiple modalities together, since each of the final detections are supported by only one modality.

Average Fusion. To actually fuse multimodal information, a straightforward strategy is to modify NMS to average confidence scores of overlapping detections from different modalities, rather than suppressing the weaker modality. Such an averaging has been proposed in prior work [32,36,52]. However, averaging scores will necessarily *decrease* the NMS score which reports the max of an overlapping set of detections (Fig. 1c). Our experiments demonstrate that averaging produces worse results than NMS and single-modal detectors. Intuitively, if two modalities agree that there exist a detection, fusion should *increase* the overall confidence rather than decrease.

Algorithm 1. Multimodal Fusion by NMS or ProbEn
___

1: Input: class priors π_k for $k \in \{1, \ldots, K\}$; the flag of fusion method (NMS or ProbEn); set $\mathcal{D}$: detections from multiple modalities. Each detection $d = (\mathbf{y}, \mathbf{z}, m) \in \mathcal{D}$ contains classification posteriors $\mathbf{y}$, box coordinates $\mathbf{z}$ and modality tag m.
2: Initialize set of fused detections $\mathcal{F} = \{\}$
3: **while** $\mathcal{D} \neq \emptyset$ **do**
4:    Find detection $d \in \mathcal{D}$ with largest posterior
5:    Find all detections in $\mathcal{D}$ that overlap d (e.g., > 0.5 IoU), denoted as $\mathcal{T} \subseteq \mathcal{D}$
6:    **if** NMS **then**
7:        $d' \leftarrow d$
8:    **else if** ProbEn **then**
9:        Find highest scoring detection in $\mathcal{T}$ of each modality, denoted as $\mathcal{S} \subseteq \mathcal{T}$
10:       Compute d' from $\mathcal{S}$ by fusing scores $\mathbf{y}$ with Eq. (4) and boxes $\mathbf{z}$ with Eq. (8)
11:    **end if**
12:    $\mathcal{F} \leftarrow \mathcal{F} + \{d'\}, \qquad \mathcal{D} \leftarrow \mathcal{D} - \mathcal{T}$
13: **end while**
14: **return** set $\mathcal{F}$ of fused detections
___

Probabilistic Ensembling (ProbEn). We derive our probabilistic approach for late-fusion of detections by starting with how to fuse detection scores (Algorithm 1). Assume we have an object with label y (e.g., a "person") and measured signals from two modalities: x_1 (RGB) and x_2 (thermal). We write out our formulation for two modalities, but the extension to multiple (evaluated in our experiments) is straightforward. Crucially, we assume measurements are conditionally independent given the object label y:

$$p(x_1, x_2|y) = p(x_1|y)p(x_2|y) \tag{1}$$

This can also be written as $p(x_1|y) = p(x_1|x_2, y)$, which may be easier to intuit. Given the person label y, predict its RGB appearance x_1; if this prediction would not change the given knowledge of the thermal signal x_2, then conditional independence holds. We wish to infer labels given multimodal measurements:

$$p(y|x_1, x_2) = \frac{p(x_1, x_2|y)p(y)}{p(x_1, x_2)} \propto p(x_1, x_2|y)p(y) \tag{2}$$

By applying the conditional independence assumption from (1) to (2), we have:

$$p(y|x_1, x_2) \propto p(x_1|y)p(x_2|y)p(y) \propto \frac{p(x_1|y)p(y)p(x_2|y)p(y)}{p(y)} \tag{3}$$

$$\propto \frac{p(y|x_1)p(y|x_2)}{p(y)} \tag{4}$$

The above suggests a simple approach to fusion that is provably optimal when single-modal features are conditionally-independent of the true object label:

1. Train independent single-modal classifiers that predict the distributions over the label y given each individual feature modality $p(y|x_1)$ and $p(y|x_2)$.

2. Produce a final score by multiplying the two distributions, dividing by the class prior distribution, and normalizing the final result (4) to sum-to-one.

To obtain the class prior $p(y)$, we can simply normalize the counts of per-class examples. Extending ProbEn (4) to M modalities is simple:

$$p(y|\{x_i\}_{i=1}^M) \propto \frac{\Pi_{i=1}^M p(y|x_i)}{p(y)^{M-1}}. \tag{5}$$

Independence Assumptions. ProbEn is optimal given the independence assumption from (1). Even when such independence assumptions do not hold in practice, the resulting models may still be effective [11] (i.e., just as assumptions of Gaussianity can still be useful even if strictly untrue [29,41]). Interestingly, many fusion methods including NMS and averaging make the same underlying assumption, as discussed in [29]. In fact, [29] points out that Average Fusion (which averages class posteriors) makes an even stronger assumption: posteriors do not deviate dramatically from class priors. This is likely not true, as corroborated by the poor performance of averaging in our experiments (despite its apparent widespread use [32,36,52]).

Relationship to Prior Work. To compare to prior fusion approaches that tend to operate on logit scores, we rewrite the single-modal softmax posterior for class-k given modality i in terms of single-modal logit score $s_i[k]$. For notational simplicity, we suppress its dependence on the underlying input modality x_i: $p(y=k|x_i) = \frac{\exp(s_i[k])}{\sum_j \exp(s_i[j])} \propto \exp(s_i[k])$, where we exploit the fact that the partition function in the denominator is not a function of the class label k. We now plug the above into Eq. (5):

$$p(y=k|\{x_i\}_{i=1}^M) \propto \frac{\Pi_{i=1}^M p(y=k|x_i)}{p(y=k)^{M-1}} \propto \frac{\exp(\sum_{i=1}^M s_i[k])}{p(y=k)^{M-1}} \tag{6}$$

ProbEn is thus equivalent to *summing logits*, dividing by the class prior and normalizing via a softmax. Our derivation (6) reveals that summing logits without the division may over-count class priors, where the over-counting grows with the number of modalities M. The supplement shows that dividing by class posteriors $p(y)$ marginally helps. In practice, we empirically find that assuming uniform priors works surprisingly well, even on imbalanced datasets. This is the default for our experiments, unless otherwise noted.

Missing Modalities. Importantly, summing and averaging behave profoundly differently when fusing across "missing" modalities (Fig. 3). Intuitively, different single-modal detectors often do not fire on the same object. This means that to output a final set of detections above a confidence threshold (e.g., necessary for computing precision-recall metrics), one will need to compare scores from fused multi-modal detections with single modal detections, as illustrated in Fig. 3. ProbEn elegantly deals with missing modalities because *probabilistically-normalized* multi-modal posteriors $p(y|x_1, x_2)$ can be directly compared with single-modal posteriors $p(y|x_1)$.

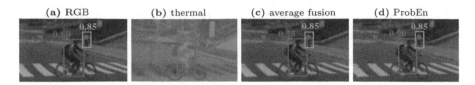

Fig. 3. Missing Modalities. The orange-person **(a)** fails to trigger a thermal detection **(b)**, resulting in a single-modal RGB detection (0.85 confidence). To generate an output set of detections (for downstream metrics such as average precision), this detection must be compared to the fused multimodal detection of the red-person (RGB: 0.80, thermal: 0.70). **(c)** averaging confidences for the red-person lowers their score (0.75) below the orange-person, which is unintuitive because additional detections should boost confidence. **(d)** ProbEn increases the red-person fused score to 0.90, allowing for proper comparisons to single-modal detections. (Color figure online)

Bounding Box Fusion. Thus far, we have focused on fusion of class posteriors. We now extend ProbEn to probabilistically fuse bounding box (bbox) coordinates of overlapping detections. We repurpose the derivation from (4) for a continuous bbox label rather than a discrete one. Specifically, we write $\mathbf{z}$ for the continuous random variable defining the bounding box (parameterized by its centroid, width, and height) associated with a given detection. We assume single-modal detections provide a posterior $p(\mathbf{z}|x_i)$ that takes the form of a Gaussian with a single variance σ_i^2, i.e., $p(\mathbf{z}|x_i) = \mathcal{N}(\boldsymbol{\mu}_i, \sigma_i^2\mathbf{I})$ where $\boldsymbol{\mu}_i$ are box coordinates predicted from modality i. We also assume a uniform prior on $p(\mathbf{z})$, implying bbox coordinates can lie anywhere in the image plane. Doing so, we can write

$$p(\mathbf{z}|x_1, x_2) \propto p(\mathbf{z}|x_1)p(\mathbf{z}|x_2) \propto \exp\left(\frac{\|\mathbf{z}-\boldsymbol{\mu}_1\|^2}{-2\sigma_1^2}\right)\exp\left(\frac{\|\mathbf{z}-\boldsymbol{\mu}_2\|^2}{-2\sigma_2^2}\right) \quad (7)$$

$$\propto \exp\left(\frac{\|\mathbf{z}-\boldsymbol{\mu}\|^2}{-2(\frac{1}{\sigma_1^2}+\frac{1}{\sigma_2^2})}\right), \quad \text{where} \quad \boldsymbol{\mu} = \frac{\frac{\boldsymbol{\mu}_1}{\sigma_1^2}+\frac{\boldsymbol{\mu}_2}{\sigma_2^2}}{\frac{1}{\sigma_1^2}+\frac{1}{\sigma_2^2}} \quad (8)$$

We refer the reader to the supplement for a detailed derivation. Equation (8) suggests a simple way to probabilistically fuse box coordinates: compute a weighted average of box coordinates, where weights are given by the inverse covariance. We explore three methods for setting σ_i^2. The first method "avg" fixes $\sigma_i^2=1$, amounting to simply averaging bounding box coodinates. The second "s-avg" approximates $\sigma_i^2 \approx \frac{1}{p(y=k|x_i)}$, implying that more confident detections should have a higher weight when fusing box coordinates. This performs marginally better than simply averaging. The third "v-avg" train the detector to predict regression *variance*/uncertainty using the Gaussian negative log likelihood (GNLL) loss [39] alongside the box regression loss. Interestingly, incorporating GNLL not only produces better variance/uncertainty estimate helpful for fusion but also improves detection performance of the trained detectors (details in supplement).

Fig. 4. RGB and thermal images are unaligned both spatially and temporally in FLIR [17], which annotates only thermal images. As a result, prior methods relies on thermal and drop the RGB modality. We find mid-fusion, taking both RGB and thermal as input, notably improves detection accuracy. When late-fusing detections computed by the mid-fusion and thermal-only detectors, our ProbEn yields much better performance (Tables 3 and 4).

4   Experiments

We validate different fusion methods on two datasets: KAIST [26] which is released under the Simplified BSD License, and FLIR [17] (Fig. 4), which allows for non-commercial educational and research purposes. Because the two datasets contain personally identifiable information such as faces and license plates, we assure that we (1) use them only for research, and (2) will release our code and models to the public without redistributing the data. We first describe implementation details and then report the experimental results on each dataset (alongside their evaluation metrics) in separate subsections.

4.1   Implementation

We conduct experiments with PyTorch [40] on a single GPU (Nvidia GTX 2080). We train our detectors (based on Faster-RCNN) with Detectron2 [50], using SGD and learning rate 5e–3. For data augmentation, we adopt random flipping and resizing. We pre-train our detector on COCO dataset [34]. As COCO has only RGB images, fine-tuning the pre-trained detector on thermal inputs needs careful pre-processing of thermal images (detailed below).

Pre-processing. All RGB and thermal images have intensity in [0, 255]. In training an RGB-based detector, RGB input images are commonly processed using the mean subtraction [50] where the mean values are computed over all the training images. Similarly, we calculate the mean value (135.438) in the thermal training data. We find using a precise mean subtraction to process thermal images yields better performance when fine-tuning the pre-trained detector.

Stage-wise Training. We fine-tune the pre-trained detector to train single-modal detectors and the early-fusion detectors. To train a mid-fusion detector, we truncate the *already-trained* single-modal detectors, concatenate features add a new detection head and train the whole model (Fig. 2a). The late-fusion methods fuse detections from (single-modal) detectors. Note that all the late-fusion

Fig. 5. Detections overlaid on two KAIST testing examples in columns. **Top**: detections by our mid-fusion model. **Bottom**: detections by our ProbEn by fusing detections of thermal-only and mid-fusion models. Green, red and blue boxes stand for true positives, false negative (miss-detection) and false positives. Visually, ProbEn performs much better than the mid-fusion model, which is already comparable to the prior work as shown in Tables 1 and 2. (Color figure online)

methods are *non-learned*. We also experimented with learning-based late-fusion methods (e.g., learning to fuse logits) but find them to be only marginally better than ProbEn (9.08 vs. 9.16 in LAMR using argmax box fusion). Therefore, we focus on the non-learned late fusion methods in the main paper and study learning-based ones in the supplement.

Post-processing. When ensembling two detectors, we find it crucial to calibrate scores particularly when we fuse detections from our in-house models and off-the-shelf models released by others. We adopt the simple temperature scaling for score calibration [21]. Please refer to the supplement for details.

4.2 Multimodal Pedestrian Detection on KAIST

Dataset. The KAIST dataset is a popular multimodal benchmark for pedestrian detection [26]. In KAIST, RGB and thermal images are aligned with a beam-splitter, and have resolutions of 640×480 and 320×256, respectively. We resize thermal images to 640×480 during training. KAIST also provides day/night tags for breakdown analysis. The original KAIST dataset contains 95,328 RGB-thermal image pairs, which are split into a training set (50,172) and a testing set (45, 156). Because the original KAIST dataset contains noisy annotations, the literature introduces cleaned version of the train/test sets: a sanitized train-set (7,601 examples) [32] and a cleaned test-set (2,252 examples) [35]. We also follow the literature [26] to evaluate under the "reasonable setting" for evaluation by ignoring annotated persons that are occluded (tagged by KAIST) or too small (<55 pixels). We follow this literature for fair comparison with recent methods.

Metric. We measure detection performance with the Log-Average Miss Rate (LAMR), which is a standard metric in pedestrian detection [15] and KAIST [26]. LAMR is computed by averaging the miss rate (false negative rate) at nine false positives per image (FPPI) rates evenly spaced in log-space from the range 10^{-2}

Table 1. Ablation study on KAIST. (LAMR↓ in %). The upper panel shows that (1) RGB-only and Thermal-only detectors perform notably better than each other on *Day* and *Night* respectively, and (2) MidFusion strikes a balance and performs better overall. In the lower panel, we focus on the very-late fusion of RGB and Thermal. We ablate methods for *score fusion* (max as in NMS, avg and ProbEn), and *box fusion* (argmax as in NMS, ProbEn that uses avg, s-avg or v-avg). Somewhat surprisingly, "max + argmax", or NMS, performs quite well on both *Day* and *Night*; average score fusion performs poorly because it double counts class prior. As for box fusion, using the learned variance/uncertainty by v-avg performs better than the heuristic methods (avg and s-avg). Our ProbEn performs significantly better and ProbEn$_3$ is the best by fusing three models: RGB, Thermal, and MidFusion.

Baselines		*Day*	*Night*	*All*
RGB		14.56	27.42	18.67
Thermal		24.59	7.76	18.99
EarlyFusion		26.30	6.61	19.36
MidFusion		17.55	9.30	14.48
Pooling		37.92	22.61	32.68
Score-fusion	*Box-fusion*	*Day*	*Night*	*All*
max	argmax	13.25	6.42	10.78
max	avg	13.25	6.65	10.89
max	s-avg	13.35	6.65	10.96
max	v-avg	13.19	6.65	10.79
avg	argmax	21.68	15.16	19.53
avg	avg	21.59	15.46	19.47
avg	s-avg	21.67	15.46	19.55
avg	v-avg	21.51	15.46	19.42
ProbEn	argmax	10.21	5.45	8.62
ProbEn	avg	10.14	5.41	8.58
ProbEn	s-avg	10.27	5.41	8.67
ProbEn	v-avg	9.93	5.41	8.50
ProbEn$_3$	argmax	13.67	6.31	11.00
ProbEn$_3$	avg	9.07	4.89	7.68
ProbEn$_3$	s-avg	**9.07**	**4.89**	7.68
ProbEn$_3$	v-avg	**9.07**	**4.89**	**7.66**

to 10^0 [26]. It does not evaluate the detections that match to ignored ground-truth [15,26]. A true positive is a detection that matches a ground-truth object with IoU>0.5 [26]; false positives are detections that do not match any ground-truth; false negatives are miss-detections.

Ablation Study on KAIST. Table 1 shows ablation studies on KAIST. Single modal detectors tend to work well in different environments, with RGB detectors working on well-lit day images while Thermal working well on nighttime images. EarlyFusion reduces the miss rate by a modest amount, while Mid-Fusion is more effective. Naive strategies for late fusion (such as pooling together detections from different modalities) are quite poor because they generate many repeated detections on the same object, which are counted as false positives. Interestingly, simple NMS that has max score fusion and argmax box fusion, is quite effective at removing overlapping detections from different modalities, already outperforming Early and MidFusion. Instead of suppressing the weaker modality, one might average the scores of overlapping detections but this is quite ineffective because it always decreases the score from NMS. Intuitively, one should increase the score when different modalities agree on a detection. ProbEn accomplishes this by probabilistic integration of information from the RGB and Thermal single-modal detectors. Moreover, it can be further improved by probabilisitcally fusing coordinates of overlapping boxes. Lastly, ProbEn$_3$ that ensembles three models (RGB, thermal and MidFusion), performs the best.

Qualitative Results are displayed in Fig. 5. Visually, ProbEn detects all persons, while the MidFusion model has multiple false negatives / miss-detections.

Quantitative Comparison on KAIST Compared Methods. Among many prior methods, we particularly compare against four recent ones: AR-CNN [57], MBNet [58], MLPD [28], and GAFF [55]. AR-CNN focuses on weakly-unaligned RGB-thermal pairs and explores multiple heuristic methods for fusing features, scores and boxes. MBNet addresses modality imbalance w.r.t illumination and features to improve detection; both MLPD and GAFF are mid-fusion methods that design sophisticated network architectures; MLPD adopts aggressive data augmentation techniques and GAFF extensively exploits attentive modules to fuse multimodal features. Table 2 lists more methods.

Results. Table 2 compares ProbEn against the prior work. ProbEn+ that ensembles three models trained in-house (RGB, Thermal, and MidFusion) achieves competitive performance (7.95 LAMR) against the prior art. When replacing our MidFusion detector with off-the-shelf mid-fusion detectors [28,55], ProbEn++ significantly outperforms all the existing methods, boosting the performance from the prior art 6.48 to 5.14! This clearly shows that ProbEn works quite well when the conditional independence assumption does not hold, i.e., fusing outputs from other fusion methods (both off-the-shelf and trained in-house). As ProbEn performs better than past work as a non-learned solution, we argue that it should serve as a new baseline for future research on multimodal detection.

Table 2. Benchmarking on KAIST measured by % LAMR↓. We report numbers from the respective papers. Results are comparable to Table 1. *Simple probabilistic ensembling of independently-trained detectors (ProbEn) outperforms $\frac{9}{12}$ methods on the leaderboard. Infact, even NMS (MaxFusion) outperforms $\frac{8}{12}$ methods, indicating the under-appreciated effectiveness of detector-ensembling as a multimodal fusion technique.* Performance further increases when adding a MidFusion detector to the probabilistic ensemble (ProbEn₃). Replacing our in-house MidFusion with off-the-shelf mid-fusion detectors MLPD [28] and GAFF [55] significantly boosts the state-of-art from 6.48 to 5.14! This shows ProbEn remains effective even when fusing models for which conditional independence does not hold.

Method	Day	Night	All
HalfwayFusion [36]	36.84	35.49	36.99
RPN+BDT [30]	30.51	27.62	29.83
TC-DET [4]	34.81	10.31	27.11
IATDNN [20]	27.29	24.41	26.37
IAF R-CNN [33]	21.85	18.96	20.95
SyNet [2]	22.64	15.80	20.19
CIAN [56]	14.77	11.13	14.12
MSDS-RCNN [32]	12.22	7.82	10.89
AR-CNN [57]	9.94	8.38	9.34
MBNet [58]	8.28	7.86	8.13
MLPD [28]	7.95	6.95	7.58
GAFF [55]	8.35	3.46	6.48
MaxFusion (NMS)	13.25	6.42	10.78
ProbEn	9.93	5.41	8.50
ProbEn₃	9.07	4.89	7.66
ProbEn₃ w/ MLPD	7.81	5.02	6.76
ProbEn₃ w/ GAFF	**6.04**	**3.59**	**5.14**

4.3   Multimodal Object Detection on FLIR

Dataset. The FLIR dataset [17] consists of RGB images (captured by a FLIR BlackFly RGB camera with 1280×1024 resolution) and thermal images (acquired by a FLIR Tau2 thermal camera 640×512 resolution). We resize all images to resolution 640×512. FLIR has $10,228$ *unaligned* RGB-thermal image pairs and annotates only for thermal (Fig. 4). Image pairs are split into trainset ($8,862$ images) and a validation set ($1,366$ images). FLIR evaluates on three classes which have imbalanced examples [8,12,27,38,54]: $28,151$ persons, $46,692$ cars, and $4,457$ bicycles. Following [54], we remove 108 thermal images in the val-set that do not have the RGB counterparts. For breakdown analysis w.r.t day/night scenes, we manually tag the validation images with "day" (768) and "night" (490). We will release our annotations to the public.

Misaligned Modalities. Because FLIR's RGB and thermal images are heavily unaligned, it labels only thermal images and does not have RGB annotations. We can still train Early and MidFusion models using multimodal inputs and the thermal annotations. These detectors might learn to internally align the unaligned modalities to predict bounding boxes according to the thermal annotations. Because we do not have an RGB-only detector, our ProbEn ensembles EarlyFusion, MidFusion, and thermal-only detectors.

Metric. We measure performance using Average Precision (AP) [16,46]. Precision is computed over testing images within a single class, with true positives that overlap ground-truth bounding boxes (e.g., IoU>0.5). Computing the average precision (AP) across all classes measures the performance in multi-class object detection. Following [8,12,27,38,54], we define a true positive as a detection that overlaps a ground-truth with IoU>0.5. Note that AP used in the multimodal detection literature is different from mAP [34], which averages over different AP's computed with different IoU thresholds.

Table 3. Ablation study on FLIR. day/night scenes (AP↑ in percentage with IoU>0.5). Compared to thermal-only detector, incorporating RGB by EarlyFusion and MidFusion notably improves performance. Late-fusion (lower panel) ensembles three detectors: Thermal, EarlyFusion and MidFusion. All the explored late-fusion methods lead to better performance than MidFusion. In particular, ProbEn performs the best. Moreover, similar to the results on KAIST, using predicted uncertainty to fuse boxes (v-avg) performs better than the other two heuristic box fusion methods, avg that naively averages box coordinates and s-avg that uses classification scores to weighted average box coordinates.

Baselines		Day	Night	All
Thermal		75.35	82.90	79.24
EarlyFusion		77.37	79.56	78.80
MidFusion		79.37	81.64	80.53
Pooling		52.57	55.15	53.66
Score-fusion	*Box-fusion*	*Day*	*Night*	*All*
max	argmax	81.91	84.42	83.14
max	avg	81.84	84.62	83.21
max	s-avg	81.85	84.48	83.19
max	v-avg	81.80	85.07	83.31
avg	argmax	81.34	84.69	82.65
avg	avg	81.26	84.81	82.91
avg	s-avg	81.26	84.72	82.89
avg	v-avg	81.26	85.39	83.03
ProbEn$_3$	argmax	82.19	84.73	83.27
ProbEn$_3$	avg	82.19	84.91	83.63
ProbEn$_3$	s-avg	82.20	84.84	83.61
ProbEn$_3$	v-avg	**82.21**	**85.56**	**83.76**

day scene   night scene

Fig. 6. Detections overlaid on two FLIR testing images (in columns) with RGB (top) and thermal images (middle and bottom). To avoid clutter, we do not mark class labels for the bounding boxes. Ground-truth annotations are shown on the RGB, emphaszing that RGB and thermal images are strongly unaligned. On the thermal images, we compare thermal-only (mid-row) and our ProbEn (bottom-row) models. Green, red and blue boxes stand for true positives, false negative (mis-detected persons) and false positives. In particular, in the second column, the thermal-only model has many false negatives (or miss-detections), which are "bicycles". Understandably, thermal cameras will not capture bicycles because they do not emit heat. In contrast, RGB capture bicycle signatures better than thermal. This explains why our fusion performs better on bicycles.

Ablation Study on FLIR. We compare our fusion methods in Table 3, along with qualitative results in Fig. 6. We analyze results using our day/night tags. Compared to the single-modal detector (Thermal), our learning-based early-fusion (EarlyFusion) and mid-fusion (MidFusion) produce better performance. MidFusion outperforms EarlyFusion, implying that end-to-end learning of fusing features better handles mis-alignment between RGB and thermal images. By applying late-fusion methods to detections of Thermal, EarlyFusion and Mid-Fusion detectors, we boost detection performance. Note that typical ensembling methods in the single-modal (RGB) detection literature [32,36,52] often use max/average score fusion, and argmax/average box fusion, which are outperformed by our ProbEn. This suggests that ProbEn should be potentially a better ensembling method for object detection.

Quantitative Comparison on FLIR Compared Methods. We compare against prior methods including ThermalDet [8], BU [27], ODSC [38], MMTOD [12], CFR [54], and GAFF [55]. As FLIR does not have aligned

Table 4. Benchmarking on FLIR measured by AP↑ in percentage with IoU>0.5 with breakdown on the three categories. Perhaps surprisingly, end-to-end training on thermal already outperforms all the prior methods, presumably because of using a better pre-trained model (Faster-RCNN). Importantly, our ProbEn increases AP from prior art 74.6% to 84.4%! These results are comparable to Table 3.

Method	Bicycle	Person	Car	All
MMTOD-CG [12]	50.26	63.31	70.63	61.40
MMTOD-UNIT [12]	49.43	64.47	70.72	61.54
ODSC [38]	55.53	71.01	82.33	69.62
CFR3 [54]	55.77	74.49	84.91	72.39
BU(AT,T) [27]	56.10	76.10	87.00	73.10
BU(LT,T) [27]	57.40	75.60	86.50	73.20
GAFF [55]	—	—	—	72.90
ThermalDet [8]	60.04	78.24	85.52	74.60
Thermal	62.63	84.04	87.11	79.24
EarlyFusion	63.43	85.27	87.69	78.80
MidFusion	69.80	84.16	87.63	80.53
ProbEn$_3$	**73.49**	**87.65**	**90.14**	**83.76**

RGB-thermal images and only annotates thermal images, many methods exploit domain adaptation that adapts a pre-trained RGB detector to thermal input. For example, MMTOD [12] and ODSC [38] adopt the image-to-image-translation technique [53,59] to generate RGB from thermal, hypothesizing that this helps train a better multimodal detector by finetuning a detector that is pre-trained over large-scale RGB images. BU [27] operates such a translation/adaptation on features that generates thermal features to be similar to RGB features. ThermalDet [8] exclusively exploits thermal images and ignores RGB images; it proposes to combine features from multiple layers for the final detection. GAFF [55] trains on RGB-thermal image with a sophisticated attention module that fuse single-modal features. Perhaps because the complexity of the attention module, GAFF is limited to using small network backbones (ResNet18 and VGG16). Somewhat surprisingly, to the best of our knowledge, there is no prior work that trained early-fusion or mid-fusion deep networks (Fig. 2a) on the heavily unaligned RGB-thermal image pairs (like in FLIR) for multimodal detection. We find directly training them performs much better than prior work (Table 4).

Results. Table 4 shows that all our methods outperform the prior art. Our single-modal detector (trained on thermal images) achieves slightly better performance than ThermalDet [8], which also exclusively trains on thermal images. This is probably because we use a better pre-trained Faster-RCNN model provided by the excellent Detectron2 toolbox. Surprisingly, our simpler EarlyFusion and MidFusion models achieve big boosts over the thermal-only model (Thermal), while MidFusion performs much better. This confirms our hypothesis that fusing features better handles mis-alignment of RGB-thermal images than the early-fusion method. Our ProbEn performs the best, significantly better than all compared methods! Notably, our fusion methods boost "bicycle" detection. We conjecture that bicycles do not emit heat to deliver strong signatures in thermal, but are more visible in RGB; fusing them greatly improves bicycle detection.

5   Discussion and Conclusions

We explore different fusion strategies for multimodal detection under both aligned and unaligned RGB-thermal images. We show that non-learned probabilistic fusion, ProbEn, significantly outperforms prior approaches. Key reasons for its strong performance are that (1) it can take advantage of highly-tuned single-modal detectors trained on large-scale single-modal datasets, and (2) it can deal with missing detections from particular modalities, a common occurrence when fusing together detections. One by-product of our diagnostic analysis is the remarkable performance of NMS as a fusion technique, precisely because it exploits the same key insights. Our ProbEn yields >**13%** relative improvement over prior work, both on aligned and unaligned multimodal benchmarks.

Acknowledgement. This work was supported by the CMU Argo AI Center for Autonomous Vehicle Research.

References

1. Akiba, T., Kerola, T., Niitani, Y., Ogawa, T., Sano, S., Suzuki, S.: PFDet: 2nd place solution to open images challenge 2018 object detection track. arXiv:1809.00778 (2018)
2. Albaba, B.M., Ozer, S.: SyNet: an ensemble network for object detection in UAV images. In: 2020 25th International Conference on Pattern Recognition (ICPR). pp. 10227–10234. IEEE (2021)
3. Bauer, E., Kohavi, R.: An empirical comparison of voting classification algorithms: Bagging, boosting, and variants. Mach. Learn. **36**(1), 105–139 (1999)
4. Kieu, M., Bagdanov, A.D., Bertini, M., del Bimbo, A.: Task-conditioned domain adaptation for pedestrian detection in thermal imagery. In: Vedaldi, A., Bischof, H., Brox, T., Frahm, J.-M. (eds.) ECCV 2020. LNCS, vol. 12367, pp. 546–562. Springer, Cham (2020). https://doi.org/10.1007/978-3-030-58542-6_33
5. Bodla, N., Singh, B., Chellappa, R., Davis, L.S.: Soft-NMS-improving object detection with one line of code. In: ICCV (2017)
6. Bolya, D., Zhou, C., Xiao, F., Lee, Y.J.: YOLACT: real-time instance segmentation. In: ICCV (2019)
7. Caesar, H., et al.: nuScenes a multimodal dataset for autonomous driving. In: CVPR (2020)
8. Cao, Y., Zhou, T., Zhu, X., Su, Y.: Every feature counts: an improved one-stage detector in thermal imagery. In: IEEE International Conference on Computer and Communications (ICCC) (2019)
9. Choi, H., Kim, S., Park, K., Sohn, K.: Multi-spectral pedestrian detection based on accumulated object proposal with fully convolutional networks. In: International Conference on Pattern Recognition (ICPR) (2016)

10. Dalal, N., Triggs, B.: Histograms of oriented gradients for human detection. In: CVPR (2005)
11. Dawid, A.P.: Conditional independence in statistical theory. J. Roy. Stat. Soc.: Ser. B (Methodol.) **41**(1), 1–15 (1979)
12. Devaguptapu, C., Akolekar, N., M Sharma, M., N Balasubramanian, V.: Borrow from anywhere: pseudo multi-modal object detection in thermal imagery. In: CVPR Workshops (2019)
13. Dietterich, T.G.: Ensemble methods in machine learning. In: Kittler, J., Roli, F. (eds.) MCS 2000. LNCS, vol. 1857, pp. 1–15. Springer, Heidelberg (2000). https://doi.org/10.1007/3-540-45014-9_1
14. Dollár, P., Wojek, C., Schiele, B., Perona, P.: Pedestrian detection: A benchmark. In: CVPR (2009)
15. Dollar, P., Wojek, C., Schiele, B., Perona, P.: Pedestrian detection: An evaluation of the state of the art. IEEE Trans. Pattern Anal. Mach. Intell. **34**(4), 743–761 (2011)
16. Everingham, M., Eslami, S.A., Van Gool, L., Williams, C.K., Winn, J., Zisserman, A.: The pascal visual object classes challenge: a retrospective. Int. J. Comput. Vision **111**(1), 98–136 (2015)
17. FLIR: Flir thermal dataset for algorithm training (2018). https://www.flir.in/oem/adas/adas-dataset-form
18. Freund, Y., et al.: Experiments with a new boosting algorithm. In: ICML, vol. 96, pp. 148–156. Citeseer (1996)
19. Geiger, A., Lenz, P., Urtasun, R.: Are we ready for autonomous driving? The KITTI vision benchmark suite. In: Conference on Computer Vision and Pattern Recognition (CVPR) (2012)
20. Guan, D., Cao, Y., Yang, J., Cao, Y., Yang, M.Y.: Fusion of multispectral data through illumination-aware deep neural networks for pedestrian detection. Inf. Fusion **50**, 148–157 (2019)
21. Guo, C., Pleiss, G., Sun, Y., Weinberger, K.Q.: On calibration of modern neural networks. arXiv:1706.04599 (2017)
22. Guo, R., et al.: 2nd place solution in google ai open images object detection track 2019. arXiv:1911.07171 (2019)
23. He, K., Gkioxari, G., Dollár, P., Girshick, R.: Mask R-CNN. In: ICCV (2017)
24. Hosang, J., Benenson, R., Schiele, B.: Learning non-maximum suppression. In: Proceedings of the IEEE Conference on Computer Vision and Pattern Recognition, pp. 4507–4515 (2017)
25. Huang, Z., Chen, Z., Li, Q., Zhang, H., Wang, N.: 1st place solutions of waymo open dataset challenge 2020–2D object detection track. arXiv:2008.01365 (2020)
26. Hwang, S., Park, J., Kim, N., Choi, Y., So Kweon, I.: Multispectral pedestrian detection: Benchmark dataset and baseline. In: CVPR (2015)
27. Kiew, M.Y., Bagdanov, A.D., Bertini, M.: Bottom-up and layer-wise domain adaptation for pedestrian detection in thermal images. ACM Transactions on Multimedia Computing Communications and Applications (2020)
28. Kim, J., Kim, H., Kim, T., Kim, N., Choi, Y.: MLPD: multi-label pedestrian detector in multispectral domain. IEEE Rob. Auto. Lett. **6**(4), 7846–7853 (2021)
29. Kittler, J., Hatef, M., Duin, R.P., Matas, J.: On combining classifiers. IEEE Trans. Pattern Anal. Mach. Intell. **20**(3), 226–239 (1998)
30. Konig, D., Adam, M., Jarvers, C., Layher, G., Neumann, H., Teutsch, M.: Fully convolutional region proposal networks for multispectral person detection. In: Proceedings of the IEEE Conference on Computer Vision and Pattern Recognition Workshops, pp. 49–56 (2017)

31. Krizhevsky, A., Sutskever, I., Hinton, G.E.: ImageNet classification with deep convolutional neural networks. Adv. Neural. Inf. Process. Syst. **25**, 1097–1105 (2012)
32. Li, C., Song, D., Tong, R., Tang, M.: Multispectral pedestrian detection via simultaneous detection and segmentation. arXiv:1808.04818 (2018)
33. Li, C., Song, D., Tong, R., Tang, M.: Illumination-aware faster r-CNN for robust multispectral pedestrian detection. Pattern Recogn. **85**, 161–171 (2019)
34. Lin, T.Y., et al.: Microsoft COCO: common objects in context. In: Fleet, D., Pajdla, T., Schiele, B., Tuytelaars, T. (eds.) ECCV 2014. LNCS, vol. 8693, pp. 740–755. Springer, Cham (2014). https://doi.org/10.1007/978-3-319-10602-1_48
35. Liu, J., Zhang, S., Wang, S., Metaxas, D.: Improved annotations of test set of KAIST (2018)
36. Liu, J., Zhang, S., Wang, S., Metaxas, D.N.: Multispectral deep neural networks for pedestrian detection. In: BMVC (2016)
37. Liu, W., Anguelov, D., Erhan, D., Szegedy, C., Reed, S., Fu, C.-Y., Berg, A.C.: SSD: single shot multibox detector. In: Leibe, B., Matas, J., Sebe, N., Welling, M. (eds.) ECCV 2016. LNCS, vol. 9905, pp. 21–37. Springer, Cham (2016). https://doi.org/10.1007/978-3-319-46448-0_2
38. Munir, F., Azam, S., Rafique, M.A., Sheri, A.M., Jeon, M.: Thermal object detection using domain adaptation through style consistency. arXiv:2006.00821 (2020)
39. Nix, D.A., Weigend, A.S.: Estimating the mean and variance of the target probability distribution. In: Proceedings of 1994 IEEE international conference on neural networks (ICNN 1994), vol. 1, pp. 55–60. IEEE (1994)
40. Paszke, A., et al.: Automatic differentiation in Pytorch (2017)
41. Pearl, J.: Probabilistic Reasoning in Intelligent Systems: Networks of Plausible Inference. Elsevier, San Mateo (2014)
42. Quigley, M., et al.: ROS: an open-source robot operating system. In: ICRA Workshop on Open Source Software, vol. 3, p. 5. Kobe, Japan (2009)
43. Redmon, J., Divvala, S., Girshick, R., Farhadi, A.: You only look once: Unified, real-time object detection. In: CVPR (2016)
44. Redmon, J., Farhadi, A.: Yolo9000: better, faster, stronger. In: CVPR (2017)
45. Ren, S., He, K., Girshick, R., Sun, J.: Faster R-CNN: towards real-time object detection with region proposal networks. In: NeurIPS (2015)
46. Russakovsky, O., et al.: ImageNet large scale visual recognition challenge. Int. J. Comput. Vis. **115**(3), 211–252 (2015)
47. Solovyev, R., Wang, W., Gabruseva, T.: Weighted boxes fusion: ensembling boxes from different object detection models. Image Vis. Comput. **107**, 104117 (2021)
48. Valverde, F.R., Hurtado, J.V., Valada, A.: There is more than meets the eye: self-supervised multi-object detection and tracking with sound by distilling multimodal knowledge. In: CVPR (2021)
49. Wagner, J., Fischer, V., Herman, M., Behnke, S.: Multispectral pedestrian detection using deep fusion convolutional neural networks. In: Proceedings of European Symposium on Artificial Neural Networks (2016)
50. Wu, Y., Kirillov, A., Massa, F., Lo, W.Y., Girshick, R.: Detectron2. https://github.com/facebookresearch/detectron2 (2019)
51. Xu, D., Ouyang, W., Ricci, E., Wang, X., Sebe, N.: Learning cross-modal deep representations for robust pedestrian detection. In: CVPR (2017)
52. Xu, P., Davoine, F., Denoeux, T.: Evidential combination of pedestrian detectors. In: British Machine Vision Conference, pp. 1–14 (2014)
53. Zhang, H., Dana, K.: Multi-style generative network for real-time transfer. arXiv:1703.06953 (2017)

54. Zhang, H., Fromont, E., Lefèvre, S., Avignon, B.: Multispectral fusion for object detection with cyclic fuse-and-refine blocks. In: IEEE International Conference on Image Processing (ICIP) (2020)
55. Zhang, H., Fromont, E., Lefèvre, S., Avignon, B.: Guided attentive feature fusion for multispectral pedestrian detection. In: WACV (2021)
56. Zhang, L., et al.: Cross-modality interactive attention network for multispectral pedestrian detection. Inf. Fus. **50**, 20–29 (2019)
57. Zhang, L., Zhu, X., Chen, X., Yang, X., Lei, Z., Liu, Z.: Weakly aligned cross-modal learning for multispectral pedestrian detection. In: ICCV (2019)
58. Zhou, K., Chen, L., Cao, X.: Improving multispectral pedestrian detection by addressing modality imbalance problems. In: Vedaldi, A., Bischof, H., Brox, T., Frahm, J.-M. (eds.) ECCV 2020. LNCS, vol. 12363, pp. 787–803. Springer, Cham (2020). https://doi.org/10.1007/978-3-030-58523-5_46
59. Zhu, J.Y., Park, T., Isola, P., Efros, A.A.: Unpaired image-to-image translation using cycle-consistent adversarial networks. In: ICCV (2017)
60. Zitnick, C.L., Dollár, P.: Edge Boxes: locating object proposals from edges. In: Fleet, D., Pajdla, T., Schiele, B., Tuytelaars, T. (eds.) ECCV 2014. LNCS, vol. 8693, pp. 391–405. Springer, Cham (2014). https://doi.org/10.1007/978-3-319-10602-1_26

Exploiting Unlabeled Data with Vision and Language Models for Object Detection

Shiyu Zhao[1]([⊠])[iD], Zhixing Zhang[1][iD], Samuel Schulter[2][iD], Long Zhao[3][iD],
B.G Vijay Kumar[2][iD], Anastasis Stathopoulos[1][iD], Manmohan Chandraker[2,4][iD],
and Dimitris N. Metaxas[1][iD]

[1] Rutgers University, New Brunswick, USA
sz553@rutgers.edu
[2] NEC Labs America, San Jose, USA
[3] Google Research, Los Angeles, USA
[4] UC San Diego, La Jolla, USA

Abstract. Building robust and generic object detection frameworks requires scaling to larger label spaces and bigger training datasets. However, it is prohibitively costly to acquire annotations for thousands of categories at a large scale. We propose a novel method that leverages the rich semantics available in recent vision and language models to localize and classify objects in unlabeled images, effectively generating pseudo labels for object detection. Starting with a generic and class-agnostic region proposal mechanism, we use vision and language models to categorize each region of an image into any object category that is required for downstream tasks. We demonstrate the value of the generated pseudo labels in two specific tasks, open-vocabulary detection, where a model needs to generalize to unseen object categories, and semi-supervised object detection, where additional unlabeled images can be used to improve the model. Our empirical evaluation shows the effectiveness of the pseudo labels in both tasks, where we outperform competitive baselines and achieve a novel state-of-the-art for open-vocabulary object detection. Our code is available at https://github.com/xiaofeng94/VL-PLM.

1 Introduction

Recent advances in object detection build on large-scale datasets [17,27,41], which provide rich and accurate human-annotated bounding boxes for many object categories. However, the annotation cost of such datasets is significant. Moreover, the long-tailed distribution of natural object categories makes it even harder to collect sufficient annotations for all categories. Semi-supervised object detection (SSOD) [44,60] and open-vocabulary object detection (OVD) [4,16,54] are two tasks to lower annotations costs by leveraging different forms of unlabeled

---

S. Zhao1 and Z. Zhang1—Equal contribution.

Supplementary Information The online version contains supplementary material available at https://doi.org/10.1007/978-3-031-20077-9_10.

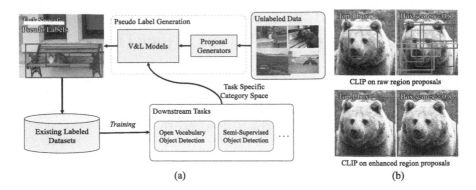

Fig. 1. (a) Overview of leveraging the semantic knowledge contained in vision and language models for mining unlabeled data to improve object detection systems for open-vocabulary and semi-supervised tasks. **(b)** Illustration of the weak localization ability when applying CLIP [37] on raw object proposals (top), compared with our improvements (bottom). The left images show the pseudo label with the highest score. The right images show all pseudo labels with scores greater than 0.8. The proposed scoring gives much cleaner pseudo labels.

data. In SSOD, a small fraction of fully-annotated training images is given along with a large corpus of unlabeled images. In OVD, a fraction of the desired object categories is annotated (the base categories) in all training images and the task is to also detect a set of novel (or unknown) categories at test time. These object categories can be present in the training images, but are not annotated with ground truth bounding boxes. A common and successful approach for leveraging unlabeled data is by generating pseudo labels. However, all prior works on SSOD only leveraged the small set of labeled data for generating pseudo labels, while most prior work on OVD does not leverage pseudo labels at all.

In this work, we propose a simple but effective way to mine unlabeled images using recently proposed vision and language (V&L) models to generate pseudo labels for both known and unknown categories, which suits both tasks, SSOD and OVD. V&L models [23,29,37] can be trained from (noisy) image caption pairs, which can be obtained at a large scale without human annotation efforts by crawling websites for images and their alt-texts. Despite the noisy annotations, these models demonstrate excellent performance on various semantic tasks like zero-shot classification or image-text retrieval. The large amount of diverse images, combined with the free-form text, provides a powerful source of information to train robust and generic models. These properties make vision and language models an ideal candidate to improve existing object detection pipelines that leverage unlabeled data, like OVD or SSOD, see Fig. 1(a).

Specifically, our approach leverages the recently proposed vision and language model CLIP [37] to generate pseudo labels for object detection. We first predict region proposals with a two-stage class-agnostic proposal generator which was trained with limited ground truth (using only known base categories in OVD and only labeled images in SSOD), but generalizes to unseen categories. For each region proposal, we then obtain a probability distribution over the desired object categories (depending on the task) with the pre-trained V&L model CLIP [37]. However, as shown in Fig. 1(b), a major challenge of V&L models is the rather low object localization quality, also observed in [57]. To improve localization, we propose two strategies where the two-stage proposal generator helps the V&L model: (1) Fusing CLIP scores and objectness scores of the two-stage proposal generator, and (2) removing redundant proposals by repeated application of the localization head (2nd stage) in the proposal generator. Finally, the generated pseudo labels are combined with the original ground truth to train the final detector. We name our method as **V&L**-guided **P**seudo-Label Mining (VL-PLM).

Extensive experiments demonstrate that VL-PLM successfully exploits the unlabeled data for open-vocabulary detection and outperforms the state-of-the-art ViLD [16] on novel categories by +6.8 AP on the COCO dataset [32]. Moreover, VL-PLM improves the performance on known categories in SSOD and beats the popular baseline STAC [44] by a clear margin, by only replacing its pseudo labels with ours. Besides, we also conduct various ablation studies on the properties of the generated pseudo labels and analyze the design choices of our proposed method. We also believe that VL-PLM can be further improved with better V&L models like ALIGN [23] or ALBEF [29].

The contributions of our work are as follows: **(1)** We leverage V&L models for improving object detection frameworks by generating pseudo labels on unlabeled data. **(2)** A simple but effective strategy to improve the localization quality of pseudo labels scored with the V&L model CLIP [37]. **(3)** State-of-the-art results for novel categories on the COCO open-vocabulary detection setting. **(4)** We showcase the benefits of VL-PLM in a semi-supervised object detection setting.

2   Related Work

The goal of our work is to improve object detection systems by leveraging unlabeled data via vision and language models that carry rich semantic information.

Vision & Language (VL) Models: Combining natural language and images has enabled many valuable applications in recent years, like image captioning [2,7, 12,25], visual question answering [1,13,20,30,36,55], referring expression comprehension [8,24,26,34,35,52,53], image-text retrieval [29,37,47] or language-driven embodied AI [3,9]. While early works proposed task-specific models, generic representation learning from vision and language inputs has gained more attention [8,19,33,34,45]. Most recent works like CLIP [37] or ALIGN [23] also propose generic vision and language representation learning approaches, but have significantly increased the scale of training data, which led to impressive results in tasks like zero-shot image classification or image-text retrieval. The training data consist of image and text pairs, typically crawled from the web at a very large scale (400M for [37] and 1.2B for [23]), but without human annotation effort. In our work, we leverage such pre-trained models to mine unlabeled data and to generate pseudo labels in the form of bounding boxes, suitable for object detection. One challenge with using such V&L models [23,37] is their limited capability in localizing objects (recall Fig. 1(b)), likely due to the lack of region-word alignment in the image-text pairs of their training data. In Sect. 3.2, we show how to improve localization quality with our proposal generator.

Vision & Language Models for Dense Prediction Tasks: The success of CLIP [37] (and others [23,29]) has motivated the extension of zero-shot classification capabilities to dense image prediction tasks like object detection [16,21, 42,54] or semantic segmentation [28,39,50,59]. These works try to map features of individual objects (detection) or pixels (segmentation) into the joint vision-language embedding space provided by models like CLIP. For example, ViLD [16] trains an object detector in the open-vocabulary regime by predicting the text embedding (from the CLIP text-encoder) of the category name for each image region. LSeg [28] follows a similar approach, but is applied to zero-shot semantic segmentation. Both works leverage task-specific insights and do not generate explicit pseudo labels. In contrast, our proposed VL-PLM is more generic by generating pseudo labels, thus enabling also other tasks like semi-supervised object detection [44]. Similar to our work, both Gao *et al.* [14] and Zhong *et al.* [57] generate explicit pseudo labels in the form of bounding boxes. In [14], the attention maps of a pretrained V&L model [29] between words of a given caption and image regions are used together with object proposals to generate pseudo labels. In contrast, our approach does not require image captions as input and we use only unlabeled images, while still outperforming [14] in an open-vocabulary setting on COCO. RegionCLIP [57] assigns semantics to region proposals via a pretrained V&L model, effectively creating pseudo labels in the form of bounding boxes. While our approach uses such pseudo labels directly for training object detectors, [57] uses them for fine-tuning the original V&L model, which then builds the basis for downstream tasks like open-vocabulary detection. We believe this contribution is orthogonal to ours as it effectively builds a better starting point of the V&L model, and can be incorporated into our framework as well. Interestingly, even without the refined V&L model, we show improved accuracy with pseudo labels specifically for novel categories as shown in Sect. 4.1.

The main focus of all the aforementioned works is to enable the dynamic expansion of the label space and to recognize novel categories. While our work also demonstrates state-of-the-art results in this open-vocabulary setting, where we mine unlabeled data for novel categories, we want to stress that our pseudo labels are applicable more generally. In particular, we also use a V&L model to mine unlabeled images for known categories in a semi-supervised object detection setting. Furthermore, by building on the general concept of pseudo labels, our approach may be extended to other dense prediction tasks like semantic segmentation in future works as well.

Object Detection From Incomplete Annotations: Pseudo labels are proven useful in many recent object detection methods trained with various forms of weak annotations: semi-supervised detection [44,60], unsupervised object discovery [43], open-vocabulary detection [14,57], weakly-supervised detection [10,58], unsupervised domain adaptation [22,51] or multi-dataset detection [56]. In all cases, an initial model trained from base information is applied on the training data to obtain the missing information. Our main proposal is to leverage V&L

models to improve these pseudo labels and have one unified way of improving the accuracy in multiple settings, see Sect. 3.3. In this work, we focus on two important forms of weak supervision: zero-shot/open-vocabulary detection (OVD) and semi-supervised object detection (SSOD). In zero-shot detection [4] a model is trained from a set of base categories. Without ever seeing any instance of a novel category during training, the model is asked to predict novel categories, typically via association in a different embedding space, like attribute or text embeddings. Recent works [16,38,54] relax the setting to include novel categories in the training data, but without bounding box annotations, which also enables V&L models to be used (via additional images that come with caption data). ViLD [16], as described above, uses CLIP [37] with model distillation losses to make predictions in the joint vision-text embedding space. In contrast, we demonstrate that explicitly creating pseudo labels for novel categories via mining the training data can significantly improve the accuracy, see Sect. 4.1. The second task we focus on is semi-supervised object detection (SSOD), where a small set of images with bounding box annotations and a large set of unlabeled images are given. In contrast to OVD, the label space does not change from train to test time. A popular and recent baseline that builds on pseudo labels is STAC [44]. This approach employs a consistency loss between predictions on a strongly augmented image and pseudo labels computed on the original image. We demonstrate the benefit of leveraging V&L models to improve the pseudo label quality in such a framework. Other works on SSOD, like [49,60] propose several orthogonal improvements which can be incorporated into our framework as well. In this work, however, we focus purely on the impact of the pseudo labels. Finally, note that our concepts may also be applicable to other tasks beyond open-vocabulary and semi-supervised object detection, but we leave this for future work.

3   Method

The goal of our work is to mine unlabeled images with vision & language (V&L) models to generate semantically rich pseudo labels (PLs) in the form of bounding boxes so that object detectors can better leverage unlabeled data. We start with a generic training strategy for object detectors with the unlabeled data in Sect. 3.1. Then, Sect. 3.2 describes the proposed VL-PLM for pseudo label generation. Finally, Sect. 3.3 presents specific object detection tasks with our PLs.

3.1   Training Object Detectors with Unlabeled Data

Unlabeled data comes in many different forms for object detectors. In semi-supervised object detection, we have a set of fully-labeled images $\mathcal{I}_L$ with annotations for the full label space $\mathcal{S}$, as well as unlabeled images $\mathcal{I}_U$, with $\mathcal{I}_L \cap \mathcal{I}_U = \varnothing$. In open-vocabulary detection, we have partly-labeled images with annotations for the set of base categories $\mathcal{S}_B$, but without annotations for the unknown/novel categories $\mathcal{S}_N$. Note that partly-labeled images are therefore contained in both $\mathcal{I}_L$ and $\mathcal{I}_U$, i.e., $\mathcal{I}_L = \mathcal{I}_U$.

A popular and successful approach to learn from unlabeled data is via pseudo labels. Recent semi-supervised object detection methods follow this approach by first training a teacher model on the limited ground truth data, then generating pseudo labels for the unlabeled data, and finally training a student model. In the following, we describe a general training strategy for object detection to handle different forms of unlabeled data.

We define a generic loss function for an object detector with parameters θ over both labeled and unlabeled images as

$$\mathcal{L}(\theta, \mathcal{I}) = \frac{1}{N_\mathcal{I}} \sum_{i=1}^{N_\mathcal{I}} [I_i \in \mathcal{I}_L] \, l_s(\theta, I_i) + \alpha [I_i \in \mathcal{I}_U] \, l_u(\theta, I_i) \,, \tag{1}$$

where α is a hyperparameter to balance supervised l_s and unsupervised l_u losses and $[\cdot]$ is the indicator function returning either 0 or 1 depending on the condition. Note again that I_i can be contained in both $\mathcal{I}_L$ and $\mathcal{I}_U$.

Object detection ultimately is a set prediction problem and to define a loss function, the set of predictions (class probabilities and bounding box estimates) need to be matched with the set of ground truth boxes. Different options exist to find a matching [6,18] but it is mainly defined by the similarity (IoU) between predicted and ground truth boxes. We define the matching for prediction i as $\sigma(i)$, which returns a ground truth index j if successfully matched or $\mathtt{nil}$ otherwise. The supervised loss l_s contains a standard cross-entropy loss for the classification l_{cls} and an ℓ_1 loss for the box regression l_{reg}. Given $I \in \mathcal{I}$, we define l_s as,

$$l_s(\theta, I) = \frac{1}{N^*} \sum_i l_{cls} \left(C_i^\theta(I), c_{\sigma(i)}^* \right) + [\sigma(i) \neq \mathtt{nil}] \, l_{reg} \left(T_i^\theta(I), \mathbf{t}_{\sigma(i)}^* \right) \,, \tag{2}$$

where N^* is the number of predicted bounding boxes. $C_i^\theta(\cdot)$ and $T_i^\theta(\cdot)$ are the predicted class distributions and bounding boxes of the object detector. The corresponding (matched) ground truth is defined as $c_{\sigma(i)}^*$ and $\mathbf{t}_{\sigma(i)}^*$, respectively.

The unsupervised loss l_u is similarly defined, but uses pseudo labels with high confidence as supervision signals:

$$l_u(\theta, I) = \frac{1}{N^u} \sum_i [\max(\mathbf{p}_{\sigma(i)}^u) \geq \tau] \cdot \left(l_{cls} \left(C_i^\theta(I), \hat{c}_{\sigma(i)}^u \right) + \right.$$
$$\left. [\sigma(i) \neq \mathtt{nil}] \, l_{reg} \left(T_i^\theta(I), \mathbf{t}_{\sigma(i)}^u \right) \right) \,. \tag{3}$$

Here, $\mathbf{p}_{\sigma(i)}^u$ defines the probability distribution over the label space of the pseudo label matched with prediction i and N^u is the number of adopted pseudo labels, i.e., $N^u = \sum_i [\max(\mathbf{p}_{\sigma(i)}^u) \geq \tau]$. Pseudo labels for the classification and the box regression losses are $\hat{c}_{\sigma(i)}^u = \arg\max(\mathbf{p}_{\sigma(i)}^u)$ and $\mathbf{t}_{\sigma(i)}^u$, respectively.

The key to successful training of object detectors from unlabeled data are accurate pseudo labels. In the next section, we will present our approach, VL-PLM, to leverage V&L models as external models to exploit unlabeled data for generating pseudo labels.

3.2   VL-PLM: Pseudo Labels from Vision & Language Models

V&L models are trained on large scale datasets with image-text pairs that cover a diverse set of image domains and rich semantics in natural text. Moreover, the

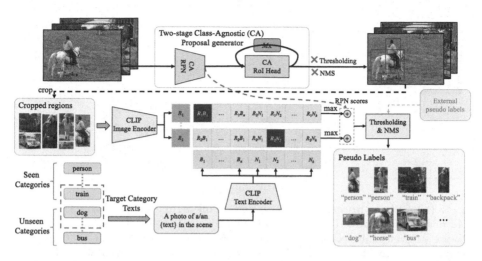

Fig. 2. Overview of the proposed VL-PLM to mine unlabeled images with vision & language models to generate pseudo labels for object detection. The top part illustrates our class-agnostic proposal generator, which improves the pseudo label localization by using the class-agnostic proposal score and the repeated application of the RoI head. The bottom part illustrates the scoring of cropped regions with the V&L model based on the target category names. The chosen category names can be adjusted for the desired downstream task. After thresholding and NMS, we get the final pseudo labels. For some tasks like SSOD, we will merge external pseudo labels for a teacher model with ours before thresholding and NMS.

image-text pairs can be obtained without costly human annotation by using web-crawled data (images and corresponding alt-texts) [23,37]. Thus, V&L models are ideal sources of external knowledge to generate pseudo labels for arbitrary categories, which can be used for downstream tasks like open-vocabulary or semi-supervised object detection.

Overview: Figure 2 illustrates the overall pipeline of our pseudo label generation with the recent V&L model CLIP [37]. We first feed an unlabeled image into our two-stage class-agnostic detector (described in the next section below) to obtain region proposals. We then crop image patches based on those regions and feed them into the CLIP image-encoder to obtain an embedding in the CLIP vision-and-language space. Using the corresponding CLIP text-encoder and template text prompts, we generate embeddings for category names that are desired for the specific task. For each region, we compute the similarities between the region embedding and the text embeddings via a dot product and use softmax to obtain a distribution over the categories. We then generate the final pseudo labels using scores from both class-agnostic detector and V&L model, which we describe in detail below.

There are two key challenges in our framework: (1) Generating robust proposals for novel categories, required by open-vocabulary detection, and (2) overcoming the poor localization quality of the raw CLIP model, see Fig. 1(b).

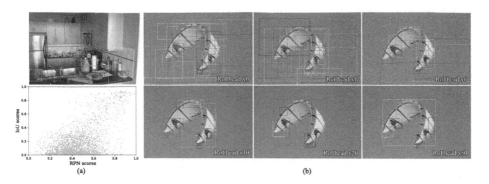

Fig. 3. (a) RPN scores indicate localization quality. Top: Top 50 boxes from RPN in an image which correctly locates nearly all objects. Bottom: A positive correlation between RPN and IoU scores for RPN boxes of 50 randomly sampled COCO images. The correlation coefficient is 0.51. **(b)** Box refinement by repeating RoI head. "×N" indicates how many times we repeat the RoI head.

We introduce simple but effective solutions to address the two challenges in the following.

Generating Robust and Class-Agnostic Region Proposals: To benefit tasks like open vocabulary detection with the unlabeled data, the proposal generator should be able to locate not only objects of categories seen during training but also of objects of novel categories. While unsupervised candidates like selective search [46] exist, these are often time-consuming and generate many noisy boxes. As suggested in prior studies [16,54], the region proposal network (RPN) of a two-stage detector generalizes well for novel categories. Moreover, we find that the RoI head is able to improve the localization of region proposals, which is elaborated in the next section. Thus, we train a standard two-stage detector, e.g., Faster-RCNN [40], as our proposal generator using available ground truth, which are annotations of base categories for open vocabulary detection and annotations from the small fraction of annotated images in semi-supervised detection. To further improve the generalization ability, we ignore the category information of the training set and train a class-agnostic proposal generator. Please refer to Sect. 4.3 and the supplement for a detailed analysis of the proposal generator.

Generating Pseudo Labels with a V&L Model: Directly applying CLIP [37] on cropped region proposals yields low localization quality, as was observed in Fig. 1(b) and also in [57]. Here, we demonstrate how to improve the localization ability with our two-stage class-agnostic proposal generator in two ways. Firstly, we find that the RPN score is a good indicator for localization quality of region proposals. Figure 3(a) illustrates a positive correlation between RPN and IoU scores. We leverage this observation and average the RPN score with those of the CLIP predictions. Secondly, we remove thresholding and NMS of the proposal generator and feed proposal boxes into the RoI head multiple times, similar to [5]. We observe that it pushes redundant boxes closer to each other by repeating the

RoI head, which can be seen in Fig. 3(b). In this way, we encounter better located bounding boxes and provide better pseudo labels. Please refer to Sect. 4.3 for a corresponding empirical analysis.

To further improve the quality of our pseudo labels, we adopt the multi-scale region embedding from CLIP as described in [16]. Moreover, as suggested in [44], we employ a high threshold to pick pseudo labels with high confidence. The confidence score of the pseudo label for the region R_i is formulated as $\bar{c}_i^u = [s_i^u \geq \tau] \cdot s_i^u$, with

$$s_i^u = \frac{S_{RPN}(R_i) + \max(\mathbf{p}_i^u)}{2} , \qquad (4)$$

where $S_{RPN}(\cdot)$ denotes the RPN score. The prediction probability distribution $\mathbf{p}_i^u$ is defined as

$$\mathbf{p}_i^u = \text{softmax}\{\phi(E_{\text{im}}(R_i) + E_{\text{im}}(R_i^{1.5\times})) \cdot E_{\text{txt}}(\text{Categories})^T\}. \qquad (5)$$

Here, $R_i^{1.5\times}$ is a region cropped by $1.5\times$ the size of R_i. E_{im} and E_{txt} are the image and text encoders of CLIP, respectively, and $\phi(\mathbf{x}) = \mathbf{x}/||\mathbf{x}||$. If $\bar{c}_i^u = 0$, we exclude R_i from our pseudo labels.

3.3   Using Our Pseudo Labels for Downstream Tasks

Finally, we briefly describe how we use the pseudo labels that are generated from unlabeled data for two specific downstream tasks that we focus on in this work.

Open-Vocabulary Detection: In this task, the detector has access to images with annotations for base categories and needs to generalize to novel categories. We leverage the data of the base categories to train a class-agnostic Mask R-CNN as our proposal generator and take the names of novel categories as the input texts of the CLIP text-encoder in aforementioned pseudo label generation process. Then, we train a standard Mask R-CNN with RestNet50-FPN [31] with both base ground truth and novel pseudo labels as described in Sect. 3.1.

Semi-supervised Object Detection: In this task, relevant methods usually train a teacher model using ground truth from the limited set of labeled images, and then generate pseudo labels with the teacher on the unlabeled images. We also generate those pseudo labels and merge them with pseudo labels from our VL-PLM. Please refer to the supplementary document for details. Thus, the student model is trained on available ground truth and pseudo labels from both our V&L-based approach and the teacher model.

4   Experiments

We experimentally evaluate the proposed VL-PLM first on open-vocabulary detection in Sect. 4.1 and then on semi-supervised object detection in Sect. 4.2. In Sect. 4.3 we ablate various design choices of VL-PLM.

Table 1. Evaluations for open vocabulary detection on the COCO 2017 [32]. Region-CLIP* indicates a model without refinement using image-caption pairs.

Method	Training source	Novel AP	Base AP	Overall AP
Bansal et al. [4]	instance-level labels in $\mathcal{S}_B$	0.31	29.2	24.9
Zhu et al. [61]		3.41	13.8	13.0
Rahman et al. [38]		4.12	35.9	27.9
OVR-CNN [54]	image-caption pairs in $\mathcal{S}_B \cup \mathcal{S}_N$ instance-level labels in $\mathcal{S}_B$	22.8	46.0	39.9
Gao et al. [14]	raw image-text pairs via Internet image-caption pairs in $\mathcal{S}_B \cup \mathcal{S}_N$	30.8	46.1	42.1
RegionCLIP [57]	instance-level labels in $\mathcal{S}_B$	31.4	57.1	50.4
RegionCLIP* [57]	raw image-text pairs via Internet	14.2	52.8	42.7
ViLD [16]	instance-level labels in $\mathcal{S}_B$	27.6	59.5	51.3
VL-PLM (Ours)		**34.4**	**60.2**	**53.5**

4.1 Open-Vocabulary Object Detection

In this task, we have a training set with annotations for known base categories $\mathcal{S}_B$. Our goal is to train a detector for novel categories $\mathcal{S}_N$. Usually, the labeled images $\mathcal{I}_L$ and the unlabeled images $\mathcal{I}_U$ are the same, i.e., $\mathcal{I}_L = \mathcal{I}_U$.

Experimental Setup: Following prior studies [4,14,16,54], we base our evaluation on COCO 2017 [32] in the zero-shot setting (COCO-ZS) where there are 48 known base categories and 17 unknown novel categories. Images from the training set are regarded as labeled for base classes and also as unlabeled for novel classes. We take the widely adopted mean Average Precision at an IoU of 0.5 (AP_{50}) as the metric and mainly compare our method with ViLD [16], the state-of-the-art method for open vocabulary detection. Thus, we follow ViLD and report AP_{50} over novel categories, base categories and all categories as Novel AP, Base AP, and Overall AP, respectively. Our supplemental material contains results for the LVIS [17] dataset.

Implementation Details: We set a NMS threshold of 0.3 for the RPN of the proposal generator. The confidence threshold for pseudo labels (PLs) is $\tau = 0.8$. Finally, we obtain an average of 4.09 PLs per image, which achieve a Novel AP of 20.9. We use the above hyperparameters for pseudo label generation in all experiments, unless otherwise specified. The proposal generator and the final detector were implemented in Detectron2 [48] and trained on a server with NVIDIA A100 GPUs. The proposal generator was trained for 90,000 iterations with a batch size of 16. Similar to ViLD, the final detector is trained from scratch for 180,000 iterations with input size of 1024×1024, large-scale jitter augmentation [15], synchronized batch normalization of batch size 128, weight decay of 4e–5, and an initial learning rate of 0.32.

Comparison to SOTA: As shown in Table 1, the detector trained with VL-PLM significantly outperforms the prior state-of-the-art ViLD by nearly +7% in Novel AP. Compared with [54] and [14], our method achieves much better performance not only on novel but also on base categories. This indicates training with our PLs has less impact on the predictions of base categories, where

Table 2. Open-vocabulary models trained with base categories from COCO are evaluated on unseen datasets. The evaluation protocol follows [14] and reports AP50

PLs	Iterations × Batch size	VOC 2007	Object365	LVIS
Gao *et al.* [14]	150K × 64	59.2	6.9	8.0
VL-PLM	180K × 16	**67.4**	**10.9**	**22.2**

previous approaches suffered a huge performance drop. Overall, we can see that using V&L models to explicitly generate PLs for novel categories to train the model can give a clear performance boost. Although this introduces an overhead compared to ViLD (and others), which can include novel categories dynamically into the label space, many practical applications easily tolerate this overhead in favor of significantly improved accuracy. Such a setup is also similar to prior works that generate synthetic features of novel categories [61]. Moreover, our method has large potential for further improvement with better V&L model. [16] demonstrates a 60% performance boost of ViLD when using ALIGN [23] as the V&L model. We expect similar improvements on VL-PLM if ALIGN is available.

Generalizing to Unseen Datasets: Following Gao *et al.*'s evaluation protocol [14], we evaluate COCO-trained models on three unseen datasets: VOC 2007 [11], Object365 [41] and LVIS [17]. To do so, we generate PLs for the novel label spaces of these datasets on the COCO dataset and train a standard Faster R-CNN model. The results of our approach on the three unseen datasets is compared to [14] in Table 2. VL-PLM significantly outperforms [14] with similar iterations and smaller batch sizes. Note that [14] requires additional image captions to generate PLs, while VL-PLM can generate PLs for any given category.

4.2 Semi-supervised Object Detection

In this task, we have annotations for all categories on a small portion of a large image set. This portion is regarded as the labeled set $\mathcal{I}_L$ and the remaining images are regarded as the unlabeled set $\mathcal{I}_U$ i.e. $\mathcal{I}_L \cap \mathcal{I}_U = \varnothing$.

Experimental Setup: Following previous studies [44,49,60], we conduct experiments on COCO [32] with 1, 2, 5, and 10% of the training images selected as the labeled data and the rest as the unlabeled data, respectively. In the supplement, we provide more results for varying numbers of unlabeled data. To demonstrate how VL-PLM improves PLs for SSOD, we mainly compare our method with the following baselines. (1) *Supervised*: A vanilla teacher model trained on the labeled set $\mathcal{I}_L$. (2) *Supervised*+PLs: We apply the vanilla teacher model on the unlabeled set $\mathcal{I}_U$ to generate PLs and train a student model with both ground truth and PLs. To compare with *Supervised*+PLs, VL-PLM generates PLs for all categories on $\mathcal{I}_U$. Then, those PLs are merged into the PLs from the vanilla teacher as the final PLs to train a student model named as *Supervised*+VL-PLM. (3) STAC [44]: A popular SSOD baseline. To compare with STAC, we

Table 3. Evaluation of pseudo labels for semi-supervised object detection on COCO [32].

Methods	1% COCO	2% COCO	5% COCO	10% COCO
Supervised	9.25	12.70	17.71	22.10
Supervised+PLs	11.18	14.88	21.20	25.98
Supervised+VL-PLM	**15.35**	**18.60**	**23.70**	**27.23**
STAC [44]	13.97	18.25	24.38	28.64
STAC+VL-PLM	**17.71**	**21.20**	**26.21**	**29.61**

only replace its PLs with ours that are used to train *Supervised*+VL-PLM. The new STAC student model is denoted as STAC+VL-PLM. Here we report the standard metric for COCO, mAP, which is an average over IoU thresholds from 0.5 to 0.95 with a step size of 0.05.

Implementation Details: We follow the same PL generation pipeline and hyperparameters as the OVD experiment, except that we take a class-agnostic Faster R-CNN [40] as our proposal generator and train it on the different COCO splits. *Supervised* and *Supervised*+PLs are implemented in Detectron2 [48] and trained for 90,000 iterations with a batch size of 16. For models related to STAC [44], we use the official code of STAC with default settings.

Results: As shown in Table 3, models with VL-PLM outperform *Supervised* + PLs and STAC by a clear margin, respectively. Since the only change to the baselines is the addition of VL-PLM's PLs, we can conclude that V&L adds clear value to the PLs and can benefit SSOD. Another interesting finding is that models with VL-PLM provide bigger gains for smaller labeled data, which is the most important regime for SSOD as it brings down annotation costs. In that regime, PLs from V&L models are likely stronger than PLs from the small amount of annotated data. We also want to mention two recent SSOD methods [49,60] that achieve higher absolute performance, however, only with additional and orthogonal contributions. VL-PLM may also improve these methods, but here we focus on a fair comparison to other PL-based methods. Moreover, we believe that with better V&L models, VL-PLM can further improve SSOD.

4.3   Analysis of Pseudo Label Generation

We base our ablation studies on the COCO-ZS setting for OVD unless otherwise specified. All models are trained for 90,000 iterations with a batch size of 16.

Understanding the Quality of PLs: Average precision (AP) is a dominant metric to evaluate object detection methods. However, AP alone does not fully indicate the quality of PLs, and the number of PLs also needs to be considered. To support this claim, we generate 5 sets of PLs as follows. (1) *PL v1*: We take the raw region proposals from RPN without RoI refinement in our pseudo label

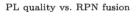

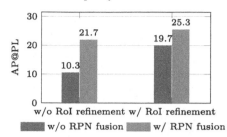

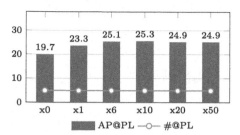

Fig. 4. The quality of PLs with different combinations of RPN and RoI head. We change the threshold τ to ensure each combination with a similar #@PL. "×N" means we apply RoI head N times to refine the proposal boxes.

Table 4. Relationship between the quality of pseudo labels and the performance of the final open vocabulary detectors.

	PL setting	Pseudo labels		Final Detector		
		AP@PL	#@PL	Base AP	Novel AP	Overall AP
PL v1	No RoI, $\tau = 0.05$	17.4	89.92	33.3	14.6	28.4
PL v2	No RoI, $\tau = 0.95$	14.6	2.88	56.1	26.0	48.2
PL v3	VL-PLM, $\tau = 0.05$	20.6	85.15	29.7	19.3	27.0
PL v4	VL-PLM, $\tau = 0.95$	18.0	2.93	55.4	**31.3**	**49.1**
PL v5	VL-PLM, $\tau = 0.99$	11.1	1.62	**56.7**	27.2	49.0

generation and set $\tau = 0.05$. (2) *PL v2*: The same as *PL v1* but with $\tau = 0.95$. (3) *PL v3*: VL-PLM with $\tau = 0.05$. (4) *PL v4*: VL-PLM with $\tau = 0.95$. (5) *PL v5*: VL-PLM with $\tau = 0.99$. In Table 4, we report AP_{50} (AP@PL) and the average per-image number (#@PL) of pseudo labels on novel categories. We also report the performance of detection models trained with the corresponding PLs as Novel AP, Base AP and Overall AP. Comparing *PL v1* with *PL v4* and *PL v2* with *PL v4*, we can see that a good balance between AP@PL and #@PL is desired. Many PLs may achieve high AP@PL, but drop the performance of the final detector. A high threshold reduces the number of PLs but degrades AP@PL as well as the final performance. We found $\tau = 0.8$ to provide a good trade-off. The table also demonstrates the benefit of VL-PLM over no RoI refinement. The supplement contains more analysis and visualizations of our pseudo labels.

Two-Stage Proposal Generator Matters: As mentioned in Sect. 3.2, we improve the localization ability of CLIP with the two-stage proposal generator in two ways: 1) we merge CLIP scores with RPN scores, and 2) we repeatedly refine the region proposals from RPN with the RoI Head. To showcase how RPN and the RoI head help PLs, we evaluate the quality of PLs from different settings in Fig. 4. As shown, RPN score fusion always improves the quality of PLs. As we increase the number of refinement steps with RoI head, the quality increases

Table 5. The quality of pseudo labels generated from different region proposals. The threshold τ is tuned to ensure a similar #@PL for each method.

	Selective search [46]	RoI Head	RPN	RPN+RoI (Ours)
τ	0.99	0.55	0.88	0.82
AP@PL	5.7	8.8	19.7	**25.3**
#@PL	34.92	5.01	4.70	**4.26**

and converges after about 10 steps. Besides proposals from our RPN with RoI refinement (RPN+RoI), we investigate region proposals from different sources, i.e. 1) Selective search [46], 2) RPN only, and 3) RoI head with default thresholding and NMS. Table 5 shows that selective search with a high τ still leads to a large #@PL with a low AP@PL for at least two reasons. First, unlike RPN, selective search does not provide objectiveness scores to improve the localization of CLIP. Second, it returns ten times more proposals than RPN, which contain too many noisy boxes. Finally, the RoI head alone also leads to a poor quality of PLs because it classifies many novel objects as background, due to its training protocol. In the supplement, we show that the proposal generator, which is trained on base categories, generalizes to novel categories.

Time Efficiency: VL-PLM sequentially generates PLs for each region proposal, which is time-consuming. For example, VL-PLM with ResNet50 takes 0.54 s per image on average. We provide two solutions to reduce the time cost. 1) Simple multithreading on 8 GPUs can generate PLs for the whole COCO training set within 6 h. 2) We provide a faster version (Fast VL-PLM) by sharing the ResNet50 feature extraction for all region proposals of the same image. This reduces the runtime by 5× with a slight performance drop. Adding multi-scale features (Multiscale Fast VL-PLM) avoids the performance drop but still reduces runtime by 3×. Please refer to the supplement for more details.

5   Conclusion

This paper demonstrates how to leverage pre-trained V&L models to mine unlabeled data for different object detection tasks, e.g., OVD and SSOD. We propose a V&L model guided pseudo label mining framework (VL-PLM) that is simple but effective, and is able to generate pseudo labels (PLs) for a task-specific labelspace. Our experiments showcase that training a standard detector with our PLs sets a new state-of-the-art for OVD on COCO. Moreover, our PLs can benefit SSOD models, especially when the amount of ground truth labels is limited. We believe that VL-PLM can be further improved with better V&L models.

Acknowledgments. This research has been partially funded by research grants to D. Metaxas from NEC Labs America through NSF IUCRC CARTA-1747778, NSF: 1951890, 2003874, 1703883, 1763523 and ARO MURI SCAN.

References

1. Agrawal, A., et al.: VQA: visual question answering. In: ICCV (2015)
2. Agrawal, H., et al.: nocaps: novel object captioning at scale. In: ICCV (2019)
3. Anderson, P., et al.: Vision-and-Language navigation: interpreting visually-grounded navigation instructions in real environments. In: CVPR (2018)
4. Bansal, A., Sikka, K., Sharma, G., Chellappa, R., Divakaran, A.: Zero-shot object detection. In: Ferrari, V., Hebert, M., Sminchisescu, C., Weiss, Y. (eds.) ECCV 2018. LNCS, vol. 11205, pp. 397–414. Springer, Cham (2018). https://doi.org/10.1007/978-3-030-01246-5_24
5. Cai, Z., Vasconcelos, N.: Cascade R-CNN: delving into high quality object detection. In: CVPR (2018)
6. Carion, N., Massa, F., Synnaeve, G., Usunier, N., Kirillov, A., Zagoruyko, S.: End-to-end object detection with transformers. In: Vedaldi, A., Bischof, H., Brox, T., Frahm, J.-M. (eds.) ECCV 2020. LNCS, vol. 12346, pp. 213–229. Springer, Cham (2020). https://doi.org/10.1007/978-3-030-58452-8_13
7. Chen, X., et al.: Microsoft COCO captions: data collection and evaluation server (2015)
8. Chen, Y.C., et al.: UNITER: UNiversal image-TExt representation learning. In: Vedaldi, A., Bischof, H., Brox, T., Frahm, J.-M. (eds.) ECCV 2020. LNCS, vol. 12375, pp. 104–120. Springer, Cham (2020). https://doi.org/10.1007/978-3-030-58577-8_7
9. Das, A., Datta, S., Gkioxari, G., Lee, S., Parikh, D., Batra, D.: Embodied question answering. In: CVPR (2018)
10. Dong, B., Huang, Z., Guo, Y., Wang, Q., Niu, Z., Zuo, W.: Boosting weakly supervised object detection via learning bounding box adjusters. In: ICCV., pp. 2876–2885 (2021)
11. Everingham, M., Eslami, S., Van Gool, L., Williams, C.K., Winn, J., Zisserman, A.: The pascal visual object classes challenge: a retrospective. Int. J. Comput. Vision 111(1), 98–136 (2015)
12. Fang, H., et al.: From captions to visual concepts and back. In: CVPR (2015)
13. Fukui, A., et al..: Multimodal compact bilinear pooling for visual question answering and visual grounding. In: EMNLP (2016)
14. Gao, M., Xing, C., Niebles, J.C., Li, J., Xu, R., Liu, W., Xiong, C.: Towards open vocabulary object detection without human-provided bounding boxes. In: ECCV 2022 (2021)
15. Ghiasi, G., et al.: : Simple copy-paste is a strong data augmentation method for instance segmentation. In: CVPR, pp. 2918–2928 (2021)
16. Gu, X., Lin, T.Y., Kuo, W., Cui, Y.: Open-vocabulary object detection via vision and language knowledge distillation. In: ICLR (2022)
17. Gupta, A., Dollár, P., Girshick, R.: LVIS: a dataset for large vocabulary instance segmentation. In: CVPR (2019)
18. He, K., Gkioxari, G., Dollár, P., Girshick, R.: Mask R-CNN. In: ICCV (2017)
19. Hu, R., Singh, A.: UniT: multimodal Multitask Learning with a unified transformer. In: ICCV (2021)
20. Hudson, D.A., Manning, C.D.: Learning by abstraction: the neural state machine. In: NeurIPS (2019)
21. Huynh, D., Kuen, J., Lin, Z., Gu, J., Elhamifar, E.: Open-vocabulary instance segmentation via robust cross-modal pseudo-labeling (2021)

22. Inoue, N., Furuta, R., Yamasaki, T., Aizawa, K.: Cross-Domain Weakly-Supervised Object Detection through Progressive Domain Adaptation. In: CVPR (2018)
23. Jia, C., et al.: Scaling up visual and vision-language representation learning with noisy text supervision. In: ICML (D2021)
24. Kamath, A., Singh, M., LeCun, Y., Synnaeve, G., Misra, I., Carion, N.: MDETR - modulated detection for end-to-end multi-modal understanding. In: ICCV (2021)
25. Karpathy, A., Fei-Fei, L.: Deep visual-semantic alignments for generating image descriptions. In: CVPR (2015)
26. Kazemzadeh, S., Ordonez, V., Matten, M., Berg, T.: ReferItGame: referring to objects in photographs of natural scenes. In: EMNLP (2014)
27. Kuznetsova, A., et al.: The open images dataset v4: Unified image classification, object detection, and visual relationship detection at scale. Int. J. Comput. Vis, **128**, 1956–1981 (2020)
28. Li, B., Weinberger, K.Q., Belongie, S., Koltun, V., Ranftl, R.: Language-driven semantic segmentation. In: ICLR (2022)
29. Li, J., Selvaraju, R.R., Gotmare, A.D., Joty, S., Xiong, C., Hoi, S.: Align before fuse: vision and language representation learning with momentum distillation. In: NeurIPS (2021)
30. Li, X., et al.: OSCAR: object-semantics aligned pre-training for vision-language tasks. In: Vedaldi, A., Bischof, H., Brox, T., Frahm, J.-M. (eds.) ECCV 2020. LNCS, vol. 12375, pp. 121–137. Springer, Cham (2020). https://doi.org/10.1007/978-3-030-58577-8_8
31. Lin, T.Y., Dollár, P., Girshick, R., He, K., Hariharan, B., Belongie, S.: Feature pyramid networks for object detection. In: CVPR (2017)
32. Lin, T.Y., et al.: Microsoft COCO: common objects in context. In: Fleet, D., Pajdla, T., Schiele, B., Tuytelaars, T. (eds.) ECCV 2014. LNCS, vol. 8693, pp. 740–755. Springer, Cham (2014). https://doi.org/10.1007/978-3-319-10602-1_48
33. Liu, Y., et al.: RoBERTa: a robustly optimized BERT pretraining approach (2019)
34. Lu, J., Batra, D., Parikh, D., Lee, S.: ViLBERT: pretraining task-agnostic visiolinguistic representations for Vision-and-Language Tasks. In: NeurIPS (2019)
35. Mao, J., Huang, J., Toshev, A., Camburu, O., Yuille, A., Murphy, K.: Generation and Comprehension of Unambiguous Object Descriptions. In: CVPR (2016)
36. Peng, G., et al.: Dynamic fusion with Intra- and inter- modality attention flow for visual question answering. In: CVPR (2019)
37. Radford, A., et al.: Learning transferable visual models from natural language supervision. In: ICML (2021)
38. Rahman, S., Khan, S., Barnes, N.: Improved visual-semantic alignment for zero-shot object detection. In: AAAI, pp. 11932–11939 (2020)
39. Rao, Y., et al.: Denseclip: Language-guided dense prediction with context-aware prompting. In: 2022 IEEE/CVF Conference on Computer Vision and Pattern Recognition (CVPR) (2021)
40. Ren, S., He, K., Girshick, R., Sun, J.: Faster R-CNN: towards real-time object detection with Region Proposal Networks. In: NeurIPS (2015)
41. Shao, S., et al.: Objects365: a large-scale. high-quality dataset for object detection. In : 2019 IEEE/CVF International Conference on Computer Vision (2019)
42. Shi, H., Hayat, M., Wu, Y., Cai, J.: ProposalCLIP: unsupervised open-category object proposal generation via exploiting clip cues. In: 2022 IEEE/CVF Conference on Computer Vision and Pattern Recognition (CVPR) (2022)
43. Siméoni, O., et al.: Localizing objects with self-supervised transformers and no labels. In: BMVC (2021)

44. Sohn, K., Zhang, Z., Li, C.L., Zhang, H., Lee, C.Y., Pfister, T.: A simple semi-supervised learning framework for object detection. In: arXiv:2005.04757 (2020)
45. Sun, C., Myers, A., Vondrick, C., Murphy, K., Schmid, C.: Videobert: A joint model for video and language representation learning. In: ICCV (2019)
46. Uijlings, J., van de Sande, K., Gevers, T., Smeulders, A.: Selective search for object recognition. Int. J. Comput. Vis. **104**, 154–171 (2013)
47. Wang, L., Li, Y., Lazebnik, S.: Learning Deep Structure-Preserving Image-Text Embeddings. In: CVPR (2016)
48. Wu, Y., Kirillov, A., Massa, F., Lo, W.Y., Girshick, R.: Detectron2. https://github.com/facebookresearch/detectron2 (2019)
49. Xu, M., et al.: End-to-end semi-supervised object detection with soft teacher. In: ICCV, pp. 3060–3069 (2021)
50. Xu, M., et al.: A simple baseline for zero-shot semantic segmentation with pre-trained vision-language model (2021)
51. Yu, F., et al.: Unsupervised domain adaptation for object detection via cross-domain semi-supervised learning. In: WACV (2022)
52. Yu, L., et al.: MAttNet: modular attention network for referring expression comprehension. In: CVPR (2018)
53. Yu, L., Poirson, P., Yang, S., Berg, A.C., Berg, T.L.: Modeling context in referring expressions. In: Leibe, B., Matas, J., Sebe, N., Welling, M. (eds.) ECCV 2016. LNCS, vol. 9906, pp. 69–85. Springer, Cham (2016). https://doi.org/10.1007/978-3-319-46475-6_5
54. Zareian, A., Rosa, K.D., Hu, D.H., Chang, S.F.: Open-vocabulary object detection using captions. In: CVPR (2021)
55. Zhang, P., et al.: VinVL: revisiting visual representations in vision-language models. In: CVPR (2021)
56. Zhao, X., Schulter, S., Sharma, G., Tsai, Y.-H., Chandraker, M., Wu, Y.: Object detection with a unified label space from multiple datasets. In: Vedaldi, A., Bischof, H., Brox, T., Frahm, J.-M. (eds.) ECCV 2020. LNCS, vol. 12359, pp. 178–193. Springer, Cham (2020). https://doi.org/10.1007/978-3-030-58568-6_11
57. Zhong, Y., et al.: RegionCLIP: Region-based language-image pretraining. In: 2022 IEEE/CVF Conference on Computer Vision and Pattern Recognition (CVPR) (2021)
58. Zhong, Y., Wang, J., Peng, J., Zhang, L.: Boosting weakly supervised object detection with progressive knowledge transfer. In: Vedaldi, A., Bischof, H., Brox, T., Frahm, J.-M. (eds.) ECCV 2020. LNCS, vol. 12371, pp. 615–631. Springer, Cham (2020). https://doi.org/10.1007/978-3-030-58574-7_37
59. Zhou, C., Loy, C.C., Dai, B.: DenseCLIP: extract free dense labels from clip. In: ECCV 2022 (2021)
60. Zhou, Q., Yu, C., Wang, Z., Qian, Q., Li, H.: Instant-teaching: an end-to-end semi-supervised object detection framework. In: CVPR (2021)
61. Zhu, P., Wang, H., Saligrama, V.: Don't even look once: synthesizing features for zero-shot detection. In: CVPR, pp. 11693–11702 (2020)

CPO: Change Robust Panorama to Point Cloud Localization

Junho Kim[1], Hojun Jang[1], Changwoon Choi[1], and Young Min Kim[1,2(✉)]

[1] Department of Electrical and Computer Engineering, Seoul National University,
Seoul, South Korea
[2] Interdisciplinary Program in Artificial Intelligence and INMC,
Seoul National University, Seoul, South Korea
youngmin.kim@snu.ac.kr

Abstract. We present CPO, a fast and robust algorithm that localizes a 2D panorama with respect to a 3D point cloud of a scene possibly containing changes. To robustly handle scene changes, our approach deviates from conventional feature point matching, and focuses on the spatial context provided from panorama images. Specifically, we propose efficient color histogram generation and subsequent robust localization using score maps. By utilizing the unique equivariance of spherical projections, we propose very fast color histogram generation for a large number of camera poses without explicitly rendering images for all candidate poses. We accumulate the regional consistency of the panorama and point cloud as 2D/3D score maps, and use them to weigh the input color values to further increase robustness. The weighted color distribution quickly finds good initial poses and achieves stable convergence for gradient-based optimization. CPO is lightweight and achieves effective localization in all tested scenarios, showing stable performance despite scene changes, repetitive structures, or featureless regions, which are typical challenges for visual localization with perspective cameras.

Keywords: Visual localization · Panorama · Point cloud

1 Introduction

The location information is a crucial building block to develop applications for AR/VR, autonomous driving, and embodied agents. Visual localization is one of the cheapest methods for localization as it could operate only using camera inputs and a pre-captured 3D map. While many existing visual localization algorithms utilize perpsective images [29,31,35], they are vulnerable to repetitive structures, lack of visual features, or scene changes. Recently, localization using panorama images [6,7,20,37] has gained attention, as devices with 360° cameras are becoming more accessible. The holistic view of panorama images

Supplementary Information The online version contains supplementary material available at https://doi.org/10.1007/978-3-031-20077-9_11.

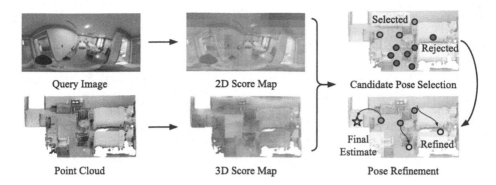

Fig. 1. Overview of our approach. CPO first creates 2D and 3D score maps that attenuate regions containing scene changes. The score maps are further used to guide candidate pose selection and pose refinement.

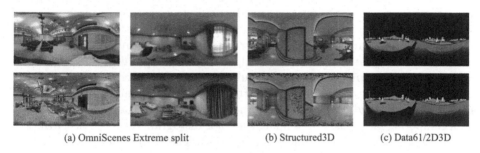

(a) OmniScenes Extreme split   (b) Structured3D   (c) Data61/2D3D

Fig. 2. Qualitative results of CPO. We show the query image (top), and the projected point cloud on the estimated pose (bottom). CPO can flexibly operate using raw color measurements or semantic labels.

has the potential to compensate for few outliers in localization and thus is less susceptible to minor changes or ambiguities compared to perspective images.

Despite the potential of panorama images, it is challenging to perform localization amidst drastic scene changes while simultaneously attaining efficiency and accuracy. On the 3D map side, it is costly to collect the up-to-date 3D map that reflects the frequent changes within the scenes. On the algorithmic side, existing localization methods have bottlenecks either in computational efficiency or accuracy. While recent panorama-based localization methods [6,7,20,37] perform accurate localization by leveraging the holistic context in panoramas, they are vulnerable to scene changes without dedicated treatment to account for changes. For perspective cameras, such scene changes are often handled by a two-step approach, using learning-based robust image retrieval [3,13] followed by feature matching [30]. However, the image retrieval step involves global feature extraction which is often costly to compute and memory intensive.

We propose CPO, a fast localization algorithm that leverages the regional distributions within the panorama images for robust pose prediction under scene changes. Given a 2D panorama image as input, we find the camera pose using a 3D point cloud as the reference map. With careful investigation on the pre-collected 3D map and the holistic view of the panorama, CPO focuses on regions with consistent color distributions. CPO represents the consistency as 2D/3D score maps and quickly selects a small set of initial candidate poses from which the remaining discrepancy can be quickly and stably optimized for accurate localization as shown in Fig. 1. As a result, CPO enables panorama to point cloud localization under scene changes without the use of pose priors, unlike the previous state-of-the-art [20]. Further, the formulation of CPO is flexible and can be applied on both raw color measurements and semantic labels, which is not possible with conventional structure-based localization relying on visual features. To the best of our knowledge, we are the first to explicitly propose a method for coping with changes in panorama to point cloud localization.

The key to fast and stable localization is the efficient color histogram generation that scores the regional consistency of candidate poses. Specifically, we utilize color histograms generated from synthetic projections of the point cloud and make comparisons with the query image. Instead of extensively rendering a large number of synthetic images, we first cache histograms in a few selected views. Then, color histograms for various other views are efficiently approximated by re-using the histograms of the nearest neighbor from the pre-computed color distribution of overlapping views. As a result, CPO generates color histograms for millions of synthetic views within a matter of milliseconds and thus can search a wide range of candidate poses within an order-of-magnitude shorter runtime than competing methods. We compare the color histograms and construct the 2D and 3D score maps, as shown in Fig. 1 (middle). The score maps impose higher scores in regions with consistent color distribution, indicating that the region did not change from the reference 3D map. The 2D and 3D score maps are crucial for change-robust localization, which is further verified with our experiments.

We test our algorithm in a wide range of scenes with various input modalities where a few exemplar results are presented in Fig. 2. CPO outperforms existing approaches by a large margin despite a considerable amount of scene change or lack of visual features. Notably, CPO attains highly accurate localization, flexibly handling both RGB and semantic labels in both indoor and outdoor scenes, without altering the formulation. Since CPO does not rely on point features, our algorithm is quickly applicable in an off-the-shelf manner without any training of neural networks or collecting pose-annotated images. We expect CPO to be a lightweight solution for stable localization in various practical scenarios.

2   Related Work

In this section, we describe prior works for localization under scene changes, and further elaborate on conventional visual localization methods that employ either a single-step or two-step approach.

Localization Under Scene Changes. Even the state-of-the-art techniques for visual localization can fail when the visual appearance of the scene changes.

This is because conventional localization approaches are often designed to find similar visual appearances from pre-collected images with ground-truth poses. Many visual localization approaches assume that the image features do not significantly change, and either train a neural network [19,19,22,35] or retrieve image features [14,18,23,31,32]. Numerous datasets and approaches have been presented in recent years to account for change-robust localization. The proposed datasets reflect day/night [25,35] or seasonal changes [5,25,33] for outdoor scenes and changes in the spatial arrangement of objects [34,36,38] for indoor scenes. To cope with such changes, most approaches follow a structure-based paradigm, incorporating a robust image retrieval method [3,10,13,17] along with a learned feature matching module [9,29,30,39]. An alternative approach utilizes indoor layouts from depth images, which stay constant despite changes in object layouts [16]. We compare CPO against various change-robust localization methods, and demonstrate that CPO outperforms the baselines amidst scene changes.

Single-Step Localization. Many existing methods [6,7,37] for panorama-based localization follow a single-step approach, where the pose is directly found with respect to the 3D map. Since panorama images capture a larger scene context, fewer ambiguities arise than perspective images, and reasonable localization is possible even without a refinement process or a pose-annotated database. Campbell *et al.* [6,7] introduced a class of global optimization algorithms that could effectively find pose in diverse indoor and outdoor environments [4,26]. However, these algorithms require consistent semantic segmentation labels for both the panorama and 3D point cloud, which are often hard to acquire in practice. Zhang *et al.* [37] propose a learning-based localization algorithm using panoramic views, where networks are trained using rendered views from the 3D map. We compare CPO with optimization-based algorithms [6,7], and demonstrate that CPO outperforms these algorithms under a wide variety of practical scenarios.

Two-Step Localization. Compared to single-step methods, more accurate localization is often acquired by two-step approaches that initialize poses with an effective search scheme followed by refinement. For panorama images, PICCOLO [20] follows a two-step paradigm, where promising poses are found and further refined using sampling loss values that measure the color discrepancy in 2D and 3D. While PICCOLO does not incorporate learning, it shows competitive performance in conventional panorama localization datasets [20]. Nevertheless, the initialization and refinement is unstable to scene changes as the method lacks explicit treatment of such adversaries. CPO improves upon PICCOLO by leveraging score maps in 2D that attenuate changes for effective initialization and score maps in 3D that guide sampling loss minimization for stable convergence.

For perspective images, many structure-based methods [13,29] use a two-step approach, where candidate poses are found with image retrieval [3] or scene coordinate regression [22] and further refined with PnP-RANSAC [11] from feature matching [29,30,39]. While these methods can effectively localize perspective images, the initialization procedure often requires neural networks that are memory and compute intensive, trained with a dense, pose-annotated database of images. We compare CPO against prominent two-step localization methods, and demonstrate that CPO attains efficiency and accuracy with an effective formulation in the initialization and refinement.

3   Method

Given a point cloud $P = \{X, C\}$, CPO aims to find the optimal rotation $R^* \in SO(3)$ and translation $t^* \in \mathbb{R}^3$ at which the image I_Q is taken. Let $X, C \in \mathbb{R}^{N \times 3}$ denote the point cloud coordinates and color values, and $I_Q \in \mathbb{R}^{H \times W \times 3}$ the query panorama image. Figure 1 depicts the steps that CPO localizes the panorama image under scene changes. First, we extensively measure the color consistency between the panorama and point cloud in various poses. We propose fast histogram generation described in Sect. 3.1 for efficient comparison. The consistency values are recorded as a 2D score map $M_{2D} \in \mathbb{R}^{H \times W \times 1}$ and a 3D score map $M_{3D} \in \mathbb{R}^{N \times 1}$ which is defined in Sect. 3.2. We use the color histograms and score maps to select candidate poses (Sect. 3.3), which are further refined to deduce the final pose (Sect. 3.4).

3.1   Fast Histogram Generation

Instead of focusing on point features, CPO relies on the regional color distribution of images to match the global context between the 2D and 3D measurements. To cope with color distribution shifts from illumination change or camera white balance, we first preprocess the raw color measurements in 2D and 3D via color histogram matching [1,8,15]. Specifically, we generate a single color histogram for the query image and point cloud, and establish a matching between the two distributions via optimal transport. While more sophisticated learning-based methods [12,24,40] may be used to handle drastic illumination changes such as night-to-day shifts, we find that simple matching can still handle a modest range of color variations prevalent in practical settings. After preprocessing, we compare the intersections of the RGB color histograms between the *patches* from the query image I_Q and the synthetic projections of the point cloud P.

The efficient generation of color histograms is a major building block for CPO. While there could be an enormous number of poses that the synthetic projections can be generated from, we re-use the pre-computed histograms from another view to accelerate the process. Suppose we have created color histograms for patches of images taken from the original view I_o, as shown in Fig. 3. Then the color histogram for the image in a new view I_n can be quickly approximated without explicitly rendering the image and counting bins of colors for pixels within the patches. Let $\mathcal{S}_o = \{S_i^o\}$ denote the image patches of I_o and $\mathcal{C}_o = \{c_i^o\}$ the 2D image coordinates of the patch centroids. $\mathcal{S}_n$ and $\mathcal{C}_n$ are similarly defined for the novel view I_n. For each novel view patch, we project the patch centroid using the relative transformation and obtain the color histogram of the nearest patch of the original image, as described in Fig. 3. To elaborate, we first map the patch centroid location c_i^n of $S_i^n \in \mathcal{S}_n$ to the original image coordinate frame,

$$p_i = \Pi(R_{\text{rel}}\Pi^{-1}(c_i^n) + t_{\text{rel}}), \tag{1}$$

$$\Pi(R_{rel}\Pi^{-1}(c_i^n) + t_{rel})$$

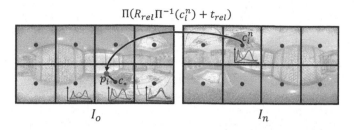

I_o I_n

Fig. 3. Illustration of fast histogram generation. For each image patch in the novel view I_n, we first project the patch centroid c_i^n to the view of the original image I_o. The color histogram of the patch in the novel view is estimated as the histogram of image patch c_* in the original view that is closest to the transformed centroid p_i.

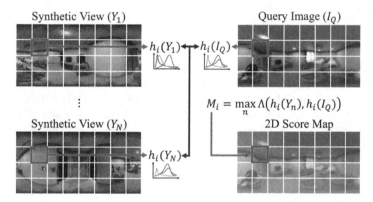

Fig. 4. Illustration of 2D score map generation. The 2D score map for the ith patch M_i is the maximum histogram intersection between the ith patch in query image I_Q and the synthetic views $Y_n \in \mathcal{Y}$.

where R_{rel}, t_{rel} is the relative pose and $\Pi^{-1}(\cdot) : \mathbb{R}^2 \to \mathbb{R}^3$ is the inverse projection function that maps a 2D coordinate to its 3D world coordinate. The color histogram for S_i^n is assigned as the color histogram of the patch centroid in I_o that is closest to p_i, namely $c_* = \arg\min_{c \in \mathcal{C}_o} \|c - p_i\|_2$.

We specifically utilize the cached histograms to generate histograms with arbitrary rotations at a fixed translation. In this case, the camera observes the same set of visible points without changes in occlusion or parallax effect due to depth. Therefore the synthetic image is rendered only once and the patch-wise histograms can be closely approximated by our fast variant with $p_i = \Pi(R_{rel}\Pi^{-1}(c_i^n))$.

3.2   Score Map Generation

Based on the color histogram of the query image and the synthetic views from the point cloud, we generate 2D and 3D score maps to account for possible changes in the measurements. Given a query image $I_Q \in \mathbb{R}^{H \times W \times 3}$, we create multiple synthetic views $Y \in \mathcal{Y}$ at various translations and rotations within the point cloud. Specifically, we project the input point cloud $P = \{X, C\}$ and assign the measured color $Y(u, v) = C_n$ at the projected location of the corresponding 3D coordinate $(u, v) = \Pi(R_Y X_n + t_Y)$ to create the synthetic view Y.

We further compare the color distribution of the synthetic views $Y \in \mathcal{Y}$ against the input image I_Q and assign higher scores to regions with high consistency. We first divide both the query image and the synthetic views into patches and calculate the color histograms of the patches. Following the notation in Sect. 3.1, we can denote the patches of the query image as $\mathcal{S}_Q = \{S_i^Q\}$ and $\mathcal{S}_Y = \{S_i^Y\}$ for each synthetic view. Then the color distribution of patch i is recorded into a histogram with B bins per channel: $h_i(\cdot) : \mathbb{R}^{H \times W \times 3} \to \cdot S_i \to \mathbb{R}^{B \times 3}$. The consistency of two patches is calculated by finding the intersection between two histograms $\Lambda(\cdot, \cdot) : \mathbb{R}^{B \times 3} \times \mathbb{R}^{B \times 3} \to \mathbb{R}$. Finally, we aggregate the consistency values from multiple synthetic views into the 2D score map for the query image M_{2D} and the 3D score map for the point cloud M_{3D}. We verify the efficacy of the score maps for CPO in Sect. 4.3.

2D Score Map. The 2D score map $M_{2D} \in \mathbb{R}^{H \times W}$ assigns higher scores to regions in the query image I_Q that are consistent with the point cloud color. As shown in Fig. 4, we split M_{2D} into patches and assign a score for each patch. We define the 2D score as the maximum histogram intersection that each patch in the input query image I_Q achieves, compared against multiple synthetic views in $\mathcal{Y}$. Formally, denoting $\mathcal{M} = \{M_i\}$ as the scores for patches in M_{2D}, the score for the ith patch is

$$M_i = \max_{Y \in \mathcal{Y}} \Lambda(h_i(Y), h_i(I_Q)). \tag{2}$$

If a patch in the query image contains scene change it will have small histogram intersections with any of the synthetic views. Note that for computing Eq. 2 we use the fast histogram generation from Sect. 3.1 to avoid the direct rendering of Y. We utilize the 2D score map to attenuate image regions with changes during candidate pose selection in Sect. 3.3.

3D Score Map. The 3D score map $M_{3D} \in \mathbb{R}^N$ measures the color consistency of each 3D point with respect to the query image. We compute the 3D score map by back-projecting the histogram intersection scores to the point cloud locations, as shown in Fig. 5. Given a synthetic view $Y \in \mathcal{Y}$, let $B_Y \in \mathbb{R}^N$ denote the assignment of patch-based intersection scores between Y and I_Q into the 3D points whose locations are projected onto corresponding patches in Y. The 3D score map is the average of the back-projected scores B_Y for individual points, namely

$$M_{3D} = \frac{1}{|\mathcal{Y}|} \sum_{Y \in \mathcal{Y}} B_Y. \tag{3}$$

If a region in the point cloud contains scene changes, one can expect the majority of the back-projected scores B_Y to be small for that region, leading to smaller 3D scores. We use the 3D score map to weigh the sampling loss for pose refinement in Sect. 3.4. By placing smaller weights on regions that contain scene changes, the 3D score map leads to more stable convergence.

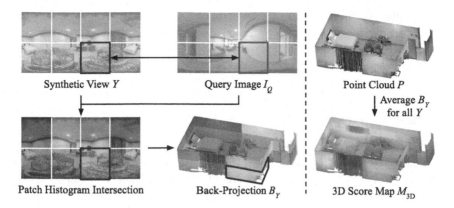

Fig. 5. Illustration of 3D score map generation. For each synthetic view $Y \in \mathcal{Y}$, the patch-wise color histogram is compared against the query image and the resulting intersection scores are back-projected onto 3D locations. The back-projected scores B_Y are averaged for all synthetic views to form the 3D score map M_{3D}.

3.3 Candidate Pose Selection

For the final step, CPO optimizes sampling loss [20] from selected initial poses, as shown in Fig. 1. CPO chooses the candidate starting poses by efficiently leveraging the color distribution of the panorama and point cloud. The space of candidate starting poses is selected in two steps. First, we choose N_t 3D locations within various regions of the point cloud, and render N_t synthetic views. For datasets with large open spaces lacking much clutter, the positions are selected from uniform grid partitions. On the other hand, for cluttered indoor scenes, we propose to efficiently handle valid starting positions by building octrees to approximate the amorphous empty spaces as in Rodenberg *et al.* [28] and select centroids of the octrees for N_t starting positions.

Second, we select the final K candidate poses out of $N_t \times N_r$ poses, where N_r is the number of rotations assigned to each translation, uniformly sampled from $SO(3)$. We only render a single view for the N_t locations, and obtain patch-wise histograms for N_r rotations using the fast histogram generation from Sect. 3.1. We select final K poses that have the largest histogram intersections with the query panorama image. The fast generation of color histograms at synthetic views enables efficient candidate pose selection, which is quantitatively verified in Sect. 4.3.

Here, we compute the patch-wise histogram intersections for $N_t \times N_r$ poses where the 2D score map M_{2D} from Sect. 3.2 is used to place smaller weights on image patches that are likely to contain scene change. Let $\mathcal{Y}_c$ denote the $N_t \times N_r$ synthetic views used for finding candidate poses. For a synthetic view $Y \in \mathcal{Y}_c$, the weighted histogram intersection $w(Y)$ with the query image I_Q is expressed as follows,

$$w(Y) = \sum_i M_i \Lambda(h_i(Y), h_i(I_Q)). \tag{4}$$

Conceptually, the affinity between a synthetic view Y and the query image I_Q is computed as the sum of each patch-wise intersection weighted by the corresponding patch M_i from the 2D score map M_{2D}. We can expect changed regions to be attenuated in the candidate pose selection process and therefore CPO can quickly compensate for possible scene changes.

3.4   Pose Refinement

We individually refine the selected K poses by optimizing a weighted variant of sampling loss [20], which quantifies the color differences between 2D and 3D. To elaborate, let $\Pi(\cdot)$ be the projection function that maps a point cloud to coordinates in the 2D panorama image I_Q. Further, let $\Gamma(\cdot; I_Q)$ indicate the sampling function that maps 2D coordinates to pixel values sampled from I_Q. The weighted sampling loss enforces each 3D point's color to be similar to its 2D projection's sampled color while placing lesser weight on points that are likely to contain change. Given the 3D score map M_{3D}, this is expressed as follows,

$$L_{\text{sampling}}(R, t) = \|M_{3D} \odot [\Gamma(\Pi(RX + t); I_Q) - C]\|_2, \tag{5}$$

where $\odot$ is the Hadamard product and $RX + t$ is the transformed point cloud under the candidate camera pose R, t. To obtain the refined poses, we minimize the weighted sampling loss for the K candidate poses using gradient descent [21]. At termination, the refined pose with the smallest sampling loss value is chosen.

4   Experiments

In this section, we analyze the performance of CPO in various localization scenarios. CPO is mainly implemented using PyTorch [27], and is accelerated with a single RTX 2080 GPU. We report the full hyperparameter setup for running CPO and further qualitative results for each tested scenario in the supplementary material. All translation and rotation errors are reported using median values, and for evaluating accuracy a prediction is considered correct if the translation error is below 0.05m and the rotation error is below 5°.

Baselines. We select five baselines for comparison: PICCOLO [20], GOSMA [7], GOPAC [6], structure-based approach, and depth-based approach. PICCOLO, GOSMA, and GOPAC are optimization-based approaches that find pose by minimizing a designated objective function. Structure-based approach [29,31] is one of the most performant methods for localization using perspective images. This baseline first finds promising candidate poses via image retrieval using global features [13] and further refines pose via learned feature matching [30]. To adapt structure-based method to our problem setup using panorama images, we construct a database of pose-annotated synthetic views rendered from the point cloud and use it for retrieval. Depth-based approach first performs learning-based monocular depth estimation on the query panorama image [2], and finds

Table 1. Quantitative results on all splits containing changes in OmniScenes [20].

Method	t-error (m)			R-error (°)			Accuracy		
	Robot	Hand	Extreme	Robot	Hand	Extreme	Robot	Hand	Extreme
PICCOLO	3.78	4.04	3.99	104.23	121.67	122.30	0.06	0.01	0.01
PICCOLO w/ prior	1.07	0.53	1.24	21.03	7.54	23.71	0.39	0.45	0.38
Structure-Based	0.04	0.05	0.06	**0.77**	0.86	0.99	0.56	0.51	0.46
Depth-Based	0.46	0.09	0.48	1.35	1.24	2.37	0.38	0.39	0.30
CPO	**0.02**	**0.02**	**0.03**	1.46	**0.37**	**0.37**	**0.58**	**0.58**	**0.57**

Table 2. Quantitative results on all splits containing changes in Structured3D [38].

Method	t-error (m)	R-error (°)	Acc. (0.05 m, 5°)	Acc. (0.02 m, 2°)	Acc. (0.01 m, 1°)
PICCOLO	0.19	4.20	0.47	0.45	0.43
Structure-Based	0.02	0.64	**0.59**	0.47	0.29
Depth-Based	0.18	1.98	0.45	0.33	0.19
CPO	**0.01**	**0.29**	0.56	**0.54**	**0.51**

the pose that best aligns the estimated depth to the point cloud. The approach is similar to the layout-matching baseline from Jenkins *et al.* [16], where it demonstrated effective localization under scene change. Additional details about implementing the baselines are deferred to the supplementary material.

4.1 Localization Performance on Scenes with Changes

We assess the robustness of CPO using the OmniScenes [20] and Structured3D [38] dataset, which allows performance evaluation for the localization of panorama images against point clouds in changed scenes.

OmniScenes. The OmniScenes dataset consists of seven 3D scans and 4121 2D panorama images, where the panorama images are captured with cameras either handheld or robot mounted. Further, the panorama images are obtained at different times of day and include changes in scene configuration and lighting. OmniScenes contains three splits (Robot, Handheld, Extreme) that are recorded in scenes with changes, where the Extreme split contains panorama images captured with extreme camera motion.

We compare CPO against PICCOLO [20], structure-based approach, and depth-based approach. The evaluation results for all three splits in OmniScenes are shown in Table 1. In all splits, CPO outperforms the baselines without the help of prior information or training neural networks. While PICCOLO [20] performs competitively with gravity direction prior, the performance largely degrades without such information. Further, outliers triggered from scene changes and motion blur make accurate localization difficult using structure-based or depth-based methods. CPO is immune to such adversaries as it explicitly models scene changes and regional inconsistencies with 2D, 3D score maps.

186   J. Kim et al.

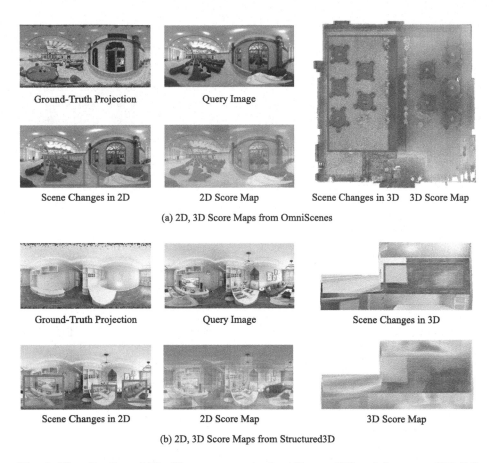

Fig. 6. Visualization of 2D, 3D score maps in OmniScenes [20] and Structured3D [38]. The 2D score map assigns lower scores to the capturer's hand and objects not present in 3D. Similarly, the 3D score map assigns lower scores to regions not present in 2D.

The score maps of CPO effectively attenuate scene changes, providing useful evidence for robust localization. Figure 6 visualizes the exemplar 2D and 3D score maps generated in the wedding hall scene from OmniScenes. The scene contains drastic changes in object layout, where the carpets are removed and the arrangement of chairs has largely changed since the 3D scan. As shown in Fig. 6, the 2D score map assigns smaller scores to new objects and the capturer's hand, which are not present in the 3D scan. Further, the 3D score map shown in Fig. 6 assigns smaller scores to chairs and blue carpets, which are present in the 3D scan but are largely modified in the panorama image.

Structured3D. We further compare CPO against PICCOLO in Structured3D, which is a large-scale dataset containing synthetic 3D models with changes in object layout and illumination, as shown in Fig. 2. Due to the large size of the dataset (21845 indoor rooms), 672 rooms are selected for evaluation. For

Table 3. Quantitative results on Stanford 2D-3D-S [4], compared against PICCOLO (PC), structure-based approach (SB), and depth-based approach (DB).

Area	t-error (m)				R-error (°)				Accuracy			
	PC	SB	DB	CPO	PC	SB	DB	CPO	PC	SB	DB	CPO
Area 1	0.02	0.05	1.39	**0.01**	0.46	0.81	89.48	**0.25**	0.66	0.51	0.28	**0.89**
Area 2	0.76	0.18	3.00	**0.01**	2.25	2.08	89.76	**0.27**	0.42	0.41	0.14	**0.81**
Area 3	0.02	0.05	1.39	**0.01**	0.49	1.01	88.94	**0.24**	0.53	0.50	0.24	**0.76**
Area 4	0.18	0.05	1.30	**0.01**	4.17	1.07	89.12	**0.28**	0.48	0.50	0.28	**0.83**
Area 5	0.50	0.10	2.37	**0.01**	14.64	1.31	89.88	**0.27**	0.44	0.47	0.18	**0.73**
Area 6	**0.01**	0.04	1.54	**0.01**	0.31	0.74	89.39	**0.18**	0.68	0.55	0.29	**0.90**
Total	0.03	0.06	1.72	**0.01**	0.63	1.04	89.51	**0.24**	0.53	0.49	0.23	**0.83**

each room, the dataset contains three object configurations (empty, simple, full) along with three lighting configurations (raw, cold, warm), leading to nine configurations in total. We consider the object layout change from empty to full, where illumination change is randomly selected for each room. We provide further details about the evaluation in the supplementary material. The median errors and localization accuracy at various thresholds is reported in Table 2. CPO outperforms the baselines in most metrics, due to the change compensation of 2D/3D score maps as shown in Fig. 6.

4.2   Localization Performance on Scenes Without Changes

We further demonstrate the wide applicability of CPO by comparing CPO with existing approaches in various scene types and input modalities (raw color / semantic labels). The evaluation is performed in one indoor dataset (Stanford 2D-3D-S [4]), and one outdoor dataset (Data61/2D3D [26]). Unlike OmniScenes and Structured3D, most of these datasets lack scene change. Although CPO mainly targets scenes with changes, it shows state-of-the-art results in these datasets. This is due to the fast histogram generation that allows for effective search from the large pool of candidate poses, which is an essential component of panorama to point cloud localization given the highly non-convex nature of the objective function presented in Sect. 3.

Localization with Raw Color. We first make comparisons with PICCOLO [20], structure-based approach, and depth-based approach in the Stanford 2D-3D-S dataset. In Table 3, we report the localization accuracy and median error, where CPO outperforms other baselines by a large margin. Note that PICCOLO is the current state-of-the-art algorithm for the Stanford 2D-3D-S dataset. The median translation and rotation error of PICCOLO [20] deviates largely in areas 2, 4, and 5, which contain a large number of scenes such as hallways that exhibit repetitive structure. On the other hand, the error metrics and accuracy of CPO are much more consistent in all areas.

Table 4. Localization performance using semantic labels on a subset of Area 3 from Stanford 2D-3D-S [4]. Q_1, Q_2, Q_3 are quartile values of each metric.

	t-error (m)			R-error ($°$)			Runtime (s)		
	Q_1	Q_2	Q_3	Q_1	Q_2	Q_3	Q_1	Q_2	Q_3
PICCOLO	**0.00**	**0.01**	0.07	**0.11**	**0.21**	0.56	14.0	14.3	16.1
GOSMA	0.05	0.08	0.15	0.91	1.13	2.18	**1.4**	1.8	4.4
CPO	0.01	**0.01**	**0.02**	0.20	0.32	**0.51**	1.5	**1.6**	**1.6**

Table 5. Localization performance on all areas of the Data61/2D3D dataset [26].

Method	t-error (m)			R-error ($°$)		
	GOPAC	PICCOLO	CPO	GOPAC	PICCOLO	CPO
Error	1.1	4.9	**0.1**	1.4	28.8	**0.3**

Localization with Semantic Labels. We evaluate the performance of CPO against algorithms that use semantic labels as input, namely GOSMA [7] and GOPAC [6]. We additionally report results from PICCOLO [20], as it could also function with semantic labels. To accommodate for the different input modality, CPO and PICCOLO use color-coded semantic labels as input, as shown in Fig. 2(c). We first compare CPO with PICCOLO and GOSMA on 33 images in Area 3 of the Stanford 2D-3D-S dataset following the evaluation procedure of Campbell *et al.* [7]. As shown in Table 4, CPO outperforms GOSMA [7] by a large margin, with the 3rd quartile values of the errors being smaller than the 1st quartile values of GOSMA [7]. Further, while the performance gap with PIC-COLO [20] is smaller than GOSMA, CPO consistently exhibits a much smaller runtime.

We further compare CPO with PICCOLO and GOPAC [6] in the Data61/2D 3D dataset [26], which is an outdoor dataset that contains semantic labels for both 2D and 3D. The dataset is mainly recorded in the rural regions of Australia, where large portions of the scene are highly repetitive and lack features as shown in Fig. 2(c). Nevertheless, CPO exceeds GOPAC [6] in localization accuracy, as shown in Table 5. Note that CPO only uses a single GPU for acceleration whereas GOPAC employs a quad-GPU configuration for effective performance [6]. Due to the fast histogram generation from Sect. 3.1, CPO can efficiently localize using a smaller number of computational resources.

4.3   Ablation Study

In this section, we ablate key components of CPO, namely histogram-based candidate pose selection and 2D, 3D score maps. The ablation study for other constituents of CPO is provided in the supplementary material.

Table 6. Ablation of various components of CPO in OmniScenes [20] Extreme split.

Method	t-error (m)	R-error (°)	Acc.
w/o Histogram initialization	3.29	75.60	0.20
w/o 2D score map	0.10	1.19	0.48
w/o 3D score map	**0.03**	1.56	0.55
Ours	**0.03**	**0.37**	**0.57**

Table 7. Average runtime for a single synthetic view in Room 3 from OmniScenes [20].

Method	PICCOLO	Structure-Based	Depth-Based	CPO
Runtime (ms)	2.135	38.70	2.745	**0.188**

Histogram-Based Candidate Pose Selection. We verify the effect of using color histograms for candidate pose selection on the Extreme split from the OmniScenes dataset [20]. CPO is compared with a variant that performs candidate pose selection using sampling loss values as in PICCOLO [20], where all other conditions remain the same. As shown in Table 6, a drastic performance gap is present. CPO uses patch-based color histograms for pose selection and thus considers larger spatial context compared to pixel-wise sampling loss. This allows for CPO to effectively overcome ambiguities that arise from repetitive scene structures and scene changes that are present in the Extreme split.

We further validate the efficiency of histogram-based initialization against various initialization methods used in the baselines. In Table 7, we report the average runtime for processing a single synthetic view in milliseconds. The histogram based initialization used in CPO exhibits an order-of-magnitude shorter runtime than other competing methods. The effective utilization of spherical equivariance in fast histogram generation allows for efficient search within a wide range of poses and quickly generate 2D/3D score maps.

Score Maps. We validate the effectiveness of the score maps for robust localization under scene changes on the Extreme split from the OmniScenes dataset [20]. Recall that we use the 2D score map for guiding candidate pose selection and the 3D score map for guiding pose refinement. We report evaluation results for variants of CPO that do not use either the 2D or 3D score map. As shown in Table 6, optimal performance is obtained by using both score maps. The score maps effectively attenuate scene changes, leading to stable pose estimation.

5   Conclusion

In this paper, we present CPO, a fast and robust algorithm for 2D panorama to 3D point cloud localization. To fully leverage the potential of panoramic images for localization, we account for possible scene changes by saving the color distribution consistency in 2D, 3D score maps. The score maps effectively attenuate regions that contain changes and thus lead to more stable camera pose estimation. With the proposed fast histogram generation, the score maps are efficiently constructed and CPO can subsequently select promising initial poses for stable optimization. By effectively utilizing the holistic context in 2D and 3D, CPO achieves stable localization results across various datasets including scenes with changes. We expect CPO to be widely applied in practical localization scenarios where scene change is inevitable.

Acknowledgements. This work was partly supported by the National Research Foundation of Korea (NRF) grant funded by the Korea government(MSIT) (No. 2020R1C1C1008195), Creative-Pioneering Researchers Program through Seoul National University, and Institute of Information & communications Technology Planning & Evaluation (IITP) grant funded by the Korea government(MSIT) (No.2021-0-02068, Artificial Intelligence Innovation Hub).

References

1. Afifi, M., Barron, J.T., LeGendre, C., Tsai, Y.T., Bleibel, F.: Cross-camera convolutional color constancy. In: The IEEE International Conference on Computer Vision (ICCV) (2021)
2. Albanis, G., et al.: Pano3d: a holistic benchmark and a solid baseline for 360° depth estimation. In: 2021 IEEE/CVF Conference on Computer Vision and Pattern Recognition Workshops (CVPRW), pp. 3722–3732 (2021). https://doi.org/10.1109/CVPRW53098.2021.00413
3. Arandjelović, R., Gronat, P., Torii, A., Pajdla, T., Sivic, J.: NetVLAD: CNN architecture for weakly supervised place recognition. In: IEEE Conference on Computer Vision and Pattern Recognition (2016)
4. Armeni, I., Sax, S., Zamir, A.R., Savarese, S.: Joint 2d–3d-semantic data for indoor scene understanding. arXiv preprint arXiv:1702.01105 (2017)
5. Badino, H., Huber, D., Kanade, T.: The CMU Visual Localization Data Set. http://3dvis.ri.cmu.edu/data-sets/localization (2011)
6. Campbell, D., Petersson, L., Kneip, L., Li, H.: Globally-optimal inlier set maximisation for camera pose and correspondence estimation. IEEE Transactions on Pattern Analysis and Machine Intelligence, June 2018. https://doi.org/10.1109/TPAMI.2018.2848650
7. Campbell, D., Petersson, L., Kneip, L., Li, H., Gould, S.: The alignment of the spheres: globally-optimal spherical mixture alignment for camera pose estimation. In: Proceedings of the 2019 IEEE/CVF Conference on Computer Vision and Pattern Recognition (CVPR). IEEE, Long Beach, USA, June 2019
8. Coltuc, D., Bolon, P., Chassery, J.M.: Exact histogram specification. IEEE Trans. Image Process. **15**, 1143–52 (2006). https://doi.org/10.1109/TIP.2005.864170
9. Dong, S., et al.: Robust neural routing through space partitions for camera relocalization in dynamic indoor environments. In: Proceedings of the IEEE/CVF Conference on Computer Vision and Pattern Recognition (CVPR), pp. 8544–8554, June 2021
10. Dusmanu, M., et al.: D2-Net: a trainable CNN for joint detection and description of local features. In: Proceedings of the 2019 IEEE/CVF Conference on Computer Vision and Pattern Recognition (2019)

11. Fischler, M.A., Bolles, R.C.: Random sample consensus: a paradigm for model fitting with applications to image analysis and automated cartography. Commun. ACM. **24**(6), 381–395 (1981). http://dblp.uni-trier.de/db/journals/cacm/cacm24. htmlFischlerB81

12. Gatys, L.A., Ecker, A.S., Bethge, M.: Image style transfer using convolutional neural networks. In: Proceedings of the IEEE Conference on Computer Vision and Pattern Recognition (CVPR), June 2016

13. Ge, Y., Wang, H., Zhu, F., Zhao, R., Li, H.: Self-supervising fine-grained region similarities for large-scale image localization. In: Vedaldi, A., Bischof, H., Brox, T., Frahm, J.-M. (eds.) ECCV 2020. LNCS, vol. 12349, pp. 369–386. Springer, Cham (2020). https://doi.org/10.1007/978-3-030-58548-8_22

14. Gee, A.P., Mayol-Cuevas, W.W.: 6d relocalisation for RGBD cameras using synthetic view regression. In: Bowden, R., Collomosse, J.P., Mikolajczyk, K. (eds.) British Machine Vision Conference, BMVC 2012, Surrey, UK, 3–7 September 2012, pp. 1–11. BMVA Press (2012). https://doi.org/10.5244/C.26.113

15. Gonzalez, R.C., Woods, R.E.: Digital Image Processing. Prentice Hall, Upper Saddle River (2008). http://www.amazon.com/Digital-Image-Processing-3rd-Edition/dp/013168728X

16. Howard-Jenkins, H., Ruiz-Sarmiento, J.R., Prisacariu, V.A.: LaLaLoc: Latent layout localisation in dynamic, unvisited environments. In: Proceedings of the IEEE/CVF International Conference on Computer Vision (ICCV), pp. 10107–10116, October 2021

17. Humenberger, M., et al.: Robust image retrieval-based visual localization using kapture (2020)

18. Irschara, A., Zach, C., Frahm, J., Bischof, H.: From structure-from-motion point clouds to fast location recognition. In: 2009 IEEE Conference on Computer Vision and Pattern Recognition, pp. 2599–2606 (2009). https://doi.org/10.1109/CVPR. 2009.5206587

19. Kendall, A., Grimes, M., Cipolla, R.: PoseNet: a convolutional network for realtime 6-DOF camera relocalization (2015)

20. Kim, J., Choi, C., Jang, H., Kim, Y.M.: PICCOLO: point cloud-centric omnidirectional localization. In: Proceedings of the IEEE/CVF International Conference on Computer Vision (ICCV), pp. 3313–3323, October 2021

21. Kingma, D.P., Ba, J.: Adam: A method for stochastic optimization. In: Bengio, Y., LeCun, Y. (eds.) 3rd International Conference on Learning Representations, ICLR 2015, San Diego, CA, USA, 7–9 May 2015, Conference Track Proceedings (2015). http://arxiv.org/abs/1412.6980

22. Li, X., Wang, S., Zhao, Y., Verbeek, J., Kannala, J.: Hierarchical scene coordinate classification and regression for visual localization. In: CVPR (2020)

23. Li, Y., Snavely, N., Huttenlocher, D.P.: Location recognition using prioritized feature matching. In: Daniilidis, K., Maragos, P., Paragios, N. (eds.) ECCV 2010. LNCS, vol. 6312, pp. 791–804. Springer, Heidelberg (2010). https://doi.org/10. 1007/978-3-642-15552-9_57

24. Luan, F., Paris, S., Shechtman, E., Bala, K.: Deep photo style transfer. arXiv preprint arXiv:1703.07511 (2017)

25. Maddern, W., Pascoe, G., Gadd, M., Barnes, D., Yeomans, B., Newman, P.: Real-time kinematic ground truth for the oxford robotcar dataset. arXiv preprint arXiv: 2002.10152 (2020), http://arxiv.org/pdf/2002.10152

26. Namin, S., Najafi, M., Salzmann, M., Petersson, L.: A multi-modal graphical model for scene analysis. In: 2015 IEEE Winter Conference on Applications of Computer Vision (WACV), pp. 1006–1013. IEEE Computer Society, Los Alamitos, CA, USA (2015). https://doi.org/10.1109/WACV.2015.139, http://doi.ieeecomputersociety.org/10.1109/WACV.2015.139
27. Paszke, A., et al.: Pytorch: an imperative style, high-performance deep learning library. In: Wallach, H., Larochelle, H., Beygelzimer, A., d' Alché-Buc, F., Fox, E., Garnett, R. (eds.) Advances in Neural Information Processing Systems, vol. 32, pp. 8024–8035. Curran Associates, Inc (2019). http://papers.neurips.cc/paper/9015-pytorch-an-imperative-style-high-performance-deep-learning-library.pdf
28. Rodenberg, O.B.P.M., Verbree, E., Zlatanova, S.: Indoor A* Pathfinding Through an Octree Representation of a Point Cloud. ISPRS Annals of Photogrammetry, Remote Sensing and Spatial Information Sciences, IV21, pp. 249–255, October 2016. https://doi.org/10.5194/isprs-annals-IV-2-W1-249-2016
29. Sarlin, P.E., Cadena, C., Siegwart, R., Dymczyk, M.: From coarse to fine: robust hierarchical localization at large scale. In: CVPR (2019)
30. Sarlin, P.E., DeTone, D., Malisiewicz, T., Rabinovich, A.: SuperGlue: Learning feature matching with graph neural networks. In: CVPR (2020)
31. Sattler, T., Leibe, B., Kobbelt, L.: Improving image-based localization by active correspondence search. In: Fitzgibbon, A., Lazebnik, S., Perona, P., Sato, Y., Schmid, C. (eds.) ECCV 2012. LNCS, vol. 7572, pp. 752–765. Springer, Heidelberg (2012). https://doi.org/10.1007/978-3-642-33718-5_54
32. Sattler, T., Leibe, B., Kobbelt, L.: Efficient & effective prioritized matching for large-scale image-based localization. IEEE Trans. Pattern Anal. Mach. Intell. **39**(9), 1744–1756 (2017)
33. Sattler, T., et al.: Benchmarking 6DOF outdoor visual localization in changing conditions. In: Conference on Computer Vision and Pattern Recognition (CVPR) (2018)
34. Taira, H., et al.: InLoc: Indoor visual localization with dense matching and view synthesis. In: CVPR 2018 - IEEE Conference on Computer Vision and Pattern Recognition. Salt Lake City, United States, June 2018. http://hal.archives-ouvertes.fr/hal-01859637
35. Walch, F., Hazirbas, C., Leal-Taixe, L., Sattler, T., Hilsenbeck, S., Cremers, D.: Image-based localization using LSTMS for structured feature correlation. In: Proceedings of the IEEE International Conference on Computer Vision (ICCV), October 2017
36. Wald, J., Sattler, T., Golodetz, S., Cavallari, T., Tombari, F.: Beyond controlled environments: 3d camera re-localization in changing indoor scenes. In: Vedaldi, A., Bischof, H., Brox, T., Frahm, J.-M. (eds.) ECCV 2020. LNCS, vol. 12352, pp. 467–487. Springer, Cham (2020). https://doi.org/10.1007/978-3-030-58571-6_28
37. Zhang, C., Budvytis, I., Liwicki, S., Cipolla, R.: Rotation equivariant orientation estimation for omnidirectional localization. In: ACCV (2020)
38. Zheng, J., et al.: Structured3D: a large photo-realistic dataset for structured 3d modeling. In: Vedaldi, A., Bischof, H., Brox, T., Frahm, J.-M. (eds.) ECCV 2020. LNCS, vol. 12354, pp. 519–535. Springer, Cham (2020). https://doi.org/10.1007/978-3-030-58545-7_30
39. Zhou, Q., Sattler, T., Leal-Taixe, L.: Patch2pix: epipolar-guided pixel-level correspondences. In: CVPR (2021)
40. Zhu, J.Y., Park, T., Isola, P., Efros, A.A.: Unpaired image-to-image translation using cycle-consistent adversarial networks. In: 2017 IEEE International Conference on Computer Vision (ICCV) (2017)

INT: Towards Infinite-Frames 3D Detection with an Efficient Framework

Jianyun Xu, Zhenwei Miao$^{(\boxtimes)}$, Da Zhang, Hongyu Pan, Kaixuan Liu, Peihan Hao, Jun Zhu, Zhengyang Sun, Hongmin Li, and Xin Zhan

Alibaba Group, Hangzhou, China
{xujianyun.xjy,zhenwei.mzw}@alibaba-inc.com

Abstract. It is natural to construct a multi-frame instead of a single-frame 3D detector for a continuous-time stream. Although increasing the number of frames might improve performance, previous multi-frame studies only used very limited frames to build their systems due to the dramatically increased computational and memory cost. To address these issues, we propose a novel on-stream training and prediction framework that, in theory, can employ an infinite number of frames while keeping the same amount of computation as a single-frame detector. This **infinite** framework (INT), which can be used with most existing detectors, is utilized, for example, on the popular CenterPoint, with significant latency reductions and performance improvements. We've also conducted extensive experiments on two large-scale datasets, nuScenes and Waymo Open Dataset, to demonstrate the scheme's effectiveness and efficiency. By employing INT on CenterPoint, we can get around 7% (Waymo) and 15% (nuScenes) performance boost with only 2~4 ms latency overhead, and currently SOTA on the Waymo 3D Detection leaderboard.

Keywords: Infinite · Multi-frame · 3D detection · Efficient · Pointcloud

1 Introduction

3D object detection from pointclouds has been proven as a viable robotics vision solution, particularly in autonomous driving applications. Many single-frame 3D detectors [10,15,20,23,26,27,36,39,42] are developed to meet the real-time requirement of the online system. Nevertheless, it is more natural for a continuous-time system to adopt multi-frame detectors that can fully take advantage of the time-sequence information. However, as far as we know, few multi-frame 3D detectors are available for long frame sequences due to the heavy computation and memory burden. It is desirable to propose a concise real-time long-sequence 3D detection framework with promising performance.

Existing works [5,11,22,32,37–39] demonstrate that multi-frame models yield performance gains over single-frame ones. However, these approaches require

Supplementary Information The online version contains supplementary material available at https://doi.org/10.1007/978-3-031-20077-9_12.

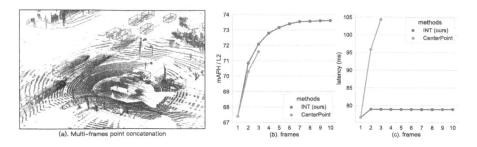

Fig. 1. Impact of frames used in detectors on Waymo *val* set. While CenterPoint's performance improves as the number of frames grows, the latency also increases dramatically. On the other hand, our INT keeps the same latency while increasing frames.

loading all the used frames at once during training, resulting in very limited frames being used due to computational, memory, or optimization difficulties. Taking the SOTA detector CenterPoint [39] as an example, it only uses two frames [39] on the Waymo Open Dataset [29]. While increasing the number of frames can boost the performance, it also leads to significant latency burst as shown in Fig. 1. Memory overflow occurs if we keep increasing the frames of CenterPoint, making both training and inference impossible. As a result, we believe that the number of frames used is the bottleneck preventing multi-frame development, and we intend to break through this barrier first.

There are two major problems that limit the number of frames in a multi-frame detector: 1) repeated computation. Most of the current multi-frame frameworks have a lot of repeated calculations or redundant data that causes computational spikes or memory overflow; 2) optimization difficulty. Some multi-frame systems have longer gradient conduction links as the number of frames increases, introducing optimization difficulties.

To alleviate the above problems, we propose INT (short for **infinite**), an on-stream system that theoretically allows training and prediction to utilize infinite number of frames. INT contains two primary components: 1) a Memory Bank (MB) for temporal information fusion and 2) a Dynamic Training Sequence Length (DTSL) strategy for on-stream training. The MB is a place to store the recursively updated historical information so that we don't have to compute past frames' features repeatedly. As a result, it only requires a small amount of memory but can fuse infinite data frames. To tackle the problem of optimization difficulty, we truncate the gradient of back propagation to the MB during training. However, an inherent flaw of iteratively updating MB on a training stream is that historical and current information are not given by the same model parameters, leading to training issues. To solve this problem, DTSL is employed. The primary idea of DTSL is to start with short sequences and quickly clear the MB to avoid excessive inconsistency between historical and current data; then gradually lengthen the sequence as training progresses since the gap between historical and current model parameters becomes negligible.

To make INT feasible, we propose three modules: SeqFusion, SeqSampler and SeqAug. SeqFusion is a module in MB for temporal fusion that proposes multiple fusion methods for two types of data commonly used in pointcloud detection, i.e., point-style and image-style. SeqSampler is a sequence index generator that DTSL uses to generate training sequences of different lengths at each epoch. Finally, SeqAug is a data augmentation for on-stream training, capable of maintaining the same random state on the same stream.

Our contributions can be summarized as:

- We present INT, an on-stream multi-frame system made up of MB and DTSL that can theoretically be trained and predicted using infinite frames while consuming similar computation and memory as a single-frame system.
- We propose three modules, SeqFusion, SeqSampler and SeqAug, to make INT feasible.
- We conduct extensive experiments on nuScenes and Waymo Open Dataset to illustrate the effectiveness and efficiency of INT.

2   Related Work

2.1   3D Object Detection

Recent studies on 3D object detection can be broadly divided into three categories: LiDAR-based [10,15,16,19,23,27,35,36,39,42,43], image-based [4,14,17,31], and fusion-based [3,18,22,24,30,40,41]. Here we focus on LiDAR-based schemes.

According to the views of pointclouds, 3D detectors can be classified as point-based, voxel-based, range-based, and hybrid. PointRCNN [27] and VoteNet [23] are two representative point-based methods that use a structure like Point-Net++ [25] to extract point-by-point features. These schemes are characterized by better preservation of pointclouds' original geometric information. Still, they are sensitive to the number of pointclouds that pose serious latency and memory issues. In contrast, voxel-based solutions, such as VoxelNet [42], PointPillars [15], Second [36], CenterPoint [39] and AFDetV2 [10] are less sensitive to the number of pointclouds. They convert the pointcloud into 2D pillars or 3D voxels first, then extract features using 2D or 3D (sparse) convolution, making them easier to deploy. Another category is rangeview-based schemes [6,16,19] that perform feature extraction and target prediction on an efficient unfolded spherical projection view. Meanwhile, they contend with target scale variation and occlusion issues, resulting in performance that is generally inferior to that of voxel-based schemes. Hybrid methods [20,26,35,43] attempt to integrate features from several views to collect complementing information and enhance performance.

We define two data styles according to the data format to facilitate the analysis of different detectors:

- *Image-style*. Well-organized data in 2D, 3D, or 4D dimensions similar to that of an image.
- *Point-style*. Disorganized data such as pointclouds and sparse 3D voxels.

The data in pointcloud-based detectors, including input, intermediate feature, and output, is generally point-style or image-style. We design the fusion

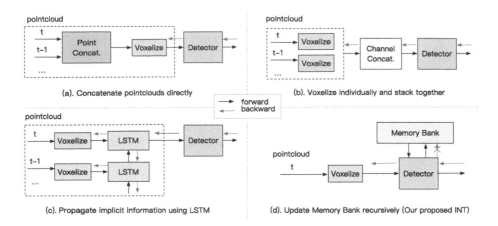

Fig. 2. Training phase of different multi-frame schemes. Operations inside dash rectangle either involve repetitive computation or raise memory burden, which leads to a very limited frame number for training.

algorithms for both point-style and image-style data in INT's Memory Bank, so that INT can be employed in most 3D detectors. In this work, we choose the recently popular CenterPoint [39] as the baseline for studies since it performs better in terms of efficiency and performance, and it is now scoring at SOTA level on the large-scale open datasets nuScenes [2] and Waymo Open Dataset [29].

2.2   Multi-frame Methods

There have been a variety of LSTM-based techniques in the field of video object detection, such as [7,13,33]. Transformer-based video detection schemes have recently emerged [9], however transformer may not be suitable for working on-stream because it naturally needs to compute the relationship between all frames, which implies a lot of repeated computations.

Recent methods for multi-frame pointclouds can be roughly divided into three categories as shown in Fig. 2(a), (b) and (c). [2,22,36] directly concatenate multi-frame pointclouds and introduce a channel indicating their relative timestamps, as shown in Fig. 2(a). While this method is simple and effective, it involves a lot of unnecessary computations and increases the memory burden, making it unsuitable for more frames. Instead of merging at the point level, MinkowskiNet [5] and MotionNet [32] combine multiple frames at the feature map level. They must voxelize multi-frame pointclouds independently before stacking the feature maps together and extracting spatio-temporal information using 3D or 4D convolution, as depicted in Fig. 2(b). Obviously, this approach requires repeated data processing and is memory intensive, thus the number of frames is very limited.

To overcome above difficulties, 2020An [11] and 3DVID [38] proposed LSTM or GRU-based solutions to solve the computational and memory issues in the inference phase. However, the gradient transfer to the history frames still results in a considerable memory overhead and introduce optimization difficulties during training, so the number of frames cannot be high, as shown in Fig. 2(c). To handle the problem more thoroughly, we propose computing the gradient for the current data and not for the historical data during training, as shown in Fig. 2(d). We then employ a Dynamic Training Sequence Length (DTSL) strategy to eliminate the potential information inconsistency problem. Similarly, 3D-MAN [37] stores historical information in a Memory Bank that does not participate in the gradient calculation. However, 3D-MAN needs to store a fixed number of frames of historical proposals and feature maps, which increases the amount of memory required for its training as the number of frames increases. To get around this problem, we propose recursively updating the Memory Bank's historical information.

To the best of our knowledge, we are the first 3D multi-frame system that can be trained and inferred with infinite frames.

3 Methodology

We present INT framework in this section. The overall architecture is detailed in Sect. 3.1. Section 3.2 gives the sequence fusion (SeqFusion) methods of Memory Bank. Sections 3.3 and 3.4 illustrate the training strategies, including sequence sampler (SeqSampler) and sequence data augmentation (SeqAug), respectively.

3.1 Overview of INT Framework

The INT framework in Fig. 3 is highly compact. The main body consists of a single-frame detector and a recursively updated Memory Bank (MB). The Dynamic Training Sequence Length (DTSL) below serves as a training strategy that is not needed for inference (inference only needs the pointclouds input in chronological order). In addition, there are no special requirements for single-frame detector selection. For example, any detector listed in Sect. 2.1 can be utilized.

Memory Bank (MB). The primary distinction between INT and a regular multi-frame detector is the MB, which stores historical data so that we do not have to compute past features repeatedly. MB is comparable to the hidden state in LSTM while it is more flexible, interpretable, and customizable. The user has complete control over where and what information should be saved or retrieved. For example, in Sect. 3.2, we show how to store and update several forms of data. Furthermore, we choose to update the MB recursively to solve the problem of excessive memory cost. To tackle the problem of optimization difficulty, we truncate the gradient of backpropagation to the MB during training.

Dynamic Training Sequence Length (DTSL). A problem with INT training on stream is the information gained from the current observation is not derived using the same model parameters as the past data in the MB. This could lead to inconsistencies in training and prediction, which is one of the key

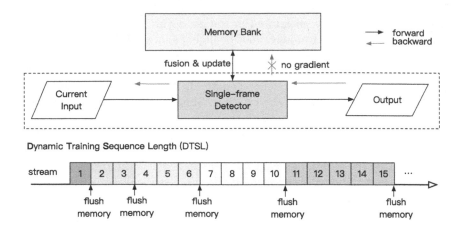

Fig. 3. Overview of INT framework. It consists of a single-frame detector and a Memory Bank. The Dynamic Training Sequence Length below serves as a training strategy.

reasons why prior multi-frame work was not trained on stream. To solve this problem, we offer the DTSL: beginning with a small sequence length and gradually increasing it, as indicated at the bottom of Fig. 3. This is based on the following observation: as the number of training steps increases, model parameter updates get slower, and the difference in information acquired from different model parameters becomes essentially trivial. As a result, when the model parameters are updated quickly, the training sequence should be short so that the Memory Bank can be cleaned up in time. Once the training is stable, the sequence length can be increased with confidence. DTSL could be defined in a variety of ways, one of which is as follows:

$$DTSL = max(1, \lfloor l_{max} \cdot min(1, \ max(0, \ 2 \cdot \frac{ep_{cur}}{ep_{all}} - 0.5))\rfloor) \tag{1}$$

where l_{max} is the maximum training sequence length, ep_{cur} and ep_{all} is current epoch and total epoch number, respectively.

3.2 SeqFusion

Temporal fusion in the Memory Bank is critical in the INT framework. As the type of data in a 3D detector is either point-style or image-style, as indicated in Sect. 2.1, we develop both the point-style and image-style fusion algorithms. In general, original pointcloud, sparse voxel, predicted object, etc., fall into the point-style category. Whereas dense voxel, intermediate feature map, final prediction map, etc., fall into the image-style category.

Point-Style Fusion. Here we propose a general and straightforward practice: concatenating past point-style data with present data directly, using a channel to identify the temporal relationship. The historical point-style data is put into a fixed length FIFO queue, and as new observations arrive, foreground data is pushed into it, while oldest data is popped out. According to the poses of ego vehicle, the position information in the history data must be spatially transformed before fusion to avoid the influence of ego movement. The point-style fusion is formulated as:

$$T_{rel} = T_{cur}^{-1} \cdot T_{last}, \tag{2}$$

$$P_f = PointConcat(P_{cur}, \ T_{rel} \cdot P_{last}) \tag{3}$$

where T_{last} and T_{cur} are the last and current frame's ego vehicle poses, respectively, while T_{rel} is the calculated relative pose between the two frames. P_{last} refers to the past point-style data in Memory Bank and P_f is the fused data of P_{last} and current P_{cur}.

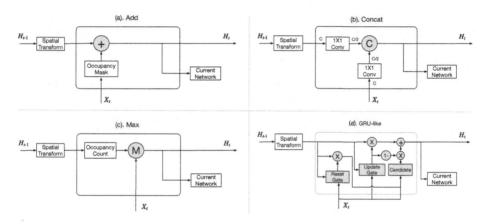

Fig. 4. Four temporal fusion methods for image-style data. Occupancy Mask and Occupancy Count in *Add* and *Max* are used to distinguish different moments.

Image-Style Fusion. We propose four fusion algorithms for the image-style data, including *Add*, *Max*, *Concat* and *GRU-like* as depicted in Fig. 4 (a), (b), (c) and (d). As the historical image-style data and current data should be identical in dimensions based on recursive updates, *Add* and *Max* are simple in design and implementation. The computational overhead of these two fusion methods is cheap. We also devise the *Concat* fusion approach, in which both the historical and the current feature channels are first compressed to 1/2 of the origin and then concatenated along channel dimension. To investigate the impact of long-term data, we develop a *GRU-like* fusion method with learnable parameters to select which data should be kept and which should be discarded. To eliminate the effect of ego vehicle motion, historical image-style data must be spatially transformed first. The image-style fusion process can be summarized as follows:

$$\tilde{I}_{last} = F_{sample}(I_{last}, \ F_{affine}(T_{rel}, \ s)), \tag{4}$$

$$I_f = Fusion(I_{cur}, \ \tilde{I}_{last}) \tag{5}$$

where T_{rel} is the same as Eq. 3. $F_{affine}(\cdot)$ and $F_{sample}(\cdot)$ refer to *affine grid* and *grid sample* operation respectively, which are proposed in [12] for image-style data transformation. I_{last} refers to the past image-style data in Memory Bank and I_f is the fused data of I_{last} and current I_{cur}. s is the shape of I_{last}. $Fusion(\cdot)$ can be *Add, Max, Concat* and *GRU-like*, as shown in Fig. 4.

3.3 SeqSampler

SeqSampler is the key to perform the training of INT in an infinite-frames manner. It is designed to split original sequences to target length, and then generate the indices of them orderly. If the sequence is infinite-long, the training or inference can go on infinitely. DTSL is formed by executing SeqSampler with different target lengths for each epoch.

The length of original sequences in a dataset generally varies, for as in the Waymo Open Dataset [29], where sequence lengths oscillate around 200. Certain datasets, such as nuScenes [2], may be interval labeled, with one frame labeled every ten frames. As a result, the SeqSampler should be designed with the idea that the source sequence will be non-fixed in length and will be annotated at intervals. The procedures of SeqSampler are as simple as *Sequence Sort* and *Sequence Split*, as indicated in Fig. 5. In *Sequence Sort*, we rearrange the random input samples orderly by sequences. Then split them to target length in *Sequence Sort*, and may padding some of them to meet the batch or iteration demands.

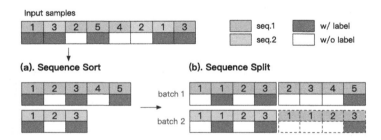

Fig. 5. An example of SeqSampler. There are two sequences: seq1 contains 5 frames and seq2 has 3, both are interval labeled. Given the desired batch size 2 and target length 4, we need to get the final iteration indices. First, the two sequences are sorted separately. Then, the original sequences are splitted to 3 segments in the target length, and a segment is randomly replicated (dashed rectangles) to guarantee that both batches have the same number of samples.

3.4 SeqAug

Data augmentation has been successful in many recent 3D detectors [15,36,39]. However, because of the shift in training paradigm, our suggested INT framework can not directly migrate current validated data augmentation methods.

One of the main reasons for this is that INT is trained on a stream with a clear association between the before and after frames, whereas data augmentation is typically random, and the before and after frames could take various augmentation procedures. To solve this problem and allow INT to benefit from data augmentation, we must verify that a certain method of data augmentation on the same stream maintains the same random state at all times. We term the data augmentation that meets this condition SeqAug. According to the data augmentation methods widely employed in pointcloud detection, SeqAug can be split into two categories: Sequence Point Transformation (flipping, rotation, translation, scaling, and so on) and Sequence GtAug (copy and paste of the ground truth pointclouds).

Sequence Point Transformation. If a pointcloud is successively augmented by flipping T_f, rotation T_r, scaling T_s, and translation T_t, the other frames in the same stream must keep the same random state to establish a reasonable temporal relationship. In addition, because of these transformations, T_{rel} in Eq. 3 must be recalculated:

$$T_{rel} = T_t \cdot T_s \cdot T_r \cdot T_f \cdot T_{cur}^{-1} \cdot T_{last} \cdot T_f \cdot T_r^{-1} \cdot T_s^{-1} \cdot T_t^{-1} \qquad (6)$$

where T_{last} and T_{cur} are the last and current frame's ego vehicle poses.

Sequence GtAug. Similarly, recording random states of the same stream is required to ensure that the sequential objects from the Gt database can be copied and pasted consecutively, as shown in Fig. 6.

a). Before Sequence GtAug   b). After Sequence GtAug

Fig. 6. An example of Sequence GtAug. The colors of pointclouds represent different moments, with red being the current frame. (Color figure online)

4   Experiments

In this paper, we build the proposed INT framework based on the highly competitive and popular detector CenterPoint [39]. In the following sections, we first briefly introduce the datasets in Sect. 4.1, followed by a description of a few critical experimental setups in Sect. 4.2. The efficiency and effectiveness of the INT framework are then illustrated in Sect. 4.3 by comparing it to the baseline CenterPoint, followed by Sect. 4.4, which compares the results of INT on the Waymo test set to other SOTAs. Finally, Sect. 4.5 is several INT ablation experiments.

4.1 Datasets

This section briefly describes the two open datasets used in this paper.

Waymo Open Dataset. Waymo [29] comprises 798, 202 and 150 sequences for train, validation and test, respectively. Each sequence lasts around 20 s and contains about 200 frames. There are three categories for detection: VEHICLE, PEDESTRIAN, and CYCLIST. The mean Average Precision (mAP) and mAP weighted by heading accuracy (mAPH) are the official 3D detection metrics. There are two degrees of difficulty: LEVEL 1 for boxes with more than five LiDAR points, and LEVEL 2 for boxes with at least one LiDAR point. In this paper, we utilize the officially prescribed mAPH on LEVEL 2 by default.

nuScenes. There are 1000 driving sequences in nuScenes [2], with 700, 150, and 150 for training, validation, and testing, respectively. Each sequence lasts about 20 s and has a LiDAR frequency of 20 frames per second. The primary metrics for 3D detection are mean Average Precision (mAP) and nuScenes Detection Score (NDS). NDS is a weighted average of mAP and other attribute measurements such as translation, scale, orientation, velocity, and other box properties. In this study, we employ mAP and NDS as experimental results.

4.2 Experimental Settings

We employ the same network designs and training schedules as CenterPoint [39] and keep the positive and negative sample strategies, post-processing settings, loss functions, etc., unchanged.

Backbone Settings. VoxelNet [36,42] and PointPillars [15] are two 3D encoders used by CenterPoint, dubbed CenterPoint-Voxel and CenterPoint-Pillar, respectively. Our INT also experiments with these two backbones, which correspond to INT-Voxel and INT-Pillar, respectively.

Frame Settings. Although INT can be trained and inferred on an infinite number of frames, the sequence length of the actual dataset is finite. To facilitate comparison with previous work and demonstrate the benefits of the INT framework, we select a few specific frames on nuScenes and Waymo Open Dataset. We use 10, 20 and 100 training frames on nuScenes, and 10 training frames on Waymo Open Dataset.

Fusion Settings. On INT, we choose three kinds of data added to Memory Bank: point-style foreground pointcloud, image-style intermediate feature map, and image-style final prediction map. For the foreground pointcloud, we fuse the historical points with the current points during the input phase and then update them based on the predictions at the end of network. For the intermediate feature map, we fuse and update its historical information at the same position before the Region Proposal Network. For the final prediction map, we fuse and update historical information simultaneously before the detection header. Appendix A.4 takes INT-Voxel as a typical example to provide a more specific explanation.

Latency Settings. To test the network's actual latency, we remove redundant parts of the data processing in CenterPoint [39] and just maintain the data IO and memory transfer (to the GPU) operations. We shift the essential voxelization component to the GPU to limit the CPU's influence. We also build up data prefetching in the dataloader to lessen IO effect and run latency tests when it is stabilized. Finally, the following test circumstances are used: CUDA Version 10.2, cudnn 7.6.5, GeForce RTX 2070 SUPER, Driver Version 460.91.03.

4.3   Effectiveness and Efficiency

As shown in Table 1 and 2, we first compare to the baseline CenterPoint to demonstrate the paper's main point, i.e., the effectiveness and efficiency of INT. In these two tables, we try two types of backbone, termed E-PointPillars and E-VoxelNet in the columns, and the unit of latency is milliseconds. The settings of INT can be referred to Table 4 and 5. CenterPoint with multiple frames refers to concatenating multi-frame pointclouds at the input level, which introduces repetitive computation and additional memory burden as analyzed in Sect. 2.2. For example, two-frames CenterPoint in Table 1 increases the latency by around 20 ms when compared to its single-frame counterpart (more details in Appendix A.6). In contrast, the latency of INT is unaffected by the number of frames used, and its performance is much better than that of multi-frame CenterPoint as the number of frames grows. As can be obviously observed in Table 1 and 2, INT shows significant improvements in both latency and performance, gaining around 7% mAPH (Waymo) and 15% NDS (nuScenes) boost while only adding 2~4 ms delay when compared to single-frame CenterPoint.

4.4   Comparison with SOTAs

In this section, we compare the results of INT on the Waymo *test* set with those of other SOTAs schemes, as shown in Table 3. The approaches are divided into two groups in the table: single-frame and multi-frame. It is seen that the multi-frame scheme is generally superior to the single-frame scheme. Most multi-frame approaches employ the original pointclouds concatenation [10,28,39], and we can see that the number of frames is used fewer due to computational and memory constraints. Finally, our suggested INT scheme outperforms other SOTA schemes by a large margin. As far as we know, INT is the best non-ensemble approach on Waymo Open Dataset leaderboard[1].

---

[1] https://waymo.com/open/challenges/2020/3d-detection/.

Table 1. Effectiveness and efficiency of INT on Waymo Open Dataset *val* set. The APH of L2 difficulty is reported. The "-2s" suffix in the rows means two-stage model. CenterPoint's mAPH results are obtained from official website, except for those with a *, which are missing from the official results and were reproduced by us.

Methods	Frames	E-PointPillars					E-VoxelNet				
		VEH↑	PED↑	CYC↑	mAPH↑	Latency↓	VEH↑	PED↑	CYC↑	mAPH↑	Latency↓
CenterPoint	1	65.5	55.1	60.2	60.3	**57.7**	66.2	62.6	67.6	65.5	**71.7**
CenterPoint	2	66.6*	61.9*	62.3*	63.6*	77.8	67.3	67.5	69.9	68.2	90.9
INT (ours)	2	66.2	60.4	64.4	63.7	61.6	69.4	69.1	72.6	70.3	74.0
INT (ours)	10	**69.6**	**66.3**	**65.7**	**67.2**	61.6	**72.2**	**72.1**	**75.3**	**73.2**	74.0
CenterPoint-2s	1	66.7	55.9	61.7	61.4	**61.7**	67.9	65.6	68.6	67.4	**76.6**
CenterPoint-2s	2	68.4*	63.0*	64.3*	65.2*	82.9	69.7	70.3	70.9	70.3	95.8
INT-2s (ours)	2	67.9	61.7	66.0	65.2	65.9	70.8	68.7	73.1	70.8	78.9
INT-2s (ours)	10	**70.8**	**67.0**	**68.1**	**68.6**	65.9	**73.3**	**71.9**	**75.6**	**73.6**	78.9

Table 2. Effectiveness and efficiency of INT on nuScenes *val* set. CenterPoint's mAP and NDS results are obtained from official website, except for those with a *, which are missing from the official results and were reproduced by us.

Methods	Frames	E-PointPillars			E-VoxelNet		
		mAP↑	NDS↑	Latency↓	mAP↑	NDS↑	Latency↓
CenterPoint	1	42.5*	46.4*	**39.2**	49.7*	50.7*	**81.1**
CenterPoint	10	50.3	60.2	49.4	59.6	66.8	117.2
INT (ours)	10	49.3	59.9	43.0	58.5	65.5	84.1
INT (ours)	20	50.7	61.0	43.0	60.9	66.9	84.1
INT (ours)	100	**52.3**	**61.8**	43.0	**61.8**	**67.3**	84.1

Table 3. Comparison with SOTAs on Waymo Open Dataset *test* set. We only present the non-emsemble approaches, and INT is currently the best non-emsemble solution on the Waymo Open Dataset leaderboard[1], to the best of our knowledge. Accessed on 2 March 2022.

Methods	Frames	VEH-APH↑		PED-APH↑		CYC-APH↑		mAPH↑	
		L1	L2	L1	L2	L1	L2	L1	L2
StarNet [21]	1	61.0	54.5	59.9	54.0	-	-	-	-
PointPillars [15]	1	68.1	60.1	55.5	50.1	-	-	-	-
RCD [1]	1	71.6	64.7	-	-	-	-	-	-
M3DeTR [8]	1	77.2	70.1	58.9	52.4	65.7	63.8	67.1	61.9
HIK-LiDAR [34]	1	78.1	70.6	69.9	64.1	69.7	67.2	72.6	67.3
CenterPoint [39]	1	79.7	71.8	72.1	66.4	-	-	-	-
3D-MAN [37]	15	78.3	70.0	66.0	60.3	-	-	-	-
RSN [28]	3	80.3	71.6	75.6	67.8	-	-	-	-
CenterPoint [39]	2	80.6	73.0	77.3	71.5	73.7	71.3	77.2	71.9
CenterPoint++ [39]	3	82.3	75.1	78.2	72.4	73.3	71.1	78.0	72.8
AFDetV2 [10]	2	81.2	73.9	78.1	72.4	75.4	73.0	78.2	73.1
INT (ours)	10	83.1	76.2	78.5	72.8	74.8	72.7	78.8	73.9
INT (ours)	100	**84.3**	**77.6**	**79.7**	**74.0**	**76.3**	**74.1**	**80.1**	**75.2**

4.5   Ablation Studies

Impact of Different Fusion Data. This section investigates the impact of various fusion data used in INT. We use one kind of point-style data, the foreground pointcloud, and two kinds of image-style data, the intermediate feature map before RPN and the final prediction map in this paper. The fusion method of foreground pointcloud is termed as *PC Fusion* which is explained in Sect. 3.2. The fusion method of the intermediate feature map and the final prediction map is *Concat*, as described in Sect. 3.2, named as *FM Fusion* and *PM Fusion*, respectively. The fusion results of these three kinds of data on Waymo Open Dataset and nuScenes are shown in Table 4 and 5. First, the tables' performance columns show that all the three fusion data have considerable performance boosts, with *PC Fusion* having the highest effect gain. Then according to the latency columns, the increase in time of different fusion data is relatively small, which is very cost-effective given the performance benefit.

Table 4. Impact of different fusion data on Waymo Open Dataset *val* set. By default, the training sequence length was set to 10 frames. In order to indicate how the final result comes in Table 1, we also add a column called "Two Stage".

PC fusion	FM fusion	PM fusion	Two stage	E-PointPillars					E-VoxelNet				
				VEH↑	PED↑	CYC↑	mAPH↑	Latency↓	VEH↑	PED↑	CYC↑	mAPH↑	Latency↓
				65.5	55.1	60.2	60.3	**57.4**	66.2	62.6	67.6	65.5	**71.5**
√				68.1	65.8	65.4	66.4	59.5	71.7	70.8	74.2	72.3	72.7
	√			63.6	63.3	64.7	63.8	59.0	66.1	67.3	73.8	69.1	72.2
		√		66.4	64.0	64.2	64.5	58.2	67.7	68.1	74.1	70.0	72.0
√	√			69.5	66.8	64.8	67.0	60.9	72.0	71.8	76.5	73.5	73.3
√	√	√		69.6	66.3	65.7	67.2	61.6	72.2	**72.1**	**76.1**	73.5	74.0
√	√	√	√	**70.8**	**67.0**	**68.1**	**68.6**	65.9	**73.3**	71.9	75.6	**73.6**	78.9

Table 5. Impact of different fusion data on nuScenes *val* set. By default, the training sequence length was set to 10 frames. In order to indicate how the final result comes in Table 2, we also add a column called "100 frames".

PC fusion	FM fusion	PM fusion	100 frames	E-PointPillars			E-VoxelNet		
				mAP	NDS	Latency	mAP	NDS	Latency
				42.5	46.4	**39.2**	49.7	50.7	**81.1**
√				47.1	58.5	41.2	56.6	64.5	82.4
	√			48.4	57.4	40.5	55.9	56.6	82.1
		√		45.3	56.0	39.7	53.9	62.7	82.0
√	√			48.7	59.8	42.4	58.4	65.2	83.3
√	√	√		49.3	59.9	43.0	58.5	65.5	84.1
√	√	√	√	**52.3**	**61.8**	43.0	**61.8**	**67.3**	84.1

Impact of Training Sequence Length. The length indicated here actually refer to the maximum length since Dynamic Training Sequence Length (DTSL) is used in training. Figure 1 depicts the relationship between frames and performance for the 2-stage INT-Voxel model on the Waymo Open Dataset. We also plot the 2-stage CenterPoint-Voxel results together to make comparisons clearer. As shown in Fig. 1(b), INT improves as the number of frames increases, although there is saturation after a certain point (See Appendix A.5 for more explanation); as for Fig. 1(c), the time consumed by INT is slightly higher than that of single-frame CenterPoint, but it does not increase with the number of frames.

Impact of Sequence Augmentation. Section 3.4 introduces SeqAug, a data augmentation technique for on-stream training, and this section examines the role of Point Transformation and GtAug in SeqAug. As seen in Table 6, both augmentation strategies result in significant performance improvements, making data augmentation essential for INT training just as regular detectors do.

Table 6. Impact of SeqAug on Waymo Open Dataset *val* set. One-stage INT-Pillar and INT-Voxel are used.

Sequence point trans.	Sequence GtAug	E-PointPillars				E-VoxelNet			
		VEL-APH↑	PED-APH↑	CYC-APH↑	mAPH↑	VEL-APH↑	PED-APH↑	CYC-APH↑	mAPH↑
		59.6	56.7	56.2	57.5	65.0	62.4	61.9	63.1
√		69.3	65.0	62.4	65.6	71.8	71.4	73.1	72.1
√	√	69.6	66.3	65.7	67.2	72.2	72.1	76.1	73.5

More Ablation Studies in Appendix. The impact of sequence length on nuScenes is shown in Appendix A.1. The performance and latency of temporal fusion methods for image-style data (proposed in Sect. 3.2) are shown in Appendix A.2. The impact of DTSL proposed in Sect. 3.1 can be found in Appendix A.3.

5 Conclusion

In this paper, we present INT, a novel on-stream training and prediction framework that, in theory, can employ an infinite number of frames while using about the same amount of computational and memory cost as a single-frame detector. To make INT feasible, we propose three key modules, i.e., SeqFusion, SeqSampler, and SeqAug. We utilize INT on the popular CenterPoint, with significant latency reductions and performance improvements, and rank **1st** currently on Waymo Open Dataset 3D Detection leaderboard among the non-ensemble SOTA methods. Moreover, the INT is a general multi-frame system, which may be used for tasks like segmentation and motion as well as detection.

Acknowledgement. This work was supported by Alibaba Group through Alibaba Innovative Research (AIR) Program and Alibaba Research Intern Program.

References

1. Bewley, A., Sun, P., Mensink, T., Anguelov, D., Sminchisescu, C.: Range conditioned dilated convolutions for scale invariant 3d object detection. arXiv preprint arXiv:2005.09927 (2020)
2. Caesar, H., et al.: nuscenes: a multimodal dataset for autonomous driving. In: Proceedings of the IEEE Conference on Computer Vision and Pattern Recognition, pp. 11621–11631 (2020)
3. Chen, X., Ma, H., Wan, J., Li, B., Xia, T.: Multi-view 3d object detection network for autonomous driving. In: Proceedings of the IEEE Conference on Computer Vision and Pattern Recognition, pp. 1907–1915 (2017)
4. Chong, Z., et al.: MonodiStill: learning spatial features for monocular 3d object detection. arXiv preprint arXiv:2201.10830 (2022)
5. Choy, C., Gwak, J., Savarese, S.: 4d spatio-temporal convnets: Minkowski convolutional neural networks. In: Proceedings of the IEEE Conference on Computer Vision and Pattern Recognition, pp. 3075–3084 (2019)
6. Fan, L., Xiong, X., Wang, F., Wang, N., Zhang, Z.: Rangedet:in defense of range view for lidar-based 3d object detection. In: Proceedings of the IEEE International Conference on Computer Vision (2021)
7. Feng, Y., Ma, L., Liu, W., Luo, J.: Spatio-temporal video re-localization by warp LSTM. In: Proceedings of the IEEE Conference on Computer Vision and Pattern Recognition, pp. 1288–1297 (2019)
8. Guan, T., et al.: M3DeTR: multi-representation, multi-scale, mutual-relation 3d object detection with transformers. In: Proceedings of the IEEE Winter Conference on Applications of Computer Vision (2021)
9. He, L., et al.: End-to-end video object detection with spatial-temporal transformers. In: Proceedings of the 29th ACM International Conference on Multimedia, pp. 1507–1516 (2021)
10. Hu, Y., et al.: Afdetv2: rethinking the necessity of the second stage for object detection from point clouds. In: Proceedings of the AAAI Conference on Artificial Intelligence (2021)
11. Huang, R., et al.: An LSTM approach to temporal 3d object detection in LiDAR point clouds. In: Vedaldi, A., Bischof, H., Brox, T., Frahm, J.-M. (eds.) ECCV 2020. LNCS, vol. 12363, pp. 266–282. Springer, Cham (2020). https://doi.org/10.1007/978-3-030-58523-5_16
12. Jaderberg, M., et al.: Spatial transformer networks. In: Advances in Neural Information Processing Systems., vol. 28 (2015)
13. Kang, K., et al.: Object detection in videos with tubelet proposal networks. In: Proceedings of the IEEE Conference on Computer Vision and Pattern Recognition, pp. 727–735 (2017)
14. Ku, J., Pon, A.D., Waslander, S.L.: Monocular 3d object detection leveraging accurate proposals and shape reconstruction. In: Proceedings of the IEEE Conference on Computer Vision and Pattern Recognition, pp. 11867–11876 (2019)
15. Lang, A.H., Vora, S., Caesar, H., Zhou, L., Beijbom, O.: PointPillars: fast encoders for object detection from point clouds. In: Proceedings of the IEEE Conference on Computer Vision and Pattern Recognition (2019)
16. Li, B., Zhang, T., Xia, T.: Vehicle detection from 3d lidar using fully convolutional network. arXiv preprint arXiv:1608.07916 (2016)
17. Li, B., Ouyang, W., Sheng, L., Zeng, X., Wang, X.: Gs3d: an efficient 3d object detection framework for autonomous driving. In: Proceedings of the IEEE Conference on Computer Vision and Pattern Recognition, pp. 1019–1028 (2019)

18. Liang, M., Yang, B., Chen, Y., Hu, R., Urtasun, R.: Multi-task multi-sensor fusion for 3d object detection. In: Proceedings of the IEEE Conference on Computer Vision and Pattern Recognition, pp. 7345–7353 (2019)
19. Meyer, G.P., Laddha, A., Kee, E., Vallespi-Gonzalez, C., Wellington, C.K.: Laser-Net: an efficient probabilistic 3d object detector for autonomous driving. In: Proceedings of the IEEE Conference on Computer Vision and Pattern Recognition, pp. 12677–12686 (2019)
20. Miao, Z., et al.: PVGNet: a bottom-up one-stage 3d object detector with integrated multi-level features. In: Proceedings of the IEEE Conference on Computer Vision and Pattern Recognition, pp. 3279–3288 (2021)
21. Ngiam, J., Caine, B., Han, W., Yang, B., Vasudevan, V.: StarNet: targeted computation for object detection in point clouds. arXiv preprint arXiv:1908.11069 (2019)
22. Piergiovanni, A., Casser, V., Ryoo, M.S., Angelova, A.: 4d-net for learned multimodal alignment. In: Proceedings of the IEEE International Conference on Computer Vision (2021)
23. Qi, C.R., Litany, O., He, K., Guibas, L.J.: Deep Hough voting for 3d object detection in point clouds. In: Proceedings of the IEEE International Conference on Computer Vision (2019)
24. Qi, C.R., Liu, W., Wu, C., Su, H., Guibas, L.J.: Frustum pointNets for 3d object detection from RGB-D data. In: Proceedings of the IEEE Conference on Computer Vision and Pattern Recognition, pp. 918–927 (2018)
25. Qi, C.R., Yi, L., Su, H., Guibas, L.J.: Pointnet++: deep hierarchical feature learning on point sets in a metric space. In: Advances in Neural Information Processing Systems, vol. 30 (2017)
26. Shi, S., Guo, C., Jiang, L., Wang, Z., Li, H.: PV-RCNN: point-voxel feature set abstraction for 3d object detection. In: Proceedings of the IEEE Conference on Computer Vision and Pattern Recognition (2020)
27. Shi, S., Wang, X., Li, H.: PointRCNN: 3d object proposal generation and detection from point cloud. In: Proceedings of the IEEE Conference on Computer Vision and Pattern Recognition (2019)
28. Sun, P.,et al.: RSN: range sparse net for efficient, accurate lidar 3d object detection. In: Proceedings of the IEEE Conference on Computer Vision and Pattern Recognition (2021)
29. Sun, P., et al.: Scalability in perception for autonomous driving: Waymo open dataset. In: Proceedings of the IEEE Conference on Computer Vision and Pattern Recognition, pp. 2446–2454 (2020)
30. Vora, S., Lang, A.H., Helou, B., Beijbom, O.: Pointpainting: sequential fusion for 3d object detection. In: Proceedings of the IEEE Conference on Computer Vision and Pattern Recognition, pp. 4604–4612 (2020)
31. Wang, Y., Chao, W.L., Garg, D., Hariharan, B., Campbell, M., Weinberger, K.Q.: Pseudo-lidar from visual depth estimation: Bridging the gap in 3d object detection for autonomous driving. In: Proceedings of the IEEE Conference on Computer Vision and Pattern Recognition, pp. 8445–8453 (2019)
32. Wu, P., Chen, S., Metaxas, D.N.: MotionNet: joint perception and motion prediction for autonomous driving based on bird's eye view maps. In: Proceedings of the IEEE Conference on Computer Vision and Pattern Recognition, pp. 11385–11395 (2020)
33. Xiao, F., Lee, Y.J.: Video object detection with an aligned spatial-temporal memory. In: European Conference on Computer Vision, pp. 485–501 (2018)
34. Xu, J., Tang, X., Dou, J., Shu, X., Zhu, Y.: CenterAtt: Fast 2-stage center attention network. arXiv preprint arXiv:2106.10493 (2021)

35. Xu, J., Zhang, R., Dou, J., Zhu, Y., Sun, J., Pu, S.: RPVNet: a deep and efficient range-point-voxel fusion network for lidar point cloud segmentation. In: Proceedings of the IEEE International Conference on Computer Vision, pp. 16024–16033 (2021)
36. Yan, Y., Mao, Y., Li, B.: Second: sparsely embedded convolutional detection. Sensors **18**(10), 3337 (2018)
37. Yang, Z., Zhou, Y., Chen, Z., Ngiam, J.: 3d-man: 3d multi-frame attention network for object detection. In: Proceedings of the IEEE Conference on Computer Vision and Pattern Recognition, pp. 1863–1872 (2021)
38. Yin, J., Shen, J., Guan, C., Zhou, D., Yang, R.: Lidar-based online 3d video object detection with graph-based message passing and spatiotemporal transformer attention. In: Proceedings of the IEEE Conference on Computer Vision and Pattern Recognition (2020)
39. Yin, T., Zhou, X., Krahenbuhl, P.: Center-based 3d object detection and tracking. In: Proceedings of the IEEE Conference on Computer Vision and Pattern Recognition (2021)
40. Yoo, J.H., Kim, Y., Kim, J., Choi, J.W.: 3D-CVF: generating joint camera and LiDAR features using cross-view spatial feature fusion for 3d object detection. In: Vedaldi, A., Bischof, H., Brox, T., Frahm, J.-M. (eds.) ECCV 2020. LNCS, vol. 12372, pp. 720–736. Springer, Cham (2020). https://doi.org/10.1007/978-3-030-58583-9_43
41. Zeng, Y., et al.: Lift: Learning 4d lidar image fusion transformer for 3d object detection. In: Proceedings of the IEEE Conference on Computer Vision and Pattern Recognition, pp. 17172–17181 (2022)
42. Zhou, Y., Tuzel, O.: VoxelNet: end-to-end learning for point cloud based 3d object detection. In: Proceedings of the IEEE Conference on Computer Vision and Pattern Recognition (2018)
43. Zhou, Y., et al.: End-to-end multi-view fusion for 3d object detection in lidar point clouds. In: Conference on Robot Learning, pp. 923–932. PMLR (2020)

End-to-End Weakly Supervised Object Detection with Sparse Proposal Evolution

Mingxiang Liao[1], Fang Wan[1(✉)], Yuan Yao[1], Zhenjun Han[1], Jialing Zou[1],
Yuze Wang[2], Bailan Feng[2], Peng Yuan[2], and Qixiang Ye[1]

[1] University of Chinese Academy of Sciences, Beijing, China
{liaomingxiang20,yaoyuan17}@mails.ucas.ac.cn,
{wanfang,hanzhj,qxye}@ucas.ac.cn
[2] Huawei Noah's Ark Lab, Bei Jing, China
{wangyuze1,fengbailan,yuanpeng126}@huawei.com

Abstract. Conventional methods for weakly supervised object detection (WSOD) typically enumerate dense proposals and select the discriminative proposals as objects. However, these two-stage "enumerate-and-select" methods suffer object feature ambiguity brought by dense proposals and low detection efficiency caused by the proposal enumeration procedure. In this study, we propose a sparse proposal evolution (SPE) approach, which advances WSOD from the two-stage pipeline with dense proposals to an end-to-end framework with sparse proposals. SPE is built upon a visual transformer equipped with a seed proposal generation (SPG) branch and a sparse proposal refinement (SPR) branch. SPG generates high-quality seed proposals by taking advantage of the cascaded self-attention mechanism of the visual transformer, and SPR trains the detector to predict sparse proposals which are supervised by the seed proposals in a one-to-one matching fashion. SPG and SPR are iteratively performed so that seed proposals update to accurate supervision signals and sparse proposals evolve to precise object regions. Experiments on VOC and COCO object detection datasets show that SPE outperforms the state-of-the-art end-to-end methods by 7.0% mAP and 8.1% AP50. It is an order of magnitude faster than the two-stage methods, setting the first solid baseline for end-to-end WSOD with sparse proposals. The code is available at https://github.com/MingXiangL/SPE.

Keywords: Weakly supervised object detection · Sparse proposals · Proposal evolution · End-to-end training

1 Introduction

Visual object detection has achieved unprecedented progress in the past decade. However, such progress heavily relies on the large amount of data annotations (*e.g.*, object bounding boxes) which require extensive human effort and time cost.

Supplementary Information The online version contains supplementary material available at https://doi.org/10.1007/978-3-031-20077-9_13.

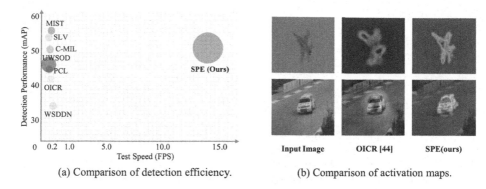

(a) Comparison of detection efficiency.

(b) Comparison of activation maps.

Fig. 1. Comparison of (a) detection efficiency and (b) activation maps between the conventional methods and the proposed SPE for weakly supervised object detection (WSOD) on VOC 2007. In (a), larger cycles denote higher proposal generation speeds. All speeds in (a) are evaluated on a NVIDIA RTX GPU.

Weakly supervised object detection (WSOD), which only requires image-level annotations indicating the presence or absence of a class of objects, significantly reduces the annotation cost [4, 14, 31–33, 52].

For the lack of instance-level annotation, WSOD methods require to localize the objects while estimate object detectors at the same time during training. To fulfill this purpose, the early WSDDN method [6] used an "enumerate-and-select" pipeline. It firstly enumerates dense proposals using empirical clues [27, 37] to ensure a high recall rate and then selects the most discriminative proposal as the pseudo object for detector training. Recent studies improved either the proposal enumeration [38, 41, 44] or the proposal selection module [19, 23, 43, 51].

However, this "enumerate-and-select" pipeline meets the performance upper bound for the following two problems: (1) The redundant and near-duplicate proposals aggregate the difficulty to localize objects and decrease the detection efficiency, Fig. 1(a). (2) During training, the labels of the dense proposals are assigned by a single pseudo object through a many-to-one matching strategy, *i.e.*, multiple proposals with large IoUs between the pseudo object are selected for detector training, which introduces ambiguity to feature representation, Fig. 1(b).

In this paper, we propose the sparse proposal evolution (SPE) approach, which advances WSOD from the enumerate-and-select pipeline with dense proposals (Fig. 2(a)) to an end-to-end framework with sparse proposals (Fig. 2(b)). SPE adopts a "seed-and-refine" approach, which first produces sparse seed proposals and then refines them to achieve accurate object localization.

SPE consists of a seed proposal generation (SPG) branch and a sparse proposal refinement (SPR) branch. During training, SPG leverages the visual transformer [46] to generate semantic-aware attention maps. By taking advantage of the cascaded self-attention mechanism born with the visual transformer, the semantic-aware attention map can extract long-range feature dependencies and activate full object extentFig. 1(b). With these semantic-aware attention

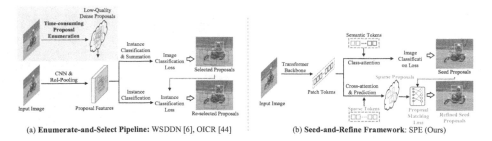

Fig. 2. Comparison of (a) the conventional "enumerate-and-select" pipeline with (b) our "seed-and-refine" framework for weakly supervised object detection.

maps, SPG can generate high-quality seed proposals. Using the seed proposals as pseudo supervisions, SPR trains a detector by introducing a set of sparse proposals that are learned to match with the seed proposals in a one-to-one matching fashion. During the proposal matching procedure, each seed proposal is augmented to multiple orientations, which provide the opportunity to refine object locations when the proposals and the detector evolve.

The contributions of this study include:

– We propose the sparse proposal evolution (SPE) approach, opening the promising direction for end-to-end WSOD with sparse proposals.
– We update many-to-one proposal selection to one-to-one proposal-proposal matching, making it possible to apply the "seed-and-refine" mechanism in the challenging WSOD problem.
– SPE significantly improves the efficiency and precision of the end-to-end WSOD methods, demonstrating the potential to be a new baseline framework.

2 Related Work

2.1 Weakly Supervised Object Detection

Enumerate-and-Select Method (Two-stage). This line of methods enumerates object locations using a stand-alone region proposal algorithm. A multiple instance learning (MIL) procedure iteratively performs proposal selection and detector estimation. Nevertheless, as the object proposals are dense and redundant, MIL is often puzzled by the partial activation problem [5,13,32,48]. WSDDN [6] built the first deep MIL network by integrating an MIL loss into a deep network. Online instance classifier refinement (OICR) [15,18,26,43,48,53] was proposed to select high-quality instances as pseudo objects to refine the instance classifier. Proposal cluster learning (PCL) [24,42] further alleviated networks from concentrating on object parts by proposal clustering [42].

In the two-stage framework, object pixel gradient [39], segmentation collaboration [15,21,28,40], dissimilarity coefficient [3], attention and self-distillation [23] and extra annotations from other domains [7,17] were introduced to optimize proposal selection. Context information [25,50] was also explored to identify the instances from surrounding regions. In [48,49], a min-entropy model was proposed to alleviate localization randomness. In [26], object-aware instance labeling was explored for accurate object localization by considering the instance completeness. In [19,51], continuation MIL was proposed to alleviate the non-convexity of the WSOD loss function.

Despite the substantial progress, most WSOD methods used a stand-alone proposal generation module, which decreases not only the overall detection efficiency but also the performance upper bound.

Enumerate-and-Select Method (End-to-End). Recent methods [38,44] attempted to break the two-stage WSOD routine. WeakRPN [44] utilized object contours in convolutional feature maps to generate proposals to train a region proposal network (RPN). However, it remains relying on proposal enumeration during the training stage. In [38], an RPN [34] was trained using the pseudo objects predicted by the weakly supervised detector in a self-training fashion. Nevertheless, it requires generating dense object proposals by sliding windows. Both methods suffer from selecting inaccurate candidates from dense proposals.

2.2 Object Proposal Generation

Empirical Enumeration Method. This line of methods enumerates dense proposals based on simple features and classifiers [2,9,37]. Constrained Parametric MinCuts (CPMC) [9] produced up to 10,000 regions based on figure-ground segments and trained a regressor to select high-scored proposals. Selective Search [37] and MCG [2] adopted hierarchical segmentation and region merging on the color and contour features for proposal generation. BING [12] generated redundant proposals with sliding windows and filtered them with a classifier. EdgeBoxes [27] estimated objectness by detecting complete contours in dense bounding proposals.

Learning-Based Method. Recent methods had tried to learn an RPN under weak supervision. In [44], an EdgeBoxes-like algorithm is embedded into DNNs. In [41], extra video datasets were used to learn an RPN [34]. In [38], the RPN was trained using the pseudo objects selected by the weakly supervised detector in a self-supervised fashion.

However, these methods required generating very dense object proposals. The problem of achieving a high recall rate using sparse (hundreds or tens of) proposals without precise supervision still remains.

3 Methodology

In this section, we first give an overview of the proposed sparse proposal evolution (SPE) approach. We then introduce the seed proposal generation (SPG) and sparse proposal refinement (SPR) modules. Finally, we describe the end-to-end training procedure based on iterative optimization of SPG and SPR.

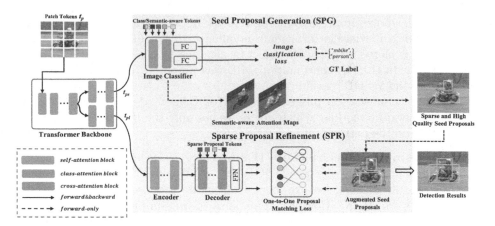

Fig. 3. Flowchart of the proposed sparse proposal evolution (SPE) approach. The diagram consists of a transformer backbone, a seed proposal generation (SPG) branch and a sparse proposal refinement (SPR) branch. During the training phase, SPG and SPR are jointly performed under a "seed-and-refine" mechanism for end-to-end WSOD with sparse object proposals.

3.1 Overview

Figure 3 presents the flowchart of SPE, which consists of a backbone network, an SPG branch, and an SPR branch. The backbone network, which is built upon CaiT [46], contains two sub-branches with l shared transformer blocks (each block has a self-attention layer and a multi-layer perception layer). The SPG branch consists of two modules, one for image classification and the other for seed proposal generation. The initial supervisions come from the image classification loss (in the SPG branch), which drive to learn the image classifiers for semantic-aware attention maps and seed proposal generation through a thresholding algorithm [54]. The SPR branch is an encoder-decoder structure [30], which is trained by the one-to-one matching loss between seed proposals and sparse proposals. During training, an input image is first divided into $w \times h$ patches to construct $N = w \times h$ patch tokens t_p. These patch tokens are fed to the transformer to extract semantic-sensitive patch embeddings t_{ps} and location-sensitive patch embeddings t_{pl}, which are respectively fed to the SPG branch and SPR branch.

3.2 Seed Proposal Generation

The core of SPE is generating sparse yet high-quality seed proposals. Visual transformer was observed to be able to extract long-range feature dependencies by taking advantage of the cascaded self-attention mechanism, which facilitated activating and localizing full object extent [20]. This inspires us to introduce it to WSOD to produce high-quality seed proposals for object localization.

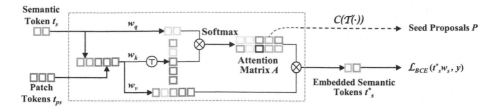

Fig. 4. Flowchart of the class-attention layer in the proposed SPG branch.

Semantic-Aware Attention Maps. As shown in Fig. 3, the SPG branch contains an image classification module and a seed proposal generation module. The image classification module contains two class-attention blocks and a fully connected (FC) layer, following CaiT [46]. Each class-attention block consists of a class-attention layer and an MLP layer with a shortcut connection. A class token $t_c \in \mathbb{R}^{1 \times D}$ is fed to the first class-attention block, where the class-attention $\text{CA}(\cdot)$ is performed on t_c and t_{ps} as

$$\begin{aligned}
t_c^* &= \text{CA}(t_c, t_{ps}, w_q, w_k, w_v) \\
&= \text{Softmax}\left((t_c w_q)([t_c, t_{ps}]w_k)^\top / \sqrt{D} \right)([t_c, t_{ps}]w_v) \\
&= A([t_c, t_{ps}]w_v),
\end{aligned} \tag{1}$$

where w_q, w_k, w_v denote weights in the class-attention layer, Fig. 4. $[t_c, t_{ps}]$ denotes concatenating t_c and t_{ps} along the first dimension. $A \in \mathbb{R}^{1 \times (N+1)}$ is the attention vector of class token t_c. In the multi-head attention layer where J heads are considered, D in Eq. 1 is updated as D_0, where $D_0 = D/J$. A is then updated as the average of attention vectors weighted by their standard deviation of the J heads. t_c^* is then projected by the MLP layer in the first class-attention layer and then further fed to the second class-attention block to calculate the final embeddings $t_c^* \in \mathbb{R}^{1 \times D}$ for image classification. The FC layer parameterized by $w_c \in \mathbb{R}^{D \times C}$ projects the class token t_c^* to a classification score.

Considering that the class token t_c is class-agnostic and cannot produce attention maps for each semantic category, we further add C semantic-aware tokens $t_s \in \mathbb{R}^{C \times D}$. C denotes the number of classes. By feeding both t_c and t_s to the class-attention blocks and applying class-attention defined in Eq. 1, we obtain the final token embeddings t_c^* and t_s^*. The attention vector A is updated to the attention matrix $\mathbf{A} \in \mathbb{R}^{(C+1) \times (C+N+1)}$. An extra FC layer parameterized with $w_s \in \mathbb{R}^{D \times 1}$ is added to classify the semantic tokens t_s^*. Given the image label $y = [y_1, y_2, ..., y_C]^T \in \mathbb{R}^{C \times 1}$, where $y_c = 1$ or 0 indicates the presence or absence of the c-th object category in the image, the loss function for SPG is defined as

$$\mathcal{L}_{spg}(t_c^*, t_s^*) = \mathcal{L}_{BCE}(t_c^* w_c, y) + \mathcal{L}_{BCE}(t_s^* w_s, y), \tag{2}$$

where $\mathcal{L}_{BCE}(\cdot)$ denotes the binary cross-entropy loss [6].

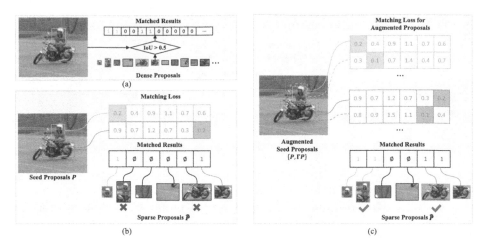

Fig. 5. Comparison of matching strategies. (a) Many-to-one matching of previous WSOD methods. (b) One-to-one matching strategy [8] applied to WSOD. (c) One-to-one matching with proposal augmentation (ours).

Seed Proposals. By optimizing Eq. 2 and executing Eq. 1 in the second class-attention block, we obtain the attention matrix $\mathbf{A} \in \mathbb{R}^{(C+1)\times(C+N+1)}$. The semantic-aware attention matrix $\mathbf{A}^* \in \mathbb{R}^{C \times N}$ is produced by indexing the first C rows and the middle N columns from $\mathbf{A}$. Attention map A_c of the c-th class is then obtained by reshaping the c-th row in $\mathbf{A}^*$ to $w \times h$ and then resized to the same resolution as the original image.

A thresholding function $\mathcal{T}(A_c, \delta_{seed})$ with a fixed threshold δ_{seed} [54] is used to binarize each semantic-aware attention map to foreground or background pixels. Based on $\mathcal{T}(A_c, \delta_{seed})$, the seed proposals are generated as

$$P = \{\mathcal{C}(\mathcal{T}(A_c, \delta_{seed}), \delta_{multi}), ...\}_{c=1}^{C} = \{B, O\} = \{(b_1, o_1), (b_2, o_2), ...\}, \quad (3)$$

where function $\mathcal{C}(\cdot)$ outputs a set of tight bounding boxes to enclose the connected regions in the binary map $\mathcal{T}(A_c, \delta_{seed})$, under the constraint that the area of each connected region is larger than δ_{multi} of the largest connected region. Consequently, we obtain a set of bounding boxes $B = [b_1, b_2, ..., b_M] \in \mathbb{R}^{M \times 4}$ for foreground categories in the image, where each category produces at least one seed proposal. The one-hot class labels for these bounding boxes are denoted as $O = [o_1, o_2, ..., o_M]^T \in \mathbb{R}^{M \times C}$.

3.3 Sparse Proposal Refinement

Although SPG can perform object localization using seed proposals, the performance is far from satisfactory due to the lack of instance-level supervision. We further propose sparse proposal refinement (SPR), with the aim of learning object detector while refining seed proposals.

Sparse Proposals. As shown in Fig. 3, the SPR branch follows recently proposed fully-supervised transformer detectors (DETR [8] and Conditional DETR [30]), which leverage a transformer encoder, a transformer decoder, and a feedforward network (FFN) to predict the object categories and locations. The location-sensitive patch embedding t_{pl} from the transformer backbone is first encoded by the transformer encoder to t_{pl}^*. In the transformer decoder, a fixed set of sparse proposal tokens $t_p \in \mathbb{R}^{K \times D}$ are defined to make conditional cross-attention [30] with the encoded location-aware embedding t_{pl}^*.

The decoded t_p^* is then fed to the FFN to predict K sparse proposals, as

$$\widehat{P} = \text{FFN}(t_p^*, w_{FFN}) = \{\widehat{B}, \widehat{O}\} = \{(\hat{b}_1, \hat{o}_1), (\hat{b}_2, \hat{o}_2), ..., (\hat{b}_K, \hat{o}_K)\}, \tag{4}$$

where w_{FFN} and K respectively denote the parameters of the FFN and the number of proposal tokens.

One-to-One Proposal Matching. Using the seed proposals defined by Eq. 3 as pseudo objects, an optimal bipartite match between seed and sparse proposals is applied. The optimal bipartite match [8] is formulated as $\widehat{\mathfrak{S}} = [\hat{\sigma}_1, \hat{\sigma}_2, ..., \hat{\sigma}_K]$, where $\hat{\sigma}_i \in \{\varnothing, 1, 2, ..., m, ..., M\}$. $\hat{\sigma}_i = m$ denotes the i-th sparse proposal is matched with the m-th seed proposal. $\hat{\sigma}_i = \varnothing$ means that the i-th sparse proposal has no matched object and is categorized to "background". The loss function of the SPR branch is defined as

$$\mathcal{L}_{spr}(P, \widehat{P}) = \sum_{i=1}^{K} \left[\lambda_{FL}\mathcal{L}_{FL}(o_i, \hat{o}_{\hat{\sigma}_i}) + \mathbb{1}_{\{\hat{\sigma}_i \neq \varnothing\}} \lambda_{L_1}\mathcal{L}_{L_1}(b_i, \hat{b}_{\hat{\sigma}_i}) \right.$$
$$\left. + \mathbb{1}_{\{\hat{\sigma}_i \neq \varnothing\}} \lambda_{GIoU}\mathcal{L}_{GIoU}(b_i, \hat{b}_{\hat{\sigma}_i}) \right], \tag{5}$$

where $\mathcal{L}_{FL}$, $\mathcal{L}_{L_1}$ and $\mathcal{L}_{GIoU}$ are Focal loss [47], L1 loss and generalized IoU loss [36], respectively. λ_{FL}, λ_{L_1} and λ_{GIoU} are regularization factors.

Seed Proposal Augmentation. The above-defined one-to-one matching breaks many-to-one label assignment, Fig. 5(a). However, the supervision signals (seed proposals) generated by attention maps contain localization noises that cannot be corrected by the one-to-one matching mechanism, Fig. 5(b). To alleviate this problem, we augment the seed proposals through a *"box jittering"* strategy, which produces randomly jittered bounding boxes on four orientations. The *box jittering* process of a bounding box $b_i = (t_x, t_y, t_w, t_h)$ is defined as

$$\Gamma b_i = (t_x, t_y, t_w, t_h) \pm (\varepsilon_x t_x, \varepsilon_y t_y, \varepsilon_w t_w, \varepsilon_h t_h), \tag{6}$$

where the coefficients $(\varepsilon_x, \varepsilon_y, \varepsilon_w, \varepsilon_h)$ are randomly sampled from a uniform distribution $U(-\delta_{aug}, +\delta_{aug})$. δ_{aug} is a small value to ensure Γb_i is around b_i.

By applying *"box jittering"* upon the boxes B, we extend the seed proposals $P = \{O, B\}$ to augmented seed proposals $\{P, \Gamma P\} = \{[O, \Gamma O], [B, \Gamma B]\}$, where the class label Γo_i is the same as o_i. With seed proposal augmentation, sparse proposals can correct noise in seed proposals, Fig. 5(c), which facilities seed proposal refinement and detection performance improvement.

Table 1. Performance with respect to δ_{seed} and δ_{multi} on VOC 2007 *test* set.

Modules	δ_{seed}	δ_{multi}	mAP	CorLoc
SPG	0.1	1	23.0	48.2
	0.2	1	**29.7**	**57.8**
	0.3	1	18.2	43.6
	0.4	1	8.9	25.9
SPE	0.2	1	37.8	56.9
	0.2	0.75	41.0	61.0
	0.2	0.5	**42.6**	61.3
	0.2	0.25	42.4	**61.5**

Table 2. Performance of SPE under SPR branch numbers on VOC 2007 *test* set.

#SPR branches	δ_{aug}	mAP	CorLoc
0 (SPG)	0	29.7	57.8
1	0	42.6	61.3
2	0	**42.9**	**61.5**
3	0	42.7	61.3
1	0.05	42.7	61.3
1	0.1	**45.6**	**64.0**
1	0.15	45.1	64.0
1	0.2	43.4	61.6

3.4 End-to-End Training

As the proposal generation and proposal refinement branches are unified upon the transformer backbone, we are able to train the seed proposal generator, the object detector, and the backbone network in an end-to-end fashion. As shown in Fig. 3, the SPG branch and the SPR branch share the transformer backbone [46]. Considering that the optimization objectives of the two network branches are not exactly the same, we separate the backbone transformer from the $(l + 1)$-th block so that they share only part of the backbone network. The two network branches are jointly optimized by the total loss defined as

$$\mathcal{L}_{spe} = \mathcal{L}_{spg} + \mathbb{1}_{\{e \geq \tau\}}\mathcal{L}_{spr}, \tag{7}$$

where e denotes the training epoch and τ is a threshold number of epochs. During end-to-end training, the SPG branch is first optimized for τ epochs as a "warm-up" step, which guarantees that the seed proposals are semantic-aware and can coarsely cover object extent. Subsequently, the transformer backbone, the SPG, and SPR branches are jointly trained under the supervision of the image classification loss and the proposal matching loss.

4 Experiment

In this section, we first introduce the experimental settings. We then conduct ablation study and quantitative and qualitative model analysis. We finally compare the proposed SPE approach with the state-of-the-art (SOTA) methods.

4.1 Experimental Setting

SPE is implemented based on the CaiT-XXS36 model [46] pre-trained on the ILSVRC 2012 dataset [1]. We evaluate SPE on the PASCAL VOC 2007, 2012 and MS COCO 2014, 2017 datasets. On VOC, we use mAP [29] and correct localization (CorLoc) [45] as the evaluation metric. The model is trained on the union set of VOC 2007 *trainval* and VOC 2012 *trainval* ("0712", containing 16551 images of 20 object classes), and evaluated on *test* set of VOC 2007 (containing 4952 images). On MS COCO datasets, we use average precision (AP) as the evaluation metric. The COCO datasets contain 80 object categories and have more challenging aspects including multi-objects and complex backgrounds. On COCO 2014 and 2017, we respectively use the 83k and 118k *train* sets for training, the 40k and 5k *val* sets for testing. Each input image is re-scaled to the fixed size and randomly horizontally flipped.

During training, we employ the AdamW gradient descent algorithm with weight decay 5e-2, and a batch size of 8 in 8 GPUs. The model respectively iterates 50 and 15 epochs on VOC and COCO datasets. During training, the learning rate for the backbone is fixed to be 1e-5. The learning rate for the rest branches is initialized to 1e-4 and drops to 1e-5 after 40 and 11 epochs on VOC and COCO datasets, respectively. The number K of proposal tokens is set to 300 following [8]. The "warm-up" time τ in Eq. 7 is empirically set to 7.

4.2   Ablation Study

We analyze SPE's hyper-parameters δ_{seed} and δ_{multi}, times of proposal refinement, matching manners, and the detection efficiency. We also study the effect of the shared backbone block numbers, the detector and backbone network. All the ablation experiments are conducted on PASCAL VOC.

SPG. Table 1 includes the detection and localization performance of SPG under different δ_{seed} and δ_{multi}. It can be seen that δ_{seed} has the key influence from the generation of seed proposals. When $\delta_{seed} = 0.2$, SPG achieves 29.7% mAP and 57.8% CorLoc. When δ_{multi} decreases, the performance first increases and then decreases. This implies that as δ_{multi} decreases SPG discovers more and more objects, which enriches the supervision signals and improves the detection performance. On the other hand, with the increase of δ_{multi}, SPG produces more noise proposals, which degenerate the detection performance.

SPR. Table 2 shows the effect of proposal refinement times by adding extra SPR branches and introducing seed proposal augmentation. When adding one SPR branch, the detection performance is significantly improved by 12.9%(29.7% vs 42.6%) and the localization performance is improved by 3.5%(57.8% vs 61.3%), which clearly demonstrates SPR's effectiveness for refining the seed proposals. When more SPR branches are added, marginal performance improvements are achieved. By introducing seed proposal augmentation, the performance is further significantly improved by 3.0%(42.6 vs 45.6%) and 2.7%(61.3 vs 64.0%) with $\delta_{aug} = 0.1$, demonstrating that the proposal augmentation mechanism can suppress the noise of seed proposals and achieve more accurate localization.

Detection Efficiency. In Table 3, we compare the proposed SPE with "enumerate-and-select" methods, including the two-stage OICR method [43] and the STOA end-to-end method UWSOD [38]. The compared terms include the number of parameters (#Params), MACs, time of proposal generation (τ) and inference speed. The experiments are carried out under image scale 512^2 on the

220   M. Liao et al.

Table 3. Comparison of parameters, MACs, time to generate proposals and inference speed on the VOC *test* set. SPE is implemented based on CaiT-XXS36. Test speeds ("speed") are evaluated on a single NVIDIA RTX GPU.

Methods	#Params (M)	MACs (G)	τ (s/img)	Speed(fps)	mAP
OICR(VGG16) [43]	120.9	304.26	3.79	0.26	44.1
UWSOD(VGG16) [38]	138.5	923.31	0.002	4.2	45.7
UWSOD(WSR18) [38]	135.0	237.97	0.002	4.3	46.9
SPE(Ours)	33.9	51.25	0	14.3	51.0

Table 4. Performance of SPE with l shared blocks on VOC 2007 *test* set.

l shared blocks	mAP	CorLoc
36	32.8	50.0
24	**45.6**	**64.0**
12	43.1	60.1

Table 5. Performance of different detectors on VOC 2007 *test* set.

Detector	Backbone	mAP
Faster RCNN	VGG16	78.3
Faster RCNN	ResNet50	80.9
Faster RCNN	CaiT-XXS36	81.4
Conditional DETR	CaiT-XXS36	77.5

PASCAL VOC dataset (0712 *trainval* for training and 07 *test* set for testing). SPE has much fewer parameters than OICR and UWSOD (only ∼1/4 of OICR and UWSOD), and uses much fewer MACs than OICR and UWSOD (only 1/20∼1/4 of OICR and UWSOD). These results show that SPE, which discards dense proposals by learning sparse proposals, is efficient for object detection. For testing, SPE directly uses the backbone and the SPR branch for object detection and does not need computational costs for proposal generation. With such high detection efficiency, SPE achieves 51.0% mAP, which respectively outperforms OICR and UWSOD by 9.8% and 7.0%.

Number of Shared Backbone Blocks. We analyze the effect of backbone blocks shared by SPG and SPR (denoted by l), Table 4. When $l = 36$, i.e., the two branches share all backbone blocks of CaiT-XXS36, the detection and localization performance are 32.8% and 50.0%, respectively. This is because the learning of regression task will interfere the attention map in SPG, and thus degenerates the quality of generated seed proposals. When $l = 24$, the above problem is largely alleviated, and the detection and localization performances respectively increase to 45.6% and 64.0%. When sharing fewer layers, the performances slightly decrease due to the increase of inductive bias.

Backbone and Detector. In Table 5, we compare Faster RCNN w/ VGG16, Faster RCNN w/ ResNet50, Faster RCNN w/ CaiT-XXS36, and Conditional DETR w/ CaiT-XXS36 on VOC 0712 under fully supervised settings. The mAP of Conditional DETR w/ CaiT-XXS36 is 77.5%, which is lower than that of Faster-RCNN w/ VGG16 (78.3%). It shows the detector is not the key factor of performance gain. The mAP of Faster R-CNN w/ CaiT-XXS36 is 81.4%, which is 3.1% higher than w/ VGG16 and 0.5% higher than w/ ResNet50. We also conducted experiments of MIST [35] w/ CaiT-XXS36, but achieved much worse results than MIST [35] w/ VGG16. Although CaiT-XXS36 is better in fully supervised detection task, it is not superior than VGG16 for traditional WSOD methods.

4.3   Visualization Analysis

Qualitative Analysis. Figure 7 shows the evolution of seed proposals and matched proposals and their corresponding attention maps (heatmaps) generated by SPG and SPR. At early training epochs, SPG activates most of the objects and can produce seed proposals for object location initialization. However, these proposals still suffer from background activation or partial activation. After matching with the sparse proposals, seed proposals are refined to more accurate object locations, which demonstrates the effectiveness of the SPR module with the proposal augmentation strategy. As training goes on, the seed proposals are gradually refined by and matched with the sparse proposals, and finally evolve to full object extent.

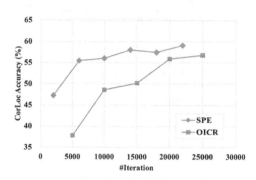

Fig. 6. Comparison of CorLoc accuracy of SPE and OICR [43] during training.

Figure 8 visualizes the seed proposals and matched sparse proposals and the corresponding attention map. With the long-range feature dependencies of

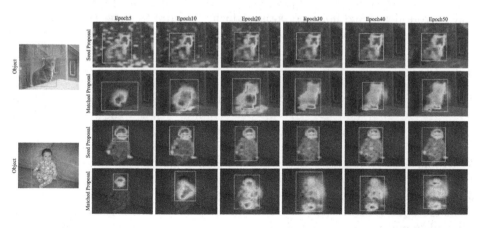

Fig. 7. Evolution of seed proposals and matched sparse proposals (yellow bounding boxes) during training. Heatmaps in the "seed proposal" column show the semantic-aware attention maps, while heatmaps in "matched proposal" column show the cross-attention maps of the matched sparse proposals. (Color figure online)

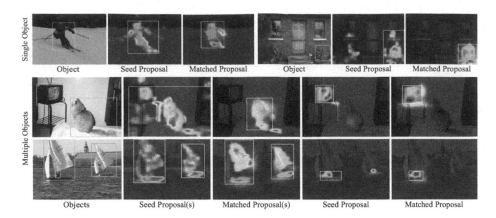

Fig. 8. Visualization of seed proposals and matched sparse proposals (yellow boxes). Heatmaps in "seed proposal" column show the semantic-aware attention maps for object classes. Heatmaps in the "matched proposal" column show the cross-attention maps of the matched sparse proposals. (Color figure online)

transformer, the semantic-aware attention maps in SPG can activate full object extent. Based on these attention maps, SPG can generate sparse yet high-quality seed proposals. By introducing SPR, the matched proposal can promote seed proposals and achieves preciser object localization. These results validate the effectiveness of the proposed SPG and SPR branches of SPE, where the seed proposals and sparse proposals evolve towards true object locations.

Quantitative Analysis. Figure 6 shows the CorLoc accuracy of SPE and OICR [43] during training iterations. By introducing transformer block, SPE can generate much preciser proposals at very early iterations. In contrast, OICR suffers from dense and noise proposals, which struggles to select the object proposals so that the localization performance deteriorates in early iterations.

4.4   Performance

PASCAL VOC. Table 6 shows the performance of SPE and the SOTA methods on VOC 2007 dataset. "07" in "Set" column denotes the *trainval* set of VOC 2007, "0712" denotes *trainval* set of VOC 2007 and 2012 datasets. "CaiT" denotes CaiT-XXS36. † refers to our implementation using the official code. With image scale 384, SPE achieves competitive 48.5% mAP and 66.4% CorLoc accuracy when training on 0712 *trainval* set. With image scale 512, SPE achieves 51.0% mAP and 70.4% CorLoc accuracy, which outperforms the two-stage methods WSDDN [6] and OICR [43] by 16.2% and 9.8%. Compared with the end-to-end methods using dense object proposals, the performance of SPE is very competitive. It also outperforms the SOTA UWSOD by 7.0% mAP.

MS COCO. In Table 7, we report the performance of SPE and the SOTA methods on the MS COCO 2014 and 2017 datasets. "14" and "17" in "Set"

Table 6. Detection Performance(%) on the PASCAL VOC 2007 *test* set.

Backbone	Set	Method	mAP	CorLoc
Enumerate-and-select methods (Two-Stage)				
VGG16	07	WSDDN [6]	34.8	53.5
	07	OICR [43]	41.2	60.6
	07	SLV [10]	53.5	**71.0**
	07	DC-WSOD [3]	52.9	70.9
	07	TS^{2}C [50]	44.3	61.0
	07	SDCN [28]	50.2	68.6
	07	C-MIL [19]	50.5	65.0
	07	PCL [42]	43.5	62.7
	07	MIST [35]	**54.9**	68.8
	0712	WSDDN† [6]	36.9	56.8
	0712	OICR† [43]	43.6	61.7
Enumerate-and-select methods (End-to-End)				
VGG16	07	OM+MIL [18]	23.4	41.2
	07	OPG [39]	28.8	43.5
	07	SPAM [22]	27.5	-
	07	UWSOD [38]	44.0	63.0
Seed-and-refine methods (End-to-end)				
CaiT	0712	SPE (ours)-384	48.5	66.4
	0712	SPE (ours)-512	**51.0**	**70.4**

Table 7. Detection Performance(%) on the MS COCO 2014 and 2017 set.

Backbone	Set	Method	AP	AP50	AP75
Enumerate-and-select methods (Two-stage)					
VGG16	14	WSDDN [6]	-	11.5	-
	14	WCCN [15]	-	12.3	-
	14	ODGA [16]	-	12.8	-
	14	PCL [42]	8.5	19.4	-
	14	WSOD^2 [53]	10.8	22.7	-
	14	C-MIDN [21]	9.6	21.4	-
	14	MIST [35]	**12.4**	**25.8**	**10.5**
	14	PG-PS [11]	-	20.7	-
Enumerate-and-select methods (End-to-end)					
VGG16	17	UWSOD [38]	2.5	9.3	1.1
WSR18	17	UWSOD [38]	3.1	10.1	1.4
Seed-and-refine methods (End-to-End)					
CaiT	14	SPE (ours)-384	5.7	15.2	3.4
	17	SPE (ours)-384	6.3	16.3	4.0
	17	SPE (ours)-512	**7.2**	**18.2**	**4.8**

column respectively denote training on MS COCO 2014 and 2017 datasets. On COCO 2014, SPE respectively achieves 5.7%, 15.2%, and 3.4% under metric AP, AP50 and AP75, which are comparable with the two-stage "enumerate-and-select" methods. On MS COCO 2017, SPE respectively achieves 6.3% AP, 16.3% AP50 and 4.0% AP75, outperforming the end-to-end UWSOD method [38] by 3.2%, 6.2% and 2.6%. When increasing the image scale to 512, the APs are further improved by 0.9%, 1.9%, and 0.8%, respectively.

5   Conclusion

We proposed the sparse proposal evolution (SPE) approach, and advanced WSOD methods with dense proposals to an end-to-end fashion with sparse proposals. SPE uses a "seed-and-refine" framework, which is efficient for both training and test. By taking advantage of the visual transformer, SPE generates sparse yet high-quality seed proposals. With the one-to-one proposal matching strategy, SPE iteratively improves seed proposals and object detectors in a self-evolution fashion. As the first end-to-end framework with sparse proposals, SPE demonstrates tremendous potential and provides a fresh insight to the challenging WSOD problem.

Acknowledgement. This work was supported by National Natural Science Foundation of China (NSFC) under Grant 62006216, 61836012, 62171431 and 62176260, the Strategic Priority Research Program of Chinese Academy of Sciences under Grant No. XDA27000000.

References

1. Alex, K., Ilya, S., Hinton, G.E.: Imagenet classification with deep convolutional neural networks. In: NeurIPS, pp. 1097–1115 (2012)
2. Arbeláez, P.A., Pont-Tuset, J., Barron, J.T., Marqués, F., Malik, J.: Multiscale combinatorial grouping. In: IEEE CVPR, pp. 328–335 (2014)
3. Arun, A., Jawahar, C.V., Kumar, M.P.: Dissimilarity coefficient based weakly supervised object detection. In: IEEE CVPR, pp. 9432–9441 (2019)
4. Bilen, H., Pedersoli, M., Tuytelaars, T.: Weakly supervised object detection with posterior regularization. In: BMVC, pp. 1997–2005 (2014)
5. Bilen, H., Pedersoli, M., Tuytelaars, T.: Weakly supervised object detection with convex clustering. In: IEEE CVPR, pp. 1081–1089 (2015)
6. Bilen, H., Vedaldi, A.: Weakly supervised deep detection networks. In: IEEE CVPR. pp. 2846–2854 (2016)
7. Cao, T., Du, L., Zhang, X., Chen, S., Zhang, Y., Wang, Y.: Cat: Weakly supervised object detection with category transfer (2021)
8. Carion, N., Massa, F., Synnaeve, G., Usunier, N., Kirillov, A., Zagoruyko, S.: End-to-end object detection with transformers. In: Vedaldi, A., Bischof, H., Brox, T., Frahm, J.-M. (eds.) ECCV 2020. LNCS, vol. 12346, pp. 213–229. Springer, Cham (2020). https://doi.org/10.1007/978-3-030-58452-8_13
9. Carreira, J., Sminchisescu, C.: CPMC: automatic object segmentation using constrained parametric min-cuts. IEEE TPAMI **34**(7), 1312–1328 (2012)
10. Carreira, J., Sminchisescu, C.: CPMC: automatic object segmentation using constrained parametric min-cuts. IEEE TPAMI **34**(7), 1312–1328 (2012)
11. Cheng, G., Yang, J., Gao, D., Guo, L., Han, J.: High-quality proposals for weakly supervised object detection. IEEE TIP **29**, 5794–5804 (2020)
12. Cheng, M., Zhang, Z., Lin, W., Torr, P.H.S.: BING: binarized normed gradients for objectness estimation at 300fps. In: IEEE CVPR, pp. 3286–3293 (2014)
13. Chong, W., Kaiqi, H., Weiqiang, R., Junge, Z., Steve, M.: Large-scale weakly supervised object localization via latent category learning. IEEE TIP **24**(4), 1371–1385 (2015)
14. Wang, C., Ren, W., Huang, K., Tan, T.: Weakly supervised object localization with latent category learning. In: Fleet, D., Pajdla, T., Schiele, B., Tuytelaars, T. (eds.) ECCV 2014. LNCS, vol. 8694, pp. 431–445. Springer, Cham (2014). https://doi.org/10.1007/978-3-319-10599-4_28
15. Diba, A., Sharma, V., Pazandeh, A., Pirsiavash, H., Van Gool, L.: Weakly supervised cascaded convolutional networks. In: IEEE CVPR, pp. 5131–5139 (2017)
16. Diba, A., Sharma, V., Stiefelhagen, R., Van Gool, L.: Object discovery by generative adversarial & ranking networks. arXiv preprint arXiv:1711.08174 (2017)
17. Dong, B., Huang, Z., Guo, Y., Wang, Q., Niu, Z., Zuo, W.: Boosting weakly supervised object detection via learning bounding box adjusters. In: IEEE ICCV (2021)
18. Dong, L., Bin, H.J., Yali, L., Shengjin, W., Hsuan, Y.M.: Weakly supervised object localization with progressive domain adaptation. In: IEEE CVPR, pp. 3512–3520 (2016)

19. Fang, W., Chang, L., Wei, K., Xiangyang, J., Jianbin, J., Qixiang, Y.: CMIL: continuation multiple instance learning for weakly supervised object detection. In: IEEE CVPR (2019)

20. Gao, W., et al.: TS-CAM: token semantic coupled attention map for weakly supervised object localization. CoRR abs/2103.14862 (2021)

21. Gao, Y., et al.: C-MIDN: coupled multiple instance detection network with segmentation guidance for weakly supervised object detection. In: IEEE ICCV (2019)

22. Gudi, A., van Rosmalen, N., Loog, M., van Gemert, J.C.: Object-extent pooling for weakly supervised single-shot localization. In: BMVC (2017)

23. Huang, Z., Zou, Y., Kumar, B.V.K.V., Huang, D.: Comprehensive attention self-distillation for weakly-supervised object detection. In: NeurIPS (2020)

24. Kantorov, V., et al.: Deep self-taught learning for weakly supervised object localization. In: IEEE CVPR, pp. 4294–4302 (2017)

25. ContextLocNet: context-aware deep network models for weakly supervised localization. In: Leibe, B., Matas, J., Sebe, N., Welling, M. (eds.) ECCV 2016. LNCS, vol. 9909, pp. 350–365. Springer, Cham (2016). https://doi.org/10.1007/978-3-319-46454-1_22

26. Kosugi, S., Yamasaki, T., Aizawa, K.: Object-aware instance labeling for weakly supervised object detection. In: IEEE ICCV (2019)

27. Zitnick, C.L., Dollár, P.: Edge boxes: locating object proposals from edges. In: Fleet, D., Pajdla, T., Schiele, B., Tuytelaars, T. (eds.) ECCV 2014. LNCS, vol. 8693, pp. 391–405. Springer, Cham (2014). https://doi.org/10.1007/978-3-319-10602-1_26

28. Li, X., Kan, M., Shan, S., Chen, X.: Weakly supervised object detection with segmentation collaboration. In: IEEE ICCV (2019)

29. Mark, E., Luc, V.G., KI, W.C., John, W., Andrew, Z.: The pascal visual object classes (VOC) challenge. IJCV. **88**(2), 303–338 (2010)

30. Meng, D., et al.: Conditional DETR for fast training convergence. In: IEEE ICCV, pp. 3651–3660, October 2021

31. Oh, S.H., Jae, L.Y., Stefanie, J., Trevor, D.: Weakly supervised discovery of visual pattern configurations. In: NeurIPS, pp. 1637–1645 (2014)

32. Oh, S.H., Ross, G., Stefanie, J., Julien, M., Zaid, H., Trevor, D.: On learning to localize objects with minimal supervision. In: ICML, pp. 1611–1619 (2014)

33. Parthipan, S., Tao, X.: Weakly supervised object detector learning with model drift detection. In: IEEE ICCV, pp. 343–350 (2011)

34. Ren, S., He, K., Girshick, R., Sun, J.: Faster R-CNN: towards real-time object detection with region proposal networks. In: NeurIPS, pp. 91–99 (2015)

35. Ren, Z., et al.: Instance-aware, context-focused, and memory-efficient weakly supervised object detection. In: IEEE CVPR, pp. 10595–10604 (2020)

36. Rezatofighi, H., Tsoi, N., Gwak, J., Sadeghian, A., Reid, I., Savarese, S.: Generalized intersection over union: a metric and a loss for bounding box regression. In: IEEE CVPR, June 2019

37. RR, U.J., de Sande Koen EA, V., Theo, G., WM, S.A.: Selective search for object recognition. IJCV. **104**(2), 154–171 (2013)

38. Shen, Y., Ji, R., Chen, Z., Wu, Y., Huang, F.: UWSOD: toward fully-supervised-level capacity weakly supervised object detection. In: NeurIPS (2020)

39. Shen, Y., Ji, R., Wang, C., Li, X., Li, X.: Weakly supervised object detection via object-specific pixel gradient. IEEE TNNLS **29**(12), 5960–5970 (2018)

40. Shen, Y., Ji, R., Wang, Y., Wu, Y., Cao, L.: Cyclic guidance for weakly supervised joint detection and segmentation. In: IEEE CVPR, pp. 697–707 (2019)

41. Singh, K.K., Lee, Y.J.: You reap what you sow: using videos to generate high precision object proposals for weakly-supervised object detection. In: IEEE CVPR, pp. 9414–9422 (2019)
42. Tang, P., et al.: PCL: proposal cluster learning for weakly supervised object detection. IEEE TPAMI **42**(1), 176–191 (2020)
43. Tang, P., Wang, X., Bai, X., Liu, W.: Multiple instance detection network with online instance classifier refinement. In: IEEE CVPR, pp. 3059–3067 (2017)
44. Tang, P., et al.: Weakly supervised region proposal network and object detection. In: Ferrari, V., Hebert, M., Sminchisescu, C., Weiss, Y. (eds.) ECCV 2018. LNCS, vol. 11215, pp. 370–386. Springer, Cham (2018). https://doi.org/10.1007/978-3-030-01252-6_22
45. Thomas, D., Bogdan, A., Vittorio, F.: Weakly supervised localization and learning with generic knowledge. IJCV **100**(3), 275–293 (2012)
46. Touvron, H., Cord, M., Sablayrolles, A., Synnaeve, G., Jégou, H.: Going deeper with image transformers. arXiv preprint arXiv:2103.17239 (2021)
47. Tsung-Yi, L., Priya, G., Ross, G., Kaiming, H., Dollár, P.: Focal loss for dense object detection. In: IEEE ICCV (2017)
48. Wan, F., Wei, P., Jiao, J., Han, Z., Ye, Q.: Min-entropy latent model for weakly supervised object detection. In: IEEE CVPR, pp. 1297–1306 (2018)
49. Wan, F., Wei, P., Jiao, J., Han, Z., Ye, Q.: Min-entropy latent model for weakly supervised object detection. IEEE TPAMI **41**(10), 2395–2409 (2019)
50. Wei, Y., et al.: TS^{2}C: tight box mining with surrounding segmentation context for weakly supervised object detection. In: Ferrari, V., Hebert, M., Sminchisescu, C., Weiss, Y. (eds.) ECCV 2018. LNCS, vol. 11215, pp. 454–470. Springer, Cham (2018). https://doi.org/10.1007/978-3-030-01252-6_27
51. Ye, Q., Wan, F., Liu, C., Huang, Q., Ji, X.: Continuation multiple instance learning for weakly and fully supervised object detection. IEEE TNNLS, pp. 1–15 (2021). https://doi.org/10.1109/TNNLS.2021.3070801
52. Ye, Q., Zhang, T., Qiu, Q., Zhang, B., Chen, J., Sapiro, G.: Self-learning scene-specific pedestrian detectors using a progressive latent model. In: IEEE CVPR, pp. 2057–2066 (2017)
53. Zeng, Z., Liu, B., Fu, J., Chao, H., Zhang, L.: WSOD2: learning bottom-up and top-down objectness distillation for weakly-supervised object detection. In: IEEE ICCV (2019)
54. Zhou, B., Khosla, A., Lapedriza, A., Oliva, A., Torralba, A.: Learning deep features for discriminative localization. In: IEEE CVPR, pp. 2921–2929 (2016)

Calibration-Free Multi-view Crowd Counting

Qi Zhang[1,2](✉)[iD] and Antoni B. Chan[2][iD]

[1] College of Computer Science & Software Engineering, Shenzhen University,
Shenzhen, China
[2] Department of Computer Science, City University of Hong Kong,
Hong Kong SAR, China
qzhang364-c@my.cityu.edu.hk, abchan@cityu.edu.hk

Abstract. Deep learning based multi-view crowd counting (MVCC) has been proposed to handle scenes with large size, in irregular shape or with severe occlusions. The current MVCC methods require camera calibrations in both training and testing, limiting the real application scenarios of MVCC. To extend and apply MVCC to more practical situations, in this paper we propose *calibration-free* multi-view crowd counting (CF-MVCC), which obtains the scene-level count directly from the density map predictions for each camera view without needing the camera calibrations in the test. Specifically, the proposed CF-MVCC method first estimates the homography matrix to align each pair of camera-views, and then estimates a matching probability map for each camera-view pair. Based on the matching maps of all camera-view pairs, a weight map for each camera view is predicted, which represents how many cameras can reliably see a given pixel in the camera view. Finally, using the weight maps, the total scene-level count is obtained as a simple weighted sum of the density maps for the camera views. Experiments are conducted on several multi-view counting datasets, and promising performance is achieved compared to calibrated MVCC methods that require camera calibrations as input and use scene-level density maps as supervision.

1 Introduction

Crowd counting has many applications in real life, such as crowd control, traffic scheduling or retail shop management, etc. In the past decade, with the strong learning ability of deep learning models, single-view image counting methods based on density map prediction have achieved good performance. However, these single-view image methods may not perform well when the scene is too large or too wide, in irregular shape, or with severe occlusions. Therefore, multi-view crowd counting (MVCC) has been proposed to fuse multiple camera views to mitigate these shortcomings of single-view image counting.

Supplementary Information The online version contains supplementary material available at https://doi.org/10.1007/978-3-031-20077-9_14.

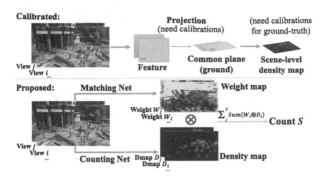

Fig. 1. The proposed calibration-free multi-view crowd counting (CF-MVCC) combines single-view predictions with learned weight maps to obtain the scene-level count.

The current MVCC methods rely on camera calibrations (both intrinsic and extrinsic camera parameters) to project features or density map predictions from the single camera views to the common ground-plane for fusion (see Fig. 1 top). The camera calibration is also required to obtain the ground-truth people locations on the ground-plane to build scene-level density maps for supervision. Although the latest MVCC method [55] handles the cross-view cross-scene (CVCS) setting, it still requires the camera calibrations during training and testing, which limits its real application scenarios. Therefore, it is important to explore *calibration-free* multi-view counting methods.

For calibration-free MVCC, the key issue is to align the camera views without pre-provided camera calibrations. However, it is difficult to calibrate the cameras online from the multi-view images in MVCC, since there are a relatively small number of cameras (less than 5) that are typically on opposite sides of the scene (i.e., large change in camera angle). It may also be inconvenient to perform multi-view counting by calibrating the camera views first if the model is tested on many different scenes. Besides, extra priors about the scenes are required to estimate camera intrinsic or extrinsic, such as in [1,2,4]. We observe that the people' heads are approximately on a plane in the 3D world, and thus the same person's image coordinates in different camera views can be roughly modeled with a homography transformation matrix. Thus, instead of using a common ground-plane for aligning all the camera views together like previous methods [53,55], we propose to align pairs of camera views by estimating pairwise homography transformations.

To extend and apply MVCC to more practical situations, in this paper, we propose a calibration-free multi-view crowd counting (CF-MVCC) method, which obtains the scene-level count as a weighted summation over the predicted density maps from the camera-views (see Fig. 1). The weight maps applied to each density map consider the number of cameras in which the given pixel is visible (to avoid double counting) and the confidence of each pixel (to avoid poorly predicted regions such as those far from the camera). The weight maps are generated using estimated pairwise homographies in the testing stage, and thus CF-MVCC can be applied to a novel scene without camera calibrations.

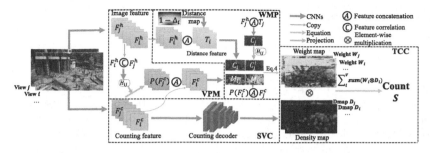

Fig. 2. Pipeline of CF-MVCC. The single-view counting (SVC) module predicts density maps D_i for each camera-view. Given a pair of camera-views (i,j), the view-pair matching (VPM) module estimates the homography H_{ij} and a matching probability map M_{ij} between them. The weight map prediction (WMP) module calculates the weight map W_i for each camera using the matching probability maps M_{ij} and confidence maps C_i, where the confidence maps are estimated from image features F_i^h and distance features T_i. Finally, the total count calculation (TCC) is obtained as a weighted sum between the density maps D_i and the weight maps W_i.

Specifically, the proposed CF-MVCC method estimates the total crowd count in the scene via 4 modules. 1) *Single-view counting module* (SVC) consists of feature extraction and density map prediction submodules. 2) *View-pair matching module* (VPM) estimates the homography between pairs of camera views. For each camera pair, the features from one camera view are then projected to the other view, concatenated, and used to estimate a matching probability map between the two camera view. 3) *Weight map prediction module* (WMP) calculates a weight map for each view using all the matching probability maps. In addition, image content and distance information are used when calculating the weight maps to adjust for the confidence from each camera view. 4) *Total count calculation module* (TCC) obtains the total count as a weighted sum of the predicted single-view density maps using the estimated weight maps. In summary, the contributions of the paper are three-fold:

1. We propose a calibration-free multi-view counting model (CF-MVCC) to further extend the application of MVCC methods to more unconstrained scenarios, which can be applied to new scenes without camera calibrations. As far as we know, this is the first work to extend multi-view counting to the calibration-free camera setting.
2. The proposed method uses single-view density map predictions to directly estimate the scene crowd count without pixel-level supervision, via a weighting map with confidence score that is guided by camera-view content and distance information.
3. We conduct extensive experiments on multi-view counting datasets and achieve better performance than calibration-free baselines, and promising performance compared to well-calibrated MVCC methods. Furthermore, our model trained on a large synthetic dataset can be applied to real novel scenes with domain adaptation.

2   Related Work

In this section, we review single-image and multi-view counting, followed by DNN-based homography estimation.

Single-Image Counting. Early research works on single-image counting rely on hand-crafted features [13,41], including detection-based [35], regression-based [6] or density map based methods [16]. Deep-learning based methods have been proposed for single image counting via estimating density maps [3,29,37,51]. Among them, many have focused on handling the scale variation and perspective change issues [12,14,17,20,40]. Unlike [38] and [47], [49] corrected the perspective distortions by uniformly warping the input images guided by a predicted perspective factor. Recent research explore different forms of supervision (e.g., regression methods or loss functions) [43,45]. [22] introduced local counting maps and an adaptive mixture regression framework to improve the crowd estimation precision in a coarse-to-fine manner. [25] proposed Bayesian loss, which adopts a more reliable supervision on the count expectation at each annotated point.

To extend the application scenarios of crowd counting, weakly supervised [5,21,50,57] or semi-supervised methods [23,36,42] have also been proposed. Synthetic data and domain adaptation have been incorporated for better performance [46]. Other modalities are also fused with RGB images for improving the counting performance under certain conditions, such as RGBD [18] or RGBT [19]. In contrast to category-specific counting methods (e.g., people), general object counting has also been proposed recently [24,31,48]. [31] proposed a general object counting dataset and a model that predicts counting maps from the similarity of the reference patches and the testing image.

Generally, all these methods aim at counting objects in single views, while seldom have targeted at the counting for whole scenes where a single camera view is not enough to cover a large or a wide scene with severe occlusions. Therefore, multi-view counting is required to enhance the counting performance for large and wide scenes.

Multi-view Counting. Multi-view counting fuses multiple camera views for better counting performance for the whole scene. Traditional multi-view counting methods consist of detection-based [8,26], regression-based [34,44] and 3D cylinder-based methods [10]. These methods are frequently trained on a small dataset like PETS2009 [9]. Since they rely on hand-crafted features and foreground extraction techniques, their performance is limited.

Recently, deep-learning multi-view counting methods have been proposed to better fuse single views and improve the counting performance. A multi-view multi-scale (MVMS) model [53] is the first DNNs based multi-view counting method. MVMS is based on 2D projection of the camera-view feature maps to a common ground-plane for predicting ground-plane scene-level density maps. However, the projection operation requires that camera calibrations are provided for training and testing. Follow-up work [54] proposed to use 3D density maps and 3D projection to improve counting performance. [55] proposed a cross-view cross-scene (CSCV) multi-view counting model by camera selection and noise injection training. [58] enhanced the performance of the late fusion model in MVMS by modeling the correlation between each pair of views.

For previous works, the single camera views (feature maps or density maps) are projected on the ground plane for fusion to predict the scene-level density maps, and thus camera calibrations are needed in the testing stage, which limits their applicability on novel scenes where camera calibrations are unavailable. In contrast, we propose a calibration-free multi-view counting method that does not require camera calibrations during testing. Our calibration-free setting is more difficult compared to previous multi-view counting methods.

Deep Homography Estimation. Our work is also related to homography estimation works [27,30], especially DNNs-based methods [7,52]. [7] proposed to estimate the 8°C-of-freedom homography from an image pair with CNNs. [28] proposed an unsupervised method that minimizes the pixel-wise intensity error between the corresponding regions, but their unsupervised loss is not applicable when the change in camera view angle is large. [52] proposed to learn an outlier mask to select reliable regions for homography estimation. [15] proposed a multi-task learning framework for dynamic scenes by jointly estimating dynamics masks and homographies.

Our proposed model estimates the homography matrix between the people head locations in the two views of each camera pair. Note that the change in view angle for camera-view pairs in the multi-view counting datasets (e.g., CityStreet) is quite large, which is in contrast to the typical setting for previous DNN-based homography estimation works where the change in angle is small. Therefore, the priors for unsupervised methods (e.g., [28]) are not applicable. Furthermore, the homography matrix in the proposed model is constructed based on the correspondence of people heads in the camera view pair, which are more difficult to observe compared to the objects in typical homography estimation datasets. Instead, we use a supervised approach to predict the homography matrix.

3   Calibration-Free Multi-view Crowd Counting

In this section we propose our model for calibration-free multi-view crowd counting (CF-MVCC). In order to avoid using the projection operation, which requires camera calibration, we could obtain the total count by summing the density maps predicted from each camera view. However, just summing all the single-view density maps would cause double counting on pixels that are also visible from other cameras. Therefore, we apply a weight map to discount the contribution of pixels that are visible from other camera views (see Fig. 1). The weight map is computed from a matching score map, which estimates the pixel-to-pixel correspondence between a pair of camera-views, and a confidence score map, which estimates the reliability of a given pixel (e.g., since predictions on faraway regions are less reliable). Specifically, our proposed CF-MVCC model consists of following 4 modules: single-image counting, view-pair matching, weight map prediction, and total count calculation. The pipeline is illustrated in Fig. 2. Furthermore, to validate the proposed method's effectiveness on novel scenes, we also train our model on a large synthetic dataset, and then apply it to real scenes via domain adaptation.

3.1 Single-View Counting Module (SVC)

The SVC module predicts the counting density map D_i for each camera-view i, based on an extracted feature map F_i^c. For fair comparison with the SOTA calibrated MVCC method CVCS [55], in our implementation, we follow CVCS [55] and use the first 7 layers of VGG-net [39] as the feature extraction subnet, and the remaining layers of CSR-net [17] as the decoder for predicting D_i. Other single-view counting models are also tested in the ablation study of the experiments and Supp. The loss used for training SVC is $l_d = \sum_{i=1}^{V} ||D_i - D_i^{gt}||_2^2$, where D_i and D_i^{gt} are the predicted and ground-truth density maps, the summation i is over cameras, and V is the number of camera-views.

3.2 View-Pair Matching Module (VPM)

The VPM module estimates the matching score M_{ij} between any 2 camera views i and j. First, we use a CNN to estimate the homography transformation matrix from camera view i to j, denoted as H_{ij}. This CNN extracts the 2 camera views' feature maps F_i^h and F_j^h. Next, the correlation map is computed between F_i^h and F_j^h, and a decoder is applied to predict the homography transformation matrix H_{ij}. For supervision, the homography matrix ground-truth H_{ij}^{gt} is calculated based on the corresponding people head locations in the 2 camera views. In the case that the camera view pair have no overlapping field-of-view, then a dummy homography matrix is used as ground-truth to indicate the 2 camera views are non-overlapped. The loss used to train the homography estimation CNN is $l_h = \sum_{i=1}^{V} \sum_{j \neq i} ||H_{ij} - H_{ij}^{gt}||_2^2$.

Next a subnetwork is used to predict the matching score map M_{ij}, whose elements indicate the probability of whether the given pixel in view i has a match *anywhere* in view j. The input into the subnet is the concatenation of features F_i^c from view i, and the aligned features from view j, $P(F_j^c, H_{ij})$, where P is the projection layer adopted from STN [11].

3.3 Weight Map Prediction Module (WMP)

The WMP module calculates the weight W_i for each view i based on the matching score maps $\{M_{ij}\}_{j \neq i}$ with other camera views. Specifically, the weight map W_i is:

$$W_i = 1/(1 + \sum_{j \neq i} M_{ij}). \tag{1}$$

Note that for pixel p, the denominator $1 + \sum_{j \neq i} M_{ij}(p)$ is the number of camera-views that see pixel p in camera-view i (including camera-view i itself). Thus the weight $W_i(p)$ will average the density map values of corresponding pixels across

Fig. 3. Example of distance map $(1 - \Delta_i)$. Usually, in surveillance cameras, the top and side areas on the image plane are faraway regions and the bottom areas are the nearer regions.

visible views, thus preventing double-counting of camera-view density maps with overlapping fields-of-view.

In (1), the contribution of each camera-view is equal. However, single-view density map prediction may not always be reliable. Generally, the confidence (reliability) for regions with occlusions is lower than regions without occlusions, and the confidence of regions far from the camera is lower than near-camera regions. Therefore, to factor in these issues, we estimate a confidence score map C_i for each camera view i, based on the image content features and pixel-wise distance information. The confidence maps are then incorporated into (1),

$$W_i = C_i / (C_i + \sum_{j \neq i} C_j^i \odot M_{ij}),\tag{2}$$

where $C_j^i = P(C_j, H_{ij})$ is the projection of confidence map C_j to camera view i. Note that in (2), the views with higher confidence will have higher contribution to the count of a given pixel.

The confidence map C_i is estimated with a CNN whose inputs are the image feature map F_i^h and distance feature map T_i. Ideally, T_i should be computed by feeding a distance map Δ_i, where each pixel is the distance-to-camera in the 3D scene, into a small CNN. We note the surveillance cameras are usually angled downward to cover the scene, where the top and side areas on the image plane are faraway regions and the bottom areas are the nearer regions. Since we do not have camera calibration to compute 3D distances, we use a simple approximation for Δ_i where the bottom-middle pixel is considered as the pixel nearest to the current camera (the value is 0), and values of other pixels are the Euclidean distance to the bottom-middle pixel (See Fig. 3). The distance map Δ_i is then normalized to $[0, 1]$, and $(1 - \Delta_i)$ is fed into a CNN to output the distance feature T_i.

Related Work. The weight map of our proposed method is different from the comparison method Dmap_weighted from [53]. Specifically, Dmap_weighted uses the camera calibrations and assumes each image pixel's height in 3D world is the average person height to calculate how many cameras can see a given pixel. Dmap_weighted also does not consider occlusion handling and prediction confidence. In contrast, our method does not use camera calibrations, but instead estimates matching scores based on estimated homographies between camera views, image contents and geometry constraints (see Eq. 1). Furthermore, we incorporate confidence scores to adjust each view's contribution, due to occlusion and distance (see Eq. 2).

3.4 Total Count Calculation Module (TCC)

With the estimated weight map W_i for each camera view i, the final count S is the weighted summation of the density map predictions D_i: $S = \sum_{i=1}^{V} \text{sum}(W_i \odot D_i)$, where $\odot$ is element-wise multiplication, and sum is the summation over the map. For training, the total count loss is the MSE of the count prediction: $l_s = ||S - S^{gt}||_2^2$, where S^{gt} is the ground-truth count. Finally, the loss for training the whole model is $l = l_s + l_d + l_h$.

3.5 Adaptation to Novel Real Scenes

To apply our model to new scenes with novel camera views, we need a large number of multi-view counting scenes for training. Therefore, we train the proposed model on a large multi-view counting dataset [55]. However, directly applying the trained model to real scenes might not achieve satisfying performance due to the domain gap between the synthetic and real data in terms of single-view counting, view-pair homography estimation and matching. To reduce the domain gap, we first fine-tune the model trained on synthetic data on each real test scene with an unsupervised domain adaptation (UDA) technique [55], where only the test images are used without counting annotations or camera calibrations. To further improve the performance, we use one image with density map annotations from the training set of the target scenes, and only fine-tune the SVC module of the proposed model with the one labeled frame. Compared to [46], we only use synthetic labels and one labeled frame from the target scene, and do not require large amounts of target scene annotations; while compared to [55], we do not need calibrations of the real scenes. Therefore, ours is a more difficult and practical setting for applying the trained multi-view counting model to real scenes.

4 Experiment

4.1 Experiment Setting

Ground-Truth. We use the single-view density maps, homography transformation matrix, and scene crowd count as ground-truth for training. The ground-truth for the single-view density maps are constructed as in typical single-image counting methods [56]. The ground-truth homography transformation matrix of a camera-view pair is calculated with the corresponded people head coordinates (normalized to $[-1, 1]$). If there are no common people in the 2 camera views (no overlapped region), a "dummy" homography matrix is used as the ground-truth: $H = [0, 0, -10; 0, 0, -10; 0, 0, 1]$. As for the ground-truth people count, we only require the total scene-level count, which is in contrast to [53], which requires scene-level people annotations on the ground-plane. Thus our setting is more difficult compared to the previous multi-view counting methods that use camera calibration and pixel-level supervision.

Training and Evaluation. The training is stage by stage: we train the SVC and homography estimation CNNs, then fix both of them and train the remaining modules. On the large synthetic dataset, we use learning rates of 10^{-3}. On the real scene datasets, the learning rate is 10^{-4}. Network settings are in the supplemental. Mean absolute error (MAE) and mean normalized absolute error (NAE) of the predicted counts are used as the evaluation metrics.

Datasets. We validate the proposed calibration-free multi-view counting on both a synthetic dataset CVCS [55] and real datasets, CityStreet [53] and PETS2009 [9]. Furthermore, we also apply the proposed model trained on CVCS dataset to real datasets CityStreet, PETS2009 and DukeMTMC [32,53].

- **CVCS** is synthetic dataset for multi-view counting task, which contains 31 scenes. Each scene contains 100 frames and about 100 camera views (280k total images). 5 camera views are randomly selected for 5 times for each scene in the training, and 5 camera views are randomly selected for 21 times for each test scene during testing. No camera calibrations are used in the training or testing. The input image resolution is 640 × 360.
- **CityStreet, PETS2009 and DukeMTMC** are 3 real scene datasets for multi-view counting. CityStreet contains 3 camera views and 300 multi-view frames (676 × 380 resolution) for training and 200 for testing. PETS2009 contains 3 camera views and 1105 multi-view frames (384 × 288) for training and 794 for testing. DukeMTMC contains 4 camera views and 700 multi-view frames (640 × 360) for training and 289 for testing. Among these 3 datasets, CityStreet is the most complicated dataset as it contains more severe occlusions and larger angle changes between camera views.

Comparison Methods. We denote our method using the weight maps in Eq. 1 as CF-MVCC, and the weight maps with confidence scores in Eq. 2 as CF-MVCC-C. As there are no previous calibration-free methods proposed, we adapt existing approaches to be calibration-free:

- **Dmap_weightedH**: This is the calibration-free version of Dmap_weighted in [53]. With Dmap_weighted, the density maps are weighted by how many times an image pixel can be seen by other camera views, based on the camera calibrations. Since camera calibrations are not available in our setting, the estimated homography H_{ij} is used to calculate the weight maps. Note that this method only considers the camera geometry, and not other factors (e.g., image contents, occlusion, and distance) when computing the weights.
- **Dmap_weightedA**: The camera-view features are concatenated and used to estimate the weight maps for summing single-view predictions, which is a self-attention operation. Compared to Dmap_weightH and our method, Dmap_weightedA only considers image contents, and no geometry constraints.

Table 1. Scene-level counting performance on synthetic multi-scene dataset CVCS.

	Method	MAE	NAE
Calibrated	CVCS_backbone	14.13	0.115
	CVCS (MVMS)	9.30	0.080
	CVCS	**7.22**	**0.062**
Calibration-free	Dmap_weightedH	28.28	0.239
	Dmap_weightedA	19.85	0.165
	Total_count	18.89	0.157
	4D_corr	17.76	0.149
	CF-MVCC (ours)	16.46	0.140
	CF-MVCC-C (ours)	**13.90**	**0.118**

– **Total_count**: Since scene-level density maps are not available in our setting, we replace scene-level density maps with total count loss in CVCS [55].
– **4D_corr**: Replacing the VPM module in CF-MVCC with a 4D correlation [33] method for estimating the matching score M_{ij} of the camera-view pair.

Finally, we compare with multi-view counting methods that use camera calibrations: MVMS [53], 3D [54], CVCS_backbone and CVCS [55], and CVF [58].

4.2 Experiment Results

Scene-Level Counting Performance. We show the scene-level counting performance of the proposed models and comparison methods on CVCS, CityStreet and PETS2009 in Tables 1 and 2. On CVCS dataset, the proposed CF-MVCC-C achieves the best performance among the calibration-free methods. The comparison methods Dmap_weightedH and Dmap_weightedA only consider the camera geometry or the image contents, and thus their performance is worse than CF-MVCC, which considers both. Including confidence score maps into the weights (CF-MVCC-C) will further improve the performance. Total_count replaces the pixel-level supervision in CVCS with the total count loss, but directly regressing the scene-level count is not accurate since the projection to the ground stretches the features and makes it difficult to learn to fuse the multi-view features without pixel-level supervision. The 4D_corr method also performs poorly because the supervision from the total-counting loss is too weak to guide the learning of the matching maps from the 4D correlation maps. Finally, our CF-MVCC-C performs worse than calibrated methods CVCS and CVCS (MVMS), but still better than CVCS_backbone, which is reasonable since our method does not use any calibrations and no pixel-wise loss is available for the scene-level prediction.

In Table 2, on both real single-scene datasets, our proposed calibration-free methods perform better than the other calibration-free methods. Furthermore, CF-MVCC-C is better than CF-MVCC, indicating the effectiveness of the confidence score in the weight map estimation. Compared to calibrated methods,

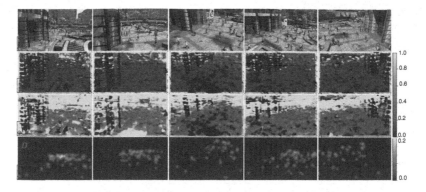

Fig. 4. Example of confidence maps C, weight maps W and density maps D.

Table 2. Scene-level counting performance on real single-scene datasets.

	Method	CityStreet		PETS2009	
		MAE	NAE	MAE	NAE
Calibrated	MVMS	8.01	0.096	3.49	0.124
	3D_counting	7.54	**0.091**	3.15	**0.113**
	CVF	**7.08**	-	**3.08**	-
Calibration-free	Dmap_weightedH	9.84	0.107	4.23	0.136
	Dmap_weightedA	9.40	0.123	6.25	0.252
	Total_count	11.28	0.152	6.95	0.265
	4D_corr	8.82	0.102	4.55	0.147
	CF-MVCC (ours)	8.24	0.103	3.84	0.125
	CF-MVCC-C (ours)	**8.06**	**0.102**	**3.46**	**0.116**

CF-MVCC-C is comparable to MVMS [53], and slightly worse than 3D [54] and CVF [58]. The reason might be that the calibrated methods can implicitly learn some specific camera geometry in the fusion step, since the methods are trained and tested on the same scenes.

Visualization Results. We show the visualization results the predicted confidence, weight, and density maps in Fig. 4. The red boxes indicate regions that cannot be seen by other cameras, and thus their predicted weights are large regardless of the confidence scores. The red circles show a person that can be seen in 3 camera views (3, 4 and 5) – the weights are small since the person can be seen by multiple cameras. This shows that the proposed method is effective at estimating weight maps with confidence information. See the supplemental for more visualizations (*eg.* projection results with ground-truth and predicted homography matrix).

Ablation Studies. Various ablation studies are evaluated on the CVCS dataset.

Table 3. Ablation study on estimating the confidence map using image features and/or distance information.

Method	Feat.	Dist.	MAE	NAE
CF-MVCC			16.46	0.140
CF-MVCC-F	✓		16.13	0.139
CF-MVCC-D		✓	16.12	0.135
CF-MVCC-C	✓	✓	**13.90**	**0.118**

Table 4. Ablation study on single-view counting networks for SVC module.

SVC	Method	MAE	NAE
CSR-Net [17]	CF-MVCC	16.46	0.140
	CF-MVCC-C	13.90	0.118
LCC [22]	CF-MVCC	14.01	0.117
	CF-MVCC-C	**12.79**	**0.109**

Ablation Study on Confidence Map. We conduct an ablation study on the confidence score estimation: 1) without the confidence scores, i.e., CF-MVCC; 2) using only image features to estimate confidence scores, denoted as CF-MVCC-F; 3) using only distance information, denoted as CF-MVCC-D; 4) using both image features and distance, i.e., our full model CF-MVCC-C. The results are presented in Table 3. Using either image features (CF-MVCC-F) or distance information (CF-MVCC-D) can improve the performance compared to not using the confidence map (CF-MVCC). Furthermore, using both image features and distance information (CF-MVCC-C) further improves the performance. Thus, the confidence map effectively adjusts the reliability of the each camera view's prediction, in order to handle occlusion and/or low resolution.

Ablation Study on Single-View Counting Network. We implement and test our proposed model with another recent single-view counting network LCC [22], which uses a larger feature backbone than CSRnet, and is trained with traditional counting density maps as in our model. The results presented in Table 4 show that the proposed CF-MVCC-C achieves better performance than CVCS when using different single-view counting networks in the SVC module.

Ablation Study on the Homography Prediction Module. We also conduct experiments to show how the homography prediction module affects the performance of the model. Here the ground-truth homography matrix is used for training the proposed model. The performance of the proposed model trained with homography prediction H_{pred} or ground-truth H_{gt} is presented in Table 5. The model with ground-truth homography achieves better performance, and CF-MVCC-C performs better than CF-MVCC.

Ablation Study on Variable Numbers of Camera-Views. The modules of the proposed models are shared across camera-views and camera-view pairs,

Table 5. Ablation study on the homography matrix input.

Homography	Method	MAE	NAE
H_{pred}	CF-MVCC	16.64	0.140
	CF-MVCC-C	13.90	0.118
H_{gt}	CF-MVCC	12.04	0.101
	CF-MVCC-C	**11.69**	**0.098**

Table 6. Ablation study on testing with different numbers of input camera-views. The model is trained on CVCS dataset with 5 camera-views as input.

No. Views	CVCS_backbone		CVCS		CF-MVCC-C	
	MAE	NAE	MAE	NAE	MAE	NAE
3	14.28	0.130	7.24	0.071	11.01	0.107
5	14.13	0.115	7.22	0.062	13.90	0.118
7	14.35	0.113	7.07	0.058	18.45	0.147
9	14.56	0.112	7.04	0.056	22.23	0.174

so our method can be applied to different numbers of camera views at test time. In Table 6, the proposed models are trained on the CVCS dataset [55] with 5 input camera views and tested on different number of views. Note that the ground-truth count is the people count covered by the multi-camera views. The performance of the proposed method CF-MVCC-C is worse than the calibrated method CVCS [55], but better than the calibrated method CVCS_backbone [55] when the number of test camera views are close to the number of training views (3 and 5). Unlike CVCS method, the performance of CF-MVCC-C degrades as the number of cameras increases. The reason is that the error in weight map prediction might increase when the number of camera views changes.

Adaptation to Novel Real Scenes. In this part, we use domain adaption to apply the proposed model CF-MVCC-C pre-trained on the synthetic CVCS dataset to the real scene datasets CityStreet, PETS2009 and DukeMTMC. We consider 3 training methods: 1) **Synth**, where pre-trained model is directly tested on the real scenes; 2) **Synth+UDA**, where unsupervised domain adaptation is applied to the pre-trained model. Specifically, 2 discriminators are added to distinguish the single-view density maps and weight maps of the source and target scenes. 3) **Synth+F**, where the models pre-trained on the synthetic dataset are fine-tuned with one labeled image set. Specifically, our pre-trained proposed model's SVC module is fine-tuned with only 1 labeled camera-view image (V) from the training set of the real dataset, denoted as "+F(V)". For comparison, the calibrated CVCS_backbone and CVCS are fine-tuned with one set of multi-view images (V) and one labeled scene-level density map (S), denoted "+F(V+S)".

The results are presented in Table 7. The first 7 methods are calibrated methods that train and test on the *same* single scene (denoted as 'RealSame'). This

Table 7. Results on real testing datasets. "Training" column indicates different training methods: "RealSame" means training and testing on the same single real scene; "Synth" means cross-scene training on synthetic dataset and directly testing on the real scenes; "+UDA" means adding unsupervised domain adaptation; "+F(V+S) means finetune the calibrated methods on a set of multi-view images (V) and one corresponding scene-level density map (S); "+F(V)" means finetuning the single-view counting with one labeled camera view image (V) from the training set of real scenes.

	Model	Training	PETS2009		DukeMTMC		CityStreet	
			MAE	NAE	MAE	NAE	MAE	NAE
Calibrated	Dmap_weighted [34]	RealSame	7.51	0.261	2.12	0.255	11.10	0.121
	Dect+ReID [53]	RealSame	9.41	0.289	2.20	0.342	27.60	0.385
	LateFusion [53]	RealSame	3.92	0.138	1.27	0.198	8.12	0.097
	EarlyFusion [53]	RealSame	5.43	0.199	1.25	0.220	8.10	0.096
	MVMS [53]	RealSame	3.49	0.124	1.03	**0.170**	8.01	0.096
	3D [54]	RealSame	3.15	**0.113**	1.37	0.244	7.54	**0.091**
	CVF [58]	RealSame	**3.08**	-	**0.87**	-	**7.08**	-
Calibrated	CVCS_backbone [55]	Synth	8.05	0.257	4.19	0.913	11.57	0.156
	CVCS_backbone [55]	Synth+UDA	5.91	0.200	3.11	0.551	10.09	0.117
	CVCS_backbone [55]	Synth+F(V+S)	5.78	0.186	2.92	0.597	9.71	0.111
	CVCS [55]	Synth	5.33	0.174	2.85	0.546	11.09	0.124
	CVCS [55]	Synth+UDA	5.17	0.165	2.83	**0.525**	9.58	0.117
	CVCS [55]	Synth+F(V+S)	5.06	0.164	2.81	0.567	9.13	0.108
Calib-free	CF-MVCC-C (ours)	Synth	14.63	0.458	5.16	0.984	48.58	0.602
	CF-MVCC-C (ours)	Synth+UDA	12.76	0.398	2.65	0.498	14.89	0.176
	CF-MVCC-C (ours)	Synth+F(V)	**4.85**	**0.162**	**1.80**	**0.293**	**8.13**	**0.095**

can be considered as the upper-bound performance for this experiment. The remaining 9 methods are calibrated and calibration-free methods using domain adaptation. The proposed method trained with Synth+F(V) achieves better performance than other training methods or CVCS [55] with domain adaptation or Synth+F(V+S). Compared to calibrated single-scene models [34,53,54,58], the CF-MVCC-C training with Synth+F(V) still achieves promising performance, and is slightly worse than MVMS and 3D. Note that Synth+F(V) only uses one frame annotated with people during fine-tuning, and does not require camera calibrations during test time. Thus, our method has practical advantage over the calibrated single-scene methods, which require much more annotations and the camera calibrations.

5   Conclusion

In this paper, we propose a calibration-free multi-view counting method that fuses the single-view predictions with learned weight maps, which consider both similarity between camera-view pairs and confidence guided by image content and distance information. The experiments show the proposed method can achieve better performance than other calibration-free baselines. Compared to previous calibrated multi-view methods, our proposed method is more practical for real applications, since our method does not need camera calibrations in the testing stage. The performance can be further improved by pre-training on a synthetic dataset, and applying domain adaptation with a single annotated image. In this case, our fine-tuned calibration-free method outperforms fine-tuned calibrated methods. Our work provides a promising step towards practical multi-view crowd counting, which requires no camera calibrations from the test scene and only one image for fine-tuning the single-view density map regressor.

Acknowledgements. This work was supported by grants from the Research Grants Council of the Hong Kong Special Administrative Region, China (CityU 11212518, CityU 11215820), and by a Strategic Research Grant from City University of Hong Kong (Project No. 7005665).

References

1. Agarwal, S., et al.: Building Rome in a day. Commun. ACM **54**(10), 105–112 (2011)
2. Ammar Abbas, S., Zisserman, A.: A geometric approach to obtain a bird's eye view from an image. In: Proceedings of the IEEE/CVF International Conference on Computer Vision Workshops (2019)
3. Bai, S., He, Z., Qiao, Y., Hu, H., Wu, W., Yan, J.: Adaptive dilated network with self-correction supervision for counting. In: Proceedings of the IEEE/CVF Conference on Computer Vision and Pattern Recognition, pp. 4594–4603 (2020)
4. Bhardwaj, R., Tummala, G.K., Ramalingam, G., Ramjee, R., Sinha, P.: Autocalib: automatic traffic camera calibration at scale. ACM Trans. Sensor Netw. (TOSN) **14**(3–4), 1–27 (2018)
5. von Borstel, M., Kandemir, M., Schmidt, P., Rao, M.K., Rajamani, K., Hamprecht, F.A.: Gaussian process density counting from weak supervision. In: Leibe, B., Matas, J., Sebe, N., Welling, M. (eds.) ECCV 2016. LNCS, vol. 9905, pp. 365–380. Springer, Cham (2016). https://doi.org/10.1007/978-3-319-46448-0_22
6. Chan, A.B., Vasconcelos, N.: Counting people with low-level features and Bayesian regression. IEEE Trans. Image Process. **21**(4), 2160–2177 (2012)
7. DeTone, D., Malisiewicz, T., Rabinovich, A.: Deep image homography estimation. arXiv preprint arXiv:1606.03798 (2016)
8. Dittrich, F., de Oliveira, L.E., Britto Jr, A.S., Koerich, A.L.: People counting in crowded and outdoor scenes using a hybrid multi-camera approach. arXiv preprint arXiv:1704.00326 (2017)
9. Ferryman, J., Shahrokni, A.: Pets 2009: dataset and challenge. In: 2009 Twelfth IEEE International Workshop on Performance Evaluation of Tracking and Surveillance, pp. 1–6. IEEE (2009)
10. Ge, W., Collins, R.T.: Crowd detection with a multiview sampler. In: Daniilidis, K., Maragos, P., Paragios, N. (eds.) ECCV 2010. LNCS, vol. 6315, pp. 324–337. Springer, Heidelberg (2010). https://doi.org/10.1007/978-3-642-15555-0_24
11. Jaderberg, M., Simonyan, K., Zisserman, A., Kavukcuoglu, K.: Spatial transformer networks. In: Advances in Neural Information Processing Systems (NIPS), pp. 2017–2025 (2015)

12. Jiang, X., et al.: Attention scaling for crowd counting. In: IEEE/CVF Conference on Computer Vision and Pattern Recognition (CVPR), June 2020
13. Junior, J.C.S.J., Musse, S.R., Jung, C.R.: Crowd analysis using computer vision techniques. IEEE Signal Process. Mag. **27**(5), 66–77 (2010)
14. Kang, D., Chan, A.: Crowd counting by adaptively fusing predictions from an image pyramid. In: BMVC (2018)
15. Le, H., Liu, F., Zhang, S., Agarwala, A.: Deep homography estimation for dynamic scenes. In: Proceedings of the IEEE/CVF Conference on Computer Vision and Pattern Recognition, pp. 7652–7661 (2020)
16. Lempitsky, V., Zisserman, A.: Learning to count objects in images. In: Advances in Neural Information Processing Systems, pp. 1324–1332 (2010)
17. Li, Y., Zhang, X., Chen, D.: CSRNET: dilated convolutional neural networks for understanding the highly congested scenes. In: Proceedings of the IEEE Conference on Computer Vision and Pattern Recognition, pp. 1091–1100 (2018)
18. Lian, D., Li, J., Zheng, J., Luo, W., Gao, S.: Density map regression guided detection network for RGB-D crowd counting and localization. In: CVPR, pp. 1821–1830 (2019)
19. Liu, L., Chen, J., Wu, H., Li, G., Li, C., Lin, L.: Cross-modal collaborative representation learning and a large-scale RGBT benchmark for crowd counting. In: Proceedings of the IEEE/CVF Conference on Computer Vision and Pattern Recognition (CVPR), pp. 4823–4833, June 2021
20. Liu, W., Salzmann, M., Fua, P.: Context-aware crowd counting. In: CVPR, pp. 5099–5108 (2019)
21. Liu, X., van de Weijer, J., Bagdanov, A.D.: Exploiting unlabeled data in CNNs by self-supervised learning to rank. IEEE Trans. Pattern Anal. Mach. Intell. **41**(8), 1862–1878 (2019)
22. Liu, X., Yang, J., Ding, W., Wang, T., Wang, Z., Xiong, J.: Adaptive mixture regression network with local counting map for crowd counting. In: Vedaldi, A., Bischof, H., Brox, T., Frahm, J.-M. (eds.) ECCV 2020. LNCS, vol. 12369, pp. 241–257. Springer, Cham (2020). https://doi.org/10.1007/978-3-030-58586-0_15
23. Liu, Y., Liu, L., Wang, P., Zhang, P., Lei, Y.: Semi-supervised crowd counting via self-training on surrogate tasks. In: Vedaldi, A., Bischof, H., Brox, T., Frahm, J.-M. (eds.) ECCV 2020. LNCS, vol. 12360, pp. 242–259. Springer, Cham (2020). https://doi.org/10.1007/978-3-030-58555-6_15
24. Lu, E., Xie, W., Zisserman, A.: Class-agnostic counting. In: Jawahar, C.V., Li, H., Mori, G., Schindler, K. (eds.) ACCV 2018. LNCS, vol. 11363, pp. 669–684. Springer, Cham (2019). https://doi.org/10.1007/978-3-030-20893-6_42
25. Ma, Z., Wei, X., Hong, X., Gong, Y.: Bayesian loss for crowd count estimation with point supervision, pp. 6141–6150 (2019)
26. Maddalena, L., Petrosino, A., Russo, F.: People counting by learning their appearance in a multi-view camera environment. Pattern Recogn. Lett. **36**, 125–134 (2014)
27. Mishkin, D., Matas, J., Perdoch, M., Lenc, K.: WXBS: wide baseline stereo generalizations. In: British Machine Vision Conference (2015)
28. Nguyen, T., Chen, S.W., Shivakumar, S.S., Taylor, C.J., Kumar, V.: Unsupervised deep homography: a fast and robust homography estimation model. IEEE Robot. Autom. Lett. **3**(3), 2346–2353 (2018)
29. Oñoro-Rubio, D., López-Sastre, R.J.: Towards perspective-free object counting with deep learning. In: Leibe, B., Matas, J., Sebe, N., Welling, M. (eds.) ECCV 2016. LNCS, vol. 9911, pp. 615–629. Springer, Cham (2016). https://doi.org/10.1007/978-3-319-46478-7_38

30. Pritchett, P., Zisserman, A.: Wide baseline stereo matching. In: International Conference on Computer Vision (1998)
31. Ranjan, V., Sharma, U., Nguyen, T., Hoai, M.: Learning to count everything. In: Proceedings of the IEEE/CVF Conference on Computer Vision and Pattern Recognition (CVPR), pp. 3394–3403, June 2021
32. Ristani, E., Solera, F., Zou, R., Cucchiara, R., Tomasi, C.: Performance measures and a data set for multi-target, multi-camera tracking. In: Hua, G., Jégou, H. (eds.) ECCV 2016. LNCS, vol. 9914, pp. 17–35. Springer, Cham (2016). https://doi.org/10.1007/978-3-319-48881-3_2
33. Rocco, I., Cimpoi, M., Arandjelović, R., Torii, A., Pajdla, T., Sivic, J.: Neighbourhood consensus networks. arXiv preprint arXiv:1810.10510 (2018)
34. Ryan, D., Denman, S., Fookes, C., Sridharan, S.: Scene invariant multi camera crowd counting. Pattern Recogn. Lett. **44**(8), 98–112 (2014)
35. Sabzmeydani, P., Mori, G.: Detecting pedestrians by learning shapelet features. In: IEEE Conference on Computer Vision and Pattern Recognition, pp. 1–8. IEEE (2007)
36. Sam, D.B., Sajjan, N.N., Maurya, H., Radhakrishnan, V.B.: Almost unsupervised learning for dense crowd counting. In: Thirty-Third AAAI Conference on Artificial Intelligence, vol. 33(1), pp. 8868–8875 (2019)
37. Sam, D.B., Surya, S., Babu, R.V.: Switching convolutional neural network for crowd counting. In: Proceedings of the IEEE Conference on Computer Vision and Pattern Recognition, vol. 1, p. 6 (2017)
38. Shi, M., Yang, Z., Xu, C., Chen, Q.: Revisiting perspective information for efficient crowd counting. In: Proceedings of the IEEE/CVF Conference on Computer Vision and Pattern Recognition, pp. 7279–7288 (2019)
39. Simonyan, K., Zisserman, A.: Very deep convolutional networks for large-scale image recognition. arXiv preprint arXiv:1409.1556 (2014)
40. Sindagi, V.A., Patel, V.M.: Generating high-quality crowd density maps using contextual pyramid CNNs. In: IEEE International Conference on Computer Vision (ICCV), pp. 1879–1888. IEEE (2017)
41. Sindagi, V.A., Patel, V.M.: A survey of recent advances in CNN-based single image crowd counting and density estimation. Pattern Recogn. Lett. **107**, 3–16 (2018)
42. Sindagi, V.A., Yasarla, R., Babu, D.S., Babu, R.V., Patel, V.M.: Learning to count in the crowd from limited labeled data. arXiv preprint arXiv:2007.03195 (2020)
43. Song, Q., et al.: Rethinking counting and localization in crowds: a purely point-based framework. arXiv preprint arXiv:2107.12746 (2021)
44. Tang, N., Lin, Y.Y., Weng, M.F., Liao, H.Y.: Cross-camera knowledge transfer for multiview people counting. IEEE Trans. Image Process. **24**(1), 80–93 (2014)
45. Wan, J., Liu, Z., Chan, A.B.: A generalized loss function for crowd counting and localization. In: Proceedings of the IEEE/CVF Conference on Computer Vision and Pattern Recognition (CVPR), pp. 1974–1983, June 2021
46. Wang, Q., Gao, J., et al.: Learning from synthetic data for crowd counting in the wild. In: CVPR, pp. 8198–8207 (2019)
47. Yan, Z., et al.: Perspective-guided convolution networks for crowd counting. In: Proceedings of the IEEE/CVF International Conference on Computer Vision, pp. 952–961 (2019)
48. Yang, S.D., Su, H.T., Hsu, W.H., Chen, W.C.: Class-agnostic few-shot object counting. In: Proceedings of the IEEE/CVF Winter Conference on Applications of Computer Vision, pp. 870–878 (2021)

49. Yang, Y., Li, G., Wu, Z., Su, L., Huang, Q., Sebe, N.: Reverse perspective network for perspective-aware object counting. In: Proceedings of the IEEE/CVF Conference on Computer Vision and Pattern Recognition, pp. 4374–4383 (2020)

50. Yang, Y., Li, G., Wu, Z., Su, L., Huang, Q., Sebe, N.: Weakly-supervised crowd counting learns from sorting rather than locations. In: Vedaldi, A., Bischof, H., Brox, T., Frahm, J.-M. (eds.) ECCV 2020. LNCS, vol. 12353, pp. 1–17. Springer, Cham (2020). https://doi.org/10.1007/978-3-030-58598-3_1

51. Zhang, C., Li, H., Wang, X., Yang, X.: Cross-scene crowd counting via deep convolutional neural networks. In: Proceedings of the IEEE Conference on Computer Vision and Pattern Recognition, pp. 833–841 (2015)

52. Zhang, J., Wang, C., Liu, S., Jia, L., Ye, N., Wang, J., Zhou, J., Sun, J.: Content-aware unsupervised deep homography estimation. In: Vedaldi, A., Bischof, H., Brox, T., Frahm, J.-M. (eds.) ECCV 2020. LNCS, vol. 12346, pp. 653–669. Springer, Cham (2020). https://doi.org/10.1007/978-3-030-58452-8_38

53. Zhang, Q., Chan, A.B.: Wide-area crowd counting via ground-plane density maps and multi-view fusion CNNs. In: Proceedings of the IEEE Conference on Computer Vision and Pattern Recognition (CVPR), pp. 8297–8306 (2019)

54. Zhang, Q., Chan, A.B.: 3d crowd counting via multi-view fusion with 3d gaussian kernels. In: AAAI Conference on Artificial Intelligence, pp. 12837–12844 (2020)

55. Zhang, Q., Lin, W., Chan, A.B.: Cross-view cross-scene multi-view crowd counting. In: Proceedings of the IEEE/CVF Conference on Computer Vision and Pattern Recognition, pp. 557–567 (2021)

56. Zhang, Y., Zhou, D., Chen, S., Gao, S., Ma, Y.: Single-image crowd counting via multi-column convolutional neural network. In: Proceedings of the IEEE Conference on Computer Vision and Pattern Recognition, pp. 589–597 (2016)

57. Zhao, Z., Shi, M., Zhao, X., Li, L.: Active crowd counting with limited supervision. arXiv preprint arXiv:2007.06334 (2020)

58. Zheng, L., Li, Y., Mu, Y.: Learning factorized cross-view fusion for multi-view crowd counting. In: 2021 IEEE International Conference on Multimedia and Expo (ICME), pp. 1–6. IEEE (2021)

Unsupervised Domain Adaptation for Monocular 3D Object Detection via Self-training

Zhenyu Li[1], Zehui Chen[2], Ang Li[3], Liangji Fang[3], Qinhong Jiang[3], Xianming Liu[1], and Junjun Jiang[1(✉)]

[1] Harbin Institute of Technology, Harbin, China
{zhenyuli17,csxm,jiangjunjun}@hit.edu.cn
[2] University of Science and Technology, Hefei, China
lovesnow@mail.ustc.edu.cn
[3] SenseTime Research, Hong Kong, China
{liang1,fangliangji,jiangqinhong}@senseauto.com

Abstract. Monocular 3D object detection (Mono3D) has achieved unprecedented success with the advent of deep learning techniques and emerging large-scale autonomous driving datasets. However, drastic performance degradation remains an unwell-studied challenge for practical cross-domain deployment as the lack of labels on the target domain. In this paper, we first comprehensively investigate the significant underlying factor of the domain gap in Mono3D, where the critical observation is a depth-shift issue caused by the geometric misalignment of domains. Then, we propose *STMono3D*, a new self-teaching framework for unsupervised domain adaptation on Mono3D. To mitigate the depth-shift, we introduce the *geometry-aligned multi-scale* training strategy to disentangle the camera parameters and guarantee the geometry consistency of domains. Based on this, we develop a teacher-student paradigm to generate adaptive pseudo labels on the target domain. Benefiting from the end-to-end framework that provides richer information of the pseudo labels, we propose the *quality-aware supervision* strategy to take instance-level pseudo confidences into account and improve the effectiveness of the target-domain training process. Moreover, the *positive focusing training* strategy and *dynamic threshold* are proposed to handle tremendous FN and FP pseudo samples. STMono3D achieves remarkable performance on all evaluated datasets and even surpasses fully supervised results on the KITTI 3D object detection dataset. To the best of our knowledge, this is the first study to explore effective UDA methods for Mono3D.

Keywords: Monocular 3D object detection · Domain adaptation · Unsupervised method · Self-training

---

Supplementary Information The online version contains supplementary material available at https://doi.org/10.1007/978-3-031-20077-9_15.

S. Avidan et al. (Eds.): ECCV 2022, LNCS 13669, pp. 245–262, 2022.
https://doi.org/10.1007/978-3-031-20077-9_15

1   Introduction

Monocular 3D object detection (Mono3D) aims to categorize and localize objects from single input RGB images. With the prevalent development of cameras for autonomous vehicles and mobile robots, this field has drawn increasing research attention. Recently, it has obtained remarkable advancements [2,7,31,32,39,40,44] driven by deep neural networks and large-scale human-annotated autonomous driving datasets [3,16,20].

However, 3D detectors trained on one specific dataset (*i.e.* source domain) might suffer from tremendous performance degradation when generalizing to another dataset (*i.e.* target domains) due to unavoidable domain-gaps arising from different types of sensors, weather conditions, and geographical locations. Especially, as shown in Fig. 1, the severe depth-shift caused by different imaging camera devices leads to totally failed locations. Hence, a monocular 3D detector trained on data collected in Singapore cities with nuScenes [3] cameras **cannot** work well (*i.e.*, average precision drops to zero) when evaluated on data from European cities captured by KITTI [16] cameras. While collecting and training with more data from different domains could alleviate this problem, it is unfortunately infeasible, given diverse real-world scenarios and expensive annotation costs. Therefore, methods for effectively adapting a monocular 3D detector trained on a labeled source domain to a novel unlabeled target domain are highly demanded in practical applications. We call this task unsupervised domain adaptation (UDA) for monocular 3D object detection.

While intensive UDA studies [9,12,15,19,26,35] on the 2D image setting are proposed, they mainly focus on handling lighting, color, and texture variations. However, in terms of the Mono3D, since detectors attend to estimate the

(a) Camera View   (b) BEV View   (c) STMono3D

Fig. 1. Depth-shift Illustration. When inferring on the target domain, models can accurately locate the objects on the 2D image but predict totally wrong object depth with tremendous shifts. Such unreliable predictions for pseudo labels cannot improve but hurt the model performance in STMono3D. GAMS guarantees the geometry consistency and enables models predict correct object depth. Best view in color: prediction and ground truth are in orange and blue. Depth-shift is shown in green arrows. (Color figure online)

spatial information of objects from monocular RGB images, the geometry alignment of domains is much more crucial. Moreover, for UDA on LiDAR-based 3D detection [27,46–48], the fundamental differences in data structures and network architectures render these approaches not readily applicable to this problem.

In this paper, we propose *STMono3D*, for UDA on monocular 3D object detection. We first thoroughly investigate the depth-shift issue caused by the tight entanglement of models and camera parameters during the training stage. Models can accurately locate the objects on the 2D image but predict totally wrong object depth with tremendous shifts when inferring on the target domain. To alleviate this issue, we develop the *geometry-aligned multi-scale* (GAMS) training strategy to guarantee the geometry consistency of domains and predict pixel-size depth to overcome the inevitable misalignment and ambiguity. Hence, models can provide effective predictions on the unlabeled target domain. Based upon this, we adopt the mean teacher [37] paradigm to facilitate the learning. The teacher model is essentially a temporal ensemble of student models, where parameters are updated by an exponential moving average window on student models of preceding iterations. It produces stable supervision for the student model without prior knowledge of the target domain.

Moreover, we observe that the Mono3D teacher model suffers from extremely low confidence scores and numerous failed predictions on the target domain. To handle these issues, we adopt *Quality-Aware Supervision* (QAS), *Positive Focusing Training* (PFT), and *Dynamic Threshold* (DT) strategies. Benefitting from the flexibility of the end-to-end mean teacher framework, we utilize the readability of each teacher-generated prediction to dynamically reweight the supervision loss of the student model, which takes instance-level qualities of pseudo labels into account, avoiding the low-quality samples interfering the training process. Since the backgrounds of domains are similar in the Mono3D UDA of the autonomous driving setting, we ignore the negative samples and only utilize positive pseudo labels to train the model. It avoids excessive FN pseudo labels at the beginning of the training process impairing the capability of the model to recognize objects. In synchronization with training, we utilize a dynamic threshold to adjust the filter score, which stabilizes the increase of pseudo labels.

To the best of our knowledge, this is the first study to explore effective UDA methods for Mono3D. Experimental results on various datasets KITTI [16], nuScenes [3], and Lyft [20] demonstrate the effectiveness of our proposed methods, where the performance gaps between source only results and fully supervised oracle results are closed by a large margin. It is noteworthy that STMono3D even outperforms the oracle results under the nuScenes→KITTI setting. Codes will be released at https://github.com/zhyever/STMono3D.

2   Related Work

2.1   Monocular 3D Object Detection

Mono3D has drawn increasing attention in recent years [2,24,29–31,33,39,40, 42,43]. Earlier work utilizes sub-networks to assist 3D detection. For instance,

3DOP [8] and MLFusion [44] use depth estimators while Deep3DBox [30] adopts 2D object detectors. Another line of research makes efforts to convert the RGB input to 3D representations like OFTNet [33] and Pseudo-Lidar [43]. While these methods have shown promising performance, they rely on the design and performance of sub-networks or dense depth labels. Recently, some methods propose to design the Mono3D framework in an end-to-end manner like 2D detection. M3D-RPN [2] implements a single-stage multi-class detector with a region proposal network and depth-aware convolution. SMOKE [25] proposes a simple framework to predict 3D objects without generating 2D proposals. Some methods [10,42] develop a DETR-like [4] bbox head, where 3D objects are predicted by independent queries in a set-to-set manner. In this paper, we mainly conduct UDA experiments based on FCOS3D [40], a neat and representative Mono3D paradigm that keeps the well-developed designs for 2D feature extraction and is adapted for this 3D task with only basic designs for specific 3D detection targets.

2.2 Unsupervised Domain Adaptation

UDA aims to generalize the model trained on a source domain to unlabeled target domains. So far, tremendous methods have been proposed for various computer vision tasks [9,12,15,19,26,35,49] (e.g., recognition, detection, segmentation). Some methods [5,28,36] employ the statistic-based metrics to model the differences between two domains. Other approaches [21,34,49] utilize the self-training strategy to generate pseudo labels for unlabeled target domains. Moreover, inspired by Generative Adversarial Networks (GANs) [17], adversarial learning was employed to align feature distributions [13,14,38], which can be explained by minimizing the H-divergence [1] or the Jensen-Shannon divergence [18] between two domains. [23,41] alleviated the domain shift on batch normalization layers by modulating the statistics in the BN layer before evaluation or specializing parameters of BN domain by domain. Most of these domain adaptation approaches are designed for the general 2D image recognition tasks, while direct adoption of these techniques for the large-scale monocular 3D object detection task may not work well due to the distinct characteristics of Mono3D, especially targes in 3D spatial coordination.

In terms of 3D object detection, [27,47,48] investigate UDA strategies for LIDAR-based detectors. SRDAN [48] adopt adversarial losses to align the features and instances with similar scales between two domains. ST3D [47] and MLC-Net [27] develop self-training strategies with delicate designs, such as random object scaling, triplet memory bank, and multi-level alignment, for domain adaptation. Following the successful trend of UDA on LIDAR-based 3D object detection, we investigate self-training strategies for Mono3D.

3   STMono3D

In this section, we first formulate the UDA task for Mono3D (Sect. 3.1), and present an overview of our framework (Sect. 3.2), followed by the self-teacher with temporal ensemble paradigm (Sect. 3.3). Then, we explain the details of

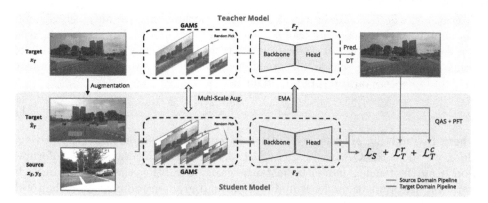

Fig. 2. Framework overview. STMono3D leverages the mean-teacher [37] paradigm where the teacher model is the exponential moving average of the student model and updated at each iteration. We design the GAMS (Sect. 3.4) to alleviate the severe depth-shift in cross domain inference and ensure the availability of pseudo labels predicted by the teacher model. QAS (Sect. 3.5) is a simple *soft-teacher* approach which leverages richer information from the teacher model to reweight losses and provide quality-aware supervision on the student model. PFT and DT are another two crucial training strategies presented in Sect. 3.6.

the geometry-aligned multi-scale training (GAMS, Sect. 3.4), the quality-aware supervision (QAS, Sect. 3.5), and some other crucial training strategies consisting of positive focusing training (PFT) and dynamic threshold (DT) (Sect. 3.6).

3.1   Problem Definition

Under the unsupervised domain adaptation setting, we access to labeled images from the source domain $\mathcal{D}_S = \{x_s^i, y_s^i, K_s^i\}_{i=1}^{N_S}$, and unlabeled images from the target domain $\mathcal{D}_T = \{x_t^i, K_t^i\}_{i=1}^{N_T}$, where N_s and N_t are the number of samples from the source and target domains, respectively. Each 2D image x^i is paired with a camera parameter K^i that projects points in 3D space to 2D image plane while y_s^i denotes the label of the corresponding training sample in the specific camera coordinate from the source domain. Label y is in the form of object class k, location (c_x, c_y, c_z), size in each dimension (d_x, d_y, d_z), and orientation θ. We aim to train models with $\{\mathcal{D}_S, \mathcal{D}_T\}$ and avoid performance degradation when evaluating on the target domain.

3.2   Framework Overview

We illustrate our STMono3D in Fig. 2. The labeled source domain data $\{x_S, y_S\}$ is utilized for supervised training of the student model F_S with a loss $\mathcal{L}_S$. In terms of the unlabeled target domain data x_T, we first perturb it by applying a strong random augmentation to obtain $\hat{x}_T$. Before passing to the models, both the target and source domain input are further augmented by the GAMS strategy in Sect. 3.4, where images and camera intrinsic parameters are cautiously aligned via simultaneously rescaling. Subsequently, the original and perturbed images are sent to the teacher and student model, respectively, where the teacher model generates intuitively reasonable pseudo labels $\hat{y}_T$ and supervises the student model via loss $\mathcal{L}_T$ on the target domain:

$$\mathcal{L}_T = \mathcal{L}_T^r + \mathcal{L}_T^c, \tag{1}$$

where $\mathcal{L}_T^r$ and $\mathcal{L}_T^c$ are the regression loss and classification loss, respectively. Here, we adopt the QAS strategy in Sect. 3.5 to further leverage richer information from the teacher model by instance-wise reweighting the loss $\mathcal{L}_T$. In each iteration, the student model is updated through gradient descent with the total loss $\mathcal{L}$, which is a linear combination of $\mathcal{L}_S$ and $\mathcal{L}_T$:

$$\mathcal{L} = \lambda \mathcal{L}_S + \mathcal{L}_T, \tag{2}$$

where λ is the weight coefficient. Then, the teacher model parameters are updated by the corresponding parameters of the student model, where we introduce the details in Sect. 3.3. Moreover, we observe that the teacher model suffers from numerous FN and FP pseudo labels on the target domain. To handle this issue, we utilize the PFT and DT strategies illustrated in Sect. 3.6.

3.3 Self-teacher with Temporal Ensemble

Following the successful trend of the mean teacher paradigm [37] in the semi-supervised learning, we adapt it to our Mono3D UDA task as illustrated in Fig. 2. The teacher model F_T and the student model F_S share the same network architecture but have different parameters θ_T and θ_S, respectively. During the training, the parameters of the teacher model are updated via taking the exponential moving average (EMA) of the student parameters:

$$\theta_T = m\theta_T + (1 - m)\theta_S, \tag{3}$$

where m is the momentum that is commonly set close to 1, $e.g.$, 0.999 in our experiments. Moreover, the input of the student model is perturbed by a strong augmentation, which ensures that the pseudo labels generated by the teacher model are more accurate than the student model predictions, thus providing available optimization directions for the parameter updating. In addition, the strong augmentation can also improve the model generalization to handle the different domain inputs. Hence, by supervising the student model with pseudo targets $\hat{y}_T$ generated by the teacher model ($i.e.$, forcing the consistency between predictions of the student and the teacher model), the student can learn domain-invariant representations to adapt to the unlabeled target domain. Figure 4 shows that the teacher model can provide effective supervision to the student model and Tables 4, 5 demonstrate the effectiveness of the mean teacher paradigm.

3.4   Geometry-Aligned Multi-scale Training

Observation. As shown in Fig. 1, depth-shift drastically harms the quality of pseudo labels on the target domain. It is mainly caused by the domain-specific geometry correspondences between 3D objects and images (*i.e.*, camera imaging process). For instance, since the pixel size (defined in Eq. 6) of the KITTI dataset is larger than the nuScenes dataset, objects in images captured by KITTI cameras are smaller than nuScenes ones. While the model can predict accurate 2D locations on image planes, it tends to estimate relatively more distant object depth based on the cue that far objects tend to be smaller in perspective view. We call the phenomenon depth-shift: models localize accurate 2D location but predict depth with tremendous shifts on the target domain. To mitigate it, we propose a straightforward yet effective augmentation strategy, *i.e.*, *geometry-aligned multi-scale* training, disentangling the camera parameters and detectors and ensuring the geometry consistency in the imaging process.

Method. Given the source input $\{x_S, y_S, K_S\}$ and the target input $\{x_T, K_T\}$, a naive geometry-aligned strategy is to rescale camera parameters to the same constant values and resize images correspondingly:

$$\mathbf{K} = \begin{bmatrix} r_x & r_y & 1 \end{bmatrix} \begin{bmatrix} f_x & 0 & p_x \\ 0 & f_y & p_y \\ 0 & 0 & 1 \end{bmatrix} \tag{4}$$

where r_x and r_y are resize rates, f and p are focal length and optical center, x and y indicate image coordinate axises, respectively. However, since the f/p cannot be changed by resizing, it is impracticable to strictly align the geometry correspondences of 3D objects and images between different domains via convenient transformations. The inevitable discrepancy and ambiguity lead to a failure on UDA.

To solve the issue, motivated by DD3D [31], we propose to predict the *pixel-size depth* d_p instead of the *metric depth* d_g:

$$d_p = \frac{s}{c} \cdot d_g, \tag{5}$$

$$s = \sqrt{\frac{1}{f_x^2} + \frac{1}{f_y^2}}, \tag{6}$$

where s and c are the pixel size and a constant, d_p is the model prediction and is scaled to the final result d_g. Therefore, while there are inevitable discrepancies between aligned geometry correspondences of two domains, the model can infer the depth from the pixel size and be more robust to the various imaging process. Moreover, we further rescale camera parameters into a multi-scale range, instead of the same constant values, and resize images correspondingly to enhance the dynamic of models. During the training, we keep ground-truth 3D bounding boxes y_S and pseudo labels $\hat{y}_T$ unchanged, avoiding changing real 3D scenes.

3.5   Quality-Aware Supervision

Observation. The cross-domain performance of the detector highly depends on the quality of pseudo labels. In practice, we have to utilize a higher threshold on the foreground score to filter out most false positive (FP) box candidates with low confidence. However, unlike the teacher model that can detect objects with high confidence in the semi-supervised 2D detection or UDA of LiDAR-based 3D detector (*e.g.*, the threshold is set to 90% and 70% in [45] and [47], respectively), we find the Mono3D cross-domain teacher **suffers from a much lower confidence** as shown in Fig. 3, which is another unique phenomenon in Mono3D UDA caused by the much worse oracle monocular 3D detection performance than 2D detection and LiDAR-based 3D detection. It indicates that though the prediction confidence surpasses the threshold, we cannot ensure the sample quality, much less for the ones near the threshold. To alleviate the impact, we propose the *quality-aware supervision* (QAS) to leverage richer information from the teacher and take instance-level quality into account.

Method. Thanks to the flexibility of the end-to-end mean teacher framework, we assess the reliability of each teacher-generated bbox to be a real foreground, which is then used to weight the foreground classification loss of the student model. Given the foreground bounding box set $\{b_i^{fg}\}_{i=1}^{N^{fg}}$, the classification loss of the unlabeled images on the target domain is defined as:

$$\mathcal{L}_T^c = \frac{\mu}{N^{fg}} \sum_{i=1}^{N^{fg}} w_i \cdot l_{cls}(b_i^{fg}, \mathcal{G}_{cls}), \tag{7}$$

where $\mathcal{G}_{cls}$ denotes the set of pseudo class labels, l_{cls} is the box classification loss, w_i is the confidence score for i^{th} foreground pseudo boxes, N^{fg} is the number of foreground pseudo box, and μ is a constant hyperparameter.

The QAS resembles a *simple positive mining* strategy, which is intuitively reasonable that there should be more severe punishment for pseudo labels with higher confidence. Moreover, compared with semi-supervised and supervised tasks that focus on simple/hard negative samples [6,45], it is more critical for UDA Mono3D models to prevent harmful influence caused by low-quality pseudo labels near the threshold. Such an instance-level weighting strategy balances the loss terms based on foreground confidence scores and significantly improves the effectiveness of STMono3D.

3.6   Crucial Training Strategies

Positive Focusing Training. Since the whole STMono3D is trained in an end-to-end manner, the teacher model can hardly detect objects with confident scores higher than the threshold at the start of the training. Tons of FN pseudo samples impair the capability of the model to recognize objects. Because backgrounds of different domains are similar with negligible domain gaps in Mono3D UDA (*e.g.*, street, sky, and house), we propose the *positive focusing training* strategy. As

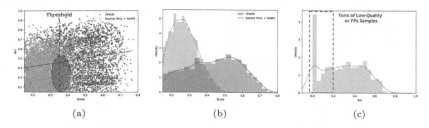

(a)   (b)   (c)

Fig. 3. (a) Correlation between confidence value and box IoU with ground-truth. (b) Distribution of confidence scores. The teacher suffers from low scores on the target domain. (c) Distribution of IoU between ground-truth and pseudo labels near the threshold (0.35–0.4). We highlight the existence of numerous low-quality and FP samples in these pseudo labels.

for the $\mathcal{L}_T^c$, we discard negative background pseudo labels and only utilize the positive samples to supervise the student model, which ensures that the model does not crash to overfit on the FN pseudo labels during the training stage.

Dynamic Threshold. In practice, we find that the mean confidence score of pseudo labels gradually increases in synchronization within training duration. Increasing false positive (FP) samples appear in the middle and late stages of training, which harshly hurts the model performance. While the QAS strategy proposed in Sect. 3.5 can reduce the negative impact of low-quality pseudo labels, the completely wrong predictions still introduce inevitable noise to the training process. To alleviate the issue, we propose a simple *progressively increasing threshold* strategy to dynamic change the threshold τ as:

$$\tau = \begin{cases} \alpha, & iter < n_1, \\ \alpha + k \cdot (iter - n_1), & n_1 \leqslant iter < n_2, \\ \alpha + k \cdot (n_2 - n_1), & iter \geqslant n_2, \end{cases} \tag{8}$$

where α is the base threshold that is set to 0.35 based on the statistics in Fig. 3(a) in our experiments, k is the slope of increasing threshold, *iter* is the iteration of training stage. The threshold is fixed to a minimum during the first n warmup steps as the teacher model can hardly detect objects with confident scores higher than the base threshold. It then linearly increases after the teacher model predicts pseudo labels with FP samples to avoid the model being blemished by increasing failure predictions. Finally, we find that the increasing of average scores tends to a saturation. Therefore, the threshold is fixed at the end of the training stage to guarantee the number of pseudo labels.

Table 1. Dataset Overview. We focus on their properties related to frontal-view cameras and 3D object detection. The dataset size refers to the number of images used in training stage. For Waymo and nuScenes, we subsample the data. See text for details.

Dataset	Size	Anno.	Loc.	Shape	FOV	Objects	Night
KITTI [16]	3712	17297	EUR	(375, 1242)	$(29°, 81°)$	8	No
nuScenes [3]	27522	252427	SG.,EUR	(900, 1600)	$(39°, 65°)$	23	Yes
Lyft [20]	21623	139793	SG.,EUR	(1024, 1224)	$(60°, 70°)$	9	No

4   Experiments

4.1   Experimental Setup

Datasets. We conduct experiments on three widely used autonomous driving datasets: KITTI [16], nuScenes [3], and Lyft [20]. Two aspects are lying in our experiments: Cross domains with different cameras (existing in all the source-target pairs) and adaptation from label rich domains to insufficient domains (*i.e.*, nuScenes→KITTI). We summarize the dataset information in detail in Table 1, and present more visualization comparisons in the *supplementary material*.

Comparison Methods. In our experiments, we compare STMono3D with three methods: (*i*) **Source Only** indicates directly evaluating the source domain trained model on the target domain. (*ii*) **Oracle** indicates the fully supervised model trained on the target domain. (*iii*) **Naive ST (with GAMS)** is the basic self-training method. We first train a model (with GAMS) on the source domain, then generate pseudo labels for the target domain, and finally fine-tuning the trained model on the target domain.

Evaluation Metric. We adopt the KITTI evaluation metric for evaluating our methods in nuScenes→KITTI and Lyft→KITTI and the NuScenes metric for Lyft→nuScenes. We focus on the commonly used car category in our experiments. For Lyft→nuScenes, we evaluate models on ring view, which is more useful in real-world applications. For KITTI, We report the average precision (AP) where the IoU thresholds are 0.5 for both the bird's eye view (BEV) IoUs and 3D IoUs. For nuScenes, since the attribute labels are different from the source domain (*i.e.*, Lyft), we discard the average attribute error (mAAE) and report the average trans error (mATE), scale error (mASE), orient error (mAOE), and average precision (mAP). Following [47], we report the closed performance gap between Source Only to Oracle.

Implementation Details. We validate our proposed STMono3D on detection backbone FCOS3D [40]. Since there is no modification to the model, our method can be adapted to other Mono3D backbones as well. We implement STMono3D based on the popular 3D object detection codebase mmDetection3D [11]. We utilize SGD [22] optimizer. Gradient clip and warm-up policy are exploited with

Table 2. Performance of STMono3D on three source-target pairs. We report AP of the car category at IoU = 0.5 as well as the domain gap closed by STMono3D. In nus→KITTI, STMono3D achieves a even better results on AP_{11} compared with the Oracle model, which demonstrates the effectiveness of our proposed method.

nus→K	AP_{11}						AP_{40}					
Method	AP_{BEV} IoU $\geqslant$ 0.5			AP_{3D} IoU $\geqslant$ 0.5			AP_{BEV} IoU $\geqslant$ 0.5			AP_{3D} IoU $\geqslant$ 0.5		
	Easy	Mod.	Hard	Easy	Mod.	Hard	Easy	Mod.	Hard	Easy	Mod.	Hard
Source Only	0	0	0	0	0	0	0	0	0	0	0	0
Oracle	33.46	23.62	22.18	29.01	19.88	17.17	33.70	23.22	20.68	28.33	18.97	16.57
STMono3D	35.63	27.37	23.95	28.65	21.89	19.55	31.85	22.82	19.30	24.00	16.85	13.66
Closed Gap	106.5%	115.8%	107.9%	98.7%	110.1%	113.8%	94.5%	98.2%	93.3%	84.7%	88.8%	82.4%

L→K	AP_{11}						L→nus	Metrics			
Method	AP_{BEV} IoU $\geqslant$ 0.5			AP_{3D} IoU $\geqslant$ 0.5			Method	AP	ATE	ASE	AOE
	Easy	Mod.	Hard	Easy	Mod.	Hard					
Source Only	0	0	0	0	0	0	Source Only	2.40	1.302	0.190	0.802
Oracle	33.46	23.62	22.18	29.01	19.88	17.17	Oracle	28.2	0.798	0.160	0.209
STMono3D	26.46	20.71	17.66	18.14	13.32	11.83	STMono3D	21.3	0.911	0.170	0.355
Closed Gap	79.0%	87.6%	79.6%	62.5%	67.0%	68.8%	Closed Gap	73.2%	77.5%	66.7%	82.9%

Table 3. Ablation study of the geometry-aligned multi-scale training.

Nus→K	AP_{11}						AP_{40}					
GAMS	AP_{BEV} IoU $\geqslant$ 0.5			AP_{3D} IoU $\geqslant$ 0.5			AP_{BEV} IoU $\geqslant$ 0.5			AP_{3D} IoU $\geqslant$ 0.5		
	Easy	Mod.	Hard	Easy	Mod.	Hard	Easy	Mod.	Hard	Easy	Mod.	Hard
	0	0	0	0	0	0	0	0	0	0	0	0
$\checkmark$	35.63	27.37	23.95	28.65	21.89	19.55	31.85	22.82	19.30	24.00	16.85	13.66

the learning rate 2×10^{-2}, the number of warm-up iterations 500, warm-up ratio 0.33, and batch size 32 on 8 T V100s. The loss weight λ of different domains in Eq. 2 is set to 1. We apply a momentum m of 0.999 in Eq. 3 following most of mean teacher paradigms [27,45]. As for the strong augmentation, we adopt the widely used image data augmentation, including random flipping, random erase, random toning, *etc.*. We subsample $\frac{1}{4}$ dataset during the training stage of NuScenes and Lyft dataset for simplicity. Notably, unlike the mean teacher paradigm or the self-training strategy used in UDA of LiDAR-based 3D detector [27,47], our STMono3D is trained in a *totally end-to-end* manner.

4.2 Main Results

As shown in Table 2, we compare the performance of our STMono3D with Source Only and Oracle. Our method outperforms the Source Only baseline on all evaluated UDA settings. Caused by the domain gap, the Source Only model cannot detect 3D objects where the mAP almost drops to 0%. Otherwise, STMono3D improves the performance on nuScenes→KITTI and Lyft→KITTI tasks by a large margin that around 110%/67% performance gap of AP_{3D} are closed. Notably, the AP_{BEV} and AP_{3D} of $AP_{11}, IoU \geqslant 0.5$ of STMono3D surpass the Oracle results, which indicates the effectiveness of our method. Furthermore, when transferring Lyft models to other domains that have full ring view annotations for evaluation (*i.e.*, Lyft→nuScenes), our STMono3D also attains a considerable performance gain which closes the Oracle and Source Only performance gap by up to 66% on AP_{3D}.

4.3   Ablation Studies and Analysis

In this section, we conduct extensive ablation experiments to investigate the individual components of our STMono3D. All experiments are conducted on the task of nuScenes→KITTI.

Effective of Geometry-Aligned Multi-scale Training. We study the effects of GAMS in the mean teacher paradigm of STMono3D and the Naive ST pipeline. Table 3 first reports the experimental results when GAMS is disabled. Caused by the depth-shift analyzed in Sect. 3.4, the teacher model generates incorrect pseudo labels on the target domain, thus leading to a severe drop in model performance. Furthermore, as shown in Table 4, GAMS is crucial for effective Naive ST as well. It is reasonable that GAMS supports the model trained on the source domain to generate valid pseudo labels on the target domain, making the fine-tuning stage helpful for the model performance. We present pseudo labels predicted by the teacher model of STMono3D in Fig. 1, which shows that the depth-shift is well alleviated. All the results highlight the importance of GAMS for effective Mono3D UDA.

Comparison of Self-training Paradigm. We compare our STMono3D with other commonly used self-training paradigms (*i.e.*, Naive ST) in Table 4. While the GAMS helps the Naive ST teacher generate effective pseudo labels on the target domain to boost UDA performance, our STMono3D still outperforms it by a significant margin. One of the primary concerns lies in low-quality pseudo

Table 4. Comparison of different self-training paradigms.

Nus→K	KITTI AP_{11}						Nus Metrics			
Method	AP_{BEV} IoU $\geqslant 0.5$			AP_{3D} IoU $\geqslant 0.5$			AP	ATE	ASE	AOE
	Easy	Mod.	Hard	Easy	Mod.	Hard				
Naive ST	0	0	0	0	0	0	–	–	–	–
Naive ST with GAMS	9.05	9.08	8.82	3.72	3.69	3.58	14.0	0.906	0.164	0.264
STMono3D	35.63	27.37	23.95	28.65	21.89	19.55	36.5	0.731	0.160	0.167

Table 5. Ablation study of the exponential moving average strategy.

Nus→K	AP_{11}						AP_{40}					
EMA	AP_{BEV} IoU $\geqslant 0.5$			AP_{3D} IoU $\geqslant 0.5$			AP_{BEV} IoU $\geqslant 0.5$			AP_{3D} IoU $\geqslant 0.5$		
	Easy	Mod.	Hard	Easy	Mod.	Hard	Easy	Mod.	Hard	Easy	Mod.	Hard
	2.55	2.41	2.38	0.82	0.82	0.82	0.45	0.31	0.25	0.06	0.03	0.02
√	35.63	27.37	23.95	28.65	21.89	19.55	31.85	22.82	19.30	24.00	16.85	13.66

Table 6. Ablation study of QAS on different loss terms.

Nus→K		AP_{11}						AP_{40}					
L_T^{reg}	L_T^{cls}	AP_{BEV} IoU $\geqslant 0.5$			AP_{3D} IoU $\geqslant 0.5$			AP_{BEV} IoU $\geqslant 0.5$			AP_{3D} IoU $\geqslant 0.5$		
		Easy	Mod.	Hard	Easy	Mod.	Hard	Easy	Mod.	Hard	Easy	Mod.	Hard
		26.33	21.92	19.57	21.17	18.14	16.46	21.66	16.64	14.03	15.55	12.06	9.88
✓		21.50	17.57	15.35	16.57	13.80	11.34	20.47	15.77	13.12	15.32	11.69	9.35
	✓	35.63	27.37	23.95	28.65	21.89	19.55	31.85	22.82	19.30	24.00	16.85	13.66
✓	✓	21.74	19.56	17.22	18.09	15.67	14.71	16.01	13.26	11.15	10.89	9.22	7.49

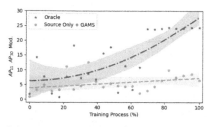 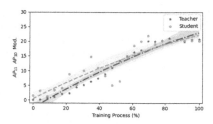

(a) Oracle *v.s.* Source Only + GAMS   (b) STMono3D Teacher *v.s.* Student

Fig. 4. Performance comparision. (a) Oracle *v.s.* Source Only with GAMS: While the Oracle performance progressively improves, the Source Only model suffers from a drasical performance fluctuation. (b) Mean Teacher *v.s.* Student on the target domain: Not only does the teacher model outperforms the student at the end of the training phase, its performance curve is also smoother and more stable.

labels caused by the domain gap. Moreover, as shown in Fig. 4(a), while the performance of Oracle improves progressively, the Source Only model on the target domain suffers from a performance fluctuation. It is also troublesome to choose a specific and suitable model from immediate results to generate pseudo labels for the student model.

In terms of our STMono3D, the whole framework is trained in an end-to-end manner. The teacher is a temporal ensemble of student models at different time stamps. Figure 4(b) shows that our teacher model is much more stable compared with the ones in Naive ST and has a better performance than the student model at the end of the training phase, where the teacher model starts to generate more predictions over the filtering score threshold. This validates our analysis in Sect. 3.3 that the mean teacher paradigm provides a more effective teacher model for pseudo label generation. Table 5 demonstrates the effectiveness of the EMA of STMono3D. The performance significantly degrades when the EMA is disabled, and the model is easily crashed during the training stage.

Effective of Quality-Aware Supervision. We study the effects of different applied loss terms of the proposed QAS strategy. Generally, the loss terms of Mono3D can be divided into two categories: (*i*) $\mathcal{L}_{cls}$ containing the object classification loss and attribute classification loss, and (*ii*) $\mathcal{L}_{reg}$ consisting of the location loss, dimension loss, and orientation loss. We separately apply the

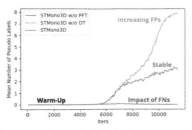

(a) Num. of pseudo labels during training

(b) Visualization examples

Fig. 5. Effects of the proposed DFT and DT. (a) Correlation between the average of the number of pseudo labels and training iters. (b) Examples of harmful FN and FP pseudo labels caused by disabling DFT and DT, respectively.

Table 7. Ablation study of PFT and DT.

Nus→K		AP_{11}						AP_{40}					
PFT	DT	AP_{BEV} IoU $\geqslant 0.5$			AP_{3D} IoU $\geqslant 0.5$			AP_{BEV} IoU $\geqslant 0.5$			AP_{3D} IoU $\geqslant 0.5$		
		Easy	Mod.	Hard	Easy	Mod.	Hard	Easy	Mod.	Hard	Easy	Mod.	Hard
		13.57	11.33	10.31	9.10	7.80	7.00	12.36	9.42	8.03	7.82	5.82	5.08
√		19.59	16.00	14.35	15.96	13.15	12.23	13.44	9.76	7.90	9.23	6.52	5.13
	√	18.90	16.57	15.75	15.15	13.73	12.85	12.74	10.35	9.42	8.41	6.81	5.96
√	√	35.63	27.37	23.95	28.65	21.89	19.55	31.85	22.82	19.30	24.00	16.85	13.66

QAS on these two kinds of losses and report the corresponding results in Table 6. Interestingly, utilizing the confidence score from the teacher to reweight the $\mathcal{L}_{reg}$ cannot improve the model performance. We speculate it is caused by a loose correlation between the IoU score and localization quality (see yellow or blue line in Fig. 3(a)), which is in line with the findings in LiDAR-based method [47]. However, we find QAS is more applicable for the $\mathcal{L}_{cls}$, where the model performance increases about 20.6% AP_{3D}. It indicates the effectiveness of our proposed QAS strategy. It is intuitively reasonable since the score of pseudo labels itself is used to measure the confidence of predicted object classification.

Effective of Crucial Training Strategies. We then further investigate the effectiveness of our proposed PFT and DT strategies. We first present the ablation results in Table 7. When we disable the strategies, model performance suffers from drastic degradations, where AP_{3D} drops 64.3%. The results demonstrate they are crucial strategies in STMono3D. As shown in Fig. 5(a), we also present the influence of them in a more intuitive manner. If we disable the PFT, the model will be severely impaired by the numerous FN predcitions (shown in Fig. 5(b) top) in the warm-up stage, leading to a failure to recognize objects in the following training iterations. On the other hand, for the teacher model w/o DT, the number of predictions abruptly increases at the end of training process, introducing more FPs predictions (shown in Fig. 5(b) down) that are harmful to the model perfomance.

5   Conclusion

In this paper, we have presented STMono3D, a meticulously designed unsupervised domain adaptation framework tailored for monocular 3D object detection task. We investigate that the depth-shift caused by the geometry discrepancy of domains leads to a drastic performance degradation when cross-domain inference. To alleviate the issue, we leverages a teacher-student paradigm for pseudo label generation and propose quality-aware supervision, positive focusing training and dynamic threshold to handle the difficulty in Mono3D UDA. Extensive experimental results demonstrate the effectiveness of STMono3D.

Acknowledgment. The research was supported by the National Natural Science Foundation of China (61971165, 61922027), and also is supported by the Fundamental Research Funds for the Central Universities.

References

1. Ben-David, S., Blitzer, J., Crammer, K., Kulesza, A., Pereira, F., Vaughan, J.W.: A theory of learning from different domains. Mach. Learn. **79**(1), 151–175 (2010)
2. Brazil, G., Liu, X.: M3D-RPN: monocular 3D region proposal network for object detection. In: International Conference on Computer Vision (ICCV), pp. 9287–9296 (2019)
3. Caesar, H., et al.: nuScenes: a multimodal dataset for autonomous driving. In: Computer Vision and Pattern Recognition (CVPR), pp. 11621–11631 (2020)
4. Carion, N., Massa, F., Synnaeve, G., Usunier, N., Kirillov, A., Zagoruyko, S.: End-to-end object detection with transformers. In: Vedaldi, A., Bischof, H., Brox, T., Frahm, J.-M. (eds.) ECCV 2020. LNCS, vol. 12346, pp. 213–229. Springer, Cham (2020). https://doi.org/10.1007/978-3-030-58452-8_13
5. Carlucci, F.M., Porzi, L., Caputo, B., Ricci, E., Bulo, S.R.: Autodial: Automatic domain alignment layers. In: International Conference on Computer Vision (ICCV), pp. 5077–5085. IEEE (2017)
6. Chen, X., Yuan, Y., Zeng, G., Wang, J.: Semi-supervised semantic segmentation with cross pseudo supervision. In: Computer Vision and Pattern Recognition (CVPR), pp. 2613–2622 (2021)
7. Chen, X., Kundu, K., Zhang, Z., Ma, H., Fidler, S., Urtasun, R.: Monocular 3D object detection for autonomous driving. In: Computer Vision and Pattern Recognition (CVPR), pp. 2147–2156 (2016)
8. Chen, X., et al.: 3D object proposals for accurate object class detection. In: Advances in Neural Information Processing Systems (NIPS) 28 (2015)
9. Chen, Y., Li, W., Sakaridis, C., Dai, D., Van Gool, L.: Domain adaptive faster R-CNN for object detection in the wild. In: Computer Vision and Pattern Recognition (CVPR), pp. 3339–3348 (2018)
10. Chen, Z., Li, Z., Zhang, S., Fang, L., Jiang, Q., Zhao, F.: Graph-DETR3D: rethinking overlapping regions for multi-view 3D object detection. arXiv preprint arXiv:2204.11582 (2022)
11. Contributors, M.: MMDetection3D: OpenMMLab next-generation platform for general 3D object detection. https://github.com/open-mmlab/mmdetection3d (2020)

12. Dubourvieux, F., Audigier, R., Loesch, A., Ainouz, S., Canu, S.: Unsupervised domain adaptation for person re-identification through source-guided pseudo-labeling. In: International Conference on Pattern Recognition (ICPR), pp. 4957–4964 (2021)
13. Ganin, Y., Lempitsky, V.: Unsupervised domain adaptation by backpropagation. In: International Conference on Machine Learning (ICML), pp. 1180–1189. PMLR (2015)
14. Ganin, Y., et al.: Domain-adversarial training of neural networks. J. Mach. Learn. Res. (JMLR) **17**(1), 2030–2096 (2016)
15. Ge, Y., et al.: Self-paced contrastive learning with hybrid memory for domain adaptive object Re-ID. Adv. Neural Inf. Process. Syst. (NIPS) **33**, 11309–11321 (2020)
16. Geiger, A., Lenz, P., Urtasun, R.: Are we ready for autonomous driving? the kitti vision benchmark suite. In: Computer Vision and Pattern Recognition (CVPR), pp. 3354–3361 (2012)
17. Goodfellow, I., et al.: Generative adversarial nets. In: Advances in Neural Information Processing Systems (NIPS) 27 (2014)
18. Gulrajani, I., Ahmed, F., Arjovsky, M., Dumoulin, V., Courville, A.C.: Improved training of wasserstein GANs. In: Advances in Neural Information Processing Systems (NIPS) 30 (2017)
19. Hoffman, J., Wang, D., Yu, F., Darrell, T.: FCNs in the wild: pixel-level adversarial and constraint-based adaptation. arXiv preprint arXiv:1612.02649 (2016)
20. Kesten, R., et al.: Level 5 perception dataset 2020. https://level-5.global/level5/data/ (2019)
21. Khodabandeh, M., Vahdat, A., Ranjbar, M., Macready, W.G.: A robust learning approach to domain adaptive object detection. In: International Conference on Computer Vision (ICCV), pp. 480–490 (2019)
22. Kingma, D.P., Ba, J.: Adam: a method for stochastic optimization. arXiv preprint arXiv:1412.6980 (2014)
23. Li, Y., Wang, N., Shi, J., Hou, X., Liu, J.: Adaptive batch normalization for practical domain adaptation. Pattern Recogn. (PR) **80**, 109–117 (2018)
24. Li, Z., et al.: SimIPU: simple 2d image and 3D point cloud unsupervised pre-training for spatial-aware visual representations. In: Proceedings of the AAAI Conference on Artificial Intelligence, vol. 36, pp. 1500–1508 (2022)
25. Liu, Z., Wu, Z., Tóth, R.: Smoke: single-stage monocular 3D object detection via keypoint estimation. In: Computer Vision and Pattern Recognition Workshops (CVPRW), pp. 996–997 (2020)
26. Long, M., Cao, Y., Wang, J., Jordan, M.: Learning transferable features with deep adaptation networks. In: International Conference on Machine Learning (ICML), pp. 97–105 (2015)
27. Luo, Z., et al.: Unsupervised domain adaptive 3d detection with multi-level consistency. In: International Conference on Computer Vision (ICCV), pp. 8866–8875 (2021)
28. Mancini, M., Porzi, L., Bulo, S.R., Caputo, B., Ricci, E.: Boosting domain adaptation by discovering latent domains. In: Computer Vision and Pattern Recognition (CVPR), pp. 3771–3780 (2018)
29. Mao, J., Shi, S., Wang, X., Li, H.: 3D object detection for autonomous driving: a review and new outlooks. arXiv preprint arXiv:2206.09474 (2022)
30. Mousavian, A., Anguelov, D., Flynn, J., Kosecka, J.: 3D bounding box estimation using deep learning and geometry. In: Computer Vision and Pattern Recognition (CVPR), pp. 7074–7082 (2017)

31. Park, D., Ambrus, R., Guizilini, V., Li, J., Gaidon, A.: Is pseudo-lidar needed for monocular 3d object detection? In: International Conference on Computer Vision (ICCV), pp. 3142–3152 (2021)
32. Reading, C., Harakeh, A., Chae, J., Waslander, S.L.: Categorical depth distribution network for monocular 3D object detection. In: Computer Vision and Pattern Recognition (CVPR), pp. 8555–8564 (2021)
33. Roddick, T., Kendall, A., Cipolla, R.: Orthographic feature transform for monocular 3D object detection. arXiv preprint arXiv:1811.08188 (2018)
34. Saito, K., Ushiku, Y., Harada, T.: Asymmetric tri-training for unsupervised domain adaptation. In: International Conference on Machine Learning (ICML), pp. 2988–2997. PMLR (2017)
35. Saito, K., Ushiku, Y., Harada, T., Saenko, K.: Strong-weak distribution alignment for adaptive object detection. In: Computer Vision and Pattern Recognition (CVPR), pp. 6956–6965 (2019)
36. Sun, B., Saenko, K.: Deep CORAL: correlation alignment for deep domain adaptation. In: Hua, G., Jégou, H. (eds.) ECCV 2016. LNCS, vol. 9915, pp. 443–450. Springer, Cham (2016). https://doi.org/10.1007/978-3-319-49409-8_35
37. Tarvainen, A., Valpola, H.: Mean teachers are better role models: weight-averaged consistency targets improve semi-supervised deep learning results. In: Advances in neural information processing systems (NIPS) 30 (2017)
38. Tzeng, E., Hoffman, J., Darrell, T., Saenko, K.: Simultaneous deep transfer across domains and tasks. In: International Conference on Computer Vision (ICCV), pp. 4068–4076 (2015)
39. Wang, T., Xinge, Z., Pang, J., Lin, D.: Probabilistic and geometric depth: detecting objects in perspective. In: Conference on Robot Learning (CoRL), pp. 1475–1485 (2022)
40. Wang, T., Zhu, X., Pang, J., Lin, D.: Fcos3d: fully convolutional one-stage monocular 3d object detection. In: International Conference on Computer Vision Workshop (ICCVW), pp. 913–922 (2021)
41. Wang, X., Jin, Y., Long, M., Wang, J., Jordan, M.I.: Transferable normalization: towards improving transferability of deep neural networks. In: Advances in Neural Information Processing Systems (NIPS) 32 (2019)
42. Wang, Y., Guizilini, V.C., Zhang, T., Wang, Y., Zhao, H., Solomon, J.: DETR3D: 3D object detection from multi-view images via 3D-to-2D queries. In: Conference on Robot Learning (CoRL), pp. 180–191 (2022)
43. Weng, X., Kitani, K.: Monocular 3D object detection with pseudo-lidar point cloud. In: International Conference on Computer Vision Workshops (ICCVW) (2019)
44. Xu, B., Chen, Z.: Multi-level fusion based 3D object detection from monocular images. In: Computer Vision and Pattern Recognition (CVPR), pp. 2345–2353 (2018)
45. Xu, M., et al.: End-to-end semi-supervised object detection with soft teacher. In: International Conference on Computer Vision (ICCV), pp. 3060–3069 (2021)
46. Yang, J., Shi, S., Wang, Z., Li, H., Qi, X.: ST3D++: denoised self-training for unsupervised domain adaptation on 3D object detection. arXiv preprint arXiv:2108.06682 (2021)
47. Yang, J., Shi, S., Wang, Z., Li, H., Qi, X.: ST3D: self-training for unsupervised domain adaptation on 3D object detection. In: Computer Vision and Pattern Recognition (CVPR), pp. 10368–10378 (2021)

48. Zhang, W., Li, W., Xu, D.: SRDAN: scale-aware and range-aware domain adaptation network for cross-dataset 3D object detection. In: Computer Vision and Pattern Recognition (CVPR), pp. 6769–6779 (2021)
49. Zou, Y., Yu, Z., Vijaya Kumar, B.V.K., Wang, J.: Unsupervised domain adaptation for semantic segmentation via class-balanced self-training. In: Ferrari, V., Hebert, M., Sminchisescu, C., Weiss, Y. (eds.) ECCV 2018. LNCS, vol. 11207, pp. 297–313. Springer, Cham (2018). https://doi.org/10.1007/978-3-030-01219-9_18

SuperLine3D: Self-supervised Line Segmentation and Description for LiDAR Point Cloud

Xiangrui Zhao[1,2] , Sheng Yang[2], Tianxin Huang[1], Jun Chen[1], Teng Ma[2], Mingyang Li[2], and Yong Liu[1(✉)]

[1] APRIL Lab, Zhejiang University, Hangzhou, Zhejiang, China
{xiangruizhao,21725129,junc}@zju.edu.cn, yongliu@iipc.zju.edu.cn
[2] Autonomous Driving Lab, DAMO Academy, Hangzhou, Zhejiang, China
damon.mt@alibaba-inc.com

Abstract. Poles and building edges are frequently observable objects on urban roads, conveying reliable hints for various computer vision tasks. To repetitively extract them as features and perform association between discrete LiDAR frames for registration, we propose the first learning-based feature segmentation and description model for 3D lines in LiDAR point cloud. To train our model without the time consuming and tedious data labeling process, we first generate synthetic primitives for the basic appearance of target lines, and build an iterative line auto-labeling process to gradually refine line labels on real LiDAR scans. Our segmentation model can extract lines under arbitrary scale perturbations, and we use shared EdgeConv encoder layers to train the two segmentation and descriptor heads jointly. Base on the model, we can build a highly-available global registration module for point cloud registration, in conditions without initial transformation hints. Experiments have demonstrated that our line-based registration method is highly competitive to state-of-the-art point-based approaches. Our code is available at https://github.com/zxrzju/SuperLine3D.git.

Keywords: 3D Line Feature · Point cloud registration

1 Introduction

Point cloud registration is an essential technique for LiDAR-based vehicle localization on urban road scenes [28]. Considering recent researches [15,18], the SLAM community [19] divides these algorithms into two categories regarding their purpose, as *local* and *global* search methods, respectively. The *local* search category [6,7] typically constructs a non-convex optimization problem by greedily associating nearest entities to align. This often relies on a good initial guess, and thus mostly used for incremental positioning modules such as the LiDAR odometry [41]

Supplementary Information The online version contains supplementary material available at https://doi.org/10.1007/978-3-031-20077-9_16.

and map-based localization [32]. The *global* search category is used for less informative conditions, i.e., relocalization and map initialization problems when the initial guess is not reliable and large positional and rotational change exists. Since nearest neighbor search methods cannot find correct matching pairs in the Euclidean space, *global* search algorithms choose to extract distinct entities and construct feature descriptors [45], to establish matches in the description space.

There exists a variety of classical hand-crafted features (e.g., FPFH [33]) for global search and registration, and recent learning-based methods [43] have improved the registration accuracy and success rate. However, the performance of some methods [25, 27] severely drops when adapting to real LiDAR scans, because the density of scanned points is inversely proportional to the scanning distance, and thus influences the coherence of point description. Considering such limitation of a single point, we propose an idea of using structural lines, analogously as previous approaches proposed for images [16, 40], to see whether a relatively stable descriptor can be concluded through a semantically meaningful group of scattered points.

In typical LiDAR point cloud scanned from urban road scenes, there are three categories of lines. 1) Intersection of planes, e.g., edge of two building facades and curbs. 2) Standalone pole objects, e.g., street lamps and road signs alongside the road. 3) Virtual line consists of edge points across multiple scan rings, generated by ray-obstacle occlusions. While the last category is not repeatable and thus inappropriate for localization, the first two types are practical landmarks suitable to be extracted and described. Since these line segments are larger targets compared to point features, they have a higher chance to be repeatably observed. Moreover, the concluded position of each line is more precise to a single corresponding point between frames due to the limited scanning resolution, which causes sampling issues.

In this paper, we propose a self-supervised learning method for line segmentation and description on LiDAR scans (Fig. 1). Following the training procedure of SuperPoint [11] to solve the lack of publicly available training data, we choose to train our line extraction model, by first construct limited synthetic data and then perform auto labeling on real scans. By sharing point cloud encoding layers and use two separate branches for decoding and application headers, we are able to jointly train two tasks on those generated data. We view such a pipeline to train and use line features for the scan registration purpose as the key contribution of our work, which includes:

- From the best of our knowledge, we propose the first learning-based line segmentation and description for LiDAR scans, bringing up an applicable feature category for global registration.
- We propose a line segment labeling method for point clouds, which can migrate the model learned from synthetic data to real LiDAR scans for automatic labeling.
- We explore the scale invariance of point cloud features, and provide a feasible idea for improving the generalization of learning-based tasks on the point cloud under scale perturbations by eliminating the scale factor in Sim(3) transformation.

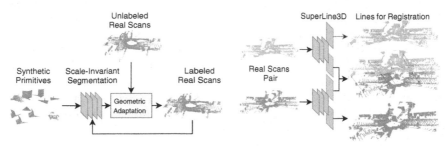

(a) Automatic Line Segments Labeling   (b) Line Segmentation and Description

Fig. 1. Pipeline overview. a): We train a scale-invariant segmentation on the synthetic data and get the precise line segment labels after multiple geometric adaptation iterations. b): We simultaneously train segmentation and description on labeled LiDAR scans, where red, purple, and green layers stand for encoders, segmentation header, and description header, respectively (Color figure online).

Extensive experimental results have shown that our line-based registration can maintain high success rate and accuracy under large-angle perturbations, and the trained model on one real scans dataset is highly adaptable to other urban scene datasets.

2 Related Work

Learning-Based Point Cloud Registration. In recent researches, there are a variety of learning-based approaches proposed for registering point clouds, and we can divide them into two groups considering whether explicit features have been extracted. End-to-end approaches use ground-truth transformation in loss calculation, and predict the transformation directly through the network: FMR [17] registers point clouds by minimizing feature-metric loss, and PCR-Net [34] evaluate the similarity of PointNet [30] features and regresses poses through fully connected layers directly. These trained end-to-end models work well on tested sequences, but they are facing a practical problem on how to perform a joint state estimation in a multi-sensor fusion system [12]. Nevertheless, knowledge of these models are hardly adaptable to different motion scheme and other datasets. Therefore, methods with explicit feature extraction and description are still an active branch in the SLAM community.

Registration with Explicit Features. Start with hand-crafted features (e.g., FPFH [33] and ISS [44]) concluding local patch appearances of point clouds, methods of extracting and describing explicit features mainly aim at the saliency of entities and coherency of description. While hand-crafted features are mostly designed for evenly sampled clouds, learning-based features [4,9,10,21,22,25] have better robustness and generalization, once trained on the target LiDAR scan datasets. D3Feat [5] uses kernel-based convolution [36] to learn feature detection and description. SpinNet [3] builds a rotation-invariant local surface descriptor through novel spatial point transformer and 3D cylindrical convolutional layer. Both D3Feat [5] and SpinNet [3] are state-of-the-art learning-based point features, but they still suffer from the inherent problem of point features, and thus requires sample consensus as a post pruning procedure to filter correct feature associations.

Line Features for SLAM. Image based line-aware approaches for detection (e.g., LSD [37], EDLines [2], and TP-LSD [16]), description (e.g., LBD [42] and SOLD2 [26]), and systematical SLAM designs (e.g., PL-SLAM [29]) have been well studied in recent years, whereas LiDAR scan based extraction and description methods, although heavily used in modern LiDAR SLAM approaches (e.g., LOAM [41] and LeGO-LOAM [35]), are under explored. To the best of our knowledge, we found Lu et al. [24] have proposed a 3D line detection method through projecting LiDAR points onto image, and thus convert the task into a 2D detection problem. Chen et al. [8] based on this work [24] to carry out a line-based registration approach for structural scenes. However, their limitations are two folds: 1) only work on organized point clouds, and 2) have not addressed line description and thus not suitable for global search registration problems. In contrast, we follow the idea of descriptor conclusion from SOLD2 [26], which has been proven to be useful in our paper for the coherency of describing a group of points.

3   Method

Considering the lack of available labeled line datasets of LiDAR scans, we follow the self-supervised idea of SuperPoint [11], to train our line segmentation model, by first constructing a simple synthetic data to initialize a base model, and then refining the model iteratively with auto-labeled real LiDAR scans from geometric adaptation (Sect. 3.1). After that, we gather line correspondences between different LiDAR scans, and jointly train the line segmentation and description in an end-to-end approach (Sect. 3.2).

3.1   Line Segmentation Model

Synthetic Data Generation. As discussed above in Sect. 1, there are two types of reliable line segments to detect: 1) intersection between planes, and 2) poles. Hence, we choose to use the following two mesh primitives shown in Fig. 2(a) for simulating their local appearances, respectively. These two mesh models are first uniformly sampled into 4,000 points as Fig. 2(b), with 5% relative 3-DOF positional perturbation added for each point. Then, to simulate possible background points nearby, we randomly cropped 40 basic primitives with each containing 1,000 points from real scans [14], and put them together to compose the final synthetic data. In total, we generated 5,000 synthetic point clouds with 5,000 points per each cloud.

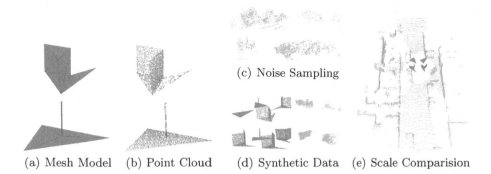

(a) Mesh Model   (b) Point Cloud   (c) Noise Sampling   (d) Synthetic Data   (e) Scale Comparision

Fig. 2. Synthetic data generation steps. We generate synthetic data through sampling primitive mesh models and augmenting real scan scattered points as noises.

Scale-Invariant Line Segmentation. We treat line detection as a point cloud segmentation problem, and the main challenge is the primitive scaling issue: In a real LiDAR frame, the density of points decreases with the scanning distance, and the voxel grid downsampling cannot fully normalize the density when the target feature is far away from the sensor. Moreover, our synthetic data generation also did not consider the scale of line segments (as visualized in Fig. 2(e) when put together). If such an issue is not handled, the model will not produce reasonable predictions when the training and test data are on different scales.

To address this issue, our network obtains scale invariance by eliminating the scale factor s of the Sim(3) transformation and using relative distances, as:

$$p' = s \cdot \mathbf{R}p + t,$$
$$f = \frac{\sum_i (p' - p'_i)}{\sum_i \|p' - p'_i\|} = \frac{s \cdot \sum_i \mathbf{R}(p - p_i)}{s \cdot \sum_i \|p - p_i\|}. \tag{1}$$

In Eq. 1, we search $k = 20$ nearest points $\{p_1, p_2, ..., p_k\}$ of a point p, and calculate the scale-invariant local feature f as the ratio of the Manhattan distance to the Euclidean distance between p and its neighbors. The trade-off of such a feature definition is that f cannot reflect the position of the original point in the Euclidean space, so the transformation has information loss. Such an influence are further evaluated in Sect. 4.3.

Model Architecture. We choose DGCNN [39] as our backbone, since it directly encodes points and their nearest neighbors without complicated operations. Equation 2 shows its local feature encoding function called *EdgeConv* [39], where $\mathbf{x}_j$ is the j-th feature, $^S\mathbf{x}_i$ is the neighbor of the $\mathbf{x}_j$ in the feature space S, and h is the learnable model.

$$h\left(\mathbf{x}_j, {}^S\mathbf{x}_i\right) = \bar{h}\left(\mathbf{x}_j, {}^S\mathbf{x}_i - \mathbf{x}_j\right). \tag{2}$$

In the first *EdgeConv* layer, x represents the point coordinates in Euclidean space. In our implementation, we gather $k = 20$ nearest neighbors of each points and calculate scale-invariant feature f. Then we turn the first *EdgeConv* layer into:

$$h\left(f_j, {}^E f_i\right) = \bar{h}\left(f_j, {}^E f_i - f_j\right). \tag{3}$$

It replaces the coordinates in the Euclidean space with scale-invariant feature f, but ${}^E f_i$ is still the feature of i-th neighbor of point p_j in Euclidean space, not the neighbor of f_j in feature space. Since part of the information in the original Euclidean space has been lost when generating scale-invariant features, preserving the neighbor relationship in the original Euclidean space can reduce further information loss.

Automatic Line Segment Labeling. There is no available labeled line dataset of LiDAR scans, and performing manual labeling on point clouds is difficult. Hence, we build an automatic line labeling pipeline (Fig. 3). Inspired by homographic adaptation in SuperPoint [11], we perform geometric adaptation on LiDAR scans. First, we train a scale-invariant segmentation model purely on the synthetic data, and apply 2D transformations with a uniform distribution of $20m$ in XOY and $360°$ in yaw to the LiDAR scans. Then, we use the trained model to predict labels on the perturbed data, aggregate the scan labels from all the perturbations and take the points that are predicted more than 80% belonging to lines as candidate points. To cluster binary points into lines, we use the region-growth algorithm. The connectivity between points is defined through a $0.5m$ KD-Tree radius search. We use the labeled points as seeds, grow to nearby labeled points, and fit lines. Once such line segments are extracted, we continue to refine the segmentation model on the obtained labeled LiDAR scans. We repeat the geometric adaptation 3 times to generate 12,989 automatically labeled LiDAR frames on the KITTI odometry sequences [14].

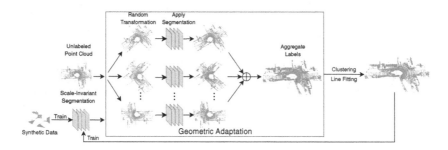

Fig. 3. Automatic line labeling pipeline. We use geometric adaptation and line fitting to reduce the network prediction noise and improve model accuracy on real LiDAR scans through iterative training.

3.2   Joint Training of Line Segmentation and Description

Definition of Line Descriptors. Different from the geometry definition which only requires two endpoints of a line segment. A descriptor for each line should convey local appearances through its all belonged points, since observed end

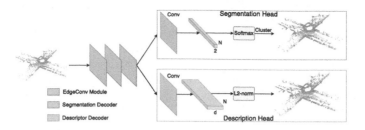

Fig. 4. Network architecture. The network uses the EdgeConv [39] module to extract features. The segmentation head and the description head predict the label and descriptor for each point, respectively.

points may be varied between frames due to possible occlusions. Therefore, we define the descriptor as an average of its all belonged points.

Network Architecture. Our network structure (Fig. 4) consists of a stacked three *EdgeConv* [39] layers for feature encoding, and two decoders for line segmentation and description, respectively. Each *EdgeConv* layer outputs a $N \times 64$ tensor used for 3-layer segmentation and description after a *MaxPooling* layer. We use *ReLU* for activation. The segmentation head turns the feature vector to a tensor sized $N \times 2$ after convolution (N for the number of input points), and then obtains a boolean label per each point through a *Softmax* layer, to predict whether it belongs to a line. The descriptor head outputs a tensor sized $N \times d$, and then performs *L2-Norm* to get a d-dimensional descriptor.

Loss Functions. Our segmentation loss $\mathbf{L}_{seg}$ is a standard cross-entropy loss, and we follow [38] and [5] to build a discrimitive loss for the descriptor. In detail, we first use the line segment label to get the mean descriptor μ of each line segment, and then use the $\mathbf{L}_{same}$ for each line to pull point descriptors towards μ. The $\mathbf{L}_{diff}$ is proposed to make the descriptors of different lines repel each other. In addition for a point cloud pair, we calculate the matched loss $\mathbf{L}_{match}$ and the loss between the non-matched lines $\mathbf{L}_{mismatch}$. Each term can be written as follows:

$$\mathbf{L}_{same} = \frac{1}{\mathbf{N}} \cdot \sum_{i}^{\mathbf{N}} \left(\frac{1}{|\mathbf{K}_i|} \cdot \sum_{j}^{\mathbf{K_i}} \left[\|\mu_i - d_j\|_1 - \delta_{\mathrm{s}} \right]_+^2 \right),$$

$$\mathbf{L}_{diff} = \frac{1}{|\mathbf{C}_{\mathbf{N}}^2|} \cdot \sum_{\langle i_a, i_b \rangle}^{\mathbf{C}_{\mathbf{N}}^2} \left[2\delta_{\mathrm{d}} - \|\mu_{i_A} - \mu_{i_B}\|_1 \right]_+^2,$$

$$\mathbf{L}_{match} = \frac{1}{\mathbf{N}} \cdot \sum_{i}^{\mathbf{N}} \left[\|\mu_i - \mu_i'\|_1 - \delta_{\mathrm{s}} \right]_+^2,$$

$$\mathbf{L}_{mismatch} = \frac{1}{|\mathbf{C}_{\mathbf{N}}^2|} \cdot \sum_{\langle i_a, i_b \rangle}^{\mathbf{C}_{\mathbf{N}}^2} \left[2\delta_{\mathrm{d}} - \|\mu_{i_A} - \mu_{i_B}'\|_1 \right]_+^2,$$

(4)

where $\mathbf{N}$ is the number of detected lines and $\mathbf{C}_{\mathbf{N}}^2$ stands for all pairs of two lines. i and j are two iterators, for lines and points on a line, respectively. μ_i is the aforementioned mean descriptor of a line, and d_j is the descriptor of its related point descriptor j. μ_i' and μ_{i_B}' are mean descriptors in another associated point cloud, and δ_{s} and δ_{d} are the positive and negative margins. $[x]_+ = \max(0, x)$, and $\|\cdot\|_1$ for the L1-distance. Finally, we use $\omega = 2$ to balance the final loss $\mathbf{L}$ as:

$$\mathbf{L} = \omega \cdot \mathbf{L}_{seg} + \mathbf{L}_{same} + \mathbf{L}_{diff} + \mathbf{L}_{match} + \mathbf{L}_{mismatch}. \quad (5)$$

Line-Based Registration. Our network outputs labels and descriptors for each point. We first extract lines using steps in Sect. 3.1. Then we perform descriptor matching to get line correspondences. The threshold of the matched descriptor is set to 0.1. The transformation $\mathbf{T}$ for registering the source cloud $\mathbb{S}$ to the target cloud $\mathbb{T}$ is optimized by minimizing point-to-line distances of all line matching cost $\xi_i, i \in \mathbf{N}$:

$$\xi_i = \sum_j^{\mathbf{N}_i} \frac{\left| \left(\mathbf{T} \cdot p_j^{\mathbb{S}} - p_{i_{e_0}}^{\mathbb{T}} \right) \times \left(\mathbf{T} \cdot p_j^{\mathbb{S}} - p_{i_{e_1}}^{\mathbb{T}} \right) \right|}{\left| p_{i_{e_0}}^{\mathbb{T}} - p_{i_{e_1}}^{\mathbb{T}} \right|} \quad (6)$$

where $p_j^{\mathbb{S}}$ is the line points in the source frame, $p_{i_{e_0}}^{\mathbb{T}}$ and $p_{i_{e_1}}^{\mathbb{T}}$ are endpoints of the matched line $\langle i_{e_0}, i_{e_1} \rangle$ of line i.

4   Experiments

4.1   Network Training

To begin with our generated synthetic data, we first train our line segmentation network using those synthetic point clouds with 50 epochs to converge. Then, to use the auto labeling method for generating sufficient and qualified real-world labeled scans, we obtain 12,989 LiDAR frames and iteratively train 100 epochs to refine these auto labeling results. Finally, we train our whole line segmentation and description network with 120 epochs to obtain the final applicable model for real-world scans.

We use scans including sequences 00–07 from the KITTI odometry dataset [14], with the last two sequences 06–07 for the validation set, and the rest 00–05 for the training set, to train our network. For each LiDAR frame, we voxelize the points cloud with $0.25m$ voxel size. We sample 20,000 points for evaluation and 15,000 points for training, since the kNN in *EdgeConv* is $O(N^2)$ space complexity and consumes large memory in the training process. We calculate point-to-line distances following Eq. 6 on the line segments in Sect. 3.1. The line pair whose mean distance is within $0.2m$ will be selected as a line correspondence to calculate descriptor loss. We implement our network in Tensorflow [1] with Adam [20] optimizer. The learning rate is set to 0.001 and decreases by 50% for every 15 epochs. The whole network is trained on 8 NVIDIA RTX 3090 GPUs.

4.2   Point Cloud Registration Test

Benchmarking. We use sequences 08–10 from the KITTI odometry dataset [14] to test the ability of our network on extracting line features and using them for point cloud registration. The preprocessing steps remain the same with our data preparation, and we choose to compare with traditional and learning-based methods for the global search registration. These traditional methods include ICP [6], RANSAC [13] and Fast Global Registration(FGR) [45], are all implemented by Open3D [46]. Specifically, The RANSAC and FGR use the FPFH [33] feature extracted from 0.25m voxel grid downsampled point clouds, and the max iteration is set to $4e^6$. Two learning-based methods include HRegNet [22] and Deep Global Registration (DGR) [9], and they use ground-truth pose to calculate loss and predict the transformation directly through the network. PointDSC [4] learns to prune outlier correspondences. D3Feat [5] and SpinNet [3] extract salient features from point clouds. Our line-based registration extracts 18 line segments with 350 points per frame on average. For fair comparisons, the number of keypoints in learning-feature-based methods is also set to 350, while other parameters remain unchanged.

Metrics. We use both the Relative Translation Error (RTE) and Relative Rotation Error (RRE) [22] to measure the registration accuracy. Additionally, as a special reference for evaluating the success rate for global search registration methods, we treat those calculated transformations with relative error w.r.t. the ground truth smaller than $2m$ and $5°$, as a successful attempt of registration.

Table 1. Registration performance on KITTI dataset. Our line segmentation and description method is highly competitive to the SOTA point-based approaches on the success rate, and both RTE and RRE can be refined with a subsequent coarse-to-fine ICP strategy.

	RTE (m)		RRE (deg)		Recall
	Mean	Std	Mean	Std	
ICP [6]	0.417	0.462	0.707	0.741	11.30%
FGR [45]	0.685	0.514	1.080	0.921	81.17%
RANSAC [13]	0.214	0.193	0.924	0.907	52.45%
HRegNet [22]	0.299	0.380	0.712	0.643	75.93%
DGR [9]	0.164	0.385	0.226	0.569	41.41%
PointDSC [4]	0.187	0.225	0.306	0.297	44.98%
SpinNet [3]	0.183	0.142	1.267	0.761	93.98%
D3Feat [5]	0.088	**0.043**	**0.343**	**0.242**	**98.90%**
SuperLine3D	**0.087**	0.104	0.591	0.444	97.68%

Results and Discussions. Table 1 shows the registration performances. Under random rotation perturbation, the recall of ICP is only 11.3%. The FGR and

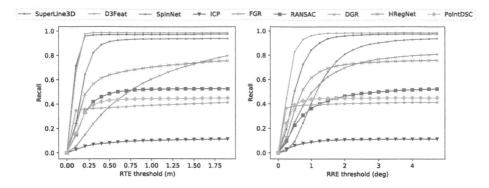

Fig. 5. Registration recall with different RRE and RTE thresholds on the KITTI dataset. The registration success rate of our line-based approach (blue) is close to the SOTA point-based approach D3Feat (orange) under different criteria. (Color figure online)

RANSAC methods based on FPFH features have higher recall but larger errors. The learning-based end-to-end methods HRegNet and DGR also drop in recall and accuracy when dealing with large perturbed scenarios. PointDSC relies on the feature model, and the features do not have full rotation invariance, so its performance also deteriorates. Figure 5 shows the registration recall with different error thresholds. SpinNet and D3Feat have better performances, with recall of over 90%. Our line-based registration achieves comparable performance to point features, with a similar mean translation error and 1.22% lower recall than D3Feat. Figure 7 shows the visualization results on KITTI test sequence. Our method successfully registers point clouds under arbitrary rotation perturbations. We will give more results in supplementary materials.

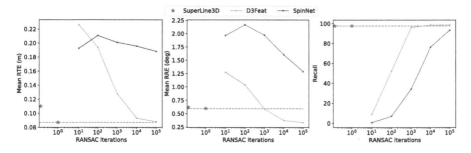

Fig. 6. Registration performance with different RANSAC iterations. There are many mismatches in point feature correspondences, which leads to unstable results when the number of iterations is small.

Ablation on RANSAC Iterations. Point feature-based registration requires RANSAC to remove outliers and calculate the correct transformation. In the Table 1 and Fig. 5, the max iteration of RANSAC in the D3Feat and SpinNet operations are set to $5e^4$. In contrast, our line-based registration does not rely on the RANSAC to filter erroneous matches: To perform outlier removal during transformation estimation, we calculate the line-to-line distances of line correspondences after the initial alignment, to remove the line correspondences with the mean distance greater than $1m$ and recalculate.

Figure 6 shows the performance of point cloud registration under different RANSAC iterations. The x-coordinates in the figure are logarithmic coordinates. Our method does not use RANSAC for outlier rejection, and we use a dashed line in blue as a reference when comparing with other methods requiring RANSAC post processing. The star near the y coordinates represents the original result, and the star with an x-coordinate of 1 is the result after outlier removal. Both D3Feat and SpinNet can not get accurate transformation without RANSAC until the max iteration exceeds 1,000.

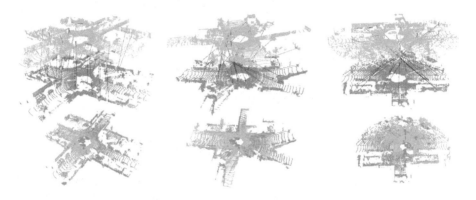

Fig. 7. Qualitative visualization on KITTI test sequence. Top: line associations between two LiDAR frames, Bottom: registration results of two frames.

4.3   Line Segmentation Evaluation

To evaluate the scale-invariance of our base segmentation model, we train Point-Net [30], PointNet++ [31] and vanilla DGCNN [39] on the synthetic dataset. The training set includes 4,000 synthetic point clouds normalized within $[0, 1]$. We test the trained model with point clouds scaled from 0.1 to 3.0.

Figure 8 shows the accuracy and mIOU of network predictions. Methods without scale adaptation suffer from performance decrease when the scale changes. The vanilla DGCNN gets best accuracy and mIOU in small scale disturbance (0.8 to 1.6), while our scale-invariant approach is stable under arbitrary scales. We can find that when the scale is determined, using the scale-invariant approach will decrease the accuracy, so we only use it in synthetic data training. In the joint training of segmentation and description, we utilize the vanilla DGCNN instead.

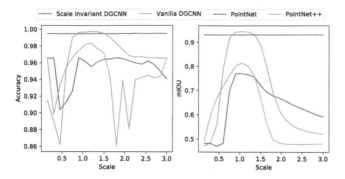

Fig. 8. Accuracy and mIOU of network predictions under different scale disturbances. Our scale-invariant approach is stable under arbitrary scales, but is a little worse than the vanilla DGCNN in the original scale.

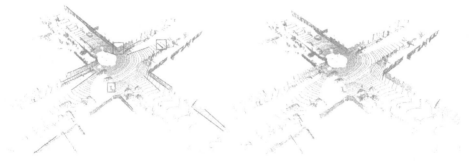

Fig. 9. Qualitative visualization of line segmentation between Lu et al. [24] (left) and ours (right). Our method segments most of the poles and building edges.

Figure 9 shows the qualitative visualization of our line segmentation compared with the only open-source 3D line detection method [24] we found. Our method segments most of the lines, while the open-source one extracts LiDAR scan lines on the ground and cannot detect the poles.

4.4 Generalization on Unseen Dataset

To compare the generalization of learning feature-based models, we test our method against state-of-the-art point feature methods on the unseen Apollo Sourthbay dataset [23] using the models trained on the KITTI dataset. We uniformly choose half of the point clouds from the SanJoseDownTown sequence as the source frames, select target frames every 5 frames, and add random yaw-axis rotation perturbances on the source frames. We get 8,296 point cloud pairs for evaluation. The data preprocessing of the point cloud is the same as the KITTI dataset.

Fig. 10. Qualitative visualization on Apollo SourthBay dataset, SanJoseDowntown sequence. The majority of the line correspondences are stable poles, which helps reduce the translation error by a large margin.

Table 2 shows the point cloud registration results. On unseen datasets, all methods show a drop in recall. D3feat has the best performance, while the mean translation error of our method is the smallest one. Fig. 10 shows qualitative visualization on the test data. There are more poles in this sequence, which is beneficial to our line-based registration.

Table 2. Test on unseen Apollo SourthBay Dataset, SanJoseDowntown sequence.

	RTE (m)		RRE (deg)		Recall
	Mean	Std	Mean	Std	
SpinNet [3]	0.199	0.203	1.207	0.874	75.66%
D3Feat [5]	0.079	**0.046**	**0.206**	**0.144**	**95.94%**
SuperLine3D	**0.045**	0.107	0.262	0.402	93.84%

4.5 Ablation Study

Skip Encoding. The receptive field is directly related to the number of encoded features in the EdgeConv module. When k is greater than 20, we can only set the batch size to 1 due to the enormous space complexity of EdgeConv. Its receptive field cannot be increased by increasing k. To this end, we utilize skip encoding. We gather $S \times k$ nearest neighbor features each time and select k features with stride size S for encoding. In this way, the receptive field increases S times without consuming too much memory (gathering $S \times k$ nearest-neighbor features will also increase a little memory usage). In the experiments, we test the cases with stride 1 (nearest neighbor encoding), 2, 4, and 6. As shown in the Table 3, adjusting the stride to 4 reaches the best performance, since the local features cannot be well encoded when the stride is too large.

Descriptor Dimension. The descriptor dimension is one of the key factors for the feature matching performance, and the matching performance is poor when the dimension is low. Our network extracts dense descriptors. Each point has a descriptor of d float numbers. It will take up a lot of storage space when its dimension is too large. Compared with the 16-dimension descriptor, the 32-dimension one has a more obvious improvement on the recall, while the 64-dimension descriptor has a small improvement. And increasing dimension to 128 only brings a smaller rotation error variance. Considering the average performances, we choose the 64-dimension implementation.

Table 3. Ablation study on stride and descriptor dimension.

		RTE (m)		RRE (m)		Recall
		Mean	Std	Mean	Std	
Stride	1	0.092	0.134	0.594	0.449	96.51%
	2	0.088	0.116	0.595	0.465	96.70%
	4	**0.087**	**0.104**	**0.591**	**0.444**	**97.68%**
	6	0.134	0.216	0.783	0.757	64.23%
Descriptordimension	16	0.115	0.175	0.627	0.510	87.56%
	32	0.095	0.132	0.597	0.462	95.28%
	64	**0.087**	**0.104**	**0.591**	0.444	**97.68%**
	128	0.090	0.120	0.593	**0.441**	96.70%

5   Conclusions

This paper proposes the first learning-based 3D line feature segmentation and description method for LiDAR scans, which achieves highly-competitive performance to the point-feature-based methods in the point cloud registration. In the future, we will explore the usage of our deep learning line features on SLAM problems such as mapping, map compression, and relocalization. We will also optimize the network structure and reduce training resource consumption.

Acknowledgments. This work is supported by the National Key R&D Program of China (Grant No: 2018AAA0101503) and Alibaba-Zhejiang University Joint Institute of Frontier Technologies.

References

1. Abadi, M., et al.: {TensorFlow}: A system for {Large-Scale} machine learning. In: 12th USENIX Symposium on Operating Systems Design and Implementation (OSDI 16), pp. 265–283 (2016)
2. Akinlar, C., Topal, C.: EDLines: a real-time line segment detector with a false detection control. Pattern Recogn. Lett. **32**(13), 1633–1642 (2011)
3. Ao, S., Hu, Q., Yang, B., Markham, A., Guo, Y.: SpinNet: learning a general surface descriptor for 3d point cloud registration. In: Proceedings of the IEEE/CVF Conference on Computer Vision and Pattern Recognition, pp. 11753–11762 (2021)

4. Bai, X., et al.: PointDSC: robust point cloud registration using deep spatial consistency. In: Proceedings of the IEEE/CVF Conference on Computer Vision and Pattern Recognition, pp. 15859–15869 (2021)
5. Bai, X., Luo, Z., Zhou, L., Fu, H., Quan, L., Tai, C.L.: D3feat: joint learning of dense detection and description of 3d local features. In: Proceedings of the IEEE/CVF Conference on Computer Vision and Pattern Recognition, pp. 6359–6367 (2020)
6. Besl, P.J., McKay, N.D.: Method for registration of 3-d shapes. In: Sensor Fusion IV: Control Paradigms and Data Structures, vol. 1611, pp. 586–606. SPIE (1992)
7. Biber, P., Straßer, W.: The normal distributions transform: a new approach to laser scan matching. In: Proceedings 2003 IEEE/RSJ International Conference on Intelligent Robots and Systems (IROS 2003) (Cat. No. 03CH37453), vol. 3, pp. 2743–2748. IEEE (2003)
8. Chen, G., Liu, Y., Dong, J., Zhang, L., Liu, H., Zhang, B., Knoll, A.: Efficient and robust line-based registration algorithm for robot perception under large-scale structural scenes. In: 2021 6th IEEE International Conference on Advanced Robotics and Mechatronics (ICARM), pp. 54–62. IEEE (2021)
9. Choy, C., Dong, W., Koltun, V.: Deep global registration. In: Proceedings of the IEEE/CVF Conference on Computer Vision and Pattern Recognition, pp. 2514–2523 (2020)
10. Choy, C., Park, J., Koltun, V.: Fully convolutional geometric features. In: Proceedings of the IEEE/CVF International Conference on Computer Vision, pp. 8958–8966 (2019)
11. DeTone, D., Malisiewicz, T., Rabinovich, A.: SuperPoint: self-supervised interest point detection and description. In: Proceedings of the IEEE Cnference on Computer Vision and Pattern Recognition Workshops, pp. 224–236 (2018)
12. Fang, F., Ma, X., Dai, X.: A multi-sensor fusion slam approach for mobile robots. In: IEEE International Conference Mechatronics and Automation, 2005. vol. 4, pp. 1837–1841. IEEE (2005)
13. Fischler, M.A., Bolles, R.C.: Random sample consensus: a paradigm for model fitting with applications to image analysis and automated cartography. Commun. ACM **24**(6), 381–395 (1981)
14. Geiger, A., Lenz, P., Urtasun, R.: Are we ready for autonomous driving? the Kitti vision benchmark suite. In: 2012 IEEE Conference on Computer Vision and Pattern Recognition, pp. 3354–3361. IEEE (2012)
15. Gu, X., Wang, X., Guo, Y.: A review of research on point cloud registration methods. IOP Conf. Ser. Mater. Sci. Eng. **782**(2), 022070 (2020)
16. Huang, S., Qin, F., Xiong, P., Ding, N., He, Y., Liu, X.: TP-LSD: tri-points based line segment detector. In: Vedaldi, A., Bischof, H., Brox, T., Frahm, J.-M. (eds.) ECCV 2020. LNCS, vol. 12372, pp. 770–785. Springer, Cham (2020). https://doi.org/10.1007/978-3-030-58583-9_46
17. Huang, X., Mei, G., Zhang, J.: Feature-metric registration: a fast semi-supervised approach for robust point cloud registration without correspondences. In: Proceedings of the IEEE/CVF Conference on Computer Vision and Pattern Recognition, pp. 11366–11374 (2020)
18. Huang, X., Mei, G., Zhang, J., Abbas, R.: A comprehensive survey on point cloud registration. arXiv preprint arXiv:2103.02690 (2021)
19. Khan, M.U., Zaidi, S.A.A., Ishtiaq, A., Bukhari, S.U.R., Samer, S., Farman, A.: A comparative survey of lidar-slam and lidar based sensor technologies. In: 2021 Mohammad Ali Jinnah University International Conference on Computing (MAJICC), pp. 1–8. IEEE (2021)

20. Kingma, D.P., Ba, J.: Adam: a method for stochastic optimization. arXiv preprint arXiv:1412.6980 (2014)
21. Li, J., Lee, G.H.: USIP: unsupervised stable interest point detection from 3d point clouds. In: Proceedings of the IEEE/CVF International Conference on Computer Vision, pp. 361–370 (2019)
22. Lu, F., et al.: HRegNet: a hierarchical network for large-scale outdoor lidar point cloud registration. In: Proceedings of the IEEE/CVF International Conference on Computer Vision, pp. 16014–16023 (2021)
23. Lu, W., Zhou, Y., Wan, G., Hou, S., Song, S.: L3-net: towards learning based lidar localization for autonomous driving. In: Proceedings of the IEEE Conference on Computer Vision and Pattern Recognition, pp. 6389–6398 (2019)
24. Lu, X., Liu, Y., Li, K.: Fast 3d line segment detection from unorganized point cloud. arXiv preprint arXiv:1901.02532 (2019)
25. Pais, G.D., Ramalingam, S., Govindu, V.M., Nascimento, J.C., Chellappa, R., Miraldo, P.: 3dregnet: a deep neural network for 3d point registration. In: Proceedings of the IEEE/CVF Conference on Computer Vision and Pattern Recognition, pp. 7193–7203 (2020)
26. Pautrat, R., Lin, J.T., Larsson, V., Oswald, M.R., Pollefeys, M.: Sold2: self-supervised occlusion-aware line description and detection. In: Proceedings of the IEEE/CVF Conference on Computer Vision and Pattern Recognition, pp. 11368–11378 (2021)
27. Perez-Gonzalez, J., Luna-Madrigal, F., Piña-Ramirez, O.: Deep learning point cloud registration based on distance features. IEEE Latin Am. Trans. **17**(12), 2053–2060 (2019)
28. Pomerleau, F., Colas, F., Siegwart, R.: A review of point cloud registration algorithms for mobile robotics. Found. Trends Robot. **4**(1), 1–104 (2015)
29. Pumarola, A., Vakhitov, A., Agudo, A., Sanfeliu, A., Moreno-Noguer, F.: Pl-slam: real-time monocular visual slam with points and lines. In: 2017 IEEE International Conference on Robotics and Automation (ICRA), pp. 4503–4508. IEEE (2017)
30. Qi, C.R., Su, H., Mo, K., Guibas, L.J.: PointNet: deep learning on point sets for 3d classification and segmentation. In: Proceedings of the IEEE Conference on Computer Vision and Pattern Recognition, pp. 652–660 (2017)
31. Qi, C.R., Yi, L., Su, H., Guibas, L.J.: Pointnet++: deep hierarchical feature learning on point sets in a metric space. In: Advances in Neural Information Processing Systems, vol. 30 (2017)
32. Rozenberszki, D., Majdik, A.L.: Lol: lidar-only odometry and localization in 3d point cloud maps. In: 2020 IEEE International Conference on Robotics and Automation (ICRA), pp. 4379–4385. IEEE (2020)
33. Rusu, R.B., Blodow, N., Beetz, M.: Fast point feature histograms (FPFH) for 3d registration. In: 2009 IEEE International Conference on Robotics and Automation, pp. 3212–3217. IEEE (2009)
34. Sarode, V., Li, X., Goforth, H., Aoki, Y., Srivatsan, R.A., Lucey, S., Choset, H.: PCRNet: point cloud registration network using pointnet encoding. arXiv preprint arXiv:1908.07906 (2019)
35. Shan, T., Englot, B.: Lego-loam: lightweight and ground-optimized lidar odometry and mapping on variable terrain. In: 2018 IEEE/RSJ International Conference on Intelligent Robots and Systems (IROS), pp. 4758–4765. IEEE (2018)
36. Thomas, H., Qi, C.R., Deschaud, J.E., Marcotegui, B., Goulette, F., Guibas, L.J.: KPConv: flexible and deformable convolution for point clouds. In: Proceedings of the IEEE/CVF International Conference on Computer Vision, pp. 6411–6420 (2019)

37. Von Gioi, R.G., Jakubowicz, J., Morel, J.M., Randall, G.: LSD: a line segment detector. Image Process. Line **2**, 35–55 (2012)
38. Wang, X., Liu, S., Shen, X., Shen, C., Jia, J.: Associatively segmenting instances and semantics in point clouds. In: Proceedings of the IEEE/CVF Conference on Computer Vision and Pattern Recognition, pp. 4096–4105 (2019)
39. Wang, Y., Sun, Y., Liu, Z., Sarma, S.E., Bronstein, M.M., Solomon, J.M.: Dynamic graph CNN for learning on point clouds. ACM Trans. Graph. (tog) **38**(5), 1–12 (2019)
40. Zhang, H., Luo, Y., Qin, F., He, Y., Liu, X.: ELSD: efficient line segment detector and descriptor. In: Proceedings of the IEEE/CVF International Conference on Computer Vision, pp. 2969–2978 (2021)
41. Zhang, J., Singh, S.: Loam: Lidar odometry and mapping in real-time. In: Robotics: Science and Systems. Berkeley, CA (2014)
42. Zhang, L., Koch, R.: An efficient and robust line segment matching approach based on LBD descriptor and pairwise geometric consistency. J. Vis. Commun. Image Representation **24**(7), 794–805 (2013)
43. Zhang, Z., Dai, Y., Sun, J.: Deep learning based point cloud registration: an overview. Virtual Reality Intell. Hardware **2**(3), 222–246 (2020)
44. Zhong, Y.: Intrinsic shape signatures: a shape descriptor for 3d object recognition. In: 2009 IEEE 12th International Conference on Computer Vision Workshops, ICCV Workshops, pp. 689–696. IEEE (2009)
45. Zhou, Q.-Y., Park, J., Koltun, V.: Fast global registration. In: Leibe, B., Matas, J., Sebe, N., Welling, M. (eds.) ECCV 2016. LNCS, vol. 9906, pp. 766–782. Springer, Cham (2016). https://doi.org/10.1007/978-3-319-46475-6_47
46. Zhou, Q.Y., Park, J., Koltun, V.: Open3d: a modern library for 3d data processing. arXiv preprint arXiv:1801.09847 (2018)

Exploring Plain Vision Transformer Backbones for Object Detection

Yanghao Li[(✉)], Hanzi Mao, Ross Girshick, and Kaiming He

Facebook AI Research, Menlo Park, USA
lyttonhao@fb.com

Abstract. We explore the *plain, non-hierarchical* Vision Transformer (ViT) as a backbone network for object detection. This design enables the original ViT architecture to be fine-tuned for object detection without needing to redesign a hierarchical backbone for pre-training. With minimal adaptations for fine-tuning, our plain-backbone detector can achieve competitive results. Surprisingly, we observe: (i) it is sufficient to build a simple feature pyramid from a single-scale feature map (without the common FPN design) and (ii) it is sufficient to use window attention (without shifting) aided with very few cross-window propagation blocks. With plain ViT backbones pre-trained as Masked Autoencoders (MAE), our detector, named ViTDet, can compete with the previous leading methods that were all based on hierarchical backbones, reaching up to 61.3 AP^{box} on the COCO dataset using only ImageNet-1K pre-training. We hope our study will draw attention to research on plain-backbone detectors. Code for ViTDet is available (https://github.com/facebookresearch/detectron2/tree/main/projects/ViTDet).

1 Introduction

Modern object detectors in general consist of a *backbone* feature extractor that is *agnostic* to the detection task and a set of necks and heads that incorporate detection-specific prior knowledge. Common components in the necks/heads may include Region-of-Interest (RoI) operations [18,23,24], Region Proposal Networks (RPN) or anchors [45], Feature Pyramid Networks (FPN) [34], *etc.* If the design of the task-specific necks/heads is decoupled from the design of the backbone, they may evolve in parallel. Empirically, object detection research has benefited from the largely independent exploration of general-purpose backbones [25,27,46,47] and detection-specific modules. For a long while, these backbones have been *multi-scale, hierarchical* architectures due to the *de facto* design of convolutional networks (ConvNet) [29], which has heavily influenced the neck/head design for detecting objects at multiple scales (*e.g.*, FPN).

R. Girshick and K. He—Equal contribution.

Supplementary Information The online version contains supplementary material available at https://doi.org/10.1007/978-3-031-20077-9_17.

hierarchical backbone, w/ FPN   **plain** backbone, w/ simple feature pyramid

Fig. 1. A typical hierarchical-backbone detector (left) *vs.*our plain-backbone detector (right). Traditional hierarchical backbones can be naturally adapted for multi-scale detection, *e.g.*, using FPN. Instead, we explore building a simple pyramid from only the last, large-stride (16) feature map of a plain backbone.

Over the past year, Vision Transformers (ViT) [12] have been established as a powerful backbone for visual recognition. Unlike typical ConvNets, the original ViT is a *plain, non-hierarchical* architecture that maintains a single-scale feature map throughout. Its "minimalist" pursuit is met by challenges when applied to object detection—*e.g.*, How can we address multi-scale objects in a downstream task with a plain backbone from upstream pre-training? Is a plain ViT too inefficient to use with high-resolution detection images? One solution, which abandons this pursuit, is to re-introduce hierarchical designs into the backbone. This solution, *e.g.*, Swin Transformers [39] and related works [15,26,31,52], can inherit the ConvNet-based detector design and has shown successful results.

In this work, we pursue a different direction: we explore object detectors that use only *plain, non-hierarchical* backbones.[1] If this direction is successful, it will enable the use of original ViT backbones for object detection; this will *decouple* the pre-training design from the fine-tuning demands, maintaining the independence of upstream *vs.*downstream tasks, as has been the case for ConvNet-based research. This direction also in part follows the ViT philosophy of "fewer inductive biases" [12] in the pursuit of universal features. As the non-local self-attention computation [51] can learn translation-equivariant features [12], they may also learn scale-equivariant features from certain forms of supervised or self-supervised pre-training.

In our study, we do *not* aim to develop new components; instead, we make *minimal* adaptations that are sufficient to overcome the aforementioned challenges. In particular, our detector builds a simple feature pyramid from only the *last* feature map of a plain ViT backbone (Fig. 1). This abandons the FPN design [34] and waives the requirement of a hierarchical backbone. To efficiently extract features from high-resolution images, our detector uses simple non-overlapping window attention (without "shifting", unlike [39]). A small number of cross-window blocks (*e.g.*, 4), which could be global attention [51] or convolutions, are used to propagate information. These adaptations are made only during fine-tuning and do not alter pre-training.

Our simple design turns out to achieve surprising results. We find that the FPN design is not necessary in the case of a plain ViT backbone and its benefit

---

[1] In this paper, "backbone" refers to architectural components that can be inherited from pre-training and "plain" refers to the non-hierarchical, single-scale property.

can be effectively gained by a simple pyramid built from a large-stride (16), single-scale map. We also find that window attention is sufficient as long as information is well propagated across windows in a small number of layers.

More surprisingly, under some circumstances, our plain-backbone detector, named ViTDet, can compete with the leading hierarchical-backbone detectors (*e.g.*, Swin [39], MViT [15,31]). With Masked Autoencoder (MAE) [22] pre-training, our plain-backbone detector can outperform the hierarchical counterparts that are pre-trained on ImageNet-1K/21K [10] with supervision (Fig. 3). The gains are more prominent for larger model sizes. The competitiveness of our detector is observed under different object detector frameworks, including Mask R-CNN [23], Cascade Mask R-CNN [3], and their enhancements. We report 61.3 AP^{box} on the COCO dataset [36] with a plain ViT-Huge backbone, using only ImageNet-1K pre-training with no labels. We also demonstrate competitive results on the long-tailed LVIS detection dataset [21]. While these strong results may be in part due to the effectiveness of MAE pre-training, our study demonstrates that plain-backbone detectors can be promising, challenging the entrenched position of hierarchical backbones for object detection.

Beyond these results, our methodology maintains the philosophy of decoupling the detector-specific designs from the task-agnostic backbone. This philosophy is in contrast to the trend of redesigning Transformer backbones to support multi-scale hierarchies [15,26,39,52]. In our case, the detection-specific prior knowledge is introduced only during fine-tuning, without needing to tailor the backbone design a priori in pre-training. This makes our detector compatible with ViT developments along various directions that are not necessarily limited by the hierarchical constraint, *e.g.*, block designs [49,50], self-supervised learning [1,22], and scaling [53]. We hope our study will inspire future research on plain-backbone object detection.[2]

2   Related Work

Object Detector Backbones. Pioneered by the work of R-CNN [19], object detection and many other vision tasks adopt a pre-training + fine-tuning paradigm: a general-purpose, task-agnostic backbone is pre-trained with supervised or self-supervised training, whose structure is later modified and adapted to the downstream tasks. The dominant backbones in computer vision have been ConvNets [29] of various forms, *e.g.*, [25,27,46,47].

Earlier neural network detectors, *e.g.*, [18,24,44,45], were based on a single-scale feature map when originally presented. While they use ConvNet backbones that are by default hierarchical, in principle, they are applicable on any plain backbone. SSD [37] is among the first works that leverage the hierarchical nature of the ConvNet backbones (*e.g.*, the last two stages of a VGG net [46]). FPN [34] pushes this direction further by using all stages of a hierarchical backbone, approached by lateral and top-down connections. The FPN design is widely

---

[2] This work is an extension of a preliminary version [32] that was unpublished and not submitted for peer review.

used in object detection methods. More recently, works including Trident Networks [30] and YOLOF [6] have revisited single-scale feature maps, but unlike our work they focus on a single-scale taken from a *hierarchical* backbone.

ViT [12] is a powerful alternative to standard ConvNets for image classification. The original ViT is a plain, non-hierarchical architecture. Various hierarchical Transformers have been presented, *e.g.*, Swin [39], MViT [15,31], PVT [52], and PiT [26]. These methods inherit some designs from ConvNets, including the hierarchical structure and the translation-equivariant priors (*e.g.*, convolutions, pooling, sliding windows). As a result, it is relatively straightforward to replace a ConvNet with these backbones for object detection.

Plain-Backbone Detectors. The success of ViT has inspired people to push the frontier of plain backbones for object detection. Most recently, UViT [8] is presented as a single-scale Transformer for object detection. UViT studies the network width, depth, and input resolution of plain ViT backbones under object detection metrics. A progressive window attention strategy is proposed to address the high-resolution inputs. Unlike UViT that modifies the architecture *during pre-training*, our study focuses on the original ViT architecture *without* a priori specification for detection. By maintaining the task-agnostic nature of the backbone, our approach supports a wide range of available ViT backbones as well as their improvements in the future. Our method *decouples* the backbone design from the detection task, which is a key motivation of pursuing plain backbones.

UViT uses single-scale feature maps for the detector heads, while our method builds a simple pyramid on the single-scale backbone. In the context of our study, it is an unnecessary constraint for the entire detector to be single-scale. Note the full UViT detector has several forms of multi-scale priors too (*e.g.*, RPN [45] and RoIAlign [23]) as it is based on Cascade Mask R-CNN [3]. In our study, we focus on leveraging pre-trained plain backbones and we do not constrain the detector neck/head design.

Object Detection Methodologies. Object detection is a flourishing research area that has embraced methodologies of distinct properties—*e.g.*, two-stage [18, 19,24,45] *vs*.one-stage [35,37,44], anchor-based [45] *vs*.anchor-free [13,28,48], and region-based [18,19,24,45] *vs*.query-based (DETR) [4]. Research on different methodologies has been continuously advancing understandings of the object detection problem. Our study suggests that the topic of "plain *vs*.hierarchical" backbones is worth exploring and may bring in new insights.

3   Method

Our goal is to remove the hierarchical constraint on the backbone and to enable explorations of plain-backbone object detection. To this end, we aim for *minimal* modifications to adapt a plain backbone to the object detection task *only during fine-tuning time*. After these adaptations, in principle one can apply any detector heads, for which we opt to use Mask R-CNN [23] and its extensions. We do *not* aim to develop new components; instead, we focus on what new insights can be drawn in our exploration.

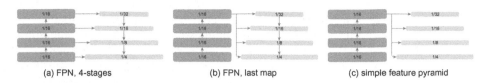

(a) FPN, 4-stages   (b) FPN, last map   (c) simple feature pyramid

Fig. 2. Building a feature pyramid on a plain backbone. **(a)** FPN-like: to mimic a hierarchical backbone, the plain backbone is artificially divided into multiple stages. **(b)** FPN-like, but using only the last feature map without stage division. **(c)** Our simple feature pyramid without FPN. In all three cases, strided convolutions/deconvolutions are used whenever the scale changes.

Simple Feature Pyramid. FPN [34] is a common solution of building an in-network pyramid for object detection. If the backbone is hierarchical, the motivation of FPN is to combine the higher-resolution features from earlier stages and the stronger features from later stages. This is realized in FPN by top-down and lateral connections [34] (Fig. 1 left).

If the backbone is non-hierarchical, the foundation of the FPN motivation is lost, as all the feature maps in the backbone are of the same resolution. In our scenario, we simply use only the *last* feature map from the backbone, which should have the strongest features. On this map, we apply a set of convolutions or deconvolutions *in parallel* to produce multi-scale feature maps. Specifically, with the default ViT feature map of a scale of $\frac{1}{16}$ (stride = 16 [12]), we produce feature maps of scales $\{\frac{1}{32}, \frac{1}{16}, \frac{1}{8}, \frac{1}{4}\}$ using convolutions of strides $\{2, 1, \frac{1}{2}, \frac{1}{4}\}$, where a fractional stride indicates a deconvolution. We refer to this as a "*simple feature pyramid*" (Fig. 1 right).

The strategy of building multi-scale feature maps from a single map is related to that of SSD [37]. However, our scenario involves *upsampling* from a deep, low-resolution feature map, unlike [37], which taps into shallower feature maps. In hierarchical backbones, upsampling is often aided by lateral connection [34]; in plain ViT backbones, we empirically find this is not necessary (Sec. 4) and simple deconvolutions are sufficient. We hypothesize that this is because ViT can rely on positional embedding [51] for encoding locations and also because the high-dimensional ViT patch embeddings do not necessarily discard information.[3]

We will compare with two FPN variants that are also built on a plain backbone (Fig. 2). In the first variant, the backbone is artificially divided into multiple stages to mimic the stages of a hierarchical backbone, with lateral and top-down connections applied (Fig. 2 (a)) [14]. The second variant is like the first one, but uses only the last map instead of the divided stages (Fig. 2 (b)). We show that these FPN variants are not necessary (Sec. 4).[4]

---

[3] With a patch size of 16 × 16 and 3 colors, a hidden dimension ≥768 (ViT-B and larger) can preserve all information of a patch if necessary.

[4] From a broader perspective, the spirit of FPN [34] is "to build a feature pyramid inside a network". Our simple feature pyramid follows this spirit. In the context of this paper, the term of "FPN" refers to the specific architecture design in [34].

Backbone Adaptation. Object detectors benefit from high-resolution input images, but computing global self-attention throughout the backbone is prohibitive in memory and is slow. In this study, we focus on the scenario where the pre-trained backbone performs global self-attention, which is then *adapted* to higher-resolution inputs during fine-tuning. This is in contrast to the recent methods that modify the attention computation directly with backbone pre-training (*e.g.*, [15,39]). Our scenario enables us to use the original ViT backbone for detection, without redesigning pre-training architectures.

We explore using *window attention* [51] with a few cross-window blocks. During fine-tuning, given a high-resolution feature map, we divide it into regular non-overlapping windows.[5] Self-attention is computed within each window. This is referred to as *"restricted"* self-attention in the original Transformer [51].

Unlike Swin, we do *not* "shift" [39] the windows across layers. To allow information propagation, we use a very few (by default, 4) blocks that can go across windows. We *evenly* split a pre-trained backbone into 4 subsets of blocks (*e.g.*, 6 in each subset for the 24-block ViT-L). We apply a propagation strategy in the last block of each subset. We study these two strategies:

(i) *Global propagation.* We perform global self-attention in the last block of each subset. As the number of global blocks is small, the memory and computation cost is feasible. This is similar to the hybrid window attention in [31] that was used jointly with FPN.

(ii) *Convolutional propagation.* As an alternative, we add an extra convolutional block after each subset. A convolutional block is a residual block [25] that consists of one or more convolutions and an identity shortcut. The last layer in this block is initialized as zero, such that the initial status of the block is an identity [20]. Initializing a block as identity allows us to insert it into any place in a pre-trained backbone without breaking the initial status of the backbone.

Our backbone adaptation is simple and makes detection fine-tuning compatible with global self-attention pre-training. As stated, it is not necessary to redesign the pre-training architectures.

Discussion. Object detectors contain components that can be task agnostic, such as the backbone, and other components that are task-specific, such as RoI heads. This model decomposition enables the task-agnostic components to be pre-trained using non-detection data (*e.g.*, ImageNet), which may provide an advantage since detection training data is relatively scarce.

Under this perspective, it becomes reasonable to pursue a backbone that involves fewer inductive biases, since the backbone may be trained effectively using large-scale data and/or self-supervision. In contrast, the detection task-specific components have relatively little data available and may still benefit from additional inductive biases. While pursuing detection heads with fewer inductive biases is an active area of work, leading methods like DETR [4] are challenging to train and still benefit from detection-specific prior knowledge [56].

---

[5] We set the window size as the pre-training feature map size by default (14 × 14 [12]).

Driven by these observations, our work follows the spirit of the original plain ViT paper with respect to the detector's backbone. While the ViT paper's discussion [12] focused on reducing inductive biases on translation equivariance, in our case, it is about having fewer or even no inductive bias on scale equivariance in the backbone. We hypothesize that the way for a plain backbone to achieve scale equivariance is to learn the prior knowledge from data, analogous to how it learns translation equivariance and locality without convolutions [12].

Our goal is to demonstrate the feasibility of this approach. Thus we choose to implement our method with standard detection specific components (*i.e.*, Mask R-CNN and its extensions). Exploring even fewer inductive biases in the detection heads is an open and interesting direction for future work. We hope it can benefit from and build on our work here.

Implementation. We use the vanilla ViT-B, ViT-L, ViT-H [12] as the pre-training backbones. We set the patch size as 16 and thus the feature map scale is $1/16$, *i.e.*, stride $= 16$.[6] Our detector heads follow Mask R-CNN [23] or Cascade Mask R-CNN [3], with architectural details described in the appendix. The input image is 1024×1024, augmented with large-scale jittering [17] during training. Due to this heavy regularization, we fine-tune for up to 100 epochs in COCO. We use the AdamW optimizer [40] and search for optimal hyper-parameters using a baseline version. More details are in the appendix.

4   Experiments

4.1   Ablation Study and Analysis

We perform ablation experiments on the COCO dataset [36]. We train on the train2017 split and evaluate on the val2017 split. We report results on bounding-box object detection (AP^{box}) and instance segmentation (AP^{mask}).

By default, we use the simple feature pyramid and global propagation described in Sec. 3. We use 4 propagation blocks, evenly placed in the backbone. We initialize the backbone with MAE [22] pre-trained on IN-1K without labels. We ablate these defaults and discuss our main observations as follows.

A Simple Feature Pyramid is Sufficient. In Table 1 we compare the feature pyramid building strategies illustrated in Fig. 2.

We study a baseline with *no feature pyramid*: both the RPN and RoI heads are applied on the backbone's final, single-scale ($\frac{1}{16}$) feature map. This case is similar to the original Faster R-CNN [45] before FPN was proposed. *All* feature pyramid variants (Table 1 a-c) are substantially better than this baseline, increasing AP by up to 3.4 points. We note that using a single-scale feature map does *not* mean the detector is single-scale: the RPN head has multi-scale anchors and the RoI heads operate on regions of multiple scales. Even so, feature

---

[6] Changing the stride affects the scale distribution and presents a different accuracy shift for objects of different scales. This topic is beyond the scope of this study. For simplicity, we use the same patch size of 16 for all of ViT-B, L, H (see the appendix).

Table 1. Ablation on feature pyramid design with plain ViT backbones, using Mask R-CNN evaluated on COCO. The backbone is ViT-B (left) and ViT-L (right). The entries (a-c) correspond to Fig. 2 (a-c), compared to a baseline without any pyramid. Both FPN and our simple pyramid are substantially better than the baseline, while our simple pyramid is sufficient.

Pyramid design	ViT-B		ViT-L	
	AP^{box}	AP^{mask}	AP^{box}	AP^{mask}
No feature pyramid	47.8	42.5	51.2	45.4
(a) FPN, 4-stage	50.3 (+2.5)	44.9 (+2.4)	54.4 (+3.2)	48.4 (+3.0)
(b) FPN, last-map	50.9 (+3.1)	45.3 (+2.8)	**54.6** (+3.4)	48.5 (+3.1)
(c) Simple feature pyramid	**51.2** (+3.4)	**45.5** (+3.0)	**54.6** (+3.4)	**48.6** (+3.2)

pyramids are beneficial. This observation is consistent with the observation in the FPN paper [34] on hierarchical backbones.

However, *the FPN design is not needed and our simple feature pyramid is sufficient* for a plain ViT backbone to enjoy the benefit of a pyramid. To ablate this design, we mimic the FPN architecture (*i.e.*, the top-down and lateral connections) as in Fig. 2 (a, b). Table 1 (a, b) shows that while both FPN variants achieve strong gains over the baseline with no pyramid (as has been widely observed with the original FPN on hierarchical backbones), they are no better than our simple feature pyramid. The original FPN [34] was motivated by combining lower-resolution, stronger feature maps with higher-resolution, weaker feature maps. This foundation is lost when the backbone is plain and has no high-resolution maps, which can explain why our simple pyramid is sufficient.

Our ablation reveals that the *set* of pyramidal feature maps, rather than the top-down/lateral connections, is the key to effective multi-scale detection. To see this, we study an even more aggressive case of the simple pyramid: we generate only the finest scale ($\frac{1}{4}$) feature map by deconvolution and then from this finest map we subsample other scales in parallel by strided *average pooling*. There are no unshared, per-scale parameters in this design. This aggressively-simple pyramid is nearly as good: it has 54.5 AP (ViT-L), 3.3 higher than the no pyramid baseline. This shows the importance of pyramidal feature maps. For any variant of these feature pyramids, the anchors (in RPN) and regions (in RoI heads) are mapped to the corresponding level in the pyramid based on their scales, as in [34]. We hypothesize that this explicit scale-equivariant mapping, rather than the top-down/lateral connection, is the main reason why a feature pyramid can greatly benefit multi-scale object detection.

Window Attention is Sufficient when Aided by a Few Propagation Blocks. Table 2 ablates our backbone adaptation approach. In short, on top of a baseline that has purely window attention and none of the cross-window propagation blocks (Table 2, "none"), various ways of propagation can show decent gains.[7]

---

[7] Even our baseline with no propagation *in the backbone* is reasonably good (52.9 AP). This can be explained by the fact that the layers beyond the backbone (the simple feature pyramid, RPN, and RoI heads) also induce cross-window communication.

Table 2. Ablation on backbone adaptation strategies using a plain ViT backbone and Mask R-CNN evaluated on COCO. All blocks perform window attention, unless modified by the propagation strategy. In sum, compared to the baseline that uses only window attention (52.9 AP^{box}) most configurations work effectively as long as information can be well propagated across windows. Here the backbone is ViT-L; the observations on ViT-B are similar (see the appendix).

prop. strategy	AP^{box}	AP^{mask}
none	52.9	47.2
4 global blocks	54.6 (+1.7)	48.6 (+1.4)
4 conv blocks	**54.8** (+1.9)	**48.8** (+1.6)
shifted win.	54.0 (+1.1)	47.9 (+0.7)

(a) Window attention with various cross-window propagation strategies.

prop. conv	AP^{box}	AP^{mask}
none	52.9	47.2
naïve	54.3 (+1.4)	48.3 (+1.1)
basic	**54.8** (+1.9)	**48.8** (+1.6)
bottleneck	54.6 (+1.7)	48.6 (+1.4)

(b) Convolutional propagation with different residual block types (4 blocks).

prop. locations	AP^{box}	AP^{mask}
none	52.9	47.2
first 4 blocks	52.9 (+0.0)	47.1 (−0.1)
last 4 blocks	54.3 (+1.4)	48.3 (+1.1)
evenly 4 blocks	**54.6** (+1.7)	**48.6** (+1.4)

(c) Locations of cross-window global propagation blocks.

prop. blks	AP^{box}	AP^{mask}
none	52.9	47.2
2	54.4 (+1.5)	48.5 (+1.3)
4	54.6 (+1.7)	48.6 (+1.4)
24†	**55.1** (+2.2)	**48.9** (+1.7)

(d) Number of global propagation blocks.
† : Memory optimization required.

Table 3. Practical performance of backbone adaptation strategies. The backbone is ViT-L. The training memory (per GPU) is benchmarked with a batch size of 1. The testing time (per image) is benchmarked on an A100 GPU. †: This 3.34× memory (49G) is estimated as if the same training implementation could be used, which is not practical and requires special memory optimization that all together slows down training by 2.2× vs.the baseline.

Prop. strategy	AP^{box}	# params	Train mem	Test time
None	52.9	1.00× (331M)	1.00× (14.6G)	1.00× (88 ms)
4 conv (bottleneck)	54.6 (+1.7)	1.04×	1.05×	1.04×
4 global	54.6 (+1.7)	1.00×	1.39×	1.16×
24 global	55.1 (+2.2)	1.00×	3.34×†	1.86×

In Table 2a, we compare our global and convolutional propagation strategies vs.the no propagation baseline. They have a gain of 1.7 and 1.9 over the baseline. We also compare with the "shifted window" (Swin [39]) strategy, in which the

Table 4. Ablation on pre-training strategies with plain ViT backbones using Mask R-CNN evaluated on COCO.

Pre-train	ViT-B		ViT-L	
	AP^{box}	AP^{mask}	AP^{box}	AP^{mask}
None (random init.)	48.1	42.6	50.0	44.2
IN-1K, supervised	47.6 (−0.5)	42.4 (−0.2)	49.6 (−0.4)	43.8 (−0.4)
IN-21K, supervised	47.8 (−0.3)	42.6 (+0.0)	50.6 (+0.6)	44.8 (+0.6)
IN-1K, MAE	**51.2** (+3.1)	**45.5** (+2.9)	**54.6** (+4.6)	**48.6** (+4.4)

window grid is shifted by a half-window size for every other block. The shifted window variant has a 1.1 gain over the baseline, but is worse than ours. Note that here we focus only on the "shifted window" aspect of Swin [39]: the backbone is still a plain ViT, adapted to shifted window attention only during fine-tuning; it is *not* the Swin architecture, which we will compare to later.

Table 2b compares different types of residual blocks for convolutional propagation. We study the basic (two 3 × 3) [25], bottleneck (1 × 1→3 × 3→1 × 1) [25], and a naïve block that has one 3 × 3 convolution. They all improve over the baseline, while the specific block design makes only marginal differences. Interestingly, even though convolution is a local operation if its receptive field covers two adjacent windows, it is sufficient in principle to connect all pixels of the two windows. This connectivity is thanks to the self-attention in both windows in the succeeding blocks. This may explain why it can perform as well as global propagation.

In Table 2c we study where cross-window propagation should be located in the backbone. By default 4 global propagation blocks are placed *evenly*. We compare with placing them in the first or last 4 blocks instead. Interestingly, performing propagation in the last 4 blocks is nearly as good as even placement. This is in line with the observation in [12] that ViT has longer attention distance in later blocks and is more localized in earlier ones. In contrast, performing propagation only in the first 4 blocks shows no gain: in this case, there is no propagation across windows in the backbone after these 4 blocks. This again demonstrates that propagation across windows is helpful.

Table 2d compares the number of global propagation blocks to use. Even using just 2 blocks achieves good accuracy and clearly outperforms the baseline. For comprehensiveness, we also report a variant where all 24 blocks in ViT-L use global attention. This has a marginal gain of 0.5 points over our 4-block default, while its training requires special memory optimization (we use memory checkpointing [7]). This requirement makes scaling to larger models (like ViT-H) impractical. Our solution of window attention plus a few propagation blocks offers a practical, high-performing tradeoff.

We benchmark this tradeoff in Table 3. Using 4 propagation blocks gives a good trade-off. Convolutional propagation is the most practical, increasing memory and time by merely ≤5%, at a small cost of 4% more parameters. Global propagation with 4 blocks is also feasible and does not increase the model size. Global self-attention in all 24 blocks is not practical.

In sum, Table 2 shows that various forms of propagation are helpful, while *we can keep using window attention in most or all blocks*. Importantly, all these architecture adaptations are performed only during fine-tuning time; they do not require a redesign of the pre-training architecture.

Masked Autoencoders Provide Strong Pre-trained Backbones. Table 4 compares backbone pre-training strategies. Supervised pre-training on IN-1K is slightly worse than no pre-training, similar to the observation in [17]. Supervised pre-training on IN-21K is marginally better for ViT-L.

In contrast, MAE [22] pre-training on IN-1K (without labels) shows massive gains, increasing AP^{box} by 3.1 for ViT-B and 4.6 for ViT-L. We hypothesize that the vanilla ViT [12], with fewer inductive biases, may require higher-capacity to learn translation and scale equivariant features, while higher-capacity models are prone to heavier overfitting. MAE pre-training can help to relieve this problem. We discuss more about MAE in context next.

4.2 Comparisons with Hierarchical Backbones

Modern detection systems involve many implementation details and subtleties. To focus on comparing backbones under as fair conditions as possible, we incorporate the Swin [39] and MViTv2 [31] backbones into our implementation.

Settings. We use the same implementation of Mask R-CNN [23] and Cascade Mask R-CNN [3] for all ViT, Swin, and MViTv2 backbones. We use FPN for the hierarchical backbones of Swin/MViTv2. We search for optimal hyperparameters separately for each backbone (see the appendix). Our Swin results are better than their counterparts in the original paper;[8] our MViTv2 results are better than or on par with those reported in [31].

Following the original papers [31,39], Swin and MViTv2 both use relative position biases [43]. For a fairer comparison, here we also adopt relative position biases in our ViT backbones as per [31], but *only* during fine-tuning, not affecting pre-training. This addition improves AP by ~1 point. Note that our ablations in Sec. 4.1 are *without* relative position biases.

Results and Analysis. Table 5 shows the comparisons. Figure 3 plots the tradeoffs. The comparisons here involve two factors: the backbone and the pre-training strategy. Our plain-backbone detector, combined with MAE pre-training, presents *better scaling behavior*. When the models are large, our method outperforms the hierarchical counterparts of Swin/MViTv2, including those using IN-21K supervised pre-training. Our result with ViT-H is 2.6 better than that with MViTv2-H. Moreover, the plain ViT has a *better* wall-clock performance (Fig. 3 right, see ViT-H *vs.* MViTv2-H), as the simpler blocks are more hardware-friendly.

---

[8] For example, Swin-B (IN-1K, Cascade Mask R-CNN) has 51.9 AP^{box} reported in the official repo. This result in our implementation is 52.7.

Table 5. Comparisons of plain *vs.* hierarchical backbones using Mask R-CNN [23] and Cascade Mask R-CNN [3] on COCO. Tradeoffs are plotted in Fig. 3. All entries are implemented and run by us to align low-level details.

Backbone	Pre-train	Mask R-CNN		Cascade Mask R-CNN	
		AP^{box}	AP^{mask}	AP^{box}	AP^{mask}
Hierarchical-backbone detectors:					
Swin-B	21K, sup	51.4	45.4	54.0	46.5
Swin-L	21K, sup	52.4	46.2	54.8	47.3
MViTv2-B	21K, sup	53.1	47.4	55.6	48.1
MViTv2-L	21K, sup	53.6	47.5	55.7	48.3
MViTv2-H	21K, sup	54.1	47.7	55.8	48.3
Our plain-backbone detectors:					
ViT-B	1K, MAE	51.6	45.9	54.0	46.7
ViT-L	1K, MAE	55.6	49.2	57.6	49.8
ViT-H	1K, MAE	**56.7**	**50.1**	**58.7**	**50.9**

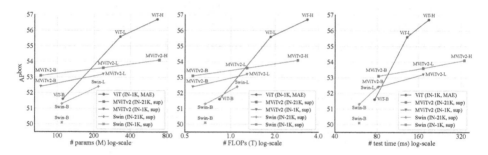

Fig. 3. Tradeoffs of accuracy *vs.* model sizes (left), FLOPs (middle), and wall-clock testing time (right). All entries are implemented and run by us to align low-level details. Swin [39] and MViTv2 [31] are pre-trained on IN-1K/21K with supervision. The ViT models are pre-trained using MAE [22] on IN-1K. Here the detector head is Mask R-CNN; similar trends are observed for Cascade Mask R-CNN and one-stage detector RetinaNet (Figure A.2 in the appendix). Detailed numbers are in the appendix (Table A.2).

We are also curious about the influence of MAE on hierarchical backbones. This is largely beyond the scope of this paper, as it involves finding good training recipes for hierarchical backbones with MAE. To provide some insight, we implement a naïve extension of MAE with the MViTv2 backbone (see the appendix). We observe that MViTv2-L with this MAE pre-training on IN-1K is 1.3 better than that with IN-21K supervised pre-training (54.9 *vs.* 53.6 AP^{box}). As a comparison, this gap is 4 points for our plain-backbone detector (Table 4). This shows that the plain ViT backbone may benefit *more* from MAE pre-training than the hierarchical backbone, suggesting that the lack of inductive biases on

Table 6. System-level comparisons with the leading results on COCO reported by the original papers. The detection framework is Cascade Mask R-CNN [3] (denoted as "Cascade"), Hybrid Task Cascade (HTC) [5], or its extension (HTC++ [39]). Here we compare results that use ImageNet data (1K or 21K); better results are reported in [9,38] using extra data. [†]: [33] combines two Swin-L backbones.

Method	Framework	Pre-train	Single-scale test		Multi-scale test	
			AP^{box}	AP^{mask}	AP^{box}	AP^{mask}
Hierarchical-backbone detectors:						
Swin-L [39]	HTC++	21K, sup	57.1	49.5	58.0	50.4
MViTv2-L [31]	Cascade	21K, sup	56.9	48.6	58.7	50.5
MViTv2-H [31]	Cascade	21K, sup	57.1	48.8	58.1	50.1
CBNetV2 [33][†]	HTC	21K, sup	59.1	51.0	59.6	51.8
SwinV2-L [38]	HTC++	21K, sup	58.9	51.2	60.2	52.1
Plain-backbone detectors:						
UViT-S [8]	Cascade	1K, sup	51.9	44.5		
UViT-B [8]	Cascade	1K, sup	52.5	44.8		
ViTDet, ViT-B	Cascade	1K, MAE	56.0	48.0	57.3	49.1
ViTDet, ViT-L	Cascade	1K, MAE	59.6	51.1	60.1	52.2
ViTDet, ViT-H	Cascade	1K, MAE	**60.4**	**52.0**	61.3	53.1

scales could be compensated by the self-supervised training of MAE. While it is an interesting future topic on improving hierarchical backbones with MAE pre-training, our plain-backbone detector enables us to use the *readily available* ViT backbones from MAE to achieve strong results.

We also note that hierarchical backbones in general involve *enhanced* self-attention block designs. Examples include the shifted window attention in Swin [39] and pooling attention in MViT v1/v2 [15,31]. These block designs, if applied to plain backbones, may also improve accuracy and parameter-efficiency. While this may put our competitors at an advantage, our method is still competitive without these enhancements.

4.3 Comparisons with Previous Systems

Next we provide *system-level* comparisons with the leading results reported in previous papers. We refer to our system as **ViTDet**, *i.e.*, ViT Detector, aiming at the usage of a ViT backbone for detection. Since these comparisons are system-level, the methods use a variety of different techniques. While we make efforts to balance the comparisons (as noted below), making a perfectly controlled comparison is infeasible in general; our goal, instead, is to situate our method in the context of current leading methods.

Comparisons on COCO. Table 6 reports the system-level comparisons on COCO. For a fairer comparison, here we make two changes following our com-

Table 7. System-level comparisons with the leading results on LVIS (v1 val) reported by the original papers. All results are without test-time augmentation. Detic [54] uses pre-trained CLIP [41] text embeddings. †: these entries use CBNetV2 [33] that combines two Swin-L backbones.

Method	Pre-train	AP^{mask}	AP^{mask}_{rare}	AP^{box}
Hierarchical-backbone detectors:				
Copy-Paste [17], Eff-B7 FPN	None (random init)	36.0	29.7	39.2
Detic [54], Swin-B	21K, sup; CLIP	41.7	41.7	–
competition winner 2021 [16] baseline, †	21K, sup	43.1	34.3	–
competition winner 2021 [16] full, †	21K, sup	**49.2**	**45.4**	–
Plain-backbone detectors:				
ViTDet, ViT-L	1K, MAE	46.0	34.3	51.2
ViTDet, ViT-H	1K, MAE	48.1	36.9	53.4

petitors: we adopt soft-nms [2] as is used by all competitors [31,33,38,39] in this table and increase the input size (from 1024 to 1280) following [33,38]. We note that we do *not* use these improvements in previous ablations. As in the previous subsection (Sec. 4.3), we use relative position biases here.

The leading systems thus far are all based on hierarchical backbones (Table 6). For the first time, we show that a *plain-backbone* detector can achieve highly accurate results on COCO and can compete with the leading systems.

We also compare with UViT [8] which is a recent plain-backbone detection method. As discussed in Sec. 2, UViT and our work have different focuses. UViT aims at designing a new plain backbone that is good for detection, while our goal here is to support general-purpose ViT backbones including the original ones in [12]. Despite the different focuses, both UViT and our work suggest that plain-backbone detection is a promising direction with strong potential.

Comparisons on LVIS. We further report system-level comparisons on the LVIS dataset [21]. LVIS contains ~2M high-quality instance segmentation annotations for 1203 classes that exhibit a natural, long-tailed object distribution. Unlike COCO, the class distribution is heavily imbalanced and many classes have very few (*e.g.*, <10) training examples.

We follow the same model and training details as used for the COCO system-level comparison plus two common LVIS practices: we use the federated loss from [55] and sample images with repeat factor sampling [21]. We fine-tune for 100 epochs on the v1 train split.

Table 7 shows the results on the v1 val split. Our plain-backbone detector achieves competitive performance *vs.* previous leading results that all use hierarchical backbones. Ours is 5.0 points higher than the 2021 competition winner's "strong baseline" [16] (48.1 *vs.* 43.1 AP^{mask}), which uses HTC with CBNetV2 [33] that combines two Swin-L backbones. A special issue in LVIS is on the long-tailed distribution, which is beyond the scope of our study. Techniques dedicated to this issue, *e.g.*, using CLIP [41] text embeddings or other advancements from

[16], can largely increase AP on the rare classes (AP_{rare}^{mask}) and thus improve overall AP. These are orthogonal to our method and could be complementary. Nevertheless, our results on LVIS again suggest that plain-backbone detectors can compete with hierarchical ones.

5   Conclusion

Our exploration has demonstrated that *plain-backbone detection is a promising research direction*. This methodology largely maintains the independence of the general-purpose backbones and the downstream task-specific designs—which had been the case for ConvNet-based research but not for Transformer-based research. We hope decoupling pre-training from fine-tuning is a methodology that will generally benefit the community, which has been shown in natural language processing [11,42]. We hope our study will also help bring the fields of computer vision and NLP closer.

References

1. Bao, H., Dong, L., Wei, F.: BEiT: BERT pre-training of image Transformers. arXiv:2106.08254 (2021)
2. Bodla, N., Singh, B., Chellappa, R., Davis, L.S.: Soft-NMS - improving object detection with one line of code. In: ICCV (2017)
3. Cai, Z., Vasconcelos, N.: Cascade R-CNN: high quality object detection and instance segmentation. TPAMI **43**(5), 1483–1498 (2019)
4. Carion, N., Massa, F., Synnaeve, G., Usunier, N., Kirillov, A., Zagoruyko, S.: End-to-end object detection with transformers. In: Vedaldi, A., Bischof, H., Brox, T., Frahm, J.-M. (eds.) ECCV 2020. LNCS, vol. 12346, pp. 213–229. Springer, Cham (2020). https://doi.org/10.1007/978-3-030-58452-8_13
5. Chen, K., et al.: Hybrid task cascade for instance segmentation. In: CVPR (2019)
6. Chen, Q., Wang, Y., Yang, T., Zhang, X., Cheng, J., Sun, J.: You only look one-level feature. In: CVPR (2021)
7. Chen, T., Xu, B., Zhang, C., Guestrin, C.: Training deep nets with sublinear memory cost. arXiv:1604.06174 (2016)
8. Chen, W., et al.: A simple single-scale vision transformer for object localization and instance segmentation. arXiv:2112.09747 (2021)
9. Dai, X., et al.: Dynamic head: unifying object detection heads with attentions. In: CVPR (2021)
10. Deng, J., Dong, W., Socher, R., Li, L.J., Li, K., Fei-Fei, L.: ImageNet: a large-scale hierarchical image database. In: CVPR (2009)
11. Devlin, J., Chang, M.W., Lee, K., Toutanova, K.: BERT: pre-training of deep bidirectional Transformers for language understanding. In: NAACL (2019)
12. Dosovitskiy, A., et al.: An image is worth 16 x 16 words: transformers for image recognition at scale. In: ICLR (2021)
13. Duan, K., Bai, S., Xie, L., Qi, H., Huang, Q., Tian, Q.: CenterNet: keypoint triplets for object detection. In: ICCV (2019)
14. El-Nouby, A., et al.: XCiT: cross-covariance image transformers. In: NeurIPS (2021)

15. Fan, H., Xiong, B., Mangalam, K., Li, Y., Yan, Z., Malik, J., Feichtenhofer, C.: Multiscale Vision Transformers. In: ICCV (2021)
16. Fu, W., Nie, C., Sun, T., Liu, J., Zhang, T., Liu, Y.: LVIS challenge track technical report 1st place solution: distribution balanced and boundary refinement for large vocabulary instance segmentation. arXiv:2111.02668 (2021)
17. Ghiasi, G., et al.: Simple copy-paste is a strong data augmentation method for instance segmentation. In: CVPR (2021)
18. Girshick, R.: Fast R-CNN. In: ICCV (2015)
19. Girshick, R., Donahue, J., Darrell, T., Malik, J.: Rich feature hierarchies for accurate object detection and semantic segmentation. In: CVPR (2014)
20. Goyal, P., et al.: Accurate, large minibatch SGD: training imagenet in 1 hour. arXiv:1706.02677 (2017)
21. Gupta, A., Dollar, P., Girshick, R.: LVIS: a dataset for large vocabulary instance segmentation. In: CVPR (2019)
22. He, K., Chen, X., Xie, S., Li, Y., Dollár, P., Girshick, R.: Masked autoencoders are scalable vision learners. arXiv:2111.06377 (2021)
23. He, K., Gkioxari, G., Dollár, P., Girshick, R.: Mask R-CNN. In: ICCV (2017)
24. He, K., Zhang, X., Ren, S., Sun, J.: Spatial pyramid pooling in deep convolutional networks for visual recognition. In: ECCV (2014)
25. He, K., Zhang, X., Ren, S., Sun, J.: Deep residual learning for image recognition. In: CVPR (2016)
26. Heo, B., Yun, S., Han, D., Chun, S., Choe, J., Oh, S.J.: Rethinking spatial dimensions of vision transformers. In: ICCV (2021)
27. Krizhevsky, A., Sutskever, I., Hinton, G.: ImageNet classification with deep convolutional neural networks. In: NeurIPS (2012)
28. Law, H., Deng, J.: CornerNet: detecting objects as paired keypoints. In: ECCV (2018)
29. LeCun, Y., et al.: Backpropagation applied to handwritten zip code recognition. Neural Comput. 1(4), 541–551 (1989)
30. Li, Y., Chen, Y., Wang, N., Zhang, Z.: Scale-aware trident networks for object detection. In: ICCV (2019)
31. Li, Y., Wu, C.Y., Fan, H., Mangalam, K., Xiong, B., Malik, J., Feichtenhofer, C.: MViTv2: improved multiscale Vision Transformers for classification and detection. arXiv:2112.01526 (2021)
32. Li, Y., Xie, S., Chen, X., Dollar, P., He, K., Girshick, R.: Benchmarking detection transfer learning with Vision Transformers. arXiv:2111.11429 (2021)
33. Liang, T., et al.: CBNetV2: a composite backbone network architecture for object detection. arXiv:2107.00420 (2021)
34. Lin, T.Y., Dollár, P., Girshick, R., He, K., Hariharan, B., Belongie, S.: Feature pyramid networks for object detection. In: CVPR (2017)
35. Lin, T.Y., Goyal, P., Girshick, R., He, K., Dollár, P.: Focal loss for dense object detection. In: ICCV (2017)
36. Lin, T.Y., et al.: Microsoft COCO: common objects in context. In: ECCV (2014)
37. Liu, W., et al.: SSD: single shot multibox detector. In: ECCV (2016)
38. Liu, Z., et al.: Swin transformer V2: scaling up capacity and resolution. arXiv:2111.09883 (2021)
39. Liu, Z., et al.: Swin transformer: hierarchical vision transformer using shifted windows. In: ICCV (2021)
40. Loshchilov, I., Hutter, F.: Decoupled weight decay regularization. In: ICLR (2019)
41. Radford, A., et al.: Learning transferable visual models from natural language supervision (2021)

42. Radford, A., Narasimhan, K., Salimans, T., Sutskever, I.: Improving language understanding by generative pre-training (2018)
43. Raffel, C., et al.: Exploring the limits of transfer learning with a unified text-to-text transformer. In: JMLR (2020)
44. Redmon, J., Divvala, S., Girshick, R., Farhadi, A.: You only look once: unified, real-time object detection. In: CVPR (2016)
45. Ren, S., He, K., Girshick, R., Sun, J.: Faster R-CNN: towards real-time object detection with region proposal networks. In: NeurIPS (2015)
46. Simonyan, K., Zisserman, A.: Very deep convolutional networks for large-scale image recognition. In: ICLR (2015)
47. Szegedy, C., et al.: Going deeper with convolutions. In: CVPR (2015)
48. Tian, Z., Shen, C., Chen, H., He, T.: FCOS: fully convolutional one-stage object detection. In: ICCV (2019)
49. Tolstikhin, I., et al.: MLP-mixer: an all-MLP architecture for vision. In: NeurIPS (2021)
50. Touvron, H., et al.: ResMLP: feedforward networks for image classification with data-efficient training. arXiv:2105.03404 (2021)
51. Vaswani, A., et al.: Attention is all you need. In: NeurIPS (2017)
52. Wang, W., et al.: Pyramid Vision transformer: a versatile backbone for dense prediction without convolutions. In: ICCV (2021)
53. Zhai, X., Kolesnikov, A., Houlsby, N., Beyer, L.: Scaling vision transformers. arXiv:2106.04560 (2021)
54. Zhou, X., Girdhar, R., Joulin, A., Krähenbühl, P., Misra, I.: Detecting twenty-thousand classes using image-level supervision. arXiv:2201.02605 (2022)
55. Zhou, X., Koltun, V., Krähenbühl, P.: Probabilistic two-stage detection. arXiv preprint arXiv:2103.07461 (2021)
56. Zhu, X., Su, W., Lu, L., Li, B., Wang, X., Dai, J.: Deformable DETR: deformable transformers for end-to-end object detection. In: ICLR (2020)

Adversarially-Aware Robust Object Detector

Ziyi Dong, Pengxu Wei$^{(\boxtimes)}$, and Liang Lin

Sun Yat-Sen University, Guangzhou, China
dongzy6@mail2.sysu.edu.cn, weipx3@mail.sysu.edu.cn, linliang@ieee.org

Abstract. Object detection, as a fundamental computer vision task, has achieved a remarkable progress with the emergence of deep neural networks. Nevertheless, few works explore the adversarial robustness of object detectors to resist adversarial attacks for practical applications in various real-world scenarios. Detectors have been greatly challenged by unnoticeable perturbation, with sharp performance drop on clean images and extremely poor performance on adversarial images. In this work, we empirically explore the model training for adversarial robustness in object detection, which greatly attributes to the conflict between learning clean images and adversarial images. To mitigate this issue, we propose a Robust Detector (RobustDet) based on adversarially-aware convolution to disentangle gradients for model learning on clean and adversarial images. RobustDet also employs the Adversarial Image Discriminator (AID) and Consistent Features with Reconstruction (CFR) to ensure a reliable robustness. Extensive experiments on PASCAL VOC and MS-COCO demonstrate that our model effectively disentangles gradients and significantly enhances the detection robustness with maintaining the detection ability on clean images. Our source code and trained models are publicly available at: https://github.com/7eu7d7/RobustDet.

Keywords: Object detection · Adversarial attack and defense · Adversarial robustness · Detection robustness bottleneck

1 Introduction

Although deep neural networks (DNNs) have achieved a remarkable progress in many visual tasks such as image classification [12], object detection [9,23] and semantic segmentation [4,37], they are vulnerable to even slight, imperceptible adversarial perturbations and yield erroneous predictions [3,10,21,31]. *A miss is as good as a mile.* Such vulnerability inspires increasing attentions on the adversarial robustness mainly in the image classification task [3,16,22,29,36]. Nevertheless, with elaborate architectures to recognize simultaneously where and which

Supplementary Information The online version contains supplementary material available at https://doi.org/10.1007/978-3-031-20077-9_18.

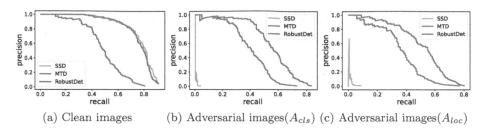

(a) Clean images   (b) Adversarial images(A_{cls}) (c) Adversarial images(A_{loc})

Fig. 1. Precision-Recall (PR) curves of non-robust detector (standard SSD), and two SSD-based robust detectors, *i.e.*, MTD [34] and our RobustDet. They are respectively evaluated under *the conventional standard setting* with clean images and *two detector attacks* whose adversarial images are generated from attacks of classification (A_{cls}) and localization (A_{loc}) [34]. It is observed that SSD has a high performance on clean images but *performs rather poorly under two attacks*. The robust detector MTD is relatively robust under attacks but *presents a significant performance drop on clean images*. Instead, *our RobustDet not only gains a reliable detection robustness on adversarial images, but also maintains a high detection performance on clean images on par with the standard SSD.*

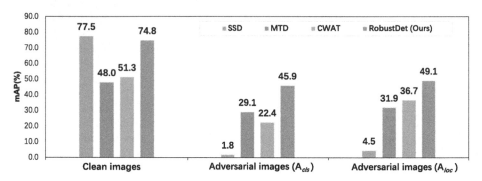

Fig. 2. Detection performance comparison on clean and adversarial images for standard SSD, MTD [34], CWAT [5] and our RobustDet.

category objects are in images, object detectors also suffers from the vulnerable robustness and are easily fooled by adversarial attacks [5,6,15,30,32]. As demonstrated in Fig. 2, standard SSD achieves only **1.8% mAP** on adversarial images, by **75.7% mAP drops**! The vulnerability of object detection models seriously raises security concerns on their practicability in security-sensitive applications, *e.g.*, autonomous driving and video surveillance.

The vulnerable robustness of object detectors has been impressively verified to attack two tasks of classification and localization [6,24,30,32], few researches focus on investigating the challenging countermeasure: *how to defend those attacks to resist the adversarial perturbations for detectors*. To address this issue, MTD [34], as an earlier attempt, regards the adversarial training of object detection as a multi-task learning and choose those adversarial images that have the largest impact on the total loss for learning. Subsequently, the second related

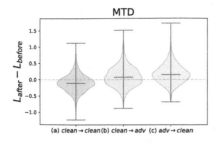
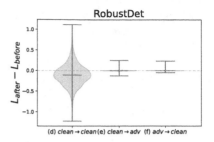

Fig. 3. Empirical analyses on the conflict between the learning of clean images and adversarial images via the statistics of loss changes (More details can be referred to our supplementary material.). (a), (b) and (c) are the loss changes on robust detector MTD [34]. (d), (e) and (f) are the loss changes on our RobustDet. For both methods under *clean → clean*, they have the decreasing loss changes for most images, indicating the favorable training. Under *clean(adv) → adv(clean)*, MTD has the increasing loss changes for most images, indicating the inverse training effects between learning clean and adversarial images. Instead, our RobustDet has almost no effects between them, indicating a better disentanglement for learning clean and adversarial images.

work, CWAT [5], points out the problem of class imbalance in the attack and proposes to attack each category as evenly as possible to generate more reasonable adversarial images. In general, these existing methods suffer from the **detection robustness bottleneck**: *a significant degradation on clean images with only a limited adversarial robustness*, shown in Fig. 1 and 2. That is, due to the introduction of adversarial perturbation during training, they reach a compromise for both the model accuracy on clean images and the robustness on adversarial images. This would inevitably make a concession of robust models with the performance sacrifice on clean images as well as a limited adversarial robustness for object detection.

In this paper, we firstly explore the aforementioned **detection robustness bottleneck** on both clean images and adversarial images for object detection. Particularly, one noteworthy difference from the adversarial robustness in the image classification task, where robust models usually only have a small amount of the performance decline on clean images [11,35], is that robust object detectors only yields a limited robustness from adversarial training and suffer from a significant performance degradation by nearly 30% on clean images (77.5% mAP for standard SSD *vs.* 48.0% mAP for MTD [34] on the PASCAL VOC dataset, as shown in Fig. 2). It indicates that, in the training phase, robust detectors hardly reach a win-win balance to trade off the robustness of adversarial images and the accuracy of clean images. *To further investigate this issue, on one hand, we inspect the individual loss changes for both images in an adversarial robust detector.* A conflict between two tasks of learning clean images and adversarial images in adversarial training is observed, which can be speculated as a pitfall to explain the aforementioned detection robustness bottleneck to a certain extent. *On the other hand, we analyze the interference between the gradients of clean images and the adversarial images for existing models.* Accordingly, strong interference is observed, indicating that an object detector has a large difficulty to distinguish no-robust and robust features. Thus, it is reasonable that models are confronted with the detection robustness bottleneck.

To mitigate this problem, we propose a Robust Detection model (RobustDet) via adversarially-aware convolution. The model learns different groups of convolution kernels and adaptively assigns weights to them based on the Adversarial Image Discriminator (AID). RobustDet also employs the Consistent Features with Reconstruction (CFR) to ensure reliable robustness. By applying reconstruction constraints to make the features extracted by the model can be reconstructed as clean images as possible, the model is drived to extract more robust features for both clean and adversarial images. Extensive experimental results on PASCAL VOC [8] and MS-COCO [18] datasets have demonstrated superior accuracy performance on clean images and promising detection robustness on adversarial images.

Overall, our contributions are summarized as follows:

1. Empirically, we analyse the detection robustness bottleneck and verify the conflict between learning clean images and adversarial images for robust object detectors.
2. Technically, we propose a robust detection model (RobustDet) based on adversarially-aware convolution to learn robust features for clean images and adversarial images. In addition, we propose Consistent Features with Reconstruction (CFR) to constrain the model to extract more robust features that can be reconstructed as clean images as possible.
3. Experimentally, we conduct comprehensive experiments to evaluate the proposed approach for adversarial detection robustness on PASCAL VOC and MS-COCO datasets, achieving state-of-the-art performance on both clean images and adversarial images. It presents a superior accuracy performance on clean images and a promising detection robustness on adversarial images.

2   Related Work

2.1   Adversarial Attack and Defense

For deep neural networks, their excellent feature representation capability has been demonstrated in various scenarios [12,13,26]. Even so, it has been criticized that neural network models easily produce totally wrong predictions under slight perturbations to inputs [28]. Especially, they are rather vulnerable to adversarial attacks. Accordingly, more and more adversarial attack methods have been proposed: gradient-based white box adversarial attack methods (e.g., FGSM [10] and PGD [21]), and black box adversarial attack methods (e.g., UPSET [24] and LeBA [33]). These methods can easily fool the classification model and even a change in just one pixel would totally fool the model [27]. To address this problem, some defense methods have been proposed [3,16,22,29,36]. Among them, adversarial training is one of the most widely used and effective methods. It allows the model to continuously learn the adversarial images and focuses more on the robust features of adversarial images and clean images to ignore non-robust features.

2.2 Attack and Robust Object Detector

In recent years, seminal object detection models have been proposed, *e.g.*, Faster RCNN [23], SSD [19], YOLOX [9], and DETR [2], building a series of profound and insightful milestones for object detection. Even so, they inevitably inherit the vulnerability to attack, with the root in deep neural networks. Existing researches have shown that attack methods for classification tasks can also be effective in attacking object detection models [34]. Object detectors have some different structures from classification models, and object detectors can be attacked more effectively for these structures. For example, DAG [32] and UEA [30] are the attack methods for object-level features by superimposing perturbation on the whole image. Dpatch [20] fools the detector by adding a patch to the image. ShapeShifter [6] attacks detectors in the physical world.

Instead, although attack methods for object detectors are becoming more and more efficient, there are few defense strategies in the object detection task. [34] proposes the MTD method based on adversarial training. At each step of adversarial training, the images that can increase the loss the most are selected from the adversarial images to learn to improve the robustness of the model. [5] explores the problem of class imbalance in the attacks for object detectors and proposes to make the attack intensity as consistent as possible for each class. Adversarial training is performed through these images to improve the robustness of the model. These methods mainly focus on the generation of adversarial images and ignore the lack of robustness caused by the structure of the model. Thus, they suffer from the detection robustness bottleneck as mentioned in Sect. 1.

Since few research works on adversarially-robust object detectors, it is almost blind to essentially explore object detection. In this paper, we will firstly explore empirically the detection robustness bottleneck to further understand the adversarial robustness in object detection in Sect. 3. Then, we will elaborate the proposed RobustDet to address the detection robustness bottleneck in Sect. 4. We will conduct extensive experiments to demonstrate the effectiveness of the proposed method In Sect. 5 and conclude the paper in Sect. 6.

Defenses against unseen attacks are customarily explored in classification tasks. However, for detection tasks we suffer from a lack of the most fundamental conception of their robustness. Thus, we focus more on more fundamental problems of the robustness of object detectors. Those more advanced problems need to be explored further based on this work.

3 Adversarial Robustness in Object Detection

3.1 Problem Setting

For a clean image x, an object detector f parameterized by $\boldsymbol{\theta}$, yields object bounding boxes $\{\hat{\boldsymbol{b}}_i = [p_i^x, p_i^y, w_i, h_i]\}$ with their predicted class probabilities $\{\hat{c}_i = [\hat{c}_i^{bg}, \hat{c}_i^1, \cdots, \hat{c}_i^C]\}$ over the background (bg) and C object categories, *i.e.*, $f(x; \boldsymbol{\theta}) \rightarrow \{\hat{\boldsymbol{b}}_i, \hat{\boldsymbol{c}}_i\}$, where p_i^x and p_i^y are the coordinates of the top left corner of $\hat{\boldsymbol{b}}_i$, w_i and h_i are the width and height of $\hat{\boldsymbol{b}}_i$. The localization loss $\mathcal{L}_{loc} = \sum_{i \in pos} L_1^{smooth}(\hat{\boldsymbol{b}}_i, \boldsymbol{b}_i)$

and the classification loss $\mathcal{L}_{cls} = -\sum_{i \in pos} c_i \log(\hat{c}_i^u) - \sum_{i \in neg} c_i \log(\hat{c}_i^{bg})$, where b_i is the Ground-Truth (GT) bounding box that matches the predicted bounding box $\hat{b}_i$ and c_i denotes its GT category, and the detection loss is $\mathcal{L}_{det} = \mathcal{L}_{loc} + \mathcal{L}_{cls}$. Following MTD [34], two types of attacks (A_{cls} and A_{loc}) for object detection are specifically steered for classification and localization, respectively:

$$
\begin{aligned}
A_{cls}(x) &= \arg\max_{\bar{x} \in \mathcal{S}_x} \mathcal{L}_{cls}(f(\bar{x}; \boldsymbol{\theta}), \{c_i, b_i\}), \\
A_{loc}(x) &= \arg\max_{\bar{x} \in \mathcal{S}_x} \mathcal{L}_{loc}(f(\bar{x}; \boldsymbol{\theta}), \{c_i, b_i\}),
\end{aligned}
\tag{1}
$$

where $\bar{x}$ is the adversarial counterpart of x, and $\mathcal{S}_x = \{\bar{x} \cap [0, 255]^{cwh} | \|\bar{x} - x\|_\infty \leq \epsilon\}$ is the adversarial image space centered on clean images x with perturbation budget of ϵ. A_{cls} denotes searching for the image x in its ϵ neighborhood that maximizes L_{cls} as the adversarial image.

3.2   Analyses of the Detection Robustness Bottleneck

(1) Conflict Between Learning Adversarial Images and Clean Images.
To defense the attacks, robust models are expected to be immune to adversarial perturbations via learning shared features between clean images and adversarial images to improve the robustness of the model. This is the conventional wisdom in prevalent adversarial training for defense, especially in the image classification task. Nevertheless, the adversarial robustness for object detection is worrisome. Namely, robust detection models perform poorly on both clean and adversarial images, as demonstrated in Fig. 1 and Fig. 2. In particular, adversarial training on both clean and adversarial images results in a significant performance drop on clean images. This may indicate a conflict between the tasks of learning clean and adversarial images; thus the model has to compromise a trade-off between adversarial and clean images. To further explore the reasons why the model cannot learn both images well, we conduct an investigation from two aspects.

Loss Changes for Clean and Adversarial Images. We inspect intuitively the loss changes for clean and adversarial images. Specifically, we perform a validation via m-step adversarial training of an adversarially-trained robust model on a batch of clean images or adversarial images and observe the loss change on another batch of images (The selection of m and algorithm details are discussed in the supplementary material). The loss change of the adversarial (clean) image after learning the clean (adversarial) image is defined as $clean \rightarrow adv$ ($adv \rightarrow clean$). From the experimental results in Fig. 3, it is observed that $clean \rightarrow adv$ and $adv \rightarrow clean$ are positive for most images compared with the most negative results of $clean \rightarrow clean$. This shows that learning clean images and adversarial images will increase the loss of each other for most images. The impact of adversarial images on clean images is greater than that of clean images on adversarial images. This validation shows that learning clean images and adversarial images are conflicting tasks for the model, to some extent. Thus, during the training phase, the model has the burden to well address this learning conflict.

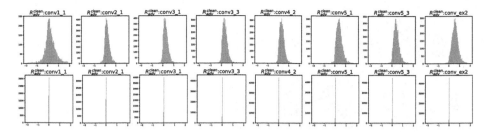

Fig. 4. The gradient entanglement degree R_{adv}^{clean} of clean images and adversarial images based on features from different convolutional layers. The upper shows the results from SSD and the second row is from our RobustDet.

Gradient Interference Analysis. The clean image and the adversarial image are from two different domains with different patterns. There are shared features between them but also have their unique features. A highly robust model must have parameters for extracting the shared features and another two part parameters for extracting unique features that are orthogonal to each other. For an adversarial trained robust model, the shared features of two kinds of images should have been well learned, and only the part processing unique features still needs reinforcement. Therefore, for this model, the gradients generated by the two kinds of images should have low correlation and be nearly orthogonal.

Accordingly, we define the intensity of gradient entanglement of one image x_1 to another image x_2: $\mathcal{R}_{g_2}^{g_1} = g_1^T g_2 / |g_2|^2$, where g_1 and g_2 are the gradient vectors of the two kind of images. The greater the gradient entanglement of the two kinds of images, the more serious the interference between them and the model does not distinguish the unique features well. Based on the experimental results of the above loss variations, the greater the gradient entanglement, the more difficult the conflict between the two kinds of images can be reconciled. The smaller gradient entanglement indicates that the model has enough ability to distinguish the shared features from their unique features and can disentangle the clean images and the adversarial images. It can be seen from the Fig. 4 that the gradient entanglement between the clean image and the adversarial image on the adversarial trained robust model is quite high, and even negative values appear in the first few layers. This shows that the updated directions of some clean images and adversarial images on the adversarial-trained model are completely opposite, which also indicates the conflict between the two kinds of images. When learning one kind of image, it will inevitably have an impact on another kind of image, which leads to a detection robustness bottleneck.

(2) The Conflict to the Robustness of Classification and Location. We compare the detection results of the non-robust model and the adversarial trained robust model on the clean image, the A_{cls} adversarial image, and the A_{loc} adversarial image. It can be seen from the Fig. 5 that the non-robust model will locate the wrong object with high confidence when applying an attack. The robust model will not completely confuse to the attack, but its classification

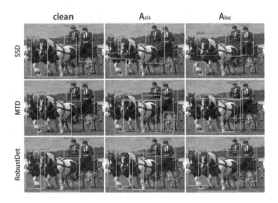

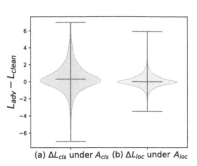

(a) ΔL_{cls} under A_{cls} (b) ΔL_{loc} under A_{loc}

Fig. 5. Left: The detection results of the standard SSD, MTD and our RobustDet on the clean image and two adversarial images attacked from classification (A_{cls}) and localization (A_{loc}). MTD and RobustDet are robust models taking SSD as their base-models. **Right:** Under the attacks of A_{cls} and A_{loc}, the corresponding loss changes between the adversarial image and the original image.

and localization accuracy on both clean images and adversarial images have greatly decreased. The robustness of localization objects is much better than classification. It can be seen from the figure that the bounding boxes predicted by the robust models do not have as large deviations as the classification.

The results in Fig. 5 shows that the variation of L_{cls} when applying A_{cls} attack compared to the variation of L_{loc} when applying A_{loc} attack is much larger. This also indicates that the classification module is less robust and more vulnerable to attack. These both shows that the conflict between the two images under the classification subtask is more serious than the localization subtask. The scores given in the classification part will also determine the selection of the bounding box. Therefore, this conflict will further damage the performance of the model.

4   Methodology

4.1   Overall Framework

Based on the aforementioned analyses in Sect. 3.2, the conflict between the learning of clean and adversarial images has adversary effects on the robustness of classification and localization. To address this problem, we propose a Robust-Det model for defenses against adversarial attacks (Fig. 6). We detect objects through adversarially-aware convolution and use an Adversarial Image Discriminator (AID) to generate the weights for the adversarially-aware convolution kernel based on the perturbations of the input image. Furthermore, inspired by VAE [14], the image reconstruction constraint via CFR is considered for reconstructing images as clean images to facilitate the model to learn robust features.

4.2   Adversarially-Aware Convolution (AAconv)

Existing models essentially utilize the shared model parameters for learning adversarial images and clean images. This inevitably makes the model suffer from a detection robustness bottleneck. There are objective distinctions between adversarial images and clean images. Admitting these distinctions rather than forcing the detector to learn these two images with the same parameters would be a better choice. Making the model explicitly distinguish these two kinds of images and detect them with different parameters will alleviate the conflict between these tasks. Inspired by [7], we propose adversarially-aware convolution in our Robust-Det model to learn robust features for clean images and adversarial images.

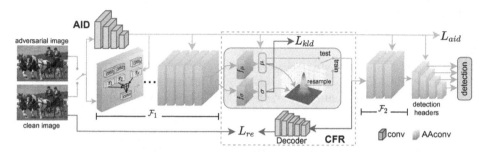

Fig. 6. The overall architecture of RobustDet based on SSD. The CFR is inserted into the SSD backbone followed by the first detection layer (conv4_3), and the two parts in front and behind this layer are named $\mathcal{F}_1$ and $\mathcal{F}_2$. The blue arrows are the data flow of AID, whose outputs are used as weights of AAconv. The purple arrows are the primary data flow when RobustDet detect objects. The teal arrows are the reconstruction data flow during training.

RobustDet employs different kernels to convolve clean images and adversarial images. Different parameters will be used for different perturbed images. The generation of the convolution kernel is controlled by an adversarial image discriminator D. Before the model detects objects in an image, the adversarial image discriminator D will first generate the M-dimensional probability vector of the image $\mathcal{P} = D(x) = \{\pi_1, \pi_2, ..., \pi_M\}$. This probability vector is used as the weights to control the convolution kernels generation. Then the parameters of the finally generated convolution kernel can be write as: $\dot{\theta}^{AAconv} = \sum_{i=1}^{M} \theta_i^{AAconv} \cdot \pi_i$, where θ_i^{AAconv} denotes parameters of dynamic convolution kernels in our AAconv module, where i indicates the index of i-th convolution kernel.

RobustDet uses adversarially-aware convolutions to adaptively detect different images with different kernels and thus it can effectively learn robust features for clean and adversarial images. It not only extracts the shared features, but also can be responsible for specific features for clean and adversarial images. Therefore, it is more effective to alleviate the detection robustness bottleneck.

4.3   Adversarial Image Discriminator (AID)

The generation of the adversarially-aware convolution kernels is controlled by the adversarial image discriminator. And this module may also be attacked and give the wrong weight. Wrong weights will lead the wrong convolution kernel to be generated, which will be a disaster for the model. Accordingly, in order to improve its robustness, we employ Online Triplet Loss [25] to the adversarial image discriminator. Specifically, we consider the probability distribution of the same kind of images (*i.e.*, clean or adversarial images) as close as possible and the different kinds of images (clean or adversarial images) as far away as possible. A margin between the probability distributions of the two kinds of images outputs is introduced to strengthen the robustness of the adversarial image discriminator. Jensen-Shannon (JS) divergence [17] is utilized to measure the distance between two probability distributions, P_1 and P_2 (two distributions as an example for JS divergence): $JS\left(P_1 \| P_2\right) = \frac{1}{2} KL\left(P_1 \| \frac{P_1+P_2}{2}\right) + \frac{1}{2} KL\left(P_2 \| \frac{P_1+P_2}{2}\right)$. Overall, the AID loss is defined as follows,

$$\mathcal{L}_{aid} = \sum_{i=1}^{N_T} \left[JS\left(D\left(x_i^a\right) \| D\left(x_i^p\right)\right) - JS\left(D\left(x_i^a\right) \| D\left(x_i^n\right)\right) + \gamma \right]_+, \quad (2)$$

where x^p (x^n) is a randomly selected image from one minibatch that has the same (opposite) type (*i.e.*, clean or adversarial image) as the anchor instance x^a in one triplet, γ is the margin between x^n and x^p, N_T is the number of triplets, and $[\cdot]_+$ clips values to $[0, +\infty]$.

4.4   Consistent Features with Reconstruction (CFR)

To alleviate the negative effects of adversarial perturbation, our RobustDet aims to ensure the feature distribution of an adversarial image in the neighbourhood of its clean image. Thus, inspired by VAE [14], our RobustDet reconstructs consistent features of clean/adversarial images with clean images via our AAconvs. Assume that the output feature map of the convolutional layer after the conv4_3 layer (VGG backbone) comes from a multivariate Gaussian distribution with an diagonal covariance matrix $\mathcal{N}(\boldsymbol{\mu} = (\mu_1, ..., \mu_N), \boldsymbol{\Sigma} = diag(\sigma_1^2, ..., \sigma_N^2))$. For simplicity, $\boldsymbol{\sigma} = (\sigma_1^2, ..., \sigma_N^2)$. Instead of directly predicting the features that are ultimately used for detection, our model predicts the mean $\boldsymbol{\mu}$ and standard deviations $\boldsymbol{\sigma}$ of its feature distribution: $\boldsymbol{\mu} = f_{\boldsymbol{\mu}}(\mathcal{F}_1(x))$, $\boldsymbol{\sigma} = f_{\boldsymbol{\sigma}}(\mathcal{F}_1(x))$, where $f_{\boldsymbol{\mu}}$ and $f_{\boldsymbol{\sigma}}$ are the two layers of the model that predict the mean and standard deviations, $\mathcal{F}_1(x)$ and $\mathcal{F}_2(x)$ is two parts of VGG that split by conv4_3. From this distribution, a N-dimensional feature vector is randomly sampled as the robust feature for the input image, which is used for subsequent CFR and object detection in the training phase. Then the reconstruction loss can be defined as:

$$\mathcal{L}_{re} = \|G\left(\boldsymbol{z}\right) - x\|^2, \quad \boldsymbol{z} \sim \mathcal{N}(\boldsymbol{\mu}, \boldsymbol{\Sigma}), \quad (3)$$

where $\| \cdot \|^2$ indicates ℓ_2 norm, and x is the clean image. Once this feature distribution is learnt, our model can generate the similar features for an adversarial image and its clean counterpart image. Thus, in the testing phase, the predicted mean $\boldsymbol{\mu}$ is directly used as the robust feature for detection.

Furthermore, similar to VAE, we also have an additional constraint to prevent the predicted distribution from collapse (*e.g.*, $\boldsymbol{\mu}$ and $\boldsymbol{\sigma}$ are approximate to zero):

$$\mathcal{L}_{kld} = \sum_{i=1}^{N} \frac{1}{2N} \left(-\log \sigma_i^2 + \mu_i^2 + \sigma_i^2 - 1 \right), \quad (4)$$

Overall, the total loss of our RobustDet is summarized as follows,

$$\mathcal{L} = \beta(\mathcal{L}_{det} + a\mathcal{L}_{aid}) + b\mathcal{L}_{re} + c\mathcal{L}_{kld}, \tag{5}$$

where β, a, b and c are the hyper-parameters.

5 Experiments

5.1 Implementation Details

Our experiments are conducted on PASCAL VOC [8] and MS-COCO [18] datasets. Mean average precision (mAP) with IoU threshold 0.5 is used for evaluating the performance of standard and robust models.

The proposed method is rooted in the one-stage detector SSD [19] with VGG16 as the backbone. Considering that Batch Normalization would increase the adversarial vulnerability [1], we make a modification on VGG16 without batch normalization layers [19]. In experiments, we use the model pre-trained on clean images for adversarial training and employ Stochastic Gradient Descent (SGD) with a learning rate of 10^{-3}, momentum 0.9, weight decay 0.0005 and batch size 32 with the multi-box loss.

For the robustness evaluation, we follow the same setting to MTD [34] and CWAT [5] for a fair comparison and use three different attacks, PGD [21], CWA [5] and DAG [32]. Among them, CWA and DAG are specifically designed for object detectors. For adversarial training, we also follow the same attack setting to MTD [34] and CWAT [5] for a fair comparison; namely, we use the PGD-20 attacker with budget $\epsilon = 8$ to generate adversarial examples [34]. And we set the margin in $\mathcal{L}_{aid}$ as $\gamma = 0.6$ and N_T is calculated from the mini-batch, and hyper-parameters in $\mathcal{L}$ as $\beta = 0.75$, $a = 3$, $b = 0.16$ and $c = 5$. RobustDet* represents RobustDet with CFR.

5.2 Detection Robustness Evaluation

In this section, we evaluate the proposed method in comparison with the state-of-the-art approaches on the PASCAL VOC and MS-COCO datasets in Table 1 and 2. The scenarios in MS-COCO are more complex than PASCAL VOC, and thus it is also more challenging to make the model robust on this dataset. Considering that the object detector has two tasks of classification and localization, we can use PGD to attack the classification (A_{cls}) and localization (A_{loc}). For DAG attacks, we perform 150 steps to make an effective attack. The experimental results are provided in Tables 1 and 2.

In Tables 1 and 2, under different datasets, in compare with standard SSD, MTD (rooted in SSD) suffers from a significant performance degradation on clean images while gaining limited robustness. For example, on the PASCAL VOC dataset, its mAP performance on clean images significantly drops from 77.5% to 1.8% and 4.5% under A_{cls} and A_{loc} attacks, respectively. It also exhibits a poor robustness under CWA and DAG attacks with only 1.2% and 4.9% mAP,

Table 1. The evaluation results using various adversarial attack method on PASCAL VOC 2007 test set[2].

Method	Clean	A_{cls}	A_{loc}	CWA	DAG
SSD	**77.5**	1.8	4.5	1.2	4.9
SSD-AT(A_{cls}) [34]	$46.7^{\downarrow 30.8}$	$21.8^{\uparrow 20.0}$	$32.2^{\downarrow 30.8}$	–	$28.0^{\uparrow 23.1}$
SSD-AT(A_{loc}) [34]	$51.9^{\downarrow 25.6}$	$23.7^{\uparrow 21.9}$	$26.5^{\uparrow 22.0}$	–	$17.2^{\uparrow 12.3}$
MTD [34]	$48.0^{\downarrow 29.5}$	$29.1^{\uparrow 27.3}$	$31.9^{\uparrow 27.4}$	$18.2^{\uparrow 17.0}$	$28.5^{\uparrow 23.6}$
CWAT(PGD-10) [5]	$51.3^{\downarrow 26.2}$	$22.4^{\uparrow 20.6}$	$36.7^{\uparrow 32.2}$	$19.9^{\uparrow 18.7}$	$50.3^{\uparrow 45.4}$
RobustDet (ours)	$75.4^{\downarrow 2.1}$	$41.5^{\uparrow 40.0}$	$45.2^{\uparrow 40.7}$	$42.4^{\uparrow 41.2}$	$52.0^{\uparrow 47.1}$
RobustDet* (ours)	$74.8^{\downarrow 2.7}$	$\mathbf{45.9}^{\uparrow 44.1}$	$\mathbf{49.1}^{\uparrow 44.6}$	$\mathbf{48.0}^{\uparrow 46.8}$	$\mathbf{56.6}^{\uparrow 51.8}$

↓ and ↑ indicate the mAP decrease or increase compared with the baseline SSD, respectively. '-' indicates the result is not provided in the existing work.

Table 2. The evaluation results using various adversarial attack method on MS-COCO 2017 test set.

Method	Clean	A_{cls}	A_{loc}	CWA	DAG
SSD	**42.0**	0.4	1.8	0.1	8.1
MTD [34]	$24.2^{\downarrow 17.8}$	$13.0^{\uparrow 12.6}$	$13.4^{\uparrow 11.6}$	$7.7^{\uparrow 7.6}$	–
CWAT(PGD-10) [5]	$23.7^{\downarrow 18.3}$	$14.2^{\uparrow 13.8}$	$15.5^{\uparrow 13.7}$	$9.2^{\uparrow 9.1}$	–
RobustDet (ours)	$36.7^{\downarrow 5.3}$	$\mathbf{20.6}^{\uparrow 20.2}$	$\mathbf{19.4}^{\uparrow 17.6}$	$\mathbf{20.5}^{\uparrow 20.4}$	$\mathbf{24.5}^{\uparrow 16.4}$
RobustDet* (ours)	$36.0^{\downarrow 6.0}$	$20.0^{\uparrow 19.6}$	$19.0^{\uparrow 17.2}$	$19.9^{\uparrow 19.8}$	$16.5^{\uparrow 8.4}$

respectively. Besides, as for existing robust methods, MTD and CWAT only gain less than 30% mAP under A_{cls} and 40% under A_{loc} and even lose almost 30% mAP on clean images compared with baseline SSD. Instead, our proposed RobustDet not only obtains a high robustness on adversarial images, but also ensures a comparable performance with standard SSD on clean images with a slight performance decrease. On the PASCAL VOC dataset, RobustDet obtains larger than 40% mAPs on adversarial images to defense detection attacks and just loses 2.7% at most on clean images, in comparison with standard SSD. Besides, it also presents a remarkable performance on the MS-COCO dataset. For instance, RobustDet achieves 24.5% under the DAG attack with only 6% mAP decline at most on clean images (RobustDet 36.7% vs. SSD 42.0%).

5.3 Model Evaluation and Analysis

Ablation Study on L_{aid}. The adversarial image discriminator may also be attacked. Thus, the AID loss is introduced to improve its robustness. As shown in Table 3, without L_{aid} RobustDet has a performance decrease on both clean and adversarial images, especially on adversarial images. For instance, it drops by 4.2% mAP under the A_{cls} attack and by 4.5% mAP under the CAW attack. The absence of L_{aid} makes it easier for AID to confuse clean and adversarial images.

Table 3. The ablation study of our model under various adversarial attack method on PASCAL VOC 2007 test set.

Method	Clean	A_{cls}	A_{loc}	CWA	DAG
RobustDet w/o L_{aid}	74.9	37.3	44.9	37.9	51.8
RobustDet* w/o L_{re}	74.6	27.5	41.8	28.6	55.9
RobustDet	**75.4**	41.5	45.2	42.4	52.0
RobustDet*	74.8	**45.9**	**49.1**	**48.0**	**56.6**

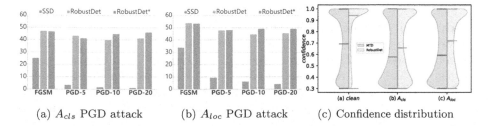

(a) A_{cls} PGD attack   (b) A_{loc} PGD attack   (c) Confidence distribution

Fig. 7. (a) and (b): The robustness of our model under attacks with $\epsilon = 8$ using different PGD steps. (c): Under the attack on L_{cls} and L_{loc} loss, the corresponding loss changes between the adversarial image and the original image.

Ablation Study on Consistent Features with Reconstruction. We compare RobustDet (without CFR) and RobustDet* (with CFR) for the ablation study on CFR. On the PASCAL VOC dataset, as shown in Table 1 and 3, the detection robustness has been improved with the CFR module by 4.1% gains at least (RobustDet 47.5% vs. RobustDet* 45.9% under CWA attack) and by 5.6% at most (RobustDet 42.4% vs. RobustDet* 46.8% under CWA attack). On MS-COCO, Table 2 shows that RobustDet* has a lower performance than RobustDet under all the attacks. This reconstruction can be treated as VAE in VGG-16 whose capacity is relatively limited to learn so many categories, thus compromising the overall training of the model and leading to the performance degradation. Besides, CFR has two losses of L_{kld} and L_{re}. In Table 3, without L_{re}, RobustDet* has a significant decrease under attacks with similar performance on clean images, compared with the baseline. This indicates the model cannot effectively predict both samples into the same distribution.

Attack Using Different PGD Steps. To verify the generalization ability of our model against different steps of PGD attacks, we follow the setting of MTD [34] and provide the performance of the model under various steps of PGD attack on PASCAL VOC in Fig. 7(a) and (b). For non-robust SSD, the performance decreases dramatically with the increase of iteration steps. Our model shows a strong robustness under a variety of PGD attacks with different number of steps. Combined with the experimental results of CWA and DAG in Table 1, it shows that our model has a promising generalization ability and can defend well even if the attacks are somewhat different from the training.

Analysis on Gradient Disentanglement. As discussed in Sect. 3.2, the detection robustness bottleneck can attribute to a conflict between learning adversarial images and clean images. It can be observed from Fig. 3, a adversarially-trained SSD model that learns adversarial (clean) images have a negative impact on the learning of clean (adversarial) images, making the loss increase. But a adversarially-trained RobustDet has almost no similar impact. The average loss variation is less than 0.1. It is also evidenced from Fig. 4 that the gradients of RobustDet on both samples are almost orthogonal. These indicate Robust-Det can effectively alleviate the detection robustness bottleneck and learn both images better.

Analysis on Confidence Distribution. To further verify our RobustDet addressing the conflict, the confidence distribution of bounding boxes that the robust model MTD and our RobustDet produce on clean and adversarial images(A_{cls} and A_{loc}), respectively, in Fig. 7(c). Here we set the filtering threshold for the confidence of the bounding box to be 0.3. From which it is evident that the confidence of the MTD robust model on both the clean and adversarial images is quite low (around 0.7 on clean, 0.6 on A_{cls} and A_{loc}), which is also a manifestation of conflict. In contrast, the confidence of our proposed RobustDet model is fairly high on clean images (around 0.95, by 0.25 higher than MTD) and the confidence on adversarial images is mostly distributed in the higher part (around 0.65 on A_{cls} and 0.7 on A_{loc}). This result can also well illustrate that our method can effectively alleviate the conflict and the detection robustness bottleneck.

6   Conclusion

In this work, we investigate the detection robustness bottleneck that the object detector discards a portion of its performance on the clean image while gaining a very limited robustness from adversarial training. Empirical analysis from the loss change and gradient interference indicate that the detection robustness bottleneck is mainly attributed to the conflict between the object detector in learning clean images and adversarial images. It is hard for object detectors to learn both images well, so it needs a learning trade-off between them.

In terms of the detection robustness bottleneck on both clean images and adversarial images, we propose the RobustDet method based on adversarially-aware convolution. RobustDet utilizes an Adversarial Image Discriminator (AID) to generate different weights to clean images and adversarial images, which guides the generation of adversarially-aware convolutional kernels to adaptively learn robust features. RobustDet also employs the Consistent Features with Reconstruction (CFR) to make the features of clean and adversarial images in the same distribution and empower the model to reconstruct the adversarial image into a clean image. This can further enhance the detection robustness. Besides, experimental results show that our method can effectively alleviate the detection robustness bottleneck. It is demonstrated that our method can significantly improve the robustness of the model without losing the performance on clean images.

Acknowledgement. This work was supported in part by NSFC (No. 62006253, U21A20470, 61876224), National Key R&D Program of China (2021ZD0111601).

References

1. Benz, P., Zhang, C., Kweon, I.S.: Batch normalization increases adversarial vulnerability and decreases adversarial transferability: a non-robust feature perspective. In: International Conference on Computer Vision (ICCV), pp. 7818–7827 (2021)
2. Carion, N., Massa, F., Synnaeve, G., Usunier, N., Kirillov, A., Zagoruyko, S.: End-to-end object detection with transformers. In: Vedaldi, A., Bischof, H., Brox, T., Frahm, J.-M. (eds.) ECCV 2020. LNCS, vol. 12346, pp. 213–229. Springer, Cham (2020). https://doi.org/10.1007/978-3-030-58452-8_13
3. Carlini, N., Wagner, D.A.: Towards evaluating the robustness of neural networks. In: IEEE Symposium on Security and Privacy, pp. 39–57 (2017)
4. Chen, L., Zhu, Y., Papandreou, G., Schroff, F., Adam, H.: Encoder-decoder with atrous separable convolution for semantic image segmentation. In: European Conference on Computer Vision (ECCV), pp. 833–851 (2018)
5. Chen, P., Kung, B., Chen, J.: Class-aware robust adversarial training for object detection. In: Computer Vision and Pattern Recognition (CVPR), pp. 10420–10429 (2021)
6. Chen, S.-T., Cornelius, C., Martin, J., Chau, D.H.P.: ShapeShifter: robust physical adversarial attack on faster R-CNN object detector. In: Berlingerio, M., Bonchi, F., Gärtner, T., Hurley, N., Ifrim, G. (eds.) ECML PKDD 2018. LNCS (LNAI), vol. 11051, pp. 52–68. Springer, Cham (2019). https://doi.org/10.1007/978-3-030-10925-7_4
7. Chen, Y., Dai, X., Liu, M., Chen, D., Yuan, L., Liu, Z.: Dynamic convolution: attention over convolution kernels. In: Computer Vision and Pattern Recognition (CVPR), pp. 11027–11036 (2020)
8. Everingham, M., Eslami, S.M.A., Van Gool, L., Williams, C.K.I., Winn, J., Zisserman, A.: The PASCAL visual object classes challenge: a retrospective. Int. J. Comput. Vision **111**(1), 98–136 (2014). https://doi.org/10.1007/s11263-014-0733-5
9. Ge, Z., Liu, S., Wang, F., Li, Z., Sun, J.: Yolox: exceeding yolo series in 2021. arXiv preprint arXiv:2107.08430 (2021)
10. Goodfellow, I.J., Shlens, J., Szegedy, C.: Explaining and harnessing adversarial examples. In: International Conference on Learning Representations (ICLR) (2015)
11. Gowal, S., Rebuffi, S., Wiles, O., Stimberg, F., Calian, D.A., Mann, T.: Improving robustness using generated data. CoRR abs/2110.09468 (2021)
12. He, K., Zhang, X., Ren, S., Sun, J.: Deep residual learning for image recognition. In: Proceedings of the IEEE Conference on Computer Vision and Pattern Recognition, pp. 770–778 (2016)
13. Howard, A., et al.: Searching for mobilenetv3. In: International Conference on Computer Vision (ICCV), pp. 1314–1324 (2019)
14. Kingma, D.P., Welling, M.: Auto-encoding variational bayes. In: International Conference on Learning Representations (ICLR) (2014)
15. Liang, S., Wu, B., Fan, Y., Wei, X., Cao, X.: Parallel rectangle flip attack: a query-based black-box attack against object detection. In: International Conference on Computer Vision (ICCV), pp. 7697–7707 (2021)
16. Liao, F., Liang, M., Dong, Y., Pang, T., Hu, X., Zhu, J.: Defense against adversarial attacks using high-level representation guided denoiser. In: Computer Vision and Pattern Recognition (CVPR), pp. 1778–1787 (2018)

17. Lin, J.: Divergence measures based on the shannon entropy. IEEE Trans. Inf. Theor. **37**(1), 145–151 (1991)
18. Lin, T.-Y., et al.: Microsoft COCO: common objects in context. In: Fleet, D., Pajdla, T., Schiele, B., Tuytelaars, T. (eds.) ECCV 2014. LNCS, vol. 8693, pp. 740–755. Springer, Cham (2014). https://doi.org/10.1007/978-3-319-10602-1_48
19. Liu, W., et al.: SSD: single shot multibox detector. In: Leibe, B., Matas, J., Sebe, N., Welling, M. (eds.) ECCV 2016. LNCS, vol. 9905, pp. 21–37. Springer, Cham (2016). https://doi.org/10.1007/978-3-319-46448-0_2
20. Liu, X., Yang, H., Liu, Z., Song, L., Chen, Y., Li, H.: DPATCH: an adversarial patch attack on object detectors. In: Workshop on Thirty-Third AAAI Conference on Artificial Intelligence (AAAI) (2019)
21. Madry, A., Makelov, A., Schmidt, L., Tsipras, D., Vladu, A.: Towards deep learning models resistant to adversarial attacks. In: International Conference on Learning Representations (ICLR) (2018)
22. Qin, C., et al.: Adversarial robustness through local linearization. In: Advances in Neural Information Processing Systems (NeurIPS), pp. 13824–13833 (2019)
23. Ren, S., He, K., Girshick, R.B., Sun, J.: Faster R-CNN: towards real-time object detection with region proposal networks. In: Advances in Neural Information Processing Systems (NeurIPS), pp. 91–99 (2015)
24. Sarkar, S., Bansal, A., Mahbub, U., Chellappa, R.: UPSET and ANGRI : breaking high performance image classifiers. CoRR abs/1707.01159 (2017)
25. Schroff, F., Kalenichenko, D., Philbin, J.: FaceNet: a unified embedding for face recognition and clustering. In: Computer Vision and Pattern Recognition (CVPR), pp. 815–823 (2015)
26. Simonyan, K., Zisserman, A.: Very deep convolutional networks for large-scale image recognition. In: International Conference on Learning Representations (ICLR) (2015)
27. Su, J., Vargas, D.V., Sakurai, K.: One pixel attack for fooling deep neural networks. IEEE Trans. Evol. Comput. **23**(5), 828–841 (2019)
28. Szegedy, C., et al.: Intriguing properties of neural networks. In: International Conference on Learning Representations (ICLR) (2014)
29. Tramèr, F., Kurakin, A., Papernot, N., Goodfellow, I.J., Boneh, D., McDaniel, P.D.: Ensemble adversarial training: attacks and defenses. In: International Conference on Learning Representations (ICLR) (2018)
30. Wei, X., Liang, S., Chen, N., Cao, X.: Transferable adversarial attacks for image and video object detection. In: International Joint Conference on Artificial Intelligence (IJCAI), pp. 954–960 (2019)
31. Xiao, C., Li, B., Zhu, J., He, W., Liu, M., Song, D.: Generating adversarial examples with adversarial networks. In: International Joint Conference on Artificial Intelligence (IJCAI), pp. 3905–3911 (2018)
32. Xie, C., Wang, J., Zhang, Z., Zhou, Y., Xie, L., Yuille, A.L.: Adversarial examples for semantic segmentation and object detection. In: International Conference on Computer Vision (ICCV), pp. 1378–1387 (2017)
33. Yang, J., Jiang, Y., Huang, X., Ni, B., Zhao, C.: Learning black-box attackers with transferable priors and query feedback. In: Advances in Neural Information Processing Systems (NeurIPS) (2020)
34. Zhang, H., Wang, J.: Towards adversarially robust object detection. In: International Conference on Computer Vision (ICCV), pp. 421–430 (2019)
35. Zhang, H., Yu, Y., Jiao, J., Xing, E.P., Ghaoui, L.E., Jordan, M.I.: Theoretically principled trade-off between robustness and accuracy. In: International Conference on Machine Learning (ICML), pp. 7472–7482 (2019)

36. Zhang, J., et al.: Attacks which do not kill training make adversarial learning stronger. In: International Conference on Machine Learning (ICML), pp. 11278–11287 (2020)
37. Zhao, H., Shi, J., Qi, X., Wang, X., Jia, J.: Pyramid scene parsing network. In: Conference on Computer Vision and Pattern Recognition (CVPR), pp. 6230–6239 (2017)

HEAD: HEtero-Assists Distillation for Heterogeneous Object Detectors

Luting Wang[1,3], Xiaojie Li[2], Yue Liao[1,3(✉)], Zeren Jiang[4], Jianlong Wu[5], Fei Wang[2,6], Chen Qian[2], and Si Liu[1,3]

[1] Institute of Artificial Intelligence, Beihang University, Beijing, China
{wangluting,liusi}@buaa.edu.cn
[2] SenseTime Research, Beijing, China
lixiaojie@senseauto.com,wangfei91@mail.ustc.edu.cn,qianchen@sensetime.com
[3] Hangzhou Innovation Institute, Beihang University, Hangzhou, China
liaoyue.ai@gmail.com
[4] ETH Zurich, Zürich, Switzerland
zeren.jiang99@gmail.com
[5] Shandong University, Jinan, China
jlwu1992@sdu.edu.cn
[6] University of Science and Technology of China, Hefei, China
https://github.com/LutingWang/HEAD

Abstract. Conventional knowledge distillation (KD) methods for object detection mainly concentrate on homogeneous teacher-student detectors. However, the design of a lightweight detector for deployment is often significantly different from a high-capacity detector. Thus, we investigate KD among heterogeneous teacher-student pairs for a wide application. We observe that the core difficulty for heterogeneous KD (hetero-KD) is the significant semantic gap between the backbone features of heterogeneous detectors due to the different optimization manners. Conventional homogeneous KD (homo-KD) methods suffer from such a gap and are hard to directly obtain satisfactory performance for hetero-KD. In this paper, we propose the HEtero-Assists Distillation (HEAD) framework, leveraging heterogeneous detection heads as assistants to guide the optimization of the student detector to reduce this gap. In HEAD, the assistant is an additional detection head with the architecture homogeneous to the teacher head attached to the student backbone. Thus, a hetero-KD is transformed into a homo-KD, allowing efficient knowledge transfer from the teacher to the student. Moreover, we extend HEAD into a Teacher-Free HEAD (TF-HEAD) framework when a well-trained teacher detector is unavailable. Our method has achieved significant improvement compared to current detection KD methods. For example, on the MS-COCO dataset, TF-HEAD helps R18 RetinaNet achieve 33.9 mAP (+2.2), while HEAD further pushes the limit to 36.2 mAP (+4.5).

Keywords: Knowledge distillation · Object detection · Heterogeneous

Supplementary Information The online version contains supplementary material available at https://doi.org/10.1007/978-3-031-20077-9_19.

1   Introduction

With the development of deep learning, the performance of object detection has achieved tremendous improvement. However, deploying detectors to edge devices often imposes constraints on the number of parameters, computation, and memory. Therefore, parameters compression and accuracy boosting are core problems for object detection towards practical application, where knowledge distillation (KD) is one of the most popular solutions. KD aims at training the compact model (student) by transferring knowledge from a high-capacity model (teacher). Recently, with the development of KD methods [17,24,33,39,49,53] in general vision models, KD in object detection has raised increasing attention.

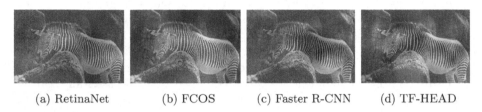

(a) RetinaNet   (b) FCOS   (c) Faster R-CNN   (d) TF-HEAD

Fig. 1. Comparison of the activation patterns from different detectors with the same backbone architecture. The intensity of the feature response increases from blue to red. These detectors produce different backbone feature representations. We use RetinaNet as the student and apply TF-HEAD to take advantage of the feature extraction abilities from an FCOS assistant and an R-CNN assistant. As a result, the activation map of TF-HEAD highlights more area of the zebra with higher intensity, indicating that the feature map contains the most information. (Color figure online)

For a clear presentation, we first give a brief definition for the general architecture of modern CNN based detectors [28,38,41], where input images are represented as feature maps and then different methods are used to decode detection results from the feature maps. In this way, a detector can be divided into a backbone including FPN [27] and a detection head. We further define detectors with the same head architecture as homogeneous, otherwise heterogeneous.

Based on this definition, we summarize object detection KD into two schemes based on the architecture of teacher-student pair: homogeneous KD (homo-KD) or heterogeneous KD (hetero-KD). The homo-KD scheme usually allows the teacher detector to have a stronger backbone than the student detector but requires same head architectures. For instance, R18 RetinaNet [28] can be taught by R50 RetinaNet by homo-KD, but not R50 RepPoints [46] or R50 Faster R-CNN [38]. Significant progress has been made in the homo-KD [3,6,11,39,43,47,54]. However, the practical application of homo-KD is limited because the student for deployment and the most powerful teacher is usually designed from different motivations and produce very different heads. Therefore, we aim to explore hetero-KD, an essential and significant topic for object detection.

We first present an analysis for heterogeneous detectors. We observe that two heterogeneous detectors share the same backbone architecture, while their backbone features representation are still very distinct. As shown in Fig. 1, activation maps from different detectors with R50 backbone, *e.g.*Faster R-CNN [38], RetinaNet [28], and FCOS [41], are different. Thus, we argue that the heterogeneous detection heads guide the backbone for different knowledge. We consider it a significant step for hetero-KD that the student mimics the teacher backbone knowledge. The intuitive idea is to perform homo-KD methods for heterogeneous detectors directly, but the accuracy improvement of the student is significantly limited. It is mainly because the backbone knowledge discrepancy enlarges the semantic gaps between the teacher and student layers.

To this end, we design a simple yet effective hetero-KD mechanism, namely HEtero-Assists Distillation (HEAD), to bridge the semantic gap between heterogeneous detectors via an adaptive assistant, thus simplifying to a homo-KD problem. For a specific teacher-student pair, we first design an additional assistant head with identical architecture with the teacher head and attach it to the student backbone. In this way, we construct a homogeneous detectors pair, *i.e.*the teacher and the student backbone equipped with the assistant. During training, the assistant and original student head process the student backbone features in parallel. Then, we propose two KD mechanisms, *i.e.*Assistant-based KD (AKD) and Cross-architecture KD (CKD), to supervise the assistant and student head learning, respectively. In AKD, we directly apply the homo-KD to the assistant and the teacher heads since they are homogeneous. Therefore, the high-level knowledge [49], *i.e.*the information flow for detection, is efficiently transferred from the teacher head to the assistant. Moreover, the teacher backbone knowledge is also transferred to the student backbone through gradient back-propagation from the assistant. Intuitively, the assistant teaches the student backbone to learn the critical knowledge reproducing the information flow [49] of the teacher. Thus, the semantic gap between heterogeneous detectors is bridged by the assistant. In CKD, we conduct a feature mimic from the student head to the teacher head. CKD plays an auxiliary role to integrate heterogeneous knowledge in the head level to compensate for AKD.

In practice, it is not always easy to obtain a suitable teacher for a specific student, limiting the application of traditional teacher-based KD methods [12,50]. Therefore, we further explore a Teacher-Free [21,23,50,52] method which accommodates our HEAD to these situations, namely TF-HEAD. TF-HEAD works by injecting diverse knowledge into the student, which helps the student to make more accurate predictions without extra computation cost at inference time. Specifically, we use the assistant to process the student backbone features, which is the same as HEAD. Since the assistant and the student heads are heterogeneous, they optimize the student backbone differently, thus enriching the knowledge inside. Although we train the assistant with ground truth labels, instead of supervision from the teacher head, the performance improvement brought by the assistant module is still significant. To push the limit further, TF-HEAD uses multiple assistants that are heterogeneous to each other.

Extensive experiments demonstrate the effectiveness of our framework. On MS-COCO dataset [29], our HEAD and TF-HEAD methods achieve state-of-the-art performance among teacher-based detection KD methods and teacher-free detection KD methods respectively. Using R50 Faster R-CNN as teacher, the mAP of R18 RetinaNet is increased from 31.7 to 36.2 (+4.5) and R18 FCOS from 32.5 to 36.0 (+3.5). Without pretrained teachers, TF-HEAD improves R18 RetinaNet from 31.7 to 33.9 (+2.2), which demonstrates that simply integrating heterogeneous knowledge helps to train better detectors, making hetero-KD advantageous compared to homo-KD.

2   Related Work

2.1   Object Detection

Object detection has three paradigms: two-stage [5,10,13,14,27,38,55], anchor-based one-stage [4,28,30,37], and anchor-free one stage [7,9,41,55,56]. Two stage detectors use an Region Proposal Network (RPN) to generate Regions of Interest (RoIs) and then adopt a region-wise prediction network (R-CNN head) to predict objects. Although two-stage architectures obtain high accuracy, their complicated pipeline hinders deployment on edge devices. In contrast, one-stage detectors get the classification and the bounding box of targets based on features extracted by the backbone directly, achieving real-time inference. Anchor-based one-stage detectors use dense anchor boxes as proposals to detect targets. However, the number of anchor boxes is far more than targets, which brings much extra computation. Anchor-free detectors learn to predict keypoints and then generate bounding boxes to detect objects without the need for predefined anchors, reaching better performance with less cost. The features extracted by different detectors are optimized by different detection heads, which will result in large semantic gaps. Thus, It's hard to mitigate the difference by traditional homo-KD methods. In this work, we introduce the adaptive assistants to effectively bridge the gap between heterogeneous teacher-student pairs.

2.2   Knowledge Distillation

General KD. KD is a technology that helps training compact student models under the supervision of powerful teacher models. Hinton *et al.* [17] propose this concept and achieve great performance improvement by training the student with class distributions generated by the teacher. Extending Hinton's work, more works [1,8,16,19,22,26,33–36,39,42,45,49,51] use intermediate representations of the teacher as hints to train the student. TAKD [32] employs intermediate-sized networks as assistants to improve the effectiveness of KD when the teacher-student capacity gap is large. Different from TAKD, our approach adopts the assistants to solve the heterogeneity between detector pairs.

Homogeneous Detection KD. Chen *et al.* [3] first apply KD to object detection by implementing feature-based and response-based loss for Faster R-CNN.

Li *et al.* [25] apply L2 loss on features sampled by proposals of the student. Wang *et al.* [43] find that mimicking features from foreground regions is more important than background and only distills the feature near object anchor locations. DeFeat [11] shows that the information of background features is also essential, so foreground and background regions are distilled simultaneously with different factors. LabelEnc [12] first trains an autoencoder to model the location-category information and then use the label representations to supervise the training of the detectors. Although these methods have achieved great success on heterogeneous backbones, heterogeneity between detection architectures are rarely explored due to the large structural and feature semantics differences.

Heterogeneous Detection KD. To transfer knowledge between heterogeneous detectors, MimicDet [31] introduces a refinement module to an one-stage detection head to imitate the workflow of two-stage heads, and then conducts KD between the aligned features from the teacher and student heads. Although MimicDet improves accuracy, it is hard to transfer the structural modification on the student head to other heterogeneous detectors. Different from MimicDet, our method is more intuitive and flexible. With minor modifications, a variety of heterogeneous detectors can be supported by our framework.

G-DetKD [48] first proposes a general distillation framework for object detectors, which performs soft matching across all pyramid levels to provide the optimal guidance to the student. However, using learned similarity scores to combine features of students at different levels before feature mimicking does not essentially reduce the semantic gap. In our work, we attach an assistant, which is same as the teacher detection head, to the student network to learn directly from the teacher. Since the assistant and the teacher have homogeneous detection heads, their feature semantic gap are smaller than the heterogeneous heads, contributing to more efficient knowledge transfer.

3 Method

In Sect. 3.1, we briefly review the pipeline of detection KD. Then we elaborate our proposed hetero-KD mechanism, HEtero-Assists Distillation (HEAD) in Sect. 3.2. Finally, we introduce a teacher-free extension of HEAD (TF-HEAD) in Sect. 3.3.

3.1 Review of Detection KD

We focus on distillation using intermediate features [39]. The distillation loss of the features can be generally formulated as

$$\mathcal{L} = \mathcal{D}\left(\mathbf{F}^T, \phi(\mathbf{F}^S)\right), \tag{1}$$

where $\mathcal{D}(\cdot)$ is a distillation loss measuring the knowledge difference between the teacher and the student. ϕ is an adaptation layer to match the dimension of the student's feature with the teacher. $\mathbf{F}^T$ and $\mathbf{F}^S$ are intermediate features of the teacher and the student respectively.

In this paper, we define $\mathcal{D}(\cdot)$ as the MSE loss. The form of ϕ depends on the shape of $\mathbf{F}^S$. For three-dimensional features with different number of channels, 1×1 convolution layers are used. For two-dimensional features with different number of dimensions, ϕ represents a linear layer.

3.2 HEAD

We elaborate the pipeline of HEAD by instantiating an example, where Faster R-CNN [10] is adopted as the teacher and RetinaNet [28] is the student. Figure 2 shows the corresponding framework. To bridge the semantic gap between teacher and student, HEAD constructs an assistant that is homogeneous with the teacher's R-CNN head. The assistant is initialized with the pretrained weight of the teacher's R-CNN head and is trained online with the student. Note that HEAD acts on the training phase only, and the assistant is unused during inference.

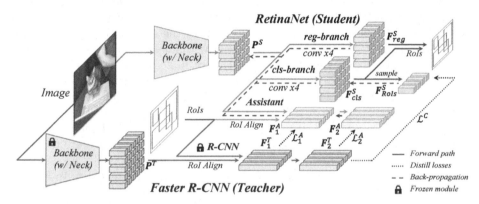

Fig. 2. Overview of HEAD, where the teacher is Faster R-CNN [38] and student is RetinaNet [28]. We construct an assistant homogeneous to the teacher's R-CNN head. We first extract the backbone features of the teacher and the student. The student backbone features are then fed into the original student head and the assistant in parallel. The teacher head processes the teacher backbone features. KD mechanism comprises an AKD between the teacher head and the assistant, and a CKD, where the teacher head directly supervises the student head.

Given an image, we first extract the backbone features of student and teacher, denoted as $\mathbf{P}^S \in \mathbb{R}^{C \times H \times W}$ and $\mathbf{P}^T \in \mathbb{R}^{C \times H' \times W'}$ respectively. We then follow the original detector pipeline to employ the student head, a RetinaNet [28] head, to calculate the student loss, denoted as $\mathcal{L}_{gt}^S$. As shown in Fig. 2, the student head comprises a regression branch and a classification branch. The student loss is calculated by summarizing losses from both branches

$$\mathcal{L}_{gt}^S = \mathcal{L}_{reg}^S + \mathcal{L}_{cls}^S. \tag{2}$$

The $\mathcal{L}_{gt}^{S}$ is calculated following the original RetinaNet. For convinience, we adopt $\mathbf{F}_{reg}^{S} \in \mathbb{R}^{C \times H \times W}$ and $\mathbf{F}_{cls}^{S} \in \mathbb{R}^{C \times H \times W}$ to denote the last intermediate feature of the regression branch and the classification branch respectively.

We next introduce the KD mechanism composed of two KD processes, *i.e.Assistant-based KD (AKD)* and *Cross-architecture KD (CKD)*. AKD is the core of HEAD. We utilize the teacher's R-CNN head and the assistant to process the corresponding backbone features $\mathbf{P}^{T}$ and $\mathbf{P}^{S}$, respectively. Meanwhile, we adopt the AKD loss $\mathcal{L}^{A}$ for the assistant to mimic the intermediate features of the teacher head. For completeness, we employ CKD, where the teacher head directly provides supervision for the student head. The CKD loss is denoted as $\mathcal{L}^{C}$. During the training phase, the overall loss is

$$\mathcal{L}^{HEAD} = \mathcal{L}_{gt}^{S} + \mathcal{L}^{A} + \mathcal{L}^{C}. \tag{3}$$

Our HEAD framework is not restricted to distillation between one-stage and two-stage detectors but can be applied to a wide range of heterogeneous detectors.

Assistant-Based KD. When the teacher is two-stage, the teacher head and the assistant perform RoI Align [13] on $\mathbf{P}^{T}$ and $\mathbf{P}^{S}$ respectively with a precomputed set of RoIs. For a two-stage student, the output of the student's RPN is used as the precomputed RoIs. For one-stage students without RPN, we take the output of the student head as a substitution. For the example in Fig. 2, we convert the classification logits of each anchor to a class-agnostic objectness logit and follow the original RPN protocol to generate RoIs. Additionally, we denote the number of RoIs as N.

We feed the backbone features $\mathbf{P}^{T}$ and $\mathbf{P}^{S}$ (or the RoI Aligned features) into the teacher head and the assistant, respectively. The intermediate features of the teacher head and the assistant is respectively denoted as $\mathbf{F}_{1}^{T}, \mathbf{F}_{2}^{T}, \ldots, \mathbf{F}_{L}^{T}$ and $\mathbf{F}_{1}^{A}, \mathbf{F}_{2}^{A}, \ldots, \mathbf{F}_{L}^{A}$. L indicates the number of intermediate features. In Fig. 2, the R-CNN head is composed of two linear layers. We use the outputs of both layers for KD, thus setting L to 2. Finally, since the teacher head is homogeneous with the assistant, we simply apply KD between intermediate features pairs

$$\mathcal{L}_{l}^{A} = \mathcal{D}\left(\mathbf{F}_{l}^{T}, \phi\left(\mathbf{F}_{l}^{S}\right)\right). \tag{4}$$

For simplicity, we use MSE loss as $\mathcal{D}(\cdot)$ and a linear layer as ϕ.

Besides the supervision from the teacher, we also use ground truth labels to supervise the assistant. In Fig. 2, we follow the original Faster R-CNN to use the standard Cross-Entropy loss and L1 loss to supervise the classification and regression output of the assistant. In general, the ground truth loss for the assistant $\mathcal{L}_{gt}^{A}$ is same as the teacher, so that the assistant learns from the ground truth labels when the teacher makes mistakes. The total AKD loss is defined as

$$\mathcal{L}^{A} = \mathcal{L}_{gt}^{A} + \frac{\lambda^{A}}{L} \sum_{l=1}^{L} \mathcal{L}_{l}^{A}, \tag{5}$$

where λ^{A} represents the loss weight.

Intuitively, $\mathcal{L}^A$ requires the assistant to reproduce the reasoning process of the teacher. For this goal, the student backbone needs to capture enough information in $\mathbf{P}^S$. Therefore, the assistant optimizes the student backbone via gradient backpropagation, so that the student backbone learns the knowledge that is critical for the assistant to reproduce the teacher's reasoning process.

Cross-Architecture KD. Though the AKD is effective and universal, it only distills knowledge into the student backbone. Hence, we design the CKD to further improve the student performance via direct supervisions from the teacher head to the student head. As shown in Fig. 2, we apply the CKD loss $\mathcal{L}^C$ between the teacher's R-CNN head and the student's RetinaNet head. Firstly, the teacher's R-CNN head generates a set of sparse RoI features $\mathbf{F}_1^T \in \mathbb{R}^{N \times C'}$, while the student's RetinaNet head generates a series of dense anchor features $\mathbf{F}_{cls}^S \in \mathbb{R}^{C \times H \times W}$. C' represents the dimensions of the R-CNN head's hidden layer. We ignore the regression feature $\mathbf{F}_{reg}^S$ following G-DetKD [48]. Secondly, inspired by MimicDet [31], we trace back to the original anchors of each RoI. Thirdly, since each anchor corresponds to a pixel on $\mathbf{F}_{cls}^S$, we sample these pixel features to form $\mathbf{F}_{RoIs}^S \in \mathbb{R}^{N \times C}$. Thereafter, we use Eq. (1) to perform CKD

$$\mathcal{L}^C = \lambda^C \mathcal{D}\left(\mathbf{F}_1^T, \phi(\mathbf{F}_{RoIs}^S)\right), \tag{6}$$

where λ^C is the loss weight, $\mathcal{D}(\cdot)$ is MSE loss, and ϕ is a linear layer mapping from C-dimensional features to C'-dimensional features.

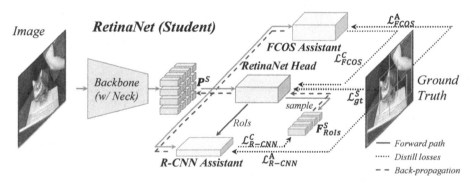

Fig. 3. An example of the TF-HEAD training pipeline. We use R-CNN head [38] and FCOS head [41] as two assistants to guide the RetinaNet [28].

If the teacher and the student are both one-stage or both two-stage, CKD simply applies MSE loss between the corresponding intermediate features of the teacher head and the student head. Suppose the teacher is FCOS [41] and the student is RetinaNet [28]. Let $\mathbf{F}_{FCOS}^T$ denote the last intermediate feature of the classification branch of the FCOS head. Then the CKD loss is denoted as

$$\mathcal{L}_{FCOS}^C = \lambda_{FCOS}^C \mathcal{D}\left(\mathbf{F}_{FCOS}^T, \phi\left(\mathbf{F}_{cls}^S\right)\right), \tag{7}$$

where λ_{FCOS}^C is the loss weight, $\mathcal{D}(\cdot)$ is MSE loss and ϕ is a 1×1 convolution layer. For both teacher and student with a two-stage pipeline, the only difference is that the adaptation layer ϕ uses a linear layer.

3.3 TF-HEAD

In practice, suitable teachers for a specific student are not always available. Traditional teacher-based KD methods, including our HEAD, fail in such situations. Therefore, we extend our HEAD to a teacher-free method, namely TF-HEAD. TF-HEAD is designed based on an experimental observation. As shown in Fig. 1, different detectors [28,38,41] have distinct activation maps, demonstrating diverse knowledge in the backbones. Heterogeneous detection architectures incorporate different human priors and adopt various backbone optimization manners. Therefore, the heterogeneous detectors produce different knowledge.

Even without the pretrained teacher in HEAD, we observe that the assistant can still learn from the ground truth labels. Based on this, we devise a teacher-free KD mechanism, TF-HEAD. As shown in Fig. 3, TF-HEAD uses assistants to transfer knowledge from the heterogeneous detectors to the student. Note that we allow more than one assistant in TF-HEAD. While the TF-HEAD framework is universal, we use the example in Fig. 3 to show its application, where the FCOS head and the R-CNN head are adopted to teach the RetinaNet head.

For each assistant, we denote its ground truth loss and CKD loss as $\mathcal{L}_\star^A$ and $\mathcal{L}_\star^C$, respectively, as described in Sect. 3.2. $\star$ indicates the name of the assistant. For the example in Fig. 3, the overall loss is

$$\mathcal{L}^{TF-HEAD} = \mathcal{L}_{gt}^S + \mathcal{L}_{FCOS}^A + \mathcal{L}_{FCOS}^C + \mathcal{L}_{R-CNN}^A + \mathcal{L}_{R-CNN}^C. \tag{8}$$

More generally, the overall loss of our TF-HEAD framework is

$$\mathcal{L}^{TF-HEAD} = \mathcal{L}_{gt}^S + \sum_\star \left(\mathcal{L}_\star^A + \mathcal{L}_\star^C \right), \tag{9}$$

where $\mathcal{L}_{gt}^S$ is the ground truth loss of the student detector. We represent the loss weights of assistant $\star$ as $\lambda_\star^A$ and $\lambda_\star^C$.

4 Experiments

Experiments are conducted on the COCO 2017 dataset [29] using the mean Average Precision (mAP) metric. We adopt the default 120k/5k split for training and validation. All distillation loss $\mathcal{D}(\cdot)$ takes the form of MSE. The adaptation layer ϕ is either a 1×1 convolution layer or a linear layer, depending on the shape of its input. For AKD, we set λ^A to 5. If the student head and the assistant are both one-stage heads, the CKD loss weight λ^C is set to 1, otherwise 2.

Training is conducted on 8 GPUs with batch size 16 in total. We use stochastic gradient descent (SGD) optimizer with 0.9 momentum and 0.0001 weight decay. 1x (12 epochs) training schedule is used. At the 8th and 11th epochs, the learning rate is divided by 10 The initial learning rate is 0.01 for one-stage detectors and 0.02 for two-stage detectors. The shorter side of the input image is scaled to 640–800 pixels, the longer side is scaled to 1333 pixels.

4.1   Main Results

Comparison with Homo-KD Methods. In this section, HEAD is compared with previous homogeneous detection KD methods. Since these methods are originally proposed for homogeneous detectors, only the backbone mimicking part can be applied. For fairness, we do not use the CKD loss $\mathcal{L}^C$, but only use the AKD loss $\mathcal{L}^A$. We conduct experiments with two student architectures (RetinaNet [28] and FCOS [41]), two student backbones (R18 [15] and MNV2 [40]), and two teacher choices (R50 Faster R-CNN [38] and R50 RepPoints [46]). On all eight teacher-student pairs, Table 1 shows that HEAD outperforms the previous methods by a large margin. Specifically, under the guidance of R50 Faster R-CNN, our HEAD framework boosts the RetinaNet [28] performance by 3.8 and 4.0 mAP for R18 and MNV2 backbones respectively. For FCOS, the performance gain is also prominent. We observe a 3.5 mAP gain on both backbones when using R50 Faster R-CNN as the teacher. Interestingly, we observe that homo-KD methods degrade the student's performance in some cases when applied to heterogeneous detector pairs. Because the semantic gap between heterogeneous detectors is much larger than homogeneous detectors, the homo-KD methods are prone to over regularize the student, which causes this phenomena [35].

Table 1. Comparison with homogeneous KD methods. † indicates that only Assistant-based KD losses are used in HEAD.

Student backbone		R18 [15]			MNV2 [40]		
Method	Teacher	mAP	mAP$_{50}$	mAP$_{75}$	mAP	mAP$_{50}$	mAP$_{75}$
RetinaNet [28]	–	31.7	49.5	33.5	28.5	44.8	29.9
FitNet [39]	R50 Faster R-CNN(40.3) [38]	34.1	52.2	36.0	31.6	48.7	33.5
FGFI [43]		34.4	52.2	36.4	30.8	47.3	32.6
DeFeat [11]		34.1	52.1	36.3	31.1	47.9	32.7
FGD [47]		34.4	52.6	36.7	31.9	48.9	34.0
HEAD† (ours)		**35.5**	**54.5**	**37.9**	**32.5**	**50.4**	**34.4**
FitNet [39]	R50 RepPoints(38.6) [46]	31.5	49.0	33.3	27.5	43.2	28.9
FGFI [43]		33.1	50.8	35.3	29.1	45.1	30.8
DeFeat [11]		30.9	48.0	32.8	28.2	44.2	29.6
FGD [47]		31.3	48.6	33.2	28.3	44.3	30.0
HEAD† (ours)		**34.2**	**52.4**	**36.6**	**30.5**	**47.1**	**32.3**
FCOS [41]	–	32.5	50.9	34.1	30.0	47.5	31.3
FitNet [39]	R50 Faster R-CNN(40.3) [38]	34.2	52.2	36.1	32.0	49.3	33.7
FGD [47]		35.4	53.8	37.3	32.9	50.5	34.6
HEAD† (ours)		**36.0**	**54.9**	**38.4**	**33.5**	**51.6**	**35.2**
FitNet [39]	R50 RepPoints(38.6) [46]	32.7	50.9	34.4	30.3	47.6	31.7
FGD [47]		33.8	52.1	35.7	31.2	48.8	32.5
HEAD† (ours)		**35.0**	**53.8**	**36.8**	**32.5**	**50.4**	**34.3**

Comparison with Hetero-KD Methods. We further compare our HEAD with the previous hetero-KD methods. When using Faster R-CNN as the teacher, we compare our HEAD with G-DetKD [48]. For RepPoints [46] teacher, since the contrastive loss in G-DetKD is not applicable to such one-stage detector, we use its backbone mimicking loss (SGFI loss) only. For fairness, we disable our CKD loss as well. As shown in Table 2, our HEAD surpasses G-DetKD and SGFI on various teacher-student pairs. Notice that Faster R-CNN uses the $2 - 6$ levels of the FPN [27] features, while RetinaNet, FCOS, and RepPoints use the $3 - 7$ levels. The result suggests that the semantic-guided feature level matching mechanism cannot effectively bridge the semantic gap between the teacher and the student if both detectors use the same FPN levels. In contrast, our HEAD bridges the semantic gap by introducing assistants to homogenize the teacher-student pair, which results in over 2.5 mAP gain on all scenarios.

Comparison with Teacher-Free Methods. Some methods have implemented teacher-free KD on object detection, such as MimicDet [31] and LabelEnc [12]. To verify the superiority of our TF-HEAD among teacher-free methods without changing the structure of the student model, we only choose LabelEnc for comparison. LabelEnc adopts a two-step training process, where both steps take 12 epochs (1x) for training. Therefore, we use a 2x (24 epoch) training schedule for TF-HEAD. Three detection architectures with R50 backbones are explored, *i.e.*RetinaNet [28], FCOS [41], and Faster R-CNN [38]. Our TF-HEAD uses two assistants for each architecture. For RetinaNet, TF-HEAD uses FCOS⋆ head and DH R-CNN head [44]. For FCOS, RetinaNet head and DH R-CNN head are used. For Faster R-CNN, we use RetinaNet head and FCOS⋆ head to guide the RPN module. As shown in Table 3, HEAD improves baselines by 1.5, 1.3, and 1.1 mAP, which is 67%, 63%, and 350% higher than the improvement of LabelEnc.

Table 2. Comparison with heterogeneous KD methods. † indicates that only AKD losses are used in HEAD.

Student backbone		R18 [15]			MNV2 [40]		
Method	Teacher	mAP	mAP$_{50}$	mAP$_{75}$	mAP	mAP$_{50}$	mAP$_{75}$
RetinaNet [28]	–	31.7	49.5	33.5	28.5	44.8	29.9
G-DetKD [48]	R50 Faster R-CNN(40.3) [38]	35.4	54.2	37.9	32.6	**50.9**	**34.5**
HEAD (ours)		**36.2**	**55.2**	**38.8**	**32.8**	50.8	34.4
SGFI [48]	R50 RepPoints(38.6) [46]	31.6	49.5	33.2	27.9	43.9	29.2
HEAD† (ours)		**34.2**	**52.4**	**36.6**	**30.5**	**47.1**	**32.3**
FCOS [41]	–	32.5	50.9	34.1	30.0	47.5	31.3
G-DetKD [48]	R50 Faster R-CNN(40.3) [38]	34.1	52.6	36.3	32.1	50.4	33.6
HEAD (ours)		**36.0**	**54.9**	**38.4**	**33.5**	**51.6**	**35.2**
SGFI [48]	R50 RepPoints(38.6) [46]	32.6	50.9	34.4	30.2	47.6	31.7
HEAD† (ours)		**35.0**	**53.8**	**36.8**	**32.5**	**50.4**	**34.3**
Faster R-CNN [38]	–	33.9	54.1	36.3	28.3	47.0	29.5
G-DetKD [48]	R50 Cascade R-CNN(43.5) [2]	36.1	57.3	39.0	33.4	54.2	35.3
HEAD (ours)		**36.7**	**58.0**	**39.3**	**33.8**	**54.4**	**35.8**

Table 3. Comparison with the teacher-free detection KD method. For fairness, we use R50 [15] backbone and 2x (24 epoch) training schedule for all experiments. $\star$ indicates FCOS with improvements including center-sampling, normalization on bbox, centerness on regression branch, and GIoU.

Method	RetinaNet [28]	FCOS$\star$ [41]	Faster R-CNN [38]
Baseline	38.7	41.0	39.4
LabelEnc [12]	39.6	41.8	39.6
TF-HEAD (ours)	**40.2**	**42.3**	**40.5**

4.2 Ablation Study

Effectiveness of HEAD. To evaluate the effectiveness of the assistant as a bridge between the teacher and the student, we conduct experiments without CKD loss. As show in Table 4, HEAD† improves R18 RetinaNet by 3.8 mAP and MNV2 RetinaNet by 4.0 mAP. Adding CKD loss further brings 0.7 mAP gain to R18 RetinaNet and 0.3 mAP gain to MNV2 RetinaNet.

Table 4. Ablation study of the HEAD. We use R50 Faster R-CNN as teacher and RetinaNet as student. $\dagger$ indicates that only AKD losses are used in HEAD.

Student Backbone		R18 [15]			MNV2 [40]		
Method	Teacher	mAP	mAP$_{50}$	mAP$_{75}$	mAP	mAP$_{50}$	mAP$_{75}$
RetinaNet [28]	–	31.7	49.5	33.5	28.5	44.8	29.9
HEAD†	R50 Faster R-CNN(40.3) [38]	35.5	54.5	37.9	32.5	50.4	**34.4**
HEAD		**36.2**	**55.2**	**38.8**	**32.8**	**50.8**	**34.4**
HEAD†	R50 RepPoints(38.6) [46]	34.2	52.4	**36.6**	30.5	47.1	**32.3**
HEAD		**34.3**	**52.8**	36.4	**30.6**	**47.7**	**32.3**

Table 5. Ablation study of TF-HEAD. The student is R18 RetinaNet [28]. We use FCOS head and R-CNN head as two assistants to guide the student.

$\mathcal{L}^A_{FCOS}$	$\mathcal{L}^C_{FCOS}$	$\mathcal{L}^A_{R-CNN}$	$\mathcal{L}^C_{R-CNN}$	mAP	mAP$_{50}$	mAP$_{75}$	mAP$_s$	mAP$_m$	mAP$_l$
				31.7	49.5	33.5	16.8	34.7	42.1
✓				32.9	51.2	34.8	17.8	36.0	43.5
✓	✓			33.0	51.4	35.0	17.3	36.3	43.9
		✓		33.4	52.1	35.1	18.1	36.4	44.8
		✓	✓	33.7	52.3	35.6	17.8	36.9	44.9
✓		✓		33.8	52.5	35.6	18.2	36.8	**45.2**
✓	✓	✓	✓	**33.9**	**52.7**	**35.9**	**18.5**	**37.4**	**45.2**

Effectiveness of TF-HEAD. Here, we investigate the effectiveness of each distillation component in Eq. (9). We use FCOS head and R-CNN head as assistants to guide an R18 RetinaNet. As shown in Table 5, our proposed TF-HEAD achieves 2.2 mAP improvement over the original RetinaNet, demonstrating the effectiveness of our TF-HEAD structure. FCOS assistant brings point-based knowledge for the backbone, boosting the baseline by 1.2 mAP. Then, CKD loss between the FCOS assistant and the RetinaNet head adds a 0.1 mAP gain. In contrast, the R-CNN assistant on its own brings 1.7 mAP gain. The CKD loss further adds 0.3 mAP. Using both assistants simultaneously reaches 33.9 mAP.

Early-Stop to Prevent Misguidance from Assistants. As shown in Fig. 4, from the 8th epoch, the CKD loss preternaturally increases while all other losses suddenly dropdown. This phenomenon suggests that the CKD loss has stopped helping the student head since then. Note that the 8th epoch is the first time to drop the learning rate. Annealing KD [20] believes that the detrimental effect is because the teacher disturbs the student from learning the ground truth labels. After the learning rate drops at the 8th epoch, the optimization direction of the assistant and the student head start to diverge, which enlarges the semantic gap in between. From this moment, CKD loss starts to over regularize [35] the student. Intuitively, the student head and the assistant have different architectures, so they should predict objects differently. Forcing the student head to mimic the assistants will impede it from learning knowledge by itself effectively. Therefore, we use early-stop to ensure that the student and assistants converge to their local optima. Table 6 shows that early-stop slightly improves the performance.

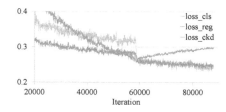

Fig. 4. Visualization of the CKD loss and ground truth losses.

Table 6. Early stopping the CKD losses increases the student performance by 0.1 mAP. Repeated experiments confirm that it is not caused by random factors.

Early-stop	mAP	mAP_s	mAP_m	mAP_l
	33.8	**18.5**	37.3	44.9
✓	**33.9**	**18.5**	**37.4**	**45.2**

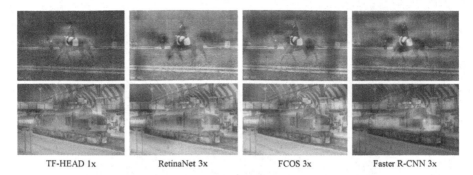

| TF-HEAD 1x | RetinaNet 3x | FCOS 3x | Faster R-CNN 3x |

Fig. 5. Visualization of backbone features from TF-HEAD, RetinaNet [28], FCOS [41], and Faster R-CNN [38]. TF-HEAD highlights more foreground area with higher intensity, while the background remains inactivated.

4.3   Visualization

Visualization of Backbone Feature Maps. By visualizing the feature maps, we verify that TF-HEAD trains stronger backbones. As shown in Fig. 5, feature maps generated by HEAD accurately identify the regions containing objects, showing that knowledge of RetinaNet [28], FCOS [41], and Faster R-CNN [38] can complement each other. Therefore, the backbone of TF-HEAD generates more informative feature maps, which helps the student to be more accurate.

Visualization of COCO Error Analysis. Fig. 6 presents analysis on *All Class* and two randomly selected classes. From RetinaNet to TF-HEAD, the *Background* error and the *False Negative* error decreases prominently, suggesting that the student has learned knowledge from heterogeneous detectors to make more accurate predictions. As a result, the *Correct* rate increases prominently. Using the pretrained teacher detector, HEAD further pushes the accuracy higher, with the *Background* error and the *False Negative* error even lower.

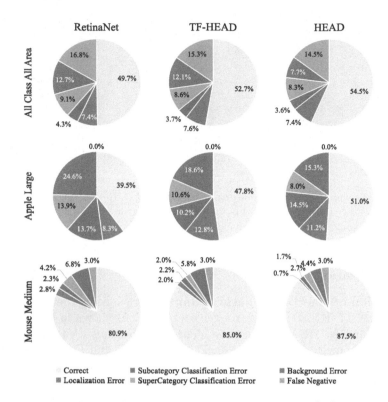

Fig. 6. COCO error analysis using tool from [18].

5 Conclusion

In this paper, we investigate KD among heterogeneous object detectors and find that the semantic gap between heterogeneous models is responsible for the difficulty of hetero-KD. Based on the observation, we design a simple yet effective HEtero-Assists Distillation (HEAD) mechanism. HEAD bridges the semantic gap between heterogeneous detectors via an adaptive assistant, thus simplifying to a homo-KD problem. For situations when the pretrained teachers are not available, we further propose a teacher-free method named TF-HEAD. Extensive experiments demonstrate the effectiveness of our framework.

Acknowledgement. This work was partly supported by the National Natural Science Foundation of China (62122010, 61876177), the Fundamental Research Funds for the Central Universities, and the Key Research and Development Program of Zhejiang Province (2022C01082).

References

1. Ahn, S., Hu, S.X., Damianou, A., Lawrence, N.D., Dai, Z.: Variational information distillation for knowledge transfer. In: CVPR, pp. 9155–9163 (2019)

2. Cai, Z., Vasconcelos, N.: Cascade R-CNN: delving into high quality object detection. In: CVPR, pp. 6154–6162 (2018)
3. Chen, G., Choi, W., Yu, X., Han, T., Chandraker, M.: Learning efficient object detection models with knowledge distillation. In: NeurIPS, pp. 743–752 (2017)
4. Chen, Q., Wang, Y., Yang, T., Zhang, X., Cheng, J., Sun, J.: You Only Look One-level Feature. In: CVPR, pp. 13034–13043 (2021)
5. Dai, J., Li, Y., He, K., Sun, J.: R-FCN: object detection via region-based fully convolutional networks. In: NeurIPS, pp. 379–387 (2016)
6. Dai, X., et al.: General instance distillation for object detection. In: CVPR, pp. 7838–7847 (2021)
7. Dong, Z., Li, G., Liao, Y., Wang, F., Ren, P., Qian, C.: CentripetalNet: pursuing high-quality keypoint pairs for object detection. In: CVPR, pp. 10516–10525 (2020)
8. Du, S., et al.: Agree to disagree: adaptive ensemble knowledge distillation in gradient space. In: NeurIPS, pp. 1–11 (2020)
9. Duan, K., Bai, S., Xie, L., Qi, H., Huang, Q., Tian, Q.: CenterNet: keypoint triplets for object detection. In: ICCV, pp. 6568–6577 (2019)
10. Girshick, R.: Fast R-CNN. In: ICCV, pp. 1440–1448 (2015)
11. Guo, J., et al.: Distilling object detectors via decoupled features. In: CVPR, pp. 2154–2164 (2021)
12. Hao, M., Liu, Y., Zhang, X., Sun, J.: LabelEnc: a new intermediate supervision method for object detection. In: ECCV, pp. 529–545 (2020)
13. He, K., Gkioxari, G., Dollar, P., Girshick, R.: Mask R-CNN. TPAMI 42(2), 386–397 (2020)
14. He, K., Zhang, X., Ren, S., Sun, J.: Spatial pyramid pooling in deep convolutional networks for visual recognition. In: ECCV, pp. 346–361 (2014)
15. He, K., Zhang, X., Ren, S., Sun, J.: Deep residual learning for image recognition. In: CVPR, pp. 770–778 (2016)
16. Heo, B., Lee, M., Yun, S., Choi, J.Y.: Knowledge transfer via distillation of activation boundaries formed by hidden neurons. AAAI 33(1), 3779–3787 (2019)
17. Hinton, G., Vinyals, O., Dean, J.: Distilling the knowledge in a neural network. In: NeurIPS (2014)
18. Hoiem, D., Chodpathumwan, Y., Dai, Q.: Diagnosing error in object detectors. In: ECCV, pp. 340–353 (2012)
19. Huang, Z., Wang, N.: Like what you like: knowledge distill via neuron selectivity transfer. arXiv preprint arXiv:1707.01219 (2017)
20. Jafari, A., Rezagholizadeh, M., Sharma, P., Ghodsi, A.: Annealing knowledge distillation. In: EACL, pp. 2493–2504 (2021)
21. Ji, M., Shin, S., Hwang, S., Park, G., Moon, I.C.: Refine myself by teaching myself: feature refinement via self-knowledge distillation. In: CVPR, pp. 10659–10668 (2021)
22. Kim, J., Park, S., Kwak, N.: Paraphrasing complex network: network compression via factor transfer. In: NeurIPS, pp. 2760–2769 (2018)
23. Kim, K., Ji, B., Yoon, D., Hwang, S.: Self-Knowledge distillation with progressive refinement of targets. In: ICCV, pp. 6567–6576 (2021)
24. Lan, X., Zhu, X., Gong, S.: Knowledge distillation by on-the-fly native ensemble. In: NeurIPS, pp. 7517–7527 (2018)
25. Li, Q., Jin, S., Yan, J.: Mimicking very efficient network for object detection. In: CVPR, pp. 7341–7349 (2017)
26. Li, X., Wu, J., Fang, H., Liao, Y., Wang, F., Qian, C.: Local correlation consistency for knowledge distillation. In: ECCV, pp. 18–33 (2020)

27. Lin, T.Y., Dollar, P., Girshick, R., He, K., Hariharan, B., Belongie, S.: Feature pyramid networks for object detection. In: CVPR, pp. 936–944 (2017)
28. Lin, T.Y., Goyal, P., Girshick, R., He, K., Dollar, P.: Focal loss for dense object detection. TPAMI **42**(2), 318–327 (2020)
29. Lin, T.Y., et al.: Microsoft COCO: common objects in context. In: ECCV, pp. 740–755 (2014)
30. Liu, W., et al.: SSD: single shot multibox detector. In: ECCV, pp. 21–37 (2016)
31. Lu, X., Li, Q., Li, B., Yan, J.: MimicDet: bridging the gap between one-stage and two-stage object detection. In: ECCV, pp. 541–557 (2020)
32. Mirzadeh, S.I., Farajtabar, M., Li, A., Levine, N., Matsukawa, A., Ghasemzadeh, H.: Improved knowledge distillation via teacher assistant. AAAI **34**(04), 5191–5198 (2020)
33. Park, W., Kim, D., Lu, Y., Cho, M.: Relational knowledge distillation. In: CVPR, pp. 3962–3971 (2019)
34. Passalis, N., Tefas, A.: Probabilistic knowledge transfer for deep representation learning. arXiv preprint arXiv:1803.10837 (2018)
35. Passalis, N., Tzelepi, M., Tefas, A.: Heterogeneous knowledge distillation using information flow modeling. In: CVPR, pp. 2336–2345 (2020)
36. Peng, B., et al.: Correlation congruence for knowledge distillation. In: CVPR, pp. 5006–5015 (2019)
37. Redmon, J., Divvala, S., Girshick, R., Farhadi, A.: You only look once: unified, real-time object detection. In: CVPR, pp. 779–788 (2015)
38. Ren, S., He, K., Girshick, R., Sun, J.: Faster R-CNN: towards real-time object detection with region proposal networks. TPAMI **39**(6), 1137–1149 (2017)
39. Romero, A., Ballas, N., Kahou, S.E., Chassang, A., Gatta, C., Bengio, Y.: FitNets: hints for thin deep nets. In: ICLR, pp. 1–13 (2015)
40. Sandler, M., Howard, A., Zhu, M., Zhmoginov, A., Chen, L.C.: MobileNetV2: inverted residuals and linear bottlenecks. In: CVPR, pp. 4510–4520 (2018)
41. Tian, Z., Shen, C., Chen, H., He, T.: FCOS: fully convolutional one-stage object detection. In: CVPR, pp. 9626–9635 (2019)
42. Tung, F., Mori, G.: Similarity-preserving knowledge distillation. In: CVPR, pp. 1365–1374 (2019)
43. Wang, T., Yuan, L., Zhang, X., Feng, J.: Distilling object detectors with fine-grained feature imitation. In: CVPR, pp. 4928–4937 (2019)
44. Wu, Y., et al.: Rethinking classification and localization for object detection. In: CVPR, pp. 10183–10192 (2020)
45. Yang, C., An, Z., Cai, L., Xu, Y.: Hierarchical self-supervised augmented knowledge distillation. In: IJCAI, pp. 1217–1223 (2021)
46. Yang, Z., Liu, S., Hu, H., Wang, L., Lin, S.: RepPoints: point set representation for object detection. In: ICCV, pp. 9656–9665 (2019)
47. Yang, Z., et al.: Focal and global knowledge distillation for detectors. In: CVPR (2022)
48. Yao, L., Pi, R., Xu, H., Zhang, W., Li, Z., Zhang, T.: G-DetKD: towards general distillation framework for object detectors via contrastive and semantic-guided feature imitation. In: ICCV (2021)
49. Yim, J., Joo, D., Bae, J., Kim, J.: A gift from knowledge distillation: fast optimization, network minimization and transfer learning. In: CVPR, pp. 7130–7138 (2017)
50. Yuan, L., Tay, F.E., Li, G., Wang, T., Feng, J.: Revisiting knowledge distillation via label smoothing regularization. In: CVPR, pp. 3902–3910 (2020)

51. Zagoruyko, S., Komodakis, N.: Paying more attention to attention: improving the performance of convolutional neural networks via attention transfer. In: ICLR, pp. 1–13 (2017)
52. Zhang, L., Song, J., Gao, A., Chen, J., Bao, C., Ma, K.: Be Your own teacher: improve the performance of convolutional neural networks via self distillation. In: ICCV, pp. 3712–3721 (2019)
53. Zhang, Y., Xiang, T., Hospedales, T.M., Lu, H.: Deep mutual learning. In: CVPR, pp. 4320–4328 (2018)
54. Zhou, C., Neubig, G., Gu, J.: Improve object detection with feature-based knowledge distillation: towards accurate and efficient detectors. In: ICLR (2021)
55. Zhou, X., Koltun, V., Krähenbühl, P.: Probabilistic two-stage detection. arXiv preprint arXiv:2103.07461 (2021)
56. Zhou, X., Wang, D., Krähenbühl, P.: Objects as points. arXiv preprint arXiv:1904.07850 (2019)

You Should Look at All Objects

Zhenchao Jin[1] , Dongdong Yu[2], Luchuan Song[3], Zehuan Yuan[2],
and Lequan Yu[1(✉)]

[1] The University of Hong Kong, Hong Kong, People's Republic of China
`blwx96@connect.hku.hk, lqyu@hku.hk`
[2] Bytedance, Beijing, China
`{yudongdong,yuanzehuan}@bytedance.com`
[3] University of Rochester, Rochester, USA
`lsong11@ur.rochester.edu`

Abstract. Feature pyramid network (FPN) is one of the key components for object detectors. However, there is a long-standing puzzle for researchers that the detection performance of large-scale objects are usually suppressed after introducing FPN. To this end, this paper first revisits FPN in the detection framework and reveals the nature of the success of FPN from the perspective of optimization. Then, we point out that the degraded performance of large-scale objects is due to the arising of improper back-propagation paths after integrating FPN. It makes each level of the backbone network only has the ability to look at the objects within a certain scale range. Based on these analysis, two feasible strategies are proposed to enable each level of the backbone to look at all objects in the FPN-based detection frameworks. Specifically, one is to introduce auxiliary objective functions to make each backbone level directly receive the back-propagation signals of various-scale objects during training. The other is to construct the feature pyramid in a more reasonable way to avoid the irrational back-propagation paths. Extensive experiments on the COCO benchmark validate the soundness of our analysis and the effectiveness of our methods. Without bells and whistles, we demonstrate that our method achieves solid improvements (more than 2%) on various detection frameworks: one-stage, two-stage, anchor-based, anchor-free and transformer-based detectors (Our code will be available at https://github.com/CharlesPikachu/YSLAO).

Keywords: Object detection · Feature pyramid network

1 Introduction

Along with the advances in deep neural networks, recent years have seen remarkable progress in object detection, which aims at detecting objects of predefined categories. A common belief for the success of the state-of-the-art detectors [2,9,14,39,45] is the use of feature pyramid network (FPN) [21]. Despite impressive, there is an unexpected phenomenon after introducing FPN that the overall detection performance improvement is built upon the *increased* Average

S. Avidan et al. (Eds.): ECCV 2022, LNCS 13669, pp. 332–349, 2022.
https://doi.org/10.1007/978-3-031-20077-9_20

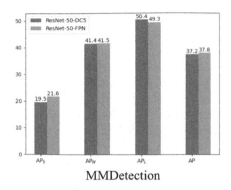
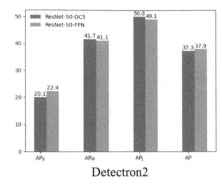

MMDetection   Detectron2

Fig. 1. Comparing the detection performance between ResNet-50-DC5 and ResNet-50-FPN based on MMDetection [4] and Detectron2 [42] toolboxes. The adopted detector is Faster R-CNN [31]. The detectors are trained on COCO 2017 train set and evaluated on COCO 2017 validation set [23].

Precision of small objects (AP_S) and the *decreased* Average Precision of large objects (AP_L). For instance, the experiments based on MMDetection [4] and Detectron2 [42] in Fig. 1 demonstrate this phenomenon. When we leverage the detection toolbox MMDetection, we can observe that AP_S increases from 19.5% to 21.6% while AP_L decreases from 50.4% to 49.3% after integrating FPN. The consistent tend can also be observed in Detectron2.

Prior to this study, there are mainly two assumptions on why the introduction of FPN works. The first is that the use of FPN helps obtain better representations by fusing multiple low-level and high-level feature maps [7,17,21,24,29]. The second is that each pyramid level can be responsible for detecting objects within a certain scale range, *i.e.*, divide-and-conquer [5]. Obviously, both assumptions should lead to the same conclusion that the increase in AP is due to the co-increase in AP_S, AP_M and AP_L. However, the unexpected drops of AP_L in Fig. 1 indicates that there are other key differences between FPN-free and FPN-based detection frameworks, while few studies have taken note of this. In this paper, we propose to investigate FPN from the perspective of optimization. Our assumption is that *except for the multi-scale feature fusion and divide-and-conquer, the back-propagation paths altered by FPN will also directly influence the performance of the detection frameworks.*

We start from explaining why FPN can benefit the detection framework by changing the back-propagation paths. Then, we point out that the back-propagation paths altered by the existing FPN paradigm will make each backbone stage only have the ability to see the objects within a certain scale range (*i.e.*, extracting features that are only fit to certain scale range objects), which is the cause of the inconsistent changes in AP_S, AP_M and AP_L in Fig. 1. Accordingly, the key insight to achieve the consistent improvements in AP of the objects with various scale ranges is to enable each backbone stage to see all objects during training. Based on this principle, we propose to expand and amend the existing back-propagation paths in FPN-based detection frameworks.

Our approach of expanding the back-propagation paths is to introduce auxiliary objective functions so that both the original signals and the extra signals can jointly supervise the learning of the corresponding backbone levels. The key technique to the success of this approach is to introduce the uncertainty [15,16] to better balance the various back-propagation signals. The strategy of amending the back-propagation paths is to build the feature pyramid in a more effective way and thereby, all levels of the backbone network can receive the sufficient signals. The key technique of this approach is the feature grouping module used to promise the space compactness of homogeneous representations.

In a nutshell, the contributions of this paper are:

– To the best of our knowledge, it is the first work to reveal the nature of the success of FPN from the perspective of optimization. Further, we provide new insight in explaining why the introduction of the traditional FPN would suppress the performance of large-scale objects from this perspective.
– We propose to introduce auxiliary objective functions guided by uncertainty to mitigate the inconsistent changes in AP_S, AP_M and AP_L. Since there are no additional computational overhead during testing in the strategy, the inference speed of the detectors can be preserved from decreasing.
– We propose a novel feature pyramid generalization paradigm. The key idea is to make the back-propagation signals of various-scale objects can directly pass to each level of the backbone network. We further design a cascade structure to achieve more robust Average Precision (AP) improvements.
– The extensive experiments on COCO benchmark validate the soundness of our principle and the effectiveness of our solutions. Without bells and whistles, our method boosts the detection performance by more than 2% AP on various frameworks: one-stage, two-stage, anchor-based, anchor-free and transformer-based detectors.

2   Related Works

Object Detection. Recent years have witnessed remarkable improvements in object detection [2,14,29,37,39]. In general, there are two leading paradigms in this area, *i.e.*, one-stage and two-stage frameworks. Two-stage pipeline is first introduced by R-CNN [8], where a set of region proposals are yielded in the first stage, and then the second stage classifies and refines the proposals. The next milestone of two-stage detector is the emergence of Faster R-CNN [31], which aims to improve the efficiency of two-stage methods and allow the detectors to be trained end-to-end. After that, plenty of algorithms have been proposed to further boost its performance, including applying multi-scale training and testing [35,36], redesigning and reforming architecture [2,3,9,41,50], introducing relation and attention mechanism [13,26,32], improving the training strategy and loss function [12,20,28,30,33], adopting more reasonable post-processing algorithms [1,11,25,40]. Different from the two-stage approaches, one-stage detectors directly predict the object category and location based on the predefined anchors. They are simpler and faster than two-stage methods but have trailed the detection performance until the emergence of RetinaNet [22]. Thereafter, lots of works [5,6,19,39] are presented to boost the detection performance of one-stage detectors and at present, one-stage methods can achieve very close performance with two-stage frameworks at a faster inference speed.

Feature Pyramids. Feature pyramids have dominated modern detectors for serval years. Recent researches on feature pyramids can be roughly categorized into three gatherings: top-down or bottom-up networks [21,24,29,34], attention based methods [14,17,44,47], and neural architecture search based approaches [7,38]. Specifically, feature pyramid network (FPN) [21] is one of the most classical paradigms to build a feature pyramid, which designs a top-down architecture with lateral connections to make each pyramid level carry the high-level semantic information. After that, several works [7,14,17,24,29,47] follow FPN and make attempts to obtain more effective representations by improving the strategy of multi-scale feature fusion. PANet [24] proposes to leverage bottom-up architecture to shorten the information interaction path between shallow layers and topmost features. SAFNet [14] aims to suppress the redundant information at all pyramid scales by introducing attention mechanism. Nas-fpn [7] proposes to construct the feature pyramids by neural architecture search. However, the starting point of the above methods is that FPN can brings two benefits, *i.e.*, leveraging multi-scale feature fusion to obtain more effective representations [7,17,21,24,29] and adopting divide-and-conquer to reduce the learning difficulty [5]. And it fails to explain why introducing FPN will suppress the performance of large-scale objects. Motivated by this, we propose to revisit FPN from the perspective of optimization, which successfully explains the anomalous phenomenon in Fig. 1. From this novel starting point, we further propose to mitigate the inconsistent changes in AP_S, AP_M and AP_L by expanding or amending the back-propagation paths in FPN-based detection frameworks. And it is the main difference between our approaches and previous works.

3 Revisit FPN

3.1 Backbone Network

In object detection, the backbone network $\mathcal{F}_B$ is used to extract the basic features $\mathcal{C}$ from the input image I. For the convenience of presentation, we assume that the adopted backbone network is ResNet [10]. It generally consists of one basic feature extractor and plenty of residual blocks, where the residual blocks can be grouped into four stages according to the resolutions of the output feature maps. Specifically, $\mathcal{C}$ is calculated as follow,

$$
\begin{aligned}
C_1 &= f_{s_0}(I), \\
C_i &= f_{s_{i-1}}(C_{i-1}),\ 2 \leq i \leq 5,
\end{aligned}
\tag{1}
$$

where $\mathcal{C}$ consists of $\{C_2, C_3, C_4, C_5\}$ and $\mathcal{F}_B$ consists of $\{f_{s_0}, f_{s_1}, f_{s_2}, f_{s_3}, f_{s_4}\}$.

3.2   FPN-free Detection Framework

For FPN-free detectors, the network usually leverages C_5 to perform the classification and regression of the objects as follow,

$$
\begin{aligned}
O_{cls} &= f_{cls}(f_{pre}(C_5)), \\
O_{reg} &= f_{reg}(f_{pre}(C_5)),
\end{aligned}
\tag{2}
$$

where f_{pre} is introduced to unify various operations between C_5 and the output results, e.g., the region proposal network [31]. O_{cls} and O_{reg} are the predicted category information and location information of the objects, respectively. f_{cls} and f_{reg} are a 1×1 convolution layer, respectively. During training, the classification and regression loss are calculated as follow,

$$
L = L_{cls}(O_{cls}, GT_{cls}) + \lambda L_{reg}(O_{reg}, GT_{reg}),
\tag{3}
$$

where the adopted objective functions L_{cls} and L_{reg} depend on the utilized detection framework. GT_{cls} and GT_{reg} are the ground-truth classification and regression information, respectively. λ is a hyper-parameter used to balance the classification and regression losses.

3.3   FPN-Based Detection Framework

For FPN-based detectors, $\mathcal{C}$ is first used to build the feature pyramid as follow,

$$
\begin{aligned}
C'_5 &= f_{lat_5}(C_5), \\
C'_4 &= f_{lat_4}(C_4) + UP_{2\times}(C'_5), \\
C'_3 &= f_{lat_3}(C_3) + UP_{2\times}(C'_4), \\
C'_2 &= f_{lat_2}(C_2) + UP_{2\times}(C'_3), \\
P_l &= f_{smo_l}(C'_l),\ 2 \le l \le 5,
\end{aligned}
\tag{4}
$$

where $\mathcal{P} = \{P_2, P_3, P_4, P_5\}$ is the constructed feature pyramid. $UP_{2\times}$ denotes for the upsampling with the scale factor of 2. $f_{lat_i}, 2 \le i \le 5$ is the lateral connections implemented by a 1×1 convolution layer, respectively, which is used to change the number of the channels of $\mathcal{C}$. $f_{smo_l}, 2 \le l \le 5$ is a linear function and is usually implemented by a 3×3 convolution layer. Without loss of generality, Eq. (4) can be rewritten as follow,

$$
P_l = \sum_{i=l}^{5} w_i \cdot C_i,\ 2 \le l \le 5,
\tag{5}
$$

where w_i is the final weights for the correspond level after polynomial expansions [17]. Then, the network uses $\mathcal{P}$ to predict the classification and regression information of the objects assigned to each pyramid level l as follow,

$$
\begin{aligned}
O_{cls,l} &= f_{cls,l}(f_{pre,l}(P_l)), \\
O_{reg,l} &= f_{reg,l}(f_{pre,l}(P_l)).
\end{aligned}
\tag{6}
$$

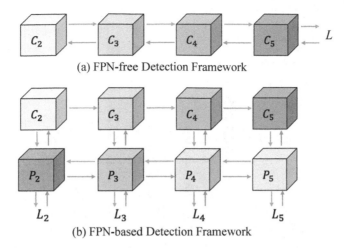

(a) FPN-free Detection Framework

(b) FPN-based Detection Framework

Fig. 2. Comparing the back-propagation paths between FPN-free detection framework and FPN-based detection framework. The blue arrows represent for forward and the orange arrows denote for back propagation. Note that, only the most significant back-propagation signals to each backbone level will be marked. (Color figure online)

The objects assignment rule is to make the low-resolution pyramid features (*e.g.*, P_5) be responsible for predicting the large-scale objects, while the high-resolution pyramid features (*e.g.*, P_2) are utilized to predict the small-scale objects. During network optimization, the losses at each pyramid level l are calculated as follow,

$$L_l = L_{cls}(O_{cls,l}, GT_{cls,l}) + \lambda L_{reg}(O_{reg,l}, GT_{reg,l}). \tag{7}$$

3.4   Analysis of FPN

From Sect. 3.2 and 3.3, we can observe that introducing FPN can alter the back-propagation paths between the objective functions and the backbone network. Figure 2 shows the detailed differences between the FPN-free and FPN-based detection framework. In the FPN-free detection pipeline, only the backbone feature C_5 is directly under the supervision of the objective functions. Since there exists the vanishing gradient problem in deep neural networks, the shallow layers (*i.e.*, $\{f_{s_0}, f_{s_1}, f_{s_2}, f_{s_3}\}$) of the backbone network will be difficult to receive effective supervision by the backward propagation. While in the FPN-based detection framework, we can observe that all the backbone features are directly under the supervision of the objective functions. Since this strategy avoids the vanishing gradient problem for the shallow layers, each level of the backbone network can receive more supervision to train its own parameters. We believe that it is the key reason why FPN-based detectors outperform FPN-free detectors from the perspective of optimization.

To further demonstrate the principle above, we conduct the empirical study and show the experimental results in Fig. 3. FPN-Aux and DC5-Aux denote

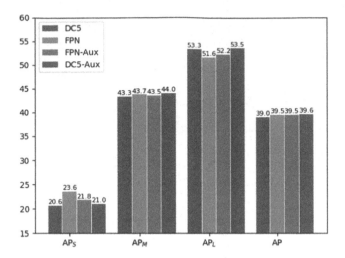

Fig. 3. The detection performance with different settings. The adopted backbone network is ResNet-101 and the utilized detector is Faster R-CNN. The models are trained on COCO 2017 train set and evaluated on COCO 2017 validation set [23].

for introducing the auxiliary losses in the shallow layers of the backbone networks [40,48]. Specifically, given $\mathcal{C}$, we first have

$$\hat{O}_{cls,i} = \hat{f}_{cls,i}(\hat{f}_{pre,i}(C_i)),\ 2 \leq i \leq 4,$$
$$\hat{O}_{reg,i} = \hat{f}_{reg,i}(\hat{f}_{pre,i}(C_i)),\ 2 \leq i \leq 4. \tag{8}$$

For the two-stage detectors [31], to avoid double calculation of the proposals, we will utilize the proposals calculated in Eq. (2) or Eq. (6) to extract the ROIs. Then, the auxiliary losses can be obtained as follow,

$$\hat{L}_i = L_{cls}(\hat{O}_{cls,i}, GT_{cls}) + \lambda L_{reg}(\hat{O}_{reg,i}, GT_{reg}). \tag{9}$$

And the final loss of the detection framework is the summation of the auxiliary losses and the original losses. Since the auxiliary losses can be used to directly supervise the learning of the shallow layers of the backbone network, if our assumption is correct, introducing auxiliary losses should own a similar function to integrating FPN from the perspective of optimization. In Fig. 3, it is observed that the auxiliary losses can boost the detection performance of FPN-free detector (from 39.0% to 39.6%) and obtain a comparable AP result to FPN-based detector (39.6% v.s. 39.5%). However, the introduction of auxiliary losses seems useless to FPN-based detector (from 39.5% to 39.5%). This result validates our assumption that from the perspective of optimization, the nature of the success of FPN is the shorten back-propagation distance between the objective losses and the shallow layers of the backbone network.

Now, the question is why the introduction of FPN will suppress the detection performance of large-scale objects. As illustrated in Fig. 2, P_2 is a linear combination of $\{C_2, C_3, C_4, C_5\}$, therefore, L_2 can directly supervise the learning of all the backbone stages. With the similar principle, L_3, L_4 and L_5 have the ability to directly constrain $\{C_3, C_4, C_5\}$, $\{C_4, C_5\}$ and C_5, respectively. However, as mentioned above, L_2 is only used to make the corresponding backbone levels focus on the objects within a small scale range. Thus, the learned feature C_2 only has the ability to detect the small-scale objects well by back propagation. Meanwhile, the backbone network also needs to utilize Eq. (1) to calculate $\{C_3, C_4, C_5\}$ with C_2 as input. Obviously, it is insufficient for f_{s_2} to extract rich semantic features of the larger objects from C_2. Worse still, the adverse effects will be further accumulated when leveraging f_{s_3} and f_{s_4} to calculate C_4 and C_5. As a result, the semantic information carried by C_5 is somehow ineffective for predicting the large-scale objects. And it is why there is always an unexpected phenomenon after introducing FPN that the overall detection performance improvement is built upon the increased AP_S and the decreased AP_L.

The empirical study in Fig. 3 also validate our assumption. In detail, we can observe that after applying the auxiliary losses to the FPN-based detection frameworks, the performance improvements among $\{AP_S, AP_M, AP_L\}$ tend to be consistent with FPN-free detectors w/ the auxiliary losses. The result shows that as the auxiliary losses can help the shallow layers of the backbone learn the features to detect various-scale objects, C_5 no longer suffers from the ineffective features for predicting large-scale objects as only integrating FPN into the detection framework. In other words, the lack of effective semantic information of large-scale objects in C_5 is the key reason for the decrease of AP_L. And the problem is derived from the inability of $f_{s_i}, 1 \leq i \leq 3$ to look at various-scale objects during training.

4   Methodology

Motivated by the finding that the inconsistent changes in $\{AP_S, AP_M, AP_L\}$ is caused by the inability of $f_{s_i}, 1 \leq i \leq 3$ to see all objects during training, we propose to make the backbone stages look at various-scale objects by expanding or amending the back-propagation paths in FPN-based detection frameworks to address the decreased AP_L problem above. Specifically, we propose two strategies, *i.e.*, introducing auxiliary objective functions and building the feature pyramid in a more reasonable manner in this section.

4.1   Auxiliary Losses

As mentioned in Sect. 3.4, introducing auxiliary losses can help $f_{s_i}, 1 \leq i \leq 3$ own the ability to see all objects. However, the simple summation of the losses may be insufficient. In order to introduce auxiliary losses more rationally, we propose to leverage the uncertainty [15,16,43] to better balance the various-type loss signals. Specifically, we incorporate the uncertainty into each classification and regression auxiliary loss as follow,

$$\mathcal{L}(p, gt) = e^{-\alpha}\hat{\mathcal{L}}(p, gt) + \tau\alpha, \tag{10}$$

where p is the predicted result and gt is the corresponding ground truth. $\hat{\mathcal{L}}$ denotes for the loss function, e.g., L_{reg} and L_{cls}. τ is a hyper-parameter used to avoid generating high uncertainty α. α is generated as follow,

$$\alpha = ReLU(w \cdot x + b), \tag{11}$$

where x is the feature map also utilized to predict p. w and b are the learnable parameters. $ReLU$ is used to promise $\alpha \geq 0$.

4.2   Feature Pyramid Generation Paradigm

Building the feature pyramid in a more reasonable way is also an effective method to achieve consistent improvements in $\{AP_S, AP_M, AP_L\}$. As analysed in Sect. 3.4, the problem in the process of constructing traditional FPN is caused by Eq. (4). Specifically, P_l should contain the feature maps from all backbone levels so that L_l can help each backbone level see the objects inputted to L_l. Accordingly, the summation of $L_l, 2 \leq l \leq 5$ can make each backbone level own the ability to look at all objects.

Feature Grouping. To select effective feature maps from $\mathcal{C}' = \{C'_2, C'_3, C'_4, C'_5\}$ for the objects assigned to the corresponding pyramid level, we first perform channel swapping on $\mathcal{C}'$ as follow,

$$X_k = R^{zhw}(M_k \otimes R^{zn}(C'_k)), \ 2 \leq k \leq 5, \tag{12}$$

where $\otimes$ denotes for matrix multiplication. R^{zn} reshapes C'_k into the size of $Z \times HW$ and R^{zhw} reshapes the input tensor into the size of $Z \times H \times W$, where Z is the number of the channels and $H \times W$ is the resolution of the feature map. M_k is a matrix of size $Z \times Z$ used to achieve channel swapping. In practice, M_k is generated as follow,

$$M_k = G_k(C'_k), \tag{13}$$

where the structure of G_k is shown in Fig. 4. We expect M_k to own the ability to make the homogeneous feature maps become compact along the channel dimension.

Then, X_k is divided into quarters along the channel dimension,

$$X_k = \{X_{k,2}, X_{k,3}, X_{k,4}, X_{k,5}\}, \tag{14}$$

where we assume that $X_{k,l}, 2 \leq l \leq 5$ only carries the effective semantic information of the objects assigned to the pyramid level l. After that, we have

$$P'_l = X_{2,l} \oplus X_{3,l} \oplus X_{4,l} \oplus X_{5,l}, \ 2 \leq l \leq 5, \tag{15}$$

where $\oplus$ denotes for the concatenation operation. Finally, the feature pyramid is constructed as follow,

$$P_l = f_{smo_l}(P'_l), \ 2 \leq l \leq 5. \tag{16}$$

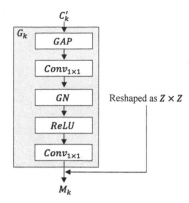

Fig. 4. An illustration of the structure of G_k. $Conv_{1\times1}$ denotes for a 1×1 convolution layer. GN means group normalization and GAP is the global average pooling operation.

Cascade Structure. To better promote the space compactness, we propose to employ a cascade structure to conduct feature grouping in a coarse-to-fine manner. Specifically, at the second stage, P'_l will first be taken as the input of the feature grouping module and thereby we can obtain $\hat{P}'_l$. Then, we have

$$P''_l = f_w(P'_l) \cdot P'_l + f_w(\hat{P}'_l) \cdot \hat{P}'_l,\ 2 \leq l \leq 5, \tag{17}$$

where f_w is a non-linear function used to generate the feature fusion weights. In our implementation, f_w consists of two convolution blocks (a block consists of a convolution, a normalization and an activation layer). Finally, Eq. (16) will be conducted to obtain the feature pyramid with the input P''_l. The same can be done for the cases when the number of the stages is greater than 2.

5   Experiments

Dataset. Our approaches are evaluated on the challenging MS COCO benchmark [23], which contains $\sim$118k images for training (*train-2017*), 5k images for validation (*val-2017*) and $\sim$20k images with no disclosed annotations for testing (*test-dev*). By default, the detection frameworks in this section are trained on *train-2017* set and evaluated on *val-2017* set.

Implementation Details. Our methods are implemented with MMDetection [4]. We train our detection frameworks on 8 NVIDIA Tesla V100 GPUs with a 32 GB memory per-card. Following previous works [21,22,31], we initialize the backbone networks using the weights pre-trained on ImageNet [18] and randomly initialize the weights of the newly added modules. The input images are resized to keep their shorter side being 800 and their longer side less or equal to 1,333. The optimizer is stochastic gradient descent (SGD) with momentum of 0.9, weight decay of 0.0001, and batch size of 16 (*i.e.*, 2 images per GPU). By default, the

Table 1. Ablation study on auxiliary losses. FPS is evaluated on a single Titan Xp.

Framework	Backbone	Auxiliary	Uncertainty	AP	AP$_{50}$	AP$_{75}$	AP$_S$	AP$_M$	AP$_L$	FPS
One-stage										
RetinaNet	ResNet-101			38.5	57.6	41.0	21.7	42.8	50.4	15.0
RetinaNet	ResNet-101	✓		38.7	57.7	41.2	21.2	43.0	51.2	15.0
RetinaNet	ResNet-101	✓	✓	40.1	61.4	43.7	23.3	44.4	52.4	15.0
Two-stage										
Faster R-CNN	ResNet-101			39.5	60.4	42.9	23.6	43.7	51.6	15.6
Faster R-CNN	ResNet-101	✓		39.5	60.0	43.3	21.8	43.5	52.2	15.6
Faster R-CNN	ResNet-101	✓	✓	40.9	62.0	44.8	24.2	45.3	53.3	15.6

Table 2. Ablation study on the feature pyramid generation paradigm.

Framework	Backbone	Feature grouping	Cascade times	AP	AP$_{50}$	AP$_{75}$	AP$_S$	AP$_M$	AP$_L$	FPS
One-stage										
RetinaNet	ResNet-101			38.5	57.6	41.0	21.7	42.8	50.4	15.0
RetinaNet	ResNet-101	✓	1×	40.2	60.1	42.6	23.3	44.5	52.7	12.2
RetinaNet	ResNet-101	✓	2×	40.8	60.5	43.6	24.0	44.8	54.4	11.7
RetinaNet	ResNet-101	✓	3×	41.2	60.8	43.8	24.1	45.2	55.2	11.1
Two-stage										
Faster R-CNN	ResNet-101			39.5	60.4	42.9	23.6	43.7	51.6	15.6
Faster R-CNN	ResNet-101	✓	1×	40.6	61.9	44.5	24.2	45.0	52.7	12.0
Faster R-CNN	ResNet-101	✓	2×	41.7	62.7	45.4	24.8	45.9	53.7	11.4
Faster R-CNN	ResNet-101	✓	3×	42.2	63.0	45.8	25.5	46.1	55.8	10.9

models are trained for 12 epochs (1× schedule), and we set the initial learning rate as 0.02 and decay it by 0.1 at epoch 9 and 11, respectively. We adopt random horizontal flip as the data augmentation. Other unmentioned hyper-parameters follow the settings in MMDetection.

In the inference phase, the input image is first resized in the same way as the training phase and then we forward it through the whole network to output the predicted bounding boxes with the category probability distribution. After that, we leverage a score 0.05 to preliminary filter out background bounding boxes and then output the top 1,000 detections per pyramid level. Finally, the non-maximum suppression (NMS) is applied with the IoU threshold 0.5 per class to output the final top 100 confident detections per image.

Evaluation Metrics. The results are evaluated with standard COCO-style metrics, including AP (averaged over IoU thresholds), AP$_{50}$ (AP for IoU threshold 50%), AP$_{75}$ (AP for IoU threshold 75%), AP$_S$ (AP on objects of small scales), AP$_M$ (AP on objects of medium scales) and AP$_L$ (AP on objects of large scales).

5.1   Ablation Studies

Auxiliary Losses. Since the auxiliary losses can build extra back-propagation paths between the objective functions and the backbone levels, we propose to

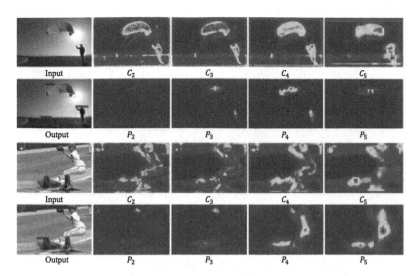

Fig. 5. Visualization of the learned features. The adopted model is Faster R-CNN with ResNet-101. The pictures are selected from MS COCO *val-2017*.

introduce auxiliary losses to address the dropped AP_L problem. Table 1 shows the ablation experiments. After introducing the auxiliary losses, it is observed that AP_L increases from 50.4% to 51.2% and from 51.6% to 52.2% in the one-stage and two-stage detector, respectively. The improvements indicate that the auxiliary losses can help $f_{s_i}, 1 \leq i \leq 3$ own the ability to see all objects and thereby C_5 can carry more effective semantic information of the large-scale objects. Furthermore, we can observe that AP_S drops a lot if simply add the auxiliary losses and the original losses linearly. The drops indicate that to some extent, the auxiliary signals will overwrite the original loss signals especially for the small objects whose effective information is the least. To this end, we introduce the uncertainty to the auxiliary losses to scale the auxiliary signals adaptively. It is observed that AP_S improves from 21.2% to 23.3% and from 21.8% to 24.2% in the one-stage and two-stage pipeline, respectively. As a result, the overall detection performance improves with the consistent changes in $\{AP_S, AP_M, AP_L\}$. These improvements well demonstrate the correctness of our speculation and the effectiveness of our method. Furthermore, since the auxiliary predictions do not participate in the model inference phase, the FPS of the detectors will not drop after the introduction of the auxiliary losses.

Feature Grouping. From the perspective of optimization, we have identified the unreasonable operation in the process of building traditional FPN. Specifically, the top-down architecture will make the shallow layers of the backbone network fail to see the large-scale objects. To mitigate the adverse effects caused, we propose to leverage a feature grouping module to construct each feature pyramid level by selecting the feature maps from all backbone stages. Table 2 demonstrates the empirical study. We can observe that the FPN with feature grouping outperforms the traditional FPN by 1.7% and 1.1% in one-stage and two-stage detection framework, respectively. And AP increases with the consistent rises in $\{AP_S, AP_M, AP_L\}$. The result indicates that the feature grouping module has the ability to make each backbone level see all objects through amending the back-propagation paths between objective functions and the backbone network.

Cascade Structure. To achieve more robust improvements by enhancing the space compactness of the homogeneous feature maps, we propose to introduce a cascade feature grouping structure. The experimental results in Table 2 demonstrate the effectiveness of this structure. It is observed that the detection performance improves steadily as the number of cascade times increases in both one-stage and two-stage frameworks. Moreover, the improvements of AP always benefit from the consistent improvements of $\{AP_S, AP_M, AP_L\}$.

Visualization of Learned Features. In Fig. 5, we visualize the feature maps outputted by the backbone levels (*i.e.*, $\mathcal{C}$) and pyramid levels (*i.e.*, $\mathcal{P}$). It is observed that $\mathcal{C}$ contain the semantic information of the whole image, while $\mathcal{P}$ only carries the effective semantics used to detect the objects within the corresponding scale range, indicating that the feature grouping module can well promise the space compactness of the homogeneous feature maps.

5.2   Performance with Various Detection Frameworks

To further prove the soundness of our principle and the robustness of our approach, we integrate the cascade feature grouping (CFG) structure into various detection frameworks. Table 3 demonstrates the experimental results. For one-stage detectors, our approach consistently improves the baseline frameworks by at least 2.3% AP. For two-stage detectors with pre-defined anchors and ResNet backbone, the baseline frameworks are increased by more than 2.5% AP. Recent academic attention has been geared toward anchor-free detectors and transformer-based backbone networks. We have also made attempts to integrate the proposed structure into these frameworks. It is observed that the cascade feature grouping structure brings more than 2.2% AP improvements to the anchor-free detectors and the transformer-based detectors. Moreover, we have also trained a strong baseline with multi-scale training, 3× schedule and ResNeXt-101-64x4d backbone. After integrating the cascade feature grouping module into the traditional FPN, the strong baseline is still improved by 3.5% AP. It is worth mentioning that the performance gains are all achieved by consistently boosting the AP of the objects within different scale ranges. The results above together show the necessity and effectiveness that each level of the backbone network should own the ability to look at all objects.

5.3   Instance Segmentation

To verify the generalization ability of our approach, we also apply the cascade feature grouping module on a more challenging instance segmentation task,

Table 3. The improvements on AP after integrating the cascade feature grouping module into various detection frameworks. The 1×, 3× training schedules follow the settings explained in MMDetection [4]. FPN-CFG denotes for applying the cascade feature grouping module into FPN.

Method	Backbone	Schedule	AP	AP_{50}	AP_{75}	AP_S	AP_M	AP_L
One-stage								
RetinaNet [22]	ResNet-101-FPN	1×	38.5	57.6	41.0	21.7	42.8	50.4
RetinaNet [22]	ResNet-101-FPN-CFG	1×	41.2 (+2.7)	60.8	43.8	24.1	45.2	55.2
FreeAnchor [46]	ResNet-101-FPN	1×	40.3	59.0	43.1	21.8	44.0	54.2
FreeAnchor [46]	ResNet-101-FPN-CFG	1×	43.2 (+2.9)	62.0	46.3	24.4	47.4	57.6
ATSS [45]	ResNet-101-FPN	1×	41.5	59.9	45.2	24.2	45.9	53.3
ATSS [45]	ResNet-101-FPN-CFG	1×	43.8 (+2.3)	62.1	47.3	26.8	48.0	57.2
Two-stage								
Faster R-CNN [31]	ResNet-101-FPN	1×	39.4	60.1	43.1	22.4	43.7	51.1
Faster R-CNN [31]	ResNet-101-FPN-CFG	1×	42.2 (+2.8)	63.0	45.8	25.5	46.1	55.8
Mask R-CNN [9]	ResNet-101-FPN	1×	40.0	60.5	44.0	22.6	44.0	52.6
Mask R-CNN [9]	ResNet-101-FPN-CFG	1×	43.3 (+3.3)	63.7	47.6	25.7	47.1	56.6
Cascade R-CNN [2]	ResNet-101-FPN	1×	42.0	60.4	45.7	23.4	45.8	55.7
Cascade R-CNN [2]	ResNet-101-FPN-CFG	1×	44.5 (+2.5)	63.1	48.4	26.1	48.5	57.8
Cascade Mask R-CNN [2]	ResNet-101-FPN	1×	42.9	61.0	46.6	24.4	46.5	57.0
Cascade Mask R-CNN [2]	ResNet-101-FPN-CFG	1×	45.4 (+2.5)	63.8	49.4	27.5	49.3	59.5
Anchor-free								
FCOS [39]	ResNet-50-FPN	1×	36.6	56.0	38.8	21.0	40.6	47.0
FCOS [39]	ResNet-50-FPN-CFG	1×	39.6 (+3.0)	58.8	42.3	22.9	43.4	51.9
Sparse R-CNN [37]	ResNet-50-FPN	1×	37.9	56.0	40.5	20.7	40.0	53.5
Sparse R-CNN [37]	ResNet-50-FPN-CFG	1×	40.1 (+2.2)	58.7	42.6	22.2	42.6	55.6
FSAF [49]	ResNet-101-FPN	1×	39.3	58.6	42.1	22.1	43.4	51.2
FSAF [49]	ResNet-101-FPN-CFG	1×	42.2 (+2.9)	62.0	44.8	24.3	45.9	56.2
Transformer								
Mask R-CNN [27]	Swin-T-FPN	1×	42.7	65.2	46.8	26.5	45.9	56.6
Mask R-CNN [27]	Swin-T-FPN-CFG	1×	46.0 (+3.3)	67.0	50.5	28.8	49.7	59.1
Strong baseline								
Cascade Mask R-CNN [2]	ResNeXt-101-64x4d-FPN	3×	46.6	65.1	50.6	29.3	50.5	60.1
Cascade Mask R-CNN [2]	ResNeXt-101-64x4d-FPN-CFG	3×	50.1 (+3.5)	68.6	54.5	32.7	53.7	64.3

which requires the prediction of object instances and their per-pixel segmentation mask simultaneously. As shown in Table 4, our method improves AP^{seg} of different detectors from 39.30% to 41.40%, 36.10% to 38.70%, and 37.30% to 39.40%, respectively. Moreover, all the improvements are built upon the consistent increases in $\{AP_S^{seg}, AP_M^{seg}, AP_L^{seg}\}$.

6   Conclusions

This work first identifies the nature of the success of FPN from the perspective of optimization. Based on the principle, we succeed in illustrating the reason why the introduction of FPN will suppress the detection performance of large objects. We further conclude that the key to address the inconsistent changes problem in $\{AP_S, AP_M, AP_L\}$ is to enable each backbone level to look at all objects. Therefrom, we propose to design two strategies to achieve this goal.

Table 4. Experimental results on instance segmentation task. The models are trained on the MS COCO *train-2017* split and evaluated on the MS COCO *val-2017* set.

Method	Backbone	Schedule	AP^{seg}	AP^{seg}_{50}	AP^{seg}_{75}	AP^{seg}_{S}	AP^{seg}_{M}	AP^{seg}_{L}
Mask R-CNN	Swin-T-FPN	1×	39.30	62.20	42.20	20.50	41.80	57.80
Mask R-CNN	Swin-T-FPN-CFG	1×	41.40 (+2.1)	64.50	44.60	21.90	44.60	58.80
Mask R-CNN	ResNet-101-FPN	1×	36.10	57.50	38.60	18.80	39.70	49.50
Mask R-CNN	ResNet-101-FPN-CFG	1×	38.70 (+2.6)	60.80	41.50	19.00	42.00	56.00
Cascade Mask R-CNN	ResNet-101-FPN	1×	37.30	58.20	40.10	19.70	40.60	51.50
Cascade Mask R-CNN	ResNet-101-FPN-CFG	1×	39.40 (+2.1)	61.30	42.60	19.70	42.60	57.10

One is to introduce the auxiliary losses so that the auxiliary signals containing the information of all objects can directly pass through the shallow layers of the backbone network. The other is to integrate the cascade feature grouping structure into the existing FPN, which can also amend the back-propagation paths between the objective functions and the shallow layers of the backbone network. Extensive experiments show the soundness of our principle and the effectiveness of our strategies. Without bells and whistles, our method brings consistent performance improvements to 12 different detection frameworks.

References

1. Bodla, N., Singh, B., Chellappa, R., Davis, L.S.: Soft-NMS-improving object detection with one line of code. In: Proceedings of the IEEE International Conference on Computer Vision, pp. 5561–5569 (2017)
2. Cai, Z., Vasconcelos, N.: Cascade R-CNN: high quality object detection and instance segmentation. IEEE Trans. Pattern Anal. Mach. Intell. **43**(5), 1483–1498 (2019)
3. Chen, K., et al.: Hybrid task cascade for instance segmentation. In: Proceedings of the IEEE/CVF Conference on Computer Vision and Pattern Recognition, pp. 4974–4983 (2019)
4. Chen, K., et al.: MMDetection: open MMLab detection toolbox and benchmark. arXiv preprint arXiv:1906.07155 (2019)
5. Chen, Q., Wang, Y., Yang, T., Zhang, X., Cheng, J., Sun, J.: You only look one-level feature. In: Proceedings of the IEEE/CVF Conference on Computer Vision and Pattern Recognition, pp. 13039–13048 (2021)
6. Ge, Z., Liu, S., Wang, F., Li, Z., Sun, J.: Yolox: exceeding yolo series in 2021. arXiv preprint arXiv:2107.08430 (2021)
7. Ghiasi, G., Lin, T.Y., Le, Q.V.: NAS-FPN: learning scalable feature pyramid architecture for object detection. In: Proceedings of the IEEE/CVF Conference on Computer Vision and Pattern Recognition, pp. 7036–7045 (2019)
8. Girshick, R., Donahue, J., Darrell, T., Malik, J.: Rich feature hierarchies for accurate object detection and semantic segmentation. In: Proceedings of the IEEE Conference on Computer Vision and Pattern Recognition, pp. 580–587 (2014)
9. He, K., Gkioxari, G., Dollár, P., Girshick, R.: Mask R-CNN. In: Proceedings of the IEEE International Conference on Computer Vision, pp. 2961–2969 (2017)

10. He, K., Zhang, X., Ren, S., Sun, J.: Deep residual learning for image recognition. In: Proceedings of the IEEE Conference on Computer Vision and Pattern Recognition, pp. 770–778 (2016)

11. He, Y., Zhang, X., Savvides, M., Kitani, K.: Softer-NMS: rethinking bounding box regression for accurate object detection. arXiv preprint arXiv:1809.08545 2(3) (2018)

12. He, Y., Zhu, C., Wang, J., Savvides, M., Zhang, X.: Bounding box regression with uncertainty for accurate object detection. In: Proceedings of the IEEE/CVF Conference on Computer Vision and Pattern Recognition, pp. 2888–2897 (2019)

13. Hu, H., Gu, J., Zhang, Z., Dai, J., Wei, Y.: Relation networks for object detection. In: Proceedings of the IEEE Conference on Computer Vision and Pattern Recognition, pp. 3588–3597 (2018)

14. Jin, Z., Liu, B., Chu, Q., Yu, N.: SAFNet: a semi-anchor-free network with enhanced feature pyramid for object detection. IEEE Trans. Image Process. **29**, 9445–9457 (2020)

15. Kendall, A., Gal, Y.: What uncertainties do we need in bayesian deep learning for computer vision? In: Advances in Neural Information Processing Systems, vol. 30 (2017)

16. Kendall, A., Gal, Y., Cipolla, R.: Multi-task learning using uncertainty to weigh losses for scene geometry and semantics. In: Proceedings of the IEEE Conference on Computer Vision and Pattern Recognition, pp. 7482–7491 (2018)

17. Kong, T., Sun, F., Tan, C., Liu, H., Huang, W.: Deep feature pyramid reconfiguration for object detection. In: Proceedings of the European conference on computer vision (ECCV), pp. 169–185 (2018)

18. Krizhevsky, A., Sutskever, I., Hinton, G.E.: ImageNet classification with deep convolutional neural networks. Adv. Neural Inf. Process. Syst. **25**, 1097–1105 (2012)

19. Li, S., Yang, L., Huang, J., Hua, X.S., Zhang, L.: Dynamic anchor feature selection for single-shot object detection. In: Proceedings of the IEEE/CVF International Conference on Computer Vision, pp. 6609–6618 (2019)

20. Li, X., et al.: Generalized focal loss: learning qualified and distributed bounding boxes for dense object detection. arXiv preprint arXiv:2006.04388 (2020)

21. Lin, T.Y., Dollár, P., Girshick, R., He, K., Hariharan, B., Belongie, S.: Feature pyramid networks for object detection. In: Proceedings of the IEEE Conference on Computer Vision and Pattern Recognition, pp. 2117–2125 (2017)

22. Lin, T.Y., Goyal, P., Girshick, R., He, K., Dollár, P.: Focal loss for dense object detection. In: Proceedings of the IEEE International Conference on Computer Vision, pp. 2980–2988 (2017)

23. Lin, T.-Y., et al.: Microsoft COCO: common objects in context. In: Fleet, D., Pajdla, T., Schiele, B., Tuytelaars, T. (eds.) ECCV 2014. LNCS, vol. 8693, pp. 740–755. Springer, Cham (2014). https://doi.org/10.1007/978-3-319-10602-1_48

24. Liu, S., Qi, L., Qin, H., Shi, J., Jia, J.: Path aggregation network for instance segmentation. In: Proceedings of the IEEE Conference on Computer Vision and Pattern Recognition, pp. 8759–8768 (2018)

25. Liu, S., Huang, D., Wang, Y.: Adaptive NMS: refining pedestrian detection in a crowd. In: Proceedings of the IEEE/CVF Conference on Computer Vision and Pattern Recognition, pp. 6459–6468 (2019)

26. Liu, Y., Wang, R., Shan, S., Chen, X.: Structure inference net: object detection using scene-level context and instance-level relationships. In: Proceedings of the IEEE Conference on Computer Vision and Pattern Recognition, pp. 6985–6994 (2018)

27. Liu, Z., et al.: Swin transformer: hierarchical vision transformer using shifted windows. arXiv preprint arXiv:2103.14030 (2021)
28. Micikevicius, P., et al.: Mixed precision training. arXiv preprint arXiv:1710.03740 (2017)
29. Pang, J., Chen, K., Shi, J., Feng, H., Ouyang, W., Lin, D.: Libra R-CNN: towards balanced learning for object detection. In: Proceedings of the IEEE/CVF Conference on Computer Vision and Pattern Recognition, pp. 821–830 (2019)
30. Qian, Q., Chen, L., Li, H., Jin, R.: DR loss: improving object detection by distributional ranking. In: Proceedings of the IEEE/CVF Conference on Computer Vision and Pattern Recognition, pp. 12164–12172 (2020)
31. Ren, S., He, K., Girshick, R., Sun, J.: Faster R-CNN: towards real-time object detection with region proposal networks. Adv. Neural Inf. Process. Syst. **28**, 91–99 (2015)
32. Shrivastava, A., Gupta, A.: Contextual priming and feedback for faster R-CNN. In: Leibe, B., Matas, J., Sebe, N., Welling, M. (eds.) ECCV 2016. LNCS, vol. 9905, pp. 330–348. Springer, Cham (2016). https://doi.org/10.1007/978-3-319-46448-0_20
33. Shrivastava, A., Gupta, A., Girshick, R.: Training region-based object detectors with online hard example mining. In: Proceedings of the IEEE Conference on Computer Vision and Pattern Recognition, pp. 761–769 (2016)
34. Shrivastava, A., Sukthankar, R., Malik, J., Gupta, A.: Beyond skip connections: top-down modulation for object detection. arXiv preprint arXiv:1612.06851 (2016)
35. Singh, B., Davis, L.S.: An analysis of scale invariance in object detection snip. In: Proceedings of the IEEE Conference on Computer Vision and Pattern Recognition, pp. 3578–3587 (2018)
36. Singh, B., Najibi, M., Davis, L.S.: Sniper: efficient multi-scale training. arXiv preprint arXiv:1805.09300 (2018)
37. Sun, P., et al.: Sparse R-CNN: end-to-end object detection with learnable proposals. In: Proceedings of the IEEE/CVF Conference on Computer Vision and Pattern Recognition, pp. 14454–14463 (2021)
38. Tan, M., Pang, R., Le, Q.V.: EfficientDet: scalable and efficient object detection. In: Proceedings of the IEEE/CVF Conference on Computer Vision and Pattern Recognition, pp. 10781–10790 (2020)
39. Tian, Z., Shen, C., Chen, H., He, T.: FCOS: fully convolutional one-stage object detection. In: Proceedings of the IEEE/CVF International Conference on Computer Vision, pp. 9627–9636 (2019)
40. Wang, J., Song, L., Li, Z., Sun, H., Sun, J., Zheng, N.: End-to-end object detection with fully convolutional network. In: Proceedings of the IEEE/CVF Conference on Computer Vision and Pattern Recognition, pp. 15849–15858 (2021)
41. Wu, Y., et al.: Rethinking classification and localization for object detection. In: Proceedings of the IEEE/CVF Conference on Computer Vision and Pattern Recognition, pp. 10186–10195 (2020)
42. Wu, Y., Kirillov, A., Massa, F., Lo, W.Y., Girshick, R.: Detectron2. https://github.com/facebookresearch/detectron2 (2019)
43. Yang, W., Zhang, T., Yu, X., Qi, T., Zhang, Y., Wu, F.: Uncertainty guided collaborative training for weakly supervised temporal action detection. In: Proceedings of the IEEE/CVF Conference on Computer Vision and Pattern Recognition, pp. 53–63 (2021)
44. Zhang, D., Zhang, H., Tang, J., Wang, M., Hua, X., Sun, Q.: Feature pyramid transformer. In: Vedaldi, A., Bischof, H., Brox, T., Frahm, J.-M. (eds.) ECCV 2020. LNCS, vol. 12373, pp. 323–339. Springer, Cham (2020). https://doi.org/10.1007/978-3-030-58604-1_20

45. Zhang, S., Chi, C., Yao, Y., Lei, Z., Li, S.Z.: Bridging the gap between anchor-based and anchor-free detection via adaptive training sample selection. In: Proceedings of the IEEE/CVF Conference on Computer Vision and Pattern Recognition, pp. 9759–9768 (2020)
46. Zhang, X., Wan, F., Liu, C., Ji, X., Ye, Q.: Learning to match anchors for visual object detection. IEEE Trans. Pattern Anal. Mach. Intell. **44**(6), 3096–3109 (2021)
47. Zhao, G., Ge, W., Yu, Y.: GraphFPN: graph feature pyramid network for object detection. In: Proceedings of the IEEE/CVF International Conference on Computer Vision, pp. 2763–2772 (2021)
48. Zhao, H., Shi, J., Qi, X., Wang, X., Jia, J.: Pyramid scene parsing network. In: Proceedings of the IEEE Conference on Computer Vision and Pattern Recognition, pp. 2881–2890 (2017)
49. Zhu, C., He, Y., Savvides, M.: Feature selective anchor-free module for single-shot object detection. In: Proceedings of the IEEE Conference on Computer Vision and Pattern Recognition, pp. 840–849 (2019)
50. Zhu, X., Hu, H., Lin, S., Dai, J.: Deformable convnets v2: more deformable, better results. In: Proceedings of the IEEE/CVF Conference on Computer Vision and Pattern Recognition, pp. 9308–9316 (2019)

Detecting Twenty-Thousand Classes Using Image-Level Supervision

Xingyi Zhou[1,2]([✉]), Rohit Girdhar[1], Armand Joulin[1], Philipp Krähenbühl[2], and Ishan Misra[1]

[1] Meta AI, Menlo Park, USA
[2] The University of Texas at Austin, Austin, USA
zhouxy@cs.utexas.edu

Abstract. Current object detectors are limited in vocabulary size due to the small scale of detection datasets. Image classifiers, on the other hand, reason about much larger vocabularies, as their datasets are larger and easier to collect. We propose *Detic*, which simply trains the classifiers of a detector on image classification data and thus expands the vocabulary of detectors to tens of thousands of concepts. Unlike prior work, Detic does not need complex assignment schemes to assign image labels to boxes based on model predictions, making it much easier to implement and compatible with a range of detection architectures and backbones. Our results show that Detic yields excellent detectors even for classes without box annotations. It outperforms prior work on both open-vocabulary and long-tail detection benchmarks. Detic provides a gain of 2.4 mAP for all classes and 8.3 mAP for novel classes on the open-vocabulary LVIS benchmark. On the standard LVIS benchmark, Detic obtains 41.7 mAP when evaluated on all classes, or only rare classes, hence closing the gap in performance for object categories with few samples. For the first time, we train a detector with all the twenty-one-thousand classes of the ImageNet dataset and show that it generalizes to new datasets without finetuning. Code is available at https://github.com/facebookresearch/Detic.

1 Introduction

Object detection consists of two sub-problems - finding the object (localization) and naming it (classification). Traditional methods tightly couple these two sub-problems and thus rely on box labels for all classes. Despite many data collection efforts, detection datasets [18,28,34,49] are much smaller in overall size and vocabularies than classification datasets [10]. For example, the recent LVIS

X. Zhou—Work done during an internship at Meta.

Supplementary Information The online version contains supplementary material available at https://doi.org/10.1007/978-3-031-20077-9_21.

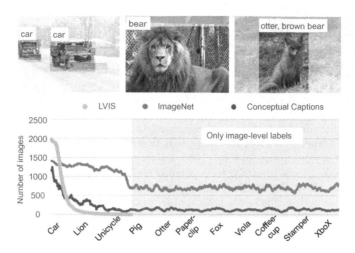

Fig. 1. Top: Typical detection results from a strong open-vocabulary LVIS detector. The detector misses objects of "common" classes. **Bottom:** Number of images in LVIS, ImageNet, and Conceptual Captions per class (smoothed by averaging 100 neighboring classes). Classification datasets have a much larger vocabulary than detection datasets.

detection dataset [18] has 1000+ classes with 120K images; OpenImages [28] has 500 classes in 1.8M images. Moreover, not all classes contain sufficient annotations to train a robust detector (see Fig. 1 Top). In classification, even the ten-year-old ImageNet [10] has 21K classes and 14M images (Fig. 1 Bottom).

In this paper, we propose **Det**ector with **i**mage **c**lasses (Detic) that uses image-level supervision in addition to detection supervision. We observe that the localization and classification sub-problems can be decoupled. Modern region proposal networks already localize many 'new' objects using existing detection supervision. Thus, we focus on the classification sub-problem and use image-level labels to train the classifier and broaden the vocabulary of the detector. We propose a simple classification loss that applies the image-level supervision to the proposal with the largest size, and do not supervise other outputs for image-labeled data. This is easy to implement and massively expands the vocabulary.

Most existing weakly-supervised detection techniques [13,22,36,59,67] use the weakly labeled data to supervise *both* the localization and classification sub-problems of detection. Since image-classification data has no box labels, these methods develop various label-to-box assignment techniques *based on model predictions* to obtain supervision. For example, YOLO9000 [45] and DLWL [44] assign the image label to proposals that have high prediction scores on the labeled class. Unfortunately, this prediction-based assignment requires good initial detections which leads to a chicken-and-egg problem—we need a good detector for good label assignment, but we need many boxes to train a good detector. Our method completely side-steps the prediction-based label assignment process by supervising the classification sub-problem alone when using classification

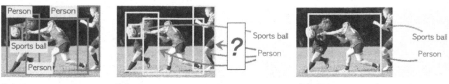

(a) Standard detection (b) Prediction-based label assignment (c) Our non-prediction-based loss

Fig. 2. Left: Standard detection requires ground-truth labeled boxes and cannot leverage image-level labels. **Center:** Existing prediction-based weakly supervised detection methods [3,44,45] use image-level labels by assigning them to the detector's predicted boxes (proposals). Unfortunately, this assignment is error-prone, especially for large vocabulary detection. **Right:** Detic simply assigns the image-labels to the *max-size* proposal. We show that this loss is both simpler and performs better than prior work.

data. This also enables our method to learn detectors for new classes which would have been impossible to predict and assign.

Experiments on the open-vocabulary LVIS [17,18] and the open-vocabulary COCO [2] benchmarks show that our method can significantly improve over a strong box-supervised baseline, on both novel and base classes. With image-level supervision from ImageNet-21K [10], our model trained without novel class detection annotations improves the baseline by 8.3 point and matches the performance of using full class annotations in training. With the standard LVIS annotations, our model reaches 41.7 mAP and 41.7 mAP_{rare}, closing the gap between rare classes and all classes. On open-vocabulary COCO, our method outperforms the previous state-of-the-art OVR-CNN [72] by 5 point with the same detector and data. Finally, we train a detector using the full ImageNet-21K with more than twenty-thousand classes. Our detector generalizes much better to new datasets [28,49] with disjoint label spaces, reaching 21.5 mAP on Objects365 and 55.2 mAP50 on OpenImages, without seeing any images from the corresponding training sets. Our contributions are summarized below:

- We identify issues and propose a simpler alternative to existing weakly-supervised detection techniques in the open-vocabulary setting.
- Our proposed family of losses significantly improves detection performance on novel classes, closely matching the supervised performance upper bound.
- Our detector transfers to new datasets and vocabularies without finetuning.
- We release our code (in supplement). It is ready-to-use for open-vocabulary detection in the real world. See examples in supplement (Fig. 2).

2   Related Work

Weakly-Supervised Object Detection (WSOD) trains object detector using image-level labels. Many works use only image-level labels without any box supervision [30,51,52,63,70]. WSDDN [3] and OIRC [60] use a subnetwork to predict per-proposal weighting and sum up proposal scores into a single image scores. PCL [59] first clusters proposals and then assign image labels at the cluster level. CASD [22] further introduces feature-level attention and self-distillation. As no bounding box supervision is used in training, these methods rely on low-level region proposal techniques [1,62], which leads to reduced localization quality.

Another line of WSOD work uses bounding box supervision together with image labels, known as **semi-supervised WSOD** [12,13,31,35,61,68,75]. YOLO9000 [45] mixes detection data and classification data in the same mini-batch, and assigns classification labels to anchors with the highest predicted scores. DLWL [44] combines self-training and clustering-based WSOD [59], and again assigns image labels to max-scored proposals. MosaicOS [73] handles domain differences between detection and image datasets by mosaic augmentation [4] and proposed a three-stage self-training and finetuning framework. In segmentation, Pinheiro *et al.* [41] use a log-sum-exponential function to aggregate pixels scores into a global classification. Our work belongs to semi-supervised WSOD. Unlike prior work, we use a simple image-supervised loss. Besides image labels, researchers have also studied complementary methods for weak localization supervision like points [7] or scribles [47].

Open-Vocabulary Object Detection, or also named **zero-shot object detection**, aims to detect objects outside of the training vocabulary. The basic solution [2] is to replace the last classification layer with language embeddings (e.g., GloVe [40]) of the class names. Rahman *et al.* [43] and Li *et al.* [33] improve the classifier embedding using external text information. OVR-CNN [72] pretrains the detector on image-text pairs. ViLD [17], OpenSeg [16] and langSeg [29] upgrade the language embedding to CLIP [42]. ViLD further distills region features from CLIP image features. We use CLIP [42] classifier as well, but do not use distillation. Instead, we use additional image-labeled data for co-training.

Large-Vocabulary Object Detection [18,45,53,69] requires detecting 1000+ classes. Many existing works focus on handling the long-tail problem [6,14,32, 39,65,74]. Equalization losses [55,56] and SeeSaw loss [64] reweights the per-class loss by balancing the gradients [55] or number of samples [64]. Federated Loss [76] subsamples classes per-iteration to mimic the federated annotation [18]. Yang *et al.* [69] detects 11K classes with a label hierarchy. Our method builds on these advances, and we tackle the problem from a different aspect: using additional image-labeled data.

Proposal Network Generalization. ViLD [17] reports that region proposal networks have certain generalization abilities for new classes by default. Dave *et al.* [9] shows segmentation and localization generalizes across classes. Kim *et al.* [25] further improves proposal generalization with a localization quality estimator. In our experiments, we found proposals to generalize well enough (see Appendix A), as also observed in ViLD [17]. Further improvements to RPNs [17, 25,27,38] can hopefully lead to better results.

3   Preliminaries

We train object detectors using both object detection and image classification datasets. We propose a simple way to leverage image supervision to learn object detectors, including for classes without box labels. We first describe the object detection problem and then detail our approach.

Problem Setup. Given an image $\mathbf{I} \in \mathbb{R}^{3 \times h \times w}$, object detection solves the two subproblems of (1) localization: find all objects with their location, represented as a box $\mathbf{b}_j \in \mathbb{R}^4$ and (2) classification: assign a class label $c_j \in \mathcal{C}^{\text{test}}$ to the j-th object. Here $\mathcal{C}^{\text{test}}$ is the class vocabulary provided by the user at test time. During training, we use a detection dataset $\mathcal{D}^{\text{det}} = \{(\mathbf{I}, \{(\mathbf{b}, c)_k\})_i\}_{i=1}^{|\mathcal{D}^{\text{det}}|}$ with vocabulary $\mathcal{C}^{\text{det}}$ that has both class and box labels. We also use an image classification dataset $\mathcal{D}^{\text{cls}} = \{(\mathbf{I}, \{c_k\})_i\}_{i=1}^{|\mathcal{D}^{\text{cls}}|}$ with vocabulary $\mathcal{C}^{\text{cls}}$ that only has image-level class labels. The vocabularies $\mathcal{C}^{\text{test}}$, $\mathcal{C}^{\text{det}}$, $\mathcal{C}^{\text{cls}}$ may or may not overlap.

Traditional Object Detection considers $\mathcal{C}^{\text{test}} = \mathcal{C}^{\text{det}}$ and $\mathcal{D}^{\text{cls}} = \emptyset$. Predominant object detectors [20,46] follow a two-stage framework. The first stage, called the *region proposal network* (RPN), takes the image $\mathbf{I}$ and produces a set of object proposals $\{(\mathbf{b}, \mathbf{f}, o)_j\}$, where $\mathbf{f}_j \in \mathbb{R}^D$ is a D-dimensional region feature and $o \in \mathbb{R}$ is the objectness score. The second stage takes the object feature and outputs a classification score and a refined box location for each object, $s_j = \mathbf{W}\mathbf{f}_j$, $\hat{\mathbf{b}}_j = \mathbf{B}\mathbf{f}_j + \mathbf{b}_j$, where $\mathbf{W} \in \mathbb{R}^{|\mathcal{C}^{\text{det}}| \times D}$ and $\mathbf{B} \in \mathbb{R}^{4 \times D}$ are the learned weights of the classification layer and the regression layer, respectively.[1] Our work focuses on improving classification in the second stage. In our experiments, the proposal network and the bounding box regressors are not the current performance bottleneck, as modern detectors use an over-sufficient number of proposals in testing (1K proposals for < 20 objects per image. See Appendix A for more details).

Open-vocabulary Object Detection allows $\mathcal{C}^{\text{test}} \neq \mathcal{C}^{\text{det}}$. Simply replacing the classification weights $\mathbf{W}$ with fixed language embeddings of class names converts a traditional detector to an open-vocabulary detector [2]. The region features are trained to match the fixed language embeddings. We follow Gu *et al.* [17] to use the CLIP embeddings [42] as the classification weights. In theory, this open-vocabulary detector can detect any object class. However, in practice, it yields unsatisfying results as shown in Fig. 1. Our method uses image-level supervision to improve object detection including in the open-vocabulary setting.

4   Detic: Detector with Image Classes

As shown in Fig. 3, our method leverages the box labels from detection datasets $\mathcal{D}^{\text{det}}$ and image-level labels from classification datasets $\mathcal{D}^{\text{cls}}$. During training, we compose a mini-batch using images from both types of datasets. For images with

---

[1] We omit the two linear layers and the bias in the second stage for notation simplicity.

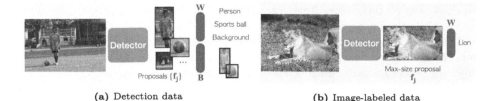

(a) Detection data   (b) Image-labeled data

Fig. 3. Approach Overview. We mix train on detection data and image-labeled data. When using detection data, our model uses the standard detection losses to train the classifier ($\mathbf{W}$) and the box prediction branch ($\mathbf{B}$) of a detector. When using image-labeled data, we only train the classifier using our modified classification loss. Our loss trains the features extracted from the largest-sized proposal.

box labels, we follow the standard two-stage detector training [46]. For image-level labeled images, we only train the features from a fixed region proposal for classification. Thus, we only compute the localization losses (RPN loss and bounding box regression loss) on images with ground truth box labels. Below we describe our modified classification loss for image-level labels.

A sample from the weakly labeled dataset $\mathcal{D}^{\text{cls}}$ contains an image $\mathbf{I}$ and a set of K labels $\{c_k\}_{k=1}^K$. We use the region proposal network to extract N object features $\{(\mathbf{b}, \mathbf{f}, o)_j\}_{j=1}^N$. Prediction-based methods try to assign image labels to regions, and aim to train both localization and classification abilities. Instead, we propose simple ways to use the image labels $\{c_k\}_{k=1}^K$ and only improve classification. Our key idea is to use a fixed way to assign image labels to regions, and side-step a complex prediction-based assignment. We allow the fixed assignment schemes miss certain objects, as long as they miss fewer objects than the prediction-based counterparts, thus leading to better performance.

Non-prediction-Based Losses. We now describe a variety of simple ways to use image labels and evaluate them empirically in Table 1. Our first idea is to use the whole image as a new "proposal" box. We call this loss **image-box**. We ignore all proposals from the RPN, and instead use an injected box of the whole image $\mathbf{b}' = (0, 0, w, h)$. We then apply the classification loss to its RoI features $\mathbf{f}'$ for all classes $c \in \{c_k\}_{k=1}^K$:

$$L_{\text{image-box}} = BCE(\mathbf{W}\mathbf{f}', c)$$

where $BCE(s, c) = -log\sigma(s_c) - \sum_{k \neq c} log(1 - \sigma(s_k))$ is the binary cross-entropy loss, and σ is the sigmoid activation. Thus, our loss uses the features from the same 'proposal' for solving the classification problem for all the classes $\{c_k\}$.

In practice, the image-box can be replaced by smaller boxes. We introduce two alternatives: the proposal with the **max object score** or the proposal with the **max size**:

$$L_{\text{max-object-score}} = BCE(\mathbf{W}\mathbf{f}_j, c), j = \text{argmax}_j o_j$$

$$L_{\text{max-size}} = BCE(\mathbf{W}\mathbf{f}_j, c), j = \text{argmax}_j (\text{size}(\mathbf{b}_j))$$

We show that all these three losses can effectively leverage the image-level supervision, while the max-size loss performs the best. We thus use the max-size loss by default for image-supervised data. We also note that the classification parameters $\mathbf{W}$ are shared across both detection and classification data, which greatly improves detection performance. The overall training objective is

$$L(\mathbf{I}) = \begin{cases} L_{\text{rpn}} + L_{\text{reg}} + L_{\text{cls}}, & \text{if } \mathbf{I} \in \mathcal{D}^{\text{det}} \\ \lambda L_{\text{max-size}}, & \text{if } \mathbf{I} \in \mathcal{D}^{\text{cls}} \end{cases}$$

where L_{rpn}, L_{reg}, L_{cls} are standard losses in a two-stage detector, and $\lambda = 0.1$ is the weight of our loss.

Relation to Prediction-Based Assignments. In traditional weakly-supervised detection [3,44,45], a popular idea is to assign the image to the proposals based on model prediction. Let $\mathbf{F} = (\mathbf{f}_1, \ldots, \mathbf{f}_N)$ be the stacked feature of all object proposals and $\mathbf{S} = \mathbf{WF}$ be their classification scores. For each $c \in \{c_k\}_{k=1}^K$, $L = BCE(\mathbf{S}_j, c), j = \mathcal{F}(\mathbf{S}, c)$, where $\mathcal{F}$ is the label-to-box assignment process. In most methods, $\mathcal{F}$ is a function of the prediction $\mathbf{S}$. For example, $\mathcal{F}$ selects the proposal with max score on c. Our key insight is that $\mathcal{F}$ should *not* depend on the prediction $\mathbf{S}$. In large-vocabulary detection, the initial recognition ability of rare or novel classes is low, making the label assignment process inaccurate. Our method side-steps this prediction-and-assignment process entirely and relies on a fixed supervision criteria.

5 Experiments

We evaluate Detic on the large-vocabulary object detection dataset LVIS [18]. We mainly use the open-vocabulary setting proposed by Gu *et al.* [17], and also report results on the standard LVIS setting. We describe our experiment setup below.

LVIS. The LVIS [18] dataset has object detection and instance segmentation labels for 1203 classes with 100K images. The classes are divided into three groups - frequent, common, rare based on the number of training images. We refer to this standard LVIS training set as *LVIS-all*. Following ViLD [17], we remove the labels of 337 rare-class from training and consider them as novel classes in testing. We refer to this partial training set with only frequent and common classes as *LVIS-base*. We report mask mAP which is the official metric for LVIS. While our model is developed for box detection, we use a standard class-agnostic mask head [20] to produce segmentation masks for boxes. We train the mask head only on detection data.

Image-Supervised Data. We use two sources of image-supervised data: ImageNet-21K [10] and Conceptual Captions [50]. ImageNet-21K (IN-21K) contains 14M images for 21K classes. For ease of training and evaluation, most of our experiments use the 997 classes that overlap with the LVIS vocabulary and denote this subset as IN-L. Conceptual Captions [50] (CC) is an image captioning dataset containing 3M images. We extract image labels from the captions using exact text-matching and keep images whose captions mention at least one LVIS class. See Appendix B for results of directly using captions. The resulting dataset contains 1.5M images with 992 LVIS classes. We summarize the datasets used below.

Notation	Definition	#Images	#Classes
LVIS-all	The original LVIS dataset [18]	100K	1203
LVIS-base	LVIS without rare-class annotations	100K	866
IN-21K	The original ImageNet-21K dataset [10]	14M	21k
IN-L	997 overlapping IN-21K classes with LVIS	1.2M	997
CC	Conceptual Captions [50] with LVIS classes	1.5M	992

5.1 Implementation Details

Box-Supervised: A Strong LVIS Baseline. We first establish a strong baseline on LVIS to demonstrate that our improvements are orthogonal to recent advances in object detection. The baseline only uses the supervised bounding box labels. We use the CenterNet2 [76] detector with ResNet50 [21] backbone. We use Federated Loss [76] and repeat factor sampling [18]. We use large scale jittering [15] with input resolution 640×640 and train for a $4\times$ (~ 48 LVIS epochs) schedule. To show our method is compatible with better pretraining, we use ImageNet-21k pretrained backbone weights [48]. As described in Sect. 3, we use the CLIP [42] embedding as the classifier. Our baseline is 9.1 mAP higher than the detectron2 baseline [66] (31.5 vs. 22.4 mAP^{mask}) and trains in a similar time (17 vs. 12 h on 8 V100 GPUs). See Appendix C for more details.

Resolution Change for Image-Labeled Images. ImageNet images are inherently smaller and more object-focused than LVIS images [73]. In practice, we observe it is important to use smaller image resolution for ImageNet images. Using smaller resolution in addition allows us to increase the batch-size with the same computation. In our implementation, we use 320×320 for ImageNet and CC and ablate this in Appendix D.

Multi-dataset Training. We sample detection and classification mini-batches in a 1 : 1 ratio, regardless of the original dataset size. We group images from the same dataset on the same GPU to improve training efficiency [77].

Training Schedules. To shorten the experimental cycle and have a good initialization for prediction-based WSOD losses [44,45], we always first train a converged base-class-only model ($4\times$ schedule) and finetune on it with additional image-labeled data for another $4\times$ schedule. We confirm finetuning the model

Table 1. Prediction-based *vs* non-prediction-based methods. We show overall and novel-class mAP on open-vocabulary LVIS [17] (with 866 base classes and 337 novel classes) with different image-labeled datasets (IN-L or CC). The models are trained using our strong baseline Sect. 5.1 (top row). This baseline is trained on boxes from the base classes and has non-zero novel-class mAP as it uses the CLIP classifier. All models in the following rows are finetuned from the baseline model and leverage image-labeled data. We repeat experiments for 3 runs and report mean/ std. All variants of our proposed non-prediction-based losses outperform existing prediction-based counterparts.

	IN-L (object-centric)		CC (non object-centric)	
	mAP^{mask}	$\text{mAP}^{\text{mask}}_{\text{novel}}$	mAP^{mask}	$\text{mAP}^{\text{mask}}_{\text{novel}}$
Box-Supervised (baseline)	$30.0_{\pm0.4}$	$16.3_{\pm0.7}$	$30.0_{\pm0.4}$	$16.3_{\pm0.7}$
Prediction-based methods				
Self-training [54]	$30.3_{\pm0.0}$	$15.6_{\pm0.1}$	$30.1_{\pm0.2}$	$15.9_{\pm0.8}$
WSDDN [3]	$29.8_{\pm0.2}$	$15.6_{\pm0.3}$	$30.0_{\pm0.1}$	$16.5_{\pm0.8}$
DLWL* [44]	$30.6_{\pm0.1}$	$18.2_{\pm0.2}$	$29.7_{\pm0.3}$	$16.9_{\pm0.6}$
YOLO9000 [45]	$31.2_{\pm0.3}$	$20.4_{\pm0.9}$	$29.4_{\pm0.1}$	$15.9_{\pm0.6}$
Non-prediction-based methods				
Detic (Max-object-score)	$32.2_{\pm0.1}$	$24.4_{\pm0.3}$	$29.8_{\pm0.1}$	$18.2_{\pm0.6}$
Detic (Image-box)	$\mathbf{32.4_{\pm0.1}}$	$23.8_{\pm0.5}$	$\mathbf{30.9_{\pm0.1}}$	$\mathbf{19.5_{\pm0.5}}$
Detic (Max-size)	$\mathbf{32.4_{\pm0.1}}$	$\mathbf{24.6_{\pm0.3}}$	$30.9_{\pm0.2}$	$\mathbf{19.5_{\pm0.3}}$
Fully-supervised (all classes)	$31.1_{\pm0.4}$	$25.5_{\pm0.7}$	$31.1_{\pm0.4}$	$25.5_{\pm0.7}$

using only box supervision does not improve the performance. The 4× schedule for our joint training consists of ∼24 LVIS epochs plus ∼4.8 ImageNet epochs or ∼3.8 CC epochs. Training our ResNet50 model takes ∼22 hours on 8 V100 GPUs. The large 21K Swin-B model trains in ∼24 hours on 32 GPUs.

5.2   Prediction-Based *vs* Non-prediction-Based Methods

Table 1 shows the results of the box-supervised baseline, existing prediction-based methods, and our proposed non-prediction-based methods. The baseline (Box-Supervised) is trained without access to novel class bounding box labels. It uses the CLIP classifier [17] and has open-vocabulary capabilities with 16.3 $\text{mAP}_{\text{novel}}$. In order to leverage additional image-labeled data like ImageNet or CC, we use prior prediction-based methods or our non-prediction-based method.

We compare a few prediction-based methods that assign image labels to proposals based on predictions. Self-training assigns predictions of Box-Supervised as pseudo-labels *offline* with a fixed score threshold (0.5). The other prediction-based methods use different losses to assign predictions to image labels online. See Appendix E for implementation details. For DLWL [44], we implement a simplified version that does not include bootstrapping and refer to it as DLWL*.

Table 1 (third block) shows the results of our non-prediction-based methods in Sect. 4. All variants of our proposed simpler method outperform the complex prediction-based counterparts, with both image-supervised datasets. On the novel classes, Detic provides a significant gain of ~ 4.2 points with ImageNet over the best prediction-based methods.

Using Non-object Centric Images from Conceptual Captions. ImageNet images typically have a single large object [18]. Thus, our non-prediction-based methods, for example image-box which considers the entire image as a bounding box, are well suited for ImageNet. To test whether our losses work with different image distributions with multiple objects, we test it with the Conceptual Captions (CC) dataset. Even on this challenging dataset with multiple objects/labels per image, Detic provides a gain of ~ 2.6 points on novel class detection over the best prediction-based methods. This suggests that our simpler Detic method can generalize to different types of image-labeled data. Overall, the results from Table 1 suggest that complex prediction-based methods that overly rely on model prediction scores do not perform well for open-vocabulary detection. Amongst our non-prediction-based variants, the max-size loss consistently performs the best, and is the default for Detic in our following experiments.

Why Does Max-Size Work? Intuitively, our simpler non-prediction methods outperform the complex prediction-based method by side-stepping a hard assignment problem. Prediction-based methods rely on strong initial detections to assign image-level labels to predicted boxes. When the initial predictions are reliable, prediction-based methods are ideal. However, in open-vocabulary scenarios, such strong initial predictions are absent, which explains the limited performance of prediction-based methods. Detic's simpler assignment does not rely on strong predictions and is more robust under the challenges of open-vocabulary setting.

We now study two additional advantages of the Detic max-size variant over prediction-based methods that may contribute to improved performance: 1) the selected max-size proposal can safely *cover* the target object; 2) the selected max-size proposal is consistent during different training iterations.

Figure 4 provides typical qualitative examples of the assigned region for the prediction-based method and our max-size variant. On an annotated subset of IN-L, Detic max-size covers 92.8% target objects, vs. 69.0% for the prediction-based method. Overall, unlike prediction-based methods, Detic's simpler assignment yields boxes that are more likely to contain the object. Indeed, Detic may miss certain objects (especially small objects) or supervise to a loose region. However, in order for Detic to yield a good detector, the selected box need not be perfect, it just needs to 1) provide meaningful training signal (cover the objects and be consistent during training); 2) be 'more correct' than the box selected by the prediction-based method. We provide details about our metrics, more quantitative evaluation, and more discussions in Appendix E.

5.3 Comparison with a Fully-Supervised Detector

In Table 1, compared with the strong baseline Box-Supervised, Detic improves the detection performance by 2.4 mAP and 8.3 $\text{mAP}_{\text{novel}}$. Thus, Detic with image-level labels leads to strong open-vocabulary detection performance and

Fig. 4. Visualization of the assigned boxes during training. We show all boxes with score > 0.5 in blue and the assigned (selected) box in red. **Top:** The prediction-based method selects different boxes across training, and the selected box may not cover the objects in the image. **Bottom:** Our simpler max-size variant selects a box that covers the objects and is more consistent across training. (Color figure online)

Table 2. Open-vocabulary LVIS compared to ViLD [17]. We train our model *using their training settings and architecture* (MaskRCNN-ResNet50, training from scratch). We report mask mAP and its breakdown to novel (rare), common, and frequent classes. Variants of ViLD use distillation (ViLD) or ensembling (ViLD-ensemble.). Detic (with IN-L) uses a single model and improves both mAP and mAP_{novel}.

	mAP^{mask}	mAP^{mask}_{novel}	mAP^{mask}_c	mAP^{mask}_f
ViLD-text [17]	24.9	10.1	23.9	**32.5**
ViLD [17]	22.5	16.1	20.0	28.3
ViLD-ensemble [17]	25.5	16.6	24.6	30.3
Detic	**26.8**	**17.8**	**26.3**	31.6

can provide orthogonal gains to existing open-vocabulary detectors [2]. To further understand the open-vocabulary capabilities of Detic, we also report the *top-line* results trained with box labels for all classes (Table 1 last row). Despite not using box labels for the novel classes, Detic with ImageNet performs favorably compared to the fully-supervised detector. This result also suggests that bounding box annotations may not be required for new classes. Detic combined with large image classification datasets is a simple and effective alternative for increasing detector vocabulary.

5.4   Comparison with the State-of-the-Art

We compare Detic's open-vocabulary object detectors with state-of-the-art methods on the open-vocabulary LVIS and the open-vocabulary COCO benchmarks. In each case, we strictly follow the architecture and setup from prior work to ensure fair comparisons.

Open-vocabulary LVIS. We compare to ViLD [17], which first uses CLIP embeddings [42] for open-vocabulary detection. We strictly follow their training

Table 3. Open-vocabulary COCO [2]. We compare Detic using the same training data and architecture from OVR-CNN [72]. We report box mAP at IoU threshold 0.5 using Faster R-CNN with ResNet50-C4 backbone. Detic builds upon the CLIP baseline (second row) and shows significant improvements over prior work. †: results quoted from OVR-CNN [72] paper or code. ‡: results quoted from the original publications.

	$mAP50_{all}^{box}$	$mAP50_{novel}^{box}$	$mAP50_{base}^{box}$
Base-only†	39.9	0	**49.9**
Base-only (CLIP)	39.3	1.3	48.7
WSDDN [3]†	24.6	20.5	23.4
Cap2Det [71]†	20.1	20.3	20.1
SB [2]‡	24.9	0.31	29.2
DELO [78]‡	13.0	3.41	13.8
PL [43]‡	27.9	4.12	35.9
OVR-CNN [72]†	39.9	22.8	46.0
Detic	**45.0**	**27.8**	47.1

setup and model architecture (Appendix G) and report results in Table 2. Here ViLD-text is exactly our Box-Supervised baseline. Detic provides a gain of 7.7 points on mAP_{novel}. Compared to ViLD-text, ViLD, which uses knowledge distillation from the CLIP visual backbone, improves mAP_{novel} at the cost of hurting overall mAP. Ensembling the two models, ViLD-ens provides improvements for both metrics. On the other hand, Detic uses a single model which improves both novel and overall mAP, and outperforms the ViLD ensemble.

Open-vocabulary COCO. Next, we compare with prior works on the popular open-vocabulary COCO benchmark [2] (see benchmark and implementation details in Appendix H). We strictly follow OVR-CNN [72] to use Faster R-CNN with ResNet50-C4 backbone and do not use any improvements from Sect. 5.1. Following [72], we use COCO captions as the image-supervised data. We extract nouns from the captions and use both the image labels and captions as supervision.

Table 3 summarizes our results. As the training set contains only 48 base classes, the base-class only model (second row) yields low mAP on novel classes. Detic improves the baseline and outperforms OVR-CNN [72] by a large margin, using exactly the same model, training recipe, and data.

Additionally, similar to Table 1, we compare to prior prediction-based methods on the open-vocabulary COCO benchmark in Appendix H. In this setting too, Detic improves over prior work providing significant gains on novel class detection and overall detection performance.

5.5 Detecting 21K Classes Across Datasets Without Finetuning

Next, we train a detector with the full 21K classes of ImageNet. We use our strong recipe with Swin-B [37] backbone. In practice, training a classification

Table 4. Detecting 21K classes across datasets. We use Detic to train a detector and evaluate it on multiple datasets *without retraining*. We report the bounding box mAP on Objects365 and OpenImages. Compared to the Box-Supervised baseline (trained on LVIS-all), Detic leverages image-level supervision to train robust detectors. The performance of Detic is 70%-80% of dataset-specific models (bottom row) that use dataset specific box labels.

	Objects365 [49]		OpenImages [28]	
	mAP^{box}	mAP$^{box}_{rare}$	mAP50^{box}	mAP50$^{box}_{rare}$
Box-Supervised	19.1	14.0	46.2	61.7
Detic w. IN-L	21.2	17.8	53.0	67.1
Detic w. IN-21k	**21.5**	**20.0**	**55.2**	**68.8**
Dataset-specific oracles	31.2	22.5	69.9	81.8

Table 5. Detic with different classifiers. We vary the classifier used with Detic and observe that it works well with different choices. While CLIP embeddings give the best performance (* indicates our default), all classifiers benefit from our Detic.

Classifier	Box-supervised		Detic	
	mAP^{mask}	mAP$^{mask}_{novel}$	mAP^{mask}	mAP$^{mask}_{novel}$
*CLIP [42]	30.2	16.4	32.4	24.9
Trained	27.4	0	31.7	17.4
FastText [24]	27.5	9.0	30.9	19.2
OpenCLIP [23]	27.1	8.9	30.7	19.4

layer of 21K classes is computationally involved.[2] We adopt a modified Federated Loss [76] that uniformly samples 50 classes from the vocabulary at every iteration. We only compute classification scores and back-propagate on the sampled classes.

As there are no direct benchmark to evaluate detectors with such large vocabulary, we evaluate our detectors on new datasets *without finetuning*. We evaluate on two large-scale object detection datasets: Objects365v2 [49] and OpenImages [28], both with around 1.8M training images. We follow LVIS to split $\frac{1}{3}$ of classes with the fewest training images as rare classes. Table 4 shows the results. On both datasets, Detic improves the Box-Supervised baseline by a large margin, especially on classes with fewer annotations. Using all the 21k classes further improves performance owing to the large vocabulary. Our single model significantly reduces the gap towards the dataset-specific oracles and reaches 70%–80% of their performance without using the corresponding 1.8M detection annotations. See Fig. 5 for qualitative results.

---

[2] This is more pronounced in detection than classification, as the "batch-size" for the classification layer is 512× image-batch-size, where 512 is #RoIs per image.

Fig. 5. Qualitative results of our 21k-class detector. We show random samples from images containing novel classes in OpenImages (top) and Objects365 (bottom) validation sets. We use the CLIP embedding of the corresponding vocabularies. We show LVIS classes in purple and novel classes in green. We use a score threshold of 0.5 and show the most confident class for each box. Best viewed on screen.

Table 6. Detic with different pretraining data. Top: our method using ImageNet-1K as pretraining and ImageNet-21K as co-training; Bottom: using ImageNet-21K for both pretraining and co-training. Co-training helps pretraining in both cases.

	Pretrain data	mAP^{mask}	mAP^{mask}_{novel}
Box-Supervised	IN-1K	26.1	13.6
Detic	IN-1K	28.8 (+2.7)	21.7 (+8.1)
Box-Supervised	IN-21K	30.2	16.4
Detic	IN-21K	32.4 (+2.2)	24.9 (+8.5)

5.6 Ablation Studies

We now ablate our key components under the open-vocabulary LVIS setting with IN-L as the image-classification data. We use our strong training recipe as described in Sect. 5.1 for all these experiments.

Classifier Weights. We study the effect of different classifier weights $\mathbf{W}$. While our main open-vocabulary experiments use CLIP [42], we show the gain of Detic is independent of CLIP. We train Box-Supervised and Detic with different classifiers, including a standard random initialized and trained classifier, and other *fixed* language models [23,24] The results are shown in Table 5. By default, a trained classifier cannot recognize novel classes. However, Detic enables novel class recognition ability even in this setting (17.4 mAP_{novel} for classes without detection labels). Using language models such as FastText [24] or an open-source version of CLIP [23] leads to better novel class performance. CLIP [42] performs the best among them.

Effect of Pretraining. Many existing methods use additional data only for pretraining [11,72,73], while we use image-labeled data for co-training. We present results of Detic with different types of pretraining in Table 6. Detic provides similar gains across different types of pretraining, suggesting that our gains are orthogonal to advances in pretraining. We believe that this is because pretraining improves the overall features, while Detic uses co-training which improves both the features and the classifier.

5.7   The Standard LVIS benchmark

Finally, we evaluate Detic on the standard LVIS benchmark [18]. In this setting, the baseline (Box-Supervised) is trained with box and mask labels for all classes while Detic uses additional image-level labels from IN-L. We train Detic with the same recipe in Sect. 5.1 and use a strong Swin-B [37] backbone and 896×896 input size. We report the mask mAP across all classes and also split into rare, common, and frequent classes. Notably, Detic achieves 41.7 mAP and 41.7 mAP_r, closing the gap between the overall mAP and the rare mAP. This suggests Detic effectively uses image-level labels to improve the performance of classes with very few boxes labels. Appendix I provides more comparisons to prior work [73] on LVIS. Appendix J shows Detic generalizes to DETR-based [79] detectors (Table 7).

Table 7. Standard LVIS. We evaluate our baseline (Box-Supervised) and Detic using different backbones on the LVIS dataset. We report the mask mAP. We also report prior work on LVIS using large backbone networks (single-scale testing) for references (not for apple-to-apple comparison). †: detectors using additional data. Detic improves over the baseline with increased gains for the rare classes.

	Backbone	mAP^{mask}	mAP_r^{mask}	mAP_c^{mask}	mAP_f^{mask}
MosaicOS† [73]	ResNeXt-101	28.3	21.7	27.3	32.4
CenterNet2 [76]	ResNeXt-101	34.9	24.6	34.7	42.5
AsyncSLL† [19]	ResNeSt-269	36.0	27.8	36.7	39.6
SeesawLoss [64]	ResNeSt-200	37.3	26.4	36.3	**43.1**
Copy-paste [15]	EfficientNet-B7	38.1	32.1	37.1	41.9
Tan et al. [57]	ResNeSt-269	38.8	28.5	39.5	42.7
Baseline	Swin-B	40.7	35.9	40.5	**43.1**
Detic†	Swin-B	**41.7**	**41.7**	**40.8**	42.6

6   Limitations and Conclusions

We present Detic which is a simple way to use image supervision in large-vocabulary object detection. While Detic is simpler than prior assignment-based weakly-supervised detection methods, it supervises all image labels to the same region and does not consider overall dataset statistics. We leave incorporating such information for future work. Moreover, open vocabulary generalization has no guarantees on extreme domains. Our experiments show Detic improves large-vocabulary detection with various weak data sources, classifiers, detector architectures, and training recipes.

Acknowledgement. We thank Bowen Cheng and Ross Girshick for helpful discussions and feedback. This material is in part based upon work supported by the National Science Foundation under Grant No. IIS-1845485 and IIS-2006820. Xingyi is supported by a Facebook PhD Fellowship.

References

1. Arbeláez, P., Pont-Tuset, J., Barron, J.T., Marques, F., Malik, J.: Multiscale combinatorial grouping. In: CVPR (2014)
2. Bansal, A., Sikka, K., Sharma, G., Chellappa, R., Divakaran, A.: Zero-shot object detection. In: Ferrari, V., Hebert, M., Sminchisescu, C., Weiss, Y. (eds.) ECCV 2018. LNCS, vol. 11205, pp. 397–414. Springer, Cham (2018). https://doi.org/10.1007/978-3-030-01246-5_24
3. Bilen, H., Vedaldi, A.: Weakly supervised deep detection networks. In: CVPR (2016)
4. Bochkovskiy, A., Wang, C.Y., Liao, H.Y.M.: Yolov4: optimal speed and accuracy of object detection. arXiv:2004.10934 (2020)
5. Cai, Z., Vasconcelos, N.: Cascade R-CNN: delving into high quality object detection. In: CVPR (2018)
6. Chang, N., Yu, Z., Wang, Y.X., Anandkumar, A., Fidler, S., Alvarez, J.M.: Image-level or object-level? A tale of two resampling strategies for long-tailed detection. In: ICML (2021)
7. Chen, L., Yang, T., Zhang, X., Zhang, W., Sun, J.: Points as queries: weakly semi-supervised object detection by points. In: CVPR (2021)
8. Dave, A., Dollár, P., Ramanan, D., Kirillov, A., Girshick, R.: Evaluating large-vocabulary object detectors: the devil is in the details. arXiv:2102.01066 (2021)
9. Dave, A., Tokmakov, P., Ramanan, D.: Towards segmenting anything that moves. In: ICCVW (2019)
10. Deng, J., Dong, W., Socher, R., Li, L.J., Li, K., Fei-Fei, L.: ImageNet: a large-scale hierarchical image database. In: CVPR (2009)
11. Desai, K., Johnson, J.: VirTex: learning visual representations from textual annotations. In: CVPR (2021)
12. Dong, B., Huang, Z., Guo, Y., Wang, Q., Niu, Z., Zuo, W.: Boosting weakly supervised object detection via learning bounding box adjusters. In: ICCV (2021)
13. Fang, S., Cao, Y., Wang, X., Chen, K., Lin, D., Zhang, W.: WSSOD: a new pipeline for weakly-and semi-supervised object detection. arXiv:2105.11293 (2021)
14. Feng, C., Zhong, Y., Huang, W.: Exploring classification equilibrium in long-tailed object detection. In: ICCV (2021)
15. Ghiasi, G., et al.: Simple copy-paste is a strong data augmentation method for instance segmentation. In: CVPR (2021)
16. Ghiasi, G., Gu, X., Cui, Y., Lin, T.Y.: Open-vocabulary image segmentation. arXiv:2112.12143 (2021)
17. Gu, X., Lin, T.Y., Kuo, W., Cui, Y.: Open-vocabulary object detection via vision and language knowledge distillation. ICLR (2022)

18. Gupta, A., Dollar, P., Girshick, R.: LVIS: a dataset for large vocabulary instance segmentation. In: CVPR (2019)
19. Han, J., Niu, M., Du, Z., Wei, L., Xie, L., Zhang, X., Tian, Q.: Joint coco and Lvis workshop at ECCV 2020: Lvis challenge track technical report: asynchronous semi-supervised learning for large vocabulary instance segmentation (2020)
20. He, K., Gkioxari, G., Dollar, P., Girshick, R.: Mask R-CNN. In: ICCV (2017)
21. He, K., Zhang, X., Ren, S., Sun, J.: Deep residual learning for image recognition. In: CVPR (2016)
22. Huang, Z., Zou, Y., Bhagavatula, V., Huang, D.: Comprehensive attention self-distillation for weakly-supervised object detection. In: NeurIPS (2020)
23. Ilharco, G., et al.: Openclip, July 2021. https://doi.org/10.5281/zenodo.5143773
24. Joulin, A., Grave, E., Bojanowski, P., Douze, M., Jégou, H., Mikolov, T.: Fasttext. Zip: compressing text classification models. arXiv:1612.03651 (2016)
25. Kim, D., Lin, T.Y., Angelova, A., Kweon, I.S., Kuo, W.: Learning open-world object proposals without learning to classify. arXiv:2108.06753 (2021)
26. Kingma, D.P., Ba, J.: Adam: a method for stochastic optimization. In: ICLR (2015)
27. Konan, S., Liang, K.J., Yin, L.: Extending one-stage detection with open-world proposals. arXiv:2201.02302 (2022)
28. Kuznetsova, A., et al.: The open images dataset v4. In: IJCV (2020)
29. Li, B., Weinberger, K.Q., Belongie, S., Koltun, V., Ranftl, R.: Language-driven semantic segmentation. In: ICLR (2022)
30. Li, X., Kan, M., Shan, S., Chen, X.: Weakly supervised object detection with segmentation collaboration. In: ICCV (2019)
31. Li, Y., Zhang, J., Huang, K., Zhang, J.: Mixed supervised object detection with robust objectness transfer. In: TPAMI (2018)
32. Li, Y., Wang, T., Kang, B., Tang, S., Wang, C., Li, J., Feng, J.: Overcoming classifier imbalance for long-tail object detection with balanced group softmax. In: CVPR (2020)
33. Li, Z., Yao, L., Zhang, X., Wang, X., Kanhere, S., Zhang, H.: Zero-shot object detection with textual descriptions. In: AAAI (2019)
34. Lin, T.-Y., Maire, M., Belongie, S., Hays, J., Perona, P., Ramanan, D., Dollár, P., Zitnick, C.L.: Microsoft COCO: common objects in context. In: Fleet, D., Pajdla, T., Schiele, B., Tuytelaars, T. (eds.) ECCV 2014. LNCS, vol. 8693, pp. 740–755. Springer, Cham (2014). https://doi.org/10.1007/978-3-319-10602-1_48
35. Liu, Y., Zhang, Z., Niu, L., Chen, J., Zhang, L.: Mixed supervised object detection by transferringmask prior and semantic similarity. In: NeurIPS (2021)
36. Liu, Y.C., et al.: Unbiased teacher for semi-supervised object detection. In: ICLR (2021)
37. Liu, Z., et al.: Swin transformer: hierarchical vision transformer using shifted windows. In: ICCV (2021)
38. Maaz, M., Rasheed, H., Khan, S., Khan, F.S., Anwer, R.M., Yang, M.H.: Multi-modal transformers excel at class-agnostic object detection. arXiv:2111.11430 (2021)
39. Pan, T.Y., et al.: On model calibration for long-tailed object detection and instance segmentation. In: NeurIPS (2021)
40. Pennington, J., Socher, R., Manning, C.D.: GloVe: global vectors for word representation. In: EMNLP (2014)
41. Pinheiro, P.O., Collobert, R.: Weakly supervised semantic segmentation with convolutional networks. In: CVPR (2015)
42. Radford, A., et al.: Learning transferable visual models from natural language supervision. arXiv:2103.00020 (2021)

43. Rahman, S., Khan, S., Barnes, N.: Improved visual-semantic alignment for zero-shot object detection. In: AAAI (2020)
44. Ramanathan, V., Wang, R., Mahajan, D.: DLWL: improving detection for lowshot classes with weakly labelled data. In: CVPR (2020)
45. Redmon, J., Farhadi, A.: Yolo9000: better, faster, stronger. In: CVPR (2017)
46. Ren, S., He, K., Girshick, R., Sun, J.: Faster R-CNN: towards real-time object detection with region proposal networks. In: NIPS (2015)
47. Ren, Z., Yu, Z., Yang, X., Liu, M.-Y., Schwing, A.G., Kautz, J.: UFO^2: a unified framework towards omni-supervised object detection. In: Vedaldi, A., Bischof, H., Brox, T., Frahm, J.-M. (eds.) ECCV 2020. LNCS, vol. 12364, pp. 288–313. Springer, Cham (2020). https://doi.org/10.1007/978-3-030-58529-7_18
48. Ridnik, T., Ben-Baruch, E., Noy, A., Zelnik-Manor, L.: Imagenet-21k pretraining for the masses. In: NeurIPS (2021)
49. Shao, S., et al.: Objects365: a large-scale, high-quality dataset for object detection. In: ICCV (2019)
50. Sharma, P., Ding, N., Goodman, S., Soricut, R.: Conceptual captions: a cleaned, hypernymed, image alt-text dataset for automatic image captioning. In: ACL (2018)
51. Shen, Y., et al.: Enabling deep residual networks for weakly supervised object detection. In: Vedaldi, A., Bischof, H., Brox, T., Frahm, J.-M. (eds.) ECCV 2020. LNCS, vol. 12353, pp. 118–136. Springer, Cham (2020). https://doi.org/10.1007/978-3-030-58598-3_8
52. Shen, Y., Ji, R., Wang, Y., Wu, Y., Cao, L.: Cyclic guidance for weakly supervised joint detection and segmentation. In: CVPR (2019)
53. Singh, B., Li, H., Sharma, A., Davis, L.S.: R-FCN-3000 at 30fps: decoupling detection and classification. In: CVPR (2018)
54. Sohn, K., Zhang, Z., Li, C.L., Zhang, H., Lee, C.Y., Pfister, T.: A simple semi-supervised learning framework for object detection. arXiv:2005.04757 (2020)
55. Tan, J., Lu, X., Zhang, G., Yin, C., Li, Q.: Equalization loss v2: a new gradient balance approach for long-tailed object detection. In: CVPR (2021)
56. Tan, J., et al.: Equalization loss for long-tailed object recognition. In: CVPR (2020)
57. Tan, J., et al.: 1st place solution of Lvis challenge 2020: a good box is not a guarantee of a good mask. arXiv:2009.01559 (2020)
58. Tan, M., Pang, R., Le, Q.V.: Efficientdet: scalable and efficient object detection. In: CVPR (2020)
59. Tang, P., et al.: PCL: proposal cluster learning for weakly supervised object detection. In: TPAMI (2018)
60. Tang, P., Wang, X., Bai, X., Liu, W.: Multiple instance detection network with online instance classifier refinement. In: CVPR (2017)
61. Uijlings, J., Popov, S., Ferrari, V.: Revisiting knowledge transfer for training object class detectors. In: CVPR (2018)
62. Uijlings, J.R., Van De Sande, K.E., Gevers, T., Smeulders, A.W.: Selective search for object recognition. In: IJCV (2013)
63. Wan, F., Liu, C., Ke, W., Ji, X., Jiao, J., Ye, Q.: C-mil:continuation multiple instance learning for weakly supervised object detection. In: CVPR (2019)
64. Wang, J., et al.: Seesaw loss for long-tailed instance segmentation. In: CVPR (2021)
65. Wu, J., Song, L., Wang, T., Zhang, Q., Yuan, J.: Forest R-CNN: large-vocabulary long-tailed object detection and instance segmentation. In: ACM Multimedia (2020)
66. Wu, Y., Kirillov, A., Massa, F., Lo, W.Y., Girshick, R.: Detectron2 (2019). https://github.com/facebookresearch/detectron2

67. Xu, M., et al.: End-to-end semi-supervised object detection with soft teacher. In: ICCV (2021)
68. Yan, Z., Liang, J., Pan, W., Li, J., Zhang, C.: Weakly-and semi-supervised object detection with expectation-maximization algorithm. arXiv:1702.08740 (2017)
69. Yang, H., Wu, H., Chen, H.: Detecting 11k classes: large scale object detection without fine-grained bounding boxes. In: ICCV (2019)
70. Yang, K., Li, D., Dou, Y.: Towards precise end-to-end weakly supervised object detection network. In: ICCV (2019)
71. Ye, K., Zhang, M., Kovashka, A., Li, W., Qin, D., Berent, J.: Cap2DET: learning to amplify weak caption supervision for object detection. In: ICCV (2019)
72. Zareian, A., Rosa, K.D., Hu, D.H., Chang, S.F.: Open-vocabulary object detection using captions. In: CVPR (2021)
73. Zhang, C., et al.: MosaicOS: a simple and effective use of object-centric images for long-tailed object detection. In: ICCV (2021)
74. Zhang, S., Li, Z., Yan, S., He, X., Sun, J.: Distribution alignment: a unified framework for long-tail visual recognition. In: CVPR (2021)
75. Zhong, Y., Wang, J., Peng, J., Zhang, L.: Boosting weakly supervised object detection with progressive knowledge transfer. In: Vedaldi, A., Bischof, H., Brox, T., Frahm, J.-M. (eds.) ECCV 2020. LNCS, vol. 12371, pp. 615–631. Springer, Cham (2020). https://doi.org/10.1007/978-3-030-58574-7_37
76. Zhou, X., Koltun, V., Krähenbühl, P.: Probabilistic two-stage detection. arXiv:2103.07461 (2021)
77. Zhou, X., Koltun, V., Krähenbühl, P.: Simple multi-dataset detection. In: CVPR (2022)
78. Zhu, P., Wang, H., Saligrama, V.: Don't even look once: Synthesizing features for zero-shot detection. In: CVPR (2020)
79. Zhu, X., Su, W., Lu, L., Li, B., Wang, X., Dai, J.: Deformable DeTR: deformable transformers for end-to-end object detection. In: ICLR (2021)

DCL-Net: Deep Correspondence Learning Network for 6D Pose Estimation

Hongyang Li[1], Jiehong Lin[1,2], and Kui Jia[1,3(✉)]

[1] South China University of Technology, Guangzhou, China
{eeli.hongyang,lin.jiehong}@mail.scut.edu.cn, kuijia@scut.edu.cn
[2] DexForce Co., Ltd., Shenzhen, China
[3] Peng Cheng Laboratory, Shenzhen, China

Abstract. Establishment of point correspondence between camera and object coordinate systems is a promising way to solve 6D object poses. However, surrogate objectives of correspondence learning in 3D space are a step away from the true ones of object pose estimation, making the learning suboptimal for the end task. In this paper, we address this shortcoming by introducing a new method of *Deep Correspondence Learning Network* for direct 6D object pose estimation, shortened as *DCL-Net*. Specifically, DCL-Net employs dual newly proposed *Feature Disengagement and Alignment (FDA) modules* to establish, in the feature space, partial-to-partial correspondence and complete-to-complete one for partial object observation and its complete CAD model, respectively, which result in aggregated pose and match feature pairs from two coordinate systems; these two FDA modules thus bring complementary advantages. The match feature pairs are used to learn confidence scores for measuring the qualities of deep correspondence, while the pose feature pairs are weighted by confidence scores for direct object pose regression. A confidence-based pose refinement network is also proposed to further improve pose precision in an iterative manner. Extensive experiments show that DCL-Net outperforms existing methods on three benchmarking datasets, including YCB-Video, LineMOD, and Oclussion-LineMOD; ablation studies also confirm the efficacy of our novel designs. Our code is released publicly at https://github.com/Gorilla-Lab-SCUT/DCL-Net.

Keywords: 6D pose estimation · Correspondence learning

1 Introduction

6D object pose estimation is a fundamental task of 3D semantic analysis with many real-world applications, such as robotic grasping [7,44], augmented reality [27], and autonomous driving [8,9,21,42]. Non-linearity of the rotation space of $SO(3)$ makes it hard to handle this nontrivial task through direct pose regression

---

H. Li and J. Lin—Equal contribution.

Supplementary Information The online version contains supplementary material available at https://doi.org/10.1007/978-3-031-20077-9_22.

370   H. Li et al.

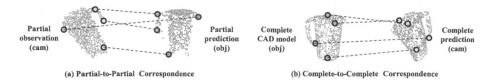

(a) Partial-to-Partial Correspondence   (b) Complete-to-Complete Correspondence

Fig. 1. Illustrations of two kinds of point correspondence between camera coordinate system (cam) and object coordinate system (obj). Best view in the electronic version.

from object observations [6,11,15,18,24–26,39,45,47]. Many of the data-driven methods [3,14,20,23,28,31,33,34,38,41] thus achieve the estimation by learning point correspondence between camera and object coordinate systems.

Given a partial object observation in camera coordinate system along with its CAD model in object coordinate one, we show in Fig. 1 two possible ways to build point correspondence: i) inferring the observed points in object coordinate system for partial-to-partial correspondence; ii) inferring the sampled points of CAD model in camera coordinate system for complete-to-complete correspondence. These two kinds of correspondence show different advantages. The partial-to-partial correspondence is of higher qualities than the complete-to-complete one due to the difficulty in shape completion, while the latter is more robust to figure out poses for objects with severe occlusions, which the former can hardly handle with.

While these methods are promising by solving 6D poses from point correspondence (*e.g.*, via a PnP algorithm), their surrogate correspondence objectives are a step away from the true ones of estimating 6D object poses, thus making their learnings suboptimal for the end task [40]. To this end, we present a novel method to realize the above two ways of correspondence establishment in the feature space via dual newly proposed *Feature Disengagement and Alignment (FDA) modules*, and directly estimate object poses from feature pairs of two coordinate systems, which are weighted by confidence scores measuring the qualities of deep correspondence. We term our method as *Deep Correspondence Learning Network*, shortened as *DCL-Net*. Figure 2 gives the illustration.

For the partial object observation and its CAD model, DCL-Net firstly extracts their point-wise feature maps in parallel; then dual Feature Disengagement and Alignment (FDA) modules are designed to establish, in feature space, the partial-to-partial correspondence and the complete-to-complete one between camera and object coordinate systems. Specifically, each FDA module takes as inputs two point-wise feature maps, and disengages each feature map into individual pose and match ones; the match feature maps of two systems are then used to learn an attention map for building deep correspondence; finally, both pose and match feature maps are aligned and paired across systems based on the attention map, resulting in pose and match feature pairs, respectively. DCL-Net aggregates two sets of correspondence together, since they bring complementary advantages, by fusing the respective pose and match feature pairs of two FDA modules. The aggregated match feature pairs are used to learn confidence scores for measuring the qualities of deep correspondence, while the pose ones are weighted by the scores to directly regress object poses. A confidence-based pose refinement network is also proposed to further improve the results of DCL-Net in an iterative manner. Extensive experiments show that DCL-Net outperforms existing methods for 6D object pose estimation on three well-acknowledged datasets, including YCB-Video [4], LineMOD [16], and Occlusion-LineMOD [3]; remarkably, on the more challenging Occlusion-LineMOD, our DCL-Net outperforms the state-of-the-art method [13] with an improvement of 4.4% on the metric of ADD(S), revealing the strength of DCL-Net on handling with occlusion. Ablation studies also confirm the efficacy of individual components of DCL-Net. Our technical contributions are summarized as follows:

- We design a novel *Feature Disengagement and Alignment (FDA) module* to establish deep correspondence between two point-wise feature maps from different coordinate systems; more specifically, FDA module disengages each feature map into individual pose and match ones, which are then aligned across systems to generate pose and match feature pairs, respectively, such that deep correspondence is established within the aligned feature pairs.
- We propose a new method of *Deep Correspondence Learning Network* for direct regression of 6D object poses, termed as DCL-Net, which employs dual FDA modules to establish, in feature space, partial-to-partial correspondence and complete-to-complete one between camera and object coordinate systems, respectively; these two FDA modules bring complementary advantages.
- Match feature pairs of dual FDA modules are aggregated and used for learning of confidence scores to measure the qualities of correspondence, while pose feature pairs are weighted by the scores for estimation of 6D pose; a confidence-based pose refinement network is also proposed to iteratively improve pose precision.

2   Related Work

6D Pose Estimation from RGB Data. This body of works can be broadly categorized into three types: i) holistic methods [11,15,18] for directly estimating object poses; ii) keypoint-based methods [28,33,34], which establish 2D-3D correspondence via 2D keypoint detection, followed by a PnP/RANSAC algorithm to solve the poses; iii) dense correspondence methods [3,20,23,31], which make dense pixel-wise predictions and vote for the final results.

Due to loss of geometry information, these methods are sensitive to lighting conditions and appearance textures, and thus inferior to the RGB-D methods.

6D Pose Estimation from RGB-D Data. Depth maps provide rich geometry information complementary to appearance one from RGB images. Traditional methods [3,16,32,37,43] solve object poses by extracting features from RGB-D data and performing correspondence grouping and hypothesis verification. Earlier deep methods, such as PoseCNN [45] and SSD-6D [19], learn coarse poses firstly from RGB images, and refine the poses on point clouds by using ICP [2] or MCN [22]. Recently, learning deep features of point clouds becomes an efficient way to improve pose precision, especially for methods [39, 47] of direct regression, which make efforts to enhance pose embeddings from deep geometry features, due to the difficulty in the learning of rotations from a nonlinear space. Wang *et al.* present DenseFusion [39], which fuses local features of RGB images and point clouds in a point-wise manner, and thus explicitly reasons about appearance and geometry information to make the learning more discriminative; due to the incomplete and noisy shape information, Zhou *et al.* propose PR-GCN [47] to polish point clouds and enhance pose embeddings via Graph Convolutional Network. On the other hand, dense correspondence methods show the advantages of deep networks on building the point correspondence in Euclidean space; for example, He *et al.* propose PVN3D [14] to regress dense keypoints, and achieve remarkable results. While promising, these methods are usually trained with surrogate objectives instead of the true ones of estimating 6D poses, making the learning suboptimal for the end task.

Our proposed DCL-Net borrows the idea from dense correspondence methods by learning deep correspondence in feature space, and weights the feature correspondence based on confidence scores for direct estimation of object poses. Besides, the learned correspondence is also utilized by an iterative pose refinement network for precision improvement.

3   Deep Correspondence Learning Network

Given the partial object observation $\mathcal{X}_c$ in the camera coordinate system, along with the object CAD model $\mathcal{Y}_o$ in the object coordinate one, our goal is to estimate the 6D pose $(\boldsymbol{R}, \boldsymbol{t})$ between these two systems, where $\boldsymbol{R} \in SO(3)$ stands for a rotation, and $\boldsymbol{t} \in \mathbb{R}^3$ for a translation.

Figure 2 gives the illustration of our proposed *Deep Correspondence Learning Network* (dubbed *DCL-Net*). DCL-Net firstly extracts point-wise features of $\mathcal{X}_c$ and $\mathcal{Y}_o$ (cf. Sect. 3.1), then establishes correspondence in feature space via *dual Feature Disengagement and Alignment modules* (cf. Sect. 3.2), and finally regresses the object pose $(\boldsymbol{R}, \boldsymbol{t})$ with confidence scores based on the learned deep correspondence (cf. Sect. 3.3). The training objectives of DCL-Net are given in Sect. 3.4. A confidence-based pose refinement network is also introduced to iteratively improve pose precision (cf. Sect. 3.5).

3.1   Point-Wise Feature Extraction

We represent the inputs of the object observation $\mathcal{X}_c$ and its CAD model $\mathcal{Y}_o$ as $(\boldsymbol{I}^{\mathcal{X}_c}, \boldsymbol{P}^{\mathcal{X}_c})$ and $(\boldsymbol{I}^{\mathcal{Y}_o}, \boldsymbol{P}^{\mathcal{Y}_o})$ with $N_{\mathcal{X}}$ and $N_{\mathcal{Y}}$ sampled points, respectively, where $\boldsymbol{P}$ denotes a point set, and $\boldsymbol{I}$ denotes RGB values corresponding to points in $\boldsymbol{P}$. As shown in Fig. 2, we use two parallel backbones to extract their point-wise features $\boldsymbol{F}^{\mathcal{X}_c}$ and $\boldsymbol{F}^{\mathcal{Y}_o}$, respectively. Following [12], both backbones are built based on 3D Sparse Convolutions [10], of which the volumetric features are then converted to point-level ones; more details about the architectures are given in the supplementary material. Note that for each object instance, $\boldsymbol{F}^{\mathcal{Y}_o}$ can be pre-computed during inference for efficiency.

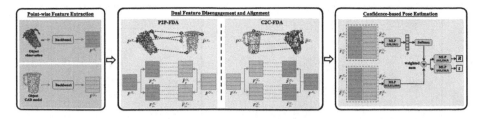

Fig. 2. An illustration of DCL-Net. Given object observation and its CAD model, DCL-Net first extracts their point-wise features $F^{\mathcal{X}_c}$ and $F^{\mathcal{Y}_o}$, separately; then dual Feature Disengagement and Alignment (FDA) modules are employed to establish, in feature space, partial-to-partial correspondence and complete-to-complete one between camera and object coordinate systems, respectively, which result in aggregated pose and match feature pairs; the match feature pairs are used to learn confidence scores s for measuring the qualities of deep correspondence, while the pose ones are weighted by s for estimating 6D object pose (R, t). Best view in the electronic version.

3.2   Dual Feature Disengagement and Alignment

The key to figure out the pose between the object observation and its CAD model lies in the establishment of correspondence. As pointed out in Sect. 1, there exist at least two ways to achieve this goal: i) learning the partial point set $\widetilde{P}^{\mathcal{X}_o}$ in object system from complete $P^{\mathcal{Y}_o}$ to pair with $P^{\mathcal{X}_c}$, e.g., $(P^{\mathcal{X}_c}, \widetilde{P}^{\mathcal{X}_o})$, for partial-to-partial correspondence; ii) inferring the complete point set $\widetilde{P}^{\mathcal{Y}_c}$ in camera coordinate system from partial $P^{\mathcal{X}_c}$ to pair with $P^{\mathcal{Y}_o}$, e.g., $(\widetilde{P}^{\mathcal{Y}_c}, P^{\mathcal{Y}_o})$, for complete-to-complete correspondence.

In this paper, we propose to establish the correspondence in the deep feature space, from which *pose feature pairs* along with *match feature pairs* can be generated for the learning of object pose and confidence scores, respectively. Figure 2 gives illustrations of the correspondence in both 3D space and feature space. Specifically, we design a novel *Feature Disengagement and Alignment (FDA) module* to learn the pose feature pairs, e.g., $(F_p^{\mathcal{X}_c}, \widetilde{F}_p^{\mathcal{X}_o})$ and $(\widetilde{F}_p^{\mathcal{Y}_c}, F_p^{\mathcal{Y}_o})$ w.r.t the above $(P^{\mathcal{X}_c}, \widetilde{P}^{\mathcal{X}_o})$ and $(\widetilde{P}^{\mathcal{Y}_c}, P^{\mathcal{Y}_o})$, respectively, and the match feature pairs, e.g., $(F_m^{\mathcal{X}_c}, \widetilde{F}_m^{\mathcal{X}_o})$ and $(\widetilde{F}_m^{\mathcal{Y}_c}, F_m^{\mathcal{Y}_o})$, which can be formulated as follows:

$$F_p^{\mathcal{X}_c}, F_m^{\mathcal{X}_c}, \widetilde{F}_p^{\mathcal{X}_o}, \widetilde{F}_m^{\mathcal{X}_o}, \widetilde{P}^{\mathcal{X}_o} = \mathrm{FDA}(F^{\mathcal{X}_c}, F^{\mathcal{Y}_o}), \tag{1}$$

$$F_p^{\mathcal{Y}_o}, F_m^{\mathcal{Y}_o}, \widetilde{F}_p^{\mathcal{Y}_c}, \widetilde{F}_m^{\mathcal{Y}_c}, \widetilde{P}^{\mathcal{Y}_c} = \mathrm{FDA}(F^{\mathcal{Y}_o}, F^{\mathcal{X}_c}). \tag{2}$$

We term the partial-to-partial (1) and complete-to-complete (2) FDA modules as P2P-FDA and C2C-FDA modules, respectively.

Feature Disengagement and Alignment Module. Feature Disengagement and Alignment (FDA) module takes point-wise feature maps of different coordinate systems as inputs, disengages each feature map into pose and match

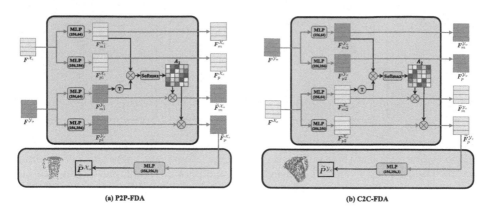

(a) P2P-FDA   (b) C2C-FDA

Fig. 3. Illustrations of dual Feature Disengagement and Alignment modules. "T" denotes matrix transposition, and "×" denotes matrix multiplication.

ones, which are then aligned across systems to establish deep correspondence. Figure 3 gives illustrations of both P2P-FDA and C2C-FDA modules, where network specifics are also given.

We take P2P-FDA module (1) as an example to illustrate the implementation of FDA. Specifically, as shown in Fig. 3, we firstly disengage $\boldsymbol{F}^{\mathcal{X}_c}$ into a pose feature $\boldsymbol{F}_{p1}^{\mathcal{X}_c}$ and a match one $\boldsymbol{F}_{m1}^{\mathcal{X}_c}$:

$$\boldsymbol{F}_{p1}^{\mathcal{X}_c} = \texttt{MLP}(\boldsymbol{F}^{\mathcal{X}_c}), \boldsymbol{F}_{m1}^{\mathcal{X}_c} = \texttt{MLP}(\boldsymbol{F}^{\mathcal{X}_c}), \tag{3}$$

where $\texttt{MLP}(\cdot)$ denotes a subnetwork of Multi-layer Perceptron (MLP). The same applies to $\boldsymbol{F}^{\mathcal{Y}_o}$, and we have $\boldsymbol{F}_{p1}^{\mathcal{Y}_o}$ and $\boldsymbol{F}_{m1}^{\mathcal{Y}_o}$. The match features $\boldsymbol{F}_{m1}^{\mathcal{X}_c}$ and $\boldsymbol{F}_{m1}^{\mathcal{Y}_o}$ is then used for the learning of an attention map $\boldsymbol{A}_1 \in \mathbb{R}^{N_\mathcal{X} \times N_\mathcal{Y}}$ as follows:

$$\boldsymbol{A}_1 = \texttt{Softmax}(\boldsymbol{F}_{m1}^{\mathcal{X}_c} \times \texttt{Transpose}(\boldsymbol{F}_{m1}^{\mathcal{Y}_o})), \tag{4}$$

where $\texttt{Transpose}(\cdot)$ denotes tensor transposition, and $\texttt{Softmax}(\cdot)$ denotes softmax operation along columns. Each element $a_{1,ij}$ in $\boldsymbol{A}_1$ indicates the match degree between i^{th} point in $\boldsymbol{P}^{\mathcal{X}_c}$ and j^{th} one in $\boldsymbol{P}^{\mathcal{Y}_o}$. Then pose and match features of the partial observation $\mathcal{X}_o$ in object system can be interpolated by matrix multiplication of $\boldsymbol{A}_1$ and those of $\boldsymbol{P}^{\mathcal{Y}_o}$, respectively, to be aligned with features of $\mathcal{X}_c$ in camera coordinate system:

$$\begin{cases} \boldsymbol{F}_p^{\mathcal{X}_c} = \boldsymbol{F}_{p1}^{\mathcal{X}_c} \\ \widetilde{\boldsymbol{F}}_p^{\mathcal{X}_o} = \boldsymbol{A}_1 \times \boldsymbol{F}_{p1}^{\mathcal{Y}_o} \end{cases}, \begin{cases} \boldsymbol{F}_m^{\mathcal{X}_c} = \boldsymbol{F}_{m1}^{\mathcal{X}_c} \\ \widetilde{\boldsymbol{F}}_m^{\mathcal{X}_o} = \boldsymbol{A}_1 \times \boldsymbol{F}_{m1}^{\mathcal{Y}_o} \end{cases}. \tag{5}$$

Through feature alignment, $\widetilde{\boldsymbol{P}}^{\mathcal{X}_o}$ is expected to be decoded out from $\widetilde{\boldsymbol{F}}_p^{\mathcal{X}_o}$:

$$\widetilde{\boldsymbol{P}}^{\mathcal{X}_o} = \texttt{MLP}(\widetilde{\boldsymbol{F}}_p^{\mathcal{X}_o}). \tag{6}$$

Supervisions on the reconstruction of $\widetilde{\boldsymbol{P}}^{\mathcal{X}_o}$ guide the learning of deep correspondence in P2P-FDA module.

P2P-FDA module (1) learns deep correspondence of the partial $\mathcal{X}$ in two coordinate systems, while C2C-FDA module (2) infers that of the complete $\mathcal{Y}$ via a same network structure, as shown in Fig. 3(b). We adopt dual FDA modules in our design to enable robust correspondence establishment, since they bring complementary functions: P2P-FDA module provides more accurate correspondence than that of C2C-FDA module, due to the difficulty in shape completion from partial observation for the latter module; however, C2C-FDA module plays a vital role under the condition of severe occlusions, which P2P-FDA module can hardly handle with.

3.3 Confidence-Based Pose Estimation

After dual feature disengagement and alignment, we construct the pose and match feature pairs as follows:

$$F_p = \begin{bmatrix} F_p^{\mathcal{X}_c}, \widetilde{F}_p^{\mathcal{X}_o} \\ \widetilde{F}_p^{\mathcal{Y}_c}, F_p^{\mathcal{Y}_o} \end{bmatrix}, F_m = \begin{bmatrix} F_m^{\mathcal{X}_c}, \widetilde{F}_m^{\mathcal{X}_o} \\ \widetilde{F}_m^{\mathcal{Y}_c}, F_m^{\mathcal{Y}_o} \end{bmatrix}. \tag{7}$$

As shown in Fig. 2, the paired match feature F_m is fed into an MLP for the learning of confidence scores $s = \{s_i\}_{i=1}^{N_{\mathcal{X}}+N_{\mathcal{Y}}}$ to reflect the qualities of deep correspondence:

$$s = \mathrm{MLP}(F_m). \tag{8}$$

The paired pose feature F_p is also fed into an MLP and weighted by s for precisely estimating the 6D pose (R, t):

$$R = \mathrm{MLP}(f), t = \mathrm{MLP}(f), \tag{9}$$
$$s.t.\ f = \mathrm{SUM}(\mathrm{SoftMax}(s) \cdot \mathrm{MLP}(F_p)),$$

where SUM denotes summation along rows.

Rather than numerical calculation from two paired point sets, we directly regress the 6D object pose from deep pair-wise features with confidence scores, which effectively weakens the negative impact of correspondence of low quality on pose estimation, and thus realizes more precise results.

3.4 Training of Deep Correspondence Learning Network

For dual FDA modules, we supervise the reconstruction of $\widetilde{P}^{\mathcal{X}_o} = \{\widetilde{p}_i^{\mathcal{X}_o}\}_{i=1}^{N_{\mathcal{X}}}$ and $\widetilde{P}^{\mathcal{Y}_c} = \{\widetilde{p}_i^{\mathcal{Y}_c}\}_{i=1}^{N_{\mathcal{Y}}}$ to guide the learning of deep correspondence via the following objectives:

$$\mathcal{L}_{p2p} = \frac{1}{N_{\mathcal{X}}} \sum_{i=1}^{N_{\mathcal{X}}} ||\widetilde{p}_i^{\mathcal{X}_o} - R^{*T}(p_i^{\mathcal{X}_c} - t^*)||, \tag{10}$$

$$\mathcal{L}_{c2c} = \frac{1}{N_{\mathcal{Y}}} \sum_{i=1}^{N_{\mathcal{Y}}} ||\widetilde{p}_i^{\mathcal{Y}_c} - (R^* p_i^{\mathcal{Y}_o} + t^*)||, \tag{11}$$

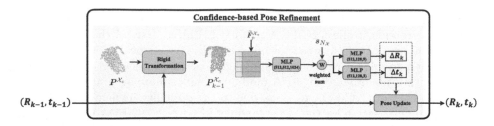

Fig. 4. An illustration of the iterative confidence-based pose estimation network.

where $\boldsymbol{P}^{\mathcal{X}_c} = \{\boldsymbol{p}_i^{\mathcal{X}_c}\}_{i=1}^{N_{\mathcal{X}}}$ and $\boldsymbol{P}^{\mathcal{Y}_o} = \{\boldsymbol{p}_i^{\mathcal{Y}_o}\}_{i=1}^{N_{\mathcal{Y}}}$ are input point sets, and $\boldsymbol{R}^*$ and $\boldsymbol{t}^*$ denote ground truth 6D pose. For the confidence-based pose estimation, we use the following objectives on top of the learning of the predicted object pose $(\boldsymbol{R}, \boldsymbol{t})$ and confidence scores $\boldsymbol{s} = \{s_i\}_{i=1}^{N_{\mathcal{X}}+N_{\mathcal{Y}}}$, respectively:

$$\mathcal{L}_{pose} = \frac{1}{N_{\mathcal{Y}}} \sum_{i=1}^{N_{\mathcal{Y}}} ||\boldsymbol{R}\boldsymbol{p}_i^{\mathcal{Y}_o} + \boldsymbol{t} - (\boldsymbol{R}^*\boldsymbol{p}_i^{\mathcal{Y}_o} + \boldsymbol{t}^*)||. \tag{12}$$

$$\mathcal{L}_{conf} = \frac{1}{N_{\mathcal{X}}} \sum_{i=1}^{N_{\mathcal{X}}} \sigma(||\widetilde{\boldsymbol{p}}_i^{\mathcal{X}_o} - \boldsymbol{R}^T(\boldsymbol{p}_i^{\mathcal{X}_c} - \boldsymbol{t})||, s_i)$$

$$+ \frac{1}{N_{\mathcal{Y}}} \sum_{j=1}^{N_{\mathcal{Y}}} \sigma(||\widetilde{\boldsymbol{p}}_j^{\mathcal{Y}_c} - (\boldsymbol{R}\boldsymbol{p}_j^{\mathcal{Y}_o} + \boldsymbol{t})||, s_{N_{\mathcal{X}}+j}), \tag{13}$$

where $\sigma(d, s) = ds - w\log(s)$, and w is a balancing hyperparameter. We note that the objectives (10), (11) and (12) are designed for asymmetric objects, while for symmetric ones, we modify them by replacing L_2 distance with Chamfer distance, as done in [39].

The overall training objective combines (10), (11), (12), and (13), resulting in the following optimization problem:

$$\min \mathcal{L} = \lambda_1 \mathcal{L}_{p2p} + \lambda_2 \mathcal{L}_{c2c} + \lambda_3 \mathcal{L}_{pose} + \lambda_4 \mathcal{L}_{conf}, \tag{14}$$

where λ_1, λ_2, λ_3 and λ_4 are penalty parameters.

3.5   Confidence-Based Pose Refinement

To take full advantages of the learned correspondence, we propose a confidence-based pose refinement network, as shown in Fig. 4, where the input point set $\boldsymbol{P}^{\mathcal{X}_c}$ is transformed with predicted pose, and paired with $\widetilde{\boldsymbol{F}}_p^{\mathcal{X}_o}$ for residual pose estimation in an iterative manner. Specifically, assuming after $k-1$ iterations of refinement, the current object pose is updated as $(\boldsymbol{R}_{k-1}, \boldsymbol{t}_{k-1})$, and we use it for transforming $\boldsymbol{P}^{\mathcal{X}_c} = \{\boldsymbol{p}_i^{\mathcal{X}_c}\}_{i=1}^{N_{\mathcal{X}}}$ to $\boldsymbol{P}_{k-1}^{\mathcal{X}_c} = \{\boldsymbol{R}_{k-1}^T(\boldsymbol{p}_i^{\mathcal{X}_c} - \boldsymbol{t}_{k-1})\}_{i=1}^{N_{\mathcal{X}}}$; for forming pair-wise pose features with the learned correspondence in dual FDA modules, we reuse $\widetilde{F}_p^{\mathcal{X}_o}$ by concatenating it with $P_{k-1}^{\mathcal{X}_c}$. Similarly to Sect. 3.3, we feed the pose feature pairs into an MLP, and weight them by reusing the confidence scores $s_{N_{\mathcal{X}}}$ (denoting the first $N_{\mathcal{X}}$ elements of s) for estimating the residual pose $(\Delta R_k, \Delta t_k)$:

$$\Delta R_k = \text{MLP}(f_k), \Delta t_k = \text{MLP}(f_k), \quad (15)$$

$$s.t. \ f_k = \text{SUM}(\text{SoftMax}(s_{N_{\mathcal{X}}}) \cdot \text{MLP}([P_{k-1}^{\mathcal{X}_c}, \widetilde{F}_p^{\mathcal{X}_o}])).$$

Finally, the pose (R_k, t_k) of the kth iteration can be obtained as follows:

$$R_k = \Delta R_k R_{k-1}, t_k = R_{k-1}\Delta t_k + t_{k-1}. \quad (16)$$

4 Experiments

Datasets. We conduct experiments on three benchmarking datasets, including YCB-Video [4], LineMOD [16], and Occlusion-LineMOD [3]. YCB-Video dataset consists of 92 RGB-D videos with 21 different object instances, fully annotated with object poses and masks. Following [39], we use 80 videos therein for training along with additional 80,000 synthetic images, and evaluate DCL-Net on 2,949 keyframes sampled from the rest 12 videos. LineMOD is also a fully annotated dataset for 6D pose estimation, containing 13 videos with 13 low-textured object instances; we follow the prior work [39] to split training and testing sets. Occlusion-LineMOD is an annotated subset of LineMOD with 8 different object instances, which handpicks RGB-D images of scenes with heavy object occlusions and self-occlusions from LineMOD, making the task of pose estimation more challenging; following [35], we use the DCL-Net trained on the original LineMOD to evaluate on Occlusion-LineMOD.

Implementation Details. For both object observations and CAD models, we sample point sets with 1,024 points as inputs of DCL-Net; that is, $N_{\mathcal{X}} = N_{\mathcal{Y}} = 1,024$. For the training objectives, we set the penalty parameters $\lambda_1, \lambda_2, \lambda_3, \lambda_4$ in (14) as 5.0, 1.0, 1.0, and 1.0, respectively; w in (13) is set as 0.01. During inference, we run twice the confidence-based pose refinement for improvement of pose precision.

Evaluation Metrics. We use the same evaluation metrics as those in [39]. For YCB-Video dataset, the average closest point distance (ADD-S) [45] is employed to measure the pose error; following [39], we report the Area Under the Curve (AUC) of ADD-S with the maximum threshold at 0.1 m, and the percentage of ADD-S smaller than the minimum tolerance at 2 cm (< 2 cm). For both LineMOD and Occlusion-LineMOD datasets, ADD-S is employed only for symmetric objects, while the Average Distance (ADD) for asymmetric objects; we report the percentage of distance smaller than 10% of object diameter. Besides, we use Chamfer Distance (CD) to measure the reconstruction results.

Table 1. Ablation studies of the use of dual FDA modules on YCB-Video dataset [4]. Experiments are conducted without confidence-based weighting and pose refinement.

P2P-FDA	C2C-FDA	AUC	<2 cm	CD ($\times 10^{-3}$)	
				P^{X_o}	P^{Y_c}
×	×	94.1	97.4	–	–
✓	×	95.0	98.7	7.1	–
×	✓	94.5	98.8	–	8.2
✓	✓	**95.3**	**99.0**	**7.0**	**8.1**

Table 2. Quantitative results obtained by least-squares optimization [1] and our proposed direct regression on YCB-Video dataset [4]. Experiments are conducted without pose refinement.

		AUC	<2 cm
w/o Conf.	Least-squares optimization [1]	94.7	98.2
	Direct pose regression	95.3	99.0
with Conf.	Least-squares optimization [1]	95.4	98.3
	Direct pose regression	**95.8**	**99.0**

4.1   Ablation Studies and Analyses

We firstly conduct ablation studies to evaluate the efficacy of novel designs proposed in our DCL-Net. These experiments are conducted on YCB-Video dataset [4].

Effects of Dual Feature Disengagement and Alignment. We conduct four experiments to evaluate the efficacy of the use of dual FDA modules: i) without any FDA modules (baseline), ii) only with P2P-FDA, iii) only with C2C-FDA, and iv) with dual modules. For simplicity, these experiments are conducted without confidence-based weighting as well as pose refinement. The quantitative results on ADD-S AUC and ADD-S< 2 cm are shown in Table 1, where the reconstruction results of asymmetric objects are also reported. From the table, methods with (one or dual) FDA modules indeed outperforms the baseline, which demonstrates the importance of deep correspondence learning on pose estimation. Single P2P-FDA module achieves more accurate results than single C2C-FDA module by making better reconstructions (7.1×10^{-3} versus 8.2×10^{-3} on CD) and deep correspondence as well, and the mixed use of them boosts the performance, indicating their complementary advantages. For the last framework, we visualize the reconstruction results along with the learned correspondence of both P2P-FDA and C2C-FDA modules in Fig. 5; shape completion can be achieved for C2C-FDA module, even with severe occlusions, to build valid deep correspondence of high quality, and thus make DCL-Net more robust and reliable.

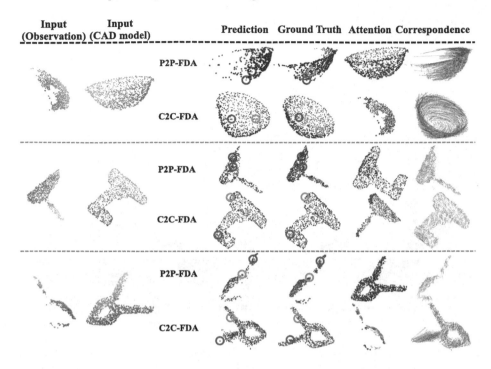

Fig. 5. Visualizations of shape predictions, attentions, and correspondence of both P2P-FDA and C2C-FDA modules on YCB-Video dataset [4]. Best view in electronic version. (Color figure online)

We also explore the attention maps of dual FDA modules in Fig. 5. Take C2C-FDA module as an example, the predicted points are learned from the features of the input observed ones via attention maps, *i.e.*, each predicted point corresponds to the observed ones with different attention weights, and we thus colorize those corresponding points with large weights in Fig. 5; as shown in the figure, for the predicted points (red) locate at the observed parts, most of the input points with larger weights (red) could locate at the corresponding local regions, showing the qualities of attention maps, while for those at the occluded parts (blue), the corresponding points (blue) may locate scatteredly, but thanks to the correspondence learning in feature space, these points could still be completed in the C2C-FDA reconstruction results.

Effects of Confidence-Based Pose Estimation. Through learning deep correspondence in feature space, DCL-Net achieves direct regression of object poses, while the predictions of dual FDA modules can also establish point correspondence *w.r.t* inputs to solve poses via least-squares optimization [1]. We compare the quantitative results obtained by these two approaches (without pose refinement) in Table 2, where results of direct regression from deep feature correspondence outperforms those from point correspondence consistently with or without

Table 3. Quantitative results of DCL-Net with or without pose refinement on YCB-Video dataset [4].

	AUC	<2 cm
w/o Pose Refinement	95.8	99.0
with Pose Refinement	**96.6**	**99.0**

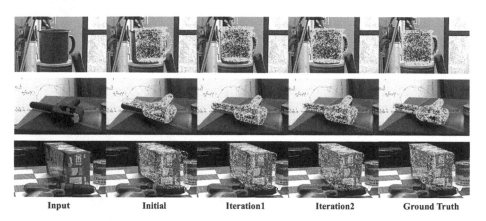

| Input | Initial | Iteration1 | Iteration2 | Ground Truth |

Fig. 6. Qualitative results of DCL-Net with or without pose refinement on YCB-Video dataset [4]. The sampled points of CAD models are transformed by the predicted poses and projected to 2D images.

confidence scores, showing that pose estimation from feature space is less sensitive to the correspondence of low qualities, thanks to the direct objectives for the end task. Besides, we also observe that the learning of confidence scores not only measures the qualities of correspondence and decreases the influence of bad correspondence, but also helps improve the qualities themselves effectively (Table 3).

Effects of Confidence-Based Pose Refinement. Table 4 demonstrates the efficiency of our confidence-based pose refinement for boosting the performance, *e.g.*, improvement by 0.8% on the metric of ADD-S AUC, which is also verified by the qualitative results shown in Fig. 6.

4.2   Comparisons with Existing Methods

We compare our proposed DCL-Net with the existing methods for 6D object pose estimation from RGB-D data, including those based on direct regression (*e.g.*, DenseFusion [39] and PR-GCN [47]), and those based on dense correspondence learning (*e.g.*, PVN3D [14] and FFB6D [13]).

Quantitative results on the three benchmarking datasets, including YCB-Video [4], LineMOD [16], and Occlusion-LineMOD [3], are reported in Table 4,

Table 4. Quantitative results of different methods on YCB-Video dataset [4]. The evaluation metrics are ADD-S AUC and ADD-S< 2 cm. Objects with bold name are symmetric.

	PoseCNN+ICP [45]		DenseFusion [39]		G2L [5]	PVN3D [14]		PR-GCN [47]		FFB6D		DCL-Net	
	AUC	<2 cm	AUC	<2 cm	AUC	AUC	<2 cm	AUC	<2 cm	AUC	<2 cm	AUC	<2 cm
002_master_chef_can	95.8	**100.0**	96.4	**100.0**	94.0	96.0	**100.0**	**97.1**	**100.0**	96.3	**100.0**	96.1	**100.0**
003_cracker_box	92.7	91.6	95.5	99.5	88.7	96.1	**100.0**	**97.6**	**100.0**	96.3	**100.0**	96.4	99.4
004_sugar_box	98.2	**100.0**	97.5	**100.0**	96.0	97.4	**100.0**	**98.3**	**100.0**	97.6	**100.0**	98.1	**100.0**
005_tomato_soup_can	94.5	96.9	94.96	96.9	86.4	**96.2**	98.1	95.3	97.6	95.6	98.2	95.8	97.7
006_mustard_bottle	98.6	**100.0**	97.2	**100.0**	95.9	97.5	**100.0**	97.9	**100.0**	97.8	**100.0**	**98.7**	**100.0**
007_tuna_fish_can	97.1	**100.0**	96.6	**100.0**	84.1	96.0	**100.0**	97.6	**100.0**	96.8	**100.0**	97.4	**100.0**
008_pudding_box	97.9	**100.0**	96.5	**100.0**	93.5	97.1	**100.0**	**98.4**	**100.0**	97.1	**100.0**	98.2	**100.0**
009_gelatin_box	98.8	**100.0**	98.1	**100.0**	96.8	97.7	**100.0**	96.2	94.4	98.1	**100.0**	**98.9**	**100.0**
010_potted_meat_can	92.7	93.6	91.3	93.1	86.2	93.3	94.6	**96.6**	**99.1**	94.7	94.3	93.1	94.7
011_banana	97.1	99.7	96.6	**100.0**	96.3	96.6	**100.0**	**98.5**	**100.0**	97.2	**100.0**	98.1	**100.0**
019_pitcher_base	97.8	**100.0**	97.1	**100.0**	91.8	97.4	**100.0**	98.1	**100.0**	97.6	**100.0**	98.0	99.8
021_bleach_cleanser	96.9	99.4	95.8	**100.0**	92.0	96.0	**100.0**	**97.9**	**100.0**	96.8	**100.0**	97.0	**100.0**
024_bowl	81.0	54.9	88.2	98.8	86.7	90.2	80.5	90.3	96.6	96.3	**100.0**	**97.3**	**100.0**
025_mug	95.0	99.8	97.1	**100.0**	95.4	97.6	**100.0**	**98.1**	**100.0**	97.3	**100.0**	97.8	**100.0**
035_power_drill	**98.2**	99.6	96.0	98.7	95.2	96.7	**100.0**	98.1	**100.0**	97.2	**100.0**	98.0	**100.0**
036_wood_block	87.6	80.2	89.7	94.6	86.2	90.4	93.8	**96.0**	**100.0**	92.6	92.1	93.9	97.5
037_scissors	91.7	95.6	95.2	**100.0**	83.8	96.7	**100.0**	**96.7**	**100.0**	97.7	**100.0**	87.6	98.3
040_large_marker	97.2	99.7	97.5	**100.0**	96.8	96.7	99.8	97.9	**100.0**	96.6	**100.0**	97.8	99.8
051_large_clamp	75.2	74.9	72.9	79.2	94.4	93.6	93.6	87.5	93.3	96.8	**100.0**	95.7	98.6
052_extra_large_clamp	64.4	48.8	69.8	76.3	**92.3**	88.4	83.6	79.7	84.6	**96.0**	**98.6**	88.8	87.2
061_foam_brick	97.2	**100.0**	92.5	**100.0**	94.7	96.8	**100.0**	**97.8**	**100.0**	97.3	**100.0**	97.5	**100.0**
MEAN	93.0	93.2	93.1	96.8	92.4	95.5	97.6	95.8	98.5	**96.6**	**99.2**	**96.6**	99.0

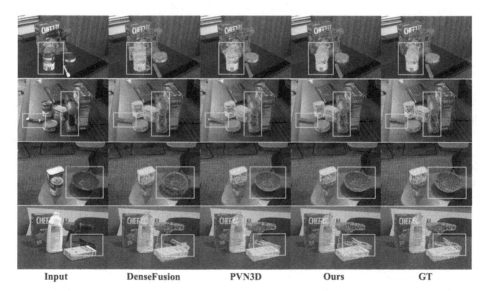

Input   DenseFusion   PVN3D   Ours   GT

Fig. 7. Qualitative results of different methods on YCB-Video dataset [4]. The sampled points of CAD models are transformed by the predicted poses and projected to 2D images.

Table 5. Quantitative results of different methods on ADD(S) on LineMOD dataset [16]. Objects with bold name are symmetric.

	Implicit+ICP [36]	SSD6D+ICP [19]	PointFusion [46]	DenseFusion [39]	DenseFusion (Iterative) [39]	G2L [5]	PR-GCN [47]	DCL-Net
Ape	20.6	65	70.4	79.5	92.3	96.8	**97.6**	97.4
Bench	64.3	80	80.7	84.2	93.2	96.1	99.2	**99.4**
Camera	63.2	78	60.8	76.5	94.4	98.2	99.4	**99.8**
Can	76.1	86	61.1	86.6	93.1	98.0	98.4	**99.9**
Cat	72.0	70	79.1	88.8	96.5	99.2	98.7	**100.0**
Driller	41.6	73	47.3	77.7	87.0	99.8	98.8	**99.9**
Duck	32.4	66	63.0	76.3	92.3	97.7	**98.9**	98.4
egg	98.6	**100**	99.9	99.9	99.8	**100.0**	99.9	**100.0**
glue	96.4	**100**	99.3	99.4	**100.0**	**100.0**	**100.0**	99.9
Hole	49.9	49	71.8	79.0	92.1	99.0	99.4	**100.0**
Iron	63.1	78	83.2	92.1	97.0	99.3	98.5	**100.0**
Lamp	91.7	73	62.3	92.3	95.3	**99.5**	99.2	**99.5**
Phone	71.0	79	78.8	88.0	92.8	98.9	98.4	**99.7**
MEAN	64.7	79	73.7	86.2	94.3	98.7	98.9	**99.5**

Table 6. Quantitative results of different methods on ADD(S) on Occlusion-LineMOD dataset [3]. Objects with bold name are symmetric.

	PoseCNN [45]	Deep-Heat [29]	SS [17]	Pix2pose [30]	PVNet [31]	Hybrid-Pose [35]	PVN3D [14]	PR-GCN [47]	FFB6D [13]	DCL-Net
Ape	9.6	12.1	17.6	22.0	15.8	20.9	33.9	40.2	47.2	**56.7**
Can	45.2	39.9	53.9	44.7	63.3	75.3	**88.6**	76.2	85.2	80.2
Cat	0.9	8.2	3.3	22.7	16.7	24.9	39.1	**57.0**	45.7	48.1
Driller	41.4	45.2	62.4	44.7	65.7	70.2	78.4	**82.3**	81.4	81.4
Duck	19.6	17.2	19.2	15.0	25.2	27.9	41.9	30.0	**53.9**	44.6
egg	22.0	22.1	25.9	25.2	50.2	52.4	80.9	68.2	70.2	**83.6**
glue	38.5	35.8	39.6	32.4	49.6	53.8	68.1	67.0	60.1	**79.1**
Hole	22.1	36.0	21.3	49.5	39.7	54.2	74.7	**97.2**	85.9	91.3
MEAN	24.9	27.0	27.0	32.0	40.8	47.5	63.2	65.0	66.2	**70.6**

Table 5, and Table 6, respectively, all of which show the superiority of our DCL-Net consistently in the regime of pose precision; qualitative results on YCB-Video dataset [4] are also provided in Fig. 7 to verify the advantages of our DCL-Net. Remarkably, on the more challenging Occlusion-LineMOD dataset, the improvements of our DCL-Net over the state-of-the-art methods of PR-GCN [47] and FFB6D [13] reach 5.6% and 4.4% on the metric of ADD(S), respectively, indicating the advantages of our DCL-Net on handling with object occlusions or self-occlusions.

Acknowledgements. This work is supported in part by Guangdong R&D key project of China (No.: 2019B010155001), and the Program for Guangdong Introducing Innovative and Enterpreneurial Teams (No.: 2017ZT07X183). We also thank Yi Li and Xun Xu for their valuable comments.

References

1. Arun, K.S., Huang, T.S., Blostein, S.D.: Least-squares fitting of two 3-D point sets. IEEE Trans. Pattern Anal. Mach. Intell. **5**, 698–700 (1987)
2. Besl, P.J., McKay, N.D.: Method for registration of 3-D shapes. In: Sensor Fusion IV: Control Paradigms and Data Structures, vol. 1611, pp. 586–606. International Society for Optics and Photonics (1992)

3. Brachmann, E., Krull, A., Michel, F., Gumhold, S., Shotton, J., Rother, C.: Learning 6D object pose estimation using 3D object coordinates. In: Fleet, D., Pajdla, T., Schiele, B., Tuytelaars, T. (eds.) ECCV 2014. LNCS, vol. 8690, pp. 536–551. Springer, Cham (2014). https://doi.org/10.1007/978-3-319-10605-2_35
4. Calli, B., Singh, A., Walsman, A., Srinivasa, S., Abbeel, P., Dollar, A.M.: The YCB object and model set: towards common benchmarks for manipulation research. In: 2015 International Conference on Advanced Robotics (ICAR), pp. 510–517. IEEE (2015)
5. Chen, W., Jia, X., Chang, H.J., Duan, J., Leonardis, A.: G2L-Net: global to local network for real-time 6D pose estimation with embedding vector features. In: Proceedings of the IEEE/CVF Conference on Computer Vision and Pattern Recognition, pp. 4233–4242 (2020)
6. Chen, W., Jia, X., Chang, H.J., Duan, J., Shen, L., Leonardis, A.: FS-Net: fast shape-based network for category-level 6d object pose estimation with decoupled rotation mechanism. In: Proceedings of the IEEE/CVF Conference on Computer Vision and Pattern Recognition, pp. 1581–1590 (2021)
7. Collet, A., Martinez, M., Srinivasa, S.S.: The moped framework: object recognition and pose estimation for manipulation. Int. J. Rob. Res. **30**(10), 1284–1306 (2011)
8. Deng, S., Liang, Z., Sun, L., Jia, K.: VISTA: boosting 3D object detection via dual cross-view spatial attention. In: Proceedings of the IEEE/CVF Conference on Computer Vision and Pattern Recognition, pp. 8448–8457 (2022)
9. Geiger, A., Lenz, P., Urtasun, R.: Are we ready for autonomous driving? The KITTI vision benchmark suite. In: 2012 IEEE Conference on Computer Vision and Pattern Recognition, pp. 3354–3361. IEEE (2012)
10. Graham, B., Engelcke, M., Van Der Maaten, L.: 3D semantic segmentation with submanifold sparse convolutional networks. In: Proceedings of the IEEE Conference on Computer Vision and Pattern Recognition, pp. 9224–9232 (2018)
11. Gu, C., Ren, X.: Discriminative mixture-of-templates for viewpoint classification. In: Daniilidis, K., Maragos, P., Paragios, N. (eds.) ECCV 2010. LNCS, vol. 6315, pp. 408–421. Springer, Heidelberg (2010). https://doi.org/10.1007/978-3-642-15555-0_30
12. He, C., Zeng, H., Huang, J., Hua, X.S., Zhang, L.: Structure aware single-stage 3D object detection from point cloud. In: Proceedings of the IEEE/CVF Conference on Computer Vision and Pattern Recognition, pp. 11873–11882 (2020)
13. He, Y., Huang, H., Fan, H., Chen, Q., Sun, J.: FFB6D: a full flow bidirectional fusion network for 6D pose estimation. In: Proceedings of the IEEE/CVF Conference on Computer Vision and Pattern Recognition, pp. 3003–3013 (2021)
14. He, Y., Sun, W., Huang, H., Liu, J., Fan, H., Sun, J.: PVN3D: a deep pointwise 3D keypoints voting network for 6dof pose estimation. In: Proceedings of the IEEE/CVF Conference on Computer Vision and Pattern Recognition, pp. 11632–11641 (2020)
15. Hinterstoisser, S., et al.: Gradient response maps for real-time detection of textureless objects. IEEE Trans. Pattern Anal. Mach. Intell. **34**(5), 876–888 (2011)
16. Hinterstoisser, S., et al.: Multimodal templates for real-time detection of textureless objects in heavily cluttered scenes. In: 2011 International Conference on Computer Vision, pp. 858–865. IEEE (2011)
17. Hu, Y., Fua, P., Wang, W., Salzmann, M.: Single-stage 6D object pose estimation. In: Proceedings of the IEEE/CVF Conference on Computer Vision and Pattern Recognition, pp. 2930–2939 (2020)

18. Huttenlocher, D.P., Klanderman, G.A., Rucklidge, W.J.: Comparing images using the Hausdorff distance. IEEE Trans. Pattern Anal. Mach. Intell. **15**(9), 850–863 (1993)

19. Kehl, W., Manhardt, F., Tombari, F., Ilic, S., Navab, N.: SSD-6D: making RGB-based 3D detection and 6D pose estimation great again. In: Proceedings of the IEEE International Conference on Computer Vision, pp. 1521–1529 (2017)

20. Kehl, W., Milletari, F., Tombari, F., Ilic, S., Navab, N.: Deep learning of local RGB-D patches for 3D object detection and 6D pose estimation. In: Leibe, B., Matas, J., Sebe, N., Welling, M. (eds.) ECCV 2016. LNCS, vol. 9907, pp. 205–220. Springer, Cham (2016). https://doi.org/10.1007/978-3-319-46487-9_13

21. Levinson, J., et al.: Towards fully autonomous driving: systems and algorithms. In: 2011 IEEE Intelligent Vehicles Symposium (IV), pp. 163–168. IEEE (2011)

22. Li, C., Bai, J., Hager, G.D.: A unified framework for multi-view multi-class object pose estimation. In: Ferrari, V., Hebert, M., Sminchisescu, C., Weiss, Y. (eds.) ECCV 2018. LNCS, vol. 11220, pp. 263–281. Springer, Cham (2018). https://doi.org/10.1007/978-3-030-01270-0_16

23. Liebelt, J., Schmid, C., Schertler, K.: Independent object class detection using 3D feature maps. In: 2008 IEEE Conference on Computer Vision and Pattern Recognition, pp. 1–8. IEEE (2008)

24. Lin, J., Li, H., Chen, K., Lu, J., Jia, K.: Sparse steerable convolutions: an efficient learning of SE(3)-equivariant features for estimation and tracking of object poses in 3D space. In: Advances in Neural Information Processing Systems, vol. 34 (2021)

25. Lin, J., Wei, Z., Ding, C., Jia, K.: Category-level 6D object pose and size estimation using self-supervised deep prior deformation networks. arXiv preprint arXiv:2207.05444 (2022)

26. Lin, J., Wei, Z., Li, Z., Xu, S., Jia, K., Li, Y.: DualPoseNet: category-level 6d object pose and size estimation using dual pose network with refined learning of pose consistency. In: Proceedings of the IEEE/CVF International Conference on Computer Vision, pp. 3560–3569 (2021)

27. Marchand, E., Uchiyama, H., Spindler, F.: Pose estimation for augmented reality: a hands-on survey. IEEE Trans. Visual Comput. Graphics **22**(12), 2633–2651 (2015)

28. Newell, A., Yang, K., Deng, J.: Stacked hourglass networks for human pose estimation. In: Leibe, B., Matas, J., Sebe, N., Welling, M. (eds.) ECCV 2016. LNCS, vol. 9912, pp. 483–499. Springer, Cham (2016). https://doi.org/10.1007/978-3-319-46484-8_29

29. Oberweger, M., Rad, M., Lepetit, V.: Making deep heatmaps robust to partial occlusions for 3D object pose estimation. In: Ferrari, V., Hebert, M., Sminchisescu, C., Weiss, Y. (eds.) ECCV 2018. LNCS, vol. 11219, pp. 125–141. Springer, Cham (2018). https://doi.org/10.1007/978-3-030-01267-0_8

30. Park, K., Patten, T., Vincze, M.: Pix2Pose: pixel-wise coordinate regression of objects for 6D pose estimation. In: Proceedings of the IEEE/CVF International Conference on Computer Vision, pp. 7668–7677 (2019)

31. Peng, S., Liu, Y., Huang, Q., Zhou, X., Bao, H.: PVNet: pixel-wise voting network for 6DoF pose estimation. In: Proceedings of the IEEE/CVF Conference on Computer Vision and Pattern Recognition, pp. 4561–4570 (2019)

32. Rios-Cabrera, R., Tuytelaars, T.: Discriminatively trained templates for 3D object detection: a real time scalable approach. In: Proceedings of the IEEE International Conference on Computer Vision, pp. 2048–2055 (2013)

33. Rothganger, F., Lazebnik, S., Schmid, C., Ponce, J.: 3D object modeling and recognition using local affine-invariant image descriptors and multi-view spatial constraints. Int. J. Comput. Vision **66**(3), 231–259 (2006)

34. Rublee, E., Rabaud, V., Konolige, K., Bradski, G.: ORB: an efficient alternative to sift or surf. In: 2011 International Conference on Computer Vision, pp. 2564–2571. IEEE (2011)
35. Song, C., Song, J., Huang, Q.: HybridPose: 6D object pose estimation under hybrid representations. In: Proceedings of the IEEE/CVF Conference on Computer Vision and Pattern Recognition, pp. 431–440 (2020)
36. Sundermeyer, M., Marton, Z.-C., Durner, M., Brucker, M., Triebel, R.: Implicit 3D orientation learning for 6D object detection from RGB images. In: Ferrari, V., Hebert, M., Sminchisescu, C., Weiss, Y. (eds.) ECCV 2018. LNCS, vol. 11210, pp. 712–729. Springer, Cham (2018). https://doi.org/10.1007/978-3-030-01231-1_43
37. Tejani, A., Tang, D., Kouskouridas, R., Kim, T.-K.: Latent-class Hough forests for 3D object detection and pose estimation. In: Fleet, D., Pajdla, T., Schiele, B., Tuytelaars, T. (eds.) ECCV 2014. LNCS, vol. 8694, pp. 462–477. Springer, Cham (2014). https://doi.org/10.1007/978-3-319-10599-4_30
38. Tian, M., Ang, M.H., Lee, G.H.: Shape prior deformation for categorical 6D object pose and size estimation. In: Vedaldi, A., Bischof, H., Brox, T., Frahm, J.-M. (eds.) ECCV 2020. LNCS, vol. 12366, pp. 530–546. Springer, Cham (2020). https://doi.org/10.1007/978-3-030-58589-1_32
39. Wang, C., et al.: DenseFusion: 6D object pose estimation by iterative dense fusion. In: Proceedings of the IEEE/CVF Conference on Computer Vision and Pattern Recognition, pp. 3343–3352 (2019)
40. Wang, G., Manhardt, F., Tombari, F., Ji, X.: GDR-Net: geometry-guided direct regression network for monocular 6d object pose estimation. In: Proceedings of the IEEE/CVF Conference on Computer Vision and Pattern Recognition, pp. 16611–16621 (2021)
41. Wang, H., Sridhar, S., Huang, J., Valentin, J., Song, S., Guibas, L.J.: Normalized object coordinate space for category-level 6D object pose and size estimation. In: Proceedings of the IEEE/CVF Conference on Computer Vision and Pattern Recognition, pp. 2642–2651 (2019)
42. Wang, Z., Jia, K.: Frustum ConvNet: sliding frustums to aggregate local pointwise features for amodal 3d object detection. In: 2019 IEEE/RSJ International Conference on Intelligent Robots and Systems (IROS), pp. 1742–1749. IEEE (2019)
43. Wohlhart, P., Lepetit, V.: Learning descriptors for object recognition and 3D pose estimation. In: Proceedings of the IEEE Conference on Computer Vision and Pattern Recognition, pp. 3109–3118 (2015)
44. Wu, C., et al.: Grasp proposal networks: an end-to-end solution for visual learning of robotic grasps. Adv. Neural. Inf. Process. Syst. 33, 13174–13184 (2020)
45. Xiang, Y., Schmidt, T., Narayanan, V., Fox, D.: PoseCNN: a convolutional neural network for 6D object pose estimation in cluttered scenes. arXiv preprint arXiv:1711.00199 (2017)
46. Xu, D., Anguelov, D., Jain, A.: PointFusion: deep sensor fusion for 3D bounding box estimation. In: Proceedings of the IEEE Conference on Computer Vision and Pattern Recognition, pp. 244–253 (2018)
47. Zhou, G., Wang, H., Chen, J., Huang, D.: PR-GCN: a deep graph convolutional network with point refinement for 6d pose estimation. In: Proceedings of the IEEE/CVF International Conference on Computer Vision, pp. 2793–2802 (2021)

Monocular 3D Object Detection with Depth from Motion

Tai Wang[1,2], Jiangmiao Pang[2(✉)], and Dahua Lin[1,2]

[1] The Chinese University of Hong Kong, Hong Kong, China
{wt019,dhlin}@ie.cuhk.edu.hk
[2] Shanghai AI Laboratory, Shanghai, China
pangjiangmiao@gmail.com

Abstract. Perceiving 3D objects from monocular inputs is crucial for robotic systems, given its economy compared to multi-sensor settings. It is notably difficult as a single image can not provide any clues for predicting absolute depth values. Motivated by binocular methods for 3D object detection, we take advantage of the strong geometry structure provided by camera ego-motion for accurate object depth estimation and detection. We first make a theoretical analysis on this general two-view case and notice two challenges: 1) Cumulative errors from multiple estimations that make the direct prediction intractable; 2) Inherent dilemmas caused by static cameras and matching ambiguity. Accordingly, we establish the stereo correspondence with a geometry-aware cost volume as the alternative for depth estimation and further compensate it with monocular understanding to address the second problem. Our framework, named Depth from Motion (DfM), then uses the established geometry to lift 2D image features to the 3D space and detects 3D objects thereon. We also present a pose-free DfM to make it usable when the camera pose is unavailable. Our framework outperforms state-of-the-art methods by a large margin on the KITTI benchmark. Detailed quantitative and qualitative analyses also validate our theoretical conclusions. The code is released at https://github.com/Tai-Wang/Depth-from-Motion.

Keywords: Monocular 3D object detection · Depth from motion

1 Introduction

3D object detection is a fundamental task for practical applications such as autonomous driving. In the past few years, LiDAR-based [16,28,42,45] and binocular-based [5,7,9,12,17] approaches have made great progress and achieved promising performance. In contrast, monocular methods [23,30,35,37] still yield unsatisfactory results as their depth estimation is naturally ill-posed. Although several works [23,29,30,35,44] made some attempts to tackle this problem, the current solutions still focus on digging out more geometry structures from *a single image*. It is still hard for them to estimate accurate *absolute* depth values.

Supplementary Information The online version contains supplementary material available at https://doi.org/10.1007/978-3-031-20077-9_23.

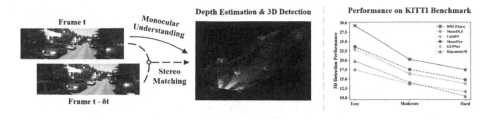

Fig. 1. In this paper, we present a framework for monocular 3D detection from videos. In contrast to previous work only relying on monocular understanding from a single image, our method integrates the stereo geometric clues from temporally adjacent images. It significantly improves depth estimation accuracy, the most critical part for camera-only 3D perception, and thus enhances the 3D detection performance.

This paper aims to use stereo geometry from a pair of images nearby in temporal to facilitate the object depth estimation. The basic principle is similar to depth estimation in binocular systems. Two cameras in binocular systems are strictly constrained on the same plane and have a fixed distance, which is known as the system's *baseline*. State-of-the-art stereo 3D object detection methods take this baseline as a critical clue and transform depth estimation to an easier disparity estimation problem. Similarly, two nearby images in temporal also have stereo correspondence, but their baseline is dynamic and relies on the ego-motion of the camera. This idea is intuitively promising, but few previous works explored it. The only recent work for 3D detection from monocular videos, Kinematic3D [3], uses a 3D Kalman Filter and an integrated ego-motion module to build the connection between frames. It focuses on the robustness and stability of detection results but still estimates depth from a single image. Our work, instead, is the first to study how to improve object depth estimation and 3D detection from the strong stereo geometry formed by ego-motion.

We first conduct a theoretical analysis on this problem to better understand the geometry relationship. It reveals that direct derivation of depth in this setting involves many estimations and thus has fundamental difficulty caused by cumulative errors. The stereo estimation also has several intrinsic dilemmas, such as no baseline formed by static cameras. We thus build our framework with a depth-from-motion module addressing these problems to construct 3D features and detect 3D objects thereon. Specifically, we first involve the complex geometry relationship in a differential cost volume as the alternative for stereo estimation. To guarantee its physical rationality for any arbitrarily augmented inputs, we devise a pipeline to ensure the pose transformation takes place in the original space, namely *canonical space*. Furthermore, we compensate it with another monocular pathway and fuse them with learnable weights. The distribution of these learned weights well demonstrates the theoretical discussion on the intrinsic weaknesses of stereo estimation.

Considering camera poses are not always available, we also introduce a pose-free method to make the framework more flexible. We first decouple the ego-pose estimation as translation and rotation. Instead of using the straightforward Euler angles, we formulate the rotation with quaternion, a more friendly representation for optimization, to avoid periodic targets. In addition, we adopt a self-supervised loss to regularize the learning of pose to make the training get rid of pose annotations and expensive loss weights tuning.

We evaluate our framework on the KITTI [8] benchmark. It achieves 1st place out of monocular methods, surpassing previous methods by a large margin, 2.6%–5.6% and 4.2%–7.5% AP higher on the 3D and bird-eye-view vehicle detection benchmark respectively. These impressive experimental results demonstrate the potential of this stream of methods in this context, which is a more interpretable and practical perception approach like that human beings rely on.

2 Related Work

Video-Based Depth Estimation. Depth estimation from monocular videos is an important problem for mobile devices and VR/AR applications. Learning-based methods can be divided into MVS-based (Multi-View-Stereo) methods [19, 34] and monocular-stereo hybrid methods [15,22,43]. The former group can not handle dynamic scenes due to the static assumption of MVS, and the latter addresses this problem by integrating a pretrained single-view depth estimator. In addition, there is another line of work [10,11] using videos as supervision to achieve self-supervised depth estimation. Although these works have made progress in this problem, there is still a notable gap between this field and camera-only 3D detection. Due to the disparity of scenarios and ultimate targets, previous work hardly attempts to tackle the object depth estimation problem in our context.

Video-Based Object Detection. Video-based object detection [1,20,39,47, 48] has been studied for several years in the 2D case. These works target a better trade-off between accuracy and efficiency by aggregating features from multiple frames. Unlike the 3D case, the main problems of 2D detection from videos are the occlusion and blur of objects. The transformation between frames is generally flow-based, without considering geometric consistency in the real world. In comparison, the only previous work [3] for monocular 3D video object detection improves the robustness of detection results with 3D Kinematic designs. This paper is different from both. We instead focus on the specific problem in the 3D case: estimating object depth more accurately from the depth-from-motion setting and further boosting the 3D detection performance.

Camera-Only 3D Object Detection. Compared to LiDAR-based approaches [16,28,36,42,45,46], camera-only methods take RGB images as the only input and need to reason the depth information without accurate measurement provided by depth sensors. Among them, monocular 3D detection is more challenging than binocular because of its ill-posed property.

Earlier learning-based monocular methods [4,24,40] used sub-networks to solve this problem. Afterward, due to the system complexity and dependence on external data and pretrained models, recent work turns to end-to-end designs [2,13,23,32,37] like 2D detection. As several works [23,30,35] point out the crucial role of depth estimation in this setting, a stream of work [18,29,35,44] attempted to address the problem with more geometric designs. Meanwhile, another line incorporates depth information to study the feature transformation approaches. Pioneer work [27,38] in this line transforms the input image to 3D representations with depth estimation and performs 3D object detection thereon. Recent CaDDN [26] merges these two stages into an end-to-end framework and achieves promising results. Our work follows this high-level pipeline while focusing on improving the depth estimation from video input.

As for binocular methods, apart from the previously mentioned Pseudo-LiDAR fashion, they can be grouped into two tracks: front-view 2D-based [17, 25,33,41] and bird-eye-view volume-based [5,12]. The volume-based methods are consistent with the feature transformation ideas of CaDDN. Our framework is also motivated by this stream. In contrast, we focus on studying a more difficult stereo setting: general multi-view cases formed by ego-motion.

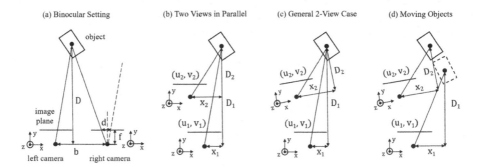

Fig. 2. Multi-view geometry for object depth estimation in the (a) binocular, (b) parallel two-view, (c) general two-view system and (d) that for moving objects.

3   Theoretical Analysis

In this section, we will first make a theoretical analysis for general stereo depth estimation. Among different multi-view settings, the binocular case is the simplest one and thus studied the most in the driving scenario [5,17,33]. We start with this setting and further discuss the connection and difference when extending it to general cases. Finally, we analyze the main challenges in the depth-from-motion setting and introduce our framework design thereon.

3.1   Object Depth from Binocular Systems

Binocular systems strictly constrain two cameras on the same plane. As shown in Fig. 2-(a), the focal length of cameras and the distance between the pair of cameras (namely *baseline* of the system) are supposed to be constant. Following the similar triangle rule under the pinhole camera model, they follow

$$\frac{d}{f} = \frac{b}{D} \Rightarrow D = f\frac{b}{d}, \tag{1}$$

where d is the horizontal disparity on the pair of images, f is the focal length of cameras, D is the object depth, b is the baseline. Following Eq. 1, object depth estimation can be transformed to a much easier disparity estimation problem.

3.2   Object Depth from General Two-View Systems

Binocular systems rely on two-view stereo geometry to estimate object depth. Intuitively, two nearby images in a video also have similar stereo correspondence. Can we use two-view geometry in this general case to predict object depth?

We step by step extend the geometry relationship in binocular systems to general two-view cases. The analysis supposes the camera is in different positions at time t_1 and t_2 respectively, and we know the camera parameters at each position. We assume all objects do not move at the beginning of this analysis and discuss the object motion at the end.

As shown in Fig. 1-(b), suppose the camera's movement only involves translation. We can obtain Δx and ΔD from the transformation of camera poses. The two-view geometry in this parallel case satisfies

$$\frac{u_1 - c_u}{f} = \frac{x_1}{D_1}, \quad \frac{u_2 - c_u}{f} = \frac{x_2}{D_2}, \quad \Delta x = x_1 - x_2, \quad \Delta D = D_1 - D_2, \tag{2}$$

where (u_1, v_1) and (u_2, v_2) are a pair of corresponding points on the images, D_1 and D_2 are their depths, x_1 and x_2 are their locations in 3D space along the x-axis. From these relationships, we can derive D_1:

$$D_1 = \frac{f(\Delta x - \frac{u_2 - c_u}{f}\Delta D)}{u_1 - u_2} \xlongequal{\Delta D = 0} \frac{f\Delta x}{u_1 - u_2}. \tag{3}$$

The geometry relationship in binocular systems is its special case when $\Delta D = 0$.

As Eq. 3 shows, in contrast to binocular system, the "baseline" in this case is no longer fixed but dynamic that relies on camera ego-motion $\Delta x, \Delta D$ and object absolute locations u_2. Accordingly, object depth estimation also relies on them apart from the disparity $u_1 - u_2$.

To better understand this case, we quantitatively compare it with the binocular system on KITTI as an example. It is well-known that a suitable baseline should not be too large or small. A too-large baseline yields small shared regions of two images, while a too-small baseline results in small disparities and large estimation errors. So we take the binocular baseline (0.54 m on KITTI) as our example target to form with $\Delta x - \frac{u_2 - c_u}{f}\Delta D$ in this case. Because the horizontal translation Δx is typically much smaller than 0.54 m, we need a large translation along the depth direction (ΔD) and a large horizontal distance from the 2D camera center ($u_2 - c_u$) to get a baseline large enough for stereo matching. For example, to form the 0.54-m baseline, when ΔD is 5.4 m, f is 700 pixels, then we need $u_2 - c_u = 70$. Accordingly, when ΔD is only 2.7 m, then we need

$u_2 - c_u = 140^1$. It means we can get more accurate estimations for objects far from central lines and may encounter problems otherwise.

On this basis, involving ego-rotation (Fig. 1-(c)) will introduce rotation coefficients entangled with object absolute positions to the disparity computation, and involving object motion (Fig. 1-(d)) will introduce *relative* translation and rotation factors. More introduction of absolute positions and motion estimation errors makes direct depth estimation more difficult. See more derivation details in the supplementary materials.

3.3 Achilles Heel of Depth from Motion

Based on the previous analysis, we can observe that direct derivation of depth in a general two-view system involves many estimations like object absolute locations and motions, thus having fundamental difficulties caused by cumulative errors. In addition, the stereo-based solution has several cases that are intrinsically hard to handle, such as no baseline formed by static cameras and the common ambiguity problem of matching on less-textured regions.

Therefore, motivated by binocular approaches [5], we involve the complex geometric relationship in a differential plane-sweep cost volume as the alternative to establish the stereo correspondence: Considering we can not directly estimate depth from disparity, we instead provide candidate depths for each pixel, reproject these 2.5D points to another frame and learn which one is most likely according to the pixel-wise feature similarity. Furthermore, to address the second challenge, we introduce another path for monocular understanding to compensate the stereo estimation. Next, we will elaborate on these designs with our framework in detail.

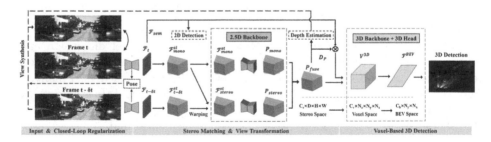

Fig. 3. An overview of our framework.

4 Methodology

A general pipeline for camera-only 3D detection methods typically consists of three stages: extracting features from input images, lifting the features to 3D

---

[1] For reference, the half-width of an image on KITTI is about 600 pixels.

space, and finally detecting 3D objects thereon. We build our framework following this approach (Fig. 3). Next, we will introduce our overall framework and present two key designs: geometry-aware cost volume construction and monocular compensation for stereo estimation. Finally, we propose a solution for pose-free cases, making the framework more flexible.

4.1 Framework Overview

2D Feature Extraction. Motivated by binocular approaches [5,12], given the input image-pair $(I_t, I_{t-\delta t})$, we first use a shared 2D backbone to extract their features $(\mathcal{F}_t, \mathcal{F}_{t-\delta t})$. Afterward, we devise two different necks to generate F_t as geometric feature for stereo matching and F_{sem} as semantic feature following [12]. To guarantee the semantic features can get correct supervision signals, they are also used to perform the auxiliary 2D detection.

Stereo Matching and View Transformation. After getting the features of two frames, we construct the stereo cost volume $\mathcal{F}_{stereo}^{st}$ with the pose transformation between them. In addition, we lift $\mathcal{F}_t$ with pre-defined discrete depth levels to get $\mathcal{F}_{mono}^{st}$ in stereo space for subsequent monocular understanding. A dual-path 3D aggregation network filters these two volumes to predict the depth distribution volume D_P. $D_P(u, v, :)$ represents the depth distribution of pixel (u, v) over the depth levels. The depth prediction is supervised with projected LiDAR points. Details of cost volume construction and the dual-path feature aggregation will be presented in Sect. 4.2 and 4.3. Subsequently, we lift the semantic feature $\mathcal{F}_{sem}$ with D_P, combine it with geometric stereo feature P_{stereo} as the final stereo feature, and sample voxel features thereon. As shown in Fig. 3, this process transforms the feature in stereo space to voxel space, which has a regular structure and is thus more convenient for us to perform object detection.

Voxel-Based 3D Detection. Next, we merge the channel dimension and height dimension to transform the 3D feature V^{3D} to bird-eye-view (BEV) space, and apply a 2D hourglass network to aggregate the BEV features. Finally, a lightweight head is appended to predict 3D bounding boxes and their categories. The training loss is composed of two parts as [12]: depth regression loss and 2D/3D detection loss. See more details in the supplemental materials.

4.2 Geometry-Aware Stereo Cost Volume Construction

The key component in the previously mentioned stereo matching is the construction of cost volume. In contrast to the binocular case, the pose transformation between two frames is a rigid transformation composed of translation and rotation. This difference affects the method to construct cost volume and makes it hard to perform data augmentation on input images. Next, we will first formulate the procedure of volume construction and then present how we make it compatible with arbitrarily augmented input.

Formally, for each position $\mathbf{x} = (u, v, w)$ in the stereo volume, we can derive the reprojection matrix $\mathcal{W}$ to warp $\mathcal{F}_{t-\delta t}$ to the space of frame t and concatenate the corresponding feature together:

$$\mathcal{F}^{st}_{stereo}(u_t, v_t, w_t) = concat\Big[\mathcal{F}_t(u_t, v_t), \mathcal{F}_{t-\delta t}(u_{t-\delta t}, v_{t-\delta t})\Big], \qquad (4)$$

$$(u_{t-\delta t}, v_{t-\delta t}, d(w_{t-\delta t}))^T = \mathcal{W}(u_t, v_t, d(w_t))^T, \quad \mathcal{W} = KTK^{-1}. \qquad (5)$$

Here (u_t, v_t, w_t) and $(u_{t-\delta t}, v_{t-\delta t}, w_{t-\delta t})$ represent the queried pixel coordinates in the stereo space of two frames. $d(w) = w \cdot \Delta d + d_{min}$ is the function to calculate the corresponding depth, where Δd is the divided depth interval and d_{min} is the minimum depth of detection range. $\mathcal{W}$ is the reprojection matrix, which is derived by multiplying intrinsic matrix K, ego-motion (rigid transformation) T and K^{-1}, assuming the intrinsic matrix does not change across two frames. We find that any data augmentation, such as image rescale or flip, can affect the physical rationality of reprojection matrix $\mathcal{W}$. Constructing a *geometry-aware* cost volume from augmented images here is not as trivial as in previous camera-only detection methods. Therefore, we devise an approach to addressing this problem. As shown in Fig. 4-(a), we need to find the corresponding features between a pair of augmented image features $(\mathcal{F}_t, \mathcal{F}_{t-\delta t})$. Our key idea is to guarantee the warping transformation is conducted in the 3D real world, namely *canonical space*. For example, if we perform flipping, rescaling, and cropping on the input two images, we first need to append pre-defined depth levels to each 2D grid coordinate of $\mathcal{F}_t$ and lift each 2.5D coordinate to 3D. During transformation, the effect of *intrinsic* augmentations like rescaling and cropping should be removed through the manipulated[2] intrinsic matrix K. Afterward, we flip the stereo grid $\tilde{G}^{st}_t$ to get G^{st}_t in the canonical space. With the recovered grid, we can further perform the pose transformation to get $G^{st}_{t-\delta t}$, project it to the 2D plane and obtain several $G_{t-\delta t}$ grid maps. Finally, we replay the image augmentations and sample the corresponding features.

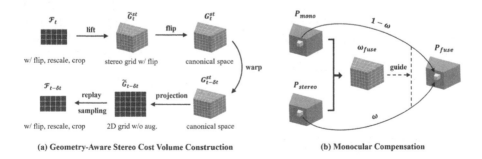

(a) Geometry-Aware Stereo Cost Volume Construction   (b) Monocular Compensation

Fig. 4. Key components in our depth-from-motion module.

---

[2] Rescaling and cropping correspond to the manipulation of focal length and camera centers proportionally.

In this way, we can exploit any data augmentation to the input images without influencing the intrinsic rationality of ego-motion transformation. Compared to the tricky image swapping for flip augmentation in the binocular case and other alternatives, our method is also generalizable for other multi-view cases.

4.3   Monocular Compensation

The underlying philosophies of stereo and monocular depth estimation are different: stereo estimation relies on matching while monocular estimation relies on the semantic and geometric understanding of a single image and data-driven priors. As analyzed in Sect. 3.3, there are multiple cases that stereo estimation approaches can not handle. Therefore, we incorporate the monocular contextual prior to compensate stereo depth estimation.

Specifically, as shown in Fig. 4-(b), we use two 3D hourglass networks to aggregate monocular and stereo features separately. The network for monocular path shares the same architecture with the other, except for the input channel is half given the $\mathcal{F}^{st}_{mono}$ is half of $\mathcal{F}^{st}_{stereo}$. Then we have two feature volumes P_{mono} and P_{stereo} in the stereo space with the same shape. To aggregate these two features, we devise a simple yet effective and interpretable scheme. First, P_{mono} and P_{stereo} are concatenated and fed into a simple 2D convolutional network composed of 1×1 kernel, and aggregated along the depth channel, e.g., compressed from $2D$ channels to D. Then the sigmoid response of this feature serves as the weight ω_{fuse} for guiding the fusion of P_{mono} and P_{stereo}. Formally, denoting the convolutional network as ϕ, this procedure is represented as follows:

$$\omega_{fuse} = \sigma(\phi(P_{mono}, P_{stereo})), \quad P_{fuse} = \omega_{fuse} \circ P_{stereo} + (1 - \omega_{fuse}) \circ P_{mono} \quad (6)$$

Here σ denotes the sigmoid function, and $\circ$ refers to element-wise multiplication. The derived stereo feature P_{fuse} is directly used to predict the depth distribution after a softmax and also fed into the subsequent networks for 3D detection.

This design is clean yet effective, as to be shown in the ablation studies of Sect. 5.4. Furthermore, it is interpretable both intuitively and empirically. The weight distribution of each position on the image is derived from monocular and stereo depth distributions of the same position. It is location-aware for different regions on the image, agnostic to specific reasons of inaccurate stereo estimation, and self-adaptive to different input cases. We can also validate this expected behavior by visualizing the weight ω_{fuse} and observe where stereo or monocular estimation is more reliable. See more visualization analysis in Sect. 5.3.

4.4   Pose-Free Depth from Motion

Now we have an integrated framework for estimating depth and detecting 3D objects from consecutive-frame images. In the framework, ego-pose serves as a critical clue like the baseline in the binocular case. We essentially estimate the metric-aware depth given the metric-aware pose transformation. Although it can be easily obtained in practical applications, here we still propose a solution for the pose-free case. It is useful for mobile devices in the wild and necessary for evaluating our final models on the KITTI [8] test set.

The target formulation is critical for camera pose estimation. It is well known that any rigid pose transformation can be decomposed as translation and rotation. Both have three Degrees of Freedom (DoF). Previous work [3,10] typically regresses the 3D translation and three Euler angles. The regression of translation $\mathbf{t}$ is straightforward. For rotation estimation, instead of estimating the periodic Euler angles, we represent the rotation target with a unit quaternion $\mathbf{q}$. It is a more friendly formulation as the network output.

Therefore, the output of our pose network is a vector including translation and unnormalized quaternion. We use the shared backbone as the encoder and add a decoder following [10]. Our baseline supervises the output with L1 loss:

$$\mathcal{L}_t = ||\mathbf{t} - \hat{\mathbf{t}}||_1, \quad \mathcal{L}_r = ||\mathbf{q} - \frac{\hat{\mathbf{q}}}{||\hat{\mathbf{q}}||}||_1, \quad \mathcal{L}_{pose} = \mathcal{L}_t + \lambda_r \mathcal{L}_r. \tag{7}$$

However, this loss design has several problems: 1) Adjusting the weight λ_r is difficult and expensive; 2) There is a domain gap for two 2D images to directly regress the 3D ego-motion; 3) We still need pose annotations during training. Therefore, we use a self-supervised loss [10,11] to replace it, considering its strength in these aspects. Specifically, the self-supervised loss is composed of an appearance matching loss $\mathcal{L}_p$ and a depth smoothness loss $\mathcal{L}_s$:

$$\mathcal{L}_{pose}(I_t, I_{t-\delta t}) = \mathcal{L}_p(I_t, I_{t-\delta t \to t}) + \lambda_s \mathcal{L}_s \tag{8}$$

Here $I_{t-\delta t \to t}$ represents the frame t synthesized with the image and depth of frame $t - \delta t$ and the predicted pose. More details are in the supplemental.

Note that in contrast to [10,11], we use the LiDAR signal to supervise the learning of depth directly and only use the self-supervised loss to learn pose. In this way, because the learning of depth is supervised by absolute depth values, we can also learn a metric-aware pose even without explicit pose annotations.

5   Experiments

5.1   Experimental Setup

Dataset. We evaluate our method on the KITTI dataset [8]. It consists of 7481/7518 frames for training/testing and the training set is generally divided into 3712/3769 samples as training/validation splits. In this paper, apart from the multi-modality input data and annotations of the current frame, we also use three temporarily preceding frames. Related pose information is extracted from the raw data following Kinematic3D [3]. We use images and pose information of these preceding frames and only use LiDAR as depth supervision during training.

Metrics. KITTI uses Average Precision (AP) for 3D object detection evaluation. It requires a 3D bounding box overlap of more than 70%/50%/50% for car/pedestrian/cyclist. We report the AP_{40} results following [32], corresponding to the AP of 40 recall points, which is more stable and fair for comparison.

Implementation Details. We randomly select one of three temporarily preceding images together with the current frame as training input while use the earliest one during inference if not specified in experiments. Other hyper-parameter settings, data augmentation methods and loss designs basically follow recent binocular methods [5,12]. See more details in the supplemental materials.

Table 1. AP_{40} results on the KITTI validation benchmark.

Methods	Venue	AP_{3D} IoU$\geq$ 0.7			AP_{BEV} IoU$\geq$ 0.7		
		Easy	Mod.	Hard	Easy	Mod.	Hard
MonoDIS [32]	ICCV 2019	11.06	7.60	6.37	18.45	12.58	10.66
MonoPair [6]	CVPR 2020	16.28	12.30	10.42	24.12	18.17	15.76
MoVi3D [31]	ECCV 2020	14.28	11.13	9.68	22.36	17.87	15.73
MonoDLE [23]	CVPR 2021	17.45	13.66	11.68	24.97	19.33	17.01
PGD [35]	CoRL 2021	19.27	13.23	10.65	26.60	18.23	15.00
CaDDN [26]	CVPR 2021	23.57	16.31	13.84	–	–	–
MonoFlex [44]	CVPR 2021	23.64	17.51	14.83	–	–	–
MonoRCNN [29]	ICCV 2021	16.61	13.19	10.65	25.29	19.22	15.30
GUPNet [21]	ICCV 2021	22.76	16.46	13.72	31.07	22.94	19.75
DFR-Net [49]	ICCV 2021	19.55	14.79	11.04	26.60	19.80	15.34
Kinematic3D [3]	ECCV 2020	19.76	14.10	10.47	27.83	19.72	15.10
DfM w/o pose	ECCV 2022	26.65	18.49	15.94	34.97	25.00	22.00
DfM w/ pose	ECCV 2022	**29.27**	**20.22**	**17.46**	**38.60**	**27.13**	**24.05**

5.2   Quantitative Analysis

Main Results. First, we compare our framework with other state-of-the-art methods on the KITTI validation benchmark (Table 1), considering the ego-pose information is not available on the test set. We observe a significant improvement in both 3D detection and bird-eye-view (BEV) performance, 2.6%–5.6% and 4.2%–7.5% higher than the previous best for all the difficulty levels respectively. We conjecture that the better improvement on BEV performance is caused by our paradigm of voxel-based 3D detector: it finally detects 3D objects from the bird-eye-view following [16,42]. In addition, even without ego-pose information, our framework still outperforms others by a notable margin. This further shows the benefits brought by temporal information and stereo estimation. Please refer to the supplemental for its performance on the test set and other categories.

Comparison with Video-Based Methods. Compared to the only previous methods using video information, Kinematic3D [3], our method also shows significant superiority. The reason is that Kinematic3D focuses more on the stability of detection and forecasting while our method pays more attention to depth estimation. Considering that the evaluation metric on KITTI requires particularly accurate localization for detected objects, our method naturally shows better performance on the benchmark. Note that our method is also compatible with some methods proposed in Kinematic3D. They can further improve the detection stability and efficiency of our framework and provide a natural integration with the downstream tasks such as tracking, prediction and planning.

Comparison with Binocular Methods. Although our approach has achieved promising progress over previous monocular methods, we still observe a large gap between ours and binocular state of the art (64.7% AP for moderate). It is partly due to intrinsic weaknesses of the depth-from-motion setting. Nevertheless, we can expect a large space for improvement as the advancement of binocular methods, from RT3DStereo [14] (23.3% AP) to LIGA-Stereo [12] (64.7% AP).

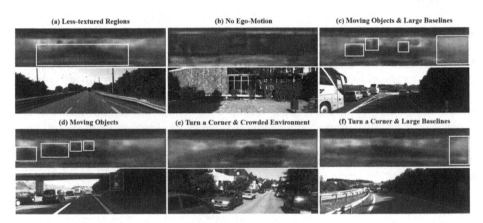

Fig. 5. Qualitative Analysis of aggregation weights in different cases. The depth estimation relies more on monocular priors for less textured regions in (a) (e), static cameras in (b) and moving objects in (c) (d) while tends to use stereo matching on other cases, especially on the background and the regions far away from camera centers in (f). Note that our analysis is still valid when the car is turning a corner in (e) because the rotation in the ego-motion is small in a short period.

5.3   Qualitative Analysis

For qualitative analysis, we show the visualization of aggregation weights (summed along the depth axis) in Sect. 4.3 with some representative cases (Fig. 5). For each sample plotted in the figure, we visualize the weight ranging from 0 to 1 above each image. Larger weights are marked with lighter regions in the weight maps, which indicates that the depth estimation relies more on stereo matching.

Next, we will discuss the inherent problems of stereo methods in the depth-from-motion setting analyzed in Sect. 3.3. In a general case, (a) shows that the estimation relies more on monocular priors for less textured regions such as the road. (b) shows a case that stereo matching will break down: no baseline is formed by static cameras. (c) and (d) show that stereo methods can not handle moving objects with the current pure design. In addition, on the right side of image (c), when the richness of texture seems similar, the regions far away from camera centers can form larger baselines. They can thus get more accurate estimations from stereo matching. A similar phenomenon can be seen in sample (f). Finally, even the driving car is turning a corner, all of our analysis is still valid because the rotation in the ego-motion can not be quite large in a short period. This weight is also learned adaptively for the crowded environment. These prove the interpretability of our method and the necessity of monocular compensation. It also points out possible directions for improving this group of the method, such as handling moving objects with customized designs in the stereo estimation.

For the visualization of 3D detection and depth estimation results from the perspective view and bird's eye view, please refer to the demo video attached in the supplementary material.

5.4   Ablation Studies

Geometry-Aware Stereo Cost Volume. First, we show the benefits of geometry-aware stereo cost volume construction in Table 2. Both flip and rescale augmentation can remarkably enhance the detector. We suspect that making the cost volume more compatible with various augmented inputs can improve the generalization ability of models for different scenes and camera intrinsic settings.

Table 2. From top to down: Ablation studies for (a) geometry-aware cost volume construction, (b) detection performance of different depth estimation approaches, (c) using different preceding frames during inference, and (d) different pose-free designs.

Methods	AP_{3D} IoU$\geq$ 0.7			AP_{BEV} IoU$\geq$ 0.7		
	Easy	Mod.	Hard	Easy	Mod.	Hard
Baseline	17.41	12.93	11.60	24.78	18.21	16.06
+Flip aug	19.13	13.92	12.62	26.89	19.48	17.52
+Rescale aug	21.47	15.32	13.83	29.22	21.22	19.51
Mono Only	20.06	15.30	14.05	27.84	21.78	19.96
Stereo Only	21.47	15.32	13.83	29.22	21.22	19.51
Mono+Stereo	26.61	18.82	16.47	36.16	26.09	23.17
Prev-1st	24.09	17.27	15.03	35.50	25.24	22.82
Prev-2nd	24.92	17.62	15.68	35.89	25.39	22.99
Prev-3rd	25.19	17.96	15.92	36.16	25.88	23.03
Euler for rotation	20.16	15.03	13.01	28.96	21.21	19.08
+ quaternion	23.88	16.93	14.47	33.23	23.75	20.72
+ reproj. supervision	26.65	18.49	15.94	34.97	25.00	22.00

Monocular Compensation We compare different approaches for depth estimation in Table 2 and Fig. 6. We turn off one of two branches in Sect. 4.3 by setting the corresponding weight to zero during training and compare their detection (Table 2) and depth estimation accuracy (Fig. 6). We can see that with only monocular context, models still achieve a decent detection performance while failing on depth estimation of the entire scene. Stereo matching performs better on both aspects, especially the latter. Because these modules compensate each other fundamentally, our aggregation design brings an impressive gain thereon.

Different Preceding Frames. As analyzed in Sect. 3.3, the distance of ego-vehicle in two frames can affect the baseline in this depth-from-motion setting and thus affect the accuracy of stereo matching. To compare the effect of using different frames, we train the model with a randomly selected previous frame for each sample and test it with a fixed one. Note that when the sample does not have the corresponding preceding frame, for instance, the third preceding one, we will use the earliest one that it has. As Table 2 shows, using the third preceding frame performs better than others up to about 1% mAP, which validates our analysis. This study has additional space for exploration: If given more previous frames, which one would be the best choice? If we involve multiple frames into stereo matching and depth estimation, what is a better frame selection design?

Pose-Free Designs. Finally, we study the specific designs for pose-free depth from motion. Our baseline uses the Euler angle as the rotation representation as [3] and directly regresses the translation and rotation with the pose supervision. We further try the quaternion representation and reprojected photometric loss as the supervision, and both show superiority than before. More importantly, we can avoid the pose annotation completely with the self-supervised paradigm, which is especially important for the practice in the real world.

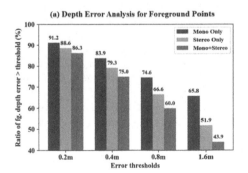
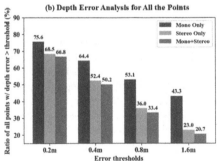

Fig. 6. We make error analysis for the depth predictions of foreground region and the entire scene by different methods, respectively, by comparing the percentage of points with depth errors greater than thresholds: 0.2 m, 0.4 m, 0.8 m, 1.6 m. The error medians of monocular/stereo/hybrid methods on the foreground region/the entire scene are 5.86/3.33/2.60 m and 1.15/0.58/0.48 m.

6   Conclusion

In this paper, we propose a framework for monocular 3D detection from videos. It lifts 2D image features to 3D space via an effective depth estimation module and detects 3D objects on top. The depth-from-motion system leverages an important ego-motion clue to estimate depth from stereo matching, which is further compensated with monocular understanding for addressing several intrinsic dilemmas. To make this framework more flexible, we further extend it to pose-free case with an effective rotation formulation and a self-supervised paradigm. Experimental results show the efficacy of our method and validate our theoretical discussion. In the future, we will optimize our framework in terms its simplicity and generalization ability. How to address the stereo estimation of moving objects is also an important problem worthy of further exploration.

Acknowledgement.. This work is supported by GRF 14205719, TRS T41-603/20-R, Centre for Perceptual and Interactive Intelligence, and CUHK Interdisciplinary AI Research Institute.

References

1. Bertasius, G., Torresani, L., Shi, J.: Object detection in video with spatiotemporal sampling networks. In: Ferrari, V., Hebert, M., Sminchisescu, C., Weiss, Y. (eds.) ECCV 2018. LNCS, vol. 11216, pp. 342–357. Springer, Cham (2018). https://doi.org/10.1007/978-3-030-01258-8_21
2. Brazil, G., Liu, X.: M3D-RPN: monocular 3D region proposal network for object detection. In: IEEE International Conference on Computer Vision (2019)
3. Brazil, G., Pons-Moll, G., Liu, X., Schiele, B.: Kinematic 3D object detection in monocular video. In: Vedaldi, A., Bischof, H., Brox, T., Frahm, J.-M. (eds.) ECCV 2020. LNCS, vol. 12368, pp. 135–152. Springer, Cham (2020). https://doi.org/10.1007/978-3-030-58592-1_9
4. Chen, X., et al.: 3D object proposals for accurate object class detection. In: Conference on Neural Information Processing Systems (2015)
5. Chen, Y., Liu, S., Shen, X., Jia, J.: DSGN: deep stereo geometry network for 3D object detection. In: Proceedings of the IEEE/CVF Conference on Computer Vision and Pattern Recognition, pp. 12536–12545 (2020)
6. Chen, Y., Tai, L., Sun, K., Li, M.: MonoPair: monocular 3D object detection using pairwise spatial relationships. In: IEEE Conference on Computer Vision and Pattern Recognition (2020)
7. Garg, R., B.G., V.K., Carneiro, G., Reid, I.: Unsupervised CNN for single view depth estimation: geometry to the rescue. In: Leibe, B., Matas, J., Sebe, N., Welling, M. (eds.) ECCV 2016. LNCS, vol. 9912, pp. 740–756. Springer, Cham (2016). https://doi.org/10.1007/978-3-319-46484-8_45
8. Geiger, A., Lenz, P., Urtasun, R.: Are we ready for autonomous driving? The KITTI vision benchmark suite. In: IEEE Conference on Computer Vision and Pattern Recognition (2012)
9. Godard, C., Aodha, O.M., Brostow, G.J.: Unsupervised monocular depth estimation with leftright consistency. In: IEEE Conference on Computer Vision and Pattern Recognition (2017)

10. Godard, C., Mac Aodha, O., Firman, M., Brostow, G.J.: Digging into self-supervised monocular depth estimation. In: Proceedings of the IEEE/CVF International Conference on Computer Vision, pp. 3828–3838 (2019)
11. Guizilini, V., Ambrus, R., Pillai, S., Raventos, A., Gaidon, A.: 3D packing for self-supervised monocular depth estimation. In: Proceedings of the IEEE/CVF Conference on Computer Vision and Pattern Recognition, pp. 2485–2494 (2020)
12. Guo, X., Shi, S., Wang, X., Li, H.: Liga-stereo: learning lidar geometry aware representations for stereo-based 3d detector. In: Proceedings of the IEEE/CVF International Conference on Computer Vision, pp. 3153–3163 (2021)
13. Jörgensen, E., Zach, C., Kahl, F.: Monocular 3d object detection and box fitting trained end-to-end using intersection-over-union loss. CoRR abs/1906.08070 (2019). https://arxiv.org/abs/1906.08070
14. Königshof, H., Salscheider, N.O., Stiller, C.: Realtime 3D object detection for automated driving using stereo vision and semantic information. In: 2019 IEEE Intelligent Transportation Systems Conference (ITSC), pp. 1405–1410. IEEE (2019)
15. Kopf, J., Rong, X., Huang, J.B.: Robust consistent video depth estimation. In: Proceedings of the IEEE/CVF Conference on Computer Vision and Pattern Recognition, pp. 1611–1621 (2021)
16. Lang, A.H., Vora, S., Caesar, H., Zhou, L., Yang, J., Beijbom, O.: PointPillars: fast encoders for object detection from point clouds. In: IEEE Conference on Computer Vision and Pattern Recognition (2019)
17. Li, P., Chen, X., Shen, S.: Stereo R-CNN based 3D object detection for autonomous driving. In: Proceedings of the IEEE/CVF Conference on Computer Vision and Pattern Recognition, pp. 7644–7652 (2019)
18. Li, P., Zhao, H., Liu, P., Cao, F.: RTM3D: real-time monocular 3d detection from object keypoints for autonomous driving. In: Vedaldi, A., Bischof, H., Brox, T., Frahm, J.-M. (eds.) ECCV 2020. LNCS, vol. 12348, pp. 644–660. Springer, Cham (2020). https://doi.org/10.1007/978-3-030-58580-8_38
19. Liu, C., Gu, J., Kim, K., Narasimhan, S.G., Kautz, J.: Neural RGB→d sensing: depth and uncertainty from a video camera. In: Proceedings of the IEEE/CVF Conference on Computer Vision and Pattern Recognition, pp. 10986–10995 (2019)
20. Liu, M., Zhu, M.: Mobile video object detection with temporally-aware feature maps. In: Proceedings of the IEEE Conference on Computer Vision and Pattern Recognition, pp. 5686–5695 (2018)
21. Lu, Y., et al.: Geometry uncertainty projection network for monocular 3D object detection. In: Proceedings of the IEEE/CVF International Conference on Computer Vision (ICCV)
22. Luo, X., Huang, J.B., Szeliski, R., Matzen, K., Kopf, J.: Consistent video depth estimation. ACM Trans. Graph. (ToG) $39(4)$, 71–1 (2020)
23. Ma, X., et al.: Delving into localization errors for monocular 3D object detection. In: Proceedings of the IEEE/CVF Conference on Computer Vision and Pattern Recognition (CVPR)
24. Mousavian, A., Anguelov, D., Flynn, J., Kosecka, J.: 3D bounding box estimation using deep learning and geometry. In: IEEE Conference on Computer Vision and Pattern Recognition (2017)
25. Peng, X., Zhu, X., Wang, T., Ma, Y.: SIDE: center-based stereo 3D detector with structure-aware instance depth estimation. In: Proceedings of the IEEE/CVF Winter Conference on Applications of Computer Vision, pp. 119–128 (2022)
26. Reading, C., Harakeh, A., Chae, J., Waslander, S.L.: Categorical depth distribution network for monocular 3D object detection. In: CVPR (2021)

27. Roddick, T., Kendall, A., Cipolla, R.: Orthographic feature transform for monocular 3D object detection. CoRR abs/1811.08188 (2018). https://arxiv.org/abs/1811.08188

28. Shi, S., Wang, X., Li, H.: PointRCNN: 3D object proposal generation and detection from point cloud. In: IEEE Conference on Computer Vision and Pattern Recognition (2019)

29. Shi, X., Ye, Q., Chen, X., Chen, C., Chen, Z., Kim, T.K.: Geometry-based distance decomposition for monocular 3D object detection. In: IEEE International Conference on Computer Vision (2021)

30. Simonelli, A., Bulo, S.R., Porzi, L., Kontschieder, P., Ricci, E.: Are we missing confidence in pseudo-lidar methods for monocular 3D object detection? In: Proceedings of the IEEE/CVF International Conference on Computer Vision, pp. 3225–3233 (2021)

31. Simonelli, A., Buló, S.R., Porzi, L., Ricci, E., Kontschieder, P.: Towards generalization across depth for monocular 3D object detection. In: Vedaldi, A., Bischof, H., Brox, T., Frahm, J.-M. (eds.) ECCV 2020. LNCS, vol. 12367, pp. 767–782. Springer, Cham (2020). https://doi.org/10.1007/978-3-030-58542-6_46

32. Simonelli, A., Buló, S.R.R., Porzi, L., López-Antequera, M., Kontschieder, P.: Disentangling monocular 3D object detection. In: IEEE International Conference on Computer Vision (2019)

33. Sun, J., et al.: Disp R-CNN: stereo 3D object detection via shape prior guided instance disparity estimation. In: Proceedings of the IEEE/CVF Conference on Computer Vision and Pattern Recognition, pp. 10548–10557 (2020)

34. Teed, Z., Deng, J.: DeepV2D: video to depth with differentiable structure from motion. arXiv preprint arXiv:1812.04605 (2018)

35. Wang, T., Xinge, Z., Pang, J., Lin, D.: Probabilistic and geometric depth: detecting objects in perspective. In: Conference on Robot Learning, pp. 1475–1485. PMLR (2022)

36. Wang, T., Zhu, X., Lin, D.: Reconfigurable voxels: a new representation for lidar-based point clouds. In: Conference on Robot Learning (2020)

37. Wang, T., Zhu, X., Pang, J., Lin, D.: FCOS3D: fully convolutional one-stage monocular 3D object detection. In: Proceedings of the IEEE/CVF International Conference on Computer Vision (ICCV) Workshops (2021)

38. Wang, Y., Chao, W.L., Garg, D., Hariharan, B., Campbell, M., Weinberger, K.Q.: Pseudo-lidar from visual depth estimation: bridging the gap in 3D object detection for autonomous driving. In: IEEE Conference on Computer Vision and Pattern Recognition (2019)

39. Xiao, F., Lee, Y.J.: Video object detection with an aligned spatial-temporal memory. In: Ferrari, V., Hebert, M., Sminchisescu, C., Weiss, Y. (eds.) ECCV 2018. LNCS, vol. 11212, pp. 494–510. Springer, Cham (2018). https://doi.org/10.1007/978-3-030-01237-3_30

40. Xu, B., Chen, Z.: Multi-level fusion based 3D object detection from monocular images. In: IEEE Conference on Computer Vision and Pattern Recognition (2018)

41. Xu, Z., et al.: ZoomNet: part-aware adaptive zooming neural network for 3D object detection. In: Proceedings of the AAAI Conference on Artificial Intelligence, vol. 34, pp. 12557–12564 (2020)

42. Yan, Y., Mao, Y., Li, B.: Second: sparsely embedded convolutional detection. Sensors **18**(10), 3337 (2018)

43. Yoon, J.S., Kim, K., Gallo, O., Park, H.S., Kautz, J.: Novel view synthesis of dynamic scenes with globally coherent depths from a monocular camera. In: Pro-

ceedings of the IEEE/CVF Conference on Computer Vision and Pattern Recognition, pp. 5336–5345 (2020)

44. Zhang, Y., Lu, J., Zhou, J.: Objects are different: flexible monocular 3D object detection. In: Proceedings of the IEEE/CVF Conference on Computer Vision and Pattern Recognition (CVPR) (2021)

45. Zhou, Y., Tuzel, O.: VoxelNet: end-to-end learning for point cloud based 3D object detection. In: IEEE Conference on Computer Vision and Pattern Recognition (2018)

46. Zhu, X., Ma, Y., Wang, T., Xu, Y., Shi, J., Lin, D.: SSN: shape signature networks for multi-class object detection from point clouds. In: Vedaldi, A., Bischof, H., Brox, T., Frahm, J.-M. (eds.) ECCV 2020. LNCS, vol. 12370, pp. 581–597. Springer, Cham (2020). https://doi.org/10.1007/978-3-030-58595-2_35

47. Zhu, X., Dai, J., Yuan, L., Wei, Y.: Towards high performance video object detection. In: Proceedings of the IEEE Conference on Computer Vision and Pattern Recognition, pp. 7210–7218 (2018)

48. Zhu, X., Wang, Y., Dai, J., Yuan, L., Wei, Y.: Flow-guided feature aggregation for video object detection. In: Proceedings of the IEEE International Conference on Computer Vision, pp. 408–417 (2017)

49. Zou, Z., et al.: The devil is in the task: exploiting reciprocal appearance-localization features for monocular 3D object detection. In: Proceedings of the IEEE/CVF International Conference on Computer Vision (ICCV) (2021)

DISP6D: Disentangled Implicit Shape and Pose Learning for Scalable 6D Pose Estimation

Yilin Wen[1(✉)], Xiangyu Li[2], Hao Pan[3(✉)], Lei Yang[1,4],
Zheng Wang[5], Taku Komura[1], and Wenping Wang[6]

[1] The University of Hong Kong, Hong Kong, China
`ylwen@hku.hk`
[2] Brown University, Providence, USA
[3] Microsoft Research Asia, Beijing, China
[4] Centre for Garment Production Limited, Hong Kong, China
[5] SUSTech, Shenzhen, China
[6] Texas A&M University, College Station, USA

Abstract. Scalable 6D pose estimation for rigid objects from RGB images aims at handling multiple objects and generalizing to novel objects. Building on a well-known auto-encoding framework to cope with object symmetry and the lack of labeled training data, we achieve scalability by disentangling the latent representation of auto-encoder into shape and pose sub-spaces. The latent shape space models the similarity of different objects through contrastive metric learning, and the latent pose code is compared with canonical rotations for rotation retrieval. Because different object symmetries induce inconsistent latent pose spaces, we re-entangle the shape representation with canonical rotations to generate shape-dependent pose codebooks for rotation retrieval. We show state-of-the-art performance on two benchmarks containing textureless CAD objects without category and daily objects with categories respectively, and further demonstrate improved scalability by extending to a more challenging setting of daily objects across categories.

Keywords: 6D pose estimation · Scalability · Disentanglement · Symmetry ambiguity · Re-entanglement · Sim-to-real

1 Introduction

Estimating the 6D pose of objects from a single RGB image is fundamental in fields like robotics and scene understanding. While efficient learning-based methods have been developed [27,45,57], a common assumption with many of

Work partially done during internships of Y. Wen and X. Li with Microsoft Research Asia. Code and data are available at: https://github.com/fylwen/DISP-6D.

Supplementary Information The online version contains supplementary material available at https://doi.org/10.1007/978-3-031-20077-9_24.

S. Avidan et al. (Eds.): ECCV 2022, LNCS 13669, pp. 404–421, 2022.
https://doi.org/10.1007/978-3-031-20077-9_24

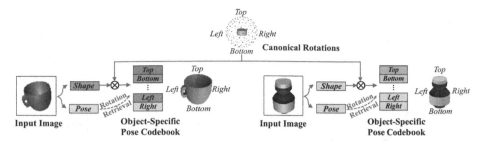

Fig. 1. Disentanglement for pose estimation. Images of objects are mapped to latent representations for object shape and pose, respectively. Due to different object symmetries, query pose codes must refer to object-specific pose codebooks (symmetries marked by code color) for rotation retrieval, which are generated by re-entangling canonical rotations with object shapes.

these works is that a specialized network is trained for each object, which makes it expensive to process multiple objects by switching and streaming to respective networks, and renders it impossible to handle novel objects without re-training.

Recent works improve the capability of a single network for processing multiple objects through different ways. For example, a series of works [7,51,54] perform category-level pose estimation, by learning to map input pixels (and point clouds) to corresponding points of a canonically aligned object, and computing pose registration based on the correspondences. However, these works assume that the space of canonically aligned objects for a given category is sufficiently regular to learn with neural networks, which does not hold for different objects across categories. Moreover, the point-wise correspondences are ambiguous under object symmetries, which may hinder the performance of these methods. On the other hand, Multipath-AAE [46] builds on the auto-encoding framework [47,48] to learn pose embeddings for different objects, by using a specific decoder for each object. Therefore Multipath-AAE is not restricted by the categorical shape alignment regularity, yet the network complexity becomes prohibitive as the number of training objects gets large. In addition, the single latent representation encoding mixed information of diverse objects under different poses may not be sufficiently accurate for pose estimation.

We present DISP6D − an approach to train a single network that processes more objects simultaneously (Fig. 2). As we build on the auto-encoding framework [48], objects do not need category labels and the symmetry ambiguity is automatically handled. Meanwhile, we extend [48] by *disentangling* object shape and pose in the latent representation; therefore we avoid per-object decoders and reduce the network training complexity significantly. The disentanglement allows the latent pose code of an arbitrary object to be compared with a pose codebook indexed by canonical rotations for retrieval of the object rotation (see Figs. 1, 2), where the learned latent poses are more accurate for RGB-based pose estimation than codes mixing shape and pose information.

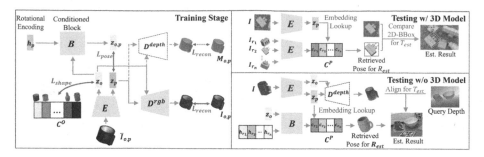

Fig. 2. Network structures in the training (left) and testing stage (right) for different settings. If testing objects have available 3D models (or not), we train an RGB decoder only (or plus a depth decoder) (left). During test stage, object rotation is *purely RGB-based estimation* by retrieving from the codebook $\mathcal{C}^P$, which is constructed by encoding the given object views (top right), or by shape code conditioned generation (bottom right). Translation is computed by pinhole camera (top right) or by depth comparison (bottom right).

Learning such a disentangled representation faces a critical challenge: the different symmetries of objects do not admit one pose codebook applicable to all objects. To understand this difficulty, consider that the cup in Fig. 1 has distinctive codes for representing the left and right views, but the rotational symmetry of the bottle demands an identical code for the two views. This exemplifies the frequent infeasibility of disentangling an input image into *independent* latent factors by a neural network [3], the factors being shape and pose in our case.

To solve this dependent disentanglement problem, we model the shape-pose dependency by introducing a module that *re-entangles* the shape and rotation and generates an object-conditioned pose codebook respecting the object symmetry, against which the query latent pose code is compared for pose retrieval. In addition, to facilitate generalization to novel objects, we take advantage of the decoupled latent shape space and apply contrastive metric learning, which encourages objects with similar geometry to have similar shape codes. By training the system with diverse shapes, novel objects can be robustly processed by referring to similar training objects with proximate latent shape codes.

We evaluate our approach by training on synthetic data only and testing on real data. Our approach allows for evaluations of two different settings proposed by previous works, i.e., the textureless CAD objects without category labels proposed by [46] and the daily objects with specified categories by [54], on which we compare favorably than state-of-the-art methods that similarly work with RGB images for rotation estimation. In addition, we extend to a more challenging setting of daily objects without leveraging the category information by mixing the objects from [54], on which our approach preserves competitive performance. These results demonstrate the improved scalability of our method. Finally, extensive ablation studies confirm the effectiveness of disentangled shape and pose learning and other design choices.

2   Related Works

6D Pose Estimation. There is a massive literature on instance-level pose estimation from RGB(D) images (see [31] for a survey). These works can be roughly classified into three streams, i.e., by direct pose regression [2,27,57], by registering 2D and 3D points [4,21,32,40,42,45,49], and by template retrieval [20,47,48,55,59]. For instance-level pose estimation, learning-based methods train a specialized network for each testing object.

Wang *et al.* [54] propose a shared 3D shape space (NOCS) for all instances from the same category, where the objects are pre-aligned and normalized into a common coordinate system. Variations among the instances in the NOCS space are expected to be smooth and predictable, to make the NOCS mapping learnable when trained on large scale categorical datasets like ShapeNet [5]. For pose estimation, the pixels of a detected object are mapped to 3D points in the NOCS space, which are registered with the input depth image to find the 6D rigid transformation along with scaling. Grabner *et al.* [14] use a similar canonical object coordinate representation for category level 3D model retrieval.

Subsequent works improve the categorical pipeline by modeling the shape differences inside a category adaptively, with many of them fusing depth with RGB input for more accurate translation and scale estimation [6,7,9,11,33,51]. Specifically, within the RGB-input domain, Chen *et al.* [11] propose an analysis-by-synthesis approach to minimize the difference between the input image and a 2D object view synthesized by neural rendering, by gradient descent on both shape and pose variables. All these category-level approaches train different network branches for each category to learn and utilize the intra-category shape consistency.

In comparison, our scalable approach can accommodate categories of different symmetries with a common network path that learns the inter- and intra-categorical features adaptively (Fig. 1). Similarly, StarMap [61] and PoseContrast [58] work on the cross-category setting for estimating only the 3D rotation; however, they do not address object symmetries. LatentFusion [39] does not assume categorical objects either, but requires multiple view images for neural reconstruction before pose estimation.

Multipath-AAE [46] works under a different assumption: the novel test objects share little shape consistency with training objects but have 3D models available, which is practical for industrial manufacturing settings. Multipath-AAE extends the augmented auto-encoder approach [48] by sharing an encoder to learn the latent pose embedding and assigning to each object a separate decoder, which bypasses the large shape differences across objects and enables auto-encoding. The shared encoder therefore learns pose-aware features that generalize to different objects. This setting is followed by Pitteri *et al.* [43] who use learned local surface embedding for pose estimation, and Nguyen *et al.* [37] who improve robustness by modeling occlusion. Compared with [46], our disentanglement of shape and pose allows the auto-encoding without multi-path decoders for different objects, thus making the framework more scalable. However, the disentanglement into independent factors is challenging to learn and we propose re-entanglement to generate shape conditioned pose codebook for feasible learning.

Disentangled Representation Learning. Disentangled representations are a key objective for interpretable and generalizable learning [1,34]. Previous works encourage disentangled representation learning by unsupervised learning [10,18]. Recently, focus has been given to the conditions under which learned representations can be disentangled [17,28,35], with the finding that quite frequently the direct mapping to disentangled independent factors is unattainable for neural networks [3]. Our discussion on scalable 6D pose estimation exemplifies the situation: the disentanglement of object shape and pose as independent factors is prevented by different object symmetries. We provide a solution to the disentanglement problem by re-entangling the independent factors so that a neural network mapping can be learned.

3   Method

As shown in Fig. 2, our overall framework is an auto-encoder that learns to encode an RGB image of the observed object to its latent shape code and object-dependent pose code separately, where the latent pose code is compared with a codebook of implicit rotation representations for fast pose estimation. Therefore, our approach obtains the object rotation purely from RGB input; depth input and reconstruction are optionally used only to remove translation/scale ambiguity when the object size is unknown (Sect. 4).

3.1   Disentangled Shape and Pose Learning

Given the input RGB image $\mathbf{I}_{o,p} \in \mathbb{R}^{3 \times H \times W}$ for an object o under pose $p \in$ SE(3), the encoder E maps $\mathbf{I}_{o,p}$ to a low-dimensional latent code $E(\mathbf{I}_{o,p}) = (\mathbf{z}_o, \mathbf{z}_p) \in \mathbb{R}^{2d}$ with $d \ll H \times W$, where $\mathbf{z}_o, \mathbf{z}_p \in \mathbb{R}^d$ encode the implicit shape and pose representations, respectively.

The decoder D^{rgb} tries to recover the input image from latent codes. Since we expect $\mathbf{z}_o$ and $\mathbf{z}_p$ to encode the overall object appearance and the view-specific appearance respectively, we borrow ideas from generative models [12,25,26] and use the AdaIN modulation [24] in the decoder to condition the per-view reconstruction on the object code; the detailed decoder structure can be found in the supplementary document. Moreover, we have tested by switching the roles of $\mathbf{z}_o$ and $\mathbf{z}_p$ for the decoder and found degraded performance (see supplemental).

Since we use only synthetic data for training, to narrow the domain gap between synthetic and real data, we follow [46,47] and adopt data augmentations that randomly change the color and scaling of an input image $\mathbf{I}$ to obtain the augmented image $\bar{\mathbf{I}}$, and aim to recover the canonical image $\mathbf{I}$ by auto-encoding. The loss function of the auto-encoding task therefore is

$$L_{recon} = \sum_{o,p} ||\mathbf{I}_{o,p} - D^{rgb}(E(\bar{\mathbf{I}}_{o,p}))||^2. \tag{1}$$

Note that our design accommodates different objects by sharing the same pair of encoder-decoder E and D^{rgb}, and hence is different from [46] that assigns to each object an individual decoder and previous instance-level approaches that train a specialized network for each object.

3.2   Contrastive Metric Learning for Object Shapes

The key to the generalization of pose estimation to a novel object is to exploit its similarity with the training objects, so that its generated pose codebook (Sect. 3.3) can capture its symmetry by referring to that of similar training objects. To learn such similarity relationships, we build a metric space for the shape codes of training objects by contrastive metric learning [8,15,38,56].

Denote the training object set as $\mathcal{O} = \{o_i\}_{i \in [N_O]}$, where N_O is the number of training objects. Similar to [56], to learn the contrastive metric among shape codes, we establish a shape embedding $\mathcal{C}^O \in \mathbb{R}^{N_O \times d}$ containing codes $\{c_i \in \mathbb{R}^d\}_{i \in [N_O]}$, each corresponding to a training object. We then define the proximity of c_i to z_o in the form of probability distribution as

$$\Pr(c_i|z_o) = \frac{\exp(\hat{c}_i \cdot \hat{z}_o/\tau)}{\sum_{j=1}^N \exp(\hat{c}_j \cdot \hat{z}_o/\tau)} \quad (2)$$

where $\tau = 0.07$ is a temperature parameter controlling the sharpness of the distribution, and $\hat{a} = \frac{a}{\|a\|}$ denotes normalized unit-length vectors.

The target distribution given o is simply a one-hot vector $w^o \in \{0,1\}^{N_O}$, with $w_i^o = 1$ if $o = o_i$ and the rest entries being zero. The contrastive metric loss for learning the shape space is then defined as

$$L_{shape} = -\sum_{o,p} \sum_{i=1}^{N_O} w_i^o \log \Pr(c_i|z_o). \quad (3)$$

To minimize the above loss, while z_o is updated by the SGD solver during each training step, we update the shape embedding $\mathcal{C}^O$ by the exponential moving average (EMA) with decay rate d_s, thus making c_o a smoothed history of z_o. Details of the EMA update can be found in the supplementary document.

3.3   Re-entanglement of Shape and Pose

The pose code z_p is compared with a codebook of sampled canonical orientations to retrieve the object rotation (Figs. 1, 2). As noted in Fig. 1, different object symmetries demand object-specific pose codebooks. To generate such a conditioned pose codebook, we propose a distributed representation of rotations and a transformation that entangles rotations with shape code in a generalizable way.

Rotational Position Encoding. We need to distinguish between different rotations in a canonical pose representation. Inspired by the positional encoding in sequence models [53], we have adopted the 4D hyper spherical harmonics

(HSH) rotation encoding. The HSH is a set of orthogonal basis functions on the 4D hypersphere that mimic the sine/cosine wave functions for positional encoding in sequence models: it is a distributed vector representation that can extend to high dimensions ($d = 128$ in our case), has a multi-spectrum structure that encodes both high frequency and low frequency variations of rotations, and has periodic structures with fixed linear transformations for relative rotations [41,60]. Denoting the HSH function as $Z_{nl}^m(\beta, \theta, \phi)$, with $\beta \in [0, 2\pi]$, $\theta \in [0, \pi]$, $\phi \in [0, 2\pi]$ as the in-plane rotation, zenith and azimuth angles respectively and l, m, n as polynomial degrees, we obtain the 128-dim vector encoding h_p by ranging over $n \in [0, \cdots, 6]$ with $0 \leq l \leq n$, $0 \leq m \leq l$. Details of the construction can be found in the supplemental document.

Conditioned Pose Code Generation. We design a conditional block B to entangle the object code z_o with the rotational position encoding h_p of rotation p and output a pose code $z_{o,p} = B(z_o, h_p)$ comparable with z_p (Fig. 2).

Entanglement is a recurring topic in machine learning, with implementation techniques like parameter generation [12,44,52] that boil down to a tensor product structure [36,50]. Therefore, we introduce a 3rd-order learnable tensor $\mathbf{W} \in \mathbb{R}^{d \times d \times d}$ and apply the following two-step transformation B to obtain the entangled pose code:

$$z'_{o,p} = \mathbf{W}(FC(sg(z_o)), FC(h_p)), \quad z_{o,p} = \text{FFN}(z'_{o,p}), \tag{4}$$

where $FC(sg(z_o)), FC(h_p) \in \mathbb{R}^d$ are the pre-processing of z_o and h_p, $sg(\cdot)$ is to stop gradient back-propagation as the shape code z_o is a pre-condition not to be updated by pose learning (see Sect. 5.5, Table 2 for an ablation), and $\mathbf{W}(\cdot, \cdot)$ denotes the tensor contraction along its first two orders. A feed-forward residual block FFN is followed to generate the final pose code $z_{o,p}$.

To synchronize the pose representation computed via the conditional block with that learned by the encoder, we minimize the cosine distance between $z_{o,p}$ and z_p during training:

$$L_{pose} = -\sum_{o,p} \hat{z}_{o,p} \cdot \hat{z}_p. \tag{5}$$

In summary, our total training loss combines the reconstruction loss (Eq. (1)), the contrastive loss for shape space (Eq. (3)) and the synchronization loss between pose representations from B and E (Eq. (5)), with weights λ_1, λ_2:

$$L = L_{recon} + \lambda_1 L_{shape} + \lambda_2 L_{pose}.$$

4 Inference Under Different Settings

In the test stage, we estimate rotation purely from RGB input, which takes three steps (Fig. 2, right): Given the query image crop $\mathbf{I}$ bounding the object of interest, we first obtain its latent shape and pose codes as $(z_o, z_p) = E(\mathbf{I})$, then build a pose embedding $\mathcal{C}^P \in \mathbb{R}^{N_P \times d}$ with each row $c_q \in \mathbb{R}^d$ corresponding to the rotation q from a set of N_P canonical rotations $\mathcal{R} \subset SO(3)$, and finally retrieve the estimated pose as $q^* = \arg\max_{q \in \mathcal{R}} \hat{z}_p \cdot \hat{c}_q$. Translation (and scale) is estimated subsequently, which may use depth data to remove scale ambiguity.

Previous works on scalable pose estimation towards novel objects have assumed two different application scenarios as discussed below, on which our framework can be flexibly adapted and achieve state-of-the-art performances. We also present an extended setting to better explore the scalability of our approach.

Setting I: Novel Objects in a Given Category. A series of works [11,51,54] assume that the novel testing objects are from a specific category but have no 3D models available. Therefore, for pose retrieval we compute $\mathcal{C}^P = \{B(z_o, h_q)\}_{q \in \mathcal{R}}$ from the sampled canonical rotations $\mathcal{R}$ and the shape code z_o.

As the testing objects have no specific sizes in this setting, to remove the 2D-3D scale ambiguity and estimate translation and scale properly, we require the input depth map and compare it with a decoded canonical depth map. The estimation of translation and scale involves a simple outlier point removal process and mean depth comparison for translation estimation and bounding box comparison for scale estimation; for details please refer to the supplemental document. As shown in Fig. 2, the depth decoder D^{depth} is simply an additional branch parallel to the RGB decoder, supervised to reconstruct a canonical depth map $\mathbf{M}_{o,p} \in \mathbb{R}^{1 \times H \times W}$ for the rotated object at a fixed distance away from the camera. The reconstruction loss in Eq. (1) is updated to be:

$$L_{recon} = \sum_{o,p} ||\mathbf{I}_{o,p} - D^{rgb}(E(\bar{\mathbf{I}}_{o,p}))||^2 + ||\mathbf{M}_{o,p} - D^{depth}(E(\bar{\mathbf{I}}_{o,p}))||^2 \quad (6)$$

Comparison in Sect. 5.2 shows our improved rotation accuracy and robustness to object symmetries.

Setting II: Novel Objects with 3D Models. Multipath-AAE [46] works with a set of CAD objects with drastic geometric differences and no specific category consistency. However, the 3D models of novel testing objects are accessible, as is common in applications like industrial manufacturing [43,46].

In this setting, we follow previous auto-encoding frameworks [46,48] to construct an offline pose codebook with the CAD model. Specifically, we first render images $\mathbf{I}_q$ of the given object under the reference orientations q and then obtain $\mathcal{C}^P = \{z_q\}_{q \in \mathcal{R}}$, with z_q the pose code part of $E(\mathbf{I}_q)$. Given the physical size and camera intrinsics, translation is obtained purely from RGB input with the pinhole camera model. The decoder D^{rgb} is not used during the test stage. As shown in Sect. 5.4, our disentangled auto-encoder learns highly discriminative pose encoding that performs even better than per-object trained auto-encoders, and generalizes well to novel objects with largely different shapes.

Setting III (Extension): Novel Objects across Categories without 3D Models. We further challenge our method on an extension of setting I by combining objects of all categories in [54] into one set. Without referring to predefined category labels in training and testing, the task has never been addressed

	NOCS [54]	Chen et al. [11]	Ours-per	Ours-all	
Only synthetic training data	×	✓	✓	✓	
Only RGB for rotation est.	×	✓	✓	✓	
Extension to cross-category	×	×	×	✓	

Fig. 3. Scope of compared methods on settings I and III (left), and qualitative cases of *Ours-per* (right). *All methods use query depth for translation estimation.*

before in previous works [11,51,54]. As shown in Sect. 5.3, our disentangled auto-encoder enables a straightforward extension to this cross-category setting with marginal performance degrading compared to setting I, which demonstrates the scalability of our approach.

5   Experiments

5.1   Setup

We resize the input images to $H \times W = 128 \times 128$, use a latent code dimension $d = 128$, and set $d_s = 0.9995$ for the EMA decay, $\lambda_1 = 0.004$, $\lambda_2 = 0.002$ for balancing the loss terms. We use the Adam optimizer [29] with default parameters and a learning rate of 0.0002, and train 50k iterations for settings I, II, and 150k iterations for setting III, with a batch size of 64 to convergence. Detailed network structure and training data preparation are in the supplementary document.

5.2   Setting I: Novel Objects in a Given Category

Dataset and Metrics. The benchmark of [54] has two parts, i.e., CAMERA containing synthetic data and REAL275 containing real data, that span 6 categories of objects (*bottle, bowl, camera, can, laptop, mug*) situated in daily indoor scenes. Furthermore, the objects in a category have diverse scales, and due to the inherent 2D-3D scale ambiguity, the estimation of translation plus scaling is only possible when additional cues like depth are given.

We use the synthetic CAMERA dataset with 1085 objects for training and evaluate on the real test set of REAL275, and follow [11] to report the average precision (AP) at different thresholds of rotation and translation errors. Note that while [11] uses input depth for improved translation estimation, it assumes a fixed scale and thus does not address scale estimation. Nevertheless, for completeness we report our scale estimation result by measuring 3D IoU precision in the supplemental document.

Baselines. The most relevant baseline is [11], as both methods train on synthetic data only and test on real data, and estimate rotation based on RGB input

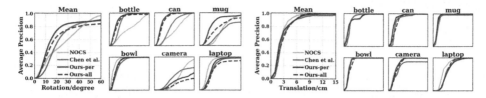

Fig. 4. Comparison on REAL275 of average precision (ranging from 0 to 1) at different rotation error (left, ranging from 0 to 60°) or translation error (right, ranging from 0 to 15 cm) thresholds. We report *Ours-per* of setting I per-category level and *Ours-all* of setting III combining all 6 categories.

only and use depth only for translation estimation. Another baseline is the earlier [54], which however trains on both real and synthetic data and relies on input depth for rotation estimation. All three methods use the same 2D detection backbone Mask-RCNN adopted from [54]. We summarize the differences in scopes of three methods in Fig. 3(left) where our method in this setting is denoted *Ours-per*, and defer an empirical discussion of more category-level methods taking RGB-D input for rotation estimation [6,7,33,51] to the supplemental.

Pose Codebook. 5K reference rotations are obtained by K-means clustering on the CAMERA training set rotations. Generating a pose codebook from 5K HSH codes takes 0.04 s on a GTX 1080 GPU and can be batched for more objects.

Results. As shown in Fig. 4, compared with Chen *et al.* [11], our rotation estimation has increased AP with a significant margin when the error threshold is below 40°; meanwhile, both methods have comparable performances on translation estimation. Compared with NOCS [54], our margin is even more significant throughout the range of 10° to 45° for rotation estimation. Qualitative results are visualized in Fig. 3. Among the different categories, we perform better in the classes of bottle, can and mug, which have strong partial symmetries and our method handles robustly. However, the camera category poses difficulty to our method; the main reason is that subtle textures are needed to distinguish vastly different poses, e.g., the front and back of a camera are quite similar for flat lens, but there are few objects out of the totally 74 objects in training set to cover such texture diversities. In comparison, both [11] and [54] use optimization to search for rotation and are more resilient to severe train/test disparities. For scale estimation, our 3D IoU accuracy is comparable to [54] (see supplemental).

5.3 Setting III (Extension): Novel Objects Across Categories Without 3D Models

We further challenge our method on the extended setting that combines all 6 categories of the NOCS benchmark into one set, without referring to category labels in training and testing; the trained network is denoted *Ours-all*. As we learn a metric shape space without the need for category labels (Sect. 3.2), we expect our method to extend to this cross-category setting without much difficulty.

As shown in Fig. 4, for rotation estimation, *Ours-all* achieves improved results than Chen *et al.* [11] for error thresholds <28°, and NOCS [54] for error thresholds in 10°–40°, even though [11,54] train per-category network modules to exploit the intra-category consistency. Meanwhile, the lower performance compared with *Ours-per* can be attributed to the confusion of shape-conditioned pose learning introduced by the increased cross-category shape variances, as for example under certain views a mug with an occluded handle looks quite similar to a can or bowl, but they are forced to generate pose codes with different symmetries. Qualitative cases are given in the supplemental.

Although none of the previous works [11,54] are designed to address this setting, for a better understanding of the challenge, we adapt and retrain NOCS [54] by using a single head for all categories (*i.e., NOCS-all*); without per-category correspondence consistency, we find that *NOCS-all* performs poorly especially for rotation estimation. We also retrain PoseContrast [58] under our setting, which is the state-of-the-art for cross-category rotation estimation. Results show that [58] does not handle objects with different symmetries as well as we do. Details are given in the supplemental.

5.4 Setting II: Novel Objects with 3D Models

Dataset and Metrics.   Following [46], we evaluate on T-LESS [22] which contains 30 textureless industrial parts with very different shapes and symmetries (see the supplementary for a visualization). Accuracy is measured by the recall rate of visible surface discrepancy metric $e_{VSD} < 0.3$ [23] at distance tolerance 20 mm, among test instances with visible portion >10%.

Baselines.   We compare with Multipath-AAE [46], Pitteri *et al.* [43], and Nguyen *et al.* [37]. All these methods share the same setting by training jointly on only the first 18 objects and testing on all 30 objects, using CAD models from TLESS.

Pose Codebook.   We follow [46–48] to build for each test object an offline pose codebook with 92232 reference rotations, that is formed by combining 36 in-plane rotations and 2562 equidistant spherical views sampled via [19].

Results.   We first report in Table 1(a) the accuracy for all test instances with 2D GT bounding boxes. We outperform Multipath-AAE [46] by 4% on average for the novel objects (*i.e.,* Obj 19–30) and 5% for the trained objects (*i.e.,* Obj 1–18), although Multipath-AAE [46] assigns separate decoders for the 18 training objects and optionally uses the GT mask to eliminate background noise for better performances. We also outperform the concurrent work by Nyugen *et al.* [37]. For a more complete evaluation, we further compare with [47,48] which train for each of the 30 objects a specific auto-encoder, and find our result still outperforms it by 3% on the 18 training objects of ours. These results show that our disentanglement learning improves the auto-encoder framework and

Table 1. Comparison on T-LESS. Reported are the average recall rates with $e_{VSD} < 0.3$. All methods were trained with only the first 18 objects, except AAE [47,48] which trains individual networks for each of the 30 objects.

(a) w/ 2D GT bboxes, † for using GT mask

Ave. on	Obj 1-18	Obj 19-30	Obj 1-30
AAE[47,48]	62.57	**66.63**	64.19
Multipath-AAE[46]	51.75	52.49	52.04
Multipath-AAE[46]†	60.75	59.89	60.41
Nguyen *et al.*[37]	59.62	57.75	58.87
Ours	**66.14**	64.42	**65.45**

(b) w/ MaskRCNN [16] detection.

Ave. on	Obj 1-30
Multipath-AAE[46]	23.51
Pitteri *et al.* [43]	23.27
Ours	**35.36**

Fig. 5. Qualitative results on T-LESS of setting II. We denote our estimations in blue (trained objects) and red (unseen objects), and GT poses in green. (Color figure online)

generalizes to objects with different shapes and symmetries (see Sect. 5.5, Fig. 6 for detailed analysis).

We then report in Table 1(b) the evaluation under the full 2D detection and pose estimation pipeline, by adopting Mask-RCNN [16] from [30] as the 2D detector and following the single object single instance protocol [23]. Our result improves over that of the comparing methods by a significant margin of around 12%. Our qualitative cases are in Fig. 5 and the per-object recall rates are given in the supplementary.

Instance-Level Estimation. Although we focus on scalable pose estimation for novel test objects, it is possible to apply our framework to an instance-level task where all test objects are given for training. We provide such a limit case study in the supplementary, and compare with more instance-level pose estimation methods on the BOP leader board [21,30,32,40,47,48]. Our approach provides fast yet accurate pose estimations that can be further improved by refinement.

5.5 Ablation Study

Shape Conditioned Pose Code Generation. We first discuss the necessity to generate shape-dependent pose codes. To this end, we separate shape codes from pose codebook generation by replacing the 3rd-order tensor $\mathbf{W}$ in Eq. (4) with a multi-layer perceptron MLP that takes only the HSH encoding as input, *i.e.* $\text{MLP}(FC(\boldsymbol{h}_p))$. The MLP has four layers of width $[1024, 1024, 1024, 128]$ and thus more trainable weights than $\mathbf{W}$. The average precision on setting III reported in Table 2 (2nd, 6th rows) shows that the performance significantly drops when

Table 2. Ablation tests on the design of shape conditioned pose code generation and contrastive learning for object shape. Reported are mAP at different rotation error thresholds (in degrees) for mixed categories of REAL275 (setting III).

Design of B	w/ L_{shape}	AP_5	AP_{10}	AP_{15}	AP_{20}	AP_{30}	AP_{60}
MLP$(FC(h_p))$	✓	4.7	15.7	28.9	36.9	47.0	72.4
MLP$(FC(sg(z_o)), FC(h_p))$	✓	7.5	27.3	47.8	61.8	74.9	84.3
$\mathbf{W}(FC(z_o), FC(h_p))$	✓	6.6	26.6	47.8	62.0	**76.6**	**87.5**
$\mathbf{W}(FC(sg(z_o)), FC(h_p))$	✗	2.8	15.2	33.6	48.9	67.6	81.3
$\mathbf{W}(FC(sg(z_o)), FC(h_p))$	✓	**9.1**	**30.9**	**50.7**	**64.4**	75.3	84.3

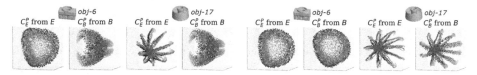

(a) w/o shape condition   (b) w/ shape condition

Fig. 6. Top three PCA projections of pose codes $\mathcal{C}_E^P$ **and** $\mathcal{C}_B^P$ from encoder E and condition block B for two T-LESS objects. Point colors (blue→green→red) encode rotations as viewpoints change from north pole to south pole. The shape conditioned pose codes well capture the symmetries and synchronize with encoder outputs (b), but unconditioned pose codes fail (a). (Color figure online)

the shape code is separated from pose code generation, indicating the difficulty of learning independent latent representations of shape and pose.

To further visualize the effectiveness of pose code generation, given an object o, we inspect two sets of latent pose representations: $\mathcal{C}_E^P = \{z_p\}_{p \in \mathcal{R}}$ generated by the encoder E and $\mathcal{C}_B^P = \{z_{o,p}\}_{p \in \mathcal{R}}$ by the conditioned block B. $\mathcal{R}$ has 8020 rotations from a combination of 20 in-plane rotations and 401 quasi-equidistant views sampled via [13]. Ideally, the two sets of latent codes should coincide with each other, so that they can be compared for effective rotation estimation.

We show in Fig. 6 for two T-LESS training objects: the box-like Obj-6 and the cylinder-like Obj-17, where with our entanglement of shape and pose information, $\mathcal{C}_B^P$ well synchronize with $\mathcal{C}_E^P$ for objects with different degrees of symmetry, though for Obj-6 a global rotation of the PCA projections between $\mathcal{C}_B^P$ and $\mathcal{C}_E^P$ exists due to the nearly isotropic distribution of latent codes. On the contrary, when the shape code is isolated from generating the pose codebook, it becomes difficult for $\mathcal{C}_B^P$ to follow the pattern of $\mathcal{C}_E^P$ for different objects. Such contrast demonstrates the necessity of our entanglement. We further discuss in the supplementary for objects with texture solving the rotational ambiguity, where our pose codes can well capture the textural difference.

We then move on to validate the design of combining pose and shape. An intuitive idea is to simply concatenate the shape and pose rotational encoding and process by an MLP, *i.e.* MLP$(FC(sg(z_o)), FC(h_p))$, with MLP having

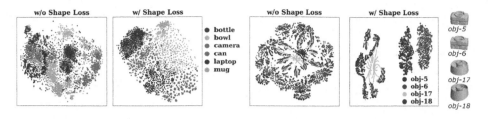

Fig. 7. t-SNE embedding of shape codes z_o for training images of six CAMERA categories (left) and four T-LESS objects (right). With contrastive metric learning the shape spaces show better regularity w.r.t. shape similarities.

four layers of width $[1024, 1024, 1024, 128]$. The comparison in Table 2 (3rd, 6th rows) shows that the 3rd-order tensor outperforms MLP, thus verifying our design choice.

Finally, we validate the necessity to treat z_o as a pre-condition for pose code generation, by allowing gradients to be backpropagated through the conditioned pose code generation module to z_o instead. Table 2, 4th and 6th rows, show that pre-conditioning by stop gradient $sg(z_o)$ performs better for rotation error thresholds $\leq 20°$, demonstrating its recognition of subtle pose differences.

Contrastive Metric Learning for Object Shapes. The mAP in Table 2 (5th, 6th rows) demonstrates our gain from the contrastive metric learning of the shape space, where with the shape loss L_{shape} the generalization to unseen objects is significantly improved. We also visualize the shape codes z_o with t-SNE in Fig. 7, for training samples from the CAMERA objects and 4 T-LESS objects. With shape space metric learning, we observe much better intra-category clustering and inter-category separation on CAMERA, though the network is unaware of category labels in this setting (setting III). For the T-LESS objects, the introduction of L_{shape} not only well separates the box-like objects (Obj-5,6) from the cylinder-like objects (Obj-17,18), but also recognizes the detailed geometric differences between Obj-5 and Obj-6; in comparison, the shape codes for different objects are mixed together without shape space metric learning.

6   Conclusion

We have presented a simple yet scalable approach for 6D pose estimation that generalizes to novel objects unseen during training. Building on an auto-encoding framework that handles object symmetry robustly, we achieve scalability by disentangling the latent code into shape and pose representations, where the shape representation forms a metric space by contrastive learning to accommodate novel objects, and the pose code is compared with canonical rotations for pose estimation. As disentanglement into independent shape and pose spaces is fundamentally difficult due to different object symmetries, we re-entangle shape code with pose codebook generation to avoid the issue. We obtain state-of-the-art results on two established settings when training with synthetic data only, and extend to a cross-category setting to further demonstrate scalability.

Limitation and Future Work. We mainly focus on learning for rotation estimation from a single RGB image, while the translation estimation can be further improved by fully exploiting the input depth with neural networks, as discussed in [33,51]. Extending to multiview input for improved robustness under severe occlusion and inaccurate 2D detection is also a promising direction.

Acknowledgements. This work was partially supported by the Innovation and Technology Commission of the HKSAR Government under the InnoHK initiative.

References

1. Bengio, Y., Courville, A., Vincent, P.: Representation learning: a review and new perspectives. IEEE Trans. Pattern Anal. Mach. Intell. **35**(8), 1798–1828 (2013)
2. Billings, G., Johnson-Roberson, M.: SilhoNet: an RGB method for 3D object pose estimation and grasp planning. arXiv preprint arXiv:1809.06893 (2018)
3. Bouchacourt, D., Ibrahim, M., Deny, S.: Addressing the topological defects of disentanglement via distributed operators (2021)
4. Brachmann, E., Michel, F., Krull, A., Ying Yang, M., Gumhold, S., et al.: Uncertainty-driven 6d pose estimation of objects and scenes from a single RGB image. In: Proceedings of the IEEE Conference on Computer Vision and Pattern Recognition, pp. 3364–3372 (2016)
5. Chang, A.X., et al.: ShapeNet: an information-rich 3D model repository (2015)
6. Chen, D., Li, J., Wang, Z., Xu, K.: Learning canonical shape space for category-level 6D object pose and size estimation. In: Proceedings of the IEEE/CVF Conference on Computer Vision and Pattern Recognition (CVPR), June 2020
7. Chen, K., Dou, Q.: SGPA: structure-guided prior adaptation for category-level 6d object pose estimation. In: Proceedings of the IEEE/CVF International Conference on Computer Vision, pp. 2773–2782 (2021)
8. Chen, T., Kornblith, S., Norouzi, M., Hinton, G.: A simple framework for contrastive learning of visual representations. In: International Conference on Machine Learning, pp. 1597–1607. PMLR (2020)
9. Chen, W., Jia, X., Chang, H.J., Duan, J., Shen, L., Leonardis, A.: FS-Net: fast shape-based network for category-level 6D object pose estimation with decoupled rotation mechanism. In: Proceedings of the IEEE/CVF Conference on Computer Vision and Pattern Recognition, pp. 1581–1590 (2021)
10. Chen, X., Duan, Y., Houthooft, R., Schulman, J., Sutskever, I., Abbeel, P.: Info-GAN: interpretable representation learning by information maximizing generative adversarial nets. In: Advances in Neural Information Processing Systems, vol. 29, pp. 2172–2180 (2016)
11. Chen, X., Dong, Z., Song, J., Geiger, A., Hilliges, O.: Category level object pose estimation via neural analysis-by-synthesis. In: Vedaldi, A., Bischof, H., Brox, T., Frahm, J.-M. (eds.) ECCV 2020. LNCS, vol. 12371, pp. 139–156. Springer, Cham (2020). https://doi.org/10.1007/978-3-030-58574-7_9
12. Dumoulin, V., et al.: Feature-wise transformations. Distill **3**(7), e11 (2018)
13. González, Á.: Measurement of areas on a sphere using Fibonacci and latitude-longitude lattices. Math. Geosci. **42**(1), 49 (2010)

14. Grabner, A., Roth, P.M., Lepetit, V.: Location field descriptors: single image 3D model retrieval in the wild. In: 2019 International Conference on 3D Vision (3DV), pp. 583–593. IEEE (2019)
15. He, K., Fan, H., Wu, Y., Xie, S., Girshick, R.: Momentum contrast for unsupervised visual representation learning. In: Proceedings of the IEEE Conference on Computer Vision and Pattern Recognition (CVPR) (2020)
16. He, K., Gkioxari, G., Dollár, P., Girshick, R.: Mask R-CNN. In: Proceedings of the IEEE International Conference on Computer Vision (ICCV), pp. 2961–2969 (2017)
17. Higgins, I., et al.: Towards a definition of disentangled representations. arXiv preprint arXiv:1812.02230 (2018)
18. Higgins, I., et al.: beta-VAE: learning basic visual concepts with a constrained variational framework. In: ICLR (2017)
19. Hinterstoisser, S., Benhimane, S., Lepetit, V., Fua, P., Navab, N.: Simultaneous recognition and homography extraction of local patches with a simple linear classifier. In: BMVC, pp. 1–10 (2008)
20. Hinterstoisser, S., et al.: Model based training, detection and pose estimation of texture-less 3D objects in heavily cluttered scenes. In: Lee, K.M., Matsushita, Y., Rehg, J.M., Hu, Z. (eds.) ACCV 2012. LNCS, vol. 7724, pp. 548–562. Springer, Heidelberg (2013). https://doi.org/10.1007/978-3-642-37331-2_42
21. Hodaň, T., Baráth, D., Matas, J.: EPOS: estimating 6D pose of objects with symmetries. In: IEEE Conference on Computer Vision and Pattern Recognition (CVPR) (2020)
22. Hodaň, T., Haluza, P., Obdržálek, Š., Matas, J., Lourakis, M., Zabulis, X.: T-LESS: an RGB-D dataset for 6D pose estimation of texture-less objects. In: IEEE Winter Conference on Applications of Computer Vision (WACV) (2017)
23. Hodaň, T., et al.: BOP: benchmark for 6D object pose estimation. In: Ferrari, V., Hebert, M., Sminchisescu, C., Weiss, Y. (eds.) ECCV 2018. LNCS, vol. 11214, pp. 19–35. Springer, Cham (2018). https://doi.org/10.1007/978-3-030-01249-6_2
24. Huang, X., Belongie, S.: Arbitrary style transfer in real-time with adaptive instance normalization. In: Proceedings of the IEEE International Conference on Computer Vision, pp. 1501–1510 (2017)
25. Karras, T., Laine, S., Aila, T.: A style-based generator architecture for generative adversarial networks. In: Proceedings of the IEEE/CVF Conference on Computer Vision and Pattern Recognition, pp. 4401–4410 (2019)
26. Karras, T., Laine, S., Aittala, M., Hellsten, J., Lehtinen, J., Aila, T.: Analyzing and improving the image quality of StyleGAN. In: Proceedings of the IEEE/CVF Conference on Computer Vision and Pattern Recognition, pp. 8110–8119 (2020)
27. Kehl, W., Manhardt, F., Tombari, F., Ilic, S., Navab, N.: SSD-6D: making RGB-based 3D detection and 6D pose estimation great again. In: Proceedings of the IEEE International Conference on Computer Vision, pp. 1521–1529 (2017)
28. Khemakhem, I., Kingma, D., Monti, R., Hyvarinen, A.: Variational autoencoders and nonlinear ICA: a unifying framework. In: Proceedings of International Conference on Artificial Intelligence and Statistics. Proceedings of Machine Learning Research, vol. 108. PMLR (2020)
29. Kingma, D.P., Ba, J.: Adam: a method for stochastic optimization. arXiv preprint arXiv:1412.6980 (2014)
30. Labbé, Y., Carpentier, J., Aubry, M., Sivic, J.: CosyPose: consistent multi-view multi-object 6D pose estimation. In: Vedaldi, A., Bischof, H., Brox, T., Frahm, J.-M. (eds.) ECCV 2020. LNCS, vol. 12362, pp. 574–591. Springer, Cham (2020). https://doi.org/10.1007/978-3-030-58520-4_34

31. Lepetit, V.: Recent advances in 3D object and hand pose estimation. arXiv preprint arXiv:2006.05927 (2020)
32. Li, Z., Wang, G., Ji, X.: CDPN: coordinates-based disentangled pose network for real-time RGB-based 6-DoF object pose estimation. In: Proceedings of the IEEE International Conference on Computer Vision, pp. 7678–7687 (2019)
33. Lin, J., Wei, Z., Li, Z., Xu, S., Jia, K., Li, Y.: DualPoseNet: category-level 6D object pose and size estimation using dual pose network with refined learning of pose consistency. arXiv preprint arXiv:2103.06526 (2021)
34. Locatello, F., Abbati, G., Rainforth, T., Bauer, S., Schölkopf, B., Bachem, O.: On the fairness of disentangled representations. In: Advances in Neural Information Processing Systems, vol. 32. Curran Associates, Inc. (2019)
35. Locatello, F., et al.: Challenging common assumptions in the unsupervised learning of disentangled representations. In: Chaudhuri, K., Salakhutdinov, R. (eds.) Proceedings of International Conference on Machine Learning. Proceedings of Machine Learning Research, vol. 97. PMLR (2019)
36. Martyn, J., Vidal, G., Roberts, C., Leichenauer, S.: Entanglement and tensor networks for supervised image classification (2020)
37. Nguyen, V.N., Hu, Y., Xiao, Y., Salzmann, M., Lepetit, V.: Templates for 3D object pose estimation revisited: generalization to new objects and robustness to occlusions. In: Proceedings of the IEEE/CVF Conference on Computer Vision and Pattern Recognition (CVPR), pp. 6771–6780, June 2022
38. van den Oord, A., Li, Y., Vinyals, O.: Representation learning with contrastive predictive coding. arXiv preprint arXiv:1807.03748 (2018)
39. Park, K., Mousavian, A., Xiang, Y., Fox, D.: LatentFusion: end-to-end differentiable reconstruction and rendering for unseen object pose estimation. In: Proceedings of the IEEE Conference on Computer Vision and Pattern Recognition (2020)
40. Park, K., Patten, T., Vincze, M.: Pix2Pose: pixel-wise coordinate regression of objects for 6d pose estimation. arXiv preprint arXiv:1908.07433 (2019)
41. Pasha Hosseinbor, A., et al.: 4D hyperspherical harmonic (HyperSPHARM) representation of surface anatomy: a holistic treatment of multiple disconnected anatomical structures. Med. Image Anal. **22**(1), 89–101 (2015)
42. Peng, S., Liu, Y., Huang, Q., Zhou, X., Bao, H.: PVNet: pixel-wise voting network for 6dof pose estimation. In: Proceedings of the IEEE Conference on Computer Vision and Pattern Recognition, pp. 4561–4570 (2019)
43. Pitteri, G., Bugeau, A., Ilic, S., Lepetit, V.: 3D object detection and pose estimation of unseen objects in color images with local surface embeddings. In: 15th Asian Conference on Computer Vision, Kyoto (virtual conference), Japan, November 2020
44. Platanios, E.A., Sachan, M., Neubig, G., Mitchell, T.: Contextual parameter generation for universal neural machine translation. In: Proceedings of the 2018 Conference on Empirical Methods in Natural Language Processing, pp. 425–435 (2018)
45. Rad, M., Lepetit, V.: BB8: a scalable, accurate, robust to partial occlusion method for predicting the 3D poses of challenging objects without using depth. In: Proceedings of the IEEE International Conference on Computer Vision, pp. 3828–3836 (2017)
46. Sundermeyer, M., et al.: Multi-path learning for object pose estimation across domains. In: Proceedings of the IEEE Conference on Computer Vision and Pattern Recognition, pp. 13916–13925 (2020)

47. Sundermeyer, M., Marton, Z.-C., Durner, M., Brucker, M., Triebel, R.: Implicit 3D orientation learning for 6D object detection from RGB images. In: Ferrari, V., Hebert, M., Sminchisescu, C., Weiss, Y. (eds.) ECCV 2018. LNCS, vol. 11210, pp. 712–729. Springer, Cham (2018). https://doi.org/10.1007/978-3-030-01231-1_43

48. Sundermeyer, M., Marton, Z.C., Durner, M., Triebel, R.: Augmented autoencoders: implicit 3D orientation learning for 6D object detection. Int. J. Comput. Vis., 1–16 (2019)

49. Tekin, B., Sinha, S.N., Fua, P.: Real-time seamless single shot 6d object pose prediction. In: Proceedings of the IEEE Conference on Computer Vision and Pattern Recognition, pp. 292–301 (2018)

50. Tenenbaum, J.B., Freeman, W.T.: Separating style and content with bilinear models. Neural Comput. **12**(6), 1247–1283 (2000). https://doi.org/10.1162/089976600300015349

51. Tian, M., Ang, M.H., Lee, G.H.: Shape prior deformation for categorical 6D object pose and size estimation. In: Vedaldi, A., Bischof, H., Brox, T., Frahm, J.-M. (eds.) ECCV 2020. LNCS, vol. 12366, pp. 530–546. Springer, Cham (2020). https://doi.org/10.1007/978-3-030-58589-1_32

52. Tian, Z., Shen, C., Chen, H.: Conditional convolutions for instance segmentation. In: Vedaldi, A., Bischof, H., Brox, T., Frahm, J.-M. (eds.) ECCV 2020. LNCS, vol. 12346, pp. 282–298. Springer, Cham (2020). https://doi.org/10.1007/978-3-030-58452-8_17

53. Vaswani, A., et al.: Attention is all you need. In: Advances in Neural Information Processing Systems, vol. 30. Curran Associates, Inc. (2017)

54. Wang, H., Sridhar, S., Huang, J., Valentin, J., Song, S., Guibas, L.J.: Normalized object coordinate space for category-level 6d object pose and size estimation. In: Proceedings of the IEEE Conference on Computer Vision and Pattern Recognition, pp. 2642–2651 (2019)

55. Wen, Y., Pan, H., Yang, L., Wang, W.: Edge enhanced implicit orientation learning with geometric prior for 6d pose estimation. IEEE Rob. Autom. Lett. (IROS) **5**(3), 4931–4938 (2020)

56. Wu, Z., Xiong, Y., Yu, S.X., Lin, D.: Unsupervised feature learning via nonparametric instance discrimination. In: Proceedings of the IEEE Conference on Computer Vision and Pattern Recognition (CVPR), pp. 3733–3742 (2018)

57. Xiang, Y., Schmidt, T., Narayanan, V., Fox, D.: PoseCNN: a convolutional neural network for 6D object pose estimation in cluttered scenes. arXiv preprint arXiv:1711.00199 (2017)

58. Xiao, Y., Du, Y., Marlet, R.: PoseContrast: class-agnostic object viewpoint estimation in the wild with pose-aware contrastive learning. In: 2021 International Conference on 3D Vision (3DV), pp. 74–84 (2021). https://doi.org/10.1109/3DV53792.2021.00018

59. Zhang, H., Cao, Q.: Detect in RGB, optimize in edge: accurate 6d pose estimation for texture-less industrial parts. In: 2019 International Conference on Robotics and Automation (ICRA), pp. 3486–3492. IEEE (2019)

60. Zhao, L.: Spherical and spheroidal harmonics: examples and computations (2017)

61. Zhou, X., Karpur, A., Luo, L., Huang, Q.: StarMap for category-agnostic keypoint and viewpoint estimation. In: Ferrari, V., Hebert, M., Sminchisescu, C., Weiss, Y. (eds.) ECCV 2018. LNCS, vol. 11205, pp. 328–345. Springer, Cham (2018). https://doi.org/10.1007/978-3-030-01246-5_20

Distilling Object Detectors with Global Knowledge

Sanli Tang[1], Zhongyu Zhang[1], Zhanzhan Cheng[1(✉)], Jing Lu[1], Yunlu Xu[1], Yi Niu[1], and Fan He[2]

[1] Hikvision Research Institute, Hangzhou, China
{tangsanli,zhangzhongyu,chengzhanzhan,lujing6,xuyunlu,
niuyi}@hikvision.com
[2] Institute of Image Processing and Pattern Recognition, Shanghai Jiao Tong University, Shanghai, China
hf-inspire@sjtu.edu.cn

Abstract. Knowledge distillation learns a lightweight student model that mimics a cumbersome teacher. Existing methods regard the knowledge as the feature of each instance or their relations, which is the instance-level knowledge only from the teacher model, i.e., the *local* knowledge. However, the empirical studies show that the *local* knowledge is much noisy in object detection tasks, especially on the blurred, occluded, or small instances. Thus, a more intrinsic approach is to measure the representations of instances w.r.t. a group of *common* basis vectors in the two feature spaces of the teacher and the student detectors, i.e., *global* knowledge. Then, the distilling algorithm can be applied as space alignment. To this end, a novel prototype generation module (PGM) is proposed to find the *common* basis vectors, dubbed *prototypes*, in the two feature spaces. Then, a robust distilling module (RDM) is applied to construct the global knowledge based on the prototypes and filtrate noisy local knowledge by measuring the discrepancy of the representations in two feature spaces. Experiments with Faster-RCNN and RetinaNet on PASCAL and COCO datasets show that our method achieves the best performance for distilling object detectors with various backbones, which even surpasses the performance of the teacher model. We also show that the existing methods can be easily combined with global knowledge and obtain further improvement. Code is available: https://github.com/hikvision-research/DAVAR-Lab-ML.

Keywords: Object detection · Knowledge distillation

S. Tang and Z. Zhang—Authors contributed equally.

Supplementary Information The online version contains supplementary material available at https://doi.org/10.1007/978-3-031-20077-9_25.

1   Introduction

Object detectors can be enhanced by applying larger networks [13,21], which, however, will increase the storage and computational cost. A promising solution for finding the sweet spot between efficiency and performance is knowledge distillation (KD) [1,16], which learns a lightweight student that mimics the behaviors of a cumbersome teacher.

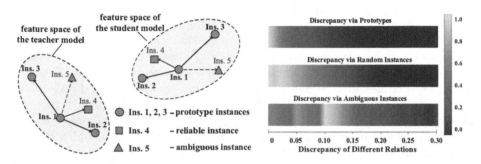

Fig. 1. Left: the prototypes are representative and play roles as a common group of basis vectors in *TS-space*. Although the absolute location of *Ins. 4* is different in *TS-space*, its representations, e.g., the relations, w.r.t. prototypes are similar while *Ins. 5* shows the representation of much dissimilar. **Right**: on COCO dataset [27] with Faster-RCNN detector [34], we show the discrepancy of relations between instances and three types of basis in *TS-space*. 10 instances are selected for each class as the bases and others are used for measuring the discrepancy of relations in *TS-space*. The relations with *prototypes* show much smaller discrepancy than others.

The knowledge can be known to be formed in three categories [10]: feature-based knowledge [15,35,41,43,44], response-based knowledge [16,23,32], and relation-based knowledge [4,24,29,32,40]. Such knowledge can be treated as the *local* knowledge, since only the instance-level knowledge from a single feature space, e.g., the teacher's, is considered. Based on these knowledge, existing methods design their distilling algorithms for object detection tasks based on some prior senses, e.g., the foreground regions [41], the decoupled background regions [11], the attention guided regions [22,44], or the discrepancy regions [4,22]. However, we find that the local knowledge is of much discrepancy between the teacher and the student in object detection tasks, especially on the ambiguous instances which are blur, truncated, or small. This is because features of ambiguous instances are susceptible to the small disturbance in feature spaces of the teacher and the student. Thus, the distilling process will suffer from the noisy local knowledge, e.g., the false positives and the localization errors, and lead to sub-optimal.

The main concerns on relieving the effect of noisy local knowledge are two folds: constructing reliable global knowledge and applying robust distilling algorithms. By viewing knowledge as the representation of feature space, a more intrinsic approach is to find a group of common basis vectors in both the feature spaces of the teacher and the student detectors. In this way, the *global* knowledge can be formed by representing the instances w.r.t. these basis vectors. Then, a more robust distilling algorithm can be designed by measuring the discrepancy of the representations in the two feature spaces. Hereafter, we name the two feature spaces of the teacher and the student detector as *TS-space* and the common basis vectors of the TS-space as *prototypes*.

In Fig. 1 (left), we illustrate that: (1) the representations of normal instances w.r.t. the prototypes are of the little discrepancy between two feature spaces, e.g., the *Ins.4*; (2) the discrepancy of the ambiguous instances is much larger than others, e.g., the *Ins. 5*. In Fig. 1 (right), we show the statistic analysis of the discrepancy of the instance representations in *TS-space* on the COCO dataset. Notice that each instance is represented by a pair of features in the *TS-space*. Thus, we first measure the cosine similarity between the bases and each of the other instances in the *TS-space*, and then calculate the discrepancy by l_1 distance as shown by the abscissa. In Fig. 1 (right), the discrepancy of relations between prototypes and other instances is much smaller than other bases, which shows a more promising representation of the knowledge in *TS-space*.

Based on the above considerations, we first propose a prototype generation module (PGM) to find a group of common basis vectors as the prototypes in *TS-space*. It selects the prototypes according to minimizing the reconstruction errors of the instances in the two feature spaces, which is inspired by the dictionary learning [20,31,39]. Then, a robust distillation module (RDM) is designed for robust knowledge construction and transfer. Based on the prototypes, the global knowledge is formed by representing the instances under the prototypes, which shows a smaller gap between the two spaces as in Fig. 1 (right). The discrepancy of the representations in *TS-space* can also be regarded as an ensemble of the two models to mitigate noisy local knowledge transferring when distilling. Experiments are carried out with both single-stage (RetinaNet [26]) and two-stage detectors (Faster R-CNN [34]) on Pascal VOC [7] and COCO [27] benchmarks. Extensive experimental results show that the proposed method can effectively improve the performance of knowledge distillation, which achieves new remarkable performance. We also show the existing methods can be further improved by the prototypes with global and local knowledge.

2 Related Works

2.1 Object Detection

Existing object detection methods based on deep neural networks can be divided into anchor-based and anchor-free detectors. The anchor-based detectors use the preset boxes as anchors, which are trained to classify their categories and regress the offsets of coordinates. They can be further divided into multi-stage [9,34] and single-stage [8,28,33] detectors. As the representative multi-stage detector, Faster R-CNN [34] uses a region proposal network to generate proposals that probably contain objects and then predicts their categories and refines the proposals in the second stage. Considering the large computation cost of the multi-stage detectors, YOLO [33], as the representative single-stage detector, is proposed to use a fully convolutional network to predict both the bounding boxes and categories. It is further improved by applying feature pyramid [28], deconvolutional layers [8] and focal loss [26] to treat the various object scales, the semantic information of features, and the unbalance of positives and negatives, respectively. Many anchor-free detectors [38,47] are proposed to avoid empirically setting and tedious calculation of the anchors. Although applying deeper and wider networks can often improve the performance of detectors, it is too computationally expensive in many resource-limited applications.

2.2 Knowledge Distillation

Knowledge distillation [14,16,45] is proposed by Hinton et al. [16] in the image classification task to transfer knowledge of a cumbersome teacher model into a compact student model. There are two main aspects of knowledge distillation: knowledge construction and knowledge transfer. For the first aspect, knowledge mainly consists of three types [10]: the feature-based knowledge, i.e., activations of intermediate feature [15,17,35,43], the relation-based knowledge, i.e., structures in the embedding space [24,29,32,37,40], and the response-based knowledge, i.e., the soft target of the output layers [16]. For the second aspect to effectively transfer the knowledge to the student. [16] applies a temperature factor to control the softness of the probability distribution over classes. [35] adds a regression layer as a bridge to match dimensions of the features. Such knowledge can be viewed as local knowledge since only the instance-level knowledge in the single feature space, e.g., the teacher's is considered.

For distilling an object detector [3,11,22,44,46], more attention is paid on *constructing knowledge* due to the extreme imbalance over the foreground/background areas and the numbers of instances among different classes. [41] aims at keeping the balance between foreground and background features by distilling on the areas around ground-truth boxes, while [23] distills on high-level features within the equivalently sampled foreground and background proposals by referring to the ground-truth boxes. [4] is recently proposed to distill features in anchors where there are the most discrepancies of confidence between the student and the teacher model. [36] proposes to gradually reduce the distillation penalty to balance the two targets of detection and distillation. However, existing methods regard the activations or the relations between all instances as the local knowledge to distill object detectors, which suffers from the noises, e.g., the ambiguous instances or the detection errors from the teacher.

3 Method

In this section, we detail the proposed framework for distilling object detectors with global knowledge. As shown in Fig. 2, the overall framework consists of two modules: a prototype generation module (PGM) to find class-wise prototypes for bridging the two feature spaces, and a robust distilling module (RDM) to construct and distill the reliable global knowledge based on the prototypes.

3.1 Prototype Generation Module

The knowledge of a deep model can be viewed as the representation of its feature space, which can be approximated by a small set of basis vectors from the view of dictionary learning [20,39], as shown in Fig 1 (left). Concretely, let $F = \{f_i\}_{i=1}^N \in \mathbb{R}^{D \times N}$ be features of N instances in the feature space of D dimensions. The K ($K \ll N$) basis vectors $G = \{g_i\}_{i=1}^K \subset F$ of a single feature space can be selected by minimizing the reconstruction errors of all instances:

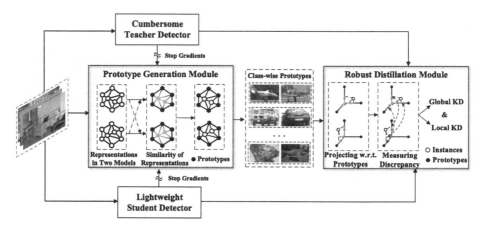

Fig. 2. The proposed framework for distilling object detectors with global knowledge. A prototype generation module (PGM) is first deployed to find the prototypes for each class based on the similarity of their representations in *TS-space*. A robust distillation module (RDM) is then designed to construct reliable global knowledge w.r.t. the prototypes and measure their discrepancy for robust knowledge distillation.

$$G,\ W = \arg\min_{G,W} ||F - GW||_2^2 + \lambda ||W||_1^2, \tag{1}$$

where $W \in \mathbb{R}^{K \times N}$ is the representation of all samples F w.r.t. the basis vectors G. The last regularized term weighted by λ helps to learn a sparse W, which makes the basis vectors G representative.

In the knowledge distillation task, there are two different feature spaces that are represented by the teacher and student detectors, namely *TS-space*. Thus, a more intrinsic approach is to find a group of common basis vectors in *TS-space*, which bridge the gap between the two spaces and reduce the difficulty of distillation. Following the above considerations, the prototype generation module (PGM) aims at finding K instances as the basis vectors, dubbed *prototypes*. In this way, other instances can be represented by prototypes with minimum reconstruction errors in each of the feature spaces. Meanwhile, the representing discrepancy based on the prototypes between two feature spaces should also be small such that it is easier to transform one feature space to another.

Let $F_t = \{f_i^t\}_{i=1}^N \in \mathbb{R}^{D_t \times N}$ and $F_s = \{f_i^s\}_{i=1}^N \in \mathbb{R}^{D_s \times N}$ be the N instances in the feature spaces of the teacher and the student detectors, respectively. D_t and D_s are the dimensions of the two feature spaces. The K prototypes can be grouped as $(G_t, G_s) = \{(g_i^t, g_i^s)\}_{i=1}^K$, where $G_t = F_{i(t)} \subset F_t$ and $G_s = F_{i(s)} \subset F_s$ are the subset of all instances in $TS\text{-}space$. $i(s)$, $i(t)$ are the indexing sets.

Notice that the prototypes are the common basis vectors of $TS\text{-}space$. Thus, they can be generated from all the instances by minimizing the reconstruction errors in both of the two feature spaces as well as a regularization of the representing consistency with a trade-off weight λ:

$$\|F_t - F_{i(t)}W_t\|_2^2 + \|F_s - F_{i(s)}W_s\|_2^2 + \lambda\|W_s - W_t\|_2^2$$
$$\text{s.t.}\quad i(s) = i(t) \quad \text{and} \quad |i(s)| = |i(t)| = K \tag{2}$$

$W_t = \{w_{j,i}^t\}_{K \times N}$ and $W_s = \{w_{j,i}^s\}_{K \times N}$ are the representations, i.e., coordinates, of the N instances w.r.t. the K prototypes in the feature spaces of the teacher and the student. The last term in Eq. 2 requires the representations of instances in $TS\text{-}space$ are similar such that the discrepancy of the relations is small, as illustrated in Fig. 1 (right). The constraint $i(s) = i(t)$ requires that a prototype is indeed one instance represented in two feature spaces, and total K prototypes are selected. In this way, representations of instances w.r.t. the prototypes can be regarded as approximations of the feature space, i.e., the global knowledge, as shown in Fig. 1 (left), which allows penalizing the difference of the relations between instances and prototypes in two feature spaces for knowledge transfer. Besides, the discrepancy of relations w.r.t. the prototypes can be used as the robustness cue for knowledge transfer, as illustrated in Fig. 1.

We show an approximate solution of the problem in Eq. 2 through a variant of matching pursuit [31], which is indeed a greedy algorithm yet very efficient. To select the $(n+1)^{\text{th}}$ prototype (g_{n+1}^t, g_{n+1}^s), we first define the residuals $r_{n,i}^t$ and $r_{n,i}^s$ w.r.t. the selected n prototypes as follows:

$$r_{n,i}^t \triangleq f_i^t - \sum_{k=1}^n g_k^t w_{k,i}^t, \quad r_{n,i}^s \triangleq f_i^s - \sum_{k=1}^n g_k^s w_{k,i}^s. \tag{3}$$

The objective in Eq. 2 w.r.t. the $(n+1)^{\text{th}}$ prototype can be written by

$$\mathcal{L}_{n+1} = \sum_{i=1}^N \|r_{n+1,i}^t\|_2^2 + \sum_{i=1}^N \|r_{n+1,i}^s\|_2^2 + \lambda \sum_{i=1}^N \sum_{k=1}^{n+1} (w_{k,i}^t - w_{k,i}^s)^2. \tag{4}$$

The optimal $w_{n+1,i}^t$ and $w_{n+1,i}^s$ can be obtained by making the derivative of the $\mathcal{L}_{n+1}$ with respect of $w_{n+1,i}^t$ and $w_{n+1,i}^s$ to zero. Then, we have

$$w_{n+1,i}^t = \frac{\langle r_{n,i}^t, g_{n+1}^t \rangle + \lambda w_{n+1,i}^s}{\lambda + \|g_{n+1}^t\|_2^2}, \quad w_{n+1,i}^s = \frac{\langle r_{n,i}^s, g_{n+1}^s \rangle + \lambda w_{n+1,i}^t}{\lambda + \|g_{n+1}^s\|_2^2}. \tag{5}$$

Algorithm 1. Algorithm for selecting prototypes in PGM.

Input:
$\{(\boldsymbol{f}_i^t, \boldsymbol{f}_i^s)\}_{i=1}^N$: features of N instances in *TS-space*;
Parameter:
K: number of prototypes to be selected;
λ: regularization weight;
Output:
$\mathcal{I}$: index set of the prototypes
1: initialize $n = 0$, the residuals $\boldsymbol{r}_{0,i}^t = \boldsymbol{f}_i^t$, and $\boldsymbol{r}_{0,i}^s = \boldsymbol{f}_i^s$ $\forall i = 1, \cdots, N$;
2: **while** $n < K$ **do**
3:     compute the optimal $w_{n+1,i}^s$ and $w_{n+1,i}^t$ by Eq. 5;
4:     compute the $\mathcal{L}_{n+1}^k$ with Eq. 4 for each instance by setting $\boldsymbol{g}_{n+1}^s = \boldsymbol{f}_k^s$ and $\boldsymbol{g}_{n+1}^t = \boldsymbol{f}_k^t$, $\forall k = 1, \cdots, N$;
5:     append the index k^* into $\mathcal{I}$ where $k^* = \arg\min_k \{\mathcal{L}_{n+1}^k\}$ $\forall$ $(\boldsymbol{g}_k^s, \boldsymbol{g}_k^t) \in \{(\boldsymbol{f}_i^s, \boldsymbol{f}_i^t)\}_{i=1}^N$; set $\boldsymbol{g}_{n+1}^t = \boldsymbol{f}_{k^*}^t$ and $\boldsymbol{g}_{n+1}^s = \boldsymbol{f}_{k^*}^s$;
6:     update the residuals $\boldsymbol{r}_{n+1,i}^t$ and $\boldsymbol{r}_{n+1,i}^s$ by Eq. 3;
7:     set $n = n + 1$;
8: **end while**
9: **Return:** $\mathcal{I}$

We detail the derivation and show the closed-form solution of Eq. 5 in the supplemental materials, where we also show more analysis about the relationship between global knowledge and relation-based knowledge. The overall algorithm for generating prototypes is summarized in Algorithm 1. Notice that we separately generate prototypes for each class.

3.2   Robust Distillation Module

In this section, we focus on *global knowledge construction* and *robust knowledge transferring* by a robust distillation module (RDM) based on the prototypes.

Identifying the Knowledge. By referring to the prototypes, the global knowledge, i.e., the representations of instances on the common basis vectors in the two feature spaces, can be naturally constructed by measuring the representation between the instances and the prototypes.

Specifically, let the features of the jth instance in the ith image be $\boldsymbol{f}_{i,j}^t$ and $\boldsymbol{f}_{i,j}^s$ in the feature spaces of the teacher and the student detectors, respectively. For an instance with a pair of features $(\boldsymbol{f}_{i,j}^t, \boldsymbol{f}_{i,j}^s)$ in *TS-space*, they can be separately projected onto the common basis vectors $(\boldsymbol{G}_t, \boldsymbol{G}_s)$ in each space as $\boldsymbol{\Lambda}_{i,j}^t = \mathcal{P}_{\boldsymbol{G}_t}(\boldsymbol{f}_{i,j}^t)$ and $\boldsymbol{\Lambda}_{i,j}^s = \mathcal{P}_{\boldsymbol{G}_s}(\boldsymbol{f}_{i,j}^s)$. $\mathcal{P}$ is the projection function. The project coefficients $\boldsymbol{\Lambda}_{i,j}^t$ and $\boldsymbol{\Lambda}_{i,j}^s$ can be calculated exactly the same as in Eq. 5.

Thus, the global knowledge can be transferred by minimizing:

$$\mathcal{L}_{\text{global}} = \frac{1}{2NK} \sum_{i=1}^{n} \sum_{j=1}^{n_i} \sigma_{i,j} \|\boldsymbol{\Lambda}_{i,j}^s - \boldsymbol{\Lambda}_{i,j}^t\|_2^2, \tag{6}$$

Algorithm 2. The proposed knowledge distilling process.

Input: teacher detector $\mathcal{T}$, student detector $\mathcal{S}$, prototype updating period T and maximum training epochs T_m.

1: let e be the current training epoch and set $e = 0$;
2: **while** $e < T_m$ **do**
3:    **if** mod$(e, \mathrm{T}) == 0$ **then**
4:        extract features of instances $\boldsymbol{F}_t$ and $\boldsymbol{F}_s$ from the teacher $\mathcal{T}$ and current student (at e-th epoch) $\mathcal{S}^e$, respectively;
5:        updating and bootstrapping prototypes $(\boldsymbol{G}_t, \boldsymbol{G}_s)$ for each class by minimizing Eq. 2 based on $\mathcal{T}$ and $\mathcal{S}^e$ (see Algorithm 1);
6:    **end if**
7:    training the student detector for one epoch by minimizing Eq. 9;
8:    set $e = e + 1$;
9: **end while**

---

where $N = \sum_{i=1}^{n} n_i$ are the total number of instances. n is the number of images and n_i is the number of instances in the i-th image. $\sigma_{i,j}$ is the weight that reveals how reliable the knowledge is and will be discussed later.

For the local feature-based knowledge, we follow [41] identifying the knowledge as the features of the regions that overlap with any ground-truth boxes larger than a threshold. Thus, the local feature-based knowledge can be defined as:

$$\mathcal{L}_{\mathrm{local}}^{\mathrm{feat}} = \frac{1}{2N} \sum_{i=1}^{n} \sum_{j=1}^{n_i} \sigma_{i,j} \|\mathcal{H}(\boldsymbol{f}_{i,j}^s) - \boldsymbol{f}_{i,j}^t\|_2^2, \tag{7}$$

where $\mathcal{H}$ is an adaptation function, e.g., a 1×1 convolutional layer with ReLU activation in our paper, that transforms the features of the student into the feature space of the same dimensions as the teacher's.

For the local response-based knowledge, we use the proposals and apply the RoI-align [34] to get the prediction inside the regions. The KL-divergence weighted by $\sigma_{i,j}$ is used on the predicting logits between the teacher and the student, and denoted as $\mathcal{L}_{\mathrm{local}}^{\mathrm{resp}}$.

Robustly Distilling the Knowledge. Since the knowledge from the teacher might be noisy, especially on ambiguous instances, a robust knowledge transferring approach is required to distinguish noisy knowledge and mitigate transferring them to the student. Inspired from co-teaching [12,18,30] to alleviate the noise from multiple views, the student might also have a voice in discriminating the noisy knowledge. Based on the observations that reliable knowledge should have similar representations under the measurement from two models, shown in Fig. 1, the robustness of knowledge can be estimated by the discrepancy of representations in *TS-space*. Thus, the weight $\sigma_{i,j}$ for fine-grained knowledge distillation can be approximated as

$$\sigma_{i,j} = 1 - \|\boldsymbol{\Lambda}_{i,j}^s - \boldsymbol{\Lambda}_{i,j}^t\|_2. \tag{8}$$

$\sigma_{i,j}$ describes the similarity of the representations between the instance and the prototypes in the *TS-space*. It is indeed heavily related to the last term in Eq. 2, where we concentrate more on the instances with small discrepancy w.r.t. the prototypes for both global and local knowledge transfer.

Table 1. Knowledge distillation results on COCO dataset with different detectors. Some results are missing since we cannot find the performance report in their papers.

Method	mAP	AP_{50}	AP_{75}	AP_s	AP_m	AP_l	mAR	AR_s	AR_m	AR_l
Faster-Res101 (teacher)	39.8	60.1	43.3	22.5	43.6	52.8	53.0	32.8	56.9	68.6
Faster-Res50 (student)	38.4	59.0	42.0	21.5	42.1	50.3	52.0	32.6	55.8	66.1
FGFI [41]	39.3	59.8	42.9	22.5	42.3	52.2	52.4	32.2	55.7	67.9
DeFeat [11]	40.3	60.9	**44.0**	23.1	44.1	**53.4**	53.7	33.3	57.7	69.1
FBKD [44]	40.2	60.4	43.6	22.8	43.8	53.2	53.4	32.7	57.1	68.8
GID [4]	40.2	60.8	43.6	**23.6**	43.9	53.0	53.7	33.6	57.7	68.6
Ours	**40.6**	**61.0**	**44.0**	23.4	**44.4**	53.3	**53.8**	**33.9**	57.9	**69.2**
Retina-Res101 (teacher)	38.9	58.0	41.5	21.0	42.8	52.4	54.8	33.4	59.3	71.2
Retina-Res50 (student)	37.4	56.7	39.6	20.0	40.7	49.7	53.9	33.1	57.7	70.2
FGFI [41]	38.6	58.7	41.3	21.4	42.5	51.5	54.6	34.7	58.2	70.4
GID [4]	39.1	**59.0**	42.3	**22.8**	43.1	52.3	55.3	**36.7**	59.1	71.1
DeFeat [11]	39.3	58.2	42.1	21.7	42.9	52.9	55.1	33.9	59.6	71.5
FBKD [44]	39.3	58.8	42.0	21.2	43.2	53.0	55.4	34.6	59.7	72.2
FR [5]	39.3	58.8	42.0	21.5	43.3	52.6	–	–	–	–
PFI [22]	39.6	–	–	21.4	44.0	52.5	–	–	–	–
Ours	**39.8**	58.6	**42.6**	21.8	**43.5**	**53.5**	**55.8**	34.1	**60.0**	**72.2**

3.3   Optimization

The overall objective for distilling object detectors can be summarized as:

$$\mathcal{L}_{kd} = \mathcal{L}_{det} + \alpha_1 \mathcal{L}_{global} + \alpha_2 \mathcal{L}_{local}^{feat} + \alpha_3 \mathcal{L}_{local}^{resp}, \tag{9}$$

where $\mathcal{L}_{det}$ is the original detection objective defined by the student detector. α_1, α_2, and α_3 weigh the global and local knowledge transfer. For detectors with FPN [25] using multiple feature maps for prediction, we independently apply the PGM and the RDM on each of the feature maps. Since the student is gradually optimized and the relations are changed, the prototypes should be updated when training the student. For efficiency, the prototypes are bootstrapped and updated every T epochs. Both the student and the teacher detectors are pretrained on the task-relevant dataset to extract features of instances and generate the prototypes. The overall proposed distilling algorithm is summarized in Algorithm 2.

4   Experiments

We perform experiments with the representative single-stage and two-stage detectors, namely, RetinaNet [26] and Faster R-CNN [34] on the PASCAL VOC [7] and COCO [27] detection benchmarks. We follow the common settings that use both VOC 07 and 12 *trainval* split for training and VOC 07 *test* split for test. For the COCO dataset, the *train* split are used for training while the *val* split are used for test. Unless otherwise specified, the hyper-parameters are set as $K = 10$, $\lambda = 10$ and $T = 1$. The distilling weights α_1, α_2, and α_3 are set to 1.0, 1.0, 5.0, respectively. The student detector is trained through 2× learning schedule on on 8 V100 32G GPUs. The input images are resized as large as 1333×800 while keeping the aspect ratio. Other standard augmentations, e.g., the photometric distortion, are applied as the settings in MMDetection [19]. The ResNet101 and ResNet50 [13] backbones are used for the teacher and the student detectors, respectively. We also validate our methods with larger teachers, e.g., Cascade Mask R-CNN [2] with ResNext-101 [42]. More implementation details are included in the supplemental material.

4.1   Comparison with Existing Methods on VOC and COCO Datasets

We first evaluate our method on VOC and COCO datasets with the representative two-stage detector (Faster R-CNN) and single-stage detector (RetinaNet). As shown in Table 1 and Table 2, all student models are significantly improved by our knowledge distillation algorithm, e.g., 2.2% and 2.4% mAP on the COCO dataset and 2.5% and 2.5% mAP on the VOC dataset for both detectors. Moreover, they even surpass the teacher detector within a large margin, e.g., 0.8%, 0.9% on COCO dataset for both detectors. As we form the global knowledge as the ensemble of both the student and the teacher detectors and use common basis vectors to bridge the two feature spaces for distilling, the proposed method shows more potential to achieve a further gain compared to the teacher detectors.

We also compare our method with the SOTA detection distillation methods with the same teacher and student detectors. Table 1 and Table 2 show that the proposed method achieves best mAP on COCO and VOC datasets. Notice that GID [4] applies all the three types of local knowledge, i.e., feature-based, relation-based, and response-based knowledge for distilling. However, the proposed method shows further improvement on both COCO and VOC datasets, e.g., 0.7% mAP gain for distilling the RetinaNet. It reveals that distilling the knowledge by forcing the student to absolutely behave the same as the teacher still leads to sub-optimal since the local knowledge represented by the ambiguous instances is hard to transfer and will hurt the distillation. The proposed method shows a more promising way by looking for a group of common basis vectors, i.e., the prototypes, for bridging the gap of the two feature spaces and forming as well as distilling the global knowledge based on the prototypes in a more robust

way. Moreover, the results in Table 1 and Table 2 demonstrate that our method
is capable to be applied to various detection frameworks.

4.2 Effects of the Prototypes in Robust Knowledge Distillation

To verify the advantages of the prototypes bridging the two feature spaces for
global and local knowledge distillation, we conduct ablation experiments on the
VOC dataset with 1× learning schedule. ResNet101-based and ResNet50-based
Faster R-CNN are used as the teacher and the student detectors, respectively.

We first separately apply $\mathcal{L}_{\text{global}}$, $\mathcal{L}_{\text{local}}^{\text{feat}}$ and $\mathcal{L}_{\text{local}}^{\text{resp}}$ in Eq. 9 for knowledge
distillation. In our framework, the global knowledge is formed as the projections
of instances w.r.t. the prototypes, while the feature-based and response-based
local knowledge is weighted through the discrepancy of the projections. Table 3
shows that the prototypes can boost the global and local knowledge distillation
by a large margin. By applying both the global and local knowledge, we show
1.6% performance gain compared to the student detector with the 1× learning
schedule, which also surpasses the teacher detector with the mAP 82.4%.

Table 2. Knowledge distillation results on Pascal VOC dataset with different detectors.

Method	Faster R-CNN Res101-50			RetinaNet Res101-50		
	mAP	AP_{50}	AP_{75}	mAP	AP_{50}	AP_{75}
Teacher	56.3	82.7	62.6	58.2	82.0	63.0
Student	54.2	82.1	59.9	56.1	80.9	60.7
FitNet [35]	55.0	82.2	61.2	56.4	81.7	61.7
FGFI [41]	55.3	82.1	61.1	55.6	81.4	60.5
FBKD [44]	55.4	82.0	61.3	56.7	81.9	61.9
ICD [22]	56.4	82.4	63.4	57.7	**82.4**	63.5
GID [4]	56.5	82.6	61.6	57.9	82.0	63.2
Ours	**56.7**	**82.9**	**61.9**	**58.6**	**82.4**	**64.2**

Table 3. Ablation experiment on separately applying the global knowledge $\mathcal{L}_{\text{global}}$, feature-based local knowledge $\mathcal{L}_{\text{local}}^{\text{feat}}$ and response-based local knowledge $\mathcal{L}_{\text{local}}^{\text{resp}}$ in Eq. 9 on VOC dataset with 1× learning schedule.

Module	Student	Faster R-CNN Res101-50					
$\mathcal{L}_{\text{local}}^{\text{feat}}$		✓			✓		✓
$\mathcal{L}_{\text{global}}$			✓			✓	✓
$\mathcal{L}_{\text{local}}^{\text{resp}}$				✓	✓	✓	✓
AP_{50}	81.3	82.0	82.4	82.2	82.6	82.4	**82.9**

Furthermore, we also extend some existing methods based on the prototypes. DeFeat [11], RKD [32] and Vanilla-KD [16] are the representative feature-
based, relation-based and response-based local knowledge distillation methods.
We directly use the released source codes of FBKD and carefully re-implement
the RKD (as RKD†) and Vanilla-KD as (Vanilla-KD†) for distilling the object
detectors. Then, we apply the prototypes separately: as for RKD [32], we form
the global knowledge by projecting the instances w.r.t. the prototypes; as for
DeFeat [11] and Vanilla-KD [16], we apply the distilling weight defined in Eq. 8,
which is measured by the discrepancy w.r.t. the prototypes. Table 4 shows the
consistent performance gain among those three knowledge distillation methods
with the prototypes, which shows the effectiveness of prototypes for both constructing more reliable global knowledge and more robust knowledge transfer.
The implementation details by combining prototypes with those distilling methods are included in the supplemental materials.

Table 4. Ablation experiment by combining the prototypes with the existing representative methods for feature-based [11], relation-based [32], and response-based [16]
local knowledge distillation, respectively.

Method	Student	DeFeat [11]		RKD† [32]		Vanilla-KD† [16]	
+prototypes			✓		✓		✓
AP$_{50}$	81.3	82.0	**82.4**	81.6	**82.0**	81.8	**82.2**

Table 5. Ablation experiments on the hyperparameters α_1, α_2, α_3, λ, K, and T.

α_1	0.1	0.5	1.0	1.2	α_2	0.5	0.8	1.0	1.5
AP$_{50}$	82.1	82.3	**82.9**	82.6	AP$_{50}$	82.3	82.4	**82.9**	82.6
α_3	1	5	10	20	λ	1	10	50	100
AP$_{50}$	82.3	**82.9**	82.3	82.2	AP$_{50}$	82.3	**82.9**	82.6	82.0
K	1	5	10	20	T	0.5	1	2	3
AP$_{50}$	82.0	82.3	**82.9**	82.5	AP$_{50}$	82.8	**82.9**	82.3	82.2

4.3   Analysis of the Hyperparameters

We investigate the updating periods T in Algorithm 2 of the prototypes for
knowledge distillation on the VOC dataset. Since the student detector is updated
during training, the prototypes and their features G_s should be updated. Table 5
shows that as the period T increasing, the performance slightly decreases. It is
because the bootstrapped prototypes are approximations of the basis vectors of
updated student detector, which results in some bias when forming the global
knowledge as well as computing the discrepancy in Eq. 8. Table 5 also shows
ablation experiments on the three weights α_1, α_2, and α_3 of the three terms

Table 6. Ablation experiments on the effect of different prototype generation methods for knowledge distillation. For the cluster-like algorithms, e.g., K-Means and DBSCAN [6], we apply them separately on the feature space of either the teacher or the student.

Method	K-Means		DBSCAN [6]		Ambiguous	Ours
Features	Student	Teacher	Student	Teacher	–	Both
AP_{50}	82.3	82.1	82.4	82.2	81.8	**82.9**

in Eq. 9, the number of selected prototypes K and the similarity regularization weight λ in Eq. 2. The results in Table 5 show that the proposed method is relatively robust to the hyperparameters, which achieves better performance than the student in a wide range of hyperparameters.

4.4   Analysis on the Prototype Generation Methods

In our framework, the prototypes play roles as the common basis vectors in both the feature spaces of the teacher and the student. They are selected by minimizing the reconstruction errors among instances in *TS-space* as defined in Eq. 2. We also compare the proposed prototype generation algorithm in Algorithm 1 with some other similar methods, e.g., the K-means and the DBSCAN [6]. Besides, we also deliberately select the same number of ambiguous instances, e.g., small or truncated instances, as the prototypes for comparison. In Table 6, we show the performance of knowledge distillation based on those prototype generation methods. We find that the cluster-like algorithms, e.g., the K-means or the DBSCAN [6], fail to improve the distillation by comparing the results in Table 3, because those algorithms are applied only in the single feature space and can hardly bridge the two feature spaces of the teacher and the student. The poor performance by selecting the ambiguous instances as the prototypes further verify the importance of selecting the representative instances as the prototypes. Otherwise, it will bring large discrepancy as shown in Fig. 1 (right), and increase the difficulty of knowledge distillation.

4.5   Distilling with Larger Teacher

The larger teacher will achieve better performance, which might also bring an extra bonus for knowledge distillation. Following the common settings with the existing methods [11,36,41], on the VOC dataset, we use the Faster R-CNN with the backbones ResNet152 and ResNet50 as the teacher and the student. For a fair comparison, we follow DeFeat [11] by using 1× learning schedule. On the COCO dataset, we follow FBKD [44] by applying ResNeXt101-based [42] Cascade Mask R-CNN [2] as the teacher detector and the ResNet50-based Faster R-CNN as the student. The 2× learning schedule is used as in FBKD [44]. In Table 8 and Table 7, we show the performance of knowledge distillation with larger teachers on VOC and COCO datasets, respectively. The proposed method can still achieve the best performance on the VOC dataset, with the 0.6% mAP advantage w.r.t. DeFeat [11]. On the COCO dataset, we achieve comparable performance as the FBKD [44] with the much larger teacher and heterogeneous backbone. The performance with larger teachers further shows the proposed method can be applied in various detection frameworks with the same hyperparameters.

4.6   Analysis of Noisy Knowledge Transferring

In Fig. 3, we also illustrate some wrong detection in red boxes, *e.g.*, false positives and inaccurately located instances, from the teacher detector that are transferred to the student. Our method shows more promising results against noisy knowledge transferring and is capable to surpass the performance of the teacher detector. More quantitative analysis is discussed in the supplementary.

Table 7. Knowledge distillation results with larger teacher on COCO dataset.

Method	Backbone	mAP	AP_{50}	AP_{75}	AP_s	AP_m	AP_l
Cascade R-CNN (teacher)	ResNext101	47.3	66.3	51.7	28.2	51.7	62.7
Faster R-CNN (student)	ResNet50	38.4	59.0	42.0	21.5	42.1	50.3
FBKD [44]	ResNet50	**41.5**	**62.2**	**45.1**	**23.5**	45.0	55.3
Ours	ResNet50	**41.5**	61.9	**45.1**	**23.5**	**45.1**	**55.4**

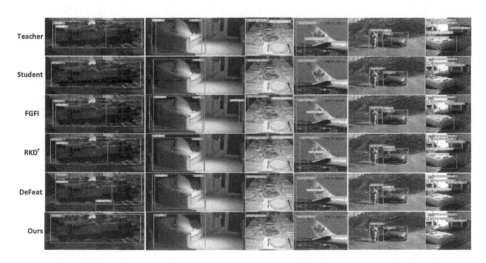

Fig. 3. Illustration of detection results via different knowledge distillation methods, e.g., FGIF [41], our re-implemented RKD [32], DeFeat [11], and ours. Some noisy knowledge of the teacher are transferred to the student (marked in red boxes). Best view in color.

Table 8. Knowledge distillation results with larger teacher on VOC dataset.

Method	Teacher	Student	Faster R-CNN ResNet152-50			
			FGFI [41]	TADF [36]	DeFeat [11]	Ours
AP_{50}	83.1	81.3	81.6	81.7	82.3	**82.9**

5 Conclusion

In this paper, we propose a novel knowledge distillation framework with global knowledge. The prototype generation module is first designed to find a group of common basis vectors, i.e., the *prototypes*, by minimizing the reconstruction errors in both the feature spaces of the teacher and the student. The robust distillation module is then applied to (1) construct the global knowledge by projecting the instances w.r.t. the prototypes, and (2) robustly distill the global and local knowledge by measuring their discrepancy in the two spaces. Experiments show that the proposed method achieves state-of-the-art performance on two popular detection frameworks and benchmarks. The extensive experimental results show that the proposed method can be easily stretched with larger teachers and the existing knowledge distillation methods to obtain further improvement.

References

1. Bucila, C., Caruana, R., Niculescu-Mizil, A.: Model compression. In: SIGKDD, pp. 535–541 (2006)
2. Cai, Z., Vasconcelos, N.: Cascade R-CNN: high quality object detection and instance segmentation. IEEE Trans. Pattern Anal. Mach. Intell. **43**(5), 1483–1498 (2021)
3. Chen, G., Choi, W., Yu, X., Han, T.X., Chandraker, M.: Learning efficient object detection models with knowledge distillation. In: NeurIPS, pp. 742–751 (2017)
4. Dai, X., et al.: General instance distillation for object detection. CoRR abs/2103.02340 (2021)
5. Du, Z., et al.: Distilling object detectors with feature richness. CoRR abs/2111.00674 (2021)
6. Ester, M., Kriegel, H., Sander, J., Xu, X.: A density-based algorithm for discovering clusters in large spatial databases with noise. In: Simoudis, E., Han, J., Fayyad, U.M. (eds.) Proceedings of the Second International Conference on Knowledge Discovery and Data Mining (KDD-96), Portland, Oregon, USA, pp. 226–231. AAAI Press (1996)
7. Everingham, M., Gool, L.V., Williams, C.K.I., Winn, J.M., Zisserman, A.: The pascal visual object classes (VOC) challenge. IJCV **88**(2), 303–338 (2010)
8. Fu, C., Liu, W., Ranga, A., Tyagi, A., Berg, A.C.: DSSD : deconvolutional single shot detector. CoRR abs/1701.06659 (2017)
9. Girshick, R.: Fast R-CNN. In: ICCV, pp. 1440–1448 (2015)
10. Gou, J., Yu, B., Maybank, S.J., Tao, D.: Knowledge distillation: a survey. CoRR abs/2006.05525 (2020)

11. Guo, J., et al.: Distilling object detectors via decoupled features. CoRR abs/2103.14475 (2021)
12. Han, B., et al.: Co-teaching: robust training of deep neural networks with extremely noisy labels. In: NeurIPS, pp. 8536–8546 (2018)
13. He, K., Zhang, X., Ren, S., Sun, J.: Deep residual learning for image recognition. In: CVPR, pp. 770–778. CS (2016)
14. Heo, B., Kim, J., Yun, S., Park, H., Kwak, N., Choi, J.Y.: A comprehensive overhaul of feature distillation. In: ICCV, pp. 1921–1930 (2019)
15. Heo, B., Lee, M., Yun, S., Choi, J.Y.: Knowledge transfer via distillation of activation boundaries formed by hidden neurons. In: AAA, pp. 3779–3787 (2019)
16. Hinton, G.E., Vinyals, O., Dean, J.: Distilling the knowledge in a neural network. CoRR abs/1503.02531 (2015)
17. Huang, Z., Wang, N.: Like what you like: knowledge distill via neuron selectivity transfer. CoRR abs/1707.01219 (2017)
18. Jiang, L., Zhou, Z., Leung, T., Li, L., Fei-Fei, L.: Mentornet: learning data-driven curriculum for very deep neural networks on corrupted labels. In: ICML, vol. 80, pp. 2309–2318 (2018)
19. Kai Chen, e.a.: Mmdetection: open mmlab detection toolbox and benchmark. CoRR abs/1906.07155 (2019)
20. Kreutz-Delgado, K., Murray, J.F., Rao, B.D., Engan, K., Lee, T., Sejnowski, T.J.: Dictionary learning algorithms for sparse representation. Neural Comput. 15(2), 349–396 (2003)
21. Le, E., Kokkinos, I., Mitra, N.J.: Going deeper with lean point networks. In: CVPR, pp. 9500–9509 (2020)
22. Li, G., Li, X., Wang, Y., Zhang, S., Wu, Y., Liang, D.: Knowledge distillation for object detection via rank mimicking and prediction-guided feature imitation. CoRR abs/2112.04840 (2021)
23. Li, Q., Jin, S., Yan, J.: Mimicking very efficient network for object detection. In: CVPR, pp. 7341–7349 (2017)
24. Li, X., Wu, J., Fang, H., Liao, Y., Wang, F., Qian, C.: Local correlation consistency for knowledge distillation. In: Vedaldi, A., Bischof, H., Brox, T., Frahm, J.-M. (eds.) ECCV 2020. LNCS, vol. 12357, pp. 18–33. Springer, Cham (2020). https://doi.org/10.1007/978-3-030-58610-2_2
25. Lin, T., Dollár, P., Girshick, R.B., He, K., Hariharan, B., Belongie, S.J.: Feature pyramid networks for object detection. In: CVPR, pp. 936–944 (2017)
26. Lin, T., Goyal, P., Girshick, R.B., He, K., Dollár, P.: Focal loss for dense object detection. In: ICCV, pp. 2999–3007 (2017)
27. Lin, T.-Y., et al.: Microsoft COCO: common objects in context. In: Fleet, D., Pajdla, T., Schiele, B., Tuytelaars, T. (eds.) ECCV 2014. LNCS, vol. 8693, pp. 740–755. Springer, Cham (2014). https://doi.org/10.1007/978-3-319-10602-1_48
28. Liu, W., et al.: SSD: single shot multibox detector. In: Leibe, B., Matas, J., Sebe, N., Welling, M. (eds.) ECCV 2016. LNCS, vol. 9905, pp. 21–37. Springer, Cham (2016). https://doi.org/10.1007/978-3-319-46448-0_2
29. Liu, Y., et al.: Knowledge distillation via instance relationship graph. In: CVPR, pp. 7096–7104 (2019)
30. Malach, E., Shalev-Shwartz, S.: Decoupling "when to update" from "how to update". In: NeurIPS, pp. 960–970 (2017)
31. Mallat, S., Zhang, Z.: Matching pursuits with time-frequency dictionaries. TIP 41(12), 3397–3415 (1993)
32. Park, W., Kim, D., Lu, Y., Cho, M.: Relational knowledge distillation. In: CVPR, pp. 3967–3976 (2019)

33. Redmon, J., Divvala, S.K., Girshick, R.B., Farhadi, A.: You only look once: unified, real-time object detection. In: CVPR, pp. 779–788 (2016)
34. Ren, S., He, K., Girshick, R.B., Sun, J.: Faster R-CNN: towards real-time object detection with region proposal networks. In: NeurIPS, pp. 91–99 (2015)
35. Romero, A., Ballas, N., Kahou, S.E., Chassang, A., Gatta, C., Bengio, Y.: Fitnets: hints for thin deep nets. In: ICLR (2015)
36. Sun, R., Tang, F., Zhang, X., Xiong, H., Tian, Q.: Distilling object detectors with task adaptive regularization. CoRR abs/2006.13108 (2020)
37. Tian, Y., Krishnan, D., Isola, P.: Contrastive representation distillation. In: ICLR (2020)
38. Tian, Z., Shen, C., Chen, H., He, T.: FCOS: fully convolutional one-stage object detection. In: ICCV, pp. 9626–9635 (2019)
39. Tosic, I., Frossard, P.: Dictionary learning. SPM (2011)
40. Tung, F., Mori, G.: Similarity-preserving knowledge distillation. In: ICCV, pp. 1365–1374 (2019)
41. Wang, T., Yuan, L., Zhang, X., Feng, J.: Distilling object detectors with fine-grained feature imitation. In: CVPR, pp. 4933–4942 (2019)
42. Xie, S., Girshick, R.B., Dollár, P., Tu, Z., He, K.: Aggregated residual transformations for deep neural networks. In: 2017 IEEE Conference on Computer Vision and Pattern Recognition, CVPR 2017, Honolulu, HI, USA, 21–26 July 2017, pp. 5987–5995. IEEE Computer Society (2017)
43. Yim, J., Joo, D., Bae, J., Kim, J.: A gift from knowledge distillation: fast optimization, network minimization and transfer learning. In: CVPR, pp. 7130–7138 (2017)
44. Zhang, L., Ma, K.: Improve object detection with feature-based knowledge distillation: towards accurate and efficient detectors. In: ICLR (2021)
45. Zhang, Y., et al.: Prime-aware adaptive distillation. In: Vedaldi, A., Bischof, H., Brox, T., Frahm, J.-M. (eds.) ECCV 2020. LNCS, vol. 12364, pp. 658–674. Springer, Cham (2020). https://doi.org/10.1007/978-3-030-58529-7_39
46. Zheng, Z., Ye, R., Wang, P., Wang, J., Ren, D., Zuo, W.: Localization distillation for object detection. CoRR abs/2102.12252 (2021)
47. Zhu, C., He, Y., Savvides, M.: Feature selective anchor-free module for single-shot object detection. In: CVPR, pp. 840–849 (2019)

Unifying Visual Perception by Dispersible Points Learning

Jianming Liang[1,2], Guanglu Song[2], Biao Leng[1], and Yu Liu[2(✉)]

[1] School of Computer Science and Engineering, Beihang University, Beijing, China
lengbiao@buaa.edu.cn
[2] SenseTime Research, Hong Kong, China
songguanglu@sensetime.com, liuyuisanai@gmail.com

Abstract. We present a conceptually simple, flexible, and universal visual perception head for variant visual tasks, e.g., classification, object detection, instance segmentation and pose estimation, and different frameworks, such as one-stage or two-stage pipelines. Our approach effectively identifies an object in an image while simultaneously generating a high-quality bounding box or contour-based segmentation mask or set of keypoints. The method, called UniHead, views different visual perception tasks as the dispersible points learning via the transformer encoder architecture. Given a fixed spatial coordinate, UniHead adaptively scatters it to different spatial points and reasons about their relations by transformer encoder. It directly outputs the final set of predictions in the form of multiple points, allowing us to perform different visual tasks in different frameworks with the same head design. We show extensive evaluations on ImageNet classification and all three tracks of the COCO suite of challenges, including object detection, instance segmentation and pose estimation. Without bells and whistles, UniHead can unify these visual tasks via a single visual head design and achieve comparable performance compared to expert models developed for each task. We hope our simple and universal UniHead will serve as a solid baseline and help promote universal visual perception research. Code and models are available at https://github.com/Sense-X/UniHead.

Keywords: Dispersible points learning · Transformer encoder · General visual perception

1 Introduction

Image classification [12], object detection [16,24], instance segmentation [8,24] and human pose estimation [1,24] are the vital visual perception tasks in computer vision. The vision community has rapidly improved results by developing

---

J. Liang—Work is done during the internship at SenseTime.

Supplementary Information The online version contains supplementary material available at https://doi.org/10.1007/978-3-031-20077-9_26.

440   J. Liang et al.

robust feature representation. Regardless of the development of the powerful backbone, in large part, these advances are inseparable from the task-aware visual head structure design, such as TSD [36], CondInst [40] and CPN [7], or the elaborate frameworks construction, *e.g.*, one-stage detectors [23,26,41] and two-stage detectors [4,34]. These methods are conceptually experienced and introduce task exclusivity, *e.g.*, TSD [36] developed in object detection cannot be migrated to pose estimation. Our goal in this work is to develop a comparably generalized feature representation learning with task-agnostic structure design for *unifying visual perception*.

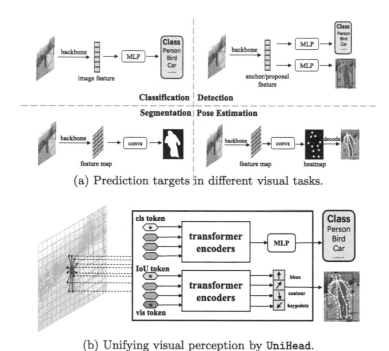

(a) Prediction targets in different visual tasks.

(b) Unifying visual perception by UniHead.

Fig. 1. (a). Illustration of the typical pipelines for different visual tasks. Different sub-tasks require different prediction targets and different feature structures. (b). Illustration of the UniHead design. Given a fixed spatial coordinate, UniHead adaptively scatters it to different spatial points and reasons about their relations by transformer encoders. It directly outputs a set of predictions in the form of multiple points to perform different visual tasks.

The main barriers behind this are: 1) As shown in Fig. 1(a), the different prediction targets force the visual perception into different sub-tasks, *i.e.*, *a class label* for image classification, *a bounding box* for object detection, *a pixel-wised mask* for instance segmentation, and *a group of landmarks* for pose estimation. 2) How to conduct a task-agnostic head module which can generalize to all sub-tasks and frameworks while achieving good results? Given this, one might expect a complex head design is required to solve these barriers. However, we show that a surprisingly simple, flexible, and universal head module can easily generalize to different visual tasks or frameworks and surpass prior expert models in each individual task.

Our method, called UniHead, can be directly migrated to variant visual frameworks, e.g., Faster RCNN [34], FCOS [41] and ATSS [50], by formulating the prediction targets as the dispersible points learning. As shown in Fig. 1(b), UniHead is built upon any network backbone and the prediction targets for different tasks can be achieved by a basic yet effective points estimation. Given a fixed spatial coordinate, UniHead adaptively scatters it to different spatial points and reasons about their relations by several stacked transformer encoders. It directly outputs the final set of predictions in the form of multiple points, which is robust to geometric variations an object can exhibit, including scale, deformation, and orientation. For *image classification*, the points directly predict the object class. For *object detection*, the points are placed along the four edges of a bounding box. For *instance segmentation*, the points are evenly distributed along the instance mask contour. For *pose estimation*, the position of points conforms to the pose distribution of the training data.

Furthermore, we found it essential to adapt the initial position of the points according to different prediction targets. This can effectively alleviate the difficulty of optimization under the requirement of fitting objects with different scales and orientations. Additionally, the UniHead only adds a small computational overhead, enabling a universal system and rapid experimentation.

Without bells and whistles, UniHead can be equipped with popular backbones on different visual tasks, such as ResNet [18], ResNeXt [46], Swin Transformer [27], etc. It excels on the ImageNet [12] classification and all three tracks of the COCO [24] suite of challenges, including object detection, instance segmentation, and human pose estimation. We conduct extensive experiments to showcase the generality of our UniHead. By viewing each task as the dispersible points learning via the transformer encoder architecture, UniHead can perform comparably without any special design for specific tasks. UniHead, therefore, can be seen more broadly as a universal head module for visual perception and easily migrated to more complex tasks.

To summarize, our contributions are as follows:

1) We develop a comparably generalized dispersible points learning method for unifying visual perception. We hope our work can inspire the vision community to explore a unified vision framework.

2) We introduce the transformer encoder to reason about the relations of dispersible points and the adaptively points initialization to handle the geometric variations an object can exhibit, including scale, deformation, and orientation.

3) Detailed experiments on ImageNet [12] and MS-COCO [24] datasets show that UniHead can easily generalize to different tasks while obtaining comparable performance compared to the expert models developed in individual tasks.

2   Related Work

Image classification [12], object detection [16,24], instance segmentation [8,24] and pose estimation [1,24] are four popular tasks in computer vision. They all benefit a lot from the development of deep neural networks [18,37]. Among them, image classification [21] was the first to be applied with CNNs. The performance was improved by a considerable margin. After that, researchers are devoted to designing powerful backbones [18,19,46], which also give lift to other instance-level tasks, such as object detection [23,34] and human pose estimation [37].

For object detection, it requires bounding box level location and category information of interested instances in an image. The methods can be roughly categorized into three types: **Two-stage, One-stage** and **DETR** detectors. **Two-stage** methods detect a series of region proposals at first and refine them in the second stage. Faster RCNN [34] is a popular pipeline of the two-stage method, which also includes R-FCN [9], Cascade RCNN [4], Grid RCNN [29], *etc.*. **One-stage** methods predict locations and class scores on a large amount of pre-defined spatial candidates. They can be further divided into two types: anchor-based and anchor-free detectors. Anchor-based methods use anchor boxes as an initial set, such as SSD [26] and RetinaNet [23]. For anchor-free methods, some methods make dense predictions on spatial points, such as CenterNet (objects as points) [51], FCOS [41] and RepPoints [47]. And some other works obtain a keypoint heatmap first and get objects by grouping them. CornerNet [22], ExtremeNet [52] and CenterNet (keypoint triplets) [14] fall into this category. **DETR** methods, such as DETR [5], Deformable DETR [53] and Conditional DETR [30], propose to detect objects by decoding a pre-defined set of object queries with transformers. These queries are optimized one-to-one with ground truths so there is no need for NMS as post-processing. Such a way of one-to-one label assignment also inspires other works like Sparse RCNN [38].

For instance segmentation, it requires mask and class information for instances. The methods can be categorized into two types: **mask-based** and **contour-based. Mask-based** methods predict binary mask directly, which can further be divided into local-mask and global-mask methods. Most local-mask methods include two stages: the first one for instance detection and the second one for instance mask generation, such as Mask RCNN [17], PANet [25] and PointRend [20]. Global-mask methods usually predict the mask for the whole image and leverage dynamic mask filters to decode masks for different instances, such as YOLACT [3] and CondInst [40]. **Contour-based** methods obtain instance masks by predicting object boundaries. PolarMask [45] and DeepSnake [31] are two typical works using this idea.

For human pose estimation, it requires the keypoint locations (*e.g.* nose, eyes, knees) for multiple humans in an image. There are mainly two kinds of approaches: **heatmap-based** and **regression-based. Heatmap-based** methods use a multi-class classifier to generate keypoint heatmaps and compose them with clustering and grouping procedures, such as CPN [7], HRNet [37] and DARK [49]. **Regression-based** methods, including Integral [39] and Center-

Net [51], *etc.*, predict coordinates of keypoints directly. It is more simple to plug them into existing end-to-end learning frameworks.

Mask R-CNN [17], PointSetNet [44] and LSNet [15] achieved merging object detection, instance segmentation and pose estimation into one network. Besides these tasks, UniHead can be extended to image classification. Furthermore, UniHead can also be simply embedded in variant types of architectures, *e.g.*, anchor-free, anchor-based, and two-stage detectors, showing powerful ability on task and framework generalization.

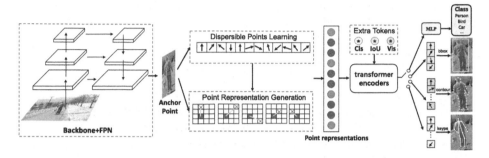

Fig. 2. A typical pipeline of UniHead. At first, most methods of location-sensitive tasks contain a backbone and the feature pyramid (not used in the image classification task) to extract feature maps. Then, for an anchor point, UniHead obtains multiple points via dispersible points learning. To generate point representations, bilinear interpolation is performed on the feature map according to point coordinates, which is denoted in dotted line. The obtained features will be concatenated with extra learnable tokens if necessary, and sent to corresponding transformer encoders to complete variant visual tasks.

3 Method

In this paper, we introduce the UniHead, a generalized visual head. It can be applied to different detection frameworks, such as Faster RCNN [34], FCOS [41] and ATSS [50], as well as different tasks including classification, object detection, instance segmentation and pose estimation. In this section, we first describe the design principle of UniHead and then detail the adaptation to different visual tasks and different visual frameworks. Finally, we delve into the inherent advantage of UniHead over other methods.

3.1   UniHead

In UniHead, given a fixed spatial coordinate $(\mathcal{A}_x, \mathcal{A}_y)$ (referred as **anchor point**), *i.e.*, *center point of a proposal or a point in the feature map*, it adaptively scatters it to different spatial points and reasons about the relations of them by several stacked transformer encoders. As shown in Fig. 2, UniHead adopts the sequentially three-stage procedure to seek for the scattered point representations. In the first stage, it will generate the anchor representation $\mathcal{F}_{x,y}$ according to the anchor coordinate or region proposal. For one-stage or anchor-free detectors, it is designated by the feature representation in the corresponding coordinate of the feature map. For the two-stage detectors, the feature generated by RoI Pooling [34] is used. In the second stage, K scattered points are generated by:

$$
\begin{aligned}
P_{x_i} &= \mathcal{A}_x + s_x \cdot \Delta x_i \\
P_{y_i} &= \mathcal{A}_y + s_y \cdot \Delta y_i,
\end{aligned}
\tag{1}
$$

where $(\Delta x_i, \Delta y_i) = f(\mathcal{F}_{x,y}; w_i)$. f is a simple multi-layer perceptron and w_i is the learnable parameter. (s_x, s_y) is the computed scalar to modulate the magnitude of the $(\Delta x_i, \Delta y_i)$. Specifically, (s_x, s_y) is the width and height of the region proposal in a two-stage detector, the anchor scale in a one-stage detector, and the model stride in an anchor-free detector. In the final stage, instead of quantizing a floating-number of (P_{x_i}, P_{y_i}), we perform bilinear interpolation to generate the point representations $\mathcal{F}_{x_i, y_i}, i \in [1, K]$.

To better reason about the relations of these scattered point representations and generate more informative features, we introduce the transformer operator to capture the correlative dependence between them. To improve the robustness of different visual tasks, we insert a task-aware token embedding by:

$$
z_0 = [\mathbf{T_{task}}; \mathcal{F}_{x_1, y_1}; \mathcal{F}_{x_2, y_2}; \ldots; \mathcal{F}_{x_K, y_K}],
\tag{2}
$$

where $\mathbf{T_{task}}$ can be $\mathbf{T_{class}}$, $\mathbf{T_{IoU}}$, and $\mathbf{T_{visibility}}$ for image classification, object detection and pose estimation, respectively. The computation in transformer encoders for point representations can be formulated as:

$$
\begin{aligned}
z_l' &= \text{MHSA}(\text{LN}(z_{l-1})) + z_{l-1}, \qquad l = 1 \ldots L, \\
z_l &= \text{MLP}(\text{LN}(z_l')) + z_l', \qquad l = 1 \ldots L, \\
[\mathbf{T_{task}'}; \mathcal{F}_{x_1, y_1}'; \mathcal{F}_{x_2, y_2}'; \ldots; \mathcal{F}_{x_K, y_K}'] &= z_L,
\end{aligned}
\tag{3}
$$

where MHSA means multi-head self attention in [43], LN indicates layer normalization [2], MLP is a multi-layer perceptron. Formally, during training, we use L transformer encoders, and the final output z_L will be adapted to different visual tasks to perform the task-aware prediction.

3.2   Adaptation to Different Visual Tasks

Image Classification. For image classification, we directly use the final feature map to perform dispersible points learning. The anchor point is set as the center of the input image and the corresponding scales are the input scale. We choose to align the classifier setting with standard vision transformers, *i.e.*, only leveraging classification token instead of all tokens in the classifier. The training can be formulated as:

$$\mathcal{L}_{cls} = \text{CrossEntropy}(\text{softmax}(\text{MLP}(\mathbf{T}'_{cls})), \mathbf{y}). \tag{4}$$

In the above $\mathbf{y}$ specifies the ground-truth class and MLP is a single fully-connected layer predicting the model's probability for the class with label $\mathbf{y}$.

Object Detection. UniHead can be applied to a variety of detectors, such as Faster R-CNN [34], FCOS [41], *etc.*, without changing the backbone network structure, and the manner of label assignment. Specially, we concatenate a learnable token $\mathbf{T}_{IoU}$ as a replacement for the IoU branch. After passing through all transformer blocks, the $\mathbf{T}'_{IoU}$ is used to predict IoU, which will be multiplied by class prediction to get final scores at inference time. The $\mathcal{F}'_{x_i,y_i}$ is used to predict the offset for point (P_{x_i}, P_{y_i}). There are:

$$(P'_{x_i}, P'_{y_i}) = (P_{x_i}, P_{y_i}) + \text{MLP}(\mathcal{F}'_{x_i,y_i}) \odot (s_x, s_y), \tag{5}$$

where $\odot$ denotes element-wise multiplication, and the MLP is a single fully-connected layer shared between different points. The predicted bounding box can be computed by $B' = (\min\{P'_{x_i}\}, \min\{P'_{y_i}\}, \max\{P'_{x_i}\}, \max\{P'_{y_i}\})$, $i \in [1, K]$.

For the classification branch, it performs the same computational manner as UniHead in image classification. For regression, it shares z_0 with the classification branch to reduce the computational cost of point representation generation. Our loss function for detection is defined as:

$$\mathcal{L}_{loc} = -\frac{1}{n} \sum_{j=1}^{n} L_1(B'_j, B_j), \tag{6}$$

where j is the index of positive samples, B'_j is the predicted box and B_j is the ground truth. Other kinds of detection loss can also be used, *e.g.*, GIoU loss [35].

Instance Segmentation. For instance segmentation, we view this task as the contour-based regression. UniHead is placed at the output of the backbone to generate the points P'_{x_i,y_i} by Eq. 1, Eq. 2, Eq. 3 and Eq. 5. To align the point number between scattered points and the contour points in training data, we uniformly add new points, or delete points with the shortest edge until the target number is met, which is similar to Deep Snake [31]. All ground truth points are clockwise arranged around the contour line. The scattered points $\{P'_{x_i,y_i}, i \in [1, K]\}$ are uniformly and clockwisely perform one-to-one matching with them.

Besides, some objects are split into several components due to occlusions. To overcome this problem, we simply follow PolarMask [45] and directly treat them as multiple objects. During training, we use L_1 loss to optimize each point:

$$\mathcal{L}_{seg} = \frac{1}{n} \sum_{i=1}^{n} L_1(P'_{x_i,y_i}, P_{x_i,y_i}), \tag{7}$$

446   J. Liang et al.

where P'_{x_i,y_i} is the predicted point and P_{x_i,y_i} is the corresponding ground truth.

Pose Estimation. The overall design of pose estimation is consistent with instance segmentation, except that an extra token $\mathbf{T_{visibility}}$ is introduced to predict the visibility of keypoints. The number K of predicted points is aligned with keypoint number in the dataset. For pose estimation, each keypoint has a clear definition, like nose, eyes, *etc.*, which makes it possible to build one-to-one connection with dispersible points. l_1 loss is adopted to train the keypoint localization branch, same as Eq. 7. For the training of keypoint visibility prediction, we use standard binary cross entropy loss.

Fig. 3. Ways of point initialization for different tasks. From left to right: image classification, object detection, instance segmentation, pose estimation.

3.3   Adaptation to Different Visual Frameworks

Two-stage Framework. UniHead is applied to region proposals in the two-stage framework. Each proposal is represented as a combination of an anchor point $(\mathcal{A}_x, \mathcal{A}_y)$ and its scale (s_x, s_y). The offsets $(\Delta x_i, \Delta y_i)$ are generated from the proposal feature extracted with RoI Pooling or RoI Align. Without other modifications, UniHead now can be directly used on a two-stage framework.

One-stage Framework. UniHead is applied on dense spatial points in the one-stage framework. For anchor-free methods, $(\mathcal{A}_x, \mathcal{A}_y)$ and (s_x, s_y) are a point and the stride of the feature map. For anchor-based methods, $(\mathcal{A}_x, \mathcal{A}_y)$ and (s_x, s_y) are the center point and the scale of an anchor. The offsets $(\Delta x_i, \Delta y_i)$ are generated using a 1×1 convolutional layer.

3.4   UniHead Initialization

To effectively alleviate the difficulty of optimization under the requirement of fitting objects with different scales and orientations, the result points are initialized in a more appropriate way for different tasks, which is illustrated in Fig. 3. For image classification, points are casually scattered around the anchor point. For object detection, points are divided into four groups placed at the bottom, top, left, and right of the anchor point, respectively. For instance segmentation, first we set a 2D reference vector that starts from the anchor point. Based on the direction of this vector, the points are uniformly and clockwise initialized on the edge of a pseudo box generated from the anchor point and its spatial scale. For pose estimation, we calculate the average positions of different keypoints in the training dataset and use them to initialize points.

The initial point position is controlled by tuning the *bias* of the last fully-connected layer in MLP used for offsets generation. Taking object detection as an example, the *bias* for points at left, right, top and bottom are set to $[-0.5, 0]$, $[0.5, 0]$, $[0, -0.5]$ and $[0, 0.5]$, respectively.

Table 1. Ablation study on extra blocks for image classification task.

Method	GFLOPs	Top-1 acc
ResNet-50	3.8	78.5
ResNet-50+extra blocks	4.2	79.0
ResNet-50+UniHead	4.1	**79.5**
Swin-T	4.5	81.2
Swin-T+extra blocks	5.2	81.7
Swin-T+UniHead	4.7	**81.8**
Swin-B	15.4	83.5
Swin-B+extra blocks	16.7	83.6
Swin-B+UniHead	15.7	**83.9**

Table 2. Ablation study on T_{task}. 'Det.' and 'Keyp.' mean detection and pose estimation, respectively.

Task	w/ T_{task}	AP	$AP_{.5}$	$AP_{.75}$	AP_s	AP_m	AP_l
Det.	x	41.6	**61.2**	**44.8**	23.4	45.1	56.2
	✓	**41.8**	60.6	44.7	**23.8**	**45.1**	**56.7**
Keyp.	x	50.4	78.8	53.9	–	44.9	58.5
	✓	**50.7**	**78.9**	**54.6**	–	**45.5**	**58.5**

4   Experiments

For image classification, experiments are conducted on the ILSVRC-2012 ImageNet [12] dataset with 1K classes and 1.3M images. We use Top-1 accuracy as the metric in classification experiments.

We also conduct experiments with different backbones on the MS-COCO 2017 [24] dataset, including object detection, instance segmentation, and human pose estimation tasks. For these tasks, training is performed on the *train* set, over 57K images for human pose estimation, and over 118K images for object detection and instance segmentation. For experiments of ablation studies, evaluation is conducted on the *val* set. We also report performance on the *test-dev* set to compare with the state-of-art methods. The mean average precision (AP) is used as the measurement in COCO experiments. But the definition of AP varies with tasks. For object detection and instance segmentation, AP is calculated under different IoU thresholds (bounding box IoU or mask IoU). For human pose estimation, AP is calculated with object keypoint similarity (OKS).

4.1   Implementation Details

In the image classification task, all models are trained using AdamW optimizer [28] with 1e-4 initial learning rate, 0.05 weight decay, $\beta_1 = 0.9$, $\beta_2 = 0.999$ and a batch size of 1024. We train classification models for 300 epochs and use consine annealing scheduler to decrease learning rate. Data augmentations in [42] are also used, *e.g.*, mix up, label smoothing, *etc.*.

For other three tasks, we use different backbones including ResNet [18], ResNeXt [46] and Swin Transformer [27] with weights pretrained on ImageNet [12]. For object detection, we use our UniHead on different detection pipelines and follow their original hyper-parameters. For instance segmentation and pose estimation, the same settings as Faster RCNN [34] are used. During training, we adopt AdamW [28] as the optimizer, with 1e-4 initial learning rate, 0.05 weight decay, $\beta_1 = 0.9$ and $\beta_2 = 0.999$. In our 1× setting, we train our model with mini-batch size 16 for 13 epochs and decrease the learning rate by a factor of 10 at epoch 9 and 12. Unless specified, the input scale of images is [800, 1333] and no data augmentations except horizontal flipping are used in training. The hyper-parameter of newly-added transformers keeps the same as [13].

Table 3. Ablation study on UniHead bias initialization strategy.

Task	UniHead Initialization?	AP	AP$_{.5}$	AP$_{.75}$
Det.	x	40.9	60.7	43.7
	✓	**41.6**	**61.2**	**44.8**
Segm.	x	29.7	**53.5**	28.9
	✓	**30.4**	53.2	**30.1**
Keyp.	x	57.0	81.9	62.4
	✓	**57.9**	**82.6**	**63.9**

Table 4. Ablation study on **point number**. Point number 8, 16, 24, 32 are tried.

K	AP	AP$_{.5}$	AP$_{.75}$	AP$_s$	AP$_m$	AP$_l$
8	40.8	59.3	43.7	22.3	44.3	54.6
16	41.8	60.6	44.7	23.8	**45.1**	56.7
24	**41.8**	**60.7**	**44.7**	**23.9**	44.8	56.5
32	41.5	60.3	44.5	22.8	44.6	**56.8**

4.2 Ablation Studies

In this section, we conduct extensive ablation studies on ImageNet and COCO *val* set to validate the effectiveness of UniHead on classification and localization tasks, respectively. Specially, for localization task, we choose object detection and all models are trained on Faster RCNN [34] baseline with AdamW optimizer [28] and ResNet-50 backbone for fair comparison. We find that AdamW can stably improve the performance by $\sim 1\%$ AP compared to SGD.

Extra Blocks. We add extra blocks to the classification backbone networks to align their FLOPs with UniHead. Specifically, we append two bottlenecks to ResNet-50 ([3,4,6,5] for four stages) and two transformer blocks to Swin-T ([2,2,6,4] for four stages), whose results are shown in Table 1. Though additional layers can boost the performance, UniHead can achieve better performance with similar FLOPs. Also, we conduct the same experiment on Swin-B. We can see that when the model becomes bigger with higher FLOPs, extra blocks can hardly bring improvement. But UniHead achieves a continual performance boost. All these results prove that improvement brought by UniHead does not only account for its transformer blocks.

Task Token. We also explore the influence of $\mathbf{T_{IoU}}$ and $\mathbf{T_{visibility}}$ on object detection and pose estimation, respectively. As is shown in Table 2, the introduction of $\mathbf{T_{task}}$ brings a slight improvement on both tasks, proving the effectiveness of task tokens. It is worth noting that though visibility prediction is not used in pose estimation evaluation, $\mathbf{T_{visibility}}$ still has a positive impact on training.

Table 5. Ablation study on **block number**. L_{cls} and L_{loc} denote transformer encoder block number of classification and localization, respectively. #params means parameters of the detection head. The training and inference time is measured on a 16GB V100 GPU.

L_{cls}	L_{loc}	#params	GFLOPs	Training (s/iter)	Inference (ms/img)	AP	AP$_{.5}$	AP$_{.75}$
baseline		14.3M	215	0.38	82	38.8	59.9	42.1
1	1	11.9M	227	0.39	85	41.6	60.3	44.3
2	2	12.7M	239	0.40	87	41.6	60.4	44.7
3	3	13.5M	251	0.40	90	41.7	60.5	44.7
4	4	14.3M	263	0.41	92	**42.0**	60.6	**45.0**

Table 6. Ablation study on **different modules**. IoU prediction is not used in this table. "HD", "MHSA" and "DPL" mean head disentanglement, multi-head self attention and dispersible points learning, respectively.

HD	MHSA	DPL	AP	AP$_{.5}$	AP$_{.75}$	AP$_s$	AP$_m$	AP$_l$
x	x	x	38.8	59.9	42.1	22.1	41.9	51.9
✓	x	x	39.3	60.0	42.5	22.0	42.9	52.6
✓	✓	x	39.9	60.5	43.4	22.4	43.2	53.4
✓	x	✓	40.7	**61.6**	44.4	23.1	43.4	55.1
✓	✓	✓	**41.6**	61.2	**44.8**	**23.4**	**45.1**	**56.2**

UniHead Initialization. We replace our task-specific bias initialization with zero initialization on different tasks. Main results are shown in Table 3. It proves that a proper initialization can help the unified architecture learn the knowledge of different tasks more quickly.

Point Number. We evaluate the performance of different point numbers in `UniHead`, which is shown in Table 4. It shows that our head can benefit from the increasing number of points. But more points may bring overfitting and more computational cost. So we choose to use $K = 16$ in our implementations.

Block Number. We also analyze the influence of the number of transformer encoder blocks. As is shown in Table 5, we compare the performances, head parameters, FLOPs, training time, and inference time with baseline under different block number settings. Our head can benefit slightly from the increase in block numbers. Considering computational costs and the head capacity, we finally use $L_{cls} = 2$ and $L_{loc} = 3$ in our implementations.

Head Disentanglement. To show that our method does not only benefit from the separated task heads, a Faster RCNN with sibling heads is given in the second row of Table 6. We simply remove the shared fully connected layers in the RCNN head and replace them with separated ones. We can observe that the improvement brought by head disentanglement (0.5 AP) is actually limited.

Dispersible Points Learning and Multi-head Self Attention. In order to demonstrate the effectiveness of dispersible points learning and multi-head self attention, we conduct experiments with different head designs and compare them with our head (without IoU prediction). First, we take the output of RoI Align [17] as tokens directly (49 in total), and process them with disentangled transformer encoders. The result is in the third row of Table 6. We can see that though more points are used, it still performs worse than DPL with $K = 16$.

Table 7. Results of UniHead with variant detection pipelines.

Method	AP	AP$_{.5}$	AP$_{.75}$
Faster RCNN [34]	38.8	59.9	42.1
+UniHead	**41.8**	**60.6**	**44.7**
Cascade RCNN [4]	42.1	60.8	45.3
+UniHead	**43.0**	**61.5**	**46.2**
ATSS (anchor-based) [50]	39.5	58.1	42.2
+UniHead	**40.6**	**58.3**	**44.2**
FCOS (w/o imprv.) [41]	37.1	56.3	39.1
+UniHead	**39.7**	**57.9**	**42.6**
Mask RCNN [17]	35.2	56.8	37.5
+UniHead (mask)	**37.0**	**57.9**	**39.9**

Table 8. Results of UniHead with variant backbones. "DCN" means deformable convolution. * means multi-scale training.

Method	Ours	AP	AP$_{.5}$	AP$_{.75}$
ResNet-50		38.8	59.9	42.1
ResNet-50	✓	**41.8**	**60.6**	**44.7**
ResNet-101		39.9	60.5	43.5
ResNet-101	✓	**42.4**	**61.4**	**45.7**
ResNeXt-101-64 × 4d		42.2	**63.4**	45.7
ResNeXt-101-64 × 4d	✓	**44.5**	63.2	**48.0**
ResNeXt-101-64 × 4d-DCN		45.4	**67.1**	49.2
ResNeXt-101-64 × 4d-DCN	✓	**47.3**	66.9	**51.3**
Swin-T*		43.7	66.4	47.7
Swin-T*	✓	**46.3**	**66.4**	**49.5**

Then, we leverage deformable RoI Pooling [10] as another form of dispersible points learning. Specifically, multiple offsets are generated in the same way and applied to deformable RoI Pooling for feature extraction. The result is shown in the fourth row of Table 6. It indicates that the combination of dispersible points learning and multi-head attention is more effective to capture semantic information within an instance.

4.3 Generalization Ability

Detection Pipeline Generalization. We evaluate the performance by transferring our UniHead to different detection pipelines. Specially, we simply replace the detection head in Mask RCNN with UniHead to build a mask-based version.

As is shown in Table 7, the `UniHead` can boost the performance of all these types of detectors, showing its generalization ability on different detection frameworks.

Backbone Generalization. We further conduct experiments with different backbones under the setting of Faster RCNN. As is shown in Table 8, our head can steadily boost the performance by $2 \sim 3\%$ AP. It demonstrates the generalization ability of our method on variant backbones.

Table 9. Results on different tasks. "*" indicates multi-scale training, multi-stage refinement and 11x scheduler. "+" is multi-scale training and 2x scheduler.

Task	Method	backbone	Top-1 acc.	AP	AP$_{.5}$	AP$_{.75}$
Cls.	baseline	R50	78.5	–	–	–
	UniHead		**79.5**	–	–	–
Det.	Faster RCNN	R50	–	38.8	59.9	42.1
	UniHead		–	**41.8**	**60.6**	**44.7**
	Mask RCNN		–	39.0	59.8	42.4
	UniHead (box)		–	**42.3**	**60.9**	**45.5**
Segm.	DeepSnake [31]	DLA34	–	30.3	–	–
	UniHead	R50	–	**30.4**	53.2	30.1
Keyp.	PointSet* [44]	R50	–	**58.0**	80.8	62.4
	UniHead$^+$		–	57.9	**82.6**	**63.9**

Task Generalization. As mentioned before, our head is a unifying perception head, which means that it can be applied to variant visual tasks. To be specific, we use $K = 16$ for image classification and object detection, $K = 36$ for instance segmentation and $K = 17$ points for human pose estimation. The baseline of classification is trained with the same setting as `UniHead` for fair comparison. The performance is evaluated on ImageNet *val* set for classification, and COCO *val* set for other three tasks. The experimental results are shown in Table 9. We can see that with a ResNet-50 backbone, the `UniHead` makes improvements on classification and object detection, and get a close performance compared with expert models for instance segmentation and pose estimation.

4.4   Comparison with State-of-the-Art

We evaluate object detection, instance segmentation and pose estimation on COCO *test-dev*, whose results are shown in Table 10. The reported AP is related to corresponding tasks, *e.g.*, mask AP for instance segmentation. We only adopt multi-scale training for data augmentation and no TTA is used. **It should be noted that we don't introduce any task-aware algorithm design, *e.g.*, multi-stage refinement for pose estimation.**

Table 10. Comparisons of for different algorithms and different tasks evaluated on the COCO *test-dev* set. "FG" and "TG" indicate that the method can be generalized to different visual frameworks and visual tasks, respectively. "*" denotes multi-scale test.

Method	FG	TG	backbone	iteration	AP	AP$_{.5}$	AP$_{.75}$	AP$_S$	AP$_M$	AP$_L$
Object Detection										
ATSS [50]	x	x	X-101-64x4d-DCN	2x	47.7	65.5	51.9	29.7	50.8	59.4
BorderDet [33]	x	x	X-101-64x4d-DCN	2x	48.0	67.1	52.1	29.4	50.7	60.5
Deformable DETR [53]	x	x	X-101-64x4d-DCN	~4x	50.1	69.7	54.6	30.6	52.8	64.7
DynamicHead [11]	✓	x	X-101-64x4d-DCN	2x	52.3	70.7	57.2	35.1	56.2	63.4
PointSet [44]	x	✓	X-101-64x4d-DCN	2x	45.1	66.1	48.9	–	–	–
LSNet [15]	x	✓	X-101-64x4d-DCN	2x	49.6	69.0	54.1	30.3	52.8	62.8
UniHead	✓	✓	X-101-64x4d-DCN	2x	50.5	70.0	54.4	31.2	53.4	64.7
UniHead	✓	✓	Swin-L	2x	**54.7**	**74.5**	**59.1**	**35.6**	**58.2**	**70.2**
Instance Segmentation										
Mask-based:										
Mask RCNN [17]	x	✓	X-101-32x4d	1x	37.1	60.0	39.4	16.9	39.9	53.5
HTC [6]	x	✓	X-101-64x4d	~2x	41.2	63.9	44.7	22.8	43.9	54.6
YOLACT [3]	x	x	ResNet-101	4x	31.2	50.6	32.8	12.1	33.3	47.1
DetectoRS [32]	x	x	X-101-32x4d	3x	45.8	69.2	50.1	27.4	48.7	59.6
UniHead (w/ mask head)	✓	✓	X-101-64x4d-DCN	3x	43.6	67.1	47.0	25.1	46.5	58.1
UniHead (w/ mask head)	✓	✓	Swin-L	3x	**46.7**	**71.2**	**50.8**	**28.2**	**50.3**	**62.1**
Contour-based:										
ExtremeNet [52]	x	✓	HG-2 stacked	~8x	18.9	44.5	13.7	10.4	20.4	28.3
DeepSnake [31]	x	x	DLA-34 [48]	~11x	30.3	–	–	–	–	–
PolarMask [45]	x	x	X-101-64x4d-DCN	2x	36.2	59.4	37.7	17.8	37.7	51.5
PointSet [44]	x	✓	X-101-64x4d-DCN	2x	34.6	60.1	34.9	45.1	66.1	48.9
LSNet [15]	x	✓	X-101-64x4d-DCN	~2x	37.6	64.0	38.3	22.1	39.9	49.1
UniHead	✓	✓	X-101-64x4d-DCN	2x	36.6	63.0	36.2	22.0	38.6	48.5
UniHead	✓	✓	Swin-L	2x	**39.4**	**67.0**	**39.3**	**24.7**	**41.7**	**52.0**
Pose Estimation										
Heatmap-based:										
CPN [7]	x	x	ResNet-Inception	–	72.1	91.4	80.0	–	68.7	77.2
HRNet [37]	x	x	HRNet-W48	~16x	75.5	92.5	83.3	–	71.9	81.5
DARK [49]	x	x	HRNet-W48	~11x	**76.2**	**92.5**	**83.6**	–	**72.5**	**82.4**
Regression-based:										
CenterNet* [51]	x	✓	HG-2 stacked	~11x	63.0	86.8	69.6	–	58.9	70.4
PointSet [44]	x	✓	X-101-64x4d-DCN	~8x	62.5	83.1	68.3	–	–	–
LSNet [15]	x	✓	X-101-64x4d-DCN	~6x	59.0	83.6	65.2	–	53.3	67.9
UniHead	✓	✓	X-101-64x4d-DCN	2x	65.4	87.3	72.6	–	60.9	72.3
UniHead	✓	✓	Swin-L	2x	**66.1**	**88.7**	**73.7**	–	**62.0**	**72.3**

For object detection, the experimental setting in multi-scale training is [480, 960] for image minimum side and 1333 for image maximum side. We can see that with stronger backbones, our UniHead can achieve competitive performance, although it is not developed just for object detection. For instance segmentation, the same augmentation strategy as object detection is used. Here we also use the mask head of Mask RCNN [17] to build a mask-based UniHead. Without bells and whistles, UniHead gets 46.7% AP with mask-based head and 39.4% AP with contour-based head. Compared with expert models, UniHead achieves comparable performance only using a simpler pipeline. For pose estimation, we use a larger resolution of input image ([480, 1200] for image minimum side and 2000 for image maximum side). With a surprisingly simple way, *i.e.*, direct keypoint regression using l_1 loss, UniHead gets a close performance compared with other regression-based methods which utilize multi-stage refinement (like [44]) and more iterations of training.

5   Conclusion

In this paper, we proposed UniHead, a unifying visual perception head. It can not only be embedded in variant detection frameworks, but also applied to different visual tasks, including image classification, object detection, instance segmentation and pose estimation. UniHead perceives instances by dispersible points learning, which is also equipped with transformer encoders to capture semantic relations of them. Though our UniHead is designed in a simple way, it achieves comparable performance on each task compared with expert models. This work shows the potential in general visual learning and we hope it can promote universal visual perception research.

Acknowledgement. The work was supported by the National Key R&D Program of China under Grant 2019YFB2102400.

References

1. Andriluka, M., Pishchulin, L., Gehler, P., Schiele, B.: 2D human pose estimation: new benchmark and state of the art analysis. In: CVPR, pp. 3686–3693 (2014)
2. Ba, J.L., Kiros, J.R., Hinton, G.E.: Layer normalization. arXiv:1607.06450 (2016)
3. Bolya, D., Zhou, C., Xiao, F., Lee, Y.J.: YOLACT: real-time instance segmentation. In: ICCV, pp. 9157–9166 (2019)
4. Cai, Z., Vasconcelos, N.: Cascade R-CNN: delving into high quality object detection. In: CVPR, pp. 6154–6162 (2018)
5. Carion, N., Massa, F., Synnaeve, G., Usunier, N., Kirillov, A., Zagoruyko, S.: End-to-end object detection with transformers. In: ECCV, pp. 213–229 (2020)
6. Chen, K., et al.: Hybrid task cascade for instance segmentation. In: CVPR, pp. 4974–4983 (2019)
7. Chen, Y., Wang, Z., Peng, Y., Zhang, Z., Yu, G., Sun, J.: Cascaded pyramid network for multi-person pose estimation. In: CVPR, pp. 7103–7112 (2018)
8. Cordts, M., et al.: The cityscapes dataset for semantic urban scene understanding. In: CVPR, pp. 3213–3223 (2016)
9. Dai, J., Li, Y., He, K., Sun, J.: R-FCN: object detection via region-based fully convolutional networks. In: NeurIPS 29 (2016)
10. Dai, J., et al.: Deformable convolutional networks. In: ICCV, pp. 764–773 (2017)
11. Dai, X., et al.: Dynamic head: unifying object detection heads with attentions. In: CVPR, pp. 7373–7382 (2021)

12. Deng, J., Dong, W., Socher, R., Li, L.J., Li, K., Fei-Fei, L.: ImageNet: a large-scale hierarchical image database. In: CVPR, pp. 248–255 (2009)
13. Dosovitskiy, A., et al.: An image is worth 16 × 16 words: transformers for image recognition at scale. arXiv:2010.11929 (2020)
14. Duan, K., Bai, S., Xie, L., Qi, H., Huang, Q., Tian, Q.: CenterNet: keypoint triplets for object detection. In: ICCV, pp. 6569–6578 (2019)
15. Duan, K., Xie, L., Qi, H., Bai, S., Huang, Q., Tian, Q.: Location-sensitive visual recognition with cross-IoU loss. arXiv:2104.04899 (2021)
16. Everingham, M., Van Gool, L., Williams, C.K., Winn, J., Zisserman, A.: The pascal visual object classes (VOC) challenge. IJCV **88**(2), 303–338 (2010)
17. He, K., Gkioxari, G., Dollár, P., Girshick, R.: Mask R-CNN. In: ICCV, pp. 2961–2969 (2017)
18. He, K., Zhang, X., Ren, S., Sun, J.: Deep residual learning for image recognition. In: CVPR, pp. 770–778 (2016)
19. Huang, G., Liu, Z., Van Der Maaten, L., Weinberger, K.Q.: Densely connected convolutional networks. In: CVPR, pp. 4700–4708 (2017)
20. Kirillov, A., Wu, Y., He, K., Girshick, R.: PointRend: image segmentation as rendering. In: CVPR, pp. 9799–9808 (2020)
21. Krizhevsky, A., Sutskever, I., Hinton, G.E.: ImageNet classification with deep convolutional neural networks. In: NeurIPS 25 (2012)
22. Law, H., Deng, J.: CornerNet: Detecting objects as paired keypoints. In: ECCV, pp. 734–750 (2018)
23. Lin, T.Y., Goyal, P., Girshick, R., He, K., Dollár, P.: Focal loss for dense object detection. In: ICCV, pp. 2980–2988 (2017)
24. Lin, T.Y., et al.: Microsoft coco: common objects in context. In: ECCV, pp. 740–755 (2014)
25. Liu, S., Qi, L., Qin, H., Shi, J., Jia, J.: Path aggregation network for instance segmentation. In: CVPR, pp. 8759–8768 (2018)
26. Liu, W., Anguelov, D., Erhan, D., Szegedy, C., Reed, S., Fu, C.Y., Berg, A.C.: SSD: single shot multibox detector. In: ECCV, pp. 21–37 (2016)
27. Liu, Z., et al.: Swin transformer: hierarchical vision transformer using shifted windows. arXiv:2103.14030 (2021)
28. Loshchilov, I., Hutter, F.: Decoupled weight decay regularization. arXiv:1711.05101 (2017)
29. Lu, X., Li, B., Yue, Y., Li, Q., Yan, J.: Grid R-CNN. In: CVPR, pp. 7363–7372 (2019)
30. Meng, D., et al.: Conditional DETR for fast training convergence. In: ICCV, pp. 3651–3660 (2021)
31. Peng, S., Jiang, W., Pi, H., Li, X., Bao, H., Zhou, X.: Deep snake for real-time instance segmentation. In: CVPR, pp. 8533–8542 (2020)
32. Qiao, S., Chen, L.C., Yuille, A.: Detectors: detecting objects with recursive feature pyramid and switchable atrous convolution. In: CVPR, pp. 10213–10224 (2021)
33. Qiu, H., Ma, Y., Li, Z., Liu, S., Sun, J.: BorderDet: border feature for dense object detection. In: ECCV, pp. 549–564 (2020)
34. Ren, S., He, K., Girshick, R., Sun, J.: Faster R-CNN: towards real-time object detection with region proposal networks. In: NeurIPS (2015)
35. Rezatofighi, H., Tsoi, N., Gwak, J., Sadeghian, A., Reid, I., Savarese, S.: Generalized intersection over union: a metric and a loss for bounding box regression. In: CVPR, pp. 658–666 (2019)
36. Song, G., Liu, Y., Wang, X.: Revisiting the sibling head in object detector. In: CVPR, pp. 11563–11572 (2020)

37. Sun, K., Xiao, B., Liu, D., Wang, J.: Deep high-resolution representation learning for human pose estimation. In: CVPR, pp. 5693–5703 (2019)
38. Sun, P., et al.: Sparse R-CNN: end-to-end object detection with learnable proposals. In: CVPR, pp. 14454–14463 (2021)
39. Sun, X., Xiao, B., Wei, F., Liang, S., Wei, Y.: Integral human pose regression. In: ECCV, pp. 529–545 (2018)
40. Tian, Z., Shen, C., Chen, H.: Conditional convolutions for instance segmentation. In: ECCV, pp. 282–298 (2020)
41. Tian, Z., Shen, C., Chen, H., He, T.: FCOS: fully convolutional one-stage object detection. In: ICCV, pp. 9627–9636 (2019)
42. Touvron, H., Cord, M., Douze, M., Massa, F., Sablayrolles, A., Jégou, H.: Training data-efficient image transformers & distillation through attention. In: ICML. pp. 10347–10357 (2021)
43. Vaswani, A., et al.: Attention is all you need. In: NeurIPS 30 (2017)
44. Wei, F., Sun, X., Li, H., Wang, J., Lin, S.: Point-set anchors for object detection, instance segmentation and pose estimation. In: ECCV, pp. 527–544 (2020)
45. Xie, E., et al.: PolarMask: single shot instance segmentation with polar representation. In: CVPR, pp. 12193–12202 (2020)
46. Xie, S., Girshick, R., Dollár, P., Tu, Z., He, K.: Aggregated residual transformations for deep neural networks. In: CVPR, pp. 1492–1500 (2017)
47. Yang, Z., Liu, S., Hu, H., Wang, L., Lin, S.: RepPoints: point set representation for object detection. In: ICCV, pp. 9657–9666 (2019)
48. Yu, F., Wang, D., Shelhamer, E., Darrell, T.: Deep layer aggregation. In: CVPR, pp. 2403–2412 (2018)
49. Zhang, F., Zhu, X., Dai, H., Ye, M., Zhu, C.: Distribution-aware coordinate representation for human pose estimation. In: CVPR, pp. 7093–7102 (2020)
50. Zhang, S., Chi, C., Yao, Y., Lei, Z., Li, S.Z.: Bridging the gap between anchor-based and anchor-free detection via adaptive training sample selection. In: CVPR, pp. 9759–9768 (2020)
51. Zhou, X., Wang, D., Krähenbühl, P.: Objects as points. arXiv:1904.07850 (2019)
52. Zhou, X., Zhuo, J., Krahenbuhl, P.: Bottom-up object detection by grouping extreme and center points. In: CVPR, pp. 850–859 (2019)
53. Zhu, X., Su, W., Lu, L., Li, B., Wang, X., Dai, J.: Deformable DETR: deformable transformers for end-to-end object detection. arXiv:2010.04159 (2020)

PseCo: Pseudo Labeling and Consistency Training for Semi-Supervised Object Detection

Gang Li[1,2], Xiang Li[1(✉)], Yujie Wang[2], Yichao Wu[2], Ding Liang[2], and Shanshan Zhang[1(✉)]

[1] Nanjing University of Science and Technology, Nanjing, China
{gang.li,xiang.li.implus,shanshan.zhang}@njust.edu.cn
[2] SenseTime Research, Hong Kong, China
{wangyujie,wuyichao,liangding}@sensetime.com

Abstract. In this paper, we delve into two key techniques in Semi-Supervised Object Detection (SSOD), namely pseudo labeling and consistency training. We observe that these two techniques currently neglect some important properties of object detection, hindering efficient learning on unlabeled data. Specifically, for pseudo labeling, existing works only focus on the classification score yet fail to guarantee the localization precision of pseudo boxes; For consistency training, the widely adopted random-resize training only considers the label-level consistency but misses the feature-level one, which also plays an important role in ensuring the scale invariance. To address the problems incurred by noisy pseudo boxes, we design Noisy Pseudo box Learning (NPL) that includes Prediction-guided Label Assignment (PLA) and Positive-proposal Consistency Voting (PCV). PLA relies on model predictions to assign labels and makes it robust to even coarse pseudo boxes; while PCV leverages the regression consistency of positive proposals to reflect the localization quality of pseudo boxes. Furthermore, in consistency training, we propose Multi-view Scale-invariant Learning (MSL) that includes mechanisms of both label- and feature-level consistency, where feature consistency is achieved by aligning shifted feature pyramids between two images with identical content but varied scales. On COCO benchmark, our method, termed PSEudo labeling and COnsistency training (PseCo), outperforms the SOTA (Soft Teacher) by 2.0, 1.8, 2.0 points under 1%, 5%, and 10% labelling ratios, respectively. It also significantly improves the learning efficiency for SSOD, e.g., PseCo halves the training time of the SOTA approach but achieves even better performance. Code is available at https://github.com/ligang-cs/PseCo.

Keywords: Semi-supervised learning · Object detection

Supplementary Information The online version contains supplementary material available at https://doi.org/10.1007/978-3-031-20077-9_27.

1   Introduction

With the rapid development of deep learning, many computer vision tasks achieve significant improvements, such as image classification [2,3], object detection [1,10,16], etc. Behind these advances, plenty of annotated data plays an important role [24]. However, labeling accurate annotations for large-scale data is usually time-consuming and expensive, especially for object detection, which requires annotating precise bounding boxes for each instance, besides category labels. Therefore, employing easily accessible unlabeled data to facilitate the model training with limited annotated data is a promising direction, named Semi-Supervised Learning, where labeled data and unlabeled data are combined together as training examples.

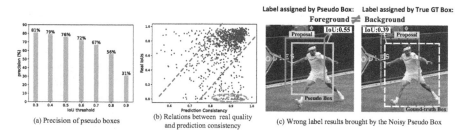

(a) Precision of pseudo boxes

(b) Relations between real quality and prediction consistency

(c) Wrong label results brought by the Noisy Pseudo Box

Fig. 1. (a) The precision of pseudo boxes under various IoU thresholds. (b) The scatter diagram of the relation between the prediction consistency and their true localization quality. Some dots falling in the orange ellipse are caused by annotation errors. Examples are attached in *supplemental material*. (c) One specific example to demonstrate that noisy pseudo boxes will mislead label assignment.

Semi-Supervised for Image Classification (SSIC) has been widely investigated in previous literature, and the learning paradigm on unlabeled data can be roughly divided into two categories: pseudo labeling [8,19] and consistency training [23,25], each of which receives much attention. Recently, some works (e.g., FixMatch [20], FlexMatch [29]) attempt to combine these two techniques into one framework and achieve state-of-the-art performance. In Semi-Supervised Object Detection (SSOD), some works borrow the key techniques (e.g. pseudo labeling, consistency training) from SSIC, and directly apply them to SSOD. Although these works [27,31] obtain gains from unlabeled data, they neglect some important properties of object detection, resulting in sub-optimal results. On the one hand, compared with image classification, pseudo labels of object detection are more complicated, containing both category and location information. On the other hand, object detection is required to capture stronger scale-invariant ability than image classification, as it needs to carefully deal with the targets with rich scales. In this work, we present a SSOD framework, termed PSEudo labeling and COnsistency training (PseCo), to integrate object detection properties into SSOD, making pseudo labeling and consistency training work better for object detection tasks.

In pseudo labeling, the model produces one-hot pseudo labels on unlabeled data by itself, and only pseudo labels whose scores are above the predefined score threshold are retained. As for object detection, the pseudo label consists of both category labels and bounding boxes. Although category labels can be guaranteed to be accurate via setting a high score threshold, the localization quality of pseudo box fails to be measured and guaranteed. It has been validated in previous works that the classification score is not strongly correlated with the precision of box localization [7,11,27,30]. In Fig. 1(a), we compute the precision of pseudo boxes under various Intersection-over-Union (IoU) thresholds, via comparing produced pseudo boxes with ground-truths. Under loose criterion (IoU=0.3), precision can reach 81%, but it will drop to 31% when we lift the IoU threshold to 0.9. This dramatic precision gap indicates coarse pseudo boxes whose IoUs belong to [0.3,0.9] account for 50%. If these noisy pseudo boxes are used as targets to train the detector, it must hinder the optimization, resulting in slow convergence and inefficient learning on unlabeled data. Furthermore, we analyze the negative effects brought by noisy pseudo boxes on classification and regression tasks as follows, respectively.

For the classification task, noisy pseudo boxes will mislead the label assignment, where labels are assigned based on IoUs between proposals and gt boxes (pseudo boxes in our case). As shown in Fig. 1(c), a background proposal is taken as foreground due to a large IoU value with a poorly localized pseudo box. As a result, the IoU-based label assignment will fail on unlabeled data and confuse decision boundaries between foreground and background. To address this issue, we design a prediction-guided label assignment strategy for unlabeled data, which assigns labels based on predictions of the teacher, instead of IoUs with pseudo boxes as before, making it robust for poorly localized pseudo boxes.

For the regression task, it is necessary to measure the localization quality of pseudo boxes. We propose a simple yet effective method to achieve this, named Positive-proposal Consistency Voting. We empirically find that regression consistency from positive proposals is capable of reflecting the localization quality of corresponding pseudo boxes. In Fig. 1(b), we visualize the relations between predicted consistency and their true IoUs, where their positive correlations can be found. Therefore, it is reasonable to employ the estimated localization quality (i.e., regression consistency from positive proposals) to re-weight the regression losses, making precise pseudo boxes contribute more to regression supervisions.

Apart from pseudo labeling, we also analyze the consistency training for SSOD. Consistency training enforces the model to generate similar predictions when fed with perturbed versions of the same image, where perturbations can be implemented by injecting various data augmentations. Through consistency training, models can be invariant to different input transformations. Current SSOD methods [15,27,31] only apply off-the-shelf, general data augmentations, most of which are borrowed from image classification. However, different from classification, object detection is an instance-based task, where object scales usually vary in a large range, and detectors are expected to handle all scale ranges. Therefore, learning strong scale-invariant ability via consistency training is important. In scale consistency, it should be allowed for the model to predict the same boxes for input images with identical contents but varied scales.

To ensure label consistency, random-resizing is a common augmentation, which resizes input images and gt boxes according to a randomly generated resize ratio. Besides label consistency, feature consistency also plays an important role in scale-invariant learning, but it is neglected in previous works. Thanks to the pyramid structure of popular backbone networks, feature alignment can be easily implemented by shifting feature pyramid levels according to the scale changes. Motivated by this, we introduce a brand new data augmentation technique, named Multi-view Scale-invariant Learning (MSL), to learn label-level and feature-level consistency simultaneously in a simple framework.

In summary, we delve into two key techniques of semi-supervised learning (e.g., pseudo labeling and consistency training) for SSOD, and integrate object detection properties into them. On COCO benchmarks, our PseCo outperforms the state-of-the-art methods by a large margin, for example, under 10% labelling ratio, it can improve a 26.9% mAP baseline to 36.1% mAP, surpassing previous methods by at least 2.0%. When labeled data is abundant, i.e., we use full COCO training set as labeled data and extra 123K unlabeled2017 as unlabeled data, our PseCo improves the 41.0% mAP baseline by +5.1%, reaching 46.1% mAP, establishing a new state of the art. Moreover, PseCo also significantly boosts the convergence speed, e.g. PseCo halves the training time of the SOTA (Soft Teacher [27]), but achieves even better performance.

2   Related Works

Semi-supervised Learning in Image Classification. Semi-supervised learning can be categorized into two groups: pseudo labeling (also called self-training) and consistency training, and previous methods design learning paradigms based on one of them. Pseudo labeling [5,8,19,26] iteratively adds unlabeled data into the training procedure with pseudo labels annotated by an initially trained network. Here, only model predictions with high confidence will be transformed into the one-hot format and become pseudo labels. Noisy Student Training [26] injects noise into unlabeled data training, which equips the model with stronger generalization through training on the combination of labeled and unlabeled data. On the other hand, consistency training [1,23,25] relies on the assumption that the model should be invariant to small changes on input images or model hidden states. It enforces the model to make similar predictions on the perturbed versions of the same image, and perturbations can be implemented by injecting noise into images and hidden states. UDA [25] validates the advanced data augmentations play a crucial role in consistency training, and observes the strong augmentations found in supervised-learning can also lead to obvious improvements in semi-supervised learning.

Recently, some works [20,29] attempt to combine pseudo labeling and consistency training, achieving state-of-the-art performance. FixMatch [20] firstly applies the weak and strong augmentations to the same input image, respectively, to generate two versions, then uses the weakly-augmented version to generate hard pseudo labels. The model is trained on strongly-augmented versions to align predictions with pseudo labels. Based on FixMatch, FlexMatch [29] proposes to adjust score thresholds for different classes during the generation of pseudo labels, based on curriculum learning. It has been widely validated that pseudo labeling and consistency training are two powerful techniques in semi-supervised image classification, hence in this work, we attempt to integrate object detection properties into them and make them work better for semi-supervised object detection.

Semi-Supervised Learning in Object Detection. STAC [21] is the first attempt to apply pseudo labeling and consistency training based on the strong data augmentations to semi-supervised object detection, however, it adopts two stages of training as Noisy Student Training [26], which prevents the pseudo labels from updating along with model training and limits the performance. After STAC, [15,22,27,28,31] borrow the idea of Exponential Moving Average (EMA) from Mean Teacher [23], and update the teacher model after each training iteration to generate instant pseudo labels, realizing the end-to-end framework. To pursue high quality of pseudo labels and overcome confirmation bias, Instant-Teaching [31] and ISMT [28] introduce model ensemble to aggregate predictions from multiple teacher models which are initialized differently; similarly, Humble Teacher [22] ensembles the teacher model predictions by taking both the image and its horizontally flipped version as input. Although these ensemble methods can promote the quality of pseudo labels, they also introduce considerable computation overhead. Unbiased Teacher [15] replaces traditional Cross-entropy loss with Focal loss [13] to alleviate the class-imbalanced pseudo-labeling issue, which shows strong performance when labeled data is scarce. Soft Teacher [27] uses teacher classification scores as classification loss weights, to suppress negative effects from underlying objects missed by pseudo labels. Different from previous methods, our work elaborately analyzes whether the pseudo labeling and consistency training can be directly applied to SSOD, but gets a negative answer. To integrate object detection properties into these two techniques, we introduce Noisy Pseudo box Learning and Multi-view Scale-invariant Learning, obtaining much better performance and faster convergence speed.

3   Method

We show the framework of our PseCo in Fig. 2. On the unlabeled data, PseCo consists of Noisy Pseudo box Learning (NPL) and Multi-view Scale-invariant Learning (MSL). In the following parts, we will introduce the basic framework, the proposed NPL and MSL, respectively.

3.1   The Basic Framework

At first, we directly apply standard pseudo labeling and consistency training to SSOD, building our basic framework. Following previous works [15,27,31], we also adopt Teacher-student training scheme, where the teacher model is built from the student model at every training iteration via Exponential Moving Average (EMA). We randomly sample labeled data and unlabeled data based on a

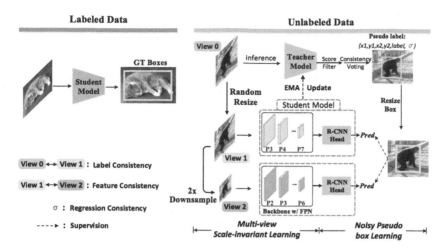

Fig. 2. The framework of our PseCo. Each training batch consists of both labeled and unlabeled images. On the unlabeled images, the student model trains on view V_1 and V_2 at the same time, taking the same pseudo boxes as supervisions. View V_0 refers to input images for the teacher model.

sample ratio to form the training batch. On the labeled data, the student model is trained in a regular manner, supervised by the ground-truth boxes:

$$\mathcal{L}^l = \mathcal{L}^l_{cls} + \mathcal{L}^l_{reg}. \tag{1}$$

On the unlabeled data, we firstly apply weak data augmentations (e.g. horizontal flip, random resizing) to input images, and then feed them to the teacher model for pseudo label generation. Considering the detection boxes tend to be dense even after NMS, we set a score threshold τ and only retain boxes with scores above τ as pseudo labels. After that, strong augmentations (e.g. cutout, rotation, brightness jitter)[1] will be performed on the input image to generate the training example for student model. Since high classification scores do not lead to precise localization, we abandon bounding box regression on unlabeled data, as done in [15]. Actually, applying the box regression loss on unlabeled data will cause unstable training in our experiments.

Foreground-background imbalance [9,13] is an intrinsic issue in object detection, and it gets worse under the semi-supervised setting. A high score threshold τ is usually adopted to guarantee the precision of pseudo labels, but it also results in scarcity of pseudo labels, aggravating the imbalance of foreground/background. Moreover, there also exists foreground-foreground imbalance, exactly, training examples from some specific categories can be limited when labeled data is scarce, which makes the model prone to predict the dominant classes, causing biased prediction. To alleviate these imbalance issues, we

---

[1] We adopt the same data augmentations as Soft Teacher [27], please refer to [27] for more augmentation details.

follow the practice of Unbiased Teacher [15], and replace the standard cross-entropy loss with focal loss [13]:

$$\mathcal{L}_{cls}^u = -\alpha_t(1-p_t)^\gamma log(p_t), \; p_t = \begin{cases} p, & if \; y = 1, \\ 1-p, & otherwise, \end{cases} \tag{2}$$

where parameters α_t and γ adopt default settings in original focal loss paper [13]. The overall loss function is formulated as:

$$\mathcal{L} = \mathcal{L}^l + \beta\mathcal{L}^u, \tag{3}$$

where β is used to control the contribution of unlabeled data. In theory, our proposed method is independent of the detection framework and can be applied on both one-stage and two-stage detectors. However, considering all previous methods are based on Faster R-CNN [18] detection framework, for a fair comparison with them, we also adopt Faster R-CNN as the default detection framework.

3.2 Noisy Pseudo Box Learning

In SSOD, pseudo labels contain both category and location. Since the score of pseudo labels can only indicate the confidence of pseudo box categories, the localization quality of pseudo boxes is not guaranteed. Imprecise pseudo boxes will mislead the label assignment and regression task, making learning on unlabeled data inefficient. Motivated by this, we introduce Prediction-guided Label Assignment and Positive-proposal Consistency Voting to reduce negative effects on the label assignment and regression task, respectively.

Prediction-guided Label Assignment. The standard label assignment strategy in Faster R-CNN [18] only takes the IoUs between proposals and gt boxes (pseudo boxes in our case) into consideration and assigns foreground to those proposals, whose IoUs are above a pre-defined threshold t (0.5 as default). This strategy relies on the assumption that gt boxes are precise, however, this assumption does not hold for unlabeled data obviously. As a result, some low-quality proposals will be mistakenly assigned as positive, confusing the classification boundaries between foreground and background. One specific example is shown in Fig. 1(c), where a proposal with the true IoU as 0.39 is mistakenly assigned as positive.

To address this problem, we propose Prediction-guided Label Assignment (PLA), which takes teacher predictions as auxiliary information and reduces dependency on IoUs. In Teacher-student training scheme, not only can the detection results (after NMS) of teacher perform as pseudo labels, but also teacher's dense predictions (before NMS) are able to provide guidance for student model training. We share the proposals generated by the teacher RPN with the student, so that teacher predictions on these proposals can be easily transferred to student. To measure the proposal quality (q) comprehensively, the classification confidence and localization precision of teacher predictions are jointly employed, concretely, $q = s^\alpha \times u^{1-\alpha}$, where s and u denote a foreground score and an IoU value between the regressed box and the ground truth, respectively. α controls the contribution of s and u in the overall quality. On unlabeled data, we first construct a candidate bag for each ground truth g by the traditional IoU-based strategy, where the IoU threshold t is set to a relatively low value, e.g., 0.4 as default, to contain more proposals. Within each candidate bag, the proposals are firstly sorted by their quality q, then top-$\mathcal{N}$ proposals are adopted as positive samples and the rest are negatives. The number $\mathcal{N}$ is decided by *the dynamic k estimation* strategy proposed in OTA [4], specifically, the IoU values over the candidate bag is summed up to represent the number of positive samples. The proposed PLA gets rid of strong dependencies on IoUs and alleviates negative effects from poorly localized pseudo boxes, leading to clearer classification boundaries. Furthermore, our label assign strategy integrates more teacher knowledge into student model training, realizing better knowledge distillation.

Positive-proposal Consistency Voting. Considering the classification score fails to indicate localization quality, we introduce a simple yet effective method to measure the localization quality, named Positive-proposal Consistency Voting (PCV). Assigning multiple proposals to each gt box (or pseudo box) is a common practice in CNN-based detectors [11,18,30], and we observe that the consistency of regression results from these proposals is capable of reflecting the localization quality of the corresponding pseudo box. Regression consistency σ^j for pseudo box (indexed by j) is formulated as:

$$\sigma^j = \frac{\sum_{i=1}^{N} u_i^j}{N}, \tag{4}$$

where u denotes an IoU value between the predicted box and the pseudo box, as defined above; N denotes the number of positive proposals, assigned to the pseudo box j. After obtaining σ^j, we employ it as the instance-wise regression loss weight:

$$\mathcal{L}_{reg}^u = \frac{1}{MN} \sum_{j=1}^{M} \sigma^j \sum_{i=1}^{N} |reg_i^j - r\hat{e}g_i^j|, \tag{5}$$

where reg and $r\hat{e}g$ refer to the regression output and ground-truth, respectively. In Fig. 1(b), we depict the scatter diagram of the relation between prediction consistency σ of pseudo boxes and their true IoUs. It is obvious that σ is positively correlated with true IoUs. Note that, some dots falling in the orange ellipse are mainly caused by annotation errors. We visualize some examples in *supplemental material*, where the pseudo boxes accurately detect some objects, which are missed by the ground truths.

3.3   Multi-view Scale-Invariant Learning

Different from image classification, in object detection, object scales vary in a large range and detectors hardly show comparable performance on all scales. Therefore, learning scale-invariant representations from unlabeled data is considerably important for SSOD. In consistency training, strong data augmentations

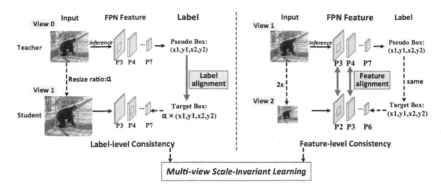

Fig. 3. Comparisons between label-level consistency learning and feature-level consistency learning. For label consistency, labels are aligned according to the resize ratio α; for feature consistency, features are aligned by shifting the feature pyramid level.

play a crucial role [25, 26] in achieving competitive performance. Through injecting the perturbations into the input images, data augmentations equip the model with robustness to various transformations. From the perspective of scale invariance, we regard the common data augmentation strategy (e.g. random-resizing) as label-level consistency since it resizes the label according to the scale changes of input images. Unfortunately, existing works only involve the widely adopted label-level consistency but fail to consider the feature-level one. Since detection network usually has designs of rich feature pyramids, feature-level consistency is easy to implement across paired inputs [17] and should be considered seriously. In this paper, we propose Multi-view Scale-invariant Learning (MSL) that combines both label- and feature-level consistency into a simple framework, where feature-level consistency is realized by aligning shifted pyramid features between two images with identical content but different scales.

To be specific, two views, namely V_1 and V_2, are used for student training in MSL. We denote the input image for the teacher model as V_0. Views V_1 and V_2 are constructed to learn label- and feature-level consistency, respectively. Among them, V_1 is implemented by vanilla random resizing, which rescales the input V_0 and pseudo boxes according to a resize ratio α randomly sampled from the range $[\alpha_{min}, \alpha_{max}]$ ([0.8, 1.3] as default). For feature consistency learning, we firstly downsample V_1 by even number times (2x as default) to produce V_2, then combine V_1 and V_2 into image pairs. Upsampling is also certainly permitted, but we only perform downsampling here for GPU memory restriction. Because the spatial sizes of adjacent FPN layers always differ by 2x, the P3-P7 layers[2] of V_1 can align well with P2-P6 layers of V_2 in the spatial dimension. Through feature alignment, the same pseudo boxes can supervise the student model training on both V_1 and V_2. Integrating label consistency and feature consistency into consistency learning leads to stronger scale-invariant learning and significantly accelerates model convergence, as we will show later in the experiments. Comparisons between label consistency and feature consistency are shown in Fig. 3.

---

[2] P_x refers to the FPN layer whose feature maps are downsampled by 2^x times.

Learning scale-invariant representation from unlabeled data is also explored by SoCo [24]. However, we claim there are two intrinsic differences between MSL and SoCo: (1) MSL models scale invariance from both label consistency and image feature consistency, while SoCo only considers object feature consistency. Through aligning **dense image features** of shifted pyramids between paired images, our MSL can provide more comprehensive and dense supervisory signals than the SoCo, which only performs consistency on **sparse objects**. (2) SoCo implements feature consistency via contrastive learning, which is designed for the pretraining; in contrast, our MSL uses bounding box supervision to implement consistency learning and can be integrated into the detection task.

4   Experiments

4.1   Dataset and Evaluation Protocol

In this section, we conduct extensive experiments to verify the effectiveness of PseCo on MS COCO benchmark [14]. There are two training sets, namely the train2017 set, containing 118k labeled images, and the unlabeled2017 set, containing 123k unlabeled images. The val2017 with 5k images is used as validation set, and we report all experiment results on val2017. The performance is measured by COCO average prevision (denoted as mAP). Following the common practice of SSOD [21], there are two experimental settings: **Partially Labeled Data** and **Fully Labeled Data**, which are described as follows:

Partially Labeled Data. We randomly sample 1, 2, 5, and 10% data from train2017 as labeled data, and use the rest as unlabeled. Under each labelling ratio, we report the mean and standard deviation over 5 different data folds.

Fully Labeled Data. Under this setting, we take train2017 as the training labeled set and unlabeled2017 as the training unlabeled set.

4.2   Implementation Details

For a fair comparison, we adopt Faster R-CNN [18] with FPN [12] as the detection framework, and ResNet-50 [6] as the backbone. The confidence threshold τ is set to 0.5, empirically. We set β as 4.0 to control contributions of unlabeled data in the overall losses. The performance is evaluated on the Teacher model. Training details for **Partially Labeled Data** and **Fully Labeled Data** are described below:

Partially Labeled Data. All models are trained for 180k iterations on 8 GPUs. The initial learning rate is set as 0.01 and divided by 10 at 120k and 160k iterations. The training batch in each GPU includes 5 images, where the sample ratio between unlabeled data and labeled data is set to 4:1.

Fully Labeled Data. All models are trained for 720k iterations on 8 GPUs. Mini-batch in each GPU is 8 with the sample ratio between unlabeled and labeled data as 1:1. The learning rate is initialized to 0.01 and divided by 10 at 480k and 680k iterations.

Table 1. Comparisons with the state-of-the-art methods on val2017 set under the **Partially Labeled Data** and **Fully Labeled Data** settings.

Method	Partially Labeled Data				Fully Labeled Data
	1%	2%	5%	10%	
Supervised baseline	12.20 ± 0.29	16.53 ± 0.12	21.17 ± 0.17	26.90 ± 0.08	41.0
STAC [21]	13.97 ± 0.35	18.25 ± 0.25	24.38 ± 0.12	28.64 ± 0.21	39.5 $\xrightarrow{-0.3}$ 39.2
Humble Teacher [22]	16.96 ± 0.35	21.74 ± 0.24	27.70 ± 0.15	31.61 ± 0.28	37.6 $\xrightarrow{+4.8}$ 42.4
ISMT [28]	18.88 ± 0.74	22.43 ± 0.56	26.37 ± 0.24	30.53 ± 0.52	37.8 $\xrightarrow{+1.8}$ 39.6
Instant-Teaching [31]	18.05 ± 0.15	22.45 ± 0.15	26.75 ± 0.05	30.40 ± 0.05	37.6 $\xrightarrow{+2.6}$ 40.2
Unbiased Teacher [15]	20.75 ± 0.12	24.30 ± 0.07	28.27 ± 0.11	31.50 ± 0.10	40.2 $\xrightarrow{+1.1}$ 41.3
Soft Teacher [27]	20.46 ± 0.39	–	30.74 ± 0.08	34.04 ± 0.14	40.9 $\xrightarrow{+3.6}$ 44.5
PseCo (ours)	**22.43** ± 0.36	**27.77** ± 0.18	**32.50** ± 0.08	**36.06** ± 0.24	41.0 $\xrightarrow{+5.1}$ **46.1**

4.3 Comparison with State-of-the-Art Methods

We compare the proposed PseCo with other state-of-the-art methods on COCO val2017 set. Comparisons under the **Partially Labeled Data** setting are first conducted, with results reported in Table 1. When labeled data is scarce (i.e., under 1% and 2% labelling ratios), our method surpasses the state-of-the-art method, Unbiased Teacher [15], by 1.7% and 3.5%, reaching 22.4 and 27.8 mAP, respectively. When more labeled data is accessible, the SOTA method is transferred to Soft Teacher [27]. Our method still outperforms it by 1.8% and 2.0% under 5% and 10% labelling ratios, respectively. Therefore, the proposed method outperforms the SOTAs by a large margin, at least 1.7%, under all labelling ratios. Compared with the supervised baseline, PseCo obtains even better performance with only 2% labeled data than the baseline with 10% labeled data, demonstrating the effectiveness of proposed semi-supervised learning techniques.

Moreover, we also compare the convergence speed with the previous best method (Soft Teacher [27]) in Fig. 4, where convergence curves are depicted under 10% and 5% labelling ratios. It is obvious that our method has a faster convergence speed, specifically, our method uses only 2/5 and 1/4 iterations of Soft Teacher to achieve the same performance under 10% and 5% labelling ratios respectively. Although we employ an extra view (V_2) to learn feature-level consistency, it only increases the training time of each iteration by 25% (from 0.72 sec/iter to 0.91 sec/iter), due to the low input resolution of V_2. In summary, we halve the training time of SOTA approach but achieve even better performance, which validates the superior learning efficiency of our method on unlabeled data.

The experimental results under the **Fully Labeled Data** setting are reported in Table 1, where both results of comparison methods and their supervised baseline are listed. Following the practice in Soft Teacher [27], we also apply weak augmentations to the labeled data and obtain a strong supervised baseline, 41.0 mAP. Although with a such strong baseline, PseCo still achieves larger improvements (+5.1%) than others and reaches 46.1 mAP, building a new state of the art. Some qualitative results are attached in *supplemental material*.

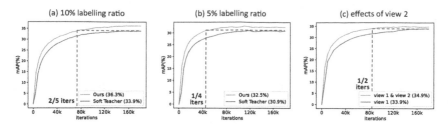

Fig. 4. Comparison of model convergence speed. In (a) and (b), we compare PseCo against Soft Teacher [27]. Here, we reproduce Soft Teacher using their source codes. (c) depicts the comparison between V_1 and $V_1 \& V_2$. In legend, the numbers in brackets refer to mAP. Performance is evaluated on the teacher.

Table 2. Ablation studies on each component of our method. MSL represents Multi-view Scale-invariant Learning; NPL represents Noisy Pseudo box Learning. In MSL, V_1 and V_2 are constructed for label- and feature-level consistency, respectively. In NPL, PCV and PLA stand for Positive-proposal Consistency Voting and Prediction-guided Label Assignment, respectively.

MSL		NPL		mAP	AP_{50}	AP_{75}
V_1	V_2	PCV	PLA			
				26.8	44.9	28.4
✓				33.9(+7.1)	55.2	36.0
✓	✓			34.9(+8.1)	56.3	37.1
✓		✓		34.8(+8.0)	55.1	37.4
✓		✓	✓	35.7(+8.9)	56.4	38.4
✓	✓	✓		36.0(+9.2)	56.9	38.7
✓	✓	✓	✓	**36.3**(+9.5)	**57.2**	**39.2**

4.4 Ablation Study

We conduct detailed ablation studies to verify key designs. All ablation studies are conducted on a single data fold from the 10% labelling ratio.

Effect of Individual Component. In Table 2, we show effectiveness of each component step by step. When only using 10% labeled data as training examples, it obtains 26.8 mAP. Next, we construct the semi-supervised baseline by applying V_1 on unlabeled data for label-level consistency learning. The baseline does not consider any adverse effects incurred by coarse pseudo boxes and obtains 33.9 mAP. Furthermore, by leveraging additional view V_2, the feature-level scale-invariant learning is enabled, and an improvement of +1.0 mAP is found. On the other hand, to alleviate the issue of coarse pseudo boxes, we introduce PCV to suppress the inaccurate regression signals, improving the baseline from 33.9 to 34.8 mAP. After that, we replace the traditional IoU-based label assignment strategy with the PLA and enjoy another +0.9 mAP gain. Finally, when combing MSL and NPL together, it achieves the best performance, 36.3 mAP.

Table 3. Analysis of Multi-view Scale-invariant learning, which contains both the label- and feature-level consistency.

(a) Study on label consistency.

Method	mAP	AP_S	AP_M	AP_L
Single-scale training	32.7	19.0	36.0	42.5
Label consistency	**33.9**	**19.1**	**37.2**	**44.4**

(b) Study on feature consistency.

Method	mAP	AP_S	AP_M	AP_L
Vanilla multi-view training	33.9	20.9	37.2	43.0
Feature consistency	**34.9**	**22.1**	**38.2**	**43.6**

Table 4. Ablation studies related to Positive-proposal Consistency Voting (PCV) and Prediction-guided Label Assignment (PLA).

(a) Comparison between our PCV and other regression methods.

Method	mAP	AP_{50}	AP_{75}
Abandon reg [15]	33.9	55.2	36.0
Reg consistency [22]	34.2	55.1	36.5
Box jittering [27]	34.5	54.9	36.9
PCV (ours)	**34.8**	**55.1**	**37.4**

(b) Study on hyper-parameter α.

α	mAP	AP_{50}	AP_{75}
0	35.2	56.1	37.8
0.5	**35.7**	**56.4**	**38.4**
1.0	35.4	55.7	38.4

(c) Study on IoU threshold t.

t	mAP	AP_{50}	AP_{75}
0.3	35.7	56.2	**38.6**
0.4	**35.7**	**56.4**	38.4
0.5	35.5	56.1	38.3

Comparison with Other Regression Methods. Scores of pseudo boxes can only indicate the confidence of predicted object category, thus they fail to reflect localization quality [11,15]. Naive confidence thresholding will introduce some coarse bounding boxes for regression tasks. To alleviate this issue, Unbiased Teacher [15] abandons regression losses on unlabeled data (denoted as "abandon reg"); Humble Teacher [22] aligns the regression predictions between the teacher and student on selected top-$\mathcal{N}$ proposals (dubbed "reg consistency"); Soft Teacher [27] introduces the box jittering to calculate prediction variance on jittered pseudo boxes, which is used to filter out poorly localized pseudo boxes. In Table 4a, we compare our Positive-proposal Consistency Voting (PCV) with these methods. PCV obtains the best performance, concretely, on AP_{75}, PCV surpasses two competitors, reg consistency and box jittering, by 0.9% and 0.5%, respectively. Although both PCV and box jittering [27] rely on prediction variance, there exist great differences. Firstly, PCV produces localization quality by intrinsic proposals, thus it avoids extra network forward on jittered boxes, enjoying higher training efficiency. Moreover, unlike the box jittering, which meticulously tunes the variance threshold, PCV is free of hyper-parameters.

Study on Different Hyper-parameters of PLA. We first investigate the performance using different α in PLA, which balances the influence of classification score (s) and localization precision (u) in the proposal quality. Through a coarse search shown in Table 4b, we find that combining s and u yields better performance than using them individually. We then carry out experiments to study the robustness of the IoU threshold t, which is used to build the candidate bag. From the Table 4c, using lower t to construct a bigger candidate bag is preferred.

Analysis of Multi-view Scale-invariant Learning. We propose the MSL to model scale invariance from the aspects of both label- and feature-level consistency. The studies on them are reported in Table 3. At first, we construct a single-scale training baseline without scale variance, where the input images for the teacher and student are kept on the same scale. It obtains 32.7 mAP. Next, we apply the different scale jitter on the teacher and student to implement label-level consistency, which surpasses the single-scale training by 1.2 mAP. Based on the label consistency, we further introduce the view V_2 to perform feature consistency learning. It obtains +1.0% improvements, reaching 34.9 mAP. Apart from performance gains, the feature consistency can also significantly boost the convergence speed as depicted in Fig. 4(c). To validate the improvements introduced by the V_2 come from comprehensive scale-invariant learning, instead of vanilla multi-view training, we also add an extra view V_2' besides the V_1, where V_2' is downsampled from V_1 by 2x and performs label consistency as V_1. From the Table 3(b), vanilla multi-view training with only label consistency hardly brings improvements against the single V_1 (33.9 vs 33.9%).

Effect of Focal Loss. In Table 5, we compare the Cross Entropy (CE) Loss and Focal Loss. Thanks to the Focal Loss, an improvement of +0.6 mAP is achieved against the CE Loss. On the other hand, even with the CE Loss, our PseCo still surpasses the Soft Teacher by a large margin, i.e., 1.7 mAP.

Table 5. Ablation study on Focal Loss.

Method	mAP	AP_{50}	AP_{75}
PseCo w/ CE Loss	35.7	55.6	38.9
PseCo w/ Focal Loss	**36.3**	**57.2**	**39.2**

5 Conclusion

In this work, we elaborately analyze two key techniques of semi-supervised object detection (e.g. pseudo labeling and consistency training), and observe these two techniques currently neglect some important properties of object detection. Motivated by this, we propose a new SSOD framework, PseCo, to integrate object detection properties into SSOD. PseCo consists of Noisy Pseudo box Learning (NPL) and Multi-view Scale-invariant Learning (MSL). In NPL, prediction-guided label assignment and positive-proposal consistency voting are proposed to perform the robust label assignment and regression task using noisy pseudo boxes, respectively. Based on the common label-level consistency, MSL additionally designs a novel feature-level scale-invariant learning, which is neglected in prior works. To validate the effectiveness of our method, extensive experiments are conducted on COCO benchmark. Experimental results validate PseCo surpasses the SOTAs by a large margin both in accuracy and efficiency.

Acknowledgements. G. Li, X. Li and S. Zhang are with PCA Lab, Key Lab of Intelligent Perception and Systems for High-Dimensional Information of Ministry of Education, and Jiangsu Key Lab of Image and Video Understanding for Social Security, School of Computer Science and Engineering, Nanjing University of Science and Technology. This work is partially supported by National Natural Science Foundation of China (Grant No. 62172225) and the Fundamental Research Funds for the Central Universities (No. 30920032201).

References

1. Berthelot, D., Carlini, N., Goodfellow, I., Papernot, N., Oliver, A., Raffel, C.A.: Mixmatch: a holistic approach to semi-supervised learning. In: Advances in Neural Information Processing Systems 32 (2019)
2. Deng, J., Dong, W., Socher, R., Li, L.J., Li, K., Fei-Fei, L.: ImageNet: a large-scale hierarchical image database. In: 2009 IEEE Conference on Computer Vision and Pattern Recognition, pp. 248–255. IEEE (2009)
3. Dosovitskiy, A., et al.: An image is worth 16×16 words: transformers for image recognition at scale. arXiv preprint arXiv:2010.11929 (2020)
4. Ge, Z., Liu, S., Li, Z., Yoshie, O., Sun, J.: OTA: optimal transport assignment for object detection. In: Proceedings of the IEEE/CVF Conference on Computer Vision and Pattern Recognition, pp. 303–312 (2021)
5. Grandvalet, Y., Bengio, Y.: Semi-supervised learning by entropy minimization. In: Advances in neural information processing systems 17 (2004)
6. He, K., Zhang, X., Ren, S., Sun, J.: Deep residual learning for image recognition. In: Proceedings of the IEEE Conference on Computer Vision and Pattern Recognition, pp. 770–778 (2016)
7. Jiang, B., Luo, R., Mao, J., Xiao, T., Jiang, Y.: Acquisition of localization confidence for accurate object detection. In: Proceedings of the European Conference on Computer Vision (ECCV), pp. 784–799 (2018)
8. Lee, D.H., et al.: Pseudo-label: The simple and efficient semi-supervised learning method for deep neural networks. In: Workshop on Challenges in Representation Learning, ICML, vol. 3, p. 896 (2013)
9. Li, B., Liu, Y., Wang, X.: Gradient harmonized single-stage detector. In: Proceedings of the AAAI Conference on Artificial Intelligence, vol. 33, pp. 8577–8584 (2019)
10. Li, G., Li, X., Wang, Y., Zhang, S., Wu, Y., Liang, D.: Knowledge distillation for object detection via rank mimicking and prediction-guided feature imitation. In: Proceedings of the AAAI Conference on Artificial Intelligence, vol. 36, pp. 1306–1313 (2022)
11. Li, X., Lv, C., Wang, W., Li, G., Yang, L., Yang, J.: Generalized focal loss: towards efficient representation learning for dense object detection. IEEE Transactions on Pattern Analysis and Machine Intelligence (2022)
12. Lin, T.Y., Dollár, P., Girshick, R., He, K., Hariharan, B., Belongie, S.: Feature pyramid networks for object detection. In: Proceedings of the IEEE Conference on Computer Vision and Pattern Recognition, pp. 2117–2125 (2017)
13. Lin, T.Y., Goyal, P., Girshick, R., He, K., Dollár, P.: Focal loss for dense object detection. In: Proceedings of the IEEE International Conference on Computer Vision, pp. 2980–2988 (2017)

14. Lin, T.Y., et al.: Microsoft COCO: common objects in context. In: Fleet, D., Pajdla, T., Schiele, B., Tuytelaars, T. (eds.) ECCV 2014. LNCS, vol. 8693, pp. 740–755. Springer, Cham (2014). https://doi.org/10.1007/978-3-319-10602-1_48

15. Liu, Y.C., et al.: Unbiased teacher for semi-supervised object detection. arXiv preprint arXiv:2102.09480 (2021)

16. Liu, Z., et al.: Swin transformer: hierarchical vision transformer using shifted windows. In: Proceedings of the IEEE/CVF International Conference on Computer Vision, pp. 10012–10022 (2021)

17. Qi, L., et al.: Multi-scale aligned distillation for low-resolution detection. In: Proceedings of the IEEE/CVF Conference on Computer Vision and Pattern Recognition, pp. 14443–14453 (2021)

18. Ren, S., He, K., Girshick, R., Sun, J.: Faster R-CNN: towards real-time object detection with region proposal networks. In: Advances in Neural Information Processing Systems 28 (2015)

19. Scudder, H.: Probability of error of some adaptive pattern-recognition machines. IEEE Trans. Inf. Theor. **11**(3), 363–371 (1965)

20. Sohn, K., et al.: FixMatch: simplifying semi-supervised learning with consistency and confidence. Adv. Neural. Inf. Process. Syst. **33**, 596–608 (2020)

21. Sohn, K., Zhang, Z., Li, C.L., Zhang, H., Lee, C.Y., Pfister, T.: A simple semi-supervised learning framework for object detection. arXiv preprint arXiv:2005.04757 (2020)

22. Tang, Y., Chen, W., Luo, Y., Zhang, Y.: Humble teachers teach better students for semi-supervised object detection. In: Proceedings of the IEEE/CVF Conference on Computer Vision and Pattern Recognition, pp. 3132–3141 (2021)

23. Tarvainen, A., Valpola, H.: Mean teachers are better role models: weight-averaged consistency targets improve semi-supervised deep learning results. In: Advances in neural information processing systems 30 (2017)

24. Wei, F., Gao, Y., Wu, Z., Hu, H., Lin, S.: Aligning pretraining for detection via object-level contrastive learning. In: Advances in Neural Information Processing Systems 34 (2021)

25. Xie, Q., Dai, Z., Hovy, E., Luong, T., Le, Q.: Unsupervised data augmentation for consistency training. Adv. Neural. Inf. Process. Syst. **33**, 6256–6268 (2020)

26. Xie, Q., Luong, M.T., Hovy, E., Le, Q.V.: Self-training with noisy student improves ImageNet classification. In: Proceedings of the IEEE/CVF Conference on Computer Vision and Pattern Recognition, pp. 10687–10698 (2020)

27. Xu, M., et al.: End-to-end semi-supervised object detection with soft teacher. In: Proceedings of the IEEE/CVF International Conference on Computer Vision, pp. 3060–3069 (2021)

28. Yang, Q., Wei, X., Wang, B., Hua, X.S., Zhang, L.: Interactive self-training with mean teachers for semi-supervised object detection. In: Proceedings of the IEEE/CVF Conference on Computer Vision and Pattern Recognition, pp. 5941–5950 (2021)

29. Zhang, B., et al.: FlexMatch: boosting semi-supervised learning with curriculum pseudo labeling. In: Advances in Neural Information Processing Systems 34 (2021)

30. Zhang, H., Wang, Y., Dayoub, F., Sunderhauf, N.: VarifocalNet: an IoU-aware dense object detector. In: Proceedings of the IEEE/CVF Conference on Computer Vision and Pattern Recognition, pp. 8514–8523 (2021)

31. Zhou, Q., Yu, C., Wang, Z., Qian, Q., Li, H.: Instant-teaching: an end-to-end semi-supervised object detection framework. In: Proceedings of the IEEE/CVF Conference on Computer Vision and Pattern Recognition, pp. 4081–4090 (2021)

Exploring Resolution and Degradation Clues as Self-supervised Signal for Low Quality Object Detection

Ziteng Cui[1], Yingying Zhu[2], Lin Gu[3,4(✉)], Guo-Jun Qi[5], Xiaoxiao Li[6], Renrui Zhang[7], Zenghui Zhang[1], and Tatsuya Harada[3,4]

[1] Shanghai Jiao Tong University, Shanghai, China
[2] University of Texas at Arlington, Arlington, USA
[3] RIKEN AIP, Chuo City, Japan
`lin.gu@riken.jp`
[4] The University of Tokyo, Tokyo, Japan
[5] Laboratory for Machine Perception and Learning, Orlando, USA
[6] The University of British Columbia, Vancouver, Canada
[7] Shanghai AI Laboratory, Shanghai, China

Abstract. Image restoration algorithms such as super resolution (SR) are indispensable pre-processing modules for object detection in low quality images. Most of these algorithms assume the degradation is fixed and known a priori. However, in practical, either the real degradation or optimal up-sampling ratio rate is unknown or differs from assumption, leading to a deteriorating performance for both the pre-processing module and the consequent high-level task such as object detection. Here, we propose a novel self-supervised framework to detect objects in degraded low resolution images. We utilizes the downsampling degradation as a kind of transformation for self-supervised signals to explore the equivariant representation against various resolutions and other degradation conditions. The Auto Encoding Resolution in Self-supervision (AERIS) framework could further take the advantage of advanced SR architectures with an arbitrary resolution restoring decoder to reconstruct the original correspondence from the degraded input image. Both the representation learning and object detection are optimized jointly in an end-to-end training fashion. The generic AERIS framework could be implemented on various mainstream object detection architectures with different backbones. The extensive experiments show that our methods has achieved superior performance compared with existing methods when facing variant degradation situations. Code is available at this link https://github.com/cuiziteng/ECCV_AERIS.

Keywords: Self-supervised learning · Computational photography · Object detection

Supplementary Information The online version contains supplementary material available at https://doi.org/10.1007/978-3-031-20077-9_28.

1   Introduction

High level vision tasks (*i.e.* image classification, object detection, and semantic segmentation) have witnessed great success thanks to the large scale dataset [10,14,35]. Images in these datasets are mainly captured by commercial cameras with higher resolution and signal-to-noise ratio (SNR). Trained and optimized on these high-quality images, high-level vision would suffer a performance drop on low resolution [9,19,53] or low quality images [1,8,38,41,45,52].

To improve the performance of vision algorithms on degraded low resolution images, Dai *et al.* [9] presented the first comprehensive study advocating pre-processing images with super resolution (SR) algorithms. Other high-level tasks like face recognition [66], face detection [2], image classification [38,55] and semantic segmentation [53], also benefit from the restoration module to extract more discriminate features.

Most existing enhancement methods, especially SR algorithms [3,59,60], assume target images are from a **known and fixed** degradation model [13,36]:

$$t(x) = (x \circledast k) \downarrow_s + n, \tag{1}$$

where $t(x)$ and x denote the degraded low resolution (LR) image and original high resolution (HR) input respectively. k is the blur kernel while $\downarrow_s$ is the down-sampling operation with ratio s. n is the additive noise. However, the performance of these enhancement algorithms would decline severely when the real degradation deviates from the assumption [18]. To make it worse, for machine perception tasks, as shown in Fig. 1b, higher resolution does not necessarily guarantee a better performance in high level tasks. Like object detection, the optimal SR ratio

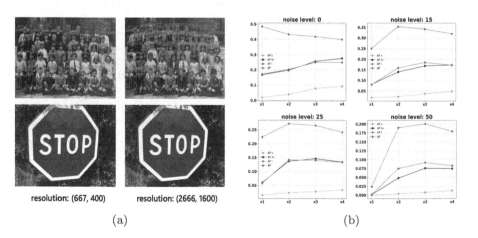

Fig. 1. Illustration of scale variance bottleneck. (a): Tiny people are well detected at high resolution while the large traffic sign is recognized in low resolution. (b): Detection result on down-sampled MS COCO [35] dataset (down scale rate: 4) with different noise level. Specifically, we up-scale the images with different ratio (2, 3, 4) before detection. X-axis is up-scale ratio and Y-axis is mAP result of CenterNet [64]. We also report the results on small, medium and large objects.

varies across the images due to the scale variance bottleneck [48,49], there is a trade off that certain high level predictions are better handled at lower resolution and others better processed at higher resolution. As illustrated in Fig. 1a, though working well on individual tiny person at high resolution (2666,1600), the detection method ignores the large traffic sign. On the contrary, in low resolution (667,400) images, detecting network's reception field could observe more global context for large structure, at the cost of sacrificing the small objects. Figure 1b also quantitatively demonstrates this bottleneck. The detection performance does not necessary increases with super resolution ratio, especially for large objects.

Instead of explicitly enhancing an input image with a fixed restoration module, we exploit the intrinsic equivariant representation against various resolutions and degradation. *I know who I was when I got up this morning, but I think I must have been changed several times since then.*[1]. Either being small enough to squeeze through the door or so big to shed a pool of tears, Alice should be encoded with a equivariant representation to show who she is in the world. Based on the encoded representation shown in Fig. 2, we propose an end-to-end framework for object detection in low quality images. To capture the complex patterns of visual structures, we utilize groups of downsampling degradation transformations under different downsampling rate, noise and degradation kernel as the self-supervised signal [16,63].

During the training, we generate a degraded LR image $t(x)$ from the original HR image x through a random degradation transformation t. As shown in Fig. 2, to train the Encoder E to learn the degradation equivariant representation $E(t(x))$, we introduce an arbitrary-resolution restoration decoder (ARRD) decoder D_r. ARRD implicitly decodes t to reconstruct the original HR data x from the representation $E(t(x))$ of various degraded LR image $t(x)$. If the self-supervised signal is reconstructed, the representation should capture the dynamics of how they change under different resolution and other degradation as much as possible [7,44,63]. The nature of reconstructing HR data also allows us to leverage the advance of the fast-growing SR research by directly using their successful architectures.

On the encoded representation $E(t(x))$, we further impose an object detection decoder D_o to supervise the encoder E to encode the image structure relevant to the consequent tasks. The object detection decoder D_o performs the detection task to get the object's location and class. During inference, the target image is directly passed through the encoder E and object detection decoder D_o in Fig. 2 for detection. Compared to pre-processing module based methods [19, 46], our inference pipeline is more computation efficient as we avoid explicitly reconstructing the image details.

To cover the diverse degradation and resolutions, in real scenario, we generate degraded $t(x)$ by randomly sampling a transformations t according to practical down-sampling degradation model [36,59]. As shown in Fig. 2, the transformation t is characterised by down-sampling ratio s, blur kernel k, and noise level n in Eq. 1.

---

[1] Chapter 5, Alice in Wonderland.

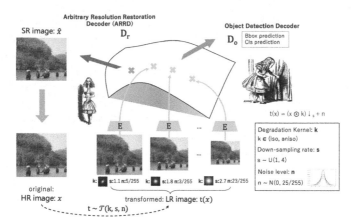

Fig. 2. A simple illustration of Auto Encoding Resolution in Self-supervision (AERIS). Encoder E encodes images transformed under various self-supervised signal into degradation equivariant representations (like Alice after drinking "Drink me"). ARRD D_r implicitly decodes the self-supervised signal to reconstruct the original image/transformation while detection decoder D_o decodes the representations for object detection task.

Our contributions could be summarised as follows:

- We propose a novel framework, Auto Encoding Resolution in Self-supervision (AERIS), to detect objects in degraded low resolution images by utilizing the resolution and degradation clues as self-supervised signal. Specifically, we learn the degradation equivariant representation that captures the dynamics of feature representations under diverse resolutions and degradation types. Our AERIS is generic and could be implemented on several mainstream object detection architecture.
- AERIS method takes the strength of advanced super resolution (SR) research by training an arbitrary resolution restoration decoder (ARRD) that reconstructs the high resolution details. Furthermore, by optimizing the representation learning and detection in a unified end-to-end training framework, the representation preserves the intrinsic visual structure that is discriminative for detection.
- We evaluate our method on mainstream public dataset MS COCO [35] and KITTI [15]. The experiment results also show that our method has achieved SOTA performance on several degradation conditions.

2   Related Works

2.1   Single Image Super Resolution

Image restoration algorithms are intuitive solutions to handle degradation, here we mainly introduce single image super-resolution (SISR), since the object detection task is sensitive to resolution, and the other low-level vision tasks (*i.e.* denoise, deblur) also have connections with SISR task.

The very first CCN-based SR was proposed by Dong *et al.* [11] with a three-layer neural network. Then Kim *et al.* [29] extended the depth of network to 20 layers with gradient clipping and residual learning. Batch normalization is later identified to impose the negative effect on the SR reconstruction. By removing this layer, EDSR [34] achieves SOTA in 2017. After ESDR, better SR architectures are designed by integrating the successful deep learning techniques such as Laplacian pyramid structure [30], dense connection [51], back projection [20], transformer blocks [33] and so on. Besides designing sophisticated architecture, losses like perceptual loss [26] and adversarial loss [31] are also demonstrated to improve the SR reconstruction quality.

SR algorithms heavily rely on the assumption of degradation model and fixed resolution. Much efforts are spent to relax the constraint. Not limited to a unfixed up-sampling scale, like Hu *et al.* [24] first proposed Meta-SR to super-resolve images with arbitrary scale factor. After that, LIIF [6] utilize implicit function to solve this task, and FuncNet [40] further been proposed also for noise and blur condition.

To deploy SR for real scenarios, blind SR methods assume the degradation information is not known. One direction is to convert the problem into non-blind SR by provide prior degradation information [62] or initially estimate the degradation parameters [3]. However, the applied non-blind SR algorithm is very sensitive to the error of the degradation estimation. Gu *et al.* [18] then proposed to iterative correct the estimated degradation with an iterative kernel correction (IKC) method. Without explicitly estimating degradation parameters, Wang *et al.* [54] introduced a contrastive loss to design the degradation-aware SR network based on the learned representations. Recently, Zhang *et al.* [59] solved the general blind SISR by designing a practical model considering complex degradation. This model has been demonstrated to cover the degradation space of real images. Therefore, we adopt this practical model to synthesize various degraded LR images as the self-supervised signal to train our model.

2.2   Image Restoration for Machine Perception

There is sufficient evidence that degraded scene would give negative impact on high-level vision tasks [9,19,27,57]. As for resolution, Dai *et al.* [9] made the first analyze on improving several vision tasks with SR as pre-process. Wang *et al.* [55] analyzed the effectiveness of SR in image classification task while DSRL [53] improved the low-resolution semantic segmentation with an additional SR block. Shermeyer and Etten [46] evaluate the effectiveness of a SR pre-process step on aerial image object detection. Recently, Haris *et al.* [19] jointly optimise object detection loss along with SR sub-network [20] to improve detection performance.

Similarly, noise and blur's effect on high-level vision have also been well-studied. Hendrycks *et al.* [22] evaluate image classification robustness under multiply degradation conditions including noise and blur. Kamann *et al.* [27] studied the impact of noise and blur on different semantic segmentation methods.

Liu *et al.* [38] combine a denoise network in classifier to improve classification's performance under noisy condition. Very recently, Mohamed and Gabriel [45] analyse motion blur and propose several methods to improve detection performance on motion blurry images.

However, most of these existing works assume the degradation parameters such as the down-sampling ratio is known and fixed. Based on the degradation equivariant representation, our framework is robust to various degradation in real-world scenarios. Without an explicit restoration module or restoration step, we directly perform the detection on low-dimension encoded features that saves much computational burden.

3   Down-sampling Degradation Transformations

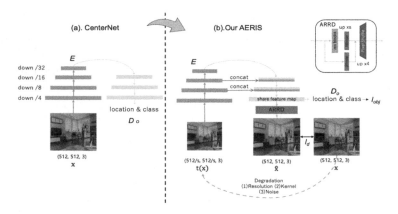

Fig. 3. An illustration of how our AERIS is implemented based on CenterNet [64]. Left is the original CenterNet while the right one is the architecture of AERIS.

In real scenarios, the image may be captured and processed in various ways. To cover these generally unknown operations, it is necessary to select a practical degradation model for the degradation transformation. This model would transform the high resolution (HR) image x to the low resolution counterpart $t(x)$ with Eq. 1.

Early restoration methods assume a simple degradation model where LR is directly down-sampled from the HR images without or with simple noise. Instead of dealing with synthetic images, recent methods now focus on more realistic degradation models. For example, [4] directly train the model on the LR and HR images pair captured by the real camera system. USRNet [60] effectively handled the degradation models with different parameters such as scale factors by unfolding the model-based energy function. Here, we adopt the practical degradation model [3,13,36,59,60] that accounts for diverse degradation in real images.

Convolution Operation: Gaussian blur kernel is the most common kernel to blur the image [3,12,37]. Here, we choose two Gaussian degradation kernels k: isotropic Gaussian kernels k_{iso} and anisotropic Gaussian kernels k_{aniso} [3,59,62]. We also consider none degradation kernel as k_{none}. Following [59], the kernel size is uniformly sampled from $\{7 \times 7, 9 \times 9, ..., 21 \times 21\}$ and the k_{iso}'s width is uniformly chosen from $(0.1, 2.4)$. For k_{aniso}, the kernel angle is uniformly chosen from $(0, \pi)$ and the longer kernel width is uniformly chosen from $(0.5, 6)$.

Noise: When dealing with the real-world scenarios, the Gaussian noise model is usually adopted to simulate the noises from camera sensor noise [28], low-light noise [56] to quantization noise [25] *etc.* Therefore, we adopt a zero-mean additive white Gaussian noise (AWGN) model $n \sim N(0, \sigma)$ in Eq. 1. The variance σ is randomly chosen from a uniform distribution $U(0, 25/255)$ (*e.g.* 13.2/255).

Down-Sampling: For the down-sampling process, the sampling ratio s is randomly chosen from uniform distribution $U(1, 4)$ (*e.g.* 1.9) while the down-sampling methods is randomly chosen from nearest method $d^s_{nearest}$, bilinear method $d^s_{bilinear}$ and bicubic method $d^s_{bicubic}$.

So the final down-sampling degradation transformation t would take from random blur kernel k, noise level n and down-sampling ratio s in the total distribution $\mathcal{T}$, as $t \sim \mathcal{T}(k, n, s)$.

4   Our Framework

Due to its concise structure, we mainly take one-stage object detector Center-Net [64] to illustrate how to implement our AERIS. More object detectors' implements and results please refer to supplementary. We think that our AERIS framework is a generic framework that could also be implemented on other popular object detectors [17,43] and various backbones [23,32,39,42].

4.1   CenterNet

CenterNet [64] is an efficient one-stage anchor-free object detector. We show its vanilla structure of [64] in Fig. 3 (a). Input image is fed to the backbone (*i.e.* ResNet18 [21]) to extract /32 bottleneck feature, and then upsampled to a /4 feature map by three ×2 deconvolution blocks. This /4 feature map is passed to scaling blocks with three independent convolution blocks to generate the final feature maps. Based on this feature map, there are prediction heads conducting class-wise bbox center detection, bbox height and width regression, offset regression respectively. For more details, please refer to [64].

The CenterNet could be decomposed into an encoder-decoder style structure. Here, we denote the network backbone part (gray part in Fig. 3.a) as encoder E. The object detection decoder D_o, comprised by three prediction heads (colored in orange in Fig. 3 (a)), decodes the object information.

4.2   Architecture and Training Pipeline

Figure 3 (b) illustrates how to implement our AERIS based on CenterNet [64]. The detailed training procedure is given in Algorithm 1. When training AERIS, we first apply the degradation transformation $t \sim \mathcal{T}(k, n, s)$ convert x to a random generated $t(x)$, covering the degradation space of real scenarios. In each batch B, the generated $t(x) \in \mathbb{R}^{B \times 3 \times \frac{H}{s} \times \frac{W}{s}}$ should keep the same downsampling rate $s \sim (1, 4)$. Then the transformed degraded LR image $t(x)$ are sent to the encoder E to encode the degradation equivariant representation $E(t(x)) \in \mathbb{R}^{B \times C \times \frac{H}{s*d} \times \frac{W}{s*d}}$. Here the encoder E refers to the backbone in detection network, and d is the down-sample rate of backbone (*i.e.* 32 for ResNet [21]).

We then input degradation equivariant representation $E(t(x))$ into upscaling blocks with three $\times 2$ deconvolution blocks to generate the final feature map for object detection decoder D_o and arbitrary resolution restoration decoder (ARRD) D_r. As illustrated by the red arrows in Fig. 3, we introduce the skip connection on /8 and /16 feature maps between the backbone encoder E and the deconvolution blocks. Fusing features from different scales is a common process in low-level vision tasks, and could enhance semantic information and contribute to the subsequent D_o and D_r.

We further regularise the representation encode E with our unique ARRD D_r that implicitly estimate the self-supervised singal t to recover HR image $\hat{x}$. Since the downsampling rate s is not a fixed integral number in the training stage, ARRD could deal with an arbitrary scale factor. ARRD D_r could force the encoder E to not only capture the dynamics of how images change under different transformations, but also extracts the complex patterns of visual structures. Since ARRD D_r aims to recover the original resolution of clean image x from $E(t(x)))$, it could also support the object detection decoder D_o with more detailed features. Inspired by the learnable resizer model [50], we design this decoder with a residual bilinear model shown in Fig. 3, which ends up with a $\times 4$ pixel shuffle layer [47]. ARRD is a light weight structure that uses fewer parameters (0.06M) compared to the backbone encoder (11.17M), upscaling blocks (3.61M) and detection decoder D_o (0.12M). The ARRD loss l_d is defined as an L1 loss between output image $\hat{x}$ and ground truth image x:

$$l_d = |\hat{x} - x|_1 = |D_r(E(t(x))) - x|_1. \tag{2}$$

We adopt the three CenterNet prediction heads as the object detection decoder D_o to conduct detection on the final feature map generated by the upscaling block.

As shown in Algorithm 1, we optimise the total loss l_{total} including detection loss l_{obj} (*i.e.* classwise bbox center loss, bbox width and height loss, bbox offset loss for CenterNet [64]), and data restoration loss l_d:

$$l_{total} = l_{obj} + \lambda \cdot l_d, \tag{3}$$

where λ is the non-negative parameters for loss balancing. Which we set to 0.4 in CenterNet experiments and 0.8 in DETR experiments, more ablation details please refer to supplementary.

Algorithm 1. AERIS Algorithm Pipeline

---

(1). Data Generation:

B: batch size, C: channel, H: image height, W: image width

inputs: HR image $x = (B, C, H, W)$, down-sample factor $s \sim (1.0, 4.0)$

outputs: degraded LR image $t(x) = (B, C, \frac{H}{s}, \frac{W}{s})$

    for i in range(B): **do**

        (1). Convolution with blur kernel k

        (2). Down-sampling with rate s

        (3). Add noise n

    end for

(2). Training:

inputs: Degraded LR image $t(x) = (B, C, \frac{H}{s}, \frac{W}{s})$

outputs: detection output, estimated SR image $\hat{x}$

encoding:

$t(x) \xrightarrow{\quad E \quad} E(t(x))$

decoding:

data restoration decoding: $\hat{x} = D_r(E(t(x))$

detection decoding: detection results $= D_o(E(t(x))$

4.3   Inference Procedure

The inference procedure only involves encoder E , upscaling block and object detection decoder D_o as illustrated in Fig. 3. Specifically, the encoder E encodes the input target image before D_o performs the detection. Compared to explicitly pre-processing image for high-level tasks [9,19,46], our AERIS saves much computational time as we avoid reconstructing HR details of data.

We could also reconstruct the HR image with our ARRD decoder D_r. Very interestingly, our restored images $\hat{x}$ are more machine vision oriented and exhibit artifacts around the center of the object, as shown in Fig. 4.

5   Experiments and Details

5.1   Datasets and Implementation Details

Dataset. We adopt two widely used object detection datasets MS COCO [35] and KITTI [15] for detection robustness evaluation. MS COCO contains ∼118k images with bounding box annotation in 80 categories. We use COCO `train2017` set as train set and use COCO `val2017` set as normal condition evaluation set. Also COCO dataset differentiates the labels of different scale level's objects, and give them specific evaluation metrics (small: AP_s, middle: AP_m, large: AP_l), which could show us different degradation conditions' influence on different scale objects, especially the down-sampling process s.

KITTI [15] is a popular small object detection dataset for autonomous driving. For KITTI dataset, we evaluate car class, and use KITTI `train` set as train

Table 1. Comparison with SOTA restoration methods and different training strategies on **COCO-d** dataset. Here **CenterNet** with **ResNet-18** backbone and **Swin-T** backbone were adopted. The inference images with **higher resolution** are in **blue** background.

Test Set	Pre-process	Training Strategy	CenterNet (ResNet-18)				CenterNet (Swin-T)			
			AP	AP_s	AP_m	AP_l	AP	AP_s	AP_m	AP_l
COCO	-	Detection	30.1	10.6	33.2	47.2	36.9	17.9	41.8	52.9
COCO-d		Detection	14.5	1.2	10.4	38.6	19.9	2.7	16.9	46.2
	bicubic (×2)		16.2	4.1	15.3	31.1	18.6	4.0	17.8	39.7
	bicubic (×4)		8.0	4.6	10.5	10.1	10.6	**5.7**	12.8	16.7
	SRGAN [31] (×2)		14.8	2.6	14.3	27.9	16.6	3.0	16.5	33.4
	DBPN [20] (×2)		15.0	3.5	14.3	27.4	16.7	3.4	16.1	32.0
	Real-SR [4] (×2)		14.2	2.6	12.4	29.5	17.3	3.6	17.0	34.1
	BSRGAN [59] (×2)		16.8	4.2	15.8	36.9	20.2	4.8	18.1	40.5
	BM3D		10.4	0.8	6.8	27.9	10.9	0.7	8.8	35.1
	Restormer [58]		11.4	1.2	7.2	34.8	11.9	1.4	8.9	33.4
	-	Deg t	17.6	2.3	15.4	41.9	20.9	3.1	20.3	47.6
		Deg t + N	17.9	2.5	15.9	42.5	21.0	3.0	20.4	48.2
		D_r + Detection	17.7	**4.8**	15.8	41.0	21.4	5.6	19.6	46.3
		AERIS	**18.4**	2.7	**16.4**	**42.5**	**21.6**	3.2	**20.4**	**49.0**

set and use KITTI `val` set as normal condition evaluation set, and show the AP rate for comparison.

Impalement Details. We build our framework based on the open-source object detection toolbox `mmdetection` [5]. Throughout the experiments, the backbone ResNet-18 [21] and Swin-T [39] are initialed with ImageNet [21] pre-train weights. We apply the data augmentation pipeline in `mmdetection` [5], specifically we adopt random crop, random flip and multi-scale test.

During training stage, all the models are trained on 4 T V100 GPUs. Same as setting in [5], for AERIS-CenterNet training, the input image shape is resized to 512×512. The model has been trained for 140 epochs with SGD optimizer. Batch size is set to 16 per GPU. Momentum and weight decay are set to 0.9 and 1e-4. Initial learning rate is 0.01 and warms up at first 500 iterations and would decays to one-tenth at 90 and 120 epoch.

Comparison Methods. To evaluate object detectors' robustness under different conditions' degradation, we separately set the multi-degradation evaluation and single-degradation evaluation (see Sect. 5.2 and Sect. 5.3 for details). We first compare our methods with SOTA image restoration methods: non-blind SR methods [20,31,33], blind SR methods [4,59], denoise methods [33,58,61]. Also in Sect. 5.3, we separately using different type of restoration methods to handle different type of degradation, for degradation specific comparison.

Table 2. Comparison with SOTA restoration methods and different training strategies on **KITTI-d** dataset. Here **CenterNet** with **ResNet-18** backbone is adopted. We also show the inference speed (FPS) in the table.

Methods	–	Bicubic (x2)	Bicubic (x4)	SRGAN [31] (x2)	DBPN [20] (x2)	BSRGAN [59] (x2)
AP	42.2	50.6	36.5	54.3	55.6	70.8
FPS	**87.4**	50.0	16.2	51.1	50.6	51.4
Methods	BM3D	Restormer [58]	Deg t	Deg t + N	D_r + Detection	**AERIS**
AP	50.9	52.6	76.0	76.6	80.0	**80.5**
FPS	86.0	86.1	**87.4**	**87.4**	43.6	**87.4**

On the other hand, we also compare with other training strategies of the network setting, to evaluate their robustness improvement on detection. As it shown in Table 1 and Table 3. "Deg t" corresponds to train the detector with the LR images $t(x)$ random generated from HR images x, with the random degradation transformations in Sect. 3. "Deg t + N" means to mix the training data of HR image x and LR images $t(x)$. "D_r + Detection" is the structure like [19] which joint optimize a pre-process SR block and following object detector.

For fairness, all comparison methods adopt the same data augmentation process and same training setting. In the testing stage, all the results are tested on a single RTX 6000 GPU. We compare the speed by reporting the frames per second (FPS) in the experiments, a simple illustration is shown in Table 2.

5.2 Multi-degradation Evaluation

To evaluate object detectors' robustness under diverse degradation of real-world images. Different from previous works [22,27,38,45] that only consider single degradation type at a time. Following the practical degradation model [13,36] in Eq. 1, we design the experiments on images with multiply degradation conditions and down-scale ratios, to verify detection robustness in real-world diverse condition. We generate **COCO-d** dataset from original COCO val2017 dataset and **KITTI-d** dataset from original KITTI val dataset. We give per-image a random blur kernel (isotropic Gaussian kernel k_{iso}, anisotropic Gaussian kernel k_{aniso}) and random noise level (AWGN noise with variance $\sigma \sim U(0, 25/255)$). As for the resolutions, we down-sample per image in COCO val2017 with a random rate $s \sim U(1.0, 4.0)$.

The experimental results are shown in Table 1 and Table 2, we add the up-scale ratio ($\times 2$, $\times 4$) after name of SR methods. We first give the detection results on original COCO val2017 and **COCO-d** dataset. The object detector is easily affected and the performance suffers a large decrease on the multi-degradation condition. Table 1 also verifies up-scale higher resolution (either by interpolate or SR pre-process) improves the detection performance on small objects, but has a negative impact on the middle and large objects. Restoration methods would also invalid if degradation types and down-sampling scales are diverse, among several restoration methods, real-world SR method BSRGAN [59] could

484 Z. Cui et al.

Table 3. Comparison with SOTA restoration methods and SSL methods on COCO val2017 with **noise, gaussian blur** condition and **low resolution** condition (down-sampling ratio: **2** and **4**). Here **CenterNet** with **ResNet-18** backbone was adopted. Higher resolution results are in **blue** background.

(a) Noise.

Method $\quad\sigma$	(5, 50)	15	25	50
-	22.8	26.8	23.8	15.4
IRCNN [61]	22.6	26.8	24.2	16.8
Swin-IR [33]	24.2	28.0	25.6	19.3
Restormer [58]	23.8	27.6	25.1	18.9
Deg t + N	24.3	27.6	25.0	18.3
D_r + Detection	24.8	28.5	25.5	19.4
AERIS	**25.1**	**28.7**	**26.5**	**20.2**

(b) Blur.

Method $\quad k$	Mix	▪	▪	▪
-	26.7	25.8	23.9	23.1
EPLL [65]	27.8	26.8	25.4	25.2
IRCNN [61]	26.7	26.9	24.1	22.8
Deg t + N	28.8	27.5	27.6	27.8
D_r + Detection	28.5	27.7	27.5	27.3
AERIS	**29.3**	**28.6**	**28.0**	**28.2**

(c) Down-sampling (Ratio: **2**).

Method $\quad$ metric	AP	AP$_s$	AP$_m$	AP$_l$
-	20.2	1.5	16.1	49.8
SRGAN [31] (×2)	24.0	6.2	25.4	39.8
DBPN [20] (×2)	25.1	7.3	27.1	41.9
Swin-IR [33] (×2)	25.4	7.6	27.0	42.4
D_r + Detection	26.0	8.4	26.2	46.5
AERIS	25.4	4.6	25.8	**49.6**
AERIS (×2)	**26.8**	**8.6**	**28.8**	45.2

(d) Down-sampling (Ratio: **4**).

Method $\quad$ metric	AP	AP$_s$	AP$_m$	AP$_l$
-	8.2	0.0	3.2	33.1
DBPN [20] (×2)	14.8	1.0	9.9	39.7
DBPN [20] (×4)	12.2	1.7	11.7	23.4
Swin-IR [33] (×2)	15.2	1.1	10.1	39.9
Swin-IR [33] (×4)	12.8	1.8	12.2	23.4
D_r + Detection	15.1	1.8	12.7	40.1
AERIS	13.0	0.8	10.2	**42.6**
AERIS (×2)	**15.8**	**2.0**	**13.2**	40.9

get satisfactory results. Our AERIS model could get best performance in most of metrics, even with a lower input resolution, but the one limitation is that AERIS could not get best performance on small object.

5.3 Degradation Specific Evaluation

To further understand the advantages of AERIS, we design the experiments on single degradation conditions. We separately make experiments on noise, gaussian blur and low-resolution conditions. For noise and blur condition, in training stage of three SSL methods, we generate $t(x)$ from x with noise n (variance $\sigma \sim U(0, 50/255)$) and blur kernel k (same as Sect. 3). As for low resolution condition, we generate $t(x)$ from x with down-sampling ratio s. Here we discuss three conditions as follow:

Table 4. Ablation results of CenterNet on **COCO-d** dataset.

CenterNet	+Deg t	+feature connect	+ARRD loc 1	+ARRD loc 2	+ARRD loc 3	mAP (COCO-d)
$\checkmark$						14.5
$\checkmark$	$\checkmark$					16.8 (+2.3)
$\checkmark$	$\checkmark$	$\checkmark$				17.5 (+3.0)
$\checkmark$	$\checkmark$			$\checkmark$		17.7 (+3.2)
$\checkmark$	$\checkmark$	$\checkmark$	$\checkmark$			18.2 (+3.7)
$\checkmark$	$\checkmark$	$\checkmark$		$\checkmark$		18.4 (+3.9)
$\checkmark$	$\checkmark$	$\checkmark$			$\checkmark$	17.9 (+3.4)

Performance *w.r.t* Noise & Blur. For noise's affect on object detection, we process COCO val2017 with random Gaussian noise $n \sim N(0, \sigma)$, we first random dom choose variance σ from uniform distribution $U(5/255, 50/255)$ for mix noise level evaluation. Then we take three different noise level: $\sigma = 15$, $\sigma = 25$ and $\sigma = 50$ for specific evaluation. We compare AERIS with SOTA denoise methods IRCNN [61], Swin-IR [33] and Restormer [58] and also compare with other training strategies. We report the average precision (AP) in Table 3a.

For blur's affect on object detection, we first process COCO val2017 with random isotropic Gaussian kernel k_{iso} and anisotropic Gaussian kernel k_{aniso} (probability both 0.5) as Mix evaluation. Then we specifically choose three degradation kernels for specific evaluation (see Table 3b). We compare with Gaussian deblur methods EPLL [65] and IRCNN [61] and other two other training strategies, then report AP value in Table 3b. Our AERIS gains **best** performance under various noise and blur conditions, among image restoration methods and other training strategies.

Performance *w.r.t* Low Resolution. To evaluate low resolution's affect on detection task, we down-scale original COCO val2017 with a fixed down-sampling ratio s. Here we set the down-sampling ratio to 2 and 4, and then compare with SOTA SISR methods SRGAN [31], DBPN [20], Swin-IR [33] and pre-stage method "D_r + Detection". We report the total AP and different level objects' detection performance (AP$_s$, AP$_m$, AP$_l$) in Table 3c and Table 3d. We also make an additional experiments to up-scale input images with ratio 2 and then send into AERIS model as **AERIS** ($\times 2$), for same resolution comparison with SR methods and pre-upsampling method.

5.4 Ablation Study

To evaluate the location of ARRD on CenterNet [64], we separately make the ablation study to evaluate each part's effectiveness, as shown in Table 4, "+Deg t" refers to adding the degradation transformation in Sect. 3. "+feature connect" means the feature connection process in Fig. 3. "+ARRD" adds the decoder

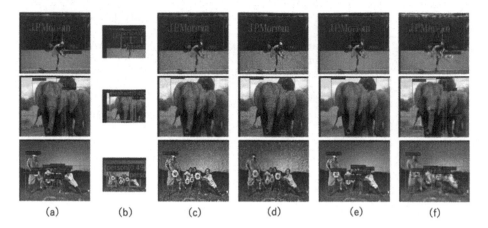

(a)	(b)	(c)	(d)	(e)	(f)

Fig. 4. Exemplar detection results on MS COCO 2017 dataset [35]. (a)/(b) is Center-Net trained on normal images and tested on normal/**COCO-d** dataset, (c)/(d)/(e) is CenterNet tested on the degraded image restored by individual SR algorithm SRGAN [31]/Real-SR [4]/BSRGan [59]. (f) is the detection result of our AERIS and we use the output of ARRD D_r as background images.

D_r upon the network structure. We also evaluate adding ARRD on different location of the up-sampling blocks, "loc 1" means the shallow up-samling layer, "loc 2" means middle up-sampling layer and "loc 3" means the final up-sampling layer ("loc 3" also connect with the detection decoder D_o), as our finding, to implement ARRD on the middle layer could get best result.

6   Conclusion

In this paper, we propose a novel self-supervised framework, AERIS, to handle object detection for arbitary degraded low resolution images. To capture the dynamics of feature representations under diverse resolution and degradation conditions, we propose a degradation equivariant representation that is generic and could be implemented on popular detection architectures. To further combine the strength of the existing progress on super resolution (SR), we also introduce an arbitrary-resolution restoration decoder that supervises the latent representation to preserve the visual structure. The extensive experiments demonstrate that our AERIS achieves SOTA results on two mainstream public datasets among different degradation conditions (resolution, noise and blur).

Acknowledgement. This work was supported by JST Moonshot R&D Grant Number JPMJMS2011 and JST ACT-X Grant Number JPMJAX190D, Japan.

References

1. Afifi, M., Brown, M.S.: What else can fool deep learning? addressing color constancy errors on deep neural network performance. In: International Conference on Computer Vision (ICCV) (2019)
2. Bai, Y., Zhang, Y., Ding, M., Ghanem, B.: Finding tiny faces in the wild with generative adversarial network. In: 2018 IEEE/CVF Conference on Computer Vision and Pattern Recognition (CVPR), pp. 21–30 (2018). https://doi.org/10.1109/CVPR.2018.00010
3. Bell-Kligler, S., Shocher, A., Irani, M.: Blind super-resolution kernel estimation using an internal-gan. In: Wallach, H., Larochelle, H., Beygelzimer, A., d' Alché-Buc, F., Fox, E., Garnett, R. (eds.) Advances in Neural Information Processing Systems. vol. 32. Curran Associates, Inc. (2019). https://proceedings.neurips.cc/paper/2019/file/5fd0b37cd7dbbb00f97ba6ce92bf5add-Paper.pdf
4. Cai, J., Zeng, H., Yong, H., Cao, Z., Zhang, L.: Toward real-world single image super-resolution: A new benchmark and a new model. In: Proceedings of the IEEE International Conference on Computer Vision (2019)
5. Chen, K., et al.: MMDetection: Open mmlab detection toolbox and benchmark. arXiv preprint arXiv:1906.07155 (2019)
6. Chen, Y., Liu, S., Wang, X.: Learning continuous image representation with local implicit image function. arXiv preprint arXiv:2012.09161 (2020)
7. Cohen, T.S., Welling, M.: Group equivariant convolutional networks. In: Proceedings of the 33rd International Conference on International Conference on Machine Learning - vol. 48. pp. 2990–2999. ICML'16, JMLR.org (2016)
8. Cui, Z., Qi, G.J., Gu, L., You, S., Zhang, Z., Harada, T.: Multitask aet with orthogonal tangent regularity for dark object detection. In: Proceedings of the IEEE/CVF International Conference on Computer Vision (ICCV), pp. 2553–2562 (2021)
9. Dai, D., Wang, Y., Chen, Y., Van Gool, L.: Is image super-resolution helpful for other vision tasks? In: IEEE Winter Conference on Applications of Computer Vision (WACV) (2016)
10. Deng, J., Dong, W., Socher, R., Li, L.J., Li, K., Fei-Fei, L.: Imagenet: A large-scale hierarchical image database. In: 2009 IEEE conference on computer vision and pattern recognition, pp. 248–255. IEEE (2009)
11. Dong, C., Loy, C.C., He, K., et al.: Learning a deep convolutional network for image super-resolution. In: Computer Vision - ECCV 2014, pp. 184–199 (2014)
12. Efrat, N., Glasner, D., Apartsin, A., Nadler, B., Levin, A.: Accurate blur models vs. image priors in single image super-resolution. In: 2013 IEEE International Conference on Computer Vision, pp. 2832–2839 (2013). https://doi.org/10.1109/ICCV.2013.352
13. Elad, M., Feuer, A.: Restoration of a single superresolution image from several blurred, noisy, and undersampled measured images. IEEE Trans. Image Process. 6(12), 1646–1658 (1997). https://doi.org/10.1109/83.650118
14. Everingham, M., Gool, L., Williams, C.K., Winn, J., Zisserman, A.: The pascal visual object classes (voc) challenge. Int. J. Comput. Vision 88(2), 303–338 (2010) https://doi.org/10.1007/s11263-009-0275-4
15. Geiger, A., Lenz, P., Urtasun, R.: Are we ready for autonomous driving? the kitti vision benchmark suite. In: Conference on Computer Vision and Pattern Recognition (CVPR) (2012)

16. Gidaris, S., Singh, P., Komodakis, N.: Unsupervised representation learning by predicting image rotations. In: International Conference on Learning Representations (2018). https://openreview.net/forum?id=S1v4N2l0-

17. Girshick, R.: Fast r-cnn. In: 2015 IEEE International Conference on Computer Vision (ICCV), pp. 1440–1448 (2015). https://doi.org/10.1109/ICCV.2015.169

18. Gu, J., Lu, H., Zuo, W., Dong, C.: Blind super-resolution with iterative kernel correction. In: Proceedings of the IEEE/CVF Conference on Computer Vision and Pattern Recognition (CVPR) (2019)

19. Haris, M., Shakhnarovich, G., Ukita, N.: Task-driven super resolution: object detection in low-resolution images. In: Mantoro, T., Lee, M., Ayu, M.A., Wong, K.W., Hidayanto, A.N. (eds.) Neural Inform. Process., pp. 387–395. Springer International Publishing, Cham (2021)

20. Haris, M., Shakhnarovich, G., Ukita, N.: Deep back-projection networks for super-resolution. In: Proceedings of the IEEE Conference on Computer Vision and Pattern Recognition (CVPR) (2018)

21. He, K., Zhang, X., Ren, S., Sun, J.: Deep residual learning for image recognition. In: 2016 IEEE Conference on Computer Vision and Pattern Recognition (CVPR), pp. 770–778 (2016). DOI: https://doi.org/10.1109/CVPR.2016.90

22. Hendrycks, D., Dietterich, T.: Benchmarking neural network robustness to common corruptions and perturbations. In: Proceedings of the International Conference on Learning Representations (2019)

23. Howard, A.G., Zhu, M., Chen, B., Kalenichenko, D., Wang, W., Weyand, T., Andreetto, M., Adam, H.: Mobilenets: Efficient convolutional neural networks for mobile vision applications. CoRR abs/1704.04861 (2017). https://arxiv.org/abs/1704.04861

24. Hu, X., Mu, H., Zhang, X., Wang, Z., Tan, T., Sun, J.: Meta-sr: A magnification-arbitrary network for super-resolution. In: Proceedings of the IEEE/CVF Conference on Computer Vision and Pattern Recognition (CVPR) (2019)

25. Irie, K., McKinnon, A.E., Unsworth, K., Woodhead, I.M.: A technique for evaluation of ccd video-camera noise. IEEE Trans. Circuits Syst. Video Technol. **18**(2), 280–284 (2008). https://doi.org/10.1109/TCSVT.2007.913972

26. Johnson, J., Alahi, A., Fei-Fei, L.: Perceptual losses for real-time style transfer and super-resolution. In: European Conference on Computer Vision (2016)

27. Kamann, C., Rother, C.: Benchmarking the robustness of semantic segmentation models. In: Proceedings of the IEEE/CVF Conference on Computer Vision and Pattern Recognition (CVPR) (2020)

28. Karaimer, H.C., Brown, M.S.: A software platform for manipulating the camera imaging pipeline. In: European Conference on Computer Vision (ECCV) (2016)

29. Kim, J., Lee, J.K., Lee, K.M.: Accurate image super-resolution using very deep convolutional networks. In: 2016 IEEE Conference on Computer Vision and Pattern Recognition (CVPR), pp. 1646–1654 (2016). https://doi.org/10.1109/CVPR.2016.182

30. Lai, W.S., Huang, J.B., Ahuja, N., Yang, M.H.: Deep laplacian pyramid networks for fast and accurate super-resolution. In: 2017 IEEE Conference on Computer Vision and Pattern Recognition (CVPR), pp. 5835–5843 (2017). https://doi.org/10.1109/CVPR.2017.618

31. Ledig, C., et al.: Photo-realistic single image super-resolution using a generative adversarial network. In: 2017 IEEE Conference on Computer Vision and Pattern Recognition (CVPR), pp. 105–114 (2017). https://doi.org/10.1109/CVPR.2017.19

32. Li, K., et al.: Uniformer: Unifying convolution and self-attention for visual recognition (2022)

33. Liang, J., Cao, J., Sun, G., Zhang, K., Van Gool, L., Timofte, R.: Swinir: Image restoration using swin transformer. In: IEEE International Conference on Computer Vision Workshops (2021)
34. Lim, B., Son, S., Kim, H., Nah, S., Lee, K.M.: Enhanced deep residual networks for single image super-resolution. In: 2017 IEEE Conference on Computer Vision and Pattern Recognition Workshops (CVPRW), pp. 1132–1140 (2017). https://doi.org/10.1109/CVPRW.2017.151
35. Lin, T.-Y., et al.: Microsoft COCO: common objects in context. In: Fleet, D., Pajdla, T., Schiele, B., Tuytelaars, T. (eds.) ECCV 2014. LNCS, vol. 8693, pp. 740–755. Springer, Cham (2014). https://doi.org/10.1007/978-3-319-10602-1_48
36. Liu, C., Sun, D.: On bayesian adaptive video super resolution. IEEE Trans. Pattern Anal. Mach. Intell. **36**(2), 346–360 (2014). https://doi.org/10.1109/TPAMI.2013.127
37. Liu, C., Sun, D.: On bayesian adaptive video super resolution. IEEE Trans. Pattern Anal. Mach. Intell. **36**(2), 346–360 (2014). https://doi.org/10.1109/TPAMI.2013.127
38. Liu, D., Wen, B., Liu, X., Wang, Z., Huang, T.S.: When image denoising meets high-level vision tasks: A deep learning approach. In: IJCAI (2018)
39. Liu, Z., et al.: Swin transformer: Hierarchical vision transformer using shifted windows. In: Proceedings of the IEEE/CVF International Conference on Computer Vision (ICCV) (2021)
40. Luo, F., Wu, X., Guo, Y.: Functional neural networks for parametric image restoration problems. In: Beygelzimer, A., Dauphin, Y., Liang, P., Vaughan, J.W. (eds.) Advances in Neural Information Processing Systems (2021). https://openreview.net/forum?id=MMZ4djXrwbu
41. Ma, X., Wang, Z., Zhan, Y., Zheng, Y., Wang, Z., Dai, D., Lin, C.W.: Both style and fog matter: Cumulative domain adaptation for semantic foggy scene understanding. In: Proceedings of the IEEE/CVF Conference on Computer Vision and Pattern Recognition (CVPR), pp. 18922–18931 (June 2022)
42. Mao, M., Peng, G., Zhang, R., Zheng, H., Ma, T., Peng, Y., Ding, E., Zhang, B., Han, S.: Dual-stream network for visual recognition. In: Beygelzimer, A., Dauphin, Y., Liang, P., Vaughan, J.W. (eds.) Advances in Neural Information Processing Systems (2021). https://openreview.net/forum?id=AjfD1JjeVKN
43. Redmon, J., Divvala, S., Girshick, R., Farhadi, A.: You only look once: Unified, real-time object detection. In: 2016 IEEE Conference on Computer Vision and Pattern Recognition (CVPR), pp. 779–788 (2016). https://doi.org/10.1109/CVPR.2016.91
44. Sabour, S., Frosst, N., Hinton, G.E.: Dynamic routing between capsules. In: Proceedings of the 31st International Conference on Neural Information Processing Systems. pp. 3859–3869. NIPS'17, Curran Associates Inc., Red Hook, NY, USA (2017)
45. Sayed, M., Brostow, G.: Improved handling of motion blur in online object detection. In: Proceedings of the IEEE/CVF Conference on Computer Vision and Pattern Recognition (CVPR), pp. 1706–1716 (2021)
46. Shermeyer, J., Van Etten, A.: The effects of super-resolution on object detection performance in satellite imagery. In: Proceedings of the IEEE/CVF Conference on Computer Vision and Pattern Recognition (CVPR) Workshops (2019)
47. Shi, W., Caballero, J., Huszár, F., Totz, J., Aitken, A.P., Bishop, R., Rueckert, D., Wang, Z.: Real-time single image and video super-resolution using an efficient sub-pixel convolutional neural network. In: 2016 IEEE Conference on Computer Vision and Pattern Recognition (CVPR), pp. 1874–1883 (2016). https://doi.org/10.1109/CVPR.2016.207

48. Singh, B., Davis, L.S.: An analysis of scale invariance in object detection snip. In: Proceedings of the IEEE Conference on Computer Vision and Pattern Recognition (CVPR) (2018)
49. Singh, B., Najibi, M., Davis, L.S.: Sniper: Efficient multi-scale training. In: Bengio, S., Wallach, H., Larochelle, H., Grauman, K., Cesa-Bianchi, N., Garnett, R. (eds.) Advances in Neural Information Processing Systems. vol. 31. Curran Associates, Inc. (2018). https://proceedings.neurips.cc/paper/2018/file/166cee72e93a992007a89b39eb29628b-Paper.pdf
50. Talebi, H., Milanfar, P.: Learning to resize images for computer vision tasks. In: Proceedings of the IEEE/CVF International Conference on Computer Vision (ICCV), pp. 497–506 (October 2021)
51. Tong, T., Li, G., Liu, X., Gao, Q.: Image super-resolution using dense skip connections. In: 2017 IEEE International Conference on Computer Vision (ICCV), pp. 4809–4817 (2017). https://doi.org/10.1109/ICCV.2017.514
52. Vasiljevic, I., Chakrabarti, A., Shakhnarovich, G.: Examining the impact of blur on recognition by convolutional networks (2017)
53. Wang, L., Li, D., Zhu, Y., Tian, L., Shan, Y.: Dual super-resolution learning for semantic segmentation. In: 2020 IEEE/CVF Conference on Computer Vision and Pattern Recognition (CVPR), pp. 3773–3782 (2020). https://doi.org/10.1109/CVPR42600.2020.00383
54. Wang, L., Wang, Y., Dong, X., Xu, Q., Yang, J., An, W., Guo, Y.: Unsupervised degradation representation learning for blind super-resolution. In: Proceedings of the IEEE/CVF Conference on Computer Vision and Pattern Recognition (CVPR), pp. 10581–10590 (2021)
55. Wang, Z., Chang, S., Yang, Y., Liu, D., Huang, T.S.: Studying very low resolution recognition using deep networks. In: Proceedings of the IEEE Conference on Computer Vision and Pattern Recognition (CVPR) (2016)
56. Wei, K., Fu, Y., Yang, J., Huang, H.: A physics-based noise formation model for extreme low-light raw denoising. In: IEEE Conference on Computer Vision and Pattern Recognition (2020)
57. Yang, W., Yuan, Y., Ren, W., et al.: Advancing image understanding in poor visibility environments: a collective benchmark study. IEEE Trans. Image Process. **29**, 5737–5752 (2020). https://doi.org/10.1109/TIP.2020.2981922
58. Zamir, S.W., Arora, A., Khan, S., Hayat, M., Khan, F.S., Yang, M.H.: Restormer: Efficient transformer for high-resolution image restoration. In: CVPR (2022)
59. Zhang, K., Liang, J., Van Gool, L., Timofte, R.: Designing a practical degradation model for deep blind image super-resolution. In: IEEE International Conference on Computer Vision (2021)
60. Zhang, K., Van Gool, L., Timofte, R.: Deep unfolding network for image super-resolution. In: IEEE Conference on Computer Vision and Pattern Recognition, pp. 3217–3226 (2020)
61. Zhang, K., Zuo, W., Gu, S., Zhang, L.: Learning deep cnn denoiser prior for image restoration. In: IEEE Conference on Computer Vision and Pattern Recognition, pp. 3929–3938 (2017)
62. Zhang, K., Zuo, W., Zhang, L.: Learning a single convolutional super-resolution network for multiple degradations. In: IEEE Conference on Computer Vision and Pattern Recognition, pp. 3262–3271 (2018)
63. Zhang, L., Qi, G.J., Wang, L., Luo, J.: Aet vs. aed: Unsupervised representation learning by auto-encoding transformations rather than data. In: Proceedings of the IEEE Conference on Computer Vision and Pattern Recognition, pp. 2547–2555 (2019)

64. Zhou, X., Wang, D., Krähenbühl, P.: Objects as points. CoRR abs/1904.07850 (2019), https://arxiv.org/abs/1904.07850
65. Zoran, D., Weiss, Y.: From learning models of natural image patches to whole image restoration. In: 2011 International Conference on Computer Vision, pp. 479–486 (2011). https://doi.org/10.1109/ICCV.2011.6126278
66. Zou, W.W.W., Yuen, P.C.: Very low resolution face recognition problem. IEEE Trans. Image Process. **21**(1), 327–340 (2012). https://doi.org/10.1109/TIP.2011.2162423

Robust Category-Level 6D Pose Estimation with Coarse-to-Fine Rendering of Neural Features

Wufei Ma[1]([⊠]), Angtian Wang[1], Alan Yuille[1], and Adam Kortylewski[1,2,3]

[1] Johns Hopkins University, Baltimore, MD 21218, USA
{wma27,angtianwang,ayuille1,akortyl1}@jhu.edu
[2] Max Planck Institute for Informatics, Saarbrücken, Germany
[3] University of Freiburg, Breisgau, Germany

Abstract. We consider the problem of category-level 6D pose estimation from a single RGB image. Our approach represents an object category as a cuboid mesh and learns a generative model of the neural feature activations at each mesh vertex to perform pose estimation through differentiable rendering. A common problem of rendering-based approaches is that they rely on bounding box proposals, which do not convey information about the 3D rotation of the object and are not reliable when objects are partially occluded. Instead, we introduce a coarse-to-fine optimization strategy that utilizes the rendering process to estimate a sparse set of 6D object proposals, which are subsequently refined with gradient-based optimization. The key to enabling the convergence of our approach is a neural feature representation that is trained to be scale- and rotation-invariant using contrastive learning. Our experiments demonstrate an enhanced category-level 6D pose estimation performance compared to prior work, particularly under strong partial occlusion.

Keywords: Category-level 6D pose estimation · Render-and-compare

1 Introduction

Estimating the 3D position and 3D orientation of objects is an important requirement for a comprehensive scene understanding in computer vision. Real-world applications, such as augmented reality (AR) or robotics, require vision systems to generalize in new environments that may contain previously unseen and partially occluded object instances. However, most prior work on 6D pose estimation focused on the "instance-level" task, where exact CAD models of the object instances are available [10,12,19,23,35]. Moreover, the few prior methods on "category-level" 6D pose estimation often either rely on a ground truth depth map [20,31], which are practically hard to obtain in many application areas, or

Supplementary Information The online version contains supplementary material available at https://doi.org/10.1007/978-3-031-20077-9_29.

rely on 2D bounding box proposals [28,38], which are not reliable in challenging occlusion scenarios [30] (see also our experimental results).

Recent work introduced generative models of neural network features for image classification [14] and 3D pose estimation [28], which have the ability to learn category-level object models that are highly robust to partial occlusion. Intuitively, these models are composed of a convolutional neural network [17] and a Bayesian generative model of the neural feature activations. The invariance properties of the neural features enable these models to generalize despite variations in instance-specific details such as changes in the object shape and texture. Moreover, the generative model can be augmented with an outlier model [11] to avoid being distorted by local occlusion patterns.

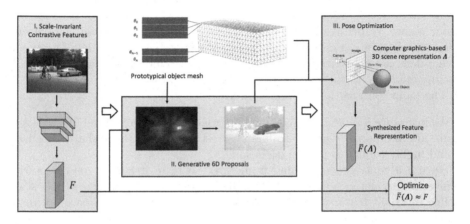

Fig. 1. Overview of our coarse-to-fine 6D pose estimation. We propose to train a neural representation that is invariant to instance-specific details, 3D rotation, and changes in the object scale. With the help of the scale-invariant contrastive features, we can efficiently search generative 6D proposals in the coarse stage and then refine the initial 6D poses with pose optimization in the fine stage.

In this work, we build on and significantly extend generative models of neural network features to perform category-level 6D pose estimation from a single RGB image. In particular, we follow neural mesh models [28] and represent an object category as a cuboid mesh and learn a generative model of the neural feature activations at each mesh vertex to perform pose estimation through a render-and-compare process. The core problem of such a rendering-based approach to pose estimation is to search efficiently through the combinatorially large space of the 6D latent parameters, because the iterative rendering process is rather costly compared to simple feed-forward regression approaches. Related work addresses this problem by first estimating 2D object bounding boxes with a proposal network [12,18,31], but these are not reliable under partial occlusion and truncation [30]. Instead, we address this problem by extending neural mesh models with scale-invariant features and a coarse-to-fine render-and-compare optimization strategy, which retains the robustness to partial occlusion (Fig. 1). In particular, we first use a coarse search strategy, in which we render the model in a set of pre-defined initial poses that are evenly distributed over the entire search space and select a sparse set of candidate initializations with low reconstruction loss. This process generates 6D object proposals robustly under occlusion, as it relies on the generative object model. Subsequently, the 6D proposals are refined with gradient-based render-and-compare optimization.

The key to making the coarse-to-fine optimization efficient and accurate (i.e., not missing out on small or partially occluded objects) is to learn a feature representation that induces large convergence basins in the optimization process. To this end, we introduce a contrastive learning framework [1,9,32] to learn features that are invariant to instance-specific details (such as changes in the shape and texture), as well as to changes in the 3D pose and scale of the object.

We evaluate our model on the PASCAL3D+ dataset [34] and the Object-Net3D dataset [33], which are challenging real-world datasets of outdoor and indoor scenes, respectively. Our experiments demonstrate that our model outperforms strong object detection and pose estimation baseline models. Our model further demonstrates exceptional robustness to partial occlusion compared to all baseline methods on the Occluded PASCAL3D+ dataset [30].

The main contributions of our work are:

1. We introduce a render-and-compare approach for category-level 6D pose estimation and adopt a coarse-to-fine pose estimation strategy that is accurate and highly robust to partial occlusion.
2. We use a contrastive learning framework to train a feature representation invariant to instance-specific details, 3D rotation, and changes in object scale.
3. The invariant features enable a coarse-to-fine render-and-compare optimization, which involves novel generative 6D object proposals and a subsequent gradient-based pose refinement.
4. Our method outperforms previous methods on the PASCAL3D+, Object-Net3D dataset, and we demonstrate the robustness of our model to partial occlusion on Occluded PASCAL3D+ dataset. We further show the efficacy of our proposed modules in the ablation study.

2   Related Work

Category-Level 3D Pose Estimation. Category-level 3D pose estimation assumes the bounding box of the object is given and predicts the 3D object pose. Previous methods can be categorized into two groups, keypoint-based methods and render-and-compare methods. Keypoint-based methods [22,38] first detect semantic keypoints and then predict 3D object pose by solving a Perspective-n-Point problem. Render-and-compare methods [28] predict the 3D pose by fitting a rigid transformation of the mesh model that minimizes the reconstruction error between a predicted feature map and a rendered feature map. 3D pose estimation methods often exploit the inductive bias that the principal points of the objects are close to the image center and the objects have a similar scale.

Category-Level 6D Pose Estimation. Category-level 6D pose estimation is a more challenging problem and involves object detection and pose estimation without knowing the accurate 3D model or the textures of the testing objects. Previous methods [3,20,31] often investigate this problem in the RGBD setting. Depth maps help these models to infer the 3D location of the objects and at the same time resolve the scale ambiguities [3]. However, depth annotations are often hard to obtain, which limits the practicality of these methods. In this work, we investigate category-level 6D pose estimation from monocular RGB images and show that our method can robustly estimate 6D object poses under partial occlusion and truncation.

Feature-Level Render-and-Compare. Render-and-compare methods minimize the reconstruction error between a predicted feature representation and a representation rendered from a 3D scene (e.g., a 3D mesh model $\mathcal{M}$ and the corresponding 3D pose m). Previous methods follow similar formulations but differ in the feature representation and the optimization algorithms. Wang et al. [31] proposed to hard-code the features as the normalized 3D coordinates and predict the object pose by solving a rigid transformation between the 3D model $\mathcal{M}$ and the predicted coordinate map with the Umeyama algorithm [27]. NeMo [28] learns contrastive features for the 3D model $\mathcal{M}$ and solves 3D object pose with the objects centered and rescaled. Iwase et al. [12] found that features with only 3 channels are sufficient for instance-level 6D pose estimation and proposed to learn the features with a differentiable Levenberg-Marquardt (LM) optimization.

In a broader context, the feature-level render-and-compare process can be interpreted as an *approximate* analysis-by-synthesis [7,8] approach to computer vision. Analysis-by-synthesis has several advantages over purely discriminative methods as it enables efficient learning [29] and largely enhances robustness in out-of-distribution situations, particularly when objects are partially occluded in image classification [15,16,36,37], object detection [30], scene understanding [21, 25], face reconstruction [5] and human detection [6], as well as when objects are viewed from unseen 3D poses [28]. Our work extends the approximate analysis-by-synthesis approach to category-level 6D pose estimation.

3 Method

This section presents our main contributions. First, we review the render-and-compare approach for pose estimation in Sect. 3.2. Then we introduce the learning of scale-invariant contrastive features in Sect. 3.3. In Sect. 3.4, we introduce a coarse-to-fine optimization strategy that uses a generative model to generate 6D object proposals in the coarse stage and then refines the initial 6D poses with a render-and-compare pose optimization. We discuss a multi-object reasoning module in Sect. 3.5 that enables our model to accurately detect occluded and truncated objects and as well as complicated multi-object scenes.

3.1 Notation

We denote a feature representation of an input image I as $\zeta(I) = F^l \in \mathbb{R}^{H \times W \times c}$. Where l is the output of layer l of a deep convolutional neural network ζ, with

c being the number of channels in layer l. $f_i^l \in \mathbb{R}^c$ is a feature vector in F^l at position i on the 2D lattice $\mathcal{P}$ of the feature map. In the remainder of this section, we omit the superscript l for notational simplicity because this is fixed a-priori in our model.

3.2   Prior Work: Render-And-Compare for Pose Estimation

Our work builds on and significantly extends neural mesh models (NMMs) [12, 28], which are themselves 3D extensions of Compositional Generative Networks [13]. Neural mesh models define a probabilistic generative models $p(F \mid \mathfrak{N})$ of the real-valued feature activations F using a 3D neural mesh representation $\mathfrak{N}$. The neural mesh $\mathfrak{N} = \{\mathcal{V}, \mathcal{E}, \mathcal{C}\}$ is represented by a set of vertices $\mathcal{V} = \{V_i \in \mathbb{R}^3\}_{i=1}^N$ and learnable features for each vertex $\mathcal{C} = \{C_i \in \mathbb{R}^c\}_{i=1}^N$, where c is the number of channels in layer l. Given the object pose (or camera viewpoint) m, we can render the neural mesh model $\mathfrak{N}$ into feature maps using rasteriation, i.e., $\bar{F}(m) = \mathfrak{R}(\mathfrak{N}, m) \in \mathbb{R}^{H \times W \times D}$. The neural mesh model defines the likelihood of a target feature map $F \in \mathbb{R}^{H \times W \times D}$ as

$$p(F \mid \mathfrak{N}, m, \mathcal{B}) = \prod_{i \in \mathcal{FG}} p(f_i \mid \mathfrak{N}, m) \prod_{i' \in \mathcal{BG}} p(f_{i'} \mid \mathcal{B}) \tag{1}$$

where the foreground $\mathcal{FG}$ is the set of all positions on the 2D lattice $\mathcal{P}$ of the feature map F that are covered by the rendered neural mesh model and the background $\mathcal{BG}$ contains those pixels that are not covered by the mesh. The foreground likelihood is defined as a Gaussian distribution $p(f_i \mid \mathfrak{N}, m) = \mathcal{N}(f_i \mid C_r, \sigma_r^2 I)$. The correspondence between the image feature f_i and the vertex feature C_r is determined through the rendering process. Background features are modeled using a simple background model that is defined by a Gaussian distribution $p(f_{i'} \mid \mathcal{B}) = \mathcal{N}(f_{i'} \mid b, \sigma^2 I)$ with $\mathcal{B} = \{b, \sigma\}$, which can be estimated with maximum likelihood from the background features. The training of the generative model parameters $\{\mathfrak{N}, B\}$ and the feature extractor is done by maximum likelihood estimation (MLE) from the training data. At test time, we can infer the object pose m by minimizing the negative log-likelihood of the model w.r.t. the pose m with gradient descent

$$\mathcal{L}_{\mathrm{NLL}}(F, \mathfrak{N}, m, \mathcal{B}) = -\ln p(F \mid \mathfrak{N}, m, \mathcal{B})$$

$$= -\sum_{i \in \mathcal{FG}} \left(\ln \left(\frac{1}{\sigma_r \sqrt{2\pi}} \right) - \frac{1}{2\sigma_r^2} \|f_i - C_r\|^2 \right)$$

$$- \sum_{i' \in \mathcal{BG}} \left(\ln \left(\frac{1}{\sigma \sqrt{2\pi}} \right) - \frac{1}{2\sigma^2} \|f_{i'} - b\|^2 \right) \tag{2}$$

Assuming unit variance [28], i.e., $\sigma_r = \sigma = 1$, the loss function reduce to the mean squared error (MSE) between vertex features and the target feature map

$$\mathcal{L}_{\mathrm{NLL}}(F, \mathfrak{N}, m, \mathcal{B}) = \frac{1}{2} \sum_{i \in \mathcal{FG}} \|f_i - C_r\|^2 + \frac{1}{2} \sum_{i' \in \mathcal{BG}} \|f_i - b\|^2 + const. \tag{3}$$

Fig. 2. Illustration of our object-centric data augmentation strategy, to generate feature activations across several scales, which are essential for our contrastive learning framework.

Previous works adopted this general framework for category-level 3D pose estimation [28,31] and instance-level 6D pose estimation [12], thereby using different types of learnable features $\mathcal{C}$ and optimization algorithms. In this work, we extend this framework to category-level 6D pose estimation from a single RGB image, which requires us to overcome additional challenges. Specifically, we need to address the challenge that the learnable feature representation $\mathcal{C}$ needs to account for the large variations in object scale, as well as the intra-category variation in terms of the object shape and texture properties.

3.3 Learning Scale-Invariant Contrastive Features

In this work, we propose to account for the variations in the object scale, shape, and appearance by learning contrastive features that are invariant to these variations. This will enable us to estimate the 6D object pose by optimizing the maximum likelihood formulation in Eq. 3 directly with gradient-based optimization. We demonstrate the efficacy of our scale-invariant contrastive features in Fig. 3 and quantitatively in Sect. 4.2.

Contrastive Learning of Scale-Invariant Features. One of the major challenges in 6D pose estimation is the variation in object scales. Due to the nature of convolution layers in the feature extractor ζ, nearby and distant objects could yield very different feature activations in F. Unfortunately, annotations of 6D poses for small objects are limited. Therefore, we use data augmentation to learn scale-invariant features from object-centric samples.

Specifically, given an image $\mathbf{I} \in \mathbb{R}^{H \times W \times 3}$, we prepare the training sample as follows. First, we resize the image with scale s and obtain a new image with size $\frac{H}{s} \times \frac{W}{s}$. Then texture images from the Describable Textures Dataset (DTD) [4] are used to pad the image back to $H \times W$. We update the distance annotation d of the object assuming a pinhole camera model, such that the distance annotation can be computed as $d' = d \cdot s$. The augmented data is depicted in Fig. 2.

In order for the CNN backbone ζ to extract feature invariant to instance-specific details and to avoid local optima in the loss landscapes of the reconstruction loss, we train the feature extractor ζ using contrastive learning to learn features that are distributed akin to the probabilistic generative model as defined in Eqs. 1–3. We achieve this by adopting a contrastive loss:

$$\mathcal{L}_{\text{contrastive}} = -\sum_{i\in\mathcal{FG}}\sum_{j\in\mathcal{FG}\setminus\{i\}}\|f_i - f_j\|^2 - \sum_{i\in\mathcal{FG}}\sum_{j\in\mathcal{BG}}\|f_i - f_j\|^2 \qquad (4)$$

which encourages the features of different vertices to be discriminative from each other and features of the object vertices distinct from the features in the background. Our full model is trained by optimizing $\mathcal{L}_{\text{contrastive}}$ in a contrastive learning framework, where we update the parameters of the feature extractor ζ and the vertices features $\mathcal{C}$ in the neural mesh model jointly.

MLE Learning of the Neural Mesh Model (NMM). We train the parameters $\mathcal{C}$ of the probabilistic generative model through maximum likelihood estimation (MLE) by minimizing the negative log-likelihood of the feature representations over the whole training set (Eq. 3). The correspondence between the feature vectors f_i and vertices r is computed using the annotated 6D pose. To reduce the computational cost of optimizing Eq. 3, we follow [1] and update $\mathcal{C}$ in a moving average manner.

Convergence properties. The benefits of the scale-invariant contrastive features are two-fold. First, the ground truth 6D pose is very close to the global minimum of the reconstruction loss in all six dimensions. We illustrate the 6D loss landscapes in Fig. 3. Each curve corresponds to one of the six dimensions of the 6D pose and is centered at the ground truth pose. The large convergence basins that can be observed allow us to search for object proposals from simply sparse sampling and to evaluate a pre-defined set of 6D poses, without the need of a first-stage model widely used by related works [12,18,31]. Second, the loss landscapes are generally smooth around the global minimum. This contrasts with the keypoint-based methods that fit a rigid transformation between two groups of keypoints [18,31] and the render-and-compare methods over RGB space [2,26] with many local minima on the optimization surface.

3.4 Coarse-to-Fine 6D Pose Estimation

Previous methods for 3D object detection or 6D pose optimization are built on top of a 2D region proposal network or refine predictions from a separate pose estimation network. Although this approach was empirically effective, the performance of the hybrid model is largely limited by the 2D region proposal network or the initial pose estimation network. The first-stage networks are unreliable for objects with out-of-distribution textures or shapes, or even miss the object if the object is partially occluded or truncated.

Therefore, we propose a coarse-to-fine 6D pose estimation strategy that searches generative 6D proposals in the coarse stage and then refines the initial 6D poses with pose optimization in the fine stage. The overview of our coarse-to-fine strategy is depicted in Fig. 4. Since the generative 6D proposals are built on the generative neural mesh models and scale-invariant contrastive features, they are robust to partial occlusion and truncation. Moreover, this coarse-to-fine strategy can largely benefit subsequent pose optimization. The generative 6D proposals are often located at regions near global optimum that makes effective

(a)   (b)   (c)   (d)

Fig. 3. We visualize the loss landscapes of the pose optimization with scale-invariant contrastive features. (a) shows the input image. (b) shows the reconstruction loss $\max_r \|C_r - f_i\|^2$ for each pixel. (c) visualizes the predicted 6D pose. Each curve in (d) corresponds to one of the six dimensions of the 6D pose and is centered at the ground truth pose. We can see with the help the scale-invariant contrastive features, the pose optimization has a clear global minimum near the ground truth pose and is easy to optimize. This further allows us to search for generative 6D proposals, as described in Sect. 3.4.

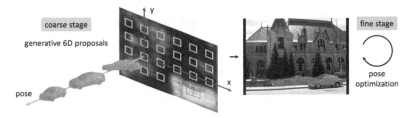

Fig. 4. Overview of our proposed coarse-to-fine 6D pose estimation. We search for generative 6D proposals in the coarse stage and then refine the initial 6D poses with pose optimization in the fine stage. Since the generative 6D proposals are built on the generative neural mesh models and the scale-invariant contrastive features, they are robust to partial occlusion and truncation and are easy to optimize. Note that the CAD models are for visualization only and are not used in any part of our model.

gradients toward the ground truth pose. We compare Faster R-CNN 6D proposals and our generative 6D proposals quantitatively in Sect. 4.4. We further visualize loss landscapes of different 6D object proposals in the supplementary material.

Coarse Stage: generative 6D proposals. With the scale-invariant contrastive features, the pose optimization has a clear global minimum near the ground truth location, and the loss landscapes are smooth with decent gradients around the global minimum (see Fig. 3). This nice property allows us to search for generative 6D proposals from a sparse sampling over six dimensions. Given a 6D pose sample, we estimate the reconstruction loss in Eq. 3 and predict generative 6D proposals with non-maximum suppression. Since the structure of the 3D model $\mathcal{M}$ and the sampled 6D poses are consistent across all testing samples, the 2D coordinates and visibility of the vertices can be pre-computed and cached. We further adopt a strategy to speed up by searching over the 2D locations first and then the other four dimensions, which is detailed in the supplementary materials. This allows us to predict generative 6D proposals that are robust to partial occlusion and truncation and are easy to optimize with a negligible complexity overhead.

Fine stage: pose optimization. The goal of pose optimization is to refine the initial 6D pose of an object, which can be either predicted by a stand-alone pose estimation network or from our generative 6D proposals. We maximize the feature correlation between the predicted features F from the feature extract ζ and the rendered features $\bar{F}$ with respect to the object pose. Since the ground truth $\mathcal{FG}$ and $\mathcal{BG}$ is unknown, we approximate the maximum likelihood problem in Eq. 3 with a one-hot map $\mathbf{Z}$ to denote the foreground and background regions in the feature map:

$$
\mathbf{Z}_i = \begin{cases} 1 & \text{if } \|f_i - C_r\|^2 \geq \|f_i - b\|^2 \\ 0 & \text{otherwise} \end{cases}
\tag{5}
$$

Finally, we minimize $\mathcal{L}_{\text{NLL}}$ with respect to object pose m with gradient descent

$$
\mathcal{L}_{\text{NLL}}(F, \mathfrak{N}, m, \mathcal{B}) = \frac{1}{2} \sum_i \left(\mathbb{1}_{Z_i=1} \|f_i - C_r\|^2 + \mathbb{1}_{Z_i=0} \|f_i - b\|^2 \right) + const.
\tag{6}
$$

3.5 Multi-object Reasoning

One challenge when extending 3D pose estimation to 6D pose estimation is the existence of multiple objects in the image. Therefore, we propose a multi-object reasoning module that can resolve mutual occlusion and can be applied on top of any render-and-compare methods. The motivation is that we need to assign the pixels in the feature maps to different instances, and our multi-object reasoning module resembles related methods in instance segmentation [37].

Given multiple generative 6D proposals, we run the pose optimization gradient descent for a small number of epochs. If the rendered feature maps of two objects overlap, we recover the occlusion order by running pixel-level competition, and for each overlapping region, only one object is considered as the foreground object and the other objects are considered as background. We use a one-hot map to record the multi-object reasoning results, where

$$
\mathbf{Z} \in \mathbb{Z}^{H \times W \times k}, \quad Z_{i,j,k} = \begin{cases} 1 & \text{if the } ktext-thobjectistheforegroundobject \\ 0 & \text{otherwise} \end{cases}
\tag{7}
$$

Then we run the pose optimization again given the occlusion ordering $\mathbf{Z}$. We visualize the results of the multi-object occlusion reasoning in Fig. 5.

4   Experiments

In this section, we investigate the performance of our approach in challenging 6D pose estimation datasets and compare its performance to related methods. We first describe the experimental setup in Sect. 4.1. Then we study the performance of our model in Sect. 4.2. We visualize some qualitative examples in Sect. 4.3. Finally, we run ablation study experiments on the generative 6D proposals and the multi-object reasoning module in Sect. 4.4.

4.1   Experimental Setup

Datasets. We evaluate our model on PASCAL3D+ dataset [34], Occluded PAS-CAL3D+ dataset [30], and ObjectNet3D dataset [33]. PASCAL3D+ dataset contains objects from 12 man-made categories, and each object is annotated with 3D pose, 2D centroid, and object distance. The ImageNet subset of the PASCAL3D+ dataset contains 11045 images for training and 10812 images for evaluation, and the PASCAL VOC subset contains 4293 images for training and 4212 images for validation. Occluded PASCAL3D+ is based on the ImageNet subset of the PASCAL3D+ dataset, and partial occlusion is simulated by superimposing occluders on top of the objects and the background. We also experimented on ObjectNet3D dataset, which consists of 100 categories with 17101 training images and 19604 testing images. Following [28,38], we compare the 6D pose estimation performance on 18 categories.

Evaluation metrics. Category-level 6D pose estimation estimates both the 3D pose (azimuth, elevation, and in-plane rotation) and the 3D location of the visible objects. In our experiments, we adopt the pose estimation error and the average distance metric (ADD) for evaluation. Following [38], the pose estimation error measures the angle between the predicted rotation matrix and the ground truth rotation matrix $\Delta(R_{\mathrm{pred}}, R_{\mathrm{gt}}) = \frac{\|\mathrm{logm}(R_{\mathrm{pred}}^{\top} R_{\mathrm{gt}})\|_{\mathcal{F}}}{\sqrt{2}}$. Average distance (ADD) is a widely used metric to measure the translation of the keypoints between the ground truth pose and the predicted pose. For the PASCAL VOC images, we also evaluate the mean average precision (mAP) at $(\pi/3, 5.0)$.

Implementation details. Our model includes a contrastive feature backbone and a corresponding neural mesh model. The feature extractor is a ResNet50 model with two upsampling layers, so the output feature map is $\frac{1}{8}$ of the input resolution. The neural mesh model is a category-wise cuboid model with around 1100 vertices. The scale of the cuboid mesh model is the average of the scales of the sub-category mesh models, and the vertices are sampled uniformly across six faces. Our model is trained for 1200 epochs with random horizontal flip and 2D translation and takes around 20 h on one NVIDIA RTX Titan GPU. During inference, the pose optimization with multi-object reasoning takes 4.1 s on average per object.

Table 1. Quantitative results of 6D pose estimation on PASCAL3D+ dataset.

Subset	Model	Pose Acc ($\frac{\pi}{6}$) ↑	Pose Acc ($\frac{\pi}{18}$) ↑	Median Pose Error ↓	Median ADD ↓	mAP ↑
ImageNet	FRCNN+Cls	78.90	37.35	0.22	0.74	–
ImageNet	FRCNN+NeMo	66.06	28.44	0.33	1.84	–
ImageNet	RTM3DExt	74.94	39.56	0.23	0.92	–
ImageNet	Ours	**81.45**	**47.68**	**0.19**	**0.53**	–
PASCAL VOC	FRCNN+Cls	38.98	15.05	1.38	2.04	0.11
PASCAL VOC	FRCNN+NeMo	40.13	**19.17**	1.40	2.14	0.32
PASCAL VOC	RTM3DExt	18.04	8.12	6.28	20.0	0.11
PASCAL VOC	Ours	**45.32**	18.09	**0.65**	**1.87**	**0.43**

Table 2. Quantitative results of 6D pose estimation on ObjectNet3D dataset.

Model	Pose Acc ($\frac{\pi}{6}$) ↑	Pose Acc ($\frac{\pi}{18}$) ↑	Median Pose Error ↓	Median ADD ↓
RTM3DExt	38.44	16.61	2.50	4.87
Ours	**52.47**	**16.65**	**0.49**	**1.95**

Baseline models. Since we know of no other 6D pose estimation methods for category-level 6D pose estimation from a single RGB image, we compare our model with related works in 3D object detection and 3D pose estimation and extend them to the 6D pose estimation setting.

RTM3D is one of the state-of-the-art models for monocular 3D object detection. It predicts a 3D bounding box (i.e., location, rotation, and scale) by minimizing the reprojection error between the regressed 2D keypoints and the corners of the 3D cuboid. To extend RTM3D to 6D pose estimation, we fix the cuboid dimensions and fit a rigid 6D transformation.

We further compare our approach with two-stage models that predict object proposals in the first stage and then estimate object poses from the proposed RoIs. We adopt Faster R-CNN [24] for object detection. Two methods are considered for pose estimation. Following previous works [28,38], we formulate the pose estimation as a classification problem and predict the object pose from the RoI features from the Faster R-CNN backbone. Based on the reported results [28,38], we also consider the state-of-the-art 3D pose estimation model, NeMo [28], where we optimize the 3D object pose from the predicted 2D bounding box. The two models are denoted as "FRCNN+Cls" and "FRCNN+NeMo" respectively.

4.2   Quantitative Results

6D pose estimation on PASCAL3D+ and ObjectNet3D dataset. Table 1 shows the 6D pose estimation results on the ImageNet and PASCAL VOC subsets of the PASCAL3D+ dataset. Compared to the ImageNet images, the PASCAL VOC subset is more challenging as there are multiple objects with occlusion, truncation, as well as a larger variance in the object scale and location. Our model outperforms all baseline models in both the pose error and the average distance metric. To show our model can be applied to different man-made in-door and out-door categories, we also experiment on the ObjectNet3D dataset, and the results are shown in Table 2. Despite the considerable number of occluded and truncated images in ObjectNet3D dataset, our model achieves reasonable accuracy and outperforms the competitive baseline by a wide margin.

Robust 6D pose estimation on the Occluded PASCAL3D+ dataset. In order to investigate the robustness under occlusion, we further evaluate each model on Occluded PASCAL3D+ dataset under different occlusion levels. The quantitative results are reported in Table 3. As we can see, our model achieves superior performance across all occlusion levels and shows a wider performance gap compared to the performance on the un-occluded images.

Table 3. Quantitative results of 6D pose estimation on the Occluded PASCAL3D+ dataset.

Subset	Level	Method	Pose Acc ($\frac{\pi}{6}$) ↑	Pose Acc ($\frac{\pi}{18}$) ↑	Median Pose Error ↓	Median ADD ↓
ImageNet	1	FRCNN+Cls	61.48	26.11	0.33	1.07
ImageNet	1	FRCNN+NeMo	48.34	17.46	0.55	1.90
ImageNet	1	RTM3DExt	43.55	17.68	0.82	3.29
ImageNet	1	Ours	**66.63**	**30.84**	**0.31**	**0.77**
ImageNet	2	FRCNN+Cls	41.95	14.75	0.75	1.47
ImageNet	2	FRCNN+NeMo	34.33	9.65	1.05	2.03
ImageNet	2	RTM3DExt	21.27	7.24	3.14	5.00
ImageNet	2	Ours	**47.95**	**16.25**	**0.56**	**1.22**
ImageNet	3	FRCNN+Cls	22.42	**5.58**	2.01	1.95
ImageNet	3	FRCNN+NeMo	18.19	3.32	2.40	2.35
ImageNet	3	RTM3DExt	10.17	3.11	3.14	19.92
ImageNet	3	Ours	**27.43**	5.30	**1.07**	**1.94**

4.3   Qualitative Examples

Fig. 5 shows some qualitative examples of our proposed model on PASCAL3D+ dataset. As we can see, our method can robustly estimate 6D poses for objects varying in scales and textures and is robust to partial occlusion.

4.4   Ablation Study

Generative 6D proposals. Unlike previous works that are based on 2D region proposal networks, we introduce generative 6D proposals that are robust to partial occlusion and truncation and are easy to optimize. We run ablation study experiments on the object proposal methods and compare the performance of our model using (1) generative 6D proposals ("Ours w/ GP"), or (ii) Faster R-CNN object proposals ("Ours w/ FRCNN"). The quantitative results on the Occluded PASCAL3D+ dataset are reported in Table 4. As we can see, we can

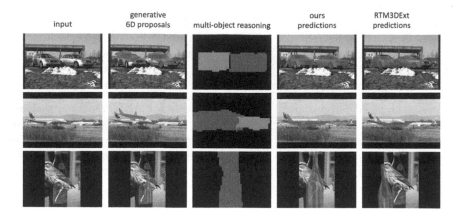

Fig. 5. Qualitative examples of our proposed model.

significantly improve the performance of our model in almost all tests with the generative 6D proposals. Note that "Ours w/ FRCNN" naturally benefits from model ensembling, and "Ours w/ FRCNN" can achieve a better pose estimation only in occlusion level 1 when the Faster R-CNN model can predict highly accurate poses without any refinement. In occlusion levels 2 and 3, "Ours w/ GP" significantly outperforms "Ours w/ FRCNN" in terms of both object location and pose estimation.

Table 4. Ablation study on the 6D proposal method. We compare the performance of our proposed model using Faster R-CNN 6D proposals and generative 6D proposals (GP) on the PASCAL3D+ dataset.

Level	Method	Pose Acc ($\frac{\pi}{6}$) ↑	Pose Acc ($\frac{\pi}{18}$) ↑	Median Pose Error ↓	Median ADD ↓
1	Ours w/FRCNN	65.79	**34.56**	**0.28**	0.95
1	Ours w/GP	**66.63**	30.84	0.31	**0.77**
2	Ours w/FRCNN	45.43	**17.46**	0.64	1.30
2	Ours w/GP	**47.95**	16.25	**0.56**	**1.22**
3	Ours w/FRCNN	23.53	5.27	1.67	2.05
3	Ours w/GP	**27.43**	**5.30**	**1.07**	**1.94**

Number of pre-defined initial poses. Far all categories, we uniformly sample a sparse set of initial poses over the space of 6D poses. In Table 5, we ablate on the number of initial poses used to search the generative 6D proposals.

Multi-object reasoning. In order to estimate 6D poses of multiple objects with render-and-compare, we propose a multi-object reasoning module to correctly assign pixels in the feature map to each object proposal. We quantitatively compare the performance of our model with and without an object reasoning module on the PASCAL subset of the PASCAL3D+ dataset. As shown in Table 6, we can

Table 5. Ablation on the number of initial poses used to search the generative 6D proposals. The default setting in the paper is bold.

Init. 3D Pose	Init. 3D Loc	Acc $(\frac{\pi}{6})$	Acc $(\frac{\pi}{18})$	Median Err	Median ADD
$12 \times 3 \times 3$	$3 \times 3 \times 3$	69.77	35.82	0.28	0.65
$6 \times 2 \times 2$	$9 \times 9 \times 9$	71.64	38.75	0.26	0.63
$\mathbf{12 \times 3 \times 3}$	$\mathbf{9 \times 9 \times 9}$	81.45	47.68	0.19	0.53
$18 \times 6 \times 6$	$9 \times 9 \times 9$	83.46	49.28	0.18	0.51
$12 \times 3 \times 3$	$12 \times 12 \times 12$	84.54	51.39	0.17	0.49

Table 6. Ablation study on the multi-object reasoning. We compare the performance of our proposed model with and without the multi-object reasoning on the PASCAL VOC subset of PASCAL3D+ dataset.

Method	Pose Acc $(\frac{\pi}{6})$ ↑	Pose Acc $(\frac{\pi}{18})$ ↑	Median Pose Error ↓	Median ADD ↓	mAP ↑
Ours w/o reasoning	44.89	17.63	0.66	**1.87**	0.41
Ours	**45.32**	**18.09**	**0.65**	1.87	**0.43**

effectively improve the performance of our model with the multi-object reasoning module.

5   Conclusions

In this work, we consider the problem of category-level 6D pose estimation from a single RGB image. We find that previous methods built on 2D region proposal networks are less robust to partial occlusion and truncation, and the predicted initial poses are harder to optimize. Therefore, we propose a coarse-to-fine 6D pose optimization strategy where we search generative 6D proposals in the coarse stage and then refine them with pose optimization in the second stage. Both stages of our coarse-to-fine 6D pose estimation are built on our scale-invariant contrastive features and are hence robust to partial occlusion and truncation. We demonstrate the superiority of our approach compared to related works on several challenging datasets.

Acknowledgements. AK acknowledges support via his Emmy Noether Research Group funded by the German Science Foundation (DFG) under Grant No. 468670075. AY acknowledges the Institute for Assured Autonomy at JHU with Grant IAA 80052272, ONR N00014-21-1-2812, NSF grant BCS-1827427.

References

1. Bai, Y., Wang, A., Kortylewski, A., Yuille, A.: CoKe: localized contrastive learning for robust keypoint detection. arXiv preprint arXiv:2009.14115 (2020)
2. Blanz, V., Vetter, T.: A morphable model for the synthesis of 3D faces. In: Proceedings of the 26th Annual Conference on Computer Graphics and Interactive Techniques, pp. 187–194. SIGGRAPH 1999, ACM Press/Addison-Wesley Publishing Co., USA (1999). https://doi.org/10.1145/311535.311556
3. Chen, X., Dong, Z., Song, J., Geiger, A., Hilliges, O.: Category level object pose estimation via neural analysis-by-synthesis. In: Vedaldi, A., Bischof, H., Brox, T., Frahm, J.-M. (eds.) ECCV 2020. LNCS, vol. 12371, pp. 139–156. Springer, Cham (2020). https://doi.org/10.1007/978-3-030-58574-7_9
4. Cimpoi, M., Maji, S., Kokkinos, I., Mohamed, S., Vedaldi, A.: Describing textures in the wild. In: Proceedings of the IEEE Conference on Computer Vision and Pattern Recognition (CVPR) (2014)
5. Egger, B., et al.: Occlusion-aware 3D morphable models and an illumination prior for face image analysis. Int. J. Comput. Vis. **126**(12), 1269–1287 (2018)
6. Girshick, R., Felzenszwalb, P., McAllester, D.: Object detection with grammar models. In: Advances in Neural Information Processing Systems 24 (2011)
7. Grenander, U.: A unified approach to pattern analysis. In: Advances in computers, vol. 10, pp. 175–216. Elsevier (1970)
8. Grenander, U.: Elements of pattern theory. JHU Press, Baltimore (1996)
9. He, K., Fan, H., Wu, Y., Xie, S., Girshick, R.: Momentum contrast for unsupervised visual representation learning. In: Proceedings of the IEEE/CVF Conference on Computer Vision and Pattern Recognition (CVPR) (2020)
10. He, Y., Sun, W., Huang, H., Liu, J., Fan, H., Sun, J.: PVN3D: a deep pointwise 3D keypoints voting network for 6DoF pose estimation. In: Proceedings of the IEEE/CVF Conference on Computer Vision and Pattern Recognition (CVPR) (2020)
11. Huber, P.J.: Robust statistics, vol. 523. Wiley (2004)
12. Iwase, S., Liu, X., Khirodkar, R., Yokota, R., Kitani, K.M.: Repose: fast 6D object pose refinement via deep texture rendering. In: Proceedings of the IEEE/CVF International Conference on Computer Vision (ICCV), pp. 3303–3312 (2021)
13. Kortylewski, A., He, J., Liu, Q., Cosgrove, C., Yang, C., Yuille, A.L.: Compositional generative networks and robustness to perceptible image changes. In: 2021 55th Annual Conference on Information Sciences and Systems (CISS), pp. 1–8. IEEE (2021)
14. Kortylewski, A., He, J., Liu, Q., Yuille, A.L.: Compositional convolutional neural networks: a deep architecture with innate robustness to partial occlusion. In: Proceedings of the IEEE/CVF Conference on Computer Vision and Pattern Recognition (CVPR) (2020)
15. Kortylewski, A., Liu, Q., Wang, A., Sun, Y., Yuille, A.: Compositional convolutional neural networks: a robust and interpretable model for object recognition under occlusion. International Journal of Computer Vision, pp. 1–25 (2020)
16. Kortylewski, A., Liu, Q., Wang, H., Zhang, Z., Yuille, A.: Combining compositional models and deep networks for robust object classification under occlusion. In: Proceedings of the IEEE/CVF Winter Conference on Applications of Computer Vision, pp. 1333–1341 (2020)
17. LeCun, Y., Bengio, Y., et al.: Convolutional networks for images, speech, and time series. Handb. Brain Theor. Neural Netw. **3361**(10), 1995 (1995)

18. Li, P., Zhao, H., Liu, P., Cao, F.: RTM3D: real-time monocular 3D detection from object keypoints for autonomous driving. In: Vedaldi, A., Bischof, H., Brox, T., Frahm, J.-M. (eds.) ECCV 2020. LNCS, vol. 12348, pp. 644–660. Springer, Cham (2020). https://doi.org/10.1007/978-3-030-58580-8_38
19. Li, Y., Wang, G., Ji, X., Xiang, Y., Fox, D.: DeepIM: deep iterative matching for 6D pose estimation. In: Proceedings of the European Conference on Computer Vision (ECCV) (2018)
20. Lin, J., Wei, Z., Li, Z., Xu, S., Jia, K., Li, Y.: DualPoseNet: category-level 6D object pose and size estimation using dual pose network with refined learning of pose consistency. In: Proceedings of the IEEE/CVF International Conference on Computer Vision (ICCV), pp. 3560–3569 (2021)
21. Moreno, P., Williams, C.K.I., Nash, C., Kohli, P.: Overcoming occlusion with inverse graphics. In: Hua, G., Jégou, H. (eds.) ECCV 2016. LNCS, vol. 9915, pp. 170–185. Springer, Cham (2016). https://doi.org/10.1007/978-3-319-49409-8_16
22. Pavlakos, G., Zhou, X., Chan, A., Derpanis, K.G., Daniilidis, K.: 6-DoF object pose from semantic keypoints. In: 2017 IEEE International Conference on Robotics and Automation (ICRA), pp. 2011–2018 (2017). https://doi.org/10.1109/ICRA.2017.7989233
23. Peng, S., Liu, Y., Huang, Q., Zhou, X., Bao, H.: PVNet: pixel-wise voting network for 6DoF pose estimation. In: Proceedings of the IEEE/CVF Conference on Computer Vision and Pattern Recognition (CVPR) (2019)
24. Ren, S., He, K., Girshick, R., Sun, J.: Faster R-CNN: towards real-time object detection with region proposal networks. IEEE Trans. Pattern Anal. Mach. Intell. **39**(6), 1137–1149 (2016)
25. Romaszko, L., Williams, C.K., Moreno, P., Kohli, P.: Vision-as-inverse-graphics: obtaining a rich 3D explanation of a scene from a single image. In: Proceedings of the IEEE International Conference on Computer Vision Workshops, pp. 851–859 (2017)
26. Schönborn, S., Egger, B., Morel-Forster, A., Vetter, T.: Markov Chain Monte Carlo for automated face image analysis. Int. J. Comput. Vis. **123**(2), 160–183 (2017)
27. Umeyama, S.: Least-squares estimation of transformation parameters between two point patterns. IEEE Trans. Pattern Anal. Mach. Intell. **13**(04), 376–380 (1991)
28. Wang, A., Kortylewski, A., Yuille, A.: NEMO: Neural mesh models of contrastive features for robust 3D pose estimation. In: International Conference on Learning Representations (2021). https://openreview.net/forum?id=pmj131uIL9H
29. Wang, A., Mei, S., Yuille, A.L., Kortylewski, A.: Neural view synthesis and matching for semi-supervised few-shot learning of 3D pose. Adv. Neural. Inf. Process. Syst. **34**, 7207–7219 (2021)
30. Wang, A., Sun, Y., Kortylewski, A., Yuille, A.L.: Robust object detection under occlusion with context-aware compositionalNets. In: Proceedings of the IEEE/CVF Conference on Computer Vision and Pattern Recognition, pp. 12645–12654 (2020)
31. Wang, H., Sridhar, S., Huang, J., Valentin, J., Song, S., Guibas, L.J.: Normalized object coordinate space for category-level 6D object pose and size estimation. In: Proceedings of the IEEE/CVF Conference on Computer Vision and Pattern Recognition (CVPR) (2019)
32. Wu, Z., Xiong, Y., Yu, S.X., Lin, D.: Unsupervised feature learning via non-parametric instance discrimination. In: Proceedings of the IEEE Conference on Computer Vision and Pattern Recognition (CVPR) (2018)
33. Xiang, Y., et al.: ObjectNet3D: a large scale database for 3D object recognition. In: Leibe, B., Matas, J., Sebe, N., Welling, M. (eds.) ECCV 2016. LNCS, vol. 9912, pp. 160–176. Springer, Cham (2016). https://doi.org/10.1007/978-3-319-46484-8_10

34. Xiang, Y., Mottaghi, R., Savarese, S.: Beyond pascal: a benchmark for 3D object detection in the wild. In: IEEE Winter Conference on Applications of Computer Vision, pp. 75–82. IEEE (2014)
35. Xiang, Y., Schmidt, T., Narayanan, V., Fox, D.: PoseCNN: a convolutional neural network for 6d object pose estimation in cluttered scenes. arXiv preprint arXiv:1711.00199 (2017)
36. Xiao, M., Kortylewski, A., Wu, R., Qiao, S., Shen, W., Yuille, A.: TDMPNet: prototype network with recurrent top-down modulation for robust object classification under partial occlusion. In: Bartoli, A., Fusiello, A. (eds.) ECCV 2020. LNCS, vol. 12536, pp. 447–463. Springer, Cham (2020). https://doi.org/10.1007/978-3-030-66096-3_31
37. Yuan, X., Kortylewski, A., Sun, Y., Yuille, A.: Robust instance segmentation through reasoning about multi-object occlusion. In: Proceedings of the IEEE/CVF Conference on Computer Vision and Pattern Recognition (CVPR), pp. 11141–11150 (2021)
38. Zhou, X., Karpur, A., Luo, L., Huang, Q.: StarMap for category-agnostic keypoint and viewpoint estimation. In: Proceedings of the European Conference on Computer Vision (ECCV), pp. 318–334 (2018)

Translation, Scale and Rotation: Cross-Modal Alignment Meets RGB-Infrared Vehicle Detection

Maoxun Yuan[1] , Yinyan Wang[1], and Xingxing Wei[2]([✉])

[1] Beijing Key Laboratory of Digital Media, Beihang University, Beijing, China
{yuanmaoxun,wangyinyan}@buaa.edu.cn
[2] Institute of Artificial Intelligence, Hangzhou Innovation Institute, Beihang
University, Beijing, China
xxwei@buaa.edu.cn

Abstract. Integrating multispectral data in object detection, especially visible and infrared images, has received great attention in recent years. Since visible (RGB) and infrared (IR) images can provide complementary information to handle light variations, the paired images are used in many fields, such as multispectral pedestrian detection, RGB-IR crowd counting and RGB-IR salient object detection. Compared with natural RGB-IR images, we find detection in aerial RGB-IR images suffers from cross-modal weakly misalignment problems, which are manifested in the position, size and angle deviations of the same object. In this paper, we mainly address the challenge of cross-modal weakly misalignment in aerial RGB-IR images. Specifically, we firstly explain and analyze the cause of the weakly misalignment problem. Then, we propose a Translation-Scale-Rotation Alignment (TSRA) module to address the problem by calibrating the feature maps from these two modalities. The module predicts the deviation between two modality objects through an alignment process and utilizes Modality-Selection (MS) strategy to improve the performance of alignment. Finally, a two-stream feature alignment detector (TSFADet) based on the TSRA module is constructed for RGB-IR object detection in aerial images. With comprehensive experiments on the public DroneVehicle datasets, we verify that our method reduces the effect of the cross-modal misalignment and achieve robust detection results.

Keywords: Multispectral object detection · Cross-modal alignment · Vehicle detection · Aerial imagery

1 Introduction

Object detection in aerial images plays an important role in computer vision field with various applications, such as urban planning, surveillance and disaster rescue. Unlike natural images that are often taken from low-altitude perspectives, aerial images are typically taken with bird views, which implies that objects in

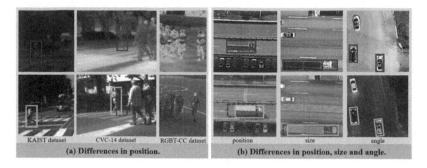

Fig. 1. Illustration of the modality weakly misalignment problem. (a) and (b) are the visualization image patches (cropped on the same position of RGB-IR image pairs) of groundtruth annotations in nature image datasets and aerial DroneVehicle dataset. The yellow and the red boxes represent annotations of same objects in the infrared images and the visible images, respectively. KAIST and CVC-14 are the pedestrian detection dataset, and RGBT-CC is the crowd counting dataset.

aerial images are always distributed with arbitrary orientation. To solve these problems, several oriented object detectors [5,25,28,41] have been proposed and obtained state-of-the-art results on challenging aerial image datasets [18,27]. However, these detectors are only designed for the visible images alone, which cannot cope with the challenges in limited illumination (nighttime).

For these reasons, infrared cameras have been invested to deal with complex scenarios. Infrared cameras can present clear silhouettes of objects even in low-light condition, due to the capability in capturing the radiated heat. This makes visible (RGB) images and infrared (IR) images complement each other. In natural images, RGB-IR images are utilized in many fields , such as multispectral pedestrian detection, RGB-IR crowd counting and RGB-IR salient object detection. However, there are few RGB-IR methods and paired image datasets specifically for aerial imagery.

Image alignment is one of the issues that should be considered in cross-modal image applications. Existing methods [6,11,16,29,38–40] usually assume that visible-infrared image pairs are perfectly geometrically aligned, and they directly perform the multi-modal fusion methods. Actually, after the image registration algorithm, the paired images are just weakly aligned (shown in Fig. 1(a)). However, objects are always arbitrary oriented in aerial images, they differ not only in position, but also in scale and angle. These three deviations (position, size and angle) of the paired arbitrary oriented objects are closely coupled, changing one will affect another one, which makes the alignment operation more complicated. As shown in Fig. 1(b), the dashed boxes represent the position of the corresponding bounding-boxes in the infrared images. We find that the same object on image pairs differs in location, scale and angle. Therefore, weakly misalignment in cross-modal aerial images is a common issue that needs to be addressed.

To solve the above problem, in this paper, we propose and analyze the cause of the weakly misalignment problem. The problem is mainly caused by two factors: hardware errors and annotation errors. To address these issues, we propose a TSRA module to calibrate the feature maps from two modality proposals through translation, scale and rotation operations. In the module, the feature maps of RGB-IR modality proposals are first subjected to the alignment process to acquire the deviation, and then we utilize a Modality-Selection strategy to select the appropriate annotations as the reference bounding-boxes. The final feature maps for classification and regression are obtained by fusing the aligned proposal features. Finally, we construct a TSRA-based oriented object detector to evaluate the effectiveness of the TSRA module.

In summary, the contributions of this paper are as follows:

- We present the cross-modal weakly misalignment problem specific to the RGB-IR object detection in aerial images. To the best of our knowledge, it is the first time to present and analyse the weakly misalignment problem in rotated object detection of RGB-IR aerial images.
- We propose a TSRA module which consists of alignment process and MS strategy to translation, scale and rotate the feature maps of two modality objects. Meanwhile, the Multi-task Jitter is designed to further improve model performance. To evaluate the validity of the TSRA module, we construct a two-stream feature alignment detector (TSFADet) for RGB-IR object detection in aerial images, which can be trained with an end-to-end manner.
- Extensive experiments on DroneVehicle dataset demonstrate that, our TSFADet outperforms previous state-of-the-art datectors and the TSRA module is effective for solving the cross-modal weakly misalignment problem.

2   Related Work

2.1   Oriented Object Detection

Aerial images are the main application scenarios of the rotation detectors. Xia et al. [27] construct a large-scale object detection benchmark with oriented annotations, named DOTA. Since then, several existing works [5,12,17,19,28,30] are mainly based on typical proposal-based frameworks to explore oriented object detection. Naturally, some methods [17,19] set numerous rotated anchors with different angles, scales and aspect ratios for better regression. These methods lead to extensive computation complexity. To avoid a large number of anchors, Ding et al. [5] designed an RoI transformer to learn the transformation from Horizontal RoIs (HRoIs) to Rotated RoI (RRoIs), which boosts the detection accuracy of oriented objects. Recently, Oriented R-CNN [28] is proposed to further improve the detection performance by replacing RROI learning module with a lighter and simpler oriented region proposal network (orientation RPN).

To improve real-time and availability of detectors, some works [7,21,26,31,34] have explored one-stage or anchor-free oriented object detection frameworks. For instance, R^3Det [31] and S^2A-Net [7] are one-stage object detector, which align

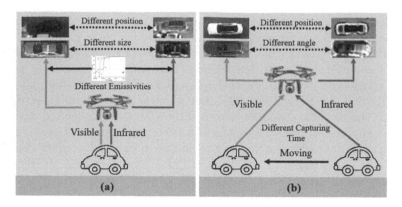

Fig. 2. The illustration of Hardware Errors. (a) and (b) are the description of radiation distortion and clock skew, respectively.

the feature between horizontal receptive fields and rotated anchors. Recently, GWD [32] and KLD [33] are proposed to use the Gaussian Wasserstein distance and KL divergence to optimize the localization of the bounding boxes, respectively. Considering that many current mainstream rotation detectors are based on the well-extended two-stage detection framework, we also build a two-stream rotation detector based on the two-stage detection framework to verify the effectiveness of our proposed method.

2.2   Cross-Modal Image Alignment

Images from different modalities usually contain scale, rotation or radiance differences so that cross-modal image alignment is required before using them simultaneously [1,42]. The aim of image alignment is to warp a sensed image into the common spatial coordinate system of a reference image so that they are matched in pixel. Existing methods are generally divided into area-based methods and feature-based methods. The area-based methods register the image pairs using a similarity metric function, while the feature-based methods include four processes: feature extraction, feature matching, transformation model estimation and image re-sampling and warping. As deep learning has great potential in feature extraction, numerous researchers have designed data-driven strategy in the field of cross-modal image alignment [4,20,35]. Although image alignment is a necessary step in many fields, it brings extra time consumption and cannot completely address the weakly misalignment problem.

Recently, a few works have been proposed to address the image alignment issue by end-to-end training network. [37] firstly addressed the alignment problem by introducing region feature alignment (RFA) module. Zhou et al. [40] designed a illumination aware feature alignment (IAFA) module to align two modality features and then construct Modality Balance Network (MBNet) based on SSD. However, these methods only consider the translation way to solve the deviation, and cannot solve complex misalignment problems in aerial images, such as angle deviation and size deviation. Inspired by [37], in this paper, we propose TSRA module to predict the offset of two objects in position, size and angle.

3 Methodology and Analysis

In this section, we first analyze the cause of modality weakly misalignment problem (Sect. 3.1). According to our analysis, we propose the TSRA module (Section 3.2) which consists of alignment process, MS strategy and multi-task jitter to solve the problem. For the same object in two modality images, we use MS strategy to select the bounding-boxes with better annotation in the two modalities as the reference modality, and then perform alignment process to calibrate the feature maps from two modalities. Finally, we put everything together into a description of the TSFADet (Sect. 3.3).

3.1 Analysis

Modality weakly misalignment is a common problem in aerial cross-modal images, since the data are collected by different sensors. Through observation and research, we find the the problem usually occurs in the three situation: hardware errors, annotation errors and both, which are explained as follows.

Hardware Errors: Hardware errors are mainly reflected in radiation distortions and clock skews. The radiation distortions often occur in the process of the sensor imaging [23]. The spectral emissivity of the ground objects is different from the real spectral emissivity. These radiation differences will cause images have different representations (*e.g.* color, intensity and texture) for the same objects (shown in Fig. 2(a)). Therefore, the same object on two modality images will have differences in scale and position caused by radiation distortion (shown in Fig. 1(a)).

As shown in Fig. 2(b), due to the different sensors' capturing time, the clock skew between two sensors (*e.g.* visible and infrared) can lead to pixel-misalignment of image pairs, especially for locally moving objects such as cars on a highway [10]. As a result, clock skew causes the position and angle of the same object to be inconsistent in different modalities, see Fig. 1(a).

Annotation Errors: Since different people have different standards for labeling data, the annotation errors are inevitable. In the process of multispectral data annotation, it is difficult to ensure that the objects are annotated accurately in different modalities. The annotations can affect the training performance of the model. Some examples of the annotation errors in DroneVehicle datasat are shown in Fig. 3(a).

Fig. 3. The visualization image patches (cropped on the same position of RGB-IR image pairs) in the DroneVehicle dataset. (a) Examples of annotation errors. (b) Examples of hardware errors and annotation errors occur simultaneously. (Color figure online)

Hardware errors and annotation errors can occur simultaneously in the same object, as shown in Fig. 3(b). That makes the deviation between two modalities cannot be simply solved by affine transformation, therefore, we need to design a module to handle the above situations and perform alignment process in a region-wise way.

3.2 Translation-Scale-Rotation Alignment Module

The proposed TSRA module can be injected into the object detection framework to solve the weakly misalignment problem. The module mainly consists of two parts: alignment process and modality-selection strategy. To improve the robustness of the TSRA module, we also present a multi-task jitter to augment the alignment process.

Alignment Process. Our RGB-IR alignment task is the process of overlaying two proposals of the same object. Refer to [1,42], we introduce the concept of the reference and sensed modality into our task. The alignment process is shown in Fig. 4. Given the two fixed region feature maps (ϕ_r and ϕ_s) pooled by rotated RoIAlign operation, we acquire a new feature map ϕ_d by direct subtraction of two modalities, $\phi_d = \phi_s - \phi_r$. Through this operation, the feature map ϕ_d can obtain the differential representation between the two modalities. Then, three sets of consecutive fully connected layers F_i are utilized to predict the position deviation p, angle deviation r and size deviation s of the region, $\{t(t_x, t_y), s(s_w, s_h), r(r_\theta)\} = F_i(\phi_d)$. Moreover, we add the predicted deviation to the proposals $p(x, y, w, h, \theta)$ and obtain the sensed proposals $p_s(x + t_x, y + t_y, w + s_w, h + s_h, \theta + r_\theta)$. Finally, we re-pool the sensed feature

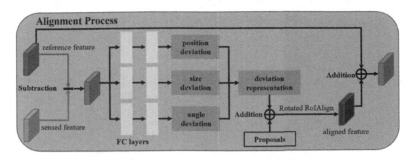

Fig. 4. The concrete structure of the alignment process uses three sets of fully connected layers to predict the deviation of position, size and angle.

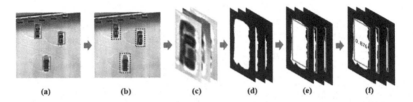

Fig. 5. Illustration of our proposed evaluation method, which can be summarized in the following steps: (a) original bounding-boxes. (b) extend bounding-boxes. (c) crop objects. (d) binarization process. (e) map original bounding-boxes to cropped images. (f) calculate score.

maps on the sensed proposals through rotated RoIAlign operation and acquire aligned feature. The final fused feature can be formulated as:

$$\phi_{fused} = \phi_r + ROIAlign(p_s) \tag{1}$$

Modality-Selection Strategy. To alleviate the influence of annotation errors during training, we design the MS strategy to select the bounding-box with better annotation in the two modalities as the reference modality, rather than simply selecting the infrared image as the reference modality [9,16,37,40]. Through this operation, we can determine which bounding-boxes should be used as the reference modality, and then determine the reference feature and sensed feature.

Specifically, we design a evaluation method (shown in Fig. 5) and perform it on the visible and infrared images separately to select reference bounding-boxes. For each paired bounding-box B_{rgb} and B_{ir}, we first extend the bounding-boxes to include the full object. The full objects C_{rgb} and C_{ir} are then cropped from their original images and subjected to color binarization F_b. Finally, we obtain the scores S_{rgb} and S_{ir} according to their corresponding binary images $F_b(C_{rgb})$ and $F_b(C_{ir})$, and select the one with the higher score as the reference bounding-box (e.g. if $S_{rgb} > S_{ir}$, choose B_{rgb}). The score S of the bounding-box

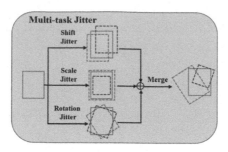

Fig. 6. Illustration of the Multi-task Jitter. Red boxes denote the sensed bounding-boxes. Blue boxes and green boxes represent jitter proposal instances. (Color figure online)

is calculated as follows:

$$S = \frac{n}{N_{\text{object}}} \times 0.5 + \frac{n}{N_{\text{bounding-box}}} \times 0.5 \tag{2}$$

In equation (2), n denotes the number of white pixels in the original bounding-box. N_{object} indicates the number of white pixels of the full object. $N_{\text{bounding-box}}$ is the total number of pixels of the original bounding-box. S is the final score, and its value range is between 0 and 1. For the ideal bounding-box annotation, S should be close to 1.

Multi-task Jitter. To improve the robustness of the TSRA module during training, we refer to the ROI jitter strategy [37] and present a novel Multi-task Jitter (MJ) to augment the deviation. Specifically, the MJ adds the translation, scale and rotation jitter to the sensed proposals, and uses the same settings as [37] to generate jitter randomly, as shown in Fig. 6.

$$
\begin{aligned}
j_x, j_y &\sim N\left(0, \sigma_x^2; 0, \sigma_y^2; 0\right), \\
j_w, j_h &\sim N\left(0, \sigma_w^2; 0, \sigma_h^2; 0\right), \\
j_\theta &\sim N\left(0, \sigma_\theta^2\right),
\end{aligned}
\tag{3}
$$

where j_x, j_y, j_w, j_h and j_θ represent location, width, height and angle of a sensed jitter proposal, respectively.

3.3   TSRA-Based Oriented Detector

To evaluate our proposed TSRA module, we construct a two-stage oriented object detector incorporating into the TSRA module, called TSFADet. The TSFADet mainly consists of two-stream backbone network, oriented RPN, oriented R-CNN head and our proposed TSRA module. The detailed architecture and description of the loss function are as follows.

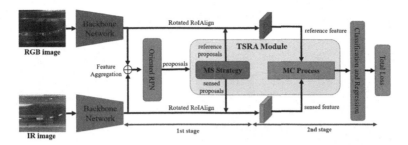

Fig. 7. Overall structure of Two-Stream Feature Alignment Detector (TSFADet), which is a two-stage detector. The first stage generates oriented proposals by oriented RPN and the second stage uses Translation-Scale-Rotation Alignment module to align the oriented features.

Overall Architecture. The overall architecture of the proposed oriented detector is shown in Fig. 7. The TSFADet extends the framework of Oriented R-CNN [28] and adopts the two-stream framework to deal with RGB-IR inputs. The backbone is built on FPN follows [13], which produces five levels of features. We aggregate feature maps from two modalities and utilize the Oriented Region Proposal Network (Oriented RPN) to generate proposals. Then we perform MS strategy and alignment process to predict the offset between two modalities. Finally, we acquire the aligned ROI feature to perform the classification and regression task.

Loss Function. The loss function used for measuring the accuracy of predicted deviation is:

$$L_{\text{deviation}} \left(\{g_i^*\}, \{t_i\}, \{t_i^*\}, \{s_i\}, \{s_i^*\}, \{r_i\}, \{r_i^*\} \right) =$$

$$\frac{1}{N_{\text{deviation}}} \sum_{i=1}^{n} g_i^* \left(\text{ smooth }_1 \left(t_i - t_i^*\right) + \text{smooth}_1 \left(s_i - s_i^*\right) + \text{smooth} L_1 \left(r_i - r_i^*\right)\right) \tag{4}$$

where i is the index of proposal in a batch, t_i, s_i, and r_i are the predicted position deviation, size deviation and angle deviation. $g_i \in \{0, 1\}$, where $g_i = 1$ if i-th proposal is positive, else negative. $N_{deviation}$ is the total number of positive proposals. t_i^*, s_i^*, and r_i^* are the associated ground-truth position deviation, size deviation and angle deviation of the i-th sensed bounding-box, which calculated as follows:

$$\begin{aligned}
t_x^* &= \left((x_s - x_r) \cos \theta_r + (y_s - y_r) \sin \theta_r \right) / w_r, \\
t_y^* &= \left((y_s - y_r) \cos \theta_r + (x_s - x_r) \sin \theta_r \right) / h_r, \\
s_w^* &= \log w_s / w_r, \quad s_h^* = \log h_s / h_r, \\
r_\theta^* &= \left((\theta_s - \theta_r) \mod 2\pi \right) / 2\pi,
\end{aligned} \tag{5}$$

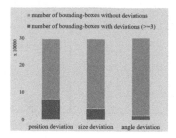

Fig. 8. The statistics of groundtruth bounding-boxes deviation within RGB-IR image pairs in DroneVehicle dataset.

In equation (5), $(x_s, y_s, w_s, h_s, \theta_s)$ and $(x_r, y_r, w_r, h_r, \theta_r)$ are the stack vector for representing location, width, height and angle of the sensed bounding-box and reference bounding-box, respectively.

Finally, the final total loss function can be represented as follows:

$$L = L_{cls} + L_{re.g.} + L_{rpn} + \lambda L_{\text{deviation}} \qquad (6)$$

where the formulations of L_{rpn}, L_{cls} and L_{reg} remain the same as Oriented R-CNN [28]. In our implementation, we set $\lambda = 1$, and thus the average gradient of each loss is at the same scale.

Implementation Details. We implement the network in one unified code library modified from MMDetection [3]. During training, we use the same hyperparameter settings of the original Oriented R-CNN model [28] and use ResNet-50 [8] as the backbone network, which is pretrained on ImageNet. Horizontal and vertical flipping are adopted as data augmentation during training. The whole network is trained by SGD algorithm with the momentum of 0.9 and the weight decay of 0.0001. We train TSFADet for a maximum of 20 epochs with a batch size of 6 and input image size 512×512. The initial learning rate is set to 0.005 and divided by 10 at epoch 16 and 19. The whole framework can be trained end-to-end and the training requires about 14 h on an NVIDIA GV100 GPU.

4 Experimental Results

In this section we show results of experiments we have made to evaluate the effectiveness of TSFADet. In Sect. 4.1, we first introduce the DroneVehicle dataset [24], and in Sect. 4.3 we carry out ablation studies for the proposed method on the DroneVehicle dataset. In Sect. 4.4 we compare it with other detection approaches.

4.1 Dataset and Evaluation Metrics

Our experiments were conducted on the DroneVehicle RGB-IR vehicle detection dataset [24]. DroneVehicle is a large-scale drone-based dataset with well-aligned visible/infrared pairs from day to night.

Table 1. Ablation experiments of TSRA module on DroneVehicle dataset. The symbols of 'P', 'S', and 'A' represent Position, Size and Angle prediction branches respectively.

	P	S	A	car	freight-car	truck	bus	van	mAP
TSFADet (full)				**89.88**	**67.87**	**63.74**	**89.81**	**53.99**	**73.06**
TSFADet w/o MJ				89.34	66.53	62.65	89.62	53.67	72.36
TSFADet w/o MS				89.78	66.26	61.44	89.60	53.17	72.05
TSFADet w/o MJ and MS	P	S	A						
	✓	✓	✓	89.69	65.11	60.39	89.43	51.01	71.13
	✓	✓		89.65	64.77	61.28	89.26	48.57	70.71
	✓		✓	89.68	62.97	60.22	88.90	49.59	70.27
	✓			89.56	62.83	58.35	89.46	47.26	69.49
Baseline				89.45	62.14	57.00	89.09	45.43	68.62

The DroneVehicle dataset collects 28,439 RGB-Infrared image pairs, covering urban roads, residential areas, parking lots, and other scenarios. Besides, the authors made rich annotations with oriented bounding boxes for the five categories (car, bus, truck, van and freight car). To verify the effectiveness of our method, we make the following improvements to the annotations of the original dataset:

- The objects that only annotated in one modality are added in same position to the other modality.
- If the bounding-box in visible image is under extremely bad illumination, we will discard this bounding-box in both modalities.
- Sort the bounding-box of the two modalities so that the same object is assigned in the same index.

The final training set contains 17,990 image pairs and the validation set contains 1,469 images pairs. We evaluate the detection performance on the validation set and adopt the mean average precision (mAP) as evaluation criteria. For mAP, an Intersection over Union (IoU) threshold of 0.5 is used to calculate True Positives (TP) and False Positives (FP).

4.2   Statistics of DroneVehicle

To demonstrate the generality of the weakly misalignment problem in aerial imagery, we also obtain the statistics information of DroneVehicle dataset. we separately count the number of bounding-boxes with deviations (position and size offset by 3 pixels, angle offset by $3\,^{\circ}C$) in the DroneVehicle dataset. As illustrated in Fig. 8, more than 20% of the bounding-boxes have the deviation problem. The results show that the weakly misalignment problem in aerial images is a common issue that needs to be considered.

Table 2. Quantitative comparisons of using different methods to demonstrate the contribution of the MS strategy.

Methods	car	truck	freight-car	bus	van	mAP
RGB Modality	89.47	65.56	60.36	89.63	52.82	71.57
IR Modality	89.78	66.26	61.44	89.60	53.17	72.05
Random strategy	89.53	66.71	62.38	89.74	53.74	72.42
MS strategy	**89.88**	**67.87**	**63.74**	**89.81**	**53.99**	**73.06**

4.3 Ablation Studies

Ablation experiments are performed on the DroneVehicle dataset for a detailed analysis in this section. Throughout the experiments, the TSFADet has been inspected by removing each key component from its full version. And the baseline is a two-stream Oriented R-CNN, which only adopts simple additional operation to fuse two modalities. Table 1 provides the performance of the different versions with/without the Modality-Selection strategy (MS) and Multi-task Jitter (MJ).

Alignment Process. 'TSFADet w/o MJ and MS' version is trained using the alignment process only. As shown in Table 1, 'TSFADet w/o MJ and MS' version obtains 71.13% mAP, which is almost 3% higher than the baseline version. Moreover, we also exclude different deviation prediction branches to train the 'TSFADet w/o MJ and MS' version. As can be seen in Table 1, adding Size and Angle prediction branches to the Position prediction branch can improve the performance of the model respectively. Specifically, with the Position and Size prediction branches, the mAP has increased by a significant 2.1% (from 68.2% to 70.71%) compared to the baseline. As a result, the performance improvement of the alignment process was noticeable in DroneVehicle dataset. We conclude that reducing the effect of the weakly misalignment problem caused by hardware errors through the alignment process can improve the multispectral detection performance.

Modality-Selection Strategy. Based on alignment process, we further add the Modality-Selection strategy and validate its contribution. As shown in Table 1, the 'TSFADet w/o MJ' version is trained with the MS strategy to further improve the detection performance and achieves 72.36% mAP. To have a deep insight of the effectiveness of Modality-Selection strategy, we investigate the performance of different design choices in Table 2. We use different strategies to select reference modality of bounding-boxes, including directly using the RGB or IR images as the reference modality, randomly selecting bounding-boxes and our MS strategy. From Table 2 we can see that our proposed MS strategy has greater advantages. The quantitative comparisons demonstrate the importance of addressing reference bounding-boxes accuracy in the weakly misalignment

Table 3. Evaluation results on the DroneVehicle dataset. The last column refers to input modalities of the approach.

Detectors	car	truck	freight-car	bus	van	mAP	Modality
Faster R-CNN(OBB) [22]	79.69	41.99	33.99	76.94	37.68	54.06	RGB
RetinaNet(OBB) [14]	78.45	34.39	24.14	69.75	28.82	47.11	
ROI Transformer [5]	61.55	55.05	42.26	85.48	44.84	61.55	
S^{2}ANet [7]	79.86	50.02	36.21	82.77	37.52	57.28	
Oriented R-CNN [28]	80.26	55.39	42.12	86.84	46.92	62.30	
Faster-R-CNN(OBB) [22]	89.68	40.95	43.10	86.32	41.21	60.27	IR
RetinaNet(OBB) [14]	88.81	35.43	39.47	76.45	32.12	54.45	
ROI Transformer [5]	89.64	50.98	53.42	88.86	44.47	65.47	
S^{2}ANet [7]	89.71	51.03	50.27	88.97	44.03	64.80	
Oriented R-CNN [28]	89.63	53.92	53.86	89.15	40.95	65.50	
Halfway Fusion(OBB) [15]	89.85	60.34	55.51	88.97	46.28	68.19	RGB +IR
CIAN(OBB) [36]	89.98	62.47	60.22	88.9	49.59	70.23	
AR-CNN(OBB) [37]	**90.08**	64.82	62.12	89.38	51.51	71.58	
TSFADet(Ours)	89.88	67.87	63.74	**89.81**	53.99	73.06	
Cascade-TSFADet (Ours)	90.01	**69.15**	**65.45**	89.70	**55.19**	**73.90**	

problem. The experiments show that the MS strategy alleviates the weakly misalignment problem and improves the performance of multispectral detection.

Multi-task Jitter. To verify that the the Multi-task Jitter is effective, we also made a comparison with/ without it (the 'TSFADet w/o MS' version) in Table 1. It is observed that performance gains can generally be achieved by the Multi-task Jitter. By introducing the Multi-task Jitter which generates various deviations to the sensed bounding-boxes, the alignment process achieves higher accuracy in predicting the deviations between sensed and referenced bounding-boxes. This demonstrates that the detection performance can be further improved by Multi-task Jitter, since it makes the network more robust to solve weakly misalignment problem.

4.4   Comparisons

Comparison Methods. We compare our proposed TSFADet with 5 state-of-the-art single-modality detectors, including Faster R-CNN [22], RetinaNet [14], ROI Transformer [5], S^{2}ANet [7] and Oriented R-CNN [28]. Since the rotation detectors are focus on detection in single-modality images at present, we re-implement three methods (Halfway Fusion [15], CIAN [36] and AR-CNN [37]) for multispectral object detection on rotation detectors. The backbone of the detectors is also ResNet-50 [8]. Other hyperparameters including training schedule and data augmentations are also same to the TSFADet to ensure the fairness of the comparisons.

Table 4. Speed versus accuracy on the DroneVehicle dataset.

Method	FPS	mAP	Input	framework
Halfway Fusion(OBB)	20.4	68.19	RGB+IR	two-stage
CIAN(OBB)	**21.7**	70.23	RGB+IR	one-stage
AR-CNN(OBB)	18.2	71.58	RGB+IR	two-stage
TSFADet(Ours)	18.6	**73.06**	RGB+IR	two-stage

Quantitative Comparison. We evaluate our method and the other eight state-of-the-art methods by using mAP metric. The results are shown in the Table 3. The multispectral methods using both RGB and IR images are superior to the single-modality methods. In single-modality methods, Oriented R-CNN and ROI Transformer both have comparable detection accuracy (65.5% mAP and 65.47% mAP) in IR images. We further exploit the advantages of Oriented R-CNN in detection performance and propose TSFADet to perform multispectral detection tasks. From Table 3 we can see that our proposed detector achieves 73.06% mAP, better than other multispectral methods. We also combine Cascade R-CNN [2] structure with our TSFADet and achieve the highest result of 73.90% mAP.

Speed Versus Accuracy. We compare the speed and accuracy of different detectors on a single NVIDIA GV100 GPU. All detectors are tested with a batch size of 1 under the same settings. During testing, the size of input images is 512×512. Table 4 reports the comparison results. Since CIAN is a one-stage detector, its speed is faster than other detectors. In addition, our detector has higher detection accuracy (73.06% mAP) than other multispectral detectors and runs with comparable speed (18.6 FPS), only 1.8fps slower than the Halfway Fusion method.

5 Conclusions

In this work, we propose and analysis the weakly misalignment problem in multispectral aerial detection. Then we explore a TSRA module based multispectral detector named TSFADet to alleviate the weakly misalignment problems. Specifically, we present a new alignment process, which predicts the deviations of position, size and angle to solve the misalignment caused by device factors. Meanwhile, the MS strategy is designed to address the problem caused by human factors. Moreover, we adapt a Multi-task Jitter to further improve the robustness of TSRA module. Our detector can be trained with an end-to-end manner and achieves state-of-the-art accuracy on the DroneVehicle dataset. The proposed method can be generalized to other multispectral detection task and facilitate potential applications.

Acknowledgments. This work was supported by National Key R&D Program of China (Grant No.2020AAA0104002) and the Project of the National Natural Science Foundation of China (No.62076018).

References

1. Brown, L.G.: A survey of image registration techniques. ACM Comput. Surv. (CSUR) **24**(4), 325–376 (1992)
2. Cai, Z., Vasconcelos, N.: Cascade R-CNN: Delving into high quality object detection. In: Proceedings of the IEEE Conference on Computer Vision and Pattern Recognition, pp. 6154–6162 (2018)
3. Chen, K., et al.: MMDetection: open MMLab detection toolbox and benchmark. arXiv preprint arXiv:1906.07155 (2019)
4. Cui, S., Ma, A., Zhang, L., Xu, M., Zhong, Y.: MAP-Net: SAR and optical image matching via image-based convolutional network with attention mechanism and spatial pyramid aggregated pooling. IEEE Trans. Geosci. Remote Sens. **60**, 1–13 (2021)
5. Ding, J., Xue, N., Long, Y., Xia, G.S., Lu, Q.: Learning ROI transformer for oriented object detection in aerial images. In: Proceedings of the IEEE/CVF Conference on Computer Vision and Pattern Recognition, pp. 2849–2858 (2019)
6. Guan, D., Cao, Y., Yang, J., Cao, Y., Yang, M.Y.: Fusion of multispectral data through illumination-aware deep neural networks for pedestrian detection. Inf. Fusion **50**, 148–157 (2019)
7. Han, J., Ding, J., Li, J., Xia, G.S.: Align deep features for oriented object detection. IEEE Trans. Geosci. Remote Sens. **60**, 1–11 (2021)
8. He, K., Zhang, X., Ren, S., Sun, J.: Deep residual learning for image recognition. In: Proceedings of the IEEE Conference on Computer Vision and Pattern Recognition, pp. 770–778 (2016)
9. Kim, J.U., Park, S., Ro, Y.M.: Uncertainty-guided cross-modal learning for robust multispectral pedestrian detection. IEEE Trans. Circuits Syst. Video Technol. **32**, 1510–1523 (2021)
10. Lee, J., Seo, S., Kim, M.: SIPSA-Net: shift-invariant pan sharpening with moving object alignment for satellite imagery. In: Proceedings of the IEEE/CVF Conference on Computer Vision and Pattern Recognition, pp. 10166–10174 (2021)
11. Li, C., Liang, X., Lu, Y., Zhao, N., Tang, J.: RGB-T object tracking: benchmark and baseline. Pattern Recogn. **96**, 106977 (2019)
12. Li, C., Xu, C., Cui, Z., Wang, D., Zhang, T., Yang, J.: Feature-attentioned object detection in remote sensing imagery. In: 2019 IEEE International Conference on Image Processing (ICIP), pp. 3886–3890. IEEE (2019)
13. Lin, T.Y., Dollár, P., Girshick, R., He, K., Hariharan, B., Belongie, S.: Feature pyramid networks for object detection. In: Proceedings of the IEEE Conference on Computer Vision and Pattern Recognition, pp. 2117–2125 (2017)
14. Lin, T.Y., Goyal, P., Girshick, R., He, K., Dollár, P.: Focal loss for dense object detection. In: Proceedings of the IEEE International Conference on Computer Vision, pp. 2980–2988 (2017)
15. Liu, J., Zhang, S., Wang, S., Metaxas, D.N.: Multispectral deep neural networks for pedestrian detection. arXiv preprint arXiv:1611.02644 (2016)

16. Liu, L., Chen, J., Wu, H., Li, G., Li, C., Lin, L.: Cross-modal collaborative representation learning and a large-scale RGBT benchmark for crowd counting. In: Proceedings of the IEEE/CVF Conference on Computer Vision and Pattern Recognition, pp. 4823–4833 (2021)
17. Liu, Z., Wang, H., Weng, L., Yang, Y.: Ship rotated bounding box space for ship extraction from high-resolution optical satellite images with complex backgrounds. IEEE Geosci. Remote Sens. Lett. **13**(8), 1074–1078 (2016)
18. Liu, Z., Yuan, L., Weng, L., Yang, Y.: A high resolution optical satellite image dataset for ship recognition and some new baselines. In: International Conference on Pattern Recognition Applications and Methods, vol. 2, pp. 324–331. SCITEPRESS (2017)
19. Ma, J., et al.: Arbitrary-oriented scene text detection via rotation proposals. IEEE Trans. Multimed. **20**(11), 3111–3122 (2018)
20. Ma, W., Zhang, J., Wu, Y., Jiao, L., Zhu, H., Zhao, W.: A novel two-step registration method for remote sensing images based on deep and local features. IEEE Trans. Geosci. Remote Sens. **57**(7), 4834–4843 (2019)
21. Pan, X., et al.: Dynamic refinement network for oriented and densely packed object detection. In: Proceedings of the IEEE/CVF Conference on Computer Vision and Pattern Recognition, pp. 11207–11216 (2020)
22. Ren, S., He, K., Girshick, R., Sun, J.: Faster R-CNN: Towards real-time object detection with region proposal networks. Adv. Neural. Inf. Process. Syst. **28**, 91–99 (2015)
23. Richards, J.A., Richards, J.: Remote sensing digital image analysis, vol. 3. Springer (1999)
24. Sun, Y., Cao, B., Zhu, P., Hu, Q.: Drone-based RGB-infrared cross-modality vehicle detection via uncertainty-aware learning. arXiv e-prints pp. arXiv-2003 (2020)
25. Wang, J., Ding, J., Guo, H., Cheng, W., Pan, T., Yang, W.: Mask OBB: a semantic attention-based mask oriented bounding box representation for multi-category object detection in aerial images. Remote Sens. **11**(24), 2930 (2019)
26. Wei, H., Zhang, Y., Chang, Z., Li, H., Wang, H., Sun, X.: Oriented objects as pairs of middle lines. ISPRS J. Photogramm. Remote. Sens. **169**, 268–279 (2020)
27. Xia, G.S., et al.: DOTA: a large-scale dataset for object detection in aerial images. In: Proceedings of the IEEE Conference on Computer Vision and Pattern Recognition, pp. 3974–3983 (2018)
28. Xie, X., Cheng, G., Wang, J., Yao, X., Han, J.: Oriented R-CNN for object detection. In: Proceedings of the IEEE/CVF International Conference on Computer Vision, pp. 3520–3529 (2021)
29. Xu, D., Ouyang, W., Ricci, E., Wang, X., Sebe, N.: Learning cross-modal deep representations for robust pedestrian detection. In: Proceedings of the IEEE Conference on Computer Vision and Pattern Recognition, pp. 5363–5371 (2017)
30. Xu, Y., et al.: Gliding vertex on the horizontal bounding box for multi-oriented object detection. IEEE Trans. Pattern Anal. Mach. Intell. **43**(4), 1452–1459 (2020)
31. Yang, X., Liu, Q., Yan, J., Li, A., Zhang, Z., Yu, G.: R3Det: refined single-stage detector with feature refinement for rotating object. arXiv preprint arXiv:1908.05612 2(4) (2019)
32. Yang, X., Yan, J., Ming, Q., Wang, W., Zhang, X., Tian, Q.: Rethinking rotated object detection with Gaussian wasserstein distance loss. In: ICML, pp. 11830–11841. PMLR (2021)
33. Yang, X., et al.: Learning high-precision bounding box for rotated object detection via Kullback-Leibler divergence. Neurips **34**, 18381–18394 (2021)

34. Yi, J., Wu, P., Liu, B., Huang, Q., Qu, H., Metaxas, D.: Oriented object detection in aerial images with box boundary-aware vectors. In: Proceedings of the IEEE/CVF Winter Conference on Applications of Computer Vision, pp. 2150–2159 (2021)

35. Zhang, H., et al.: Explore better network framework for high resolution optical and SAR image matching. IEEE Trans. Geosci. Remote Sens. **60**, 1–18 (2021)

36. Zhang, L., et al.: Cross-modality interactive attention network for multispectral pedestrian detection. Inf. Fusion **50**, 20–29 (2019)

37. Zhang, L., Zhu, X., Chen, X., Yang, X., Lei, Z., Liu, Z.: Weakly aligned cross-modal learning for multispectral pedestrian detection. In: Proceedings of the IEEE/CVF International Conference on Computer Vision, pp. 5127–5137 (2019)

38. Zhang, Q., Huang, N., Yao, L., Zhang, D., Shan, C., Han, J.: RGB-T salient object detection via fusing multi-level CNN features. IEEE Trans. Image Process. **29**, 3321–3335 (2019)

39. Zhang, Q., Zhao, S., Luo, Y., Zhang, D., Huang, N., Han, J.: ABMDRNet: adaptive-weighted bi-directional modality difference reduction network for RGB-T semantic segmentation. In: Proceedings of the IEEE/CVF Conference on Computer Vision and Pattern Recognition, pp. 2633–2642 (2021)

40. Zhou, K., Chen, L., Cao, X.: Improving multispectral pedestrian detection by addressing modality imbalance problems. In: Vedaldi, A., Bischof, H., Brox, T., Frahm, J.-M. (eds.) ECCV 2020. LNCS, vol. 12363, pp. 787–803. Springer, Cham (2020). https://doi.org/10.1007/978-3-030-58523-5_46

41. Zhou, L., Wei, H., Li, H., Zhao, W., Zhang, Y., Zhang, Y.: Arbitrary-oriented object detection in remote sensing images based on polar coordinates. IEEE Access **8**, 223373–223384 (2020)

42. Zitova, B., Flusser, J.: Image registration methods: a survey. Image Vis. Comput. **21**(11), 977–1000 (2003)

RFLA: Gaussian Receptive Field Based Label Assignment for Tiny Object Detection

Chang Xu[1], Jinwang Wang[2], Wen Yang[1(✉)], Huai Yu[1], Lei Yu[1], and Gui-Song Xia[3]

[1] School of Electronic Information, Wuhan University, Wuhan, China
{xuchangeis,yangwen,yuhuai,ly.wd}@whu.edu.cn
[2] Huawei Technologies Co., Ltd., Shenzhen, China
wangjinwang3@huawei.com
[3] School of Computer Science, Wuhan University, Wuhan, China
guisong.xia@whu.edu.cn

Abstract. Detecting tiny objects is one of the main obstacles hindering the development of object detection. The performance of generic object detectors tends to drastically deteriorate on tiny object detection tasks. In this paper, we point out that either box prior in the anchor-based detector or point prior in the anchor-free detector is sub-optimal for tiny objects. Our key observation is that the current anchor-based or anchor-free label assignment paradigms will incur many outlier tiny-sized ground truth samples, leading to detectors imposing less focus on the tiny objects. To this end, we propose a Gaussian Receptive Field based Label Assignment (RFLA) strategy for tiny object detection. Specifically, RFLA first utilizes the prior information that the feature receptive field follows Gaussian distribution. Then, instead of assigning samples with IoU or center sampling strategy, a new Receptive Field Distance (RFD) is proposed to directly measure the similarity between the Gaussian receptive field and ground truth. Considering that the IoU-threshold based and center sampling strategy are skewed to large objects, we further design a Hierarchical Label Assignment (HLA) module based on RFD to achieve balanced learning for tiny objects. Extensive experiments on four datasets demonstrate the effectiveness of the proposed methods. Especially, our approach outperforms the state-of-the-art competitors with 4.0 AP points on the AI-TOD dataset. Codes are available at https://github.com/Chasel-Tsui/mmdet-rfla.

Keywords: Tiny object detection · Gaussian receptive field · Label assignment

1 Introduction

Tiny object, featured by its extremely limited amount of pixels (less than 16×16 pixels defined in AI-TOD [49]), is always *a hard nut to crack* in the computer

---

Supplementary Information The online version contains supplementary material available at https://doi.org/10.1007/978-3-031-20077-9_31.

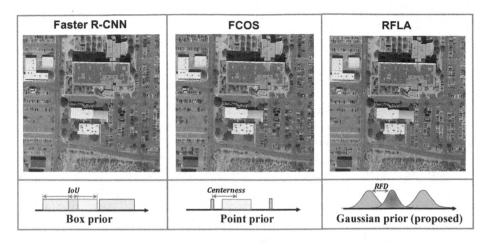

Fig. 1. Comparison between detection results of different label assignment schemes. The detection results are listed in the first row. The green, blue and red boxes denote true positive (TP), false positive (FP) and false negative (FN) predictions. The schematic diagram of different prior is in the second row, where the green region is *gt*, grey, red and yellow regions denote box, point and Gaussian prior respectively. (Color figure online)

vision community. Tiny Object Detection (TOD) is one of the most challenging tasks, and generic object detectors usually fail to provide satisfactory results on TOD tasks [49,57], resulting from tiny object's lack of discriminative features. Considering the particularity of tiny objects, several customized TOD benchmarks are proposed (*e.g.* AI-TOD [49], TinyPerson [57], and AI-TOD-v2 [51]), facilitating a series of downstream tasks including driving assistance, traffic management, and maritime rescue. Recently, TOD has gradually become a popular yet challenging direction independent of generic object detection [13,25].

Generic object detectors can be divided into two factions: the anchor-based and the anchor-free paradigms. For anchor-based detectors, prior boxes of discrete locations, scales, and aspect ratios are heuristically preset. Then, label assignment strategies (*e.g.* Max IoU Strategy [39], ATSS [58]) are constructed mainly based on IoU to find the appropriate matching relationship between anchors and ground truth (*gt*). Anchor-free detectors change the prior from boxes to points. Usually the point prior covered by *gt* is regarded as a positive sample (with the centerness in FCOS [46]), saving the effort of anchor box fine-tuning.

Despite the outstanding performance of the above two factions on generic object detection tasks, their performance on TOD tasks commonly suffers a drastic drop [49,57]. In this paper, we argue that the current prior box and point along with their corresponding measurement strategies are sub-optimal for tiny objects, which will further hinder the process of label assignment. Specifically, we take the individual prior box and point as instances and rethink them from the perspective of distribution.

$$p(v|x, y) = \frac{\varepsilon(x - x_1)\varepsilon(x_2 - x)\varepsilon(y - y_1)\varepsilon(y_2 - y)}{(x_2 - x_1)(y_2 - y_1)} \qquad (1)$$

where $p(v|x, y)$ is the probability density function of prior information, (x, y) is the location on the image, v is the weight of the corresponding location, $\varepsilon(\cdot)$ is a step function that equals to 1 when the input is larger than 0, otherwise equals to 0. $[(x_1, y_1), (x_2, y_2)]$ is the region of prior information, for anchor-based detectors $x_2 - x_1 = $ width, $y_2 - y_1 = $ height, while for anchor-free detectors $x_2 - x_1 = 1$, $y_2 - y_1 = 1$. The schematic diagram of different prior is shown in the second row of Fig. 1, existing prior information combing with its corresponding measurement strategy has the following problems for tiny objects.

First, the individual box prior and point prior both have a limited prior domain (where $p(v|x, y) > 0$), while existing label assignment metrics are highly dependent on the overlap of domain. In other words, when a particular gt has no overlap with a specific prior, their positional relationship cannot be solved by IoU or centerness. For tiny objects, it is often the case that the gt box has no overlap with almost all anchor boxes (*i.e.* IoU = 0) or does not contain any anchor points [52], leading to tiny objects' lack of positive samples [52]. To this end, heuristics are usually deployed to guarantee more positive samples for tiny objects [58,59]. However, the assigner often fails to compensate positive samples for tiny objects based on the zero-valued IoU or centerness. Therefore, the network will impose less attention on tiny object learning. Details about this point are analyzed in Sect. 4.5. Second, current prior region mainly follows a uniform distribution and treats each location inside the prior region equally ($v = constant$). However, prior information is essentially leveraged to assist the label assignment or feature point assignment process [58]. In this process, one implicit rule is assigning feature points with appropriate receptive field to gt [39,46]. As theoretically analyzed in previous work [29], when remapping the receptive field of feature point back onto the input image, the effective receptive field is actually Gaussian distributed. The gap between the uniformly distributed prior and the Gaussian distributed receptive field will lead to the mismatch between gt and the receptive field of the feature points assigned to it.

To mitigate the above problems, we introduce a novel prior based on Gaussian distribution and build a Gaussian Receptive Field based Label Assignment (RFLA) strategy that is more conducive to tiny objects. Specifically, we propose to directly measure the similarity between the Gaussian receptive field and gt region with a newly designed Receptive Field Distance (RFD). Leveraging the Gaussian receptive field as prior information can elegantly address the issues incurred by box and point prior. On the one hand, the Gaussian distribution is not step changed. The domain of each individual prior is the entire image, where the weight of each location gradually decays from the center to the periphery with a value higher than 0. It is thus feasible to model the positional relationship between any feature point and any gt on the whole image, making it possible to obtain balanced positive samples for different sized objects. On the other hand, Gaussian prior can better fit the property of Gaussian effective receptive field, thereby alleviating receptive field mismatch problem, especially for tiny objects.

Moreover, since IoU and RFD are not in the same dimension, directly applying the new metric to the existing threshold-based label assignment structure is not rational. Instead, we introduce to rank the priority of each feature point *w.r.t.* their RFD scores, based on which we further design a Hierarchical Label Assigner (HLA) which progressively alleviates outlier *gt* samples and obtain sufficient training for tiny objects.

The contributions of this paper are summarized as follows:

(1) We experimentally reveal that current anchor-based and anchor-free detectors exist scale-sample imbalance problem in tiny object label assignment.
(2) To mitigate the above problem, we introduce a simple but effective Receptive Field-based Label Assignment (RFLA) strategy. The RFLA is easy to replace the standard box and point-based label assignment strategies in mainstream detectors, boosting their performance on TOD.
(3) Extensive experiments on four datasets validate the performance superiority of our proposed method. The introduced method significantly outperforms the state-of-the-art competitors on the challenging AI-TOD dataset without additional costs in the inference stage.

2   Related Work

2.1   Object Detection

The mainstream object detection methods include anchor-based detectors and anchor-free detectors. Classic anchor-based detectors include Faster R-CNN [39], Cascade R-CNN [4], RetinaNet [24], YOLO series [3,37,38] *etc.* It is commonly believed that one fundamental defect of the anchor-based paradigm is its requirement of tuning *w.r.t* the specific task [46]. Moreover, the IoU-based label assignment strategy [39] that is built upon anchor boxes also introduces additional hyper-parameters, showing a significant impact on the detection performance.

Anchor-free detectors get rid of the constraints of anchor-boxes, and seek to directly predict objects from center points like FCOS [46] and FoveaBox [19], or seek to predict objects from key-points such as CornerNet [20], Grid R-CNN [28] and RepPoints [55]. The recently published anchor-free detectors mainly follow the end-to-end paradigm, they merely preset a set of boxes without shape or location prior information, and then directly reason about the final predictions, such as DETR [5], Deformable DETR [64], and Sparse R-CNN [44]. Despite the success of the end-to-end paradigm on generic object detection tasks, their performance on TOD tasks require further investigation.

Unlike box and point prior-based detectors, we introduce another prior information based on the receptive field. Combining the Gaussian receptive field and its customized label assignment strategy can significantly alleviate the imbalance problem raised by existing prior and measurement for tiny objects.

2.2 Tiny Object Detection

Most of the existing tiny object detection methods can be roughly grouped into the following four classes: Data augmentation, Multi-scale learning, Customized training strategy for tiny objects, and Feature enhancement strategy.

Data Augmentation. A simple yet effective way is to collect more tiny object data. Another way is to use simple data augmentations include rotating, image flipping, and up-sampling. Krisantal *et al.* [18] seek to enhance TOD performance by oversampling images that contain tiny objects and copy-pasting them.

Multi-scale Learning. The multi-resolution image pyramid is a basic way of multi-scale learning. To reduce the computation cost, some works [23,27,61] propose to construct feature-level pyramid. After that, lots of methods attempt to further improve FPN, some of them are PANet [26], BiFPN [45], Recursive-FPN [35]. Besides, TridentNet [22] constructs multi-branch detection heads with different receptive fields to generate scale-specific feature maps. Multi-scale learning strategies commonly boost TOD performance with additional computation.

Customized Training Strategy for Tiny Objects. Object detectors usually cannot get satisfactory performance on tiny objects and large objects simultaneously. Inspired by this fact, SNIP [42] and SNIPER [43] are designed to selectively train objects within a certain scale range. In addition, Kim *et al.* [17] introduces a Scale-Aware Network (SAN) and maps the features of different spaces onto a scale-invariant subspace, making detectors more robust to scale variation.

Feature Enhancement Strategy. Some works propose to enhance the feature representation of small objects by super-solution or GAN. PGAN [21] makes the first attempt to apply GAN to small object detection. Moreover, Bai *et al.* [1] propose an MT-GAN which trains an image-level super-resolution model for enhancing the small RoI features. Feature-level super-resolution [32] is proposed to improve small object detection performance for proposal based detectors. Also, there are some other super-solution based methods including [2,8,36].

Most of the methods dedicated to TOD will bring about additional annotation or computation costs. In contrast, our proposed method attempts to push forward TOD from the perspective of label assignment, and our proposed strategy will not bring any additional cost in the inference stage.

2.3 Label Assignment in Object Detection

As revealed by ATSS [58], the essential difference between the anchor-free and anchor-based detector is the way of defining training samples. The selection of positive and negative (*pos/neg*) training samples will notably affect the detector's performance. Recently, many works have been proposed for better label assignment in generic object detection tasks. FreeAnchor [60] decides positive anchors based on a detection-customized likelihood. PAA [16] proposes to use GMM to model the distribution of anchors and divide *pos/neg* samples based on the center of GMM. OTA [14] models the label assignment process as an optimal transport problem and seeks to solve the optimal assignment strategy. ATSS [58] adaptively adjusting the *pos/neg* samples *w.r.t.* their statistics characteristics. AutoAssign [62] and IQDet [30] reweight and sample high-quality regions based on the predicted IoU and confidence.

Unlike the above-mentioned general object detection strategies, this paper focuses on the design of prior information and its corresponding label assignment strategy for TOD.

3   Method

3.1   Receptive Field Modelling

One basic principle that mainstream object detectors obey is *dividing and conquering*, namely detecting objects of different scales on the different layers of FPN [7,23]. Specifically, anchor-based detectors tile prior boxes of different scales on different layers of FPN to assist label assignment, and objects of different scales are thus detected on the different layers of FPN. For anchor-free detectors, they group objects in different scale ranges (*e.g.* [0, 64] for P_3) onto different levels of FPN for detection. Despite label assignment strategy varies, one common ground of anchor-based and anchor-free detectors is to assign feature points of an appropriate receptive field to objects of different scales [39,46]. Thus, the receptive field can directly serve as a founded and convincing prior for label assignment without the designing of heuristic anchor box preset or scale grouping.

In this paper, we propose to directly measure the matching degree between the Effective Receptive Field (ERF) and the *gt* region for label assignment, getting rid of the box or point prior that deteriorates TOD. Previous work has pointed out that the ERF can be theoretically derived as Gaussian distribution [29]. In this work, we follow this paradigm and seek to model the ERF of each feature point as Gaussian distribution, and we first derive the Theoretical Receptive Field (TRF) of the *n-th* layer on a standard convolution neural network [15] by the following formula as tr_n:

$$tr_n = tr_{n-1} + (k_n - 1) \prod_{i=1}^{n-1} s_i \qquad (2)$$

where tr_n denotes the TRF of each point on the *n-th* convolution layer, k_n and s_n denotes the kernel size and stride of the convolution operation on the *n-th* layer.

As studied in [29], the ERF and TRF have the same center points but the ERF of each feature point only occupies part of the full TRF. Therefore, we use the location of each feature point (x_n, y_n) as the mean vector of a standard 2-D Gaussian distribution. As it is hard to get the precise ERF, we approximate the ERF radius er_n with half the radius of TRF. The square of er_n serves as the co-variance of 2-D Gaussian distribution for a standard square-like convolution kernel. To sum up, we model the range of ERF into a 2-D Gaussian distribution $N_e(\boldsymbol{\mu}_e, \boldsymbol{\Sigma}_e)$ with

$$\boldsymbol{\mu}_e = \begin{bmatrix} x_n \\ y_n \end{bmatrix}, \boldsymbol{\Sigma}_e = \begin{bmatrix} er_n^2 & 0 \\ 0 & er_n^2 \end{bmatrix}. \qquad (3)$$

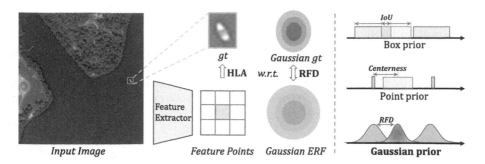

Fig. 2. The process of RFLA. In RFLA, we directly calculate the RFD between Gaussian ERF and *gt*, then assign labels with HLA.

3.2   Receptive Field Distance

Obtaining the Gaussian ERF, the following key step is to measure the matching degree between the ERF of feature points and a certain *gt*. As discussed in the introduction, the step-changed uniform distribution is not conducive to tiny objects, it is also necessary to model *gt* into another distribution.

Observing that the main body of object is aggregated in the center of bounding box [48,50], we also model the *gt* box (x_g, y_g, w_g, h_g) into a standard 2-D Gaussian distribution $N_g(\boldsymbol{\mu}_g, \boldsymbol{\Sigma}_g)$, where the center point of each annotated box serves as the mean vector of Gaussian and the square of half side length serves as the co-variance matrix, namely,

$$\boldsymbol{\mu_g} = \begin{bmatrix} x_g \\ y_g \end{bmatrix}, \boldsymbol{\Sigma_g} = \begin{bmatrix} \frac{w_g^2}{4} & 0 \\ 0 & \frac{h_g^2}{4} \end{bmatrix}. \tag{4}$$

In this paper, we investigate three types of classic distances between Gaussian distributions as Receptive Field Distance Candidates (RFDC). These distance measurement include Wasserstein distance [34,53], K-L divergence [11,54] and J-S divergence [12]. The J-S divergence between Gaussian distributions has no closed-form solution [12,31], enormous computation will be introduced when approximating its solution, thus, the J-S divergence is not used. Herein, we will first analyze their closed form solutions in our task, then discuss their pros and cons for the TOD task.

Wasserstein Distance. The Wasserstein Distance comes from Optimal Transport theory [34].

Given the Gaussian ERF $n_e = N_e(\boldsymbol{\mu}_e, \boldsymbol{\Sigma}_e)$ and Gaussian *gt* $n_g = N_g(\boldsymbol{\mu}_g, \boldsymbol{\Sigma}_g)$, the 2nd Wasserstein distance can be simplized as Eq. 5 [53].

$$W_2^2(n_e, n_g) = \left\| \left([x_n, y_n, er_n, er_n]^T, \left[x_g, y_g, \frac{w_g}{2}, \frac{h_g}{2} \right]^T \right) \right\|_2^2. \tag{5}$$

The main advantage of Wasserstein Distance is that it can measure two non-overlapping distributions [34]. It is always the case that the *gt* box has no overlap with most prior box and points, and the assigner fails to rank the priority of these candidates to a certain *gt*. Thus, it is easy to say the characteristic of Wasserstein distance is conducive to TOD, which can consistently reflect the matching degree between all feature points and a certain *gt* box, making the assigner feasible to compensate more positive samples for tiny objects according to a rational priority. However, the Wasserstein distance is not scale invariant and might be sub-optimal when the dataset contains objects of large-scale variance [54].

Kullback-Leibler Divergence. Kullback-Leibler Divergence (KLD) is a classic statistical distance which measures how one probability distribution is different from another.

KLD between two Gaussian distributions also has a closed form solution, the KLD between ERF n_e and *gt* region n_g is as follows:

$$D_{\mathrm{KL}}\left(n_e \| n_g\right) = \frac{1}{2}(\mathrm{tr}\left(\boldsymbol{\Sigma}_g^{-1}\boldsymbol{\Sigma}_e\right) + \left(\boldsymbol{\mu}_g - \boldsymbol{\mu}_e\right)^\top \boldsymbol{\Sigma}_g^{-1}\left(\boldsymbol{\mu}_g - \boldsymbol{\mu}_e\right) + \ln\frac{|\boldsymbol{\Sigma}_g|}{|\boldsymbol{\Sigma}_e|} - 2), \quad (6)$$

Eq. 6 can be further simplified as:

$$D_{\mathrm{KL}}\left(n_e \| n_g\right) = \frac{er_n^2}{8w_g^2} + \frac{er_n^2}{8h_g^2} + \frac{2(x_n - x_g)^2}{w_g^2} + \frac{2(y_n - y_g)^2}{h_g^2} + \ln\frac{2w_g}{er_n} + \ln\frac{2h_g}{er_n} - 1. \quad (7)$$

As demonstrated by the work [54], KLD has the property of scale invariance between two 2-D Gaussian distributions, and the scale invariance is crucial for the detection [56]. While the main disadvantage of KLD is that it cannot consistently reflect the distance between two distributions when their overlap is negligible. Hence, the KLD between ERF and *gt* is selected as another RFDC in this paper.

In summary, we investigate three classic ways of probability distribution measurement, while Wasserstein distance and KLD are selected as RFDC. Then, we apply a non-linear transformation into RFDC and get the RFD with a normalized value range between (0, 1) as follows:

$$\mathrm{RFD} = \frac{1}{1 + \mathrm{RFDC}} \quad (8)$$

3.3 Hierarchical Label Assignment

Some anchor-based detectors set a threshold based on IoU to decide *pos/neg* samples [4,24,39], while anchor-free detectors mainly divide *pos/neg* samples by the spatial location between point prior and *gt* region. Since tiny objects are usually unwelcome in both threshold-based and *gt* region-based strategies, we propose to hierarchically assign labels to tiny objects by score ranking.

To guarantee that the positional relationship between any feature point and any *gt* can be solved, the proposed Hierarchical Label Assignment (HLA) strategy is built on the proposed RFD. Before assigning, an RFD score matrix between feature points and *gt* is computed based on the above method. In the first stage, we rank each feature point to its RFD score with a certain *gt*. Then, positive labels are assigned to feature points with top k RFD scores with a certain *gt*. Finally, we get the assigning result r_1 and the corresponding mask m of features that have been assigned, where m is binary-valued (0/1). In the second stage, to improve the overall recall and alleviate outliers, we slight decay the effective radius er_n by multiplying a stage factor β, then repeat the above ranking strategy and supplement one positive sample to each gt, getting the assigning result r_2. We obtain the final assigning result r by the following rule:

$$r = r_1 m + r_2(1 - m), \qquad (9)$$

where the mask operation m is taken to avoid introducing too many low-quality samples for those gt which have already been assigned with sufficient samples. Not that the occluded sample will be assigned to the smaller gt. Combining the RFD with the HLA strategy, we can get the complete Receptive Field based Label Assignment (RFLA) strategy for TOD.

3.4   Application to Detectors

The proposed RFLA strategy can easily be applied to anchor-based and anchor-free frameworks. Without losing generality, we take the classic Faster R-CNN [39] and FCOS [46] as examples. Concretely, for Faster R-CNN, RFLA can be used to replace the standard anchor tiling and MaxIoU anchor assigning process. For FCOS, we remove the constraint of limiting feature points inside gt box because the tiny box only covers an extremely limited region which commonly holds much fewer feature points than the large object. Then, it is easy to replace the point based assigning with RFLA for balanced learning. Note that we modify the centerness [46] loss into the following formula to avoid gradient explosion:

$$\text{centerness}^* = \sqrt{\frac{\varepsilon[\min(l^*, r^*)]\min(l^*, r^*) + c}{\max(l^*, r^*)} \times \frac{\varepsilon[\min(t^*, b^*)]\min(t^*, b^*) + c}{\max(t^*, b^*)}},$$
$$(10)$$

where l^*, t^*, r^*, b^* are regression targets defined in FCOS, $\varepsilon(\cdot)$ is a step function same as that in Eq. 1, c is a factor set to 0.01 to avoid gradient vanishing problem when the center point of regression target is outside the gt box. In the following part, extensive experiments will show RFLA's outstanding robustness to TOD.

4   Experiment

4.1   Dataset

Experiments are conducted on four datasets. The main experiments are performed on the challenging AI-TOD [49] dataset, which has the smallest average absolute object size of 12.8 pixels and contains 28,036 images. Furthermore, we test the proposed method on TinyPerson [57], VisDrone2019 [10] and DOTA-v2.0 [9]. Note that the selected datasets all contain a great amount of tiny objects (smaller than 16×16 pixels).

4.2   Experiment Settings

All the experiments are conducted on a computer with 1 NVIDIA RTX 3090 GPU, and the model training is based on PyTorch [33], the core codes are built

Table 1. Comparison between different ways of measuring receptive-field distance. Note that in this experiment, all distances are built on HLA.

Distance	AP	$AP_{0.5}$	AP_{vt}	AP_t
GIoU	17.9	45.1	5.5	16.7
WD	**21.1**	**52.2**	6.6	**21.5**
KLD	**21.1**	51.6	**9.5**	21.2

Table 2. Influence of different designs. Note that RFD denotes only using the first stage of HLA, HLA means using all stages of HLA.

RFD	HLA	AP	$AP_{0.5}$	AP_{vt}	AP_t
		11.1	26.3	0.0	7.2
✓		20.7	50.6	7.6	20.5
✓	✓	**21.1**	**51.6**	**9.5**	**21.2**

Table 3. Influence of the stage factor β in the Hierarchical Label Assigner (HLA). The KLD is used as RFD.

β	AP	$AP_{0.5}$	AP_{vt}	AP_t
0.95	**21.1**	51.1	8.4	21.1
0.9	**21.1**	**51.6**	**9.5**	**21.2**
0.85	20.8	51.4	7.4	21.0
0.8	19.7	49.0	5.6	19.2

Table 4. Gaussian anchor and receptive anchor. GA means Gaussian Anchor and RA means Receptive Anchor.

Method	AP	$AP_{0.5}$	AP_{vt}	AP_t
GA	19.6	49.2	8.2	19.7
RA	18.9	47.5	6.1	19.1
baseline	11.1	26.3	0.0	7.2

upon MMdetection [6]. The ImageNet [41] pre-trained model is used as the backbone. All models are trained using the Stochastic Gradient Descent (SGD) optimizer for 12 epochs with 0.9 momenta, 0.0001 weight decay, and 2 batch size. The initial learning rate is set to 0.005 and decays at the 8th and 11th epochs. Besides, the number of RPN proposals is set to 3000. In the inference stage, the confidence score is set to 0.05 to filter out background bounding boxes, and the NMS IoU threshold is set to 0.5 with top 3000 bounding boxes. All the other parameters are set the same as default in MMdetection. The evaluation metric follows AI-TOD benchmark [49] except for experiments on TinyPerson. The above parameters are used in all experiments unless specified otherwise.

4.3 Ablation Study

Effectiveness of Different RFD. In this part, we respectively apply Wasserstein distance (WD) and Kullback-Leibler divergence (KLD) to measure the distance between Gaussian ERF and *gt* region as discussed in Sect. 3.2. We also test the performance of GIoU [40] by setting the prior as ERF sized box. Note that all experiments are conducted based on Faster R-CNN w/ HLA since RFD and HLA are interdependent. As shown in Table 1, it can be seen that GIoU is inferior to RFD since it fails to distinguish the locations of mutually inclusive boxes, while the performance of WD and KLD are comparable. The KLD surpasses WD in AP_{vt}, while slightly lower than WD under AP_t metric. As mentioned in Sect. 3.2, the KLD is scale-invariant, thus it is better for *very tiny* objects. Note that in the following experiments, we use KLD as the default RFD.

Effectiveness of Individual Component. The core designs in this paper are interdependent, whilst they can be separated into two parts: the Hierarchical

Table 5. Main results on AI-TOD. Note that models are trained on the `trainval set` and validated on the `test set`. Note that FCOS* means using P2-P6 of FPN.

Method	Backbone	AP	$AP_{0.5}$	$AP_{0.75}$	AP_{vt}	AP_t	AP_s	AP_m
TridentNet [22]	ResNet-50	7.5	20.9	3.6	1.0	5.8	12.6	14.0
Faster R-CNN [39]	ResNet-50	11.1	26.3	7.6	0.0	7.2	23.3	33.6
Cascade RPN [47]	ResNet-50	13.3	33.5	7.8	3.9	12.9	18.1	26.3
Cascade R-CNN [4]	ResNet-50	13.8	30.8	10.5	0.0	10.6	25.5	26.6
DetectoRS [35]	ResNet-50	14.8	32.8	11.4	0.0	10.8	28.3	28.0
DotD [52]	ResNet-50	16.1	39.2	10.6	8.3	17.6	18.1	22.1
DetectoRS w/ NWD [48]	ResNet-50	20.8	49.3	14.3	6.4	19.7	29.6	38.3
SSD-512 [27]	ResNet-50	7.0	21.7	2.8	1.0	4.7	11.5	13.5
RetinaNet [24]	ResNet-50	8.7	22.3	4.8	2.4	8.9	12.2	16.0
PAA [16]	ResNet-50	10.0	26.5	6.7	3.5	10.5	13.1	22.1
ATSS [58]	ResNet-50	12.8	30.6	8.5	1.9	11.6	19.5	29.2
RepPoints [55]	ResNet-50	9.2	23.6	5.3	2.5	9.2	12.9	14.4
OTA [14]	ResNet-50	10.4	24.3	7.2	2.5	11.9	15.7	20.9
AutoAssign [62]	ResNet-50	12.2	32.0	6.8	3.4	13.7	16.0	19.1
FCOS [46]	ResNet-50	12.6	30.4	8.1	2.3	12.2	17.2	25.0
M-CenterNet [49]	DLA-34	14.5	40.7	6.4	6.1	15.0	19.4	20.4
FCOS*	ResNet-50	15.4	36.3	10.9	6.0	17.6	18.5	20.7
RetinaNet w/ RFLA	ResNet-50	9.1	23.1	5.2	4.1	10.5	10.5	12.3
AutoAssign w/ RFLA	ResNet-50	14.2	37.8	6.9	6.4	14.9	17.4	21.8
FCOS* w/ RFLA	ResNet-50	16.3	39.1	11.3	7.3	18.5	19.8	21.8
Faster R-CNN w/ RFLA	ResNet-50	21.1	51.6	13.1	**9.5**	21.2	26.1	31.5
Cascade R-CNN w/ RFLA	ResNet-50	22.1	51.6	15.6	8.2	22.0	27.3	35.2
DetectoRS w/ RFLA	ResNet-50	**24.8**	**55.2**	**18.5**	9.3	**24.8**	**30.3**	**38.2**

Label Assignment (HLA) strategy and the Receptive Field Distance (RFD) built upon the HLA. Note that the validation of RFD requires using the first stage of HLA, we do not assign labels based on the threshold of RFD since the original threshold in the baseline detector is designed for IoU, which is not in the same dimension as RFD. We progressively apply RFD and HLA into the Faster R-CNN. Results are listed in Table 2, AP improves progressively, the individual effectiveness is thus verified. When switching the IoU-based assignment strategy to the RFD-based one, a notable improvement of 9.6 AP points is obtained. This can be explained that the limited domain of box prior leads to the remarkably low IoU between anchors and gt, many gt fail to match with any anchor. With Gaussian prior and RFD, the assigner is capable of measuring the priority (RFD score) of all feature points to a particular gt. Thus, even though the gt has no overlap with any box prior, some positive samples can be compensated for the gt with a rational receptive field, leading to the sufficient training of tiny objects.

Performance of Different Decay Factor β. As in Sect. 3.3, in the HLA, we design a stage factor β to the ERF for mitigating the outlier effect. In Table 3,

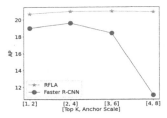 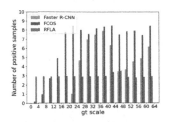

Fig. 3. Comparison between top k in Faster R-CNN w/ HLA and anchor fine-tuning in Faster R-CNN baseline.

Fig. 4. Scale-sample imbalance problems of different detectors. Base anchor scale is set to 8 for Faster R-CNN.

we keep all other parameters fixed and experimentally show that 0.9 is the best choice. Setting β to a lower value will introduce too many low-quality samples.

Performance of Different k. In the HLA, the hyper-parameter k is designed to adjust the number of positive samples assigned to each instance. Herein, we keep all other parameters fixed and set k from 1 to 4. Their performance is 20.7, 21.1, 21.1, and 20.9 AP, respectively. When setting k to 2 or 3, the best performance can be attained. Thus 3 is recommended as the default setting. Moreover, the AP only waves by a small margin under the tested k. Moreover, we compare the AP under different k with the result of anchor size tuning, as shown in Fig. 3. It is easy to find that the performance of box prior based detector is quite sensitive to the box size on TOD tasks, while in our design, the performance is quite robust to the chosen of k, which consistently keeps a high level over box prior.

Gaussian Anchor and Receptive Anchor. We directly model the anchors into Gaussian distributions, calculate the RFD score between gt, and then assign labels with HLA. Results are shown in Table 4. The results show a great advantage of Gaussian prior and its combination with HLA. The Gaussian prior has a broader domain, making sample compensation possible. In addition, we change the anchor scale to the ERF scale, then assign labels with the MaxIoU strategy. The improvement over baseline further indicates the sensitivity of the box prior to detection performance for TOD. It also reveals that the current anchor will potentially introduce the receptive field mismatch problem for tiny objects.

4.4 Main Result

We compare our method with other state-of-the-art detectors on AI-TOD benchmark [49]. As shown in Table 5, DetectoRS w/ RFLA achieves 24.8 AP, which has 4.0 AP above the state-of-the-art competitors. Notably, the improvement of RFLA with multi-stage anchor-based detectors is particularly significant. We think it mainly owes to the multi-stage detectors' mechanism of *looking and thinking twice*. In the first stage, the combination of the proposed RFLA with RPN can improve the recall of tiny objects to a great extent. In the second stage, proposals are refined for precise location and classification. Besides, improvements can also be expected on one-stage anchor-based or anchor-free detectors,

Table 6. Results on TinyPerson.

Method	AP_{50}^{tiny}	AP_{50}^{tiny1}	AP_{50}^{tiny2}	AP_{50}^{tiny3}	AP_{50}^{small}	AP_{25}^{tiny}	AP_{75}^{tiny}
FCOS	23.4	9.8	22.7	34.7	39.2	43.8	1.7
Faster R-CNN	48.7	32.3	54.5	58.8	64.7	68.9	**6.0**
FCOS w/ RFLA	$26.5^{+3.1}$	$10.0^{+0.2}$	$24.4^{+1.7}$	$40.6^{+5.9}$	$50.5^{+11.3}$	$50.0^{+6.2}$	$2.9^{+1.2}$
Faster R-CNN w/ RFLA	$\mathbf{50.1^{+1.4}}$	$\mathbf{32.8^{+0.5}}$	$\mathbf{55.6^{+1.1}}$	$\mathbf{60.6^{+1.8}}$	$\mathbf{65.3^{+0.6}}$	$\mathbf{69.9^{+1.0}}$	$5.9^{-0.1}$

Table 7. Results on VisDrone2019. The train, val sets are used for training and validation. FR, DR denote Faster R-CNN, DetectoRS, * means *with RFLA*.

Method	AP	$AP_{0.5}$	AP_{vt}	AP_t
FCOS	14.1	25.5	0.1	2.1
FR	22.3	38.0	0.1	6.2
DR	25.7	41.7	0.5	7.6
FCOS*	$15.1^{+1.0}$	$27.3^{+1.8}$	$0.4^{+0.3}$	$3.8^{+1.7}$
FR*	$23.4^{+1.1}$	$41.4^{+3.4}$	$\mathbf{4.8^{+4.7}}$	$11.7^{+5.5}$
DR*	$\mathbf{27.4^{+1.7}}$	$\mathbf{45.3^{+3.6}}$	$4.5^{+4.0}$	$\mathbf{12.9^{+5.3}}$

Table 8. Results on DOTA-v2.0. The train, val sets are used for training and validation. FR, DR denote Faster R-CNN, DetectoRS, * means *with RFLA*.

Method	AP	$AP_{0.5}$	AP_{vt}	AP_t
FCOS	31.8	55.4	0.3	4.0
FR	35.6	59.5	0.0	7.1
DR	40.8	62.6	0.0	7.0
FCOS*	$32.1^{+0.3}$	$55.6^{+0.2}$	$0.7^{+0.4}$	$6.8^{+2.8}$
FR*	$36.3^{+0.7}$	$61.5^{+2.0}$	$1.9^{+1.9}$	$\mathbf{11.7^{+4.6}}$
DR*	$\mathbf{41.3^{+0.5}}$	$\mathbf{64.2^{+1.6}}$	$\mathbf{2.1^{+2.1}}$	$10.8^{+3.8}$

and the improvement in AP_{vt} is more obvious, 1.7 points for RetinaNet and 1.3 points for FCOS*. The gap between one-stage and multi-stage detectors is common for TOD [10,57,63]. It mainly results from the lack of multi-stage regression, which is crucial for TOD.

4.5   Analysis

We conduct a group of analysis experiments to delve into different prior designs and assigners for tiny objects. In the first step, we respectively deploy the way of prior tiling in Faster R-CNN [39], FCOS [46] and RFLA. In the second step, we randomly generate different *gt* in different locations of the image and simulate the process of label assignment for statistics. Concretely, the *gt* scales are randomly picked from 0 to 64. After that, we divide the scale range into 16 intervals, as shown in Fig. 4, and calculate the average number of positive samples assigned to each *gt* in different scale ranges. Observations in Fig. 4 indicate severe scale-sample imbalance problems for existing detectors. For anchor-based detectors, objects in the tiny scale and the interval between box scales become outliers. Anchor-free detectors somewhat alleviate this problem. However, tiny objects are still outliers since tiny object covers an extremely limited region. The number of prior points inside *gt* is much smaller than that of large objects. The scale-sample imbalance problem will mislead the network towards unbalanced optimization, where less focus is imposed on outlier samples. In contrast, the number of positive samples assigned to *gt* in different scale ranges is greatly reconciled with RFLA, achieving a balanced optimization for tiny objects.

4.6 Experiment on More Datasets

We conduct experiments on another TOD dataset TinyPerson [57]. The dataset setting and evaluation all follow TinyPerson benchmark [57]. The results are in Table 6, 3.1 and 1.4 AP_{50}^{tiny} improvement can be obtained when applying RFLA into FCOS and Faster R-CNN. We also tested the RFLA on AI-TOD-v2 [51], whose performance is listed in GitHub. We further verify the effectiveness of RFLA on datasets which simultaneously hold a large scale variance and contain many tiny objects (*i.e.* VisDrone2019, DOTA-v2.0). The results are in Tables 7 and 8. The improvement of AP_{vt} and AP_t is quite obvious for both datasets. The consistent improvement on various datasets indicates RFLA's generality. Finally, visualization results on the AI-TOD dataset are shown in Fig. 5. When applying RFLA into Faster R-CNN, FN predictions can be greatly eliminated.

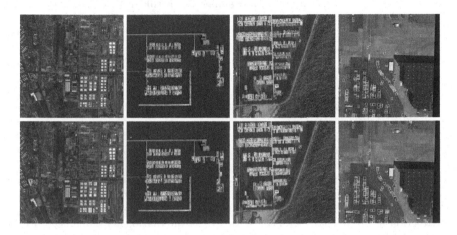

Fig. 5. Visualization results on AI-TOD. The first row is the result of Faster R-CNN and the second row is the result of Faster R-CNN w/ RFLA.

5 Conclusion

In this paper, we point out that box and point prior do not work well for TOD, leading to scale-sample imbalance problems when assigning labels. To this end, we introduce a new Gaussian receptive field prior. Then, we further design a new Receptive Field Distance (RFD), which measures the similarity between ERF and *gt* to conquer the shortages of IoU and centerness on TOD. The RFD works with the HLA strategy, obtaining balanced learning for tiny objects. Experiments on four datasets show the superiority and robustness of the RFLA.

Acknowledgement. This work was partly supported by the Fundamental Research Funds for the Central Universities under Grant 2042022kf1010, and the National Natural Science Foundation of China under Grant 61771351 and 61871297. The numerical calculations were conducted on the supercomputing system in the Supercomputing Center, Wuhan University.

References

1. Bai, Y., Zhang, Y., Ding, M., Ghanem, B.: SOD-MTGAN: small object detection via multi-task generative adversarial network. In: Ferrari, V., Hebert, M., Sminchisescu, C., Weiss, Y. (eds.) ECCV 2018. LNCS, vol. 11217, pp. 210–226. Springer, Cham (2018). https://doi.org/10.1007/978-3-030-01261-8_13

2. Bashir, S.M.A., Wang, Y.: Small object detection in remote sensing images with residual feature aggregation-based super-resolution and object detector network. Remote Sens. 13(9), 1854 (2021)

3. Bochkovskiy, A., Wang, C.Y., Liao, H.Y.M.: YOLOv4: optimal speed and accuracy of object detection. CoRR arXiv:2004.10934 (2020)

4. Cai, Z., Vas., N.: Cascade R-CNN: delving into high quality object detection. In: IEEE Conference on Computer Vision and Pattern Recognition, pp. 6154–6162 (2018)

5. Carion, N., Massa, F., Synnaeve, G., Usunier, N., Kirillov, A., Zagoruyko, S.: End-to-end object detection with transformers. In: Vedaldi, A., Bischof, H., Brox, T., Frahm, J.-M. (eds.) ECCV 2020. LNCS, vol. 12346, pp. 213–229. Springer, Cham (2020). https://doi.org/10.1007/978-3-030-58452-8_13

6. Chen, K., Wang, J., Pang, J., et al.: MMDetection: Open MMLab detection toolbox and benchmark. CoRR arXiv:1906.07155 (2019)

7. Chen, Q., Wang, Y., Yang, T., Zhang, X., Cheng, J., Sun, J.: You only look one-level feature. In: IEEE Conference on Computer Vision and Pattern Recognition, pp. 13039–13048 (2021)

8. Courtrai, L., Pham, M.T., Lefèvre, S.: Small object detection in remote sensing images based on super-resolution with auxiliary generative adversarial networks. Remote Sens. 12(19), 3152 (2020)

9. Ding, J., et al.: Object detection in aerial images: a large-scale benchmark and challenges. IEEE Trans. Pattern Anal. Mach. Intell. 44, 7778–7796 (2021)

10. Du, D., Zhu, P., Wen, L., et al.: VisDrone-DET2019: the vision meets drone object detection in image challenge results. In: IEEE International Conference on Computer Vision Workshops, pp. 213–226 (2019)

11. Duchi, J.: Derivations for linear algebra and optimization 3(1), 2325–5870. Berkeley, California (2007)

12. Endres, D.M., Schindelin, J.E.: A new metric for probability distributions. IEEE Trans. Inf. Theor. 49(7), 1858–1860 (2003)

13. Everingham, M., Eslami, S.A., Van Gool, L., Williams, C.K., Winn, J., Zisserman, A.: The pascal visual object classes challenge: a retrospective. Int. J. Comput. Vis. 111(1), 98–136 (2015)

14. Ge, Z., Liu, S., Li, Z., Yoshie, O., Sun, J.: OTA: optimal transport assignment for object detection. In: IEEE Conference on Computer Vision and Pattern Recognition (2021)

15. He, K., Zhang, X., Ren, S., Sun, J.: Deep residual learning for image recognition. In: IEEE Conference on Computer Vision and Pattern Recognition, pp. 770–778 (2016)

16. Kim, K., Lee, H.S.: Probabilistic anchor assignment with IoU prediction for object detection. In: Vedaldi, A., Bischof, H., Brox, T., Frahm, J.-M. (eds.) ECCV 2020. LNCS, vol. 12370, pp. 355–371. Springer, Cham (2020). https://doi.org/10.1007/978-3-030-58595-2_22

17. Kim, Y., Kang, B.-N., Kim, D.: SAN: learning relationship between convolutional features for multi-scale object detection. In: Ferrari, V., Hebert, M., Sminchisescu, C., Weiss, Y. (eds.) ECCV 2018. LNCS, vol. 11209, pp. 328–343. Springer, Cham (2018). https://doi.org/10.1007/978-3-030-01228-1_20

18. Kisantal, M., Wojna, Z., Murawski, J., Naruniec, J., Cho, K.: Augmentation for small object detection. arXiv preprint arXiv:1902.07296 (2019)

19. Kong, T., Sun, F., Liu, H., Jiang, Y., Li, L., Shi, J.: Foveabox: beyound anchor-based object detection. IEEE Trans. Image Process. **29**, 7389–7398 (2020)

20. Law, H., Deng, J.: CornerNet: detecting objects as paired keypoints. In: Ferrari, V., Hebert, M., Sminchisescu, C., Weiss, Y. (eds.) Computer Vision – ECCV 2018. LNCS, vol. 11218, pp. 765–781. Springer, Cham (2018). https://doi.org/10.1007/978-3-030-01264-9_45

21. Li, J., Liang, X., Wei, Y., Xu, T., Feng, J., Yan, S.: Perceptual generative adversarial networks for small object detection. In: IEEE Conference on Computer Vision and Pattern Recognition, pp. 1222–1230 (2017)

22. Li, Y., Chen, Y., Wang, N., Zhang, Z.: Scale-aware trident networks for object detection. In: IEEE International Conference on Computer Vision, pp. 6054–6063 (2019)

23. Lin, T.Y., Dollar, P., Girshick, R., He, K., Hariharan, B., Belongie, S.: Feature pyramid networks for object detection. In: IEEE Conference on Computer Vision and Pattern Recognition, pp. 2117–2125 (2017)

24. Lin, T.Y., Goyal, P., Girshick, R., He, K., Dollar, P.: Focal loss for dense object detection. In: IEEE International Conference on Computer Vision, pp. 2980–2988 (2017)

25. Lin, T.Y., et al.: Microsoft COCO: common objects in context. In: Fleet, D., Pajdla, T., Schiele, B., Tuytelaars, T. (eds.) ECCV 2014. LNCS, vol. 8693, pp. 740–755. Springer, Cham (2014). https://doi.org/10.1007/978-3-319-10602-1_48

26. Liu, S., Qi, L., Qin, H., Shi, J., Jia, J.: Path aggregation network for instance segmentation. In: IEEE Conference on Computer Vision and Pattern Recognition, pp. 8759–8768 (2018)

27. Liu, W., et al.: SSD: single shot multibox detector. In: Leibe, B., Matas, J., Sebe, N., Welling, M. (eds.) ECCV 2016. LNCS, vol. 9905, pp. 21–37. Springer, Cham (2016). https://doi.org/10.1007/978-3-319-46448-0_2

28. Lu, X., Li, B., Yue, Y., Li, Q., Yan, J.: Grid R-CNN. In: IEEE Conference on Computer Vision and Pattern Recognition, pp. 7363–7372 (2019)

29. Luo, W., Li, Y., Urtasun, R., Zemel, R.: Understanding the effective receptive field in deep convolutional neural networks. In: Advances in Neural Information Processing Systems 29 (2016)

30. Ma, Y., Liu, S., Li, Z., Sun, J.: IQDet: instance-wise quality distribution sampling for object detection. In: Proceedings of the IEEE/CVF Conference on Computer Vision and Pattern Recognition, pp. 1717–1725 (2021)

31. Nielsen, F.: On the jensen-shannon symmetrization of distances relying on abstract means. Entropy **21**(5), 485 (2019). https://doi.org/10.3390/e21050485

32. Noh, J., Bae, W., Lee, W., Seo, J., Kim, G.: Better to follow, follow to be better: towards precise supervision of feature super-resolution for small object detection. In: IEEE International Conference on Computer Vision, pp. 9725–9734 (2019)

33. Paszke, A., Gross, S., Massa, F., Lerer, A., et al.: PyTorch: an imperative style, high-performance deep learning library. In: Advances in Neural Information Processing Systems, pp. 8024–8035 (2019)

34. Peyré, G., Cuturi, M., et al.: Computational optimal transport: with applications to data science. Found. Trends Mach. Learn. **11**(5–6), 355–607 (2019)

35. Qiao, S., Chen, L.C., Yuille, A.: DetectoRS: detecting objects with recursive feature pyramid and switchable atrous convolution. In: IEEE Conference on Computer Vision and Pattern Recognition (2021)
36. Rabbi, J., Ray, N., Schubert, M., Chowdhury, S., Chao, D.: Small-object detection in remote sensing images with end-to-end edge-enhanced GAN and object detector network. Remote Sens. **12**(9), 1432 (2020)
37. Redmon, J., Farhadi, A.: YOLO9000: Better, faster, stronger. In: IEEE Conference on Computer Vision and Pattern Recognition, pp. 7263–7271 (2017)
38. Redmon, J., Farhadi, A.: YOLOv3: an incremental improvement. arXiv preprint arXiv:1804.02767 (2018)
39. Ren, S., He, K., Girshick, R., Sun, J.: Faster R-CNN: towards real-time object detection with region proposal networks. In: Advances in Neural Information Processing Systems, pp. 91–99 (2015)
40. Rezatofighi, H., Tsoi, N., Gwak, J., Sadeghian, A., Reid, I., Savarese, S.: Generalized intersection over union: a metric and a loss for bounding box regression. In: IEEE Conference on Computer Vision and Pattern Recognition, pp. 658–666 (2019)
41. Bernstein, M., et al.: ImageNet large scale visual recognition challenge. Int. J. Comput. Vis. **115**(3), 211–252 (2015)
42. Singh, B., Davis, L.S.: An analysis of scale invariance in object detection snip. In: IEEE Conference on Computer Vision and Pattern Recognition, pp. 3578–3587 (2018)
43. Singh, B., Najibi, M., Davis, L.S.: Sniper: efficient multi-scale training. In: Advances in Neural Information Processing Systems, pp. 9310–9320 (2018)
44. Sun, P., et al.: Sparse R-CNN: end-to-end object detection with learnable proposals. In: IEEE Conference on Computer Vision and Pattern Recognition, pp. 14454–14463 (2021)
45. Tan, M., Pang, R., Le, Q.V.: EfficientDet: scalable and efficient object detection. In: IEEE Conference on Computer Vision and Pattern Recognition, pp. 10781–10790 (2020)
46. Tian, Z., Shen, C., Chen, H., He, T.: FCOS: fully convolutional one-stage object detection. In: IEEE International Conference on Computer Vision, pp. 9627–9636 (2019)
47. Vu, T., Jang, H., Pham, T.X., Yoo, C.: Cascade RPN: delving into high-quality region proposal network with adaptive convolution **32**, 1432–1442 (2019)
48. Wang, J., Xu, C., Yang, W., Yu, L.: A normalized Gaussian wasserstein distance for tiny object detection. arXiv preprint arXiv:2110.13389 (2021)
49. Wang, J., Yang, W., Guo, H., Zhang, R., Xia, G.S.: Tiny object detection in aerial images. In: International Conference on Pattern Recognition, pp. 3791–3798 (2021)
50. Wang, J., Yang, W., Li, H.C., Zhang, H., Xia, G.S.: Learning center probability map for detecting objects in aerial images. IEEE Trans. Geosci. Remote Sens. **59**(5), 4307–4323 (2021)
51. Xu, C., Wang, J., Yang, W., Yu, H., Yu, L., Xia, G.S.: Detecting tiny objects in aerial images: a normalized wasserstein distance and a new benchmark. ISPRS J. Photogramm. Remote. Sens. **190**, 79–93 (2022)
52. Xu, C., Wang, J., Yang, W., Yu, L.: Dot distance for tiny object detection in aerial images. In: IEEE Conference on Computer Vision and Pattern Recognition Workshops, pp. 1192–1201 (2021)
53. Yang, X., Yan, J., Ming, Q., Wang, W., Zhang, X., Tian, Q.: Rethinking rotated object detection with Gaussian wasserstein distance loss. In: International Conference on Machine Learning, vol. 139, pp. 11830–11841 (2021)

54. Yang, X., Yang, X., Yang, J., Ming, Q., Wang, W., Tian, Q., Yan, J.: Learning high-precision bounding box for rotated object detection via Kullback-Leibler divergence. In: Advances in Neural Information Processing Systems 34 (2021)
55. Yang, Z., Liu, S., Hu, H., Wang, L., Lin, S.: RepPoints: point set representation for object detection. In: IEEE International Conference on Computer Vision, pp. 9657–9666 (2019)
56. Yu, J., Jiang, Y., Wang, Z., Cao, Z., Huang, T.: UnitBox: an advanced object detection network, pp. 516–520 (2016)
57. Yu, X., Gong, Y., Jiang, N., Ye, Q., Han, Z.: Scale match for tiny person detection. In: IEEE Workshops on Applications of Computer Vision, pp. 1257–1265 (2020)
58. Zhang, S., Chi, C., Yao, Y., Lei, Z., Li, S.Z.: Bridging the gap between anchor-based and anchor-free detection via adaptive training sample selection. In: IEEE Conference on Computer Vision and Pattern Recognition, pp. 9759–9768 (2020)
59. Zhang, S., Zhu, X., Lei, Z., Shi, H., Wang, X., Li, S.Z.: S3FD: single shot scale-invariant face detector. In: IEEE Conference on Computer Vision and Pattern Recognition, pp. 192–201 (2017)
60. Zhang, X., Wan, F., Liu, C., Ji, X., Ye, Q.: Learning to match anchors for visual object detection. IEEE Trans. Pattern Anal. Mach. Intell. **44**, 3096–3109 (2021)
61. Zhao, Q., et al.: M2Det: a single-shot object detector based on multi-level feature pyramid network. In: AAAI Conference on Artificial Intelligence, pp. 9259–9266 (2019)
62. Zhu, B., et al.: AutoAssign: differentiable label assignment for dense object detection. arXiv preprint arXiv:2007.03496 (2020)
63. Zhu, P., et al.: VisDrone-DET2018: the vision meets drone object detection in image challenge results. In: Leal-Taixé, L., Roth, S. (eds.) ECCV 2018. LNCS, vol. 11133, pp. 437–468. Springer, Cham (2019). https://doi.org/10.1007/978-3-030-11021-5_27
64. Zhu, X., Su, W., Lu, L., Li, B., Wang, X., Dai, J.: Deformable DETR: deformable transformers for end-to-end object detection. In: International Conference on Learning Representations (2021)

Rethinking IoU-based Optimization
for Single-stage 3D Object Detection

Hualian Sheng[1,2,3], Sijia Cai[2], Na Zhao[3(✉)], Bing Deng[2], Jianqiang Huang[2],
Xian-Sheng Hua[2], Min-Jian Zhao[1], and Gim Hee Lee[3]

[1] College of Information Science and Electronic Engineering, Zhejiang University,
Hangzhou, China
{hlsheng,mjzhao}@zju.edu.cn
[2] Alibaba Cloud Computing Ltd., Hangzhou, China
{stephen.csj,dengbing.db,jianqiang.hjq,xiansheng.hxs}@alibaba-inc.com
[3] Department of Computer Science, National University of Singapore, Singapore,
Singapore
{nazhao,gimhee.lee}@comp.nus.edu.sg

Abstract. Since Intersection-over-Union (IoU) based optimization
maintains the consistency of the final IoU prediction metric and losses,
it has been widely used in both regression and classification branches
of single-stage 2D object detectors. Recently, several 3D object detection methods adopt IoU-based optimization and directly replace the
2D IoU with 3D IoU. However, such a direct computation in 3D is
very costly due to the complex implementation and inefficient backward operations. Moreover, 3D IoU-based optimization is sub-optimal
as it is sensitive to rotation and thus can cause training instability
and detection performance deterioration. In this paper, we propose a
novel Rotation-Decoupled IoU (RDIoU) method that can mitigate the
rotation-sensitivity issue, and produce more efficient optimization objectives compared with 3D IoU during the training stage. Specifically, our
RDIoU simplifies the complex interactions of regression parameters by
decoupling the rotation variable as an independent term, yet preserving
the geometry of 3D IoU. By incorporating RDIoU into both the regression and classification branches, the network is encouraged to learn more
precise bounding boxes and concurrently overcome the misalignment
issue between classification and regression. Extensive experiments on the
benchmark KITTI and Waymo Open Dataset validate that our RDIoU
method can bring substantial improvement for the single-stage 3D object
detection. The code is available at https://github.com/hlsheng1/RDIoU.

Keywords: 3D object detection · Single-stage · Rotation-Decoupled
IoU

Supplementary Information The online version contains supplementary material
available at https://doi.org/10.1007/978-3-031-20077-9_32.

1   Introduction

Point cloud-based 3D object detection is an important task in robotics and autonomous driving. In contrast to the image-based object detection task, 3D object detection needs to predict 3D bounding boxes with higher degrees-of-freedom and allocate confidence map in a larger search space. This causes difficulties in predicting accurate 3D bounding boxes with reliable confidence.

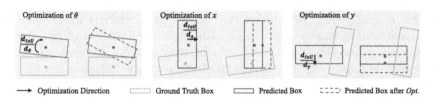

Fig. 1. Illustration of direct 3D IoU optimization between the ground truth box (red) and predicted box (green) in Bird's Eye View (BEV), compared to the post-optimized bounding box (dotted green). We see that optimizing the 3D IoU over the bounding box parameters does not bring the predicted boxes closer to the ground truths. (Color figure online)

State-of-the-art 3D detection approaches can be generally divided into single-stage and two-stage methods. Two-stage methods [1,17,22,23,36] usually perform a second feature extraction or multi-scale feature aggregation based on the proposals generated by the region proposal network (RPN). As a result, the second-stage network can focus on the partial positive areas to avoid the sparsity of the whole point cloud. Furthermore, the second-stage network can utilize Intersection-over-Union (IoU) guided supervision to generate more reliable confidence predictions. In contrast to the coarse-to-fine pipeline in the two-stage methods, single-stage methods [9,10,31,36–38] adopt an end-to-end pipeline that designs one dense object detector to directly predict pixel-level object categories and bounding boxes. The end-to-end one-stage pipeline is much more elegant and effective than the two-stage pipeline. Nevertheless, the performance of single-stage methods is usually inferior to the two-stage methods. The performance gap is mainly caused by inaccurate regression precision and confidence assignment of the single-stage methods since they independently predict the 3D bounding box center, size and rotation with the Smooth-$\ell 1$ loss [6], which results in inconsistency between the loss and the final IoU-based evaluation metric.

To maintain the consistency between the loss and IoU-based evaluation metric, IoU-based optimization [11,12,20,40] has been widely studied and shown impressive performance improvements in image-based single-stage object detection. Inspired by this, several single-stage 3D object detection approaches [38,41] adopt the IoU-based optimization by replacing the 2D IoU with the 3D IoU. Despite their impressive performance gain in the axis-aligned cases, the computation of intersection area between two rotated 3D bounding boxes is much more complex than their 2D counterparts without rotation. A number of efforts [2,32,33,39] have been made to simplify the computation of rotated IoU intersection by approximations. For example, PIoU [2] only counts the pixels in the intersection area. However, none of these methods can be directly utilized to solve the **negative coupling effect of rotation on the 3D IoU**. As illustrated in Fig. 1, optimizing the 3D IoU over the bounding box parameters can lead to further misalignment between the predicted and ground truth bounding boxes. This problem is caused by the coupling between the rotation and the center and size parameters of the 3D bounding box. In contrast, the issue of negative coupling effect of rotation does not exist in the 2D IoU counterpart under common settings as the optimization over the center and size parameters directly minimizes the 2D IoU without rotation. To this end, we propose a new high-performance and efficient 3D bounding box optimization objective that satisfies the following three conditions: it must 1) be differentiable; 2) satisfy the consistency between the evaluation metric and optimization objective; 3) circumvent the negative coupling effect of rotation on the 3D IoU.

In this paper, we propose a Rotation-Decoupled IoU (RDIoU) method to model the interaction of two arbitrary-oriented 3D bounding boxes while stabilize the training process. Our main idea is to disentangle dependencies of the bounding box parameters by decoupling and handling the rotation individually at a loss level. Specifically, we utilize a 4-dimensional representation of the box to calculate the IoU-like criterion and remove complex rotation-edge variations. A fixed hyperparameter is introduced to further control the weights of rotation change in the computation of our RDIoU. Our proposed RDIoU formulation addresses the non-differentiable and instability issues caused by the rotation change while preserving the geometry of 3D IoU. By incorporating RDIoU into the regression and classification branches, we propose a RDIoU-guided DIoU loss [40] and a RDIoU-guided quality focal loss [11,12]. These two enhanced losses guide the optimization towards high-performance box localization and alleviate the misalignment between classification and regression, and thus significantly improve the single-stage 3D detection performance over other existing losses.

Based on our proposed RDIoU, we build a simple and elegant single-stage 3D detector. In the training phase, our RDIoU-based optimization guides the 3D CNN backbone to achieve better feature alignment and get more accurate box parameters without encountering the rotation-sensitive issues. Furthermore, our RDIoU-based single-stage 3D detector also enables us to effectively train the entire network in an end-to-end manner without the need of hyperparameter-sensitive, stage-wise training or time-consuming backward operations. Our main contributions in this paper are: 1) We propose the RDIoU-based optimization for 3D object detectors, which brings a more robust training process as compared to the 3D IoU-based optimization strategy. 2) We incorporate RDIoU into regression supervision and present the RDIoU-guided DIoU loss, which exhibits significantly better performance as compared to the 3D IoU-guided DIoU loss [38]. 3) We incorporate RDIoU into classification supervision and present the RDIoU-guided quality focal loss, which is able to help generate more reasonable confidence maps. 4) We conduct extensive experiments on two benchmark datasets (*i.e.,* KITTI and Waymo), and the promising results validate that our RDIoU can attain top performance with the commonly used backbone networks.

2   Related Work

Single-Stage Detectors. Single-stage detectors predict the location and category from predefined anchor boxes or points over different spatial positions in a single-shot manner such as SECOND [31] and PointPillar [10]. SECOND [31] is the first to apply 3D sparse convolution [7,8] to process the 3D voxel features, which are averaged by voxel-enclosed points. PointPillar [10] collapses the points in vertical pillars with a simplified PointNet [18,19], followed by a typical 2D CNN backbone. Point-GNN [25] proposes a graph neural network to learn better point features. 3DSSD [34] develops F-FPS as a supplement of D-FPS to build an anchor-free 3D object detector. SA-SSD [9] applies an auxiliary segment network to assist the voxel feature learning. CIA-SSD [37] utilizes an IoU-aware confidence rectification to improve the classification. SE-SSD [38] proposes a self-ensembling training schedule to improve the performance of a pretrained CIA-SSD model. These single-stage detectors are usually of high speed.

Two-Stage Detectors. Two-stage detectors can be seen as the extension of single-stage detectors. These methods first generate high-quality proposals with categories based on RPN, and then refine each proposal's location and output the prediction confidence. PointRCNN [23] generates proposals based on segmented foreground objects and then refines the bounding box via a regression branch. Part A^2 [24] extends PointRCNN with an intra-object part supervision. PV-RCNN [22] first utilizes voxel-based backbone to generate high-quality proposals, and then devotes a point-based approach to aggregate multi-scale voxel features along with raw point features. Its variant Voxel-RCNN [4] proposes an accelerated point-based module to capture multi-scale voxel features without raw point features. LiDAR-RCNN [13] introduces a plug-and-play point-based module to refine the RPN proposals based on simple PointNet-like approach. CenterPoint [36] suggests an anchor-free method to improve the RPN detect head, and then learns more accurate bounding box regression based on BEV features within given proposals. Transformer architecture [28] recently appears in the 3D detection area. VoTr [16] improves the region proposal network by introducing Transformer into sparse convolution. CT3D [21] proposes a novel channel-wise Transformer for proposal refinement. These two-stage detectors usually exhibit high performance but suffer the problem of having too many hyperparameters and high latency, and thus limiting their usefulness in the industrial application. In comparison, it is imperative to improve the single-stage detector for the better trade-off between performance and latency.

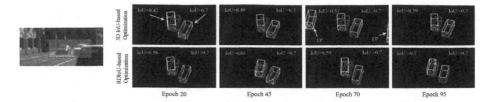

Fig. 2. Qualitative comparison between the 3D IoU-based and RDIoU-based optimization strategies on the KITTI *train* set. The predicted and ground truth bounding boxes are shown in green and blue, respectively. The 3D IoU-based strategy is difficult to handle the hard sample, and the IoU is eventually stagnant under 0.7. In contrast, RDIoU-based strategy finally makes the prediction much closer to the ground truth. (Color figure online)

IoU-Based Optimization. IoU-based optimization has been effectively validated and implemented in 2D object detection without rotation, e.g. GIoU loss [20], DIoU/CIoU loss [40], quality focal loss [11,12], etc. These methods aim to directly optimize the final evaluation metric and have achieved promising performance. Recently, several 3D rotated object detection works study a direct extension of the 2D IoU to 3D domain and yield the 3D IoU loss [41] and ODIoU loss [38]. However, these 3D IoU-based losses usually need high resource cost such as huge GPU memory cost due to brute-force search or time-consuming back-propagation on the CPU. Moreover, it is sub-optimal to set the 3D IoU as the optimization objective as shown in Fig. 1. Instead, we propose a more effective optimization objective, *i.e.* the RDIoU, to achieve both high-performance training and efficient back-propagation on the GPU.

3 Method

Our main contribution is the RDIoU, which is a better optimization objective than the existing 3D IoU in alleviating the negative coupling effect of the rotation during the training stage. In the following, we first discuss the details of our RDIoU and the comparison with 3D IoU. Subsequently, we insert our RDIoU into the regression and classification branches of existing 3D object detectors.

3.1 Our RDIoU

The optimization strategies for object detection generally fall into two types:

1. Non IoU-based: Each box parameter is individually optimized without considering their spatial connection. Typically, Smooth-$\ell 1$ loss [6] and focal loss [14] are used for regression and classification, respectively.
2. IoU-based: The box parameters are jointly optimized via maintaining consistency with the IoU evaluation metric. Typically, DIoU/CIoU loss [40] and quality focal loss [11] are used for regression and classification, respectively.

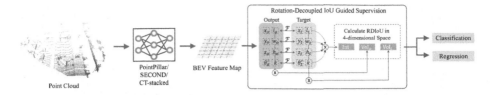

Fig. 3. The illustration of RDIoU method. We advocate a Rotation-Decoupled IoU to model the intersection of two rotated 3D bounding boxes. This design is further set as the optimization target to guide the classification and regression learning, respectively.

Compared to non IoU-based optimization, the IoU-based optimization strategy usually exhibits better performance due to the end-to-end metric learning. However, a naive application of this strategy on 3D object detection causes potential instability issue in the optimization due to the negative coupling effect of the rotation and thus affects the final convergence of the network, as shown in the first row of Fig. 2. In view of this problem, we construct a more efficient optimization strategy that considers both the stability of the training process and the preservation of the geometry from the IoU on the bounding box. Figure 3 illustrates our proposed RDIoU method.

Let $(x_o, y_o, z_o, l_o, w_o, h_o, \theta_o)$ denotes the 3D bounding box parameters of the regression vector from the regression branch and $(x_t, y_t, z_t, l_t, w_t, h_t, \theta_t)$ denotes its corresponding target regression vector. (x, y, z) is the center coordinate, (l, w, h) is the size, and θ is the rotation of the bounding box. Furthermore, we use $(x_a, y_a, z_a, l_a, w_a, h_a, \theta_a)$ to denote the selected anchor box from the 3D object detector and $(x_g, y_g, z_g, l_g, w_g, h_g, \theta_g)$ to denote the ground truth 3D bounding box. Following the previous works [31], the regression target can be encoded as:

$$x_t = \frac{x_g - x_a}{d}, y_t = \frac{y_g - y_a}{d}, z_t = \frac{z_g - z_a}{h_a}, \tag{1}$$

$$l_t = \frac{l_g}{l_a}, \quad w_t = \frac{w_g}{w_a}, \quad h_t = \frac{h_g}{h_a}, \quad \theta_t = \theta_g - \theta_a, \tag{2}$$

where $d = \sqrt{(l_a)^2 + (w_a)^2}$ is the diagonal of the base of anchor.

Since the negative coupling effect of rotation is the main source of inaccuracies in the 3D IoU-based optimization, we decouple the rotation into an independent dimension to avoid its complex coupling relationship with the other bounding box parameters. Specifically, the rotation is decoupled into the $4\text{-}th$ dimension with a fixed edge k. As a result, the center of the optimized bounding box is transformed from (x_t, y_t, z_t) to $(x_t, y_t, z_t, \theta_t)$, and thus we can easily calculate the IoU in this 4-dimensional space. Consequently, the RDIoU of two rotated 3D bounding boxes can be formulated with a regular IoU [20] as:

$$\text{RDIoU} = \text{Int}/(\text{Vol}_o + \text{Vol}_t - \text{Int}), \quad \text{where} \tag{3}$$

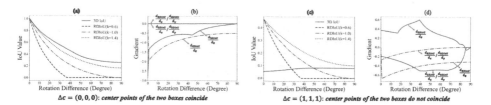

Fig. 4. Simulation experiments. We initialize two 3D boxes of size equal to the predefined anchor size, *i.e.*, (3.9,1.6,1.56). Here, Δc is the box center distance. The gradients of RDIoU are computed with $k = 1$.

$$\text{Int} = \mathcal{F}(x_o, x_t, l_o, l_t) * \mathcal{F}(y_o, y_t, w_o, w_t) * \mathcal{F}(z_o, z_t, h_o, h_t) * \mathcal{F}(\theta_{o'}, \theta_{t'}, k, k),$$

$$\text{Vol}_o = l_o * w_o * h_o * k, \quad \text{Vol}_t = l_t * w_t * h_t * k,$$

$$\text{and} \quad \mathcal{F}(a_o, a_t, b_o, b_t) = \min(a_o + \frac{b_o}{2}, a_t + \frac{b_t}{2}) - \max(a_o - \frac{b_o}{2}, a_t - \frac{b_t}{2}).$$

Following the common setting [31], we set $\theta_{o'} = \sin\theta_o\cos\theta_t$ and $\theta_{t'} = \cos\theta_o\sin\theta_t$. "Int" denotes the intersection volume between the two 4-dimensional bounding boxes. k is side length of the fourth dimension corresponding to center θ, which we empirically set as $k = 1$ to achieve the best performance.

Our proposed RDIoU inherits the geometry constraints from the 3D IoU through an IoU-like formulation in the 4-dimensional space. Every variable is differentiable with our RDIoU as the regression target, and thus can be trained with the regular gradient-based back-propagation on the GPU. Furthermore, the decoupling of the rotation as an independent variable in our RDIoU leads to the right optimization direction for each individual variable with the increasing IoU during optimization.

3.2 More Comparison Between RDIoU and 3D IoU

To further investigate the intrinsic difference, we simulate the values of 3D IoU and our RDIoU under increasing rotation differences. As shown in Fig. 4(a), the values of RDIoU and 3D IoU are similar when the center points of the two boxes coincide. In contrast, as shown in Fig. 4(c), the values become distinct when the center points of the two boxes do not coincide. Specifically, we can see that the 3D IoU yields unreasonable dynamics in Fig. 4(c), where the computed IoU value increases even when the rotation difference becomes larger. We utilize the hyperparameter k to control the weight of rotation change. As can be seen from Fig. 4(a) and (c), a smaller k results in a steeper curve. Furthermore, we plot the gradient changes of x, y and θ with increasing rotation difference in Fig. 4(b) and (d) corresponding to Fig. 4(a) and (c), respectively. From Fig. 4(b), we can see that the gradients of 3D IoU and RDIoU are close when the center points of the two boxes coincide. However, as shown in Fig. 4(d), the gradient over rotation of 3D IoU is obviously misdirected ($\frac{d_{3DIoU}}{d_\theta} > 0$) when the center points of the two boxes do not coincide. In this case, the gradient of 3D IoU changes drastically, while RDIoU still performs in a relatively smooth manner.

3.3 Incorporating RDIoU into Regression Supervision

We modify the DIoU loss [40] for 2D object detection to take our RDIoU for 3D object detection with rotation. Specifically, the modified regression loss aims to maximize the intersection volume, *i.e.* the RDIoU and minimize the normalized center distance in the 4-dimensional space. Let $c_o = [x_o, y_o, z_o, \theta_{o'}]$ and $c_t = [x_t, y_t, z_t, \theta_{t'}]$, the center distance penalty is:

$$\rho_c = \frac{\delta(c_o, c_t)}{\text{Diag}}, \tag{4}$$

where $\delta(\cdot)$ denotes the square of Euclidean distance and

$$\text{Diag} = \mathcal{G}(x_o, x_t, l_o, l_t) + \mathcal{G}(y_o, y_t, w_o, w_t) + \mathcal{G}(z_o, z_t, h_o, h_t) + \mathcal{G}(\theta_{o'}, \theta_{t'}, k, k),$$

where $\mathcal{G}(a_o, a_t, b_o, b_t) = \left(\max(a_o + \frac{b_o}{2}, a_t + \frac{b_t}{2}) - \min(a_o - \frac{b_o}{2}, a_t - \frac{b_t}{2}) \right)^2$. As a result, the final RDIoU-guided DIoU loss for 3D bounding box regression is:

$$\mathcal{L}_{RL} = 1 - \text{RDIoU} + \rho_c. \tag{5}$$

Compared with the existing 3D variants of DIoU losses [38,41] that directly maximize the 3D intersection volume and minimize the 3D center distance, our RDIoU-guided DIoU loss has the advantages of more efficient learning and low resource cost. The rotation decoupling operator transforms the rotated 3D bounding box into a 4-dimensional latent space, which leads to stable optimization direction for each variable. Unlike [38,41] that need huge GPU memory cost or necessary pre-trained model, our RDIoU-guided DIoU loss can be easily implemented in GPU with a small cost. In the ablation studies, we show RDIoU-guided DIoU loss can surpass the 3D IoU-guided DIoU loss by a large margin.

3.4 Incorporating RDIoU into Classification Supervision

Solving the misalignment problem is also a crucial issue for object detection. Thus, we derive a RDIoU-guided quality focal loss to jointly supervise the classification and the bounding box quality estimation. The quality focal loss [11,12] has achieved good performance in 2D image detection, where the IoUs between predicted and ground truth boxes are set as the quality targets. For 3D detection with rotated 3D bounding boxes, an intuitive thought is to apply the quality focal loss with 3D IoU-guided quality supervision. However, 3D IoU can cause confusion when the higher prediction error corresponds to a larger 3D IoU (see Fig. 1), and therefore it leads to bad dynamics during the optimization.

On the contrary, our RDIoU is less susceptible to the change of regression variables and thus it can be seen as a better measure of the regression quality. Consequently, we utilize our RDIoU as the quality estimation target. Similar to GFLV2 [11], we adopt joint representation targets with the quality focal loss for both classification and bounding box quality prediction. Specifically, the target for each sample can be expressed as $t = r \times e$, where $r = [r_1, r_2, \ldots, r_m], r_i \in \{0, 1\}$ is the classification representation with m classes and $e \in [0, 1]$ is the scalar RDIoU representation. Taking the joint estimation as y, the RDIoU-guided quality focal loss is given by:

$$\mathcal{L}_{RQFL} = -\beta_1 |\text{RDIoU} - y|^{\beta_2} \left((1 - \text{RDIoU}) \log(1 - y) + \text{RDIoU} \log(y) \right), \quad (6)$$

where $\beta_1 = 0.25$ and $\beta_2 = 2$ follow the setting of focal loss. In this way, the predicted values of classification head model both the category probability and the corresponding bounding box confidence. Furthermore, we use the cross-entropy loss for direction classification ($\mathcal{L}_d$). Finally, the overall loss for training is:

$$\mathcal{L} = \mathcal{L}_{RQFL} + \gamma_1 \mathcal{L}_d + \gamma_2 \mathcal{L}_{RL}, \quad (7)$$

where γ_1 and γ_2 are hyperparameters to weigh the loss terms.

Backbone Network. Following the previous works [10,31], we voxelize the point cloud to produce a regular representation. In each voxel, we calculate the mean coordinates and intensities of the raw points as the voxel feature. Subsequently, the 3D backbone network gradually converts the initial voxel features into high-dimensional feature volumes, and the 3D features along Z-axis are stacked into 2D BEV feature maps. A 2D backbone network is designed to enhance the extraction of the BEV features for the final location and classification tasks. Motivated by the success of Transformer [28] in computer vision-related tasks, we adopt a stacked architecture that contains both the convolution block and the Transformer block to generate the final detection features. Specifically, the convolution block first extracts the BEV features while keeping the dimensions (both the number of channels and the size of feature map) unchanged. A convolution layer with stride two is then adopted to further reduce the spatial size. The Transformer block then processes the high-level features without changing the feature dimensions. Our designed conv-trans-stacked (CT-stacked) architecture shows better performance as compared to the pure convolution based network. The whole framework of our RDIoU is illustrated in Fig. 3. The final feature map is 8× downsampling of the input resolution. The classification, quality estimation, and regression are performed at pixel-level.

4   Experiments

In this section, we compare our RDIoU to other state-of-the-art methods on two popular benchmarks: KITTI [5] and Waymo Open Dataset [26]. Furthermore, we conduct extensive ablation studies to investigate the performance on different backbone networks and on each component of RDIoU to validate our design.

4.1   Datasets

KITTI. This dataset consists of 7,481 LiDAR samples for training and 7,518 LiDAR samples for testing. We further follow the common protocol [10,31] to split the original training data into 3,712 training samples and 3,769 validation samples for experimental studies.

Waymo Open Dataset. This dataset consists of 798 training sequences with 158,361 LiDAR samples, and 202 validation sequences with 40,077 LiDAR samples. Five LiDAR sensors are used for full 360-degree annotation instead of 90-degree as in KITTI. Currently, it is the largest dataset for autonomous driving.

4.2   Implementation Details

For KITTI, the raw point clouds are first clipped into $(0, 70.4)$m, $(-40, 40)m$, $(-3, 1)$m for X, Y, Z axis ranges with voxel size $(0.05, 0.05, 0.1)$m. For Waymo Open Dataset, the corresponding axis ranges are $(-75.2, 75.2)$m, $(-75.2, 75.2)$m, $(-2, 4)$m, and the voxel size is $(0.1, 0.1, 0.15)$m. We conduct all experiments based on the OpenPCDet [27] toolbox.

Table 1. Performance comparisons with state-of-the-art methods on the KITTI *val* set with 11 recall positions. M : ✓ means training on three classes. M : ✗ means training only on car. Mod.* is the most important metric. The top-1 of two-stage and single-stage methods are bold, respectively.

Type	Method	M	Car-3D (IoU = 0.7)			Ped.-3D (IoU = 0.5)			Cyc.-3D (IoU = 0.5)		
			Easy	Mod.*	Hard	Easy	Mod.	Hard	Easy	Mod.	Hard
Two-stage	Part-A^2 [24]	✓	**89.56**	79.41	78.84	65.69	**60.05**	55.45	85.50	69.90	65.49
	STD [35]	✗	89.70	79.80	**79.30**	–	–	–	–	–	–
	PV-RCNN [22]	✓	89.35	83.69	78.70	63.12	54.84	51.78	**86.06**	69.48	64.50
	Voxel-RCNN [4]	✗	89.41	84.52	78.93	–	–	–	–	–	–
	VoTr-TSD [16]	✗	89.04	84.04	78.68	–	–	–	–	–	–
	CT3D [21]	✓	89.11	85.04	78.76	64.23	59.84	**55.76**	85.04	**71.71**	**68.05**
	CT3D [21]	✗	89.54	86.06	78.99	–	–	–	–	–	–
	BtcDet [30]	✗	–	**86.57**	–	–	–	–	–	–	–
Single-stage	VoxelNet [43]	✓	81.97	65.46	62.85	57.86	53.42	48.87	67.17	47.65	45.11
	SECOND [31]	✓	88.61	78.62	77.22	56.55	52.98	47.73	80.59	67.16	63.11
	PointPillar [10]	✓	86.46	77.28	74.65	57.75	52.29	47.91	80.06	62.69	59.71
	3DSSD [34]	✓	89.71	79.45	78.67	–	–	–	–	–	–
	SA-SSD [9]	✗	**90.15**	79.91	78.78	–	–	–	–	–	–
	CIA-SSD [37]	✗	90.04	78.91	78.80	–	–	–	–	–	–
	SE-SSD [38]	✗	–	85.71	–	–	–	–	–	–	–
	VoTr-SSD [16]	✗	87.86	78.27	76.93	–	–	–	–	–	–
	RDIoU (Ours)	✓	89.16	85.24	78.41	63.26	**57.47**	52.53	83.32	68.39	63.63
	RDIoU (Ours)	✗	89.76	**86.62**	79.04	–	–	–	–	–	–

The 3D backbone has four levels with feature dimensions $(16, 32, 64, 64)$, $(16, 32, 64, 128)$ for KITTI and Waymo Open Dataset, respectively. The 2D backbone contains two blocks, the first block is implemented by 5 CNN layers for

KITTI and 6 CNN layers for Waymo Open Dataset to keep the same resolution with the output of 3D backbone. The second block is implemented by 1 CNN layer and 4 Transformer (using the setting of 4× expansion in FFN layers and 4 attention heads) layers [15,28] with half the resolution. Finally, one fractionally-strided convolution layer is adopted to double the resolution.

All the evaluated models are trained from scratch in an end-to-end manner with the ADAM optimizer. The learning rate is decayed with a cosine annealing strategy, and the maximum is $3.5 \times e^{-4}$. We use a batch size of 32. For the hyperparameters of the overall loss, we set $\gamma_1 = 0.2$ and $\gamma_2 = 2$.

4.3 Results on Real-world Datasets

KITTI. KITTI is relatively small as compared to the Waymo Open Dataset. We follow the previous works to train models on *train* set, and report the results on *val* set. Furthermore, we report the detection results on KITTI *test* server by training the model with *train+val* set. All the evaluated models are reported in three difficulty levels (*i.e.*, *easy, moderate, hard*). Table 1 reports the results on the KITTI *val* set. For the most important 3D object detection metric on *moderate* level of car, our proposed RDIoU method surpasses the current best single-stage models CIA-SSD [37], SE-SSD [38], VoTr-SSD [16] with +7.71%AP, +0.91%AP, +8.35%AP, respectively. Furthermore, our RDIoU even outperforms the best two-stage models VoTr-TSD [16], CT3D [21] BtcDet [30] with +2.58%AP, +0.56%AP, +0.05%AP, respectively. This superior performance strongly manifests the effectiveness of our proposed method.

Table 2. Performance comparisons with state-of-the-art methods for car detection on the KITTI *test* benchmark with 40 recall positions. The top-1 of two-stage and single-stage methods are bold, respectively.

Method	Reference	Stage	3D AP (IoU = 0.7)		
			Easy	Moderate*	Hard
Part-A^2 [24]	TPAMI 2020	Two	87.81	78.49	73.51
STD [35]	ICCV 2019	Two	87.95	79.71	75.09
Point-GNN [25]	CVPR2020	Two	88.33	79.47	72.29
PV-RCNN [22]	CVPR 2020	Two	90.25	81.43	76.82
LiDAR-RCNN [13]	CVPR 2021	Two	85.97	74.21	69.18
VoTr-TSD [16]	ICCV 2021	Two	89.90	82.09	**79.14**
CT3D [21]	ICCV 2021	Two	87.83	81.77	77.16
BtcDet [30]	AAAI 2022	Two	**90.64**	**82.86**	78.09
VoxelNet [43]	CVPR 2018	Single	77.82	64.17	57.51
SECOND [31]	Sensors 2018	Single	83.34	72.55	65.82
PointPillar [10]	CVPR 2019	Single	82.58	74.31	68.99
3DSSD [34]	CVPR 2020	Single	88.36	79.57	74.55
SA-SSD [9]	CVPR 2020	Single	88.75	79.79	74.16
SE-SSD [38]	CVPR 2021	Single	**91.49**	**82.54**	77.15
RDIoU (Ours)	–	Single	90.65	82.30	**77.26**

For pedestrian and cyclist detection, we perform a three-class training for our RDIoU method and compare to the state-of-the-art methods with the same settings. It can be seen that our RDIoU leads a large margin compared with these single-stage methods (VoxelNet [43], SECOND [31] and PointPillar [10]). At the *moderate* level, our RDIoU outperforms SECOND with +4.49%AP and +1.23%AP on pedestrian and cyclist detection, respectively. This also proves that our RDIoU has the superior ability of detecting small objects. Note that the performances on small objects are marginally lower compared to the other two-stage methods such as Part-A^2 [24] and CT3D [21]. This is because single-stage methods usually assign more attention to the main objects (*i.e.*, car) compared to the two-stage methods which have the inherent advantage from the proposals.

Table 2 shows the car-3D detection results by submitting to the KITTI *test* server. Our RDIoU achieves 82.30%AP on the most important *moderate* level, surpassing the state-of-the-art methods of LiDAR-RCNN [13], VoTr-TSD [16], CT3D [21] by +8.09%AP, +0.21%AP, +0.53%AP, respectively. Note that these are all two-stage methods such that RDIoU has the absolute advantage of inference speed. Compared to SE-SSD [38] and BtcDet [30], our RDIoU is slightly lower by -0.24%AP and -0.56%AP, respectively. One possible reason is the mismatched data distributions between the KITTI *val* set and *test* set [13,24]. Moreover, SE-SSD requires extra data augmentation and complex self-ensembling procedure while the two-stage method BtcDet requires a further box refinement module. Overall, the results on both *test* and *val* sets consistently reveal that RDIoU method is highly effective.

Table 3. Performance comparisons with state-of-the-art methods for the vehicle detection on the Waymo validation dataset. Here PointPillars* is implemented in mmdetection3D [3]. The top-1 of two-stage and single-stage methods are bold, respectively.

Method	Stage	3D AP/APH (IoU = 0.7)				BEV AP/APH (IoU = 0.7)			
		Overall	0–30 m	30–50 m	50 m-Inf	Overall	0–30 m	30–50 m	50 m-Inf
LEVEL_1									
MVF [42]	Two	62.9/–	86.3/–	60.0/–	36.0/–	80.4/–	93.6/–	79.2/–	63.1/–
PV-RCNN [22]	Two	70.3/69.7	91.9/91.3	69.2/68.5	42.2/41.3	80.0/82.1	97.4/96.7	83.0/82.0	65.0/63.2
Voxel-RCNN [4]	Two	75.6/–	92.5/–	74.1/–	53.2/–	88.2/–	97.6/–	87.3/–	77.7/–
LiDAR-RCNN [13]	Two	76.0/75.5	92.1/91.6	74.6/74.1	54.5/53.4	90.1/89.3	97.0/96.5	**89.5/88.6**	**78.9/77.4**
CenterPoint [36]	Two	76.7/76.2	–/–	–/–	–/–		–/–	–/–	–/–
VoTr-TSD [16]	Two	75.0/74.3	92.3/91.7	73.4/72.6	51.1/50.0	–/–	–/–	–/–	–/–
CT3D [21]	Two	76.3/–	92.5/–	75.1/–	**55.4/–**	**90.5/–**	**97.6/–**	88.1/–	78.9/–
BtcDet [30]	Two	**78.6/78.1**	**96.1/–**	**77.6/–**	54.5/–	–/–	–/–	–/–	–/–
PointPillar* [10]	Single	72.1/71.5	88.3/87.8	69.9/69.3	48.0/47.3	87.9/87.1	96.6/96.0	87.1/86.2	78.1/76.5
Pillar-OD [29]	Single	69.8/–	88.5/–	66.5/–	42.9/–	87.1/–	95.8/–	84.7/–	72.1/–
VoTr-SSD [16]	Single	69.0/68.4	88.2/87.6	66.7/66.1	42.1/41.4	–/–	–/–	–/–	–/–
RDIoU (Ours)	Single	**78.4/78.0**	**93.0/92.6**	**75.4/74.9**	**56.2/55.6**	**91.6/91.0**	**98.1/97.7**	**90.8/90.2**	**82.4/81.1**
LEVEL_2									
PV-RCNN [22]	Two	65.4/64.8	91.6/91.0	65.1/64.5	36.5/35.7	77.5/76.6	94.6/94.0	80.4/79.4	55.4/53.8
Voxel-RCNN [4]	Two	66.6/–	91.7/–	67.9/–	40.8/–	81.1/–	97.0/–	81.4/–	63.3/–
LiDAR-RCNN [13]	Two	68.3/67.9	91.3/90.9	68.5/68.0	42.4/41.8	81.7/81.0	94.3/93.9	**82.3/81.5**	**65.8/64.5**
CenterPoint [36]	Two	68.8/68.3	–/–	–/–	–/–	–/–	–/–	–/–	–/–
VoTr-TSD [16]	Two	65.9/65.3	–/–	–/–	–/–	–/–	–/–	–/–	–/–
CT3D [21]	Two	69.0/–	91.8/–	68.9/–	42.6/–	**81.7/–**	**97.1/–**	82.2/–	64.3/–
BtcDet [30]	Two	**70.1/69.6**	**96.0/–**	**70.1/–**	**43.9/–**	–/–	–/–	–/–	–/–
PointPillars* [10]	Single	63.6/63.1	87.4/86.9	62.9/62.3	37.2/36.7	81.3/80.4	94.0/93.5	81.7/80.8	65.5/64.1
VoTr-SSD [16]	Single	60.2/59.7	–/–	–/–	–/–	–/–	–/–	–/–	–/–
RDIoU (Ours)	Single	**69.5/69.1**	**92.3/91.9**	**69.3/68.9**	**43.7/43.1**	**83.1/82.5**	**97.5/97.1**	**85.2/84.6**	**68.3/67.2**

Waymo Open Dataset. All methods for comparison are evaluated with AP and average precision by heading (APH) at two difficulty levels defined in the official evaluation, where the *LEVEL_1* objects contain at least 5 points while the *LEVEL_2* objects contain 1~5 inside points. The rotated IoU threshold is set to 0.7 for vehicle detection. We also report the detection results based on the different distances of the objects for adequate comparison. Table 3 reports the results on validation sequences of Waymo Open Dataset. It can be clearly seen that RDIoU achieves excellent performance on this large-scale, diverse, and challenging dataset. Our RDIoU beats almost all state-of-the-arts including the two-stage methods on all evaluation metrics by a large margin in a number of settings. Specifically, our RDIoU outperforms the latest state-of-the-art methods CenterPoint [36], VoTr-TSD [16], CT3D [21] with +1.7%, +3.4%, +2.1% on 3D AP of *LEVEL_1*, respectively, and achieves fairly close performance as compared to BtcDet [30] (only -0.2%AP performance drop). These inspired results further affirm the strong ability of our RDIoU method.

4.4 Ablation Studies

In this section, we detail the influence of each component that contributes to the final RDIoU design. All models are trained on the KITTI *train* set from scratch, and evaluated on the KITTI *val* set for fair comparison. We use CT-stacked backbone network as the default setting. The final performance is reported on 3D *moderate* level of car with 11 and 40 recall positions.

Effect of Different Backbone Networks. In Table 4, we plug RDIoU into another two commonly used 3D object detection backbone networks SEC-OND [31] and PointPillar [10]. It can be seen that RDIoU can help different backbone networks to achieve significant performance improvement. Specifically, plugging our RDIoU into PointPillar, SECOND and our CT-stacked backbone networks brings $3D_{R40}+2.54\%$, $3D_{R40}+2.95\%$ and $3D_{R40}+3.19\%$ improvements on *moderate* level, respectively. The contributing factor is that our RDIoU method can be integrated into any existing backbone networks to assist the model learning for better performance.

Table 4. Ablation study on different backbone networks. (+RDIoU) means replacing the classification and regression losses in baseline models with our proposed RDIoU.

Method	$3D_{R11}$			$3D_{R40}$	FPS (Hz)
	Easy	Mod.	Hard	Mod.	
PointPillar [10]	87.08	77.74	76.24	79.88	33.8
PointPillar (+RDIoU)	**88.89**	**78.89**	**78.02**	**82.42**	33.8
SECOND [31]	88.78	78.74	77.51	82.85	30.5
SECOND (+RDIoU)	**89.24**	**86.10**	**78.60**	**85.80**	30.5
CT-stacked	88.93	78.91	77.63	83.01	26.6
CT-stacked (+RDIoU)	**89.76**	**86.62**	**79.04**	**86.20**	26.6

Table 5. Ablation study on RDIoU-guided regression loss. All models utilize RDIoU-guided quality focal loss for classification.

Method	3D IoU Guided	RDIoU Guided	$3D_{R11}$ Easy	Mod.	Hard	$3D_{R40}$ Mod.
Smooth−$\ell1$ loss [14]			89.19	78.86	77.53	83.14
IoU loss [41]	✓		88.80	81.94	77.67	83.60
		✓	**89.40**	**85.60**	**78.76**	**85.73**
CIoU loss [40]	✓		88.82	83.20	77.48	84.01
		✓	**89.43**	**86.21**	**78.90**	**85.98**
DIoU loss [40]	✓		88.83	83.59	77.93	84.20
		✓	**89.76**	**86.62**	**79.04**	**86.20**

Table 6. Ablation study on RDIoU-guided classification loss. Traditional focal loss is adopted as the default setting. All models utilize RDIoU-guided DIoU loss.

3D IoU Guided QFL	RDIoU Guided QFL	$3D_{R11}$ Easy	Mod.	Hard	$3D_{R40}$ Mod.
		89.16	84.78	78.15	85.12
✓		89.33	86.07	78.79	85.79
	✓	**89.76**	**86.62**	**79.04**	**86.20**

Effect of RDIoU-Guided Regression Branch. As shown in Fig. 5, although 3D IoU-based regression losses show better performance than the Smooth-$\ell1$ loss, our RDIoU-based regression losses can still further boost the performance by a large margin. Specifically, RDIoU-guided IoU loss [41], CIoU loss [40], DIoU loss [40] surpass the 3D IoU-guided losses with $3D_{R40}+2.13\%$, $3D_{R40}+1.97\%$, $3D_{R40}+2.00\%$, respectively. These gains in AP strongly prove the effectiveness of our proposed method, which encourages the network to learn more precise 3D bounding boxes. DIoU loss performs better than IoU loss due to the direct minimization for the normalized distance between predicted and ground truth bounding boxes. Note that the aspect ratio of the 3D real-world category is relatively stable, and thus CIoU loss does not bring performance improvement as compared to the DIoU loss.

Effect of RDIoU-Guided Classification Branch. In Table 6, we investigate the influence of RDIoU-guided quality focal loss by replacing it with the traditional focal loss [14] and the 3D IoU-guided quality foal loss [12], respectively. As seen in 1st and 2nd rows of Table 6, the 3D IoU-guided quality focal loss performs better than the traditional focal loss due to the extra quality estimation for each predicted bounding box. 2nd row and 3rd row of Table 6 demonstrate that RDIoU-guided quality focal loss can also obviously exceed 3D IoU-guided quality focal loss ($3D_{R11}+0.55\%$, $3D_{R40}+0.41\%$). This significant improvement comes from the stable measurement of the predicted bounding boxes, which subsequently facilitates the generation of more reliable confidence maps.

5   Conclusion

This paper presents a novel RDIoU method to model the intersection of two arbitrary-oriented 3D bounding boxes for improving the single-stage point cloud detectors. RDIoU decouples the rotation variable as an independent term while preserving the geometry of 3D IoU. It exhibits robustness to the rotation change compared with the 3D IoU. Based on RDIoU, we propose the RDIoU-guided DIoU loss to enable stable optimization process and efficient back-propagation during training, and it achieves the best performance among the latest 3D regression losses. Moreover, we introduce the RDIoU-guided quality focal loss to address the misalignment problem between the regression results and the confidence maps, and it also exhibits much better than the 3D IoU-guided quality focal loss. The experimental results show that our RDIoU method can help the commonly used backbone networks to achieve state-of-the-art performance.

Acknowledgements. This work was supported by the National Key R&D Program of China under Grant 2020AAA0103902; Zhejiang Provincial Key Laboratory of Information Processing, Communication and Networking (IPCAN), Hangzhou 310027, China; Fundamental Research Funds for the Central Universities 226-2022-00195; The National Research Foundation, Singapore under its AI Singapore Programme (AISG Award No: AISG2-RP-2021-024); The Tier 2 grant MOE-T2EP20120-0011 from the Singapore Ministry of Education.

References

1. Chen, X., Ma, H., Wan, J., Li, B., Xia, T.: Multi-view 3D object detection network for autonomous driving. In: Proceedings of the IEEE/CVF Conference on Computer Vision and Pattern Recognition (CVPR), pp. 1907–1915 (2017)
2. Chen, Z., et al.: PIoU loss: towards accurate oriented object detection in complex environments. In: Vedaldi, A., Bischof, H., Brox, T., Frahm, J.-M. (eds.) ECCV 2020. LNCS, vol. 12350, pp. 195–211. Springer, Cham (2020). https://doi.org/10.1007/978-3-030-58558-7_12
3. Contributors, M.: MMDetection3D: OpenMMLab next-generation platform for general 3D object detection. https://github.com/open-mmlab/mmdetection3d (2020)
4. Deng, J., Shi, S., Li, P., Zhou, W., Zhang, Y., Li, H.: Voxel r-cnn: towards high performance voxel-based 3D object detection. arXiv preprint arXiv:2012.15712 (2020)
5. Geiger, A., Lenz, P., Stiller, C., Urtasun, R.: Vision meets robotics: the kitti dataset. Int. J. Rob. Res. **32**(11), 1231–1237 (2013)
6. Girshick, R.: Fast r-cnn. In: Proceedings of the IEEE/CVF International Conference on Computer Vision (ICCV), pp. 1440–1448 (2015)
7. Graham, B.: Sparse 3D convolutional neural networks. arXiv preprint arXiv:1505.02890 (2015)

8. Graham, B., van der Maaten, L.: Submanifold sparse convolutional networks. arXiv preprint arXiv:1706.01307 (2017)
9. He, C., Zeng, H., Huang, J., Hua, X.S., Zhang, L.: Structure aware single-stage 3D object detection from point cloud. In: Proceedings of the IEEE/CVF Conference on Computer Vision and Pattern Recognition (CVPR), pp. 11873–11882 (2020)
10. Lang, A.H., Vora, S., Caesar, H., Zhou, L., Yang, J., Beijbom, O.: Pointpillars: fast encoders for object detection from point clouds. In: Proceedings of the IEEE/CVF Conference on Computer Vision and Pattern Recognition (CVPR), pp. 12697–12705 (2019)
11. Li, X., Wang, W., Hu, X., Li, J., Tang, J., Yang, J.: Generalized focal loss v2: learning reliable localization quality estimation for dense object detection. In: Proceedings of the IEEE/CVF Conference on Computer Vision and Pattern Recognition (CVPR), pp. 11632–11641 (2021)
12. Li, X., et al.: Generalized focal loss: learning qualified and distributed bounding boxes for dense object detection. Adv. Neural Inf. Process. Syst. (NIPS) **33**, 21002–21012 (2020)
13. Li, Z., Wang, F., Wang, N.: Lidar r-cnn: an efficient and universal 3D object detector. In: Proceedings of the IEEE/CVF Conference on Computer Vision and Pattern Recognition (CVPR), pp. 7546–7555 (2021)
14. Lin, T.Y., Goyal, P., Girshick, R., He, K., Dollár, P.: Focal loss for dense object detection. In: Proceedings of the IEEE/CVF International Conference on Computer Vision (ICCV), pp. 2980–2988 (2017)
15. Liu, Z., et al.: Swin transformer: hierarchical vision transformer using shifted windows. arXiv preprint arXiv:2103.14030 (2021)
16. Mao, J., et al.: Voxel transformer for 3D object detection. In: Proceedings of the IEEE/CVF International Conference on Computer Vision (ICCV), pp. 3164–3173 (2021)
17. Qi, C.R., Liu, W., Wu, C., Su, H., Guibas, L.J.: Frustum pointnets for 3D object detection from rgb-d data. In: Proceedings of the IEEE/CVF Conference on Computer Vision and Pattern Recognition (CVPR), pp. 918–927 (2018)
18. Qi, C.R., Su, H., Mo, K., Guibas, L.J.: Pointnet: deep learning on point sets for 3D classification and segmentation. In: Proceedings of the IEEE/CVF Conference on Computer Vision and Pattern Recognition (CVPR), pp. 652–660 (2017)
19. Qi, C.R., Yi, L., Su, H., Guibas, L.J.: Pointnet++: deep hierarchical feature learning on point sets in a metric space. Adv. Neural Inf. Process. Syst. (NIPS) **30**, 5099–5108 (2017)
20. Rezatofighi, H., Tsoi, N., Gwak, J., Sadeghian, A., Reid, I., Savarese, S.: Generalized intersection over union: a metric and a loss for bounding box regression. In: Proceedings of the IEEE/CVF Conference on Computer Vision and Pattern Recognition (CVPR), pp. 658–666 (2019)
21. Sheng, H., et al.: Improving 3D object detection with channel-wise transformer. In: Proceedings of the IEEE/CVF International Conference on Computer Vision (ICCV), pp. 2743–2752 (2021)
22. Shi, S., et al.: Pv-rcnn: point-voxel feature set abstraction for 3D object detection. In: Proceedings of the IEEE/CVF Conference on Computer Vision and Pattern Recognition (CVPR), pp. 10529–10538 (2020)
23. Shi, S., Wang, X., Li, H.: Pointrcnn: 3D object proposal generation and detection from point cloud. In: Proceedings of the IEEE/CVF Conference on Computer Vision and Pattern Recognition (CVPR), pp. 770–779 (2019)

24. Shi, S., Wang, Z., Shi, J., Wang, X., Li, H.: From points to parts: 3D object detection from point cloud with part-aware and part-aggregation network. IEEE Trans. Pattern Anal. Mach. Intell. (TPAMI) **43**, 2647–2664 (2020)
25. Shi, W., Rajkumar, R.: Point-gnn: graph neural network for 3D object detection in a point cloud. In: Proceedings of the IEEE/CVF Conference on Computer Vision and Pattern Recognition (CVPR), pp. 1711–1719 (2020)
26. Sun, P., et al.: Scalability in perception for autonomous driving: waymo open dataset. In: Proceedings of the IEEE/CVF Conference on Computer Vision and Pattern Recognition (CVPR), pp. 2446–2454 (2020)
27. Team, O.D.: Openpcdet: an open-source toolbox for 3D object detection from point clouds (2020). https://github.com/open-mmlab/OpenPCDet
28. Vaswani, A., et al.: Attention is all you need. Adv. Neural Inf. Process. Syst. (NIPS), 5998–6008 (2017)
29. Wang, Y., et al.: Pillar-based object detection for autonomous driving. In: Proceedings of the European Conference on Computer Vision (ECCV), pp. 18–34 (2020)
30. Xu, Q., Zhong, Y., Neumann, U.: Behind the curtain: learning occluded shapes for 3D object detection. arXiv preprint arXiv:2112.02205 (2021)
31. Yan, Y., Mao, Y., Li, B.: Second: sparsely embedded convolutional detection. Sensors **18**(10), 3337 (2018)
32. Yang, X., Yan, J., Ming, Q., Wang, W., Zhang, X., Tian, Q.: Rethinking rotated object detection with gaussian wasserstein distance loss. arXiv preprint arXiv:2101.11952 (2021)
33. Yang, X., et al.: Scrdet: towards more robust detection for small, cluttered and rotated objects. In: Proceedings of the IEEE/CVF International Conference on Computer Vision (ICCV), pp. 8232–8241 (2019)
34. Yang, Z., Sun, Y., Liu, S., Jia, J.: 3DSSD: point-based 3D single stage object detector. In: Proceedings of the IEEE/CVF Conference on Computer Vision and Pattern Recognition (CVPR), pp. 11040–11048 (2020)
35. Yang, Z., Sun, Y., Liu, S., Shen, X., Jia, J.: Std: sparse-to-dense 3D object detector for point cloud. In: Proceedings of the IEEE/CVF International Conference on Computer Vision (ICCV), pp. 1951–1960 (2019)
36. Yin, T., Zhou, X., Krahenbuhl, P.: Center-based 3D object detection and tracking. In: Proceedings of the IEEE/CVF Conference on Computer Vision and Pattern Recognition (CVPR), pp. 11784–11793 (2021)
37. Zheng, W., Tang, W., Chen, S., Jiang, L., Fu, C.W.: Cia-ssd: confident iou-aware single-stage object detector from point cloud. arXiv preprint arXiv:2012.03015 (2020)
38. Zheng, W., Tang, W., Jiang, L., Fu, C.W.: SE-SSD: self-ensembling single-stage object detector from point cloud. In: Proceedings of the IEEE/CVF Conference on Computer Vision and Pattern Recognition (CVPR), pp. 14494–14503 (2021)
39. Zheng, Yu., Zhang, D., Xie, S., Lu, J., Zhou, J.: Rotation-robust intersection over union for 3D object detection. In: Vedaldi, A., Bischof, H., Brox, T., Frahm, J.-M. (eds.) ECCV 2020. LNCS, vol. 12365, pp. 464–480. Springer, Cham (2020). https://doi.org/10.1007/978-3-030-58565-5_28
40. Zheng, Z., Wang, P., Liu, W., Li, J., Ye, R., Ren, D.: Distance-iou loss: faster and better learning for bounding box regression. In: Proceedings of the AAAI Conference on Artificial Intelligence (AAAI), vol. 34, pp. 12993–13000 (2020)
41. Zhou, D., et al.: Iou loss for 2D/3D object detection. In: International Conference on 3D Vision (3DV), pp. 85–94. IEEE (2019)

42. Zhou, Y., et al.: End-to-end multi-view fusion for 3D object detection in lidar point clouds. In: Conference on Robot Learning (CoRL), pp. 923–932 (2020)
43. Zhou, Y., Tuzel, O.: Voxelnet: end-to-end learning for point cloud based 3D object detection. In: Proceedings of the IEEE/CVF Conference on Computer Vision and Pattern Recognition (CVPR), pp. 4490–4499 (2018)

TD-Road: Top-Down Road Network Extraction with Holistic Graph Construction

Yang He$^{(\boxtimes)}$, Ravi Garg, and Amber Roy Chowdhury

Amazon Last Mile, New York, USA
{yanhea,ravigarg,amberch}@amazon.com

Abstract. Graph-based approaches have been becoming increasingly popular in road network extraction, in addition to segmentation-based methods. Road networks are represented as graph structures, being able to explicitly define the topology structures and avoid the ambiguity of segmentation masks, such as between a real junction area and multiple separate roads in different heights. In contrast to the bottom-up graph-based approaches, which rely on orientation information, we propose a novel top-down approach to generate road network graphs with a holistic model, namely TD-Road. We decompose road extraction as two subtasks: key point prediction and connectedness prediction. We directly apply graph structures (i.e., locations of node and connections between them) as training supervisions for neural networks and generate road graph outputs in inference, instead of learning some intermediate properties of a graph structure (e.g., orientations or distances for the next move). Our network integrates a relation inference module with key point prediction, to capture connections between neighboring points and outputs the final road graphs with no post-processing steps required. Extensive experiments are conducted on challenging datasets, including *City-Scale* and *SpaceNet* to show the effectiveness and simplicity of our method, that the proposed method achieves remarkable results compared with previous state-of-the-art methods.

Keywords: Road network extraction · Relation inference · End-to-end appoach · Remote sensing

1 Introduction

Road network extraction from satellite imagery is a fundamental component for automatically constructing rich and accurate maps, and enabling further route planning and navigation applications. High quality maps require several good properties, including road connectivity, precise localization on junctions and multiple interactive roads, and large coverage of the physical world. To resolve the above challenges, a large variety of methods have been proposed, which are typically categorized into segmentation-based [2,28] and graph-based methods [1,10,23]. While segmentation based methods are good at modeling

S. Avidan et al. (Eds.): ECCV 2022, LNCS 13669, pp. 562–577, 2022.
https://doi.org/10.1007/978-3-031-20077-9_33

Image   Segmentation-based methods   Previous graph-based methods   Ours

Fig. 1. Supervision signals for various road extraction methods. Different from prior work, we directly leverage graph structures to supervise the training of our network, and then our network produces graphs in a straightforward manner during inference.

contextual dependencies, segmentation masks are vague in representing complex structures [10] and require various post-processing heuristics to convert road masks into road networks. In this work, we focus on the second category and propose a novel top-down approach for road graph construction.

Previous graph-based methods make use of the orientation clue to construct a road graph iteratively [1,3,23] or simultaneously [10]. In each location of a road, they estimate the orientation to explore and move forward, and add the next location to the graph, which are bottom-up approaches and gradually extend a road graph. In the end, road graph extraction is completed when no orientation can be found from all the locations of the current graph. Furthermore, a recent work [10] improves the iterative graph construction scheme by encoding key point locations and orientations to extend as the outputs of neural networks. Similar to segmentation, it performs graph construction using a dense prediction network, integrating more context dependencies and avoiding expensive iterative scanning of satellite images. However, this method still relies on orientations to establish edges for graph construction.

In spite of the success of previous methods in building road graphs, we question if orientation-based methods are the best way to generate road graphs from satellite images? This question is from the observation that orientation prediction in these methods is quantized and can cause imperfection in geometries and node localization in the resultant road graph. Besides, orientation is not a direct matching, hence a post-processing is indispensable to convert the intermediate results into final graphs, which might introduce further errors and cause mismatch between different locations. In this paper, we propose a simple alternative approach to generate road graphs, where we aim to learn the connectedness between different points and output graphs directly. The proposed method of predicting the connectedness not only helps us to emit road graph structures, but also allows our network to train using graph supervision (i.e., location of nodes and connected edges between them), which is completely different to other approaches, as shown in Fig. 1.

Relation reasoning has attracted much attention in learning the relation between multiple instances, achieving broad applications such as answering complicated questions from images [19], learning non-maximum suppression in object detection [12]. In our work, we introduce a relation reasoning module into road network extraction, and apply it to learn the connectedness between two locations from the key point prediction component of our network. Finally, the whole network can produce a set of points on a road as well as their connections with a holistic scheme.

This paper introduces a novel holistic graph construction method using neural networks. We highlight the key novelties of our work below:

- We propose a new road network extraction framework, TD-Road, which regards road network extraction as key point prediction and connectedness prediction subtasks. Our model learns to generate a road graph end-to-end using graph supervision, as compared to intermediate information used to generate graphs in previous graph-based methods. Our method is extremely simple that it outputs a graph structure without any further post-processing.
- We introduce relation inference into road network extraction, which shows appealing capability to model the relations between different locations of a map. In our work, we leverage a relation reasoning module to learn the connectedness between two points on a road. Further, we propose a neighbor-guided relation reasoning module to boost our framework.
- Extensive experiments and comparisons show the effectiveness and advantages of our new scheme for road extraction. We demonstrate that the proposed method localizes crucial graph nodes precisely and performs better in dealing with ambiguous regions.

2 Related Work

2.1 Road Network Extraction

Graph-Based Approaches: As an early study of graph-based model, Road-Tracer [1] formulates road network extraction as a graph growing procedure, which starts from initial seeds and extracts roads iteratively by predicting the orientations to extend the graph. Further, VecRoad [23] aims to overcome the imprecise graph exploration with a fixed step size, and boost the iterative graph construction by using a flexible step size and segmentation cues. Besides, These graph-growing approaches also suffer from inefficiencies since they need to feed-forward an image patch to CNN to obtain the orientations in each step. To overcome the low-efficiency of single prediction, Sat2Graph [10] represents the graph as tensor coding, which encodes the key points and orientations at the same time with a dense prediction network, which directly produces the prediction over a large area. Besides, Sat2Graph shows inspiring results in handling ambiguous regions, such as multiple parallel roads and challenging highways with bridge interactions at different layers. Further, graph convolution networks have been exploited in similar tasks to learn the attribute for each road segments [13] or locations [11].

Segmentation-Based Approaches: In addition to graph-based methods, other approaches consider the road extraction as a segmentation task to output road masks. These methods can model global context, but find it hard to represent complex structures well using a simple road mask. Many previous works focus on designing network architectures for road segmentation [6,9,16,20,24,28], which can capture long and narrow shapes, as well as large variances of layout structures. In particular, DlinkNet [28] is a successful architecture designed for road segmentation, which leverages skip connection over different stages and dilated convolutions in the bottleneck. Deep layer aggregation has also been shown to be an effective architecture for this task [10]. To improve connectivity, joint orientation learning [2] has been combined with segmentation, and orientations are demonstrated as a crucial clue for road segmentation.

Observing the prior work, orientation is important and exploited by most methods, either graph-based or segmentation-based approaches. However, very few works directly models the connections between adjacent locations. Besides, graph-based methods still require a post-processing step to convert the outputs of networks into graphs, based on the orientations or moves for the next points. Different from others [1,10,23], our network can output a graph structure in a holistic way and allows optimization using graph structures (i.e., nodes and edges) directly.

2.2   Relation Network

Relation network is a neural network component, aiming to infer the relationship among multiple instances, which could be objects [19], images [7,21] etc. For example, it is proposed to answer complex questions regarding multiple objects in visual question answering [19]. By incorporating a relation reasoning module, it is able to answer more complicated questions, for example "What is the color of the object behind the blue cube?". Relation network is also utilized to learn the similarity scores between images for few-shot learning [22], which shows strong capability to learn complex manifolds. Besides, relation inference has been employed in object detection for learning non-maximum suppression [12], which picks the best bounding box from all the region proposals and allows for training end-to-end, integrated with other components of object detection.

Inspired by relation reasoning in prior work, we design a new model for road network extraction by representing roads as graphs. Differently, we learn pixelwise and pairwise relations from a dense feature map, for constructing graph structures from image inputs. As far as we know, there is no previous work on road network extraction modeling the relation between different locations of a map and output a road network graph directly from a network.

3   A Holistic Model for Direct Graph Construction

3.1   Overview

We depict our model for holistic road graph construction from satellite images. Our approach leverages graphs to supervise the training of our network. We decompose the graph construction into two sub-tasks: **key point prediction** and **connectedness prediction** between key points. Figure 2 draws the

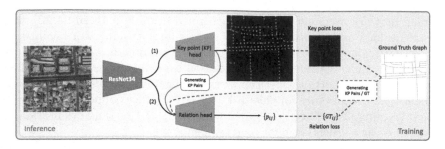

Fig. 2. Overview of TD-Road model. The model outputs a set of key points as well as their connections as the extracted road graph. Our network has two branches, consisting of key point prediction and relation reasoning over key points. For each key point, the relation reasoning module computes the probabilities between each key point and its neighboring pairs, which takes a dense feature map and neighbor information of key points as inputs. In training, the ground truth graph provides the pairs regarding the connectedness between key points. In inference, our network uses the predicted key points and corresponding generated neighbors to perform relation reasoning, and then at the end outputs a road graph.

overview of our model, and we discuss the details of the two components as follows. Particularly, we highlight that our graph generation is trained end-to-end from input satellite imagery to generated graphs. To build our model, ResNet is applied as our backbone to extract dense features and different heads for individual sub-tasks are designed. First, the key point prediction head outputs a 2-d heatmap indicating the location of key points of roads, which can be trained using a segmentation-like loss and will be discussed with more details in Sect. 3.3. Second, we generate key point pairs if two points are close enough, and classify each pair as connected or not based on our relation reasoning module, as followed in Sect. 3.2. In model training, we create positive/negative pairs using the key point locations as well as their connectedness from ground truth graphs. In inference, we first run the key point branch and apply the outputs from key point prediction as the inputs of relation branch to predict the connectedness between predicted key points.

3.2   Relation Reasoning for Graph Edges

As the main contribution of this work, we first introduce our relation reasoning module for connecting key points and constructing a graph. To build a relation reasoning module for establishing edges between graph nodes, we create a separate decoder with a shared encoder to key point prediction, as illustrated in Fig. 2. The decoder first outputs a dense feature, and feature extraction of key points over the dense features is processed for classifying the key point pair. Let $F_R \in \mathbf{R}^{C \times H_0 \times W_0} = \mathbf{\Theta}(\mathbf{E}(I))$ be the output of a decoder $\mathbf{\Theta}$ followed with a feature extractor $\mathbf{E}$ performed on the input image I. $\{(x_i, y_i)\}_{i=1}^{K}$ are the predicted key points, and then our goal is to know if there is an edge between points (x_i, y_i) and (x_j, y_j).

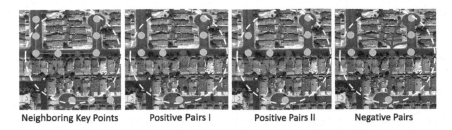

Neighboring Key Points   Positive Pairs I   Positive Pairs II   Negative Pairs

Fig. 3. Training examples for relation reasoning module. We perform binary classification for each pair between a candidate (blue) and its neighbors (orange). Positive pairs are regarded as the key point pairs, which are connected through a straight line. Otherwise, it will be regarded as negative pairs. (Color figure online)

Naive Relation Reasoning: To reach the above goal, we check the edges between a candidate point and all of its neighbors, relying on a distance threshold, as shown in Fig. 3. During training, graph annotation provides us the correct edges, therefore, we know the connectedness of each key point pair. And thus we can easily build a binary classifier to predict the connectedness between two key points. Specifically, we consider all the neighbors of a candidate point as potential connections, and assign labels to them. Clearly, a direct edge between two points is a valid positive example, as shown in the second plot of Fig. 3. Further, even two points are not directly connected, but they are routable in the same direction through the intermediate connecting point, we also consider this is a positive pair, as shown in the third plot of Fig. 3. Last, the negative pairs are the points not traversed, or not in a same direction, as shown in the last plot of Fig. 3 (Fig. 4).

To learn the relation between two points, we extract pixelwise features from F_R at the locations (x_i, y_i) and (x_j, y_j). Since the feature map might be in a low resolution format, we apply bilinear interpolation operations to extract features, where the operations are differentiable, resulting in features $F_i^* = \text{Interpolation}(F_R, x_i, y_i)$ and $F_j^* = \text{Interpolation}(F_R, x_j, y_j)$. And then, we apply a linear projection on the concatenation of F_i^* and F_j^* (i.e., $\text{Cat}(F_i^*, F_j^*)$)to produce the connectedness score. To augment the training and boost the inference, we

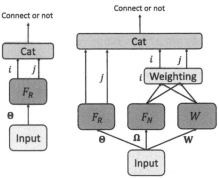

Fig. 4. Illustration of the naive relation reasoning module (left) and the neighbor-enhanced relation module (right).

predict the probability by switching the order of two points. Finally, the probability to establish the edge can be calculated as

$$P = (\text{Linear}(2C, 1)(\text{Cat}(F_i^*, F_j^*)) + \text{Linear}(2C, 1)(\text{Cat}(F_j^*, F_i^*)))/2, \quad (1)$$

and the model parameters Θ, $\mathbf{E}$ and the above linear classifier can be learned by using binary cross entropy loss, which is denoted as $\mathcal{L}_R$ for the relation module.

Neighbor-Enhanced Relation Reasoning: Observing the relation module mentioned above, we realize that feature extractions for the key points are separately accomplished. Hence, it fails to model context information in relation reasoning. Accordingly, it is interesting to know if contexts, in particular other key points, help relation reasoning and determining connectedness. To aggregate the context information over key points, we learn additional projection Ω and weighting function $\mathbf{W}$, outputting features of C and 1 channels, respectively. Therefore, we project the feature map from the encoder and obtain $F_N = \Omega(\mathbf{E}(I))$ and $W = \mathbf{W}(\mathbf{E}(I))$, where $F_N \in \mathbf{R}^{C \times H_0 \times W_0}$ and $W \in \mathbf{R}^{H_0 \times W_0}$. The context of neighbors for a key point at (x_i, y_i) can be weighted by F_N and W, which is formulated as

$$\hat{F}_i = \frac{\sum_{(x_j, y_j) \in S_{x_i, y_i}} F_N(:, x_j, y_j) * W(x_j, y_j)}{\sum_{(x_j, y_j) \in S_{x_i, y_i}} W(x_j, y_j)}, \tag{2}$$

where S_{x_i, y_i} are the locations which are the neighbors of the point at (x_i, y_i). Similar to Eq.(1), the final prediction can be computed by concatenating them: $P = (\text{Linear}(4C, 1)(\text{Cat}(F_i^*, F_j^*, \hat{F}_i, \hat{F}_j)) + \text{Linear}(4C, 1)(\text{Cat}(F_j^*, F_i^*, \hat{F}_j, \hat{F}_i)))/2$.

3.3   Key Point Prediction for Graph Nodes

To predict the locations of key points, we create a dense prediction model based on an encoder-decoder architecture and carefully design a suitable loss based on road mask and key points. In the following, we present our decoder used in this work, which is inspired by deep layer aggregation architectures [27] and All-MLP decoder [26].

DLA-MLP Decoder as Task Heads: Key point prediction is a task focusing on local information and semantics. Key points usually appear in the junction areas or abrupt blending locations and interpolated locations between others. Therefore, propagating very wide context is likely unreasonable for this task, therefore, we present a simple decoder based on Multi-Layer Perceptron (MLP) which performs prediction over individual pixels. Since the encoder already compresses long range context information into feature maps, we do not aggregate further contextual semantics in the decoder. Further, recent state-of-the-art segmentation model [26] shows that competitive results with MLP decoder can be achieved when encoder is able to capture representative features, which further motivates us to design our decoder with MLP to infer individual road key points.

Deep layer aggregation (DLA) [27] is a network scheme, which summarizes CNN features across layers and augments a base model to model what and where better. With fewer parameters, it shows better accuracy with iterative and hierarchical feature fusion, compared to skip connections with concatenation. In this work, we present our MLP-based decoder with DLA to effectively aggregate low-level localizable features as well as high-level contextual semantics.

By combining MLP decoder [26] and DLA architectures [27], our DLA-MLP decoder fuses the hierarchical features gradually with MLP components. Let $\{F_{i,0}\}_{i=1}^{N}$ be the multiscale hierarchical features from the encoder, where we have N stages in total. For each feature map $F_{i,0}$, it has a size of $C_i \times H_i \times W_i$. Formally, we formulate the steps of our DLA-MLP decoder with C embedding dimensions, and the decoder outputs a feature map with size of $C \times H_0 \times W_0$ as follows.

$$F_{i,j}' = \text{Linear}(C_{i,j}, C)(F_{i,j}), \tag{3}$$

$$F_{i,j}' = \text{Upsampling}(H_{i-1}, W_{i-1})(F_{i,j}'), \tag{4}$$

$$F_{i,j+1} = \text{Linear}(C_{i-1,j} + C, C)(\text{Cat}(F_{i-1,j}, F_{i,j}')), \tag{5}$$

where $j = [0, ..., N-2]$, $i = [N-j-1, ..., N]$, and finally a feature map $F_{N,N-1} \in \mathbf{R}^{C \times H_0 \times W_0}$ is obtained as the fused representation. And then we apply a 1×1 convolution to project the representations to a heatmap of one channel for key point prediction. Furthermore, we apply our DLA-MLP decoder as a component (Ω in Sect. 3.2) of our relation head to aggregate features similarly, in addition to key point prediction. In this work, we apply the same embedding dimension for key point prediction and relation reasoning module with $C = 128$.

3.4   Loss Function

As a binary classification problem, key point prediction can be also trained using binary cross entropy (BCE) loss. However, it needs to address the extreme imbalanced training example for key points. When vanilla BCE loss is applied, we observe poor results in that very few key points are detected and the performance of our overall model is restricted.

The reasons are two aspects. First, the background non-road pixels are a lot, therefore, the training is likely dominated by the negative pixels. Second, the key point ground truths are conceptually contradictory, in that many road pixels are labeled negative, even though they share similar visual patterns with the positively labeled pixels, such as colors, shapes, contexts, etc.

Since our approach relies on the key points to construct a graph, we need to deal with the challenges mentioned

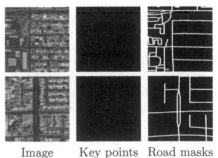

Image   Key points   Road masks

Fig. 5. Ground truth examples in computing loss function. We leverage road mask to help more effective key point prediction.

above. In this work, we weight the different pixels for key point predictions, based on BCE loss. We consider there are three types of pixels: key point pixels; road pixels but not key points; background pixels. Specifically, we set different loss weights for those pixels. Formally, given the ground truth label y_t for key points and prediction p_t over location t, our road mask driven BCE loss for key point prediction can be computed by

$$\mathcal{L}_{KP} = -\sum_t w_t \cdot (y_t \cdot \log(p_t) + (1 - y_t) \cdot \log(1 - p_t)), \qquad (6)$$

where $w_t \in \{w_{kp}, w_r, w_b\}$ are the loss weights for individual pixels depending on their types, where Fig. 5 shows an example of ground truth used for loss function computation.

Regularization: To further exploit the road information, we learn an additional decoder to predict binary road masks and orientations of neighboring key points, which are widely adopted in prior work for road extraction. In our work, we highlight that our approach does not reply to segmentation masks or orientations to construct our road graph, but we still observe this information is useful and compatible with our framework. Therefore, we regard this additional task as a regularization term $\mathcal{L}_{reg}$ to train our full model.

Finally, the loss for overall system is in a combination between key point, relation and regularization heads:

$$\mathcal{L} = \mathcal{L}_{KP} + \mathcal{L}_R + \mathcal{L}_{reg}. \qquad (7)$$

Our method is embarrassingly simple in generating road graphs from satellite images using neural networks, that we only need two hyperparameters to filter incorrect key points and connections out. It is allowed to tune the thresholds to achieve higher precision or recall.

4 Experiments and Results

4.1 Datasets and Evaluation Settings

City-Scale: This dataset [10] provides satellite imagery focusing on 20 US cities. The dataset covers downtown areas with complex structures such as the overlaid highways and bridges. Each image has a resolution of 2048×2048, and every pixel corresponds to 1 m in the real world. Therefore, this is a challenging scenario, where multiple parallel roads or complicated structures appear in the images. In addition, the dataset also provides the key points used to train a graph-based model. We follow previous work [10] to use the same key points and connections to learn our model. Finally, we use 144 images to train our model, and evaluate different approaches on 27 examples.

SpaceNet: This dataset [25] contains 2780 satellite images. We follow the data split of [10] and experimental setup to resize the images to 1 m per pixel. This split contains 2040, 358, 382 examples for training, validation and testing. The dataset provides the ground truths in the format of line strings, indicating the center of roads. To train our method, we first convert the line strings into the graph format with key points (nodes) and connections (edges). In particular, we linearly interpolate the key points with 20 pixels in case the original connecting key points in the dataset are very far from each other.

Evaluation Metrics: First, we adopt the widely used APLS (i.e., average path length similarity), introduced by [25], to evaluate the performance of each model. The APLS metric computes the shortest path length between road network pairs, which captures the overall performance of extracted roads. Second, we report the TOPO scores [4] of precision (P), recall (R) and F1-score of extracted roads in topology. We utilize the implmentation of TOPO scores from [10] to compare our approach with others, which is very strict to penalize the details of extracted roads.

Comparison Methods: We compare our approach with previous popular methods and recent state-of-the-art models including graph-based model Road-Tracer [1], Sat2Graph [10] as well as segmentation-based model UNet [18], DlinkNet [28], DeepRoadTracer [17] and orientation-learning based method [2].

4.2 Implementation Details

In this work, all the models are trained with 1024×1024 cropped image patches for both datasets, and we use whole images to infer road networks. During training, we crop image patches at random locations and then apply flipping operations vertically and horizontally at 50% probability. Further, we rotate image/graph pairs in the range of $(-15°, 15°)$ and a photometric distortion [5] is leveraged including brightness, contrast, saturation changes of an image. Specifically, we implement our models using PyTorch and mmseg package [8], and train the model with 8 T V100 GPUs. AdamW [15] is applied to optimize the training, where initial learning rate is 1×10^{-3}, and betas is $(0.9, 0.999)$, and weight decay is 0.01. Further, we set the learning rate of key point prediction and relation inference heads as $10\times$ of the backbone. We use 1×10^{-6} to warm up the training with 200 iterations. Following many previous work [1,2,28], all of our models are implemented with ResNet-34 as the backbone, and the model weights are initialized using the ImageNet-1k pretrained representation. 30k and 150k training iterations are applied for *City-Scale* and *SpaceNet* datasets, and learning rates are adjusted using cosine-based schedulers. We set $\{w_{kp}, w_r, w_b\}$ as $\{200, 20, 1\}$ for key point prediction loss in both datasets.

4.3 Comparison Results

In Table 1 and Table 2, comparison results with other state-of-the-art methods are listed. From the tables, we observe the proposed graph-based road extraction method performs comparable with previous state-of-the-art method, Sat2Graph [10], whereas Sat2Graph adopt a stronger backbone DLA [27]. In Table 1, our best model obtains 65.74 APLS, which outperforms all the other methods. Further, our best model also obtains higher precision than other methods, which indicates the effectiveness of relation reasoning which builds connections properly. Regarding recall, the proposed model is slightly worse than

Table 1. Comparison results on *City-Scale* dataset.

Method	Backbone	Type	Topo			APLS
			P	R	F-1	
UNet [18]	CNN	Seg.	78.00	57.44	66.16	57.29
DeepRoadMapper [17]	ResNet-50		75.34	65.99	70.36	52.50
Orientation [2]	ResNet-34		75.83	68.90	72.20	55.34
DLinkNet [28]	ResNet-34		78.63	48.07	57.42	54.08
DLA [10,27]	DLA		75.59	72.26	73.89	57.22
RoadTracer [1]	CNN	Graph	78.00	57.44	66.16	57.29
Sat2Graph [10]	DLA		80.70	**72.28**	76.26	63.14
Ours (Naive)	ResNet-34		77.82	68.44	72.83	62.17
Ours (Neighbors)			**81.94**	71.63	**76.43**	**65.74**

DLA [27] and Sat2Graph [10], but clearly better than all the other segmentation-based methods and graph-growing-based method RoadTracer [1]. In particular, we notice that the segmentation-based method using DLA already provides 73.89 recall, which indicates the capability of DLA to detect more roads than ResNet-34 or similar architectures. Similar to *City-Scale*, we achieve more favorable results in *SpaceNet* when the same backbone is applied compared with other methods. We also highlight that our full model achieves competing results with previous state-of-the-art model Sat2Graph [10] with a DLA backbone.

Further, we also compare our models using different relation reasoning modules with other approaches. By using naive relation reasoning mentioned in Sec 3.2, our method already outperforms other segmentation-based methods in APLS and recall of TOPO evaluation. Obviously, we can see the effectiveness of incorporating neighbor information into each key points, that all the evaluation metrics are consistently improved by using neighbors-based relation reasoning in both datasets.

In addition to quantitative comparison, we also visualize the extracted roads from different approaches in Fig. 6. For the graph-based methods, we first convert the results of graph formats into binary road masks. From this plot, we would like to highlight several points. First, we clearly observe the advantages of our method over DLinkNet, which suffers from the connectivity issues in some areas with rich vegetation or low-contrast appearances, as shown in the 1^{-st}, 2^{-nd}, 5^{-th}, 6^{-th} rows of the plot. Second, comparing our method with Sat2Graph, we can see our method handles junctions better, because our method directly considers two key points are supposed to connect or not. However, Sat2Graph relies on the orientations between different key points, which are not accurate. And the heuristic post-processing might also introduce errors. In contrast, we link different key points by learning a binary classifier, which is a straightforward solution. Besides, our neighbors-based relation reasoning module can help to aggregate useful context information in constructing graph edges, and achieves more precise results than our naive reasoning.

Table 2. Comparison results on *SpaceNet* dataset.

Method	Backbone	Type	Topo			APLS
			P	R	F-1	
UNet [18]	CNN	Seg.	68.96	66.32	67.61	53.77
DeepRoadMapper [17]	ResNet-50		82.79	72.56	77.34	62.26
Orientation [2]	ResNet-34		81.56	71.38	76.13	58.82
DLinkNet [28]	ResNet-34		**88.42**	60.06	68.80	56.93
DLA [10, 27]	DLA		78.99	69.80	74.11	56.36
RoadTracer [1]	CNN	Graph	78.61	62.45	69.60	56.03
Sat2Graph [10]	DLA		85.93	76.55	80.97	64.43
Ours (Naive)	ResNet-34		82.45	73.54	77.74	60.91
Ours (Neighbors)			84.81	**77.80**	**81.15**	**65.15**

Table 3. Comparison results on *City-Scale* dataset in association with different loss functions for key point prediction.

Loss	Topo			APLS
	P	R	F-1	
BCE	75.71	68.81	71.89	60.32
Focal [14]	80.82	62.16	69.79	47.95
Ours	77.82	68.44	72.54	62.17

4.4   Ablation Studies and Analysis

How Important is the Loss Function for Key Point Prediction? Key point prediction plays an important role, which provides inputs to the relation reason module. Hence, we show the results of using different loss function for key point prediction. To avoid the negative impact of imbalanced pixels, focal loss [14] is another option. Therefore, we compare our road mask weighting strategy with standard BCE loss and focal loss. For BCE loss, we set loss weight for positive and negative examples are 100 and 2. For focal loss, we set the loss weights as 100 and 5, we set γ in focal loss as 1. In Table 3, we list the comparison results on *City-Scale* dataset, which is trained using naive relation module. From this table, it is apparent that mask-driven loss is beneficial to reach higher performance, owing to the more accurate key point localization. Even though focal loss is widely used in handling imbalanced data distribution, we cannot observe a successful application in our case. We can see focal loss achieves 80.82 precision, but performs not so well in road coverages and capturing road structures, that recall and APLS are significantly worse than other losses.

Further, we show an example of predicted key points from standard BCE loss and our version in Fig. 7. From this figure, we can see standard BCE and our version capture similar structures of roads, and both loss functions help isolate key points successfully, which are not very close to other points. However, our version can distinguish the key points better when many of them fall into a small region. as highlighted by the red bounding box in Fig. 7.

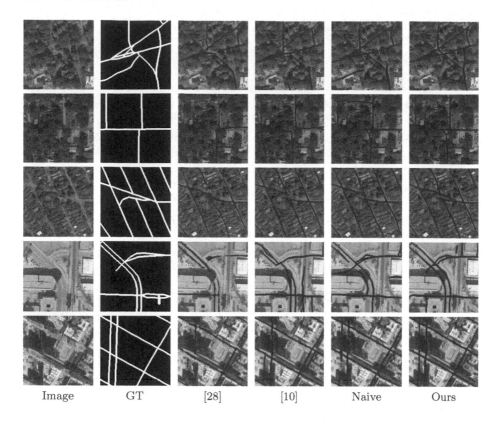

Image   GT   [28]   [10]   Naive   Ours

Fig. 6. Qualitative results on the extracted roads in *City-Scale* dataset. We compare our models with naive and neighbors-based relation reasoning modules with DLinkNet [28] and Sat2Graph [10].

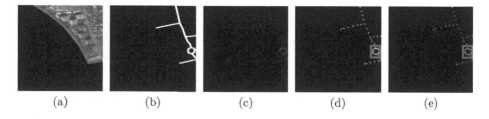

(a)   (b)   (c)   (d)   (e)

Fig. 7. Example of key point prediction using different losses. (a) Image. (b) Mask for the loss. (c) Key point GT. (d) Prediction w/o mask-based loss. (e) Prediction with our mask-driven loss.

Is the Model Sensitive to the Thresholds for Determining Graph Nodes and Edges? We perform road extraction by using different thresholds for key point prediction and connectedness prediction, varying from 0.3 to 0.5 with step 0.1. Figure 8 shows the results by fixing each threshold and changing another. From this figure, we can see the model is less sensitive to the

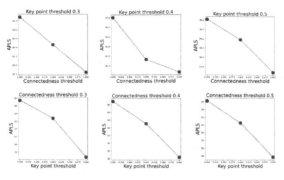

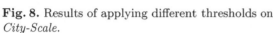

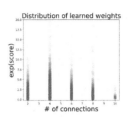

Fig. 8. Results of applying different thresholds on *City-Scale.*

Fig. 9. Scatter plot of learned weights in neighbors-based relation reasoning module.

connectedness prediction. In other words, it gives us similar predictions once a relation reasoning module is learned. In contrast, the key point prediction is crucial in providing an initial point set for the relation module, and drastically affects the performance, which sheds the light for future directions, that we need to improve the key point prediction with a stronger encoder and specific decoder for key points.

What does the Neighbors-Based Relation Learn? In our neighbor-enhanced relation reasoning module, we learn to weight individual key points. To understand the learned relation, we show the statistics about the key points on *City-Scale.* In Fig. 9, the x-axis shows the number of connections for key points. For example, a point with 4 connections is a junction and the one with 2 connections is a common key point. From this plot, we can see the weights for 4 connections are larger than others, therefore, the information from junctions could be propagated to other locations and affect the relation reasoning more than other points. In contrast, the naive relation reasoning cannot leverage junction information to determine connectedness, and obtain less accurate results.

5   Conclusions

In this paper, we present TD-Road, a simple-yet-novel graph-based method for road network extraction. Different from most previous work, we directly learn and emit graph structures with neural networks, instead of producing intermediate representations such as orientations, next moves, etc. Our method is extremely simple, in that we regard the graph generation as key point prediction and connectedness learning problems. By integrating a pixel-level relation module into a dense prediction network, our approach is able to produce graph structures in a holistic way. We also present an effective relation reasoning module with neighbors for each detected key point, and the overall model achieves more favorable results than other methods using the same network backbone.

Acknowledgment. The authors sincerely thank Dr. Songtao He for providing the ground truth of SpaceNet3 dataset used in [10].

References

1. Bastani, F., et al.: Roadtracer: automatic extraction of road networks from aerial images. In: 2018 IEEE/CVF Conference on Computer Vision and Pattern Recognition, pp. 4720–4728 (2018). https://doi.org/10.1109/CVPR.2018.00496
2. Batra, A., Singh, S., Pang, G., Basu, S., Jawahar, C., Paluri, M.: Improved road connectivity by joint learning of orientation and segmentation. In: Proceedings of the IEEE/CVF Conference on Computer Vision and Pattern Recognition (2019)
3. Belli, D., Kipf, T.: Image-conditioned graph generation for road network extraction. arXiv preprint arXiv:1910.14388 (2019)
4. Biagioni, J., Eriksson, J.: Inferring road maps from global positioning system traces: survey and comparative evaluation. Transp. Res. Rec. **2291**, 61–71 (2012)
5. Bochkovskiy, A., Wang, C.Y., Liao, H.Y.M.: Yolov4: optimal speed and accuracy of object detection. arXiv preprint arXiv:2004.10934 (2020)
6. Chaurasia, A., Culurciello, E.: Linknet: exploiting encoder representations for efficient semantic segmentation. In: 2017 IEEE Visual Communications and Image Processing (VCIP), pp. 1–4. IEEE (2017)
7. Chen, N., Zhou, Q.Y., Prasanna, V.: Understanding web images by object relation network. In: Proceedings of the 21st International Conference on World Wide Web, pp. 291–300 (2012)
8. Contributors, M.: MMSegmentation: openmmlab semantic segmentation toolbox and benchmark (2020). https://github.com/open-mmlab/mmsegmentation
9. Ding, L., Bruzzone, L.: Diresnet: direction-aware residual network for road extraction in VHR remote sensing images. IEEE Trans. Geosci. Remote Sens. **59**, 10243–10254 (2020)
10. He, S., et al.: Sat2Graph: road graph extraction through graph-tensor encoding. In: Vedaldi, A., Bischof, H., Brox, T., Frahm, J.-M. (eds.) ECCV 2020. LNCS, vol. 12369, pp. 51–67. Springer, Cham (2020). https://doi.org/10.1007/978-3-030-58586-0_4
11. He, S., et al.: Roadtagger: robust road attribute inference with graph neural networks. In: AAAI (2020)
12. Hosang, J., Benenson, R., Schiele, B.: Learning non-maximum suppression. In: CVPR (2017)
13. Jepsen, T.S., Jensen, C.S., Nielsen, T.D.: Graph convolutional networks for road networks. In: ACM SIGSPATIAL (2019)
14. Lin, T.Y., Goyal, P., Girshick, R., He, K., Dollár, P.: Focal loss for dense object detection. In: Proceedings of the IEEE International Conference on Computer Vision, pp. 2980–2988 (2017)
15. Loshchilov, I., Hutter, F.: Decoupled weight decay regularization. In: International Conference on Learning Representations (2018)
16. Lu, X., Zhong, Y., Zhao, J.: Multi-scale enhanced deep network for road detection. In: IGARSS 2019–2019 IEEE International Geoscience and Remote Sensing Symposium (2019)
17. Máttyus, G., Luo, W., Urtasun, R.: Deeproadmapper: extracting road topology from aerial images. In: Proceedings of the IEEE International Conference on Computer Vision (2017)

18. Ronneberger, O., Fischer, P., Brox, T.: U-Net: convolutional networks for biomedical image segmentation. In: Navab, N., Hornegger, J., Wells, W.M., Frangi, A.F. (eds.) MICCAI 2015. LNCS, vol. 9351, pp. 234–241. Springer, Cham (2015). https://doi.org/10.1007/978-3-319-24574-4_28
19. Santoro, A., et al.: A simple neural network module for relational reasoning. Adv. Neural Inf. Process. Syst. (2017)
20. Shamsolmoali, P., Zareapoor, M., Zhou, H., Wang, R., Yang, J.: Road segmentation for remote sensing images using adversarial spatial pyramid networks. IEEE Trans. Geosci. Remote Sens. **59**, 4673–4688 (2020)
21. Sun, C., Shrivastava, A., Vondrick, C., Murphy, K., Sukthankar, R., Schmid, C.: Actor-centric relation network. In: Proceedings of the European Actor-Centric Relation Network Conference on Computer Vision (ECCV), pp. 318–334 (2018)
22. Sung, F., Yang, Y., Zhang, L., Xiang, T., Torr, P.H., Hospedales, T.M.: Learning to compare: relation network for few-shot learning. In: CVPR (2018)
23. Tan, Y.Q., Gao, S.H., Li, X.Y., Cheng, M.M., Ren, B.: Vecroad: point-based iterative graph exploration for road graphs extraction. In: Proceedings of the IEEE/CVF Conference on Computer Vision and Pattern Recognition (2020)
24. Tao, C., Qi, J., Li, Y., Wang, H., Li, H.: Spatial information inference net: road extraction using road-specific contextual information. ISPRS J. Photogram. Remote Sens. **158**, 155–166 (2019)
25. Van Etten, A., Lindenbaum, D., Bacastow, T.M.: Spacenet: a remote sensing dataset and challenge series. arXiv preprint arXiv:1807.01232 (2018)
26. Xie, E., Wang, W., Yu, Z., Anandkumar, A., Alvarez, J.M., Luo, P.: Segformer: simple and efficient design for semantic segmentation with transformers. Adv. Neural Inf. Process. Syst. **34**, 12077–12090 (2021)
27. Yu, F., Wang, D., Shelhamer, E., Darrell, T.: Deep layer aggregation. In: CVPR (2018)
28. Zhou, L., Zhang, C., Wu, M.: D-linknet: linknet with pretrained encoder and dilated convolution for high resolution satellite imagery road extraction. In: Proceedings of the IEEE Conference on Computer Vision and Pattern Recognition (CVPR) Workshops (2018)

Multi-faceted Distillation of Base-Novel Commonality for Few-Shot Object Detection

Shuang Wu[2], Wenjie Pei[2(✉)], Dianwen Mei[2], Fanglin Chen[2], Jiandong Tian[3], and Guangming Lu[1,2(✉)]

[1] Guangdong Provincial Key Laboratory of Novel Security Intelligence Technologies, Shenzhen, China
[2] Harbin Institute of Technology, Shenzhen, China
wenjiecoder@outlook.com, luguangm@hit.edu.cn
[3] Shenyang Institute of Automation, Chinese Academy of Sciences, Shenyang, China
tianjd@sia.cn

Abstract. Most of existing methods for few-shot object detection follow the fine-tuning paradigm, which potentially assumes that the class-agnostic generalizable knowledge can be learned and transferred implicitly from base classes with abundant samples to novel classes with limited samples via such a two-stage training strategy. However, it is not necessarily true since the object detector can hardly distinguish between class-agnostic knowledge and class-specific knowledge automatically without explicit modeling. In this work we propose to learn three types of class-agnostic commonalities between base and novel classes explicitly: recognition-related semantic commonalities, localization-related semantic commonalities and distribution commonalities. We design a unified distillation framework based on a memory bank, which is able to perform distillation of all three types of commonalities jointly and efficiently. Extensive experiments demonstrate that our method can be readily integrated into most of existing fine-tuning based methods and consistently improve the performance by a large margin.

Keywords: Few-shot · Object detection · Knowledge distillation · Commonality

1 Introduction

Few-shot object detection aims to learn effective object detectors for novel classes with limited samples, leveraging the generalizable prior knowledge learned from abundant data of base classes. Compared to general object detection [8,27], few-shot object detection is supposed to be able to generalize across different classes rather than just across different samples within a class. It is also more

Supplementary Information The online version contains supplementary material available at https://doi.org/10.1007/978-3-031-20077-9_34.

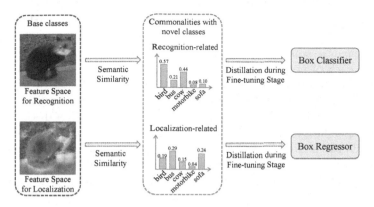

Fig. 1. Given a cat sample from the base class 'Cat', we measure the semantic similarities between it and each of novel classes in the optimized feature space for both object recognition and localization, which are interpreted as the recognition- and localization-related semantic commonalities, respectively. These learned commonalities are distilled during the fine-tuning stage to improve the performance of the object detector on novel classes. Note that the visualizations by Grad-CAM++ [2] show that the learned features for recognition focus on the local salient regions while the localization pays more attention to the global boundary or shape features.

challenging than few-shot classification [7,31,34] in that it demands to learn the transferable knowledge not only on recognition, but also on localization.

A prominent modeling paradigm for few-shot object detection is fine-tuning framework [6,26,32,35,40], which first pre-trains the object detector using the samples from base classes, then fine-tunes the model on novel classes. Based on such two-stage training strategy, many methods are proposed to deal with a specific challenge in few-shot object detection, such as MPSR [40] which tackles the problem of scale variation, FSCE [32] for alleviating confusion between novel classes, and Retentive R-CNN [6] suppressing the performance degradation on base classes during fine-tuning. A potential hypothesis of such fine-tuning paradigm is that the class-agnostic prior knowledge for object detection could be transferred from base classes to novel classes implicitly. Nevertheless, the object detector can hardly distinguish between class-agnostic knowledge and class-specific knowledge automatically without explicit modeling.

In this work we propose to learn multi-faceted commonalities between base classes and novel classes explicitly in the fine-tuning framework, which is class-agnostic and can be transferred across different classes. Then we perform distillation on the learned commonalities to circumvent the scarcity of novel classes and thereby improve the performance of the object detector on novel classes. To be specific, we aim to learn three types of base-novel commonalities: 1) the recognition-related semantic commonalities like similar appearance features shared among semantically close classes; 2) the localization-related semantic commonalities such as the similar object shape or boundary features between different classes; 3) the distribution commonalities in feature space shared between similar classes like close mean and variance of features in a presumed Gaussian distribution [30]. Consider the example in Fig. 1, we first learn the optimized feature spaces for object recognition and localization respectively. Then we measure the semantic similarities between a given cat sample (from the base class 'Cat') and each of novel classes in each feature space. The obtained similarity distribution in the feature space for recognition is interpreted as the recognition-related semantic commonalities, and the same applies to the localization-related semantic commonalities. The learned commonalities are further distilled towards their corresponding tasks respectively during fine-tuning of the object detector on novel classes, namely recognition-related commonalities for object classification and localization-related commonalities for object bounding box regression. Consequently, all samples in base classes that share commonalities with a novel class can be leveraged to train the object detector on this novel class, which is equivalent to augment the training data for novel classes. Note that the learned features for recognition and localization focus on different object areas: the recognition captures the local salient regions (e.g., the head of cat in Fig. 1) whilst the localization pays more attention to the global boundaries as shown in Fig. 1. Thus we decouple the feature spaces for object recognition and localization and learn the corresponding commonalities in the decoupled feature spaces separately. Inspired by Distribution Calibration [45], we learn the distribution commonalities by estimating the feature variance for a novel class via reference to the closed base classes, and distill the obtained commonalities by sampling for data augmentation. To conclude, we make following contributions.

- We learn three types of generalizable commonalities between base and novel classes explicitly, which can be transferred from base classes to novel classes.
- We design a unified distillation framework based on a memory bank, which is able to distill all three types of learned commonalities jointly and efficiently in an end-to-end manner during the fine-tuning stage.
- Our method can be integrated into most of fine-tuning based methods. Extensive experiments show that our method leads to substantial improvements when integrated into various classical methods. As a result, our method advances the state-of-the-art performance by a large margin.

2   Related Work

Few-Shot Image Classification. Few-shot image classification, which aims to recognize novel categories with limited annotated instances, has received increased attention in the recent past. Optimization-based approaches [7,20,24] modify the classical gradient-based optimization for fast adaption to new tasks. Metric-based approaches [31,33,34,48] learn a metric space where instances could be recognized by comparing the distance to the prototype of each category. Hallucination-based approaches [11,36,45] learn to generate novel samples to deal with data scarcity. Compared to image classification, few-shot object detection which has to consider localization in addition, is still under-explored.

Few-Shot Object Detection. Early works of few-shot object detection focus on the meta-learning paradigm [5,10,15,16,21,22,37,42,44,50], which introduces a meta-learner to leverage meta-level knowledge that can be transferred from base classes to novel classes. Recently, researchers find out that the simple fine-tuning based approaches [1,6,23,26,32,35,38–40,51,52] could outperform most of meta-learning based approaches. TFA [35] proposes a two-stage fine-tuning process that only fine-tunes the prediction layer. FSCE [32] rescues misclassifications between novel classes by supervised contrastive learning. UP-FSOD [38] devises universal prototypes to enhance the generalization of object features. Retentive R-CNN [6] regularizes the adaptation during fine-tuning to maintain the performance on base classes. DeFRCN [26] proposes to decouple the features for RPN and R-CNN. All these methods learn to detect novel instances by implicitly exploiting the class-agnostic knowledge learned from base classes. Instead, we address few-shot object detection by distilling the multi-faceted commonalities between base classes and novel classes.

Knowledge Distillation. Classical knowledge distillation aims at transferring knowledge from a model (teacher) to the other (student). [14] introduces the soft prediction of the teacher network as dark knowledge for distillation. [28] leverages the intermediate representations learned by teacher to guide student. [19] proposes to transfer attention information of teacher. Several works [9,18, 43,47,49] use the student itself as a teacher, named self-distillation. Inspired by these works, we design a novel distillation framework to distill commonalities between base classes and novel classes based on a memory bank.

3 Multi-faceted Distillation of Base-Novel Commonality

In this section, we start with the preliminary of few-shot object detection, then we introduce our method which distills the multi-faceted base-novel commonalities to circumvent the scarcity of training samples in few-shot object detection.

3.1 Preliminary

We follow the standard few-shot object detection settings introduced in [16, 35] and split classes into two sets: base classes C_b with abundant annotated instances, and novel classes C_n with only K (usually less than 30) instances per category. Our proposed method involves the two-stage training procedure [35]. In the first stage, the Faster R-CNN [27] detector is trained with all the available samples of base classes. In the second stage, the pre-trained detector is fine-tuned on samples of both base and novel classes.

Different from existing works [6,26,32,35,40] that create a small balanced training set with K novel samples and K base samples in the second stage, we fine-tune the detector with abundant samples of base classes which are used in the first stage (the training details are described in the supplementary materials). Thus, we are able to distill the multi-faceted commonalities that can be transferred from abundant samples of base classes to limited samples of novel classes to circumvent the data scarcity. Specifically, we distill three types of base-novel commonalities to learn robust detector for novel classes, including 1) the

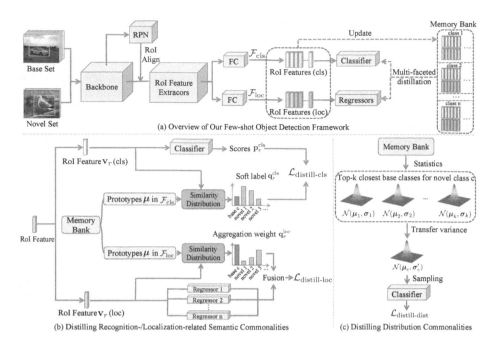

Fig. 2. The framework of our approach. (a) The RoI features are decoupled into two separate feature spaces for classification $\mathcal{F}_{\text{cls}}$ and bounding box regression $\mathcal{F}_{\text{loc}}$, respectively. During the fine-tuning stage, the recognition-related and distribution commonalities are learned in $\mathcal{F}_{\text{cls}}$ while the localization-related commonalities are learned in $\mathcal{F}_{\text{loc}}$. All three types of commonalities are distilled in a unified framework based on a memory bank. (b) The recognition-related commonalities are distilled by viewing them as the soft labels to supervise the classifier whereas the localization-related commonalities are used as aggregation weights to fuse all regressors. (c) We distill the variance for a novel class via reference to the top-k closest base classes, and sample examples from the calibrated distribution to train the classifier.

recognition-related semantic commonalities 2) the localization-related semantic commonalities, and 3) the distribution commonalities. Figure 2 illustrates the overall framework of our method.

3.2   Distilling Recognition-Related Semantic Commonalities

Semantically close categories tend to share similar high-level semantic commonalities that is related to object recognition, such as similar appearance between cow and horse. We aim to distill such semantic commonalities between base and novel classes to guide the learning of the object detector on novel classes.

Classical knowledge distillation [14] transfers knowledge from a larger teacher model to a student model. The transferred knowledge is represented as the predicted probabilistic distribution on all classes by the teacher model, which can be interpreted as the similarities of current sample to each class. The knowledge distillation is performed by using such probabilistic distribution as the soft labels to supervise the learning of the model together with the one-hot hard labels.

We draw inspiration from such classical way of knowledge distillation but conduct distillation in a different way. To distill the recognition-related semantic commonalities between base and novel classes, we measure the similarities of samples in base classes to each novel class. Since there is no sufficient samples from novel classes for learning a teacher model, we calculate such similarities in a pre-learned feature space $\mathcal{F}_{cls}$ directly instead of predicting class probabilities by a teacher model. Formally, given a foreground region proposal r from a base class, which is generated by the region proposal network (RPN), we define the similarity of it to a novel class c as the cosine distance between its RoI feature $\mathbf{v}_r$ and the prototype $\boldsymbol{\mu}_c$ of the class c in the pre-learned feature space $\mathcal{F}_{cls}$:

$$d_r^c = \alpha \cdot \frac{\mathbf{v}_r^T \boldsymbol{\mu}_c}{\|\mathbf{v}_r\| \|\boldsymbol{\mu}_c\|}, c \in \mathcal{C}_n. \tag{1}$$

Herein, $\mathcal{C}_n$ is the set of novel classes and $\alpha > 0$ is the scaling factor. The prototype $\boldsymbol{\mu}_c$ is obtained by averaging the object features of a candidate set (implemented as a memory bank, will be elaborated on in Sect. 3.5) in the novel class c:

$$\boldsymbol{\mu}_c = \frac{1}{n_c} \sum_{i=1}^{n_c} \mathbf{f}_c^i, \tag{2}$$

where $\mathbf{f}_c^i$ is the vectorial feature for the i-th object in the candidate set and n_c is size of the set. Since we focus on distilling the base-novel commonalities to circumvent the scarcity of training samples in novel classes, the base-base commonalities are ignored to allocate all model capacity to base-novel commonalities. As a result, the similarities of a region proposal r from a base class to other base classes are defined as a small constant value:

$$d_r^c = -\alpha, c \in \mathcal{C}_b \setminus \{c_{gt}\}, \tag{3}$$

where $\mathcal{C}_b$ denotes the set of base classes and α is the same scaling factor as in Eq. 1. Note that we also calculate the cosine similarity between r and its groundtruth class c_{gt} following Eq. 1 to guarantee the predicting accuracy (w.r.t. c_{gt}). Finally we normalize the similarities of sample r to all classes by a softmax function:

$$q_{r,c}^{cls} = \frac{\exp(d_r^c)}{\sum_{i=1}^{C} \exp(d_r^i)}, c \in \mathcal{C}_n \cup \mathcal{C}_b. \tag{4}$$

Assuming that a foreground region proposal r has 0 commonality with background c_{bg}, we obtain the complete similarity distribution for r: $\mathbf{q}_r^{cls} = [\mathbf{q}_r^{cls}; 0]$.

Similar to the classical knowledge distillation, we utilize the obtained similarities of a region proposal as soft labels to supervise the learning of our object detector. In particular, we perform such distillation during the fine-tuning stage of the detector. Formally, for the region proposal r from a base class, we minimize the Kullback-Leibler (KL) divergence between the soft labels $\mathbf{q}_r^{cls}$ and the predicted class probabilities $\mathbf{p}_r^{cls}$ by the object detector:

$$\mathcal{L}_{distill\text{-}cls} = \sum_{c \in \mathcal{C}_n \cup \mathcal{C}_b \cup \{c_{bg}\}} (\mathbf{q}_{r,c}^{cls} \log \mathbf{q}_{r,c}^{cls} - \mathbf{q}_{r,c}^{cls} \log \mathbf{p}_{r,c}^{cls}). \tag{5}$$

Rationale. We learn the semantic commonalities that are related to object recognition by measuring the similarities of samples from base classes to each novel class in a pre-defined feature space. Then the learned commonalities (after normalization) are viewed as soft labels to supervise the fine-tuning of the object detector. Consequently, all samples in base classes that share recognition-related semantics with a novel class can be leveraged to train the object detector on this novel class. In this sense, the proposed commonality distillation significantly augments the training data for novel classes, thereby improving the performance of the object detector on novel classes.

3.3   Distilling Localization-Related Semantic Commonalities

Besides the recognition-related semantic commonalities, similar categories also share semantic commonalities that is related to object localization such as similar shape or boundary features. Distilling such commonalities between similar base and novel classes enables the object detector to learn transferable knowledge on localization from abundant base class samples, thereby improving its performance of object detection on novel classes.

The localization-related semantic commonalities are distilled in a similar way as the recognition-related commonalities in Sect. 3.2. We also learn the localization-related commonalities by measuring the similarities of samples in base classes to each novel class in a pre-learned feature space $\mathcal{F}_{loc}$. One of the key differences between distillation of two different types of commonalities (recognition- or localization-related) is that they are learned in different pre-learned feature spaces: each feature space should be learned by optimizing the corresponding task (object classification or localization), as illustrated in Fig. 1. We present an efficient implementation in Sect. 3.5.

The learned localization-related commonalities is represented as the normalized similarities in the same form shown in Eq. 4. In contrast to viewing the recognition-related commonalities as soft labels for supervision, the localization-related commonalities are leveraged as normalized weights to aggregate all class-specific bounding box regressors for object localization. This is based on the intuition that an object can be localized by not only the bounding box regressor for its groundtruth class, but also the regressors for the similar classes, more similarities leading to more confidence. Formally, given a region proposal r from a base class, its bounding box is predicted as offsets $\mathbf{t} = (t_x, t_y, t_w, t_h)$ to the groundtruth position by aggregating the predictions of all regressors for C classes. Then the detector is optimized by minimizing the error between the aggregated prediction and the groundtruth using the smoothed L1 loss [8]:

$$\mathcal{L}_{\text{distill-loc}} = \sum_{c=1}^{C} \mathbf{q}_{r,c}^{loc} \cdot \sum_{i \in \{x,y,w,h\}} \text{Smooth}_{L1}(t_i^c - u_i), \qquad (6)$$

where $\mathbf{q}_r^{loc}$ is the normalized similarities representing the localization-related commonalities. u_i is the bounding-box regression groundtruth for r while t_i^c is the prediction of box regressor for the class c.

Rationale. The similarities between samples from base classes to each novel class in a pre-learned feature space $\mathcal{F}_{\text{loc}}$ towards localization are learned as the localization-related commonalities, and are further used as aggregation weights to fuse regressors for all classes. To be specific, a sample (object) from a base class is localized by referring to the predictions of all regressors for the novel classes sharing localization-related commonalities with this sample. It is equivalent to training these regressors with the sample. As a result, all regressors for novel classes are optimized with a lot of additional training samples from base classes, which yields better performance of localization.

3.4   Distilling Distribution Commonalities

Semantically similar categories usually follow similar data distributions, such as close mean and variance of features in a presumed Gaussian distribution between these categories [30]. Hence, the third type of commonalities between base and novel classes that we aim to distill is the distribution commonalities. Inspired by Distribution Calibration [45] in few-shot image classification, we distill the distributional statistics from base classes to calibrate the distribution of those similar novel classes. Consequently, we can sample sufficient examples for these novel classes to improve the performance of the object detector on novel classes.

Unlike Distribution Calibration which transfers both the mean and variance of base classes to novel classes, we only distill the variance of base classes while preserving the mean values of novel classes. This is because transferring both the mean and variance of base classes would result in the distributional overlapping between the base and novel classes, making it harder to distinguish between them during object detection. In contrast, the classification between base and novel classes is not required in the few-shot classification setting.

Assuming that each feature dimension follows a Gaussian distribution, which is consistent with Distribution Calibration [45], we first calculate the mean and variance per feature dimension for both base and novel classes in a pre-learned feature space, and select the top-k semantically closest base classes for each novel class according to the Euclidean distance w.r.t. the mean values (equivalent to the class prototype in Eq. 2). Then we can approximate the variance of a novel class using the averaged variance over its top-k closest base classes. Formally, the calibrated variance of a novel class c is estimated by:

$$\boldsymbol{\sigma}'_c = \frac{1}{k} \sum_{i \in S_c} \boldsymbol{\sigma}_i. \qquad (7)$$

Herein, $\boldsymbol{\sigma}_i$ is the variance of the base class i and S_c is the set of top-k closest base classes to the novel class c. In this way we are able to sample more examples in this pre-learned feature space for the novel class c following the obtained Gaussian distribution $\mathcal{N}(\boldsymbol{\mu}_c, \boldsymbol{\sigma}'_c)$:

$$\mathbb{S}_c = \{\mathbf{v} | \mathbf{v} \sim \mathcal{N}(\boldsymbol{\mu}_c, \boldsymbol{\sigma}'_c)\}, \qquad (8)$$

where μ_c is mean of the novel class c. $\mathbb{S}_c$ is the set of sampled features, which are further used to train the classifier f_θ of the object detector using the Cross-Entropy loss:

$$\mathcal{L}_{\text{distill-dist}} = \frac{1}{|\mathbb{S}_c|} \sum_{\mathbf{v} \in \mathbb{S}_c} \text{CE}(c, f_\theta(\mathbf{v})). \tag{9}$$

3.5 Unified Distillation Framework Based on Memory Bank

We propose a unified distillation framework, which is able to distill all three commonalities jointly in an end-to-end manner during the fine-tuning stage.

Both the recognition-related commonalities and the localization-related commonalities are obtained by calculating the similarities between samples of base classes to each of novel classes in their corresponding (but different) pre-learned feature spaces. Typically such pre-learned feature spaces are independent from the feature space for learning the detector, which is achieved by pre-learning the feature spaces based on other data or other networks. Doing so enables the knowledge distillation between two different feature spaces. However, such implementation has two limitations: 1) the commonalities calculated in the pre-learned feature space may not be accurate since the extracted features for samples of both base and novel classes are potentially not optimized; 2) the whole training is performed in two separated stages, which is not efficient.

We propose to learn the commonalities in the same feature space as that for learning the detector. As shown in Fig. 2, we only learn one feature space by the typical feature learning backbone together with the RoI feature extractor based on the training data for current task. Then we decouple the feature space into two separate feature spaces by two projection heads: one (denoted as $\mathcal{F}_{\text{cls}}$) is connected to the classification head and is used for learning the recognition-related commonalities, the other one (denoted as $\mathcal{F}_{\text{loc}}$) is connected to the regression head and is used for learning the localization-related commonalities. Each projection head consists of a fully connected layer and a ReLU layer. We first pre-train the detector based on the samples from base classes. Then in the fine-tuning stage, we learn each type of commonalities and perform the commonality distillation jointly in the corresponding feature space. Note that the distribution commonalities are also learned in the feature space $\mathcal{F}_{\text{cls}}$ since the distribution similarities are intuitively more related to the recognition-related semantics.

Commonality Distillation. During the fine-tuning of the detector, the feature space is evolving all the time. Thus all types of commonalities are also evolving with the update of the feature space. Meanwhile, the commonality distillation is performed in two aspects. First, the commonalities learned based on the previous training state of feature space are further used to optimize the feature space in the next iteration (state). In this sense, the commonalities are distilled between different training states in the same feature space, which is similar to Self-Knowledge Distillation [18]. Second, the recognition-related and distribution commonalities are also distilled from the feature space $\mathcal{F}_{\text{cls}}$ to the classification head while the localization-related commonalities are distilled from $\mathcal{F}_{\text{loc}}$ to the localization head, yielding more precise classifier and regressors.

Memory Bank. During the fine-tuning of the detector, the commonalities are evolving with the update of the feature space. However, calculating the prototype for each class (including base and novel classes) from scratch using all available samples in the training set, which is involved in learning all three types of commonalities, is quite computationally expensive due to the feature extraction for all samples. To address this problem, we maintain a dynamic memory bank to store the features (in both $\mathcal{F}_{\mathrm{loc}}$ and $\mathcal{F}_{\mathrm{cls}}$) of a maximum number of L RoI features for each class to improve the efficiency. Denoting the memory bank as $\mathbf{M} = \{\mathbf{m}_c\}_{c=1}^{C}$ where C is the class number, the RoI features of each class are stored as a queue. During each training iteration, we update the memory bank by enqueuing the current batch of samples to the corresponding class queue and dequeuing the same amount of oldest samples for the same class. Then we can calculate the prototype for each class using the RoI features stored in $\mathbf{M}$. As a result, we do not need to extract features for all samples from scratch each time the feature space is updated, and the operating efficiency is thereby improved significantly. Using memory bank for efficiency has been previously explored in unsupervised learning [12,41].

Parameter Learning. In the pre-training stage using samples from base classes, we train the object detector with standard Faster R-CNN [27] losses:

$$\mathcal{L}_{\mathrm{det}} = \mathcal{L}_{\mathrm{rpn}} + \mathcal{L}_{\mathrm{cls}} + \mathcal{L}_{\mathrm{reg}}, \tag{10}$$

where $\mathcal{L}_{\mathrm{rpn}}$ is the loss of the RPN to distinguish foreground from background, $\mathcal{L}_{\mathrm{cls}}$ is the Cross-Entropy loss for classification, and $\mathcal{L}_{\mathrm{reg}}$ is the smoothed L1 loss [8] for the regression of bounding boxes. In the fine-tuning stage, the model is supervised with both the Faster R-CNN loss $\mathcal{L}_{\mathrm{det}}$ and the losses for the distillation of three types of commonalities, in an end-to-end manner:

$$\mathcal{L} = \mathcal{L}_{\mathrm{det}} + \lambda_c \mathcal{L}_{\mathrm{distill\text{-}cls}} + \lambda_l \mathcal{L}_{\mathrm{distill\text{-}loc}} + \lambda_d \mathcal{L}_{\mathrm{distill\text{-}dist}}, \tag{11}$$

where λ_c, λ_l and λ_d are hyper-parameters to balance among losses.

4   Experiments

4.1   Experimental Setup

Datasets. Our approach is evaluated on PASCAL VOC [4] and MS COCO [25] datasets. We follow the consistent data construction and evaluation protocol in [16,35]. For PASCAL VOC, the overall 20 classes are split into 15 base classes and 5 novel classes. We utilize the same three partitions of base classes and novel classes introduced in [16]. All base class instances from PASCAL VOC (07+12) trainval sets are available. Each novel class has K instances available where K is set to 1, 2, 3, 5 and 10. We report AP50 of novel classes (nAP50) on PASCAL VOC 07 test set. For the 80 classes in MS COCO, the 20 classes overlapped with PASCAL VOC are selected as novel classes, the remaining 60 classes are selected as base classes. Similarly, we report COCO-style AP and AP75 of novel classes on COCO 2014 validation set with $K = 1, 2, 3, 5, 10, 30$.

Table 1. Comparison of different few-shot object detection methods in terms of nAP50 on three PASCAL VOC Novel Split sets.

Method/Shots	Novel split 1					Novel split 2					Novel split 3				
	1	2	3	5	10	1	2	3	5	10	1	2	3	5	10
LSTD [3]	8.2	1.0	12.4	29.1	38.5	11.4	3.8	5.0	15.7	31.0	12.6	8.5	15.0	27.3	36.3
FSRW [16]	14.8	15.5	26.7	33.9	47.2	15.7	15.3	22.7	30.1	40.5	21.3	25.6	28.4	42.8	45.9
MetaDet [37]	18.9	20.6	30.2	36.8	49.6	21.8	23.1	27.8	31.7	43.0	20.6	23.9	29.4	43.9	44.1
Meta R-CNN [44]	19.9	25.5	35.0	45.7	51.5	10.4	19.4	29.6	34.8	45.4	14.3	18.2	27.5	41.2	48.1
RepMet [17]	26.1	32.9	34.4	38.6	41.3	17.2	22.1	23.4	28.3	35.8	27.5	31.1	31.5	34.4	37.2
NP-RepMet [46]	37.8	40.3	41.7	47.3	49.4	41.6	43.0	43.4	47.4	49.1	33.3	38.0	39.8	41.5	44.8
TFA w/cos [35]	39.8	36.1	44.7	55.7	56.0	23.5	26.9	34.1	35.1	39.1	30.8	34.8	42.8	49.5	49.8
MPSR [40]	41.7	–	51.4	55.2	61.8	24.4	–	39.2	39.9	47.8	35.6	–	42.3	48.0	49.7
HallucFsDet [51]	47.0	44.9	46.5	54.7	54.7	26.3	31.8	37.4	37.4	41.2	40.4	42.1	43.3	51.4	49.6
Retentive R-CNN [6]	42.4	45.8	45.9	53.7	56.1	21.7	27.8	35.2	37.0	40.3	30.2	37.6	43.0	49.7	50.1
FSCE [32]	44.2	43.8	51.4	61.9	63.4	27.3	29.5	43.5	44.2	50.2	37.2	41.9	47.5	54.6	58.5
FSCN [23]	40.7	45.1	46.5	57.4	62.4	27.3	31.4	40.8	42.7	46.3	31.2	36.4	43.7	50.1	55.6
SRR-FSD [52]	47.8	50.5	51.3	55.2	56.8	32.5	35.3	39.1	40.8	43.8	40.1	41.5	44.3	46.9	46.4
SQMG [50]	48.6	51.1	52.0	53.7	54.3	41.6	45.4	45.8	46.3	48.0	46.1	51.7	52.6	54.1	55.0
CME [22]	41.5	47.5	50.4	58.2	60.9	27.2	30.2	41.4	42.5	46.8	34.3	39.6	45.1	48.3	51.5
Dictionary [39]	46.1	43.5	48.9	60.0	61.7	25.6	29.9	44.8	47.5	48.2	39.5	45.4	48.9	53.9	56.9
FADI [1]	50.3	54.8	54.2	59.3	63.2	30.6	35.0	40.3	42.8	48.0	45.7	49.7	49.1	55.0	59.6
UP-FSOD [38]	43.8	47.8	50.3	55.4	61.7	31.2	30.5	41.2	42.2	48.3	35.5	39.7	43.9	50.6	53.3
QA-FewDet [10]	42.4	51.9	55.7	62.6	63.4	25.9	37.8	46.6	48.9	51.1	35.2	42.9	47.8	54.8	53.5
DeFRCN [26]	57.0	58.6	64.3	67.8	67.0	35.8	42.7	51.0	54.5	52.9	52.5	56.6	55.8	60.7	62.5
Ours	**63.4**	**66.3**	**67.7**	**69.4**	**68.1**	**42.1**	**46.5**	**53.4**	**55.3**	**53.8**	**56.1**	**58.3**	**59.0**	**62.2**	**63.7**

Implementation Details. As a plug-and-play module, our approach can be easily integrated into other fine-tuning based methods. we evaluate our approach on four baselines: TFA [35], Retentive R-CNN [6], FSCE [32] and DeFRCN [26]. We train the detector with a mini-batch of 16 on 8 GPUs, 2 images per GPU. ResNet-101 [13] pre-trained on ImageNet [29] is used as the backbone. The maximum queue size L in our memory bank is tuned to be 2048. The scaling factor α is tune to be 5. For distribution distillation, we transfer the variance of top $k = 2$ base classes, and sample $|\mathbb{S}_c| = 10$ instances from the calibrated distribution for novel class c during each iteration. The weights of each loss are tuned to be $\lambda_c = 0.1$, $\lambda_l = 1.0$, $\lambda_d = 0.1$. Moreover, We begin the distillation after 200 iterations in the fine-tuning stage to perform a basic optimization of the feature space on novel classes. Code is available at: https://github.com/WuShuang1998/MFDC.

4.2   Comparison with State-of-the-Art Methods

We integrate our method based on DeFRCN [26], a state-of-the-art method for few-shot object detection, to compare with other latest methods.

Results on PASCAL VOC. Table 1 shows the results on PASCAL VOC. It can be observed that our approach outperforms other methods in all novel splits with different numbers of training shots. In particular, our method achieves much larger performance gain in extremely low-shot settings. For instance, for novel split 1, our approach surpasses the previously best method by 6.4% and 7.7% in

Table 2. Few-shot object detection performance on MS COCO.

Method	1-shot		2-shot		3-shot		5-shot		10-shot		30-shot	
	nAP	nAP75	nAP	nAP75	nAP	nAP75	nAP	nAP75	nAP	nAP75	nAP	nAP75
FSRW [16]	–	–	–	–	–	–	–	–	5.6	4.6	9.1	7.6
SRR-FSD [52]	–	–	–	–	–	–	–	–	11.3	9.8	14.7	13.5
FSCE [32]	–	–	–	–	–	–	–	–	11.9	10.5	16.4	16.2
UP-FSOD [38]	–	–	–	–	–	–	–	–	11.0	10.7	15.6	15.7
SQMG [50]	–	–	–	–	–	–	–	–	13.9	11.7	15.9	14.3
CME [22]	–	–	–	–	–	–	–	–	15.1	16.4	16.9	17.8
TFA w/cos [35]	3.4	3.8	4.6	4.8	6.6	6.5	8.3	8.0	10.0	9.3	13.7	13.4
MPSR [40]	2.3	2.3	3.5	3.4	5.2	5.1	6.7	6.4	9.8	9.7	14.1	14.2
QA-FewDet [10]	4.9	4.4	7.6	6.2	8.4	7.3	9.7	8.6	11.6	9.8	16.5	15.5
FADI [1]	5.7	6.0	7.0	7.0	8.6	8.3	10.1	9.7	12.2	11.9	16.1	15.8
DeFRCN [26]	6.5	6.9	11.8	12.4	13.4	13.6	15.3	14.6	18.6	17.6	22.5	22.3
Ours	**10.8**	**11.6**	**13.9**	**14.8**	**15.0**	**15.5**	**16.4**	**17.3**	**19.4**	**20.2**	**22.7**	**23.2**

Table 3. Performance of integrating our method with different classical methods in term of nAP50 on Novel Split 1 of PASCAL VOC.

Baseline method	Ours	1-shot	2-shot	3-shot	5-shot	10-shot
TFA w/cos [35]		39.8	36.1	44.7	55.7	56.0
	✓	**45.2**	**47.3**	**50.6**	**58.2**	**58.4**
Retentive R-CNN [6]		42.4	45.8	45.9	53.7	56.1
	✓	**47.8**	**48.1**	**51.4**	**58.2**	**58.9**
FSCE [32]		44.2	43.8	51.4	61.9	63.4
	✓	**48.0**	**51.6**	**55.3**	**63.8**	**66.2**
DeFRCN [26]		57.0	58.6	64.3	67.8	67.0
	✓	**63.4**	**66.3**	**67.7**	**69.4**	**68.1**

1-shot and 2-shot scenarios, respectively. It is reasonable because the distillation of commonalities plays more important role in fewer-shot settings.

Results on MS COCO. Similar performance improvements by our method can be observed on the MS COCO benchmark. As shown in Table 2, our approach consistently outperforms other state-of-the-art methods in all settings although MS COCO is quite challenging. Particularly, for 1-shot scenarios, our approach pushes forward the current state-of-the-art performance from 6.5% to 10.8% in nAP. Besides, the improvement from 6.9% to 11.6% in nAP75 demonstrates the effectiveness of our approach on localization.

4.3 Integration with Different Baseline Methods

We further integrate our method with different baseline methods to evaluate the robustness of our method. Table 3 presents the performance of four different baselines and our method on Novel Split 1 of PASCAL VOC. Our method consistently boosts the performance distinctly. For instance, when integrated with TFA w/cos [35], our method achieves substantial performance gains: 5.4%, 11.2%, 5.9%, 2.5% and 2.4% from 1-shot to 10-shot respectively. These results reveal the strong robustness of our approach on different baseline methods.

Table 4. Effectiveness of each type of commonality. 'Recog', 'Local', 'Dist' refer to the recognition-related, localization-related and distribution commonalities, respectively.

Recog	Local	Dist	nAP50		
			1-shot	2-shot	3-shot
			58.5	62.6	65.4
✓			62.3	64.8	67.3
	✓		59.9	64.1	65.7
		✓	62.6	65.1	66.2
✓		✓	63.2	65.9	67.7
✓	✓		62.8	65.6	67.2
✓	✓	✓	**63.4**	**66.3**	**67.7**

Table 5. Effect of using different feature spaces from the object detector to learn commonalities. 'Independent' denotes the feature space pre-optimized on ImageNet, and 'uniform' denotes the same feature space as the object detector.

Feature space	nAP50		
	1-shot	2-shot	3-shot
Baseline	58.5	62.6	65.4
Independent	59.6	63.8	66.1
Uniform (ours)	**62.3**	**64.8**	**67.3**

4.4   Ablation Studies

In this section, we conduct ablation studies by integrating our method with DeFRCN [26]. All experiments are performed on Novel Split 1 of PASCAL VOC. Note that more ablation studies on other hyper-parameters are provided in the supplementary materials.

Effectiveness of Each Type of Commonality. Table 4 shows the effectiveness of each type of commonality. Compared with the baseline in the first line, each individual type of commonality improves the performance distinctly. Combining all three types of commonalities achieves larger performance gain than any individual one.

Learning Commonalities in an Independent Feature Space from the Object Detector. Our method learns commonalities in the same (uniform) feature space as the object detector, which allows our model to 1) achieve more accurate commonalities due to more optimized features for current data and 2) perform commonality distillation in an end-to-end manner. To validate the first merit, we conduct experiments to learn commonalities in an independent feature space from the object detector, which is pre-optimized on ImageNet dataset. All class prototypes and cosine similarities for learning commonalities are calculated in this independent feature space. The results in Table 5 show that the performance gain in such way is smaller than that of using the same space feature as the object detector (denoted as 'Uniform').

Qualitative Evaluation. To have a qualitative evaluation, we visualize the instances from base classes that have most recognition- and localization-related commonalities (interpreted as semantic similarities) with the novel class 'Bird' respectively in Fig. 3(a). The instances from the semantically similar base classes

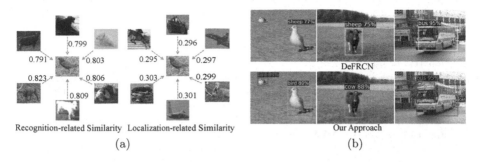

Recognition-related Similarity   Localization-related Similarity   Our Approach

(a)   (b)

Fig. 3. (a) Visualization of base instances with highest recognition-related similarity and localization-related similarity to the novel class 'Bird'. (b) 1-shot object detection results of randomly selected test samples by DeFRCN [26] and our approach on PASCAL VOC Novel Split 1. More examples can be found in the supplementary materials.

to 'Bird', such as 'Dog' and 'sheep', tend to have more recognition-related commonalities with 'Bird' than other base classes. In contrast, instances from the base classes bearing more shape similarities to 'Bird', like 'Plane', have more localization-related commonalities with 'Bird' than other classes. Such observations are consistent with the different attention distributions in feature space between recognition and localization shown in Fig. 1. By distilling the multi-faceted commonalities, our object detector is able to perform recognition and localization more accurately, as shown in Fig. 3(b).

5   Conclusion

In this paper, we propose the multi-faceted distillation for few-shot object detection. The key insight is to learn three types of commonalities between base and novel classes explicitly: recognition-related semantic commonalities, localization-related semantic commonalities and distribution commonalities. Then these commonalities are distilled during the fine-tuning stage based on the memory bank. Our method improves the state-of-the-art performance of few-shot object detection by a large margin.

Acknowledgements. This work was supported in part by the NSFC fund (U2013210, 62006060, 62176077), in part by the Guangdong Basic and Applied Basic Research Foundation under Grant (2019Bl515120055, 2021A1515012528, 2022A1515010306), in part by the Shenzhen Key Technical Project under Grant 2020N046, in part by the Shenzhen Fundamental Research Fund under Grant (JCYJ20210324132210025), in part by the Shenzhen Stable Support Plan Fund for Universities (GXWD20201230155427003-20200824125730001, GXWD202012 30155427003-20200824164357001), in part by CAAI-Huawei MindSpore Open Fund(CAAIXSJLJJ-2021-003B), in part by the Medical Biometrics Perception and Analysis Engineering Laboratory, Shenzhen, China, and in part by the Guangdong Provincial Key Laboratory of Novel Security Intelligence Technologies (2022B1212010005).

References

1. Cao, Y., et al.: Few-shot object detection via association and discrimination. In: NeurIPS (2021)
2. Chattopadhay, A., Sarkar, A., Howlader, P., Balasubramanian, V.N.: Grad-cam++: generalized gradient-based visual explanations for deep convolutional networks. In: WACV (2018)
3. Chen, H., Wang, Y., Wang, G., Qiao, Y.: Lstd: a low-shot transfer detector for object detection. In: AAAI (2018)
4. Everingham, M., Van Gool, L., Williams, C.K., Winn, J., Zisserman, A.: The pascal visual object classes (voc) challenge. Int. J. Comput. Vision **88**(2), 303–338 (2010)
5. Fan, Q., Zhuo, W., Tang, C.K., Tai, Y.W.: Few-shot object detection with attention-rpn and multi-relation detector. In: CVPR (2020)
6. Fan, Z., Ma, Y., Li, Z., Sun, J.: Generalized few-shot object detection without forgetting. In: CVPR (2021)
7. Finn, C., Abbeel, P., Levine, S.: Model-agnostic meta-learning for fast adaptation of deep networks. In: ICML (2017)
8. Girshick, R.: Fast r-cnn. In: ICCV (2015)
9. Hahn, S., Choi, H.: Self-knowledge distillation in natural language processing. arXiv preprint arXiv:1908.01851 (2019)
10. Han, G., He, Y., Huang, S., Ma, J., Chang, S.F.: Query adaptive few-shot object detection with heterogeneous graph convolutional networks. In: ICCV (2021)
11. Hariharan, B., Girshick, R.: Low-shot visual recognition by shrinking and hallucinating features. In: ICCV (2017)
12. He, K., Fan, H., Wu, Y., Xie, S., Girshick, R.: Momentum contrast for unsupervised visual representation learning. In: CVPR (2020)
13. He, K., Zhang, X., Ren, S., Sun, J.: Deep residual learning for image recognition. In: CVPR (2016)
14. Hinton, G., Vinyals, O., Dean, J., et al.: Distilling the knowledge in a neural network. arXiv preprint arXiv:1503.02531 2(7) (2015)
15. Hu, H., Bai, S., Li, A., Cui, J., Wang, L.: Dense relation distillation with context-aware aggregation for few-shot object detection. In: CVPR (2021)
16. Kang, B., Liu, Z., Wang, X., Yu, F., Feng, J., Darrell, T.: Few-shot object detection via feature reweighting. In: ICCV (2019)
17. Karlinsky, L., et al.: Repmet: representative-based metric learning for classification and few-shot object detection. In: CVPR (2019)
18. Kim, K., Ji, B., Yoon, D., Hwang, S.: Self-knowledge distillation with progressive refinement of targets. In: ICCV (2021)
19. Komodakis, N., Zagoruyko, S.: Paying more attention to attention: improving the performance of convolutional neural networks via attention transfer. In: ICLR (2017)
20. Lee, K., Maji, S., Ravichandran, A., Soatto, S.: Meta-learning with differentiable convex optimization. In: CVPR (2019)
21. Li, A., Li, Z.: Transformation invariant few-shot object detection. In: CVPR (2021)
22. Li, B., Yang, B., Liu, C., Liu, F., Ji, R., Ye, Q.: Beyond max-margin: class margin equilibrium for few-shot object detection. In: CVPR (2021)
23. Li, Y., et al.: Few-shot object detection via classification refinement and distractor retreatment. In: CVPR (2021)
24. Li, Z., Zhou, F., Chen, F., Li, H.: Meta-sgd: learning to learn quickly for few-shot learning. arXiv preprint arXiv:1707.09835 (2017)

25. Lin, T.-Y., et al.: Microsoft COCO: common objects in context. In: Fleet, D., Pajdla, T., Schiele, B., Tuytelaars, T. (eds.) ECCV 2014. LNCS, vol. 8693, pp. 740–755. Springer, Cham (2014). https://doi.org/10.1007/978-3-319-10602-1_48
26. Qiao, L., Zhao, Y., Li, Z., Qiu, X., Wu, J., Zhang, C.: Defrcn: decoupled faster r-cnn for few-shot object detection. In: ICCV (2021)
27. Ren, S., He, K., Girshick, R., Sun, J.: Faster r-cnn: towards real-time object detection with region proposal networks. In: NeurIPS (2015)
28. Romero, A., Ballas, N., Kahou, S.E., Chassang, A., Gatta, C., Bengio, Y.: Fitnets: hints for thin deep nets. arXiv preprint arXiv:1412.6550 (2014)
29. Russakovsky, O., et al.: Imagenet large scale visual recognition challenge. Int. J. Comput. Vision 115(3), 211–252 (2015)
30. Salakhutdinov, R., Tenenbaum, J., Torralba, A.: One-shot learning with a hierarchical nonparametric bayesian model. In: ICML Workshop (2012)
31. Snell, J., Swersky, K., Zemel, R.: Prototypical networks for few-shot learning. In: NeurIPS (2017)
32. Sun, B., Li, B., Cai, S., Yuan, Y., Zhang, C.: Fsce: few-shot object detection via contrastive proposal encoding. In: CVPR (2021)
33. Sung, F., Yang, Y., Zhang, L., Xiang, T., Torr, P.H., Hospedales, T.M.: Learning to compare: relation network for few-shot learning. In: CVPR (2018)
34. Vinyals, O., Blundell, C., Lillicrap, T., Wierstra, D., et al.: Matching networks for one shot learning. In: NeurIPS (2016)
35. Wang, X., Huang, T., Gonzalez, J., Darrell, T., Yu, F.: Frustratingly simple few-shot object detection. In: ICML (2020)
36. Wang, Y.X., Girshick, R., Hebert, M., Hariharan, B.: Low-shot learning from imaginary data. In: CVPR (2018)
37. Wang, Y.X., Ramanan, D., Hebert, M.: Meta-learning to detect rare objects. In: ICCV (2019)
38. Wu, A., Han, Y., Zhu, L., Yang, Y.: Universal-prototype enhancing for few-shot object detection. In: ICCV (2021)
39. Wu, A., Zhao, S., Deng, C., Liu, W.: Generalized and discriminative few-shot object detection via svd-dictionary enhancement. In: NeurIPS (2021)
40. Wu, J., Liu, S., Huang, D., Wang, Y.: Multi-scale positive sample refinement for few-shot object detection. In: Vedaldi, A., Bischof, H., Brox, T., Frahm, J.-M. (eds.) ECCV 2020. LNCS, vol. 12361, pp. 456–472. Springer, Cham (2020). https://doi.org/10.1007/978-3-030-58517-4_27
41. Wu, Z., Xiong, Y., Yu, S.X., Lin, D.: Unsupervised feature learning via nonparametric instance discrimination. In: CVPR (2018)
42. Xiao, Y., Marlet, R.: Few-shot object detection and viewpoint estimation for objects in the wild. In: Vedaldi, A., Bischof, H., Brox, T., Frahm, J.-M. (eds.) ECCV 2020. LNCS, vol. 12362, pp. 192–210. Springer, Cham (2020). https://doi.org/10.1007/978-3-030-58520-4_12
43. Xu, T.B., Liu, C.L.: Data-distortion guided self-distillation for deep neural networks. In: AAAI (2019)
44. Yan, X., Chen, Z., Xu, A., Wang, X., Liang, X., Lin, L.: Meta r-cnn: towards general solver for instance-level low-shot learning. In: ICCV (2019)
45. Yang, S., Liu, L., Xu, M.: Free lunch for few-shot learning: distribution calibration. In: ICLR (2020)
46. Yang, Y., Wei, F., Shi, M., Li, G.: Restoring negative information in few-shot object detection. In: NeurIPS (2020)
47. Yun, S., Park, J., Lee, K., Shin, J.: Regularizing class-wise predictions via self-knowledge distillation. In: CVPR (2020)

48. Zhang, C., Cai, Y., Lin, G., Shen, C.: Deepemd: few-shot image classification with differentiable earth mover's distance and structured classifiers. In: CVPR (2020)
49. Zhang, L., Song, J., Gao, A., Chen, J., Bao, C., Ma, K.: Be your own teacher: improve the performance of convolutional neural networks via self distillation. In: ICCV (2019)
50. Zhang, L., Zhou, S., Guan, J., Zhang, J.: Accurate few-shot object detection with support-query mutual guidance and hybrid loss. In: CVPR (2021)
51. Zhang, W., Wang, Y.X.: Hallucination improves few-shot object detection. In: CVPR (2021)
52. Zhu, C., Chen, F., Ahmed, U., Shen, Z., Savvides, M.: Semantic relation reasoning for shot-stable few-shot object detection. In: CVPR (2021)

PointCLM: A Contrastive Learning-based Framework for Multi-instance Point Cloud Registration

Mingzhi Yuan[1,3] , Zhihao Li[1,3] , Qiuye Jin[1,3] , Xinrong Chen[1,2,3(✉)] ,
and Manning Wang[1,3(✉)]

[1] Digital Medical Research Center, School of Basic Medical Sciences,
Fudan University, Shanghai 200032, China
{mzyuan20,lizhihao21,qyjin18,chenxinrong,mnwang}@fudan.edu.cn
[2] Academy for Engineering and Technology, Fudan University,
Shanghai 200032, China
[3] Shanghai Key Laboratory of Medical Image Computing and Computer Assisted
Intervention, Shanghai 200032, China

Abstract. Multi-instance point cloud registration is the problem of estimating multiple poses of source point cloud instances within a target point cloud. Solving this problem is challenging since inlier correspondences of one instance constitute outliers of all the other instances. Existing methods often rely on time-consuming hypothesis sampling or features leveraging spatial consistency, resulting in limited performance. In this paper, we propose PointCLM, a contrastive learning-based framework for mutli-instance point cloud registration. We first utilize contrastive learning to learn well-distributed deep representations for the input putative correspondences. Then based on these representations, we propose a outlier pruning strategy and a clustering strategy to efficiently remove outliers and assign the remaining correspondences to correct instances. Our method outperforms the state-of-the-art methods on both synthetic and real datasets by a large margin. The code will be made publicly available at http://github.com/phdymz/PointCLM.

Keywords: Multi-instance point cloud registration · Multi-model fitting · Contrastive learning

1 Introduction

3D point cloud registration is a fundamental task in computer vision [9, 21, 50], and most studies mainly focus on pairwise registration. However, in real applications, target scene may contain multiple repeated instances, and we need to estimate multiple rigid transformations between a source point cloud and these repeated instances in the target point cloud. An example is illustrated in

---

Supplementary Information The online version contains supplementary material available at https://doi.org/10.1007/978-3-031-20077-9_35.

Fig. 1. This problem is named as multi-instance point cloud registration and it is more challenging than pairwise point cloud registration.

There exist two solutions to the multi-instance point cloud registration problem. One solution is to use an instance detector [32,37] to detect instances in the target point cloud, and turn this problem into multiple pairwise registrations. However, this approach can only detect known classes in the training set, and the registration performance is limited by the instance detector. Another solution is via multi-model fitting [23,29,31,42]. This approach starts from building putative correspondences based on local features, followed by estimating multiple transformations from noisy correspondences using multi-model fitting algorithms. Multi-model fitting problem has been studied for decades. The basic idea of most multi-model fitting methods is to sample a series of hypotheses and then perform preference analysis [15,16,48,54] or consensus analysis [29,30,35,43]. Most of these multi-model fitting algorithms are traditional methods, which rely on a large number of sampling for generating hypotheses and sophisticated strategies for selecting real models, resulting in large computational cost.

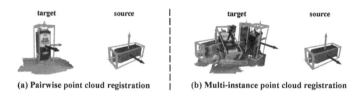

(a) Pairwise point cloud registration | (b) Multi-instance point cloud registration

Fig. 1. Given a source point cloud of a 3d object, pairwise point cloud registration (left) focuses on estimating a single rigid transformation between the source point cloud and the target point cloud, while multi-instance point cloud registration (right) aims to estimate the 6d poses of the same objects within the target point cloud.

Recently, a series of deep learning-based methods have achieved excellent performance in pairwise point cloud registration, including feature matching [4,13,20,46], outlier correspondences rejection [3,12,24,52], etc. Multi-instance point cloud registration also faces the interference of outliers, which inspires researchers to extend deep learning-based methods to the multi-instance case. However, in the multi-instance case, the inliers of one instance constitute outliers of all the other instances, so we need not only to identify outliers, but also to predict which instance the inliers belong to. To the best of our knowledge, the only existing deep learning-based method [23] that can be used in multi-instance point cloud registration is by sequential binary classification. However, this method has limited performance because it does not fully explore the interaction between correspondences. There is also a traditional method [42] which clusters the correspondences based on spatial consistency [25]. However, due to the ambiguity of spatial consistency, this method cannot assign the correspondences very efficiently when outliers are located close to inliers. Therefore, an intuitive idea is to learn a more discriminative representation for correspondence so that not only the outliers can be easily pruned but also the inliers of different instances are separable in the feature space.

In this paper, we propose a contrastive learning-based method to learn deep representations for correspondences, based on which, we can not only remove outliers in the putative correspondences, but also correctly assign inliers to each instance. Specifically, we first select inlier correspondences belonging to the same instance to build positive pairs and select one correspondence from an instance and another correspondence not belonging to that instance to build negative pairs. Then we train a feature extractor with contrastive loss to make the correspondences in positive pairs near each other and the correspondences in negative pairs fall apart from each other in the feature space. This makes the inliers of each instance form a certain scale of clusters in the feature space, while the outliers are scattered. Based on this distribution, we prune the input putative correspondences according to the density over the feature space and obtain a correspondence set that has little outliers. After that, we perform a spectral clustering based on feature similarity and spatial consistency [3,25], in which the number of instances can be automatically determined and the remaining correspondences can be correctly assigned to each instance. Finally, we calculate the transformation for each instance using the correspondences assigned to it. Our main contributions are as follows:

- We propose a contrastive learning-based strategy that makes inlier correspondences and outlier correspondences well distributed in the feature space;
- We propose a pruning strategy based on feature similarity and spatial consistency to remove outliers and then utilize spectral clustering to assign the remaining correspondences to correct instances;
- Our method outperforms existing state-of-the-art methods in multi-instance point cloud registration on both synthetic and real datasets.

2   Related Work

Point cloud registration has long been a fundamental task in computer vision and robotic, which can be roughly divided into direct methods [1,9,36,39] and feature-based methods [4,17,20,46]. In recent years, thanks to the development of deep learning, many feature-based methods achieved state-of-the-art performance. These methods commonly produce correspondences by feature matching and then remove outliers to estimate transformations robustly. Despite the rapid development of deep features [4,13,20,46], the correspondences generated by feature matching still contain outliers. Therefore, removing outliers is of great significance in point cloud registration. In the past, many traditional methods have been proposed to remove outliers, including RANSAC-based methods [5,15,26], branch and bound-based methods [10], and many others [40,49]. A comprehensive review of these methods can be found in [21,50,51]. Recently, a series of learning-based methods [3,12,24,52] have been proposed and achieved remarkable results in outlier removal. For example, Yi et al. used a PointNet-style [38] network with instance normalization to predict outliers [52], which has been widely used as a backbone network for predicting outliers [41,53]. Choy et al. used a sparse convolution-based network to classify putative correspondences into inliers and outliers [12]. Based on the assumption of spatial compatibility between inliers, Bai et al. incorporated geometric prior into deep neural network and designed a non-local layer [3] to better aggregate features, which achieved outstanding results. The above methods are all designed for pairwise registration. However, unlike pairwise registration, inliers of one instance constitute outliers of all the other instances in multi-instance point cloud registration. Such pseudo outliers make it difficult to directly generalize the above binary classification models to the case of multi-instance point cloud registration. Inspired by success of previous works in pairwise registration, we introduce deep learning into multi-instance point cloud registration and propose a method that can not only remove outliers but also assign inlier correspondences to each instance.

Multi-model fitting aims to fit multiple models from noisy data, such as fitting multiple planes [6] in a point cloud, estimating fundamental matrices in motion segmentation [18], calculating rigid transformations in multi-instance point cloud registration [42], etc. Since inliers of one instance constitute outliers of all the other instances, multi-model fitting is more challenging than single-model fitting. Existing multi-model fitting methods can be roughly divided into two categories. The first category fits models sequentially [7,8,22,23], which relies on repeatedly sampling and selecting models. For example, sequential RANSAC [22] detects instances in a sequential manner by repeatedly running RANSAC to recover a single instance and then removing its inliers from the input. Progressive-X and Progressive-X+ [7,8] use a better performing Graph-cut RANSAC [5] as a sampler to generate hypotheses. CONSAC [23] introduced deep models into multi-model fitting for the first time, using a network similar to PointNet [38] to guide sampling. The second category fits multiple models simultaneously [29–31,42,43]. For example, many preference analysis-based methods [29,30,43] initially sample a series of hypotheses and then cluster input points according to the residuals of the hypotheses. RansaCov [31] formulates the multi-model fitting as a maximum coverage problem and provides two strategies to solve it approximately. ECC [42] utilizes the spatial consistency [25] of point cloud rigid transformation and clusters correspondences in a bottom-up manner based on a distance-invariant matrix. Although spatial consistency performs efficiently in [42], the lack of orientation constraints makes the distance-invariant matrix still ambiguous in some cases, especially when outliers are close to inliers. In this paper, a novel deep representation is integrated with the spatial consistency to achieve better results.

3   Problem Formulation

We use X and Y to denote the source and target point clouds, respectively. The source point cloud consists of an instance of a 3D model, and the target point cloud contains M instances of the same model, where these instances may be sampled from a part of the 3D model. By matching local features [4,13,20, 46], we can generate putative correspondences between the two point clouds. A correspondence is denoted $c_i = (x_i, y_i) \in \mathbb{R}^6$, where $x_i \in X$, $y_i \in Y$ are the coordinates of a pair of 3D keypoints from the two point clouds. Our objective is to divide the putative correspondence set $C = \{c_i\}_{i=1}^{N}$ into $M + 1$ subsets $C_o, C_1, \ldots, C_M$ satisfying $C = C_o \cup C_1 \cup \ldots \cup C_M$, where C_o denotes the predicted outlier set and C_m denotes the inlier set for the m-th predicted instance. When we know the true instance number is M, recovering M rigid transformations $\{R_m, t_m\}_{m=1}^{M}$ from the two point clouds is to minimize the objective function:

$$\min_{\{R_m, t_m\}_{m=1}^{M}} \frac{1}{M} \sum_{m=1}^{M} \sum_{(x_{mi}, y_{mi}) \in C_m^{gt}} \frac{1}{|C_m^{gt}|} \|y_{mi} - R_m x_{mi} - t_m\|^2 \quad (1)$$

where C_m^{gt} denotes the ground truth inlier set of the m-th instance, and $|C_m^{gt}|$ denotes the number of inliers in C_m^{gt}. The above problem is very challenging, because the inliers in C_i^{gt} constitute outliers in C_j^{gt} for $i \neq j$. In practice, the problem becomes even more difficult because the true instance number in the target point cloud is often unknown in prior, which is the case that we deal with in this paper.

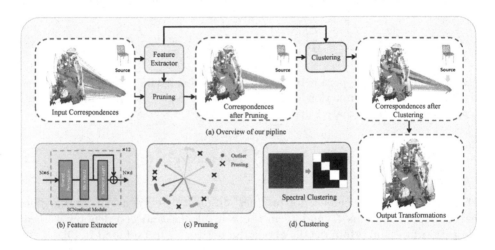

(a) Overview of our pipline

(b) Feature Extractor   (c) Pruning   (d) Clustering

Fig. 2. The pipeline of the proposed multi-instance point cloud registration framework PointCLM. It takes putative correspondence as input, and output M rigid transformations. The green lines and red lines represent inliers and outliers, respectively. After clustering, the correspondences in different clusters are visualized in different colors. The green bounding boxes in output transformations represent the ground truth poses of instances in the target point cloud and the red bounding boxes represent our predictions. The transformed point clouds in the target point cloud are visualized in blue. (Color figure online)

4   Method

In this section, we present our framework for multi-instance point cloud registration, which is illustrated in Fig. 2. Our framework takes the putative correspondences generated by feature matching as input, and it first uses the Feature

Extractor trained by contrastive learning to extract deep representations for the input correspondences (Sect. 4.1). Then, we prune the correspondences according to both spatial consistency and the similarity of their deep representations (Sect. 4.2). Finally, we cluster the remaining correspondences and estimate the transformations for multiple instances using the clustering results (Sect. 4.3).

4.1   Feature Extractor

The first stage of our framework embeds the N input putative correspondences $C = \{c_i\}_{i=1}^N$ into a feature space to obtain well-distributed d-dimension representations $F = \{f_i \in \mathbb{R}^d\}_{i=1}^N$ for the following pruning and clustering. Here, we adopt the SCNonlocal module in [3] as our feature extractor, which consists of 12 repetitive blocks. As shown in Fig. 2(b), each block consists of a shared Perceptron layer, a BatchNorm layer with ReLU and a nonlocal layer. The nonlocal layer integrates the spatial consistency [25] of rigid transformation. Before calculating the features of each layer, a spatial consistency matrix β is first calculated:

$$\beta_{ij} = \left[1 - \frac{d_{ij}^2}{\sigma_d^2}\right]_+, d_{ij} = \left| \|x_i - x_j\| - \|y_i - y_j\| \right| \tag{2}$$

where σ_d is a distance parameter to control the sensitivity to length difference, $[.]_+$ denotes a clamp function $max(x, 0)$ to make $\beta_{ij} \geq 0$. The nonlocal layers aggregate the intermediate features using β:

$$f_i^{k+1} = f_i^k + MLP \left(\sum_{j=1}^{|C|} \text{soft} \max_j (\alpha\beta) g\left(f_j^k\right) \right) \tag{3}$$

where α denotes the embed dot-product similarity between the intermediate feature representations f_i^k and f_j^k in the k-th blocks, and $g(\cdot)$ denotes a linear projection function. More details about the network can be found in [3].

We utilize contrastive learning to train our feature extractor to obtain well-distributed deep representations $F = \{f_i \in \mathbb{R}^d\}_{i=1}^N$. Concretely, for an anchor correspondence $c_{mi} \in C_m^{gt}$, we define the other correspondences in C_m^{gt} as its positive samples, and define the correspondences in $C \backslash C_m^{gt}$ as its negative samples. We define the negative sample with the smallest Euclidean distance to the anchor correspondence in the feature space as the hardest negative sample. During each iteration, we exhaust all inliers as anchors and select their hardest negative samples to build hardest negative pair set $\mathcal{N}$ and randomly select positive samples to build positive pair set $\mathcal{P}$. Our contrastive loss is formulated as:

$$\mathcal{L} = \sum_{(i,j)\in\mathcal{P}} [D\left(f_i, f_j\right) - m_p]_+^2 / |\mathcal{P}| + \sum_{(i,j)\in\mathcal{N}} [m_n - D\left(f_i, f_j\right)]_+^2 / |\mathcal{N}| \tag{4}$$

where m_p and m_n are margins for positive and negative pairs, which prevent the network from overfitting [28]. Since the inlier rate of input correspondences is commonly not high and we can downsample the input correspondences to a suitable scale, our exhaustion over all negative samples to find the hardest one for each minibatch is feasible. Our ablation experiments show that utilizing hardest negative pairs plays an important role in the high performance of the proposed method.

By optimizing the loss in Eq. 4, the representations of correspondences belonging to different instances are easily separable in the feature space, while the representations of correspondences belonging to the same instance are clustered together. We then use these well-distributed representations for both pruning and clustering. Our experiments show that the deep representations provide information that spatial consistency does not have, which makes pruning and clustering more effective.

4.2 Pruning

The input correspondences tend to contain a large proportion of outliers, which severely devastates the following inlier correspondence clustering and transformation estimation. Therefore, an intuitive idea is to first prune the input correspondences to remove outliers. A series of pruning strategies have been proposed in the past. For example, the input can be pruned based on similarity threshold [19] or confidence [53]. In this paper, we propose a density-based pruning strategy which prunes the input correspondences according to the deep representation learned in Sect. 4.1 along with spatial consistency constraints.

As introduced in Sect. 4.1, through contrastive learning, correspondences satisfying the same rigid transformation have similar representations in the feature space and they are far away from other correspondences. This means that the feature density around inliers are higher than that around outliers [44]. Based on this idea, we design a density-based pruning strategy as shown in Fig. 2(c). We treat the isolated points in red as outliers and remove it, while the clustered points in other colors are reserved. The detail of our pruning method is as follows.

We first calculate the feature similarity matrix S^F between correspondences using the extracted deep representations $F = \left\{ f_i \in \mathbb{R}^d \right\}_{i=1}^N$:

$$S_{ij}^F = < f_i, f_j > \tag{5}$$

where $< \cdot >$ represents dot product. After that, we use the feature similarity matrix S^F and the spatial consistency matrix β to calculate the similarity matrix S:

$$S = S^F \otimes \beta \tag{6}$$

where $\otimes$ represents element-wise product, and the spatial consistency matrix β has been calculated before.

Second, we set a threshold τ_S and use it to binarize the similarity matrix S to a binary similarity matrix $\hat{S}$. When the i-th correspondence and the j-th correspondence satisfy sufficient spatial consistency and similarity in the feature space at the same time, $\hat{S}_{ij} = 1$, otherwise $\hat{S}_{ij} = 0$. Now, we can treat the input correspondences as the nodes of a graph, and $\hat{S}$ as the graph's adjacency matrix. The inlier sets can be regarded as subgraphs with a certain scale while outliers appear as isolated points or small-scale subgraphs.

Finally, we sum the rows of the binary similarity matrix $\hat{S}$, and select the correspondences with row-sum values larger than a threshold τ_N. As illustrated in Fig. 2(a), our pruning method can effectively remove most or even all outliers. Our experiments also demonstrate that the pruning step is crucial for our method. We also provide details about how to select the thresholds τ_S and τ_N and ablation experiments in Supplementary Material.

4.3   Clustering and Transformations Estimation

After pruning, we obtain a clean set of correspondences, which is almost free of outliers. The next step is to divide these correspondences into multiple subsets belonging to different instances and estimate the final rigid transformations for all the instances. The correspondence division can be considered as a clustering problem, and the number of instances should be equal to the number of clusters. Here, we use a spectral clustering algorithm [27,45], which can determine the number of clusters automatically. The algorithm consists of the following steps:

Step 1: Recompute the binary similarity matrix $\hat{S}_n$ using the feature similarity and spatial consistency of the remaining correspondences, where n represents the number of correspondences after pruning;

Step 2: Calculate the normalized Laplacian matrix $\hat{L}_n$ of the matrix $\hat{S}_n$, and calculate the eigenvalues $\lambda_1\left(\hat{L}_n\right) \leq \lambda_2\left(\hat{L}_n\right) \leq \ldots \leq \lambda_n\left(\hat{L}_n\right)$ of the normalized Laplacian matrix;

Step 3: Determine the number of clusters M by the following formula:

$$M = \arg\max_{k}\left\{\lambda_{k+1}\left(\hat{L}_n\right) - \lambda_k\left(\hat{L}_n\right)\right\} \tag{7}$$

Step 4: Apply spectral clustering [45] with M clusters.

Since the deep representations have a good distribution in the feature space, the binary similarity matrix $\hat{S}_n$ conforms to the ideal matrix defined in [27]. Therefore, the number of clusters determined by Eq. 7 is reliable, which is proved in [27].

After the above steps, the remaining correspondences are assigned to different clusters as shown in Fig. 2(a), and then we can use a solver such as RANSAC [15] to estimate the rigid transformation of each instance. Because our pruning and clustering strategy are very efficient, the inlier rate of each instance is high, and only a few dozen RANSAC iterations are enough to achieve outstanding performance.

5   Experiment

We conduct experiments on both synthetic and real datasets and compare our PointCLM to state-of-the-art methods [23,29,31,42]. The following sections are organized as follows. First, we illustrate our experimental settings including our implementation, datasets, competitors and evaluation metrics in Sect. 5.1. Next, we conduct experiments on the synthetic and the real datasets in Sect. 5.2 and 5.3, respectively. We further conduct comprehensive ablation studies in Sect. 5.4 to illustrate the efficiency of our PointCLM and the importance of each component. More details are provided in the supplementary material, including the construction of the datasets, more qualitative evaluation and some experiments for hyperparameter choices.

5.1   Experimental Settings

Implementation: We implement our network in Pytorch [33] and implement spectral clustering with sklearn [34]. We randomly downsample the input correspondences to 1000. The distance parameter σ_d is set to 0.05 for the synthetic dataset and 0.1 for the real dataset. We set the dimension d of the deep representation to 128. Threshold τ_S is set to 0.85. Threshold τ_N is set to 10 for the synthetic dataset and 20 for the real dataset. The margins m_p and m_n are set to 0.1 and 1.4, respectively. Our batchsize is set to 16. We optimize the network using the ADAM optimizer with an initial learning rate of 0.01 and train the network for 15K iterations. All the experiments are conducted on a single RTX1080Ti graphic card with Intel Core i7-7800X CPU.

Datasets: We conduct experiments on both synthetic and real datasets. Our synthetic dataset is constructed from ModelNet40 [47], which consists of 12311 meshed CAD models from 40 categories. To construct our synthetic dataset, for each model, we uniformly downsample 1024 points from it to form the source point cloud, and then rotate and translate it 5–10 times repeatedly to generate multiple instances. The instances are mixed with noise points to form the target point cloud as shown in Fig. 3. The rotation along each axis is uniformly sampled in [0,180°] and the translation is in [0,5]. Our input correspondences for synthetic dataset are randomly generated by mixing the ground truth correspondences with outliers. We control the inlier ratio per instance at approximate 2%. We generate 12311 such synthetic source-target point cloud pairs using 12311 models. We use 9843 pairs for training and 2468 pairs for testing. We randomly set aside 10% pairs in the training set for validation.

Our real dataset is Scan2CAD [2], which is constructed using ShapeNet [11] and ScanNet [14]. This dataset uses the CAD models in ShapeNet to replace the point clouds in the real scanned scene and provides accurate annotations, including models' categories, rotations and translations, etc. The dataset provides 1506 annotated scenes, and each scene contains at least one class of instances. Therefore, we make full use of these annotations and split the scenes containing multiple kinds of instances into multiple source-target point cloud pairs for multi-instance registration. In this way, we get 2184 pairs of point clouds, most of which contain 2–5 instances of the same class in the target point clouds. We divide the samples into training set, validation set and test set according to the ratio of 7:1:2. We use fine-tuned FCGF [13] to produce local features and generate putative correspondences by feature matching. More details about our dataset construction are provided in the supplementary material.

Competitors: We compare our PointCLM with four state-of-the-art methods, including T-linkage [29], RansaCov [31], CONSAC [23] and ECC [42]. T-linkage is a typical algorithm based on preference analysis, which samples a series of hypotheses and clusters the inputs based on the residuals of the hypotheses. RansaCov regards multi-model fitting as a maximum coverage problem, which can be approximately solved in greedy strategy or using relaxed linear programming. Here we use the former strategy due to its effectiveness. CONSAC uses a deep network to guide the sampling process, and we train this network using the same training set as our network. ECC clusters the input correspondences based on spatial consistency and doesn't need hypothesis sampling as above methods. For a fair comparison, we not only use the same input, but also fine-tune the above methods both on GPU and CPU, and choose the ones with the best performance for comparison.

Evaluation Metrics: We first define rotation error RE and translation error TE as follow:

$$RE(R) = \arccos \left(\frac{\mathrm{Tr}\left(R^\mathrm{T} R^* \right) - 1}{2} \right), TE(t) = \| t - t^* \|_2 \qquad (8)$$

where R^* and t^* are the ground truth rotation and translation. We consider the instances with both rotation error and translation error below the thresholds to be successfully registered and our thresholds for RE and TE are 15° and 0.1, respectively. Since both our method and the above comparing methods predict multiple rigid transformations, we use mean recall (MR), mean precision (MP) and mean F1 Score (MF) as evaluation metric. For a pair of source point cloud and target point cloud, we define instance recall as $\frac{n_{success}^{pred}}{M^{gt}}$ and instance precision as $\frac{n_{success}^{pred}}{M^{pred}}$, where $n_{success}^{pred}$ denotes the number of successfully registered instances in prediction, M^{gt} denotes the ground truth number of instances, and M^{pred} denotes the number of predicted transformations. The instance F1 Score is the harmonic mean of the instance precision and instance recall. We calculate the instance precision, instance recall, and instance F1 Score of each sample in test set and average them to obtain our final evaluation metrics, the mean recall (MR), the mean precision (MP), and the mean F1 Score (MF).

5.2   Experiment on Synthetic Dataset

We first compare our method with other competitors on the synthetic dataset and the results are show in Table 1. The sampling-based methods such as T-Linkage, RansaCov, and CONSAC do not achieve good performance due to extremely low inlier ratio. Benefiting from spatial consistency, ECC performs effectively. Nevertheless, our PointCLM surpasses the second best method ECC by a large margin in all evaluation metrics.

Table 1. Registration results on synthetic dataset (left) and real dataset (right).

	ModelNet40 (synthetic dataset)				Scan2CAD (real dataset)			
	MR(%)	MP(%)	MF(%)	Time(s)	MR(%)	MP(%)	MF(%)	Time(s)
T-linkage [29]	0.61	1.48	0.87	3.89	34.99	46.86	40.07	6.64
RansaCov [31]	0.73	5.33	1.29	0.14	60.50	33.28	42.94	**0.07**
CONSAC [23]	1.00	7.45	1.77	0.61	55.48	53.34	54.39	0.39
ECC [42]	82.90	92.92	87.63	3.56	64.66	69.73	67.10	1.84
PointCLM	**92.60**	**99.69**	**96.01**	**0.06**	**78.10**	70.64	**74.18**	0.10

We provide a set of visualizations to qualitatively evaluate our PointCLM and compare it with other competitors in Fig. 3. The first row of Fig. 3 shows the input correspondences, and our pruning and clustering results. Figure 3(b) shows that our PointCLM surprisingly removes all outliers, and the remaining correspondences are well clustered as shown in Fig. 3 (c). The second row of Fig. 3 shows the registration results of our proposed method and the competitors. It can be seen that both T-Linkage and RansaCov fail to register any instances. For the six instances in the target point cloud, CONSAC only registers one instance successfully. It is worth noting that although ECC register four instances successfully, but it fails to register the two tables in the lower right corner. This is because the two tables are mixed together and spatial consistency is not enough to distinguish them. However, our method successfully registers all instances.

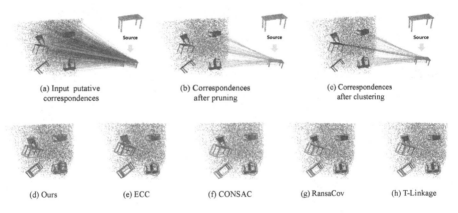

(a) Input putative correspondences   (b) Correspondences after pruning   (c) Correspondences after clustering

(d) Ours   (e) ECC   (f) CONSAC   (g) RansaCov   (h) T-Linkage

Fig. 3. Results on synthetic dataset. In (a) and (b), the green lines and red lines represent inlier correspondences and outlier correspondences, respectively. In (c), the correspondences in each clusters after clustering are visualized in different colors. In (d-f), the green bounding boxes represent the ground truth poses of instances in the target point cloud and the red bounding boxes represent predictions. The transformed point clouds in the target point cloud are visualized in blue. (Color figure online)

5.3   Experiment on Real Dataset

We then compare our PointCLM with other competitors on Scan2CAD [2]. As shown in Table 1, our PointCLM outperforms all the competitors on all three evaluation metrics, MR, MP, and MF and it is also competitive in speed. The performance of ECC and PointCLM is lower than that on the synthetic dataset while the performance of the other methods is higher than that on the synthetic dataset. This is due to the change of the distribution of the instances' inlier ratio.

We also provide a set of visualizations to qualitatively evaluate our Point-CLM and compare it with the other competitors. The first row of Fig. 4 shows the input correspondences, and our pruning and clustering results. Figure 4(b) shows that our method removes almost all outliers, ensuring that the following clustering performs efficiently as shown in Fig. 4(c). For the five instances contained in the target point cloud, T-Linkage and CONSAC successfully register two instances, but one prediction of T-Linkage has large errors. RansaCov successfully registers three instances. Since three chairs in the target point cloud are close to each other, ECC does not successfully register all these instances. Our method successfully accomplishes the registration of all instances.

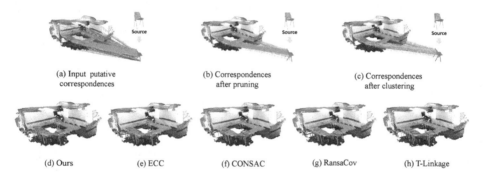

Fig. 4. Results on real dataset. In (a) and (b), the green lines and red lines represent inlier correspondences and outlier correspondences, respectively. In (c), the correspondences in each clusters after clustering are visualized in different colors. In (d-f), the green bounding boxes represent the ground truth poses of instances in the target point cloud and the red bounding boxes represent predictions. The transformed point clouds in the target point cloud are visualized in blue. (Color figure online)

5.4   Ablation Studies

In this section we provide comprehensive ablation studies to illustrate the effectiveness of each component. All our ablation studies are performed on Scan2CAD.

Ablation on Deep Representation: To study the effectiveness of our adopted deep representations, we compare the performance of our framework with and

Table 2. Ablation study results on deep representation and pruning.

Deep representatoin	Pruning	MR(%)	MP(%)	MF(%)	Time(s)
	✓	76.61	65.05	70.36	0.17
✓		62.23	32.77	42.93	1.24
✓	✓	**78.10**	**70.64**	**74.18**	**0.10**

without deep representation. The version without deep representation deletes Feature Extractor and set $S = \beta$, which relies only on spatial consistency for pruning and clustering. The comparison results are shown in Table 2. It can be seen that both the accuracy and the speed metrics are improved by using the deep representations. Without deep representations, less correspondences are pruned and more correspondences need to be clustered, which increase the runtime of our method. Although the framework without deep representations has lower performance in MR, MP and MF, it is still a competitive baseline, which is suitable for the case without training data. This indicates the effectiveness of the pruning and clustering strategies proposed in this paper.

Ablation on Pruning: To quantitatively study the effectiveness of our pruning strategy, we simply remove the pruning strategy in our method, and then compare the performance before and after removal. Table. 2 shows that the performance of our method drops sharply if the pruning step is removed, which is due to the fact that the noisy binary similarity matrix does not conform to the ideal matrix defined in [27] and spectral clustering cannot group the correspondences correctly. This result reveals that pruning is crucial for subsequent clustering.

Ablation on RANSAC Iterations: In addition, we also test the performance of our model with different numbers of RANSAC iterations and the results are shown in Table 3. It can be seen that fairly good results can be achieved with only five iterations, and the performances with 50 and 500 iterations are very close. These results indicate that the pruning and clustering steps greatly improve the inlier ratio of each instance, so reliable results can be estimated using only a small number of iterations.

Table 3. Influence of the number of RANSAC iterations.

RANSAC iterations	MR(%)	MP(%)	MF(%)
5	77.39	67.76	72.26
50	78.10	**70.64**	74.18
500	**79.33**	**70.64**	**74.73**

Ablation on Hardest Negative Pairs: Exhausting the negative pairs to find the hardest ones for each minibatch incurs larger computational overhead, but our ablation shows it worthwhile. We compare it with the same model trained using randomly selected negative pairs. The results of using the hardest negative pairs as in the proposed method and using randomly selected negative pairs are shown in Table 4. All accuracy metrics are improved by using hardest negative pairs in contrastive learning. By comparing Table 4 and Table 2, we can find that using random negative pairs in contrastive representative learning achieves better results than not using the deep representation, but the margin is small. In addition, we collect the average cosine similarity within positive pairs and top-K hardest negative pairs in the feature space in Table 4. The result shows the representation trained using hardest negative pairs are better separated in the feature space, which is more discriminative.

Table 4. Ablation experiment results on training with hardest negative pairs.

	MR(%)	MP(%)	MF(%)	Positive(%)	Top-1(%)	Top-10(%)
Random	76.85	67.50	71.87	95.43	96.91	91.37
Hardest	**78.10**	**70.64**	**74.18**	83.96	61.32	49.65

6 Conclusion

In this paper, we propose a novel framework to address the multi-instance point cloud registration problem. We use contrastive learning to learn well-distributed deep representations for input correspondences, based on which we develop a pruning and a clustering strategy to remove outlier correspondences efficiently and assign the remaining inlier correspondences to correct instances. Then, the transformation from the source point cloud to each instance can be easily estimated. Extensive experiments on both synthetic and real datasets demonstrate the effectiveness of our framework and its superiority over existing solutions. We think the proposed representation learning and the outlier pruning strategy has the potential to be used in pairwise point cloud registration.

Acknowledgements. This work was supported by the National Natural Science Foundation of China under Grant 62076070.

References

1. Aoki, Y., Goforth, H., Srivatsan, R.A., Lucey, S.: Pointnetlk: robust & efficient point cloud registration using pointnet. In: Proceedings of the IEEE/CVF Conference on Computer Vision and Pattern Recognition, pp. 7163–7172 (2019)
2. Avetisyan, A., Dahnert, M., Dai, A., Savva, M., Chang, A.X., Nießner, M.: Scan2cad: learning cad model alignment in rgb-d scans. In: Proceedings of the IEEE/CVF Conference on Computer Vision and Pattern Recognition, pp. 2614–2623 (2019)

3. Bai, X., et al.: Pointdsc: robust point cloud registration using deep spatial consistency. In: Proceedings of the IEEE/CVF Conference on Computer Vision and Pattern Recognition, pp. 15859–15869 (2021)

4. Bai, X., Luo, Z., Zhou, L., Fu, H., Quan, L., Tai, C.L.: D3feat: joint learning of dense detection and description of 3D local features. In: Proceedings of the IEEE/CVF Conference on Computer Vision and Pattern Recognition, pp. 6359–6367 (2020)

5. Barath, D., Matas, J.: Graph-cut ransac. In: Proceedings of the IEEE Conference on Computer Vision and Pattern Recognition, pp. 6733–6741 (2018)

6. Barath, D., Matas, J.: Multi-class model fitting by energy minimization and mode-seeking. In: Proceedings of the European Conference on Computer Vision (ECCV), pp. 221–236 (2018)

7. Barath, D., Matas, J.: Progressive-x: efficient, anytime, multi-model fitting algorithm. In: Proceedings of the IEEE/CVF International Conference on Computer Vision, pp. 3780–3788 (2019)

8. Barath, D., Rozumny, D., Eichhardt, I., Hajder, L., Matas, J.: Progressive-x+: clustering in the consensus space. arXiv preprint arXiv:2103.13875 (2021)

9. Besl, P.J., McKay, N.D.: Method for registration of 3-d shapes. In: Sensor Fusion IV: Control Paradigms and Data Structures, vol. 1611, pp. 586–606. SPIE (1992)

10. Bustos, A.P., Chin, T.J.: Guaranteed outlier removal for point cloud registration with correspondences. IEEE Trans. Pattern Anal. Mach. Intell. **40**(12), 2868–2882 (2017)

11. Chang, A.X., et al.: Shapenet: an information-rich 3D model repository. arXiv preprint arXiv:1512.03012 (2015)

12. Choy, C., Dong, W., Koltun, V.: Deep global registration. In: Proceedings of the IEEE/CVF Conference on Computer Vision and Pattern Recognition, pp. 2514–2523 (2020)

13. Choy, C., Park, J., Koltun, V.: Fully convolutional geometric features. In: Proceedings of the IEEE/CVF International Conference on Computer Vision, pp. 8958–8966 (2019)

14. Dai, A., Chang, A.X., Savva, M., Halber, M., Funkhouser, T., Nießner, M.: Scannet: richly-annotated 3D reconstructions of indoor scenes. In: Proceedings of the IEEE Conference on Computer Vision and Pattern Recognition, pp. 5828–5839 (2017)

15. Fischler, M.A., Bolles, R.C.: Random sample consensus: a paradigm for model fitting with applications to image analysis and automated cartography. Commun. ACM **24**(6), 381–395 (1981)

16. Fouhey, D.F., Scharstein, A.D.: Multi-model estimation in the presence of outliers. Bachelorsthesis, Middlebury College, Middlebury (2011)

17. Fu, K., Liu, S., Luo, X., Wang, M.: Robust point cloud registration framework based on deep graph matching. In: Proceedings of the IEEE/CVF Conference on Computer Vision and Pattern Recognition, pp. 8893–8902 (2021)

18. Hartley, R.I.: In defense of the eight-point algorithm. IEEE Trans. Pattern Anal. Mach. Intell. **19**(6), 580–593 (1997)

19. Heckel, R., Bölcskei, H.: Subspace clustering via thresholding and spectral clustering. In: 2013 IEEE International Conference on Acoustics, Speech and Signal Processing, pp. 3263–3267. IEEE (2013)

20. Huang, S., Gojcic, Z., Usvyatsov, M., Wieser, A., Schindler, K.: Predator: registration of 3D point clouds with low overlap. In: Proceedings of the IEEE/CVF Conference on Computer Vision and Pattern Recognition, pp. 4267–4276 (2021)

21. Huang, X., Mei, G., Zhang, J., Abbas, R.: A comprehensive survey on point cloud registration. arXiv preprint arXiv:2103.02690 (2021)

22. Kanazawa, Y., Kawakami, H.: Detection of planar regions with uncalibrated stereo using distributions of feature points. In: BMVC, pp. 1–10. Citeseer (2004)
23. Kluger, F., Brachmann, E., Ackermann, H., Rother, C., Yang, M.Y., Rosenhahn, B.: Consac: robust multi-model fitting by conditional sample consensus. In: Proceedings of the IEEE/CVF Conference on Computer Vision and Pattern Recognition, pp. 4634–4643 (2020)
24. Lee, J., Kim, S., Cho, M., Park, J.: Deep hough voting for robust global registration. In: Proceedings of the IEEE/CVF International Conference on Computer Vision, pp. 15994–16003 (2021)
25. Leordeanu, M., Hebert, M.: A spectral technique for correspondence problems using pairwise constraints (2005)
26. Li, J., Hu, Q., Ai, M.: Gesac: robust graph enhanced sample consensus for point cloud registration. ISPRS J. Photogram. Remote Sens. **167**, 363–374 (2020)
27. Li, Z., Liu, J., Chen, S., Tang, X.: Noise robust spectral clustering. In: 2007 IEEE 11th International Conference on Computer Vision, pp. 1–8. IEEE (2007)
28. Lin, J., Morere, O., Chandrasekhar, V., Veillard, A., Goh, H.: Deephash: getting regularization, depth and fine-tuning right. arXiv preprint arXiv:1501.04711 (2015)
29. Magri, L., Fusiello, A.: T-linkage: a continuous relaxation of j-linkage for multi-model fitting. In: Proceedings of the IEEE Conference on Computer Vision and Pattern Recognition, pp. 3954–3961 (2014)
30. Magri, L., Fusiello, A.: Robust multiple model fitting with preference analysis and low-rank approximation. In: BMVC, vol. 20, p. 12 (2015)
31. Magri, L., Fusiello, A.: Multiple model fitting as a set coverage problem. In: Proceedings of the IEEE Conference on Computer Vision and Pattern Recognition, pp. 3318–3326 (2016)
32. Misra, I., Girdhar, R., Joulin, A.: An end-to-end transformer model for 3D object detection. In: Proceedings of the IEEE/CVF International Conference on Computer Vision, pp. 2906–2917 (2021)
33. Paszke, A., et al.: Automatic differentiation in pytorch (2017)
34. Pedregosa, F., et al.: Scikit-learn: machine learning in python. J. Mach. Learn. Res. **12**, 2825–2830 (2011)
35. Pham, T.T., Chin, T.J., Yu, J., Suter, D.: The random cluster model for robust geometric fitting. IEEE Trans. Pattern Anal. Mach. Intell. **36**(8), 1658–1671 (2014)
36. Pomerleau, F., Colas, F., Siegwart, R.: A review of point cloud registration algorithms for mobile robotics. Found. Trends Rob. **4**(1), 1–104 (2015)
37. Qi, C.R., Litany, O., He, K., Guibas, L.J.: Deep hough voting for 3D object detection in point clouds. In: Proceedings of the IEEE/CVF International Conference on Computer Vision, pp. 9277–9286 (2019)
38. Qi, C.R., Su, H., Mo, K., Guibas, L.J.: Pointnet: deep learning on point sets for 3D classification and segmentation. In: Proceedings of the IEEE Conference on Computer Vision and Pattern Recognition, pp. 652–660 (2017)
39. Rusinkiewicz, S., Levoy, M.: Efficient variants of the ICP algorithm. In: Proceedings Third International Conference on 3-D Digital Imaging and Modeling, pp. 145–152. IEEE (2001)
40. Stechschulte, J., Ahmed, N., Heckman, C.: Robust low-overlap 3-D point cloud registration for outlier rejection. In: 2019 International Conference on Robotics and Automation (ICRA), pp. 7143–7149. IEEE (2019)
41. Sun, W., Jiang, W., Trulls, E., Tagliasacchi, A., Yi, K.M.: ACNE: attentive context normalization for robust permutation-equivariant learning. In: Proceedings of the IEEE/CVF Conference on Computer Vision and Pattern Recognition, pp. 11286–11295 (2020)

42. Tang, W., Zou, D.: Multi-instance point cloud registration by efficient correspondence clustering. arXiv preprint arXiv:2111.14582 (2021)
43. Toldo, R., Fusiello, A.: Robust multiple structures estimation with J-linkage. In: Forsyth, D., Torr, P., Zisserman, A. (eds.) ECCV 2008. LNCS, vol. 5302, pp. 537–547. Springer, Heidelberg (2008). https://doi.org/10.1007/978-3-540-88682-2_41
44. Torr, P.H., Nasuto, S.J., Bishop, J.M.: Napsac: high noise, high dimensional robust estimation-it's in the bag. In: British Machine Vision Conference (BMVC), vol. 2, p. 3 (2002)
45. Von Luxburg, U.: A tutorial on spectral clustering. Stat. Comput. **17**(4), 395–416 (2007)
46. Wang, H., Liu, Y., Dong, Z., Wang, W., Yang, B.: You only hypothesize once: point cloud registration with rotation-equivariant descriptors. arXiv preprint arXiv:2109.00182 (2021)
47. Wu, Z., et al.: 3D shapenets: a deep representation for volumetric shapes. In: Proceedings of the IEEE Conference on Computer Vision and Pattern Recognition, pp. 1912–1920 (2015)
48. Xu, L., Oja, E., Kultanen, P.: A new curve detection method: randomized hough transform (rht). Pattern Recogn. Lett. **11**(5), 331–338 (1990)
49. Yang, H., Shi, J., Carlone, L.: Teaser: fast and certifiable point cloud registration. IEEE Trans. Rob. **37**(2), 314–333 (2020)
50. Yang, J., Xian, K., Wang, P., Zhang, Y.: A performance evaluation of correspondence grouping methods for 3D rigid data matching. IEEE Trans. Pattern Anal. Mach. Intell. **43**(6), 1859–1874 (2019)
51. Yang, J., Xian, K., Xiao, Y., Cao, Z.: Performance evaluation of 3D correspondence grouping algorithms. In: 2017 International Conference on 3D Vision (3DV), pp. 467–476. IEEE (2017)
52. Yi, K.M., Trulls, E., Ono, Y., Lepetit, V., Salzmann, M., Fua, P.: Learning to find good correspondences. In: Proceedings of the IEEE Conference on Computer Vision and Pattern Recognition, pp. 2666–2674 (2018)
53. Zhao, C., Ge, Y., Zhu, F., Zhao, R., Li, H., Salzmann, M.: Progressive correspondence pruning by consensus learning. In: Proceedings of the IEEE/CVF International Conference on Computer Vision, pp. 6464–6473 (2021)
54. Zuliani, M., Kenney, C.S., Manjunath, B.: The multiransac algorithm and its application to detect planar homographies. In: IEEE International Conference on Image Processing 2005, vol. 3, pp. III-153. IEEE (2005)

Weakly Supervised Object Localization via Transformer with Implicit Spatial Calibration

Haotian Bai⬤, Ruimao Zhang(✉)⬤, Jiong Wang⬤, and Xiang Wan

Shenzhen Research Institute of Big Data, The Chinese Univeristy of Hong Kong (Shenzhen), Shenzhen, China
zhangruimao@cuhk.edu.cn

Abstract. Weakly Supervised Object Localization (WSOL), which aims to localize objects by only using image-level labels, has attracted much attention because of its low annotation cost in real applications. Recent studies leverage the advantage of self-attention in visual Transformer for long-range dependency to re-active semantic regions, aiming to avoid partial activation in traditional class activation mapping (CAM). However, the long-range modeling in Transformer neglects the inherent spatial coherence of the object, and it usually diffuses the semantic-aware regions far from the object boundary, making localization results significantly larger or far smaller. To address such an issue, we introduce a simple yet effective Spatial Calibration Module (SCM) for accurate WSOL, incorporating semantic similarities of patch tokens and their spatial relationships into a unified diffusion model. Specifically, we introduce a learnable parameter to dynamically adjust the semantic correlations and spatial context intensities for effective information propagation. In practice, SCM is designed as an external module of Transformer, and can be removed during inference to reduce the computation cost. The object-sensitive localization ability is implicitly embedded into the Transformer encoder through optimization in the training phase. It enables the generated attention maps to capture the sharper object boundaries and filter the object-irrelevant background area. Extensive experimental results demonstrate the effectiveness of the proposed method, which significantly outperforms its counterpart TS-CAM on both CUB-200 and ImageNet-1K benchmarks. The code is available at https://github.com/164140757/SCM.

Keywords: Weakly supervised object localization · Image context modeling · Class activation mapping · Transformer · Semantic propagation

H. Bai—Research done when Haotian Bai was a Research Assistant at Shenzhen Research Institute of Big Data, The Chinese Univeristy of Hong Kong (Shenzhen).

Supplementary Information The online version contains supplementary material available at https://doi.org/10.1007/978-3-031-20077-9_36.

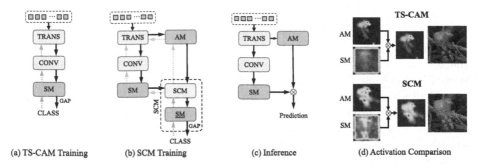

(a) TS-CAM Training   (b) SCM Training   (c) Inference   (d) Activation Comparison

Fig. 1. Transformer-based localization pipelines in WSOL. The dashed arrows indicate the module parameters update during backpropagation. (a) TS-CAM [7]: the training pipeline encodes the feature maps into semantic maps (SM) through a convolution head, then applies a GAP to receive gradients from the image-label supervision. (b) SCM(Ours): our training pipeline incorporates external SCM to produce new semantic maps SM refined with the learned spatial and semantic correlation. Then it updates the Transformer backbone through backpropagation to obtain better attention maps and semantic representations for WOLS. (c) Inference: SCM is dropped out, and we couple attention maps (AM) and SM just like TS-CAM for final localization prediction. (d) Comparison of AM, SM, and final activation maps of TS-CAM and proposed SCM.

1   Introduction

Weakly supervised object localization (WSOL), which learns to localize objects by only using image-level labels, has attracted much attention recently for its low annotation cost. The representative study of WSOL, Class Activation Map (CAM) [36] generates localization results using features from the last convolutional layer. However, the model trained for classification usually focuses on the discriminative regions, resulting insufficient activation for object localization. To solve such an issue, there are many CNN-based methods have been proposed in the literature, including regularization [18,28,30,33], adversarial training [5,18,33], and divergent activation [25,30,31], but the CNN's inherent limitation of local activation dampens their performance. Although discriminative activation is optimal for minimizing image classification loss, it suffers from the inability to capture object boundaries precisely.

Recently, visual Transformer has succeeded in computer vision due to its superior ability to capture long-range feature dependency. Vision Transformer [24] splits an input image into patches with the positional embedding, then constructs a sequence of tokens as its visual representation. The self-attention mechanism enables Transformer to learn long-range semantic correlations, which is pivotal for object localization. A representative study is Token Semantic Coupled Attention Map (TS-CAM) [7] which replaces traditional CNN with Transformer and takes full advantage of long-range dependencies to solve the partial activation problem. It localizes objects by semantic-awarded attention maps from patch tokens. However, we argue that only using a Transformer is not an optimal choice in practice. Firstly, Transformer attends to long-range global dependency while inevitably it cannot capture local structure well, which is critical in describing the boundaries of objects. In addition, Transformer splits images into discrete patches. Thus it may not attend to the inherent spatial coherence of objects, which makes it unable to predict the complete activation. As shown in Fig. 1(d), the activation map obtained from TS-CAM captures the global structure. Still, it concentrates in a small semantic-rich region like the bird's upper body, failing to solve partial activation completely. Furthermore, we observe that the fur has no abrupt change in neighboring space, and its semantic context may favor propagating the activated regions to provide a more accurate result covering the whole body.

Inspired by this potential continuity, we propose a novel external module named Spatial Calibration Module (SCM), tailored for Transformers to produce activation maps with sharper boundaries. As shown in Fig. 1(a)–(b), instead of directly applying Global Average Pooling (GAP) on semantic maps to calculate loss as TS-CAM [7], we insert an external SCM to refine both semantic and attention maps and then use the calibrated features to calculate the semantic loss. Precisely, it implicitly calibrates attention representation of Transformer and produces more meaningful activation maps to cover functional areas based on spatial and contextual coherence. Our core design, a unified diffusion model, is introduced to incorporate semantic similarities of patch tokens and their local spatial relations during training. While in the inference phase, SCM can be dropped out to maintain the model's simplicity, as shown in Fig. 1(c). Then, we use the calibrated Transformer backbone to predict the localization results by coupling SM and AM. The main contributions of this paper are as follows:

1. We propose a novel spatial calibration module (SCM) as an external Transformer module to solve the partial activation problem in WSOL by leveraging the spatial correlation. Specifically, SCM is designed to optimize Transformers implicitly and will be dropped out during inference.
2. We propose a novel information propagation methodology that provides a flexible way to integrate spatial and semantic relationships to enlarge the semantic-rich regions and cover objects completely. In practice, we introduce learnable parameters to adjust the diffusion range and filter the noise dynamically for flexible control and better adaptability.
3. Extensive experiments demonstrate that the proposed framework outperforms its counterparts in the two challenging WSOL benchmarks.

2   Related Work

2.1   Weakly Supervised Object Localization

The weakly supervised object localization aims to localize objects by solely image-level labels. The seminar work CAM [36] demonstrates the effectiveness of localizing objects using feature maps from CNNs trained initially for classification. Despite its simplicity, CAM-based methods suffer from limited discriminative regions, which cannot cover objects completely. The field has focused on how to expand the activation with various attempts. Firstly, the dropout strategy is proposed to guide the model to attend to more significant regions. For instance, HaS [25] hides patches in training images randomly to force the network to seek other relevant parts; CutMix [31] adopts the same way to drop out patches but further augment the area of the patches with ground-truth labels to reduce information loss. Similarly, ADL [5] adopts an importance map to maintain the informative regions' classification power. Instead of dropping out patches, people leverage the pixels correlations to fulfill objects as they often share similar patterns. SPG [34] learns to sense more areas with similar distribution and expand the attention scope. I^2C [35] exploits inter-and-cross images' pixel-level consistency to improve the quality of localization maps. Furthermore, the predicted masks can be enhanced to become complete. GC-Net [16] highlights tight geometric shapes to fit the masks. SPOL [27] fuses shallow features and deep features from CNN that filter the background noise and generates sharp boundaries.

Instead of applying only CNN as the backbone for WSOL, Transformer can be another candidate to alleviate the problem of partial activation as it captures long-range feature dependency. A recent study TS-CAM [7] utilizes attention maps from patches coupled with reallocated semantics to predict localization maps, surpassing most of its CNN counterparts in WSOL. Recent work LCTR [2] adopted a similar framework with Transformer while inserting their tailored module in each Transformer block to strengthen the global features. However, we observe that using Transformer alone cannot solve the partial activation completely as it fails to capture the local structure and ignores spatial coherence. What is more, it is cumbersome to insert a module for each Transformer block like LCTR [2]. To address the issue, we propose a simple external module termed spatial calibration module (SCM) that calibrates Transformer by incorporating spatial and semantic relations to provide more complete feature maps and erase background noise.

2.2   Graph Diffusion

Pixels in natural images generally exhibit strong correlation, and constructing graph structure to capture such relationships has attracted much attention. In semantic segmentation, studies like [13,14] build graphs on images to obtain contextual information and long-term dependencies to model label distribution jointly. In image preprossessing, Gene et.al [3] analyses graphs constructed from 2D images in spectral and succeeds in many traditional processing areas, including image compression, restoration filtering, and segmentation. The graph structure enables many classic graph algorithms and leads to new insights and understanding of image properties.

Similarly, in WSOL, the limited activation regions share semantic coherence with neighboring locations, making it possible to expand the area by information flow to cover objects precisely. In our study, we revise the classic Graph Diffusion Kernel (GDK) algorithm [11] to infer complete pseudo masks based on partial activation results. GDK is initially adopted in graph analysis like social networks [1], search engines [17], and biology [22] to inference pathway membership in genetic interaction networks. GDK's strategy to explore graphs via random walk

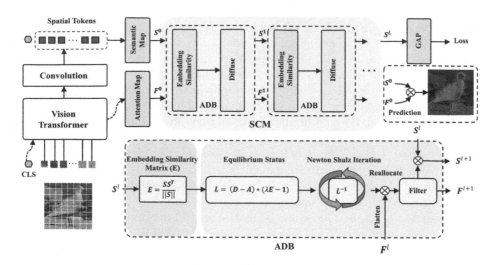

Fig. 2. The overall framework consists of two parts. (Left) Vision Transformer provides the original attention map F_0 and semantic map S_0, (Right) They are dynamically adjusted by stacked activation diffusion blocks (ADBs). The detail of the layer design is shown at the bottom-right corner (the residual connections for F_l and S_l are omitted for simplicity). Once model optimized, F_0 and S_0 are directly element-wise multiplied for final prediction.

inspires us to modify it to incorporate information from the image context, enabling dynamical adjustment by semantic similarity.

3   Methodology

This section describes the Spatial Calibration Module (SCM), which is built by stacking multiple activation diffusion blocks (ADB). ADB consists of several submodules, including semantic similarity estimation, activation diffusion, diffuse matrix approximation, and dynamic filtering. At the end of the section, we show how to predict the final localization results by using the proposed framework during the inference.

3.1   Overall Architecture

In WSOL, the attention maps from models trained on image-level labels mainly concentrate on discriminative parts, which fail to cover the whole objects. Our proposed SCM aims to diffuse activation at small areas outwards to alleviate the partial activation problem in WSOL. In a broad view, the whole framework is supervised by image-level labels during training. As shown in Fig. 1(b), Transformer learns to calibrate both attention maps and semantic maps through the semantic loss from SCM implicitly. To infer the prediction, as described in Fig. 1(c), we drop SCM and use the element-wise product of revised maps to localize objects.

As shown in Fig. 2, an input image is split into $N = H \times W$ patches with each represented as a token, where (H, W) is the patch resolution. After grouping these patch tokens and CLS token into a sequence, we send it into I cascaded Transformer blocks for further representation learning. Similar as TS-CAM [7], to build the initial attention map $\boldsymbol{F}^0 \in \mathbb{R}^{H \times W}$, the self-attention matrix $\boldsymbol{W}_i \in \mathbb{R}^{(N+1) \times (N+1)}$ at i^{th} layer is averaged over the multiple self-attention heads. Denote $\boldsymbol{M}_i \in \mathbb{R}^{H \times W}$ as attention weights that corresponds to the class token in $\boldsymbol{W}_i$, we average $\{\boldsymbol{M}_i\}_{i=1}^I$ across all intermediate layers to get the attention map $\boldsymbol{F}^0$ of Transformer.

$$\boldsymbol{F}^0 = \frac{1}{I} \sum_{i=1}^I \boldsymbol{M}_i \tag{1}$$

To obtain the semantic map $\boldsymbol{S}^0 \in \mathbb{R}^{H \times W \times C}$, where C denotes the number of categories, we extract all spatial tokens $\{\boldsymbol{t}_n\}_{n=1}^N$ from the last Transformer layer and then encode them by a convolution head,

$$\boldsymbol{S}^0 = \text{reshape}(\boldsymbol{t}_1...\boldsymbol{t}_N) * \boldsymbol{k} \tag{2}$$

where $*$ is the convolution operation, $\boldsymbol{k}$ is a 3×3 convolution kernel, and reshape$(\cdot)$ is an operation that converts a sequence of tokens into 2D feature maps. Then we send both $\boldsymbol{F}^0$ and $\boldsymbol{S}^0$ into SCM to refine them.

As illustrated in Fig. 2, for the lth ADB, denote $\boldsymbol{S}^l$ and $\boldsymbol{F}^l$ as the inputs, and $\boldsymbol{S}^{l+1}$ and $\boldsymbol{F}^{l+1}$ as the outputs. Firstly, to guide the propagation, we estimate embedding similarity $\boldsymbol{E}$ between pairs of patches in $\boldsymbol{S}^l$. To enlarge activation $\boldsymbol{F}^l$, we apply $\boldsymbol{E}$ to diffuse $\boldsymbol{F}^l$ towards the equilibrium status indicated by the inverse of Laplacian matrix $\boldsymbol{L}^l$. In practice, we re-activate $\boldsymbol{F}^l$ by approximating $(\boldsymbol{L}^l)^{-1}$ with Newton Shulz Iteration. Afterward, a dynamic filtering module is applied to remove over-diffused parts. Finally, the refined $\boldsymbol{F}^l$ updates $\boldsymbol{S}^l$ via an element-wise multiplication.

In general, by stacking multiple ADBs, the intensity of both maps is dynamically adjusted to balance semantic and spatial features. In the training phase, we apply GAP to $\boldsymbol{S}^L$ to get classification logits and calculate semantic loss with the ground truth. During inference, SCM will be dropped out, and the element-wise product of newly extracted $\boldsymbol{F}^0$ and $\boldsymbol{S}^0$ is used to obtain the localization result.

3.2 Activation Diffusion Block

In this subsection, we dive into Activation Diffusion Block (ADB). Under the assumption of continuity of visual content, we calculate the semantic and spatial relationships of patches in $\boldsymbol{S}^L$, then diffuse it outwards dynamically to alleviate the partial activation problem in WSOL.

Semantic Similarity Estimation. Within the lth activation diffusion block, $l \in \{1, 2, ..., L\}$, we need semantic and spatial relationships between any pair of

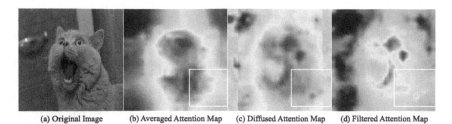

(a) Original Image   (b) Averaged Attention Map   (c) Diffused Attention Map   (d) Filtered Attention Map

Fig. 3. Illustration of activation diffusion pipeline with a hand-crafted example. (a) Input image. (b) Original Transformer's attention map. (c) Diffused attention map. (d) Filtered attention map. As the spatial coherence is embedded into the attention map via our SCM, the obtained attention map by using proposed method captures a complete object boundary with less noise.

patches for propagation. To achieve it, we construct an undirected graph with each v_i^l connected with its first-order neighbors. Please refer to Fig. 5 at the Appendix for details. Given token representation of S^l, we build an N-node graph G^l. Denote the ith node as $v_i^l \in \mathbb{R}^Q$. Then, we can infer the semantic similarity E^l, where the specific element $E_{i,j}^l$ is defined as the cosine distance between v_i^l and v_j^l:

$$E_{i,j}^l = \frac{v_i^l(v_j^l)^{\mathsf{T}}}{||v_i{}^l||||v_j{}^l||} \tag{3}$$

where v_i^l and v_j^l are flattened vectors, and the larger value $E_{i,j}^l$ denotes the higher similarity shared by v_i^l and v_j^l.

Activation Diffusion. To present spatial relationship, we define a binary adjacency matrix $A^l \in \mathbb{R}^{N \times N}$, whose element $A_{i,j}^l$ indicates whether v_i^l and v_j^l are connected. We further introduce a diagonal degree matrix $D^l \in \mathbb{R}^{N \times N}$, where $D_{i,i}^l$ corresponds to the summation of all the degrees related to v_i^l. Then, we obtain Laplacian matrix $\hat{L}^l = D^l - A^l$, with each element $(L^l)_{i,j}^{-1}$ describes the correlation of v_i^l and v_j^l at the equilibrium status.

Recent studies [6,13,14] on graph representation inspire us that the inverse of the Laplacian matrix leads to the global diffusion, which allows each unit to communicate with the rest. To enhance the diffusion with semantic relationships, we incorporate $\hat{L}^l$ with node contextual information E^l. Intuitively, we take advantage of the spatial connectivity and semantic coherence to split the tokens into the semantic-awarded foreground objects and the background environment. In practice, we use a learnable parameter λ to dynamically adjust the semantic intensity, which makes the diffusion process more flexible and easier to fit various situations. The Laplacian matrix L^l with semantics is defined as,

$$L^l = (D^l - A^l) \odot (\lambda E^l - 1) \tag{4}$$

where $\odot$ represents element-wise multiplication, and $\mathbf{1}$ denotes the information flow exchange with neighboring vertexes. $(\boldsymbol{D}^l - \boldsymbol{A}^l)$ denotes the spatial connectivity, $(\lambda \boldsymbol{E}^l - \mathbf{1})$ represents the semantic coherence, and $\odot$ incorporates them for diffusion. Please refer to Appendix for full details of Eq. (4). After the global propagation, the reallocated activation score map can be calculated as follows,

$$\boldsymbol{F}^{l+1} = (\boldsymbol{L}^l)^{-1}\Gamma(\boldsymbol{F}^l) \tag{5}$$

where $\boldsymbol{F}^{l+1}$ is the output re-allocated attention map and Γ is a flattening operation that reshapes $\boldsymbol{F}^l$ into a patch sequence.

Diffuse Matrix Approximation. In practice, directly using $(\boldsymbol{L}^l)^{-1}$ may be impractical since $\boldsymbol{L}^l$ is not guaranteed to be positive-definite and its inverse may not exist. Meanwhile, as observed in our initial experiments, directly applying the inverse produced unwanted artifacts. To deal with the problems, we exploit Newton Schulz Iteration [20,21] to solve $(\boldsymbol{L}^l)^{-1}$ to approximate the global diffusion result,

$$\begin{aligned} X_0 &= \alpha(\boldsymbol{L}^l)^{\mathsf{T}} \\ X_{p+1} &= X_p(2\boldsymbol{I} - \boldsymbol{L}^l X_p), \end{aligned} \tag{6}$$

where X_0 is initialized as $(\boldsymbol{L}^l)^{\mathsf{T}}$ multiplied by a small constant value α. The subscript p denotes the number of iterations, and $\boldsymbol{I}$ is the identity matrix. As discussed above, we only need $(\boldsymbol{L}^l)^{-1}$ to thrust propagation instead of obtaining the equilibrium result, so we just iterate the Eq. (6) for p times then take the approximated $(\boldsymbol{L}^l)^{-1}$ back to Eq. (5). Then we obtain the diffused activation of $\boldsymbol{F}^l$, which is visualized in Fig. 3(c). We can see that diffusion has redistributed the averaged attention map with more boundary details, such as the *ear* and the *mouth*, which are beneficial for final object localization.

Dynamic Filtering. As depicted in Fig. 3(c), we found that the reallocated score map $\boldsymbol{F}^{l+1}$ provides a sharper boundary, but there is a side-effect that it diffuses the activation out of object boundaries, which may make the unnecessary background context back into $\boldsymbol{S}^{l+1}$ or result in over-estimation of bounding box. Therefore, we propose a soft-threshold filter, depicted as Eq. (7), to increase density contrast between the objects and the surrounding background to depress the outside noise.

$$\mathcal{T}(\boldsymbol{F}^l, \beta) = \beta \cdot \text{tanhShrink}(\frac{\boldsymbol{F}^l}{\beta}) \tag{7}$$

where $\beta \in (0,1)$ is a threshold parameter for more flexible control. $\mathcal{T}$ denotes a soft-threshold function, and $\text{tanhShrink}(x) = x - \tanh(x)$ is used to depress activation under β. Then $\boldsymbol{S}^{l+1} = \boldsymbol{S}^l \odot \mathcal{T}(\boldsymbol{F}^l, \beta)$. As shown in Fig. 3(d), the filter operation removes noise and provides sharper contrast.

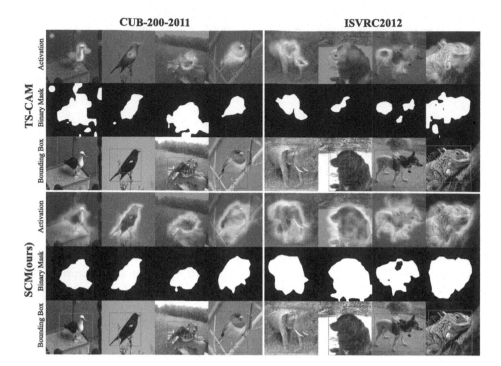

Fig. 4. Visual comparison of TS-CAM and SCM on 4 samples from CUB-200-2011 and ISVRC2012. Here we use three rows for each method to show activation maps, binary map predictions, and bounding box predictions, respectively. The threshold value γ is set to be the optimal values proposed in TS-CAM and SCM.

3.3   Prediction

After optimizing the model through backpropagation, the calibrated Transformer can generate the object-boundary-aware activation maps. Thus, we drop SCM during inference to obtain the final bounding box. Specifically, the bounding box prediction is generated by coupling S^0 and F^0 as depicted in Fig. 2. As $S^0 \in \mathbb{R}^{H \times W \times C}$ is a C-channel 2D semantic map, each channel represents an activation map for a specific class c. To obtain the prediction from score maps, we carry out the following procedures: (1) Pass S^0 through a GAP to calculate classification scores. (2) Select i^{th} map $S_i^0 \in \mathbb{R}^{H \times W}$ corresponding to the highest classification score from S^0. (3) Calculate the element-wise product $F^0 \odot S_i^0$. The coupled result is then up-sampled to the same size as the input for bounding box prediction.

4   Experiments

4.1   Experiment Settings

Datasets. We evaluate SCM on two commonly used benchmarks, CUB-200-2011 [29] and ILSVRC2012 [23]. CUB-200-2011 is an image dataset with photos of 200 bird species, containing a training set of 5,994 images and a test set of 5,794 images. ILSVRC contains about 1.2 million images with 1,000 categories for training and 50,000 images for validation. Our SCM is trained on the training set and evaluated on the validation set from which we only use the bounding box annotations for evaluation.

Evaluation Metrics. We evaluate the performance by the commonly used metric GT-Known and save models with the best performance. For GT-Known, a bounding box prediction is positive if its Intersection-over-Union (IoU) δ with at least one of the ground truth boxes is over 50% . Furthermore, for a fair comparison with previous works, we apply the commonly reported Top1/5 Localization Accuracy(Loc Acc) and Classification Accuracy(Cls Acc). Compared with GT-Known, Loc Acc requires the correct classification result besides the condition of GT-Known. Please refer to the appendix for more strict measures like MaxboxAccV1 and MaxboxAccV2 as recommended by [4] to evaluate localization performance only.

Implementation Details. The Transformer module is built upon the Deit [26] pretrained on ILSVRC. In detail, we initialize λ, β in ABDs to constant values (1 and 0.5 respectively), and choose $p = 4$ and $\alpha = 0.002$ in Eq. (6). For input images, each sample is re-scaled to a size of 256×256, then randomly cropped to 224×224. The MLP head in the pretrained Transformer is replaced by a 2D convolution head with kernel size of 3, stride of 1, and padding of 1 to encode feature maps into semantic maps S^0 (200 output units for CUB-200-2011, and 1000 for ILSVRC). The new head is initialized with He's approach [9]. During training, we use AdamW [15] with $\epsilon = 1e^{-8}$, $\beta_1 = 0.9$, $\beta_2 = 0.99$ and weight decay of 5e-4. On CUB-200-2011, the training lasts 30 epochs with an initial learning rate of 5e-5 and batch size of 256. On ILSVRC, the training procedure carries out 20 epochs with a learning rate of 1e-6 and batch size of 512. We measure model performance on the validation set after every epoch. At last, we save the parameters with the best GT-Known performance on the validation set.

4.2   Performance

To demonstrate the effectiveness of the proposed SCM, we compare it against previous methods on CUB-200-2011 and ILSVRC2012 in Table 1. From GT-Known in CUB, SCM outperforms baseline method TS-CAM [7] with a large margin, yielding GT-known 96.6% with a performance gain of 8.9%. Compared with other CNN counterparts, SCM is competitive and outperforms the state-of-the-art SPOL [27] using only about 24% parameters. As for ILSVRC, SCM surpasses TS-CAM by 1.2% on GT-Known and 5.1% on Top-1 Loc Acc and is competitive against SPOL built on the multi-stage CNN models. Compared with SPOL, SCM has the following advantages, (1) **Simple**: SPOL produces semantic maps and attention maps on two different modules separately, while SCM is only finetuned on a single backbone. (2) **Light-weighted**: SPOL is built on a multi-stage model with huge parameters, while SCM is built on a small Transformer

Table 1. Comparison of SCM with state-of-the-art methods in both classification and localization on CUB [29] and ILSVRC [23] test set. The column Params indicates the number of parameters in backbone on which models are built. Values in bracket show improvement of our method compared with TS-CAM [7]. GT-K. stands for ground truth known.

Model	Backbone	Params (M)	CUB					ILSVRC				
			Cls acc.		Loc acc.			Cls acc.		Loc acc.		
			Top-1	Top-5	Top-1	Top-5	GT-K.	Top-1	Top-5	Top-1	Top-5	GT-K.
CAM[36]	VGG16	138	–	–	34.4	–	–	68.8	88.6	42.8	54.9	–
ACoL[33]	VGG16	138	71.9	–	45.9	61.0	–	67.5	88.0	45.8	63.3	–
MEIL[18]	VGG16	138	74.8	–	57.5	–	–	73.3	–	49.5	–	–
SPG[34]	InceptionV3	24		–	46.6	59.4	–	**84.5**	**97.3**	**56.1**	**70.6**	64.7
I²C[35]	InceptionV3	24	–		55.9	68.3	**72.6**	73.3	91.6	53.1	64.1	68.5
GC-Net[16]	GoogleNet	6.8	76.8	**92.3**	**63.2**	**75.5**	–	77.4	93.6	49.1	58.1	–
ADL[5]	ResNet50-SE	28	80.3	–	62.3	–	–	75.9	–	48.5	–	–
BGC[10]	ResNet50	25.6	–	–	53.8	65.8	69.9	–	–	53.8	65.8	**69.9**
PDM[19]	ResNet50	25.6	**81.3**	–	54.4	65.5	69.6	75.6	91.6	54.4	65.5	69.6
LCTR[2]	Deit-S	22	**85.0**	**97.1**	**79.2**	89.9	92.4	**77.1**	**93.4**	**56.1**	65.8	68.7
TS-CAM[7]	Deit-S	22	80.3	94.8	71.3	83.8	87.7	74.3	82.1	53.4	64.3	67.6
SCM(ours)	Deit-S	22	78.5	94.5	76.4(5.1↑)	**91.6(7.8↑)**	**96.6(8.9↑)**	76.7(2.4↑)	93.0(10.9↑)	**56.1(2.7↑)**	**66.4(2.1↑)**	**68.8(1.2↑)**
PSOL[32]	DenseNet161 + EfficientNet-B7	95.0	–	–	77.4	89.5	93.0	–	–	56.4	66.5	**69.0**
SPOL[32]	ResNet50 + EfficientNet-B7	91.6	–	–	**80.1**	**93.4**	**96.5**	–	–	**59.1**	**67.2**	**69.0**

* CNN-based models are listed above. Transformer-based models are given at the center. Both PSOL [32] and SPOL [27] are composed of multiple-stage models are listed below. The best performance is shown as **bold** for CNN-based, Transformer, and multi-stage models, respectively.

with only about 24% parameters of the former. (3) **Convenient**: SPOL has to infer the prediction with the complex network design, but SCM is dropped out during the inference stage. Furthermore, compared with the recent Transformer-based works like LCTR [2], with the same backbone Deit-S, we surpass it by a large margin 4.2% in terms of GT-Known in CUB and obtain comparable performance on Loc Acc for both CUB and ISVRC. We achieve this without additional parameters during inference, while other recent proposed methods add carefully designed modules or processes to improve the performance. The models are saved with the best GT-Known performance and achieve satisfactory Loc Acc and Cls Acc. Please refer to Sect. 4.3 for more details.

The visual comparison of SCM and TS-CAM is shown in Fig. 4. We observe that TS-CAM preserves the global structure but still suffers from the partial activation problem that degrades its localization ability. Specifically, it cannot predict a complete component from the activation map. We notice that minor and sporadic artifacts appear on the binary threshold maps, and most of them include half parts of the objects. After adding SCM as a simple external adaptor, the masks become integral and accurate, so we believe that SCM is necessary for Transformers to find their niche in WSOL.

4.3   Ablation Study

In this section, we first illustrate the trade-off between localization and classification given the pre-determined backbone. Then we explore why SCM can reallocate and enlarge activation from two perspectives. Specifically, we show

Model	Opt_epoch	GT-Known
conformer-small	5	96.1
vit-small	3	91.0
deit-small	20	96.8
deit-tiny	22	91.8
deit-base	5	93.8

(a) Overview   (b) Loc best   (c) Cls best   (d) Ablation study on adaptability

Fig. 5. (a) The overview of the activation scores propagation, which is a process that evolves from the raw attention regions to the semantic rich regions. (b) Status with the best Loc Acc at the relatively early training stage. (c) Status with the best CLS Acc at the later training stage. (d) The comparison between SCM on different Transformers and various scales. We record GT-known and the epoch number at which the best GT-known performance is obtained.

the visual results of both semantic maps S^l and attention maps F^l across all layers, and analyze them with the learnable parameters' trend during training. Next, we illustrate the influence of module scale by stacking a different number of ADBs. At last, we apply SCM to other Transformers like ViT [24], and Conformer [8] to prove SCM's adaptability. If not mentioned specifically, We carry out all the experiments on Deit-small with SCM consisting of four ADBs and all the experiments share the same implementation discussed above.

Trade-off Between Classification and Localization. SCM is an external module and will be dropped out during inference, adding no additional computational burden. Thus there is a trade-off between performance of localization and classification when the backbone is pre-determined. As shown in Fig. 5(a), SCM aims to calibrate the raw attention to localize the bird. Specifically, Transformer trained with SCM localizes objects well while suffers from sub-optimal CLS Acc in Fig. 5(b). In contrast, as training process continues, it classifies objects better but only focuses on the discriminant part of the whole object, resulting in worse localization result in Fig. 5(c). To clearly show the advantage of SCM for localization, we saved the model with the highest GT-Known as depicted in Fig. 5(b).

Visualization Result of S^l and F^l. Implicit attention of models trained on image-level labels is blessed with remarkable localization ability as shown in CAM [36]. However, due to the effect of label-wise semantic loss, the models would finally be driven to gather around semantic-rich regions, causing the problem of partial activation. TS-CAM [7] suffers from a similar issue despite improving the localization performance by Transformer's long-range feature dependency. In Fig. 6, we display both S^l and F^l at each layer of SCM. We observe that F^0 and S^0 have already covered the object completely, demonstrating that SCM can calibrate Transformer to cover objects. As the layer gets deeper, S^l and F^l concentrate more on semantic-rich regions, and S^L at the last layer is further used to calculate the loss. It explains why we drop out SCM instead of appending it to Transformer, as sharper boundaries are provided at S^0 and F^0.

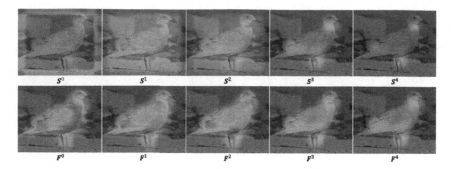

Fig. 6. Visualization of both semantic maps S^l (upper) and attention maps F^l (lower) input to the lth ADB block for a sample from CUB-200-2011 test set.

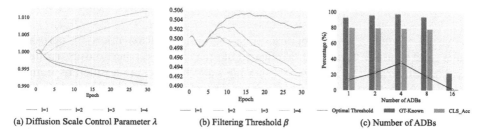

(a) Diffusion Scale Control Parameter λ (b) Filtering Threshold β (c) Number of ADBs

Fig. 7. The learnable parameters update when trained on Deit-small. The layer number l is shown below. (a) λ is used for the diffusion scale control, and lower λ means the wilder scale of diffusion. (b) β determines the threshold under which the activation maps should be filtered. (c) Evaluation of GT-known, Cls Acc (top-1) for different numbers of ADBs. γ (here in percentage format) denotes the threshold above which the bounding box is predicted from the score maps.

Propagating and Filtering. To understand the effect of propagating and filtering, we analyze parameters λ and β in each layer of SCM. As shown in Fig. 7, the training record tells that λ in deeper layers increases, while λ in shallow layers is reduced. It indicates that SCM learns to diffuse activation at front layers while concentrating it in latter layers, verifying that SCM can enlarge partially activated regions with label-wise supervision. On the other hand, β at all layers drops at the beginning, possibly because the activation provided by Transformer is sparse. It takes time for the model to shift its focus from classification to localization, as Transformer is pretrained for classification. Then it starts climbing and goes down again, indicating that attention becomes more concentrated at beginning and then turns sparse to fit the demand across layers. For instance, the front layer prefers a higher filtering threshold to reduce noise, while other layers prefer a smaller threshold to get more semantic context.

Stacking ADBs. We further investigate the effect of module scale by stacking different numbers of ADBs. As shown in Fig. 7(c), we find out that the trend of GT-known and the optimal threshold almost fits the bell curve. It indicates that setting the suitable scale for SCM is essential, as when SCM becomes too deep, it fails to classify and localize objects precisely. On the other hand, the classification accuracy drops as the number of ADBs increases, while the localization performance increases first and drops later. It tells us that classification and localization are two different tasks, and we cannot obtain the optimal for both.

Adapting SCM to More Situations. To evaluate SCM's performance with other Transformers, we select ViT [24], Conformer [8] to testify SCM. Next, we compare SCM on various model scales on Deit. As shown in Fig. 5(d), we record the localization performance with the optimal epoch at which the best model is saved. It turns out that SCM is successfully adapted to ViT and Conformer, which achieves satisfactory performance 91.8% and 96.1% on CUB-200-2011 respectively. On the other hand, we test SCM on Deit with different scales. Surprisingly the larger models don't perform as well as Deit-small. It turns out that increasing model parameter size may not be optimal for SCM to obtain better performance, and the dropped optimal epoch number indicates that it may need a lower learning rate in training for better result.

Discussions. Our study presents a novel way to calibrate the Transformer for WSOL. Although we prove its adaptability to ViT [24], Conformer [8], we cannot calibrate Transformers without CLS token such as Swin [12], since CLS token is required to obtain F^0. Furthermore, it's heuristic to choose the number of iterations used in Eq. (6), and we simplify it as a constant number. Future research may explore methods such as Deep Reinforcement Learning to search the parameter space for the optimal diffusion policy. Furthermore, the equilibrium status Eq. (4) is a patch-wise correlation like the self-attention matrix. It may indicate a new way to find the regions of interest by diffusion.

5 Conclusions

We proposed a simple external spatial calibration module (SCM) to refine attention and semantic representations of Vision Transformer for weakly supervised object localization (WSOL). SCM exploits the spatial and semantic coherence in images and calibrates Transformers to address the issue of partial activation. To dynamically incorporate semantic similarities and local spatial relationships of patch tokens, we propose a unified diffusion model to capture sharper object boundaries and inhibit irrelevant background activation. SCM is designed to be removed during the inference phase, and we use Transformers' calibrated attention and semantic representations to predict localization results. Experiments on CUB-200-2011 and ILSVRC2012 datasets prove that SCM effectively covers the full objects and significantly outperforms its counterpart TS-CAM. As the first Transformer external calibration module on WSOL, we hope SCM could shed light on refining Transformers for the more challenging WSOL scenarios.

Acknowledgement. The work is supported in part by the Young Scientists Fund of the National Natural Science Foundation of China under grant No. 62106154, by Natural Science Foundation of Guangdong Province, China (General Program) under grant No. 2022A1515011524, by Shenzhen Science and Technology Program ZDSYS20211021111415025, and by the Guangdong Provincial Key Laboratory of Big Data Computing, The Chinese Univeristy of Hong Kong (Shenzhen).

References

1. Bourigault, S., Lagnier, C., Lamprier, S., Denoyer, L., Gallinari, P.: Learning social network embeddings for predicting information diffusion. In: Proceedings of the 7th ACM International Conference on Web Search and Data Mining, pp. 393–402 (2014)
2. Chen, Z., et al.: On awakening the local continuity of transformer for weakly supervised object localization. In: Proceedings of the AAAI Conference on Artificial Intelligence (2022)
3. Cheung, G., Magli, E., Tanaka, Y., Ng, M.K.: Graph spectral image processing. Proc. IEEE **106**(5), 907–930 (2018)
4. Choe, J., Oh, S.J., Lee, S., Chun, S., Akata, Z., Shim, H.: Evaluating weakly supervised object localization methods right. In: Proceedings of the IEEE/CVF Conference on Computer Vision and Pattern Recognition, pp. 3133–3142 (2020)
5. Choe, J., Shim, H.: Attention-based dropout layer for weakly supervised object localization. In: Proceedings of the IEEE/CVF Conference on Computer Vision and Pattern Recognition, pp. 2219–2228 (2019)
6. Gao, S., Tsang, I.W.H., Chia, L.T.: Laplacian sparse coding, hypergraph laplacian sparse coding, and applications. IEEE Trans. Pattern Anal. Mach. Intell. **35**(1), 92–104 (2013)
7. Gao, W., et al.: Ts-cam: token semantic coupled attention map for weakly supervised object localization. In: Proceedings of the IEEE/CVF International Conference on Computer Vision, pp. 2886–2895 (2021)
8. Gulati, A., et al.: Conformer: convolution-augmented transformer for speech recognition. arXiv preprint arXiv:2005.08100 (2020)
9. He, K., Zhang, X., Ren, S., Sun, J.: Delving deep into rectifiers: surpassing human-level performance on imagenet classification. In: Proceedings of the IEEE International Conference on Computer Vision, pp. 1026–1034 (2015)
10. Kim, E., Kim, S., Lee, J., Kim, H., Yoon, S.: Bridging the gap between classification and localization for weakly supervised object localization. arXiv preprint arXiv:2204.00220 (2022)
11. Kondor, R.I., Lafferty, J.: Diffusion kernels on graphs and other discrete structures. In: Proceedings of the 19th International Conference on Machine Learning, vol. 2002, pp. 315–322 (2002)
12. Liu, Z., et al.: Swin transformer: hierarchical vision transformer using shifted windows. 2021 IEEE/CVF International Conference on Computer Vision (ICCV), pp. 9992–10002 (2021)
13. Liu, Z., Li, X., Luo, P., Loy, C.C., Tang, X.: Semantic image segmentation via deep parsing network. In: Proceedings of the IEEE International Conference on Computer Vision, pp. 1377–1385 (2015)
14. Liu, Z., Li, X., Luo, P., Loy, C.C., Tang, X.: Deep learning Markov random field for semantic segmentation. IEEE Trans. Pattern Anal. Mach. Intell. **40**(8), 1814–1828 (2017)
15. Loshchilov, I., Hutter, F.: Fixing weight decay regularization in adam (2018)

16. Lu, W., Jia, X., Xie, W., Shen, L., Zhou, Y., Duan, J.: Geometry constrained weakly supervised object localization. In: Vedaldi, A., Bischof, H., Brox, T., Frahm, J.-M. (eds.) ECCV 2020. LNCS, vol. 12371, pp. 481–496. Springer, Cham (2020). https://doi.org/10.1007/978-3-030-58574-7_29

17. Ma, H., King, I., Lyu, M.R.: Mining web graphs for recommendations. IEEE Trans. Knowl. Data Eng. **24**(6), 1051–1064 (2011)

18. Mai, J., Yang, M., Luo, W.: Erasing integrated learning: a simple yet effective approach for weakly supervised object localization. In: Proceedings of the IEEE/CVF Conference on Computer Vision and Pattern Recognition, pp. 8766–8775 (2020)

19. Meng, M., Zhang, T., Yang, W., Zhao, J., Zhang, Y., Wu, F.: Diverse complementary part mining for weakly supervised object localization. IEEE Trans. Image Process. **31**, 1774–1788 (2022)

20. Pan, V.: Fast and efficient parallel algorithms for the exact inversion of integer matrices. In: Maheshwari, S.N. (ed.) FSTTCS 1985. LNCS, vol. 206, pp. 504–521. Springer, Heidelberg (1985). https://doi.org/10.1007/3-540-16042-6_29

21. Pan, V., Reif, J.: Efficient parallel solution of linear systems. In: Proceedings of the Seventeenth Annual ACM Symposium on Theory of Computing, pp. 143–152 (1985)

22. Qi, Y., Suhail, Y., Lin, Y.Y., Boeke, J.D., Bader, J.S.: Finding friends and enemies in an enemies-only network: a graph diffusion kernel for predicting novel genetic interactions and co-complex membership from yeast genetic interactions. Genome Res. **18**(12), 1991–2004 (2008)

23. Russakovsky, O., et al.: Imagenet large scale visual recognition challenge. Int. J. Comput. Vision **115**(3), 211–252 (2015)

24. Sharir, G., Noy, A., Zelnik-Manor, L.: An image is worth 16×16 words, what is a video worth? arXiv preprint arXiv:2103.13915 (2021)

25. Singh, K.K., Lee, Y.J.: Hide-and-seek: forcing a network to be meticulous for weakly-supervised object and action localization (2017)

26. Touvron, H., Cord, M., Douze, M., Massa, F., Sablayrolles, A., Jégou, H.: Training data-efficient image transformers & distillation through attention. In: International Conference on Machine Learning, pp. 10347–10357. PMLR (2021)

27. Wei, J., Wang, Q., Li, Z., Wang, S., Zhou, S.K., Cui, S.: Shallow feature matters for weakly supervised object localization. In: Proceedings of the IEEE/CVF Conference on Computer Vision and Pattern Recognition, pp. 5993–6001 (2021)

28. Wei, J., Wang, S., Zhou, S.K., Cui, S., Li, Z.: Weakly supervised object localization through inter-class feature similarity and intra-class appearance consistency. In: European Conference on Computer Vision. Springer, Heidelberg (2022)

29. Welinder, P., et al.: Caltech-ucsd birds 200. Technical report (2010)

30. Xue, H., Liu, C., Wan, F., Jiao, J., Ji, X., Ye, Q.: Danet: divergent activation for weakly supervised object localization. In: Proceedings of the IEEE/CVF International Conference on Computer Vision, pp. 6589–6598 (2019)

31. Yun, S., Han, D., Oh, S.J., Chun, S., Choe, J., Yoo, Y.: Cutmix: regularization strategy to train strong classifiers with localizable features. In: Proceedings of the IEEE/CVF International Conference on Computer Vision, pp. 6023–6032 (2019)

32. Zhang, C.L., Cao, Y.H., Wu, J.: Rethinking the route towards weakly supervised object localization. In: Proceedings of the IEEE/CVF Conference on Computer Vision and Pattern Recognition, pp. 13460–13469 (2020)

33. Zhang, X., Wei, Y., Feng, J., Yang, Y., Huang, T.S.: Adversarial complementary learning for weakly supervised object localization. In: Proceedings of the IEEE Conference on Computer Vision and Pattern Recognition, pp. 1325–1334 (2018)

34. Zhang, X., Wei, Y., Kang, G., Yang, Y., Huang, T.: Self-produced guidance for weakly-supervised object localization. In: Proceedings of the European Conference on Computer Vision (ECCV), pp. 597–613 (2018)
35. Zhang, X., Wei, Y., Yang, Y.: Inter-image communication for weakly supervised localization. In: Vedaldi, A., Bischof, H., Brox, T., Frahm, J.-M. (eds.) ECCV 2020. LNCS, vol. 12364, pp. 271–287. Springer, Cham (2020). https://doi.org/10.1007/978-3-030-58529-7_17
36. Zhou, B., Khosla, A., Lapedriza, A., Oliva, A., Torralba, A.: Learning deep features for discriminative localization. In: Proceedings of the IEEE Conference on Computer Vision and Pattern Recognition, pp. 2921–2929 (2016)

MTTrans: Cross-domain Object Detection with Mean Teacher Transformer

Jinze Yu[1], Jiaming Liu[2], Xiaobao Wei[2], Haoyi Zhou[1], Yohei Nakata[3], Denis Gudovskiy[3], Tomoyuki Okuno[3], Jianxin Li[1], Kurt Keutzer[4], and Shanghang Zhang[2(✉)]

[1] Beihang University, Beijing, China
yujinze@buaa.edu.cn
[2] Peking University, Beijing, China
shanghang@pku.edu.cn
[3] Panasonic Holdings Corporation, Osaka, Japan
[4] University of California, Berkeley, USA

Abstract. Recently, DEtection TRansformer (DETR), an end-to-end object detection pipeline, has achieved promising performance. However, it requires large-scale labeled data and suffers from domain shift, especially when no labeled data is available in the target domain. To solve this problem, we propose an end-to-end cross-domain detection Transformer based on the mean teacher framework, **MTTrans**, which can fully exploit unlabeled target domain data in object detection training and transfer knowledge between domains via pseudo labels. We further propose the comprehensive multi-level feature alignment to improve the pseudo labels generated by the mean teacher framework taking advantage of the cross-scale self-attention mechanism in Deformable DETR. Image and object features are aligned at the local, global, and instance levels with domain query-based feature alignment (DQFA), bi-level graph-based prototype alignment (BGPA), and token-wise image feature alignment (TIFA). On the other hand, the unlabeled target domain data pseudo-labeled and available for the object detection training by the mean teacher framework can lead to better feature extraction and alignment. Thus, the mean teacher framework and the comprehensive multi-level feature alignment can be optimized iteratively and mutually based on the architecture of Transformers. Extensive experiments demonstrate that our proposed method achieves state-of-the-art performance in three domain adaptation scenarios, especially the result of Sim10k to Cityscapes scenario is remarkably improved from 52.6 mAP to 57.9 mAP. Code will be released https://github.com/Lafite-Yu/MTTrans-OpenSource.

Keywords: Unsupervised domain adaptation · Object detection · Mean teacher transformer

Supplementary Information The online version contains supplementary material available at https://doi.org/10.1007/978-3-031-20077-9_37.

1   Introduction

Object detection is one of the fundamental computer vision tasks which has been improved dramatically in the last decades. Methods based on Convolutional Neural Networks (CNN) [21,23,24] achieve satisfying results but rely heavily on certain hand-crafted operations and are not fully end-to-end. Recently, Transformer-based approaches [3,47] have been introduced as a promising one-stage detector. Although Transformer-based detectors have shown superior detection and generalization performance compared with CNN-based ones [1,41], they still suffer significant performance degradation caused by domain shift or variation of data distribution when tested in scenarios with domain gaps. These motivate the study of unsupervised domain adaptive (UDA) on transformer object detectors [33,42].

The pivot of UDA is to deal with domain shifts between source and target domains. It empowers the learned model to be transferred from the source to the unlabeled target domain. Most previous works are based on cross-domain feature alignment techniques, which rarely use target data in object detection training due to the lack of labels, thus causing insufficient use of data. In this paper, inspired by the prevalent mean teacher mechanism in semi-supervised learning (SSL) tasks [29,35], we innovatively design MTTrans, a cross-domain detection Transformer based on the mean teacher framework. By extending the mean teacher framework to UDA, we can sufficiently exploit unlabeled target data and transfer the knowledge between domains via pseudo labels.

However, directly incorporating the mean teacher framework to UDA object detection often results in degressive performance: the framework is proposed initially to solve the SSL task, in which the labeled and unlabeled data are in the same data distribution. The goal of UDA is to remove domain-specific components from the extracted features, and the mean teacher does not have such an ability. Such domain-specific features increase the divergence between source and target features and degrade the quality of pseudo labels generated by the mean teacher. Therefore, it is crucial to exploit cross-domain feature alignments

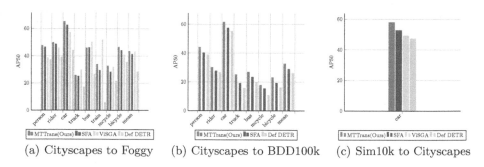

(a) Cityscapes to Foggy   (b) Cityscapes to BDD100k   (c) Sim10k to Cityscapes

Fig. 1. The performance of our proposed MTTrans compared with previous works on different datasets. Our method consistently outperforms the SOTA baseline with a large margin on the scene adaptation and the synthetic to real adaptation, and the performance of each individual category.

to learn domain-invariant features and improve the quality of pseudo labels in the target domain, which is the critical factor for better domain adaptation.

To address the issues above, we propose **MTTrans**, an end-to-end cross-domain detection Transformer framework, and the first Transformer-based study that utilizes the mean teacher structure to transfer knowledge between domains. MTTrans transfer domain-invariant task-relevant knowledge between domains and better utilize the unlabeled data via **pseudo label generation by the mean teacher framework** and the **comprehensive multi-level cross-domain feature alignment** based on the cross-scale attention mechanism in Deformable DETR [47]. With pseudo label generation, the unlabeled target domain data are pseudo-labeled and available in the object detection training. In contrast, in previous works, such data are rarely used due to the lack of labels. The multi-level feature alignment aligns both images and object proposals features at the global, instance, and local levels to enhance the reliability and the quality of the generated pseudo labels under domain shift. On the other hand, with target domain images in object detection training, better feature extraction and alignment can be achieved. Therefore, the mean teacher framework and the feature alignment act as a whole and can be optimized iteratively and mutually.

The comprehensive feature alignment strategy includes **domain query-based feature alignment (DQFA)** to align image and object features at the global level, **bi-level graph-based prototype alignment (BGPA)** which builds prototypes with the object features, and a simple **token-wise image feature alignment (TIFA)** technique for the local-level image features. Inspired by SFA [33], DQFA extracts a feature for each of the entire image and all the object proposals via cross-scale attention and shrinks global domain gaps in scene layout. However, it still suffers from the domain shift caused by object visual layout changing. Therefore, we then propose the novel BGPA technique to build and aggregate prototypes for object features based on their visual similarity, which can better learn categorical and spatial correlations (since objects in the same category and spatially connected tend to be visually similar [25]) and achieve more accurate alignment. Finally, TIFA is performed on the local-level image tokens. The quality of pseudo labels is largely improved with the comprehensive multi-level feature alignment, as shown in Fig. 5. A more detailed visualization analysis will be performed in Sect. 4.4.

Finally, the proposed MTTrans framework achieves promising performance on three challenging domain adaptation benchmarks, as shown in Fig. 1. In the weather adaptation scenario, MTTrans outperforms both end-to-end and two-stage detection algorithms by improving the result to 43.4 mAP (Cityscapes to Foggy Cityscapes). In the scene adaptation scenario, the proposed method surpasses the previous state-of-the-art result [33] by +3.7 mAP, improving the result to 32.6 mAP (Cityscapes to BDD100k). In the synthetic to real adaptation scenario, we achieve an improvement of +5.3 mAP (Sim10k to Cityscapes) over the previous state-of-the-art (SFA [33]), achieving 57.9 mAP.

2   Related Work

2.1   Object Detection

Object detection is one of the fundamental tasks of computer vision [12,19,43]. Recently, CNN-based methods with large-scale labeled training data have become the mainstream object detection approaches, categorized into stronger two-stage methods [20,24,39] and faster, lighter one-stage methods [21,23,31]. However, these methods extremely depend on handcrafted components, notably the non-maximum suppression (NMS) post-processing, and thus cannot be trained end-to-end. It was recently achieved by DETR [3] and its follow-up work Deformable DETR [47], with the vision Transformers [32]. Deformable DETR proposes a novel deformable multi-head attention mechanism to provide sparsity in attention and multi-scale feature aggregation without feature pyramid structure, allowing for faster training and better performance. In this work, we choose Deformable DETR as the base detector for its simple yet powerful working flow and the great potential of the attention mechanism for cross-domain feature extraction.

2.2   Unsupervised Domain Adaptive Object Detection

Domain Adaptive Faster R-CNN [4] is the first work to study domain-adaptive object detection. Most later works follow the cross-domain feature alignment with the adversarial training approach. These works propose to aggregate image or instance features based on their categorical predictions [34,36] or spatial correlations [2,36], and the features are aligned hierarchically at one or some levels in global, local, instance and category levels [2,22,26,34,36]. More recent works include PICA [44], which focuses on Few-shot Domain Adaptation, and Visually Similar Group Alignment (ViSGA) [25], which proposes to aggregate instance features based on their visual similarity with similarity-based hierarchical agglomerative clustering, which achieves state-of-the-art performance on some benchmarks. Other methods focus on applying other domain adaptation techniques or other base detectors, such as Mean Teacher with Object Relations (MTOR) [2] and Unbiased Mean Teacher (UMT) [8]. Regarding the Transformer-based models, Sequence Feature Alignment (SFA) [33] proposes a domain adaptive end-to-end object detector based on Deformable DETR. DA-DETR [42] proposes an alignment technique based on convolutions and spatial and channel attention for DETR. CDTrans [37] and TVT [38] are proposed for cross-domain classification. In this paper, we propose cooperating the mean teacher framework with multi-level cross-domain feature alignment based on Deformable DETR to achieve end-to-end UDA object detection.

3   Method

This section introduces our MTTrans framework for domain adaptive detection Transformer. In unsupervised domain adaptation (UDA), the data include the labeled source images and the unlabeled target images. Our goal is to transfer object detection task-specific domain-invariant knowledge from the source to the target domain and make the target domain pseudo-labeled and thus available for object detection training with the mean teacher framework and the multi-level source-target feature alignment.

In Sect. 3.1, based on the mean teacher, we propose an end-to-end cross-domain detection Transformer framework, **MTTrans**, which learns similarities between the source and target domain with pseudo labels. We then propose multi-level source-target feature alignment in Sect. 3.2 to address the domain shift problem and further improve the reliability of the pseudo labels generated by the mean teacher for the target domain. Finally, in Sect. 3.3, we elaborate on the training policy of our framework. The overall pipeline is shown in Fig. 2.

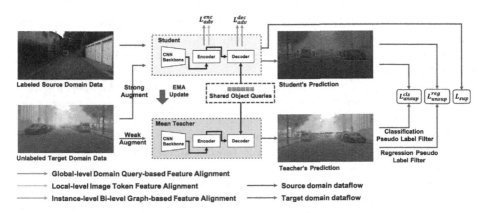

Fig. 2. The framework of MTTrans, composed of a *student model* which is the actual task model, and a temporal ensembled version of the student model called the *teacher model*. The teacher model is updated by EMA of the student model to generate pseudo labels for the target domain. To improve the quality of the pseudo labels on the target domain and reduce the source-target discrepancy, we additionally design multi-level feature alignment strategies.

3.1   Mean Teacher-Based Knowledge Transfer Framework

MTTrans is based on Deformable DETR [47] and is derived from the mean teacher framework, consisting of two models with the same architecture and identical initialization weights. The student model is updated with back-propagation, while the teacher model is updated by student's weights with exponential moving average (EMA). Thus, the teacher model can be considered as multiple temporal ensembled student models: for weights of the teacher model θ'_t at time step t, it is the EMA of successive student's weights θ_t:

$$\theta'_t = \alpha\theta'_{t-1} + (1 - \alpha)\theta_t \tag{1}$$

where α is a smoothing coefficient hyperparameter. All of the teacher's weights are updated according to Eq. 1, except for object query embeddings, which are kept the same between the two models to further enhance consistency

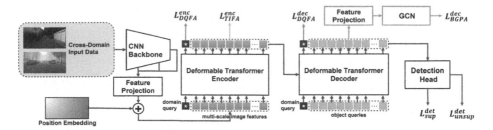

Fig. 3. The detailed structure of the student model, which is composed of a detection Transformer backbone, and the proposed multi-level feature alignment.

between them. The object queries are trainable embeddings, initialized with the normal distribution at the start of the training procedure. Then we use the temporally ensembled teacher model to guide the student model's training in the target domain via pseudo labels.

As a crucial factor for the teacher-student framework, pseudo labels are tactfully generated in our work. Object proposals with any foreground category score higher than a pre-defined threshold are assigned as pseudo labels. In addition, the unlabeled target images are strongly augmented for the student model (denoted as I_{tgt}) and weakly augmented for the teacher model (denoted as I'_{tgt}) [28]. In such a way, the teacher model's prediction can be more accurate, enabling the student model to learn from the generated pseudo labels. Although directly applying the mean teacher to the UDA task improves the results, the pseudo labels generated on the target domain are still of low quality because of the data distribution shift. The temporal ensembled model tends to accumulate errors and collapse.

3.2   Multi-level Cross-domain Adversarial Feature Alignment

To address the issue above, we design the comprehensive multi-level cross-domain feature alignment based on the cross-scale self-attention mechanism of Deformable DETR [47] to strengthen the reliability of the pseudo labels generated when faced with domain shift. The alignment is performed on different parts and at three levels of the student model, including **domain query-based feature alignment (DQFA)** for global-level image and instance features on encoder and decoder outputs, **bi-level graph-based prototype alignment (BGPA)** for instance-level object proposal features on decoder outputs, and **token-wise image feature alignment (TIFA)** for local-level image features on encoder outputs, as shown in Fig. 3.

Global-Level Domain Query-Based Feature Alignment (DQFA). Inspired by the global memory [9,11] and the sparse attention mechanism [5,45], we adopt DQFA in SFA [33] to extract and align global-level context features for images or object proposals. Besides, the domain query provides a global

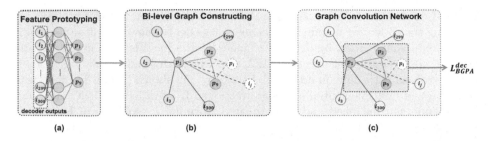

Fig. 4. The proposed bi-level graph-based prototype alignment (BGPA) for instance-level object proposal features. M prototypes (set as 9 in our work) for instance features are first generated with decoder output by an MLP. The prototype features are then aggregated before alignment by constructing a bi-level graph and a GCN.

link between any other local feature tokens, through which any two tokens can attend to each other. The two global-level feature tokens generated by the two domain queries are further classified by two domain discriminators, respectively. The domain discriminators' optimization goal is to make the extracted features more domain-specific and distinguishable, which is opposite to the purpose of the cross-domain model, which tries to learn more domain-invariant features. Therefore, the domain adversarial training method [10] is adopted to insert gradient reversal layers and reverse back-propagated gradients from domain discriminators to optimize the detection model to extract domain-invariant features.

Instance-Level Bi-level Graph-Based Prototype Alignment (BGPA).
The above DQFA can effectively shrink global domain gaps in scene layout, but it still suffers from domain shift caused by object visual layout changing. Previous work proposes aggregating and further aligning instance features based on their visual similarities [25]. In MTTrans, we propose BGPA to build and aggregate prototypes for object features based on their feature similarities with prototyping and graph construction, which can learn from categorical and spatial correlations (since objects in the same category and spatially connected tend to be visually similar [25]) and achieve a more accurate alignment. As illustrated in Fig. 4(a), M prototypes (set as 9 in this work) for object proposals are generated by an MLP with the output feature tokens of the decoder. In Fig. 4(b), we construct an undirected bi-level graph with the prototypes and the decoder outputs. The prototypes are connected to each other and the decoder outputs, while edges' weights are calculated by the nodes' cosine similarity. As shown in Fig. 4(c), the created graph is then processed with a graph convolutional network (GCN) [18,30]. Finally, the graph-aggregated prototypes are aligned with a domain discriminator to alleviate domain shift at the instance level.

Local-Level Token-Wise Image Feature Alignment (TIFA). Though adopting the above two alignments, the mean teacher framework still suffers from the domain shift caused by detailed changes at the local level. Thus, we additionally add a simple yet effective TIFA that aligns the multi-scale image local feature tokens with domain adversarial training. As shown in Fig. 3, image feature maps of multiple spatial scales are retrieved from different CNN backbone layers and then flattened and concatenated, forming a sequence of local-level image feature tokens. The feature tokens are aggregated with each other by the cross-scale self-attention mechanism in the encoder, obtaining context-enriched local-level features. TIFA aligns these tokens one by one with the domain discriminator. There exist some more complex feature alignment methods at the local level, and BGPA proposed above can also be applied to these feature tokens. However, these methods may result in performance degradation compared with the simple TIFA, as shown in Sect. 4.3.

3.3 Progressive Cross-domain Knowledge Transfer with Mean Teacher and Adversarial Feature Alignment

Compared with previous mean teacher Transformer works that focus on semi-supervised learning, we propose not only the comprehensive multi-level feature alignment described above to strengthen the reliability of the cross-domain pseudo labels but also a two-step progressive transfer training policy.

First of all, the model needs to learn from the labeled source domain data first and then be able to generate informative pseudo labels. Moreover, it is difficult to simultaneously train a randomly initialized model to perform well on both two distinctly different datasets. Therefore, we divide the mean teacher training procedure into a burn-in and a transfer training step. In the first burn-in step, we train the student model in the labeled source domain with object detection and feature alignment tasks. The loss function is a combination of both tasks:

$$\mathcal{L}_{sup} = \mathcal{L}_{det}(I_{src}, y_{src}) - \mathcal{L}_{adv} \tag{2}$$

Given a source domain image $I_{src} \in \mathcal{D}_{src}$, the backbone G and the encoder Enc of the Transformer produce the image features f_{src}, then the decoder Dec produces the features for the object proposals g, and finally, the detection head H obtains the bounding boxes and the object category predictions. The supervised detection loss is defined as follows:

$$\mathcal{L}_{det}(I_{src}, y_{src}) = l(H(g), y_{src}) \tag{3}$$

where $l(\cdot)$ denotes the supervised object detection loss which keeps the same with Deformable DETR [47].

The cross-domain adversarial feature alignment loss $\mathcal{L}_{adv}$ comprises four parts: DQFA loss on image features $\mathcal{L}_{enc}^{DQFA}$, DQFA loss on object features $\mathcal{L}_{dec}^{DQFA}$, BGPA loss $\mathcal{L}_{dec}^{BGPA}$, and TIFA loss $\mathcal{L}_{enc}^{TIFA}$:

$$\mathcal{L}_{adv} = \lambda_1 \mathcal{L}_{enc}^{DQFA}(f) + \lambda_2 \mathcal{L}_{dec}^{DQFA}(g) + \lambda_3 \mathcal{L}_{dec}^{BGPA}(g) + \lambda_4 \mathcal{L}_{enc}^{TIFA}(f) \tag{4}$$

$\mathcal{L}_{enc}^{DQFA}$ is computed in the following way, and the other three parts are computed in the same way:

$$\mathcal{L}_{enc}^{DQFA}(f) = \mathbb{E}_{f \in \mathcal{D}_{src}} \log D(f) + \mathbb{E}_{f \in \mathcal{D}_{tgt}} \log(1 - D(f)) \tag{5}$$

where D denotes the domain discriminator.

Then, in the transfer training step, both the student and the teacher model are initialized with the model trained in the first step. The student model is trained on the source and the target domain alternatively, one epoch for each domain, to maintain the object detection performance and learn to transfer between domains. The student model is updated with back-propagation, and the teacher model is updated by the student model's weights after each source domain trained epoch. The loss for target domain training is made up of two components: UDA object detection loss and adversarial feature alignment loss:

$$\mathcal{L}_{unsup} = \mathcal{L}_{det}(I_{tgt}, \hat{y}_{tgt}) - \mathcal{L}_{adv} \tag{6}$$

where $\mathcal{L}_{adv}$ is denoted in Eq. 4, I_{tgt} is the unlabeled target domain images, $\hat{y}_{tgt}$ is the generated pseudo labels, and $\mathcal{L}_{det}(I_{tgt}, \hat{y}_{tgt})$ is the pseudo-supervised object detection loss on the target domain.

To summarize, let T denote the object detector and D denote the domain discriminators, the final training objective of MTTrans is defined as :

$$\min_{T} \max_{D} \mathcal{L}_{det}^{src}(T) + \mathcal{L}_{det}^{tgt}(T) - \mathcal{L}_{adv}(T, D) \tag{7}$$

4   Evaluation

In this section, we conduct extensive experiments to demonstrate the advantages of our proposed method. In Sect. 4.1, the details of the experimental setup are given. In Sect. 4.2, we demonstrate the performance of MTTrans in three challenging domain adaptation scenarios, including Weather, Scene, and Synthetic to Real Adaptation. We also conduct comprehensive ablation studies to investigate the impact of each component in Sect. 4.3. Finally, we conduct qualitative analysis to provide a better understanding in Sect. 4.4.

4.1   Experimental Setup

Datasets. We evaluate our method on four public datasets, including Cityscapes [6], Foggy Cityscapes [27], Sim10k [15], and BDD100k [40]. We present the performance of MTTrans in three domain adaptation scenarios according to these datasets:

- **Weather adaptation.** In this scenario, we use Cityscapes collected from urban scenes as the source dataset. It consists of 3,475 images with pixel-level annotation, and 2,975 of them are used for training, the other 500 are for evaluation. Foggy Cityscapes constructed from Cityscapes by a fog synthesis algorithm is used as the target dataset.

- **Scene Adaptation.** In this condition, Cityscapes still serves as the source dataset. We utilize the daytime subset of BDD100k as the target dataset, which consists of 36,728 training images and 5,258 validation images annotated with bounding boxes.
- **Synthetic to Real Adaptation.** In this scenario, we utilize Sim10k created by the Grand Theft Auto game engine as the source domain. It is designed to conclude 10,000 training images with 58,701 bounding box annotations for cars. Car instances in Cityscapes are for target domain training and evaluation.

Implementation Details. Our method is built on the basis of Deformable DETR [47]. We set ImageNet [7] pre-trained ResNet-50 [13] as CNN backbone in all experiments. In the burn-in step, we adopt Adam optimizer [17] during training for 50 epochs. We initialize the learning rate as 2×10^{-4} which decayed by 0.1 after 40 epochs. The batch size is set to 4 for all domain adaptation scenarios. In the second cross-domain training step, the model is trained for 40 epochs, and the initial learning rate is 2×10^{-6}. The learning rate is decayed by 0.1 after 20 epochs. The batch size in this step is set to 2. In addition, we adopt Mean Average Precision (mAP) with a threshold of 0.5 as the evaluation metric. The filtering threshold for pseudo label generation is set to 0.5. All experiments are conducted on NVIDIA Tesla A100 GPUs.

4.2   Comparisons with Other Methods

The proposed MTTrans framework is assessed in three different domain adaptation scenarios, and the results obtained are compared with prior works in this section. SOTA results are achieved in all three scenarios.

Weather Adaptation. Variations in weather conditions are common, yet challenging, and object detectors must be reliable under all conditions. As a result, we evaluate the robustness of models under weather changes by transferring from Cityscapes to Foggy Cityscapes. As shown in Table 1, MTTrans outperforms other end-to-end methods by a significant margin (43.4% vs. 41.3% by the closest and SOTA end-to-end model, SFA). In addition, it achieves competitive results when compared with two-stage approaches.

Scene Adaptation. Scene layouts are not static and frequently change in real-world applications, especially in autonomous driving scenarios. As a result, model performance under scene adaptation is critical. As shown in Table 2, MTTrans obtains SOTA results (32.6%) with significant improvements over previous works. In addition, the performance of six out of seven categories in the target domain dataset has been improved. (As the SOTA method in the weather adaptation scenario ViSGA [25] did not open-source their code and did not report performance in the scene adaptation scenario, it is not included here.)

Table 1. Results of different methods for weather adaptation, that is, from cityscapes to fog cityscapes. FRCNN and DefDETR are abbreviations for Faster R-CNN and Deformable DETR, respectively.

Method	Detector	Person	Rider	Car	Truck	Bus	Train	Mcycle	Bicycle	mAP
FasterRCNN [24] (Source)	FRCNN	26.9	38.2	35.6	18.3	32.4	9.6	25.8	28.6	26.9
DivMatch [16]	FRCNN	31.8	40.5	51.0	20.9	41.8	34.3	26.6	32.4	34.9
SWDA [26]	FRCNN	31.8	44.3	48.9	21.0	43.8	28	28.9	35.8	35.3
SCDA [46]	FRCNN	33.8	42.1	52.1	26.8	42.5	26.5	29.2	34.5	35.9
MTOR [2]	FRCNN	30.6	41.4	44.0	21.9	38.6	40.6	28.3	35.6	35.1
CR-DA [34]	FRCNN	30.0	41.2	46.1	22.5	43.2	27.9	27.8	34.7	34.2
CR-SW [34]	FRCNN	34.1	44.3	53.5	24.4	44.8	38.1	26.8	34.9	37.6
GPA [36]	FRCNN	32.9	46.7	54.1	24.7	45.7	41.1	32.4	38.7	39.5
ViSGA [25]	FRCNN	38.8	45.9	57.2	**29.9**	**50.2**	**51.9**	31.9	40.9	43.3
FCOS [31] (Source)	FCOS	36.9	36.3	44.1	18.6	29.3	8.4	20.3	31.9	28.2
EPM [14]	FCOS	44.2	46.6	58.5	24.8	45.2	29.1	28.6	34.6	39.0
Def DETR [47] (Source)	DefDETR	37.7	39.1	44.2	17.2	26.8	5.8	21.6	35.5	28.5
SFA [33]	DefDETR	46.5	48.6	62.6	25.1	46.2	29.4	28.3	44.0	41.3
MTTrans(Ours)	DefDETR	**47.7**	**49.9**	**65.2**	25.8	45.9	33.8	**32.6**	**46.5**	**43.4**

Table 2. Results of different methods for the scene adaptation, i.e., Cityscapes to BDD100k daytime subset.

Methods	Detector	Person	Rider	Car	Truck	Bus	Mcycle	Bicycle	mAP
FasterR-CNN [24](Source)	FRCNN	28.8	25.4	44.1	17.9	16.1	13.9	22.4	24.1
DAF [4]	FRCNN	28.9	27.4	44.2	19.1	18.0	14.2	22.4	24.9
SWDA [26]	FRCNN	29.5	29.9	44.8	20.2	20.7	15.2	23.1	26.2
SCDA [46]	FRCNN	29.3	29.2	44.4	20.3	19.6	14.8	23.2	25.8
CR-DA [34]	FRCNN	30.8	29.0	44.8	20.5	19.8	14.1	22.8	26.0
CR-SW [34]	FRCNN	32.8	29.3	45.8	22.7	20.6	14.9	**25.5**	27.4
FCOS [31](Source)	FCOS	38.6	24.8	54.5	17.2	16.3	15.0	18.3	26.4
EPM [14]	FCOS	39.6	26.8	55.8	18.8	19.1	14.5	20.1	27.8
Def DETR [47](Source)	DefDETR	38.9	26.7	55.2	15.7	19.7	10.8	16.2	26.2
SFA [33]	DefDETR	40.2	27.6	57.5	19.1	23.4	15.4	19.2	28.9
MTTrans(Ours)	DefDETR	**44.1**	**30.1**	**61.5**	**25.1**	**26.9**	**17.7**	23.0	**32.6**

Synthetic to Real Adaptation. Images and their corresponding annotations can be created by video games such as GTA, which can considerably minimize the manual cost of data collection and annotating. As a result, it is worthwhile to enable the object detector to learn from synthetic images and then adapt to generic real-world images. Therefore, as shown in Table 3, we test MTTrans in the synthetic to real adaptation scenario, obtaining an accuracy of 57.9%, outperforming the previous state-of-the-art by 5.3%.

4.3 Ablation Studies

To better analyze each component in our proposed MTTrans framework, we conduct ablation studies by removing parts of the components in MTTrans.

Table 3. Results of different methods for the synthetic to real adaptation, i.e. Sim10k to Cityscapes.

Methods	Detector	carAP
FasterRCNN [24](Source)	FRCNN	34.6
DAF [4]	FRCNN	41.9
DivMatch [16]	FRCNN	43.9
SWDA [26]	FRCNN	44.6
SCDA [46]	FRCNN	45.1
MTOR [2]	FRCNN	46.6
CR-DA [34]	FRCNN	43.1
CR-SW [34]	FRCNN	46.2
GPA [36]	FRCNN	47.6
ViSGA [25]	FRCNN	49.3
FCOS [31](Source)	FCOS	42.5
EPM [14]	FCOS	47.3
DefDETR [47](Source)	DefDETR	47.4
SFA [33]	DefDETR	52.6
MTTrans(Ours)	DefDETR	**57.9**

Table 4. Ablation studies on the weather adaptation scenario, with Cityscapes to Foggy Cityscapes. MT stands for the mean teacher framework and SharedQE denotes the shared object queries of decoder inputs. Components of other models that differ from MTTrans are marked in red.

Methods	MT	SharedQE	DQFA		TIFA		BGPA		mAP50
			enc	dec	enc	dec	enc	dec	
Deformable DETR (Source)	✗	✗	✗	✗	✗	✗	✗	✗	28.5
MTTrans-AS0(MT-DefDETR)	✓	✓	✗	✗	✗	✗	✗	✗	35.843
MTTrans-AS11	✓	✓	✗	✓	✓	✗	✗	✓	43.183
MTTrans-AS12	✓	✓	✓	✗	✓	✗	✗	✓	42.962
MTTrans-AS13	✓	✓	✓	✓	✗	✗	✗	✓	43.013
MTTrans-AS14	✓	✓	✓	✓	✓	✗	✗	✗	43.003
MTTrans-AS15	✓	✗	✓	✓	✓	✗	✗	✓	42.797
MTTrans-AS21	✓	✓	✓	✓	✓	✓	✗	✗	42.953
MTTrans-AS22	✓	✓	✓	✓	✗	✗	✓	✓	43.068
MTTrans	✓	✓	✓	✓	✓	✗	✗	✓	43.413

From Table 4, we can observe: (1) Adding the mean teacher framework directly to Deformable DETR (MTTrans-AS0, MT-DefDETR)) can improve its performance on the target domain (+7.34 mAP). We can notice that it is critical to introduce the mean teacher framework in cross-domain adaptation, but there is still much space for improvement due to the poor quality of pseudo labels. (2) Removing any aspect of MTTrans (MTTrans-AS11 to MTTrans-AS14)will result in performance degradation. Removing DQFA for the encoder (MTTrans-AS11) results in the slightest performance drop (–0.230mAP), while removing DQFA for the decoder (MTTrans-AS12) results in the highest drop (–0.451 mAP); (3) Altering the alignment technique for the decoder from BGPA to TIFA (MTTrans-AS21, –0.460 mAP), or replacing TIFA for the encoder with BGPA (MTTrans-AS22, –0.345 mAP) both result in performance drop; (4) Removing the shared object queries between the teacher and student models (MTTrans-AS15) will also decrease MTTrans's performance (–0.616 mAP).

4.4   Visualization and Analysis

Pseudo Label Visualization. We show some visualization results of the generated pseudo labels and student model's prediction, produced by MTTrans and the mean teacher version of Deformable DETR, as shown in Fig. 5. It should be noted that input images are augmented randomly during training, and the student model's performance can not be compared between the two model's predictions in the figure. However, the teacher model's inputs are almost the same, and the pseudo labels generated by MT-DefDETR are of lower quality than MTTrans's. Furthermore, the pseudo labels generated by the teacher model are better than the student model's predictions, ensuring that the student model can learn to improve via pseudo labels.

Fig. 5. Visualization results of the generated pseudo labels, ground truth annotations, and student model predictions. As seen in the visualization result, MTTrans can generate pseudo labels of higher quality compared with MT-DefDETR; and the teacher model performs better than the student model. MT-DefDETR stands for directly applying the mean teacher framework to Deformable DETR.

Detection Results. We show some visualization results of MTTrans on the Foggy Cityscapes dataset, accompanied by ground truth, baseline, and previous state-of-the-art (SOTA) methods. As shown in Fig. 6, MTTrans can better detect complex objects covered by fog in the distance compared with Deformable DETR

Fig. 6. Visualization of detection results on the Foggy Cityscapes dataset, from left to right, are ground truth, results obtained by Deformable DETR, SFA, and MTTrans. The predicted category and prediction confidence can be seen in the bounding box labels. Recommend to read with computers, and the original image files are attached with supplement materials.

and SFA. The results are consistent with the numerical assessment results, indicating that MTTrans manages to mitigate the domain shift problem in the UDA Transformer detector. Furthermore, as detection confidence scores are shown in the left-top corner of the bounding box (best zoom in ×8), MTTrans can slightly boost the scores of true positive predictions, further indicating its strength. As shown in the third row of Fig. 6, MTTrans manages to retrieve objects ignored by SFA but discovered by Deformable DETR. From the last row in Fig. 6, even though our proposed MTTrans fails to discover the blurry and indistinguishable person, it succeeds in detecting cars that are not labeled in the ground truth. More visualization of other datasets is presented in the supplement materials.

5 Conclusions

This paper introduces an end-to-end cross-domain object detection Transformer named MTTrans based on the mean teacher framework and the comprehensive multi-level feature alignment. The mean teacher framework is adopted in MTTrans to fully utilize the unlabeled target domain dataset, making it pseudo-labeled and available in the training of the object detection task. To compensate for the lack of explicit cross-domain ability of the mean teacher framework and to further improve the quality of the generated pseudo labels under domain shift, we propose the multi-level feature alignment which aligns image and object features at local, instance, and global levels based on the cross-scale self-attention mechanism in Deformable DETR [47], including domain query-based feature alignment for global-level image and object features, bi-level graph-based prototype alignment for instance-level object features, and token-wise image feature alignment for local-level image features, respectively. Experimental results demonstrate the effectiveness of our MTTrans. We hope that this paper can inspire future work on cross-domain object detection.

Acknowledgment. We thank Xiaoqi Li and Zhaoqing Wang for their help with the manuscript revision and the anonymous reviewers for their helpful comments to improve the paper. The authors of this paper are supported by the NSFC through grant No.U20B2053, and we also thanks the support from Beijing Advanced Innovation Center for Future Blockchain and Privacy Computing.

References

1. Bai, Y., Mei, J., Yuille, A.L., Xie, C.: Are transformers more robust than cnns? Adv. Neural Inf. Process. Syst. **34**, 26831–26843 (2021)
2. Cai, Q., et al.: Exploring object relation in mean teacher for cross-domain detection. In: Proceedings of the IEEE/CVF Conference on Computer Vision and Pattern Recognition, pp. 11457–11466 (2019)
3. Carion, N., Massa, F., Synnaeve, G., Usunier, N., Kirillov, A., Zagoruyko, S.: End-to-end object detection with transformers. In: Vedaldi, A., Bischof, H., Brox, T., Frahm, J.-M. (eds.) ECCV 2020. LNCS, vol. 12346, pp. 213–229. Springer, Cham (2020). https://doi.org/10.1007/978-3-030-58452-8_13
4. Chen, Y., Li, W., Sakaridis, C., Dai, D., Van Gool, L.: Domain adaptive faster r-cnn for object detection in the wild. In: Proceedings of the IEEE Conference on Computer Vision and Pattern Recognition, pp. 3339–3348 (2018)
5. Child, R., Gray, S., Radford, A., Sutskever, I.: Generating long sequences with sparse transformers. arXiv preprint arXiv:1904.10509 (2019)
6. Cordts, M., et al.: The cityscapes dataset for semantic urban scene understanding. In: Proceedings of the IEEE Conference on Computer Vision and Pattern Recognition, pp. 3213–3223 (2016)
7. Deng, J., Dong, W., Socher, R., Li, L.J., Li, K., Fei-Fei, L.: Imagenet: a large-scale hierarchical image database. In: 2009 IEEE Conference on Computer Vision and Pattern Recognition, pp. 248–255. Ieee (2009)
8. Deng, J., Li, W., Chen, Y., Duan, L.: Unbiased mean teacher for cross-domain object detection. In: Proceedings of the IEEE/CVF Conference on Computer Vision and Pattern Recognition, pp. 4091–4101 (2021)
9. Devlin, J., Chang, M.W., Lee, K., Toutanova, K.: Bert: pre-training of deep bidirectional transformers for language understanding. arXiv preprint arXiv:1810.04805 (2018)
10. Ganin, Y., et al.: Domain-adversarial training of neural networks. J. Mach. Learn. Res. **17**(1), 2030–2096 (2016)
11. Guo, Q., Qiu, X., Liu, P., Shao, Y., Xue, X., Zhang, Z.: Star-transformer. arXiv preprint arXiv:1902.09113 (2019)
12. He, K., Gkioxari, G., Dollár, P., Girshick, R.: Mask r-cnn. In: Proceedings of the IEEE International Conference on Computer Vision, pp. 2961–2969 (2017)
13. He, K., Zhang, X., Ren, S., Sun, J.: Deep residual learning for image recognition. In: Proceedings of the IEEE Conference on Computer Vision and Pattern Recognition, pp. 770–778 (2016)
14. Hsu, C.-C., Tsai, Y.-H., Lin, Y.-Y., Yang, M.-H.: Every pixel matters: center-aware feature alignment for domain adaptive object detector. In: Vedaldi, A., Bischof, H., Brox, T., Frahm, J.-M. (eds.) ECCV 2020. LNCS, vol. 12354, pp. 733–748. Springer, Cham (2020). https://doi.org/10.1007/978-3-030-58545-7_42

644   J. Yu et al.

15. Johnson-Roberson, M., Barto, C., Mehta, R., Sridhar, S.N., Rosaen, K., Vasudevan, R.: Driving in the matrix: can virtual worlds replace human-generated annotations for real world tasks? arXiv preprint arXiv:1610.01983 (2016)
16. Kim, T., Jeong, M., Kim, S., Choi, S., Kim, C.: Diversify and match: a domain adaptive representation learning paradigm for object detection. In: Proceedings of the IEEE/CVF Conference on Computer Vision and Pattern Recognition, pp. 12456–12465 (2019)
17. Kingma, D.P., Ba, J.: Adam: a method for stochastic optimization. arXiv preprint arXiv:1412.6980 (2014)
18. Kipf, T.N., Welling, M.: Semi-supervised classification with graph convolutional networks. arXiv preprint arXiv:1609.02907 (2016)
19. Kirillov, A., He, K., Girshick, R., Rother, C., Dollár, P.: Panoptic segmentation. In: Proceedings of the IEEE/CVF Conference on Computer Vision and Pattern Recognition, pp. 9404–9413 (2019)
20. Lin, T.Y., Dollár, P., Girshick, R., He, K., Hariharan, B., Belongie, S.: Feature pyramid networks for object detection. In: Proceedings of the IEEE Conference on Computer Vision and Pattern Recognition, pp. 2117–2125 (2017)
21. Liu, W., Anguelov, D., Erhan, D., Szegedy, C., Reed, S., Fu, C.-Y., Berg, A.C.: SSD: single shot multibox detector. In: Leibe, B., Matas, J., Sebe, N., Welling, M. (eds.) ECCV 2016. LNCS, vol. 9905, pp. 21–37. Springer, Cham (2016). https://doi.org/10.1007/978-3-319-46448-0_2
22. Luo, Z., et al.: Unsupervised domain adaptive 3D detection with multi-level consistency. In: Proceedings of the IEEE/CVF International Conference on Computer Vision, pp. 8866–8875 (2021)
23. Redmon, J., Divvala, S., Girshick, R., Farhadi, A.: You only look once: unified, real-time object detection. In: Proceedings of the IEEE Conference on Computer Vision and Pattern Recognition, pp. 779–788 (2016)
24. Ren, S., He, K., Girshick, R., Sun, J.: Faster r-cnn: towards real-time object detection with region proposal networks. Adv. Neural Inf. Process. Syst. **28** (2015)
25. Rezaeianaran, F., Shetty, R., Aljundi, R., Reino, D.O., Zhang, S., Schiele, B.: Seeking similarities over differences: similarity-based domain alignment for adaptive object detection. In: Proceedings of the IEEE/CVF International Conference on Computer Vision, pp. 9204–9213 (2021)
26. Saito, K., Ushiku, Y., Harada, T., Saenko, K.: Strong-weak distribution alignment for adaptive object detection. In: Proceedings of the IEEE/CVF Conference on Computer Vision and Pattern Recognition, pp. 6956–6965 (2019)
27. Sakaridis, C., Dai, D., Van Gool, L.: Semantic foggy scene understanding with synthetic data. Int. J. Comput. Vision **126**(9), 973–992 (2018)
28. Sohn, K., et al.: Fixmatch: simplifying semi-supervised learning with consistency and confidence. Adv. Neural Inf. Process. Syst. **33**, 596–608 (2020)
29. Sohn, K., Zhang, Z., Li, C.L., Zhang, H., Lee, C.Y., Pfister, T.: A simple semi-supervised learning framework for object detection. arXiv preprint arXiv:2005.04757 (2020)
30. Sun, Q., et al.: Sugar: subgraph neural network with reinforcement pooling and self-supervised mutual information mechanism. In: Proceedings of the Web Conference 2021, pp. 2081–2091 (2021)
31. Tian, Z., Shen, C., Chen, H., He, T.: Fcos: fully convolutional one-stage object detection. In: Proceedings of the IEEE/CVF International Conference on Computer Vision, pp. 9627–9636 (2019)
32. Vaswani, A., et al.: Attention is all you need. Adv. Neural Inf. Process. Syst. **30** (2017)

33. Wang, W., et al.: Exploring sequence feature alignment for domain adaptive detection transformers. In: Proceedings of the 29th ACM International Conference on Multimedia, pp. 1730–1738 (2021)
34. Xu, C.D., Zhao, X.R., Jin, X., Wei, X.S.: Exploring categorical regularization for domain adaptive object detection. In: Proceedings of the IEEE/CVF Conference on Computer Vision and Pattern Recognition, pp. 11724–11733 (2020)
35. Xu, M., et al.: End-to-end semi-supervised object detection with soft teacher. In: Proceedings of the IEEE/CVF International Conference on Computer Vision, pp. 3060–3069 (2021)
36. Xu, M., Wang, H., Ni, B., Tian, Q., Zhang, W.: Cross-domain detection via graph-induced prototype alignment. In: Proceedings of the IEEE/CVF Conference on Computer Vision and Pattern Recognition, pp. 12355–12364 (2020)
37. Xu, T., Chen, W., Wang, P., Wang, F., Li, H., Jin, R.: Cdtrans: cross-domain transformer for unsupervised domain adaptation. arXiv preprint arXiv:2109.06165 (2021)
38. Yang, J., Liu, J., Xu, N., Huang, J.: Tvt: transferable vision transformer for unsupervised domain adaptation. arXiv preprint arXiv:2108.05988 (2021)
39. Yang, Z., Liu, S., Hu, H., Wang, L., Lin, S.: Reppoints: point set representation for object detection. In: Proceedings of the IEEE/CVF International Conference on Computer Vision, pp. 9657–9666 (2019)
40. Yu, F., et al.: Bdd100k: a diverse driving video database with scalable annotation tooling, vol. 2, no. 5, p. 6. arXiv preprint arXiv:1805.04687 (2018)
41. Zhang, C., et al.: Delving deep into the generalization of vision transformers under distribution shifts. In: Proceedings of the IEEE/CVF Conference on Computer Vision and Pattern Recognition, pp. 7277–7286 (2022)
42. Zhang, J., Huang, J., Luo, Z., Zhang, G., Lu, S.: Da-detr: domain adaptive detection transformer by hybrid attention. arXiv preprint arXiv:2103.17084 (2021)
43. Zheng, L., Shen, L., Tian, L., Wang, S., Wang, J., Tian, Q.: Scalable person re-identification: a benchmark. In: Proceedings of the IEEE International Conference on Computer Vision, pp. 1116–1124 (2015)
44. Zhong, C., Wang, J., Feng, C., Zhang, Y., Sun, J., Yokota, Y.: Pica: point-wise instance and centroid alignment based few-shot domain adaptive object detection with loose annotations. In: Proceedings of the IEEE/CVF Winter Conference on Applications of Computer Vision, pp. 2329–2338 (2022)
45. Zhou, H., et al.: Informer: beyond efficient transformer for long sequence time-series forecasting. In: Proceedings of the AAAI Conference on Artificial Intelligence, vol. 35, pp. 11106–11115 (2021)
46. Zhu, X., Pang, J., Yang, C., Shi, J., Lin, D.: Adapting object detectors via selective cross-domain alignment. In: Proceedings of the IEEE/CVF Conference on Computer Vision and Pattern Recognition, pp. 687–696 (2019)
47. Zhu, X., Su, W., Lu, L., Li, B., Wang, X., Dai, J.: Deformable detr: deformable transformers for end-to-end object detection. arXiv preprint arXiv:2010.04159 (2020)

Multi-domain Multi-definition Landmark Localization for Small Datasets

David Ferman[1,2]($\boxtimes$) and Gaurav Bharaj[1]

[1] AI Foundation, Baltimore, USA
davidcferman@gmail.com
[2] UT Austin, Austin, USA

Abstract. We present a novel method for multi image domain and multi-landmark definition learning for small dataset facial localization. Training a small dataset alongside a large(r) dataset helps with robust learning for the former, and provides a universal mechanism for facial landmark localization for new and/or smaller standard datasets. To this end, we propose a Vision Transformer encoder with a novel decoder with a definition agnostic shared landmark semantic group structured prior, that is learnt, as we train on more than one dataset concurrently. Due to our novel definition agnostic group prior the datasets may vary in landmark definitions and domains. During the decoder stage we use cross- and self-attention, whose output is later fed into domain/definition specific heads that minimize a Laplacian-log-likelihood loss. We achieve state-of-the-art performance on standard landmark localization datasets such as COFW and WFLW, when trained with a bigger dataset. We also show state-of-the-art performance on several varied image domain small datasets for animals, caricatures, and facial portrait paintings. Further, we contribute a small dataset (150 images) of pareidolias to show efficacy of our method. Finally, we provide several analysis and ablation studies to justify our claims.

Keywords: Landmarks · Multi-domain learning · Vision transformers

1 Introduction

With the rising need for novel AR/VR, telepresence, character animation filter applications (e.g., adding props and effects in live video streams of humans, pets, etc.), arises the need for facial localization for multiple image domains. While, supervised landmark localization has made great strides for the *in-the-wild* human faces domain, it is often hard to create such datasets for new image domains – animals Khan *et al.* [22], art [49], cartoons, and more recently, pareidolias Song *et al.* [39] that abstractly resemble human faces, Wardle *et al.* [46].

Supplementary Information The online version contains supplementary material available at https://doi.org/10.1007/978-3-031-20077-9_38.

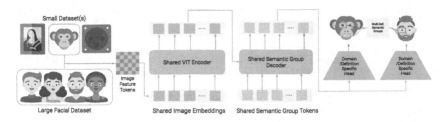

Fig. 1. System overview (left to right): Our method takes a small dataset with a landmark definition, and a larger facial dataset with a different landmark definition, and relies on common semantic group definitions to learn for both dataset concurrently.

Building a dataset for supervised learning of landmarks is hard due to the cumbersome hand-labeling process, where, hand-labels can lead to noisy and inconsistent landmarks [11], and is often very time consuming for new domains[1].

Due to varied new domains, Fig. 2, and subsequent specific applications, there's no preset definition for facial landmarks. For example, a landmark definition set that works for humans faces may not work for animal faces and vice-versa and thus makes cross-domain learning infeasible. Additionally, within human face localization problems, different datasets have different definitions of landmarks, see Fig. 2 (Humans), and certain applications can require unique landmark definitions, e.g., landmarks which correspond to mesh vertices, Wei *et al.* [49]. The landmark datasets necessitated by a particular new application are either small or non-existent. As a result, novel applications that need localization for new image domains and/or definitions becomes infeasible. Image domain localization problems have been previously approached with domain transfer methods. For example, Yaniv *et al.* [56] use domain transfer to approach learning for facial portrait artwork, Wei *et al.* [49] learn landmark correspondences as an auxiliary aspect of mesh fitting. Such methods need a specialized larger dataset and/or landmark definitions from a previous dataset, which might be sub-optimal for the candidate domain. In this work, we create a method that learns robust landmarks for new domains for which small datasets may exist, or for which a small set of labeled images can be obtained, inexpensively, while being landmark definition agnostic.

Poggio *et al.* [33] and White *et al.* [50] observe that shapes share abstract similarities while domains vary. Inspired by this observation and unlike most landmark localization methods [4,37,45,48] our approach models shared *abstract similarities*, i.e., learns together groups of facial landmark semantic groups, Fig. 2, rather than learn landmarks directly. The facial landmark semantic group learning can be shared across domains and definitions. Thus, while image domains and localization definitions vary, learning a single representation for each semantic facial group enables generalization of learning across domains and definitions.

Transformers [44] were introduced for natural language processing problems, that model word sequences, e.g., "[The] [quick] [brown] [fox] ...", as densely

---

[1] Labeling a landmark dataset for animal faces can take up to 6,833 h [22].

Fig. 2. Our method works for multiple domains and multiple definitions of facial landmark localization problems. The red box represents a *landmark semantic group* shared across different domains and landmark definitions. (Color figure online)

meaningful tokenized vectors. These vectors are initially indexed from a learned embedding matrix which captures each token's definition, learned across training instances, while instance-specific representations are built contextually via a series of attention layers. Inspired by the success of transformers in NLP, the flexible handling of multiple tasks and language domains, Raffel *et al.* [35], we consider modeling faces analogously, as a fixed "sentence" of tokens representing facial landmark semantic groups. We seek for our model to learn general definitions via semantic group embeddings, as an implicit facial prior, for predicting semantic group information from image feature contexts.

To this end, we design a novel vision transformer (ViT) [12] architecture for the multiple domain and multi facial landmark definition localization problem. As shown in Fig. 1, we first pass the image through our ViT encoder to obtain image feature tokens. These tokens are fed into our novel facial landmark semantic group decoder, which builds contextualized representations of semantic group tokens via cross-attention with image feature tokens and inter-group self-attention. Finally, each facial landmark semantic group vector is passed through definition/dataset specific heads to regress to the final landmarks. Thus, our method treats the facial landmark semantic groups in a general manner, while being capable of predicting landmarks for a variety of domains and definition.

We train our model in a *multi-domain multi-dataset* fashion for small datasets and achieve state-of-the-art performance on COFW [5], a small dataset with only 1345 images and a 29 landmark definition and very competitive performance on WFLW [52]. Additionally, we display our method's versatility in adapting to very small (roughly 100 image) datasets of animals (monkeys), caricatures, artwork image domains, and contribute a small novel dataset for pareidolias. We show great improvements via multi-domain multi-dataset learning with ablation, qualitative, and quantitative analysis. To summarize, our contributions include:

1. We introduce multi-domain multi-definition learning for the small dataset facial landmark localization problem.
2. We introduce a novel vision transformer encoder-decoder architecture which enables multi-domain (dataset) multi-definition learning via decoding landmark information via shared facial component queries in the decoder.
3. Our method achieves state-of-the-art performance on standard multiple domain facial localization datasets, along with never before seen facial localization domain small datasets, such as, pareidolias.

2   Related Works

Multi-domain Learning. Multi-domain learning predicts instance labels given both instance features and domain labels, where the goal is to learn a model that improves over a baseline that trains solely on the domain [21,51]. Similar to our work, several studies utilize multi-domain learning to boost performance on a domain with few labeled examples via concurrent training with a domain with plentiful labels [2,13,15,51]. Joshi *et al.* [21] note two approaches for multi-domain learning: domain-specific parameters and modeling inter-domain relations; our approach utilizes both simultaneously. For the image classification task, Dvornik *et al.* [13] propose a feature selection approach, while Zheng *et al.* [59] propose a domain confusion loss to encourage the network to learn domain invariant representations for image classification [15]. For facial landmarks, there may exist domain-specific biases in the outputs between domains, so this property is less desired [56]. Most similar to our approach, Nam *et al.* [30] introduce multi-domain learning for sequence tracking, where their network shares weights for the bulk of the architecture, with domain specific final layers. Our approach utilizes separate final layers for each domain, while exploiting the relations between domains in our decoder by learning shared representations for facial components.

Multi-definition Learning. The multi-definition problem for facial landmarks solves for inconsistencies between landmark labels to improve model robustness via multi-dataset training [53]. Multi-definition learning is similar to multi-domain in the sense that there is a target dataset for which performance is optimized with shared learning from a source dataset [38]. Smith *et al.* [38] propose to predict a super-set of landmark definitions, while Zhu *et al.* [60] propose an alignment module to estimate pseudo-labels in schema of a target dataset. Motivated by cross-dataset input variation and definition mismatch, Zhang *et al.* [57] propose an intermediate shape regression module that regresses shared sparse definitions that helps inform final regression to the landmark super-set. Wu *et al.* [53] utilize a shared CNN-backbone, prior to dataset/definition specific final direct regression heads. As recent state-of-the-art methods have been heatmap-based, Zhu *et al.* [60] propose separate definition-specific heatmap decoders that tightly couple the decoder architectures with output heatmap definitions [20]. Our method shares abstract similarity to [57]'s shape regression. We include sparse intermediate predictions that are latent vectors rather than explicit landmarks. Similar to [53,57], we also employ definition-specific regression heads, see Sect. 3.

CNN and Heatmap-Based Landmark Learning. Wei *et al.* [48] introduce heatmap-based estimation of 2D landmarks for human pose estimation, later Kowalski *et al.* [24] adapt it for facial landmarks. While heatmaps provide intrinsic spatial generalization [32], they induce quantization errors [3,18,26]. Stacked hourglass networks [4,31,55] or multi-scale processing [40] are then used for building global context. Jin *et al.* [18] note that connecting CNN features to fully connected layers provides a global predictive capacity that leads to inaccurate predictions due to immediate spatial connections, however, this does lead to more consistent predictions.

CoordConv [27] connect CNN features with positional information by injecting a fixed spatial bias through two additional image channels that provide global positional information of {x, y} coordinates respectively. It was adopted by previous state-of-the-art [45] and LAB [52] to capture global information in CNNs via boundary heatmaps that connect semantic groups of landmarks, e.g., eyes, mouth, etc., into semantically grouped heatmaps on a single global boundary heatmap. Chandran *et al.* [8] propose a hard-attention cropping derived from an initial global pass to consider each semantic region of the face and obtain regional heatmaps for each region for high-resolution images.

Transformers for Landmark Learning. Transformers [44] were introduced for vision tasks by DETR [7]'s use of a transformer encoder-decoder over CNN-encoded features for the object detection. Vision Transformers (ViT) [12] show promising performance for vision tasks without the use of CNNs, while DEiT [42] use a CNN for knowledge distillation for further improvements. Swin [29], inspired by CNN architectures, propose a hierarchically processed shifted window attention approach. However, we adopt a simple vanilla ViT [12], and employ a transformer decoder for predicting the latent landmark information for facial semantic group regression.

HiH [26] resolve for heatmap quantization errors and study a CNN-based versus transformer-based heatmap prediction network with a CNN-backbone. LOTR [47] show that transformers can be used to break the direct spatial dependencies induced by CNN-MLP architectures for performant direct regression. They employ a CNN-backbone followed by a transformer-encoder decoder, where the decoder queries correspond to individual landmarks, followed by MLP regression heads. Recently, FarRL [1] introduce a BERT/BEiT-like transformer pre-training equivalent on faces, pre-training self-supervisedly on 20 million facial images, and predicting facial landmarks, with heatmap prediction, as one of three facial tasks in a multi-task setup.

Our method combines transformer-based (cross and self-attention) direct regression with the semantic group intuition of LAB, as our novel transformer decoder predicts representations for the semantic groups prior to explicitly regressing landmarks contained in the semantic group. Our method is most similar to LOTR, except that while LOTR is DETR-like [7] with its full CNN-backbone, our method is ViT-like, using projection patchification, and no CNN feature backbone. Also, LOTR queries each individual landmark from the encoded image features, whereas our method queries semantic landmark groupings, e.g., nose, for multi-domain/definition learning purposes, and regresses both landmark mean and covariance information.

Multi-dataset Learning. In order to address the small-datasets common among facial landmark problems, several approaches have been devised. These include semi-supervised learning [3,16], self-supervised learning [59], and multi-dataset learning [3,59]. Zheng *et al.* [59], inspired by BERT-inspired [10] BEiT [1], use self-supervised pre-training techniques to learn general facial representations, employing both a contrastive learning approach using textual labels as well as a masked image prediction methodology on 20 million facial images. Qian*et al.* [34] introduce a synthetic data creation methodology which employs self-supervised learning to translate labeled faces into the style of other images, achieving large performance boosts over purely supervised methods. Jin *et al.* [19] introduce cross-protocol network training, where multiple facial landmark datasets are trained simultaneously by sharing a backbone feature encoder and using a different heatmap decoder network for each dataset and thus only shares weights in the CNN feature backbone, but not in the landmark heatmap decoders. Our work is similar to Jin *et al.* in that we train on multi-definition facial landmark datasets as our model's source of additional data. However, rather than decoding each dataset separately, our definition agnostic decoder shares weights across datasets by modeling shared semantic groupings of landmarks.

3   Method

Our goal is to create a robust landmark localization solution for small data regime problems, where due to varied circumstances acquiring a large dataset is infeasible or expensive. We approach this problem via a multi-domain multi-definition (MDMD) facial landmark localization formulation with a transformer-based encoder-decoder architecture. The MDMD problem consists of predicting facial landmarks for target image domain(s) or landmark definition(s), while training on one or more source domains/definitions. Our novel transformer-based architecture is shown in Fig. 1. We select n image domain datasets, which may have different landmark definitions as our MDMD input. The various landmark definitions map to a standard semantic grouping which we define for each dataset, Sect. 3.2. These n domain datasets are then fed into a ViT [12] encoder that builds image feature representations from the input images, Sect. 3.1. Pre-defined shared semantic group tokens act as a learnt structure "prior" to the shared semantic group decoder, that takes as input the encoder's output feature tokens. Then, the decoder builds representations of these definition-agnostic semantic groups by attending to both the image features via cross-attention and the other groups via self-attention, Sect. 3.3. Finally, the semantic group tokens – output of the decoder, each of which individually correspond to a unique set of landmarks (out of n), are then fed into regression heads that predict the final landmarks, Sect. 3.4.

3.1   ViT Encoder

We employ a pre-trained ViT [12] encoder that is shared across images from all input domains. The model first patchifies the input image to transform the initial image $I \in \mathbb{R}^{224 \times 224 \times 3}$ into a grid $G \in \mathbb{R}^{14 \times 14 \times D}$, with $D = 768$, and is then flattened, appended with a global token, and combined with positional encodings to obtain the ViT input tokens $X_{in} \in \mathbb{R}^{(196+1) \times D}$. The input tokens X are then passed through a series of ViT layers consisting of self-attention and MLPs. The final feature tokens are then obtained and passed to the shared decoder to extract landmark information from these generic facial features.

3.2   Facial Landmark Semantic Group (FLSG)

In-order to have a universal mechanism for support-
ing various landmark definitions, we propose a novel
facial landmarks semantic group prior. This abstract
view of the face leads to definition and domain generalization through the relaxation of strict spatial dependencies, such as in boundary heatmaps [52]. We divide
the facial landmarks for each definition into a set of
12 shared FLSGs, as shown in Fig. 3. FLSGs are mod-
eled as an embedding matrix $F_{in} \in \mathbb{R}^{12 \times D}$, where each
$F_{in}^{(i)} \in \mathbb{R}^D$ represents learned prior information for
a particular semantic group of facial landmarks. The
decoder exploits the learned FLSG representations F_{in}

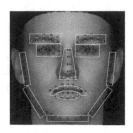

Fig. 3. Facial Landmark
Semantic Group. Image
source: [52]

that are used to initialize the FLSG tokens that act as input to the decoder.
While, different FLSGs may have a different number landmarks depending on
the definitions, our model does not explicitly differentiate between them until the
final prediction head stage, Sect. 3.4. Thus, our FLSGs unlock MDMD learning
via a standard general facial representation.

3.3   Definition Agnostic Decoder

We want FLSGs to collect information from the image features that it deems
relevant (cross-attention) and also collect information about its context wrt other
FLSGs (self-attention). We achieve this via a novel definition agnostic decoder,
where given initial FLSG tokens $F_{in} \in \mathbb{R}^{12 \times D}$ and the encoded image feature
tokens $X_{out} \in \mathbb{R}^{(196+1) \times D}$, the decoder seeks to infuse the "structured prior"
FLSG tokens with information from both the input image and other FLSG
tokens. The decoder is composed of three decoder blocks that consist of self-
and cross-attention. Each decoder block contains cross-attention in which the
FLSG tokens act as "queries" and the image features as "keys" and "values" [44].
This is followed by self-attention, where the FLSG tokens can perform message
passing. Explicitly, given the input FLSG tokens, F_{in}, each decoder block is as
follows:

$$F_{hidden}^1 = \mathsf{MHCA}(\mathsf{LN}(F_{in}), \mathsf{LN}(X_{out}))) + F_{in} \tag{1}$$

$$F_{hidden}^2 = \mathsf{MHSA}(\mathsf{LN}(F_{hidden}^1)) + F_{hidden}^1 \tag{2}$$

$$F_{out} = \mathsf{FFN}(\mathsf{LN}(F_{hidden}^2)) \tag{3}$$

where MHCA, MHSA, LN, and FFN are the standard transformer multi-head
cross-attention, multi-head self-attention, layer normalization, and feed-forward
network respectively [44]. Thus, decoder layers infuse the FLSG tokens with
image feature information as well as inter-FLSG contextual information, so that
they contain information pertaining to localizing the landmarks contained in the
given semantic group. The final FLSG tokens $F_{out} \in \mathbb{R}^{12 \times D}$, output by decoder,
are then plugged into the definition specific prediction heads.

3.4   Definition/Domain-Specific Prediction Heads

Finally, we employ definition/domain specific prediction heads, that directly regress the landmarks that correspond to each FLSG. An image I_j is provided to our model, where j is the dataset (definition) index. The dataset index is simply used to route the FLSG tokens to the head that corresponds to that dataset (see pseudocode in the supplementary). Each dataset's landmark head, regresses from an FLSG vector $F_{out}^i \in \mathbb{R}^D$ via two-layer $\mathsf{MLP}_{\mathsf{lm}j}{}^i$ to output landmarks $L_j^i \in \mathbb{R}^{N_j^i \times 2}$, where N_j^i is the number of landmarks for the ith FLSG and the jth dataset.

Rather than predict landmarks alone, following Kumar et al. [25], we also predict the covariance information via a Cholesky estimation head, $\mathsf{MLP}_{\mathsf{chol}j}{}^i$, obtaining a second output corresponding to each FLSG, $C_j^i \in \mathbb{R}^{N_j^i \times 3}$, corresponding to the parameters of the Cholesky factorization of a predicted covariance matrix. While Kumar et al.'s Cholesky estimation network regresses from the latent bottleneck vector of their CNN, and use heatmap-based prediction for the mean estimate, supervising outputs from several stacked hourglass layers of their DU-NET [41], we utilize a shared FLSG vector to predict both mean and covariance information. The final minimization loss function we use to train our model is as follows:

$$\mathcal{L}_{\mathsf{MDMD}} = \frac{1}{|\mathsf{FLSG}|} \sum_{i=1}^{|\mathsf{FLSG}|} \left[\frac{1}{N_j^i} \sum_{k=1}^{N_j^i} \mathcal{L}_{lll}(L_j^i, C_j^i, {L_{GT}}_j^i)_k \right] \tag{4}$$

Here, L_{lll} is the Laplacian log-likelihood (see supplementary) and ${L_{GT}}_j^i$ is the ground truth landmarks.

4   Experiments and Results

We evaluate our model's multi-domain and multi-definition learning capabilities on novel domains with small datasets: AnimWeb [22], ArtFace [56], CariFace [58] and PARE dataset [New], as well as standard benchmark datasets: COFW [5] and WFLW [52] (and 300W [36], LaPa [28]), see supplementary material for details on datasets.

For each experiment, we report normalized mean error (NME) with inter-ocular normalization as well as inter-pupil, where comparison necessitates. Additionally, we report Area Under The Curve (AUC) and FR (Failure Rate) scores, considering a failure as mean NME greater than 10% for a given face. While 256×256 input crops are most commonly used [34], our ViT [12] encoder was pre-trained with 224×224 input crops, that we adopt. All models are trained with the Adam [23] optimizer with learning rate $1e^{-4}$ and linear learning rate decay. For each experiment, we consider performance for our model training with a single domain and definition, and then compare its performance when training with an additional dataset in the multi-domain and multi-definition fashion. In order to train concurrently across datasets, for each mini-batch, we uniformly

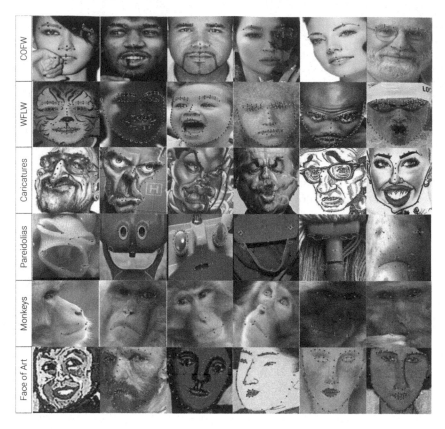

Fig. 4. Qualitative results for our method across several datasets. Key: GT landmarks, predicted landmarks, error vectors, uncertainty estimation

sample a dataset from which we draw batch samples. We include additional implementation details, including augmentation strategy, in the supplementary materials. In the following, we discuss various qualitative (Fig. 4), and quantitative results on various datasets:

4.1 COFW [5]

We evaluate our method on the COFW dataset that contains 1,345 training images, and 500 testing images. We note that among standard benchmark datasets, COFW is most similar to our problem for its unique 29 landmark definition as well as its relatively small size. We train our model with two settings: COFW, and COFW concurrently trained with LaPa. We evaluate our model with inter-pupil normalization, following [17,45], surpassing state-of-the-art, Table 1. We also note that for each dataset on which we train our model, concurrent training with a larger dataset shows significant performance improvements.

Table 1. Comparison against SOTA for COFW [5]

Method	$NME_{ip}(\%)$	$FR_{10\%}$	$AUC_{10\%}$
Wing [14]	5.44	3.75	–
DCFE [43]	5.27	7.29	35.86
AWing [45]	4.94	.99	48.82
ADNet [17]	4.68	.59	53.17
MDMD Base	4.82	**.39**	51.84
MDMD w/LaPa	**4.65**	.59	**53.49**

4.2 WFLW [52]

We further evaluate our method on the WFLW dataset, which consists of 7,500 training images and 2,500 testing images, with a 98 landmark definition. We train our model in the multi-definition manner with two settings: WFLW and WFLW concurrently with LaPa, where LaPa presents 19,000 faces with a 106 landmark definition. As 300W and COFW are relatively small with 3837 and 1345 training faces respectively, we do not consider the concurrently training with these smaller datasets, as this runs contrary to our goal of boosting performance from training with larger datasets. We compare our results with other methods for NME, FR, and AUC on the full test set along with subsets which test for robustness on large poses, expression, illumination, make-up, occlusion, and blur, in Table 2. Our method outperforms all previous state-of-the-art methods for overall scores aside from two concurrent works [3,59]. Our method also achieves SOTA performance compared to previously reported methods for the majority of subsets for NME, FR, and AUC. See qualitative comparisons for our method in Fig. 4.

4.3 Small Dataset Experiments

We consider our methods performance for small datasets of novel domains and landmark definitions. For each of these experiments, we train both a baseline model on the small dataset only as well as a multi-domain and multi-definition model, for which we employ the moderately sized 300W dataset. Per Williams *et al.* [51], the goal of multi-domain learning is to show improvement over a single domain baseline. While for previous experiments, our focus was primarily on how our method compares with previous methods, here, we compare against a baseline single-domain training. Where applicable we draw rough comparisons with previous works for these datasets. We report relative NME, FR, and AUC for all small dataset experiments in Table 3. We observe large performance gains for each dataset through the generalized learning via our multi-domain and multi-definition approach.

AnimWeb [22]
While the AnimWeb [22] dataset features 21,900 animal faces across 334 species, we select a single specie, the Japanese Macaque, containing 133 examples which

Table 2. Comparison against SOTA for WFLW [52]. *Concurrent works, Key: best, second

Metric	Method	Testset	Pose subset	Expression subset	Illumination subset	Make-up subset	Occlusion subset	Blur subset
NME(%)	ESR [6]	11.13	25.88	11.47	10.49	11.05	13.75	12.20
	SDM [54]	10.29	24.10	11.45	9.32	9.38	13.03	11.28
	CFSS [61]	9.07	21.36	10.09	8.30	8.74	11.76	9.96
	DVLN [53]	6.08	11.54	6.78	5.73	5.98	7.33	6.88
	LAB [52]	5.27	10.24	5.51	5.23	5.15	6.79	6.12
	Wing [14]	5.11	8.75	5.36	4.93	5.41	6.37	5.81
	DeCaFA [9]	4.62	8.11	4.65	4.41	4.63	5.74	5.38
	AWing [45]	4.36	7.38	4.58	4.32	4.27	5.19	4.96
	LUVLi [25]	4.37	-	-	-	-	-	-
	AWing [45]	4.36	7.38	4.58	4.32	4.27	5.19	4.96
	HiH [26]	4.18	7.20	4.19	4.45	3.97	5.00	4.81
	ADNet [17]	4.14	6.96	4.38	4.09	4.05	5.06	4.79
	FaRL [59]*	3.96	6.91	4.21	3.97	3.80	4.71	4.57
	SH-FAN Base [3]*	4.20	-	-	-	-	-	
	SH-FAN [3]*	3.72	-	-	-	-	-	
	MDMD Base*	4.06	7.11	4.21	3.88	4.04	4.86	4.63
	MDMD w/LaPa*	3.97	6.90	4.13	3.80	3.90	4.78	4.49
FR$_{10}$(%)	ESR [6]	35.24	90.18	42.04	30.80	38.84	47.28	41.40
	SDM [54]	29.40	84.36	33.44	26.22	27.67	41.85	35.32
	CFSS [61]	20.56	66.26	23.25	17.34	21.84	32.88	23.67
	DVLN [53]	10.84	46.93	11.15	7.31	11.65	16.30	13.71
	LAB [52]	7.56	28.83	6.37	6.73	7.77	13.72	10.74
	Wing [14]	6.00	22.70	4.78	4.30	7.77	12.50	7.76
	DeCaFA [9]	4.84	21.40	3.73	3.22	6.15	9.26	6.61
	AWing [45]	2.84	13.50	2.23	2.58	2.91	5.98	3.75
	LUVLi [25]	3.12	-	-	-	-	-	-
	HiH [26]	2.84	14.41	2.55	2.15	1.46	5.71	3.49
	ADNet [17]	2.72	12.72	2.15	2.44	1.94	5.79	3.54
	FaRL [59]*	1.76	-	-	-	-	-	-
	SH-FAN [3]*	1.55	-	-	-	-	-	-
	MDMD Base*	2.63	14.11	1.91	1.71	2.43	4.89	2.98
	MDMD w/LaPa*	2.2	11.96	1.27	1.58	1.46	1.35	3.59
AUC$_{10\%}$	ESR [6]	0.2774	0.0177	0.1981	0.2953	0.2485	0.1946	0.2204
	SDM [54]	0.3002	0.0226	0.2293	0.3237	0.3125	0.2060	0.2398
	CFSS [61]	0.3659	0.0632	0.3157	0.3854	0.3691	0.2688	0.3037
	DVLN [53]	0.4551	0.1474	0.3889	0.4743	0.4494	0.3794	0.3973
	LAB [52]	0.5323	0.2345	0.4951	0.5433	0.5394	0.4490	0.4630
	Wing [14]	0.5504	0.3100	0.4959	0.5408	0.5582	0.4885	0.4918
	DeCaFA [9]	0.5630	0.2920	0.5460	0.5790	0.5750	0.4850	0.4940
	AWing [45]	0.5719	0.3120	0.5149	0.5777	0.5715	0.5022	0.5120
	LUVLi [25]	0.5770	-	-	-	-	-	-
	HiH [26]	0.597	0.342	0.590	0.606	0.604	0.527	0.549
	ADNet [17]	0.6022	0.3144	0.5234	0.5805	0.6007	0.5295	0.5480
	FaRL [59]*	0.6116	-	-	-	-	-	-
	SH-FAN [3]*	.6310	-	-	-	-	-	-
	MDMD Base*	.6010	.3316	.5870	.6179	.5998	.4978	.5476
	MDMD w/LaPa*	.6083	.3438	.5933	.6252	.6127	.5354	.5582

Table 3. Evaluation of multi-domain and multi-definition learning capabilities across small datasets for novel domains and landmark definitions

Dataset	Method	NME$_{ic}$	FR$_{10\%}$	AUC$_{10\%}$	# Landmarks
AnimWeb [22]	MDMD Base	6.88	**15.15**	.4233	9
	MDMD w/300W	**6.55**	**15.15**	**.4388**	9
ArtFace [56]	MDMD Base	4.46	2.08	.5549	68
	MDMD w/300W	**3.75**	**0.0**	**.63**	68
CariFace [58]	MDMD Base	7.81	19.04	.2941	68
	MDMD w/300W	**5.85**	**6.41**	**.4357**	68
PARE	MDMD Base	9.12	28.0	.2365	9
	MDMD w/300W	**8.59**	**22.0**	**.2871**	9

Table 4. Comparison against previous work for AnimWeb [22] (left) and ArtFace [56] (middle). Following Khan, NME scores for AnimWeb are normalized by bounding box size. Comparison against previous work for CariFace [58](right).

Method	NME$_{box}$	Method	NME$_{ic}$	Method	NME	Trn Imgs
Khan *et al.* [22]	5.23	Yaniv *et al.* [56]	4.52[2]	Zhang*et al.* [58]	**5.83**	6,420
MDMD Base	3.66	MDMD Base	4.46	MDMD Base	7.81	148
MDMD 300W	**3.44**	MDMD 300W	**3.72**	MDMD 300W	5.85	148

we split into 100 training and 33 testing monkey faces for our experiment. We train jointly between 300W and the monkey domains and definitions. We note that the animals are labeled with 9 landmarks, while 300W is labeled with 68. For comparison against previous work, we cannot compare directly, as Khan *et al.* [22] train on a variety of species on a dataset with significantly large amount of training data. Furthermore, their scores represent a wide variety of animals, while ours are a subset of just one animal. Nevertheless, we report our scores for ballpark comparison in Table 4 (left).

ArtFace [56]
We compare our model's performance on 'faces in artworks' domain, utilizing the ArtFace [56] dataset, consisting of 160 faces, 10 faces per 16 artists, with a 300W-like 68 landmark definition. While Yaniv *et al.* [56] utilize an elaborate geometric-aware and style transfer to augment 300W images for training, and perform generalization to the artworks domain for testing, we split each artist by taking the first 7 image indices for training with the other 3 for testing.[2]
CariFace [58]

---

[2] We compare our results against previous work, with a caveat that our evaluation is on a subset of the dataset rather than the full dataset, and achieve SOTA performance for the ArtFace dataset, as shown in Table 4 (right).

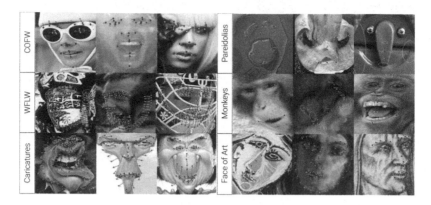

Fig. 5. Qualitative results for displaying the limitations our method across several datasets. Key: GT landmarks, predicted landmarks, error vectors, uncertainty estimation

Table 5. Ablation studies

Method	NME_{ip}	$FR_{10\%}$	$AUC_{10\%}$
MDMD Single w/Euclidean loss	4.90	.79	.5100
MDMD Single w/landmark tokens	4.73	.59	.5278
MDMD Single	4.82	.59	.5184
MDMD w/LaPa	**4.64**	**.39**	**.5349**

Zhang *et al.* [58] introduce an interesting problem of localizing landmarks on the domain of human caricatures, introducing the `CariFace` dataset that they train on 6,240 images and test on 1,560. Rather than train on the full set, we simulate the small dataset problem for this novel domain by taking the first 148 images for training and evaluating on the full test set. Similar to `ArtFace` [56], `CariFace` [58] uses the same `300W` landmark definition. We compare our NME scores trained on 40X less data from the caricature domain, and achieve slightly lower performance than Zhang *et al.*, as shown in Table 4.

PARE

Finally, we consider a unique dataset of illusory faces, also known as pareidolias, that we obtained from [46], and labeled 150 images with 9 landmarks each. This domain is particularly interesting, as the face pictures are only abstractly similar to the human faces from the `300W` dataset with which the model trains concurrently. As shown in Table 3, performance greatly improves with multi-domain and multi-definition learning.

4.4 Ablation Analysis

In addition to training with and without an additional dataset, we perform ablation studies for a several architectural components of our model. For each study, we test performance on the COFW dataset alone. First, we remove our facial landmark semantic grouping tokens from our decoder, and replace them with individual landmark tokens. Next, we train with simple Euclidean loss, rather than Lapalacian log-likelihood. We show our comparisons for against the baseline model in Table 5.

Small Datasets with v. without 300W [36]. We compare our model's performance with and without an additional dataset when training on small datasets of novel domains and definitions. We observe that for each dataset, training without the additional data leads to severe performance reductions, Table 3. Thus, we conclude that our multi-domain and multi-domain learning strategy is effective at exploiting additional labeled data for small datasets of novel domains and definitions.

Laplacian Log-Likelihood v. Euclidean Loss. To evaluate the effectiveness of our Laplacian log-likelihood training objective, we compare against a simple baseline of Euclidean distance loss. We train our model on COFW [5] and show that performance severely deteriorates when we use Euclidean loss, Table 5.

Facial Landmark Semantic Group (FLSG) v. Explicit Landmark Modeling. Lastly, we seek to evaluate the effectiveness of our FLSG modeling when compared to a simple baseline of modeling each landmark with its own token. As our MDMD method relies on FLSGs to accomplish multi-definition learning, and thus, cannot be removed while still accomplishing the same task, we instead consider its effectiveness when training with a single dataset, COFW [5]. We observe a decrease in performance when training with the FLSG in the standard scenario of a single dataset, Table 5. However, this decrease is overcome by multi-dataset learning. Thus, FLSG acts as a strategy for achieving performance gains in the multi-domain/definition scenario, while landmark queries was better for the single dataset case, in this case.

5   Limitations and Conclusion

We introduced a method for multi-domain and multi-definition landmark localization, that employs a transformer that models facial landmark semantic groups (FLSGs) as opposed to individual landmarks, in-order to share learning across domains and definitions. Our method achieves state-of-the-art performance, as well as successfully improves over baselines of single-domain learning for both small and large datasets. We note however, that our model still struggles with certain difficult circumstances, such as extreme pose and occlusions, as shown in Fig. 5. Another limitation is extremely deformed face shapes, for example, the middle caricature face, Fig. 5.

We also note that FLSGs aid in multi-definition learning, but hurt performance for the single dataset scenario (Table 5). Thus, in the future, we want to explore exploitation of explicit landmark modeling jointly with FLSGs to obtain the best of both worlds. We also note that the proposed FLS-Grouping (after several test permutations) works well for all domains/definitions and helps with generalization, in the future we want to explore domain/definition specific grouping. Additional future work may consider extending these ideas to multi-task learning, temporal modeling, or toward zero-shot and few-shot learning.

References

1. Bao, H., Dong, L., Wei, F.: Beit: Bert pre-training of image transformers. ArXiv abs/2106.08254 (2021)
2. Ben-David, S., Blitzer, J., Crammer, K., Kulesza, A., Pereira, F., Vaughan, J.W.: A theory of learning from different domains. Machine Learning, pp. 151–175 (2009). https://doi.org/10.1007/s10994-009-5152-4
3. Bulat, A., Sanchez, E., Tzimiropoulos, G.: Subpixel heatmap regression for facial landmark localization. In: Proceedings of the British Machine Vision Conference (BMVC) (2021)
4. Bulat, A., Tzimiropoulos, G.: How far are we from solving the 2d & 3d face alignment problem?(and a dataset of 230,000 3d facial landmarks). In: Proceedings of the IEEE International Conference on Computer Vision, pp. 1021–1030 (2017)
5. Burgos-Artizzu, X.P., Perona, P., Dollár, P.: Robust face landmark estimation under occlusion. In: Proceedings of the IEEE International Conference on Computer Vision, pp. 1513–1520 (2013)
6. Cao, X., Wei, Y., Wen, F., Sun, J.: Face alignment by explicit shape regression. Int. J. Comput. Vis. **107**, 177–190 (2012)
7. Carion, N., Massa, F., Synnaeve, G., Usunier, N., Kirillov, A., Zagoruyko, S.: End-to-end object detection with transformers. In: European Conference on Computer Vision. pp. 213–229. Springer (2020)
8. Chandran, P., Bradley, D., Gross, M.H., Beeler, T.: Attention-driven cropping for very high resolution facial landmark detection. 2020 IEEE/CVF Conference on Computer Vision and Pattern Recognition (CVPR), pp. 5860–5869 (2020)
9. Dapogny, A., Bailly, K., Cord, M.: Decafa: deep convolutional cascade for face alignment in the wild. 2019 IEEE/CVF International Conference on Computer Vision (ICCV), pp. 6892–6900 (2019)
10. Devlin, J., Chang, M.W., Lee, K., Toutanova, K.N.: Bert: Pre-training of deep bidirectional transformers for language understanding (2018). arxiv.org/abs/1810.04805
11. Dong, X., Yu, S.I., Weng, X., Wei, S.E., Yang, Y., Sheikh, Y.: Supervision-by-registration: an unsupervised approach to improve the precision of facial landmark detectors. 2018 IEEE/CVF Conference on Computer Vision and Pattern Recognition, pp. 360–368 (2018)
12. Dosovitskiy, A., et al.: An image is worth 16×16 words: transformers for image recognition at scale. arXiv preprint arXiv:2010.11929 (2020)
13. Dvornik, N., Schmid, C., Mairal, J.: Selecting relevant features from a multi-domain representation for few-shot classification. In: Vedaldi, A., Bischof, H., Brox, T., Frahm, J.-M. (eds.) ECCV 2020. LNCS, vol. 12355, pp. 769–786. Springer, Cham (2020). https://doi.org/10.1007/978-3-030-58607-2_45
14. Feng, Z.H., Kittler, J., Awais, M., Huber, P., Wu, X.J.: Wing loss for robust facial landmark localisation with convolutional neural networks. In: Proceedings of the IEEE Conference on Computer Vision and Pattern Recognition, pp. 2235–2245 (2018)

15. Hoffman, J., Tzeng, E., Darrell, T., Saenko, K.: Simultaneous deep transfer across domains and tasks. 2015 IEEE International Conference on Computer Vision (ICCV), pp. 4068–4076 (2015)
16. Honari, S., Molchanov, P., Tyree, S., Vincent, P., Pal, C., Kautz, J.: Improving landmark localization with semi-supervised learning. In: Proceedings of the IEEE Conference on Computer Vision and Pattern Recognition, pp. 1546–1555 (2018)
17. Huang, Y., Yang, H., Li, C., Kim, J., Wei, F.: Adnet: Leveraging error-bias towards normal direction in face alignment. arXiv preprint arXiv:2109.05721 (2021)
18. Jin, H., Liao, S., Shao, L.: Pixel-in-pixel net: towards efficient facial landmark detection in the wild. Int. J. Comput. Vision 129(12), 3174–3194 (2021)
19. Jin, S., Feng, Z., Yang, W., Kittler, J.: Separable batch normalization for robust facial landmark localization with cross-protocol network training. arXiv preprint arXiv:2101.06663 (2021)
20. Jin, S., Feng, Z., Yang, W., Kittler, J.: Separable batch normalization for robust facial landmark localization with cross-protocol network training. ArXiv abs/2101.06663 (2021)
21. Joshi, M., Dredze, M., Cohen, W.W., Rosé, C.P.: Multi-domain learning: When do domains matter? In: EMNLP (2012)
22. Khan, M.H., et al.: Animalweb: a large-scale hierarchical dataset of annotated animal faces. In: 2020 IEEE/CVF Conference on Computer Vision and Pattern Recognition (CVPR), pp. 6937–6946 (2020)
23. Kingma, D.P., Ba, J.: Adam: a method for stochastic optimization. arXiv preprint arXiv:1412.6980 (2014)
24. Kowalski, M., Naruniec, J., Trzciński, T.: Deep alignment network: a convolutional neural network for robust face alignment. In: 2017 IEEE Conference on Computer Vision and Pattern Recognition Workshops (CVPRW), pp. 2034–2043 (2017)
25. Kumar, A., et al.: Luvli face alignment: estimating landmarks' location, uncertainty, and visibility likelihood. In: Proceedings of the IEEE/CVF Conference on Computer Vision and Pattern Recognition, pp. 8236–8246 (2020)
26. Lan, X., Hu, Q., Cheng, J.: Hih: Towards more accurate face alignment via heatmap in heatmap. arXiv preprint arXiv:2104.03100 (2021)
27. Liu, R., Lehman, J., Molino, P., Such, F.P., Frank, E., Sergeev, A., Yosinski, J.: An intriguing failing of convolutional neural networks and the coordconv solution. In: NeurIPS (2018)
28. Liu, Y., Shi, H., Si, Y., Shen, H., Wang, X., Mei, T.: A high-efficiency framework for constructing large-scale face parsing benchmark. arXiv preprint arXiv:1905.04830 (2019)
29. , Liu, Z., et al.: Swin transformer: hierarchical vision transformer using shifted windows. In: Proceedings of the IEEE/CVF International Conference on Computer Vision pp. 10012–10022 (2021)
30. Nam, H., Han, B.: Learning multi-domain convolutional neural networks for visual tracking. In: 2016 IEEE Conference on Computer Vision and Pattern Recognition (CVPR), pp. 4293–4302 (2016)
31. Newell, A., Yang, K., Deng, J.: Stacked hourglass networks for human pose estimation. In: Leibe, B., Matas, J., Sebe, N., Welling, M. (eds.) ECCV 2016. LNCS, vol. 9912, pp. 483–499. Springer, Cham (2016). https://doi.org/10.1007/978-3-319-46484-8_29
32. Nibali, A., He, Z., Morgan, S., Prendergast, L.: Numerical coordinate regression with convolutional neural networks. ArXiv abs/1801.07372 (2018)
33. Poggio, T., Torre, V., Koch, C.: Computational vision and regularization theory. Readings in Computer Vision, pp. 638–643 (1987)

34. Qian, S., Sun, K., Wu, W., Qian, C., Jia, J.: Aggregation via separation: boosting facial landmark detector with semi-supervised style translation. In: Proceedings of the IEEE/CVF International Conference on Computer Vision, pp. 10153–10163 (2019)
35. Raffel, C., et al.: Exploring the limits of transfer learning with a unified text-to-text transformer. arXiv preprint arXiv:1910.10683 (2019)
36. Sagonas, C., Tzimiropoulos, G., Zafeiriou, S., Pantic, M.: 300 faces in-the-wild challenge: The first facial landmark localization challenge. In: Proceedings of the IEEE international conference on computer vision workshops. pp. 397–403 (2013)
37. Saragih, J.M., Lucey, S., Cohn, J.F.: Face alignment through subspace constrained mean-shifts. In: 2009 IEEE 12th International Conference on Computer Vision, pp. 1034–1041. IEEE (2009)
38. Smith, B.M., Zhang, L.: Collaborative facial landmark localization for transferring annotations across datasets. In: Fleet, D., Pajdla, T., Schiele, B., Tuytelaars, T. (eds.) ECCV 2014. LNCS, vol. 8694, pp. 78–93. Springer, Cham (2014). https://doi.org/10.1007/978-3-319-10599-4_6
39. Song, L., Wu, W., Fu, C., Qian, C., Loy, C.C., He, R.: Everything's talkin': Pareidolia face reenactment. arXiv preprint arXiv:2104.03061 (2021)
40. Sun, K., et al.: High-resolution representations for labeling pixels and regions. arXiv preprint arXiv:1904.04514 (2019)
41. Tang, Z., Peng, X., Li, K., Metaxas, D.N.: Towards efficient u-nets: a coupled and quantized approach. IEEE Trans. Pattern Anal. Mach. Intell. **42**, 2038–2050 (2020)
42. Touvron, H., Cord, M., Douze, M., Massa, F., Sablayrolles, A., Jégou, H.: Training data-efficient image transformers & distillation through attention. In: International Conference on Machine Learning, pp. 10347–10357. PMLR (2021)
43. Valle, R., Buenaposada, J.M., Valdés, A., Baumela, L.: A deeply-initialized coarse-to-fine ensemble of regression trees for face alignment. In: Ferrari, V., Hebert, M., Sminchisescu, C., Weiss, Y. (eds.) Computer Vision – ECCV 2018. LNCS, vol. 11218, pp. 609–624. Springer, Cham (2018). https://doi.org/10.1007/978-3-030-01264-9_36
44. Vaswani, A., et al.: Attention is all you need. In: Advances in Neural Information Processing Systems, pp. 5998–6008 (2017)
45. Wang, X., Bo, L., Fuxin, L.: Adaptive wing loss for robust face alignment via heatmap regression. In: Proceedings of the IEEE/CVF International Conference on Computer Vision, pp. 6971–6981 (2019)
46. Wardle, S.G., Paranjape, S., Taubert, J., Baker, C.I.: Illusory faces are more likely to be perceived as male than female. Proceedings of the National Academy of Sciences 119(5) (2022)
47. Watchareeruetai, U., et al.: Lotr: face landmark localization using localization transformer. arXiv preprint arXiv:2109.10057 (2021)
48. Wei, S.E., Ramakrishna, V., Kanade, T., Sheikh, Y.: Convolutional pose machines. In: Proceedings of the IEEE conference on Computer Vision and Pattern Recognition, pp. 4724–4732 (2016)
49. Wei, S.E., Saragih, J.M., Simon, T., Harley, A.W., Lombardi, S., Perdoch, M., Hypes, A., Wang, D., Badino, H., Sheikh, Y.: Vr facial animation via multiview image translation. ACM Trans. Graph. (TOG) **38**, 1–16 (2019)
50. White, T.: Shared visual abstractions. ArXiv abs/1912.04217 (2019)
51. Williams, J.: Multi-domain learning and generalization in dialog state tracking. In: SIGDIAL Conference (2013)
52. Wu, W., Qian, C., Yang, S., Wang, Q., Cai, Y., Zhou, Q.: Look at boundary: a boundary-aware face alignment algorithm. In: CVPR (2018)

53. Wu, W., Yang, S.: Leveraging intra and inter-dataset variations for robust face alignment. 2017 IEEE Conference on Computer Vision and Pattern Recognition Workshops (CVPRW) pp. 2096–2105 (2017)
54. Xiong, X., la Torre, F.D.: Supervised descent method and its applications to face alignment. In: 2013 IEEE Conference on Computer Vision and Pattern Recognition, pp. 532–539 (2013)
55. Yang, J., Liu, Q., Zhang, K.: Stacked hourglass network for robust facial landmark localisation. In: Proceedings of the IEEE Conference on Computer Vision and Pattern Recognition Workshops, pp. 79–87 (2017)
56. Yaniv, J., Newman, Y.: The face of art: landmark detection and geometric style in portraits (2019)
57. Zhang, J., Kan, M., Shan, S., Chen, X.: Leveraging datasets with varying annotations for face alignment via deep regression network. In: 2015 IEEE International Conference on Computer Vision (ICCV), pp. 3801–3809 (2015)
58. Zhang, J., Cai, H., Guo, Y., Peng, Z.: Landmark detection and 3d face reconstruction for caricature using a nonlinear parametric model. Graph. Model. **115**, 101103 (2021)
59. Zheng, Y., et al.: General facial representation learning in a visual-linguistic manner. CoRR (2021)
60. Zhu, S., Li, C., Loy, C.C., Tang, X.: Transferring landmark annotations for cross-dataset face alignment. ArXiv abs/1409.0602 (2014)
61. Zhu, S., Li, C., Loy, C.C., Tang, X.: Face alignment by coarse-to-fine shape searching. 2015 IEEE Conference on Computer Vision and Pattern Recognition (CVPR), pp. 4998–5006 (2015)

DEVIANT: Depth EquiVarIAnt NeTwork for Monocular 3D Object Detection

Abhinav Kumar[1(✉)], Garrick Brazil[2], Enrique Corona[3], Armin Parchami[3], and Xiaoming Liu[1]

[1] Michigan State University, East Lansing, USA
{kumarab6,liuxm}@msu.edu
[2] Meta AI, Menlo Park, USA
brazilga@fb.com
[3] Ford Motor Company, Detroit, USA
{ecoron18,mparcham}@ford.com
https://www.github.com/abhi1kumar/DEVIANT

Abstract. Modern neural networks use building blocks such as convolutions that are equivariant to arbitrary 2D translations. However, these vanilla blocks are not equivariant to arbitrary 3D translations in the projective manifold. Even then, all monocular 3D detectors use vanilla blocks to obtain the 3D coordinates, a task for which the vanilla blocks are not designed for. This paper takes the first step towards convolutions equivariant to arbitrary 3D translations in the projective manifold. Since the depth is the hardest to estimate for monocular detection, this paper proposes Depth EquiVarIAnt NeTwork (DEVIANT) built with existing scale equivariant steerable blocks. As a result, DEVIANT is equivariant to the depth translations in the projective manifold whereas vanilla networks are not. The additional depth equivariance forces the DEVIANT to learn consistent depth estimates, and therefore, DEVIANT achieves state-of-the-art monocular 3D detection results on KITTI and Waymo datasets in the image-only category and performs competitively to methods using extra information. Moreover, DEVIANT works better than vanilla networks in cross-dataset evaluation.

Keywords: Equivariance · Projective manifold · Monocular 3D detection

1 Introduction

Monocular 3D object detection is a fundamental task in computer vision, where the task is to infer 3D information including depth from a single monocular image. It has applications in augmented reality [2], gaming [58], robotics [60], and more recently in autonomous driving [4,63] as a fallback solution for LiDAR.

Supplementary Information The online version contains supplementary material available at https://doi.org/10.1007/978-3-031-20077-9_39.

Most of the monocular 3D methods attach extra heads to the 2D Faster-RCNN [59] or CenterNet [93] for 3D detections. Some change architectures [37, 40,71] or losses [4,13]. Others incorporate augmentation [66], or confidence [5, 40]. Recent ones use in-network ensembles [44,91] for better depth estimation.

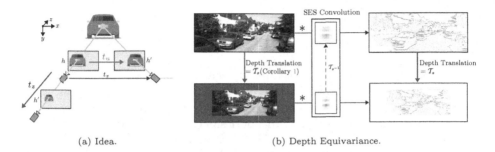

(a) Idea.   (b) Depth Equivariance.

Fig. 1. (a) Idea. Vanilla CNN is equivariant to projected 2D translations t_u, t_v of the ego camera. The ego camera moves in 3D in driving scenes which breaks this assumption. We propose DEVIANT which is additionally equivariant to depth translations t_z in the projective manifold. **(b) Depth Equivariance.** DEVIANT enforces additional consistency among the feature maps of an image and its transformation caused by the ego depth translation. $\mathcal{T}_s =$ scale transformation, $* =$ vanilla convolution.

Most of these methods use vanilla blocks such as convolutions that are *equivariant* to arbitrary 2D translations [6,56]. In other words, whenever we shift the ego camera in 2D (See t_u of Fig. 1), the new image (projection) is a translation of the original image, and therefore, these methods output a translated feature map. However, in general, the camera moves in depth in driving scenes instead of 2D (See t_z of

Table 1. Equivariance comparisons. [Key: Proj.= Projected, ax= axis].

	3D			Proj. 2D	
Translation →	x–ax (t_x)	y–ax (t_y)	z–ax (t_z)	u–ax (t_u)	v–ax (t_v)
Vanilla CNN	–	–	–	✓	✓
Log-polar [97]	–	–	✓	–	–
DEVIANT	–	–	✓	✓	✓
Ideal	✓	✓	✓	–	–

Fig. 1). So, the new image is not a translation of the original input image due to the projective transform. Thus, using vanilla blocks in monocular methods is a mismatch between the assumptions and the regime where these blocks operate. Additionally, there is a huge generalization gap between training and validation for monocular 3D detection (See Table 14 in the supplementary). Modeling translation equivariance in the correct manifold improves generalization for tasks in spherical [15] and hyperbolic [25] manifolds. Monocular detection involves processing pixels (3D point projections) to obtain the 3D information, and is thus a task in the projective manifold. Moreover, the depth in monocular detection is ill-defined [71], and thus, the hardest to estimate [48]. Hence, using building blocks *equivariant to depth translations in the projective manifold* is a natural choice for improving generalization and is also at the core of this work (See Appendix A1.8).

Table 2. Equivariances known in the literature.

Transformation → Manifold ↓	Translation	Rotation	Scale	Flips	Learned
Euclidean	Vanilla CNN [36]	Polar, Steerable [84]	Log-polar[29], Steerable [27]	ChiralNets [88]	Transformers [20]
Spherical	Spherical CNN [15]	–	–	–	–
Hyperbolic	Hyperbolic CNN [25]	–	–	–	–
Projective	Monocular Detector	–	–	–	–

Recent monocular methods use flips [4], scale [44,66], mosaic [3,72] or copy-paste [38] augmentation, depth-aware convolution [4], or geometry [42,44,62,90] to improve generalization. Although all these methods improve performance, a major issue is that their backbones are not designed for the projective world. This results in the depth estimation going haywire with a slight ego movement [94]. Moreover, data augmentation, e.g., flips, scales, mosaic, copy-paste, is not only limited for the projective tasks, but also does not guarantee desired behavior [24].

To address the mismatch between assumptions and the operating regime of the vanilla blocks and improve generalization, we take the first step towards convolutions equivariant to arbitrary 3D translations in the projective manifold. We propose Depth EquiVarIAnt NeTwork (DEVIANT) which is additionally equivariant to depth translations in the projective manifold as shown in Table 1. Building upon the classic result from [28], we simplify it under reasonable assumptions about the camera movement in autonomous driving to get scale transformations. The scale equivariant blocks are well-known in the literature [27,30,69,95], and consequently, we replace the vanilla blocks in the backbone with their scale equivariant steerable counterparts [69] to additionally embed equivariance to depth translations in the projective manifold. Hence, DEVIANT learns consistent depth estimates and improves monocular detection.

In summary, the main contributions of this work include:

- We study the modeling error in monocular 3D detection and propose depth equivariant networks built with scale equivariant steerable blocks as a solution.
- We achieve state-of-the-art (SOTA) monocular 3D object detection results on the KITTI and Waymo datasets in the image-only category and perform competitively to methods which use extra information.
- We experimentally show that DEVIANT works better in cross-dataset evaluation suggesting better generalization than vanilla CNN backbones.

2   Literature Review

Equivariant Neural Networks. The success of convolutions in CNN has led people to look for their generalizations [17,80]. Convolution is the unique solution to 2D translation equivariance in the Euclidean manifold [6,7,56]. Thus, convolution in CNN is a prior in the Euclidean manifold. Several works explore other group actions in the Euclidean manifold such as 2D rotations [16,18,50,81], scale

[32,49], flips [88], or their combinations [76,84]. Some consider 3D translations [83] and rotations [73]. Few [20,82,92] attempt learning the equivariance from the data, but such methods have significantly higher data requirements [83]. Others change the manifold to spherical [15], hyperbolic [25], graphs [51], or arbitrary manifolds [31]. Monocular 3D detection involves operations on pixels which are projections of 3D point and thus, works in a different manifold namely projective manifold. Table 2 summarizes all these equivariances known thus far.

Scale Equivariant Networks. Scale equivariance in the Euclidean manifold is more challenging than the rotations because of its acyclic and unbounded nature [56]. There are two major lines of work for scale equivariant networks. The first [21,29] infers the global scale using log-polar transform [97], while the other infers the scale locally by convolving with multiple scales of images [32] or filters [86]. Several works [27,30,69,95] extend the local idea, using steerable filters [23]. Another work [85] constructs filters for integer scaling. We compare the two kinds of scale equivariant convolutions on the monocular 3D detection task and show that steerable convolutions are better suited to embed depth (scale) equivariance. Scale equivariant networks have been used for classification [21,27,69], 2D tracking [68] and 3D object classification [21]. We are the first to use scale equivariant networks for monocular 3D detection.

3D Object Detection. Accurate 3D object detection uses sparse data from LiDARs [61], which are expensive and do not work well in severe weather [71] and glassy environments. Hence, several works have been on monocular camera-based 3D object detection, which is simplistic but has scale/depth ambiguity [71]. Earlier approaches [11,22,54,55] use hand-crafted features, while the recent ones use deep learning. Some change architectures [37,40,41,71] or losses [4,13]. Some use scale [44,66], mosaic [72] or copy-paste [38] augmentation. Others incorporate depth in convolution [4,19], or confidence [5,34,40]. More recent ones use in-network ensembles to predict the depth deterministically [91] or probabilistically [44]. A few use temporal cues [5], NMS [33], or corrected camera extrinsics [94] in the training pipeline. Some also use CAD models [10,43] or LiDAR [57] in training. Another line of work called Pseudo-LiDAR [45,47,52,64,77] estimates the depth first, and then uses a point cloud-based 3D object detector. We refer to [46] for a detailed survey. Our work is the first to use scale equivariant blocks in the backbone for monocular 3D detection.

3   Background

We first provide the necessary definitions which are used throughout this paper. These are not our contributions and can be found in the literature [8,28,83].

Equivariance. Consider a group of transformations G, whose individual members are g. Assume Φ denote the mapping of the inputs h to the outputs y. Let the inputs and outputs undergo the transformation $\mathcal{T}_g^h$ and $\mathcal{T}_g^y$ respectively. Then, the mapping Φ is equivariant to the group G [83] if $\Phi(\mathcal{T}_g^h h) = \mathcal{T}_g^y(\Phi h), \forall\, g \in G$. Thus, equivariance provides an explicit relationship between input transformations and feature-space transformations at each layer of the neural network [83], and intuitively makes the learning easier. The mapping Φ is the vanilla convolution when the $\mathcal{T}_g^h = \mathcal{T}_g^y = \mathcal{T}_t$ where $\mathcal{T}_t$ denotes the translation $\mathbf{t}$ on the discrete grid [6,7,56]. These vanilla convolution introduce weight-tying [36] in fully connected neural networks resulting in a greater generalization. A special case of equivariance is the invariance [83] which is given by $\Phi(\mathcal{T}_g^h h) = \Phi h, \forall\, g \in G$.

Projective Transformations. Our idea is to use equivariance to depth translations in the projective manifold since the monocular detection task belongs to this manifold. A natural question to ask is whether such equivariants exist in the projective manifold. [8] answers this question in negative, and says that such equivariants do not exist in general. However, such equivariants exist for special classes, such as planes. An intuitive way to understand this is to infer the rotations and translations by looking at the two projections (images). For example, the result of [8] makes sense if we consider a car with very different front and back sides as in Fig. 6. A 180° ego rotation around the car means the projections (images) are its front and the back sides, which are different. Thus, we can not infer the translations and rotations from these two projections. Based on this result, we stick with **locally** planar objects *i.e.* we assume that a 3D object is made of several *patch planes*. (See last row of Fig. 2b as an example). It is important to stress that we do **NOT** assume that the 3D object such as car is planar. The local planarity also agrees with the property of manifolds that manifolds locally resemble n-dimensional Euclidean space and because the projective transform maps planes to planes, the patch planes in 3D are also locally planar. We show a sample planar patch and the 3D object in Fig. 5 in the appendix.

Planarity and Projective Transformation. Example 13.2 from [28] links the planarity and projective transformations. Although their result is for stereo with two different cameras $(\mathbf{K}, \mathbf{K}')$, we substitute $\mathbf{K} = \mathbf{K}'$ to get Theorem 1.

Theorem 1 *[28]. Consider a 3D point lying on a patch plane $mx + ny + oz + p = 0$, and observed by an ego camera in a pinhole setup to give an image h. Let $\mathbf{t} = (t_x, t_y, t_z)$ and $\mathbf{R} = [r_{ij}]_{3\times 3}$ denote a translation and rotation of the ego camera respectively. Observing the same 3D point from a new camera position leads to an image h'. Then, the image h is related to the image h' by the projective transformation*

$$\mathcal{T} : h(u - u_0, v - v_0) \tag{1}$$

$$= h'\left(f\frac{\left(r_{11} + \bar{t}_x\frac{m}{p}\right)(u - u_0) + \left(r_{21} + \bar{t}_x\frac{n}{p}\right)(v - v_0) + \left(r_{31} + \bar{t}_x\frac{o}{p}\right)f}{\left(r_{13} + \bar{t}_z\frac{m}{p}\right)(u - u_0) + \left(r_{23} + \bar{t}_z\frac{n}{p}\right)(v - v_0) + \left(r_{33} + \bar{t}_z\frac{o}{p}\right)f}, \right.$$

$$\left. f\frac{\left(r_{12} + \bar{t}_y\frac{m}{p}\right)(u - u_0) + \left(r_{22} + \bar{t}_y\frac{n}{p}\right)(v - v_0) + \left(r_{32} + \bar{t}_y\frac{o}{p}\right)f}{\left(r_{13} + \bar{t}_z\frac{m}{p}\right)(u - u_0) + \left(r_{23} + \bar{t}_z\frac{n}{p}\right)(v - v_0) + \left(r_{33} + \bar{t}_z\frac{o}{p}\right)f} \right),$$

where f and (u_0, v_0) denote the focal length and principal point of the ego camera, and $(\bar{t}_x, \bar{t}_y, \bar{t}_z) = \mathbf{R}^T\mathbf{t}$.

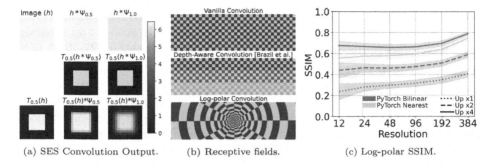

(a) SES Convolution Output.   (b) Receptive fields.   (c) Log-polar SSIM.

Fig. 2. (a) Scale Equivariance. We apply SES convolution [69] with two scales on a single channel toy image h. **(b) Receptive fields** of convolutions in the Euclidean manifold. Colors represent different weights, while shades represent the same weight. **(c) Impact of discretization on log-polar convolution.** SSIM is very low at small resolutions and is not 1 even after upscaling by 4. [Key: Up= Upscaling].

4   Depth Equivariant Backbone

The projective transformation in Eq. 1 from [28] is complicated and also involves rotations, and we do not know which convolution obeys this projective transformation. Hence, we simplify Eq. 1 under reasonable assumptions to obtain a familiar transformation for which the *convolution* is known.

Corollary 1. *When the ego camera translates in depth without rotations* $(\mathbf{R} = \mathbf{I})$, *and the patch plane is "approximately" parallel to the image plane, the image h locally is a scaled version of the second image h' independent of focal length, i.e.*

$$\mathcal{T}_s : h(u - u_0, v - v_0) \approx h' \left(\frac{u - u_0}{1 + t_z \frac{o}{p}}, \frac{v - v_0}{1 + t_z \frac{o}{p}} \right). \tag{2}$$

where f and (u_0, v_0) denote the focal length and principal point of the ego camera, and t_z denotes the ego translation.

See Appendix A1.6 for the detailed explanation of Theorem 1. Theorem 1 says

$$\mathcal{T}_s : h(u - u_0, v - v_0) \approx h' \left(\frac{u - u_0}{s}, \frac{v - v_0}{s} \right), \tag{3}$$

where, $s = 1 + t_z \frac{o}{p}$ denotes the scale and $\mathcal{T}_s$ denotes the scale transformation. The scale $s < 1$ suggests downscaling, while $s > 1$ suggests upscaling. Theorem 1 shows that the transformation $\mathcal{T}_s$ is independent of the focal length and that scale is a linear function of the depth translation. Hence, the depth translation in the projective manifold induces scale transformation and thus, the depth equivariance in the projective manifold is the scale equivariance in the Euclidean manifold. Mathematically, the desired equivariance is $[\mathcal{T}_s(h) * \Psi] = \mathcal{T}_s [h * \Psi_{s^{-1}}]$, where Ψ denotes the filter (See Appendix A1.7). As CNN is not a scale equivariant (SE) architecture [69], we aim to get SE backbone which makes the architecture equivariant to depth translations in the projective manifold. The scale transformation is a familiar transformation and SE convolutions are well known [27,30,69,95].

Scale Equivariant Steerable (SES) Blocks. We use the existing SES blocks [68,69] to construct our Depth EquiVarIAnt NeTwork (DEVIANT) backbone. As [68] does not construct SE-DLA-34 backbones, we construct our DEVIANT backbone as follows. We replace the vanilla convolutions by the SES convolutions [68] with the basis as Hermite polynomials. SES convolutions result in multi-scale representation of an input tensor. As a result, their output is five-dimensional instead of four-dimensional. Thus, we replace the 2D pools and batch norm (BN) by 3D pools and 3D BN respectively. The Scale-Projection layer [69] carries a max over the extra (scale) dimension to project five-dimensional tensors to four dimensions (See Fig. 9 in the supplementary). Ablation in Sect. 5.2 confirms that BN and Pool (BNP) should also be SE for the best performance.

The SES convolutions [27,69,95] are based on steerable-filters [23]. Steerable approaches [27] first pre-calculate the non-trainable multi-scale basis in the Euclidean manifold and then build filters by the linear combinations of the trainable weights $\mathbf{w}$ (See Fig. 9). The number of trainable weights $\mathbf{w}$ equals the number of filters at one particular scale. The linear combination of multi-scale basis ensures that the filters are also multi-scale. Thus, SES blocks bypass grid conversion and do not suffer from sampling effects.

We show the convolution of toy image h with a SES convolution in Fig. 2a. Let Ψ_s denote the filter at scale s. The convolution between downscaled image and filter $\mathcal{T}_{0.5}(h) * \Psi_{0.5}$ matches the downscaled version of original image convolved with upscaled filter $\mathcal{T}_{0.5}(h * \Psi_{1.0})$. Figure 2a (right column) shows that the output of a CNN exhibits aliasing in general and is therefore, not scale equivariant.

Log-polar Convolution: Impact of Discretization. An alternate way to convert the depth translation t_z of Eq. 2 to shift is by converting the images to log-polar space [97] around the principal point (u_0, v_0), as

$$h(\ln r, \theta) \approx h'\left(\ln r - \ln\left(1 + t_z\frac{o}{p}\right), \ \theta\right),\tag{4}$$

with $r = \sqrt{(u-u_0)^2 + (v-v_0)^2}$, and $\theta = \tan^{-1}\left(\frac{v-v_0}{u-u_0}\right)$. The log-polar transformation converts the scale to translation, so using convolution in the log-polar space is equivariant to the logarithm of the depth translation t_z. We show the receptive field of log-polar convolution in Fig. 2b. The log-polar convolution uses a smaller receptive field for objects closer to the principal point, while a larger field away from the principal point. We implemented log-polar convolution and found that its performance (See Table 11) is not acceptable, consistent with [69]. We attribute this behavior to the discretization of pixels and loss of 2D translation equivariance. Equation 4 is perfectly valid in the continuous world (Note the use of parentheses instead of square brackets in Eq. 4). However, pixels reside on discrete grids, which gives rise to sampling errors [35]. We discuss the impact of discretization on log-polar convolution in Sect. 5.2 and show it in Fig. 2c. Hence, we do not use log-polar convolution for the DEVIANT backbone.

Comparison of Equivariances for Monocular 3D Detection. We now compare equivariances for monocular 3D detection task. An ideal monocular detector should be equivariant to arbitrary 3D translations (t_x, t_y, t_z). However, most monocular detectors [33,44] estimate 2D projections of 3D centers and the depth, which they back-project in 3D world via known camera intrinsics. Thus, a good enough detector shall be equivariant to 2D translations (t_u, t_v) for projected centers as well as equivariant to depth translations (t_z).

Existing detector backbones [33,44] are only equivariant to 2D translations as they use vanilla convolutions that produce 4D feature maps. Log-polar backbones is equivariant to logarithm of depth translations but not to 2D translations. DEVIANT uses SES convolutions to produce 5D feature maps. The extra dimension in 5D feature map captures the changes in scale (for depth), while these feature maps individually are equivariant to 2D translations (for projected centers). Hence, DEVIANT augments the 2D translation equivariance (t_u, t_v) of the projected centers with the depth translation equivariance. We emphasize that although DEVIANT is **not** equivariant to arbitrary 3D translations in the projective manifold, DEVIANT **does** provide the equivariance to depth translations (t_z) and is thus a first step towards the ideal equivariance. Our experiments (Sect. 5) show that even this additional equivariance benefits monocular 3D detection task. This is expected because depth is the hardest parameter to estimate [48]. Table 1 summarizes these equivariances. Moreover, Table 10 empirically shows that 2D detection does not suffer and therefore, confirms that DEVIANT indeed augments the 2D equivariance with the depth equivariance. An idea similar to DEVIANT is the optical expansion [87] which augments optical flow with the scale information and benefits depth estimation.

5   Experiments

Our experiments use the KITTI [26], Waymo [70] and nuScenes datasets [9]. We modify the publicly-available PyTorch [53] code of GUP Net [44] and use the GUP Net model as our baseline. For DEVIANT, we keep the number of scales as three [68]. DEVIANT takes 8.5 hours for training and 0.04s per image for inference on a single A100 GPU. See Appendix A2.2 for more details.

Evaluation Metrics. KITTI evaluates on three object categories: Easy, Moderate and Hard. It assigns each object to a category based on its occlusion, truncation, and height in the image space. KITTI uses $AP_{3D|R_{40}}$ percentage metric on the Moderate category to benchmark models [26] following [63,65].

Waymo evaluates on two object levels: Level_1 and Level_2. It assigns each object to a level based on the number of LiDAR points included in its 3D box. Waymo uses APH_{3D} percentage metric which is the incorporation of heading information in AP_{3D} to benchmark models. It also provides evaluation at three distances $[0, 30)$, $[30, 50)$ and $[50, \infty)$ meters.

Data Splits. We use the following splits of the KITTI,Waymo and nuScenes:

- *KITTI Test (Full) split*: Official KITTI 3D benchmark [1] consists of 7,481 training and 7,518 testing images [26].

- *KITTI Val split*: It partitions the 7,481 training images into 3,712 training and 3,769 validation images [12].
- *Waymo Val split*: This split [57,75] contains 52,386 training and 39,848 validation images from the front camera. We construct its training set by sampling every third frame from the training sequences as in [57,75].
- *nuScenes Val split:* It consists of 28,130 training and 6,019 validation images from the front camera [9]. We use this split for evaluation [62].

5.1   KITTI Test Monocular 3D Detection

Cars. Table 3 lists out the results of monocular 3D detection and BEV evaluation on KITTI Test cars. Table 3 results show that DEVIANT outperforms the GUP Net and several other SOTA methods on both tasks. Except DD3D[52] and MonoDistill [14], DEVIANT, an image-based method, also outperforms other methods that use extra information.

Cyclists and Pedestrians. Table 4 lists out the results of monocular 3D detection on KITTI Test Cyclist and Pedestrians. The results show that DEVIANT achieves SOTA results in the image-only category on the challenging Cyclists, and is competitive on Pedestrians.

Table 3. Results on KITTI Test cars at $IoU_{3D} \geq 0.7$. Previous results are from the leader-board or papers. We show 3 methods in each Extra category and 6 methods in the image-only category. [Key: Best, **Second Best**]

Method	Extra	$AP_{3D|R_{40}}[\%](\blacktriangle)$			$AP_{BEV|R_{40}}[\%](\blacktriangle)$		
		Easy	Mod	Hard	Easy	Mod	Hard
AutoShape [43]	CAD	22.47	14.17	11.36	30.66	20.08	15.59
PCT [75]	Depth	21.00	13.37	11.31	29.65	19.03	15.92
DFR-Net [96]	Depth	19.40	13.63	10.35	28.17	19.17	14.84
MonoDistill [14]	Depth	22.97	16.03	13.60	31.87	22.59	19.72
PatchNet-C [64]	LiDAR	22.40	12.53	10.60	–	–	–
CaDDN [57]	LiDAR	19.17	13.41	11.46	27.94	18.91	17.19
DD3D [52]	LiDAR	23.22	16.34	14.20	30.98	22.56	20.03
MonoEF [94]	Odometry	21.29	13.87	11.71	29.03	19.70	17.26
Kinematic [5]	Video	19.07	12.72	9.17	26.69	17.52	13.10
GrooMeD-NMS [33]	–	18.10	12.32	9.65	26.19	18.27	14.05
MonoRCNN [62]	–	18.36	12.65	10.03	25.48	18.11	14.10
MonoDIS-M [63]	–	16.54	12.97	11.04	24.45	19.25	16.87
Ground-Aware [42]	–	**21.65**	13.25	9.91	29.81	17.98	13.08
MonoFlex [91]	–	19.94	13.89	12.07	28.23	**19.75**	**16.89**
GUP Net [44]	–	20.11	**14.20**	11.77	–	–	–
DEVIANT (Ours)	–	21.88	14.46	**11.89**	**29.65**	20.44	17.43

Table 4. Results on KITTI Test cyclists and pedestrians (Cyc/Ped) at $IoU_{3D} \geq$ 0.5. Previous results are from the leader-board or papers. [Key: Best, **Second Best**]

Method	Extra	Cyc $AP_{3D\|R_{40}}[\%](\uparrow)$			Ped $AP_{3D\|R_{40}}[\%](\uparrow)$		
		Easy	Mod	Hard	Easy	Mod	Hard
DDMP-3D[74]	Depth	4.18	2.50	2.32	4.93	3.55	3.01
DFR-Net [96]	Depth	5.69	3.58	3.10	6.09	3.62	3.39
MonoDistill [14]	Depth	5.53	2.81	2.40	12.79	8.17	7.45
CaDDN [57]	LiDAR	7.00	3.41	3.30	12.87	8.14	6.76
DD3D [52]	LiDAR	2.39	1.52	1.31	13.91	9.30	8.05
MonoEF [94]	Odometry	1.80	0.92	0.71	4.27	2.79	2.21
MonoDIS-M [63]	–	1.17	0.54	0.48	7.79	5.14	4.42
MonoFlex [91]	–	3.39	2.10	1.67	11.89	8.16	6.81
GUP Net [44]	–	**4.18**	**2.65**	**2.09**	14.72	9.53	7.87
DEVIANT (Ours)	–	5.05	3.13	2.59	**13.43**	**8.65**	**7.69**

5.2 KITTI Val Monocular 3D Detection

Cars. Table 5 summarizes the results of monocular 3D detection and BEV evaluation on KITTI Val split at two IoU_{3D} thresholds of 0.7 and 0.5 [13,33]. We report the **median** model over 5 runs. The results show that DEVIANT outperforms the GUP Net [44] baseline by a significant margin. The biggest improvements shows up on the Easy set. Significant improvements are also on the Moderate and Hard sets. Interestingly, DEVIANT also outperforms DD3D[52] by a large margin when the large-dataset pretraining is not done (denoted by DD3D$^-$).

Table 5. Results on KITTI Val cars. Comparison with bigger CNN backbones in Tab. 16. [Key: Best, **Second Best**, $^-$ = No pretrain]

Method	Extra	$IoU_{3D} \geq 0.7$						$IoU_{3D} \geq 0.5$					
		$AP_{3D\|R_{40}}[\%](\uparrow)$			$AP_{BEV\|R_{40}}[\%](\uparrow)$			$AP_{3D\|R_{40}}[\%](\uparrow)$			$AP_{BEV\|R_{40}}[\%](\uparrow)$		
		Easy	Mod	Hard	Easy	Mod	Hard	Easy	Mod	Hard	Easy	Mod	Hard
DDMP-3D [74]	Depth	28.12	20.39	16.34	–	–	–	–	–	–	–	–	–
PCT [75]	Depth	38.39	27.53	24.44	47.16	34.65	28.47	–	–	–	–	–	–
MonoDistill [14]	Depth	24.31	18.47	15.76	33.09	25.40	22.16	65.69	49.35	43.49	71.45	53.11	46.94
CaDDN [57]	LiDAR	23.57	16.31	13.84	–	–	–	–	–	–	–	–	–
PatchNet-C [64]	LiDAR	24.51	17.03	13.25	–	–	–	–	–	–	–	–	–
DD3D (DLA34) [52]	LiDAR	–	–	–	33.5	26.0	22.6	–	–	–	–	–	–
DD3D$^-$(DLA34) [52]	LiDAR	–	–	–	26.8	20.2	16.7	–	–	–	–	–	–
MonoEF [94]	Odometry	18.26	16.30	15.24	26.07	25.21	21.61	57.98	51.80	49.34	63.40	61.13	53.22
Kinematic [5]	Video	19.76	14.10	10.47	27.83	19.72	15.10	55.44	39.47	31.26	61.79	44.68	34.56
MonoRCNN [62]	–	16.61	13.19	10.65	25.29	19.22	15.30	–	–	–	–	–	–
MonoDLE [48]	–	17.45	13.66	11.68	24.97	19.33	17.01	55.41	43.42	37.81	60.73	46.87	41.89
GrooMeD-NMS [33]	–	19.67	14.32	11.27	27.38	19.75	15.92	55.62	41.07	32.89	61.83	44.98	36.29
Ground-Aware [42]	–	23.63	16.16	12.06	–	–	–	**60.92**	42.18	32.02	–	–	–
MonoFlex [91]	–	**23.64**	17.51	14.83	–	–	–	–	–	–	–	–	–
GUP Net (Reported) [44]	–	22.76	16.46	13.72	**31.07**	**22.94**	**19.75**	57.62	42.33	37.59	61.78	47.06	40.88
GUP Net (Retrained) [44]	–	21.10	15.48	12.88	28.58	20.92	17.83	58.95	**43.99**	**38.07**	**64.60**	**47.76**	**42.97**
DEVIANT (Ours)	–	24.63	**16.54**	**14.52**	32.60	23.04	19.99	61.00	46.00	40.18	65.28	49.63	43.50

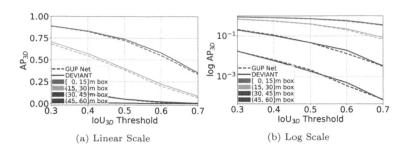

(a) Linear Scale   (b) Log Scale

Fig. 3. AP$_{3D}$ at different depths and IoU$_{3D}$ thresholds on KITTI Val Split.

Table 6. Cross-dataset evaluation of the KITTI Val model on KITTI Val and nuScenes frontal Val cars with depth MAE (↓). [Key: Best, **Second Best**]

Method	KITTI Val				nuScenes frontal Val			
	$0-20$	$20-40$	$40-\infty$	All	$0-20$	$20-40$	$40-\infty$	All
M3D-RPN [4]	0.56	1.33	2.73	1.26	0.94	3.06	10.36	2.67
MonoRCNN [62]	0.46	1.27	2.59	1.14	0.94	2.84	8.65	2.39
GUP Net [44]	**0.45**	**1.10**	**1.85**	**0.89**	**0.82**	**1.70**	**6.20**	**1.45**
DEVIANT	0.40	1.09	1.80	0.87	0.76	1.60	4.50	1.26

AP$_{3D}$ at Different Depths and IoU$_{3D}$ Thresholds. We next compare the AP$_{3D}$ of DEVIANT and GUP Net in Fig. 3 at different distances in meters and IoU$_{3D}$ matching criteria of 0.3 → 0.7 as in [33]. Figure 3 shows that DEVIANT is effective over GUP Net [44] at all depths and higher IoU$_{3D}$ thresholds.

Cross-Dataset Evaluation. Table 6 shows the result of our KITTI Val model on the KITTI Val and nuScenes [9] frontal Val images, using mean absolute error (MAE) of the depth of the boxes [62]. More details are in Appendix A3.1. DEVIANT outperforms GUP Net on most of the metrics on both the datasets, which confirms that DEVIANT generalizes better than CNNs. DEVIANT performs exceedingly well in the cross-dataset evaluation than [4,44,62]. We believe this happens because [4,44,62] rely on data or geometry to get the depth, while DEVIANT is equivariant to the depth translations, and therefore, outputs consistent depth. So, DEVIANT is more robust to data distribution changes.

Table 7. Scale Augmentation vs Scale Equivariance on KITTI Val cars. [Key: Best, Eqv = Equivariance, Aug = Augmentation]

Method	Scale Eqv	Scale Aug	IoU$_{3D} \geq 0.7$						IoU$_{3D} \geq 0.5$					
			AP$_{3D\|R_{40}}[\%](\uparrow)$			AP$_{BEV\|R_{40}}[\%](\uparrow)$			AP$_{3D\|R_{40}}[\%](\uparrow)$			AP$_{BEV\|R_{40}}[\%](\uparrow)$		
			Easy	Mod	Hard	Easy	Mod	Hard	Easy	Mod	Hard	Easy	Mod	Hard
GUP Net [44]			20.82	14.15	12.44	29.93	20.90	17.87	**62.37**	44.40	39.61	**66.81**	48.09	43.14
		✓	21.10	15.48	12.88	28.58	20.92	17.83	58.95	43.99	38.07	64.60	47.76	42.97
DEVIANT	✓		21.33	14.77	12.57	28.79	20.28	17.59	59.31	43.25	37.64	63.94	47.02	41.12
	✓	✓	**24.63**	**16.54**	**14.52**	**32.60**	**23.04**	**19.99**	61.00	**46.00**	**40.18**	65.28	**49.63**	**43.50**

Table 8. Comparison of Equivariant Architectures on KITTI Val cars. [Key: **Best**, Eqv= Equivariance, †= Retrained]

Method	Eqv	$\text{IoU}_{3D} \geq 0.7$						$\text{IoU}_{3D} \geq 0.5$					
		$\text{AP}_{3D\|R_{40}}[\%](\uparrow)$			$\text{AP}_{BEV\|R_{40}}[\%](\uparrow)$			$\text{AP}_{3D\|R_{40}}[\%](\uparrow)$			$\text{AP}_{BEV\|R_{40}}[\%](\uparrow)$		
		Easy	Mod	Hard	Easy	Mod	Hard	Easy	Mod	Hard	Easy	Mod	Hard
DETR3D† [78]	Learned	1.94	1.26	1.09	4.41	3.06	2.79	20.09	13.80	12.78	26.51	18.49	17.36
GUP Net [44]	2D	21.10	15.48	12.88	28.58	20.92	17.83	58.95	43.99	38.07	64.60	47.76	42.97
DEVIANT	2D+Depth	**24.63**	**16.54**	**14.52**	**32.60**	**23.04**	**19.99**	**61.00**	**46.00**	**40.18**	**65.28**	**49.63**	**43.50**

Table 9. Comparison with Dilated Convolution on KITTI Val cars. [Key: **Best**]

Method	Extra	$\text{IoU}_{3D} \geq 0.7$						$\text{IoU}_{3D} \geq 0.5$					
		$\text{AP}_{3D\|R_{40}}[\%](\uparrow)$			$\text{AP}_{BEV\|R_{40}}[\%](\uparrow)$			$\text{AP}_{3D\|R_{40}}[\%](\uparrow)$			$\text{AP}_{BEV\|R_{40}}[\%](\uparrow)$		
		Easy	Mod	Hard	Easy	Mod	Hard	Easy	Mod	Hard	Easy	Mod	Hard
D4LCN [19]	Depth	22.32	16.20	12.30	31.53	22.58	17.87	–	–	–	–	–	–
DCNN [89]	–	21.66	15.49	12.90	30.22	22.06	19.01	57.54	43.12	38.80	63.29	46.86	42.42
DEVIANT	–	**24.63**	**16.54**	**14.52**	**32.60**	**23.04**	**19.99**	**61.00**	**46.00**	**40.18**	**65.28**	**49.63**	**43.50**

Alternatives to Equivariance. We now compare with alternatives to equivariance in the following paragraphs.

(a) Scale Augmentation. A withstanding question in machine learning is the choice between equivariance and data augmentation [24]. Table 7 compares scale equivariance and scale augmentation. GUP Net [44] uses scale-augmentation and therefore, Table 7 shows that equivariance also benefits models which use scale-augmentation. This agrees with Tab. 2 of [69], where they observe that both augmentation and equivariance benefits classification on MNIST-scale dataset.

(b) Other Equivariant Architectures. We now benchmark adding depth (scale) equivariance to a 2D translation equivariant CNN and a transformer which learns the equivariance. Therefore, we compare DEVIANT with GUP Net [44] (a CNN), and DETR3D[78] (a transformer) in Tab. 8. As DETR3D does not report KITTI results, we trained DETR3D on KITTI using their public code. DEVIANT outperforms GUP Net and also surpasses DETR3D by a large margin. This happens because learning equivariance requires more data [83] compared to architectures which hardcode equivariance like CNN or DEVIANT.

(c) Dilated Convolution. DEVIANT adjusts the receptive field based on the object scale, and so, we compare with the dilated CNN (DCNN) [89] and D4LCN [19] in Table 9. The results show that DCNN performs sub-par to DEVIANT. This is expected because dilation corresponds to integer scales [85] while the scaling is generally a float in monocular detection. D4LCN [19] uses monocular depth as input to adjust the receptive field. DEVIANT (without depth) also outperforms D4LCN on Hard cars, which are more distant.

(d) Other Convolutions. We now compare with other known convolutions in literature such as Log-polar convolution [97], Dilated convolution [89] convolution and DISCO [67] in Table 11. The results show that the log-polar con-

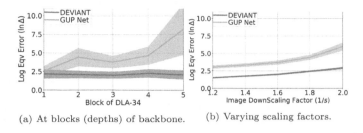

(a) At blocks (depths) of backbone.   (b) Varying scaling factors.

Fig. 4. Log Equivariance Error (Δ) comparison for DEVIANT and GUP Net at **(a)** different blocks with random image scaling factors **(b)** different image scaling factors at depth 3. DEVIANT shows **lower** scale equivariance error than vanilla GUP Net [44].

volution does not work well, and SES convolutions are better suited to embed depth (scale) equivariance. As described in Sect. 4, we investigate the behavior of log-polar convolution through a small experiment. We calculate the SSIM [79] of the original image and the image obtained after the upscaling, log-polar, inverse log-polar, and downscaling blocks. We then average the SSIM over all KITTI Val images. We repeat this experiment for multiple image heights and scaling factors. The ideal SSIM should have been one. However, Fig. 2c shows that SSIM does not reach 1 even after upscaling by 4. This result confirms that log-polar convolution loses information at low resolutions resulting in inaccurate detection.

Next, the results show that dilated convolution [89] performs sub-par to DEVIANT. Moreover, DISCO [67] also does not outperform SES convolution which agrees with the 2D tracking results of [67].

(e) Feature Pyramid Network (FPN). Our baseline GUP Net [44] uses FPN [39] and Table 5 shows that DEVIANT outperforms GUP Net. Hence, we conclude that equivariance also benefits models which use FPN.

Comparison of Equivariance Error. We next quantitatively evaluate the scale equivariance of DEVIANT vs. GUP Net [44], using the equivariance error metric [69]. The equivariance error Δ is the normalized difference between the scaled feature map and the feature map of the scaled image, and is given by $\Delta = \frac{1}{N} \sum_{i=1}^{N} \frac{||\mathcal{T}_{s_i} \Phi(h_i) - \Phi(\mathcal{T}_{s_i} h_i)||_2^2}{||\mathcal{T}_{s_i} \Phi(h_i)||_2^2}$, where Φ denotes the neural network, $\mathcal{T}_{s_i}$ is the scaling transformation for the image i, and N is the total number of images. The equivariance error is zero if the scale equivariance is perfect. We plot the log of this error at different blocks of DEVIANT and GUP Net backbones and also plot at different downscaling of KITTI Val images in Fig. 4. The plots show that DEVIANT has low equivariance error than GUP Net. This is expected since the feature maps of the proposed DEVIANT are additionally equivariant to scale transformations (depth translations). We also visualize the equivariance error for a validation image and for the objects of this image in Fig. 12 in the supplementary. The qualitative plots also show a lower error for the proposed DEVIANT, which agrees with Fig. 4. Figure 12a shows that equivariance error

Table 10. 3D and 2D detection on KITTI Val cars

Method	IoU ≥ 0.7						IoU ≥ 0.5					
	$AP_{3D|R_{40}}[\%](\uparrow)$			$AP_{2D|R_{40}}[\%](\uparrow)$			$AP_{3D|R_{40}}[\%](\uparrow)$			$AP_{2D|R_{40}}[\%](\uparrow)$		
	Easy	Mod	Hard	Easy	Mod	Hard	Easy	Mod	Hard	Easy	Mod	Hard
GUP Net [44]	21.10	15.48	12.88	96.78	88.87	79.02	58.95	43.99	38.07	99.52	91.89	81.99
DEVIANT (Ours)	24.63	16.54	14.52	96.68	88.66	78.87	61.00	46.00	40.18	97.12	91.77	81.93

Table 11. Ablation studies on KITTI Val cars

Change from DEVIANT :		$IoU_{3D} \geq 0.7$						$IoU_{3D} \geq 0.5$					
Changed	From → To	$AP_{3D|R_{40}}[\%](\uparrow)$			$AP_{BEV|R_{40}}[\%](\uparrow)$			$AP_{3D|R_{40}}[\%](\uparrow)$			$AP_{BEV|R_{40}}[\%](\uparrow)$		
		Easy	Mod	Hard	Easy	Mod	Hard	Easy	Mod	Hard	Easy	Mod	Hard
Convolution	SES→Vanilla	21.10	15.48	12.88	28.58	20.92	17.83	58.95	43.99	38.07	64.60	47.76	42.97
	SES→Log-polar [97]	9.19	6.77	5.78	16.39	11.15	9.80	40.51	27.62	23.90	45.66	31.34	25.80
	SES→Dilated [89]	21.66	15.49	12.90	30.22	22.06	19.01	57.54	43.12	38.80	63.29	46.86	42.42
	SES→DISCO [67]	20.21	13.84	11.46	28.56	19.38	16.41	55.22	39.76	35.37	59.46	43.16	38.52
Downscale	10% → 5%	24.24	16.51	14.43	31.94	22.86	19.82	60.64	44.46	40.02	64.68	49.30	43.49
α	10% → 20%	22.19	15.85	13.48	31.15	23.01	19.90	61.24	44.93	40.22	67.46	50.10	43.83
BNP	SE→ Vanilla	24.39	16.20	14.36	32.43	22.53	19.70	62.81	46.14	40.38	67.87	50.23	44.08
Scales	3 → 1	23.20	16.29	13.63	31.76	23.23	19.97	61.90	46.66	40.61	67.37	50.31	43.93
	3 → 2	24.15	16.48	14.55	32.42	23.17	20.07	61.05	46.34	40.46	67.36	50.32	44.07
—	**DEVIANT (best)**	24.63	16.54	14.52	32.60	23.04	19.99	61.00	46.00	40.18	65.28	49.63	43.50

is particularly low for nearby cars which also justifies the good performance of DEVIANT on Easy (nearby) cars in Tables 3 and 5.

Does 2D Detection Suffer? We now investigate whether 2D detection suffers from using DEVIANT backbones in Table 10. The results show that DEVIANT introduces minimal decrease in the 2D detection performance. This is consistent with [68], who report that 2D tracking improves with the SE networks.

Ablation Studies. Table 11 compares the modifications of our approach on KITTI Val cars based on the experimental settings of Sect. 5.

(a) Floating or Integer Downscaling? We next investigate the question that whether one should use floating or integer downscaling factors for DEVIANT. We vary the downscaling factors as $(1+2\alpha, 1+\alpha, 1)$ and therefore, our scaling factor $s = \left(\frac{1}{1+2\alpha}, \frac{1}{1+\alpha}, 1\right)$. We find that α of 10% works the best. We again bring up the dilated convolution (Dilated) results at this point because dilation is a scale equivariant operation for integer downscaling factors [85] ($\alpha = 100\%, s = 0.5$). Table 11 results suggest that the downscaling factors should be floating numbers.

(b) SE BNP. As described in Sect. 4, we ablate DEVIANT against the case when only convolutions are SE but BNP layers are not. So, we place Scale-Projection[69] immediately after every SES convolution. Table 11 shows that such a network performs slightly sub-optimal to our final model.

(c) Number of Scales. We next ablate against the usage of Hermite scales. Using three scales performs better than using only one scale especially on Mod and Hard objects, and slightly better than using two scales.

Table 12. Results on Waymo Val vehicles. [Key: Best, **Second Best**]

IoU$_{3D}$	Difficulty	Method	Extra	AP$_{3D}$ [%](↑)				APH$_{3D}$ [%](↑)			
				All	0-30	30-50	50-∞	All	0-30	30-50	50-∞
0.7	Level_1	CaDDN [57]	LiDAR	5.03	14.54	1.47	0.10	4.99	14.43	1.45	0.10
		PatchNet [45] in [75]	Depth	0.39	1.67	0.13	0.03	0.39	1.63	0.12	0.03
		PCT [75]	Depth	0.89	3.18	0.27	0.07	0.88	3.15	0.27	0.07
		M3D-RPN [4] in [57]	–	0.35	1.12	0.18	0.02	0.34	1.10	0.18	0.02
		GUP Net (Retrained) [44]	–	**2.28**	**6.15**	**0.81**	0.03	**2.27**	**6.11**	**0.80**	0.03
		DEVIANT (Ours)	–	2.69	6.95	0.99	**0.02**	2.67	6.90	0.98	**0.02**
0.7	Level_2	CaDDN [57]	LiDAR	4.49	14.50	1.42	0.09	4.45	14.38	1.41	0.09
		PatchNet [45] in [75]	Depth	0.38	1.67	0.13	0.03	0.36	1.63	0.11	0.03
		PCT [75]	Depth	0.66	3.18	0.27	0.07	0.66	3.15	0.26	0.07
		M3D-RPN [4] in [57]	–	0.33	1.12	0.18	0.02	0.33	1.10	0.17	0.02
		GUP Net (Retrained) [44]	–	**2.14**	**6.13**	**0.78**	0.02	**2.12**	**6.08**	**0.77**	0.02
		DEVIANT (Ours)	–	2.52	6.93	0.95	0.02	2.50	6.87	0.94	0.02
0.5	Level_1	CaDDN [57]	LiDAR	17.54	45.00	9.24	0.64	17.31	44.46	9.11	0.62
		PatchNet [45] in [75]	Depth	2.92	10.03	1.09	0.23	2.74	9.75	0.96	0.18
		PCT [75]	Depth	4.20	14.70	1.78	0.39	4.15	14.54	1.75	0.39
		M3D-RPN [4] in [57]	–	3.79	11.14	2.16	0.26	3.63	10.70	2.09	**0.21**
		GUP Net (Retrained) [44]	–	**10.02**	**24.78**	**4.84**	**0.22**	**9.94**	**24.59**	**4.78**	0.22
		DEVIANT (Ours)	–	10.98	26.85	5.13	0.18	10.89	26.64	5.08	0.18
0.5	Level_2	CaDDN [57]	LiDAR	16.51	44.87	8.99	0.58	16.28	44.33	8.86	0.55
		PatchNet [45] in [75]	Depth	2.42	10.01	1.07	0.22	2.28	9.73	0.97	0.16
		PCT [75]	Depth	4.03	14.67	1.74	0.36	4.15	14.51	1.71	0.35
		M3D-RPN [4] in [57]	–	3.61	11.12	2.12	0.24	3.46	10.67	2.04	0.20
		GUP Net (Retrained) [44]	–	**9.39**	**24.69**	**4.67**	**0.19**	**9.31**	**24.50**	**4.62**	0.19
		DEVIANT (Ours)	–	10.29	26.75	4.95	0.16	10.20	26.54	4.90	0.16

5.3 Waymo Val Monocular 3D Detection

We also benchmark our method on the Waymo dataset [70] which has more variability than KITTI. Table 12 shows the results on Waymo Val split. The results show that DEVIANT outperforms the baseline GUP Net [44] on multiple levels and multiple thresholds. The biggest gains are on the nearby objects which is consistent with Tables 3 and 5. Interestingly, DEVIANT also outperforms PatchNet [45] and PCT [75] without using depth. Although the performance of DEVIANT lags CaDDN[57], it is important to stress that CaDDN uses LiDAR data in training, while DEVIANT is an image-only method.

6 Conclusions

This paper studies the modeling error in monocular 3D detection in detail and takes the first step towards convolutions equivariant to arbitrary 3D translations in the projective manifold. Since the depth is the hardest to estimate for this task, this paper proposes Depth EquiVarIAnt NeTwork (DEVIANT) built with existing scale equivariant steerable blocks. As a result, DEVIANT is equivariant to the depth translations in the projective manifold whereas vanilla networks are not. The additional depth equivariance forces the DEVIANT to learn consistent depth estimates and therefore, DEVIANT achieves SOTA detection results on KITTI and Waymo datasets in the image-only category and performs competitively to methods using extra information. Moreover, DEVIANT works better than vanilla networks in cross-dataset evaluation. Future works include applying the idea to Pseudo-LiDAR [77], and monocular 3D tracking.

References

1. The KITTI Vision Benchmark Suite. https://www.cvlibs.net/datasets/kitti/eval_object.php?obj_benchmark=3d. Accessed 03 July 2022
2. Alhaija, H., Mustikovela, S., Mescheder, L., Geiger, A., Rother, C.: Augmented reality meets computer vision: efficient data generation for urban driving scenes. IJCV (2018)
3. Bochkovskiy, A., Wang, C.Y., Liao, H.Y.M.: YOLOv4: Optimal speed and accuracy of object detection. arXiv preprint arXiv:2004.10934 (2020)
4. Brazil, G., Liu, X.: M3D-RPN: monocular 3D region proposal network for object detection. In: ICCV (2019)
5. Brazil, G., Pons-Moll, G., Liu, X., Schiele, B.: Kinematic 3D object detection in monocular video. In: ECCV (2020)
6. Bronstein, M.: Convolution from first principles. htpps://towardsdatascience.com/deriving-convolution-from-first-principles-4ff124888028. Accessed 13 Aug 2021
7. Bronstein, M., Bruna, J., Cohen, T., Veličković, P.: Geometric deep learning: gGrids, groups, graphs, geodesics, and gauges. arXiv preprint arXiv:2104.13478 (2021)
8. Burns, B., Weiss, R., Riseman, E.: The non-existence of general-case view-invariants. In: Geometric Invariance in Computer Vision (1992)
9. Caesar, H., et al.: nuScenes: a multimodal dataset for autonomous driving. In: CVPR (2020)
10. Chabot, F., Chaouch, M., Rabarisoa, J., Teuliere, C., Chateau, T.: Deep MANTA: a coarse-to-fine many-task network for joint 2D and 3D vehicle analysis from monocular image. In: CVPR (2017)
11. Chen, X., Kundu, K., Zhang, Z., Ma, H., Fidler, S., Urtasun, R.: Monocular 3D object detection for autonomous driving. In: CVPR (2016)
12. Chen, X., Kundu, K., Zhu, Y., Berneshawi, A., Ma, H., Fidler, S., Urtasun, R.: 3D object proposals for accurate object class detection. In: NeurIPS (2015)
13. Chen, Y., Tai, L., Sun, K., Li, M.: MonoPair: Monocular 3D object detection using pairwise spatial relationships. In: CVPR (2020)
14. Chong, Z., et al.: MonoDistill: learning spatial features for monocular 3D object detection. In: ICLR (2022)
15. Cohen, T., Geiger, M., Köhler, J., Welling, M.: Spherical CNNs. In: ICLR (2018)
16. Cohen, T., Welling, M.: Learning the irreducible representations of commutative lie groups. In: ICML (2014)
17. Cohen, T., Welling, M.: Group equivariant convolutional networks. In: ICML (2016)
18. Dieleman, S., De Fauw, J., Kavukcuoglu, K.: Exploiting cyclic symmetry in convolutional neural networks. In: ICML (2016)
19. Ding, M., Huo, Y., Yi, H., Wang, Z., Shi, J., Lu, Z., Luo, P.: Learning depth-guided convolutions for monocular 3D object detection. In: CVPR Workshops (2020)

20. Dosovitskiy, A., et al.: An image is worth 16x16 words: transformers for image recognition at scale. In: ICLR (2021)
21. Esteves, C., Allen-Blanchette, C., Zhou, X., Daniilidis, K.: Polar transformer networks. In: ICLR (2018)
22. Fidler, S., Dickinson, S., Urtasun, R.: 3D object detection and viewpoint estimation with a deformable 3D cuboid model. In: NeurIPS (2012)
23. Freeman, W., Adelson, E.: The design and use of steerable filters. TPAMI (1991)
24. Gandikota, K., Geiping, J., Lähner, Z., Czapliński, A., Moeller, M.: Training or architecture? how to incorporate invariance in neural networks. arXiv preprint arXiv:2106.10044 (2021)
25. Ganea, O.E., Bécigneul, G., Hofmann, T.: Hyperbolic neural networks. In: NeurIPS (2017)
26. Geiger, A., Lenz, P., Urtasun, R.: Are we ready for autonomous driving? the KITTI vision benchmark suite. In: CVPR (2012)
27. Ghosh, R., Gupta, A.: Scale steerable filters for locally scale-invariant convolutional neural networks. In: ICML Workshops (2019)
28. Hartley, R., Zisserman, A.: Multiple view geometry in computer vision. Cambridge University Press (2003)
29. Henriques, J., Vedaldi, A.: Warped convolutions: Efficient invariance to spatial transformations. In: ICML (2017)
30. Jansson, Y., Lindeberg, T.: Scale-invariant scale-channel networks: deep networks that generalise to previously unseen scales. IJCV (2021)
31. Jing, L.: Physical symmetry enhanced neural networks. Ph.D. thesis, Massachusetts Institute of Technology (2020)
32. Kanazawa, A., Sharma, A., Jacobs, D.: Locally scale-invariant convolutional neural networks. In: NeurIPS Workshops (2014)
33. Kumar, A., Brazil, G., Liu, X.: GrooMeD-NMS: grouped mathematically differentiable NMS for monocular 3D object detection. In: CVPR (2021)
34. Kumar, A., et al.: LUVLi face alignment: estimating landmarks' location, uncertainty, and visibility likelihood. In: CVPR (2020)
35. Kumar, A., Prabhakaran, V.: Estimation of bandlimited signals from the signs of noisy samples. In: ICASSP (2013)
36. LeCun, Y., Bottou, L., Bengio, Y., Haffner, P.: Gradient-based learning applied to document recognition. Proceedings of the IEEE (1998)
37. Li, P., Zhao, H., Liu, P., Cao, F.: RTM3D: real-time monocular 3d detection from object keypoints for autonomous driving. In: Vedaldi, A., Bischof, H., Brox, T., Frahm, J.-M. (eds.) ECCV 2020. LNCS, vol. 12348, pp. 644–660. Springer, Cham (2020). https://doi.org/10.1007/978-3-030-58580-8_38
38. Lian, Q., Ye, B., Xu, R., Yao, W., Zhang, T.: Geometry-aware data augmentation for monocular 3D object detection. arXiv preprint arXiv:2104.05858 (2021)
39. Lin, T.Y., Dollár, P., Girshick, R., He, K., Hariharan, B., Belongie, S.: Feature pyramid networks for object detection. In: CVPR (2017)
40. Liu, L., Lu, J., Xu, C., Tian, Q., Zhou, J.: Deep fitting degree scoring network for monocular 3D object detection. In: CVPR (2019)
41. Liu, X., Xue, N., Wu, T.: Learning auxiliary monocular contexts helps monocular 3D object detection. In: AAAI (2022)
42. Liu, Y., Yixuan, Y., Liu, M.: Ground-aware monocular 3D object detection for autonomous driving. Robotics and Automation Letters (2021)
43. Liu, Z., Zhou, D., Lu, F., Fang, J., Zhang, L.: AutoShape: real-time shape-aware monocular 3D object detection. In: ICCV (2021)

44. Lu, Y., et al.: Geometry uncertainty projection network for monocular 3D object detection. In: ICCV (2021)
45. Ma, X., Liu, S., Xia, Z., Zhang, H., Zeng, X., Ouyang, W.: Rethinking pseudo-LiDAR representation. In: Vedaldi, A., Bischof, H., Brox, T., Frahm, J.-M. (eds.) ECCV 2020. LNCS, vol. 12358, pp. 311–327. Springer, Cham (2020). https://doi.org/10.1007/978-3-030-58601-0_19
46. Ma, X., Ouyang, W., Simonelli, A., Ricci, E.: 3D object detection from images for autonomous driving: a survey. arXiv preprint arXiv:2202.02980 (2022)
47. Ma, X., Wang, Z., Li, H., Zhang, P., Ouyang, W., Fan, X.: Accurate monocular 3D object detection via color-embedded 3D reconstruction for autonomous driving. In: ICCV (2019)
48. Ma, X., et al.: Delving into localization errors for monocular 3D object detection. In: CVPR (2021)
49. Marcos, D., Kellenberger, B., Lobry, S., Tuia, D.: Scale equivariance in CNNs with vector fields. In: ICML Workshops (2018)
50. Marcos, D., Volpi, M., Komodakis, N., Tuia, D.: Rotation equivariant vector field networks. In: ICCV (2017)
51. Micheli, A.: Neural network for graphs: a contextual constructive approach. IEEE Trans. Neural Networks (2009)
52. Park, D., Ambrus, R., Guizilini, V., Li, J., Gaidon, A.: Is Pseudo-LiDAR needed for monocular 3D object detection? In: ICCV (2021)
53. Paszke, A., et al.: PyTorch: an imperative style, high-performance deep learning library. In: NeurIPS (2019)
54. Payet, N., Todorovic, S.: From contours to 3D object detection and pose estimation. In: ICCV (2011)
55. Pepik, B., Stark, M., Gehler, P., Schiele, B.: Multi-view and 3D deformable part models. TPAMI (2015)
56. Rath, M., Condurache, A.: Boosting deep neural networks with geometrical prior knowledge: a survey. arXiv preprint arXiv:2006.16867 (2020)
57. Reading, C., Harakeh, A., Chae, J., Waslander, S.: Categorical depth distribution network for monocular 3D object detection. In: CVPR (2021)
58. Rematas, K., Kemelmacher-Shlizerman, I., Curless, B., Seitz, S.: Soccer on your tabletop. In: CVPR (2018)
59. Ren, S., He, K., Girshick, R., Sun, J.: Faster R-CNN: towards real-time object detection with region proposal networks. In: NeurIPS (2015)
60. Saxena, A., Driemeyer, J., Ng, A.: Robotic grasping of novel objects using vision. IJRR (2008)
61. Shi, S., Wang, X., Li, H.: PointRCNN: 3D object proposal generation and detection from point cloud. In: CVPR (2019)
62. Shi, X., Ye, Q., Chen, X., Chen, C., Chen, Z., Kim, T.K.: Geometry-based distance decomposition for monocular 3D object detection. In: ICCV (2021)
63. Simonelli, A., Bulò, S., Porzi, L., Antequera, M., Kontschieder, P.: Disentangling monocular 3D object detection: from single to multi-class recognition. TPAMI (2020)
64. Simonelli, A., Bulò, S., Porzi, L., Kontschieder, P., Ricci, E.: Are we missing confidence in Pseudo-LiDAR methods for monocular 3D object detection? In: ICCV (2021)
65. Simonelli, A., Bulò, S., Porzi, L., López-Antequera, M., Kontschieder, P.: Disentangling monocular 3D object detection. In: ICCV (2019)
66. Simonelli, A., Bulò, S., Porzi, L., Ricci, E., Kontschieder, P.: Towards generalization across depth for monocular 3D object detection. In: ECCV (2020)

67. Sosnovik, I., Moskalev, A., Smeulders, A.: DISCO: accurate discrete scale convolutions. In: BMVC (2021)
68. Sosnovik, I., Moskalev, A., Smeulders, A.: Scale equivariance improves siamese tracking. In: WACV (2021)
69. Sosnovik, I., Szmaja, M., Smeulders, A.: Scale-equivariant steerable networks. In: ICLR (2020)
70. Sun, P., et al.: Scalability in perception for autonomous driving: waymo open dataset. In: CVPR (2020)
71. Tang, Y., Dorn, S., Savani, C.: Center3D: center-based monocular 3D object detection with joint depth understanding. arXiv preprint arXiv:2005.13423 (2020)
72. Thayalan-Vaz, S., M, S., Santhakumar, K., Ravi Kiran, B., Gauthier, T., Yogamani, S.: Exploring 2D data augmentation for 3D monocular object detection. arXiv preprint arXiv:2104.10786 (2021)
73. Thomas, N., Smidt, T., Kearnes, S., Yang, L., Li, L., Kohlhoff, K., Riley, P.: Tensor field networks: rotation-and translation-equivariant neural networks for 3D point clouds. arXiv preprint arXiv:1802.08219 (2018)
74. Wang, L., Du, L., Ye, X., Fu, Y., Guo, G., Xue, X., Feng, J., Zhang, L.: Depth-conditioned dynamic message propagation for monocular 3D object detection. In: CVPR (2021)
75. Wang, L., Zhang, L., Zhu, Y., Zhang, Z., He, T., Li, M., Xue, X.: Progressive coordinate transforms for monocular 3D object detection. In: NeurIPS (2021)
76. Wang, R., Walters, R., Yu, R.: Incorporating symmetry into deep dynamics models for improved generalization. In: ICLR (2021)
77. Wang, Y., Chao, W.L., Garg, D., Hariharan, B., Campbell, M., Weinberger, K.: Pseudo-LiDAR from visual depth estimation: bridging the gap in 3D object detection for autonomous driving. In: CVPR (2019)
78. Wang, Y., Guizilini, V., Zhang, T., Wang, Y., Zhao, H., Solomon, J.: DETR3D: 3D object detection from multi-view images via 3D-to-2D queries. In: CoRL (2021)
79. Wang, Z., Bovik, A., Sheikh, H., Simoncelli, E.: Image quality assessment: from error visibility to structural similarity. TIP (2004)
80. Weiler, M., Forré, P., Verlinde, E., Welling, M.: Coordinate independent convolutional networks-isometry and gauge equivariant convolutions on riemannian manifolds. arXiv preprint arXiv:2106.06020 (2021)
81. Weiler, M., Hamprecht, F., Storath, M.: Learning steerable filters for rotation equivariant CNNs. In: CVPR (2018)
82. Wilk, M.v.d., Bauer, M., John, S., Hensman, J.: Learning invariances using the marginal likelihood. In: NeurIPS (2018)
83. Worrall, D., Brostow, G.: CubeNet: equivariance to 3D rotation and translation. In: Ferrari, V., Hebert, M., Sminchisescu, C., Weiss, Y. (eds.) ECCV 2018. LNCS, vol. 11209, pp. 585–602. Springer, Cham (2018). https://doi.org/10.1007/978-3-030-01228-1_35
84. Worrall, D., Garbin, S., Turmukhambetov, D., Brostow, G.: Harmonic networks: deep translation and rotation equivariance. In: CVPR (2017)
85. Worrall, D., Welling, M.: Deep scale-spaces: equivariance over scale. In: NeurIPS (2019)
86. Xu, Y., Xiao, T., Zhang, J., Yang, K., Zhang, Z.: Scale-invariant convolutional neural networks. arXiv preprint arXiv:1411.6369 (2014)
87. Yang, G., Ramanan, D.: Upgrading optical flow to 3D scene flow through optical expansion. In: CVPR (2020)
88. Yeh, R., Hu, Y.T., Schwing, A.: Chirality nets for human pose regression. NeurIPS (2019)

89. Yu, F., Koltun, V.: Multi-scale context aggregation by dilated convolutions. In: ICLR (2015)
90. Zhang, Y., Ma, X., Yi, S., Hou, J., Wang, Z., Ouyang, W., Xu, D.: Learning geometry-guided depth via projective modeling for monocular 3D object detection. arXiv preprint arXiv:2107.13931 (2021)
91. Zhang, Y., Lu, J., Zhou, J.: Objects are different: flexible monocular 3D object detection. In: CVPR (2021)
92. Zhou, A., Knowles, T., Finn, C.: Meta-learning symmetries by reparameterization. In: ICLR (2021)
93. Zhou, X., Wang, D., Krähenbühl, P.: Objects as points. arXiv preprint arXiv:1904.07850 (2019)
94. Zhou, Y., He, Y., Zhu, H., Wang, C., Li, H., Jiang, Q.: MonoEF: extrinsic parameter free monocular 3D object detection. TPAMI (2021)
95. Zhu, W., Qiu, Q., Calderbank, R., Sapiro, G., Cheng, X.: Scale-equivariant neural networks with decomposed convolutional filters. arXiv preprint arXiv:1909.11193 (2019)
96. Zou, Z., et al.: The devil is in the task: exploiting reciprocal appearance-localization features for monocular 3D object detection. In: ICCV (2021)
97. Zwicke, P., Kiss, I.: A new implementation of the mellin transform and its application to radar classification of ships. TPAMI (1983)

Label-Guided Auxiliary Training
Improves 3D Object Detector

Yaomin Huang[1](ID), Xinmei Liu[1](ID), Yichen Zhu[2](ID), Zhiyuan Xu[2](ID),
Chaomin Shen[1(✉)](ID), Zhengping Che[2](ID), Guixu Zhang[1], Yaxin Peng[3](ID),
Feifei Feng[2], and Jian Tang[2(✉)](ID)

[1] School of Computer Science, East China Normal University, Shanghai, China
{51205901049,51205901078}@stu.ecnu.edu.cn,
{cmshen,gxzhang}@cs.ecnu.edu.cn
[2] AI Innovation Center, Midea Group, Beijiao, China
{zhuyc25,xuzy70,chezp,feifei.feng,tangjian22}@midea.com
[3] Department of Mathematics, School of Science, Shanghai University,
Shanghai, China
yaxin.peng@shu.edu.cn

Abstract. Detecting 3D objects from point clouds is a practical yet challenging task that has attracted increasing attention recently. In this paper, we propose a Label-Guided auxiliary training method for 3D object detection (LG3D), which serves as an auxiliary network to enhance the feature learning of existing 3D object detectors. Specifically, we propose two novel modules: a Label-Annotation-Inducer that maps annotations and point clouds in bounding boxes to task-specific representations and a Label-Knowledge-Mapper that assists the original features to obtain detection-critical representations. The proposed auxiliary network is discarded in inference and thus has no extra computational cost at test time. We conduct extensive experiments on both indoor and outdoor datasets to verify the effectiveness of our approach. For example, our proposed LG3D improves VoteNet by 2.5% and 3.1% mAP on the SUN RGB-D and ScanNetV2 datasets, respectively. The code is available at https://github.com/FabienCode/LG3D.

1 Introduction

3D object detection is one of the fundamental tasks toward precisely and adaptively understanding the real 3D world. Specifically, 3D object detection processes point clouds (as shown in Fig. 1a) to identify the types of objects and localize their bounding boxes (as shown in Fig. 1b). While challenging and computationally expensive, 3D object detection has attracted wide attention with an

---

Y. Huang and X. Liu—Equal contributions; work done during internships at Midea Group.

Supplementary Information The online version contains supplementary material available at https://doi.org/10.1007/978-3-031-20077-9_40.

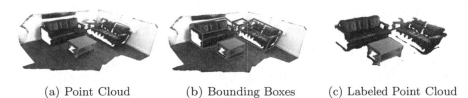

(a) Point Cloud   (b) Bounding Boxes   (c) Labeled Point Cloud

Fig. 1. An example of (a) original point cloud, (b) bounding box annotations, and (c) the label point cloud extracted from the annotated bounding boxes

increasing amount of excellent works [1–3, 13, 14, 16–18, 25, 26, 28, 35, 36]. Existing 3D object detection methods mostly focus on improving the feature extraction in point clouds and making better predictions on objects' locations, such as fusing 2D image and 3D data information [16], leveraging a shape attention graph convolution operator (SA-GConv) [1] to capture local shape features and relative geometric positions between points, and introducing a strong backbone for better feature learning ability [13]. Nevertheless, one of the most critical issues is that inference speed is typically sacrificed in order to maintain a high performance of 3D object detectors.

Balancing the inference speed and detection performance is challenging due to the nature of point clouds, i.e., the number of points in practical scenarios is huge, which slows down the forward pass. One can bypass such obstacles by applying aggressive sampling strategies, but it severely hurts the quality of detectors. Instead of modifying the architecture of the existing 3D object detectors, in this paper we resolve this issue by introducing a model-agnostic auxiliary training approach, which dramatically improves the detection performance and brings no extra computational cost at test time. Our proposed method is motivated by the assumption that the input labels (i.e., points within bounding boxes) contain rich semantic information if one could find a proper way to extract its latent features. These features can be considered an auxiliary information source, provide supervision to 3D object detectors during training, and, more importantly, can be removed after the training stage. As such, 3D object detectors can be optimized more effectively without hampering the inference speed.

The previous approach adopts learnable modules to extract features from labels in the 2D tasks. For instance, Mostajabi et al. [15] used an auto-encoder on the semantic masks to help the image segmentation model learn better pixel-level features. Similarly, LabelEnc [6] and LGD [34] formulate the bounding box along with its class identity as an extra source of information to supervise the student model. However, despite these previous attempts at learning label information, applying it to 3D detection is non-trivial due to the fundamental difference in input structure between 2D and 3D tasks, i.e., the image in the 2D task versus point clouds in 3D detection. Moreover, besides the categorical information, the point clouds inside the bounding box, i.e., the label point clouds shown in Fig. 1c, contain rich semantic and position information of each target object in the scene, which have been overlooked in the prior work.

Motivated by the above analysis, in this paper, we propose a Label-Guided auxiliary training approach for 3D object detection (LG3D), which serves as an auxiliary network to enhance the feature learning ability of vanilla 3D object detectors. To better utilize the 3D label information, we introduce two novel modules in our method. First, the Label-Annotation-Inducer (LAI) module parameterizes the bounding box label and then maps them to task-specific representations. It aims to fuse the point clouds of particular objects into the sparse, original point clouds input such that the detectors can realize the object's localization, along with other critical but unexplored high-dimensional features, learned particularly by a tiny label encoder. The Label-Knowledge-Mapper (LKM) module is followed up to obtain optimal representations. Despite the simple design of our proposed modules, it tremendously improves the performance of 3D object detectors. It's also worth noting that our proposed LG3D is only used in the training stage and is completely cost-free during the inference.

We summarize our contributions as follows:

- We propose LG3D, a new way to utilize 3D labels by using the label point clouds (i.e., point clouds inside bounding boxes) as an auxiliary network to assist the feature representation learning of the vanilla network.
- Two novel modules, LAI and LKM, are used to fuse label point clouds, annotations, and original point clouds to a single feature embedding, which can effectively compensate for the missing information of target objects caused by data sampling.
- The proposed LG3D can be simply inserted into existing 3D object detectors and removed after training. LG3D improves the state-of-the-art 3D object detectors by a large margin on both indoor and outdoor datasets.

2 Related Works

2.1 3D Object Detection

We briefly introduce the 3D object detection approaches in this section, and refer reader to Qian et al. [19] for more detailed description. ImVoteNet [16] proposes to use 2D image RGB, geometric coordinates, semantics, and pixel texture information to assist 3D point clouds object detection. PointPainting [21] proposes to use 2D semantic segmentation information to fuse the transformation matrix of LiDAR information and image information to the point. Cross-modal information fusion is proposed in the PointAugmenting [22] method, point features of corresponding points in 2D images are extracted by mapping between 3D and 2D. BRNet [3] proposes to solve the problem that VoteNet [17] cannot effectively represent the object structure information, adding a back-tracing module for resampling the more informative seed points. HGNet [1] describes the shape of an object by simulating the relative geometric position of the point. H3DNet [35] votes for center points on three dimensions of the bounding box, bounding box surface, and bounding box edges to add more detailed constraints to bounding box predictions. The backtracking module [3] is added based on VoteNet [17] to resample the seed points with richer information. 3DSSD [27] achieves a good balance between accuracy and efficiency by using the fusion sampling strategy in the downsampling process. In GroupFree3D [13], the transformer adaptively determines the relationship between points and obtains an object proposal by point aggregation. DETR3D [24] uses DETR for 3D object detection, extracting 2D features from multiple camera images, then indexing these 2D features using a set of sparse 3D target queries, using a camera transform matrix to establish connections between 3D positions and multi-view images, and finally connecting 2D feature extraction and 3D box prediction by alternating between 2D and 3D calculations. 3DETR-m [14] improves detection performance by applying mask to self-attention in transformer. However, the calculation cost of object detection increases with the increment in the use of transformers.

Despite the evolutionary development of 3D object detectors, current approaches still require overwhelming computational costs at test time to maintain satisfactory performance. Thus, we provide a novel perspective to harness the semantic information in the label to assist the training of a 3D object detector, which is the first work demonstrating the powerful yet unexplored information in the point clouds that, if handled properly, can significantly boost the existing 3D detector. Our approach is also detector agnostic and robust to different kinds of datasets.

2.2 Auxiliary Task and Knowledge Distillation

Auxiliary Task. Auxiliary task [33] is a well-studied topic that aims to assist the model with a lightweight module during training or testing. For example, in SA-SSD [8], the original point cloud features are complemented with down-sampled features with an auxiliary task. While auxiliary training in 3D detection has not raised attention, it has developed fast in 2D object detection. For instance, LabelEnc [6] proposes directly introducing auxiliary intermediate supervision to the trunk to provide feasible supervision in the training stage. It is further modified [34] into a teacher-free approach that incorporates bounding box and class information to the student network.

Knowledge Distillation. Knowledge distillation (KD) is another highly closed topic in our approach. It was initially proposed to leverage a large teacher network that transfers its representative knowledge to a compact student network. Its success has spread over numerous domain in computer vision, i.e., image classification [9,37], object detection [10,32], semantic segmentation [12], and image-to-image translation [29,30].

For 3D object detection, SE-SSD [36] uses the idea of knowledge distillation to optimize student networks through a combination of hard and soft targets. Wang et al. [23] uses KD to compensate for the gap between the model of training high-quality input and the model of testing low-quality input in reasoning. Chong et al. [4] leverage point clouds to assist monocular 3D object detection with depth information. More recently, PointDistiller [31] leverages the dynamic graph convolution to transfer the local geometric structure of point clouds.

This work combines two advantages in the auxiliary task and knowledge distillation. Namely, our approach does not require a heavy, cumbersome teacher model to perform distillation. At the same time, we still enjoy the improvement in performance without extra computational cost at test time, which is normally unavoidable in training with the auxiliary task.

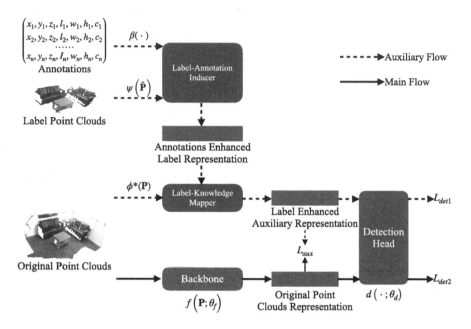

Fig. 2. Our LG3D framework. It includes an LKM module and an LAI module. The whole framework can be simply inserted into a 3D object detection network, and the LKM module shares the detection head with the backbone network. LG3D is removed directly in the inference phase, so it does not increase the computational cost. As shown in the figure, data flow in the training stage contains dotted and solid arrows, while data flow in the inference stage only contains solid arrows

3 Method

In this section, we present our method in detail. Figure 2 gives an overview of our method. In Sect. 3.1, we introduce LKM supplements the original point clouds representation with label point clouds to obtain the label enhanced auxiliary representation. In Sect. 3.2, LAI encodes the annotations and maps it to a latent semantic space for the annotation enhanced label representation that aim to get a better label enhanced auxiliary representation. In Sect. 3.3, a separable auxiliary task uses the label enhanced auxiliary representation to supervise the representation outputs from the backbone with original point clouds.

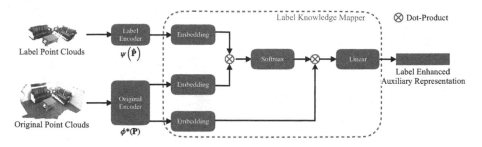

Fig. 3. The dashed box indicates the entire LKM module

3.1   Label-Knowledge Mapper

The features of the original point clouds are usually extracted by the sampling method. This way, more or fewer point clouds of the object will be lost, affecting the feature extraction. Thus we design the LKM module to induce instance features from label point clouds, then fuse it with the original point clouds representation. This module can well supplement the key information lost during the point clouds samplings, especially for the information loss of small objects.

Original point clouds and label point clouds can be represented as disordered point set $\boldsymbol{P} = \{\boldsymbol{p}_i\}_{i=1}^{n}$ with $\boldsymbol{p}_i \in \mathbb{R}^d$ and $\hat{\boldsymbol{P}} = \{\hat{\boldsymbol{p}}_j\}_{j=1}^{m}$ with $\hat{\boldsymbol{p}}_j \in \mathbb{R}^d$ respectively, where n and m is the number of original point clouds and label point clouds, respectively. d represents the (x, y, z) coordinate plus extra feature channels such as color, normal, etc. As shown in Fig. 3, in the training stage, we obtain the label point clouds by annotation information in the dataset and feed it into the label encoder. Given a training set $(\boldsymbol{P}, \hat{\boldsymbol{P}})$ and a well-trained original encoder function $\phi^*(\boldsymbol{P})$, instead of fine-tuning the original feature representation to the task-specific label space, we fix $\phi^*(\cdot)$ and learn a separate label encoder $\psi(\hat{\boldsymbol{P}})$ to extract the feature from label point clouds. Then we use a label fusion function $\mathcal{H}((\boldsymbol{P}, \hat{\boldsymbol{P}}), \theta_\mathcal{H})$ to fuse the original point clouds and the label point clouds. We find the optimal representation and function by

$$\theta_f^*, \theta_d^* = \arg\min_{\theta_f, \theta_d} \mathbb{L}_{\det}^1(d(\mathcal{H}((\boldsymbol{P}, \hat{\boldsymbol{P}}), \theta_\mathcal{H}); \theta_d), y) + \mathbb{L}_{\det}^2(d(f(\boldsymbol{P}; \theta_f); \theta_d), y)$$

$$+ \lambda \mathbb{L}_{\mathrm{aux}}, \tag{1}$$

where $y \in \mathbb{R}^{N \times V}$ is the ground-truth label, N is the number of objects, and V is the label length of each objects. $f(\boldsymbol{P}; \theta_f)$ is the function realized by the backbone. $\mathcal{H}((\boldsymbol{P}, \hat{\boldsymbol{P}}), \theta_\mathcal{H}) \in \mathbb{R}^{n' \times C}$ represents the output of the LKM module, where n' is the number of sampled points and C is the number of feature channels. $\mathbb{L}_{\mathrm{aux}}$ represents the auxiliary loss attached to the outputs of the backbone, which is independent of the detection head $d(\cdot, \theta_d)$ thus it is not affected by the latter's convergence progress. λ is the balanced coefficient.

The design of $\mathbb{L}_{\mathrm{aux}}$ is one of the most important factor of our approach and we will explain its design in Sect. 3.3. $\mathbb{L}_{\mathrm{aux}}$ aims to minimize the distance

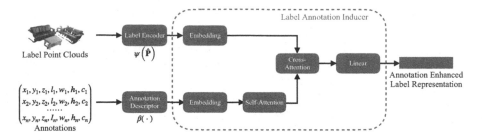

Fig. 4. In the training phase, label point clouds and annotations are fed into the LAI module

between the original point clouds feature representation and an ideal representation, which in our method is the label enhanced auxiliary representation. In order to make sure that the original point clouds features can be well combined with the features of the label point clouds, we adopt the attention mechanism [20]. Let the matrix representations of the key $(\boldsymbol{K}_l)$ and value $(\boldsymbol{V}_l)$ be $\phi^*(\boldsymbol{P};\theta_p) \in \mathbb{R}^{M \times C}$ from the original point clouds representation, query be $\boldsymbol{Q}_l = \psi(\hat{\boldsymbol{P}};\theta_{\hat{P}}) \in \mathbb{R}^{M \times C}$, with the label point clouds representation. Here M and C denotes length and dimensions of query, key and value, respectively. The query, key and value are transformed by linear layers $f_{\mathcal{Q}_l}$, $f_{\mathcal{K}_l}$, $f_{\mathcal{V}_l}$ before conducting attention. To induce the feature from label point clouds, we apply the cross-attention mechanism [20] to fetch original point clouds representation from label point clouds representation. So the ideal representation output of LKM is:

$$\mathcal{H}\left((\boldsymbol{P},\hat{\boldsymbol{P}}),\theta_{\mathcal{H}}\right) = \mathrm{Softmax}\left(\frac{f_{\mathcal{Q}_l}(\boldsymbol{Q}_l)f_{\mathcal{K}_l}(\boldsymbol{K}_l)^\top}{\sqrt{D_k}}\right)f_{\mathcal{V}_l}(\boldsymbol{V}_l), \qquad (2)$$

where D_k denotes the dimensions of the key, and $\mathrm{Softmax}(\cdot)$ is applied row-wise.

3.2   Label-Annotation-Inducer

Using the proposed Label-Knowledge Mapper described in Sect. 3.1, we obtain the enhanced point clouds representation $\mathcal{H}$. However, the rich information in the annotations has not been fully utilized. To use the label annotations information as an important form of ground truth, we propose the LAI module, as shown in Fig. 4, to complement the features of the label point clouds. Specifically, we extract the label annotations information to obtain an ideal representation $\mathcal{G}$.

Label Embedding. In a 3D object detection task, the label information of an object usually contains the center, the size and category, and it may have the head angle. Given an object label, we represent each labeled bounding box of the target object in the point clouds as $\boldsymbol{\alpha}_i = (x_i,y_i,z_i,l_i,w_i,h_i,c_i)$, where i represents the i-th bounding box, (x_i,y_i,z_i) represents the center point of the i-th bounding box, (l_i,w_i,h_i) represents the length, width and height of the i-th bounding box, and c_i represents the object category corresponding to the i-th bounding box. The initial label representation is

$$\mathcal{A} = \{\boldsymbol{\alpha}_1, \cdots, \boldsymbol{\alpha}_i, \cdots, \boldsymbol{\alpha}_N\}, \quad \boldsymbol{\alpha}_i \in \mathbb{R}^{C_L}, \tag{3}$$

where i indicates the object index, C_L is the array length of the bounding box parameter information and N is the object number.

Annotation Augmentation. We perform some information dropping for these determined annotations. When describing bounding boxes, we interpret them with rough scale indices. The centers of the approximate fields (x_i', y_i', z_i') are obtained by random dithering as

$$\begin{aligned} x_i' &= x_i + \eta_x l_i, \\ y_i' &= y_i + \eta_y w_i, \\ z_i' &= z_i + \eta_z h_i, \end{aligned} \tag{4}$$

where η_x, η_y, η_z are sampled from a uniform distribution $\eta \sim U[-B_\eta, B_\eta]$, where B_η is a scale factor whose value is set to be 0.1. Furthermore, we generate fake instances for the recognition task based on the dataset distribution. Note that we need to identify the objectiveness of each instance, that is, to determine the authenticity of a given label. We use the binary cross-entropy function to determine whether the given label is a real label in the point clouds scene or a pseudo label that we add manually and increase the robustness of learning knowledge from the real label by determining the virtual label:

$$\mathbb{L}_{\text{idf}} = -\frac{1}{N} \sum_{i=1}^{N} \delta_{\text{obj}}(\boldsymbol{\alpha}_i) \log\left(\mathcal{P}_{\text{obj}}(\boldsymbol{e}_i)\right) + (1 - \delta_{\text{obj}}(\boldsymbol{\alpha}_i)) \log\left(1 - \mathcal{P}_{\text{obj}}(\boldsymbol{e}_i)\right), \tag{5}$$

where $\mathcal{P}_{\text{obj}}(\cdot)$ is a prediction function with a full connection layer and sigmoid function, and $\delta_{\text{obj}}(\boldsymbol{\alpha}_i)$ encodes the binary classification labels, denoting whether the instance is randomly generated ($\delta_{\text{obj}}(\boldsymbol{\alpha}_i) = 0$) or manually annotated ($\delta_{\text{obj}}(\boldsymbol{\alpha}_i) = 1$).

We then introduce the annotations descriptor $\beta(\cdot)$, which could induce the new label representation $\mathcal{A}$ to the task-specific latent feature space. We adopt a relatively simple multi-layer perceptron [7] as the label annotation encoding module, so the optimization seems not difficult. The new label annotation representation is:

$$\beta_{\mathcal{A}} = \{\boldsymbol{e}_1, \cdots, \boldsymbol{e}_i, \cdots, \boldsymbol{e}_N\}, \quad \boldsymbol{e}_i \in \mathbb{R}^C, \tag{6}$$

where C is the intermediate feature dimension, and $\boldsymbol{e}_i = \beta(\boldsymbol{\alpha}_i)$ is the encoded label annotation information.

Label Information Interactions. Since the annotation representation $\beta_{\mathcal{A}}$ is relatively independent, we first model it globally by a self-attention to obtain the global annotation representation $\boldsymbol{Q}_\alpha \in \mathbb{R}^{N \times C}$. We then use this as a query condition to apply the cross attention mechanism to the label point clouds' features, so that the label point clouds can be combined with the annotation information to produce better annotation enhanced label representation.

Specifically, given the matrix representations of query $\boldsymbol{Q}_\alpha \in \mathbb{R}^{M \times C}$, key $\boldsymbol{K}_\alpha \in \mathbb{R}^{M \times C}$ and value $\boldsymbol{V}_\alpha \in \mathbb{R}^{M \times C}$ are from the label point clouds representation. Before conducting cross attention, the query, key, and value are transformed by linear layers $f_{\mathcal{Q}_\alpha}$, $f_{\mathcal{K}_\alpha}$, $f_{\mathcal{V}_\alpha}$,

$$\mathcal{F}_A\left(\boldsymbol{Q}_\alpha, \boldsymbol{K}_\alpha, \boldsymbol{V}_a\right) = \text{Softmax}\left(\frac{f_{\mathcal{Q}_a}(\boldsymbol{Q}_\alpha) f_{\mathcal{K}_\alpha}(\boldsymbol{K}_\alpha)^\top}{\sqrt{D_k}}\right) f_{\mathcal{V}_\alpha}(\boldsymbol{V}_\alpha). \tag{7}$$

With the LAI making label point clouds representation perceive label annotations information, the new label fusion function is:

$$\mathcal{G}\left(\boldsymbol{P}, (\hat{\boldsymbol{P}}, \mathcal{A}); \theta_{\mathcal{G}}\right) = \mathcal{G}\left(\phi^*\left(\boldsymbol{P}; \theta_P\right), \left(\psi(\hat{\boldsymbol{P}}; \theta_{\hat{P}}), \beta(\mathcal{A}; \theta_{\mathcal{A}})\right)\right). \tag{8}$$

3.3 Separable Auxiliary Tasks

In Sect. 3.1, we propose to use label point clouds to supplement the original point clouds representation. In Sect. 3.2, the label point clouds representation is further enriched by label annotations information. After these modules, we obtain an ideal representation $\mathcal{G}$ which can supervise the representation outputs from the backbone with original point clouds. We propose a separable auxiliary network using the above modules. It can be simply insert into various 3D object detection networks to improve the detection accuracy during the training.

It is clear that Eq. (1) directly corresponds to a multi-task training paradigm with three loss terms: the first one is label information encoder loss ($\mathbb{L}_{\text{det}}^1$) for the label information embedding; the second term is the common detection loss ($\mathbb{L}_{\text{det}}^2$), which enforces $d\left(\cdot; \theta_d'\right)$ to be a valid detection head; the third loss ($\mathbb{L}_{\text{aux}}$) minimizes the gap between the two latent spaces (namely the outputs of the backbone $f(\cdot; \theta_f')$ and the label enhanced auxiliary representation $\mathcal{G}((\boldsymbol{P}, (\hat{\boldsymbol{P}}, \mathcal{A})), \theta_{\mathcal{G}})$.

By sharing the detection head for supervision, we ensure the instructive representation quality and consistency with the original point clouds representation. The overall detection loss is:

$$\mathbb{L}_{\text{det}} = \mathbb{L}_{\text{det}}^1 + \mathbb{L}_{\text{det}}^2 + \mathbb{L}_{idf}. \tag{9}$$

In addition to the common detection loss $\mathbb{L}_{\text{det}}$, we introduce an auxiliary supervision loss $\mathbb{L}_{\text{aux}}$ that uses outputs from LKM directly to supervise the detection backbone, as flow:

$$\mathbb{L}_{\text{aux}} = \min_{\theta_f}\left\| f\left(\boldsymbol{P}, \theta_f\right) - \mathcal{G}\left((\boldsymbol{P}, (\hat{\boldsymbol{P}}, \mathcal{A})), \theta_{\mathcal{G}}\right) \right\|_2, \tag{10}$$

where $\| \cdot \|_2$ is L2-distance to minimize the difference between original point clouds representation and label enhanced auxiliary representation. It is worth noticing that the gradients of $\mathbb{L}_{aux}$ only update the backbone module. Above all, the overall loss with a coefficient λ can be summarised as follows:

$$\mathbb{L}_{total} = \mathbb{L}_{det} + \lambda\mathbb{L}_{aux}. \tag{11}$$

In summary, we use label-guided auxiliary training to motivate the underlying network to learn better feature representations. As Fig. 2 shows, during the testing phase, all dotted arrow flow lines are removed, so no additional computational overhead is incurred.

4 Experiments

4.1 Experiment Settings

Dataset. To illustrate the generalization of our method, we have conducted experiments on indoor and outdoor datasets. For indoor datasets, the SUN RGB-D dataset consists of 10,355 single-view indoor RGB-D images annotated with over 64,000 3D bounding boxes and semantic labels for 37 categories. The ScanNetV2 dataset is a 3D mesh dataset with about 1,500 3D reconstructed indoor scenes with 40 semantic classes. We follow the commonly-used settings, selecting 10 classes of SUN RGB-D and 18 classes of ScanNetV2. For outdoor datasets, we choose the KITTI dataset for evaluation. The KITTI dataset contains 7481 training samples and 7518 test samples with three categories: Car, Pedestrian and Cyclist.

Data Preparation. In the training stage, our network has two different inputs. On the one hand, we feed the full point clouds into the main branch to extract feature representation. On the other hand, we feed the point clouds inside in the bounding box and label information into the auxiliary network. The point clouds are randomly sub-sampled from the raw data of each dataset, i.e., 20,000 points from point clouds in the SUN RGB-D dataset and 40,000 point clouds from a 3D mesh in the ScanNetV2 dataset. Additionally, we perform data augmentation by randomly flipping, rotating, and scaling the point clouds.

Training and Evaluation. We implement our LG3D using MMdetection3D [5] framework. For different networks with different datasets, we followed the basic settings in MMdetection3D without additional parameter tuning. The evaluation for indoor datasets follows the same protocol as [17] using mean average precision mAP@0.25 and mAP@0.50. We only evaluate our model on the class 'Car' for the KITTI dataset due to its large amount of data and complex scenarios, just as most state-of-the-art methods test their models. We follow the official KITTI evaluation protocol during the evaluation stage, and the IoU threshold is set to 0.7 for the class 'Car'.

Table 1. Results on indoor datasets

Method	SUN RGB-D		ScanNetV2	
	mAP@0.25	mAP@0.5	mAP@0.25	mAP@0.5
VoteNet [17]	57.7	–	58.6	33.5
Reimpl. [5]	59.1	35.8	62.9	39.9
VoteNet+Ours	61.7	38.3	65.1	43.0
GroupFree3D [13]	63.0	45.2	69.1	52.8
GroupFree3D+Ours	**64.3**	**47.5**	**70.9**	**54.1**

Table 2. Results on the KITTI dataset

Method	AP_3d(%)		
	Easy	Moderate	Hard
PointPillars	82.58	74.31	68.99
PointPillars+LG3D	**84.38**	**76.42**	**69.88**
3DSSD	88.36	79.57	74.55
3DSSD+LG3D	**88.96**	**81.47**	**76.72**

4.2 Main Results

Results on Indoor Datasets. For indoor datasets, we evaluate our method on VoteNet [17] and GroupFree3D [13]. VoteNet is a classic and representative 3D object detection method, while GroupFree3D is the state-of-the-art method on indoor datasets. Results are presented in Table 1. The results show that our method significantly improve both frameworks. Compared with the baseline of VoteNet, our method achieves performance gains of 2.6% on the SUN RGB-D with mAP@0.25 and 2.5% with mAP@0.5. As for ScanNetV2, our model achieves performance gains of 2.2% and 3.1% on mAP@0.25 and mAP@0.5, respectively. Similarly, our method works for Group-Free 3D, which achieves performance gains of 1.8% mAP@0.25 and 1.3% mAP@0.5.

Results on the Outdoor KITTI Dataset. To fully illustrate the generalization of our approach, we have added our module to 3DSSD [27] and PointPillars [11] and carried out experiments on the KITTI dataset. The comparison results on the KITTI test set are shown in Table 2. Compared with the baseline, our LG3D outperforms its original version. In terms of the main metric, i.e., AP on "moderate" instances, our method outperforms PointPillars and 3DSSD by 2.11% and 1.9%, respectively.

Table 3. Ablation study results of the LKM and LAI modules

	SUN RGB-D		ScanNetV2	
	mAP@0.25	mAP@0.5	mAP@0.25	mAP@0.5
Baseline (Reimpl.)	59.1	35.8	62.9	39.9
Baseline+LKM	61.1	37.3	64.0	41.3
Baseline+LKM+LAI	**61.7**	**38.3**	**65.1**	**43.0**

Table 4. Ablation study results of the two-stage training strategy

Method	mAP@0.25	mAP@0.5
Baseline	62.9	39.9
One-Stage	64.4	42.4
Two-Stage	**65.1**	**43.0**

4.3 Ablation Studies

In this section, we discuss the designed choices in LG3D and investigate their independent impact on final metrics in ablation studies. If not specified, all models are designed on VoteNet of ScanNetV2.

Label-Guided Module. To better understand the role of our method, we conduct experiments to evaluate the contribution of each sub-task. Specifically, our LKM module comprises a label point clouds encoder and a supervision loss $L2$-distance. As shown in Table 3. Even if the LKM module alone is used to supplement the original representation with label point clouds, our method achieves some performance gains. When the LAI module is used to further complement the label point clouds representation, our method achieves a further performance improvement, which shows that our main modules significantly contribute to the overall network. For more ablation studies on label annotation augmentation strategies, please refer to the appendix.

Two Steps Training. In our method, we use a two-step training strategy. First of all, we load the well-trained function $\phi^* (P; \theta_P)$, but do not freeze its parameters. We use a joint optimization method to optimize it together with $\psi(\hat{P}; \theta_{\hat{P}})$ and $\beta(\mathcal{A}; \theta_{\mathcal{A}})$. By the first step, we obtain optimized $\phi^{*'}(P; \theta_P)$, $\psi^*(\hat{P}; \theta_{\hat{P}})$ and $\beta^*(\mathcal{A}; \theta_{\mathcal{A}})$. In the second step, we load the functions obtained in the first step, freeze all parameters, and perform the second training step to obtain the final optimized $f(\cdot; \theta_f)$ and $d(\cdot; \theta_d)$. We show the ablation in Table 4.

Training with More Epochs. The performance gain is from the proposed module, not the long training epochs. To verify that, we conduct additional experiments to train both methods with equivalent epochs (72 on VoteNet and

Table 5. Performance comparisons with different numbers of training epochs

Dataset	Method	mAP@0.25	mAP@0.50	# of Epochs
ScanNetV2	VoteNet	62.90	39.90	36
		62.50	40.10	72
	VoteNet+LG3D	**65.10**	**43.00**	72
	GroupFree3D	69.10	52.80	80
		68.50	52.80	160
	GroupFree3D+LG3D	**70.90**	**54.10**	160
SUN RGB-D	VoteNet	59.10	35.80	80
		59.20	35.70	160
	VoteNet+LG3D	**61.70**	**38.30**	160

160 on GroupFree3D). The results in Table 5 indicate that training baseline detectors for a long time are not helpful, which validates the effectiveness of our approach.

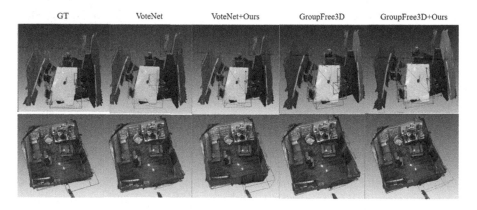

Fig. 5. Result visualizations on the ScanNetV2 dataset. GT means ground truth. The bounding box color denotes the object category. (Color figure online)

4.4 Qualitative Results and Discussion

Figure 5 shows several representative results on ScanNetV2. Our method has a good improvement effect on the detections of missing small objects and imprecision large objects. Figure 6 shows that our method is particularly effective in detecting small objects and has an improvement for other objects. In addition, due to the limitation of the ball query radius during feature processing, the perceptual field is naturally limited, especially for objects with large aspect ratio differences, such as shower curtains and curtains. The initial VoteNet is affected

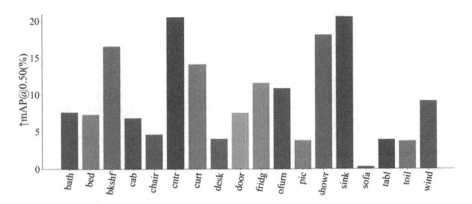

Fig. 6. The mAP@0.5 score improvement by LG3D applied to VoteNet of each category on the ScanNetV2 dataset.

by the backbone's natural limitation and the clustering operation in the detection head part by presetting the 3D spherical boundary. Our LAI module can effectively complement the effect of this problem by using the size information in the label annotations. The results show that the performance on shower curtains and curtains in the ScanNetV2 dataset are improved by about 15%. For more results on per-category performance comparisons, please refer to the appendix.

5   Conclusion

In this work, we have designed a novel label-guided auxiliary approach for 3D object detection networks to facilitate the training process. A novel point clouds label encoding module is introduced to map real labels into potential embeddings that serve as auxiliary intermediate supervision of the detection backbone during training. A knowledge refinement-like idea is used to simplify our auxiliary module. The processed label information is fed into the upper branch auxiliary network for encoding in the experiments. The distance information represented by the 3D features is used to directly optimize the feature embedding of the detection backbone. Experiments show that this method greatly improves the detection performance of the original network while maintaining the detection speed of the original network.

Acknowledgement. This work was done when Yaomin Huang and Xinmei Liu took internships at Midea Group. This work was supported in part by National Science Foundation of China (61731009 and 11771276) and Shanghai Pujiang Program (21PJ1420300).

References

1. Chen, J., Lei, B., Song, Q., Ying, H., Chen, D.Z., Wu, J.: A hierarchical graph network for 3D object detection on point clouds. In: Proceedings of the IEEE/CVF Conference on Computer Vision and Pattern Recognition, pp. 392–401 (2020)
2. Chen, Q., Sun, L., Wang, Z., Jia, K., Yuille, A.: Object as hotspots: an anchor-free 3D object detection approach via firing of hotspots. In: European Conference on Computer Vision, pp. 68–84. Springer (2020)
3. Cheng, B., Sheng, L., Shi, S., Yang, M., Xu, D.: Back-tracing representative points for voting-based 3D object detection in point clouds. In: Proceedings of the IEEE/CVF Conference on Computer Vision and Pattern Recognition, pp. 8963–8972 (2021)
4. Chong, Z., Ma, X., Zhang, H., Yue, Y., Li, H., Wang, Z., Ouyang, W.: Monodistill: learning spatial features for monocular 3d object detection. In: International Conference on Learning Representations (2022)
5. Contributors, M.: MMDetection3D: OpenMMLab next-generation platform for general 3D object detection (2020). https://github.com/open-mmlab/mmdetection3d
6. Hao, M., Liu, Y., Zhang, X., Sun, J.: LabelEnc: A New Intermediate Supervision Method for Object Detection. In: Vedaldi, A., Bischof, H., Brox, T., Frahm, J.-M. (eds.) ECCV 2020. LNCS, vol. 12370, pp. 529–545. Springer, Cham (2020). https://doi.org/10.1007/978-3-030-58595-2_32
7. Hastie, T., Tibshirani, R., Friedman, J.H., Friedman, J.H.: The elements of statistical learning: data mining, inference, and prediction, vol. 2. Springer (2009)
8. He, C., Zeng, H., Huang, J., Hua, X.S., Zhang, L.: Structure aware single-stage 3D object detection from point cloud. In: Proceedings of the IEEE/CVF Conference on Computer Vision and Pattern Recognition, pp. 11873–11882 (2020)
9. Hinton, G.E., Vinyals, O., Dean, J.: Distilling the knowledge in a neural network. CoRR abs/1503.02531 (2015)
10. Kang, Z., Zhang, P., Zhang, X., Sun, J., Zheng, N.: Instance-conditional knowledge distillation for object detection. Adv. Neural. Inf. Process. Syst. **34**, 16468–16480 (2021)
11. Lang, A.H., Vora, S., Caesar, H., Zhou, L., Yang, J., Beijbom, O.: Pointpillars: fast encoders for object detection from point clouds. In: Proceedings of the IEEE/CVF Conference on Computer Vision and Pattern Recognition (CVPR), June 2019
12. Liu, Y., Chen, K., Liu, C., Qin, Z., Luo, Z., Wang, J.: Structured knowledge distillation for semantic segmentation. In: Proceedings of the IEEE/CVF Conference on Computer Vision and Pattern Recognition, pp. 2604–2613 (2019)
13. Liu, Z., Zhang, Z., Cao, Y., Hu, H., Tong, X.: Group-free 3D object detection via transformers. In: Proceedings of the IEEE/CVF International Conference on Computer Vision, pp. 2949–2958 (2021)
14. Misra, I., Girdhar, R., Joulin, A.: An end-to-end transformer model for 3D object detection. In: Proceedings of the IEEE/CVF International Conference on Computer Vision, pp. 2906–2917 (2021)
15. Mostajabi, M., Maire, M., Shakhnarovich, G.: Regularizing deep networks by modeling and predicting label structure. In: Proceedings of the IEEE Conference on Computer Vision and Pattern Recognition, pp. 5629–5638 (2018)
16. Qi, C.R., Chen, X., Litany, O., Guibas, L.J.: Imvotenet: boosting 3D object detection in point clouds with image votes. In: Proceedings of the IEEE/CVF Conference on Computer Vision and Pattern Recognition, pp. 4404–4413 (2020)

17. Qi, C.R., Litany, O., He, K., Guibas, L.J.: Deep Hough voting for 3D object detection in point clouds. In: Proceedings of the IEEE/CVF International Conference on Computer Vision, pp. 9277–9286 (2019)
18. Qi, C.R., Liu, W., Wu, C., Su, H., Guibas, L.J.: Frustum pointnets for 3D object detection from RGB-D data. In: Proceedings of the IEEE Conference on Computer Vision and Pattern Recognition, pp. 918–927 (2018)
19. Qian, R., Lai, X., Li, X.: 3d object detection for autonomous driving: a survey. Pattern Recognition, p. 108796 (2022)
20. Vaswani, A., et al.: Attention is all you need. In: Advances in Neural Information Processing Systems 30 (2017)
21. Vora, S., Lang, A.H., Helou, B., Beijbom, O.: PointPainting: sequential fusion for 3D object detection. In: Proceedings of the IEEE/CVF Conference on Computer Vision and Pattern Recognition, pp. 4604–4612 (2020)
22. Wang, C., Ma, C., Zhu, M., Yang, X.: PointAugmenting: cross-modal augmentation for 3D object detection. In: Proceedings of the IEEE/CVF Conference on Computer Vision and Pattern Recognition, pp. 11794–11803 (2021)
23. Wang, Y., Fathi, A., Wu, J., Funkhouser, T., Solomon, J.: Multi-frame to single-frame: Knowledge distillation for 3d object detection. In: The Workshop on Perception for Autonomous Driving at the European Conference on Computer Vision (2020)
24. Wang, Y., Guizilini, V.C., Zhang, T., Wang, Y., Zhao, H., Solomon, J.: DETR3D: 3D object detection from multi-view images via 3D-to-2D queries. In: Conference on Robot Learning, pp. 180–191. PMLR (2022)
25. Wang, Z., et al.: Multi-stage fusion for multi-class 3d lidar detection. In: IEEE/CVF International Conference on Computer Vision Workshops, ICCVW 2021, pp. 3113–3121 (2021)
26. Xu, Q., Zhou, Y., Wang, W., Qi, C.R., Anguelov, D.: SPG: unsupervised domain adaptation for 3D object detection via semantic point generation. In: Proceedings of the IEEE/CVF International Conference on Computer Vision pp. 15446–15456 (2021)
27. Yang, Z., Sun, Y., Liu, S., Jia, J.: 3DSSD: Point-based 3D single stage object detector. In: Proceedings of the IEEE/CVF conference on computer vision and pattern recognition. pp. 11040–11048 (2020)
28. Yoo, J.H., Kim, Y., Kim, J., Choi, J.W.: 3D-CVF: Generating Joint Camera and LiDAR Features Using Cross-view Spatial Feature Fusion for 3D Object Detection. In: Vedaldi, A., Bischof, H., Brox, T., Frahm, J.-M. (eds.) ECCV 2020. LNCS, vol. 12372, pp. 720–736. Springer, Cham (2020). https://doi.org/10.1007/978-3-030-58583-9_43
29. Zhang, L., Chen, X., Dong, R., Ma, K.: Region-aware knowledge distillation for efficient image-to-image translation. arXiv preprint arXiv:2205.12451 (2022)
30. Zhang, L., Chen, X., Tu, X., Wan, P., Xu, N., Ma, K.: Wavelet knowledge distillation: towards efficient image-to-image translation. In: Proceedings of the IEEE/CVF Conference on Computer Vision and Pattern Recognition, pp. 12464–12474 (2022)
31. Zhang, L., Dong, R., Tai, H.S., Ma, K.: Pointdistiller: structured knowledge distillation towards efficient and compact 3d detection. In: Proceedings of the IEEE/CVF Conference on Computer Vision and Pattern Recognition (2022)
32. Zhang, L., Ma, K.: Improve object detection with feature-based knowledge distillation: towards accurate and efficient detectors. In: International Conference on Learning Representations (2020)

33. Zhang, L., Yu, M., Chen, T., Shi, Z., Bao, C., Ma, K.: Auxiliary training: towards accurate and robust models. In: Proceedings of the IEEE/CVF Conference on Computer Vision and Pattern Recognition, pp. 372–381 (2020)

34. Zhang, P., Kang, Z., Yang, T., Zhang, X., Zheng, N., Sun, J.: Lgd: label-guided self-distillation for object detection. In: Proceedings of the AAAI Conference on Artificial Intelligence, vol. 36, pp. 3309–3317 (2022)

35. Zhang, Z., Sun, B., Yang, H., Huang, Q.: H3DNet: 3D object detection using hybrid geometric primitives. In: Vedaldi, A., Bischof, H., Brox, T., Frahm, J.-M. (eds.) ECCV 2020. H3DNet: 3D object detection using hybrid geometric primitives, vol. 12357, pp. 311–329. Springer, Cham (2020). https://doi.org/10.1007/978-3-030-58610-2_19

36. Zheng, W., Tang, W., Jiang, L., Fu, C.W.: SE-SSD: self-ensembling single-stage object detector from point cloud. In: Proceedings of the IEEE/CVF Conference on Computer Vision and Pattern Recognition, pp. 14494–14503 (2021)

37. Zhu, Y., Wang, Y.: Student customized knowledge distillation: bridging the gap between student and teacher. In: Proceedings of the IEEE/CVF International Conference on Computer Vision, pp. 5057–5066 (2021)

PromptDet: Towards Open-Vocabulary Detection Using Uncurated Images

Chengjian Feng[1], Yujie Zhong[1], Zequn Jie[1], Xiangxiang Chu[1], Haibing Ren[1], Xiaolin Wei[1], Weidi Xie[2(✉)], and Lin Ma[1]

[1] Meituan Inc., Beijing, China
[2] Shanghai Jiao Tong University, Shanghai, China
weidi@sjtu.edu.cn

Abstract. The goal of this work is to establish a scalable pipeline for expanding an object detector towards novel/unseen categories, using *zero manual annotations*. To achieve that, we make the following four contributions: (i) in pursuit of generalisation, we propose a two-stage open-vocabulary object detector, where the class-agnostic object proposals are classified with a text encoder from pre-trained visual-language model; (ii) To pair the visual latent space (of RPN box proposals) with that of the pre-trained text encoder, we propose the idea of *regional prompt learning* to align the textual embedding space with regional visual object features; (iii) To scale up the learning procedure towards detecting a wider spectrum of objects, we exploit the available online resource via a novel self-training framework, which allows to train the proposed detector on a large corpus of noisy uncurated web images. Lastly, (iv) to evaluate our proposed detector, termed as **PromptDet**, we conduct extensive experiments on the challenging LVIS and MS-COCO dataset. PromptDet shows superior performance over existing approaches with *fewer additional training images* and *zero manual annotations* whatsoever. Project page with code: https://fcjian.github.io/promptdet.

1 Introduction

Object detection has been one of the most widely researched problems in computer vision, with the goal of simultaneously localising and categorising objects in the image. In the recent literature, the detection community has witnessed tremendous success by training on large-scale datasets, *e.g.* PASCAL VOC [6], MS-COCO [20], with objects of certain category being exhaustively annotated with bounding box and category labels. However, the scalability of such training regime is clearly limited, as the model can only perform well on a closed and small set of categories for which large-scale data is easy to collect and annotate.

On the other hand, the recent large-scale visual-language pre-training has shown tremendous success in open-vocabulary image classification, which opens up the opportunity for expanding the vocabulary a detector can operate on. In

---

Supplementary Information The online version contains supplementary material available at https://doi.org/10.1007/978-3-031-20077-9_41.

S. Avidan et al. (Eds.): ECCV 2022, LNCS 13669, pp. 701–717, 2022.
https://doi.org/10.1007/978-3-031-20077-9_41

Fig. 1. The proposed PromptDet is a framework for expanding the vocabulary of an object detector without human annotation. The figure depicts detection examples produced by our model on LVIS validation set, with blue and green boxes denoting the objects from **base** and novel categories respectively. Despite no ground truth annotation is provided for the novel categories, PromptDet is still able to reliably localise and recognise these objects with high accuracy. (Color figure online)

specific, these visual-language models (for example, CLIP [22] and ALIGN [15]) are often trained on billion-scale noisy image-text pairs, with noise contrastive learning, and has demonstrated a basic understanding on 'what' generally are the salient objects in an image. However, training detectors in the same manner, *i.e.* using image-text pairs, clearly poses significant challenge on scalability, as it would require the captions to not only include semantics (*i.e.* 'what'), but also the spatial information (*i.e.* 'where') of the objects. As a result, the community considers a slightly conservative scenario in open-vocabulary object detection [11,36]: **given an existing object detector trained on abundant data for some base categories, we wish to expand the detector's ability to localise and recognise novel categories, with minimal human effort.**

This paper describes a simple idea for pairing the visual latent space with a pre-trained language encoder, *e.g.* inheriting the CLIP's text encoder as a 'classifier' generator, and only train the detector's visual backbone and class-agnostic region proposal. The novelty of our approach is in the two steps for aligning the visual and textual latent spaces. Firstly, we propose to learn a certain number prompt vectors on the textual encoder side, termed as regional prompt learning (RPL), such that its latent space can be transformed to better pair with the visual embeddings from the object-centric feature. Secondly, by leveraging a large corpus of uncurated web images, we further iteratively optimise the prompt vectors by retrieving a set of candidate images from the Internet, and self-train the detector with the pseudo-labels generated on the sourced candidate images. The resultant detector is named **PromptDet**. Experimentally, despite the noise in the image candidates, such self-training regime has shown a noticeable improvement on the open-vocabulary generalisation, especially on the categories where no box annotations are available. Detection examples produced by PromptDet are illustrated in Fig. 1.

To summarise, we make the following contributions: (i) We investigate the problem of open-vocabulary detection based on a simple idea, namely, equipping a standard two-stage object detector with a frozen textual encoder from a pre-trained visual-language model. (ii) We propose a regional prompt learning approach for transforming the embedding space of the text encoder to better fit the object-centric feature proposed by the RPN of the detector. (iii) We introduce a novel learning framework, which allows to iteratively update the prompts and source high-quality external images from the web using the updated prompts, and finally self-train the detector. (iv) PromptDet substantially outperforms previous state-of-the-art on the LVIS [12] and MS-COCO [20], despite only using uncurated web images and much fewer training costs, i.e. smaller image resolution and fewer epochs.

2   Related Work

Object Detection. Generally speaking, modern object detection frameworks can be divided into two-stage [9,13,26] and one-stage ones [8,19,29,34]. The two-stage detectors first generate a set of region proposals, and then classify and refine these proposals. In contrast, the one-stage detectors directly predict the category and bounding box at each location. The majority of existing detectors require a large number of training data with bounding box annotations, and can only recognise a fixed set of categories that are present in the training data. Recently, several works develop few-shot detection [7,16,17] and zero-shot detection [11,36] to relax the restriction from expensive data annotations. In specific, few-shot detection aims to detect novel categories by adjusting the detector with one or few annotated samples. Zero-shot detection aims to identify novel categories without any additional examples.

Open-Vocabulary Object Detection. In the recent literature, open-vocabulary detection has attracted increasingly more interest within the community. The goal is to detect objects beyond a closed set, in [2], the authors propose to replace the last classification layer with language embeddings of the class names. [18,23] introduce the external text information while computing the classifier embedding. OVR-CNN [32] trains the detector on image-text pairs with contrastive learning. ViLD [11] and ZSD-YOLO [31] propose to explicitly distill the knowledge from the pre-trained CLIP visual embedding into the visual backbone of a Faster RCNN. One closely related work is the Detic [36], which seeks to self-train the detector on ImageNet21K, to expand the vocabulary of detector. Nonetheless, it still requires a tremendous amount of human effort for annotating these ImageNet21K images. In contrast, our proposed self-training framework poses less limitations, and enables to directly train on uncurated web images.

Zero-Shot Learning. Zero-shot learning aims to transfer the learned knowledge from some seen object classes to novel classes. In object recognition, early works exploit the visual attribution such as class hierarchy, class similarity and object parts to generalize from seen classes to unseen classes [1,5,14,27,33]. Other line of research learns to map visual samples and the semantic descriptors to a joint embedding space, and compute the similarity between images and free form texts in the embedding space [4,10].

Vision-Language Pre-training. In computer vision, joint visual-textual learning has been researched for a long time. In the early work from Mori et al. [21], connections between image and words in paired text documents were first explored, [30] learnt a joint image-text embedding for the case of class name annotations. In the recent literature, CLIP [22] and ALIGN [15] collect a million/billion-scale image-caption pairs from the Internet, and jointly train an image encoder and a text encoder with simple noise contrastive learning, which has shown to be extremely effective for a set of downstream tasks, such as zero-shot image classification.

3   Methodology

In this paper, we aim to expand the vocabulary of a standard two-stage object detector, to localise and recognise objects from novel categories with minimal manual effort. This section is organized as follows, we start by introducing the basic blocks for building an open-vocabulary detector, that can detect objects of arbitrary category, beyond a closed set; In Sect. 3.2, we describe the basic idea for pairing the visual backbone with a frozen language model, by inheriting CLIP's text encoder as a classifier generator; In Sect. 3.3, to encourage alignment between the object-centric visual representation and textual representation, we introduce the regional prompt learning (RPL); In Sect. 3.4, we introduce an iterative learning scheme, that can effectively leverage the uncurated web images, and source high-quality candidate images of novel categories. As a consequence, our proposed open-vocabulary detector, termed as **PromptDet**, can be self-trained on these candidate images in a scalable manner.

3.1   Open Vocabulary Object Detector

Here, we consider the same problem setup as in [11]. Assuming we are given an image detection dataset, $\mathcal{D}_{\text{train}}$, with exhaustive annotations on a set of base categories, $\mathcal{C}_{\text{train}} = \mathcal{C}_{\text{base}}$, $i.e.$ $\mathcal{D}_{\text{train}} = \{(I_1, y_1), \ldots, (I_n, y_n)\}$, where $I_i \in \mathbb{R}^{H \times W \times 3}$ refers to the i-th image, and $y_i = \{(b_i, c_i)\}^m$ denotes the coordinates ($b_i^k \in \mathbb{R}^4$) and category label ($c_i^k \in \mathbb{R}^{\mathcal{C}_{\text{base}}}$) for a total of m objects in such image. The goal is to train an object detector that can successfully operate on a test set, $\mathcal{D}_{test}$, with objects beyond a closed set of base categories, $i.e.$ $\mathcal{C}_{\text{test}} = \mathcal{C}_{\text{base}} \cup \mathcal{C}_{\text{novel}}$, thus termed as an open-vocabulary detector. In particular, we conduct the experiments on LIVS dataset [12], and treat the union of common and frequent classes as $base$ categories, and the rare classes as $novel$ categories.

Generally speaking, a popular two-stage object detector, for example, Mask-RCNN, is consisted of a visual backbone encoder, a region proposal network (RPN) and classification module:

$$\{\hat{y}_1, \ldots, \hat{y}_n\} = \Phi_{\text{CLS}} \circ \Phi_{\text{RPN}} \circ \Phi_{\text{ENC}}(I) \tag{1}$$

Constructing an open-vocabulary detector would therefore require to solve two subsequent problems: (1) to effectively generate class-agnostic region proposals, and (2) to accurately classify each of these proposed regions beyond a close set of visual categories, $i.e.$ open-vocabulary classification.

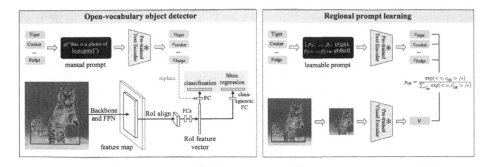

Fig. 2. Left: the proposed open-vocabulary object detector. We inherit the category embeddings as an open-vocabulary classifier, and train the visual backbone to align with the classifier. **Right**: the procedure for the off-line regional prompt learning. We take crops for all base categories, and use their visual embeddings to optimise the learnable prompt (Sect. 3.3 has detailed description).

Class-Agnostic Region Proposal Networks (Φ_{RPN}): refers to the ability of proposing all regions that are likely to have objects, regardless of their categories. Here, we parametrise the anchor classification, bounding box regression and mask prediction in a class-agnostic manner, *i.e.* sharing parameters for all the categories. This is also in line with the discovery in recent work [17,36].

Open-Vocabulary Classification (Φ_{CLS}): aims to categorise the visual object beyond a fixed-size vocabulary. We make the assumption that, there exists a common latent space between vision and natural language, classifying any visual object can thus be achieved by looking for its closest embedding in the language latent space, for example, to classify a region as "*almond*" or "*dog*", the classification probability for being "*almond*" can be computed:

$$c_{\text{almond}} = \phi_{\text{text}}(g(\text{"this is a photo of [\underline{almond}]"})) \tag{2}$$

$$c_{\text{dog}} = \phi_{\text{text}}(g(\text{"this is a photo of [\underline{dog}]"})) \tag{3}$$

$$p_{\text{almond}} = \frac{\exp(<v, c_{\text{almond}}>/\epsilon)}{\exp(<v, c_{\text{almond}}>/\epsilon) + \exp(<v, c_{\text{dog}}>/\epsilon)} \tag{4}$$

where $v \in \mathbb{R}^D$ denotes the ROI pooled features from region proposal network, $g(\cdot)$ refers to a simple tokenisation procedure, with no trainable parameters, ϕ_{text} denotes a hyper-network that maps the natural language to its corresponding latent embedding, note that, the input text usually requires to use a template with manual prompts, *e.g.* "this is a photo of [category]", which converts the classification tasks into the same format as that used during pre-training. As both visual and textual embedding have been L2 normalised, a temperature parameter ϵ is also introduced. The visual backbone is trained by optimising the classification loss, to pair the regional visual embedding and its textual embedding of the corresponding category.

Discussion: Despite the simplicity in formulating an open-vocabulary detector, training such models would suffer from great challenges, due to the lack of exhaustive annotations for large-scale dataset. Until recently, the large-scale visual-language models, such as CLIP and ALIGN, have been trained to align the latent space between vision and language, using simple noise contrastive learning at the image level. Taking benefit from the rich information in text descriptions, *e.g.* actions, objects, human-object interactions, and object-object relationships, these visual-language models have demonstrated remarkable 'zero-shot' generalisation for various image classification tasks, which opens up the opportunity for expanding the vocabulary of an object detector.

3.2   Naïve Alignment via Detector Training

In this section, we aim to train an open-vocabulary object detector (based on Mask-RCNN) on $\mathcal{D}_{\text{train}}$, *i.e.* only *base* categories, by optimising the visual backbone and the class-agnostic RPN to align with the object category classifier, that is inherited from the pre-trained frozen text encoder from CLIP, as shown in Fig. 2 (left). Note that, such training regime has also been investigated in several previous work, for example, [2,11].

However, as indicated by our experiments, naïvely aligning the visual latent space to textual ones only yields very limited open-vocabulary detection performance. We conjecture that the poor generalisation mainly comes from three aspects: Firstly, computing the category embedding with only class name is suboptimal, as they may not be precise enough to describe a visual concept, leading to the lexical ambiguity, For example, *"almond"* either refers to an edible oval nut with a hard shell or the tree that it grows on; Secondly, the web images for training CLIP are scene-centric, with objects occupying only a small portion of the image, whereas the object proposals from RPNs often closely localise the object, leading to an obvious domain gap on the visual representation; Thirdly, the base categories used for detector training are significantly less diverse than those used for training CLIP, thus, may not be sufficient to guarantee a generalisation towards novel categories. In the following sections, we propose a few simple steps to alleviate the above issues.

3.3   Alignment via Regional Prompt Learning

Comparing with the scene-centric images used for training CLIP, the output features from RPNs are local and object-centric. Naïvely aligning the regional visual representation to the *frozen* CLIP text encoder would therefore encourage each proposal to capture more context than it is required. To this end, we propose a simple idea of **regional prompt learning** (RPL), steering the textual latent space to better fit object-centric images.

Specifically, while computing the category classifier or embedding, we prepend and append a sequence of learnable vectors to the textual input, termed as 'continuous prompt vectors'. These prompt vectors do not correspond to any real concrete words, and will be attended at the subsequent layers as if they were a sequence of 'virtual tokens'. Additionally, we also include more detailed description into the prompt template to alleviate the lexical ambiguity, for instance, {category: *"almond"*, description: *"oval-shaped edible seed of the almond tree"*}.

Note that, the description can often be easily sourced from Wikipedia or meta data from the dataset. The embedding for each individual category can thus be generated as:

$$c_{\text{almond}} = \phi_{\text{text}}([p_1, \ldots, p_j, g(\underline{\text{category}}), p_{j+1} \ldots, p_{j+h}, g(\underline{\text{description}})]) \qquad (5)$$

where p_i ($i \in \{1, 2, ..., j + h\}$) denote the learnable prompt vectors with the same dimension as word embedding, $[\underline{\text{category}}]$ and $[\underline{\text{description}}]$ are calculated by tokenising the category name and detailed description. As the learnable vectors are class-agnostic, and shared for all categories, they are expected to be transferable to novel categories after training.

Optimising Prompt Vectors. To save computations, we consider to learn the prompt vectors in an off-line manner, specifically, we take the object crops of *base* categories from LVIS, resize them accordingly and pass through the frozen CLIP visual encoder, to generate the image embeddings. To optimise the prompt vectors, we keep both the visual and textual encoder frozen, and only leave the learnable prompt vectors to be updated, with a standard cross-entropy loss to classify these image crops. The process of RPL is displayed in Fig. 2 (right).

Discussion. With the proposed RPL, the textual latent space is therefore re-calibrated to match the object-centric visual embeddings. Once trained, we can re-compute all the category embeddings, and train the visual backbone to align with the prompted text encoder, as described in Fig. 2 (left). In our experiments, we have confirmed the effectiveness of RPL in Sect. 4.3, which indeed leads noticeable improvements on the open-vocabulary generalisation.

3.4 PromptDet: Alignment via Self-training

Till here, we have obtained an open-vocabulary object detector by aligning the visual backbone to prompted text encoder. However, RPL has only exploited limited visual diversity, *i.e.* only with base categories. In this section, we unleash such limitation and propose to leverage the large-scale, uncurated, noisy web images to further improve the alignment. Specifically, as shown in Fig. 3, we describe a learning framework that iterates the procedure of RPL and candidate images sourcing, followed by generating pseudo ground truth boxes, and self-training the open-vocabulary detector.

Sourcing Candidate Images. We take the LAION-400M dataset as an initial corpus of images, with the visual embeddings pre-computed by CLIP's visual encoder. To acquire candidate images for each category, we compute the similarity score between the visual embedding and the category embedding, which are computed with the learnt regional prompt. We keep the images with highest similarity (an ablation study on the selection of the number of the images has been conducted in Sect. 4.3). As a consequence, an additional set of images is constructed with both *base* and *novel* categories, with no ground truth bounding boxes available, *e.g.* $\mathcal{D}_{\text{ext}} = \{(I_{\text{ext}})_i\}_{i=1}^{|\mathcal{D}_{\text{ext}}|}$.

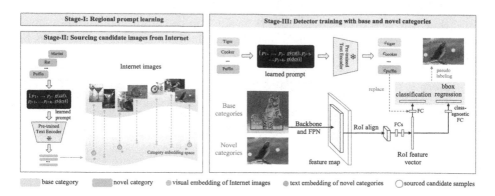

Fig. 3. Illustration of the self-training framework. **Stage-I**: we use the base categories to learn regional prompts, as already demonstrated in Fig. 2 (right). **Stage-II**: we source and download the Internet images with the learned prompt. **Stage-III**: we self-train the detector with both LVIS images of base categories and the sourced images of novel categories. Note that, the prompt learning and image sourcing can be iteratively conducted to better retrieve relevant images.

Iterative Prompt Learning And Image Sourcing. Here, we can alternate the procedure of the regional prompt learning (Fig. 3 Stage-I) and sourcing Internet images with the learned prompt with high precision (Fig. 3 Stage-II). Experimentally, such iterative sourcing procedure has shown to be beneficial for mining object-centric images with high precision. It enables to generate more accurate pseudo ground truth boxes and, as a result, largely improves the detection performance on novel categories after self-training.

Bounding Box Generation. For each image in $\mathcal{D}_{ext}$, we run the inference with our open-vocabulary detector. Since these sourced candidate images are often object-centric, the output object proposals from class-agnostic RPN usually guarantee a decent precision and recall. We retain the top-K proposals with max objectness scores (experiments are conducted on selecting the value of K), then keep the box with the maximal classification score as the pseudo ground truth for each image. Note that, despite an image may contain multiple objects of interest, we only pick the one box as pseudo ground truth. Overall, such procedure would successfully mine a large set of previously unlabeled instances with pseudo ground truth, which are later used for re-training the visual backbone and RPN (including regression head) in Mask-RCNN, effectively resembling the self-training procedure.

Discussion. Recent Detic [36] also attempts to train an open-vocabulary detector by exploiting external data, our proposed approach differs in three major aspects: (1) in Detic, the ImageNet21K is used as the initial image corpus, which have already been well-curated with manual annotations, in contrast, we advocate more challenging and scalable scenario, with all external images uncurated; (2) Detic uses a heuristic to pseudo-label the bounding boxes, *i.e.* to always pick the max-sized proposal; while in our case, we choose the box with most confident prediction; (3) our image sourcing and self-training can be iteratively conducted, and shown to lead significant performance boost, as indicated in Sect. 4.3.

4   Experiment

4.1   Dataset and Evaluation Metrics

Here, we describe the open-vocabulary detection setup on LVIS [12], more details for MS-COCO benchmark can be found in supplementary material.

LVIS.   The latest LVIS v1.0 [12] contains 1203 categories with both bounding box and instance mask annotations. The categories are divided into three groups based on the number of the images that each category appears in the *train* set: rare (1–10 images), common (11–100 images), and frequent (>100 images). We follow the same problem setting as in ViLD [11] and Detic [36], where the frequent and common classes are treated as base categories ($\mathcal{C}_{base}$), and the rare classes as the novel categories ($\mathcal{C}_{novel}$).

LAION-400M and LAION-Novel.   For self-training, we also use an external dataset, LAION-400M [28], which consists of 400 million image-text pairs filtered by pre-trained CLIP. It provides the pre-computed CLIP embedding for all the images, and we search for the images by using its 64G *knn* indices and download about 300 images for each novel category, as illustrated by Stage-II in Fig. 3. We refer to this subset of LAION-400M as LAION-novel.

While training an initial open-vocabulary object detector, we use LVIS-base. For self-training, we use a combination of LVIS-base and LAION-novel datasets, we summarise the dataset statistics in Table 1. For evaluation on LVIS v1.0 *minival* set, we mainly consider the mask Average Precision for novel categories, *i.e.* AP_{novel}. However, to complete the AP metric, we also report AP_c (for common classes) and AP_f (for frequent classes). Lastly, the mask Average Precision for all categories is denoted by AP, which is computed as the mean of all the APs ranging from 0.5 to 0.95 IoU threshold (in a step of 0.05).

Table 1. A summary of dataset statistics. The numbers in bracket refer to the number of base and novel categories

Dataset	Train	Eval	Definition	#Images	#Categories
LVIS	–	–	original LVIS dataset	0.1M	1203
LAION-400M	–	–	image-text pairs filtered by CLIP	400M	unlabeled
LVIS-base	✓	✗	common and frequent categories	0.1M	866
LAION-novel	✓	✗	image subset of novel categories	0.1M	337 (noisy)
LVIS *minival*	✗	✓	standard LVIS validation set	20K	1203 (866+337)

4.2   Implementation Details

Detector Training.   We conduct all the experiments using Mask-RCNN [13] with a ResNet-50-FPN backbone. Similar to Detic [36], we use *sigmoid* activation and binary cross-entropy loss for classification. We adopt the Stochastic Gradient Descent (SGD) optimizer with a weight decay of 0.0001 and a momentum of 0.9. Unless specified, the models are trained for 12 epochs (1× learning schedule) and the initial learning rate is set to 0.02 and then reduced by a factor of 10 at the 8-th epoch and the 11-th epoch. This detector training schedule is used for both the naïve alignment (Sect. 3.2) and self-training (Sect. 3.4). In terms of the data augmentation for the naïve alignment, we use 640–800 scale jittering and horizontal flipping.

Regional Prompt Learning. We train the learnable prompt vectors for 6 epochs. Empirically, we find that the model is not sensitive to the number of prompt vectors, we therefore use two vectors, one before $g(\text{category})$ as a prefix vector, and one after $g(\text{category})$ as a suffix vector.

One-Iteration Prompt Learning and Image Sourcing. For the first iteration, we train the prompt using the image crops from LVIS-base. Specifically, we expand the ground truth box to triple the height or width for each side, and take crops from the images based on the extended bounding box. Then we randomly select up to 200 image crops for each base class to train the prompt vectors. At the stage of image sourcing, we search for the web images on LAION-400M using the learned prompt via the *knn* indices of LAION-400M, and download about 300 images for each novel class, forming LAION-novel for later self-training.

Multi-Iteration Prompt Learning and Image Sourcing. If we perform the prompt learning and image sourcing for more than one iteration, we start the prompt learning using LVIS-base, and search more images for base categories from LAION-400M. Combining the original LVIS-base and newly sourced images, we can again update the prompt vectors, and used to search images for novel categories later on, constructing the external LAION-novel dataset.

Self-training. We first train the detector using the LVIS-base images for 6 epochs, and then train on both LVIS-base and LAION-novel for another 6 epochs. For the LAION-novel images, they are often object-centric due to the regional prompt learning, we use a smaller resolution and do 160–800 scale jittering. To guarantee high-quality of pseudo labels, we adopt a multi-scale inference scheme to generate the pseudo ground truth bounding boxes for images from LAION-novel. Specifically, one image scale is randomly selected from 160–360, and the other is randomly selected from 360–800. The two images of different scales are fed into the detector, and one pseudo bounding box is generated for each of them. We select the most confident prediction from both images as the final pseudo bounding boxes, and use them to further self-train the detector.

Training for More Epochs. To compare with state-of-the-art detectors, we train the models with a batchsize of 64 on 8 GPUs, for 72 epochs (6× learning schedule), with 100–1280 scale jittering.

4.3 Ablation Study

In this section, we conduct ablation studies on the LVIS dataset, to thoroughly validate the effectiveness of the proposed components, including the RPL, iterative candidate sourcing, and self-training. In addition, as for studying other hyper-parameters, we also conduct comparison experiment to other heuristics for box selection, effect of sourced candidate images, and finally on the training detail for whether to update the class-agnostic region proposal during self-training.

Regional Prompt Learning (RPL). To demonstrate the effectiveness of training open-vocabulary detector, by aligning the visual and textual latent space, we compare the learned prompt with the manual prompt. For simplicity, we only use two learnable vectors (one for prefix, and one for suffix) in RPL. When using more prompt vectors, we did not observe clear benefits.

As shown in Table 2, we first investigate the performance with the manual prompt of "a photo of [category]", which has also been used in previous works [11,35,36]. However, it only brings a limited generalisation, yielding a 7.4 AP on novel categories; Secondly, after adding more detailed description to the prompt template, *i.e.* use the "a photo of [category], which is [description]", the lexical ambiguity can be alleviated, and lead to an improvement of 1.6 AP on novel categories; Lastly, we verify the effectiveness of our proposed prompt learning, which further brings a performance improvement by 3.7 AP and 2.1 AP on novel categories, comparing to the two manual prompts respectively.

Table 2. Comparison on manually designed and learned prompt. Here, we only use two learnable prompt vectors in PRL, *i.e.* $[1 + 1]$ refers to using one vector for prefix, and one vector for suffix

	Prompt	AP_{novel}	AP_c	AP_f	AP
"a photo of [category]"	manual	7.4	17.2	26.1	19.0
"a photo of [category], which is [description]"	manual	9.0	18.6	26.5	20.1
regional prompt learning	[1+1]	11.1	18.8	26.6	20.3

Self-training. We evaluate the performance of after self-training the detector, both with and without the iterative candidate image sourcing. As shown in Table 3, it can always bring a noticeable improvement with different prompts, for example, from 9.0 to 15.3 AP for manual prompt, and 11.1 to 15.9 AP for learnt prompt. Additionally, while conducting a second-round regional prompt learning and image sourcing, our proposed PromptDet really shines, significantly outperforming the manually designed prompt, reaching 19.0 AP on novel categories. It demonstrates the effectiveness of self-training and iterative prompt learning for sourcing higher quality images. We also conduct a third-round regional prompt learning, and it yields 19.3 AP on novel categories. For simplicity, we iterate the prompt learning twice in the following experiments.

Box Generation. As for pseudo labeling the boxes, we show some visualisation examples by taking the most confident predictions on the sourced candidate images, as shown in Fig. 4.

Table 3. Effectiveness of self-training with different prompts. 1-iter, 2-iter and 3-iter denote that Stage-I (*i.e.* RPL) and Stage-II (*i.e.* image sourcing) are performed for one, two or three iterations, respectively

Prompt method	Self-training	AP_{novel}	AP_c	AP_f	AP
"a photo of [category], which is [description]"		9.0	18.6	26.5	20.1
	✓	15.3	17.7	25.8	20.4
Regional prompt learning		11.1	18.8	26.6	20.3
PromptDet (1-iter)	✓	15.9	17.6	25.5	20.4
PromptDet (2-iter)	✓	19.0	18.5	25.8	21.4
PromptDet (3-iter)	✓	19.3	18.3	25.8	21.4

Fig. 4. Visualisation of the generated pseudo ground truth for the sourced images.

Quantitatively, we compare with three different heuristic strategies for box generation, as validated in Detic [36]: (1) use the whole image as proposed box; (2) the proposal with max size; (3) the proposal with max RPN score.

As shown in Table 4 (left), we observe that using the most confident predictions as pseudo ground truth significantly outperforms the other strategies. Specifically, we conjecture this performance gap between ours and the max-size boxes (used in Detic) might be due to the difference on the external data. Detic exploits ImageNet21K with images being manually verified by human annotators, however, we only adopt the noisy, uncurated web images, training on the bounding boxes generated by heuristic may thus incur erroneous supervision in the detector training.

Sourcing Variable Candidate Images. We investigate the performance variation while increasing the number of uncurated web images for self-training. As shown in Table 4 (right), 0 image denotes the training scenario with no self-training involved, and when increasing the number of sourced images from 50 to 300, the performance tends to be increasing monotonically, from 14.6 to 19.0 AP on novel categories, showing the scalability of our proposed self-training mechanism. However, we found the LAION-400M dataset can only support at most 300 images for most categories, and sourcing more images would require to use a larger corpus, we leave this as a future work.

Updating Class-Agnostic RPN and Box Head. Here, we conduct the ablation study on updating or freezing the class-agnostic RPN or box regression

Table 4. Left: the comparison on different box generation methods. **Right**: the effect on increasing the sourced candidate images.

Method	AP_{novel}	AP_c	AP_f	AP
w/o self-training	10.4	19.5	26.6	20.6
image	9.9	18.8	26.0	20.1
max-size	9.5	18.8	26.1	20.1
max-obj.-score	11.3	18.7	26.0	20.3
max-pred.-score (ours)	19.0	18.5	25.8	21.4

#Web images	AP_{novel}	AP_c	AP_f	AP
0	10.4	19.5	26.6	20.6
50	14.6	19.3	26.2	21.2
100	15.8	19.3	26.2	21.4
200	17.4	19.1	26.0	21.5
300	19.0	18.5	25.8	21.4

during self-training. As shown in Table 5 (left), we find that freezing these two components can be detrimental, leading to a 1.8 AP (from 19.0 to 17.2) performance drop on detecting the novel categories.

Top-K Proposals for Pseudo Labeling. We investigate the performance by varying the number of box proposal in the pseudo-labeling procedure. As shown in Table 5 (right), selecting the most confident prediction among the top-20 proposals yields the best performance, and taking all object proposals presents the worst performance (10.4 AP *vs.* 19.0 AP) for novel categories. The other options are all viable, though with some performance drop. We set K = 20 for our experiments.

Table 5. Left: the ablation study on updating class-agnostic RPN and box regression during self-training. **Right**: the analysis on the effect of generating variable pseudo boxes from RPN

RPN classifier	Box head	AP_{novel}	AP_c	AP_f	AP
		17.2	18.2	25.8	21.0
✓		18.1	18.3	25.7	21.2
✓	✓	19.0	18.5	25.8	21.4

#Proposals	AP_{novel}	AP_c	AP_f	AP
10	17.2	18.7	25.7	21.2
20	19.0	18.5	25.8	21.4
30	16.1	18.8	25.9	21.1
1000 (all)	10.4	19.5	26.6	20.6

4.4 Comparison with the State-of-the-Art

In Table 6, we compare the proposed method with other open-vocabulary object detectors [11,36] on the LIVS v1.0 validation set. Limited by the computational resource, our best model is only trained for 72 epochs, and achieving 21.4 AP for the novel categories, surpassing the recent state-of-the-art ViLD-ens [11] and Detic [36] by 4.8 AP and 3.6 AP respectively. Additionally, we observe that training for longer schedule can significantly improve the detection performance on *common* and *frequent* categories, from 18.5 AP to 23.3 AP and 25.8 AP to 29.3 AP respectively.

Additionally, we compare with previous works on open-vocabulary COCO benchmark. Following [2,36], we apply the 48/17 base/novel split setting on

C. Feng et al.

Table 6. Detection results on the LVIS v1.0 validation set. Both Detic and our proposed approach have exploited the external images. However, in Detic, the images are manually annotated and thus indicated by '*'. Notably, PromptDet does not require a knowledge distillation from the CLIP visual encoder at the detector training, which is shown to prominently boost the performance but significantly increase the training costs

Method	Epochs	Scale Jitter	Input Size	#External	AP_{novel}	AP_c	AP_f	AP
ViLD-text [11]	384	100~2048	1024×1024	0	10.1	23.9	32.5	24.9
ViLD [11]	384	100~2048	1024×1024	0	16.1	20.0	28.3	22.5
ViLD-ens. [11]	384	100~2048	1024×1024	0	16.6	24.6	30.3	25.5
Detic [36]	384	100~2048	1024×1024	1.2M*	17.8	26.3	31.6	26.8
PromptDet	12	640~800	800×800	0.1M	19.0	18.5	25.8	21.4
PromptDet	72	100~1280	800×800	0.1M	**21.4**	23.3	29.3	25.3

MS-COCO, and report the box Average Precision at the IoU threshold 0.5. As Table 7 shows, PromptDet trained for 24 epochs outperforms Detic on both novel-class mAP (26.6 AP *vs.* 24.1 AP) and overall mAP (50.6 AP *vs.* 44.7 AP) with the same input image resolution (*i.e.* 640×640).

Table 7. Results on open-vocabulary COCO. Numbers are copied from [36]

Method	Epochs	Input size	$AP50_{novel}^{box}$	$AP50_{all}^{box}$
WSDDN [3]	96	640×640	5.9	39.9
DLWL [24]	96	640×640	19.6	42.9
Predicted [25]	96	640×640	18.7	41.9
Detic [36]	96	640×640	24.1	44.7
PromptDet	24	640×640	**26.6**	50.6

5 Conclusion

In this work, we propose an open-vocabulary object detector PromptDet, which is able to detect novel categories without any manual annotations. Specifically, we first use the pretrained, frozen CLIP text encoder, as an "off-the-shelf" classifier generator in two-stage object detector. Then we propose a regional prompt learning method to steer the textual latent space towards the task of object detection, *i.e.*, transform the textual embedding space, to better align the visual representation of object-centric images. In addition, we further develop a self-training regime, which enables to iteratively high-quality source candidate images from a large corpus of uncurated, external images, and self-train the detector. With these improvements, PromptDet achieved a 21.4 AP of novel classes on LVIS, surpassing the state-of-the-art open-vocabulary object detectors by a large margin, with much lower training costs.

References

1. Akata, Z., Malinowski, M., Fritz, M., Schiele, B.: Multi-cue zero-shot learning with strong supervision. In: Proceedings of the IEEE Conference on Computer Vision and Pattern Recognition, pp. 59–68 (2016)
2. Bansal, A., Sikka, K., Sharma, G., Chellappa, R., Divakaran, A.: Zero-shot object detection. In: Proceedings of the European Conference on Computer Vision. pp. 384–400 (2018)
3. Bilen, H., Vedaldi, A.: Weakly supervised deep detection networks. In: CVPR, pp. 2846–2854 (2016)
4. Cacheux, Y.L., Borgne, H.L., Crucianu, M.: Modeling inter and intra-class relations in the triplet loss for zero-shot learning. In: Proceedings of the IEEE Conference on Computer Vision and Pattern Recognition, pp. 10333–10342 (2019)
5. Elhoseiny, M., Zhu, Y., Zhang, H., Elgammal, A.: Link the head to the " beak": zero shot learning from noisy text description at part precision. In: Proceedings of the IEEE Conference on Computer Vision and Pattern Recognition, pp. 5640–5649 (2017)
6. Everingham, M., Eslami, S., Van Gool, L., Williams, C.K., Winn, J., Zisserman, A.: The pascal visual object classes challenge: a retrospective. Int. J. Comput. Vision $111(1)$, 98–136 (2015)
7. Fan, Q., Zhuo, W., Tang, C.K., Tai, Y.W.: Few-shot object detection with attention-rpn and multi-relation detector. In: Proceedings of the IEEE Conference on Computer Vision and Pattern Recognition, pp. 4013–4022 (2020)
8. Feng, C., Zhong, Y., Gao, Y., Scott, M.R., Huang, W.: Tood: task-aligned one-stage object detection. In: Proceedings of the International Conference on Computer Vision, pp. 3490–3499. IEEE Computer Society (2021)
9. Feng, C., Zhong, Y., Huang, W.: Exploring classification equilibrium in long-tailed object detection. In: Proceedings of the International Conference on Computer Vision, pp. 3417–3426 (2021)
10. Frome, A., et al.: Devise: a deep visual-semantic embedding model. In: Advances in Neural Information Processing Systems 26 (2013)
11. Gu, X., Lin, T.Y., Kuo, W., Cui, Y.: Open-vocabulary object detection via vision and language knowledge distillation. arXiv preprint arXiv:2104.13921 (2021)
12. Gupta, A., Dollar, P., Girshick, R.: Lvis: a dataset for large vocabulary instance segmentation. In: Proceedings of the IEEE Conference on Computer Vision and Pattern Recognition, pp. 5356–5364 (2019)
13. He, K., Gkioxari, G., Dollár, P., Girshick, R.: Mask r-cnn. In: Proceedings of the International Conference on Computer Vision, pp. 2961–2969 (2017)
14. Ji, Z., Fu, Y., Guo, J., Pang, Y., Zhang, Z.M., et al.: Stacked semantics-guided attention model for fine-grained zero-shot learning. In: Advances in Neural Information Processing Systems 31 (2018)
15. Jia, C., et al.: Scaling up visual and vision-language representation learning with noisy text supervision. In: Proceedings of the International Conference on Machine Learning, pp. 4904–4916. PMLR (2021)

16. Kang, B., Liu, Z., Wang, X., Yu, F., Feng, J., Darrell, T.: Few-shot object detection via feature reweighting. In: Proceedings of the International Conference on Computer Vision, pp. 8420–8429 (2019)
17. Kaul, P., Xie, W., Zisserman, A.: Label, verify, correct: a simple few shot object detection method. In: Proceedings of the IEEE Conference on Computer Vision and Pattern Recognition (2022)
18. Li, Z., Yao, L., Zhang, X., Wang, X., Kanhere, S., Zhang, H.: Zero-shot object detection with textual descriptions. In: Proceedings of the AAAI Conference on Artificial Intelligence (2019)
19. Lin, T.Y., Goyal, P., Girshick, R., He, K., Dollár, P.: Focal loss for dense object detection. In: Proceedings of the International Conference on Computer Vision, pp. 2980–2988 (2017)
20. Lin, T.Y., et al.: Microsoft coco: common objects in context. In: Proceedings of the European Conference on Computer Vision, pp. 740–755 (2014)
21. Mori, Y., Takahashi, H., Oka, R.: Image-to-word transformation based on dividing and vector quantizing images with words. In: MISRM (1999)
22. Radford, A., et al.: Learning transferable visual models from natural language supervision. In: Proceedings of the International Conference on Machine Learning, pp. 8748–8763. PMLR (2021)
23. Rahman, S., Khan, S., Barnes, N.: Improved visual-semantic alignment for zero-shot object detection. In: Proceedings of the AAAI Conference on Artificial Intelligence (2020)
24. Ramanathan, V., Wang, R., Mahajan, D.: Dlwl: improving detection for lowshot classes with weakly labelled data. In: CVPR, pp. 9342–9352 (2020)
25. Redmon, J., Farhadi, A.: Yolo9000: better, faster, stronger. In: CVPR, pp. 7263–7271 (2017)
26. Ren, S., He, K., Girshick, R., Sun, J.: Faster r-cnn: towards real-time object detection with region proposal networks. arXiv preprint arXiv:1506.01497 (2015)
27. Rohrbach, M., Stark, M., Schiele, B.: Evaluating knowledge transfer and zero-shot learning in a large-scale setting. In: Proceedings of the IEEE Conference on Computer Vision and Pattern Recognition (2011)
28. Schuhmann, C., et al.: Laion-400m: open dataset of clip-filtered 400 million image-text pairs. arXiv preprint arXiv:2111.02114 (2021)
29. Tian, Z., Shen, C., Chen, H., He, T.: Fcos: fully convolutional one-stage object detection. In: Proceedings of the International Conference on Computer Vision, pp. 9627–9636 (2019)
30. Weston, J., Bengio, S., Usunier, N.: Wsabie: scaling up to large vocabulary image annotation. In: IJCAI (2011)
31. Xie, J., Zheng, S.: Zsd-yolo: zero-shot yolo detection using vision-language knowledgedistillation. arXiv preprint arXiv:2109.12066 (2021)
32. Zareian, A., Rosa, K.D., Hu, D.H., Chang, S.F.: Open-vocabulary object detection using captions. In: Proceedings of the IEEE Conference on Computer Vision and Pattern Recognition (2021)
33. Zhao, H., Puig, X., Zhou, B., Fidler, S., Torralba, A.: Open vocabulary scene parsing. In: Proceedings of the International Conference on Computer Vision, pp. 2002–2010 (2017)
34. Zhong, Y., Deng, Z., Guo, S., Scott, M.R., Huang, W.: Representation sharing for fast object detector search and beyond. In: Vedaldi, A., Bischof, H., Brox, T., Frahm, J.-M. (eds.) ECCV 2020. LNCS, vol. 12364, pp. 471–487. Springer, Cham (2020). https://doi.org/10.1007/978-3-030-58529-7_28

35. Zhou, K., Yang, J., Loy, C.C., Liu, Z.: Learning to prompt for vision-language models. arXiv preprint arXiv:2109.01134 (2021)
36. Zhou, X., Girdhar, R., Joulin, A., Krähenbühl, P., Misra, I.: Detecting twenty-thousand classes using image-level supervision. arXiv preprint arXiv:2201.02605 (2022)

Densely Constrained Depth Estimator for Monocular 3D Object Detection

Yingyan Li[1,2,4,5], Yuntao Chen[3], Jiawei He[1,2,4], and Zhaoxiang Zhang[1,2,3,4,5(✉)]

[1] Institute of Automation, Chinese Academy of Sciences (CASIA), Beijing, China
{liyingyan2021,hejiawei2019,zhaoxiang.zhang}@ia.ac.cn
[2] University of Chinese Academy of Sciences (UCAS), Beijing, China
[3] Centre for Artificial Intelligence and Robotics, HKISI_CAS, Hong Kong, China
[4] National Laboratory of Pattern Recognition (NLPR), Beijing, China
[5] School of Future Technology, University of Chineses Academy of Sciences, Beijing, China

Abstract. Estimating accurate 3D locations of objects from monocular images is a challenging problem because of lacking depth. Previous work shows that utilizing the object's keypoint projection constraints to estimate multiple depth candidates boosts the detection performance. However, the existing methods can only utilize vertical edges as projection constraints for depth estimation. So these methods only use a small number of projection constraints and produce insufficient depth candidates, leading to inaccurate depth estimation. In this paper, we propose a method that utilizes *dense* projection constraints from edges of any direction. In this way, we employ much more projection constraints and produce considerable depth candidates. Besides, we present a graph matching weighting module to merge the depth candidates. The proposed method *DCD* (Densely Constrained Detector) achieves state-of-the-art performance on the KITTI and WOD benchmarks. Code is released at https://github.com/BraveGroup/DCD.

Keywords: Monocular 3D object detection · Dense geometric constraint · Message passing · Graph matching

1 Introduction

Monocular 3D detection [7,17,44,50] has become popular because images are large in number, easy to obtain, and have dense information. Nevertheless, the lack of depth information in monocular images is a fatal problem for 3D detection. Some methods [2,22] use deep neural networks to regress the 3D bounding boxes directly, but it is challenging to estimate the 3D locations of the objects from 2D images. Another line of work [8,29,43] employs a pre-trained depth estimator. However, training the depth estimator is separated from the

---

Supplementary Information The online version contains supplementary material available at https://doi.org/10.1007/978-3-031-20077-9_42.

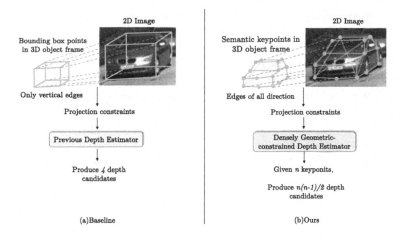

Fig. 1. The object's depth is estimated by 2D-3D edge projection constraints. This figure compares the involved edges in the object's depth estimation between (a) previous work and (b) ours. The previous work only deals with vertical edges. Our work is able to handle the edges of any direction.

detection part, requiring a large amount of additional data. In addition, some works [17,23,50] use geometric constraints, i.e., regresses the 2D/3D edges, and then estimates the object's depth from the 2D-3D edge projection constraints. These works employ 3D shape prior information and exhibit state-of-the-art performance, which is worthy of future research.

A problem of the previous work is that their geometric constraints are insufficient. Specifically, some existing methods [25,49,50] estimate the height of the 2D bounding box and the 3D bounding box, and then generate the depth candidates of an object from 2D-3D height projection constraints. The final depth is produced by weighting all the depth candidates. As Fig. 1 shows, this formulation is only suitable for the vertical edges, which means they only utilize a tiny amount of constraints and 3D prior, leading to inaccurate depth estimations.

Some of the depth candidates are of low quality, so weighting is needed. However, the previous work's weighting methods are suboptimal. Since the final depth is derived from the weighted average of depth candidates, the weight should reflect the quality of each depth candidate. Existing methods [23] use a branch to regress the weight of each depth candidate directly, and this branch is paralleled to the keypoints regression branch. So the weighting branch does not know each keypoint's quality. Some work predicts the uncertainty of each depth to measure the quality of the depth and use the uncertainty to weight [25,50]. However, they obtain the uncertainty of each depth candidate independently, and they do not supervise the weight explicitly.

To address the problem of insufficient geometric constraints, we propose a *Densely Geometric-constrained Depth Estimator (DGDE)*. *DGDE* can estimate depth candidates from projection constraints provided by edges of any direction, no more limited to the vertical edges. This estimator allows better use of the shape information of the object. In addition, training the neural network with abundant 2D-3D projection constraints helps the neural network understand the mapping relationship from the 2D plane to the 3D space.

To weight the depth candidates properly, we propose a new depth candidates weighting module that employs graph matching, named *Graph Matching Weighting module*. We construct *complete graphs* based on 2D and 3D semantic keypoints. In a 2D keypoint graph, the 2D keypoint coordinates are placed on the vertices, and an edge represents a pair of 2D keypoints. The 3D keypoint graph is constructed in the same way. We then match the 2D edges and 3D edges and produce the matching scores. The 2D-3D edge matching score is used as the weight of the corresponding depth candidate. These weights are explicitly supervisable. Moreover, the information of the entire 2d/3d edges is used to generate each 2d-3d edge matching score.

In summary, our main contributions are:

1. We propose a *Dense Geometric-constrained Depth Estimator (DGDE)*. Different from the previous methods, *DGDE* estimates depth candidates utilizing projection constraints of edges of any direction. Therefore, considerable 2D-3D projection constraints are used, producing considerable depth candidates. We produce high-quality final depth based on these candidates.
2. We propose an effective and interpretable *Graph Matching Weighting module (GMW)*. We construct the 2D/3D graph from 2D/3D keypoints respectively. Then we regard the graph matching score of the 2D-3D edge as the weight of the corresponding depth candidate. This strategy utilizes all the keypoints' information and produces explicitly supervised weights.
3. We localize each object more accurately by weighting the estimated depth candidates with corresponding matching scores. Our *Densely Constrained Detector (DCD)* achieves state-of-the-art performance on the KITTI and Waymo Open Dataset (WOD) benchmarks.

2   Related Work

Monocular 3D Object Detection. Monocular 3D object detection [5,7,13,16] becomes more and more popularity because monocular images are easy to obtain. The existing methods can be divided into two categories: single-center-point-based and multi-keypoints-based.

Single-center-point-based methods [22,51,53] use the object's center point to represent an object. In detail, M3D-RPN [2] proposes a depth-aware convolutional layer with the estimated depth. MonoPair [7] discovers that the relationships between nearby objects are useful for optimizing the final results. Although single-center-point-based methods are simple and fast, location regression is unstable because only one center point is utilized. Therefore, the multi-keypoints-based methods [17,23,50] are drawing more and more attention recently.

Multi-keypoints-based methods predict multiple keypoints for an object. More keypoints provide more projection constraints. The projection constraints are useful for training the neural network because constraints build the mapping relationship from the 2D image plane to the 3D space. Deep MANTA [5] defines 4 wireframes as templates for matching cars, while 3D-RCNN [16] proposes a render-and-compare loss. Deep3DBox [28] utilizes 2D bounding boxes as constraints to refine 3D bounding boxes. KM3D [17] localizes the objects utilizing eight bounding boxes points projection. MonoJSG [20] constructs an adaptive cost volume with semantic features to model the depth error. AutoShape [23], highly relevant to this paper, regresses 2D and 3D semantic keypoints and weighs them by predicted scores from a parallel branch. MonoDDE [19] is a concurrent work. It uses more geometric constraints than MonoFlex [50]. However, it only uses geometric constraints based on the object's center and bounding box points, while we use dense geometric constraints derived from semantic keypoints. In this paper, we propose a novel edge-based depth estimator. The estimator produces depth candidates by projection constraints, consisting of edges of any direction. We weight each edge by graph matching to derive the final depth of the object.

Graph Matching and Message Passing. Graph matching [36] is defined as matching vertices and edges between two graphs. This problem is formulated as a Quadratic Assignment Problem (QAP) [3] originally. It has been widely applied in different tasks, such as multiple object tracking [14], semantic keypoint matching [52] and point cloud registration [10]. In the deep learning era, graph matching has become a differentiable module. The spectral relaxation [48], quadratic relaxation [14] and Lagrange decomposition [31] are common in use. However, one simple yet effective way to implement the graph matching layer is using the Sinkhorn [4,32,41] algorithm, which is used in this paper. This paper utilizes a graph matching module to achieve the message passing between keypoints. This means that we calculate the weighting score not only from the keypoint itself but also by taking other keypoints' regression quality into consideration, which is a kind of message passing between keypoints. All the keypoints on the object help us judge each keypoint's importance from the perspective of the whole object. Message passing [12] is a popular design, e.g., in graph neural network [1] and transformer [38]. The message passing module learns to aggregate features between nodes in the graph and brings the global information to each node. In the object detection task, Relation Networks [15] is a pioneer work utilizing message passing between proposals. Message passing has also been used for 3D vision. Message passing between frames [45], voxels [9] and points [33] is designed for LiDAR-based 3D object detection. However, for monocular 3D object detection, message passing is seldom considered. In recent work, PGD [42] conducts message passing in the geometric relation graph. But it does not consider the message passing within the object.

3   Methodology

The overview of our framework is in Fig. 2. We employ a single-stage detector [50] to detect the object's 3D attributes from the monocular image. We propose the *Densely Geometric-constrained Depth Estimator (DGDE)*, which can calculate the depth from any direction' 2D-3D edge. The *DGDE* can effectively utilize the

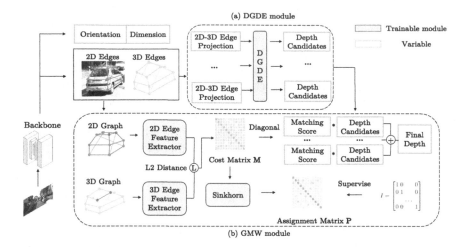

Fig. 2. Overview of our framework. (a) We propose a method *Densely Geometric-constrained Depth Estimator* (DGDE). DGDE is able to estimate the object's depth candidates from 2D-3D projection constraints of edges of any direction. (b) *Graph Matching Weighting module* (GMW) obtains the weights of estimated depth candidates by Graph Matching. A robust depth is derived from combing the multiply depth candidates with corresponding weights

semantic keypoints of the object and produce many depth candidates. Besides, we utilize the regressed 2D edges, 3D edges, and orientation as the input for our 2D-3D edge Graph Matching network. Our *Graph Matching Weighting module (GMW)* matches each 2D-3D edge and produces a matching score. By combining the multiple depths with their corresponding matching scores, we can finally generate a robust depth for the object.

3.1   Geometric-Based 3D Detection Definition

The geometric-based monocular 3D object detection estimates the object's location by 2D-3D projection constraints. Specifically, the network predicts the object's dimension (h, w, l), rotation r_y, since autonomous driving datasets generally assume that the ground is flat. Assuming an object has n semantic keypoints, we regress the i-th$(i = 1, 2, \ldots, n)$ keypoint's 2D coordinate (u^i, v^i) in image coordinate and 3D coordinate (x_o^i, y_o^i, z_o^i) in object frame. The object frame's coordinate origin is the object's center point. The i-th 2D-3D keypoint projection constraint is established from $(u^i, v^i, x_o^i, y_o^i, z_o^i, r_y)$. Given n semantic 2D-3D keypoint projection constraints, it is an overdetermined problem for solving 3D object location (x_c, y_c, z_c), which is the translation vector for transforming the points from the object frame into the camera frame. The method of generating semantic keypoints of each object is adapted from [23]. We establish a few car models by PCA and refine the models by the 3D points segmented from the points cloud and 2D masks. After we obtain the keypoints, we can use our *DGDE* to estimate the object's depth from the keypoint projection constraints.

3.2   Densely Geometric-Constrained Depth Estimation

While previous depth estimation methods [50] only take vertical edges into account, our *DGDE* can handle edges of any direction. Therefore, we are able to utilize much more constraints to estimate the depth of each depth candidate.

Next, we will show the details of estimating dense depth candidates of an object from 2D-3D keypoint projection constraints. The solution is based on the keypoint's projection relationship from 3D space to the 2D image. The i-th($i = 1, 2, \ldots, n$) keypoint's 3D coordinate (x_o^i, y_o^i, z_o^i) is defined in the object frame and is projected on a 2D image plane by the equation:

$$s_i[u_i, v_i, 1]^T = \mathbf{K}[\mathbf{R}|\mathbf{t}][x_o^i, y_o^i, z_o^i, 1]^T, \tag{1}$$

where s_i is the i-th keypoint's depth, $\mathbf{K}$ is the camera intrinsic matrix and $\mathbf{K}, \mathbf{R}, \mathbf{t}$ is represented as:

$$\mathbf{K} = \begin{bmatrix} f_x & 0 & c_x \\ 0 & f_y & c_y \\ 0 & 0 & 1 \end{bmatrix}, \mathbf{R} = \begin{bmatrix} \cos r_y & 0 & \sin r_y \\ 0 & 1 & 0 \\ -\sin r_y & 0 & \cos r_y \end{bmatrix}, \mathbf{t} = [x_c, y_c, z_c]^t. \tag{2}$$

By Eq. (1) and Eq. (2), the equation of i-th keypoint's projection constraint is denoted as:

$$\begin{cases} s_i = z_c - x_o^i \sin r_y + z_o^i \cos r_y, \\ \tilde{u}_i(z_c - x_o^i \sin r_y + z_o^i \cos r_y) = x_c + x_o^i \cos r_y + z_o^i \sin r_y, \\ \tilde{v}_i(z_c - x_o^i \sin r_y + z_o^i \cos r_y) = y_c + y_o^i, \end{cases} \tag{3}$$

where $\tilde{u}_i = \frac{u_i - c_x}{f_x}, \tilde{v}_i = \frac{v_i - c_y}{f_y}$. Intuitively, $(z_c - x_o^i \sin r_y + z_o^i \cos r_y)$ means an object's i-th 3D keypoint's Z coordinate (i.e., depth) in the camera coordinate. $(x_c + x_o^i \cos r_y + z_o^i \sin r_y)$ means 3D keypoint's X coordinate while $(y_c + y_o^i)$ means its Y coordinate.

Similarly, the j-th($j = 1, 2, \ldots, n$) projection constraint is denoted as:

$$\begin{cases} s_j = z_c - x_o^j \sin r_y + z_o^j \cos r_y, \\ \tilde{u}_j(z_c - x_o^j \sin r_y + z_o^j \cos r_y) = x_c + x_o^j \cos r_y + z_o^j \sin r_y, \\ \tilde{v}_j(z_c - x_o^j \sin r_y + z_o^j \cos r_y) = y_c + y_o^j. \end{cases} \tag{4}$$

From Eq. (3) and Eq. (4), we can densely obtain the z_c from the i-th, j-th, $i \neq j$ keypoint(i.e., $edge_{ij}$) projection constraints as:

$$z_c^{ij} = \begin{cases} \dfrac{l_i - l_j}{\tilde{u}_i - \tilde{u}_j}, & (5) \\[2mm] \dfrac{h_i - h_j}{\tilde{v}_i - \tilde{v}_j}, & (6) \end{cases}$$

where $l_i = x_o^i \cos(r_y) + z_o^i \sin(r_y) + u^i(x_o^i \sin(r_y) - z_o^i \cos(r_y))$ and $h_i = y_o^i + v^i(x_o^i \sin(r_y) - z_o^i \cos(r_y))$. This equation reveals that depth can be calculated by the projection constraints of an edge of any direction. Given z_c, we can estimate x_c, y_c from Eq. (3) as $x_c^i = u_i z_c - l_i, y_c^i = v_i z_c - h_i$.

We generate $m = n(n-1)/2$ depth candidates given n keypoints. It is inevitable to meet some low-quality depth candidates in such a large number of depths. Therefore, an appropriate weighting method is necessary to ensemble these depth candidates.

3.3   Depth Weighting by Graph Matching

As we estimate the depth candidate $z_c^{ij}(i, j = 1, \cdots, n)$ for the object o from $DGDE$, the final depth z_c of the object can be weighted from these depth estimations according to the estimation quality $w_{i,j}$, as

$$z_c = \sum_{i<j} w_{i,j} z_c^{ij}. \tag{7}$$

In this section, we propose a new weighting method, called *Graph Matching Weighting module (GMW)*.

Graph Construction and Edge Feature Extraction. We construct 2D keypoint graph $\mathcal{G}_{2d} = (\mathcal{V}_{2d}, \mathcal{E}_{2d})$ and 3D keypoint graph $\mathcal{G}_{3d} = (\mathcal{V}_{3d}, \mathcal{E}_{3d})$. In $\mathcal{G}_{2d}$, each vertex $i \in \mathcal{V}_{2d}$ denotes a predicted keypoint $^{(2d)}\mathbf{p}^i = [u^i, v^i]$ in image coordinate and the edge $^{(2d)}e^{i,j} \in \mathcal{E}_{2d}$ denotes the pair of $^{(2d)}\mathbf{p}^i$ and $^{(2d)}\mathbf{p}^j$, the edge feature $^{(2d)}\mathbf{f}^{i,j}$ is extracted from the 2D coordinate $^{(2d)}\mathbf{p}^i$ and $^{(2d)}\mathbf{p}^j$. The 3D keypoint graph is almost similar to the 2D keypoint graph. The only difference is that the vertex $i' \in \mathcal{V}_{3d}$ denotes the 3D coordinate $^{(3d)}\mathbf{p}^{i'} = [x_o^{i'}, y_o^{i'}, z_o^{i'}]$.

Following [46], the 2D and 3D edge feature extractor are as

$$^{(2d)}\mathbf{f}_k^{i,j} = \text{ReLU}_k(\text{BN}_k(\text{CN}_k(^{(2d)}\text{FC}_k(^{(2d)}\mathbf{f}_{k-1}^{i,j})))), \tag{8}$$

$$^{(3d)}\mathbf{f}_k^{i',j'} = \text{ReLU}_k(\text{BN}_k(\text{CN}_k(^{(3d)}\text{FC}_k(^{(3d)}\mathbf{f}_{k-1}^{i',j'})))), \tag{9}$$

where $k \in \{1, \cdots, K\}$ denotes the index of layers, and FC, CN, BN, ReLU denote fully-connected layer, Context Normalization [46], Batch Normalization, and ReLU, respectively. It is worth mentioning that Context Normalization extracts the global information of all edges. The input of the edge feature extractor is $\mathbf{f}_0^{i,j} = [\mathbf{p}^i, \mathbf{p}^j]$, where $[\cdot]$ denotes the concatenation of the vectors. The output of edge feature extractor $^{(2d)}\mathbf{f}^{i,j}$ and $^{(3d)}\mathbf{f}^{i',j'}$ should be L2-normalized to $[0, 1]$.

Graph Matching Layer. Given the extracted 2D and 3D edge features, the Cost Matrix $\mathbf{M} \in \mathbb{R}^{m \times m}$ is calculated from the L2 distance between each 2D edge feature $^{(2d)}\mathbf{f}^{i,j}$ on the edge s and 3D edge feature $^{(3d)}\mathbf{f}^{i',j'}$ on the edge t:

$$\mathbf{M}_{s,t} = \text{L2}(^{(2d)}\mathbf{f}^{i,j}, ^{(3d)}\mathbf{f}^{i',j'}), (s, t \in \{1, \cdots, m\}), \tag{10}$$

where m denotes the number of edges. Then we take $\mathbf{M}$ as the input of declarative Sinkhorn layer [4] to gain the Assignment Matrix $\mathbf{P}$. The Sinkhorn layer iteratively optimizes $\mathbf{P}$ by minimizing the objective function:

$$\mathcal{F}(\mathbf{M}, \mathbf{P}) = \sum_{s=1}^m \sum_{t=1}^m (\mathbf{M}_{s,t}\mathbf{P}_{s,t} + \alpha\mathbf{P}_{s,t}(\log \mathbf{P}_{s,t} - 1)), \tag{11}$$

where $\mathbf{P}_{s,t}(\log \mathbf{P}_{s,t} - 1)$ is a regularization term and α is the coefficient. $\mathbf{P} \in U(\mathbf{a}, \mathbf{b})$ as:

$$U(\mathbf{a}, \mathbf{b}) = \{\mathbf{X} \in \mathbb{R}_+^{m \times m} | \mathbf{X}\mathbf{1}^m = \mathbf{1}^m, \mathbf{X}^T\mathbf{1}^m = \mathbf{1}^m\}, \qquad (12)$$

where $\mathbf{1}^m$ is an m-dimensional vector with all values to be 1. Note that, Sinkhorn is a differentiable graph matching solver that can make the whole pipeline learnable. When calculating the final depth z_c according to Eq. (7), the weight $\mathbf{w} = \texttt{Softmax}(1/Diag(\mathbf{M}))$, where $Diag(\mathbf{M})$ means the vector consisting of diagonal elements of matrix $\mathbf{M}$. Intuitively, it means that we take the similarity of the 2D and 3D edges with the same semantic label as the prediction quality.

Loss Function. We design regression loss $\mathcal{L}_m^r$ to supervise the final weighted depth z_c, and classification loss $\mathcal{L}_m^c$ to supervise the assignment matrix $\mathbf{P}$ of graph matching output to be an identity matrix. Specifically, $\mathcal{L}_m^c$ is the Binary Entropy Loss (BCE), $\mathcal{L}_m^r$ is an L1 loss:

$$\mathcal{L}_m^c = \sum_{s=1}^{m}\sum_{t=1}^{m} BCE(\mathbf{P}_{s,t}, \mathbf{P}_{s,t}^*), \mathcal{L}_m^r = |\sum_{i<j} w_{i,j}z_c^{ij} - z_c^*|, \qquad (13)$$

where $\mathbf{P}^* = \mathbf{I}$ is the ground truth assignment matrix, z_c^* is the ground truth depth of the object. The final matching loss is $\mathcal{L}_m = \mathcal{L}_m^c + \beta\mathcal{L}_m^r$, where β is a hyper-parameter.

4   Experiments

4.1   Setup

Dataset. We evaluate our method on the KITTI [11] and Waymo Open Dataset v1.2 (WOD) [37]. The KITTI [11] dataset is collected from Europe Streets. It consists of 7481 images for training and 7518 images for testing. We divide the training data into a train set (3712 images) and a validation set (3769 images) as in [54]. Waymo Open Dataset (WOD) [37] has 798 training sequences, 202 validation sequences, and 150 test sequences. The dataset contains images captured by 5 high-resolution cameras in complex environments and is much more challenging than KITTI [11] dataset. We only use the images from the FRONT camera for training and evaluation. The training set has 158,081 images and the validation set has 39,848 images.

Evaluation Metrics. For the KITTI dataset, we compare our methods with previous methods on the *test* set using $AP_{3D|R_{40}}$ result from the test server. In ablation studies, the results on *val* set are reported. For the WOD, we focus on the category of vehicle. Following the official evaluation criteria, we compare the performance with the state-of-the-art methods using average precision (AP) and average precision weighted by heading (APH) metrics. The results are shown in Table 3. The objects are classified into two difficulty levels (LEVEL_1, LEVEL_2) according to the object's points' number under the LiDAR sensor.

Table 1. The result on the KITTI test server compared with other public methods in recent years

Methods	Reference	Category	$AP_{3D|R40|IoU@0.7}$			$AP_{BEV|R40|IoU@0.7}$		
			Easy	Mod	Hard	Easy	Mod	Hard
PatchNet [26]	ECCV20	Pretrained depth	15.68	11.12	10.17	22.97	16.86	14.97
D4LCN [8]	CVPR20		16.65	11.72	9.51	22.51	16.02	12.55
DDMP-3D [39]	CVPR21		19.71	12.78	9.80	28.08	17.89	13.44
CaDDN [30]	CVPR21	LiDAR auxiliary	19.17	13.41	11.46	27.94	18.91	17.19
RTM3D [18]	ECCV20	Directly regress	14.41	10.34	8.77	19.17	14.20	11.99
Movi3D [35]	ECCV20		15.19	10.90	9.26	22.76	17.03	14.85
Ground-Aware [21]	RAL21		21.65	13.25	9.91	29.81	17.98	13.08
MonoDLE [27]	CVPR21		17.23	12.26	10.29	24.79	18.89	16.00
MonoRCNN [34]	ICCV21		18.36	12.65	10.03	25.48	18.11	14.10
MonoEF [55]	CVPR21		21.29	13.87	11.71	29.03	19.70	17.26
MonoRUn [6]	CVPR21	Geometric-based	19.65	12.30	10.58	27.94	17.34	15.24
AutoShape [23]	ICCV21		22.47	14.17	11.36	30.66	20.08	15.59
GUPNet [25]	ICCV21		22.20	15.02	13.12	30.29	21.19	18.20
MonoFlex (Baseline) [50]	CVPR21		19.94	13.89	12.07	28.23	19.75	16.89
DCD (Ours)	ECCV22		**23.81**	**15.90**	**13.21**	**32.55**	**21.50**	**18.25**

4.2   Implementation Details

Detection Framework. We apply the 3D object detection framework following [50], which uses DLA-34 [47] as backbone. We use MultiBin loss [28] for rotation. L1 loss is adopted to estimate dimension, 2D/3D keypoints and depth.

Keypoints. The source of keypoints is discussed in Sect. 3.1. We use 73 keypoints in total consisting of the following parts: (1) 63 semantic keypoints; (2) 8 bounding box corners and the top center and the bottom center of the 3D bounding box. There are 2628 unique keypoint pairs that can be generated from 73 keypoints, so we can obtain 2628 depth estimations at most for each object. For robustness, we select 1500 depth estimations as the final candidates for weighting. The details of the selection strategy are in Sect. 4.4.

Training and Inference. For the KITTI dataset, all the input images are padded into 1280 × 384. We train the model using AdamW [24] optimizer with an initial learning rate of 3e−4 for 100 epochs. The learning rate decays by 10× at 80 and 90 epochs. We train the model on 2 RTX2080Ti GPUs and the batch size is 8. We train the weighting network (i.e., matching network) separately. The weighting network employs the AdamW optimizer with learning rate 1e−4 and weight decay 1e−5. We first train using the classification loss in the weighting network for 50 epochs and add the regression loss for another 50 epochs. During inference, only monocular images are needed. For the WOD, the input size of the images is 1920×1280. We ignore objects whose 2D bounding box's width or height is less than 20 pixels. We train our detection model for 20 epochs with 8 RTX2080Ti GPUs. The batch size is 8 and the learning rate is set to 8e-5, decayed 10× at the 18-th epoch. The rest of the experiment settings are the same as KITTI.

Fig. 3. The qualitative results on the KITTI *val* set. Rather than representing an object as a bounding box, we utilize semantic keypoints to represent an object. The red boxes represent the ground truth, while the green boxes represent the prediction (Color figure online)

4.3   Comparison with State-of-the-Art Methods

Table 1 shows the comparison with other state-of-the-art methods on the KITTI [11] test set. Our method (DCD) achieves state-of-the-art performance on both AP_{3D} and AP_{BEV}. We surpass the directly-regress-depth-based method and pretrain-depth-estimator-based methods by a large margin. It reveals that geometric constraints are critical to accurately locating objects. Compared with other geometric-based methods, we still have a significant improvement. We outperform our baseline MonoFlex [50] by **2.01** in AP_{3D} Mod. level, which reveals the importance of sufficient geometric constraints for monocular 3D detection. We also surpass other geometric-based methods such as AutoShape [23] and GUPNet [25] thanks to the dense geometric constraints and effective weighting method. The result of Pedestrian and Cyclist is in Table 2. Using only bounding box corners as input, we can still observe an improvement over MonoFlex [50]. It shows that our method can handle the problem that some objects are hard to obtain semantic keypoints (without CAD models or non-rigid). The qualitative result is in Fig. 3.

We also achieve state-of-the-art performance on WOD [37] as Table 3 shows. We surpass the previous state-of-the-art methods such as CaDDN [30] and PCT [40]. We also re-implement MonoFlex [50] on WOD [37] for a fair comparison. Compared with the baseline method, we improve the AP IoU@0.7 by **0.87**.

4.4   Ablation Studies

Keypoints Enable Better Depth Estimation. We utilize multiple keypoints rather than bounding boxes to represent an object. The keypoints can accurately reflect the object's outline, which provides meaningful shape prior and abundant information for depth estimation. To show the benefits gained from dense geometric constraints, we visualize the predicted depths' error on KITTI *val* set as Fig. 4 shows.

Table 2. The $AP_{3D|R40}$ results for Pedestrian and Cyclist on KITTI *test* set. We use the bounding box corners as the input of *DGDE*

Method	Pedestrian			Cyclist		
	Easy	Mod	Hard	Easy	Mod	Hard
M3D-RPN [2]	4.92	3.48	2.94	0.94	0.65	0.47
MonoPair [7]	10.02	6.68	5.53	3.79	2.12	1.83
MonoFlex [50]	9.43	6.31	5.26	4.17	2.35	2.04
AutoShape [23]	5.46	3.74	3.03	**5.99**	**3.06**	**2.70**
Ours	**10.37**	**6.73**	**6.28**	4.72	2.74	2.41

Table 3. The result on WOD [37] *val* set. *Italics*: These methods utilize the whole *train* set, while the others use 1/3 amount of images in *train* set. ‡: M3D-RPN is re-implemented by [30]. †: PatchNet is re-implemented by [40]. *: MonoFlex is our baseline and re-implemented ourselves

Difficulty	Method	3D AP (IoU@0.7)	3D APH (IoU@0.7)	3D AP (IoU@0.5)	3D APH (IoU@0.5)
LEVEL_1/LEVEL_2	M3D-RPN‡ [2]	0.35/0.33	0.34/0.33	3.79/3.61	3.63/3.46
	PatchNet†[26]	0.39/0.38	0.37/0.36	2.92/2.42	2.74/2.28
	PCT [40]	0.89/0.66	0.88/0.66	4.20/4.03	4.15/3.99
	CaDDN [30]	5.03/4.49	4.99/4.45	17.54/16.51	17.31/16.28
	*MonoFlex** [50]	11.70/10.96	11.64/10.90	32.26/30.31	32.06/30.12
	DCD (Ours)	**12.57/11.78**	**12.50/11.72**	**33.44/31.43**	**33.24/31.25**

The Effectiveness of DGDE. To discover the inner workings of multiple 2D-3D keypoints projection constraints, we apply the DGDE on the state-of-the-art method MonoFlex [50]. MonoFlex predicts eight bounding box corners and two top-down center points. In addition to the ten keypoints, we add another regression branch on MonoFlex to predict 63 semantic keypoints. Basically, they are sampled from the model surface representing the rough skeletons.

In Table 4, the improvements from (d) to (e) are significant (+**1.30** on the Hard level) even with only 10 keypoints. With more keypoints ((c) and (f)), DGDE achieves holistic improvements on both the uncertainty-based weighting method and our matching-based method.

The More Keypoints, the Better Performances. Our depth estimator can produce depth candidates by edge projection constraints of arbitrary directions. To fully realize the potential of our depth estimator, we use all the extra 63 semantic keypoints. Thus, it is easy to generate numerous edges and obtain considerable depth candidates (2628). With such a large number of depth candidates, it is more likely to generate an accurate and robust final depth. In Table 4, the model (f) with all keypoints outperforms our baseline by a large margin of **2.31** AP on Easy level and **1.51** AP on Mod. level.

The Effectiveness of *Graph Matching Weighting module (GMW)*. As the number of projection constraints increases, it is urgent to weigh the constraints appropriately since some are of low quality. To this end, we apply *GMW*

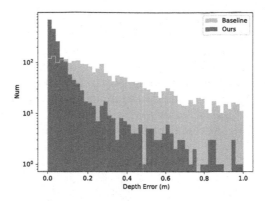

Fig. 4. This figure is the histogram of the depth error on the KITTI *val* set. X-axis represents the distance from the predicted final depth to the GT depth, and Y-axis represents the number of depths of objects with log scale. As the figure shows, our method can estimate depth much more accurately than baseline

and compare it with uncertainty-based methods. The uncertainty-based methods ((a), (b) and (c)) estimate uncertainty independently for each edge. Thus they are not capable of exploiting the global instance information of all edge projection constraints. Different from that, *GMW* is able to exploit the global information and achieve much better results. For example, model (f) (w/ GMW) surpasses model (c) (w/o GMW) by **1.55** AP on the Hard level, where the model is provided with global information to deal with severe occlusions.

Table 4. Quantitative results using the state-of-the-art method MonoFlex [50] as baseline. This table shows the effectiveness of *DGDE* and *GMW*. The Sect. 4.4 explains the strategy of choosing 1500 depth candidates

	Weighting method	$DGDE$	#Keypoints	#Depth candidates	$AP_{3D\mid R40\mid IoU@0.7}$		
					Easy	Mod	Hard
(a)	Uncertainty (Baseline) [50]		10	5	21.63	15.87	13.38
(b)	Uncertainty	✓	10	45	21.72	16.09	13.35
(c)	Uncertainty	✓	73	1500	22.84	16.53	13.77
(d)	GMW		10	5	22.58	16.14	13.63
(e)	GMW	✓	10	45	23.30	16.91	14.93
(f)	GMW	✓	73	1500	**23.94**	**17.38**	**15.32**

Study of Supervision Priority in *GMW*. In Table 5, we find that enabling depth regression supervision at the beginning detriments the performance. There is a straightforward explanation: when the match is incorrect, supervising the weighted depth will make the gradients noisy.

The Number of Edges. The numerical calculation of the depth by Eq. (6) is very unstable when the denominator is too close to zero. We made a histogram for the analysis. As shown in Fig. 5, the vast majority of these small-denominator depths are of poor quality. For this reason, we use a mask to ignore the depth candidates with extremely small denominators. This ablation study shows how the number of selected depth candidates influences the model performance. As Table 6 shows, the $AP|_{R40}$ increases when the number of selected depths is from 50 to 1500, peaks when the number of depths is 1500 and decreases afterward.

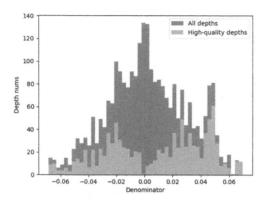

Fig. 5. The horizontal axis represents the value of the denominator of Eq. (6) for an object. The heights of green bins represent the number of depth candidates computed by *DGDE*, while the heights of red bins represent the number of high-quality depth candidates whose distance from ground truth depth is less than 0.5 m (Color figure online)

Table 5. Ablation of supervision priority of *GMW* module

Reg loss	Cls loss	Reg loss start	$AP_{3D|R40|IoU@0.7}$		
			Easy	Mod	Hard
	✓	–	23.38	17.03	15.01
✓	✓	0 epoch	22.93	16.83	14.72
✓	✓	50 epochs	**23.94**	**17.38**	**15.32**

Table 6. Ablation of the different number of edges

#Edges	$AP_{3D|R40|IoU@0.7}$		
	Easy	Mod	Hard
50	23.35	16.93	15.01
500	23.58	17.11	15.13
1500	**23.94**	**17.38**	**15.32**
2628	23.37	16.98	14.98

4.5 Disscussion About DCD and AutoShape

Although both of our method and AutoShape [23] utilize multiple keypoints to estimate the object's location, there are three critical differences:

– AutoShape directly uses all 2D-3D *keypoints* projection constraints to solve the object depth. Our method solves a depth candidate from each *edge* constraint. Thus, our edge constraints are not only in a larger number but also in higher order than the keypoint constraints.

- AutoShape generates keypoint weights independently without explicit inter-action between keypoints. Our method uses a learnable graph matching mod-ule to model the edge constraints, so we produce each depth's weight based on all the edge constraints, leading to better weighting.

We re-implement Autoshape's depth estimation and weighting method on our baseline and the experiment result is in Table 7.

Table 7. We re-implement the AutoShape's depth estimation and weighting regres-sion methods on our baseline. The combined depth estimator combines all keypoint projection constraints as input and produces one depth as output

Method	#Keypoints	Depth estimatior	#Depth candidates	$AP_{3D|R40|IoU@0.7}$		
				Easy	Mod	Hard
Autoshape [23]	73	Combined	1	22.37	16.48	14.58
DCD (Ours)	73	*DGDE*	1500	**23.94**	**17.38**	**15.32**

5   Conclusion

This paper proposes a method that can densely calculate an object's depth from 2D-3D projection constraints of edges of any direction. Therefore, we can obtain $n(n-1)/2$ depths for an object with n keypoints. Moreover, we propose a novel framework that can generate reliable weights for each depth by matching the 2D-3D edges. We finally produce a robust depth by combing each depth candidate with its weight. The experiments show the effectiveness of our method, where we outperform all the existing methods in the KITTI and WOD benchmarks.

Acknowledgement. This work was supported in part by the Major Project for New Generation of AI (No. 2018AAA0100400), the National Natural Science Foundation of China (No. 61836014, No. U21B2042, No. 62072457, No. 62006231). Also, our sincere and hearty appreciations go to Lue Fan, who polishes our paper and offers many valuable suggestions.

References

1. Battaglia, P.W., et al.: Relational inductive biases, deep learning, and graph net-works. arXiv preprint arXiv:1806.01261 (2018)
2. Brazil, G., Liu, X.: M3D-RPN: monocular 3d region proposal network for object detection. In: Proceedings of the IEEE/CVF International Conference on Com-puter Vision, pp. 9287–9296 (2019)
3. Burkard, R.E., Çela, E., Pardalos, P.M., Pitsoulis, L.S.: The Quadratic Assignment Problem, pp. 1713–1809. Springer, Boston (1998)
4. Campbell, D., Liu, L., Gould, S.: Solving the blind perspective-n-point prob-lem end-to-end with robust differentiable geometric optimization. In: Vedaldi, A., Bischof, H., Brox, T., Frahm, J.-M. (eds.) ECCV 2020. LNCS, vol. 12347, pp. 244–261. Springer, Cham (2020). https://doi.org/10.1007/978-3-030-58536-5_15

5. Chabot, F., Chaouch, M., Rabarisoa, J., Teuliere, C., Chateau, T.: Deep manta: a coarse-to-fine many-task network for joint 2d and 3d vehicle analysis from monocular image. In: Proceedings of the IEEE Conference on Computer Vision and Pattern Recognition, pp. 2040–2049 (2017)

6. Chen, H., Huang, Y., Tian, W., Gao, Z., Xiong, L.: MonoRUn: monocular 3d object detection by reconstruction and uncertainty propagation. In: Proceedings of the IEEE/CVF Conference on Computer Vision and Pattern Recognition, pp. 10379–10388 (2021)

7. Chen, Y., Tai, L., Sun, K., Li, M.: MonoPair: monocular 3d object detection using pairwise spatial relationships. In: Proceedings of the IEEE/CVF Conference on Computer Vision and Pattern Recognition, pp. 12093–12102 (2020)

8. Ding, M., et al.: Learning depth-guided convolutions for monocular 3d object detection. In: Proceedings of the IEEE/CVF Conference on Computer Vision and Pattern Recognition Workshops, pp. 1000–1001 (2020)

9. Fan, L., et al.: Embracing single stride 3d object detector with sparse transformer. arXiv preprint arXiv:2112.06375 (2021)

10. Fu, K., Liu, S., Luo, X., Wang, M.: Robust point cloud registration framework based on deep graph matching. In: Proceedings of the IEEE/CVF Conference on Computer Vision and Pattern Recognition, pp. 8893–8902 (2021)

11. Geiger, A., Lenz, P., Stiller, C., Urtasun, R.: Vision meets robotics: the kitti dataset. Int. J. Robot. Res. **32**(11), 1231–1237 (2013)

12. Gilmer, J., Schoenholz, S.S., Riley, P.F., Vinyals, O., Dahl, G.E.: Neural message passing for quantum chemistry. In: International Conference on Machine Learning, pp. 1263–1272. PMLR (2017)

13. Grabner, A., Roth, P.M., Lepetit, V.: 3d pose estimation and 3d model retrieval for objects in the wild. In: Proceedings of the IEEE Conference on Computer Vision and Pattern Recognition, pp. 3022–3031 (2018)

14. He, J., Huang, Z., Wang, N., Zhang, Z.: Learnable graph matching: incorporating graph partitioning with deep feature learning for multiple object tracking. In: Proceedings of the IEEE/CVF Conference on Computer Vision and Pattern Recognition (CVPR), pp. 5299–5309, June 2021

15. Hu, H., Gu, J., Zhang, Z., Dai, J., Wei, Y.: Relation networks for object detection. In: Proceedings of the IEEE Conference on Computer Vision and Pattern Recognition, pp. 3588–3597 (2018)

16. Kundu, A., Li, Y., Rehg, J.M.: 3D-RCNN: instance-level 3d object reconstruction via render-and-compare. In: Proceedings of the IEEE Conference on Computer Vision and Pattern Recognition, pp. 3559–3568 (2018)

17. Li, P., Zhao, H.: Monocular 3d detection with geometric constraint embedding and semi-supervised training. IEEE Robot. Autom. Lett. **6**(3), 5565–5572 (2021)

18. Li, P., Zhao, H., Liu, P., Cao, F.: RTM3D: real-time monocular 3d detection from object keypoints for autonomous driving. arXiv preprint arXiv:2001.03343 2 (2020)

19. Li, Z., Qu, Z., Zhou, Y., Liu, J., Wang, H., Jiang, L.: Diversity matters: fully exploiting depth clues for reliable monocular 3d object detection. CoRR abs/2205.09373 (2022)

20. Lian, Q., Li, P., Chen, X.: MonoJSG: joint semantic and geometric cost volume for monocular 3d object detection. In: Proceedings of the IEEE/CVF Conference on Computer Vision and Pattern Recognition, pp. 1070–1079 (2022)

21. Liu, Y., Yixuan, Y., Liu, M.: Ground-aware monocular 3d object detection for autonomous driving. IEEE Robot. Autom. Lett. **6**(2), 919–926 (2021)

22. Liu, Z., Wu, Z., Tóth, R.: Smoke: single-stage monocular 3d object detection via keypoint estimation. In: Proceedings of the IEEE/CVF Conference on Computer Vision and Pattern Recognition Workshops, pp. 996–997 (2020)
23. Liu, Z., Zhou, D., Lu, F., Fang, J., Zhang, L.: Autoshape: real-time shape-aware monocular 3d object detection. In: Proceedings of the IEEE/CVF International Conference on Computer Vision, pp. 15641–15650 (2021)
24. Loshchilov, I., Hutter, F.: Decoupled weight decay regularization. arXiv preprint arXiv:1711.05101 (2017)
25. Lu, Y., et al.: Geometry uncertainty projection network for monocular 3d object detection. In: Proceedings of the IEEE/CVF International Conference on Computer Vision, pp. 3111–3121 (2021)
26. Ma, X., Liu, S., Xia, Z., Zhang, H., Zeng, X., Ouyang, W.: Rethinking pseudo-LiDAR representation. In: Vedaldi, A., Bischof, H., Brox, T., Frahm, J.-M. (eds.) ECCV 2020. LNCS, vol. 12358, pp. 311–327. Springer, Cham (2020). https://doi.org/10.1007/978-3-030-58601-0_19
27. Ma, X., et al.: Delving into localization errors for monocular 3d object detection. In: CVPR, pp. 4721–4730 (2021)
28. Mousavian, A., Anguelov, D., Flynn, J., Kosecka, J.: 3d bounding box estimation using deep learning and geometry. In: Proceedings of the IEEE conference on Computer Vision and Pattern Recognition, pp. 7074–7082 (2017)
29. Park, D., Ambrus, R., Guizilini, V., Li, J., Gaidon, A.: Is pseudo-lidar needed for monocular 3d object detection? In: Proceedings of the IEEE/CVF International Conference on Computer Vision, pp. 3142–3152 (2021)
30. Reading, C., Harakeh, A., Chae, J., Waslander, S.L.: Categorical depth distribution network for monocular 3d object detection. arXiv preprint arXiv:2103.01100 (2021)
31. Rolínek, M., Swoboda, P., Zietlow, D., Paulus, A., Musil, V., Martius, G.: deep graph matching via blackbox differentiation of combinatorial solvers. In: Vedaldi, A., Bischof, H., Brox, T., Frahm, J.-M. (eds.) ECCV 2020. LNCS, vol. 12373, pp. 407–424. Springer, Cham (2020). https://doi.org/10.1007/978-3-030-58604-1_25
32. Sarlin, P.E., DeTone, D., Malisiewicz, T., Rabinovich, A.: SuperGlue: learning feature matching with graph neural networks. In: Proceedings of the IEEE/CVF Conference on Computer Vision and Pattern Recognition, pp. 4938–4947 (2020)
33. Sheng, H., et al.: Improving 3d object detection with channel-wise transformer. In: Proceedings of the IEEE/CVF International Conference on Computer Vision, pp. 2743–2752 (2021)
34. Shi, X., Ye, Q., Chen, X., Chen, C., Chen, Z., Kim, T.K.: Geometry-based distance decomposition for monocular 3d object detection. arXiv preprint arXiv:2104.03775 (2021)
35. Simonelli, A., Buló, S.R., Porzi, L., Ricci, E., Kontschieder, P.: Towards generalization across depth for monocular 3d object detection. In: Vedaldi, A., Bischof, H., Brox, T., Frahm, J.-M. (eds.) ECCV 2020. LNCS, vol. 12367, pp. 767–782. Springer, Cham (2020). https://doi.org/10.1007/978-3-030-58542-6_46
36. Sun, H., Zhou, W., Fei, M.: A survey on graph matching in computer vision. In: Zheng, Q., Zheng, X., Zhao, X., Yan, W., Zhang, N., Wang, L. (eds.) 13th International Congress on Image and Signal Processing, BioMedical Engineering and Informatics, CISP-BMEI 2020, Chengdu, China, 17–19 October 2020, pp. 225–230. IEEE (2020)
37. Sun, P., et al.: Scalability in perception for autonomous driving: Waymo open dataset. In: Proceedings of the IEEE/CVF Conference on Computer Vision and Pattern Recognition (CVPR), June 2020

38. Vaswani, A., et al.: Attention is all you need. In: Advances in Neural Information Processing Systems, vol. 30 (2017)
39. Wang, L., et al.: Depth-conditioned dynamic message propagation for monocular 3d object detection. In: CVPR, pp. 454–463 (2021)
40. Wang, L., et al.: Progressive coordinate transforms for monocular 3d object detection. In: Advances in Neural Information Processing Systems, vol. 34 (2021)
41. Wang, R., Yan, J., Yang, X.: Learning combinatorial embedding networks for deep graph matching. In: Proceedings of the IEEE/CVF International Conference on Computer Vision, pp. 3056–3065 (2019)
42. Wang, T., Xinge, Z., Pang, J., Lin, D.: Probabilistic and geometric depth: detecting objects in perspective. In: Conference on Robot Learning, pp. 1475–1485. PMLR (2022)
43. Weng, X., Kitani, K.: Monocular 3d object detection with pseudo-lidar point cloud. In: Proceedings of the IEEE/CVF International Conference on Computer Vision Workshops, p. 0 (2019)
44. Yan, C., Salman, E.: Mono3d: open source cell library for monolithic 3-d integrated circuits. IEEE Trans. Circuits Syst. I Regul. Pap. **65**(3), 1075–1085 (2017)
45. Yang, Z., Zhou, Y., Chen, Z., Ngiam, J.: 3d-man: 3d multi-frame attention network for object detection. In: Proceedings of the IEEE/CVF Conference on Computer Vision and Pattern Recognition, pp. 1863–1872 (2021)
46. Yi, K.M., Trulls, E., Ono, Y., Lepetit, V., Salzmann, M., Fua, P.: Learning to find good correspondences. In: Proceedings of the IEEE Conference on Computer Vision and Pattern Recognition, pp. 2666–2674 (2018)
47. Yu, F., Wang, D., Shelhamer, E., Darrell, T.: Deep layer aggregation. In: Proceedings of the IEEE Conference on Computer Vision and Pattern Recognition, pp. 2403–2412 (2018)
48. Zanfir, A., Sminchisescu, C.: Deep learning of graph matching. In: Proceedings of the IEEE Conference on Computer Vision and Pattern Recognition, pp. 2684–2693 (2018)
49. Zhang, Y., et al.: Learning geometry-guided depth via projective modeling for monocular 3d object detection. arXiv preprint arXiv:2107.13931 (2021)
50. Zhang, Y., Lu, J., Zhou, J.: Objects are different: flexible monocular 3d object detection. In: IEEE Conference on Computer Vision and Pattern Recognition, CVPR 2021, Virtual, 19–25 June 2021, pp. 3289–3298. Computer Vision Foundation/IEEE (2021)
51. Zhou, D., et al.: IAFA: instance-aware feature aggregation for 3d object detection from a single image. In: Ishikawa, H., Liu, C.-L., Pajdla, T., Shi, J. (eds.) ACCV 2020. LNCS, vol. 12622, pp. 417–435. Springer, Cham (2021). https://doi.org/10.1007/978-3-030-69525-5_25
52. Zhou, F., De la Torre, F.: Factorized graph matching. In: 2012 IEEE Conference on Computer Vision and Pattern Recognition, pp. 127–134. IEEE (2012)
53. Zhou, X., Wang, D., Krähenbühl, P.: Objects as points. arXiv preprint arXiv:1904.07850 (2019)
54. Zhou, Y., Tuzel, O.: VoxelNet: end-to-end learning for point cloud based 3d object detection. In: Proceedings of the IEEE Conference on Computer Vision and Pattern Recognition, pp. 4490–4499 (2018)
55. Zhou, Y., He, Y., Zhu, H., Wang, C., Li, H., Jiang, Q.: Monocular 3d object detection: an extrinsic parameter free approach. In: Proceedings of the IEEE/CVF Conference on Computer Vision and Pattern Recognition, pp. 7556–7566 (2021)

Polarimetric Pose Prediction

Daoyi Gao, Yitong Li, Patrick Ruhkamp[(✉)], Iuliia Skobleva,
Magdalena Wysocki, HyunJun Jung, Pengyuan Wang, Arturo Guridi,
and Benjamin Busam

Technical University of Munich, Munich, Germany
{d.gao,y.li,p.ruhkamp,i.skobleva,m.wysocki,h.jung,
p.wang,a.guridi,b.busam}@tum.de

Abstract. Light has many properties that vision sensors can passively measure. Colour-band separated wavelength and intensity are arguably the most commonly used for monocular 6D object pose estimation. This paper explores how complementary polarisation information, i.e. the orientation of light wave oscillations, influences the accuracy of pose predictions. A hybrid model that leverages physical priors jointly with a data-driven learning strategy is designed and carefully tested on objects with different levels of photometric complexity. Our design significantly improves the pose accuracy compared to state-of-the-art photometric approaches and enables object pose estimation for highly reflective and transparent objects. A new multi-modal instance-level 6D object pose dataset with highly accurate pose annotations for multiple objects with varying photometric complexity is introduced as a benchmark.

1 Introduction

"Fiat lux".[1] Light has always fascinated humanity. It is not only the inherent centre of attention for many of the most significant scientific discoveries in the last century but also plays a crucial role in society and even sets the basis for religions. Typical light sensors in computer vision send or receive pulses and waves for which the wavelength and energy are measured to retrieve colour and intensity within a specified spectrum. However, intensity and wavelength are not the only properties of an electromagnetic (EM) wave. The oscillation direction of the EM-field relative to the light ray defines its polarisation. Most natural light sources such as the sun, a lamp or a candle emit unpolarised light, which means that the light wave oscillates in a multitude of directions. Light becomes perfectly or partially polarised when a wave is reflected off an object.

---

[1] Latin for "let there be light".

D. Gao, Y. Li, P. Ruhkamp, I. Skobleva and M. Wysocki—Equal contribution; Alphabetical order.

Supplementary Information The online version contains supplementary material available at https://doi.org/10.1007/978-3-031-20077-9_43.

S. Avidan et al. (Eds.): ECCV 2022, LNCS 13669, pp. 735–752, 2022.
https://doi.org/10.1007/978-3-031-20077-9_43

Polarisation, therefore, carries information on surface structure, material and reflection angle, which can complement passively retrieved texture information from a scene [28]. These additional measurements are particularly interesting for photometrically challenging objects with metallic, reflective or transparent materials, which pose challenges to vision pipelines and effectively hamper their use for automation.

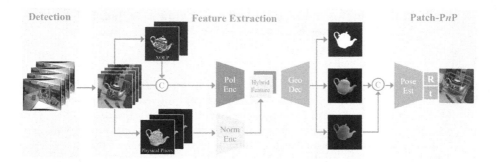

Fig. 1. PPP-Net. Our **P**olarimetric **P**ose **P**rediction Pipeline utilises the RGBP images - a quadruple of four differently polarised RGB images - to compute AOLP/DOLP and polarised normal maps through our physical model. The polarised information and the physical cues are individually encoded and fused in our hybrid model. The decoder predicts object mask, normal map and NOCS, and finally the 6D object pose is predicted by Patch-PnP [52].

While robust pipelines [9,12,21,39] have been designed for 6D pose estimation and texture-less [13,23] objects have been successfully predicted, photometrically challenging objects with reflectance and partial transparency have just recently become the focus of research [37]. These objects pose challenges to RGB-D sensing, and the field still lacks methods to cope with these problems. To address these limitations, we move beyond previous methods based on light intensity and exploit the polarisation properties of light as an additional prior for surface normals. This allows us to build a hybrid method combining a physical model with a data-driven learning approach to facilitate 6D pose estimation. We show that this not only supports pose estimation for photometrically challenging objects but also improves the pose accuracy for classical objects. To this end, our core contributions are[2]:

1. We propose **polarisation** as a new modality **for object pose estimation** and explore its advantages over previous modalities.
2. We design a **hybrid pipeline** for instance-level 6D pose estimation that leverages polarisation cues through a **combination of physical model with learning**, which shows significant improvement for **photometrically challenging objects with high reflectance and translucency**.

---

[2] Dataset and code publicly available at: https://daoyig.github.io/PPPNet/.

3. We construct the first **polarimetric instance-level 6D object pose estimation dataset** with highly accurate annotations.

2   Related Work

2.1   Polarimetric Imaging

Polarisation for 2D. Polarisation cues provide valuable complementary information for various tasks in 2D computer vision that involve photometrically challenging objects. This has inspired a series of works on semantic [58] and instance [28] segmentation for reflective and transparent objects. The absence of strong glare behind specific polarisation filters further helps to remove reflections from images [34]. While one polarisation camera can already provide significant improvements compared to photometric acquisition setups, multispectral polarimetric light fields [26] boost the performance even more.

Polarisation for 3D. Due to the inherent connection of polarisation with the object's surface, previous works on shape from polarisation (SfP) investigated the estimation of surface normals and depth from polarimetric data. However, intrinsic model ambiguities constrained setups in early works. Classical methods leverage an orthographic camera model and restrict the investigations to lab scenarios with controlled environment conditions [3,16,46,56]. Yu et al. [56] mathematically connect polarisation intensity with surface height and optimise for depth in a controlled scenario, while Atkinson et al. [3] recover surface orientation for fully diffuse surfaces. While these methods rely on monocular polarisation, more than one view can be combined with physical models for SfP [2,10], which can also be leveraged for self-supervision [50]. Some works also explore the use of complementary photometric stereo [1] and hybrid RGB+P approaches [61], which complement each other and allow for metrically accurate depth estimates if the light direction is known. If an initial depth map exists, polarimetric cues can further refine the measurements [27]. Furthermore, the polarimetric sensing model helps estimate the relative transformation of a moving polarisation sensor [11] assuming the scene is fully diffuse. Data-driven approaches can mitigate any assumptions on surface properties, light direction and object shapes. Ba et al. [4] estimate surface normals by presenting a set of plausible cues to a neural network which uses these ambiguous cues for SfP. We take inspiration from this approach to complement our pose estimation pipeline with physical priors. In contrast to these works, we are interested in the object poses in an unconstrained setup without further assuming the reflection properties or lighting. The insights of previous works enable, for the first time, to design a pipeline which addresses pose prediction for photometrically challenging objects.

2.2   6D Pose Prediction

Monocular RGB. Methods that predict 6D pose from a single image can be separated into three main categories: the ones that directly optimise for the pose, learn a pose embedding, or establish correspondences between the 3D model and the 2D image. Works that leverage pose parameterisation either directly regress the 6D pose [33,35,39,55] or discretise the regression task and solve for classification [9,30]. Networks trained this way directly predict pose parameters in the form of $SE(3)$ elements given the parameterisation used for training. Pose parameterisation can also be implicitly learnt [60]. The second branch of methods [48,49,54] utilises this to learn an implicit space to encode the pose from which the predictions can be decoded. The latest and also currently best-performing methods follow a two-stage approach. A network is used to predict 2D-3D correspondences between image and 3D model, which are used by a consecutive RANSAC/PnP pipeline that optimises the displacement robustly. Some methods in this field use sparse correspondences [25,41,43,47], while others establish dense 2D-3D pairs [22,36,40,57]. While these methods typically learn the correspondences alone, some works learn the task end-to-end [12,24,52].

RGB-D and Refinement. Since the task of monocular pose estimation from RGB is an inherently ill-posed problem, depth maps serve as a geometrical rescue. The spatial cue given by the depth map can be leveraged to establish point pairs for pose estimation [14] which can be further improved with RGB [6]. In general, the pose can be recovered from depth or combined RGB-D, and most RGB-only methods (e.g. [33,36,40,49]) benefit from a depth-driven refinement using ICP [5] or indirect multi-view cues [33]. The complementary information of RGB and depth has also inspired the seminal work DenseFusion [51] in which deeply encoded features from both modalities are fused. FFB6D [18] further improves this through a tight coupling strategy with cross-modal information exchanges in multiple feature layers combined with a keypoint extraction [19] that leverages geometry and texture cues. These works, however, crucially depend on input quality, and depth-sensing suffers in photometrically challenging regions, where polarisation cues for depth could expedite the pose prediction. To the best of our knowledge, this has not been proposed yet.

Photometric Challenges. The field of 6D pose estimation usually tests on well-established datasets with RGB-D input [7,21,29,55]. Photometrically challenging objects such as texture-less and reflective industrial parts are also part of publically available datasets [13,23]. While most of these datasets are carefully annotated for the pose, polarisation input is unavailable. Transparency is a further challenge addressed already in the pioneering work of Saxena et al. [45] where the robotic grasp point of objects is determined from RGB stereo without a 3D model. Philipps et al. [42] demonstrate how transparent objects with rotation symmetry can be reconstructed from two views using an edge detector and contour fitting. More recently, KeyPose [38] investigates instance and category level pose prediction from RGB stereo. Since their depth sensor fails on transparent objects, they leverage an opaque-transparent object pair to establish ground truth depth. ClearGrasp [44] constitutes an RGB-D method that can be used on transparent objects. The recently available StereOBJ-1M dataset includes transparent, reflective and translucent objects with variations in illumination and symmetry using a binocular stereo RGB camera for pose estimation. However, none of these datasets comprised RGBP data.

To this end, the next natural step connects the shape cues from polarisation to recover object geometry in challenging environments. We further ask the question of how to do so by starting with a look into polarimetric image formation.

3 Polarimetric Pose Prediction

In contrast to RGBP sensors (see Fig. 2), RGB-D sensors enjoy wide use in the pose estimation field. Their cost-efficiency and tight integration in many devices present many possibilities in the vision field, but their design also comes with a few drawbacks.

3.1 Photometric Challenges for RGB-D

Commercial depth sensors typically use active illumination either by projecting a pattern (e.g. Intel RealSense D series) or using time-of-flight (ToF) measurements (e.g. Kinect v2/Azure Kinect, Intel RealSense L series). While the former triangulates depth using stereo vision principles on projected or scene textures, the latter measures the roundtrip time of a light pulse that reflects from the scene. Since the measurement principle is photometric, both suffer on photometrically challenging surfaces where reflections artificially extend the roundtrip time of photons and translucent objects deteriorate the projected pattern to the extent that makes depth estimation infeasible. Figure 3 illustrates such an example for a set of common household objects. The semi-transparent vase becomes almost invisible to the used ToF sensor (RealSense L515). The reflections on both cutlery can lead to incorrect depth estimates significantly further than the correct value, while strong reflections at boundaries invalidate pixel distances.

3.2 Surface Normals from Polarisation

Before working with RGBP data, we introduce some physics behind polarimetric imaging. Natural light and most artificially emitted light is unpolarised, meaning that the electromagnetic wave oscillates along all planes perpendicular to the

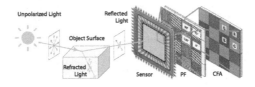

Fig. 2. Polarisation Camera. When unpolarised light hits a surface, the refracted and reflected parts are partially polarised. A polarisation sensor captures the reflected light. In front of every pixel are four polarisation filters (PF) arranged at angles 0°, 45°, 90°, 135°. The colour filter array (CFA) separates light into different wavebands.

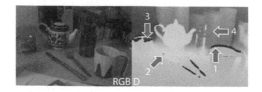

Fig. 3. Depth Artifacts. A depth sensor miscalculates depth values for typical household objects. Reflective boundaries (1,3) invalidate pixels, while strong reflections (2,3) lead to incorrect values too far away. Semi-transparent objects (4) become partly invisible to the depth sensor, which measures the distance to the objects behind.

direction of propagation of light [15]. When unpolarised light passes through a linear polariser or is reflected at Brewster's angle from a surface, it becomes perfectly polarised. How fast light travels through the material and how much of it is reflected is determined by the *refractive index*. It also determines Brewster's angle of that medium. When light is reflected at the same angle to the surface normal as the incident ray, we speak of *specular reflection*. The remaining part penetrates the object as refracted light. As the light wave traverses through the medium, it becomes partially polarised. Following this, it escapes from the object and creates *diffuse reflection*. For all real physical objects, the resulting reflection is a combination of specular and diffuse reflection, where the ratio largely depends on the refractive index and the angle of the incident light, as exemplified in Fig. 4.

Light reaches the sensor with a specific intensity I and wavelength λ. The sensor's colour filter array then separates the incoming light into RGB wavebands, as illustrated in Fig. 2. The incoming light also has a degree of linear polarisation (DOLP) ρ and a direction (angle) of polarisation (AOLP) ϕ. The measured intensity behind a polariser with an angle $\varphi_{pol} \in \{0°, 45°, 90°, 135°\}$ depends on these parameters and the unpolarised intensity I_{un} [28]:

$$I_{\varphi_{pol}} = I_{un} \cdot (1 + \rho \, \cos(2(\phi - \varphi_{pol}))). \tag{1}$$

We find φ and ρ from the over-determined system of linear equations in Eq. 1 using linear least squares. Depending on the surface properties, AOLP is

Fig. 4. DOLP. Polarisation changes for the reflection of diffuse light on a translucent surface. Note the indicated differences in the polarimetric image quadruplet that directly relate to the surface normal. The degree of linear polarisation (DOLP) for the translucent and reflective surfaces is considerably higher than for the rest of the image.

calculated as:

$$\begin{cases} \phi_d[\pi] = \alpha & \text{for diffuse reflection} \\ \phi_s[\pi] = \alpha - \frac{\pi}{2} & \text{for specular reflection} \end{cases}, \tag{2}$$

where $[\pi]$ indicates the π-ambiguity and α is the azimuth angle of the surface normal **n**. We can further relate the viewing angle $\theta \in [0, \pi/2]$ to the degree of polarisation by considering Fresnel coefficients thus DOLP is similarly given by [3]:

$$\begin{cases} \rho_d = \dfrac{(\eta - 1/\eta)^2 \sin^2(\theta)}{2 + 2\eta^2 - (\eta + 1/\eta)^2 \sin^2(\theta) + 4\cos(\theta)\sqrt{\eta^2 - \sin^2(\theta)}} \\[2ex] \rho_s = \dfrac{2\sin^2(\theta)\cos(\theta)\sqrt{\eta^2 - \sin^2(\theta)}}{\eta^2 - \sin^2(\theta) - \eta^2 \sin^2(\theta) + 2\sin^4(\theta)} \end{cases}, \tag{3}$$

with the refractive index of the observed object material η. Solving Eq. 3 for θ, we retrieve three solutions $\theta_d, \theta_{s1}, \theta_{s2}$, one for the diffuse case and two for the specular case. For each of the cases, we can now find the 3D orientation of the surface by calculating the surface normals:

$$\mathbf{n} = (\cos\alpha\sin\theta, \sin\alpha\sin\theta, \cos\theta)^{\mathrm{T}}. \tag{4}$$

We use these plausible normals $\mathbf{n}_d, \mathbf{n}_{s1}, \mathbf{n}_{s2}$ as physical priors per pixel to guide our neural network to estimate the 6D object pose.

3.3   Hybrid Polarimetric Pose Prediction Model

This section presents our **P**olarimetric **P**ose **P**rediction **N**etwork, short **PPP-Net**. Given polarimetric images at four angles $I_0, I_{45}, I_{90}, I_{135}$, together with the calculated AOLP ϕ, DOLP ρ, and normal maps N_d, N_{s1}, N_{s2} as physical priors, we aim to utilise a network to learn a pose $\mathbf{P} = [\mathbf{R}|\mathbf{t}]$ transforms a target object from the object frame to the camera frame given a 3D CAD model of the object.

Network Architecture. Our network architecture is depicted in Fig. 1. The first part of the network consists of two encoders with disjoint responsibilities. The first encodes joint polarisation information from native polarimetric images and the calculated AOLP/DOLP maps. The second one processes physical priors, i.e. the physical normals calculated from polarimetric images using the physical model. In both cases, we zoom in to a region of interest (ROI) of size 256×256 pixels. Then, the encoding is fused and passed to a decoder. The decoder receives the directly combined encoded information from both encoders enhanced by information from skip connections from different hierarchical levels of the encoders. Subsequently, it decodes an object mask, normal map, and a 3-channel dense correspondence map (NOCS) which creates a correspondence between each pixel and its normalised 3D coordinate. The predicted normal map and NOCS concatenated with corresponding 2D pixel coordinates are consecutively fed into a pose estimator as in [52]. The pose estimator comprises convolutional layers and fully connected layers and outputs the final estimated 3D rotation and translation.

Pose Parametrisation. Inspired by recent works [36,52,60] we parameterise the rotation as allocentric continuous 6D representation. Similarly, for translation we use a scale-invariant representation [12,36,52].

The continuous 6D representation $\mathbf{R}_{6d}$ for rotation comes from the first two columns of an original rotation matrix $\mathbf{R}$ [60] and we further turn it into allocentric representation [12,52]. The allocentric representation is viewpoint-independent, and as such, it is favoured by our network, which only perceives the ROI of a target object. By reducing the scene to the zoomed-in ROI, we concentrate on the most relevant information in the image, i.e. our target object, which can facilitate improvement in the pose estimation. To overcome the limitations of a direct translation vector regression, we estimate the scale-invariant translation composed of relative differences between projected object centroids and the detected bounding box center location with respect to the bounding box size. The latter is given by δ_x, δ_y and the relative zoomed-in depth, δ_z, where:

$$\begin{cases} \delta_x = (o_x - b_x)/b_w \\ \delta_y = (o_y - b_y)/b_h \\ \delta_z = t_z/r \end{cases} \tag{5}$$

with (o_x, o_y) and (b_x, b_y) being the projected object centroids and bounding box center coordinates. The size of the bounding box (b_w, b_h) is also used for calculating the zoomed-in ratio $r = s_{out}/s_{in}$ where $s_{in} = \max(b_w, b_h)$ and s_{out} is the size of the output. Note that we can recover both the rotation matrix and translation vector with known camera intrinsics K [32,36].

Object Normal Map. The surface normal map contains the surface orientation at each discrete pixel coordinate and thus encodes the shape of an object. Inspired by the previous works in SfP [4], we take a data-driven approach to retrieve the surface normal map. To better encode the geometric cue from the input physical priors apart from the polarisation cue, we do not concatenate the physical normals with the polarised images as Ba et al. [4], but encode them separately into two ResNet encoders. The decoder then learns to produce object shape encoded by the surface normal map. The estimated normals are L2-normalised to unit length. As shown in Table 1, with the given physical normals as shape prior, we can achieve high-quality normal map prediction, bringing a performance boost for the pose estimator.

Dense Correspondence Map. NOCS stores normalised 3D object coordinates given associated poses. This explicitly models correspondences between object 3D coordinates and projected 2D pixel locations. As shown by Wang et al. [52], this representation helps a consecutive differentiable pose estimator achieve higher accuracy than RANSAC/PnP.

3.4   Learning Objectives

The overall objective is composed of both geometrical features learning and pose optimisation, as: $\mathcal{L} = \mathcal{L}_{pose} + \mathcal{L}_{geo}$, with:

$$\mathcal{L}_{pose} = \mathcal{L}_R + \mathcal{L}_{center} + \mathcal{L}_z \tag{6}$$

$$\mathcal{L}_{geo} = \mathcal{L}_{mask} + \mathcal{L}_{normals} + \mathcal{L}_{xyz}. \tag{7}$$

Specifically, we employ separate loss terms for given ground truth rotation $\mathbf{R}$, (δ_x, δ_y) and δ_z as:

$$\begin{cases} \mathcal{L}_R & = \underset{\mathbf{x} \in \mathcal{M}}{\mathrm{avg}} \|\mathbf{R}\mathbf{x} - \hat{\mathbf{R}}\mathbf{x}\|_1 \\ \mathcal{L}_{center} & = \|(\delta_x - \hat{\delta}_x, \delta_y - \hat{\delta}_y)\|_1 \\ \mathcal{L}_z & = \|\delta_z - \hat{\delta}_z\|_1 \end{cases} \tag{8}$$

where $\hat{\bullet}$ denotes prediction. For symmetrical objects, the rotation loss is calculated based on the smallest loss from all possible ground-truth rotations under symmetry.

To learn the intermediate geometrical features, we employ $L1$ losses for a mask and dense correspondences map learning and a cosine similarity loss for surface normal estimation:

$$\begin{cases} \mathcal{L}_{mask} & = \|\mathbf{M} - \hat{\mathbf{M}}\|_1 \\ \mathcal{L}_{xyz} & = \mathbf{M} \odot \|\mathbf{M}_{xyz} - \hat{\mathbf{M}}_{xyz}\|_1 \\ \mathcal{L}_{normal} & = 1 - \langle \mathbf{n}, \hat{\mathbf{n}} \rangle \end{cases} \tag{9}$$

where $\odot$ indicates the Hadamard product of element-wise multiplication, and $\langle \bullet, \bullet \rangle$ denotes the dot product.

4   Polarimetric Data Acquisition

We propose the first benchmark for 6D pose estimation through physical cues from polarimetric images for photometrically challenging objects. The objects in the dataset are chosen to cover a broad spectrum of photometric difficulties to yield scientifically meaningful insights: from matte to reflective and transparent.

We follow the same data acquisition and annotation process as PhoCaL [53], which is a category-level pose estimation dataset that comprises 60 household objects with high-quality 3D models scanned by a structured light 3D stereo scanner (EinScan-SP 3D Scanner, SHINING 3D Tech. Co., Ltd., Hangzhou, China). The scanning accuracy of the device is ≤ 0.05 mm which generates highly accurate models. We select the models *cup, teapot, can, fork, knife, bottle*, because of their increasing photometric complexity, as illustrated in Fig. 5. The last three models do not include texture due to their surface structure. Therefore we used a vanishing 3D scanning spray that made the surface temporarily opaque. To acquire RGB-D images, we use a direct Time-of-Flight (dToF) camera, Intel RealSense LiDAR Camera L515 (Intel, Santa Clara, California, USA), which captures RGB and Depth data at 640×480 pixel resolution.

RGBP data is acquired using the polarisation camera Phoenix 5.0 MP PHX 050S1-QC comprising a Sony IMX264MYR CMOS (Color) Polarsens sensor (LUCID Vision Labs, Inc., Richmond B.C, Canada) through a Universe Compact C-Mount 5MP 2/3" 6mm f/2.0 lens (Universe, New York, USA) at 612×512 pixel resolution. Demosaicing is performed as part of the typical image signal processor (ISP) hardware pipeline, which is usually closed source (also for the commercial camera used here). Both cameras are mounted jointly to a KUKA iiwa (KUKA Roboter GmbH, Augsburg, Germany) 7 DoF robotic arm that guarantees a positional reproducibility of ± 0.1 mm. Intrinsic and extrinsic calibration is performed following a standard pinhole camera model [59] with five distortion coefficients [20]. For pose annotation, we leverage a mechanical pose annotation method proposed in PhoCal [53] where a robot manipulator is used to tip the object of interest and extract a point cloud. This point cloud is consecutively aligned to the 3D model using ICP [5] to allow for highly accurate pose labels even for photometrically challenging objects. We plan a robot trajectory and use this setup to acquire four scenes with four different trajectories each and utilise a total of 8740 image sets for the dataset.

5   Experimental Results

The motivation of our proposed pipeline is to show the advantage of leveraging pixelwise physical priors from polarised light (RGBP) for accurate 6D pose estimation of photometrically challenging objects - for which RGB-only and RGB-D methods often fail. For this purpose, we train and test **PPP-Net** with different modalities first on two exemplary objects with very different levels of photometric complexity, i.e. a plastic *cup*, and a photometrically very challenging, reflective and textureless stainless steel cutlery *fork*. As detailed later, we find that polarimetric information yields significant performance gain for photometrically challenging objects.

5.1   Experiments Setup

Implementation Details. We initially refine an off-the-shelf detector Mask RCNN [17] directly on the polarised images I_0 to provide useful object crops on

Fig. 5. 3D Models. Objects with increasing photometric complexity (left to right). Three objects have no texture due to reflection (cutlery) or transparency (bottle).

Table 1. PPP-Net Modalities Evaluation. Different combinations of input and output modalities are used for training to study their influence on pose estimation accuracy ADD for objects with different photometric complexity. Where applicable, metrics for estimated normals are reported. Results for other objects in Supp. Mat

Object	Photo.Chall.	Input Modalities			Output Variants		Normal Metrics					Pose Metric
		RGB	Polar RGB	Physical N	Normals	NOCS	mean↓	med.↓	11.25°↑	22.5°↑	30°↑	ADD
Cup		✓				✓	-	-	-	-	-	91.1
			✓			✓	-	-	-	-	-	91.3
			✓		✓	✓	7.3	5.5	86.2	96.1	97.9	91.3
			✓	✓	✓	✓	**4.5**	**3.5**	**94.7**	**99.1**	**99.6**	**97.2**
Fork	††	✓				✓	-	-	-	-	-	85.4
			✓			✓	-	-	-	-	-	86.1
			✓		✓	✓	11.0	7.3	72.6	90.7	93.9	92.9
			✓	✓	✓	✓	**6.5**	**4.3**	**87.6**	**95.9**	**97.6**	**95.9**

our data (as is needed for the RGB-only benchmark and ours). We follow a similar training/testing split strategy as commonly used for the public datasets [8] and employ $\approx$ 10% of the RGBP images for training and 90% for testing. We train our network end-to-end with Adam optimiser [31] for 200 epochs. The initial learning rate is set to 1e-4, halved every 50 epochs. As the depth sensor has a different field of view and is placed beneath the polarisation camera on a customised camera rig, the RGB-D benchmark split differs from the RGB training/testing split.

Evaluation Metrics. To establish our proposed novel 6D pose estimation approach, we report the pose estimation accuracy per object as the commonly used average distance (ADD), and its equivalent for symmetrical objects (ADD-S) [21] for different benchmarks. For the surface normal estimation, we calculate mean and median errors (in degrees) and the percentage of pixels where the estimated normals vary less than 11.25°, 22.5° and 30° from the ground truth.

5.2 PPP-Net Evaluation

Here, we perform a series of experiments to study the influence of the input modality on the pose estimation accuracy (see Table 1 for quantitative results,

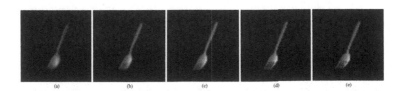

Fig. 6. Visualization of Ablations on NOCS. The quality of the geometrical representations improves when incorporating physical priors. The NOCS prediction from left to right follows the same order as the ablation experiments in Table 1: (a) unpolarised RGB input, with NOCS output; (b) polarisation input, with NOCS output; (c) polarisation input, NOCS and normals output; (d) **ours:** full model with polarisation and physical priors input, NOCS and normals output; (e) GT NOCS.

Table 2. Benchmark comparisons. We compare our method against recent RGB-D (FFB6D [18]) and RGB-only (GDR-Net [52]) methods on a variety of objects with different level of photometric challenges (†), and depth map quality (good: + to low:−) which serves as input for FFB6D. RGB-D and RGB-only comparisons are trained and tested on different splits due to different field of view of depth camera (see Sect. 5 for details). We report the Average Recall of ADD(-S)

Object	Photo. Chall.	Reflective	Metallic	Textureless	Transparent	Symmetric	Depth Quality	FFB6D	Ours	GDR	Ours
				Properties				RGB-D Split		RGB Split	
Cup							(+)	99.4	98.1	96.7	**97.2**
Teapot	†	(*)					++	86.8	**94.2**	99.0	**99.9**
Can	†	*	*				−	80.4	**99.7**	96.5	**98.4**
Fork	††	*	*	*			−−	37.0	**72.4**	86.6	**95.9**
Knife	††	*	*	*			−−−	36.7	**87.2**	92.6	**96.4**
Bottle	†††	*		*	*	*	None	61.5	**93.6**	94.4	**97.5**
Mean								67.0	**90.9**	94.3	**97.6**

Fig. 6 for qualitative improvement of NOCS), where we specifically analyse the influence of polarimetric image information for the task of 6D pose estimation. To identify the direct influence of polarisation imaging for the task of accurate object pose estimation, we first establish an RGB-only baseline by neglecting our contributions of **PPP-Net**. To compute the unpolarised RGB image, we average over polarimetric images at complementary angles and use this as input for an RGB-only network. As shown in the first two rows in Table 1 for each object (RGB against Polar RGB), the polarisation modality yields more considerable accuracy gains for the photometrically challenging object *fork* as compared to *cup*.

The accuracy of the pose estimator can be further improved when the network is guided to extract additional shape information of the object, which is implicitly encoded in the polarisation images (Table 1: 2nd to 3rd row). However, the quality of the output normals is limited. With the input of physically-induced normals from polarisation images, the network is provided with a plausible prior to encode shape information directly. Thus, it yields a much better normals prediction, significantly improving the pose performance (Table 1: 3rd to 4th row). The comparison of NOCS prediction shown in Fig. 6 reveals the fact that, given polarisation and direct shape cues, the network is guided to establish a more accurate and delicate geometrical representation, which is aligned with the quantitative improvement.

5.3   Comparison with Established Benchmarks

The input modality experiments already demonstrate the robust capabilities of polarimetric imaging inputs for **PPP-Net** to successfully learn reliable 6D pose prediction with high accuracy for photometrically challenging objects. The depth map of an RGB-D sensor can also provide geometric information that can be utilised for the task of 6D object pose estimation. We compare our method against FFB6D [18], which has a unique design that learns to combine appearance and depth information as well as local and global information from the two individual modalities.

We train FFB6D on our data for each object individually and report the best ADD(-S) metric for all objects in Table 2. The photometric challenge that each object constitutes is summarised in Table 2 and detailed by its properties (compare with Fig. 5). The objects are categorised into three classes based on the depth map quality of the depth sensor (also compare Fig. 3). We observe that objects with good depth maps and minor photometric challenges achieve high ADD values for FFB6D [18]. The increase in photometric complexity (and worse depth map quality) correlates with a decrease in ADD for challenging objects. The transparent *Bottle* object is an exception to this pattern. The depth map is completely invalid (compare Fig. 3), but FFB6D still achieves high ADD. We hypothesise that the network successfully learns to ignore the depth map input from early training onward (see Sect. 6 for details). **PPP-Net** achieves comparable results for easy objects and outperforms the strong benchmark for photometrically complex objects. Our method does not suffer from reduced ADD due to noisy or inaccurate depth maps but instead leverages the orthogonal surface information from RGBP data.

As **PPP-Net** profits vastly from physical priors from polarisation, we thoroughly investigate to which extent this additional information impacts the improvement of estimated poses, especially for photometrically challenging objects, by comparing the results also against the monocular RGB-only method GDR-Net [52]. We observe that while using polarimetric information slightly improves pose estimation accuracy for non-challenging objects, we can achieve superior performance for items with inconsistent photometric information due to reflection or transparency. In Table 2 the accuracy gain of **PPP-Net** against GDR-Net increases proportionally to the photometric complexity since our physical priors provide additional information about the geometry of an object.

6   Discussion

Limitations of Current Geometric Methods. As mentioned earlier, we postulate that the RGB-D method ignores invalid depth data already in the early stages of training (e.g. for the transparent *bottle)* and eventually learns to ignore noisy or corrupted depth information. To prove this assumption, we perform attacks on the input depth map for the FFB6D [18] encoder to analyse which parts of input modalities the network relies on when making a prediction. For this purpose, we add small Gaussian noise to the depth-related feature embedding in the bottleneck of the network and compare the ADD under this attack. We observe that the relative decrease is smaller for photometrically challenging objects as compared to objects with accurate depth maps (27% drop in ADD for *knife* and 63% for *cup*). These findings suggest that the network indeed ignores the geometrical cues of inaccurate depth inputs.

Benefits of Polarisation. We have shown that physical priors can significantly improve 6D pose estimation results for photometrically challenging objects.

RGB-only methods do not incorporate any geometric information and therefore show worse results in scenarios with objects of little texture. Methods which try to leverage geometric priors from RGB-D [18] often cannot reliably recover the 6D pose of such objects, as the depth map is usually degenerated and corrupt. Our **PPP-Net**, as the first RGBP 6D object pose estimation method, successfully achieves learning accurate poses even for very challenging objects by extracting geometric information from physical priors. Qualitative results are shown in Figs. 1 and 7, and additionally in the supplementary material. Another benefit of using RGBP lies in the sensor itself: as the polarisation filter is directly integrated on the same sensor as the Bayer filter, both modalities are intrinsically calibrated, and the image can be acquired passively, paving the way to sensor integration on low-energy and mobile devices. RGB-D cameras, on the contrary, often require energy-expensive active illumination and extrinsic calibration, which prevents simple integration and introduces additional uncertainty to the final RGB-D image.

Limitations. Our physical model requires the knowledge of the refractive index to compute the physical priors reliably. To explore the potential of the physical model, unlike prior works [4,46] which fixed the refractive index to $\eta = 1.5$ for all experiments, we use physically plausible values according to the materials (we approximate the refractive index by using the look-up table provided by https://refractiveindex.info/). This means one needs to manually choose such parameters, which would limit the performance of the physical model when using objects with unknown composite materials. Moreover, substantial changes in texture also affect the reflection of light and thus DOLP calculation which, in turn, influences our physical priors.

Fig. 7. Qualitative Results. Input image with 2D detections are shown. Predicted and GT 6D poses are illustrated by *blue* and *green* bounding boxes, respectively.

7   Conclusion

We have presented **PPP-Net**, the first learning-based 6D object pose estimation pipeline, which leverages geometric information from polarisation images through physical cues. Our method outperforms current state-of-the-art RGB-D and RGB methods for photometrically challenging objects and demonstrates at par performance for ordinary objects. Extensive ablations show the importance of complementary polarisation information for accurate pose estimation - specifically for objects without texture, i.e. reflective or transparent surfaces.

References

1. Atkinson, G.A.: Polarisation photometric stereo. Comput. Vis. Image Underst. **160**, 158–167 (2017)
2. Atkinson, G.A., Hancock, E.R.: Multi-view surface reconstruction using polarization. In: IEEE International Conference on Computer Vision (ICCV), pp. 309–316 (2005)
3. Atkinson, G.A., Hancock, E.R.: Recovery of surface orientation from diffuse polarization. Trans. Image Process. **15**(6), 1653–1664 (2006)
4. Ba, Y., Gilbert, A., Wang, F., Yang, J., Chen, R., Wang, Y., Yan, L., Shi, B., Kadambi, A.: Deep shape from polarization. In: Vedaldi, A., Bischof, H., Brox, T., Frahm, J.-M. (eds.) ECCV 2020. LNCS, vol. 12369, pp. 554–571. Springer, Cham (2020). https://doi.org/10.1007/978-3-030-58586-0_33
5. Besl, P.J., McKay, N.D.: Method for registration of 3d shapes. In: Sensor Fusion IV: Control Paradigms and Data Structures, vol. 1611, pp. 586–606. International Society for Optics and Photonics (1992)
6. Birdal, T., Ilic, S.: Point pair features based object detection and pose estimation revisited. In: IEEE International Conference on 3D Vision (3DV), pp. 527–535 (2015)
7. Brachmann, E., Krull, A., Michel, F., Gumhold, S., Shotton, J., Rother, C.: Learning 6D object pose estimation using 3D object coordinates. In: Fleet, D., Pajdla, T., Schiele, B., Tuytelaars, T. (eds.) ECCV 2014. LNCS, vol. 8690, pp. 536–551. Springer, Cham (2014). https://doi.org/10.1007/978-3-319-10605-2_35
8. Brachmann, E., Michel, F., Krull, A., Yang, M.Y., Gumhold, S., et al.: Uncertainty-driven 6d pose estimation of objects and scenes from a single rgb image. In: Proceedings of the IEEE Conference on Computer Vision and Pattern Recognition (CVPR), pp. 3364–3372 (2016)
9. Busam, B., Jung, H.J., Navab, N.: I like to move it: 6d pose estimation as an action decision process. arXiv preprint arXiv:2009.12678 (2020)
10. Cui, Z., Gu, J., Shi, B., Tan, P., Kautz, J.: Polarimetric multi-view stereo. In: Proceedings of the IEEE Conference on Computer Vision and Pattern Recognition (CVPR), pp. 1558–1567 (2017)
11. Cui, Z., Larsson, V., Pollefeys, M.: Polarimetric relative pose estimation. In: Proceedings of the IEEE/CVF International Conference on Computer Vision (ICCV), pp. 2671–2680 (2019)
12. Di, Y., Manhardt, F., Wang, G., Ji, X., Navab, N., Tombari, F.: So-pose: exploiting self-occlusion for direct 6d pose estimation. In: Proceedings of the IEEE/CVF International Conference on Computer Vision (ICCV), pp. 12396–12405 (2021)
13. Drost, B., Ulrich, M., Bergmann, P., Hartinger, P., Steger, C.: Introducing mvtec itodd-a dataset for 3d object recognition in industry. In: Proceedings of the IEEE International Conference on Computer Vision (ICCV) Workshops, pp. 2200–2208 (2017)

14. Drost, B., Ulrich, M., Navab, N., Ilic, S.: Model globally, match locally: efficient and robust 3d object recognition. In: IEEE Conference on Computer Vision and Pattern Recognition (CVPR), pp. 998–1005 (2010)
15. Fließbach, T.: Elektrodynamik: Lehrbuch zur Theoretischen Physik II, vol. 2. Springer-Verlag (2012)
16. Garcia, N.M., De Erausquin, I., Edmiston, C., Gruev, V.: Surface normal reconstruction using circularly polarized light. Opt. Express **23**(11), 14391–14406 (2015)
17. He, K., Gkioxari, G., Dollár, P., Girshick, R.: Mask r-cnn. In: Proceedings of the IEEE International Conference on Computer Vision (ICCV), pp. 2961–2969 (2017)
18. He, Y., Huang, H., Fan, H., Chen, Q., Sun, J.: Ffb6d: a full flow bidirectional fusion network for 6d pose estimation. In: IEEE/CVF Conference on Computer Vision and Pattern Recognition (CVPR) (2021)
19. He, Y., Sun, W., Huang, H., Liu, J., Fan, H., Sun, J.: Pvn3d: A deep point-wise 3d keypoints voting network for 6dof pose estimation. In: IEEE/CVF Conference on Computer Vision and Pattern Recognition (CVPR) (2020)
20. Heikkila, J., Silvén, O.: A four-step camera calibration procedure with implicit image correction. In: Proceedings of IEEE Computer Society Conference on Computer Vision and Pattern Recognition (CVPR), pp. 1106–1112 (1997)
21. Hinterstoisser, S., et al.: Model based training, detection and pose estimation of texture-less 3d objects in heavily cluttered scenes. In: Asian Conference on Computer Vision (ACCV), pp. 548–562 (2012)
22. Hodan, T., Barath, D., Matas, J.: Epos: estimating 6d pose of objects with symmetries. In: Proceedings of the IEEE/CVF Conference on Computer Vision and Pattern Recognition (CVPR), pp. 11703–11712 (2020)
23. Hodan, T., Haluza, P., Obdržálek, Š., Matas, J., Lourakis, M., Zabulis, X.: T-less: An rgb-d dataset for 6d pose estimation of texture-less objects. In: IEEE Winter Conference on Applications of Computer Vision (WACV), pp. 880–888 (2017)
24. Hu, Y., Fua, P., Wang, W., Salzmann, M.: Single-stage 6d object pose estimation. In: Proceedings of the IEEE/CVF Conference on Computer Vision and Pattern Recognition (CVPR), pp. 2930–2939 (2020)
25. Hu, Y., Hugonot, J., Fua, P., Salzmann, M.: Segmentation-driven 6d object pose estimation. In: Proceedings of the IEEE/CVF Conference on Computer Vision and Pattern Recognition (CVPR), pp. 3385–3394 (2019)
26. Islam, M.N., Tahtali, M., Pickering, M.: Specular reflection detection and inpainting in transparent object through msplfi. Remote Sens **13**(3), 455 (2021)
27. Kadambi, A., Taamazyan, V., Shi, B., Raskar, R.: Depth sensing using geometrically constrained polarization normals. Int. J. Comput. Vis. (IJCV) **125**(1–3), 34–51 (2017)
28. Kalra, A., Taamazyan, V., Rao, S.K., Venkataraman, K., Raskar, R., Kadambi, A.: Deep polarization cues for transparent object segmentation. In: Proceedings of the IEEE/CVF Conference on Computer Vision and Pattern Recognition, pp. 8602–8611 (2020)
29. Kaskman, R., Zakharov, S., Shugurov, I., Ilic, S.: Homebreweddb: Rgb-d dataset for 6d pose estimation of 3d objects. In: International Conference on Computer Vision (ICCV) Workshops (2019)
30. Kehl, W., Manhardt, F., Tombari, F., Ilic, S., Navab, N.: Ssd-6d: Making rgb-based 3d detection and 6d pose estimation great again. In: Proceedings of the IEEE International Conference on Computer Vision (ICCV). pp. 1521–1529 (2017)
31. Kingma, D.P., Ba, J.: Adam: a method for stochastic optimization. arXiv preprint arXiv:1412.6980 (2014)

32. Kundu, A., Li, Y., Rehg, J.M.: 3d-rcnn: instance-level 3d object reconstruction via render-and-compare. In: Proceedings of the IEEE Conference on Computer Vision and Pattern Recognition (CVPR), pp. 3559–3568 (2018)

33. Labbé, Y., Carpentier, J., Aubry, M., Sivic, J.: CosyPose: consistent multi-view multi-object 6D pose estimation. In: Vedaldi, A., Bischof, H., Brox, T., Frahm, J.-M. (eds.) ECCV 2020. LNCS, vol. 12362, pp. 574–591. Springer, Cham (2020). https://doi.org/10.1007/978-3-030-58520-4_34

34. Lei, C., Huang, X., Zhang, M., Yan, Q., Sun, W., Chen, Q.: Polarized reflection removal with perfect alignment in the wild. In: Proceedings of the IEEE/CVF Conference on Computer Vision and Pattern Recognition (CVPR), pp. 1750–1758 (2020)

35. Li, Y., Wang, G., Ji, X., Xiang, Yu., Fox, D.: DeepIM: deep iterative matching for 6D pose estimation. In: Ferrari, V., Hebert, M., Sminchisescu, C., Weiss, Y. (eds.) ECCV 2018. LNCS, vol. 11210, pp. 695–711. Springer, Cham (2018). https://doi.org/10.1007/978-3-030-01231-1_42

36. Li, Z., Wang, G., Ji, X.: Cdpn: coordinates-based disentangled pose network for real-time rgb-based 6-dof object pose estimation. In: Proceedings of the IEEE/CVF International Conference on Computer Vision (ICCV), pp. 7678–7687 (2019)

37. Liu, X., Iwase, S., Kitani, K.M.: Stereobj-1m: large-scale stereo image dataset for 6d object pose estimation. In: Proceedings of the IEEE/CVF International Conference on Computer Vision (ICCV), pp. 10870–10879 (2021)

38. Liu, X., Jonschkowski, R., Angelova, A., Konolige, K.: Keypose: multi-view 3d labeling and keypoint estimation for transparent objects. In: Proceedings of the IEEE/CVF Conference on Computer Vision and Pattern Recognition (CVPR), pp. 11602–11610 (2020)

39. Manhardt, F., et al.: Explaining the ambiguity of object detection and 6d pose from visual data. In: Proceedings of the IEEE/CVF International Conference on Computer Vision (ICCV), pp. 6841–6850 (2019)

40. Park, K., Patten, T., Vincze, M.: Pix2pose: pixel-wise coordinate regression of objects for 6d pose estimation. In: Proceedings of the IEEE/CVF International Conference on Computer Vision (ICCV), pp. 7668–7677 (2019)

41. Peng, S., Liu, Y., Huang, Q., Zhou, X., Bao, H.: Pvnet: pixel-wise voting network for 6dof pose estimation. In: Proceedings of the IEEE/CVF Conference on Computer Vision and Pattern Recognition, pp. 4561–4570 (2019)

42. Phillips, C.J., Lecce, M., Daniilidis, K.: Seeing glassware: From edge detection to pose estimation and shape recovery. In: Robotics: Science and Systems, vol. 3 (2016)

43. Rad, M., Lepetit, V.: Bb8: a scalable, accurate, robust to partial occlusion method for predicting the 3d poses of challenging objects without using depth. In: Proceedings of the IEEE International Conference on Computer Vision (ICCV), pp. 3828–3836 (2017)

44. Sajjan, S., et al.: Clear grasp: 3d shape estimation of transparent objects for manipulation. In: IEEE International Conference on Robotics and Automation (ICRA), pp. 3634–3642 (2020)

45. Saxena, A., Driemeyer, J., Ng, A.Y.: Robotic grasping of novel objects using vision. Int. J. Robot. Res. **27**(2), 157–173 (2008)

46. Smith, W.A., Ramamoorthi, R., Tozza, S.: Height-from-polarisation with unknown lighting or albedo. IEEE Trans. Pattern Anal. Mach. Intell. (T-PAMI) **41**(12), 2875–2888 (2018)

47. Song, C., Song, J., Huang, Q.: Hybridpose: 6d object pose estimation under hybrid representations. In: Proceedings of the IEEE/CVF Conference on Computer Vision and Pattern Recognition (CVPR), pp. 431–440 (2020)
48. Sundermeyer, M., Durner, M., Puang, E.Y., Marton, Z.C., Vaskevicius, N., Arras, K.O., Triebel, R.: Multi-path learning for object pose estimation across domains. In: Proceedings of the IEEE/CVF Conference on Computer Vision and Pattern Recognition (CVPR). pp. 13916–13925 (2020)
49. Sundermeyer, M., Marton, Z.C., Durner, M., Brucker, M., Triebel, R.: Implicit 3d orientation learning for 6d object detection from rgb images. In: Proceedings of the European Conference on Computer Vision (ECCV), pp. 699–715 (2018)
50. Verdie, Y., Song, J., Mas, B., Benjamin, B., Leonardis, A., McDonagh, S.: Cromo: cross-modal learning for monocular depth estimation. In: IEEE/CVF Conference on Computer Vision and Pattern Recognition (CVPR) (2022)
51. Wang, C., et al.: Densefusion: 6d object pose estimation by iterative dense fusion. In: Proceedings of the IEEE/CVF Conference on Computer Vision and Pattern Recognition (CVPR), pp. 3343–3352 (2019)
52. Wang, G., Manhardt, F., Tombari, F., Ji, X.: Gdr-net: geometry-guided direct regression network for monocular 6d object pose estimation. In: Proceedings of the IEEE/CVF Conference on Computer Vision and Pattern Recognition (CVPR), pp. 16611–16621 (2021)
53. Wang, P., et al.: Phocal: a multimodal dataset for category-level object pose estimation with photometrically challenging objects. In: IEEE/CVF Conference on Computer Vision and Pattern Recognition (CVPR) (2022)
54. Wohlhart, P., Lepetit, V.: Learning descriptors for object recognition and 3d pose estimation. In: Proceedings of the IEEE Conference on Computer Vision and Pattern Recognition (CVPR), pp. 3109–3118 (2015)
55. Xiang, Y., Schmidt, T., Narayanan, V., Fox, D.: Posecnn: a convolutional neural network for 6d object pose estimation in cluttered scenes. arXiv preprint arXiv:1711.00199 (2017)
56. Yu, Y., Zhu, D., Smith, W.A.: Shape-from-polarisation: a nonlinear least squares approach. In: Proceedings of the IEEE International Conference on Computer Vision (ICCV) Workshops, pp. 2969–2976 (2017)
57. Zakharov, S., Shugurov, I., Ilic, S.: Dpod: 6d pose object detector and refiner. In: Proceedings of the IEEE/CVF International Conference on Computer Vision (ICCV), pp. 1941–1950 (2019)
58. Zhang, Y., Morel, O., Blanchon, M., Seulin, R., Rastgoo, M., Sidibé, D.: Exploration of deep learning-based multimodal fusion for semantic road scene segmentation. In: VISIGRAPP (5: VISAPP), pp. 336–343 (2019)
59. Zhang, Z.: A flexible new technique for camera calibration. Transactions on Pattern Analysis and Machine Intelligence (T-PAMI) 22(11), 1330–1334 (2000)
60. Zhou, Y., Barnes, C., Lu, J., Yang, J., Li, H.: On the continuity of rotation representations in neural networks. In: Proceedings of the IEEE/CVF Conference on Computer Vision and Pattern Recognition (CVPR), pp. 5745–5753 (2019)
61. Zhu, D., Smith, W.A.: Depth from a polarisation + rgb stereo pair. In: Proceedings of the IEEE/CVF Conference on Computer Vision and Pattern Recognition, pp. 7586–7595 (2019)

Author Index

Bai, Haotian   612
Bharaj, Gaurav   646
Brazil, Garrick   664
Busam, Benjamin   735

Cai, Sijia   544
Cao, Yang   88
Chan, Antoni B.   227
Chandraker, Manmohan   159
Che, Zhengping   684
Chen, Fanglin   578
Chen, Jun   263
Chen, Pengfei   51
Chen, Xinrong   595
Chen, Yi-Ting   139
Chen, Yuntao   718
Chen, Zehui   245
Cheng, Zhanzhan   422
Choi, Changwoon   176
Chowdhury, Amber Roy   562
Chu, Xiangxiang   701
Corona, Enrique   664
Crowley, Elliot J.   123
Cui, Ziteng   473

Dai, Jifeng   1
Deng, Bing   544
Ding, Changxing   19
Dong, Ziyi   297

Fang, Liangji   245
Feng, Bailan   210
Feng, Chengjian   701
Feng, Feifei   684
Ferman, David   646
Fu, Qichen   68
Furuta, Ryosuke   68

Gao, Daoyi   735
Garg, Ravi   562
Ge, Zheng   35
Girdhar, Rohit   350
Girshick, Ross   280

Gu, Lin   473
Gudovskiy, Denis   629
Guridi, Arturo   735

Han, Xumeng   51
Han, Zhenjun   51, 210
Hao, Peihan   193
Harada, Tatsuya   473
Hassan, Najmul   51
He, Fan   422
He, Jiawei   718
He, Kaiming   280
He, Yang   562
Hua, Xian-Sheng   544
Huang, Chen   106
Huang, Jianqiang   544
Huang, Tianxin   263
Huang, Yaomin   684

Jang, Hojun   176
Jia, Kui   19, 369
Jiang, Junjun   245
Jiang, Qinhong   245
Jiang, Zeren   314
Jie, Zequn   701
Jin, Qiuye   595
Jin, Zhenchao   332
Joulin, Armand   350
Jung, HyunJun   735

Keutzer, Kurt   629
Kim, Junho   176
Kim, Young Min   176
Kitani, Kris M.   68
Komura, Taku   404
Kong, Shu   139
Kortylewski, Adam   492
Krähenbühl, Philipp   350
Kumar, Abhinav   664

Lee, Gim Hee   544
Leng, Biao   439
Li, Ang   245

Li, Gang   457
Li, Hongmin   193
Li, Hongyang   1, 369
Li, Jiachen   51
Li, Jianxin   629
Li, Mingyang   263
Li, Wei   106
Li, Xiang   457
Li, Xiangyu   404
Li, Xiaojie   314
Li, Xiaoxiao   473
Li, Yanghao   280
Li, Yingyan   718
Li, Yitong   735
Li, Yu-Jhe   68
Li, Zeming   35
Li, Zhenyu   245
Li, Zhihao   595
Li, Zhiqi   1
Liang, Ding   457
Liang, Jianming   439
Liao, Mingxiang   210
Liao, Yue   314
Lin, Dahua   386
Lin, Jiehong   19, 369
Lin, Liang   297
Liu, Jiaming   629
Liu, Kaixuan   193
Liu, Si   314
Liu, Songtao   35
Liu, Xianming   245
Liu, Xiaoming   664
Liu, Xinmei   684
Liu, Yong   263
Liu, Yu   439
Loy, Chen Change   106
Lu, Guangming   578
Lu, Jing   422
Lu, Tong   1

Ma, Lin   701
Ma, Teng   263
Ma, Wufei   492
Mao, Hanzi   280
Mao, Weixin   35
Mei, Dianwen   578
Mertz, Christoph   139
Metaxas, Dimitris N.   159
Miao, Zhenwei   193
Misra, Ishan   350

Nakata, Yohei   629
Niu, Yi   422

Ochal, Mateusz   123
Ohkawa, Takehiko   68
Okuno, Tomoyuki   629

Pan, Hao   404
Pan, Hongyu   193
Pang, Jiangmiao   386
Parchami, Armin   664
Pei, Wenjie   578
Peng, Yaxin   684

Qi, Guo-Jun   473
Qian, Chen   314
Qiao, Yu   1

Ramanan, Deva   139
Ren, Haibing   701
Ruhkamp, Patrick   735

Sato, Yoichi   68
Schulter, Samuel   159
Shen, Chaomin   684
Shen, Yongliang   88
Sheng, Hualian   544
Shi, Humphrey   51
Shi, Jinghao   139
Sima, Chonghao   1
Skobleva, Iuliia   735
Song, Guanglu   439
Song, Luchuan   332
Stathopoulos, Anastasis   159
Storkey, Amos   123
Sun, Jian   35
Sun, Zhengyang   193

Tang, Jian   684
Tang, Sanli   422
Tao, Dacheng   88
Tian, Jiandong   578

Vijay Kumar, B.G   159

Wan, Fang   210
Wan, Xiang   612
Wang, Angtian   492
Wang, Fei   314
Wang, Jinwang   526
Wang, Jiong   612
Wang, Kai   51

Wang, Luting   314
Wang, Manning   595
Wang, Pengyuan   735
Wang, Tai   386
Wang, Wen   88
Wang, Wenhai   1
Wang, Wenping   404
Wang, Yinyan   509
Wang, Yujie   457
Wang, Yuze   210
Wang, Zheng   404
Wei, Pengxu   297
Wei, Xiaobao   629
Wei, Xiaolin   701
Wei, Xingxing   509
Wei, Zewei   19
Wen, Yilin   404
Wu, Jianlong   314
Wu, Shuang   578
Wu, Yichao   457
Wysocki, Magdalena   735

Xia, Gui-Song   526
Xie, Enze   1
Xie, Weidi   701
Xu, Chang   526
Xu, Jianyun   193
Xu, Yunlu   422
Xu, Zhiyuan   684

Yang, Chenhongyi   123
Yang, Lei   404
Yang, Sheng   263
Yang, Wen   526
Yao, Yuan   210
Ye, Qixiang   51, 210
Ye, Zelin   139
Yu, Dongdong   332
Yu, Haiyan   35
Yu, Huai   526

Yu, Jinze   629
Yu, Lei   526
Yu, Lequan   332
Yu, Xuehui   51
Yuan, Maoxun   509
Yuan, Mingzhi   595
Yuan, Peng   210
Yuan, Zehuan   332
Yuille, Alan   492

Zang, Yuhang   106
Zhan, Xin   193
Zhang, Renrui   473
Zhang, Da   193
Zhang, Guixu   684
Zhang, Jing   88
Zhang, Qi   227
Zhang, Ruimao   612
Zhang, Shanghang   629
Zhang, Shanshan   457
Zhang, Zenghui   473
Zhang, Zhaoxiang   718
Zhang, Zhixing   159
Zhang, Zhongyu   422
Zhao, Jian   51
Zhao, Long   159
Zhao, Min-Jian   544
Zhao, Na   544
Zhao, Shiyu   159
Zhao, Xiangrui   263
Zhong, Yujie   701
Zhou, Haoyi   629
Zhou, Hongyu   35
Zhou, Kaiyang   106
Zhou, Xingyi   350
Zhu, Jun   193
Zhu, Yichen   684
Zhu, Yingying   473
Zou, Jialing   210

Printed in the United States
by Baker & Taylor Publisher Services